P9-CDH-855

PHILIP KOTLER
NORTHWESTERN UNIVERSITY

KEVIN LANE KELLER
DARTMOUTH COLLEGE

PEGGY H. CUNNINGHAM
QUEEN'S UNIVERSITY

MARKETING MANAGEMENT CANADIAN 12TH EDITION

PEARSON
Prentice
Hall

Toronto

Library and Archives Canada Cataloguing in Publication

Kotler, Philip
    Marketing management/Philip Kotler, Kevin Lane Keller, Peggy Cunningham.—
    Canadian 12th ed.

ISBN 0-13-128640-4

1. Marketing—Management—Textbooks. I. Cunningham, Margaret H. II. Keller, Kevin
Lane, 1956– III. Title.

HF5415.13.K68 2006   658.8   C2005-904880-8

Copyright © 2006, 2004, 2001, 1998, 1991, 1988, 1984, 1980, 1976, 1972, 1967 Pearson
Education Canada Inc., Toronto, Ontario.

Pearson Prentice Hall. All rights reserved. This publication is protected by copyright, and
permission should be obtained from the publisher prior to any prohibited reproduction,
storage in a retrieval system, or transmission in any form or by any means, electronic,
mechanical, photocopying, recording, or likewise. For information regarding permission,
write to the Permissions Department.

Original edition published by Pearson Education, Inc., Upper Saddle River, New Jersey,
USA. Copyright © 2006 by Pearson Education, Inc. This edition is authorized for sale only
in Canada.

For permission to reproduce copyrighted material, the publisher gratefully acknowledges
the copyright holders listed on page 812, which is considered an extension of this copyright
page.

ISBN 0-13-128640-4

Vice-President, Editorial Director: Michael J. Young
Editor-in-Chief: Gary Bennett
Acquisitions Editor: Laura Paterson Forbes
Marketing Manager: Eileen Lasswell
Developmental Editor: Paul Donnelly
Production Editor: Cheryl Jackson
Copy Editor: Valerie Adams
Proofreader: Karen Alliston
Production Coordinator: Andrea Falkenberg
Page Layout: Nelson Gonzalez
Permissions Researcher: Lisa Brant
Art Director: Julia Hall
Cover and Interior Design: Miguel Acevedo

1 2 3 4 5   10 09 08 07 06

Printed and bound in United States of America

Statistics Canada information is used with the permission of the Minister of Industry, as
Minister responsible for Statistics Canada. Information on the availability of the wide
range of data from Statistics Canada can be obtained from Statistics Canada's Regional
Offices, its World Wide Web site at http://www.statcan.ca, and its toll-free access number
1-800-263-1136.

ABOUT THE AUTHORS

Philip Kotler is one of the world's leading authorities on marketing. He is the S. C. Johnson & Son Distinguished Professor of International Marketing at the Kellogg School of Management, Northwestern University. He received his master's degree at the University of Chicago and his Ph.D. at MIT, both in economics. He did postdoctoral work in mathematics at Harvard University and in behavioral science at the University of Chicago.

Dr. Kotler is the co-author of *Principles of Marketing* and *Marketing: An Introduction*. His *Strategic Marketing for Nonprofit Organizations*, now in its sixth edition, is the best seller in that specialized area. Dr. Kotler's other books include *Marketing Models; The New Competition; Marketing Professional Services; Strategic Marketing for Educational Institutions; Marketing for Health Care Organizations; Marketing Congregations; High Visibility; Social Marketing; Marketing Places; The Marketing of Nations; Marketing for Hospitality and Tourism; Standing Room Only—Strategies for Marketing the Performing Arts; Museum Strategy and Marketing; Marketing Moves; Kotler on Marketing; Lateral Marketing: Ten Deadly Marketing Sins;* and *Corporate Social Responsibility.*

In addition, he has published more than one hundred articles in leading journals, including the *Harvard Business Review, Sloan Management Review, Business Horizons, California Management Review,* the *Journal of Marketing,* the *Journal of Marketing Research, Management Science,* the *Journal of Business Strategy,* and *Futurist.* He is the only three-time winner of the coveted Alpha Kappa Psi award for the best annual article published in the *Journal of Marketing.*

Professor Kotler was the first recipient of the American Marketing Association's (AMA) Distinguished Marketing Educator Award (1985). The European Association of Marketing Consultants and Sales Trainers awarded him their Prize for Marketing Excellence. He was chosen as the Leader in Marketing Thought by the Academic Members of the AMA in a 1975 survey. He also received the 1978 Paul Converse Award of the AMA, honoring his original contribution to marketing. In 1995, the Sales and Marketing Executives International (SMEI) named him Marketer of the Year. In 2002, Professor Kotler received the Distinguished Educator Award from The Academy of Marketing Science. He has received honorary doctoral degrees from Stockholm University, the University of Zurich, Athens University of Economics and Business, DePaul University, the Cracow School of Business and Economics, Groupe H.E.C. in Paris, the Budapest School of Economic Science and Public Administration, and the University of Economics and Business Administration in Vienna.

Professor Kotler has been a consultant to many major U.S. and foreign companies, including IBM, General Electric, AT&T, Honeywell, Bank of America, Merck, SAS Airlines, Michelin, and others in the areas of marketing strategy and planning, marketing organization, and international marketing.

He has been Chairman of the College of Marketing of the Institute of Management Sciences, a Director of the American Marketing Association, a Trustee of the Marketing Science Institute, a Director of the MAC Group, a member of the Yankelovich Advisory Board, and a member of the Copernicus Advisory Board. He was a member of the Board of Governors of the School of the Art Institute of Chicago and a member of the Advisory Board of the Drucker Foundation. He has traveled extensively throughout Europe, Asia, and South America, advising and lecturing to many companies about global marketing opportunities.

Kevin Lane Keller is the E. B. Osborn Professor of Marketing at the Tuck School of Business at Dartmouth College. Professor Keller has degrees from Cornell, Carnegie-Mellon, and Duke universities. At Dartmouth, he teaches an MBA elective on strategic brand management and lectures in executive programs on that topic. Previously, Professor Keller was on the faculty of the Graduate School of Business at Stanford University, where he also served as the head of the marketing group. Additionally, he has been on the marketing faculty at the University of California at Berkeley and the University of North Carolina at Chapel Hill, been a visiting professor at Duke University and the Australian Graduate School of Management, and has two years of industry experience as Marketing Consultant for Bank of America.

Professor Keller's general area of expertise is in consumer marketing. His specific research interest is in how understanding theories and concepts related to consumer behavior can improve marketing strategies. The research has been published in over fifty papers in three of the major marketing journals—the *Journal of Marketing,* the *Journal of Marketing Research,* and the *Journal of Consumer Research.* He also has served on the Editorial Review Boards of those journals. His research has been widely cited and has received numerous awards.

Professor Keller is acknowledged as one of the international leaders in the study of brands, branding, and strategic brand management. Actively involved with industry, he has worked on a host of different types of marketing projects. He has served as brand confidant to marketers for some of the world's most successful brands, including Accenture, American Express, Disney, Ford, Intel, Levi Strauss, Miller Brewing, Procter & Gamble, and Starbucks. He has done additional brand consulting with other top companies such as Allstate, Beiersdorf (Nivea), Blue Cross Blue Shield, Campbell Soup, General Mills, Goodyear, Kodak, The Mayo Clinic, Nordstrom, Shell Oil, Unilever, and Young & Rubicam. He is also an academic trustee for the Marketing Science Institute. A popular speaker, he has conducted marketing seminars and workshops with top executives in a variety of forums.

Professor Keller is currently conducting studies that address marketing strategies and tactics to build, measure, and manage brand equity. His textbook on those subjects, *Strategic Brand Management,* the second edition of which was published September 2002 by Prentice-Hall, has been heralded as the "bible of branding."

An avid sports, music, and film enthusiast, in his spare time, he helps to manage and market one of Australia's great rock and roll treasures, *The Church.* Professor Keller lives in New Hampshire with his wife, Punam (also a Tuck marketing professor), and his two daughters, Carolyn and Allison.

Peggy Cunningham is the Marie Shantz Teaching Associate Professor of Marketing at Queen's School of Business. She received her undergraduate degree from Queen's University, her MBA from the University of Calgary, and her Ph.D. from Texas A&M University. She was the founding Director of the Accelerated MBA program for business graduates (2001–2004). She previously was the Co-Chair of the E-Commerce Research Program (1998–2001), and she is currently one of the founding members of the Global Responsible Leadership Initiative (2004–present). She has considerable international experience and has been a visiting professor at universities and government training programs in France, Germany, China, the U.K., and the U.S. Her experience in industry and consulting helps her bring the perspective of the practitioner to the study of marketing. Her research interests centre on two related themes: marketing ethics and marketing partnerships (international strategic alliances and partnerships between for-profit and not-for-profit organizations). While these may seem like totally divergent areas of study, they are linked by their focus on the concepts of trust, integrity, and commitment which are the core elements to both ethical behaviour and successful partnership behaviour. She has received a number of awards for this work including the ANBAR citation award for her Strategic Alliances article written with Rajan Varadarajan and a nomination for the 2006 Accenture Award for her work in Social Alliances with Ida Berger and Meme Drumwright. Her research is published in a number of journals including the *Journal of the Academy of Marketing Science,* the *California Management Review,* and the *Journal of International Marketing.* She is a devoted teacher who tries to inspire her students to realize their full and unique potential. She currently teaches courses in marketing management and strategy, marketing ethics, and branding in the B.Comm., M.Sc., Ph.D., and Executive training programs. She is one of Queen's University's most acclaimed and awarded teaching professors. In 2004, she received the PriceWaterhouseCoopers Leaders in Management Education award. She was named the Academy of Marketing Science's Outstanding Teacher in 2001. She has been nominated twice for the Frank Knox Award for Teaching Excellence, one of the most prestigious awards given at Queen's for undergraduate teaching. She won this award in 1993. Dr. Cunningham also does a considerable amount of research and writing to further educational practice. She has written over 40 cases that have been used in case competitions and have been published in a number of leading North American marketing textbooks.

This book is dedicated to my wife and best friend, Nancy, with love. **PK**

This book is dedicated to my wife, Punam, and my two daughters, Carolyn and Allison, with much love and thanks. **KLK**

This book is dedicated to my family. They are my cheerleaders, friends, and helpmates and the centre of my world. **PC**

BRIEF CONTENTS

CONTENTS

Marketing Management is the leading MBA marketing text because its content and organization consistently reflect changes in marketing theory and practice. The very first edition of *Marketing Management*, published in 1967, introduced the concept that companies must be customer-and-market driven. But there was no mention of what have become fundamental topics, such as segmentation, targeting, and positioning. Concepts such as brand equity, customer value analysis, database marketing, e-commerce, value networks, hybrid channels, supply chain management, and integrated marketing communications were not even part of the marketing vocabulary then. Firms now sell goods and services through a variety of direct and indirect channels. Mass advertising is not nearly as effective as it was. Companies are exploring new forms of communication, such as experiential, entertainment, and viral marketing. Customers are increasingly telling companies what types of product or services they want and when, where, and how they want to buy them.

In response, companies have shifted gears from managing product portfolios to managing customer portfolios, compiling databases on individual customers so they can understand them better, and constructing individualized offerings and messages. They are doing less product and service standardization and more niching and customization. They are replacing monologues with customer dialogues. They are improving their methods of measuring customer profitability and customer lifetime value. They are intent on measuring the return on their marketing investment and its impact on shareholder value. They are also concerned with the ethical and social implications of their marketing decisions.

As companies change, so does their marketing organization. Marketing is no longer a company department charged with a limited number of tasks—it is a company-wide undertaking. It drives the company's vision, mission, and strategic planning. Marketing includes decisions like who the company wants as its customers; which needs to satisfy; what products and services to offer; what prices to set; what communications to send and receive; what channels of distribution to use; and what partnerships to develop. Marketing succeeds only when all departments work together to achieve goals: when engineering designs the right products, finance furnishes the required funds, purchasing buys quality materials, production makes quality products on time, and accounting measures the profitability of different customers, products, and areas.

And as marketing techniques and organization have changed, so has this text. The biggest change is the addition of a new co-author. Kevin Lane Keller is one of the top marketing academics of his generation. He has conducted ground-breaking research and written a highly successful text, *Strategic Brand Management*. He has also worked with marketing executives from companies around the globe to help them become better marketers. He brings fresh thinking and new perspectives to *Marketing Management*.

The Canadian twelfth edition reflects a collaborative effort among the three authors with a goal of creating the best edition of *Marketing Management* ever. Extensive focus groups were conducted to fully understand the course and classroom needs of the instructor. Based on this input, the new edition is designed to preserve the strengths of previous editions while introducing new material and organization to further enhance learning. It is dedicated to helping companies, groups, and individuals adapt their marketing strategies and management to the marketplace realities of the twenty-first century.

Revision Strategy for the Canadian Twelfth Edition

Marketing is of interest to everyone, whether they are marketing goods, services, properties, persons, places, events, information, ideas, or organizations. As the "ultimate authority" for students and educators, *Marketing Management* must be kept up-to-date and contemporary. Students (and instructors) should feel that the book is talking to them directly in terms of both content and delivery.

The success of *Marketing Management* can be attributed to its ability to maximize three dimensions that characterize the best marketing texts—depth, breadth, and relevance—as reflected by the following questions.

- *Depth.* Does the book have solid academic grounding? Does it contain important theoretical concepts, models, and frameworks? Does it provide conceptual guidance to solve practical problems?
- *Breadth.* Does the book cover all the right topics? Does it provide the proper amount of emphasis on those topics?
- *Relevance.* Does the book engage the reader? Is the book interesting to read? Does it have lots of compelling examples?

The Canadian twelfth edition builds on the fundamental strengths of past editions:

- *Managerial Orientation.* The book focuses on the major decisions that marketing managers and top management face in their efforts to harmonize the organization's objectives, capabilities, and resources with marketplace needs and opportunities.
- *Analytical Approach.* This book presents conceptual tools and frameworks for analyzing recurrent problems in marketing management. Cases and examples illustrate effective marketing principles, strategies, and practices.
- *Multidisciplinary Perspective.* This book draws on the rich findings of various scientific disciplines—economics, behavioural science, management theory, and mathematics—for fundamental concepts and tools.
- *Universal Applications.* This book applies strategic thinking to the complete spectrum of marketing: products and services, consumer and business markets, profit and nonprofit organizations, domestic and foreign companies, small and large firms, manufacturing and intermediary businesses, and low- and high-tech industries.
- *Comprehensive and Balanced Coverage.* This book covers all the topics an informed marketing manager needs to understand to execute strategic, tactical, and administrative marketing.

New Themes: Holistic Marketing

One major new theme in this edition is holistic marketing. *Holistic marketing* can be seen as the development, design, and implementation of marketing programs, processes, and activities that recognize the breadth and interdependencies involved today's marketing environment. Holistic marketing recognizes that *everything matters* with marketing and that a broad, integrated perspective is often necessary. Holistic marketing has four key dimensions:

- *Internal marketing,* which means ensuring everyone in the organization embraces appropriate marketing principles, especially senior management.
- *Integrated marketing,* which means ensuring that multiple means of creating, delivering, and communicating value are employed and combined in the optimal manner.
- *Relationship marketing* and having rich, multi-faceted relationships with customers, channel members, and other marketing partners.
- *Socially responsible marketing* in understanding the ethical, environmental, legal, and social effects of marketing.

These four dimensions are woven throughout the book and at times spelled out explicitly. Two additional themes of this text are *marketing personalization* and *marketing accountability*. The former reflects all the attempts to make marketing more individually relevant; the latter reflects the need to understand and justify the return on marketing investments within organizations.

Organization

This edition preserves the major topics of its predecessor, but reorganizes them into a new modular structure. There are now eight parts as compared to five to allow for greater flexibility in the classroom.

1. Understanding Marketing Management
2. Capturing Marketing Insights
3. Connecting with Customers
4. Building Strong Brands
5. Shaping Market Offerings
6. Communicating Value

7. Delivering Value

8. Creating Long-Term Growth

The most significant organizational changes are:

- A new part on *Capturing Marketing Insights* that includes the two research-oriented chapters, placed even earlier in the book (Chapters 3 and 4)

- A new section on *Creating Long-Term Growth* that brings together chapters on new products and new markets (global) as well as a revised concluding chapter, placed at the end of the book (Chapters 20–22)

- Chapters 16 and 17 are now aligned more definitely in terms of mass and personal communications.

- The marketing plan material has been upgraded and moved into Chapter 2 to help students gain concrete marketing skills. This includes an illustrative example of an actual company marketing plan for Pegasus Sports International.

- A glossary containing all the key terms and definitions has been added at the end of the book.

Chapter by Chapter Changes

This edition has been both streamlined and expanded to bring essentials and classic examples into sharper focus, while covering new concepts and ideas in depth. Some chapters received more extensive revisions than others. Here is an overview of the chapter changes:

- Chapter 1, *Defining Marketing for the Twenty-First Century,* now consolidates the "big picture" material from the first two chapters of the eleventh edition to introduce key marketing topics, and how they have changed and are likely to change in the future.

- Chapter 2, *Developing Marketing Strategies and Plans,* provides more discussion on holistic marketing and more detail on marketing plans, including a sample marketing plan.

- Chapter 3, *Gathering Information and Scanning the Environment,* is now couched in terms of macro approaches to marketing research.

- Chapter 4, *Conducting Marketing Research and Forecasting Demand,* is framed in terms of micro approaches and includes a new section on Marketing Productivity.

- Chapter 5, *Creating Customer Value, Satisfaction and Loyalty,* consolidates material from several chapters related to customers and introduces new material on Customer Equity.

- Chapter 6, *Analyzing Consumer Markets,* introduces a new section on Other Theories of Consumer Decision-Making.

- Chapter 7, *Business-to-Business Markets,* contains a section on Managing Business-to-Business Customer Relationships.

- Chapter 8, *Identifying Market Segments and Targets,* adds new material on local marketing, conversion marketing, experiential marketing, and marketing to Generation Y.

- Chapter 9, *Building Brand Equity,* has been completely reworked and expanded to capture more of the important concepts in building, measuring, and managing brand equity.

- Chapter 10, *Crafting the Brand Positioning,* introduces a contemporary approach to positioning based on the concepts of points-of-parity and points-of-difference.

- Chapter 11, *Dealing with Competition,* includes fresh material on how to increase product consumption.

- Chapter 12, *Shaping Market Offerings,* has been reorganized to cover material on sources of differentiation.

- Chapter 13, *Designing and Managing Services,* introduces a new section on Managing Service Brands.

- Chapter 14, *Developing Pricing Strategies and Programs,* contains a new section on understanding pricing with material on consumer psychology and pricing.

- Chapter 15, *Designing and Managing Marketing Channels and Value Networks,* includes material on e-commerce marketing practices and new material on channel power, conflict, and cooperation.

- Chapter 16, *Managing Retailing, Wholesaling, and Logistics,* includes relevant material on store activities and experiences and has been reorganized to include private labels.

- Chapter 17, *Designing and Managing Integrated Marketing Communications,* introduces a section on the Role of Marketing Communications and information on coordinating media.
- Chapter 18, *Managing Mass Communications: Advertising, Sales Promotions, Events, and Public Relations,* includes a new section on Events and Experiences Marketing.
- Chapter 19, *Managing Personal Communications: Personal Selling and Direct Marketing,* introduces new material on interactive marketing.
- Chapter 20, *Introducing New Market Offerings,* includes material on idea generation.
- Chapter 21, *Tapping into Global Markets,* covers new material on country-of-origin effects.
- Chapter 22, *Managing a Holistic Marketing Organization,* contains new sections on social marketing and the future of marketing.

Additional concepts that have been added or explored in greater detail include brand management principles, cause-related marketing, consumer decision heuristics, consumer involvement, consumer memory models, events and experiences, innovation and creativity, qualitative research techniques, marketing metrics, mental accounting, reference prices, and sponsorships.

Chapter Pedagogy

Each chapter includes:

- *Chapter Introduction,* which includes brief commentary and a major vignette on a Canadian company that sets the stage for the chapter material to follow. By covering topical brands or companies, the vignettes serve as great discussion starters.
- *Marketing Insight* boxes that delve into important marketing topics, often highlighting current research findings. New and updated Marketing Insight boxes include such topics as "Views on Marketing from Chief Executive Officers," "Progress and Priorities in Customer Equity Management," "Consumer Trends for the Future," and "Small Business, Big Sales: The Burgeoning Small-Midsize Business Market."
- *Marketing Memo* boxes that offer practical advice and directions in dealing with various decisions at all stages of the marketing management process. New and updated Marketing Memo boxes include "Managing Customer Knowledge," "Decision Traps," "Average American Consumer Quiz," and "Guidelines for Selling to Small Businesses."
- *Text Examples* Each chapter also includes 10–15 in-text examples that provide vivid illustrations of chapter concepts using actual companies and situations. Virtually all these examples of good and bad company marketing practices are new to the twelfth edition and cover a variety of products, services, and markets. Many have accompanying illustrations in the form of ads or product shots.
- *End-of-Chapter Exercises* These include Marketing Applications and the Marketing Spotlight.
- The *Marketing Applications* section has two practical exercises to challenge students: *Marketing Debate* and *Marketing Discussion. Marketing Debate* suggests opposing points-of-view on an important marketing topic from the chapter and asks student to take a side. *Marketing Discussion* identifies provocative marketing issues and allows for a personal point-of-view.
- The *Marketing Spotlight,* an in-depth examination of one of the world's most successful marketing companies, includes questions for class discussion or student assignments.

The Teaching and Learning Package

Marketing Management is an entire package of materials available to students and instructors. This edition includes a number of ancillaries designed to make the marketing management course an exciting, dynamic, interactive experience.

INSTRUCTOR'S RESOURCE CD-ROM. One source for all of your supplement needs. Includes all the same supplements hosted at our online catalogue; however, the PowerPoint Media Rich set is provided only on this CD-ROM due to its larger file size and embedded video clips. The CD-ROM also contains many images from the textbook, which you may incorporate into your lectures.

INSTRUCTOR RESOURCES ON THE ONLINE CATALOGUE. The Pearson Education Canada online catalogue at http://vig.pearsoned.ca is where instructors can access our complete array of teaching materials. Simply go to the catalogue page for this text and click on the Instructor link to download the Instructor's Manual, TestGen, PowerPoint slides (Basic only), and more.

INSTRUCTOR'S RESOURCE MANUAL. The Instructor's Resource Manual includes chapter/summary overviews, key teaching objectives, answers to end-of-chapter materials, Harvard Business School case suggestions, exercises, projects, and detailed lecture outlines. A new feature, "Professors on the Go!", was created with the busy professor in mind. It brings key material upfront, where an instructor who is short on time can find key points and assignments that can be incorporated into the lecture, without having to page through all the material provided for each chapter.

TESTGEN. The TestGen contains more than 3,000 multiple-choice, true-false, short-answer, and essay questions, with page reference and difficulty level provided for each question. *A new feature is an entire section of application questions.* These real-life situations take students beyond basic chapter concepts and vocabulary and ask them to apply marketing skills. Available on the IRCD and from the online catalogue.

POWERPOINTS. When it comes to PowerPoints, Pearson Education Canada knows one size does not fit all. That's why *Marketing Management,* Canadian Twelfth Edition, offers instructors two options.

- **PowerPoint BASIC.** This simple presentation includes only basic outlines and key points from each chapter. No animation or forms of rich media are integrated, which makes the total file size manageable and easier to share online or via email. BASIC was also designed for instructors who prefer to customize PowerPoints or want to avoid having to strip out animation, embedded files, or other media rich features.

- **PowerPoint MEDIA RICH.** This media-rich alternative includes basic outlines and key points from each chapter, plus advertisements and art from the text, images from outside the text, discussion questions, Web links, and embedded video snippets. It's the best option if you want a complete presentation solution. Instructors can further customize this presentation using the image library featured on the IRCD.

Aside from these three PowerPoint options, a select number of slides, based on the media-rich version, are also available as overhead transparencies.

CBC/PEARSON EDUCATION CANADA LIBRARY. This supplement features eight segments from the acclaimed *Venture* and *Marketplace* programs. Accompanying cases are provided on the Companion Website.

COMPANION WEBSITE. This site offers students valuable resources. Two quizzes are offered per chapter. The Concept Check Quiz is to be administered prior to reviewing the chapter, in order to assess students' initial understanding. The Concept Challenge Quiz is to be administered after reviewing the chapter. New to the Companion Website, the Marketing Plan module provides detailed information on how to develop a marketing plan and includes a series of exercises to help students develop a formal marketing plan using the hypothetical example of Sonic PDA. Also featured is the text glossary, plus links to the video segments and cases, and to the Instructor's Resources.

MARKETING MANAGEMENT CASES. Prentice Hall Custom Business Resources can provide instructors and students with all of the cases and articles needed to enhance and maximize learning in a marketing course. Instructors can create Custom CoursePacks or Custom CaseBooks. Resources include top-tier cases from Darden, Harvard, Ivey, NACRA, and Thunderbird, plus full access to a database of articles. For details on how to order these value-priced packages, contact your local rep.

MARKETING PLAN: A HANDBOOK, SECOND EDITION, WITH MARKETINGPLAN PRO 6.0. Marketing PlanPro is a highly rated commercial software program that guides students through the entire marketing plan process. The software is totally interactive and features 10 sample marketing plans, step-by-step guides, and customizable charts. Customize your marketing plan to fit your marketing needs by following easy-to-use plan wizards. Follow the clearly outlined steps from strategy to implementation. Click to print, and your text, spreadsheet, and charts come together to create a powerful marketing plan. The new *Marketing Plan: A Handbook*, by Marian Burk Wood, supplements the in-text marketing plan material with an in-depth guide to what student marketers really need to know. A structured learning process leads to a complete and actionable marketing plan. Also included are timely, real-world examples that illustrate key points, sample marketing plans, and Internet resources. The Handbook and Marketing PlanPro software are available as value-pack items at a discounted price. Contact your local Pearson representative for more information.

Acknowledgments

Without excellent students and exciting and productive colleagues, no instructor or author can stay vibrant and connected. I wish to thank the following colleagues at other schools who reviewed this edition:

- Lilly Buchwitz, Brock University
- Sheldon Deitcher, McGill University
- Bill Lucas, Mohawk College
- John Milne, York University
- Doug Olsen, University of Alberta
- Charles Royce, McGill University
- David Smith, Lakehead University

This book is truly a team effort rather than the product of any single person's work. I first wish to thank Mr. Philip Connell, who worked diligently on this edition and provided many insightful Canadian examples. I also wish to thank the entire Pearson team who worked so hard to make this book a success: Paul Donnelly, Laura Forbes, Michael Young, Cheryl Jackson, and Andrea Falkenberg. I am grateful for their hard work, patience, efficiency, and good humour. My overriding debt continues to be to my husband, Paul, who provides me with the love, time, support, and inspiration needed to prepare this edition. I also wish to thank my daughter, Krista, a former business student and marketing practitioner, who critiques my work with a user's vigilant eye.

Peggy H. Cunningham
Marie Shantz Teaching Associate Professor of Marketing
Queen's School of Business Kingston, Ontario

A Great Way to Learn and Instruct Online

The Pearson Education Canada Companion Website is easy to navigate and is organized to correspond to the chapters in this textbook. Whether you are a student in the classroom or a distance learner you will discover helpful resources for in-depth study and research that empower you in your quest for greater knowledge and maximize your potential for success in the course.

Companion
Website

[www.pearsoned.ca/kotler]

Enter

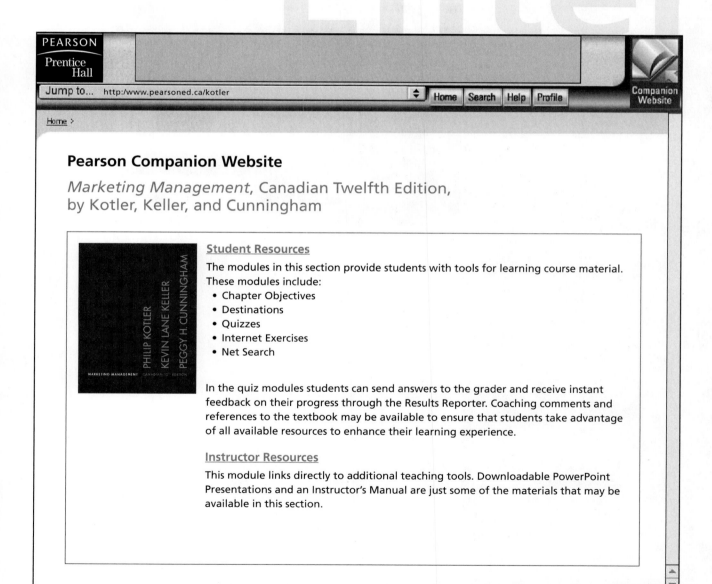

PEARSON
Prentice
Hall

Companion
Website

Jump to... http:/www.pearsoned.ca/kotler ▲▼ Home | Search | Help | Profile

Home >

Pearson Companion Website

Marketing Management, Canadian Twelfth Edition,
by Kotler, Keller, and Cunningham

Student Resources

The modules in this section provide students with tools for learning course material. These modules include:

- Chapter Objectives
- Destinations
- Quizzes
- Internet Exercises
- Net Search

In the quiz modules students can send answers to the grader and receive instant feedback on their progress through the Results Reporter. Coaching comments and references to the textbook may be available to ensure that students take advantage of all available resources to enhance their learning experience.

Instructor Resources

This module links directly to additional teaching tools. Downloadable PowerPoint Presentations and an Instructor's Manual are just some of the materials that may be available in this section.

1

UNDERSTANDING MARKETING MANAGEMENT

IN THIS CHAPTER, WE WILL ADDRESS THE FOLLOWING QUESTIONS:

- Why is marketing important?

- What is the scope of marketing?

- What are some fundamental marketing concepts?

- How has marketing management changed?

- What are the tasks necessary for successful marketing management?

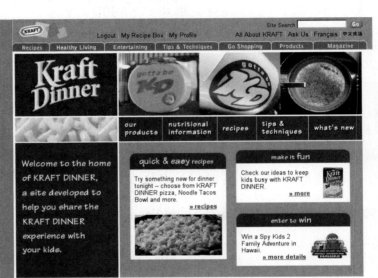

1

CHAPTER 1

Defining Marketing for the Twenty-First Century

PROFILE: CANADIAN MARKETING EXCELLENCE

Marketing is everywhere. Formally or informally, people and organizations engage in a vast number of activities that could be called marketing. Good marketing has become an increasingly vital ingredient for business success. No firm understands this better than Kraft Canada Inc.—a firm that is on the forefront when it comes to using customer information to provide solutions to consumers' meal problems. It's done this so well that *Marketing Magazine* included Kraft in its annual top-ten list of "Marketers that Mattered."

Kraft won this praise because of its new focus on developing personal relationships with Canadian consumers—a philosophy that is at the very heart of marketing. To build better consumer relationships, Kraft had to work to better understand the dilemmas busy working families face each and every day in preparing school lunches, family meals, and special occasion dinners. And Kraft wants to partner with its consumers to find solutions to these problems. Under its new customer relationship marketing (CRM) initiatives, Kraft is increasingly becoming a service provider that helps consumers shop more efficiently, prepare meals on the run with simple ingredients, and impress guests with that special dinner—even giving them advice on the wine to buy. Providing food solutions is at the heart of its strategy—"Family. Food. Simple." While Kraft's brands are incorporated into many of the solutions, other products and information provided are often beyond the Kraft brand portfolio.

The effort began about five years ago when Kraft Canada employed both marketing insight and leading-edge technologies to better understand consumers and encourage their involvement and interaction with the company. Kraft knew that consumers had more and more product choices, but less and less time. Many Canadian food retailers produced their own store brands, and spoke directly to consumers with their own magazines and at their retail outlets. Thus, Kraft realized it had to take action and build its own database upon which to found strong relationships with consumers. Up to this time, Kraft, like other packaged goods manufacturers, had focused on building relationships with retail channel members and it had very little interaction with end-consumers.

Today, all this has changed. Consumers buy Kraft products like Shake 'n' Bake coating mix and Philadelphia cream cheese because they feel close to a company that has offered them no-fuss help in the kitchen and great ideas to amuse the kids at Halloween. Many have picked up the phone and talked to someone at Kraft. Customers feel that Kraft "listens to me" and "gets me." In other words, Kraft has developed relationships with consumers the likes of which have never before been experienced.

Acting on its new knowledge, Kraft uses integrated, permission-based communications to offer solutions to over two million Canadian households in targeted mailings—its *What's Cooking* magazine in English Canada (*Qu'est-ce qui mijote* in French Canada) is the largest circulating magazine in Canada. Customers are contacted through its weekly opt-in e-mail program, which was recently selected by Forrester Research as the best in North America. Kraft has also redesigned its Web site (www.kraftcanada.com), to better meet consumers' key food needs, and it now consistently ranks as the number-one food site for Canadians. Thousands of Canadians also call Kraft's 1-800 help line seeking suggestions and cooking tips. Kraft has partnered with Food TV to deliver simple food solutions through the popular food network as well as created a half-hour TV cooking show in Quebec that is the number one food show in the province.

Kraft's marketing efforts weren't just focused on external audiences, however. It also needed an internal marketing program. Managers of the new CRM organization had to convince brand managers that a "solutions" marketing approach could complement their traditional brand programs and communications. It has had to make the case to senior management that the investment in the CRM system would pay off. Finally, Kraft has had to communicate with key retail partners to illustrate the power of this customer-focused strategy to drive sales at the store level.

Sources: Peggy Cunningham interview with Gannon Jones, Customer Relationship Manager, Kraft Canada, May 5, 2002; Bernadette Johnson, "Kraft Connects the CRM Dots: Packaged Goods Kingpin Nears Completion of Long-Term DM Strategy," *Strategy: The Canadian Marketing Report*, January 28, 2002, p. D7; "Nine More Marketers That Mattered," *Marketing Magazine Online*, **www.marketingmag.ca**, February 11, 2002 (viewed February 11, 2002); and Lesley Young, "One Bite at a Time," *Marketing Magazine Online*, **www.marketingmag.ca**, November 5, 2001 (viewed November 5, 2001).

As evident in the Kraft Canada example, good marketing is no accident, but a result of careful planning and execution. Marketing practices are continually being refined and reformed in virtually all industries to increase the odds of success. But marketing excellence is rare and difficult to achieve. Marketing is both an "art" and a "science"—there is constant tension between the formulated side of marketing and the creative side. It is easier to learn the formulated side, which will occupy most of our attention in this book; but we will also describe how real creativity and passion operate in many companies. This book will help to improve your understanding of marketing and your ability to make the right marketing decisions. In this chapter, we lay the foundation for our study by reviewing a number of important marketing concepts, tools, frameworks, and issues.

The Importance of Marketing

Financial success often depends on marketing ability. Finance, operations, accounting, and other business functions will not really matter if there is not sufficient demand for products and services so the company can make a profit. There must be a top line for there to be a bottom line. Many companies have now created a chief marketing officer, or CMO, position to put marketing on a more equal footing with other C-level executives, such as the chief executive officer (CEO) and chief financial officer (CFO). For example, Alan Berdowski is the chief marketing officer of the Ontario Lottery and Gaming Corporation, Jamie McClelland is the chief marketing officer for E*Trade Canada, and Laurie Coots is the chief marketing officer of TBWA\Worldwide. Press releases from organizations of all kinds—from consumer goods makers to insurers and from nonprofit organizations to industrial product manufacturers—trumpet their latest marketing achievements and can be found on their Web sites. In the business press, countless articles are devoted to marketing strategies and tactics.

Marketing is tricky, however, and it has been the Achilles' heel of many formerly prosperous companies. Large, well-known businesses such as Nortel, Bombardier, Sears, Levi's, General Motors, Kodak, and Xerox have confronted newly empowered customers and new competitors, and have had to rethink their business models. Even market leaders such as Microsoft, Wal-Mart, Intel, and Nike recognize that they cannot afford to relax. Jack Welch, GE's brilliant former CEO, repeatedly warned his company: "Change or die." Small companies must also pay close attention to how they market themselves and their products.

But making the right decisions is not always easy. Marketing managers must make major decisions such as what features to design into a new product, what prices to offer customers, where to sell products, and how much to spend on advertising or sales. They must also make more detailed decisions such as the exact wording or colour for new packaging. (The "Marketing Memo: Marketers' Frequently Asked Questions" is a good checklist for the questions marketing managers ask, all of which we examine in this book.) The companies at greatest risk are those that fail to carefully monitor their customers and competitors and to continuously improve their value offerings. They take a short-term, sales-driven view of their business and ultimately, they fail to satisfy their stockholders, their employees, their suppliers, and their channel partners. Skillful marketing is a never-ending pursuit.

Marketing Memo

Marketers' Frequently Asked Questions

1. How can we spot and choose the right market segment(s)?
2. How can we differentiate our offerings?
3. How should we respond to customers who buy on price?
4. How can we compete against lower-cost, lower-price competitors?
5. How far can we go in customizing our offering for each customer?
6. How can we grow our business?
7. How can we build stronger brands?
8. How can we reduce the cost of customer acquisition?
9. How can we keep our customers loyal for longer?
10. How can we tell which customers are more important?
11. How can we measure the payback from advertising, sales promotion, and public relations?
12. How can we improve sales force productivity?
13. How can we establish multiple channels and yet manage channel conflict?
14. How can we get the other company departments to be more customer-oriented?

Big Rock Brewery

Big Rock Brewery of Calgary (www.bigrockbeer.com) was the inspiration of one man, Ed McNally, who began the brewery in 1984. He founded his business on one guiding principle: "The marketplace will take notice of a superior product backed by superior service." He soon learned, however, that even high-quality products don't sell themselves. In 2005, he decided he needed to totally revamp his product packaging and launching the company's first multimedia advertising campaign in years to get the attention of drinkers in Alberta's increasingly crowded premium beer market. Paradoxically, the company is looking back to its roots in order to move ahead. It is hoping to touch westerners' sense of nostalgia by using the best of the labels created two decades ago by local artist Dirk van Wyk. "They were great designs originally used to make our beer look very different," says Jessica Barrie, the brewery's marketing manager. Big Rock is running its largest ever multimedia campaign for its Grasshopper wheat ale. Promoting Grasshopper as "the local import," the ads play on the beer's German-style brewing roots. The campaign also includes scratch-and-win labels for a variety of prizes and Grasshopper merchandise.[1]

Many large companies get stuck in formulated marketing, poring over the latest Nielsen numbers, scanning market research reports, and trying to fine-tune dealer relations and advertising messages. These companies lack the creativity and passion of marketers in the first or entrepreneurial stage like Ed McNally. Their brand and product managers need to get out of the office, start living with their customers, and visualize new ways to add value to their customers' lives.

The Scope of Marketing

To prepare to be marketers, you need to understand what marketing is, how it works, what is marketed, and who does the marketing.

In designing its new labels, Big Rock went back to its roots.

What Is Marketing?

Marketing deals with identifying and meeting human and social needs. One of the shortest definitions of marketing is "meeting needs profitably." When eBay recognized that people were unable to locate some of the items they desired most and created an online auction clearing-house or when IKEA noticed that people want good furniture at a substantially lower price and created knock-down furniture, they demonstrated marketing savvy and turned a private or social need into a profitable business opportunity.

In 2004, the American Marketing Association, the largest professional and academic association in North America, developed a new definition of marketing: *Marketing is an organizational function and a set of processes for creating, communicating, and delivering value to customers and for managing customer relationships in ways that benefit the organization and its stakeholders.* This new definition reflects many of the recent changes in marketing practice and the relationship focus that is essential to marketing today. Instead of marketing *to* customers, marketers co-create value by working *with* customers. Furthermore, the new definition reflects the fact that marketing affects and must benefit more than just customers. It must consider the value it creates for all stakeholders including shareholders, company employees, members of the channel of distribution, and society as a whole.

We see **marketing management** as *the art and science of choosing target markets and getting, keeping, and growing customers through creating, delivering, and communicating superior customer and stakeholder value.*

Although the new definition of marketing has more of a social focus than the previous definition, we can still distinguish between a social and a managerial definition of marketing. A social definition shows the role marketing plays in society. One marketer said that marketing's role is to "deliver a higher standard of living." Here is a social definition that serves our purpose: *Marketing is a societal process by which individuals and groups obtain what they need and want through creating, offering, and freely exchanging products and services of value with others.*[2] For a managerial definition, marketing has often been described as "the art of selling products," but people are surprised when they hear that the most important part of marketing is not selling! Selling is only the tip of the marketing iceberg. Peter Drucker, a leading management theorist, puts it this way:

> There will always, one can assume, be a need for some selling. But the aim of marketing is to make selling superfluous. The aim of marketing is to know and understand the customer so well that the product or service fits him and sells itself. Ideally, marketing should result in a customer who is ready to buy. All that should be needed then is to make the product or service available.[3]

When Sony designed its Play Station, when Gillette launched its Mach III razor, and when Toyota introduced its Lexus automobile, these manufacturers were swamped with orders because they had designed the "right" product based on careful marketing homework.

Exchange and Transactions

A person can obtain a product in one of four ways. One can self-produce the product or service, as when one hunts, fishes, or gathers fruit. One can use force to get a product, as in a hold-up or burglary. One can beg, as happens when a homeless person asks for food. Or one can offer a product, a service, or money in exchange for something he or she desires.

Exchange, which is the core concept of marketing, is the process of obtaining a desired product from someone by offering something in return. For exchange potential to exist, five conditions must be satisfied:

1. There are at least two parties.
2. Each party has something that might be of value to the other party.
3. Each party is capable of communication and delivery.
4. Each party is free to accept or reject the exchange offer.
5. Each party believes it is appropriate or desirable to deal with the other party.

WE COULD HAVE LEFT WELL ENOUGH ALONE.

BUT THAT WOULD HARDLY BE VERY CHARACTERISTIC.

NOW WOULD IT?

Lexus ads, and its campaign slogan, "The Passionate Pursuit of Perfection," express the company's marketing philosophy: only the best is good enough for its customers.

Whether exchange actually takes place depends on whether the two parties can agree on terms that will leave them both better off (or at least not worse off) than before. Exchange is a value-creating process because it normally leaves both parties better off.

Two parties are engaged in exchange if they are negotiating—trying to arrive at mutually agreeable terms. When an agreement is reached, we say that a transaction takes place. A **transaction** is a trade of values between two or more parties: A gives X to B and receives Y in return. Smith sells Jones a television set and Jones pays $400 to Smith. This is a classic monetary transaction; but transactions do not require money as one of the traded values. A barter transaction involves trading goods or services for other goods or services, as when lawyer Jones writes a will for dentist Smith in return for a dental examination.

A transaction involves several dimensions: at least two things of value, agreed-upon conditions, a time of agreement, and a place of agreement. A legal system supports and enforces compliance on the part of the transactors. Without a law of contracts, people would approach transactions with some distrust, and everyone would lose.

A transaction differs from a transfer. In a **transfer**, A gives X to B but does not receive anything tangible in return. Gifts, subsidies, and charitable contributions are all transfers. Transfer behaviour can also be understood through the concept of exchange. Typically, the transferor expects to receive something in exchange for his or her gift—for example, gratitude or seeing changed behaviour in the recipient. Professional fund-raisers provide benefits to donors, such as thank-you notes, donor magazines, and invitations to events. Marketers have broadened the concept of marketing to include the study of transfer behaviour as well as transaction behaviour.

In the most generic sense, marketers seek to elicit a behavioural response from another party. A business firm wants a purchase, a political candidate wants a vote, a church wants an active member, and a social-action group wants the passionate adoption of some cause. Marketing consists of actions undertaken to elicit desired responses from a target audience.

To make successful exchanges, marketers analyze what each party expects from the transaction. Simple exchange situations can be mapped by showing the two actors and the wants and offerings flowing between them. Suppose John Deere, a worldwide leader in agricultural equipment, researches the benefits that a typical large-scale farm enterprise wants when it buys tractors, combines, planters, and sprayers. These benefits include high-quality equipment, a fair price, on-time delivery, good financing terms, and good parts and service. The items on this want list are not equally important and may vary from buyer to buyer. One of John Deere's tasks is to discover the relative importance of these different wants to the buyer.

John Deere also has a want list. It wants a good price for the equipment, on-time payment, and good word of mouth. If there is a sufficient match or overlap in the want lists, a basis for a transaction exists. John Deere's task is to formulate an offer that motivates the farm enterprise to buy John Deere equipment. The farm enterprise might in turn make a counteroffer. This process of negotiation leads to mutually acceptable terms or a decision not to transact.

What Is Marketed?

Marketing people are involved in marketing ten types of entities: goods, services, experiences, events, persons, places, properties, organizations, information, and ideas.

GOODS Physical goods constitute the bulk of most countries' production and marketing effort. For example, despite Canada's history as a resource-based economy, today primary industries (agriculture, fishing, forestry, and mining, petroleum) constitute only 6 percent of the gross domestic product (GDP).[4]

SERVICES As economies advance, a growing proportion of their activities is focused on the production of services. As of 2004, the services sector in Canada accounted for 69 percent of the GDP, while goods-producing industries accounted for 31 percent (of which manufacturing accounted for only 17 percent).[5] Service industries in Canada grow faster than both goods-producing industries and the economy as a whole. Service industries in Canada grew 4.0 percent between 1997 and 2003, while goods-producing industries only grew 3.0 percent and overall GDP grew 3.6 percent during that same period. Some service sectors, such as wholesale trade and information and cultural services, grew at rates between 6 percent and 7 percent.

EVENTS Marketers promote time-based events, such as major trade shows, artistic performances, and company anniversaries. Global sporting events such as the Olympics or World Cup are promoted aggressively to both companies and fans. There is a whole profession of meeting planners who work out the details of an event and make sure it comes off perfectly.

EXPERIENCES By orchestrating several services and goods, a firm can create, stage, and market experiences. Walt Disney World's Magic Kingdom represents experiential marketing: customers visit a fairy kingdom, a pirate ship, or a haunted house. So does the Hard Rock Café, where customers can enjoy a meal or see a band in a live concert. So is skiing at Whistler or visiting the Toronto Zoo. There is also a market for customized experiences, such as spending a week at a baseball camp playing with some retired baseball greats, or climbing Mount Everest.[6]

PERSONS Celebrity marketing is a major business. Today, every major film star has an agent, a personal manager, and ties to a public relations agency. Artists, musicians, CEOs, physicians, high-profile lawyers and financiers, and other professionals are also getting help from celebrity marketers.[7] Some people have done a masterful job of marketing themselves——think of Wayne Gretzky, Avril Lavigne, Sarah McLachlan, the Tragically Hip, and Oprah Winfrey. Management consultant Tom Peters, himself a master at self-branding, has advised each person to become a "brand."

PLACES Cities, provinces, regions, and whole nations compete actively to attract tourists, factories, company headquarters, and new residents.[8] Stratford, Ontario, had one asset: its association (through its name and situation on the Avon River) with the English birthplace of William Shakespeare. This became the basis for the annual Shakespeare festival that put Stratford on the tourist map. Similarly, Ireland has performed as an outstanding place marketer, having attracted over 500 companies to locate their plants in Ireland through programs operated by the Irish Development Board (for inward investment), the Irish Tourist Board, and the Irish Export Board. Place marketers include economic development specialists, real estate agents, commercial banks, local business associations, and advertising and public relations agencies.

PROPERTIES Properties are intangible rights of ownership of either real property (real estate) or financial property (stocks and bonds). Properties are bought and sold, and this requires marketing. Real estate agents work for property owners or sellers or buy residential or commercial real estate. Investment companies and banks are involved in marketing securities to both institutional and individual investors.

ORGANIZATIONS Organizations actively work to build a strong, favourable, and unique image in the minds of their target publics. Companies spend money on corporate identity ads. Philips, the Dutch electronics company, puts out ads with the tag line "Let's Make Things Better." In the United Kingdom, Tesco's "Every Little Bit Helps" marketing program has vaulted it to the top of the supermarket chains in that country. The Body Shop and the Royal Bank gain attention by promoting social causes. Universities, museums, performing arts organizations, and not-for-profits all use marketing to boost their public images and to compete for audiences and funds.

INFORMATION   Information can be produced and marketed as a product. This is essentially what schools and universities produce and distribute at a price to parents, students, and communities. Encyclopedias and most nonfiction books market information. Magazines such as *Road and Track* and *Byte* supply information about the car and computer worlds, respectively. The production, packaging, and distribution of information are one of our society's major industries.[9] Even companies that sell physical products attempt to add value through the use of information. For example, the CEO of Siemens Medical Systems, Tom McCausland, says "[our product] is not necessarily an X-ray or an MRI, but information. Our business is really health-care information technology, and our end product is really an electronic patient record: information on lab tests, pathology, and drugs as well as voice dictation."[10]

IDEAS   Every market offering includes a basic idea. Charles Revson of Revlon observed: "In the factory, we make cosmetics; in the store we sell hope." Products and services are platforms for delivering some idea or benefit. Social marketers are busy promoting such ideas as "Friends Don't Let Friends Drive Drunk" and "A Mind Is a Terrible Thing to Waste." Seasonal public health ads in Ontario urge people in the community to protect themselves against potential harmful viruses such as influenza in the winter months and West Nile in the summer months.

Who Markets?

MARKETERS AND PROSPECTS   A **marketer** is someone seeking a response (attention, a purchase, a vote, a donation) from another party, called the **prospect**. If two parties are seeking to sell something to each other, we call them both marketers.

Marketers are skilled in stimulating demand for a company's products, but this is too limited a view of the tasks they perform. Just as production and logistics professionals are responsible for

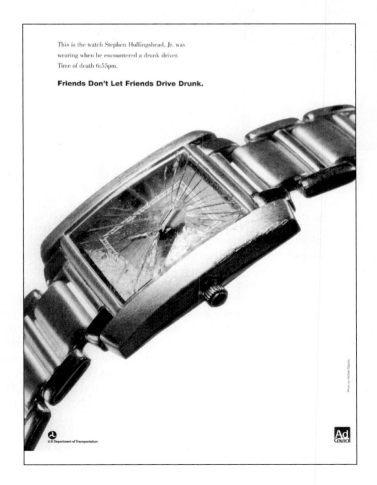

This is the watch Stephen Hollingshead, Jr. was wearing when he encountered a drunk driver.
Time of death 6:55pm.

Friends Don't Let Friends Drive Drunk.

U.S. Department of Transportation

Ad Council

An ad from the "Friends Don't Let Friends Drive Drunk" campaign promotes an idea, not a product.

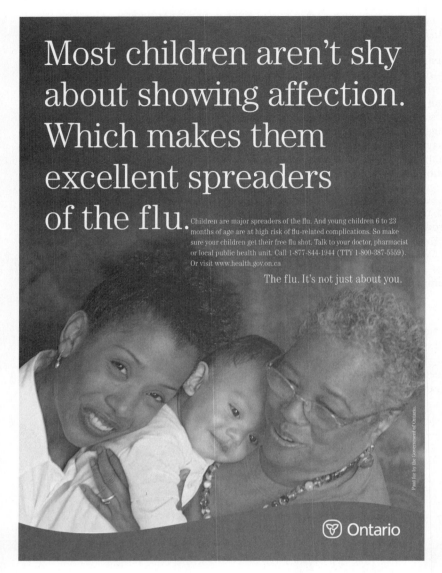

Organizations market ideas as well as products, as is done in this ad from the Government of Ontario.

supply management, marketers are responsible for demand management. Marketing managers seek to influence the level, timing, and composition of demand to meet the organization's objectives. Eight demand states are possible:

1. *Negative demand*—Consumers dislike the product and may even pay a price to avoid it.

2. *Nonexistent demand*—Consumers may be unaware or uninterested in the product.

3. *Latent demand*—Consumers may share a strong need that cannot be satisfied by an existing product.

4. *Declining demand*—Consumers begin to buy the product less frequently or not at all.

5. *Irregular demand*—Consumer purchases vary on a seasonal, monthly, weekly, daily, or even hourly basis.

6. *Full demand*—Consumers are adequately buying all products put into the marketplace.

7. *Overfull demand*—Too many consumers would like to buy the product than can be satisfied.

8. *Unwholesome demand*—Consumers may be attracted to products that have undesirable social consequences.

In each case, marketers must identify the underlying cause(s) of the demand state and then determine a plan for action to shift the demand to a more desired state.

MARKETS Traditionally, a "market" was a physical place where buyers and sellers gathered to buy and sell goods. Economists describe a market as a collection of buyers and sellers who transact over a particular product or product class (e.g., the housing market or grain market). Modern economies abound in such markets. Five basic markets and their connecting flows are shown in Figure 1.1. Manufacturers go to resource markets (raw-material markets, labour markets, money markets), buy resources and turn them into goods and services, and then sell finished products to intermediaries, who sell them to consumers. Consumers sell their labour and receive money with which they pay for goods and services. The government collects tax revenues to buy goods from resource, manufacturer, and intermediary markets and uses these goods and services to provide public services. Each nation's economy and the global economy consist of complex interacting sets of markets linked through exchange processes.

On the other hand, marketers often use the term *market* to cover various groupings of customers. They view the sellers as constituting the industry and the buyers as constituting the market. They talk about need markets (the diet-seeking market), product markets (the shoe market), demographic markets (the youth market), and geographic markets (the French market); or they extend the concept to cover other markets, such as voter markets, labour markets, and donor markets. Figure 1.2 shows the relationship between the industry and the market. Sellers and buyers are connected by four flows. The sellers send goods and services and communications (ads, direct mail) to the market; in return they receive money and information (attitudes, sales data). The inner loop shows an exchange of money for goods and services; the outer loop shows an exchange of information.

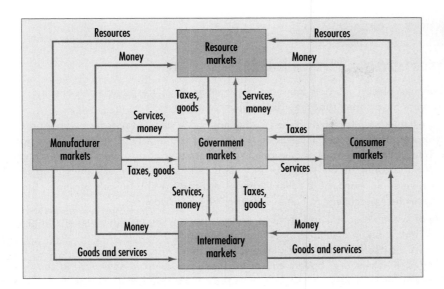

FIGURE 1.1

Structures of Flows in a
Modern Exchange Economy

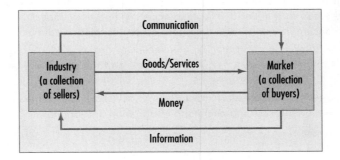

FIGURE 1.2

A Simple Marketing System

KEY CUSTOMER MARKETS   Consider the following key customer markets: consumer, business, global, and nonprofit.

Consumer Markets Companies selling mass consumer goods and services such as soft drinks, cosmetics, air travel, and athletic shoes and equipment spend a great deal of time trying to establish a superior brand image. Much of a brand's strength depends on developing a superior product and packaging, ensuring its availability, and backing it with engaging communications and reliable service. Complicating this task is the always-changing consumer market (see "Marketing Insight: New Consumer Capabilities").

Business Markets Companies selling business goods and services often face well-trained and well-informed professional buyers who are skilled in evaluating competitive offerings. Business buyers buy goods to enable themselves to make or resell a product to others at a profit. Business marketers must demonstrate how their products will help these buyers achieve higher revenue or lower costs. Advertising can play a role, but a stronger role may be played by the sales force, price, and the company's reputation for reliability and quality.

Global Markets Companies selling goods and services in the global marketplace face additional decisions and challenges. They must decide which countries to enter; how to enter each country (as an exporter, licenser, joint venture partner, contract manufacturer, or solo manufacturer); how to adapt their product and service features to each country; how to price their products in different countries; and how to adapt their communications to fit different cultures. These decisions must be made in the face of different requirements for buying, negotiating, owning, and disposing of property; different culture, language, and legal and political systems; and a currency that might fluctuate in value.

Nonprofit and Governmental Markets Companies selling their goods to nonprofit organizations such as churches, universities, charitable organizations, or government agencies need to price

New Consumer Capabilities

The digital revolution has placed a whole new set of capabilities in the hands of consumers and businesses. Consider what consumers have today that they didn't have yesterday:

- *A substantial increase in buying power.* Buyers today are only a click away from comparing competitor prices and product attributes. They can get answers on the Internet in a matter of seconds. They don't need to drive to stores, park, wait in line, and hold discussions with salespeople. Consumers can even name the price they want to pay for a hotel room, airline ticket, or mortgage, and see if there are any willing suppliers. Business buyers can run a reverse auction where sellers compete to capture the buyer's business. Buyers can join with others to aggregate their purchases to achieve deeper volume discounts.

- *A greater variety of available goods and services.* Today a person can order almost anything over the Internet: furniture (Ethan Allen), washing machines (Sears), management consulting ("Ernie"), medical advice (WebMD). Amazon.com advertises itself as the world's largest bookstore, with over 3 million books; no physical bookstore can match this. Furthermore, buyers can order these goods from anywhere in the world, which helps people living in countries with very limited local offerings to achieve great savings. It also means that buyers in countries with high prices can reduce their costs by ordering in countries with lower prices.

- *A great amount of information about practically anything.* People can read almost any newspaper in any language from anywhere in the world. They can access online encyclopedias, dictionaries, medical information, movie ratings, consumer reports, and countless other information sources.

- *A greater ease in interacting and placing and receiving orders.* Today's buyers can place orders from home, office, or mobile phone 24 hours a day, 7 days a week, and the orders will be delivered to their home or office quickly.

- *An ability to compare notes on products and services.* Today's customers can enter a chat room centred on some area of common interest and exchange information and opinions.

carefully because these organizations have limited purchasing power. Lower prices affect the features and quality that the seller can build into the offering. Much government purchasing calls for bids, with the lowest bid being favoured, in the absence of extenuating factors.

MARKETPLACES, MARKETSPACES, AND METAMARKETS   Today we can distinguish between a *marketplace* and *marketspace*. The marketplace is physical, as when you shop in a store; marketspace is digital, as when you shop on the Internet.[11]

Mohan Sawhney, a professor at the Kellogg School of Management, has proposed the concept of a *metamarket* to describe a cluster of complementary products and services that are closely related in the minds of consumers but are spread across a diverse set of industries. The automobile metamarket consists of automobile manufacturers, new car and used car dealers, financing companies, insurance companies, mechanics, spare-parts dealers, service shops, auto magazines, classified auto ads in newspapers, and auto sites on the Internet. In purchasing a car, a buyer will get involved in many parts of this metamarket, and this has created an opportunity for metamediaries to assist buyers to move seamlessly through these groups, although they are disconnected in physical space. One example is Edmund's (www.edmunds.com), a Web site where a car buyer can find the stated features and prices of different automobiles and easily click to other sites to search for the lowest-price dealer, for financing, for car accessories, and for used cars at bargain prices. Metamediaries can also serve other metamarkets such as the home ownership market, the parenting and baby-care market, and the wedding market.[12]

How Business and Marketing Are Changing

A recent book entitled *Beyond Disruption* praises companies such as Apple, Sony, and TAG Heuer for achieving exponential sales growth despite being in established but stagnant markets.[13] The explanation offered for these success stories was that these companies adopted a clear vision of the proper direction to take their brands and challenged marketing convention through product innovation,

Global marketing: Wall climbing on a Coke ad to attract attention (and customers) at the first China International Beverage Festival in Beijing in 2003.

advertising, or some other aspect of marketing. Another influential book entitled *Radical Marketing* spotlights companies such as Harley-Davidson, Virgin Atlantic Airways, and Boston Beer for adopting a different approach to marketing that focuses on stretching limited resources, staying in close contact with customers, and creating more satisfying solutions to customer needs. (See "Marketing Memo: The Ten Rules of Radical Marketing.")

We can say with some confidence that "the marketplace isn't what it used to be." It is radically different as a result of major, sometimes interlinking societal forces that have created new behaviours, new opportunities, and new challenges:

- *Changing technology.* The digital revolution has created an Information Age. The Industrial Age was characterized by mass production and mass consumption, stores stuffed with inventory, ads everywhere, and rampant discounting. The Information Age promises to lead to more accurate levels of production, more targeted communications, and more relevant pricing. Moreover, much of today's business is carried over electronic networks: intranet, extranets, and the Internet.

- *Globalization.* Technological advances in transportation, shipping, and communication have made it easier for companies to market in other countries and easier for consumers to buy products and services from marketers in other countries.

- *Deregulation.* Many countries have deregulated industries to create greater competition and growth opportunities. Bell Canada was a regulated, marketing-naïve telephone company until the 1970s, when the government began allowing other companies to sell telecommunications equipment. Bell plunged into the marketing waters and hired the best marketers it could find to help it compete. Companies in deregulated industries all find it necessary to build up marketing expertise.

Marketing Memo

The Ten Rules of Radical Marketing

In their book *Radical Marketing*, Sam Hill and Glenn Rifkin lay out a set of guidelines that can help other companies emulate the radical marketers:

1. *The CEO must own the marketing function.* CEOs of radical marketers never delegate marketing responsibility.

2. *The marketing department must start small and flat and stay small and flat.* CEOs of radical marketers must not allow layers of management to grow between them and the market.

3. *Get face-to-face with the people who matter most—the customers.* Radical marketers know the advantages of direct interaction with customers.

4. *Use market research cautiously.* Radical marketers prefer grassroots techniques.

5. *Hire only passionate missionaries, not marketers.* Radical marketers "don't have marketers, they have missionaries."

6. *Love and respect customers as individuals, not as numbers on a spreadsheet.* Radical marketers recognize that the core customers are responsible for the bulk of their companies' successes.

7. *Create a community of consumers.* Radical marketers "encourage their customers to think of themselves as a community, and of the brand as a unifier of that community."

8. *Rethink the marketing mix.* For example, radical marketers use "surgical strike advertising" characterized by short, targeted ad campaigns.

9. *Celebrate common sense and compete with larger competitors through fresh and different marketing ideas.* Radical marketers, for example, limit distribution in order to create loyalty and commitment among distributors and customers.

10. *Be true to the brand.* Radical marketers "are obsessive about brand integrity, and they are fixated on quality."

Source: Sam Hill and Glenn Rifkin, *Radical Marketing* (New York: HarperCollins, 1999), pp. 19–31.

- *Privatization.* Many countries have converted public companies to private ownership and management to increase their efficiency, such as Air Canada and British Telecom.

- *Customer empowerment.* Customers increasingly expect higher quality and service and some customization. They are more and more time-starved and want more convenience. They perceive fewer real product differences and show less brand loyalty. They can obtain extensive product information from the Internet and other sources, which permits them to shop more intelligently. They are showing greater price sensitivity in their search for value.

- *Customization.* The company is able to produce individually differentiated goods whether ordered in person, on the phone, or online. By going online, companies essentially enable consumers to design their own goods. The company also has the capacity to interact with each customer personally, to *personalize* messages, services, and the relationship. For example, Roots Canada, based in Toronto, introduced customizable handbags in 2003 available at Roots stores and on its Web store. Customers can select the style and colour of the bag they want and have the bag embroidered with an initial. As a result of considerable success with the bags, Roots has expanded its customizable offerings to include jackets, accessories, and even sweatshirts.[14]

- *Heightened competition.* Brand manufacturers are facing intense competition from domestic and foreign brands, which is resulting in rising promotion costs and shrinking profit margins. They are being further buffeted by powerful retailers who command limited shelf space and are putting out their own store brands in competition with national brands.

- *Industry convergence.* Industry boundaries are blurring at an incredible rate as companies are recognizing that new opportunities lie at the intersection of two or more industries. Pharmaceutical companies, at one time essentially chemical companies, are now adding biogenetic research capacities in order to formulate new drugs, new cosmetics (cosmoneuticals) and new foods (nutriceuticals). Shiseido, the Japanese cosmetics firm, now markets a portfolio of dermatology drugs. Christmas 2003 saw the convergence of the computing and consumer electronics industries as the giants of the computer world such as Dell, Gateway, and Hewlett-Packard released a stream of entertainment devices—from MP3 players to plasma TVs and camcorders. The shift to digital technology, in which devices needed to play entertainment content are more and more like PCs, is fuelling this massive convergence.[15]

- *Retail transformation.* Small retailers are succumbing to the growing power of giant retailers and "category killers." Store-based retailers are facing growing competition from catalogue houses; direct-mail firms; newspaper, magazine, and TV direct-to-customer ads; home shopping TV; and e-commerce on the Internet. In response, entrepreneurial retailers are building entertainment into stores with coffee bars, lectures, demonstrations, and performances. They are marketing an "experience" rather than a product assortment.

Cosmoneuticals: An ad for dermatology drugs marketed by Shiseido, the Japanese cosmetics firm. The WH/SIS product line targets spots and freckles, and includes cleanser, lotion, emulsion, day/night whitening beauty essence, and medication to be taken orally. It is sold only in Japan, mainly in drugstores.

■   *Disintermediation.* Disintermediation is a popular buzzword, which means removing the intermediaries. The amazing success of early dot-coms such as AOL, Chapters.ca, Yahoo, eBay, TD Waterhouse, and dozens of others who created disintermediation in the delivery of products and services struck terror in the hearts of many established manufacturers and retailers as they started to sell products directly to customers rather than going through traditional intermediaries or retail channels. For example, travel-based Web sites, such as **www.travelocity.ca**, put the business of many traditional travel agencies in jeopardy. In response to disintermediation, many traditional companies engaged in *reintermediation* and became "brick-and-click," adding online services to their existing offerings. Many brick-and-click competitors became stronger contenders than the pure-click firms, since they had a larger pool of resources to work with and well-established brand names.

Company Orientations toward the Marketplace

What philosophy should guide a company's marketing efforts? What relative weights should be given to the interests of the organization, the customers, and society? Very often these interests conflict. The competing concepts under which organizations have conducted marketing activities include the production concept, product concept, selling concept, marketing concept, and holistic marketing concept.

The Production Concept

The production concept is one of the oldest concepts in business. The production concept holds that consumers will prefer products that are widely available and inexpensive. Managers of production-oriented businesses concentrate on achieving high production efficiency, low costs, and mass distribution. This orientation makes sense in developing countries such as China where the largest PC manu-facturer, Legend, and domestic appliances giant, Haier, take advantage of the country's huge inexpensive labour pool to dominate the market. It is also used when a company wants to expand the market.[16]

The Product Concept

The product concept holds that consumers will favour those products that offer the most quality, performance, or innovative features. Managers in these organizations focus on making superior products and improving them over time. However, these managers are sometimes caught up in a love affair with their products. They might commit the "better-mousetrap" fallacy, believing that a better mousetrap will lead people to beat a path to their door. A new or improved product will not necessarily be successful unless the product is priced, distributed, advertised, and sold properly.

The Selling Concept

The selling concept holds that consumers and businesses, if left alone, will ordinarily not buy enough of the organization's products. The organization must, therefore, undertake an aggressive selling and promotion effort. The selling concept is epitomized by the thinking of Sergio Zyman, Coca-Cola's former vice-president of marketing: The purpose of marketing is to sell more stuff to more people more often for more money in order to make more profit.[17]

The selling concept is practised most aggressively with unsought goods, goods that buyers normally do not think of buying, such as insurance, encyclopedias, and funeral plots. Most firms practise the selling concept when they have overcapacity. Their aim is to sell what they make rather than make what the market wants. However, marketing based on hard selling carries high risks. It assumes that customers who are coaxed into buying a product will like it; and that if they do not, they will not return it or bad-mouth it or complain to consumer organizations and will buy it again.

The Marketing Concept

The marketing concept emerged in the mid-1950s.[18] Instead of a product-centred, "make-and-sell" philosophy, we shifted to a customer-centred, "sense-and-respond" philosophy. Instead of "hunting," marketing is "gardening." The job is not to find the right customers for your product, but the right products for your customers. The marketing concept holds that the key to achieving organizational goals consists of the company being more effective than competitors in creating, delivering, and communicating superior customer value to its chosen target markets.

Theodore Levitt of Harvard drew a perceptive contrast between the selling and marketing concepts:

> Selling focuses on the needs of the seller; marketing on the needs of the buyer. Selling is preoccupied with the seller's need to convert his product into cash; marketing with the idea of satisfying the needs of the customer by means of the product and the whole cluster of things associated with creating, delivering and finally consuming it.[19]

Several scholars have found that companies who embrace the marketing concept achieve superior performance.[20] This was first demonstrated for companies practising a *reactive market orientation*—understanding and meeting customers' expressed needs. Some critics say this means companies develop only low-level innovations. Narver and his colleagues argue that high-level innovation is possible if the focus is on customers' latent needs. He calls this a *proactive marketing orientation*.[21] Companies such as 3M, HP, and Motorola have made a practice of researching or imagining latent needs through a "probe-and-learn" process. Companies that practise both a reactive and proactive marketing orientation are implementing a *total market orientation* and are likely to be the most successful.

Nestlé Canada

In response to consumer demand for more nut products, Nestlé Canada began to incorporate peanuts into more of its confectionary items. However, it had to rethink this move when it was swamped by protests from people (especially children) with peanut allergies. The concern arose because Nestlé made both nut and nut-free products in the same facilities, thus potentially contaminating the "nut-free" products. For Nestlé, it wasn't a case of not being market sensitive; it was a case of which market to pursue. Seeing the potential for harm to one audience, Nestlé went back to its original formulations and removed the peanuts.[22]

In the course of converting to a marketing orientation, a company faces three hurdles: organized resistance, slow learning, and fast forgetting. Some company departments (often manufacturing, finance, and R&D) believe a stronger marketing function threatens their power in the organization. Initially, the marketing function is seen as one of several equally important functions in a check-and-balance relationship. Marketers argue that their function is more important. A few enthusiasts go further and say marketing is the major function of the enterprise, for without customers there is no company. Enlightened marketers clarify the issue by putting the customer at the centre of the company. They argue for a customer orientation in which all functions work together to respond to, serve, and satisfy the customer.[23]

The Holistic Marketing Concept

A whole set of forces that appeared in the last decade call for new marketing and business practices. Companies have new capabilities that can transform the way they have been doing marketing (see "Marketing Insight: The Internet Advantage"). Companies need fresh thinking about how to operate and compete given a new marketing environment. Marketers in the twenty-first century are increasingly recognizing the need to have a more complete, cohesive approach that goes beyond traditional applications of the marketing concept. Look at Puma.

Puma

German athletic footwear company Puma has used holistic marketing to bring the company back from being a sentimental mainstay of the 1970s to one of the trendiest athletic shoes around. Puma uses multiple marketing approaches that work synergistically to set Puma apart as an edgy, trend-setting brand. Puma designs products with distinct customer groups in mind—such as snowboarders, car-racing fans, and yoga enthusiasts—using market research generated by its retailer partners. Puma also targets the armchair athlete—its two most popular models are the Mostro, a walking shoe with a nubbed wraparound sole, and the Speed Cat, a flat sneaker modelled on shoes worn by Formula One race car drivers. It generates word of mouth or "viral marketing" by clever promotions—from partnering with BMW/Mini, Terence Conran Design Shop, and the Jamaican Olympic team, or holding promotional events at sushi restaurants during the 2002 World Cup, to outfitting Serena Williams and showcasing products in well-chosen TV shows and movies. The approach is working: Puma's sales have increased for ten straight years from 1994 to 2004, tripling in total.[24]

Holistic marketing can be seen as the development, design, and implementation of marketing programs, processes, and activities that recognizes the breadth and interdependencies of their effects. Holistic marketing recognizes that "everything matters" with marketing—the consumer, employees, other companies, competition, as well as society as a whole—and that a broad, integrated perspective is often necessary. Marketers must attend to a host of different issues, and must be sure that decisions in any one area are consistent with decisions in other areas.

Holistic marketing is thus an approach to marketing that attempts to recognize and reconcile the scope and complexities of marketing activities. Figure 1.3 provides a schematic overview of four broad themes characterizing holistic marketing.

RELATIONSHIP MARKETING Increasingly, a key goal of marketing is to develop deep, enduring relationships with all people or organizations that could directly or indirectly affect the success of the firm's marketing activities. **Relationship marketing** has the aim of building mutually satisfying long-term relations with key parties—customers, suppliers, distributors, and other marketing partners—in order to earn and retain their business.[25] Relationship marketing builds strong economic, technical, and social ties among the parties.

Relationship marketing involves cultivating the right kind of relationships with the right constituent groups. Marketing must not only do customer relationship management (CRM) but also partner relationship management (PRM). Four key constituents for marketing are customers, employees, marketing partners (channels, suppliers, distributors, dealers, agencies), and members of the financial community (shareholders, investors, analysts).

The ultimate outcome of relationship marketing is the building of a unique company asset called a marketing network. A **marketing network** consists of the company and its supporting stake-

MARKETING INSIGHT

The Internet Advantage

The Internet gives today's companies a new set of capabilities:

- Companies can operate a powerful new information and sales channel, the Internet, with augmented geographical reach to inform and promote their businesses and products worldwide. By establishing one or more Web sites, a company can list its products and services, its history, its business philosophy, its job opportunities, and other information of interest to visitors. Unlike the ads and brochures of the past, the Internet permits them to transmit an almost unlimited amount of information.

- Companies can collect fuller and richer information about markets, customers, prospects, and competitors. They can also conduct fresh marketing research using the Internet to arrange for focus groups, send out questionnaires, and gather primary data in several other ways.

- Companies can facilitate and speed up internal communication among their employees by using the Internet as a private intranet. Employees can query one another, seek advice, and download or upload needed information from and to the company's main computer.

- Companies can have two-way communications with customers and prospects, and more efficient transactions. The Internet makes it easy for individuals to e-mail companies and receive replies, and more companies today are developing extranets with suppliers and distributors for sending and receiving information, placing orders, and making payments more efficiently.

- Companies are now able to send ads, coupons, samples, and information to customers who have requested these items or have given the company permission to send them.

- Companies can customize offerings and services by using database information on the number of visitors to their Web sites and visit frequency.

- Companies can improve purchasing, recruiting, training, and internal and external communications. Companies can achieve substantial savings by using the Internet to compare sellers' prices, and to purchase materials at auction or by posting their own terms. Companies can recruit new employees. Many are also preparing Internet training products that can be downloaded to employees, dealers, and agents.

- Companies can improve logistics and operations for substantial cost savings while improving accuracy and service quality. The Internet provides a more accurate and faster way to send and receive information, orders, transactions, and payments between companies, their business partners, and their customers.

FIGURE 1.3

Holistic Marketing Dimensions

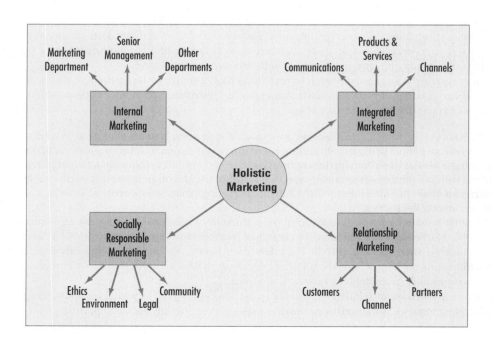

holders (customers, employees, suppliers, distributors, retailers, ad agencies, university scientists, and others) with whom it has built mutually profitable business relationships. Increasingly, competition is not between companies but between marketing networks, with the prize going to the company that has built the better network. The operating principle is simple: Build an effective network of relationships with key stakeholders, and profits will follow.[26]

Developing strong relationships requires understanding the capabilities and resources of different groups, as well as their needs, goals, and desires. A growing number of today's companies are now shaping separate offers, services, and messages to individual customers. These companies collect information on each customer's past transactions, demographics, psychographics, and media and distribution preferences. They hope to achieve profitable growth through capturing a larger share of each customer's expenditures by building high customer loyalty and focusing on customer lifetime value.

The ability of a company to deal with customers one at a time has become practical as a result of advances in factory customization, computers, the Internet, and database marketing software. BMW's technology now allows buyers to design their own model from 350 variations, 500 options, 90 exterior colours, and 170 trims. The company claims that 80 percent of the cars bought by individuals in Europe and up to 30 percent in the United States are built to order. British supermarket giant Tesco is outpacing its rival store, Sainsbury, by using its Clubcard data to personalize offers according to individual customer attributes.[27]

Yet the practice of one-to-one marketing is not for every company: The required investment in information collection, hardware, and software may exceed the payout. It works best for companies that normally collect a great deal of individual customer information, carry a lot of products that can be cross-sold, carry products that need periodic replacement or upgrading, and sell products of high value.

Rich, multifaceted relationships with key constituents create the foundation for a mutually beneficial arrangement for both parties. As described at the beginning of this chapter, Kraft Canada has invested considerably in the development of marketing relationships. One such initiative was Kraft Canada's partnership with Canadian film and television broadcaster/distributor Alliance Atlantis to launch the "Food in the Fast Lane" show on the Food Network in 2002.[28]

INTEGRATED MARKETING The marketer's task is to devise marketing activities and assemble fully integrated marketing programs to create, communicate, and deliver value for consumers. The marketing program consists of numerous decisions on which value-enhancing marketing activities to use. Marketing activities come in all forms. One traditional depiction of marketing activities is in terms of the marketing mix, which has been defined as the set of marketing tools the firm uses to pursue its marketing objectives.[29] McCarthy classified these tools into four broad groups that he called *the four Ps* of marketing: product, price, place, and promotion.[30]

The particular marketing variables under each P are shown in Figure 1.4. Marketing-mix decisions must be made for influencing the trade channels as well as the final consumers. Figure 1.5 shows the company preparing an offering mix of products, services, and prices, and utilizing a communications mix of sales promotion, advertising, sales force, public relations, direct mail, telemarketing, and interactive marketing to reach the trade channels and the target customers.

The firm can change its price, sales force size, and advertising expenditures in the short run. It can develop new products and modify its distribution channels only in the long run. Thus the firm typically makes fewer period-to-period marketing-mix changes in the short run than the number of marketing-mix decision variables might suggest.

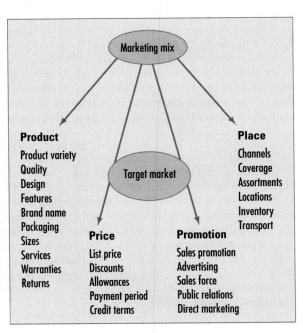

FIGURE 1.4

The Four P Components of the Marketing Mix

FIGURE 1.5

Marketing-Mix Strategy

The four Ps represent the sellers' view of the marketing tools available for influencing buyers. From a buyer's point of view, each marketing tool is designed to deliver a customer benefit. Robert Lauterborn suggested that the sellers' four Ps correspond to the customers' four Cs.[31]

Four Ps	Four Cs
Product	Customer solution
Price	Customer cost
Place	Convenience
Promotion	Communication

Winning companies will be those that can meet customer needs economically and conveniently and with effective communication.

Two key themes of integrated marketing are that (1) many different marketing activities are employed to communicate and deliver value and (2) all marketing activities are coordinated to maximize their joint effects. In other words, the design and implementation of any one marketing activity is done with all other activities in mind. Businesses must integrate their systems for demand management, resource management, and network management.

For example, an integrated communication strategy involves choosing communication options that reinforce and complement each other. A marketer might selectively employ television, radio, and print advertising, public relations and events, and PR and Web site communications so that each contributes on its own as well as improves the effectiveness of others. Because there was already a buzz for its remake of the cult 1974 film *The Texas Chainsaw Massacre*, New Line Cinema relied on a combination of both traditional TV ads and trailers, as well as interactive marketing via AOL's Instant Messenger and "bots"—robot agents—to help spread the word and get teens talking about the film. Their goal was to create a peer-to-peer communication (i.e., getting teens to do the marketing for them!).[32] Integrated channel strategy involves ensuring that direct (e.g., online sales) and indirect channels (e.g., retail sales) work together to maximize sales and brand equity.

INTERNAL MARKETING   Holistic marketing incorporates *internal marketing*, ensuring that everyone in the organization embraces appropriate marketing principles, especially senior management. Internal marketing is the task of hiring, training, and motivating able employees who want to serve customers well. Smart marketers recognize that marketing activities within the company can be as important—if not even more so—than marketing activities directed outside the company. It makes no sense to promise excellent service before the company's staff is ready to provide it.

Internal marketing must take place on two levels. At one level, the various marketing functions—sales force, advertising, customer service, product management, marketing research—must work together. Too often, the sales force thinks product managers set prices or sale quotas "too high," or the advertising director and a brand manager cannot agree on an advertising campaign. All these marketing functions must be coordinated from the customer's point of view. The following example highlights the coordination problem:

The marketing vice president of a major European airline wants to increase the airline's traffic share. His strategy is to build up customer satisfaction through providing better food, cleaner cabins, better-trained cabin crews, and lower fares; yet he has no authority in these matters. The catering department chooses food that keeps down food costs; the maintenance department uses cleaning services that keep down cleaning costs; the human resources department hires people without regard to whether they are naturally friendly; the finance department sets the fares. Because these departments generally take a cost or production point of view, the vice president of marketing is stymied in creating an integrated marketing mix.

At another level, marketing must be embraced by the other departments; they must also "think customer." Marketing is not a department so much as a company orientation. Marketing thinking must be pervasive throughout the company (see Table 1.1). Xerox goes so far as to include in every job description an explanation of how that job affects the customer. Xerox factory managers know that visits to the factory can help sell a potential customer if the factory is clean and efficient. Xerox accountants know that customer attitudes are affected by Xerox's billing accuracy and promptness in returning calls.

SOCIAL MARKETING   Holistic marketing incorporates *social marketing* and understanding broader concerns and the ethical, environmental, legal, and social context of marketing activities and programs. The cause-and-effects of marketing clearly extend beyond the company and the consumer to society as whole. Social responsibility also requires that marketers carefully consider the role that they are playing and could play in terms of social welfare.

Are companies that do an excellent job of satisfying consumer wants necessarily acting in the best long-run interests of consumers and society? Consider the following criticism:

> The fast-food hamburger industry offers tasty but unhealthy food. The hamburgers have a high fat content, and the restaurants promote fries and pies, two products high in starch and fat. The products are wrapped in convenient packaging, which leads to much waste. In satisfying consumer wants, these restaurants may be hurting consumer health and causing environmental problems.

Recognizing these criticisms, companies like McDonald's have added healthier items to their menu (e.g., salads) and introduced environmental initiatives (e.g., replacing polystyrene foam sandwich clamshells with paper wraps and lightweight recycled boxes). Recently McDonald's announced its largest environmental initiative to date. McDonald's Corp., which buys more than 1 billion kilograms of poultry, beef, and pork a year for its 30 000 restaurants worldwide, ordered its suppliers to eliminate the use of antibiotics also given to humans, specifically when those drugs are used to make chickens, pigs, and, less often, cattle, grow faster. "We saw lots of evidence that showed the declining rate of effectiveness of antibiotics in human medicine," said Bob Langert, McDonald's senior director of social responsibility. "We started to look at what we could do."[33]

Situations like this one call for a new term that enlarges the marketing concept. Among those suggested are "humanistic marketing" and "ecological marketing." We propose calling it the societal marketing concept. The *societal marketing concept* holds that the organization's task is to determine the needs, wants, and interests of target markets and to deliver the desired satisfactions more effectively and efficiently than competitors in a way that preserves or enhances the consumer's and the society's well-being.

The societal marketing concept calls upon marketers to build social and ethical considerations into their marketing practices. They must balance and juggle the often-conflicting criteria of company profits, consumer want satisfaction, and public interest. Table 1.2 displays some different types of corporate social initiatives, as illustrated with McDonald's.

Yet a number of companies—including the Body Shop, Ben & Jerry's, Loblaws, and Patagonia—have achieved notable sales and profit gains by adopting and practising a form of the societal marketing concept called *cause-related marketing*. Pringle and Thompson define this as activity by which a company with an image, product, or service to market builds a relationship or partnership with a "cause," or a number of "causes," for mutual benefit."[34]

Companies see cause-related marketing as an opportunity to enhance their corporate reputation, raise brand awareness, increase customer loyalty, build sales, and increase press coverage. They believe that customers will increasingly look for signs of good corporate citizenship that go beyond supplying rational and emotional benefits. Consider the Canadian Imperial Bank of Commerce.

| TABLE 1.1 | ASSESSING WHICH COMPANY DEPARTMENTS ARE CUSTOMER-MINDED |

R&D

- They spend time meeting customers and listening to their problems.
- They welcome the involvement of marketing, manufacturing, and other departments to each new project.
- They benchmark competitors' products and seek "best of class" solutions.
- They solicit customer reactions and suggestions as the project progresses.
- They continuously improve and refine the product on the basis of market feedback.

Purchasing

- They proactively search for the best suppliers.
- They build long-term relations with fewer but more reliable high-quality suppliers.
- They don't compromise quality for price savings.

Manufacturing

- They invite customers to visit and tour their plants.
- They visit customer plants.
- They willingly work overtime to meet promised delivery schedules.
- They continuously search for ways to produce goods faster and/or at lower cost.
- They continuously improve product quality, aiming for zero defects.
- They meet customer requirements for "customization" where possible.

Marketing

- They study customer needs and wants in well-defined market segments.
- They allocate marketing effort in relation to the long-run profit potential of the targeted segments.
- They develop winning offers for each target segment.
- They measure company image and customer satisfaction on a continuous basis.
- They continuously gather and evaluate ideas for new products, product improvements, and services.

- They urge all company departments and employees to be customer-centred.

Sales

- They have specialized knowledge of the customer's industry.
- They strive to give the customer "the best solution."
- They make only promises that they can keep.
- They feed back customers' needs and ideas to those in charge of product development.
- They serve the same customers for a long period of time.

Logistics

- They set a high standard for service delivery time and meet this standard consistently.
- They operate a knowledgeable and friendly customer service department that can answer questions, handle complaints, and resolve problems in a satisfactory and timely manner.

Accounting

- They prepare periodic "profitability" reports by product, market segment, geographic areas (regions, sales territories), order sizes, channels, and individual customers.
- They prepare invoices tailored to customer needs and answer customer queries courteously and quickly.

Finance

- They understand and support marketing expenditures (e.g., image advertising) that produce long-term customer preference and loyalty.
- They tailor the financial package to the customers' financial requirements.
- They make quick decisions on customer creditworthiness.

Public Relations

- They send out favourable news about the company and "damage control" unfavourable news.
- They act as an internal customer and public advocate for better company policies and practices.

Source: Philip Kotler, *Kotler on Marketing* (New York: The Free Press, 1999), pp. 21–22.

TABLE 1.2	CORPORATE SOCIAL INITIATIVES	
Type	**Description**	**Example**
Corporate social marketing	Supporting behaviour change campaigns	McDonald's promotion of a childhood immunization campaign in the U.S.
Cause marketing	Promoting social issues through efforts such as sponsorships, licensing agreements, and advertising	McDonald's sponsorship of Forest (a gorilla) at Sydney's Zoo—a ten-year sponsorship commitment, aimed at preserving this endangered species
Cause-related marketing	Donating a percentage of revenues to a specific cause based on the revenue occurring during the announced period of support	McDonald's earmarking of $1 for Ronald McDonald Children's Charities from the sale of every Big Mac and pizza sold on McHappy Day
Corporate philanthropy	Making gifts of money, goods, or time to help nonprofit organizations, groups, or individuals	McDonald's contributions to Ronald McDonald House Charities
Corporate community involvement	Providing in-kind or volunteer services in the community	McDonald's catering meals for firefighters in the December 1997 bushfires in Australia
Socially responsible business practices	Adapting and conducting business practices that protect the environment, and human and animal rights	McDonald's requirement that suppliers increase the amount of living space for laying hens on factory farms

Source: Philip Kotler and Nancy Lee, *Corporate Social Responsibility* (Wiley, 2004).

CIBC Run for the Cure

CIBC Run for the Cure is an annual event that raises money for the Canadian Breast Cancer Foundation (in 2005, the event raised more than $21 million) through bringing together more than 170 000 people in 40 communities across Canada. CIBC has been the title sponsor since 1997. Since approximately 70 percent of CIBC's 37 000 employees are women, it is an event that garners significant support from within the organization. In response to such strong internal support, CIBC became convinced that its involvement could benefit the company and the cause.[35] Indeed, it was also a significant societal marketing opportunity for the organization.

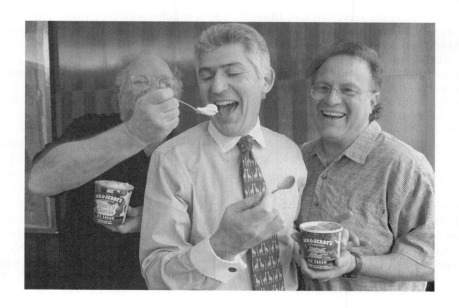

Ben & Jerry's co-founders Ben Cohen (left) and Jerry Greenfield (right) feed Unilever U.S. CEO Richard Goldstein in May 2000, when Ben & Jerry's was bought by Unilever. Cohen and Greenfield agreed to the deal after months of negotiations to ensure that the company's high standards and corporate social consciousness would be maintained.

CIBC has partnered with the Canadian Breast Cancer Foundation, successfully raising funds for this worthy cause while building its own standing in the communities in which it operates.

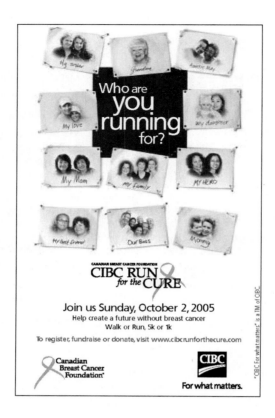

Fundamental Marketing Concepts, Trends, and Tasks

To understand the marketing function, we need to understand certain fundamental concepts and tasks, along with current trends.

Core Concepts

A core set of concepts creates a foundation for marketing management and a holistic marketing orientation.

NEEDS, WANTS, AND DEMANDS   The marketer must try to understand the target market's needs, wants, and demands. *Needs* are the basic human requirements. People need food, air, water, clothing, and shelter to survive. People also have strong needs for recreation, education, and entertainment. These needs become *wants* when they are directed to specific objects that might satisfy the need. A Canadian needs food but may want a hamburger, French fries, and a soft drink. A person in Mauritius needs food but may want a mango, rice, lentils, and beans. Wants are shaped by one's society. *Demands* are wants for specific products backed by an ability to pay. Many people want a Mercedes; only a few are able and willing to buy one. Companies must measure not only how many people want their product but also how many would actually be willing and able to buy it.

These distinctions shed light on the frequent criticism that "marketers create needs" or "marketers get people to buy things they don't want." Marketers do not create needs: Needs pre-exist marketers. Marketers, along with other societal factors, influence wants. Marketers might promote the idea that a Mercedes would satisfy a person's need for social status. They do not, however, create the need for social status.

Understanding customer needs and wants is not always simple. Some customers have needs of which they are not fully conscious, or they cannot articulate these needs, or they use words that require some interpretation. What does it mean when the customer asks for a "powerful" lawnmower, a "fast" lathe, an "attractive" bathing suit, or a "restful" hotel? Consider the customer who says he wants an "inexpensive car." The marketer must probe further. We can distinguish among five types of needs:

1. Stated needs (the customer wants an inexpensive car).

2. Real needs (the customer wants a car whose operating cost, not its initial price, is low).

3. Unstated needs (the customer expects good service from the dealer).

4. Delight needs (the customer would like the dealer to include an onboard navigation system).

5. Secret needs (the customer wants to be seen by friends as a savvy consumer).

Responding only to the stated need may short-change the customer. Many consumers do not know what they want in a product. Consumers did not know much about cellular phones when they were first introduced. Nokia and Ericsson fought to shape consumer perceptions of cellular phones. Consumers were in a learning mode and companies forged strategies to shape their wants. As stated by Carpenter, "Simply giving customers what they want isn't enough anymore—to gain an edge companies must help customers learn what they want."[36]

In the past, "responding to customer needs" meant studying customer needs and making a product that fit these needs on the average, but some of today's companies instead respond to each customer's individual needs. Dell Computer does not prepare a perfect computer for its target market. Rather, it provides product platforms on which each customer customizes the features he or she desires in the computer. This is a change from a "make-and-sell" philosophy to a philosophy of "sense and respond."

Positioning: "The First SUV with Anti-Rollover Technology." This Volvo ad focuses on the company's central benefit, safety.

TARGET MARKETS, POSITIONING, AND SEGMENTATION   A marketer can rarely satisfy everyone in a market. Not everyone likes the same cereal, hotel room, restaurant, automobile, university, or movie. Therefore, marketers start by dividing up the market into segments. They identify and profile distinct groups of buyers who might prefer or require varying product and services mixes by examining demographic, psychographic, and behavioural differences among buyers. The marketer then decides which segments present the greatest opportunity—which are its *target markets*. For each chosen target market, the firm develops a *market offering*. The offering is *positioned* in the minds of the target buyers as delivering some central benefit(s). For example, Volvo develops its cars for buyers to whom automobile safety is a major concern. Volvo, therefore, positions its car as the safest a customer can buy. Companies do best when they choose their target market(s) carefully and prepare tailored marketing programs.

OFFERINGS AND BRANDS   Companies address needs by putting forth a value proposition, a set of benefits they offer to customers to satisfy their needs. The intangible value proposition is made physical by an *offering*, which can be a combination of products, services, information, and experiences.

A *brand* is an offering from a known source. A brand name such as McDonald's carries many associations in the minds of people: hamburgers, fun, children, fast food, convenient, and Golden Arches. These associations make up the brand image. All companies strive to build brand strength—that is, a strong, favourable, and unique brand image.

VALUE AND SATISFACTION   The offering will be successful if it delivers value and satisfaction to the target buyer. The buyer chooses between different offerings on the basis of which is perceived to deliver the most value. *Value* reflects the perceived tangible and intangible benefits and costs to customers. Value can be seen as primarily a combination of quality, service, and price (qsp), called the customer value triad. Value increases with quality and service and decreases with price, although other factors can also play an important role.

Value is a central marketing concept. Marketing can be seen as the identification, creation, communication, delivery, and monitoring of customer value. *Satisfaction* reflects a person's comparative judgments resulting from a product's perceived performance (or outcome) in relation to his or her expectations. If the performance falls short of expectations, the customer is dissatisfied and disappointed. If the performance matches the expectations, the customer is satisfied. If the performance exceeds expectations, the customer is highly satisfied or delighted.

MARKETING CHANNELS   To reach a target market, the marketer uses three kinds of marketing channels. *Communication channels* deliver and receive messages from target buyers, and include newspapers, magazines, radio, television, mail, telephone, billboards, posters, flyers, CDs, audiotapes, and the Internet. Beyond these, communications are conveyed by facial expressions and clothing, the look of retail stores, and many other media. Marketers are increasingly adding dialogue channels (e-mail and toll-free numbers) to counterbalance the more normal monologue channels (such as ads).

The marketer uses *distribution channels* to display, sell, or deliver the physical product or service(s) to the buyer or user. They include distributors, wholesalers, retailers, and agents.

The marketer also uses *service channels* to carry out transactions with potential buyers. Service channels include warehouses, transportation companies, banks, and insurance companies that facilitate transactions. Marketers clearly face a design problem in choosing the best mix of communication, distribution, and service channels for their offerings.

SUPPLY CHAIN   Whereas marketing channels connect the marketer to the target buyers, the supply chain describes a longer channel stretching from raw materials to components to final products that are carried to final buyers. The supply chain for women's purses starts with hides, and moves through tanning operations, cutting operations, manufacturing, and the marketing channels bringing products to customers. The supply chain represents a value delivery system. Each company captures only a certain percentage of the total value generated by the supply chain. When a company acquires competitors or moves upstream or downstream, its aim is to capture a higher percentage of supply chain value.

COMPETITION   Competition includes all the actual and potential rival offerings and substitutes that a buyer might consider. Suppose a company like Hamilton, Ontario–based steel-maker Dofasco (**www.dofasco.ca**) is hoping to sell steel to a car manufacturer. (Figure 1.6 shows several levels of competitors.) Algoma, Dofasco, and Stelco are all large, integrated steel mills and thus are close rivals.

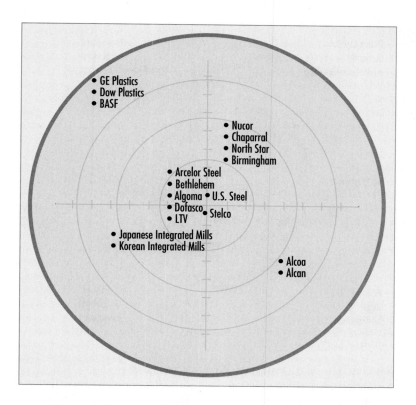

FIGURE 1.6

Dofasco Radar Screen

Source: Adapted from Adrian V. Slywotzky, *Value Migration* (Boston, MA: Harvard Business School Press, 1996), p. 99.

Together they produce three-fifths of Canada's steel. Clearly Dofasco would be thinking too narrowly of competition if it thought only of other integrated steel companies. Canada also has ten smaller mills that use electric arc furnaces to produce specialized items, such as carbon steel, bar and rod products, and specialty steels. However, since 90 percent of Canada's steel exports go to the United States, Dofasco cannot ignore its American rivals in this increasingly integrated market. Rivalry is further increased by the fact that automobile manufacturers are replacing steel with other materials like plastic, aluminum, magnesium, and carbon fibre. In fact, Dofasco is more likely to be hurt in the long run by substitutes than by its immediate rivals. Thus, it may have to closely watch the moves of Alcan (**www.alcan.com**), the aluminum manufacturer that has been investing in research to develop components and parts that will lighten the cars' weight.

MARKETING ENVIRONMENT   Competition represents only one force in the environment in which the marketer operates. The marketing environment consists of the task environment and the broad environment.

The *task environment* includes the immediate actors involved in producing, distributing, and promoting the offering. The main actors are the company, suppliers, distributors, dealers, and the target customers. Included in the supplier group are material suppliers and service suppliers such as marketing research agencies, advertising agencies, banking and insurance companies, transportation, and telecommunications companies. Included with distributors and dealers are agents, brokers, manufacturer representatives, and others who facilitate finding and selling to customers.

The *broad environment* consists of six components: demographic environment, economic environment, natural environment, technological environment, political-legal environment, and social-cultural environment. These environments contain forces that can have a major impact on the actors in the task environment. Market actors must pay close attention to the trends and developments in these environments and make timely adjustments to their marketing strategies.

MARKETING PLANNING   In practice, there is a logical process that marketing follows. The marketing planning process consists of analyzing marketing opportunities; selecting target markets; designing marketing strategies; developing marketing programs; and managing the marketing effort. Figure 1.7 presents a grand summary of the marketing process and the forces shaping the company's marketing strategy.

FIGURE 1.7

Factors Influencing Company
Marketing Strategy

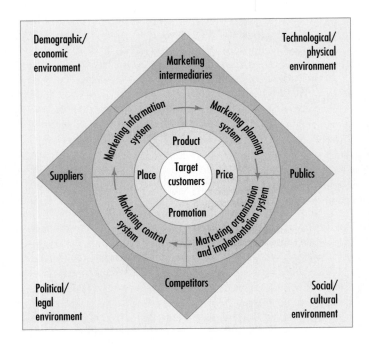

Shifts in Marketing Management

A number of important trends and forces are eliciting a new set of beliefs and practices on the part of business firms. Marketers are fundamentally rethinking their philosophies, concepts, and tools. Here are 14 major shifts in marketing management that smart companies have been making in the twenty-first century. These major themes will be examined throughout this book to help marketers and companies sail safely through the rough but promising waters ahead. Successful companies will be those who can keep their marketing changing with the changes in their marketplace—and marketspace.

FROM MARKETING DOES THE MARKETING TO EVERYONE DOES THE MARKETING
Companies generally establish a marketing department to be responsible for creating and delivering customer value. But as the late David Packard of Hewlett-Packard observed, "Marketing is far too important to leave to the marketing department." Companies now know that marketing is not done only by marketing, sales, and customer support personnel—every employee has an impact on the customer and must see the customer as the source of the company's prosperity. Consequently, companies are beginning to emphasize interdepartmental teamwork to manage key processes. More emphasis is also being placed on the smooth management of core business processes, such as new product realization, customer acquisition and retention, and order fulfillment.

FROM ORGANIZING BY PRODUCT UNITS TO ORGANIZING BY CUSTOMER SEGMENTS
Some companies are now switching from being solely product-centred with product managers and product divisions to manage them to being more customer-segment–centred. In late 1999, Royal Bank of Canada reorganized itself around customer segments, not products or territories. By studying these segments carefully, Royal Bank developed a number of new profit-generating products and services such as first mortgages and estate settlements. As a result, revenues increased by $1 billion over the next three years and the stock price rose 100 percent in the midst of a stagnant bear market.[37]

FROM MAKING EVERYTHING TO BUYING MORE GOODS AND SERVICES FROM OUTSIDE More companies are choosing to own brands rather than physical assets. Companies are also increasingly subcontracting activities to outsourcing firms. Their maxim: Outsource those activities that others can do cheaper and better, but retain core activities.

FROM USING MANY SUPPLIERS TO WORKING WITH FEWER SUPPLIERS IN A "PARTNERSHIP" Companies are deepening partnering arrangements with key suppliers and distributors. Such companies have shifted from thinking of intermediaries as customers to treating them as partners in delivering value to final customers.

FROM RELYING ON OLD MARKET POSITIONS TO UNCOVERING NEW ONES In highly competitive marketplaces, companies must always be moving forward with marketing programs, innovating products and services, and staying in touch with customer needs. Companies must always be seeking new advantages rather than just relying on their past strengths.

FROM EMPHASIZING TANGIBLE ASSETS TO EMPHASIZING INTANGIBLE ASSETS Companies are recognizing that much of their market value comes from intangible assets, particularly their brands, customer base, employees, distributor and supplier relations, and intellectual capital.

FROM BUILDING BRANDS THROUGH ADVERTISING TO BUILDING BRANDS THROUGH PERFORMANCE AND INTEGRATED COMMUNICATIONS Marketers are moving from an over-reliance on one communication tool such as advertising or sales force to blending several tools to deliver a consistent brand image to customers at every brand contact.

FROM ATTRACTING CUSTOMERS THROUGH STORES AND SALESPEOPLE TO MAKING PRODUCTS AVAILABLE ONLINE Consumers can access pictures of products, read the specs, shop among online vendors for the best prices and terms, and click to order and pay. Business-to-business purchasing is growing fast on the Internet. Personal selling can increasingly be conducted electronically, with buyer and seller seeing each other on their computer screens in real time.

FROM SELLING TO EVERYONE TO TRYING TO BE THE BEST FIRM SERVING WELL-DEFINED TARGET MARKETS Target marketing is being facilitated by the proliferation of special-interest magazines, TV channels, and Internet newsgroups. Companies are also making substantial investments in information systems as the key to lowering costs and gaining a competitive edge. They are assembling information about individual customers' purchases, preferences, demographics, and profitability.

FROM FOCUSING ON PROFITABLE TRANSACTIONS TO FOCUSING ON CUSTOMER LIFETIME VALUE Companies normally would aim to make a profit on each transaction. Now companies are focusing on their most profitable customers, products, and channels. They estimate individual customer lifetime value and design market offerings and prices to make a profit over the customer's lifetime. Companies now are placing much more emphasis on customer retention. Attracting a new customer may cost five times as much as doing a good job to retain existing customers.

FROM A FOCUS ON GAINING MARKET SHARE TO A FOCUS ON BUILDING CUSTOMER SHARE A bank aims to increase its share of the customer's wallet; the supermarket aims to capture a larger share of the customer's "stomach." Companies build customer share by offering a larger variety of goods to existing customers. They train their employees in cross-selling and up-selling.

FROM BEING LOCAL TO BEING "GLOCAL"—BOTH GLOBAL AND LOCAL Firms are adopting a combination of centralization and decentralization to better balance local adaptation and global standardization. The goal is to encourage more initiative and "intrepreneurship" at the local level, while preserving the necessary global guidelines and standards.[38]

FROM FOCUSING ON THE FINANCIAL SCORECARD TO FOCUSING ON THE MARKETING SCORECARD Top management is going beyond sales revenue alone to examine the marketing scorecard to interpret what is happening to market share, customer loss rate, customer satisfaction, product quality, and other measures. They know that changes in marketing indicators predict changes in financial results.

FROM FOCUSING ON SHAREHOLDERS TO FOCUSING ON STAKEHOLDERS Top management respects the importance of creating co-prosperity among all business partners and customers. These managers develop policies and strategies to balance the returns to all the key stakeholders.

Marketing Management Tasks

These core concepts and others provide the input for a set of tasks that make up successful marketing management. We'll use the following situation to illustrate these tasks in the context of the plan of the book.

Zeus, Inc. (name disguised) operates in several industries, including chemicals, cameras, and film. The company is organized into SBUs. Corporate management is considering what to do with its Atlas camera division. At present, Atlas produces a range of 35 mm and digital cameras. The market for cameras is intensely competitive. Although Zeus has a sizable market share and is producing much revenue for the company, the 35 mm market itself is growing very slowly and its market share is slipping. In the faster-growing digital camera segment, Zeus is facing strong competition and has been slow to gain sales. Zeus's corporate management wants Atlas's marketing group to produce a strong turnaround plan for the division. Marketing management has to come up with a convincing marketing plan, sell corporate management on the plan, and then implement and control it.

DEVELOPING MARKETING STRATEGIES AND PLANS The first task facing Atlas is to identify its potential long-run opportunities given its market experience and core competencies (see Chapter 2). Atlas can design its cameras with better features. It can also consider making a line of video cameras, or it can use its core competency in optics to design a line of binoculars and telescopes. Whichever direction it chooses, it must develop concrete marketing plans that specify the marketing strategy and tactics going forward.

CONNECTING WITH CUSTOMERS Atlas must consider how to best create value for its chosen target markets and develop strong, profitable, long-term relationships with customers (see Chapter 3). To do so, Atlas needs to understand consumer markets (see Chapter 4). How many households plan to buy cameras? Who buys and why do they buy? What are they looking for in the way of features and prices? Where do they shop? What are their images of different brands? How does the digital segment differ from the 35 mm segment? Atlas also sells cameras to business markets, including large corporations, professional firms, retailers, and government agencies (see Chapter 5). Purchasing agents or buying committees make the decisions. Atlas needs to gain a full understanding of how organizational buyers buy. It needs a sales force that is well trained in presenting product benefits.

Atlas will not want to market to all possible customers. Modern marketing practice calls for dividing the market into major market segments, evaluating each segment, and targeting those market segments that the company can best serve (see Chapter 6).

BUILDING STRONG BRANDS Atlas must understand the strengths and weaknesses of the Zeus brand with customers (see Chapter 7). Is it so strongly associated with certain technologies that it could not be used to brand new products in related categories? Is its 35 mm film heritage a detriment in the digital camera market? Suppose Atlas decides to focus on the consumer market and develop a positioning strategy (see Chapter 8). Should Atlas position its cameras as the "Cadillac" brand, offering superior cameras at a premium price with excellent service and strong advertising? Should it build a simple, low-price camera aimed at more price-conscious consumers? Should it develop a medium-quality, medium-price camera? After launch the product's strategy will need modification at the different stages in the product life cycle: introduction, growth, maturity, and decline. Furthermore, strategy choice will depend on whether the firm is a market leader, challenger, follower, or nicher. Atlas must also pay close attention to competitors (see Chapter 9), anticipating its competitors' moves and knowing how to react quickly and decisively. It may want to initiate some surprise moves, in which case it needs to anticipate how its competitors will respond.

SHAPING THE MARKET OFFERINGS At the heart of the marketing program is the product—the firm's tangible offering to the market, which includes the product quality, design, features, and packaging (see Chapter 10). As part of its product offering, Atlas may provide various services, such as leasing, delivery, repair, and training (see Chapter 11). Such support services can provide a competitive advantage in the global marketplace.

A critical marketing decision relates to price (see Chapter 12). Atlas has to decide on wholesale and retail prices, discounts, allowances, and credit terms. Its price should be commensurate with the offer's perceived value; otherwise, buyers will turn to competitors' products.

DELIVERING VALUE Atlas must also determine how to properly deliver the value embodied by these products and services to the target market. Channel activities include the various activities the company undertakes to make the product accessible and available to target customers (see Chapter 13). Atlas must identify, recruit, and link various marketing facilitators to supply its products and services efficiently to the target market. It must understand the various types of retailers, wholesalers, and physical-distribution firms and how they make their decisions (see Chapter 14).

COMMUNICATING VALUE Atlas must also adequately communicate the value embodied by its products and services to the target market. Marketing communications activities are the means by which firms attempt to inform, persuade, and remind consumers—directly or indirectly—about the brands that they sell. Atlas has to develop an integrated marketing communication program that maximizes the individual and collective contribution of all communication activities (see Chapter 15). Atlas has to set up mass communication programs consisting of advertising, sales promotion, events, and public relations (see Chapter 16). It also has to set up more personal communications in the form of direct and interactive marketing and must also hire, train, and motivate salespeople (see Chapter 17).

CAPTURING MARKETING INSIGHTS AND PERFORMANCE To understand what is happening inside and outside the company, Atlas needs a reliable marketing information system. Atlas will want to closely monitor its marketing environment. Atlas's microenvironment consists of all the players who affect the company's ability to produce and sell cameras—suppliers, marketing intermediaries, customers, and competitors. Its macroenvironment consists of demographic, economic, physical, technological, political-legal, and social-cultural forces that affect sales and profits (see Chapter 18).

Atlas also needs a dependable marketing research system. Marketing research is an indispensable marketing tool for assessing buyer wants and behaviour and actual and potential market size. An important part of gathering environmental information includes measuring market potential and forecasting future demand. To transform marketing strategy into marketing programs, marketing managers must make basic decisions on marketing expenditures, marketing activities, and marketing allocation.[39] How many dollars should support Atlas's two or three camera lines? Direct versus distributor sales? Direct-mail advertising versus trade-magazine advertising? East Coast markets versus West Coast markets? To make these allocations, marketing managers may use sales-response functions that show how sales and profits would be affected by the amount of money spent in each application (see Chapter 19).

CREATING SUCCESSFUL LONG-TERM GROWTH Atlas must also take a long-term view of its products and brands and how its profits should be grown. Based on its product positioning, it must initiate new-product development, testing, and launching (see Chapter 20). Strategy also will have to take into account changing global opportunities and challenges (see Chapter 21).

Finally, Atlas must organize its marketing resources and implement and control the marketing plan. The company must build a marketing organization that is capable of implementing the marketing plan (see Chapter 22). Because of surprises and disappointments that can occur as marketing plans are implemented, Atlas will need feedback and control.[40] Marketing evaluation and control processes are necessary to understand the efficiency and effectiveness of marketing activities and how both could be improved.

SUMMARY

1. From a managerial point of view, marketing is the process of planning and executing the conception, pricing, promotion, and distribution of ideas, goods, and services to create exchanges that satisfy individual and organizational goals. Marketing management is the art and science of choosing target markets and getting, keeping, and growing customers through creating, delivering, and communicating superior customer value.

2. Marketers are skilled at managing demand: They seek to influence the level, timing, and composition of demand. Marketers are involved in marketing many types of entities: goods, services, events, experiences, persons, places, properties, organizations, information, and ideas. They also operate in four different marketplaces: consumer, business, global, and nonprofit.

3. Businesses today face a number of challenges and opportunities, including globalization, the effects of advances in technology, and deregulation. They have responded by changing how they conduct marketing in very fundamental ways.

4. There are five competing concepts under which organizations can choose to conduct their business: the production concept, product concept, selling concept, marketing concept, and the holistic marketing concept. The first three are of limited use today.

5. The holistic marketing concept is based on the development, design, and implementation of marketing programs, processes, and activities that recognizes their breadth and interdependencies. Holistic marketing recognizes that "everything matters" with marketing and that a broad, integrated perspective is often necessary.

Four components of holistic marketing are relationship marketing, integrated marketing, internal marketing, and social marketing.

6. Marketing management has experienced a number of shifts in recent years as companies seek marketing excellence.

7. The set of tasks necessary for successful marketing management includes developing marketing strategies and plans, connecting with customers, building strong brands, shaping the market offerings, delivering and communicating value, capturing marketing insights and performance, and creating successful long-term growth.

APPLICATIONS

Marketing Debate: Does Marketing Create or Satisfy Needs?

Marketing has often been defined in terms of satisfying customers' needs and wants. Critics, however, maintain that marketing does much more than that and creates needs and wants that did not exist before. According to these critics, marketers encourage consumers to spend more money than they should on goods and services they really do not need.

Take a position: Marketing shapes consumer needs and wants versus Marketing merely reflects the needs and wants of consumers.

Marketing Discussion

Consider the broad shifts in marketing. Are there any themes that emerge in these shifts? Can they be related to the major societal forces? Which force contributed to which shift?

Marketing Spotlight: Coca-Cola

Coca-Cola is the most ubiquitous brand in history. Each day, people in 200 countries around the world drink some 1.2 billion 8-oz (237 mL) servings of the cola.

Marketing for the twenty-first century means leveraging the long-time marketing principles that work, while inventing new ways to stay relevant. Coca-Cola, which got its start in 1883, has successfully kept its brand relevant for over 100 years. Revenues in 2003 topped US$21 billion.

Coke's first president, Asa Candler, instituted many of the marketing tactics that are entrenched principles now. To gain new customers, he printed coupons offering free first tastes of the Coca-Cola drink. To build brand recognition, he gave Coca-Cola–logoed clocks, calendars, and weighing scales to pharmacists who sold the drink. He hired the company's first celebrity, Music Hall performer Hilda Clark, in the 1890s.

During the heyday of mass-market TV advertising, Coke was the master of the 30-second TV spot. Its legendary "I'd like to buy the world a Coke" and "Mean Joe Greene" ads were rated as two of the best ads ever by *Advertising Age*.

Coca-Cola also expanded overseas. During World War II, when the U.S. Army shipped Cokes to soldiers in Europe and Asia, Coke cemented its image as the "All-American beverage." But over time, Coke realized it would need a more local feel in each country. So, although it uses its signature red and white wave and lettering worldwide, the company uses different ad agencies in different countries in order to make the brand feel local. For example, the local versions of the "Mean Joe Greene" ad used sports figures famous in those regions, such as soccer stars. Similarly, ads for Coca-Cola in Spain show it as a mixer with wine, reflecting how consumers use the product in that country.

Coke also sells a wide range of different-flavoured soft drinks in different countries. Visitors to the company's museum in Atlanta, Georgia, can try these beverages—everything from cool watermelon (China), to an intensely bitter herbal soda (Italy), to a zingy ginger soda (South Africa). In 2004, Coke launched a beer-flavoured carbonated beverage in Japan.

Coca-Cola now gets two-thirds of its revenues from outside the United States. It's easier to name the countries where Coke is not: Myanmar, Cuba, and Syria. Everywhere else—including such tricky markets as Pakistan, Cambodia, Liberia, Zimbabwe, and Colombia—Coke is a beloved consumer staple. In fact, the brand is so strong and so entrenched that even the anti-American sentiments of 9/11 and after have not hurt sales. Coca-Cola's brand valuation actually increased from US$68.95 billion in August 2001 to US$70.45 billion in August 2003. (By comparison, rival Pepsi-Cola's brand value is a mere US$11.78 billion.) Coca-Cola remains the top global brand, achieving the top ranking in *Business Week*'s Global Brand Scorecard once again in 2003.

Despite its powerhouse status, Coke must continue to evolve its marketing. For example, the effectiveness of TV ads is declining due to media fragmentation and use of devices like TiVO that let viewers zap commercials. Ads that reached 70 percent of North Americans during prime time in the 1960s only reached about 15 percent in 2004. So Coke is diverting money previously spent on TV toward more experiential activities. For example, it's testing Coke Red Lounge gathering areas for teens in malls. The lounges offer exclusive music videos and video games and sell Coke drinks from a see-through Coke machine. In Britain, Coke's mycokemusic.com's Web site lets surfers legally download over 250 000 songs.

Chris Lowe, a Coke marketing executive, explained how the company stays on top: "You can never betray the core values of the brand, but you can work to make those values fresh and relevant. If you can't speak to people in these times, then you become an old icon." Lowe described the iterative steps of generating a fresh ad campaign: "There's the communication strategy that you want to put across. You test it with consumers for validity and resonance. Then you take that core meaning and make it come alive with advertising. Then you take it back to consumers to test it again."

The results of Coke's latest marketing shift aren't known yet, but in 2003 Coke's then-chairman Douglas Daft told investors that Coca-Cola Co. has "arguably the strongest and most pervasive marketing and distribution system in the world." And with Coke being the first soft drink drunk in outer space, even the sky may not be the limit.

DISCUSSION QUESTIONS

1. What have been the key success factors for Coca-Cola?

2. Where is Coca-Cola vulnerable? What should they watch out for?

3. What recommendations would you make to their senior marketing executives going forward? What should they be sure to do with their marketing?

Sources: Dean Faust, "Coke: Wooing the TiVo Generation," *Business Week*, March 1, 2004, p. 77; Paul Klebnikov, "Coke's Sinful World," *Forbes*, December 22, 2003, p. 86; "Coca-Cola Japan to Debut Beer-flavored Soda Next Month," *AsiaPulse News*, February 13, 2004; "How Coke Moulded Our View of Santa Claus to Fuel Winter Sales," *Marketing*, December 18, 2003; "The Top 100 Brands," *Business Week*, August 4, 2003; Fara Warner, "Chris Lowe Time to Get Real," *Fast Company* April 2003; **www.coca-cola.com**.

IN THIS CHAPTER, WE ADDRESS THE FOLLOWING QUESTIONS:

- How does marketing affect customer value?

- How is strategic planning carried out at different levels of the organization?

- What does a marketing plan include?

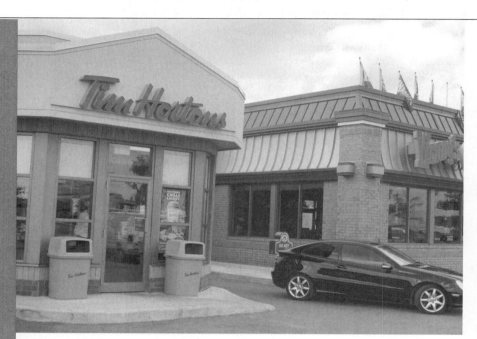

CHAPTER 2

Developing Marketing Strategies and Plans

PROFILE: CANADIAN MARKETING EXCELLENCE

It began as a one-store shop in Hamilton in 1964 founded by legendary hockey player Tim Horton. By 1967, there were three Tim Hortons stores open for business under the first successful franchisee, Ron Joyce (who currently serves as chairman emeritus of the TDL Group). Since then, Tim Hortons has grown to 2527 stores (2343 in Canada, 184 in the United States) and over US$800 million in revenue. With a 13-year cumulative average growth in sales of 7.1 percent in Canada and 17.5 percent in the United States, Tim Hortons is one very successful coffee and doughnut shop. How this local operation turned into an international franchise company and a major Canadian cultural icon, with a rapidly expanding U.S. presence, has everything to do with a very well-planned and carefully executed marketing strategy.

Tim Hortons' core strategy is the reason for its success. On its most basic level, the Tim Hortons' marketing team has created a brand that represents an idealized image of the Canadian national character: friendly, neighbourly, unpretentious, gently playful, frugal, trustworthy, and clean. The company measures everything it does against this list of brand values. "In everything we do, we've always focused on the concept of being that friendly, unpretentious, good neighbour you'd want living down the block from you," says Cathy Whelan Molloy, TDL's vice-president of brand advertising and merchandising. It also uses extensive customer and franchisee surveys, and other consumer research, to make sure its products, service, and communications fit the ideals. Furthermore, the organization has shown unwavering commitment to this vision and strategy for over 30 years.

Tim Hortons has executed this core strategy through many years of innovative marketing campaigns. It was one of the first Canadian organizations to tap into the benefits of sports marketing. Its first stores were painted blue and white to capitalize on the fame of Tim Horton himself—a Toronto Maple Leafs legend. It has developed a major presence in local communities with the creation of the nonprofit Tim Hortons Children's Foundation. The foundation sponsors an estimated 33 000 children in Timbit hockey leagues annually and operates five camps at which underprivileged Canadian and American children enjoy ten summer days and five winter days of activities.

All of the company's campaigns are designed to communicate a positive and believable truth about the Canadians who go to Tim Hortons. Effectively, "Tim Hortons dares to hold a mirror up to Canadians and challenges them to like what they see," says Philippe Garneau, a partner at Toronto's Garneau Würstlin Philp Brand Engineering. For example, in 2002, the company ran a television ad campaign called "True Stories." These were a series of vignettes based on hundreds of suggestions the company receives from its customers every year. The campaign featured Canadian sailors and students abroad trying to get their fix of Tim Hortons coffee. In 1976, Tim Hortons changed the face of doughnut consumption forever with the introduction of Timbits. It has been able to use this product in the company's marketing strategy to continue to build the playful, friendly nature of the brand. Of course, no discussion of Tim Hortons would be complete without one of the most successful annual promotional tools in Canadian history: the "Roll Up the Rim to Win" customer reward program that offers prizes ranging from coffee and doughnuts to luxury cars. In one of the best examples of how Tim Hortons used this program to build the brand, the company aired a TV spot featuring a Canadian citizen crossing over the U.S. border. When asked to prove his nationality to the immigration officer, the character simply rolls his Rs while speaking the phrase "roll up the rim to win."

These investments have paid off. Of those surveyed in the *Canadian Business* poll of Canada's best and worst brands, Tim Hortons was the clear winner, with 42 percent of those who responded to the poll (conducted by the Strategic Counsel and Spencer Francey Peters). What is more impressive is that 95 percent of the company's 2500-plus outlets are owned by franchisees, which may have independent ideas about what Tim Hortons is about. However, creating programs to ensure that the organization builds the brand and develops the business together has been crucial to the overall strategy. New franchisees must complete a seven-week training program before taking ownership of stores. Furthermore, the company has strict quality control standards. It routinely surveys and inspects stores, including checking everything from how fast and friendly the staff is to whether the trash in the parking lot has been cleared. But it is not through hierarchical, heavy-handed intervention that it creates strong brand commitment from the franchisees, it is through a well-developed internal strategy that works to ensure the success of each franchisee. For example, the "Roll Up the Rim to Win" promotion was created specifically to boost coffee sales in the warmer spring months. While franchisees end up giving away thousands of free coffees and doughnuts (in 2004, winners redeemed over 20 million food prizes), the promotion drives sales growth.

Consistently keeping customers coming back every day (sometimes two or three times a day) is Tim Hortons' challenge. In this intensely competitive market, it does not take much more than a stale doughnut or a cup of cold coffee to lose a customer. Yet consumers keep lining up. (Tim Hortons had a 68 percent share of the "most often" coffee purchases in the first quarter of 2004, while Starbucks and Second Cup had 7 percent and 3 percent respectively.) Part of this success is believed to stem from Tim Hortons' decision in the 1980s to drop the "Doughnuts" from its name and carve out a niche as a "break-time" restaurant. Now the company appeals to consumers who want to stop in for soup and sandwiches as well as those simply looking for a coffee.

Interestingly, one of the brands that Canadians seem to identify with most closely is actually owned by Americans. In 1995, Ron Joyce sold the company for US$450 million to Ohio-based Wendy's International Inc. In 2003, Tim Hortons sales represented nearly 20 percent of the fast-food giant's retail sales, and the Tim Hortons operations in both

Canada and the United States posted the best same-store sales growth in the entire organization.

Sources: John Gray, "King of the Cruller: Our Survey Crowns Tim Hortons the Best-Managed Brand in the Country," *Canadian Business Magazine Online*, **www.canadianbusiness.com**, June 6, 2004 (viewed July 12, 2004); "Before Tims Was Tims," abridged and excerpted from "Tales from Under the Rim: The Marketing of Tim Hortons" by Ron Buist, *Marketing Magazine Online*, **www.marketmag.ca**, September 22, 2003, (viewed July 12, 2004); Terry Poulton, "Long Live the Double Double," *Strategy Magazine Online*, **www.strategymag.com**, July 29, 2002, p. 19 (viewed July 12, 2004); Wendy's International Inc. Investor Presentation, June 2004, **www.wendys-invest.com** (viewed July 12, 2004); Tim Hortons Web site, **www.timhortons.com** (viewed July 12, 2004).

A key ingredient of the marketing management process is insightful, creative marketing strategies and plans that can guide marketing activities. Developing the right marketing strategy over time requires a blend of discipline and flexibility. Firms must stick to a strategy but must also find new ways to constantly improve it.[1] Marketing strategy also requires a clear understanding of how marketing works.[2]

Walk into a trendy boutique and you might see high-fashion T-shirts selling for $250. Go into an H&M clothing store and you can see a version of the same style for $25. Founded 55 years ago as a provincial Swedish clothing company, H&M—for Hennes and Mauritz—has morphed into a clothing colossus with 900 stores in 17 countries and an ambitious plan to expand by 100 stores a year. The reason H&M has reached this point while so many other stores—such as once-hot Italian retailer Benetton—have floundered is that the company has a clear mission and the creative marketing strategies and concrete plans with which to carry it out. "Our business concept is to give the customer unbeatable value by offering fashion and quality at the best price," is the H&M mission as expressed on the company's Web site. Nothing could sound simpler. Yet, fulfilling that mission requires a well-coordinated set of marketing activities. For instance, it takes H&M an average of three months to go from a designer's idea to a product on a store shelf, and that "time to market" falls to three weeks for "high-fashion" products. H&M is able to put products out quickly and inexpensively by:

- having few middlemen and owning no factories
- buying large volumes
- having extensive experience of the clothing industry
- having a great knowledge of which goods should be bought from which markets
- having efficient distribution systems
- being cost-conscious at every stage

This chapter begins by examining some of the strategic marketing implications involved in creating customer value. It then provides several perspectives on planning and describes how to draw up a formal marketing plan.

Marketing and Customer Value

Marketing involves satisfying consumers' needs and wants. The task of any business is to deliver customer value at a profit. In a hypercompetitive economy with increasingly rational buyers faced with abundant choices, a company can win only by fine-tuning the value delivery process and choosing, providing, and communicating superior value.

The Value Delivery Process

The traditional view of marketing is that the firm makes something and then sells it (Figure 2.1a). In this view, marketing takes place in the second half of the process. The company knows what to make and the market will buy enough units to produce profits. Companies that subscribe to this view have the best chance of succeeding in economies marked by goods shortages where consumers are not fussy about quality, features, or style—for example, with basic staple goods in developing markets.

The traditional view of the business process, however, will not work in economies where people face abundant choices. There, the "mass market" is actually splintering into numerous micro-markets, each with its own wants, perceptions, preferences, and buying criteria. The smart competitor must design and deliver offerings for well-defined target markets. This belief is at the core of the

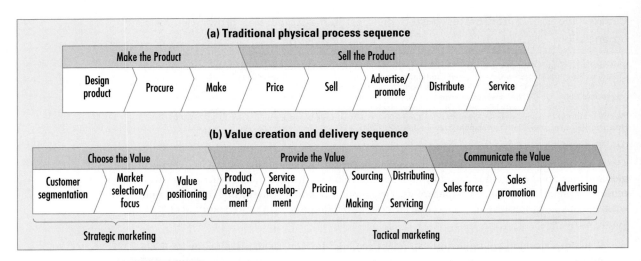

FIGURE 2.1

Two Views of the Delivery Process

Source: Michael J. Lanning and Edward G. Michaels, "A Business Is a Value Delivery System," McKinsey staff paper No. 41, June 1988. © McKinsey & Co., Inc.

new view of business processes, which places marketing at the beginning of planning. You can see this in action at your local mall. In the struggle to grow, retail chains are creating spin-offs that appeal to ever-smaller micro-markets:

Spin-offs

Gap Inc., with nearly 3000 stores in the United States, United Kingdom, Canada, France, and Japan, has successfully aimed at related segments of people seeking casual unisex clothing. Not only has it launched brand extensions like BabyGap, GapKids, and GapMaternity, it has also developed unique retail brands aimed at different but related segments of the market—Old Navy and Banana Republic. Old Navy first steamed into Canada in the summer of 2001. As one analyst noted, "Opening day resembled the chaos at an Eminem concert." To keep the brand distinct, the stores were more warehouse-like and featured cinema-style signage pointing out the bargains. Furthermore, stores were located in strip malls instead of shopping malls, which are the Gap's home turf.[3] Instead of emphasizing making and selling, all of these retailers see themselves as part of a value delivery process.

Figure 2.1(b) illustrates the value creation and delivery sequence. The process consists of three parts. The first phase, *choosing the value*, represents the "homework" marketing must do before any product exists. The marketing staff must segment the market, select the appropriate market target, and develop the offering's value positioning. The formula "segmentation, targeting, positioning" is the essence of strategic marketing. Once the business unit has chosen the value, the second phase is *providing the value*. Marketing must determine specific product features, prices, and distribution. The task in the third phase is *communicating the value* by utilizing the sales force, sales promotion, advertising, and other promotional tools to inform and promote the product. Each of these value phases has cost implications.

A pair of Nike shoes.

Nike

Critics of Nike often complain that its shoes cost almost nothing to make yet cost the consumer so much. True, the raw materials and manufacturing costs involved in the making of a sneaker are relatively cheap, but selling the product to the consumer is expensive. Materials, labour, shipping, equipment, import duties, and suppliers' costs generally total less than US$25 a pair. Compensating its sales team, its distributors, its administration, and its endorsers, as well as paying for advertising and R&D, adds US$15 or so to the total. Nike sells its product to retailers to make a profit of US$7. The retailer therefore pays roughly US$47 to put a pair of Nikes on the shelf. When the retailer's overhead (typically US$30 covering personnel, lease, and equipment) is factored in along with a US$10 profit, the shoe costs the consumer over US$80.

As Figure 2.1(b) shows, the value delivery process begins before there is a product and continues while it is being developed and after it becomes available. The Japanese have further refined this view with the following concepts:

- *Zero customer feedback time.* Customer feedback should be collected continuously after purchase to learn how to improve the product and its marketing.

- *Zero product-improvement time.* The company should evaluate all improvement ideas and introduce the most valued and feasible improvements as soon as possible.

- *Zero purchasing time.* The company should receive the required parts and supplies continuously through just-in-time arrangements with suppliers. By lowering its inventories, the company can reduce its costs.

- *Zero set-up time.* The company should be able to manufacture any of its products as soon as they are ordered, without facing high set-up time or costs.

- *Zero defects.* The products should be of high quality and free of flaws.

Nirmalya Kumar has put forth a "3 Vs" approach to marketing: (1) define the *value segment* or customers (and his or her needs); (2) define the *value proposition*; and (3) define the *value network* that will deliver the promised service.[4] Dartmouth's Frederick Webster views marketing in terms of (1) *value defining processes* (e.g., market research and company self-analysis), (2) *value developing processes* (e.g., new product development, sourcing strategy, and vendor selection), and (3) *value delivering processes* (e.g., advertising and managing distribution).[5]

The Value Chain

Michael Porter of Harvard has proposed the **value chain** as a tool for identifying ways to create more customer value (see Figure 2.2).[6] According to this model, every firm is a synthesis of activities performed to design, produce, market, deliver, and support its product. The value chain identifies nine strategically relevant activities that create value and cost in a specific business. These nine value-creating activities consist of five primary activities and four support activities.

The *primary activities* cover the sequence of bringing materials into the business (inbound logistics), converting them into final products (operations), shipping out final products (outbound

FIGURE 2.2

The Generic Value Chain

Source: Reprinted with the permission of the Free Press, an imprint of Simon & Schuster, from *Competitive Advantage: Creating and Sustaining Superior Performance*, by Michael E. Porter. Copyright © 1985 by Michael E. Porter.

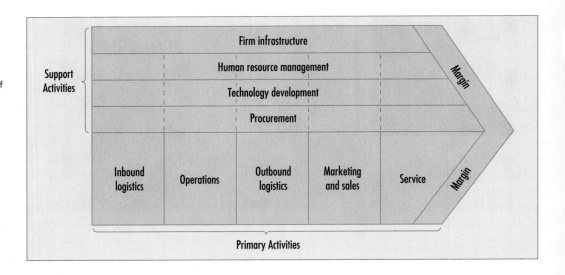

logistics), marketing them (marketing and sales), and servicing them (service). The *support activities*—procurement, technology development, human resource management, and firm infrastructure—are handled in certain specialized departments, as well as elsewhere. Several departments, for example, may do procurement and hiring. The firm's infrastructure covers the costs of general management, planning, finance, accounting, legal, and government affairs.

The firm's task is to examine its costs and performance in each value-creating activity and to look for ways to improve it. The firm should estimate its competitors' costs and performances as *benchmarks* against which to compare its own costs and performance. It should go further and study the "best of class" practices of the world's best companies.[7]

The firm's success depends not only on how well each department performs its work, but also on how well the various departmental activities are coordinated to conduct *core business processes*.[8] These core business processes include:

■ *The market sensing process.* All the activities involved in gathering market intelligence, disseminating it within the organization, and acting on the information.

■ *The new offering realization process.* All the activities involved in researching, developing, and launching new high-quality offerings quickly and within budget.

■ *The customer acquisition process.* All the activities involved in defining target markets and prospecting for new customers.

■ *The customer relationship management process.* All the activities involved in building deeper understanding, relationships, and offerings to individual customers.

■ *The fulfillment management process.* All the activities involved in receiving and approving orders, shipping the goods on time, and collecting payment.

Strong companies develop superior capabilities in managing and linking their core business processes. For example, Wal-Mart has superior strength in its stock replenishment process. As Wal-Mart stores sell their goods, sales information flows via computer not only to Wal-Mart's headquarters, but also to Wal-Mart's suppliers, who ship replacement merchandise to the stores almost at the rate it moves off the shelf.[9] The idea is to manage flows of goods, not stocks of goods. Wal-Mart has turned over this responsibility to its leading vendors in a system known as vendor-managed inventories (VMI).

Strong companies are also re-engineering the workflows and building cross-functional teams responsible for each process.[10] At Xerox, a Customer Operations Group links sales, shipping, installation, service, and billing so that these activities flow smoothly into one another. Winning companies are those that excel at managing core business processes through cross-functional teams. AT&T, Polaroid, and Motorola have reorganized their employees into cross-functional teams; cross-functional teams are also found in nonprofits and government organizations. U.S. drug store chain Rite Aid is using cross-functional teams to try to push its store from third to first place in the drug store hierarchy. The company has created teams to focus on sales and margin growth, operational

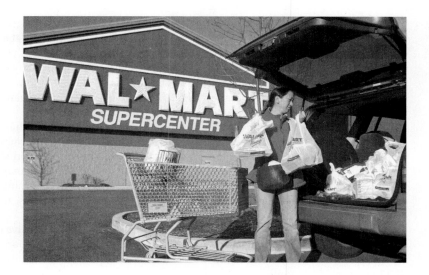

With Wal-Mart's superior stock replenishing process, replacement merchandise is shipped almost immediately.

excellence, market optimization, continued supply chain improvements, and continued cost control.[11]

To be successful, a firm also needs to look for competitive advantages beyond its own operations, into the value chains of suppliers, distributors, and customers. Many companies today have partnered with specific suppliers and distributors to create a superior **value-delivery network** (also called a **supply chain**).[12]

Canadian Tire

In late 2002, Canadian Tire entered into an agreement with NAPA Canada, a distributor of automotive replacement parts, to supply Canadian Tire stores with emergency parts and automotive products not normally kept in stock using parts-ordering and automated inventory technology. The purpose of the agreement is to allow Canadian Tire to continue growing its automotive product and service organization without adding the infrastructure and inventory costs associated with low-volume products. The agreement allows Canadian Tire to significantly enhance the services it offers automotive customers. Parts represented in this agreement make up approximately 15 percent of Canadian Tire's total automotive hard part sales.[13]

An agreement with NAPA Canada allows Canadian Tire to grow its automotive product and service organization without adding infrastructure and inventory costs associated with low-volume products.

Core Competencies

To carry out its core business processes, a company needs resources—labour power, materials, machines, information, and energy. Traditionally, companies owned and controlled most of the resources that entered their businesses, but this situation is changing. Many companies today outsource less critical resources if they can be obtained at better quality or lower cost. Frequently, outsourced resources include cleaning services, landscaping, and auto fleet management. Kodak even turned over the management of its data processing department to IBM.

The key, then, is to own and nurture the resources and competencies that make up the essence of the business. Nike, for example, does not manufacture its own shoes, because certain Asian manufacturers are more competent in this task; Nike nurtures its superiority in shoe design and shoe merchandising, its two core competencies. We can say that a **core competency** has three characteristics: (1) It is a source of competitive advantage in that it makes a significant contribution to perceived customer benefits, (2) it has applications in a wide variety of markets, and (3) it is difficult for competitors to imitate.[14]

Competitive advantage also accrues to companies that possess distinctive capabilities. Whereas core competencies tend to refer to areas of special technical and production expertise, *distinctive capabilities* tend to describe excellence in broader business processes. Consider the Hospital for Sick Children, located in Toronto.

Hospital for Sick Children

As Canada's most research-intensive hospital and the largest centre dedicated to improving children's health in the country, Sick Kids (to which it is commonly referred) is widely recognized as one of the best children's health-care and research institutions in the world. It is one of a handful of children's hospitals that is capable of both developing and administering treatments for children with very severe and complex medical problems, which otherwise would be untreatable. Its incredible reputation is based upon a set of unique and distinct capabilities that are unavailable anywhere else in the world, giving Sick Kids its competitive advantage in the realm of children's hospitals. Among these capabilities are the ability to attract and retain world-class faculty and research trainees; create state-of-the-art, high-quality, large-scale shared facilities; capitalize on intellectual property and technology commercialization opportunities; maximize opportunities for discovery and innovation; develop internationally competitive, cutting-edge infrastructure; and provide exceptional training and development opportunities. This set of capabilities has led to the development of many breakthrough treatments, helping Sick Kids maintain a level of public and private funding that is the envy of other hospitals.[15]

George Day sees market-driven organizations as excelling in three distinctive capabilities: market sensing, customer linking, and channel bonding.[16]

Competitive advantage ultimately derives from how well the company has fitted its core competencies and distinctive capabilities into tightly interlocking "activity systems." Competitors find it hard to imitate companies such as WestJet Airlines, Dell, or IKEA because they are unable to copy their activity systems.

A Holistic Marketing Orientation and Customer Value

A holistic marketing orientation can also provide insight into the process of capturing customer value. One conception of holistic marketing views it as "integrating the value exploration, value creation, and value delivery activities with the purpose of building long-term, mutually satisfying relationships and co-prosperity among key stakeholders."[17] According to this view, holistic marketers succeed by managing a superior value chain that delivers a high level of product quality, service, and speed. Holistic marketers achieve profitable growth by expanding customer share, building customer loyalty, and capturing customer lifetime value. Figure 2.3, the holistic marketing framework, shows how the interaction between relevant actors (customers, company, and collaborators) and value-based activities (value exploration, value creation, and value delivery) helps to create, maintain, and renew customer value.

The holistic marketing framework is designed to address three key management questions:

1. *Value exploration.* How can a company identify new value opportunities?

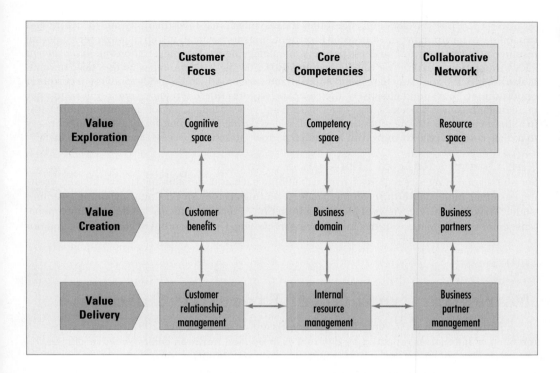

FIGURE 2.3

A Holistic Marketing Framework

Source: P. Kotler, D.C. Jain, and S. Maesincee, "Formulating a Market Renewal Strategy," in *Marketing Moves* (Part 1), Fig. 1-1 (Boston: Harvard Business School Press, 2002), p. 29.

2. *Value creation*. How can a company efficiently create more promising new value offerings?
3. *Value delivery*. How can a company use its capabilities and infrastructure to deliver the new value offerings more efficiently?

VALUE EXPLORATION Because value flows within and across markets that are themselves dynamic and competitive, companies need a well-defined strategy for value exploration. Developing such a strategy requires understanding the relationships and interactions among three spaces: (1) the customer's cognitive space; (2) the company's competence space; and (3) the collaborator's resource space. The customer's *cognitive space* reflects existing and latent needs and includes dimensions such as the need for participation, stability, freedom, and change.[18] The company's *competency space* can be described in terms of breadth (broad versus focused scope of business) and depth (physical versus knowledge-based capabilities). The collaborator's *resource space* involves horizontal partnerships, where companies choose partners based on their ability to exploit related market opportunities, and vertical partnerships, where companies choose partners based on their ability to serve their value creation.

VALUE CREATION To exploit a value opportunity, the company needs value-creation skills. Marketers need to identify new customer benefits from the customer's view, utilize core competencies from its business domain, and select and manage business partners from its collaborative networks. To craft new customer benefits, marketers must understand what the customer thinks about, wants, does, and worries about. Marketers must also observe who customers admire, who they interact with, and who influences them.

Business realignment may be necessary to maximize core competencies. It involves three steps: (1) (re)defining the business concept (the "big idea"); (2) (re)shaping the business scope (the lines of business); and (3) (re)positioning the company's brand identity (how customers should see the company). This is what Kodak is doing as sales from its traditional core businesses of film, camera, paper, and photo development have sagged, and consumers have abandoned film cameras for increasingly cheaper digital equipment, products, and services. On September 25, 2003, Chairman and Chief Executive Daniel A. Carp stood in front of shareholders and unveiled the company's new strategy. He announced that Kodak was "determined to win in these new digital markets." In order to do that, the company plans to expand its line of digital cameras, printers, and other equipment for consumers, who are now using the Internet to transmit and display their digital images. Kodak also is stepping up efforts to deliver on-demand, colour printing products for business and wants to increase its market share of the lucrative medical images and information services business.[19]

VALUE DELIVERY   Delivering value often means substantial investment in infrastructure and capabilities. The company must become proficient at customer relationship management, internal resource management, and business partnership management. *Customer relationship management* allows the company to discover who its customers are, how they behave, and what they need or want. It also enables the company to respond appropriately, coherently, and quickly to different customer opportunities. To respond effectively, the company requires *internal resource management* to integrate major business processes (e.g., order processing, general ledger, payroll, and production) within a single family of software modules. Finally, *business partnership management* allows the company to handle complex relationships with its trading partners to source, process, and deliver products.

The Central Role of Strategic Planning

Successful marketing thus requires having capabilities such as understanding customer value, creating customer value, delivering customer value, capturing customer value, and sustaining customer value. "Marketing Insight: Views of Marketing from Chief Executive Officers" addresses some important senior management priorities in improving marketing. Only a handful of companies stand out

MARKETING INSIGHT

Views on Marketing from Chief Executive Officers

Marketing faces a number of challenges in the twenty-first century. Based on an extensive 2002 research study, McKinsey identified three main challenges as reflected by differences in opinion between chief executive officers (CEOs) and their most senior marketing executives or chief marketing officers (CMOs).

- *Doing more with less.* CEOs need and expect all areas of their organizations to be more efficient; CMOs indicate that they anticipate that their budgets will grow.
- *Driving new business development.* CEOs want marketing to play a more active role in driving new business development—not just new products but also new markets, channels, and lines of business; CMOs cited new product development as their primary concern.
- *Becoming a full business partner.* CEOs look for marketing to become a more central business partner that helps to drive profits; CMOs are unsure that their groups have the skills to do so.

McKinsey suggests that bridging these gaps will require changes in spending, organization skills, and culture for many marketers. To accommodate the pressure to simultaneously grow revenues while also reducing marketing costs as a percentage of sales, they offer three recommendations:

1. Link spending priorities to profit potential, for example, as measured by size and anticipated growth rate of current customers—not historical performance;
2. Focus spending on brand drivers (features and benefits truly important to customers), not antes (features and benefits that a brand needs to stay in the game); and
3. Deepen insights on how customers get product information and make buying decisions.

Based on research on companies that successfully develop big ideas, McKinsey identifies three characteristics that help to position marketers as business development leaders:

1. Force the widest view when defining their business, assets, and competencies;
2. Combine multiple perspectives—for example, using attitudinal and need profiles as well as behaviour-based segments—to identify market opportunities or sweet spots; and
3. Focus idea generation through a combination of marketing insight and business analysis—but identify profitable unmet needs before they brainstorm creative solutions.

Finally, McKinsey offers two recommendations to overcome CEOs' concerns about the role and performance of marketing:

1. Marketers must test and develop programs more quickly as they enhance planning processes and research approaches; and
2. Marketers must more effectively evaluate the performance and profit impact of investments in the expanding marketing arena (e.g., CRM technology, sponsorships, Internet marketing, and word of mouth).

Source: David Court, Tom French, and Gary Singer, "How the CEO Sees Marketing," *Advertising Age*, March 3, 2003, p. 28.

as master marketers: Molson, Tim Hortons, Bombardier, Procter & Gamble, WestJet Airlines, Nike, Disney, Wal-Mart, McDonald's, and several Japanese (Sony, Toyota, Canon) and European (IKEA, Club Med, Bang & Olufsen, Nokia) companies. These companies focus on the customer and are organized to respond effectively to changing customer needs. They all have well-staffed marketing departments, and all their other departments—manufacturing, finance, research and development, personnel, purchasing—also accept the concept that the customer is king. (See "Marketing Insight: Keys to Long-Term Market Leadership.")

Creating, providing, and communicating value requires many different marketing activities. To ensure that the proper activities are selected and executed, strategic planning is paramount. Strategic planning calls for action in three key areas: The first is managing a company's businesses as an investment portfolio. The second involves assessing each business's strength by considering the market's growth rate and the company's position and fit in that market. The third is establishing a strategy. For each business, the company must develop a game plan for achieving its long-run objectives.

Marketing plays a critical role in this process. At Samsung Electronics America, strategic marketing could be considered a religion. When Samsung executives, engineers, marketers, and designers consider new products, they must answer one central question, "Is it wow?" If "wow" is the

MARKETING INSIGHT

Keys to Long-Term Market Leadership

The question of what accounts for the success of long-lasting, successful companies was addressed in a six-year study by Collins and Porras called *Built to Last*. The Stanford researchers identified two companies in each of 18 industries, one that they called a "visionary company" and one that they called a "comparison company." The visionary companies were acknowledged as the industry leaders and widely admired; they set ambitious goals, communicated them to their employees, and embraced a high purpose beyond making money. They also outperformed the comparison companies by a wide margin. The visionary companies included General Electric, Hewlett-Packard, and Boeing; the corresponding comparison companies were Westinghouse, Texas Instruments, and McDonnell Douglas.

The authors found three commonalities among the 18 market leaders. First, the visionary companies each held a distinctive set of values from which they did not deviate. Thus, IBM has held to the principles of respect for the individual, customer satisfaction, and continuous quality improvement throughout its history; and Johnson & Johnson holds to the principle that its first responsibility is to its customers, its second to its employees, its third to its community, and its fourth to its stockholders. The second commonality is that visionary companies express their purpose in enlightened terms. Xerox wants to improve "office productivity" and Monsanto wants to "help end hunger in the world." According to Collins and Porras, a company's core purpose should not be confused with specific business goals or strategies and should not be simply a description of a company's product line. The third commonality is that visionary companies have developed a vision of their future and act to implement it. IBM is now working to establish leadership as a "network-centric" company and not simply as the leading computer manufacturer.

In his next book, *Good to Great*, Collins provided additional insight into enduring leadership. He defined a "good-to-great" transition as a 10-year fallow period followed by 15 years of increased profits. Examining every company that ever made the Fortune 500—approximately 1400—he found 11 that met the criteria: Abbott, Circuit City, Fannie Mae, Gillette, Kimberly-Clark, Kroger, Nucor, Philip Morris, Pitney Bowes, Walgreens, and Wells Fargo. Contrasting these 11 to the appropriate comparison companies again led to some clear conclusions. While the companies that achieved greatness were all in different industries, he found that making the transition from good to great didn't require a high-profile outside CEO, cutting-edge technology, or even a fine-tuned business strategy per se. Rather, a corporate culture that identified and promoted disciplined people to think and act in a disciplined manner was found to be the key. Leaders with a blend of personal humility and professional integrity were the most effective, and good-to-great companies were driven by core values and purpose that went beyond simply making money.

Sources: James C. Collins and Jerry I. Porras, *Built to Last: Successful Habits of Visionary Companies* (New York: HarperBusiness, 1994); F. G. Rodgers and Robert L. Shook, *The IBM Way: Insights into the World's Most Successful Marketing Organization* (New York: Harper and Row, 1986); James C. Collins, *Good to Great: Why Some Companies Make the Leap . . . and Others Don't* (New York: HarperCollins 2001).

company mantra, then the high priest of "wow" is Peter Weedfald, the company's vice-president of strategic marketing. His realm includes marketing, advertising, customer and partner relations, research, the consumer information centre, and B2B and B2C commerce. He is responsible for crafting marketing strategies that reach across five different divisions: consumer electronics, information technology, telecom, semiconductors, and home appliances. Unlike many other companies, such as Sony, in which each division has its own marketing strategy, Samsung unifies strategy for all five divisions. "In most companies," says Weedfald, "there is a vice president of CRM [customer relationship management] that doesn't even talk to the person in charge of TV advertising. . . . We're threaded holistically from global marketing in Korea to the last three feet of the sale." That last three feet is where the "Wow" needs to kick in—when the consumer is still an arm's length away from the product, either literally, in the store, or online.[20]

To understand marketing management, we must understand strategic planning. Most large companies consist of four organizational levels: the corporate level, the division level, the business unit level, and the product level. Corporate headquarters is responsible for designing a corporate strategic plan to guide the whole enterprise; it makes decisions on the amount of resources to allocate to each division, as well as on which businesses to start or eliminate. Each division establishes a plan covering the allocation of funds to each business unit within the division. Each business unit develops a strategic plan to carry that business unit into a profitable future. Finally, each product level (product line, brand) within a business unit develops a marketing plan for achieving its objectives in its product market.

The **marketing plan** is the central instrument for directing and coordinating the marketing effort. The marketing plan operates at two levels: strategic and tactical. The **strategic marketing plan** lays out the target markets and the value proposition that will be offered, based on an analysis of the best market opportunities. The **tactical marketing plan** specifies the marketing tactics, including product features, promotion, merchandising, pricing, sales channels, and service.

Today, teams develop the marketing plan with inputs and sign-offs from every important function. These plans are then implemented at the appropriate levels of the organization. Results are monitored, and necessary corrective action taken. The complete planning, implementation, and control cycle is shown in Figure 2.4. We next consider planning at each of these four levels of the organization.

FIGURE 2.4

The Strategic-Planning, Implementation, and Control Processes

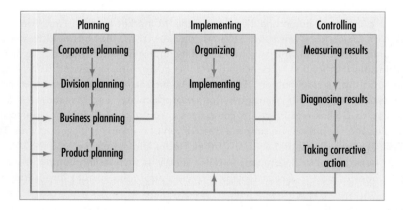

Corporate and Division Strategic Planning

By preparing statements of mission, policy, strategy, and goals, headquarters establishes the framework within which the divisions and business units prepare their plans. Some corporations give their business units a lot of freedom to set their own sales and profit goals and strategies. Others set goals for their business units but let them develop their own strategies. Still others set the goals and participate in developing individual business unit strategies.[21]

All corporate headquarters undertake four planning activities:

1. Defining the corporate mission
2. Establishing strategic business units (SBUs)
3. Assigning resources to each SBU
4. Assessing growth opportunities

Defining the Corporate Mission

An organization exists to accomplish something: to make cars, lend money, provide a night's lodging, and so on. Its specific mission or purpose is usually clear when the business starts. Over time the mission may change, to take advantage of new opportunities or respond to new market conditions. Amazon.com changed its mission from being the world's largest online bookstore to aspiring to become the world's largest online store. eBay changed its mission from running online auctions for collectors to running online auctions covering all kinds of goods.

To define its mission, the company should address Peter Drucker's classic questions:[22] What is our business? Who is the customer? What is of value to the customer? What will our business be? What should our business be? These simple-sounding questions are among the most difficult the company will ever have to answer. Successful companies continuously raise these questions and answer them thoughtfully and thoroughly. A company must redefine its mission if that mission has lost credibility or no longer defines an optimal course for the company.[23]

Organizations develop **mission statements** to share with managers, employees, and (in many cases) customers. A clear, thoughtful mission statement provides employees with a shared sense of purpose, direction, and opportunity. The statement guides geographically dispersed employees to work independently and yet collectively toward realizing the organization's goals.

Mission statements are at their best when they are guided by a vision, an almost "impossible dream" that provides a direction for the company for the next 10 to 20 years. Sony's former president, Akio Morita, wanted everyone to have access to "personal portable sound," so his company created the Walkman and portable CD player. Fred Smith wanted to deliver mail anywhere in the United States before 10:30 A.M. the next day, so he created FedEx. Figure 2.5 gives examples of three mission statements.

Good mission statements have three major characteristics. First, they focus on a limited number of goals. The statement, "We want to produce the highest-quality products, offer the most service, achieve the widest distribution, and sell at the lowest prices" claims too much. Second, mission statements stress the company's major policies and values. They narrow the range of individual discretion so that employees act consistently on important issues. Third, they define the major competitive spheres within which the company will operate:

■ *Industry.* The range of industries in which a company will operate. Some companies will operate in only one industry; some only in a set of related industries; some only in industrial goods, consumer goods, or services; and some in any industry. For example, DuPont prefers to operate in the industrial market, whereas Dow is willing to operate in the industrial and consumer markets. 3M will get into almost any industry where it can make money.

■ *Products and applications.* The range of products and applications a company will supply. Draxis Health Inc. of Mississauga, for example, is "focused on the development, production and distribution of radio-pharmaceutical products for diagnostic and therapeutic nuclear

---

Stelco Inc.

Stelco is a market-driven, technologically advanced group of businesses that are committed to maintaining leadership roles as steel producers and fabricators. These businesses are dedicated to meeting the requirements of their customers as well as collectively providing an appropriate return for Stelco shareholders. The people in these business units will achieve these objectives in healthy and safe environments through maximum development of their skills; by the creation and application of innovative process and product technology; through the identification and pursuit of new market opportunities; and by providing superior levels of quality and service.

Cara Operations Limited

One of Canada's leading integrated restaurant companies (including Swiss Chalet, Harvey's, Second Cup, Kelsey's Neighbourhood Bar & Grill, and others) has the vision and mission "to be Canada's leading integrated restaurant company while enhancing stakeholder value and building leading businesses, by maximizing our resources and living our values and principles."

Mountain Equipment Co-op

"Mountain Equipment Co-op provides quality products and services for self-propelled wilderness-oriented recreation, such as hiking and mountaineering, at the lowest reasonable price in an informative, respectful manner. We are a member-owned co-operative striving for social and environmental leadership."

FIGURE 2.5

Sample Mission Statements

Sources: Stelco Web site, **www.stelco.ca/mission/** (viewed August 22, 2005); Inco Ltd.'s Web site, **www.inco.com** (viewed July 7, 2004); Cara Operations Ltd.'s Web site, **www.cara.com** (viewed July 7, 2004); Mountain Equipment Co-op Web site, **www.mec.ca** (viewed July 7, 2004).

medicine plus contract manufacturing services for the pharmaceutical and biotechnology industries."[24]

- *Competence.* The range of technological and other core competencies that a company will master and leverage. Japan's NEC has built its core competencies in computing, communications, and components to support production of laptop computers, television receivers, and handheld telephones.

- *Market-segment.* The type of market or customers a company will serve. For example, Porsche makes only expensive cars. Gerber serves primarily the baby market.

- *Vertical.* The number of channel levels from raw material to final product and distribution in which a company will participate. At one extreme are companies with a large vertical scope; at one time Ford owned its own rubber plantations, sheep farms, glass manufacturing plants, and steel foundries. At the other extreme are "hollow corporations" or "pure marketing companies" consisting of a person with a phone, fax, computer, and desk who contracts out for every service, including design, manufacture, marketing, and physical distribution.[25]

- *Geographical.* The range of regions, countries, or country groups in which a company will operate. At one extreme are companies that operate in a specific city. At the other are multinationals such as Unilever and Caterpillar, which operate in almost every country in the world.

Defining the Business

Companies often define their businesses in terms of products: They are in the "auto business" or the "clothing business." But Levitt argues that market definitions of a business are superior to product definitions.[26] A business must be viewed as a customer-satisfying process, not a goods-producing process. Products are transient; basic needs and customer groups endure forever. Transportation is a need: the horse and carriage, the automobile, the railroad, the airline, and the truck are products that meet that need.

Levitt encouraged companies to redefine their businesses in terms of needs, not products. Pitney Bowes Inc., an old-line manufacturer of postage meters, is in the process of doing just that. With old-fashioned paper mail under siege, Pitney Bowes can no longer afford to be defined by its main product, even though it currently holds 80 percent of the North American and 62 percent of the global postage-meter market. The company is redefining itself as a leading service provider in the much larger mail and document management industry. With its wealth of engineers, cryptographers,

A Caterpillar ad in French, with the focus on users' confidence in CAT products: "Pascal knows very well that his clients won't accept any excuses. He has been in the business long enough to know that what's important is to do the work well, without delays and within budget. People say he's a perfectionist. He answers that he is simply a good professional and that's why clients depend on him. . . . Pascal uses CAT." Multinationals such as Caterpillar operate in almost every country in the world.

and even workplace anthropologists, as well as 2300 patents and several labs, Pitney Bowes is well positioned to help companies organize their communications. In a new series of ads in business publications such as *Fortune*, Pitney Bowes is spreading the word about its new mission. For instance, one ad boasts that " . . . we can generate remarkable changes across your entire business, including a sizeable increase in profits. A good example: BP. Our document solution helped them shorten billing cycles and enabled rapid receipt of payments, freeing millions in working capital." The tagline: "Pitney Bowes: Engineering the flow of communication."[27]

IBM redefined itself from a hardware and software manufacturer to a "builder of networks." Table 2.1 gives several examples of companies that have moved from a product to a market definition of their business. It highlights the difference between a target market definition and a strategic market definition. A *target market definition* tends to focus on selling a product or service. Pepsi could define its target market as everyone who drinks a cola beverage, and competitors would therefore be other cola companies. A *strategic market definition* could be everyone who might drink something to quench his or her thirst. Suddenly, Pepsi's competition would then include noncola soft drinks, bottled water, fruit juices, tea, and coffee. To better compete, Pepsi might decide to sell additional beverages whose growth rate appears to be promising.

A business can be defined in terms of three dimensions: customer groups, customer needs, and technology.[28] Consider a small company that defines its business as designing incandescent lighting systems for television studios. Its customer group is television studios; the customer need is lighting; and the technology is incandescent lighting. The company might want to expand. It could make lighting for other customer groups, such as homes, factories, and offices; or it could supply other services needed by television studios, such as heating, ventilation, or air conditioning. It could design other lighting technologies for television studios, such as infrared or ultraviolet lighting.

Large companies normally manage quite different businesses, each requiring its own strategy. General Electric classified its businesses into 49 **strategic business units (SBUs)**. An SBU has three characteristics:

1. It is a single business or collection of related businesses that can be planned separately from the rest of the company.

2. It has its own set of competitors.

3. It has a manager who is responsible for strategic planning and profit performance and who controls most of the factors affecting profit.

The purpose of identifying the company's strategic business units is to develop separate strategies and assign appropriate funding. Senior management knows that its portfolio of businesses usually includes a number of "yesterday's has-beens" as well as "tomorrow's breadwinners." Yet it cannot rely on impressions; it needs analytical tools to classify its businesses by profit potential.[29]

Assessing Growth Opportunities

Assessing growth opportunities involves planning new businesses, downsizing, or terminating older businesses. The company's plans for existing businesses allow it to project total sales and profits. If there is a gap between future desired sales and projected sales, corporate management will have to develop or acquire new businesses to fill it.

Figure 2.6 illustrates this strategic-planning gap for a major manufacturer of blank compact disks called Musicale (name disguised). The lowest curve projects the expected sales over the next five years from the current business portfolio. The highest curve describes desired sales over the same

TABLE 2.1	PRODUCT-ORIENTED VERSUS MARKET-ORIENTED DEFINITIONS OF A BUSINESS	
Company	**Product Definition**	**Market Definition**
Canadian National Railroad	We run a railroad.	We are a people-and-goods mover.
Xerox	We make copying equipment.	We help improve office productivity.
Imperial Oil	We sell gasoline.	We supply energy.
Columbia Pictures	We make movies.	We market entertainment.
Encyclopaedia Britannica	We sell encyclopedias.	We distribute information.
Carrier	We make air conditioners and furnaces.	We provide climate control in the home.

FIGURE 2.6

The Strategic Planning Gap

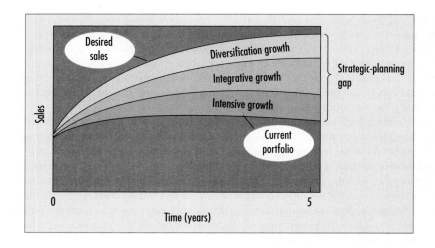

period. Evidently, the company wants to grow much faster than its current businesses will permit. How can it fill the strategic-planning gap?

The first option is to identify opportunities to achieve further growth within current businesses (intensive opportunities). The second is to identify opportunities to build or acquire businesses that are related to current businesses (integrative opportunities). The third is to identify opportunities to add attractive businesses that are unrelated to current businesses (diversification opportunities).

FIGURE 2.7

Three Intensive Growth
Strategies: Ansoff's
Product–Market Expansion
Grid

Source: Adapted from Igor Ansoff,
"Strategies for Diversification,"
Harvard Business Review
(September–October 1957): 114.
Copyright © 1957 by the President
and Fellows of Harvard College—
All rights reserved.

	Current Products	New Products
Current Markets	1. Market-penetration strategy	3. Product-development strategy
New Markets	2. Market-development strategy	(Diversification strategy)

INTENSIVE GROWTH Corporate management's first course of action should be a review of opportunities for improving existing businesses. Ansoff proposed a useful framework for detecting new intensive growth opportunities called a "product–market expansion grid" (Figure 2.7).[30]

The company first considers whether it could gain more market share with its current products in their current markets (market-penetration strategy). Next it considers whether it can find or develop new markets for its current products (market-development strategy). Then it considers whether it can develop new products of potential interest to its current markets (product-development strategy). Later it will also review opportunities to develop new products for new markets (diversification strategy).

Starbucks

Starbucks is a company that has achieved growth in many different ways. When Howard Schultz, Starbucks' CEO until 2000, came to the company in 1982, he recognized an unfilled niche for cafés serving gourmet coffee directly to customers. This became Starbucks' market-penetration strategy, and helped the company attain a loyal customer base in Seattle, Washington. The market-development strategy marked the next phase in Starbucks' growth: It applied the same successful formula that had worked wonders in Seattle first to other cities in the Pacific Northwest, then throughout North America, and finally, across the globe. Once the company established itself as a presence in thousands of cities internationally, Starbucks sought to increase the number of purchases by existing customers with a product-development strategy that led to new in-store merchandise, including compilation CDs, a Starbucks Duetto Visa card that allows customers to receive points toward Starbucks purchases whenever they use it, and high-speed wireless Internet access at thousands of Starbucks "HotSpots" through a deal with T-Mobile. Finally, Starbucks pursued diversification into grocery store aisles with Frappuccino® bottled drinks, Starbucks brand ice cream, and the purchase of tea retailer Tazo® Tea.[31]

Howard Schultz of Starbucks waves after cutting the ribbon to inaugurate Starbucks' first store outside North America, in the Ginza in Tokyo, August 1996. Today Starbucks has stores across the globe.

How might Musicale use these three major intensive growth strategies to increase its sales? Musicale could try to encourage its current customers to buy more. This could work if its customers could be shown the benefits of using more compact disks for recording music or for data storage. Musicale could try to attract competitors' customers. This could work if Musicale noticed major weaknesses in competitors' product or marketing programs. Finally, Musicale could try to convince nonusers of compact disks to start using them. This could work if there are still enough people who are not able to or do not know how to burn a compact disk.

How can Musicale use a product-development strategy? First, it might try to identify potential user groups in the current sales areas. If Musicale has been selling compact disks only to consumer markets, it might go after office and factory markets. Second, Musicale might seek additional distribution channels in its present locations. If it has been selling its disks only through stereo-equipment dealers, it might add mass-merchandising channels. Third, the company might consider selling in new locations in its home country or abroad. If Musicale sold only in North America, it could consider entering the European market.

Management should also consider new-product possibilities. Musicale could develop new features, such as additional data storage capabilities or greater durability. It could offer the CD at two or more quality levels, or it could research an alternative technology such as digital audiotape.

By examining these intensive growth strategies, management may discover several ways to grow. Still, that growth may not be enough. In that case, management must also look for integrative growth opportunities.

INTEGRATIVE GROWTH A business's sales and profits may be increased through backward, forward, or horizontal integration within its industry. For example, drug company giant Merck has gone beyond just developing and selling ethical pharmaceuticals. It purchased Medco, a mail-order pharmaceutical distributor, in 1993, formed a joint venture with DuPont to establish more basic research, and formed another joint venture with Johnson & Johnson to bring some of its ethical products into the over-the-counter market.

Media companies have long reaped the benefits of integrative growth. Here is how one business writer explains the potential that NBC could reap from its merger with Vivendi Universal Entertainment to become NBC Universal. Admittedly, it's a far-fetched example, but it gets across the possibilities inherent in this growth strategy:[32]

> [When] the hit movie *Seabiscuit* (produced by Universal Pictures) comes to television, it would air on Bravo (owned by NBC) or USA Network (owned by Universal), followed by the inevitable bid to make the movie into a TV series (by Universal Television Group), with the pilot being picked up by NBC, which passes on the show, but it's then revived in the "Brilliant But Cancelled" series on cable channel Trio (owned by Universal) where its cult status leads to a Spanish version shown on Telemundo (owned by NBC) and the creation of a popular amusement-park attraction at Universal Studios.

How might Musicale achieve integrative growth? The company might acquire one or more of its suppliers (such as plastic-material producers) to gain more control or generate more profit (backward integration). It might acquire some wholesalers or retailers, especially if they are highly profitable (forward integration). Finally, Musicale might acquire one or more competitors, provided that the government does not bar this move (horizontal integration). However, these new sources may still not deliver the desired sales volume. In that case, the company must consider diversification.

DIVERSIFICATION GROWTH Diversification growth makes sense when good opportunities can be found outside the present businesses. A good opportunity is one in which the industry is highly attractive and the company has the right mix of business strengths to be successful. For example, from its origins as an animated film producer, Walt Disney Company has moved into licensing characters for merchandised goods, entering the broadcast industry with its own Disney Channel as well as ABC and ESPN acquisitions, and developed theme parks and vacation and resort properties.

Several types of diversification are possible. First, the company could seek new products that have technological or marketing synergies with existing product lines, even though the new products themselves may appeal to a different group of customers (concentric strategy). It might start a minidisk manufacturing operation because it knows how to manufacture compact disks. Second, the company might search for new products that could appeal to current customers even though the new products are technologically unrelated to its current product line (horizontal strategy). Musicale might produce compact disk cases, even though producing them requires a different manufacturing process. Finally, the company might seek new businesses that have no relationship to its current technology, products, or markets (conglomerate strategy). Musicale might want to consider such new businesses as making application software or personal organizers.

DOWNSIZING AND DIVESTING OLDER BUSINESSES Companies must not only develop new businesses, they must also carefully prune, harvest, or divest tired old businesses in order to release needed resources and reduce costs. Weak businesses require a disproportionate amount of managerial attention. Managers should focus on growth opportunities, not fritter away energy and resources trying to salvage hemorrhaging businesses. Heinz sold its 9-Lives and Kibbles 'n Bits pet food after years of stagnant sales to allow it to better focus on its core brands in ketchup, sauces, and frozen foods.

CanWest Global Communications

CanWest of Winnipeg, Manitoba, exists to "inform, enlighten and entertain people everywhere so as to improve the quality of their lives" through its 16 broadcast television stations, specialty cable television stations, 10 metropolitan newspapers (including the *National Post*), and more than 20 nondaily publications. With so many localized assets, CanWest must prune any asset that doesn't contribute to its core business. For example, in February 2003, CanWest sold a number of its smaller daily and community newspapers in southern Ontario to Osprey Media. In July 2003, the company sold SBS Broadcasting, and in July 2004, it decided to sell Ulster Television (UTV) of London—a wholly owned subsidiary and part of CanWest's international portfolio. "While valuable in its own right, CanWest's investment in UTV was no longer considered to be of strategic importance in terms of the Company's overall media strategy," said Leonard Asper, CanWest's president and CEO.[33]

Organization and Organizational Culture

Strategic planning is done within the context of the organization. A company's **organization** consists of its structures, policies, and corporate culture, all of which can become dysfunctional in a rapidly changing business environment. Whereas structures and policies can be changed (with difficulty), the company's culture is very hard to change. Yet changing a corporate culture is often the key to successfully implementing a new strategy.

What exactly is a **corporate culture**? Most businesspeople would be hard-pressed to find words to describe this elusive concept, which some define as "the shared experiences, stories, beliefs, and norms that characterize an organization." Yet, walk into any company and the first thing that strikes you is the corporate culture—the way people are dressed, how they talk to one another, the way they greet customers.

Sometimes corporate culture develops organically and is transmitted directly from the CEO's personality and habits to the company employees. Such is the case with computer giant Microsoft, which began as an entrepreneurial upstart. Even as it grew to a US$32 billion company in 2003, Microsoft did not lose the hard-driving culture established by founder Bill Gates. In fact, most feel that Microsoft's ultra-competitive culture is the biggest key to its success and to its much-criticized dominance in the computing industry.[34]

What happens when entrepreneurial companies grow and need to create a tighter structure? This was the case with Yahoo! Inc. When the Internet icon was foundering in 2001, new CEO Terry Semel imposed a more conservative, button-down culture on the freewheeling Internet start-up. At the new Yahoo!, spontaneity is out and order is in. Whereas new initiatives used to roll ahead following free form brainstorming sessions and a gut check, now they wind their way through tests and formal analysis. Ideas either rise or fall at near-weekly meetings of a group called the Product Council. The group sizes up business plans to make sure all new projects bring benefits to Yahoo!'s existing businesses.[35]

What happens when companies with clashing cultures enter a joint venture or merger? In a study by Coopers & Lybrand of 100 companies with failed or troubled mergers, 855 of executives polled said that differences in management style and practices were the major problem.[36] Conflict was certainly the case when Germany's Daimler merged with Chrysler in 1998.

DaimlerChrysler

Daimler-Benz AG and Chrysler Corp. merged in 1998 to form DaimlerChrysler. Executives from both companies thought a host of synergies would enable DaimlerChrysler to swiftly build a global automotive empire. Fundamental differences in the way the two corporations did business, however, contributed to early departures by executives, a stock price slide, management restructuring, and even considerable losses by the American manufacturer. The two companies had contrasting management styles, Daimler preferring to operate a classic bureaucracy and Chrysler traditionally giving decision-making ability to managers lower in the ranks.[37]

Successful companies may need to adopt a new view of how to craft their strategy. The traditional view is that senior management hammers out the strategy and hands it down. Gary Hamel offers the contrasting view that imaginative ideas on strategy exist in many places within a company.[38] Senior management should identify and encourage fresh ideas from three groups who tend to be underrepresented in strategy making: employees with youthful perspectives; employees who are far removed from company headquarters; and employees who are new to the industry. Each group is capable of challenging company orthodoxy and stimulating new ideas.

Nokia

Finnish mobile-phone giant Nokia has managed to stay the frontrunner in the mobile phone industry, with annual sales of US$30.8 billion across 130 countries and a global market share of 38 percent, by installing a culture of innovation at all levels, using small, nimble creative units to let new ideas bubble up through the ranks. Innovations are as likely to come from a junior application designer as from a seasoned engineer. One example of how the company creates its culture can be seen in the company cafeteria where employees view a slide show as they eat. It's not just any slide show, but one of pictures taken with camera phones by some of Nokia's 1500 employees—part of an internal corporate competition that rewards staff creativity. Nokia even has a watchword for its culture of continuous innovation: "renewal."[39]

Strategy must be developed by identifying and selecting among different views of the future. The Royal Dutch/Shell Group has pioneered scenario analysis. A **scenario analysis** consists of developing plausible representations of a firm's possible future that make different assumptions about forces driving the market and include different uncertainties. Managers need to think through each scenario with the question: "What will we do if it happens?" They need to adopt one scenario as the most probable and watch for signposts that might confirm or disconfirm that scenario.[40]

Business Unit Strategic Planning

The business unit strategic-planning process consists of the steps shown in Figure 2.8. We examine each step in the sections that follow.

The Business Mission

Each business unit needs to define its specific mission within the broader company mission. Thus, a television studio-lighting-equipment company might define its mission as "The company aims to target major television studios and become their vendor of choice for lighting technologies that represent the most advanced and reliable studio lighting arrangements." Notice that this mission does not attempt to win business from smaller television studios, win business by being lowest in price, or venture into nonlighting products.

SWOT Analysis

The overall evaluation of a company's strengths, weaknesses, opportunities, and threats is called SWOT analysis. It involves monitoring the external and internal marketing environment.

EXTERNAL ENVIRONMENT (OPPORTUNITY AND THREAT) ANALYSIS A business unit has to monitor key *macroenvironment forces* (demographic-economic, natural, technological, political-legal, and social-cultural) and significant *microenvironment actors* (customers, competitors, suppliers, distributors, dealers) that affect its ability to earn profits. The business unit should set up a marketing intelligence system to track trends and important developments. For each trend or development, management needs to identify the associated opportunities and threats.

A major purpose of environmental scanning is to discern new opportunities. In many ways, good marketing is the art of finding, developing, and profiting from opportunities.[41] A **marketing opportunity** is an area of buyer need and interest in which there is a high probability that a company can profitably satisfy that need.[42] There are three main sources of market opportunities. The first is to supply something in short supply. This requires little marketing talent, as the need is fairly obvious. The second is to supply an existing product or service in a new or superior way. There are several ways to uncover possible product or service improvements: by asking consumers for their suggestions (*problem detection method*); by asking consumers to imagine an ideal version of the product or service (*ideal method*); and by asking consumers to chart their steps in acquiring, using, and disposing of a product (*consumption chain method*). The third source often leads to a totally new product or service.

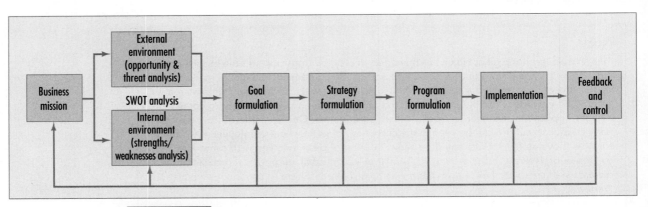

FIGURE 2.8

The Business Unit Strategic-Planning Process

Toolkit Productions Inc.

In 2001, four graduates from Queen's University saw an opportunity for a new kind of theatre business in the Toronto market. While the city was already saturated with hundreds of small theatre companies seeking to fulfill particular artistic objectives, the founders of TKP decided to take a different approach. The small group of entrepreneurs believed there was an opportunity to create productions aimed at the 20- to 30-year-old demographic—an age group that traditionally rarely attended theatre events in significant numbers. Toolkit Productions set out to engage this target market by offering less dramatic and more entertaining productions. It delivered its products in nontraditional theatrical venues such as bars and nightclubs. This tactic had the added advantage that all shows were supported by live rock bands. For example, their first show was *Cannibal! The Musical* by Trey Parker (of *South Park* fame). Megan McCoy, the executive producer, states, "While we still firmly believe in the market need we have identified, we are competing in a far more complex market than theatre alone. We are competing in the entertainment business where everyone wants a piece of the 20- to 30-year-old market." Only time will tell if the young entrepreneur's insight can truly make waves in this highly competitive market.[43]

Opportunities can take many forms, and marketers have to be good at spotting them. Consider the following:

- A company may benefit from converging industry trends and introduce hybrid products or services that are new to the market. Example: At least five major cell phone manufacturers released phones with digital photo capabilities.

- A company may make a buying process more convenient or efficient. Example: Consumers can now use the Internet to find more books than ever and search for the lowest price with a few clicks.

- A company can meet the need for more information and advice. Example: Guru.com facilitates finding professional experts in a wide range of fields.

- A company can customize a product or service that was formerly offered only in a standard form. Example: P&G's Reflect.com Web site is capable of producing a customized skin-care or hair-care product to meet a customer's need.

- A company can introduce a new capability. Example: Consumers can now create and edit digital "iMovies" with the new iMac and upload them to an Apple Web server to share with friends around the world.

- A company may be able to deliver a product or a service faster. Example: FedEx discovered a way to deliver mail and packages much more quickly than the U.S. Post Office.

- A company may be able to offer a product at a much lower price. Example: Pharmaceutical firms have created generic versions of brand-name drugs.

To evaluate opportunities, companies can use **Market Opportunity Analysis (MOA)** to determine the attractiveness and probability of success:

1. Can the benefits involved in the opportunity be articulated convincingly to a defined target market(s)?

2. Can the target market(s) be located and reached with cost-effective media and trade channels?

3. Does the company possess or have access to the critical capabilities and resources needed to deliver the customer benefits?

4. Can the company deliver the benefits better than any actual or potential competitors?

5. Will the financial rate of return meet or exceed the company's required threshold for investment?

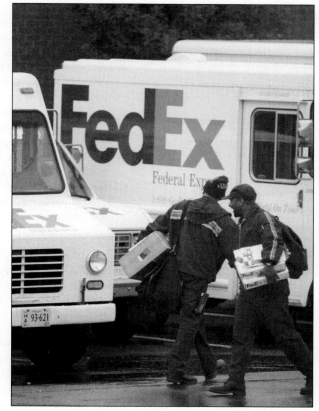

FedEx employees walk to their trucks on the first Sunday delivery at the company's suburban Washington centre. The new service was introduced based on customer request and market demand.

FIGURE 2.9

Opportunity and Threat
Matrices

In the opportunity matrix in Figure 2.9(a), the best marketing opportunities facing the TV-lighting-equipment company are listed in the upper-left cell (#1). The opportunities in the lower-right cell (#4) are too minor to consider. The opportunities in the upper-right cell (#2) and lower-left cell (#3) should be monitored in the event that any improve in attractiveness and success probability.

Some developments in the external environment represent threats. An **environmental threat** is a challenge posed by an unfavourable trend or development that would lead, in the absence of defensive marketing action, to lower sales or profit. Threats should be classified according to seriousness and probability of occurrence. Figure 2.9(b) illustrates the threat matrix facing the TV-lighting-equipment company. The threats in the upper-left cell are major, because they can seriously hurt the company and they have a high probability of occurrence. To deal with them, the company needs contingency plans that spell out changes it can make before or during the threat. The threats in the lower-right cell are very minor and can be ignored. The threats in the upper-right and lower-left cells need to be monitored carefully in the event that they grow more serious.

Once management has identified the major threats and opportunities facing a specific business unit, it can characterize that business's overall attractiveness.

INTERNAL ENVIRONMENT (STRENGTHS/WEAKNESSES) ANALYSIS It is one thing to find attractive opportunities and another to be able to take advantage of them. Each business needs to evaluate its internal strengths and weaknesses. It can do so by using a form like the one shown in "Marketing Memo: Checklist for Strengths/Weaknesses Analysis."

Clearly, the business does not have to correct all its weaknesses, nor should it gloat about all its strengths. The big question is whether the business should limit itself to those opportunities where it possesses the required strengths or whether it should consider opportunities that mean it might have to acquire or develop certain strengths. For example, managers at Texas Instruments (TI) were split between those who wanted TI to stick to industrial electronics (where it has clear strength) and those who wanted the company to continue introducing consumer products (where it lacks some required marketing strengths).

Marketing Memo

Checklist for Strengths/Weaknesses Analysis

	Performance					Importance		
	Major Strength	Minor Strength	Neutral	Minor Weakness	Major Weakness	Hi	Med	Low
Marketing								
1. Company reputation	_____	_____	_____	_____	_____	_____	_____	_____
2. Market share	_____	_____	_____	_____	_____	_____	_____	_____
3. Customer satisfaction	_____	_____	_____	_____	_____	_____	_____	_____
4. Customer retention	_____	_____	_____	_____	_____	_____	_____	_____
5. Product quality	_____	_____	_____	_____	_____	_____	_____	_____
6. Service quality	_____	_____	_____	_____	_____	_____	_____	_____
7. Pricing effectiveness	_____	_____	_____	_____	_____	_____	_____	_____
8. Distribution effectiveness	_____	_____	_____	_____	_____	_____	_____	_____
9. Promotion effectiveness	_____	_____	_____	_____	_____	_____	_____	_____
10. Sales force effectiveness	_____	_____	_____	_____	_____	_____	_____	_____
11. Innovation effectiveness	_____	_____	_____	_____	_____	_____	_____	_____
12. Geographical coverage	_____	_____	_____	_____	_____	_____	_____	_____
Finance								
13. Cost or availability of capital	_____	_____	_____	_____	_____	_____	_____	_____
14. Cash flow	_____	_____	_____	_____	_____	_____	_____	_____
15. Financial stability	_____	_____	_____	_____	_____	_____	_____	_____
Manufacturing								
16. Facilities	_____	_____	_____	_____	_____	_____	_____	_____
17. Economies of scale	_____	_____	_____	_____	_____	_____	_____	_____
18. Capacity	_____	_____	_____	_____	_____	_____	_____	_____
19. Able, dedicated workforce	_____	_____	_____	_____	_____	_____	_____	_____
20. Ability to produce on time	_____	_____	_____	_____	_____	_____	_____	_____
21. Technical manufacturing skill	_____	_____	_____	_____	_____	_____	_____	_____
Organization								
22. Visionary, capable leadership	_____	_____	_____	_____	_____	_____	_____	_____
23. Dedicated employees	_____	_____	_____	_____	_____	_____	_____	_____
24. Entrepreneurial orientation	_____	_____	_____	_____	_____	_____	_____	_____
25. Flexible or responsive	_____	_____	_____	_____	_____	_____	_____	_____

Sometimes a business does poorly not because its people lack the required strengths, but because they do not work together as a team. In one major electronics company, the engineers look down on the salespeople as "engineers who couldn't make it," and the salespeople look down on the service people as "salespeople who couldn't make it." It is therefore critical to assess interdepartmental working relationships as part of the internal environmental audit. Honeywell does exactly this.

> **Honeywell**
>
> Each year, Honeywell asks each department to rate its own strengths and weaknesses and those of the other departments with which it interacts. The notion is that each department is a supplier to some departments and a customer of other departments. If Honeywell engineers frequently underestimate the cost and completion time of new products, for example, their "internal customers" (manufacturing, finance, and sales) will be hurt.

George Stalk, a leading management consultant, suggests that winning companies are those that have achieved superior in-company capabilities, not just core competencies.[44] Every company must manage some basic processes, such as new-product development, sales generation, and order fulfillment. Each process creates value and requires interdepartmental teamwork. Although each department may possess specific core competencies, the challenge is to develop superior competitive capability in managing the company's key processes. Stalk calls this *capabilities-based competition*.

Goal Formulation

Once the company has performed a SWOT analysis, it can proceed to develop specific goals for the planning period. This stage of the process is called **goal formulation**. Managers use the term *goals* to describe objectives that are specific with respect to magnitude and time.

Most business units pursue a mix of objectives including profitability, sales growth, market-share improvement, risk containment, innovation, and reputation. The business unit sets these objectives and then manages by objectives (MBO). For an MBO system to work, the unit's objectives must meet four criteria:

1. *They must be arranged hierarchically, from the most to the least important.* For example, the business unit's key objective for the period may be to increase the rate of return on investment. This can be accomplished by increasing the profit level and reducing the amount of invested capital. Profit itself can be increased by increasing revenue and reducing expenses. Revenue can be increased by increasing market share and prices. By proceeding this way, the business can move from broad to specific objectives for specific departments and individuals.

2. *Objectives should be stated quantitatively whenever possible.* The objective "increase the return on investment (ROI)" is better stated as the goal "increase ROI to 15 percent within two years."

3. *Goals should be realistic.* They should arise from an analysis of the business unit's opportunities and strengths, not from wishful thinking.

4. *Objectives must be consistent.* It is not possible to maximize both sales and profits simultaneously.

Other important trade-offs include short-term profit versus long-term growth, deep penetration of existing markets versus developing new markets, profit goals versus nonprofit goals, and high growth versus low risk. Each choice in this set of trade-offs calls for a different marketing strategy.

Many believe that adopting the goal of strong market share growth may mean having to forgo strong short-term profits. For years, Compaq priced aggressively in order to build its market share in the computer market. Subsequently, Compaq decided to pursue profitability at the expense of growth. Yet Charan and Tichy believe that most businesses can be a growth business and can grow profitably.[45] They cite success stories such as GE Medical, Citibank, and GE Capital, all enjoying profitable growth. Some so-called trade-offs may not be trade-offs at all.

Strategic Formulation

Goals indicate what a business unit wants to achieve; **strategy** is a game plan for getting there. Every business must design a strategy for achieving its goals, consisting of a *marketing strategy*, and a compatible *technology strategy* and *sourcing strategy*.

PORTER'S GENERIC STRATEGIES Michael Porter has proposed three generic strategies that provide a good starting point for strategic thinking: overall cost leadership, differentiation, and focus.[46]

- *Overall cost leadership.* The business works hard to achieve the lowest production and distribution costs so that it can price lower than its competitors and win a large market share. Firms pursuing this strategy must be good at engineering, purchasing, manufacturing, and physical distribution. They need less skill in marketing. The problem with this strategy is that other firms will usually compete with still-lower costs and hurt the firm that rested its whole future on cost.

- *Differentiation.* The business concentrates on achieving superior performance in an important customer benefit area valued by a large part of the market. The firm cultivates those strengths that will contribute to the intended differentiation. Thus the firm seeking quality leadership, for example, must make products with the best components, put them together expertly, inspect them carefully, and effectively communicate their quality.

- *Focus.* The business focuses on one or more narrow market segments. The firm gets to know these segments intimately and pursues either cost leadership or differentiation within the target segment.

The online air travel industry provides a good example of these three strategies: Travelocity is pursuing a differentiation strategy by offering the most comprehensive range of services to the traveller. Lowestfare is pursuing a lowest-cost strategy; and Last Minute is pursuing a niche strategy in focusing on travellers who have the flexibility to travel on very short notice.

According to Porter, firms pursuing the same strategy directed to the same target market constitute a **strategic group**. The firm that carries out that strategy best will make the most profits. Firms that do not pursue a clear strategy and try to be good on all strategic dimensions do the worst. Eaton's fell upon hard times because it did not stand out in its industry as lowest in cost, highest in perceived value, or best in serving some market segment. Porter drew a distinction between operational effectiveness and strategy.[47]

Many companies believe they can win by performing the same activities more effectively than their competitors; but competitors can quickly copy the operationally effective company using benchmarking and other tools, thus diminishing the advantage of operational effectiveness. Porter defines strategy as "the creation of a unique and valuable position involving a different set of activities." A company can claim that it has a strategy when it "performs different activities from rivals or performs similar activities in different ways." Companies such as IKEA, WestJet Airlines, Dell Computer, Shopper's Drug Mart, Mountain Equipment Co-op, and Canadian Tire run their businesses much differently from their competitors; and these competitors would find it hard to copy and synchronize all the different activities that a strategically differentiated company carries out.

STRATEGIC ALLIANCES Companies are also discovering that they need strategic partners if they hope to be effective. Even giant companies—AT&T, IBM, Philips, Siemens—often cannot achieve leadership, either nationally or globally, without forming alliances with domestic or multinational companies that complement or leverage their capabilities and resources.

Just doing business in another country may require the firm to license its product, form a joint venture with a local firm, or buy from local suppliers to meet "domestic content" requirements. As a result, many firms are rapidly developing global strategic networks, and victory is going to those who build the better global network. The Star Alliance, for example, brings together 16 airlines—Lufthansa, United Airlines, Mexicana, Air Canada, ANA, Austrian Airlines, British Midland, Singapore Airlines, Tyrolean, Lauda, SAS, Thai Airways, Varig, Air New Zealand, Asiana Airlines, and Spanair—into a huge global partnership that allows travellers to make nearly seamless connections to about 700 destinations.

Many strategic alliances take the form of marketing alliances. These fall into four major categories.

1. *Product or service alliances.* One company licenses another to produce its product, or two companies jointly market their complementary products or a new product. For instance, H&R Block and Hyatt Legal Services—two service businesses—have also joined together in a marketing alliance.

2. *Promotional alliances.* One company agrees to carry a promotion for another company's product or service. For example, after several years' absence from Grand Prix racing, Michelin (Canada), headquartered in Laval, Quebec, formed a promotional alliance with the Air Canada Grand Prix for the summer of 2002. All teams racing at the Gilles Villeneuve circuit in Montreal used Michelin tires. To promote the partnership, its products, and the events, Michelin decided to use transit advertising. Not only did it place ads inside Montreal subway cars and on pillars in the stations, it also decorated a Michelin train with images of the company's spokes-character Bibendum.[48]

Star Alliance is a service alliance formed by Air Canada and its partner airlines as the first true global alliance.

3. *Logistics alliances.* One company offers logistical services for another company's product. For example, Abbott Laboratories warehouses and delivers all of 3M's medical and surgical products to hospitals across the United States.

4. *Pricing collaborations.* One or more companies join in a special pricing collaboration. Hotel and rental car companies often offer mutual price discounts.

Companies need to give creative thought to finding partners that might complement their strengths and offset their weaknesses. Well-managed alliances allow companies to obtain a greater sales impact at less cost. To keep their strategic alliances thriving, corporations have begun to develop organizational structures to support them and have come to view the ability to form and manage partnerships as core skills (called **partner relationship management, PRM**).[49]

Both pharmaceutical and biotech companies are starting to make partnership a core competency. In the 1980s and 1990s pharmaceutical and biotech firms were vertically integrated, doing all the research, development, and marketing and sales themselves. Now they are joining forces and leveraging their respective strengths. For example, Erbitux, a new drug to aid treatment of colorectal cancer, is the result of just such a partnership. The drug was originally discovered in biotech company ImClone Systems' clinical labs, but will be marketed via ImClone's partnership with pharmaceutical giant Bristol-Meyers Squibb.[50]

Program Formulation and Implementation

Once the business unit has developed its principal strategies, it must work out detailed support programs. A great marketing strategy can be sabotaged by poor implementation. If the unit has decided to attain technological leadership, it must plan programs to strengthen its R&D department, gather technological intelligence, develop leading-edge products, train the technical sales force, and develop ads to communicate its technological leadership.

Once the marketing programs are formulated, the marketing people must estimate their costs. Questions arise: Is participating in a particular trade show worth it? Will a specific sales contest pay for itself? Will hiring another salesperson contribute to the bottom line? Activity-based cost (ABC) accounting should be applied to each marketing program to determine whether it is likely to produce sufficient results to justify the cost.[51]

In implementing strategy, companies also must not lose sight of their multiple stakeholders and their needs. Traditionally, most businesses focused on shareholders. Today's businesses are increasingly recognizing that unless they nurture other stakeholders—customers, employees, suppliers, distributors—the business may never earn sufficient profits for the shareholders. A company can aim to deliver satisfaction levels above the minimum for different stakeholders. For example, it might aim to delight its customers, perform well for its employees, and deliver a threshold level of satisfaction to its suppliers. In setting these levels, a company must be careful not to violate the various stakeholder groups' sense of fairness about the relative treatment they are getting.[52]

There is a dynamic relationship connecting the stakeholder groups. A smart company creates a high level of employee satisfaction, which leads to higher effort, which leads to higher-quality products and services, which creates higher customer satisfaction, which leads to more repeat business, which leads to higher growth and profits, which leads to high shareholder satisfaction, which leads to more investment, and so on. This is the virtuous circle that spells profits and growth. "Marketing Insight: Marketing's Contribution to Shareholder Value" highlights the increasing importance of the proper bottom-line view to marketing expenditures.

According to McKinsey & Company, strategy is only one of seven elements in successful business practice.[53] The first three elements—strategy, structure, and systems—are considered the "hardware" of success. The next four—style, skills, staff, and shared values—are the "software."

The first "soft" element, *style,* means that company employees share a common way of thinking and behaving. Tim Hortons employees smile at the customer, and IBM employees are very professional in their customer dealings. The second, *skills,* means that the employees have the skills needed to carry out the company's strategy. The third, *staffing,* means that the company has hired able people, trained them well, and assigned them to the right jobs. The fourth, *shared values,* means that the employees share the same guiding values. When these elements are present, companies are usually more successful at strategy implementation.[54]

MARKETING INSIGHT

Marketing's Contribution to Shareholder Value

Companies normally focus on profit maximization rather than on shareholder value maximization. Doyle, in his *Value-Based Marketing,* charges that profit maximization leads to short-term planning and underinvestment in marketing. It leads to a focus on building sales, market share, and current profits. It leads to cost cutting and shedding assets to produce quick improvements in earnings, and erodes a company's long-term competitiveness by neglecting to invest in new market opportunities.

Companies normally measure their profit performance using ROI (return on investment, calculated by dividing profits by investment). This has two problems:

1. Profits are arbitrarily measured and subject to manipulation. Cash flow is more important. As someone observed: "Profits are a matter of opinion; cash is a fact."

2. Investment ignores the real value of the firm. More of a company's value resides in its intangible marketing assets—brands, market knowledge, customer relationships, and partner relationships—than in its balance sheet. These assets are the drivers of long-term profits.

Doyle argues that marketing will not mature as a profession until it can demonstrate the impact of marketing on shareholder value, the market value of a company minus its debt. The market value is the share price times the number of shares outstanding. The share price reflects what investors estimate is the present value of the future lifetime earnings of a company. When management is choosing a marketing strategy, Doyle wants it to apply shareholder value analysis (SVA) to see which alternative course of action will maximize shareholder value.

If Doyle's arguments are accepted, marketing will finally get the attention it deserves in the boardroom. Instead of seeing marketing as a specific function concerned only with increasing sales or market share, senior management will see it as an integral part of the whole management process. It will judge marketing by how much it contributes to shareholder value.

Source: Peter Doyle, *Value-Based Marketing: Marketing Strategies for Corporate Growth and Shareholder Value* (Chichester, England: John Wiley & Sons, 2000).

Another study of management practices found that superior performance over time depended on flawless execution, a company culture based on aiming high, a structure that is flexible and responsive, and a strategy that is clear and focused.[55]

Feedback and Control

As it implements its strategy, the firm needs to track the results and monitor new developments. Some environments are fairly stable from year to year. Other environments evolve slowly in a fairly predictable way. Still other environments change rapidly in major and unpredictable ways. Nonetheless, the company can count on one thing: The marketplace will change; and when it does, the company will need to review and revise its implementation, programs, strategies, or even objectives.

A company's strategic fit with the environment will inevitably erode because the market environment changes faster than the company's seven Ss. Thus, a company might remain efficient while it loses effectiveness. Peter Drucker pointed out that it is more important to "do the right thing" (effectiveness) than "to do things right" (efficiency). The most successful companies excel at both.

Once an organization fails to respond to a changed environment, it becomes increasingly hard to recapture its lost position. Consider what happened to Lotus Development Corporation. Its Lotus 1-2-3 software was once the world's leading software program, and now its market share in desktop software has slipped so low that analysts do not even bother to track it.

Lotus

Sales of the original IBM-PC were driven by Lotus 1-2-3, which combined an accounting spreadsheet with a program that could turn rows of numbers into charts and graphs. Yet Lotus ultimately did not keep pace as the PC evolved, missing opportunities with Apple Macintosh, Microsoft Windows, and suite applications. Following IBM's acquisition of the company in 1995, Lotus capitalized on the growing popularity of corporate e-mail systems with its Notes software, but Microsoft's ability to tie applications to operating systems gave it an unbeatable advantage. The company now works in concert with Microsoft to make sure its latest Smart Suite software takes full advantage of Windows software.[56]

Organizations, especially large ones, are subject to inertia. Inertia has been affecting giant Kraft Foods Inc., a company renowned for its expertise in creating brand extensions.

Kraft

While the company was busy rolling out products like Jell-O gel cups, Mini Oreos, and Ooey Gooey Warm N' Chewy Chips Ahoy!, it missed some important trends in supermarket food. As supermarkets' own private labels put out deeply discounted cheeses and cookies and other processed foods (e.g., President's Choice and Master's Choice), Kraft has become increasingly perceived as too high-priced. More important, Kraft neglected the trend toward healthier products with organic ingredients and less fat and has begun looking more like an expensive producer of processed junk food. It will be difficult for the company to catch up.[57]

Organizations are set up as efficient machines, and it is difficult to change one part without adjusting everything else. Yet organizations can be changed through strong leadership, preferably in advance of a crisis. The key to organizational health is willingness to examine the changing environment and to adopt new goals and behaviours.

Product Planning: The Nature and Contents of a Marketing Plan

To carry out their responsibilities, marketing managers follow a marketing process. Working within the plans set by the levels above them, product managers come up with a marketing plan for individual products, lines, brands, channels, or customer groups. Each product level (product line, brand) must develop a marketing plan for achieving its goals. A **marketing plan** is a written document that summarizes what the marketer has learned about the marketplace and indicates how the firm plans to reach its marketing objectives.[58] It contains tactical guidelines for the marketing programs and financial allocations over the planning period.[59] It is one of the most important outputs of the marketing process.

Marketing plans are becoming more customer- and competitor-oriented and better reasoned and more realistic than in the past. The plans draw more inputs from all the functions and are team-developed. Marketing executives increasingly see themselves as professional managers first, and specialists second. Planning is becoming a continuous process to respond to rapidly changing market conditions.

Sony

Sony originally planned to sell 10 million PlayStation 2 units worldwide within the first year of introduction. The marketing plan called for an aggressive presale promotional campaign to build demand and overshadow competitive game units from Nintendo and other rivals. Sony initially launched the new product in Japan, where the planned hype caused a buying frenzy in which almost 1 million units were sold within the first three days. However, unexpected components shortages kept the company from building enough units to stay on schedule. As a result, Sony was forced to revise its marketing plan by delaying the European launch and reducing the number of PlayStation 2 units shipped to stores; this delay, in turn, prevented Sony from reaching its corporate sales and profit objectives for the year.[60]

At the same time, marketing planning procedures and content vary considerably among companies. The plan is variously called a "business plan," a "marketing plan," and sometimes a "battle plan." Most marketing plans cover one year. The plans vary in length from under 5 to over 50 pages. Some companies take their plans very seriously, whereas others see them only as a rough guide to action. The most frequently cited shortcomings of current marketing plans, according to marketing executives, are lack of realism, insufficient competitive analysis, and a short-run focus. (See "Marketing Memo: Marketing Plan Criteria" for some guideline questions to ask in developing marketing plans.)

What, then, does a marketing plan look like? What does it contain?

Contents of the Marketing Plan

- *Executive summary and table of contents.* The marketing plan should open with a brief summary of the main goals and recommendations. The executive summary permits senior management to grasp the plan's major thrust. A table of contents should follow the executive summary that outlines the rest of the plan and all the supporting rationale and operational detail.

- *Situation analysis.* This section presents relevant background data on sales, costs, the market, competitors, and the various forces in the macroenvironment. How is the market defined, how big is it and how fast is it growing? What are the relevant trends affecting the market? What is the product offering and what are the critical issues facing the company? Pertinent historical information can be included to provide context. All this information is used to carry out a SWOT (strengths, weaknesses, opportunities, threats) analysis.

- *Marketing strategy.* Here the product manager defines the mission and marketing and financial objectives. The manager also defines those groups and needs that the market offerings are intended to satisfy. The manager then establishes the product line's

Marketing Memo

Marketing Plan Criteria

Here are some questions to ask in evaluating a marketing plan.

1. *Is the plan simple?* Is it easy to understand and act on? Does it communicate its content easily and practically?

2. *Is the plan specific?* Are its objectives concrete and measurable? Does it include specific actions and activities, each with specific dates of completion, specific persons responsible, and specific budgets?

3. *Is the plan realistic?* Are the sales goals, expense budgets, and milestone dates realistic? Has a frank and honest self-critique been conducted to raise possible concerns and objections?

4. *Is the plan complete?* Does it include all the necessary elements?

Source: Tim Berry and Doug Wilson, *On Target: The Book on Marketing Plans* (Eugene, OR, Palo Alto Software, 2000).

competitive positioning, which will inform the "game plan" to accomplish the plan's objectives. All this is done with inputs from other organizational areas, such as purchasing, manufacturing, sales, finance, and human resources, to ensure that the company can provide proper support for effective implementation. The marketing strategy should be specific about the branding strategy and customer strategy that will be employed.

- *Financial projections.* Financial projections include a sales forecast, an expense forecast, and a break-even analysis. On the revenue side, the projections show the forecasted sales volume by month and product category. On the expense side, the projections show the expected costs of marketing, broken down into finer categories. The break-even analysis shows how many units must be sold monthly to offset the monthly fixed costs and average per-unit variable costs.

- *Implementation controls.* The last section of the marketing plan outlines the controls for monitoring and adjusting implementation of the plan. Typically, the goals and budget are spelled out for each month or quarter so management can review each period's results and take corrective action as needed. A number of different internal and external measures will need to be taken to assess progress and suggest possible modifications. Some organizations include contingency plans outlining the steps management would take in response to specific environmental developments, such as price wars or strikes.

Sample Marketing Plan: Pegasus Sports International*

1.0 Executive Summary

Pegasus Sports International is a start-up aftermarket inline skating accessory manufacturer. In addition to the aftermarket products, Pegasus is developing SkateTours, a service that takes clients out, in conjunction with a local skate shop, and provides them with an afternoon of skating using inline skates and some of Pegasus' other accessories such as SkateSails. The aftermarket skate accessory market has been largely ignored. Although there are several major manufacturers of the skates themselves, the accessory market has not been addressed. This provides Pegasus with an extraordinary opportunity for market growth. Skating is a booming sport. Currently most of the skating is recreational. There are, however, a growing number of skating competitions, including team-orientated competitions such as skate hockey as well as individual competitions such as speed skate racing. Pegasus will work to grow these markets as well as develop the skate transportation market, a more utilitarian use of skating. Several of Pegasus' currently developed products have patents pending, and local market research indicates that there is great demand for these products. Pegasus will achieve fast, significant market penetration through a solid business model, long-range planning, and a strong management team that will be able to execute on this exciting opportunity. The three principals on the manage-

*Sample plan provided by and copyright Palo Alto Software, Inc. Find more complete sample marketing plans at www.mplans.com.

ment team have over 30 years of combined personal and industry experience. This extensive experience provides Pegasus with the empirical information as well as the passion to provide the skating market with much-needed aftermarket products. Pegasus will sell its products initially through its Web site. This "Dell" direct-to-the-consumer approach will allow Pegasus to achieve higher margins and maintain a close relationship with the customers, which is essential for producing products that have a true market demand. By the end of the year, Pegasus will have also developed relationships with different skate shops and will begin to sell some of its products through the use of retailers.

TABLE 1.0	SALES FORECAST		
	Sales Forecast		
Sales	**2003**	**2004**	**2005**
Recreational	$455 740	$598 877	$687 765
Competitive	$ 72 918	$ 95 820	$110 042
Total Sales	$528 658	$694 697	$797 807
Direct Cost of Sales	**2003**	**2004**	**2005**
Recreational	$ 82 033	$107 798	$123 798
Competitive	$ 13 125	$ 17 248	$ 19 808
Subtotal Cost of Sales	$ 95 158	$125 046	$143 606

2.0 Situation Analysis

Pegasus is entering its first year of operation. Its products have been well received, and marketing will be key to develop brand and product awareness as well as grow the customer base. Pegasus International offers several different aftermarket skating accessories, serving the growing inline skating industry.

2.1 Market Summary

Pegasus possesses good information about the market and knows a great deal about the common attributes of the most prized customer. This information will be leveraged to better understand who is served, what their specific needs are, and how Pegasus can better communicate with them.

Target Markets

Recreational
Fitness
Speed
Hockey
Extreme

2.1.1 Market Demographics

The profile for the typical Pegasus customer consists of the following geographic, demographic, and behaviour factors:

Geographics

- Pegasus has no set geographic target area. By leveraging the expansive reach of the Internet and multiple delivery services, Pegasus can serve both domestic as well as international customers.

- The total targeted population is 31 000 000 users.

Demographics

- Male and female users. An almost equal ratio between the two.

- Ages 13–46, with 48 percent clustering around the ages 23–34. The recreational users tend to cover the widest age range, including young users through active adults. The fitness users tend to be ages 20–40. The speed users tend to be in their late 20s and early 30s. The hockey players are generally in their teens through their early 20s. The extreme segment is of similar age to the hockey players.

- Of the users who are over 20, 65 percent have an undergraduate degree or substantial undergraduate coursework.

- The adult users have a median personal income of $47 000.

Behaviour Factors

- Users enjoy fitness activities not as a means for a healthy life, but as an intrinsically enjoyable activity in itself.

TABLE 2.1	TARGET MARKET FORECAST						
		Target Market Forecast					
Potential Customers	**Growth**	**2003**	**2004**	**2005**	**2006**	**2007**	**CAGR**
Recreational	10%	19 142 500	21 056 750	23 162 425	25 478 668	28 026 535	10.00%
Fitness	15%	6 820 000	7 843 000	9 019 450	10 372 368	11 928 223	15.00%
Speed	10%	387 500	426 250	468 875	515 763	567 339	10.00%
Hockey	6%	2 480 000	2 628 800	2 786 528	2 953 720	3 130 943	6.00%
Extreme	4%	2 170 000	2 256 800	2 347 072	2 440 955	2 538 593	4.00%
Total	10.48%	31 000 000	34 211 600	37 784 350	41 761 474	46 191 633	10.48%

- Users spend money on gear, typically sports equipment.
- Users have active lifestyles that include some sort of recreation at least 2–3 times a week.

2.1.2 Market Needs

Pegasus is providing the skating community with a wide range of accessories for all variations of skating. Pegasus seeks to fulfill the following benefits that are important to its customers:

- *Quality craftsmanship*. The customers work hard for their money and do not enjoy spending it on disposable products that only work for a year or two.
- *Well thought-out designs*. The skating market has not been addressed by well thought-out products that serve skaters' needs. Pegasus' industry experience and personal dedication to the sport will provide Pegasus with the needed information to produce insightfully designed products.
- *Customer service*. Exemplary service is required to build a sustainable business that has a loyal customer base.

2.1.3 Market Trends

Pegasus will distinguish itself by marketing products not previously available to skaters. The emphasis in the past has been to sell skates and very few replacement parts. The number of skaters is not restricted to any one single country, continent, or age group, so there is a world market. Pegasus has products for virtually every group of skaters. The fastest-growing segment of this sport is the fitness skater. Therefore, the marketing is being directed to service this group. BladeBoots will enable users to enter establishments without having to remove their skates. BladeBoots will be aimed at the recreational skater, the largest segment. SkateAids, on the other hand, are great for everyone.

The sport of skating will also grow through SkateSailing. This sport is primarily for the medium-to-advanced skater. The growth potential for this sport is tremendous. The sails that Pegasus has manufactured have been sold in Europe, following a pattern similar to windsurfing. Windsailing originated in Santa Monica, California, but did not take off until it had already grown big in Europe.

Another trend is group skating. More and more groups are getting together on skate excursions in cities all over the world. For example, San Francisco has night group skating that numbers in the hundreds of people. The market trends are showing continued growth in all directions of skating.

2.1.4 Market Growth

With the price of skates going down due to competition by so many skate companies, the market has had steady growth throughout the world, with 22.5 million units sold in 1999 to over 31 million in 2002. The growth statistics for 2003 are estimated to be over 35 million units. More and more people are discovering—and in many cases rediscovering—the health benefits and fun of skating.

2.2 SWOT Analysis

The following SWOT analysis captures the key strengths and weaknesses within the company, and describes the opportunities and threats facing Pegasus.

2.2.1 Strengths

- In-depth industry experience and insight.
- Creative, yet practical product designers.
- The use of a highly efficient, flexible business model utilizing direct customer sales and distribution.

2.2.2 Weaknesses

- The reliance of outside capital necessary to grow the business.
- A lack of retailers who can work directly face-to-face with the customer to generate brand and product awareness.
- The difficulty in developing brand awareness as a start-up company.

2.2.3 Opportunities

- Participation within a growing industry.
- Decreased product costs through economies of scale.
- The ability to leverage other industry participants' marketing efforts to help grow the general market.

2.2.4 Threats

- Future/potential competition from an already established market participant.
- A slump in the economy that could have a negative effect on people's spending of discretionary income on fitness/recreational products.
- The release of a study that calls into question the safety of skating or the inability to prevent major skating-induced traumas.

2.3 Competition

Pegasus Sports International is forming its own market. Although there are a few companies that do make sails and foils that a few skaters are using, Pegasus is the only one that is truly designed for and by skaters. The few competitors' sails on the market are not designed for skating, but for windsurfing or for skateboards. In the case of foils, storage and carrying are not practical. There are different indirect competitors who are manufacturers of the actual skates. After many years in the market, these companies have yet to become direct competitors by manufacturing accessories for the skates that they make.

2.4 Product Offering

Pegasus Sports International now offers several products:

- The first product that has been developed is BladeBoots, a cover for the wheels and frame of inline skates, which allow skaters to enter places that normally would not allow them in with skates on. BladeBoots come with a small pouch and belt that converts to a well-designed skate carrier.

- The second product is SkateSails. These sails are specifically designed for use while skating. Feedback that Pegasus has received from skaters indicates skatesailing could become a very popular sport. Trademarking this product is currently in progress.

- The third product, SkateAid, will be in production by December. Other ideas for products are under development, but will not be disclosed until Pegasus can protect them through pending patent applications.

2.5 Keys to Success

The keys to success are designing and producing products that meet market demand. In addition, Pegasus must ensure total customer satisfaction. If these keys to success are achieved, Pegasus will become a profitable, sustainable company.

2.6 Critical Issues

As a start-up business, Pegasus is still in the early stages. The critical issues are for Pegasus to:

- Establish itself as the premier skating accessory company.

- Pursue controlled growth that dictates that payroll expenses will never exceed the revenue base. This will help protect against recessions.

- Constantly monitor customer satisfaction, ensuring that the growth strategy will never compromise service and satisfaction levels.

3.0 Marketing Strategy

The key to the marketing strategy is focusing on the speed, health and fitness, and recreational skaters. Pegasus can cover about 80 percent of the skating market because it produces products geared toward each segment. Pegasus is able to address all of the different segments within the market because, although each segment is distinct in terms of its users and equipment, Pegasus' products are useful to all of the different segments.

3.1 Mission

Pegasus Sports International's mission is to provide the customer with the finest skating accessories available. We exist to attract and maintain customers. With a strict adherence to this maxim, success will be ensured. Our services and products will exceed the expectations of the customers.

3.2 Marketing Objectives

- Maintain positive, strong growth each quarter (notwithstanding seasonal sales patterns).

- Achieve a steady increase in market penetration.

- Decrease customer acquisition costs by 1.5 percent per quarter.

3.3 Financial Objectives

- Increase the profit margin by 1 percent per quarter through efficiency and economy-of-scale gains.

- Maintain a significant research and development budget (as a percentage relative to sales) to spur future product developments.

- A double- to triple-digit growth rate for the first three years.

3.4 Target Markets

With a world skating market of over 31 million and steadily growing (statistics released by the Sporting Goods Manufacturers Association), the niche has been created. Pegasus' aim is to expand this market by promoting SkateSailing, a new sport that is popular in both Santa Monica and Venice Beach in California. The Sporting Goods Manufacturers Association survey indicates that skating now has more participation than football, softball, skiing, and snowboarding combined. The breakdown of participation of skating is as follows: 1+ percent speed (growing), 8 percent hockey (declining), 7 percent extreme/aggressive (declining), 22 percent fitness (nearly 7 million—the fastest growing), and 61 percent recreational (first-timers). Our products are targeting the fitness and recreational groups, because they are the fastest growing. These groups are gearing themselves toward health and fitness, and combined, they can easily grow to 85 percent (or 26 million) of the market in the next five years.

3.5 Positioning

Pegasus will position itself as the premier aftermarket skating accessory company. This positioning will be achieved by leveraging Pegasus' competitive edge: industry experience and passion. Pegasus is a skating company formed by skaters for skaters. Pegasus management is able to use its vast experience and personal passion for the sport to develop innovative, useful accessories for a broad range of skaters.

3.6 Strategies

The single objective is to position Pegasus as the premier skating accessory manufacturer, serving both the domestic market as well as the international market. The marketing strategy will seek to first create customer awareness concerning the offered products and services and then develop the customer base. The message that Pegasus will seek to communicate is that Pegasus offers the best-designed, most useful skating accessories. This message will be communicated through a variety of methods. The first will be the Pegasus Web site. The Web site will provide a rich source of product information and offer consumers the opportunity to purchase. A lot of time and money will be invested into the site to provide the customer with the perception of total professionalism and utility for Pegasus' products and services.

The second marketing method will be advertisements placed in numerous industry magazines. The skating industry is supported by several different glossy magazines designed to promote the industry as a whole. In addition, a number of smaller periodicals serve the smaller market segments within the skating industry. The last method of communication is the use of printed sales literature. The two previously mentioned marketing methods will create demand for the sales literature that will be sent out to customers. The cost of the sales literature will be fairly minimal, because it will use the already-compiled information from the Web site.

3.7 Marketing Mix

Pegasus' marketing mix is comprised of the following approaches to pricing, distribution, advertising and promotion, and customer service.

- *Pricing.* This will be based on a per-product retail price.
- *Distribution.* Initially, Pegasus will use a direct-to-consumer distribution model. Over time, Pegasus will use retailers as well.
- *Advertising and promotion.* Several different methods will be used for the advertising effort.
- *Customer service.* Pegasus will strive to achieve benchmarked levels of customer care.

3.8 Marketing Research

Pegasus is blessed with the good fortune of being located in the centre of the skating world: Venice, California. Pegasus will be able to leverage this opportune location by working with many of the different skaters that live in the area. Pegasus was able to test all of its products not only with its principals, who are accomplished skaters, but also with the many other dedicated and "newbie" users located in Venice. The extensive

product testing by a wide variety of users provided Pegasus with valuable product feedback and has led to several design improvements.

4.0 Financials

This section will offer the financial overview of Pegasus related to marketing activities. Pegasus will address break-even analysis, sales forecast, and expense forecast, and indicate how these activities link to the marketing strategy.

4.1 Break-Even Analysis

The break-even analysis indicates that $7760 will be required in monthly sales revenue to reach the break-even point.

Monthly Break-Even Point

Break-even point = where the line intersects with 0

TABLE 4.1	BREAK-EVEN ANALYSIS
Break-Even Analysis:	
Monthly Units Break-Even	62
Monthly Sales Break-Even	$ 7760
Assumptions:	
Average Per-Unit Revenue	$125.62
Average Per-Unit Variable Cost	$ 22.61
Estimated Monthly Fixed Cost	$ 6363

4.2 Sales Forecast

Pegasus feels that the sales forecast figures are conservative. Pegasus will steadily increase sales as the advertising budget allows. Although the target market forecast (Table 2.1) listed all of the potential customers divided into separate groups, the sales forecast groups customers into two categories: recreational and competitive. Reducing the number of categories allows the reader to quickly discern information, making the chart more functional.

Monthly Sales Forecast

TABLE 4.2	SALES FORECAST		
	Sales Forecast		
Sales	**2003**	**2004**	**2005**
Recreational	$455 740	$598 877	$687 765
Competitive	$ 72 918	$ 95 820	$110 042
Total Sales	$528 658	$694 697	$797 807
Direct Cost of Sales	**2003**	**2004**	**2005**
Recreational	$ 82 033	$107 798	$123 798
Competitive	$ 13 125	$ 17 248	$ 19 808
Subtotal Cost of Sales	$ 95 159	$125 046	$143 605

Monthly Expense Budget

TABLE 4.3	MARKETING EXPENSE BUDGET		
Marketing Expense Budget	**2003**	**2004**	**2005**
Web site	$25 000	$8 000	$10 000
Advertisements	$8 050	$15 000	$20 000
Printed Material	$1 725	$2 000	$3 000
Total Sales and Marketing Expenses	$34 775	$25 000	$33 000
Percent of Sales	6.58%	3.60%	4.14%
Contribution Margin	$398 725	$544 652	$621 202
Contribution Margin/Sales	75.42%	78.40%	77.86%

4.3 Expense Forecast

The expense forecast will be used as a tool to keep the department on target and provide indicators when corrections/modifications are needed for the proper implementation of the marketing plan.

5.0 Controls

The purpose of Pegasus' marketing plan is to serve as a guide for the organization. The following areas will be monitored to gauge performance:

- Revenue: monthly and annual.
- Expenses: monthly and annual.
- Customer satisfaction.
- New product development.

5.1 Implementation

The following milestones identify the key marketing programs. It is important to accomplish each one on time and on budget.

Milestones

TABLE 5.1	MILESTONES				
Milestones			**Plan**		
Milestone	**Start Date**	**End Date**	**Budget**	**Manager**	**Department**
Marketing plan completion	1/1/03	2/1/03	$0	Stan	Marketing
Web site completion	1/1/03	3/15/03	$20 400	outside firm	Marketing
Advertising campaign #1	1/1/03	6/30/03	$3 500	Stan	Marketing
Advertising campaign #2	3/1/99	12/30/03	$4 550	Stan	Marketing
Development of the retail channel	1/1/03	11/30/03	$0	Stan	Marketing
Totals			$28 450		

5.2 Marketing Organization

Stan Blade will be responsible for the marketing activities.

5.3 Contingency Planning

Difficulties and Risks

- Problems generating visibility, a function of being an Internet-based start-up organization.

- An entry into the market by an already established market competitor.

Worst Case Risks Include

- Determining that the business cannot support itself on an ongoing basis.
- Having to liquidate equipment or intellectual capital to cover liabilities.

SUMMARY

1. The value delivery process involves choosing (or identifying), providing (or delivering), and communicating superior value. The value chain is a tool for identifying key activities that create value and costs in a specific business.

2. Strong companies develop superior capabilities in managing core business processes such as new-product realization, inventory management, and customer acquisition and retention. Managing these core processes effectively means creating a marketing network in which the company works closely with all parties in the production and distribution chain, from suppliers of raw materials to retail distributors. Companies no longer compete—marketing networks do.

3. Holistic marketing maximizes value exploration by understanding the relationships between the customer's cognitive space, the company's competence space, and collaborator's resource space; maximizes value creation by identifying new customer benefits from the customer's cognitive space, utilizing core competencies from its business domain, and selecting and managing business partners from its collaborative networks; and maximizes value delivery by becoming proficient at customer relationship management, internal resource management, and business partnership management.

4. Market-oriented strategic planning is the managerial process of developing and maintaining a viable fit between the organization's objectives, skills, and resources and its changing market opportunities. The aim of strategic planning is to shape the company's businesses and products so that they yield target profits and growth. Strategic planning takes place at four levels: corporate, division, business unit, and product.

5. The corporate strategy establishes the framework within which the divisions and business units prepare their strategic plans. Setting a corporate strategy entails four activities: defining the corporate mission, establishing strategic business units (SBUs), assigning resources to each SBU based on its market attractiveness and business strength, and planning new businesses and downsizing older businesses.

6. Strategic planning for individual businesses entails the following activities: defining the business mission, analyzing external opportunities and threats, analyzing internal strengths and weaknesses, formulating goals, formulating strategy, formulating supporting programs, implementing the programs, and gathering feedback and exercising control.

7. Each product level within a business unit must develop a marketing plan for achieving its goals. The marketing plan is one of the most important outputs of the marketing process.

APPLICATIONS

Marketing Debate: What Good Is a Mission Statement?

Virtually all firms have mission statements to help guide and inspire employees as well as signal what is important to the firm to those outside the firm. Mission statements are often the product of much deliberation and discussion. At the same time, some critics claim that mission statements sometimes lack "teeth" and specificity. Moreover, critics also maintain that in many cases, mission statements do not vary much from firm to firm and make the same empty promises.

Take a position: Mission statements are critical to a successful marketing organization versus Mission statements rarely provide useful marketing value.

Marketing Discussion

Consider Porter's value chain and the holistic marketing orientation model. What implications do they have for marketing planning? How would you structure a marketing plan to incorporate some of their concepts?

Marketing Spotlight: Nike

Nike hit the ground running in 1962. Originally known as Blue Ribbon Sports, the company focused on providing high-quality running shoes designed especially for athletes by athletes. Founder Philip Knight believed that high-tech shoes for runners could be manufactured at competitive prices if imported from abroad. The company's commitment to designing innovative footwear for serious athletes helped it build a cult following among North American consumers. By 1980, Nike had become the number one athletic shoe company in the United States.

From the start, Nike's marketing campaigns featured winning athletes as spokespeople. The company signed on its first spokesperson, runner Steve Prefontaine, in 1973. Prefontaine's irreverent attitude matched Nike's spirit. Marketing campaigns featuring winning athletes made sense. Nike saw a "pyramid of influence"—it saw that product and brand choices are influenced by the preferences and behaviour of a small percentage of top athletes. Using professional athletes in its advertising campaigns was both efficient and effective for Nike.

In 1985, Nike signed up then-rookie guard Michael Jordan as a spokesperson. Jordan was still an up-and-comer, but he personified superior performance. Nike's bet paid off: The Air Jordan line of basketball shoes flew off the shelves, with Nike selling over US$100 million in the first year alone. Jordan also helped build the psychological image of the Nike brand. Phil Knight said: "Sports are at the heart of American culture, so a lot of emotion already exists around it. Emotions are always hard to explain, but there's something inspira-tional about watching athletes push the limits of performance. You can't explain much in 60 seconds, but when you show Michael Jordan, you don't have to."

In 1988, Nike aired its first ads in the "Just Do It" ad campaign. The US$20 million month-long blitz—subtly encouraging people to participate more actively in sports—featured 12 TV spots in all. The campaign challenged a generation of athletic enthusiasts to chase their goals; it was a natural manifestation of Nike's attitude of self-empowerment through sports. The campaign featured celebrities and noncelebrities. One noncelebrity ad featured Walt Stack, an 80-year-old long distance runner, running across the Golden Gate Bridge as part of his morning routine. The "Just Do It" trailer appeared on the screen as the shirtless Stack ran on a chilly morning. Talking to the camera as it zoomed in and while still running, Stack remarked, "People ask me how I keep my teeth from chattering when it's cold." Pausing, Stack matter-of-factly replied, "I leave them in my locker."

As Nike began expanding overseas to Europe, it found that its American-style ads were seen as too aggressive. The brand image was perceived as too fashion-oriented. Nike realized that it had to "authenticate" its brand in Europe the way it had in North America. That meant building credibility and relevance in European sports, especially soccer. Nike became actively involved as a sponsor of soccer youth leagues, local clubs, and national teams. Authenticity required that consumers see the product being used by athletes, especially by athletes who win. The big break came in 1994, when the Brazilian team (the only national team for which Nike had any real sponsorships) won the World Cup. The victory led Nike to sign other winning teams, and by 2003 overseas revenues surpassed U.S. revenues for the first time. Nike also topped US$10 billion in sales for the first time in that year as well.

Today, Nike dominates the athletic footwear market. Nine of the ten top-selling basketball shoes, for example, are Nikes. Nike introduces hundreds of shoes each year for 30 sports—averaging one new shoe style every day of the year. Swooshes abound on everything from wristwatches to golf clubs to swimming caps.

DISCUSSION QUESTIONS

1. What have been the key success factors for Nike?
2. Where is Nike vulnerable? What should it watch out for?
3. What recommendations would you make to senior marketing executives going forward? What should they be sure to do with its marketing?

Sources: Justin Ewers and Tim Smart, "A Designer Swooshes In," *U.S. News & World Report,* January 26, 2004, p. 12; "Corporate Media Executive of the Year," *Delaney Report,* January 12, 2004, p. 1; "10 Top Nontraditional Campaigns," *Advertising Age,* December 22, 2003, p. 24; Chris Zook and James Allen, "Growth Outside the Core," *Harvard Business Review* (December 2003): 66–74.

2 PART TWO

CAPTURING MARKETING INSIGHTS

IN THIS CHAPTER, WE WILL ADDRESS THE FOLLOWING QUESTIONS:

- What are the components of a modern marketing information system?

- What are useful internal records?

- What is involved with a marketing intelligence system?

- What are the key methods for tracking and identifying opportunities in the macroenvironment?

- What are some important macro-environment developments?

3

CHAPTER 3

Gathering Information and Scanning the Environment

PROFILE: CANADIAN MARKETING EXCELLENCE

Understanding the dynamics of the market environment is imperative for marketers. Trends in the consumer (and hence the business) marketplace are constant and unstoppable. As a result, the need to continuously and rigorously gather information about the market in which you operate is crucial for success and sustainability. Consider how concern about obesity has revolutionized the tactics of some of Canada's well-known marketers.

The World Health Organization recently called obesity "the greatest neglected public health problem of our time." The organization's report stated that chronic diseases, including cardiovascular diseases, cancers, diabetes, and obesity, are rising and contribute to 59 percent of the total reported deaths in the world. Statistics Canada reports that 48 percent of Canadians are overweight—and that percentage is higher in some provinces. Of even more concern to many Canadians is the fact that many of today's kids are fat. Thirty-seven percent of children between two and 11 are overweight, and half of these are obese.

Dr. Sheela Basrur, Ontario's chief medical officer, notes that obesity rates among children ages seven to 13 tripled between 1981 and 1996. Claiming that empty calories and inactive lifestyles are creating an "obesity epidemic," she calls for action on the part of government, individuals, and companies. In particular, she notes that Aboriginals, low-income earners, and rural and northern residents are most vulnerable to the ill effects of obesity. The issue is clearly top of mind among Canadians, with the number of newspaper articles mentioning obesity doubling between 2002 and 2004. A recent Ipsos-Reid poll found that 93 percent of Canadians try to make healthy eating decisions.

One Toronto marketing executive compared the issue to the alcohol and tobacco megatrends of the 1990s, adding that while there is a concern from a litigation and legislation point of view, the "whole health and wellness issue is my number-one opportunity." In a similar vein, Paul Morrison, senior litigation partner at McCarthy Tétrault in Toronto, notes, "While it took about 900 lawsuits before tobacco manufacturers in the United States were forced to change their marketing, in many respects this paved the legal way for the anti-fat movement. Even Wall Street has warned that anti-obesity measures will curb the ability of fast food, soft drink, confectionery and snack companies to grow revenues in the future."

It's not surprising, then, that food and beverage marketers are taking notice. Firms throughout the industry certainly have their antennas up and they are all closely monitoring the evolving opinions of global health organizations, national and international governments, and consumer attitudes. They have reason to be concerned. Experts like Bruce Holub, a professor of nutritional sciences at the University of Guelph in Ontario, would like to see hazard warnings about food composition on visible surfaces in fast food outlets: "We allow for no smoking signs in these facilities, so I don't see why we're not doing something similar for food. People can ignore it or not, but at least it's there for people who want it."

How have Canadian food and beverage marketers responded to this major societal trend? There are almost as many strategies as there are companies. Kraft Foods was one of the first firms to go into damage control mode. In 2003, it made a series of public announcements about its commitment to fighting child obesity through better labelling, smaller portion sizes, and an end to in-school marketing. Thus, it's no surprise that Canadians chose Kraft as the most trusted brand in the food-manufacturing category in an Ipsos-Reid poll that same year. To accomplish a similar end, McCain Foods, one of the world's largest producers of French fries, debuted a nonhydrogenated version of its product.

Coca-Cola, another highly trusted brand, chose quite a different tactic. To increase awareness of the choices consumers have, the company launched new ads, which showed the whole line of Coke beverage brands, including fruit juices and Dasani water. Pepsi was quick to respond. It first announced that 50 percent of its product innovation efforts and those of its subsidiary, Frito-Lay, would be focused on developing healthier snack choices. In 2004, it launched its first product resulting from this effort—Rold Gold Heartzels (heart-in-heart shaped pretzels). Frito-Lay also worked in collaboration with the American Heart Association. The new snack was the first pretzel to meet the association's "Heart-check mark" guidelines as a heart-healthy food. Frito-Lay also ran full-page newspaper ads demonstrating the variety of its Frito-Lay brand snack foods that are free of trans fats. Frito-Lay Canada went on to relaunch some healthier alternatives of its popular snacks, including baked Doritos, Ruffles, Tostitos, and Lays. Dale Hooper, Frito-Lay's Toronto-based vice-president of marketing, says, "The whole goal is to provide choices and assist Canadians, in terms of their habits, to lead healthier and happier lives through products and education."

Unilever Canada also thinks Canadians should have more options on the grocery shelf. Thus, in 2004, it launched its new Carb Options line-up. Its research, however, showed that consumers were worried about taste when it came to choosing "low-fat," "light," or "low-carb" foods. Furthermore, Unilever realized that most Canadians just don't want to give up their usual peanut butter for something unknown. Thus, Unilever's solution was to bring together familiar brand names like Knorr, Skippy, and Hellmann's, but offer low-carb versions of these mainstay products. Through advertising and relabelling, the company worked to convince consumers to give the reformulated products a try. Geoff Craig, a Unilever marketing director, explains, "It's always tough launching a new brand—and it's expensive. So that's where I think people trust our brands in terms of offering them taste and variety." Unilever took a gamble that the low-carb obsession wasn't just a fad. The odds weren't in their favour, however, and the line was dropped.

Even vendors in fast food courts are starting to respond. In December 2004, Toronto-based New York Fries eliminated trans fats from its gravy and cheese, making its poutine trans fat free. Earlier that year, the company had removed trans fats from its fries by switching to sunflower oil. According to Jay Gould, president of New York Fries, "Our mantra has always been if we can make a better product than we do now, we will." Unlike fad diets like Atkins, trans fat "was becoming more and more of an issue," he adds. "And inasmuch as we could do something about it, we did."

Even beer companies are responding to the trend. After an Ipsos-Reid poll found that 35 percent of Canadians would try a low-carb beer, Sleeman Breweries launched a new low-carb beer in 2003. The company held a press conference before the launch, which resulted in extensive TV and radio coverage.

Rather than waiting for government legislation to force change, proactive companies are changing their advertising tactics as well as their products, says Robin Garrett, vice-president of Food and Consumer Products Canada. For example, in early 2005 Kraft Foods announced that it's phasing out ads aimed at six- to 11-year-olds that feature snack foods such as Oreos and Chips Ahoy! cookies and regular Kool-Aid. Garrett notes that companies like Kraft are "certainly aware of consumer interest." He went on to say, "This is the business that we're in—to serve the needs of consumers—and it only is a positive move for companies to focus on promoting foods that have an improved nutritional value or already have a high nutritional value."

Despite all of these positive efforts, some marketers believe that some of the proposed product solutions may be as harmful as the problem of obesity itself. A young brand manager from a large Canadian packaged goods firm recently refused to accept a promotion when he was asked to manage a low-carbohydrate line of products. "People don't understand how harmful low-carb diets can be," he notes. "Without carbs in the diet, the body begins using protein as its fuel; but protein is an 'inefficient' fuel source, since its real purpose is for rebuilding, not for fuel. In severely restricted diets, this protein breakdown can also include muscle and heart tissue, leading to serious health problems, even death. Another danger is that overconsumption of protein can be hard on the kidneys."

In response to all these concerns, Canada's packaged goods industry association says the anti-fat movement should focus on bad diets, not just on bad foods. "All foods can fit in a diet, but it's how you make your choices over the long term that is important," says Carolyn O'Brien, director of scientific and regulatory affairs at the Food and Consumer Products and Manufacturers of Canada. Thus, there is no doubt that meeting the challenge of obesity is far from over, but hopefully marketers will be part of the solution.

Sources: Sara Minogue, "The War on Fat," *Strategy Magazine*, October 20, 2003, p. 15; Rebecca Harris, "Will Ad Limits Help Kids?" *Marketing Magazine*, January 24, 2005; Lesley Young, "In the Fat Seat," *Marketing Magazine*, August 11, 2003; Lisa D'Innocenzo, "Unilever's Carb Options: Will Canadians Bite?" *Strategy Magazine*, June 14, 2004, p. 3; Roberta Lenard, "Body Talk: Low-Carb Fact and Fiction," *Africana*, June 10, 2004, **www.africana.com/columns/lenard/hb20040610carb.asp** (viewed January 28, 2005).

Marketers must have comprehensive, up-to-date information if they are to develop insightful and inspirational marketing plans for serving their target audiences. As the preceding discussion shows, they must understand both the broad trends influencing their marketplace as well as the unique attitudes and habits of their buyers. In this chapter, we consider how firms can develop processes to track such trends. In Chapter 4 we will see how marketers conduct more customized research that addresses specific marketing problems or issues.

Components of a Modern Marketing Information System

The major responsibility for identifying significant marketplace changes falls to the company's marketers. More than any other group in the company, they must be the trend trackers and opportunity seekers. Although every manager in an organization needs to observe the outside environment, marketers have two advantages: They have disciplined methods for collecting information and they also spend more time interacting with customers and observing competition.

Some firms have developed marketing information systems that provide management with rich detail about buyer wants, preferences, and behaviour.

DuPont

DuPont commissioned marketing studies to uncover personal pillow behaviour for its Dacron Polyester unit, which supplies filling to pillow makers and sells its own Comforel brand. One challenge is that people don't give up their old pillows: 37 percent of one sample described their relationship with their pillow as like "an old married couple" and an additional 13 percent characterized it as like a "childhood friend." They found that people fell into distinct groups in terms of pillow behaviour: stackers (23 percent), plumpers (20 percent), rollers or folders (16 percent), cuddlers (16 percent), and smashers, who pound their pillows into a more comfy shape (10 percent). Women were more likely to plump, whereas men were more likely to fold. The prevalence of stackers led the company to sell more pillows packaged as pairs, as well as to market different levels of softness or firmness.[1]

Marketers also have extensive information about how consumption patterns vary across countries. On a per capita basis within Western Europe, for example, the Swiss consume the most chocolate, the Greeks eat the most cheese, the Irish drink the most tea, and the Austrians smoke the most cigarettes.

Nevertheless, many business firms are not sophisticated about gathering information. Many do not have a marketing research department. Others have a department that limits its work to routine forecasting, sales analysis, and occasional surveys. Many managers complain about not knowing where critical information is located in the company; getting too much information that they cannot use and too little that they really need; getting important information too late; and doubting the information's accuracy. Companies with superior information enjoy a competitive advantage. The company can choose its markets better, develop better offerings, and execute better marketing planning.

Every firm must organize and distribute a continuous flow of information to its marketing managers. Companies study their managers' information needs and design marketing information systems to meet these needs. A **marketing information system (MIS)** consists of people, equipment, and procedures to gather, sort, analyze, evaluate, and distribute needed, timely, and accurate information to marketing decision makers. A marketing information system is developed from internal company records, marketing intelligence activities, and marketing research. The first two topics are discussed here; the latter topic is reviewed in the next chapter.

The company's marketing information system should be a cross between what managers think they need, what managers really need, and what is economically feasible. An internal MIS committee can interview a cross-section of marketing managers to discover their information needs. Table 3.1 displays some useful questions.

Internal Records and Marketing Intelligence

Marketing managers rely on internal reports on orders, sales, prices, costs, inventory levels, receivables, payables, and so on. By analyzing this information, they can spot important opportunities and problems.

The Order-to-Payment Cycle

The heart of the internal records system is the order-to-payment cycle. Sales representatives, dealers, and customers send orders to the firm. The sales department prepares invoices and transmits copies

TABLE 3.1	INFORMATION NEEDS PROBES

1. What decisions do you regularly make?
2. What information do you need to make these decisions?
3. What information do you regularly get?
4. What special studies do you periodically request?
5. What information would you want that you are not getting now?
6. What information would you want daily? Weekly? Monthly? Yearly?
7. What magazines and trade reports would you like to see on a regular basis?
8. What topics would you like to be kept informed of?
9. What data analysis programs would you want?
10. What are the four most helpful improvements that could be made in the present marketing information system?

to various departments. Out-of-stock items are back ordered. Shipped items are accompanied by shipping and billing documents that are sent to various departments.

Today's companies need to perform these steps quickly and accurately. Customers favour firms that can promise timely delivery. Customers and sales representatives fax or e-mail their orders. Computerized warehouses quickly fill these orders. The billing department sends out invoices as quickly as possible. An increasing number of companies are using the Internet and extranets to improve the speed, accuracy, and efficiency of the order-to-payment cycle.

Sales Information Systems

Marketing managers need timely and accurate reports on current sales. Wal-Mart, for example, knows the sales of each product by store and total each evening. This enables it to transmit nightly orders to suppliers for new shipments of replacement stock. Wal-Mart shares its sales data with its larger suppliers such as P&G and expects P&G to re-supply Wal-Mart stores in a timely manner. Wal-Mart has entrusted P&G with the management of its inventory.[2]

Companies must carefully interpret the sales data so as not to get the wrong signals. Michael Dell gave this illustration: "If you have three yellow Mustangs sitting on a dealer's lot and a customer wants a red one, the salesman may be really good at figuring out how to sell the yellow Mustang. So the yellow Mustang gets sold, and a signal gets sent back to the factory that, hey, people want yellow Mustangs."

Technological gadgets are revolutionizing sales information systems and allowing representatives from companies like insurance giant Clarica of Waterloo, Ontario, to have up-to-the-second information. Clarica's system allows agents to complete 90 percent of the applications for insurance electronically and enables the company to deliver policies to clients the day after they apply.[3]

Databases, Data Warehouses, and Data Mining

Today companies organize their information in databases—customer databases, product databases, salesperson databases—and then combine data from the different databases. For example, the customer database will contain every customer's name, address, past transactions, and even demographics and psychographics (activities, interests, and opinions) in some instances. Instead of a company sending a mass "carpet bombing" mailing of a new offer to every customer in its database, it will score the different customers according to purchase recency, frequency, and monetary value. It will send the offer only to the highest-scoring customers. Besides saving on mailing expenses, this will often achieve a double-digit response rate.

Companies warehouse these data and make them easily accessible to decision makers. Furthermore, by hiring analysts skilled in sophisticated statistical methods, they can "mine" the data and garner fresh insights into neglected customer segments, recent customer trends, and other useful information. The customer information can be cross-tabbed with product and salesperson information to yield still deeper insights. To manage all the different databases efficiently and effectively, more firms are using business integration software (see "Marketing Insight: Putting Data to Work with Business Integration Software").

Putting Data to Work with Business Integration Software

In the 1990s, companies spent billions installing giant databases and data warehouses and then enormous sums on consultants trying to make sense of it all. A typical large retailer now has 80 terabytes worth of stored information—equivalent to 16 million digital photos or 500 kilometres of bookshelves. Wal-Mart has a staggering 285 terabytes in its data warehouse.

But data have value only if they can be used. As one analyst put it, "It's like having a bank account with millions of dollars in it but no ATM card. If you can't get it out and can't make it work for you, then it is not really useful." Business integration (BI) software is designed to analyze and interpret massive quantities of data. Typical BI applications cull information out of giant databases and put it into "data marts"—smaller clusters of similar information. Breaking data down in this way helps to more easily and thoroughly diffuse information through the organization.

Consider how business integration software allows Ben & Jerry's to monitor a carton of ice cream from inception to consumption. At Ben & Jerry's headquarters, each container of ice cream is stamped after manufacture and its tracking number put in an Oracle database. Using Business Objects software, the sales team can then see which flavours are generating the most sales (Cherry Garcia is a perennial favourite). The marketing department can check to see whether orders online require additional philanthropic donations. The finance people are able to record sales and close their books more quickly. Consumer affairs can match up the cartons of ice cream with the roughly 225 calls and e-mails the company receives each week to make sure there are no systematic problems with any particular ingredients.

BI software is seen as relatively inexpensive and convenient to install, and the results can show up quickly. The Sesame Workshop installed the software for the holiday 2003 season to track its Elmo dolls and was able to cut its back orders by a third. Red Robin Gourmet Burgers, a 196-location chain, used BI software to fine-tune its marketing and operations. It found it was wasting thousands on unused sauces. Staples long devoted space to high-margin furniture. With BI, it found that small items were more profitable. Successes like these are why the market for business integration software is expected to reach US$7.5 billion in 2006.

Source: Adapted from Julie Schlosser, "Looking for Intelligence in Ice Cream," *Fortune*, March 17, 2003, pp. 114–120.

The Hudson Bay Company

As a member of the HBC group of companies, Zellers was able to mine the large HBC customer database when it launched the Mossimo fashion line in its stores. The company was able to identify customers who typically did not purchase fashion clothing lines from discount department stores such as Zellers to inform them that, in fact, the store was carrying a brand that they might consider purchasing. The effort won Zellers and its agency a silver award at the Canadian Marketing Association awards in 2003. HBC has found data mining and database marketing so useful that it is beginning to leverage the technique beyond marketing to such matters as store layout and merchandise planning.[4]

The Marketing Intelligence System

The internal records system supplies *results* data, but the marketing intelligence system supplies *happenings* data. A **marketing intelligence system** is a set of procedures and sources managers use to obtain everyday information about developments in the marketing environment. Marketing managers collect marketing intelligence by reading books, newspapers, and trade publications; talking to customers, suppliers, and distributors; and meeting with other company managers.

A company can take several steps to improve the quality of its marketing intelligence:

■ *A company can train and motivate the sales force to spot and report new developments.* Sales representatives are positioned to pick up information missed by other means, yet they often fail to pass on that information. The company must "sell" its sales force on their importance as intelligence gatherers. Sales reps should know which types of information to send to which managers. For instance, the Pearson sales reps who sell this textbook let their editors know what is going on in each discipline, who is doing exciting research, and who plans to write cutting-edge textbooks.

■ *A company can motivate distributors, retailers, and other intermediaries to pass along important intelligence.* Many companies hire specialists to gather marketing intelligence. Service providers often send mystery shoppers to their stores to assess how employees treat customers. Mystery shoppers for McDonald's discovered that only 46 percent of its restaurants met internal speed-of-service standards, forcing the company to rethink processes and training.[5] Retailers also use mystery shoppers. Neiman Marcus employs a professional shopper agency to shop at its stores. It finds stores that consistently score high on the service have the best sales. Typical questions their mystery shoppers report on are: How long before a sales associate greeted you? Did the sales associate act as if he or she wanted your business? Was the sales associate knowledgeable about products in stock?[6]

■ *A company can network externally.* It can purchase competitors' products; attend open houses and trade shows; read competitors' published reports; attend shareholders' meetings; talk to employees, dealers, distributors, suppliers, and freight agents; collect competitors' ads; and look up news stories about competitors. Software developer Cognos created an internal Web site called Street Fighter where any of the firm's 3000 workers can submit scoops about competitors and win prizes.[7] Competitive intelligence must be done legally and ethically, though. Procter & Gamble reportedly paid a multi-million dollar settlement to Unilever when some external operatives hired as part of a P&G corporate intelligence program to learn about Unilever's hair-care products were found to have engaged in such unethical behaviour as "dumpster diving."[8]

■ *A company can set up a customer advisory panel.* Members might include representative customers or the company's largest customers or its most outspoken or sophisticated customers. Many business schools have advisory panels made up of alumni and recruiters who provide valuable feedback on the curriculum.

■ *A company can take advantage of government data resources.* The 2001 Canadian census performed by Statistics Canada provides an in-depth look at population growth and change, demographic groups, family structure, and many other useful facts about Canadians.[9]

■ *A company can purchase information from outside suppliers.* Well-known data suppliers include A.C. Nielsen Canada and Information Resources, Inc. (see Table 3.2). These research firms gather consumer-panel data at a much lower cost than the company could manage on its own. Biz360 has specialized databases to provide reports from 7000 sources on the extent and nature of media coverage a company is receiving.[10]

■ *A company can use online customer feedback systems to collect competitive intelligence.* Online customer feedback facilitates collection and dissemination of information on a global scale, usually at low cost. Through online customer review boards or forums, one customer's evaluation of a product or a supplier can be distributed to a large number of other potential buyers and, of course, to marketers seeking information on the competition. Currently existing channels for feedback include message boards; threaded discussion forums that allow users to post new and follow up existing posts; discussion forums, which are more like bulletin boards; opinion forums, which feature more in-depth, lengthy reviews; and chat rooms. While chat rooms have the advantage of allowing users to share experiences and impressions, their unstructured nature makes it difficult for marketers to find relevant messages. To address this issue, various companies have adopted structured systems, such as customer discussion boards or customer reviews. See "Marketing Memo: Clicking on the Competition" for a summary of the major categories of structured online feedback systems.[11]

Some companies circulate marketing intelligence. The staff scans the Internet and major publications, abstracts relevant news, and disseminates a news bulletin to marketing managers. It collects and files relevant information and assists managers in evaluating new information.

TABLE 3.2	SECONDARY COMMERCIAL DATA SOURCES

- *Ipsos-Reid*, www.ipsos-reid.com. A weekly omnibus poll of more than 125 000 household and Internet panels, and syndicated studies such as *The Ipsos Trend Report Canada* and the *Inter@ctive Reid Report*.
- *NDP Group*, www.ndp.com. Online panels that track purchasing behaviour in Canadian and world markets.
- *A.C. Nielsen Canada*, www.acnielsen.ca. Data on products and brands sold through retail outlets (Retail Index Services), supermarket scanner data (Scantrack), and others.
- *Information Resources, Inc.*, www.infores.com. Supermarket scanner data (InfoScan) and data on the impact of supermarket promotions (PromotioScan).
- *SAMI/Burke* (acquired by the PDI partnership—Promotion Decisions Inc. and Knowledge Networks). A range of research services, including the National Shopper Lab (a household panel of 10 million for consumer diagnostics), as well as controlled store testing and market mix modelling.
- *Simmons Market Research Bureau (MRB Group)*, www.smrb.com. Annual reports covering television markets, sporting goods, and proprietary drugs, with demographic data by sex, income, age, and brand preferences (selective markets and media reaching them).
- *NOP World* (includes Roper ASW). One of the world's largest market research and business information companies,

serving North America, Europe, and Asia; offers an extensive range of both custom and syndicated research including media studies, industry specific studies, and analytic CRM services.
- *Market Facts* (a subsidiary of Aegis Group Plc.). A leading global marketing research and information company that provides services to many consumer packaged goods companies, as well as the automotive, financial, telecommunications, pharmaceuticals, and government sectors.
- *Canadian Marketing Association*, www.the-cma.org. Publishes reports on a variety of topics of interest to professional marketers.
- *Retail Council of Canada*, www.retailcouncil.org. Publishes publicly accessible and proprietary reports for retailers.
- *ESOMAR*, www.esomar.nl. The World Association of Opinion and Marketing Research Professionals, uniting over 4000 members in 100 countries. By using its directory, marketers can locate member agencies that specialize in providing market research for specific markets and countries.
- Other commercial research houses selling data to subscribers include the Audit Bureau of Circulations, Arbitron, Dun & Bradstreet's, and Starch.

Analyzing the Macroenvironment

Successful companies recognize and respond profitably to unmet needs and trends. Companies could make a fortune if they could solve any of these problems: a cure for cancer; chemical cures for mental diseases; desalinization of seawater; nonfattening, tasty nutritious food; practical electric cars; and affordable housing.

Needs and Trends

Enterprising individuals and companies manage to create new solutions to unmet needs. FedEx was created to meet the need for next-day mail delivery. Dockers was created to meet the needs of baby boomers who could no longer really wear—or fit into!—their jeans and wanted a physically and psychologically comfortable pair of pants. Amazon was created to offer more choice and information for books and other products.

We can draw distinctions among fads, trends, and megatrends. A **fad** is "unpredictable, short-lived, and without social, economic, and political significance." A company can cash in on a fad such as Beanie Babies, Furbies, and Tickle Me Elmo dolls, but this is more a matter of luck and good timing than anything else.[12]

A **trend** is a direction or sequence of events that has some momentum and durability. Trends are more predictable and durable than fads. A trend reveals the shape of the future and provides many opportunities. For example, the percentage of people who value physical fitness and well-being has risen steadily. Yoga is experiencing a rebirth. Vancouver-based Lululemon was born to serve people following this trend, particularly upscale young women in the under-30 group. See what DeBoer's Furniture did to respond to another trend.

Marketing Memo

Clicking on the Competition

There are four main ways marketers can find relevant online information on competitors' product strengths and weaknesses, as well as summary comments and overall performance rating of a product, service or supplier.

- *Independent customer goods and service review forums.* These forums include well-known Web sites such as Epinions.com, Rateital.com, Consumerreview.com, and Bizrate.com. Bizrate.com combines consumer feedback from two sources: its 1.2 million members who have volunteered to provide ratings and feedback to assist other shoppers, and survey results on service quality collected from customers of stores listed in Bizrate. These sites have the advantage of being independent from the goods and service providers, which may reduce bias.

- *Distributor or sales agent feedback sites.* These sites offer both positive and negative product or service reviews, but the stores or distributors have built the sites themselves. Chapters.Indigo.ca, for instance, offers an interactive feedback opportunity through which buyers, readers, editors, and others may review all products listed on the site, especially books. Elance.com is an online professional services provider that allows contractors to describe their level of satisfaction with subcontractors and provide details of their experiences.

- *Combo-sites offering customer reviews and expert opinions.* This type of site is concentrated in financial services and high-tech products that require professional knowledge. Zdnet.com, an online advisor on technology products, offers customer comments and evaluations based on ease of use, features, and stability, along with expert reviews. Zdnet summarizes the number of positive and negative evaluations and total download numbers within a certain period (commonly a week or a month) for each software program. The advantage of this type of review site lies in the fact that a product supplier can compare opinions from the experts with those from consumers.

- *Customer complaint sites.* These forums are designed mainly for dissatisfied customers. Reviewers at most opinion sites tend to offer positive comments due to financial incentives and potential lawsuits for slanderous or libellous negative comments. In contrast, some Web sites offer a complaining forum with a moderator. For instance, Planetfeedback.com allows customers to voice unfavourable experiences with specific companies. Another site, Complaints.com, is devoted to customers who want to vent their frustrations with particular firms or their offerings.

Source: Adapted from Robin T. Peterson and Zhilin Yang, "Web Product Reviews Help Strategy," *Marketing News*, April 7, 2004, p. 18.

DeBoer's Furniture

DeBoer's Furniture, headquartered in Concord, Ontario, operates five retail outlets in the Greater Toronto Area and one in Ottawa. In 2003, as Canada began to legitimize gay marriage, many same-sex couples flocked to get married. Since many gay and lesbian couples earn above average incomes, and have professional jobs and expensive habits, they represent a lucrative market. Working from the premise that "everybody needs a new sofa," DeBoer's Furniture is one company that created advertising designed to attract this market. In its newest campaign, labelled "Stressless," DeBoer's takes aim at another trend—harried two-income families who just want to step away from the pressures of their daily lives and enjoy their children and home, furnished, of course, with DeBoer's fine furnishings. The text in the ad (which builds a link with the Toronto International Film festival) promises people that they can get the best seat in the house any day of the year, not just when the festival is running.[13]

Megatrends have been described as "large social, economic, political and technological changes [that] are slow to form, and once in place, they influence us for some time—between seven and ten years, or longer."[14] See "Marketing Insight: Ten Megatrends Shaping the Consumer Landscape" for a look into the forces in play during the next decade or so.

Trends and megatrends merit close attention. A new product or marketing program is likely to be more successful if it is in line with strong trends rather than opposed to them, but detecting a new market opportunity does not guarantee success, even if it is technically feasible. For example, today some companies sell portable "electronic books"; but there may not be a sufficient number of people

DeBoer's has been highly successful at communicating with different target markets through the use of precise media selection.

MARKETING INSIGHT

Megatrends Shaping the Consumer Landscape

- *Aging boomers.* As baby boomers grow older, their impact on consumer spending can hardly be overstated. In 1961, only 8 percent of Canadians were aged 65 or older. In 2002, this proportion had risen to 13 percent, and it is projected to reach as high as 21 percent in 2026.

- *Delayed retirement.* Baby boomers have delayed every life stage transition, such as getting married and having children. So it's highly likely that they will also delay their retirement.

- *The changing nature of work.* Demand for highly skilled workers has changed the labour market. From 1991 to 2001, people in highly skilled labour occupations, which normally require a university education, accounted for almost half of the growth in the total labour force. In 2001, these workers accounted for 16 percent of the total labour force, up from 13 percent a decade earlier.

- *Greater educational attainment.* With so many jobs requiring intellectual skills, the number of high school graduates pursuing higher levels of education is rising. Fifty years ago, just over half the adult population had less than a Grade 9 education. By 2002, however, 45 percent of Canadians aged 15 and older had completed some form of post-secondary education.

- *Labour shortages.* As a result of an aging population, an increasingly skilled population, and increasing urbanization, many labour shortages are expected in various sectors of the economy in years to come. For example, the health sector is expected to be particularly affected, given rising demand and, in some cases, declining supply (e.g., general practitioners).

- *Increased immigration.* In 2001, a whopping 18 percent of all Canadians were foreign born. Between 2001 and 2002, Canada's population increase from immigration was almost twice as much as from natural growth. Immigration has always been an important factor in Canadian growth given our low birth rate, and it is expected to remain so.

- *Continued urbanization.* Canadians and new Canadians alike continue to gravitate toward towns and cities, particularly large cities. Almost all census metropolitan areas in Canada have seen growth since 1990.

Sources: Adapted from Peter Francese, "Top Trends for 2003," *American Demographics*, December 2002/January 2003, pp. 48–51; Statistics Canada, "Canada e-Book: The People," **http://142.206.72.67/r000_e.htm** (viewed November 4, 2004).

interested in reading a book on a computer screen or willing to pay the required price. This is why market research is necessary to determine an opportunity's profit potential.

To help marketers spot cultural shifts that might bring new opportunities or threats, several firms offer social-cultural forecasts. The Yankelovich Monitor interviews 2500 people each year and has tracked 35 social trends since 1971, such as "anti-bigness," "mysticism," "living for today," "away from possessions," and "sensuousness." It describes the percentage of the population who share the attitude as well as the percentage who do not.

Identifying the Major Forces

Companies and their suppliers, marketing intermediaries, customers, competitors, and publics all operate in a macroenvironment of forces and trends that shape opportunities and pose threats. These forces represent "noncontrollables" that the company must monitor and respond to. In the economic arena, companies and consumers are increasingly affected by global forces (see Table 3.3).

The beginning of the new century brought a series of new challenges: the steep decline of the stock market, which affected savings, investment, and retirement funds; increasing unemployment; corporate scandals; and, of course, the rise of terrorism. These dramatic events were accompanied by the continuation of other, already-existing longer-term trends that have profoundly influenced the global landscape.

Within the rapidly changing global picture, the firm must monitor six major forces: demographic, economic, social-cultural, natural, technological, and political-legal. Although these forces will be described separately, marketers must pay attention to their interactions, because these will lead to new opportunities and threats. For example, explosive population growth (demographic) leads to more resource depletion and pollution (natural), which leads consumers to call for more laws (political-legal), which stimulate new technological solutions and products (technological), which, if they are affordable (economic), may actually change attitudes and behaviour (social-cultural).

Demographic Environment

Demographic trends are highly reliable for the short and intermediate run. There is little excuse for a company's being suddenly surprised by demographic developments. The Singer Company should have known for years that its sewing machine business would be hurt by smaller families and more working wives, yet it was slow in responding.

TABLE 3.3	GLOBAL FORCES AFFECTING MARKETING

1. The substantial speedup of international transportation, communication, and financial transactions, leading to the rapid growth of world trade and investment, especially tripolar trade (North America, Western Europe, Asia).
2. The movement of manufacturing capacity and skills to lower-cost countries.
3. The rise of trade blocs such as the European Union and the NAFTA signatories.
4. The severe debt problems of a number of countries, along with the increasing fragility of the international financial system.
5. The increasing use of barter and countertrade to support international transactions.
6. The move toward market economies in formerly socialist countries along with rapid privatization of publicly owned companies.
7. The rapid dissemination of global lifestyles.
8. The development of emerging markets, namely China, India, Eastern Europe, the Arab countries, and Latin America.
9. The increasing tendency of multinationals to transcend locational and national characteristics and become transnational firms.
10. The increasing number of cross-border corporate strategic alliances—for example, airlines.
11. The increasing ethnic and religious conflicts in certain countries and regions.
12. The growth of global brands across a wide variety of industries such as automobiles, food, clothing, and electronics.

The main demographic force that marketers monitor is *population*, because people make up markets. Marketers are keenly interested in the size and growth rate of population in cities, regions, and nations; age distribution and ethnic mix; educational levels; household patterns; and regional characteristics and movements.

Worldwide Population Growth

The world population is showing explosive growth: it totalled 6.1 billion in 2000 and will exceed 7.9 billion by the year 2025.[15] In early 2005, Canada's population was estimated by Statistics Canada to be over 32 million people. Canada's population growth exceeds that of many other developed nations; however, the population grew by only 4 percent during the 1996–2001 census period. This is a remarkable decline, given the 13 to 14 percent growth Canada experienced during the late 1940s to 1950s.[16]

Here is an interesting picture:

> If the world were a village of 1000 people, it would consist of 520 women and 480 men, 330 children and 60 people over age 65, 10 college graduates and 335 illiterate adults. The village would contain 52 North Americans, 55 Russians, 84 Latin Americans, 95 East and West Europeans, 124 Africans, and 584 Asians. Communication would be difficult because 165 people would speak Mandarin, 86 English, 83 Hindi/Urdu, 64 Spanish, 58 Russian, and 37 Arabic, and the rest would speak one of over 200 other languages. There would be 329 Christians, 178 Moslems, 132 Hindus, 62 Buddhists, 3 Jews, 167 nonreligious, 45 atheists, and 86 others.[17]

The population explosion has been a source of major concern. Unchecked population growth and consumption could eventually result in insufficient food supply, depletion of key minerals, overcrowding, pollution, and an overall deterioration in the quality of life. Moreover, population growth is highest in countries and communities that can least afford it. The less developed regions of the world currently account for 76 percent of the world population and are growing at 2 percent per year, whereas the population in the more developed countries is growing at only 0.6 percent per year. In developing countries, the death rate has been falling as a result of modern medicine, but the birthrate has remained fairly stable. Feeding, clothing, and educating children, while also providing a rising standard of living, is nearly impossible in these countries.

Explosive population growth has major implications for business. A growing population does not mean growing markets unless these markets have sufficient purchasing power. Nonetheless, companies that carefully analyze their markets can find major opportunities. For example, to curb its skyrocketing population, the Chinese government has passed regulations limiting families to one child. One consequence of these regulations: These children are spoiled and fussed over as never before. Known in China as "little emperors," Chinese children are being showered with everything from candy to computers as a result of the "six pocket syndrome." As many as six adults—parents, grandparents, great-grandparents, and aunts and uncles—may be indulging the whims of each child. This trend has encouraged toy companies, such as Japan's Bandai Company, Denmark's Lego Group, and the U.S.'s Hasbro and Mattel, to aggressively enter the Chinese market.[18]

Population Age Mix

National populations vary in their age mix. At one extreme is Mexico, a country with a very young population and rapid population growth. At the other extreme is Japan, a country with one of the world's oldest populations. Milk, diapers, school supplies, and toys would be important products in Mexico. Japan's population would consume many more adult products.

However, there is a global trend toward an aging population. According to a survey in *The Economist*, more people will grow old in this century than ever before. In 2004 or 2005, the population of people aged 60 or over will surpass the proportion of under fives, and there are unlikely to ever again be more toddlers than seniors. It is the start of what the Japanese are calling the "Silver Century." The greying of the population is affected by another trend, the widespread fall in fertility rates. In most countries, women are not having enough babies to replace the people who die. The result will be fewer working people to replace those who retire. In a decade's time, many countries—Japan, the United States, Canada, and the European countries, for instance—will face the huge problem of having to support a vastly larger population of elderly people.[19]

A population can be subdivided into six age groups: preschool, school-age children, teens, young adults aged 25 to 40, middle-aged adults aged 40 to 65, and older adults aged 65 and up. For marketers, the most populous age groups shape the marketing environment. Thus, baby boomers are one of the most powerful forces shaping the marketplace.

A Mattel ad in Chinese for its Hot Wheels toy. The headline reads: "Hot Wheels Performance Tracks—Great Varieties, Great Challenges!"

Although there was a baby boom in both Canada and the United States, it is important for Canadian marketers to note that our baby boom was unique. It started later than the one in the United States (in 1947 versus 1946) and it lasted for a more prolonged period. (The American boom ended in 1964; the Canadian boom continued until 1966). The size of the boomer population in Canada is almost 10 million.[20] Furthermore, the baby boom was not a worldwide phenomenon. No developed countries, other than Australia and New Zealand, experienced the same expansion in the birth rate. In Europe, there was no baby boom, and in Japan, the birth rate declined during the baby boom years, explaining why these countries have a higher proportion of older people in their societies.

The age groups that will experience the most rapid growth in Canada in the coming decades will be older adults and teenagers—not good news for products aimed at other market segments. Consider what one organization did to respond to population age shifts.

Chatelaine

"How do you stay healthy if you don't add new readers to the franchise?" This is an important question if you are the editor of *Chatelaine*, Canada's most-read women's magazine. The magazine had traditionally been aimed at the baby boom generation, but with the aging of this group, Chatelaine found that it had few readers in the 20 to 30 age group. A $2 million makeover of the venerable magazine was undertaken. Care had to be taken, however, so that new readers were added without replacing current readers. The new *Chatelaine* is glossier and more sophisticated. Not only has it drawn new readers, it has also lured new advertisers—not just more cosmetics and packaged goods firms, but also telecommunications and entertainment firms that, like the revamped magazine, have a younger target audience.[21]

Chatelaine underwent a successful makeover to attract a younger demographic.

Baby boomers are fixated on their youth, not their age. Boomers grew up with TV advertising, so they are an easier market to reach than those born between 1965 and 1976, dubbed Generation X (and also the shadow generation and baby busters).[22] GenerationXers are typically cynical about hard-sell marketing pitches that promise more than they can deliver, but some marketers have been able to break through.

VW

U.S. Volkswagen sales rose from under 50 000 cars in 1993 to over 300 000 a decade later partly as a result of a "Drivers Wanted" ad campaign that targeted fun-loving or youthful drivers. Rather than appealing to the mass market, VW went after a younger demographic willing to spend a little extra on a Volkswagen because of the car's German engineering, sportier image, and versatility. The voiceover on the introductory TV spot identifies the target audience by saying, "On the road of life, there are passengers and there are drivers."[23]

Both baby boomers and GenerationXers will be passing the torch to the latest demographic group, Generation Y or the echo boomers, born between 1977 and 1994. Totalling approximately 8.6 million Canadians, this group is almost equal in size to baby boomers. One distinguishing characteristic of this age group is their utter fluency and comfort with computer and Internet technology. Don Tapscott has christened them "Net-Gens" for this reason. He says: "To them, digital technology is no more intimidating than a VCR or a toaster."[24]

Ethnic and Other Markets

Countries also vary in ethnic and racial makeup. At one extreme is Japan, where almost everyone is Japanese; at the other extreme are Canada and the United States, whose populations are drawn from virtually all nations. Canada's population, which exceeded 32 million by the end of 2005, is becoming increasingly diverse. In addition to its founding nations (English 5.9 million, French 4.7 million, and Aboriginal peoples 1.0 million), there is a rich mix of people from around the globe (e.g., Scottish 4.2 million, German 2.7 million, Italian 1.3 million, Chinese 1.1 million, Russian 0.3 million, and Jamaican 0.2 million).[25]

Visible minorities in Canada almost doubled during the period from 1991 to 2000. This group is comprised of 4.0 million people (about 13.4 percent of the population). The largest groups of visible minorities include Chinese (26 percent), South Asians (23 percent), blacks (17 percent), and Filipinos (8 percent).

More than 80 percent of Canada's visible minorities make census metropolitan areas their homes: 43 percent live in Toronto, 18 percent in Vancouver, 12 percent choose Montreal, while Calgary/Edmonton draws 8 percent. Toronto is Canada's most diverse city—in fact, the United Nations has proclaimed it as the most ethnically diverse city in the world. To understand where Toronto's population is headed, just consider the following statistics. Each year, over 200 000 landed immigrants enter Canada. Thus, in the last decade alone, more than 2 million people were welcomed. Almost 50 percent of these people settled in Toronto. As a result of this wave of immigration, 45 percent of Toronto's population will have a mother tongue and cultural background that is not English, French, or Aboriginal by the year 2011.

Migration patterns are also changing. Whereas Chinese immigrants used to come mainly from Hong Kong, today they come from mainland China. Thus they speak Mandarin instead of Cantonese. A second important trend is the growth in immigration from South Asia. Between the 1996 and 2001 census, the South Asian community in Toronto grew by 44 percent. The diversity of this community is witnessed by the range of languages spoken: Punjabi, Hindi, Urdu, Gujarati, Sinhalese, Tamil, Bengali, and, of course, English.

Marketing to new immigrants is both an opportunity and a challenge. It must be remembered that when people arrive in a new country, they often have no preconceptions of where to buy furniture or appliances, what car to buy, or even where to find personal hygiene products. They are new consumers looking for information. Culturally sensitive firms have an opportunity to build relationships and develop brand loyalty.

Marketers must be careful not to overgeneralize about ethnic groups. Asian Canadians, for example, are not a homogeneous group. The identities and values of Filipinos, Sri Lankans, Chinese, and Koreans are as different from each other as they are from Canadians of European background. Bobby Siu, president of Infoworth Consulting, an agency specializing in ethnic markets, emphasizes that "each Asian ethnic group has its own identity, values, and lifestyle; yet they share common experiences as Asians in Canada."[26] Stereotypes must be avoided when approaching visible minorities, especially if they are second-generation Canadians. Research has shown that people become integrated into Canada's cultural mainstream in a single generation.

The needs of visible minorities are often underserved. Asian consumers, for example, often complain that the off-the-rack clothing found in most Canadian stores does not fit them well. Even the colours are wrong for Asian complexions. A more serious concern is that small Asian Canadians often find that they experience side effects when they take the recommended dosages of over-the-counter drugs.

Some firms are starting to listen to these voices. Until recently, many black women had to mix their own cosmetic shades to obtain the right tones, but now Revlon Canada offers a line of products specifically for black women. Neilson Dairies has launched Soy Delight, a product that is an alternative to milk for lactose-intolerant Asians. And when Nike, a global sponsor of the World Cup soccer tournament, wanted to promote its affiliation in Canada, it turned toward the Italian and Portuguese communities of Toronto. In Nike's view, they represented the most passionate devotees of the sport in Canada. As Jeff Spreit, Nike Canada's advertising manager, noted, "We ended up delivering a very relevant message to a very passionate consumer."[27]

The French-Canadian minority deserves special attention because of its large size and its dispersion through several provinces. Comprising 81 percent of Quebec households and 23 percent of Canadian households, this minority (6.7 million) cannot be ignored by national marketers. Canada is officially a bicultural country, and Canadian marketers need to be sensitive to cultural differences between English and French Canadians. French Canadians have traditionally emphasized family, home, and church, but in recent decades, a growing secularism has weakened these ties in favour of materialism and nationalism.

The question of whether French-Canadian consumers are becoming more like other Canadians is debatable. But most marketers would agree that existing differences make it hazardous to employ a uniform promotional strategy across Canada. Differences in lifestyle, attitudes, and product usage make separate copy strategy and media decisions essential.

Diversity goes beyond ethnic markets. Persons with disabilities constitute almost 16 percent of Canada's population. The majority of these people are employed (65 percent of men, 50 percent of women). Since almost 60 percent of these people report mobility or agility problems, they are often a prime market for delivery and home-care services.[28]

Educational Groups

Canadian society falls into five educational groups: people with no degree, certificate, or diploma (33 percent of the population); people with a high school certificate (23 percent); people with a certificate from a trade school or community college (26 percent); people with a university degree or diploma (13 percent); and people with a graduate degree (5 percent).[29] Increasingly, people keep upgrading their education and skills after they leave school. In 2002, 4.8 million adult workers (aged 25 to 64) participated in formal, job-related training. This represents about 35 percent of all adult Canadian workers, up from 29 percent in 1997. However, the sad fact remains that those who may need the training the most don't get it, either due to lack of opportunity or income-related constraints like the lack of affordable child-care. Specifically, only 20 percent of workers with high school or less participated in formal job-related training, whereas 55 percent of workers with university education engaged in such training.[30]

Education and literacy are also highly correlated. Being able to read is a key skill in today's information-based society. It isn't surprising that people with literacy problems also have employment difficulties and tend to be low-income earners. According to Adult Literacy Canada, 22 percent of adult Canadians have serious problems dealing with any printed materials, and an additional 24 percent of Canadians can deal only with simple reading tasks. It is not surprising that the 10 percent of the Canadian population with less than a Grade 9 education faces most of the literacy challenges.[31]

Household Patterns

The "traditional household" consists of a husband, wife, and children (and sometimes grandparents). Yet, in Canada today household living arrangements are becoming more diverse. Of Canada's 11 562 980 households, couples with children still make up the largest proportion—30.5 percent of the total. However, couples with no children comprise the next largest segment at 28 percent, single person households make up another 25.7 percent, and other family household types equal 15.7 percent.[32] More people are divorcing or separating, choosing not to marry, marrying later, or marrying without the intention to have children. While the number of married couples in Canada increased 4 percent between 1991 and 2001, the number of common-law couples increased 61 percent and the number of single-parent families increased 37 percent. In some cases, these trends are even more pronounced within provincial boundaries. For example, in Quebec, the number of married couples declined over 10 percent between 1991 and 2001. In British Columbia, the increase in single-parent households was the highest at 57 percent; even more dramatic was the increase in male single-parent households by almost 70 percent.[33] Furthermore, the number of children people are having is declining. This, in combination with a growing number of single-parent homes, has resulted in a decline in the average family size from 3.7 persons in 1971 to 3.0 persons in 2004. Each group has a distinctive set of needs and buying habits. For example, people in the SSWD group (single, separated, widowed, divorced) need smaller apartments; inexpensive and smaller appliances, furniture, and furnishings; and smaller-size food packages. Marketers must increasingly consider the special needs of nontraditional households, because they are now growing more rapidly than traditional households.

A study by Cava Research Group at the University of Leeds in the United Kingdom emphasizes that single doesn't necessarily mean "alone." Researchers interviewed hundreds of people between the ages of 25 and 60 and concluded that "friends are the new family." They observed a growing trend for "neo tribes" of twenty-somethings to live communally. At the other end of the spectrum, older divorced people were seen centring their lives on their children and friends and keeping their romantic lives separate. This emphasis on friendship can influence marketers in everything from whom they target to how they craft their marketing messages. Travel with friends or with a group, for instance, now appeals to a wider swath of singles than college students on spring break or seniors going off to an elder hostel.[34] Online services are recognizing this trend.

Friendster.com

Friendster connects people for dating, making friends, business propositions, and plain old online voyeurism. The founder of Friendster created it after trying an online dating service and finding that he was not "keen on messaging random weirdoes." The premise of Friendster is that it's better to connect to new people through people you already know. It's the old friend of a friend of a friend strategy for meeting and dating. Users can browse through the profiles of their friends, friends' friends, and so on in their network. With just 20 friends, a user can be linked to 50 000 or more people. The profiles include photos, favourite books and other interests, along with pictures of their friends on the network. When users find someone interesting, they can see how they are connected and write a note. It's like being the star of your own game of "Six Degrees of Separation"—the notion that anyone can be linked to anyone else in the world via six connections. The site, which is free to members, has about 7 million users and has spawned a number of knock-off social networking sites such as Tribe, Rise, and Google's Orkut.[35]

The gay market is thought to be a particularly lucrative segment. In 2003, Statistics Canada conducted its first survey that queried people on sexual orientation. Among Canadians aged 18 to 59, 1.0 percent reported that they consider themselves to be homosexual and 0.7 percent considered themselves bisexual. About 1.3 percent of men considered themselves homosexual, about twice the proportion of women.[36] However, these results are thought to underestimate the actual gay and lesbian population, given, for example, that academics and marketing experts estimate that the gay and lesbian population ranges between 4 percent and 8 percent of the total North American population, with an even higher percentage in urban areas.[37] *Marketing Magazine* reported in 2004 that there are approximately 3.2 million gay and lesbian consumers in Canada. The statistics suggest that they are a market worth pursuing. For example, 46 percent describe themselves as trend-setters, 36 percent are usually the first people to buy new products, 57 percent are decision makers in either professional or management roles, and 94 percent would go out of their way to purchase products and services marketed directly to them. Furthermore, they report a much higher average income of $72 800 compared to the national average of $47 600. Moreover, 84 percent have no children, increasing the disposable portion of their income to well above that of the average family. In total, the gay and lesbian market is estimated to be a mind-blowing $75 billion group of consumers.[38]

Geographical Shifts in Population

This is a period of great migratory movements between and within countries. Forward-looking companies and entrepreneurs are taking advantage of the growth in immigrant populations and marketing their wares specifically to these new members of the population.

Population movement also occurs nationally as people migrate from one region of the country to another. Each year, about 12 in 1000 Canadians have itchy feet and swap provinces. For the last few years, Alberta and Ontario have been the top two choices when it came to inter-provincial moves. Alberta experienced the highest population growth rate at 10.3 percent and Ontario gained 6.1 percent, while British Columbia rose 4.9 percent. The population of Nunavut increased 8.1 percent, while Newfoundland lost almost 40 of every 1000 residents in the same period. Recent research has shown that inter-provincial moves and income are correlated. People who moved from one province to another tended to increase their earnings, especially if they moved away from a "have not" province. The effects were especially strong for men and younger people.[39]

Population movement also occurs as people migrate from rural to urban areas, and then to suburban areas. This movement has been going on for more than half a century. According to the 2001 census, 80 percent of Canadians live in urban areas. Cities like Montreal, Toronto, and Vancouver are characterized by a faster pace of living, higher incomes, and a greater variety of goods, services, and cultural offerings than can be found in Canada's small towns and rural areas.

Some people are countering the trend toward urbanization and are moving out to the "country" or to small towns, away from apartment living and the hectic pace found in many cities. Kelowna, British Columbia, and its subdivision, Central Okanagan, is Canada's second-fastest-growing town. It has been the destination of choice for West Coasters fleeing Victoria and Vancouver. Such relocation makes a difference in goods and service preferences. Businesses with potential to cash in on the rural rebound might be those that cater to the growing SOHO (small office/home office) segment.

Kinko's Copy Centres

Founded in the 1970s as a campus photocopying business, Kinko's is now reinventing itself as the well-appointed office outside the home. Where once there were copy machines, the 1200 Kinko's stores in Canada, the United States, and abroad now feature a mix of fax machines, ultra-fast colour printers, and networks of computers equipped with popular software programs and high-speed Internet connections. Kinko's is now a US$2 billion company that offers an unprecedented array of office services. People can come to a Kinko's store to do all their office jobs: copy, send, and receive faxes, use various programs on the computer, go on the Internet, order stationery and other printed supplies, and even teleconference. And as more people work at home, Kinko's offers an escape from the isolation of the home office. Kinko's acquisition by FedEx in early 2004 resulted in further integration with the overnight delivery pioneer.[40]

Other Major Macroenvironments

Other macroenvironment forces profoundly affect the fortunes of marketers. Here we review developments in the economic, social-cultural, natural, technological, and political-legal environments.

Economic Environment

Markets require purchasing power as well as people. The available purchasing power in an economy depends on current income, prices, savings, debt, and credit availability. Marketers must pay careful attention to trends affecting purchasing power because they can have a strong impact on business, especially for companies whose products are geared to high-income and price-sensitive consumers.

INCOME DISTRIBUTION Nations vary greatly in level and distribution of income and industrial structure. There are four types of industrial structures: *subsistence economies* (few opportunities for marketers); *raw-material-exporting economies* like Zaire (copper) and Saudi Arabia (oil), with good markets for equipment, tools, supplies, and luxury goods for the rich; *industrializing economies*, like India, Egypt, and the Philippines, where a new rich class and a growing middle class demand new types of goods; and *industrial economies*, which are rich markets for all sorts of goods.

In a global economy, marketers need to pay attention to the shifting income distribution in countries around the world, particularly countries where affluence levels are rising.

India

With its surfeit of low-cost, high-IQ, English-speaking employees, India is snapping up programming and call-centre jobs once held by North Americans in a wave of outsourcing that shows no signs of stopping. By 2008, IT services and back-office work in India will swell five-fold, to a US$57 billion annual export industry employing 4 million people and accounting for 7 percent of India's gross domestic product. While India's ascendance inevitably means lost jobs and anguish for North American white-collar workers, it also means a larger market for Western goods—and anguish for traditional Indian families. Along with training in North American accents and geography, India's legions of call-centre employees are absorbing new ideas about family, material possessions, and romance. "I call these kids 'liberalization children,'" says Rama Bijapurkar, a Bombay-based marketing consultant. "This generation has a hunger in the belly for achievement." Liberalization children are questioning conservative traditions such as arranged marriages and no public kissing. They want to watch Hollywood movies, listen to Western music, chat on cell phones, buy on credit—rather than saving—and eat out in restaurants or cafés. And they are being targeted relentlessly by companies that have waited to see India develop a Western-style consumer class.[41]

Marketers often distinguish countries with five different income-distribution patterns: (1) very low incomes; (2) mostly low incomes; (3) very low, very high incomes; (4) low, medium, high incomes; and (5) mostly medium incomes. Consider the market for Lamborghinis, an automobile costing more than US$150 000. The market would be very small in countries with type (1) or (2) income patterns. One of the largest single markets for Lamborghinis turns out to be Portugal (income pattern 3)—one of the poorer countries in Western Europe, but one with enough wealthy families to afford expensive cars.

Statistics Canada reports that the median income of Canadian families as of 2000 was $55 016. This represented very little change from the same figure in 1990, $54 560. However, the same is not true for specific income groups. For example, throughout the 1990s the wealthiest Canadian families (top 10 percent) got even wealthier. As of 2000, the combined income of the richest Canadian families accounted for 28 percent of the total Canadian family income, whereas in 1990 it accounted for 26 percent. These families had incomes greater than $117 850. In contrast, the poorest Canadian families (bottom 10 percent) made up less than 2 percent of the total Canadian family income, with incomes less than $18 990. Put into context, this means that for every $1 earned by the bottom 10 percent, the top 10 percent earned $18.

Not surprisingly, the income of Canadian families is not consistent across provincial boundaries. The Northwest Territories has the highest median family income at $69 046. Furthermore, Ontario, Alberta, the Yukon, and the Northwest Territories are the only regions where the median family income is above the national median, whereas all other provinces and territories are below. Alberta's median family income experienced the largest increase over the 1990s, growing over 5 percent to $60 142, while Nunavut and Newfoundland experienced the largest declines of 6.1 percent and 3.7 percent respectively ($39 424 and $41 214).[42]

Consider how the Gap has segmented its market around income differences.

The Gap

The Gap pursues a segmented market strategy with three tiers of retail clothing stores: the upscale Banana Republic, the mid-market Gap, and the budget-priced Old Navy. Jeans sell for US$70 at Banana Republic stores and for as much as US$50 at Gap stores. Old Navy jeans sell for under US$25. Each store has its own look, its own clothing lines, and its own in-house advertising. This segmented strategy helped the Gap grow from a US$7 billion to a US$14 billion business between 1996 and 2003.[43]

However, the spread of wealth may not be as useful to marketers as it once was. While it seems to make perfectly logical sense to segment markets along income boundaries, marketers are increasingly finding that income simply does not tell the whole story. More specifically, in Canada (and the broader North American market) the middle class is becoming increasingly rich in their taste and, as a result, their purchases. According to experts, Canadians are increasingly seeking more expensive products, thus causing a major redefinition of the luxury customer. Consumers want to feel rich regardless of whether or not their income actually supports the notion. Retailers like Holt Renfrew are finding that their customer base is growing. The Liquor Control Board of Ontario is finding that it is selling increasing volumes of higher-priced wines. The trend even applies to some of the biggest-ticket items such as

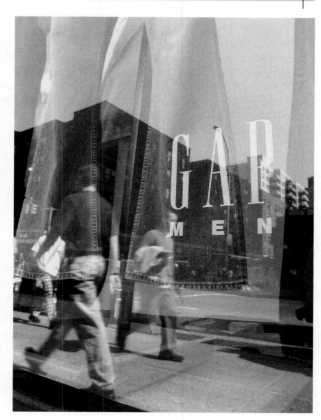

A Gap storefront displays the familiar, recognizable Gap "look."

cars. Sales of luxury vehicles such as Jaguars, BMWs, and Mercedes-Benzes have grown substantially over the last several years.[44]

SAVINGS, DEBT, AND CREDIT AVAILABILITY   Consumer expenditures are affected by savings, debt, and credit availability. Over the past ten years in Canada, savings rates have been declining. In addition, with consistently lower interest rates over the 1990s and a more relaxed attitude toward consumer debt, the amount of household indebtedness is on the rise. This is consistent with the increasing availability of credit in Canada. The number of credit cards in circulation was over 55 million in 2005. Almost half of these credit cards have outstanding balances, and the size of those balances has increased in aggregate almost 16 percent since 1993. Even though that debt is on the rise and saving is down, overall household net worth in Canada has continued to increase. This means that while Canadians are saving less and spending more, their total assets still outpace their liabilities. This suggests that as long as net worth grows faster than liabilities, an increasing level of household debt is sustainable, providing the ability of households to service this debt remains stable.[45]

OUTSOURCING AND FREE TRADE An economic issue of increasing importance is the migration of manufacturers and service jobs off-shore. Outsourcing is seen as a competitive necessity by many firms, but as a cause of unemployment by many domestic workers. For example, in December 2003, IBM decided to move the jobs of nearly 5000 programmers to India and China. GE has moved much of its research and development overseas. Microsoft, Dell, American Express, and virtually every major multinational from Accenture to Yahoo! have already offshored work or are considering doing so.

The savings are dramatic, with companies cutting 20–70 percent of their labour costs, assuming the work is of comparable quality. However, beyond the short-term gain for employers and pain for displaced domestic white-collar employees is the scarier long-term prospect. The exodus of programming work, in particular, throws the future of North America's tech dominance into doubt. Many wonder whether the West can continue to lead the industry as software programming spreads around the globe from India to Bulgaria. In Bombay, for example, there is high-speed Internet access, a world-class university, and a venture capital industry—all the ingredients you need to spawn the next earthshaking technology innovation.[46]

Outside the labour market, advocates for and against free trade debate the merits of protective tariffs.

Fair Trade Coffee

Activist group Global Exchange, a human rights organization dedicated to promoting environmental, political, and social justice around the world, has pressured the coffee industry to support Fair Trade Certified coffee. More than 500 000 farmers around the world produce and sell more than 77 million kilograms of coffee each year through the Fair Trade network. Over 100 Fair Trade coffee brands are sold worldwide in approximately 35 000 retail outlets. To become Fair Trade certified, an importer must meet stringent international criteria, such as paying a minimum price per pound of US$1.26 (US$2.77 per kilogram). Global Exchange chose to target Starbucks to participate in the network given its high profile. A grassroots campaign led to the introduction of whole bean Fair Trade Certified coffee at over 2300 Starbucks stores as part of a broader corporate social responsibility initiative on the part of the company.[47]

Social-Cultural Environment

Purchasing power is directed toward certain goods and services and away from others according to people's tastes and preferences. Society shapes the beliefs, values, and norms that largely define these tastes and preferences. People absorb, almost unconsciously, a worldview that defines their relationships to themselves, to others, to organizations, to society, to nature, and to the universe.

■   *Views of themselves.* People vary in the relative emphasis they place on self-gratification. During the 1960s and 1970s, "pleasure seekers" sought fun, change, and escape. Others sought "self-realization." People bought dream cars and dream vacations and spent more time in health activities (jogging, tennis), in introspection, and in arts and crafts. Today, some people are adopting more conservative behaviours and ambitions. Marketers must recognize that there are many different groups with different views of themselves.

- *Views of others.* People are concerned about the homeless, crime and victims, and other social problems. They would like to live in a more humane society. At the same time, people are seeking out their "own kind" and avoiding strangers. They hunger for serious and long-lasting relationships with a few others. These trends portend a growing market for social-support products and services that promote direct relations between human beings, such as health clubs, cruises, and religious activity. They also suggest a growing market for "social surrogates," things that allow people who are alone to feel that they are not, such as television, home video games, and chat rooms on the Internet.

- *Views of organizations.* People vary in their attitudes toward corporations, government agencies, trade unions, and other organizations. Most people are willing to work for these organizations, but there has been an overall decline in organizational loyalty. The massive wave of company downsizings and corporate accounting scandals such as those at Nortel, Enron, WorldCom, and Tyco has bred cynicism and distrust.[48] Many people today see work not as a source of satisfaction, but as a required chore to earn money to enjoy their nonwork hours. This outlook has several marketing implications. Companies need to find new ways to win back consumer and employee confidence. They need to make sure that they are good corporate citizens and that their consumer messages are honest.

- *Views of society.* People vary in their attitudes toward their society. Some defend it (preservers), some run it (makers), some take what they can from it (takers), some want to change it (changers), some are looking for something deeper (seekers), and some want to leave it (escapers).[49] Consumption patterns often reflect social attitude. Makers tend to be high achievers who eat, dress, and live well. Changers usually live more frugally, drive smaller cars, and wear simpler clothes. Escapers and seekers are a major market for movies, music, surfing, and camping.

- *Views of nature.* People vary in their attitudes toward nature. Some feel subjugated by it, others feel in harmony with it, and still others seek mastery over it. A long-term trend has been humankind's growing mastery of nature through technology. More recently, however, people have awakened to nature's fragility and finite resources. They recognize that nature can be destroyed by human activities. Business has responded to increased interest in camping, hiking, boating, and fishing with hiking boots, tenting equipment, and other gear. Tour operators are packaging tours to wilderness areas and to places like Antarctica.

- *Views of the universe.* People vary in their beliefs about the origin of the universe and their place in it. Most North Americans are monotheistic, although religious conviction and practice have been waning through the years. Certain evangelical movements are reaching out to bring people back into organized religion. Some of the religious impulse has been redirected into an interest in Eastern religions, mysticism, the occult, and the human potential movement.

As people lose their religious orientation, they seek self-fulfillment and immediate gratification. At the same time, every trend seems to breed a countertrend, as indicated by a worldwide rise in religious fundamentalism. Here are some other cultural characteristics of interest to marketers: the persistence of core cultural values, the existence of subcultures, and shifts of values through time.

HIGH PERSISTENCE OF CORE CULTURAL VALUES The people living in a particular society hold many *core beliefs* and values that tend to persist. Core beliefs and values are passed on from parents to children and are reinforced by major social institutions—schools, churches, businesses, and governments. *Secondary beliefs* and values are more open to change. While marketers have little influence over core values, their efforts may result in the change of some secondary beliefs. For instance, the nonprofit organization Mothers Against Drunk Drivers (MADD) does not try to stop the sale of alcohol, but it does promote the idea of appointing a designated driver who will not drink that evening. It has undertaken some interesting partnerships to help further its responsible drinking agenda.

MADD, LCBO, and Shoppers Drug Mart

In November 2004, MADD worked with two partners, the Liquor Control Board of Ontario (LCBO) and Shoppers Drug Mart, to help deter drinking and driving over the holiday season. They developed *Good Host* kits for unexpected overnight guests. The attractive, clear plastic carrying bags include sample-size toiletry items such as shampoo, conditioner, soap, toothpaste, toothbrush, deodorant, and a razor, as well as a MADD Canada red ribbon and LCBO responsible hosting tips. The $25 retail value kit is sold for $9.95, and $4.50 from each sale was donated to MADD Canada. LCBO chairman and CEO Andrew Brandt stressed, "Of course, the best strategy for responsible hosts is to pre-plan and prevent guests from drinking too much, and for guests to take a cab, transit, or arrange for a designated driver if they plan on drinking, but this doesn't always happen. This convenient kit provides handy solutions for caring hosts who want to make unexpected overnight guests feel more comfortable and make holiday gatherings enjoyable and safe."[50]

Research has shown that Canadians and Americans, especially those who live along the border between the two countries, hold many values in common. Both believe in freedom, equality, and striving for happiness, mature love, self-respect, and true friendship. Canadian researcher and author Michael Adams notes, however, that Canadians operate by a fundamentally different set of social values than Americans do, and marketers need to be sensitive to these differences:

> For example, Americans are much more outer-directed, risk-taking, and yet are more concerned with maintaining social order and tradition. In contrast, Canadians are more inner-directed, more security-seeking, and yet are more socially liberal and tolerant of individual diversity. Americans celebrate those who have lived the American Dream—working hard, taking chances, and striking it rich—so visual markers of success such as expensive cars, homes, and vacations become important indicators of one's status on the social hierarchy. Canadians, on the other hand, believe in greater interdependence, achieving equitable balances, and the "fair" distribution of the wealth.[51]

Canadians are also less trusting of business and are more skeptical of advertising. Canadians, therefore, seek to do business with companies perceived as being more ethical. Adams believes that this difference in social values results in more understated consumption. Canadians focus less on what products and brands say about us and more on what the products do for us. In fact, Canadians are more likely to agree that a car is just an appliance for getting from A to B than that a car makes a statement about their personal style and image (57 percent versus 39 percent). Canadians, therefore, prefer smaller, more affordable, and more practical cars. It was for this reason that BMW chose to subtly change its slogan "The Ultimate Driving Machine" to "The Ultimate Driving Experience" for Canada.[52]

EXISTENCE OF SUBCULTURES Each society contains **subcultures**, groups with shared values emerging from their special life experiences or circumstances. Members of subcultures share common beliefs, preferences, and behaviours. To the extent that subcultural groups exhibit different wants and consumption behaviour, marketers can choose particular subcultures as target markets.

Marketers sometimes reap unexpected rewards in targeting subcultures. Marketers have always loved teenagers because they are society's trendsetters in fashion, music, entertainment, ideas, and attitudes. Marketers also know that if they attract someone as a teen, there is a good chance they will keep the person as a customer later in life. Frito-Lay, which draws 15 percent of its sales from teens, said it saw a rise in chip-snacking by grown-ups. "We think it's because we brought them in as teenagers," said Frito-Lay's marketing director.[53]

SHIFTS OF SECONDARY CULTURAL VALUES THROUGH TIME Although core values are fairly persistent, cultural swings do take place. In the 1960s, hippies, the Beatles, Elvis Presley, and other cultural phenomena had a major impact on young people's hairstyles, clothing, sexual norms, and life goals. Today's young people are influenced by new heroes and new activities: U2's Bono, golf's Tiger Woods, and extreme sports.

Natural Environment

The deterioration of the natural environment is a major global concern. In many world cities, air and water pollution have reached dangerous levels. There is great concern about "greenhouse gases" in the atmosphere due to the burning of fossil fuels, about the depletion of the ozone layer due to certain chemicals, and about growing shortages of water. In Western Europe, "green" parties have vigorously pressed for public action to reduce industrial pollution. In North America, experts have documented ecological deterioration, and watchdog groups such as the Sierra Club and Friends of the Earth carry these concerns into political and social action.

New regulations hit certain industries very hard. Steel companies and public utilities have had to invest billions of dollars in pollution-control equipment and more environmentally friendly fuels. The auto industry has had to introduce expensive emission controls in cars. The soap industry has had to increase its products' biodegradability. The major hope is that companies will adopt practices that will protect the natural environment. Great opportunities await companies and marketers who can create new solutions that promise to reconcile prosperity with environmental protection.

Consumers often appear conflicted about the natural environment. One research study showed that although 80 percent of consumers stated that whether or not a product is safe for the environment influenced their decision to buy that product, only a little over half asserted that they bought recycled or environmentally safe products.[54] Young people especially were more likely to feel that nothing they did personally made a difference. Increasing the number of green products that are bought requires breaking consumers' loyalty habits, overcoming consumer skepticism about the motives behind the introduction of green products and their quality level, and changing consumer attitudes about the role they play in environmental protection. (See "Marketing Insight: Green Marketing.")

Marketers need to be aware of the threats and opportunities associated with four trends in the natural environment: the shortage of raw materials, especially water; the increased cost of energy; increased pollution levels; and the changing role of governments.

SHORTAGE OF RAW MATERIALS   The earth's raw materials consist of the infinite, the finite renewable, and the finite nonrenewable. *Infinite resources*, such as air and water, are becoming a problem. Water shortages are already a political issue, and the danger is no longer long term. *Finite renewable resources*, such as forests and food, must be used wisely. Forestry companies are required to reforest timberlands in order to protect the soil and to ensure sufficient wood to meet future demand. Because the amount of arable land is fixed and urban areas are constantly encroaching on farmland, food supply can also be a major problem. *Finite nonrenewable resources*—oil, coal, platinum, zinc, silver—will pose a serious problem as the point of depletion approaches. Firms making products that require these increasingly scarce minerals face substantial cost increases. Firms engaged in research and development have an excellent opportunity to develop substitute materials.

INCREASED ENERGY COSTS   One finite nonrenewable resource, oil, has created serious problems for the world economy. Over the past few years, oil prices have shot up dramatically, surpassing US$65 per barrel in 2005, and thus reinforcing the need for alternative energy forms. Companies are searching for practical means to harness solar, nuclear, wind, and other forms of energy. In the solar energy field alone, hundreds of firms introduced first-generation products to harness solar energy for heating homes and other uses. Other firms are engaged in building practical electric automobiles, with a potential prize of billions for the winner. Practical combination vehicles, like the Toyota Prius, *Motor Trend* magazine's 2004 Car of the Year, are already available.

ANTI-POLLUTION PRESSURES   Some industrial activity will inevitably damage the natural environment. Consider the dangerous mercury levels in the ocean, the quantity of DDT and other chemical pollutants in the soil and food supply, and the littering of the environment with bottles, plastics, and other packaging materials. Environment Canada is responsible for ensuring that Canadians, and Canadian companies in particular, comply with the Canadian Environmental Protection Act (CEPA), which has the mandate to "contribute to sustainable development through pollution prevention and to protect the environment, human life and health from the risks associated with toxic substances."[55] A survey conducted in 24 different countries found that Canadians are second on the list in terms of their concern about the environment. New Zealand tops the ranking. In fact, Canadians said protecting the environment was more important than promoting economic growth. Some companies are responding in a positive way to such concerns.[56]

Green Marketing

Although environmental issues have long affected marketing practices, especially in Europe, their relevance has increased in the last decade or so. With the well-publicized Earth Day activities in April 1990, the "green marketing" movement was born. An explosion of "environmentally friendly" products and marketing programs appeared as firm after firm tried to capitalize on consumers' perceived increased sensitivity to environmental issues.

From a branding perspective, however, green marketing programs have not been entirely successful. For example, in 1994, Philips Electronics NV branded its eco-friendly, energy-saving fluorescent bulbs as "Earthlight." Due to a lack of sales success, the product was repackaged in 2000 as convenient, seven-year life "Marathon" bulbs, and sales grew steadily at 7 percent annually. Faced with slumping sales, Ben & Jerry's dropped its "Rainforest Crunch" flavour of ice cream, introduced on Earth Day in 1990 to tout conservation and nuts from rainforest trees. Despite a concerted marketing effort, Green Mountain Energy has found it difficult to sell electricity from eco-friendly power plants.

Many other marketers tried and failed with green sales pitches over the last decade. What obstacles did this movement encounter?

- *Overexposure and lack of credibility.* So many companies made environmental claims that the public became skeptical of their validity. Government investigations into some "green" claims (e.g., the degradability of trash bags) and media reports of the spotty environmental track records behind others only increased consumers' doubts. This backlash resulted in many consumers thinking environmental claims were just marketing gimmicks.

- *Consumer behaviour.* Research studies have shown that consumers as a whole may not be willing to pay a premium for environmental benefits, although certain market segments will be. Most consumers appear unwilling to give up the benefits of other alternatives to choose green products. For example, some consumers dislike the performance, appearance, or texture of recycled paper and household products. And some consumers are unwilling to give up the convenience of disposable products such as diapers.

- *Poor implementation.* In jumping on the green marketing bandwagon, many firms did a poor job implementing their marketing program. Products were poorly designed in terms of environmental worthiness, overpriced, and inappropriately promoted. Some ads failed to make the connection between what the company was doing for the environment and how it affected individual consumers.

To get around these obstacles and make sure environmental initiatives are implemented, some companies recommend relying on the efforts of a "Green Champion"—an environmentalist who works internally to make companies greener. Jean Palmateer, an environmental engineer, is a "green champion" for DePuy Orthopaedics, a division of Johnson & Johnson. She recommends getting broad goals accomplished by personalizing the issue. For instance, when Palmeteer wanted to keep the medical device maker's wastewater tanks clean, she told workers that better maintained tanks would not just help the earth, but save them from 3:00 A.M. phone calls when the tanks failed to discharge. Now the tanks are cleaner and workers are sleeping better at night.

There have been some notable green marketing successes through the years. McDonald's has introduced a number of well-publicized environmental initiatives, such as unbleached paper carry-out bags and replacing polystyrene foam sandwich clamshells with paper wraps and lightweight recycled boxes. McDonald's received the U.S. Environmental Protection Agency–sponsored WasteWise Partner of the Year award for waste reduction efforts that (1) conserved 2900 tonnes of paper and cardboard by replacing sandwich containers with single-layer flexible sandwich wraps; (2) eliminated 1000 tonnes of cardboard materials that would have been used for shipping by switching to light drink cups; and (3) resulted in spending US$355 million on recycled content products.

Sources: Jacquelyn Ottman, *Green Marketing: Opportunity for Innovation*, 2nd ed. (Chicago: NTC/Contemporary Publishing Company, 1998); Geoffrey Fowler, "'Green' Sales Pitch Isn't Moving Many Products," *Wall Street Journal*, March 6, 2002, p. B4; Lynn J. Cook, "Our Electrons Are Greener," *Forbes*, June 23, 2003, p. 101; Kevin Lane Keller, *Strategic Brand Management*, 2nd ed. (Upper Saddle River, NJ: Prentice-Hall, 2003); Maggie Jackson, "Earth-Friendly Company Changes Come from One 'Green Champion' at a Time," *Boston Globe*, May 9, 2004, p. G1.

CHANGING ROLE OF GOVERNMENTS   Governments vary in their concern and efforts to promote a clean environment. For example, the German government is vigorous in its pursuit of environmental quality, partly because of the strong green movement in Germany and partly because of the ecological devastation in the former East Germany. Many poor nations are doing little about pollution, largely because they lack the funds or the political will. It is in the richer nations' interest to help the poorer nations control their pollution, but even the richer nations today lack the necessary funds.

Technological Environment

One of the most dramatic forces shaping people's lives is technology. Technology has released such wonders as penicillin, open-heart surgery, and the birth control pill. It has released such horrors as the hydrogen bomb, nerve gas, and the submachine gun. It has also released such mixed blessings as the automobile and video games.

Every new technology is a force for "creative destruction." Transistors hurt the vacuum-tube industry, xerography hurt the carbon paper business, autos hurt the railroads, and television hurt the newspapers. Instead of moving into the new technologies, many old industries fought or ignored them, and their businesses declined. Yet it is the essence of market capitalism to be dynamic and tolerate the creative destructiveness of technology as the price of progress.

Look out Dell, HP, Apple, and Microsoft: According to some seers, "smart" mobile phones will eventually eclipse the PC.

Smart Phones

"One day, 2 or 3 billion people will have cell phones, and they are all not going to have PCs," says Jeff Hawkins, inventor of the Palm Pilot and chief technology officer for PalmOne. "The mobile phone will become their digital life," Hawkins predicts. After a slow start, mobile phones have become more ubiquitous—there are 1.5 billion in the world today—and smarter. Today's most sophisticated phones already have the processing power of a mid-1990s PC while consuming 100 times less electricity. The phones are used to send e-mail, browse the Web, take pictures, and play video games. Hawkins predicts that within the next few decades all phones will be mobile phones, capable of receiving voice and Internet signals at broadband speeds, and that mobile phone bills will shrink to a few dollars a month as phone companies pay off their investment in new networks. New smart phones in the works include Palm's pocket-size Treo600, with a tiny keyboard, a built-in digital camera, and slots for added memory, and Motorola's MPx, which features a "dual-hinge" design. The handset opens in one direction and appears to be a regular phone, but it also flips open on another axis to look like an e-mail device, with the expanded phone keypad serving as a small, conventional QWERTY keypad.[57]

The economy's growth rate is affected by how many major new technologies are discovered. Unfortunately, technological discoveries do not arise evenly through time—the railroad industry created a lot of investment, and then investment petered out until the auto industry emerged. Later, radio created a lot of investment, which then petered out until television appeared. In the time between major innovations, an economy can stagnate. In the meantime, minor innovations fill the gap: freeze-dried coffee, combination shampoo and conditioner, antiperspirants and deodorants, and the like. They involve less risk, but they also divert research effort away from major breakthroughs.

A recent Statistics Canada study revealed that more than 70 percent of successful new companies are high-tech in that they innovate, use advanced technologies, employ skilled workers, or emphasize training. They operate in all sectors of the economy, including publishing and farm services, not just in those industries usually thought of as high-tech, such as biotechnology and information technology. For example, the dairy farming industry has adopted very high-tech processes. Technology is what helps the one or two farmers manage dozens or hundreds of highly productive dairy cattle. From computer-generated algorithms for designing feeding programs, to laboratory testing for determining the digestibility of feed ingredients, to computer chips and databases that track milk production, technology is used in all aspects of milk production.[58]

New technology also creates major long-run consequences that are not always foreseeable. The contraceptive pill, for example, led to smaller families, more working wives, and larger discretionary incomes—resulting in higher expenditures on vacation travel, durable goods, and luxury items.

The marketer should monitor the following trends in technology: the pace of change, the opportunities for innovation, varying R&D budgets, and increased regulation.

ACCELERATING PACE OF CHANGE Many of today's common products were not available 40 years ago. Your parents did not have personal computers, digital wristwatches, video recorders, fax machines, personal digital assistants, or the Internet; nor has the pace of technological change slowed down. The Human Genome project promises to usher in the Biological Century as biotech workers create new medical cures, new foods, and new materials. Electronic researchers are building smarter chips to make our cars, homes, and offices more responsive to changing conditions. The blending of personal computers, scanners, fax and copy machines, wireless phones, the Internet, and e-mail has made it possible for people to *telecommute*—that is, work at home or on the road instead of travelling to an office. This trend may reduce auto pollution, bring the family closer together, and create more home-centred shopping and entertainment.

An increasing number of ideas are being worked on, and the time between the appearance of new ideas and their successful implementation is all but disappearing. So is the time between introduction and peak production. Ninety percent of all the scientists who ever lived are alive today, and technology feeds upon itself.

UNLIMITED OPPORTUNITIES FOR INNOVATION Scientists today are working on a startling range of new technologies that will revolutionize products and production processes. Some of the most exciting work is being done in biotechnology, computers, microelectronics, telecommunications, robotics, and designer materials. Researchers are working on AIDS cures, happiness pills, painkillers, totally safe contraceptives, and nonfattening foods. They are designing robots for firefighting, underwater exploration, and home nursing. In addition, scientists work on fantasy products, such as small flying cars, three-dimensional television, and space colonies. The challenge in each case is to develop affordable versions of these products.

Samsung

In an ambitious endeavour, Samsung has launched a digital home business. In Korea, Samsung has 6000 networked homes that are outfitted with Internet-enabled ovens, refrigerators, security cameras, and wall-mounted flat panel displays. Samsung is looking to take the idea abroad. Wiring homes will cost from US$2000 to US$10 000, making adoption relatively affordable. Besides overcoming a few technical challenges, however, Samsung must also contend with consumers who worry about the complexity or even need for such products. But experts look to the further penetration of broadband access to propel the adoption of the digital home as consumers learn to access digital media and commerce from more devices.[59]

Companies are already harnessing the power of *virtual reality (VR)*, the combination of technologies that allows users to experience three-dimensional, computer-generated environments through sound, sight, and touch. Virtual reality has already been applied to gathering consumer reactions to new automobile designs, kitchen layouts, exterior home designs, and other potential offerings.

VARYING R&D BUDGETS In 2002, Canada spent 1.8 percent of its gross domestic product (GDP) on R&D. Both business and government expenditures contribute to this effort. Canada, however, trails a number of other OECD countries. For example, Sweden spends 4.2 percent of its domestic product on R&D, Japan spends just over 3 percent, and the United States spends 2.8 percent.[60] Because of the size of its GDP, the United States leads the world in annual R&D expenditures. The top five companies in terms of R&D expenditures in Canada are Nortel Networks, Magna International, Pratt & Whitney Canada, JDS Uniphase, and IBM Canada.[61]

INCREASED REGULATION OF TECHNOLOGICAL CHANGE As products become more complex, the public needs to be assured of their safety. Consequently, government agencies' powers to investigate and ban potentially unsafe products have been expanded. Canada has a complex web of legislation. Consider, for example, some of the legislation focused on food safety. Agriculture Canada is responsible for the safety of food products, but Health Canada also has a food and product safety division. Health Canada also administers the new nutrition labelling regulations, which were brought into effect in 2003. To complicate matters further, the Department of Justice regulates the Food and Drug Act and the Hazardous Products Act. The Canadian Standards Association (**www.csa.ca**), a not-for-profit organization, also works with business, government, and consumers to develop standards to enhance public safety and health. You will find its seal on products that have passed its safety tests and meet its rigorous standards. Marketers must be aware of these regulations when proposing, developing, and launching new products.

GreenDisk, a company that produces high-quality recycled disks.

Political-Legal Environment

Marketing decisions are strongly affected by developments in the political and legal environment. This environment is composed of laws, government agencies, and pressure groups that influence and limit various organizations and individuals. Sometimes these laws also create new opportunities for business. For example, mandatory recycling laws have given the recycling industry a major boost and spurred the creation of dozens of new companies making new products from recycled materials. Two major trends deal with the increase in business legislation and the growth of special interest groups.

INCREASE IN BUSINESS LEGISLATION Business legislation has three main purposes: to protect companies from unfair competition, to protect consumers from unfair business practices, and to protect the interests of society from unbridled business behaviour. A major purpose of business legislation and enforcement is to charge businesses with the social costs created by their products or production processes. A central concern is this: At what point do the costs of regulation exceed the benefits? The laws are not always administered fairly; regulators and enforcers may be lax or overzealous. Although each new law may have a legitimate rationale, it may have the unintended effect of sapping initiative and retarding economic growth.

Legislation affecting business has increased steadily over the years. As noted earlier, Canada has a complex web of regulatory agencies. In addition to the federal departments noted already with regard to food safety, the Department of Transport governs road and vehicle safety, Environment Canada focuses on pollution prevention, and the Competition Act covers such diverse topics as mergers (section 33), pricing (sections 34 and 38), advertising (section 37), and country of origin claims (sections 52 and 74). Canadian business is also subject to provincial regulations and may come up against rulings by Canada's marketing boards. Regulations established in the North American Free Trade Agreement (NAFTA) also have to be respected. It is no wonder that most Canadian firms have large legal departments to help marketers stay within the law!

The European Commission has been active in establishing a new framework of laws covering competitive behaviour, product standards, product liability, and commercial transactions for the 25 member nations of the European Union. The United States has many laws on its books covering such issues as competition, product safety and liability, fair trade and credit practices, and packaging and labelling.[62] Several countries have gone further than the United States and Canada in passing strong consumer-protection legislation. Norway bans several forms of sales promotion—trading stamps, contests, premiums—as inappropriate or "unfair" instruments for promoting products. Thailand requires food processors selling national brands to market low-price brands also, so that low-income consumers can find economy brands. In India, food companies need special approval to launch brands that duplicate what already exists on the market, such as another cola drink or brand of rice.

Marketers must have a good working knowledge of the major laws protecting competition, consumers, and society. Companies generally establish legal review procedures and promulgate ethical standards to guide their marketing managers, and as more business takes place in cyberspace, marketers must establish new parameters for doing electronic business ethically.

GROWTH OF SPECIAL-INTEREST GROUPS The number and power of special-interest groups have increased over the past three decades. Political action committees (PACs) lobby government

More and more consumers
are checking nutrition labels
on the food products they
purchase.

officials and pressure business executives to pay more attention to consumers' rights, women's rights, senior citizens' rights, minority rights, and gay rights.

Many companies have established public affairs departments to deal with these groups and issues. An important force affecting business is the **consumerist movement**—an organized movement of citizens and government to strengthen the rights and powers of buyers in relation to sellers. Consumerists have advocated and won the right to know the true interest cost of a loan, the true cost per standard unit of competing brands (unit pricing), the basic ingredients in a product, the nutritional quality of food, the freshness of products, and the true benefits of a product.

With consumers increasingly willing to swap personal information for customized products from firms—as long as they can be trusted—privacy issues will continue to be a public policy hot button.[63] Consumer concerns are that they will be robbed or cheated; that private information will be used against them; that someone will steal their identity; that they will be bombarded with solicitations; and that children will be targeted.[64] Several companies have established consumer affairs departments to help formulate policies and respond to consumer complaints. Companies are careful to answer their e-mail and to resolve and learn from any customer complaints.

Clearly, new laws and growing numbers of pressure groups have put more restraints on marketers. Marketers have to clear their plans with the company's legal, public relations, public affairs, and consumer affairs departments. Insurance companies directly or indirectly affect the design of smoke detectors; scientific groups affect the design of spray products by condemning aerosols. In essence, many private marketing transactions have moved into the public domain.

SUMMARY

1. To carry out their analysis, planning, implementation, and control responsibilities, marketing managers need a marketing information system (MIS). The role of the MIS is to assess the managers' information needs, develop the needed information, and distribute that information in a timely manner.

2. An MIS has three components: (a) an internal records system, which includes information on the order-to-payment cycle and sales reporting systems; (b) a marketing intelligence system, a set of procedures and sources used by managers to obtain everyday information about pertinent developments in the marketing environment; and (c) a marketing research system that allows for the systematic design, collection, analysis, and reporting of data and findings relevant to a specific marketing situation.

3. Many opportunities are found by identifying trends (directions or sequences of events that have some momentum and durability) and megatrends (major social, economic, political, and technological changes that have long-lasting influence).

4. Within the rapidly changing global picture, marketers must monitor six major environmental forces: demographic, economic, social-cultural, natural, technological, and political-legal.

5. In the demographic environment, marketers must be aware of worldwide population growth; changing mixes of age, ethnic composition, and educational levels; the rise of nontraditional families; large geographic shifts in population; and the move to micromarketing and away from mass marketing.

6. In the economic arena, marketers need to focus on income distribution and levels of savings, debt, and credit availability.

7. In the social-cultural arena, marketers must understand people's views of themselves, others, organizations, society, nature, and the universe. They must market products that correspond to society's core and secondary values, and address the needs of different subcultures within a society.

8. In the natural environment, marketers need to be aware of raw materials shortages, increased energy costs and pollution levels, and the changing role of governments in environmental protection.

9. In the technological arena, marketers should take account of the accelerating pace of technological change, opportunities for innovation, varying R&D budgets, and the increased governmental regulation brought about by technological change.

10. In the political-legal environment, marketers must work within the many laws regulating business practices and with various special-interest groups.

APPLICATIONS

Marketing Debate: Is Consumer Behaviour More a Function of a Person's Age or Generation?

One of the widely debated issues in developing marketing programs that target certain age groups is how much consumers change over time. Some marketers maintain that age differences are critical and that the needs and wants of a 25-year-old in 2005 are not that different from those of a 25-year-old in 1975. Others dispute that contention and argue that cohort and generation effects are critical and that marketing programs must therefore suit the times.

Take a position: Age differences are fundamentally more important than cohort effects versus Cohort effects can dominate age differences.

Marketing Discussion

What brands and products do you feel successfully "speak to you" and effectively target your age group? Why? Which ones do not? What could they do better?

Marketing Spotlight: Budweiser

Budweiser Lager was first brewed in 1876 by E. Anheuser & Co., St. Louis. Today, Anheuser-Busch is the largest brewer in the world in terms of volume, and it competes across a diverse range of markets. Canada is the largest beer market for Anheuser-Busch outside the United States. It entered a local brewing agreement with Labatt Breweries of Canada in 1980. Labatt brews, distributes, and markets Budweiser, Bud Light, Busch, and Busch Light in Canada. O'Doul's, the Anheuser-Busch premium nonalcoholic brew, is available in Canada as an import. The power of this partnership is shown by the fact that Budweiser, Anheuser-Busch's flagship brand, has become the leading packaged beer in Canada.

While retaining its brewing traditions, the company has adopted new technological traditions that improve its business and marketing effectiveness. In 1997, chairman August Busch III vowed to make his company a leader in mining its customers' buying patterns. The key to Anheuser-Busch's real-time analysis of marketing effectiveness is timely data:

getting information back from wholesalers and retailers on what is selling where and when.

"Wholesaler and store-level data has become the lifeblood of our organization," said Joe Patti, Anheuser's vice president for retail planning and category management. Therefore, Anheuser-Busch created BudNET to connect to wholesalers, retailers, and other Anheuser-Busch business partners. The system handles sales reporting, customer development, retail promotion notices, and weekly sales forecasting, as well as a wide array of logistics-related functions. BudNET is the information channel for an Anheuser-Busch system called WEARS (Wholesaler Equity Agreement Reporting System). Through BudNET, the delivery people of the 700 U.S. distributors of Budweiser can become the eyes and ears of the brewer.

WEARS and BudNET do much more than just keep tabs on the flow of icy-cold Bud off retailers' refrigerated shelves. Using portable transaction computers, the delivery people also log data on competing products, identifying what else is on the retailers' shelves. At the end of the day, Anheuser-Busch gets the data and looks for trends. "If Anheuser-Busch loses shelf space in a store in Clarksville, Tennessee, they know it right away," said Joe Thompson, president of Independent Beverage Group, a research and consulting firm. "They're better at this game than anyone, even Coca-Cola."

Understanding consumers means more than just gathering data on your own product or on your competitor's product. Anheuser-Busch also analyzes syndicated bar-code scan data gathered by Information Resources Inc. (IRI) to track consumer purchasing behaviour across a full range of products. Anheuser-Busch successfully launched low-carb Michelob Ultra after seeing data on consumer shifts in dietary habits in other food groups.

Timely, fine-grain data also helps sharpen Anheuser-Busch's marketing and product assortment. Demographic data help Anheuser-Busch know where cans sell better than bottles (blue-collar neighbourhoods). With store-level data, the company can create targeted marketing materials. For example, gay models appear on posters in San Francisco's Castro district but not on those in the Mission district. Better data also help predict local sales during holidays, such as knowing that Calgarians celebrate Stampede week more than St. Patrick's Day. It's not surprising that Budweiser sought to be a lead sponsor of rodeo events across western Canada, including the Calgary Stampede, which hosts 1 million people in its ten-day run. Marketing insights gained from its data also help Budweiser tailor events to the tastes of other regions. For example, to build a connection with beer drinkers in British Columbia, Budweiser sponsors the Merritt Mountain Music Festival, while it hosts the Budweiser Rock Tour in Quebec.

Anheuser-Busch uses a variety of internal and external data sources—including consumer demographics, POS, and market data—to guide product assortment decisions. Anheuser-Busch uses the six-step, industry-standard, best practice called Efficient Item Assortment (EIA) that is published by the Food Marketing Institute. Software, co-developed with an outside software vendor, creates a top-line master assortment product list for individual stores and store clusters. This tool won a Technology Leadership Award from *Consumer Goods Technology (CGT)* magazine.

Anheuser-Busch's use of IT extends overseas. Budexchange.co.uk, hosted on BudNET, tracks key data and sales of 5000 British outlets. The system rewards the loyalty of trade customers with Budweiser-branded support materials. Anheuser-Busch uses the data provided by the outlets in its proactive segmented marketing communications program. In a market in which overall sales are down 5.7 percent, Budweiser sales are up 7 percent.

Anheuser-Busch continues to expand its use of datalinks, using its market clout to improve data gathering and data sharing. August Busch IV, president for domestic operations, promised that "brewers and wholesalers with a clear, data-driven focus will have a distinct competitive advantage." Market share data confirm the success of the company's strategy—Anheuser-Busch's 2003 market share was 50.1 percent, up from 48.9 percent in 2002.

DISCUSSION QUESTIONS

1. What have been the key success factors for Anheuser-Busch?

2. Where is Anheuser-Busch vulnerable? What should it watch out for?

3. What recommendations would you make to senior marketing executives going forward? What should the company be sure to do with its marketing?

Sources: Kevin Kelleher, "66,207,896 Bottles of Beer on the Wall: Anheuser-Busch's Top-Secret Data Network Tracks Inventory," *Business 2.0*, February 25, 2004; "Website Development, Reward Systems and eCRM," **Skybridgegroup.com**; **www.anheuser-busch.com/overview/ABIICanada.htm**; **www.budnet.com**.

4

IN THIS CHAPTER, WE WILL ADDRESS THE FOLLOWING QUESTIONS:

- What constitutes good marketing research?

- What are good metrics for measuring marketing productivity?

- How can marketers assess their return on investment of marketing expenditures?

- How can companies more accurately measure and forecast demand?

4

CHAPTER 4

Conducting Marketing Research and Forecasting Demand

PROFILE: CANADIAN MARKETING EXCELLENCE

Marketers need timely, accurate, and actionable information on consumers, competition, and their brands. They need to make the best possible tactical decisions in the short run and strategic decisions in the long run. Discovering a consumer insight and understanding its marketing implications can often lead to a successful product launch or spur the growth of a brand.

However, in a world that is increasingly saturated with media and information, distilling the market and environment into understandable and digestible pieces of information upon which decisions can be based is an enormous challenge for marketers. Market researchers, consulting and communications firms, and internal marketing departments are constantly searching for new ways to gather information and analyze their environment in a meaningful way.

In today's digital age marketers often find themselves drowning in data and face the constant struggle of finding the right information and turning it into powerful marketing insights. However, it has also created many opportunities for the emergence of new techniques. Toronto-based Delvinia Interactive is one firm that is taking advantage of the increasing online activity to create unique market research products.

Over a period of two years, Delvinia developed an applied market research product called AskingMedia™. The product is an advanced media platform and tool for testing creative materials online, effectively serving as a digital survey administrator. In combination with proprietary Canadian and global Web panels maintained by Delvinia, the AskingMedia™ platform allows researchers to obtain input quickly from a targeted and geographically dispersed research sample. It also has the advantage of being able to recruit panels from numerous geographic areas, thus creating better, more representative samples, whereas traditional methods typically only drew samples from one geographic area or city centre.

AskingMedia™ also allows advertisers to show consumers virtually anything—TV pilots, 3D images of products under development, or radio jingles. More importantly, it can do it faster than traditional methods, recording the results in real time. The process works like this: Participants receive a commercial or other material a company wants to test via the Internet. The research participant is also presented with a video guide that leads him or her through the particular test. After viewing the commercial once, participants watch it a second time using the AskingMedia™ "mood bar" where they indicate whether they like or dislike the ad on a "moment-to-moment" basis just by sliding their mouse. Once viewing is completed, participants are given a standard online questionnaire to complete. All research information (usually collected within 24 to 48 hours)—real-time reporting data, participant profiles, and mood bar results—can be downloaded by the research firm for analysis. Although digital research methods are not new, the ability to test TV advertising in this fashion is an innovation that offers a very compelling benefit to clients.

The tool is proving to be a success. Recently, Delvinia partnered with Toronto research firm Millward Brown and its clients Nissan and Expedia.ca to do a comparative study of the research results obtained using AskingMedia™ versus those obtained using traditional focus group methods. The study found that AskingMedia™ was able to recruit panellists faster (100 panellists were recruited within 24 hours, a process that can usually take up to two weeks for a focus group). What's more, over half the panellists found the online tool gave them a better survey experience. As a result of the project, Delvinia received an Excellence in Research award at the annual Professional Marketing Research Society conference. *Marketing Magazine* predicts that within five years, broadband ad testing like AskingMedia™ will be the norm.

Sources: Paula Baker, "What Next: Online Research—Faster, Easier . . . Better?," *Strategy Magazine Online*, **www.strategymag.com**, October 15, 2004 (viewed November 4, 2004); Adam Froman, "Real Time Research," *Marketing Magazine Online*, **www.marketmag.ca**, June 7, 2004 (viewed November 4, 2004); Delvinia Interactive, **www.delvinia.com** (viewed November 4, 2004).

In this chapter, we review the steps involved in the marketing research process. We also consider how marketers can develop effective metrics for measuring marketing productivity. Finally, we outline how marketers can develop good sales forecasts.

The Marketing Research System

Marketing managers often commission formal marketing studies of specific problems and opportunities. They may request a market survey, a product-preference test, a sales forecast by region, or an advertising evaluation. It is the job of the marketing researcher to produce insight into the customer's attitudes and buying behaviour. We define **marketing research** as the systematic design, collection, analysis, and reporting of data and findings relevant to a specific marketing situation facing the company. Marketing research is now about a US$16.5 billion industry globally, according to ESOMAR, the World Association of Opinion and Market Research Professionals.

A company can obtain marketing research in a number of ways. Most large companies have their own marketing research departments, which often play crucial roles within the organization.[1]

Procter & Gamble

P&G's large market research function is called Consumer & Market Knowledge (CMK). Its goal is to bring consumer insight to decision making at all levels. Dedicated CMK groups work for P&G businesses around the world, including Global Business Units (GBUs), which focus on long-term brand equity and initiative development, and Market Development Organizations (MDOs), which focus on local market expertise and retail partnerships. There is also a relatively smaller, centralized corporate CMK group which, in partnership with the line businesses, focuses on three kinds of work: (1) proprietary research methods development, (2) expert application of, and cross-business learning from, core research competencies, and (3) shared services and infrastructure. CMK leverages traditional research basics such as brand tracking. CMK also finds, invents, or co-develops leading edge research approaches such as experiential consumer contacts, proprietary modelling methods, and scenario-planning or knowledge synthesis events. CMK professionals connect market insights from all these sources to shape company strategies and decisions. They influence day-to-day operational choices, such as which product formulations are launched, as well as long-term plans, such as which corporate acquisitions best round out the product portfolio.

Yet, marketing research is not limited to large companies with big budgets and marketing research departments. At much smaller companies, marketing research is often carried out by everyone in the company—and by customers, too.

Karmaloop.com

Karmaloop bills itself as an online urban boutique, and it has built its reputation as a top shop for fashionistas because of its relentless tracking of trendsetters. The five-year-old Boston company has made streetwear fashion a science by keeping tabs on young tastemakers' buying habits. In addition to its crew of 15 moonlighting artists, DJs, and designers, Karmaloop recruits street team members to ferret out new trends and to spread the word about Karmaloop brands. The street teams, which now boast 3000 reps, pass out fliers and stickers at nightclubs, concerts, and on the street, but also report on what they see at events, in the way of trends.[2]

Companies normally budget marketing research at 1 to 2 percent of company sales. A large percentage of that is spent on the services of outside firms. Marketing research firms fall into three categories:

1. *Syndicated-service research firms.* These firms gather consumer and trade information, which they sell for a fee. Examples: Nielsen Media Research, Forrester, Market Facts, SAMI/Burke.
2. *Custom marketing research firms.* These firms are hired to carry out specific projects. They design the study and report the findings.
3. *Specialty-line marketing research firms.* These firms provide specialized research services. The best example is the field-service firm, which sells field interviewing services to other firms.

Small companies can hire the services of a marketing research firm or conduct research in creative and affordable ways, such as:

1. *Engaging students or professors to design and carry out projects.* One Boston University MBA project helped American Express develop a successful advertising campaign geared toward young professionals. The cost: US$15 000.
2. *Using the Internet.* A company can collect considerable information at very little cost by examining competitors' Web sites, monitoring chat rooms, and accessing published data.
3. *Checking out rivals.* Many small companies routinely visit their competitors. Tom Coohill, a chef who owns two Atlanta restaurants, gives managers a food allowance to dine out and bring back ideas. Atlanta jeweller Frank Maier Jr., who often visits out-of-town rivals, spotted and copied a dramatic way of lighting displays.[3]

Most companies, such as Fuji Photo Film, use a combination of marketing research resources to study their industries, competitors, audiences, and channel strategies.

> ### Fuji Photo Film
>
> At the highest level, Fuji relies on data from market research syndicate NDP Group to study the market for products ranging from digital cameras to ink jet photo paper. Fuji also does custom research with a variety of research partners, and it conducts internal research for projects requiring quick information, such as changes to package design. Regardless of how the marketing research data are collected, it is a top priority for Fuji, which has had to adapt its film and digital imaging products to a rapidly changing marketplace. "If you don't have market research to help you figure out what is changing and what the future will be, you will be left behind," says Fuji's director of category management and trade marketing.[4]

The Marketing Research Process

Effective marketing research involves the six steps shown in Figure 4.1. We will illustrate these steps with the following situation:

> Air Canada is constantly looking for new ways to serve its passengers; it was one of the first companies to install phone handsets. Now it is reviewing many new ideas, especially to cater to its first-class passengers on very long flights, many of whom are businesspeople whose high-priced tickets pay most of the freight. Among these ideas are: (1) to supply an Internet connection with limited access to Web pages and e-mail messaging; (2) to offer 24 channels of satellite cable TV; and (3) to offer a 50-CD audio system that lets each passenger create a customized play list of music and movies to enjoy during the flight. The marketing research manager was assigned to investigate how first-class passengers would rate these services and how much extra they would be willing to pay if a charge was made. He was asked to focus specifically on the Internet connection. One estimate says that airlines might realize revenues of $70 billion over the next decade from in-flight Internet access, if enough first-class passengers would be willing to pay $25 for it. Air Canada could thus recover its costs in a reasonable time. Making the connection available would cost the airline $90 000 per plane.[5]

FIGURE 4.1

The Marketing Research Process

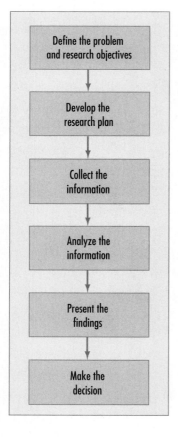

- Define the problem and research objectives
- Develop the research plan
- Collect the information
- Analyze the information
- Present the findings
- Make the decision

Step 1: Define the Problem, the Decision Alternatives, and the Research Objectives

Marketing management must be careful not to define the problem too broadly or too narrowly for the marketing researcher. A marketing manager who instructs the marketing researcher to "Find out everything you can about first class air travellers' needs" will collect a lot of unnecessary information. One who says, "Find out if enough passengers aboard a B747 flying direct between Vancouver and Tokyo would be willing to pay $25 for an Internet connection so that Air Canada would break even in one year on the cost of offering this service" is taking too narrow a view of the problem. The marketing researcher might even raise this question: "Why does the Internet connection have to be priced at $25 as opposed to $10, $50, or some other price? Why does Air Canada have to break even on the cost of the service, especially if it attracts new users?"

In discussing the problem, Air Canada's managers discover another issue. If the new service were successful, how fast could other airlines copy it? Airline marketing research is replete with examples of new services that have been so quickly copied by competitors that no airline has gained a sustainable competitive advantage. How important is it to be first, and how long could the lead be sustained?

The marketing manager and marketing researcher agreed to define the problem as follows: "Will offering an in-flight Internet service create enough incremental preference and profit for Air Canada to justify its cost against other possible investments it might make?" To help in designing the research, management should first spell out the decisions it might face and then work backward. Suppose management spells out these decisions: (1) Should Air Canada offer an Internet connection? (2) If so, should the service be offered to first-class only, or include business class, and possibly economy class? (3) What price(s) should be charged? (4) On what types of planes and lengths of trips should it be offered?

Now management and marketing researchers are ready to set specific research objectives: (1) What types of first-class passengers would respond most to using an in-flight Internet service? (2) How many first-class passengers are likely to use the Internet service at different price levels? (3) How many extra first-class passengers might choose Air Canada because of this new service? (4) How much long-term goodwill will this service add to the company's image? (5) How important is Internet service to first-class passengers relative to providing other services such as a power plug, or enhanced entertainment?

Not all research projects can be this specific. Some research is exploratory—its goal is to shed light on the real nature of the problem and to suggest possible solutions or new ideas. Some research is descriptive—it seeks to ascertain certain magnitudes, such as how many first-class passengers would purchase in-flight Internet service at $25. Some research is causal—its purpose is to test a cause-and-effect relationship.

Step 2: Develop the Research Plan

The second stage of marketing research calls for developing the most efficient plan for gathering the needed information. The marketing manager needs to know the cost of the research plan before approving it. Suppose the company made a prior estimate that launching the in-flight Internet service would yield a long-term profit of $50 000. The manager believes that doing the research would lead to an improved pricing and promotional plan and a long-term profit of $90 000. In this case, the manager should be willing to spend up to $40 000 on this research. If the research would cost more than $40 000, it is not worth doing.[6] Designing a research plan calls for decisions on the data sources, research approaches, research instruments, sampling plan, and contact methods.

DATA SOURCES The researcher can gather secondary data, primary data, or both. *Secondary data* are data that were collected for another purpose and already exist somewhere. *Primary data* are data freshly gathered for a specific purpose or for a specific research project.

Researchers usually start their investigation by examining some of the rich variety of secondary data to see whether the problem can be partly or wholly solved without collecting costly primary data. Secondary data provide a starting point and offer the advantages of low cost and ready availability. When the needed data do not exist or are dated, inaccurate, incomplete, or unreliable, the researcher will have to collect primary data. Most marketing research projects involve some primary-data collection. The normal procedure is to interview some people individually or in groups, to get a sense of how people feel about the topic in question, and then develop a formal research instrument, debug it, and carry it into the field.

RESEARCH APPROACHES Primary data can be collected in five main ways: through observation, focus groups, surveys, behavioural data, and experiments.

Observational Research Fresh data can be gathered by observing the relevant actors and settings.[7] Consumers can be unobtrusively observed as they shop or as they consume products. Ogilvy & Mather's Discovery Group creates documentary-style videos by sending researchers into consumers' homes with handheld video cameras. Hours of footage are edited to a 30-minute "highlight reel," which the group uses to analyze consumer behaviour. Other researchers equip consumers with pagers and instruct them to write down what they are doing whenever prompted, or hold more informal interview sessions at a café or bar. The Air Canada researchers might meander around first-class lounges to hear how travellers talk about the different carriers and their features. They can fly on competitors' planes to observe in-flight service.

Focus Group Research A **focus group** is a gathering of six to ten people who are carefully selected based on certain demographic, psychographic, or other considerations and brought together to discuss various topics of interest at length. Participants are normally paid a small sum for attending. A professional research moderator provides questions and probes based on a discussion guide or agenda prepared by the responsible marketing managers to ensure that the right material gets covered.

Moderators attempt to track down potentially useful insights as they try to discern the real motivations of consumers and why they are saying and doing certain things. The sessions are typically recorded in some fashion, and marketing managers often remain behind one-way mirrors in the next room. In the Air Canada research, the moderator might start with a broad question, such as "How do you feel about first-class air travel?" Questions then move to how people view the different airlines, different existing services, different proposed services, and specifically, Internet service. Although focus-group research has been shown to be a useful exploratory step, researchers must avoid generalizing the reported feelings of the focus-group participants to the whole market, because the

A focus group in session, with marketing people observing through a one-way mirror.

sample size is too small and the sample is not drawn randomly. "Marketing Insight: Conducting Informative Focus Groups" has some practical tips to improve the quality of focus groups.

Survey Research Companies undertake surveys to learn about people's knowledge, beliefs, preferences, and satisfaction, and to measure these magnitudes in the general population. A company such as Air Canada might prepare its own survey instrument to gather the information it needs, or it might add questions to an omnibus survey that carries the questions of several companies at a much lower cost. It can also put the questions to an ongoing consumer panel run by itself or another company. It may do a mall intercept study by having researchers approach people in a shopping mall and ask them questions.

Behavioural Data Customers leave traces of their purchasing behaviour in store scanning data, catalogue purchases, and customer databases. Much can be learned by analyzing these data. Customers' actual purchases reflect preferences and often are more reliable than statements they offer to market researchers. People may report preferences for popular brands, and yet the data show them actually buying other brands. For example, grocery-shopping data show that high-income people do not necessarily buy the more expensive brands, contrary to what they might state in interviews; and many low-income people buy some expensive brands. Clearly, Air Canada can learn many useful things about its passengers by analyzing ticket purchase records.

Experimental Research The most scientifically valid research is experimental research. The purpose of experimental research is to capture cause-and-effect relationships by eliminating competing explanations of the observed findings. To the extent that the design and execution of the experiment eliminate alternative hypotheses that might explain the results, research and marketing managers can have confidence in the conclusions.

Experiments call for selecting matched groups of subjects, subjecting them to different treatments, controlling extraneous variables, and checking whether observed response differences are statistically significant. To the extent that extraneous factors are eliminated or controlled, the observed effects can be related to the variations in the treatments. Air Canada might introduce in-flight Internet service on one of its regular flights from Vancouver to Tokyo. It might charge $25 one week and charge only $15 the next week. If the plane carried approximately the same number of first-class passengers each week and the particular weeks made no difference, any significant difference in the number of passengers buying the service could be related to the different prices charged. The experimental design could be elaborated by trying other prices and including other air routes.

RESEARCH INSTRUMENTS Marketing researchers have a choice of three main research instruments in collecting primary data: questionnaires, qualitative measures, and mechanical devices.

Questionnaires A questionnaire consists of a set of questions presented to respondents. Because of its flexibility, the questionnaire is by far the most common instrument used to collect primary data. Questionnaires need to be carefully developed, tested, and debugged before they are administered on a large scale. In preparing a questionnaire, the researcher carefully chooses the questions and

MARKETING INSIGHT

Conducting Informative Focus Groups

Focus groups allow marketers to observe how and why consumers accept or reject concepts, ideas, or any specific notion. The key to using focus groups successfully is to *listen*. It is critical to eliminate biases as much as possible. Although many useful insights can emerge from thoughtfully run focus groups, there can be questions as to their validity, especially in today's marketing environment.

Some researchers believe that consumers have been so bombarded with ads, they unconsciously (or perhaps cynically) parrot back what they have already heard as compared to what they think. There is also always a concern that participants are just trying to maintain their self-image and public persona or have a need to identify with the other members of the group. Participants may not be willing to admit in public—or may not even recognize— their behaviour patterns and motivations. There is also always the "loudmouth" problem—when one highly opinionated person drowns out the rest of the group. It may be expensive to recruit qualified subjects ($3000 to $5000 per group), but getting the right participants is crucial.

Even when multiple groups are involved, it may be difficult to generalize the results to a broader population. For example, focus group findings often vary from region to region. One U.S. firm specializing in focus group research claimed that the best city to conduct focus groups was Minneapolis because it could get a fairly well-educated sample of people who were honest and forthcoming about their opinions. Many marketers interpret focus groups carefully in New York and other Northeastern U.S. cities because the people in these areas tend to be highly critical and generally do not report that they like much. Too often, managers become comfortable with a particular focus group format and apply it generally and automatically to every circumstance. Europeans typically need more time than North American marketers typically are willing to give—a focus group there rarely takes less than two hours and often more than four.[8]

Participants must feel as relaxed as possible and feel a strong obligation to "speak the truth." Physical surroundings can be crucial. Researchers at one agency knew they had a problem when a fight broke out between participants at one of their sessions. As one executive noted, "we wondered why people always seemed grumpy and negative—people were resistant to any idea we showed them." The problem was the room itself: cramped, stifling, forbidding: "It was a cross between a hospital room and a police interrogation room." To fix the problem, the agency gave the room a makeover. Other firms are adapting the look of the room to fit the theme of the topic—like designing the room to look like a playroom when speaking to children.

Although many firms are substituting observational research for focus groups, ethnographic research can be expensive and tricky: Researchers have to be highly skilled, participants have to be on the level, and mounds of data have to be analyzed. The beauty of focus groups, as one marketing executive noted, is that "it's still the most cost-effective, quickest, dirtiest way to get information in rapid time on an idea." In analyzing the pros and cons, Wharton's Americus Reed might have said it best: "A focus group is like a chain saw. If you know what you're doing, it's very useful and effective. If you don't, you could lose a limb."

Sources: Sarah Stiansen, "How Focus Groups Can Go Astray," *Adweek*, December 5, 1988, pp. FK 4–6; Jeffrey Kasner, "Fistfights and Feng Shui," *Boston Globe*, July 21, 2001, pp. C1–C2; Leslie Kaufman, "Enough Talk," *Newsweek*, August 18, 1997, pp. 48–49; Linda Tischler, "Every Move You Make," *Fast Company*, April 2004, pp. 73–75; Alison Stein Wellner, "The New Science of Focus Groups," *American Demographics*, March 2003, pp. 29–33; Dennis Rook, "Out-of-Focus Groups," *Marketing Research*, Summer 2003, 15 (2), p. 11.

their form, wording, and sequence. The form of the question can influence the response. Marketing researchers distinguish between closed-end and open-end questions. Closed-end questions specify all the possible answers and provide answers that are easier to interpret and tabulate. Open-end questions allow respondents to answer in their own words and often reveal more about how people think. They are especially useful in exploratory research, where the researcher is looking for insight into how people think rather than measuring how many people think a certain way. Table 4.1 provides examples of both types of questions. Also refer to "Marketing Memo: Questionnaire Dos and Don'ts."

Qualitative Measures Some marketers prefer more qualitative methods for gauging consumer opinion because consumer actions do not always match their answers to survey questions. *Qualitative research techniques* are relatively unstructured measurement approaches that permit a

TABLE 4.1	TYPES OF QUESTIONS

Name	Description	Example
A. Closed-end Questions		
Dichotomous	A question with two possible answers.	In arranging this trip, did you personally phone Air Canada? Yes No
Multiple choice	A question with three or more answers.	With whom are you travelling on this flight? ☐ No one ☐ Children only ☐ Spouse ☐ Business associates/friends/relatives ☐ Spouse and children ☐ An organized tour group
Likert scale	A statement with which the respondent shows the amount of agreement/disagreement.	Small airlines generally give better service than large ones. Strongly disagree 1___ Disagree 2___ Neither agree nor disagree 3___ Agree 4___ Strongly agree 5___
Semantic differential	A scale connecting two bipolar words. The respondent selects the point that represents his or her opinion.	Air Canada Large----------------------------------Small Experienced------------------------Inexperienced Modern-------------------------------Old-fashioned
Importance scale	A scale that rates the importance of some attribute.	Airline food service to me is Extremely important 1___ Very important 2___ Somewhat important 3___ Not very important 4___ Not at all important 5___
Rating scale	A scale that rates some attribute from "poor" to "excellent."	Air Canada food service is Excellent 1___ Very Good 2___ Good 3___ Fair 4___ Poor 5___
Intention-to-buy scale	A scale that describes the respondent's intention to buy.	If an in-flight telephone were available on a long flight, I would Definitely buy 1___ Probably buy 2___ Not sure 3___ Probably not buy 4___ Definitely not buy 5___
B. Open-end Questions		
Completely unstructured	A question that respondents can answer in an almost unlimited number of ways.	What is your opinion of Air Canada?
Word association	Words are presented, one at a time, and respondents mention the first word that comes to mind.	What is the first word that comes to your mind when you hear the following? Airline _____ Air Canada _____ Travel _____
Sentence completion	An incomplete sentence is presented and respondents complete the sentence.	When I choose an airline, the most important consideration in my decision is _____.
Story completion	An incomplete story is presented, and respondents are asked to complete it.	"I flew Air Canada a few days ago. I noticed that the exterior and interior of the plane had very bright colours. This aroused in me the following thoughts and feelings. . . ." Now complete the story.
Picture	A picture of two characters is presented, with one making a statement. Respondents are asked to identify with the other and fill in the empty balloon.	
Thematic Apperception Test (TAT)	A picture is presented and respondents are asked to make up a story about what they think is happening or may happen in the picture.	

range of possible responses. Qualitative research techniques are a creative means of ascertaining consumer perceptions that may otherwise be difficult to uncover. The range of possible qualitative research techniques is limited only by the creativity of the marketing researcher. Here are seven techniques employed by design firm IDEO for understanding the customer experience:[9]

- *Shadowing*—observing people using products, shopping, going to hospitals, taking the train, using their cell phones.

- *Behaviour mapping*—photographing people within a space, such as a hospital waiting room, over two or three days.

- *Consumer journey*—keeping track of all the interactions a consumer has with a product, service, or space.

- *Camera journals*—asking consumers to keep visual diaries of their activities and impressions relating to a product.

- *Extreme user interviews*—talking to people who really know—or know nothing—about a product or service and evaluating their experience using it.

- *Storytelling*—prompting people to tell personal stories about their consumer experiences.

- *Unfocus groups*—interviewing a diverse group of people: To explore ideas about sandals, IDEO gathered an artist, a bodybuilder, a podiatrist, and a shoe fetishist.

Because of the freedom afforded both researchers in their probes and consumers in their responses, qualitative research can often be a useful first step in exploring consumers' brand and product perceptions. There are also drawbacks to qualitative research. The indepth insights that emerge have to be tempered by the fact that the samples involved are often very small and may not necessarily generalize to broader populations. Moreover, given the qualitative nature of the data, there may also be questions of interpretation. Different researchers examining the same results from a qualitative research study may draw very different conclusions. "Marketing Insight: Getting into Consumers' Heads with Qualitative Research" describes some popular approaches.

Marketing Memo

Questionnaire Dos And Don'ts

1. *Ensure that questions are without bias.* Do not lead the respondent into an answer.

2. *Make the questions as simple as possible.* Questions that include multiple ideas or two questions in one will confuse respondents.

3. *Make the questions specific.* Sometimes it is advisable to add memory cues. For example, it is good practice to be specific with time periods.

4. *Avoid jargon or shorthand.* Avoid trade jargon, acronyms, and initials not in everyday use.

5. *Steer clear of sophisticated or uncommon words.* Only use words in common speech.

6. *Avoid ambiguous words.* Words such as "usually" or "frequently" have no specific meaning.

7. *Avoid questions with a negative in them.* It is better to say "Do you ever . . . ?" than "Do you never . . . ?"

8. *Avoid hypothetical questions.* It is difficult to answer questions about imaginary situations. Answers cannot necessarily be trusted.

9. *Do not use words that could be misheard.* This is especially important when the interview is administered over the telephone. "What is your opinion of sects?" could yield interesting but not necessarily relevant answers.

10. *Desensitize questions by using response bands.* For questions that ask people their age or companies their turnover, it is best to offer a range of response bands.

11. *Ensure that fixed responses do not overlap.* Categories used in fixed response questions should be sequential and not overlap.

12. *Allow for "other" in fixed response questions.* Pre-coded answers should always allow for a response other than those listed.

Source: Adapted from Paul Hague and Peter Jackson, *Market Research: A Guide to Planning, Methodology, and Evaluation* (London: Kogan Page, 1999). See also Hans Baumgartner, Jan Benedict, and E. M. Steenkamp, "Response Styles in Marketing Research: A Cross-National Investigation," *Journal of Marketing Research*, May 2001, pp. 143–156.

may also be questions of interpretation. Different researchers examining the same results from a qualitative research study may draw very different conclusions. "Marketing Insight: Getting into Consumers' Heads with Qualitative Research" describes some popular approaches.

Mechanical Devices Mechanical devices are occasionally used in marketing research. For example, galvanometers can measure the interest or emotions aroused by exposure to a specific ad or picture. The tachistoscope flashes an ad to a subject with an exposure interval that may range from less than one hundredth of a second to several seconds. After each exposure, the respondent describes everything he or she recalls. Eye cameras study respondents' eye movements to see where their eyes land first, how long they linger on a given item, and so on. As one would expect, in recent years technology has advanced to such a degree that now devices like skin sensors, brain wave scanners, and full body scanners are being used to get consumer responses.[10]

Technology has replaced the diaries that participants in media surveys used to have to keep. Audiometers can be attached to television sets in participating homes to record when the set is on and to which channel it is tuned. Electronic devices can record the number of radio programs a

MARKETING INSIGHT

Getting into Consumers' Heads with Qualitative Research

Here are some commonly used qualitative research approaches to get inside consumers' minds and find out what they are thinking or feeling about brands and products:

1. *Word associations.* People can be asked what words come to mind when they hear the brand's name. "What does the Timex name mean to you? Tell me what comes to mind when you think of Timex watches." The primary purpose of free association tasks is to identify the range of possible brand associations in consumers' minds. But they may also provide some rough indication of the relative strength, favourability, and uniqueness of brand associations.

2. *Projective techniques.* People are presented an incomplete stimulus and asked to complete it or given an ambiguous stimulus that may not make sense in and of itself and are asked to make sense of it. The argument is that people will reveal their true beliefs and feelings. One such approach is "bubble exercises" based on cartoons or photos. Different people are depicted buying or using certain products or services. Empty bubbles, like those found in cartoons, are placed in the scenes to represent the thoughts, words, or actions of one or more of the participants. People are then asked to "fill in the bubble" by indicating what they believe is happening or being said. Another technique is comparison tasks. People are asked to convey their impressions by comparing brands to people, countries, animals, activities, fabrics, occupations, cars, magazines, vegetables, nationalities, or even other brands.

3. *Visualization.* People can be asked to create a collage from magazine photos or drawings to depict their perceptions. ZMET is a research technique that starts with a group of participants who are asked in advance to select a minimum of 12 images from their own sources (e.g., magazines, catalogues, and family photo albums) that represent their thoughts and feelings about the research topic. The participants bring these images to a personal one-on-one interview with a study administrator, who uses advanced interview techniques to explore the images with the participant and reveal hidden meanings. Finally, the participants use a computer program to create a collage with these images that communicates their subconscious thoughts and feelings about the topic. One ZMET study probed what women thought of pantyhose. Twenty hose-wearing women were asked to collect pictures that captured their feelings about wearing pantyhose. Some of the pictures showed fence posts encased in plastic wrap or steel bands strangling trees, suggesting that pantyhose are tight and inconvenient. Another picture showed tall flowers in a vase, suggesting that the product made a woman feel thin, tall, and sexy.

4. *Brand personification.* People can be asked to describe what kind of person they think of when the brand is mentioned: "If the brand were to come alive as a person, what would it be like, what would it do, where would it live, what would it wear, who would it talk to if it went to a party (and what would it talk about)?" For example, they may say that the John Deere brand makes them think of a rugged small-town male who is hardworking and trustworthy. The brand personality delivers a picture of the more human qualities of the brand.

5. *Laddering.* A series of increasingly more specific "why" questions can be used to gain insight into consumer motivation and consumers' deeper, more abstract goals. Ask why someone wants to buy a Nokia cellular phone. "They look well built" (attribute). "Why is it important that the phone be well built?" "It suggests that the Nokia is reliable" (a functional benefit). "Why is reliability important?" "Because my colleagues or family can be sure to reach me" (an emotional benefit). "Why must you be available to them at all times?" "I can help them if they are in trouble" (brand essence). The brand makes this person feel like a Good Samaritan, ready to help others.

Sources: Allen Adamson, "Why Traditional Brand Positioning Can't Last," *Brandweek*, November 17, 2003, pp. 38–40; Todd Wasserman, "Sharpening the Focus," *Brandweek*, November 3, 2003, pp. 28–32; Linda Tischler, "Every Move You Make," *Fast Company*, April 2004, pp. 73–75; Gerald Zaltman, *How Customers Think: Essential Insights Into the Mind of the Market* (Boston: Harvard Business School Press, 2003).

person is exposed to during the day or, using global positioning system (GPS) technology, how many billboards a person may walk by or drive by during a day.

SAMPLING PLAN   After deciding on the research approach and instruments, the marketing researcher must design a sampling plan. This calls for three decisions:

1. *Sampling unit: Who is to be surveyed?* The marketing researcher must define the target population that will be sampled. In the Air Canada survey, should the sampling unit be only first-class business travellers, first-class vacation travellers, or both? Should travellers under age 18 be interviewed? Should both husbands and wives be interviewed? Once the sampling unit is determined, a sampling frame must be developed so that everyone in the target population has an equal or known chance of being sampled.

2. *Sample size: How many people should be surveyed?* Large samples give more reliable results than small samples. However, it is not necessary to sample the entire target population or even a substantial portion to achieve reliable results. Samples of less than 1 percent of a population can often provide good reliability, with a credible sampling procedure.

3. *Sampling procedure: How should the respondents be chosen?* To obtain a representative sample, a probability sample of the population should be drawn. Probability sampling allows the calculation of confidence limits for sampling error. Thus, one could conclude after the sample is taken that "the interval 5 to 7 trips per year has 95 chances in 100 of containing the true number of trips taken annually by first-class passengers flying between Vancouver and Tokyo." Three types of probability sampling are described in Table 4.2 part A. When the cost or time involved in probability sampling is too high, marketing researchers will take nonprobability samples. Table 4.2 part B describes three types. Some marketing researchers feel that nonprobability samples are very useful in many circumstances, even though they do not allow sampling error to be measured.

CONTACT METHODS   Once the sampling plan has been determined, the marketing researcher must decide how the subject should be contacted: mail, telephone, personal, or online interview.

Mail Questionnaire The *mail questionnaire* is the best way to reach people who would not give personal interviews or whose responses might be biased or distorted by the interviewers. Mail questionnaires require simple and clearly worded questions. Unfortunately, the response rate is usually low or slow.

Telephone Interview *Telephone interviewing* is the best method for gathering information quickly; the interviewer is also able to clarify questions if respondents do not understand them. The response rate is typically higher than in the case of mailed questionnaires. The main drawback is that the interviews have to be short and not too personal. Telephone interviewing is getting more difficult because of consumers' growing antipathy toward telemarketers calling them in their homes and interrupting their lives.

TABLE 4.2	PROBABILITY AND NONPROBABILITY SAMPLES
A. Probability Sample	
Simple random sample	Every member of the population has an equal chance of selection.
Stratified random sample	The population is divided into mutually exclusive groups (such as age groups), and random samples are drawn from each group.
Cluster (area) sample	The population is divided into mutually exclusive groups (such as city blocks), and the researcher draws a sample of the groups to interview.
B. Nonprobability Sample	
Convenience sample	The researcher selects the most accessible population members.
Judgment sample	The researcher selects population members who are good prospects for accurate information.
Quota sample	The researcher finds and interviews a prescribed number of people in each of several categories.

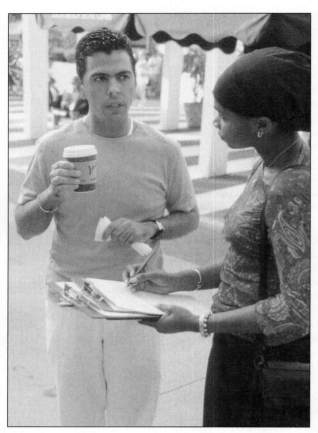

An intercept interview at a mall.

Personal Interview *Personal interviewing* is the most versatile method. The interviewer can ask more questions and record additional observations about the respondent, such as dress and body language. At the same time, personal interviewing is the most expensive method and requires more administrative planning and supervision than the other three. It is also subject to interviewer bias or distortion. Personal interviewing takes two forms. In *arranged interviews,* respondents are contacted for an appointment, and often a small payment or incentive is offered. *Intercept interviews* involve stopping people at a shopping mall or busy street corner and requesting an interview. Intercept interviews can have the drawback of being nonprobability samples, and the interviews must not require too much time.

Online Interview Today, 70 percent of Canadian households and 95 percent of businesses are online. Furthermore, over 30 percent of Canadian households and businesses have broadband access. Therefore, it is not surprising that there is increased use of online research methods.[11] Online research was up 20–30 percent in 2003, and was expected to continue along the same growth trajectory in 2004. Furthermore, online research is estimated to make up 25 percent of all survey-based research in 2004.[12]

There are so many ways to use the Internet to do research. A company can include a questionnaire on its Web site and offer an incentive to answer the questionnaire; or it can place a banner on some frequently visited site such as Yahoo!, inviting people to answer some questions and possibly win a prize. The company can sponsor a chat room or bulletin board and introduce questions from time to time, or host a real-time panel or virtual focus group. A company can learn about individuals who visit its site by following how they *clickstream* through the Web site and move to other sites. A company can post different prices, use different headlines, offer different product features on different Web sites or at different times to learn the relative effectiveness of its offerings.

Online product testing, in which companies float trial balloons for new products, is also growing and providing information much faster than traditional marketing research techniques used to develop new products. For instance, marketers for Mattel's Hot Wheels toys rely heavily on the Web to interact with collectors to help develop new products, promotions, and licensed goods. Following one fan survey, marketing executives learned that they could expand licensed offerings to boys ages 11 to 16 to keep them into the brand franchise, resulting in extended partnerships with Bell Motorcycles and BMX bikes.[13]

Hershey's Food Corp.

Candymaker Hershey was an early innovator in the area of online product testing. In 1999 through 2000, the company moved its new product testing online along with its entire historical product testing. It combined more than 1200 historical concept tests with about 300 to 400 online test results to create an online "turnkey" system that works both as a reporting tool and as an archival system. The move to online product testing has cut Hershey's new product development process by two-thirds—a strategic advantage in a mature market—and keeps a wealth of institutional data on hand even as research personnel change over the years.[14]

Not everyone is on the Web, however, and online market researchers must find creative ways to reach certain population segments, such as older Canadians, French Canadians, or the disabled. One option is to combine offline sources with the online findings, as Ipsos-Reid has done.

Ipsos-Reid[15]

The Vancouver-headquartered Ipsos-Reid Corporation, which started out as the Angus Reid Group over 20 years ago, is now a global heavyweight, with 11 offices around the world. It conducts surveys in more than 80 countries. To become a leader in the marketing research field, Ipsos-Reid needed reliable techniques and representative samples. One way it has done so in Canada is through its Canadian Online Panel, composed of over 35 000 households. This panel can also be divided into a number of subpanels, such as teens on the Web, online purchasers, small office/home office owners, Canadians who suffer from specific medical conditions, and affluent Canadians. To capture information from Canadians who may not be connected to the Web, it also utilizes its Canadian Consumer Panel, composed of 80 000 pre-selected households and over 150 000 individuals, to help companies better understand Canadian consumers. Together these two panels allow Ipsos-Reid's clients to do everything from concept, product, and ad testing to segmentation and forecasting studies.

While marketers are right to be infatuated with the possibilities of online research, it's important to remember that the field is still in its infancy and is constantly evolving to meet the needs of companies, advertising agencies, and consumers. "Marketing Memo: Pros and Cons of Online Research" outlines some of the advantages and disadvantages of online research thus far.

Step 3: Collect the Information

The data collection phase of marketing research is generally the most expensive and the most prone to error. In the case of surveys, four major problems arise. Some respondents will not be at home and must be contacted again or replaced. Other respondents will refuse to cooperate. Still others will give biased or dishonest answers. Finally, some interviewers will be biased or dishonest. Getting the right respondents is critical.

Mediamark Research

Mediamark Research interviews 26 000 U.S. residents in their homes on the kind of media they use, the brands and products they use, and their attitudes toward topics such as sports and politics. Up until 2002, however, the company had tended to exclude non–English-speaking Hispanics from the research. As the Hispanic population increased in numbers and buying power, the company recognized that it could no longer afford this limiting and potentially biased approach. Mediamark recruited a bilingual travelling task force so that when interviewers come to a Hispanic household, respondents can answer the survey in English or Spanish. They also are creating a more seamless interviewing database by asking the same questions to all people no matter what language they speak and what level of acculturation they have.[19]

Thanks to computers and telecommunications, data collection methods are rapidly improving. Some research firms interview from a centralized location. Professional interviewers sit in booths and draw telephone numbers at random. When the phone is answered, the interviewer reads a set of questions from a monitor and types the respondent's answers into a computer. This procedure eliminates editing and coding, reduces errors, saves time, and produces all the required statistics. Other research firms have set up interactive terminals in shopping centres. Persons willing to be interviewed sit at a terminal, read the questions from the monitor, and type in their answers.

Consider what one Canadian research firm is doing with technology to improve the effectiveness of online focus groups while at the same time cutting its costs.

Marketing Memo

Pros and Cons of Online Research

Advantages

- *Online research is inexpensive.* The cost of gathering survey information electronically is much less expensive than by traditional means. A typical e-mail survey costs about half what a conventional survey costs, and return rates can be as high as 50 percent.[16] For instance, Virgin.net used online research to launch its broadband service in the United Kingdom in 2002. Now the company does all its research online. The brand has seen an increase in response rates from 17 percent with paper-based research to almost 72 percent, and costs have dropped 90 percent.[17]

- *Online research is faster.* Online surveys are faster to complete since the survey can automatically direct respondents to applicable questions and be sent electronically to the research supplier once finished. One estimate is that 75 to 80 percent of a survey's targeted response can be generated in 48 hours using online methods, as compared to a telephone survey that can take 70 days to obtain 150 interviews.[18]

- *People tend to be more honest online than they are in personal or telephone interviews.* Britain's online polling company YouGov.com took 500 people and surveyed half via intercom in a booth and the other half online, asking them politically correct questions such as "Should there be more aid to Africa?" Online answers were deemed much more honest. People may be more open about their opinions when they can respond to a survey privately and not to another person who they feel might be judging them, especially on sensitive topics.

- *Online research is more versatile.* The multimedia applications of online research are especially advantageous. For instance, virtual reality software lets visitors inspect 3-D models of products such as cameras, cars, and medical equipment, and product characteristics can be easily manipulated online. Even at the most basic level, online surveys make answering a questionnaire easier and more fun than paper-and-pencil versions.

Disadvantages

- *Samples can be small and skewed.* Perhaps the largest criticism levelled against online research is that not everyone is online. Research subjects who respond to online surveys are more likely to be tech-savvy middle-class males. These people are likely to differ in socioeconomic and education levels from those online. While marketers can be certain that more and more people will go online, it is important for online market researchers to find creative ways to reach certain population segments that are less likely to be online, such as older Canadians. One option is to combine offline sources with online findings. Providing temporary Internet access at locations such as malls and recreation centres is another strategy. Some research firms use statistical models to fill in the gaps in market research left by offline consumer segments.

- *Online market research is prone to technological problems and inconsistencies.* Because online research is a relatively new method, many market researchers have not gotten survey designs right. A common error is transferring a written survey to the screen. Others overuse technology, concentrating on the bells and whistles and graphics while ignoring basic survey design guidelines. Problems also arise because browser software varies. The Web designer's final product may be seen very differently depending upon the research subject's screen and operating system.

Sources: Catherine Arnold, "Not Done Net; New Opportunities Still Exist in Online Research," *Marketing News*, April 1, 2004, p. 17; Nima M. Ray and Sharon W. Tabor, "Contributing Factors; Several Issues Affect e-Research Validity," *Marketing News*, September 15, 2003, p. 50; Louella Miles, "Online, on Tap," *Marketing*, June 16, 2004, pp. 39–40.

Tangency

Toronto-based PR firm Tangency recently began an interactive market research division after identifying a new market opportunity in data collection. Tangency believes that marketers are interested in online research, given the growth in broadband users, but they are uncomfortable with not having the research participants present. As a result, Tangency began a panellist-recruiting effort and is giving each participant a Webcam. As a result, its clients can view participants during online research efforts while also enjoying the benefits of being online. For example, focus group members can be spread across a wide geography without travelling, and clients can observe the interaction from their offices, also without travelling. Pressing queries can be answered almost immediately—and, of course, it is all more affordable. The one drawback of the system is that some technological knowledge is required, which may limit possible participants to younger, technologically savvy individuals.[20]

It is important to recognize that not everyone in the sample population will be online. (See "Marketing Insight: Global Online Market Research Challenges.")

Step 4: Analyze the Information

The next-to-last step in the process is to extract findings from the collected data. The researcher tabulates the data and develops frequency distributions. Averages and measures of dispersion are computed for the major variables. The researcher will also apply some advanced statistical techniques and decision models in the hope of discovering additional findings.

Step 5: Present the Findings

As the last step, the researcher presents the findings. The researcher should present findings that are relevant to the major marketing decisions facing management. The main survey findings for the Air Canada case show that:

1. The chief reasons for using in-flight Internet service are to pass the time surfing, and to send and receive messages from colleagues and family. The charge would be put on passengers' charge accounts and paid by their companies.

2. About 5 first-class passengers out of every 10 during a flight would use the Internet service at $25; about 6 would use it at $15. Thus, a charge of $15 would produce less revenue ($90 = 6 × $15) than $25 ($125 = 5 × $25). By charging $25, Air Canada would collect $125 per flight. Assuming that the same flight takes place 365 days a year, the company would collect $45 625 (= $125 × 365) annually. Since the investment is $90 000, it will take approximately two years before Air Canada breaks even.

3. Offering in-flight service would strengthen the public's image of Air Canada as an innovative and progressive airline. It would gain some new passengers and customer goodwill.

Step 6: Make the Decision

The managers who commissioned the research need to weigh the evidence. If their confidence in the findings is low, they may decide against introducing the in-flight Internet service. If they are predisposed to launching the service, the findings support their inclination. They may even decide to study the issues further and do more research. The decision is theirs, but hopefully the research provided them with insight into the problem. (See Table 4.3.)[21]

A growing number of organizations are using a marketing decision support system to help their marketing managers make better decisions. The Massachusetts Institute of Technology's John Little defines a **marketing decision support system (MDSS)** as a coordinated collection of data, systems, tools, and techniques with supporting software and hardware by which an organization gathers and interprets relevant information from business and environment and turns it into a basis for marketing action.[22]

A classic MDSS example is the CALLPLAN model, which helps salespeople determine the number of calls to make per period to each prospect and current client. The model takes into account travel time as well as selling time. When launched, the model was tested at United Airlines with an experimental group that managed to increase its sales over a matched control group by 8 percentage points.[23] Once a year, *Marketing News* lists hundreds of current marketing and sales software programs that assist in designing marketing research studies, segmenting markets, setting prices and advertising budgets, analyzing media, and planning sales force activity.

MARKETING INSIGHT

Global Online Market Research Challenges

When chipmaker Intel Research wanted to know how people in countries around the world use technology, it sent an anthropologist to find out. Dr. Genevieve Bell visited 100 households in 19 cities in 7 countries in Asia and the Pacific. She came back to Intel with 20 gigabytes of digital photos, 19 field notebooks, and insights about technology, culture, and design that would challenge company assumptions about digital technology.

It stands to reason that Intel—a global tech powerhouse—would want to know how technology is used in its international markets. Yet all companies have a stake in knowing how the rest of the world sees and uses what most Westerners take for granted: Internet technology. With online research becoming the fastest-growing market research tool, marketers with global ambitions need to know which countries are online and why or why not.

Internet penetration is low in most parts of Asia, Latin America, and Central and Eastern Europe. In Brazil, for example, only 7 percent of the population is online. While most people assume that the low penetration is due to economies that don't support an expensive technological infrastructure, there are other factors involved. There's climate, for one. In Malaysia, power surges caused by monsoons can fry computer motherboards. Government is also a powerful spur or barrier to Internet penetration. While the Chinese economy is zooming ahead, it's unlikely the authoritarian Chinese government will feel comfortable with market researchers gathering information from its citizens via the Internet. Contrast this with South Korea, where the government has made widespread broadband Internet access a priority, and has provided incentives to PC makers to bring cheaper models to market.

Other significant factors that can keep computers and Wi-Fi and data ports from crossing the threshold are religion and culture. Dr. Bell found that values of humility and simplicity are deemed incompatible with Internet technology and make it less welcome in some Hindu homes in India or Muslim homes in Malaysia and Indonesia. She also noted that while North Americans have private space in the home for leisure activities, Japan's tighter quarters afford little privacy. This may explain the huge popularity of text messaging on mobile phones among Japan's young people.

Dr. Bell's findings on global responses to technology point out one of the biggest obstacles to conducting international research, whether online or not: a lack of consistency. Nan Martin, global accounts director for Synovate Inc., a market research firm with offices in 46 countries, says: "In global research, we have to adapt culturally to how, where and with whom we are doing the research. . . . A simple research study conducted globally becomes much more complicated as a result of the cultural nuances, and it's necessary for us to be sensitive to those nuances in data collection and interpretation." For instance, suppose Internet penetration is equal. In Latin America, where consumers are uncomfortable with the impersonal nature of the Internet, researchers might need to incorporate interactive elements into a survey so participants feel they are talking to a real person. In Asia, focus groups are challenging because of the cultural tendency to conform. Online surveys may bring more honest responses and keep respondents from "losing face."

And what if a researcher collects data face-to-face in Mexico, but by Internet in the United States and Canada? Nan Martin says that, "Not only are the subjects answering the question differently because of cultural difference, but the data is being collected by a different method. That can shake the underpinnings of how research scientists feel about collecting data: that every time you change a variable, you're making interpretation of the results more challenging. It is so challenging, in fact, that some say this is an area where global marketers are best served by hiring an expert—an outside research firm with an expertise in acquiring and analyzing international data."

Sources: Arundhati Parmar, "Stumbling Blocks: Net Research Is Not Quite Global," *Marketing News*, March 3, 2003, p. 51; Catherine Arnold, "Global Perspective: Synovate Exec Discusses Future of International Research," *Marketing News*, May 15, 2004, p. 43; Michael Erard, "For Technology, No Small World After All," *The New York Times*, May 6, 2004, p. G5; Deborah L. Vence, "Global Consistency: Leave It to the Experts," *Marketing News*, April 28, 2003, p. 37.

Overcoming Barriers to the Use of Marketing Research

In spite of the rapid growth of marketing research, many companies still fail to use it sufficiently or correctly, for several reasons:[24]

- *A narrow conception of the research.* Many managers see marketing research as a fact-finding operation. They expect the researcher to design a questionnaire, choose a sample, conduct interviews, and report results, often without a careful definition of the problem or of the deci-

TABLE 4.3	THE SEVEN CHARACTERISTICS OF GOOD MARKETING RESEARCH
1. Scientific method.	Effective marketing research uses the principles of the scientific method: careful observation, formulation of hypotheses, prediction, and testing.
2. Research creativity.	At its best, marketing research develops innovative ways to solve a problem: a clothing company catering to teenagers gave several young men video cameras, then used the videos for focus groups held in restaurants and other places teens frequent.
3. Multiple methods.	Marketing researchers shy away from overreliance on any one method. They also recognize the value of using two or three methods to increase confidence in the results.
4. Interdependence of models and data.	Marketing researchers recognize that data are interpreted from underlying models that guide the type of information sought.
5. Value and cost of information.	Marketing researchers show concern for estimating the value of information against its cost. Costs are typically easy to determine, but the value of research is harder to quantify. It depends on the reliability and validity of the findings and management's willingness to accept and act on those findings.
6. Healthy skepticism.	Marketing researchers show a healthy skepticism toward glib assumptions made by managers about how a market works. They are alert to the problems caused by "marketing myths."
7. Ethical marketing.	Marketing research benefits both the sponsoring company and its customers. The misuse of marketing research can harm or annoy consumers, increasing resentment at what consumers regard as an invasion of their privacy or a disguised sales pitch.

sions facing management. When fact-finding fails to be useful, management's idea of the limited usefulness of marketing research is reinforced.

- *Uneven calibre of researchers.* Some managers view marketing research as little more than a clerical activity and treat it as such. Less competent marketing researchers are hired, and their weak training and deficient creativity lead to unimpressive results. The disappointing results reinforce management's prejudice against marketing research. Management continues to pay low salaries to its market researchers, thus perpetuating the basic problem.

- *Poor framing of the problem.* In the famous case where Coca-Cola introduced the New Coke after much research, the failure of the New Coke was largely due to not setting up the research problem correctly from a marketing perspective. The issue was how consumers felt about Coca-Cola as a brand and not necessarily the taste in isolation.

- *Late and occasionally erroneous findings.* Managers want results that are accurate and conclusive. They may want the results tomorrow. Yet good marketing research takes time and money. Managers are disappointed when marketing research costs too much or takes too much time.

- *Personality and presentational differences.* Differences between the styles of line managers and marketing researchers often get in the way of productive relationships. To a manager who wants concreteness, simplicity, and certainty, a marketing researcher's report may seem abstract, complicated, and tentative. Yet in the more progressive companies, marketing researchers are being included as members of the product management team, and their influence on marketing strategy is growing.

Failure to use marketing research properly has led to numerous gaffes, including this historic one:

Star Wars

In the 1970s, a successful research executive left General Foods for a daring gambit: bring market research to Hollywood to give film studios access to the same research that had spurred General Foods' success. A major studio handed him a science-fiction film proposal and asked him to research and predict its success or failure: his views would inform their decision whether to back the film. He concluded the film would fail. For one, he argued, the Watergate scandal had made the United States less trusting of its institutions and, as a result, Americans in the 1970s prized realism and authenticity over science fiction. This particular film also had the word "war" in its title; he reasoned that the United States, suffering from its post-Vietnam hangover, would stay away in droves. The film was *Star Wars*. What this researcher delivered was information, not insight. He failed to study the script itself, to see that it was a fundamentally human story—of love, conflict, loss, and redemption—that merely played out against the backdrop of space.[25]

Measuring Marketing Productivity

An important task of marketing research is to assess the efficiency and effectiveness of marketing activities. Marketers increasingly are being held accountable for their investments and must be able to justify marketing expenditures to senior management.[26] In a recent Accenture survey, 70 percent of marketing executives stated that they did not have a handle on the return on their marketing investments.[27] Another study revealed that 63 percent of senior management said they were dissatisfied with their marketing performance measurement system and wanted marketing to supply prior and posterior estimates of the impact of marketing programs.[28] With marketing costs already high and continuing to rise, senior executives are tired of seeing what they consider to be wasteful marketing—failed new products and lavish ad campaigns, extensive sales calls, and expensive promotions that are unable to move the sales needle.

Marketing research can help address this increased need for accountability. Two complementary approaches to measure marketing productivity are (1) marketing metrics to assess marketing effects and (2) marketing mix modelling to estimate causal relationships and how marketing activity affects outcomes. Some developments in the financial tools that can be used to measure key marketing assets are described in "Marketing Insight: Seeing the Big Picture and Getting to the Bottom Line in Marketing."

Marketing Metrics

Marketers employ a wide variety of measures to assess marketing effects. **Marketing metrics** is the set of measures that help firms to quantify, compare, and interpret their marketing performance. Marketing metrics can be used by brand managers to design marketing programs and by senior management to decide on financial allocations. When marketers can estimate the dollar contribution of marketing activities, they are better able to justify the value of marketing investments to senior management.[29]

Many marketing metrics relate to customer-level concerns such as their attitudes and behaviour; others relate to brand-level concerns such as market share, relative price premium, or profitability.[30] Companies can also monitor an extensive set of metrics internal to the company. One important set of measures relates to a firm's innovativeness. For example, 3M tracks the proportion of sales resulting from its recent innovations. Another key set relates to employees. Table 4.4 summarizes a list of popular internal and external marketing metrics from a survey in the United Kingdom.[31]

Amazon.com is a firm renowned for constantly monitoring its marketing activities. CEO Jeff Bezos wants to know average customer contacts per order, average time per contact, the breakdown of e-mail versus telephone contacts, and the total cost to the company of each. The man in charge of Amazon's customer service and its warehouse and distribution operations looks at about 300 charts a week for his division.[32]

MARKETING INSIGHT

Seeing the Big Picture and Getting to the Bottom Line in Marketing

To provide a financial overview of marketing activity, several authors have developed new approaches to thinking about marketing. Here are three notable ones.

Peter Doyle maintains that:

> value-based marketing is not primarily about numbers. . . . [Rather,] it consists of three main elements. First is a set of beliefs about the objectives of marketing. The . . . primary task is to develop strategies that will maximize shareholder return. . . . Second is a set of principles for choosing marketing strategies and making marketing decisions that are consistent with these beliefs. These principles are based on estimating the future cash flow associated with a strategy to calculate the shareholder value added. Finally, it is a set of processes that ensure that marketing develops, selects, and implements a strategy that is consistent with these beliefs and principles. These processes concern management of the financial, marketing, and organizational value drivers of the business. The financial value drivers are those key ratios that have the most significant impact on shareholder value. The marketing drivers are the customer-oriented plans necessary to drive improvement in the financial ratios. The organizational value drivers are the core capabilities, systems, and leadership styles needed to create and implement the shareholder value orientation in the business.

According to Doyle, financial value drivers relate to sales growth, operating margin, and investment; marketing value drivers relate to strong brands, customer loyalty, strategic relationships, market selection, and differential advantage.

Roger Best maintains that:

> Market-based management is at the base of a business with a strong market orientation. A strong market orientation translates into a strong customer focus, competitor orientation, and a team approach that cuts across organizational functions. The result is a market-based business that is in a strong position to develop and deliver market-based strategies designed to attract, satisfy, and retain customers. Implemented successfully across a wide range of market situations, a market-based approach . . . will deliver higher levels of profitability, cash flow, and shareholder value than will a cost-based approach.

Best maintains that the only source of positive cash flow is the customer and therefore the customer must be the focus of market-based management.

Tim Ambler suggests that if firms think they are already measuring marketing performance adequately, they should ask themselves five questions:

1. Do you routinely research consumer behaviour (retention, acquisition, usage, etc.) and why consumers behave that way (awareness, satisfaction, perceived quality, etc.)?

2. Are the results of this research routinely reported to the board in a format integrated with financial marketing metrics?

3. In those reports, are the results compared with the levels previously forecasted in the business plans?

4. Are they also compared with the levels achieved by your key competitor using the same indicators?

5. Is short-term performance adjusted according to the change in your marketing-based asset(s)?

Ambler believes firms must give priority to measuring and reporting marketing performance through marketing metrics. He believes evaluation can be split into two parts: (1) short-term results and (2) changes in brand equity. Short-term results often reflect profit and loss concerns as shown by sales turnover, shareholder value, or some combination of the two. Brand-equity measures include awareness, market share, relative price, number of complaints, distribution and availability, total number of customers, perceived quality, and loyalty/retention. Ambler also recommends developing employee measures and metrics, arguing that "End users are the ultimate customers, but your own staff are your first; you need to measure the health of the internal market."

Sources: Peter Doyle, *Value-Based Marketing: Marketing Strategies for Corporate Growth and Shareholder Value* (Chichester, England: John Wiley & Sons, 2000); Roger J. Best, *Market-Based Management: Strategies for Growing Customer Value and Profitability*, 2nd ed. (Upper Saddle River, NJ: Prentice Hall, 2000); Tim Ambler, *Marketing and the Bottom Line: The New Methods of Corporate Wealth* (London: Financial Times/Prentice Hall, 2000).

TABLE 4.4 ‡	SAMPLE MARKETING METRICS
I. External	**II. Internal**
Awareness	Awareness of goals
Market share (volume or value)	Commitment to goals
Relative price (market share value/volume)	Active innovation support
Number of complaints (level of dissatisfaction)	Resource adequacy
Consumer satisfaction	Staffing/skill levels
Distribution/availability	Desire to learn
Total number of customers	Willingness to change
Perceived quality/esteem	Freedom to fail
Loyalty/retention	Autonomy
Relative perceived quality	Relative employee satisfaction

Source: Tim Ambler, "What Does Marketing Success Look Like?" *Marketing Management*, Spring 2001, pp. 13–18.

Firms are also employing organizational processes and systems to make sure that the value of all these different metrics is maximized by the firm. A summary set of relevant internal and external measures can be assembled in a *marketing dashboard* for synthesis and interpretation. Some companies are also appointing marketing controllers to review budget items and expenses. Increasingly, these controllers are using business intelligence software to create digital versions of marketing dashboards that aggregate data from disparate internal and external sources.

Keystone Industries

Montreal-based Keystone Industries, maker of the French Dressing Jeans clothing line, recently implemented marketing dashboard software technology "C-Trak." The software was developed by Unisys and Calgary-based marketing firm Venture Communications. The software works by having the user set goals and then measure quantitative objectives. For example, Keystone wanted to acquire 400 new accounts. To acquire new accounts, Keystone's marketing strategy involved using prospective customer lists and making trade show appearances. The C-Trak software allows Keystone to directly attribute any new customer acquisitions to a particular activity through user-friendly software-generated reports. This helps Keystone understand how effective its lists and trade show appearances actually are.

Information generated by the software has already led the company to make a significant change to the business. Historically, the company had only marketed to its channel partners such as retail stores. The software demonstrated that Keystone should be putting more emphasis on its consumer accounts. As a result, for the first time in the company's history, they are going to begin advertising directly to consumers.[33]

As input to the marketing dashboard, companies can prepare two market-based scorecards that reflect performance and provide possible early warning signals. A **customer-performance scorecard** records how well the company is doing year after year on such customer-based measures as shown in Table 4.5. Norms should be set for each measure, and management should take action when results get out of bounds.

The second measure is called a **stakeholder-performance scorecard**. Companies need to track the satisfaction of various constituencies who have a critical interest in and impact on the company's performance: employees, suppliers, banks, distributors, retailers, and shareholders. Again, norms should be set for each group and management should take action when one or more groups register increased levels of dissatisfaction.[34] Consider Hewlett-Packard's program.

TABLE 4.5	SAMPLE CUSTOMER-PERFORMANCE SCORECARD MEASURES

- Percentage of new customers to average number of customers.
- Percentage of lost customers to average number of customers.
- Percentage of win-back customers to average number of customers.
- Percentage of customers falling into very dissatisfied, dissatisfied, neutral, satisfied, and very satisfied categories.
- Percentage of customers who say they would repurchase the product.
- Percentage of customers who say they would recommend the product to others.
- Percentage of target market customers who have brand awareness or recall.
- Percentage of customers who say that the company's product is the most preferred in its category.
- Percentage of customers who correctly identify the brand's intended positioning and differentiation.
- Average perception of company's product quality relative to chief competitor.
- Average perception of company's service quality relative to chief competitor.

Hewlett-Packard

Each division of Hewlett-Packard evaluates its performance on a customer-based scorecard that monitors 18 to 20 "business fundamentals." Some, such as customer satisfaction and on-time delivery, are rated for all divisions; other indicators are tracked according to the nature of the division's business. The company is thus able to gauge the effects of its marketing strategies on sales and profits and to identify areas where improvements in performance can lead to improved quantitative results.[35]

Measuring Marketing Plan Performance

Marketers today have better marketing metrics for measuring the performance of marketing plans.[36] They can use four tools to check on plan performance: sales analysis, market-share analysis, marketing expense-to-sales analysis, and financial analysis.

SALES ANALYSIS **Sales analysis** consists of measuring and evaluating actual sales in relation to goals. Two specific tools are used in sales analysis.

Sales-variance analysis measures the relative contribution of different factors to a gap in sales performance. Suppose the annual plan called for selling 4000 widgets in the first quarter at $1 per widget, for total revenue of $4000. At quarter's end, only 3000 widgets were sold at $0.80 per widget, for total revenue of $2400. How much of the sales performance is due to the price decline and how much to the volume decline? The following calculation answers this question:

$$
\begin{aligned}
\textit{Variance due to price decline} &= (\$1.00 - \$0.80)\ (3000) = \$\ 600 \quad 37.5\% \\
\textit{Variance due to volume decline} &= (\$1.00)\ (4000 - 3000) = \underline{\$1000} \quad \underline{62.5\%} \\
&\qquad\qquad\qquad\qquad\qquad\quad \$1600 \quad 100.0\%
\end{aligned}
$$

Almost two-thirds of the variance is due to failure to achieve the volume target. The company should look closely at why it failed to achieve expected sales volume.

Microsales analysis looks at specific products, territories, and so forth that failed to produce expected sales. Suppose the company sells in three territories and expected sales were 1500 units, 500 units, and 2000 units, respectively. The actual sales volume was 1400 units, 525 units, and 1075 units, respectively. Thus territory 1 showed a 7 percent shortfall in terms of expected sales; territory 2, a 5 percent improvement over expectations; and territory 3, a 46 percent shortfall! Territory 3 is causing most of the trouble. The sales vice-president needs to check into territory 3: maybe territory 3's sales rep is underperforming; a major competitor has entered this territory; or business is in a recession in this territory.

MARKET-SHARE ANALYSIS   Company sales do not reveal how well the company is performing relative to competitors. For this purpose, management needs to track its market share.

Market share can be measured in three ways: **Overall market share** is the company's sales expressed as a percentage of total market sales. **Served market share** is its sales expressed as a percentage of the total sales to its served market. Its **served market** is all the buyers who are able and willing to buy its product. Served market share is always larger than overall market share. A company could capture 100 percent of its served market and yet have a relatively small share of the total market. **Relative market share** can be expressed as market share in relation to its largest competitor. A relative market share over 100 percent indicates a market leader. A relative market share of exactly 100 percent means that the company is tied for the lead. A rise in relative market share means a company is gaining on its leading competitor.

Conclusions from market-share analysis, however, are subject to certain qualifications:

- *The assumption that outside forces affect all companies in the same way is often not true.* Health Canada's ad campaign on the harmful consequences of cigarette smoking caused total cigarette sales to falter, but not equally for all companies.

- *The assumption that a company's performance should be judged against the average performance of all companies is not always valid.* A company's performance should be judged against the performance of its closest competitors.

- *If a new firm enters the industry, then every existing firm's market share might fall.* A decline in market share might not mean that the company is performing any worse than other companies. Share loss depends on the degree to which the new firm hits the company's specific markets.

- *Sometimes a market-share decline is deliberately engineered to improve profits.* For example, management might drop unprofitable customers or products.

- *Market share can fluctuate for many minor reasons.* For example, it can be affected by whether a large sale occurs on the last day of the month or at the beginning of the next month. Not all shifts in market share have marketing significance.[37]

A useful way to analyze market-share movements is in terms of four components:

$$\text{Overall market share} = \text{Customer penetration} \times \text{Customer loyalty} \times \text{Customer selectivity} \times \text{Price selectivity}$$

where:

Customer penetration is the percentage of all customers who buy from the company.

Customer loyalty is the purchases from the company by its customers expressed as a percentage of their total purchases from all suppliers of the same products.

Customer selectivity is the size of the average customer purchase from the company expressed as a percentage of the size of the average customer purchase from an average company.

Price selectivity is the average price charged by the company expressed as a percentage of the average price charged by all companies.

Now suppose the company's dollar market share falls during the period. The overall market-share equation provides four possible explanations: The company lost some of its customers (lower customer penetration); existing customers are buying less from the company (lower customer loyalty); the company's remaining customers are smaller in size (lower customer selectivity); or the company's price has slipped relative to competition (lower price selectivity).

MARKETING EXPENSE-TO-SALES ANALYSIS   Annual-plan control requires making sure that the company is not overspending to achieve sales goals. The key ratio to watch is *marketing expense-to-sales.* In one company, this ratio was 30 percent and consisted of five component expense-to-sales ratios: sales force-to-sales (15 percent); advertising-to-sales (5 percent); sales promotion-to-sales (6 percent); marketing research-to-sales (1 percent); and sales administration-to-sales (3 percent).

Management needs to monitor these ratios. Fluctuations outside the normal range are cause for concern. The period-to-period fluctuations in each ratio can be tracked on a *control chart* (see Figure 4.2). This chart shows that the advertising expense-to-sales ratio normally fluctuates between 8 percent and 12 percent, say 99 out of 100 times. In the fifteenth period, however, the ratio exceeded the upper control limit. One of two hypotheses can explain this occurrence: (1) The company still

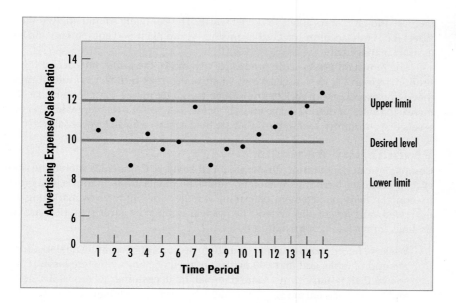

FIGURE 4.2

The Control-Chart Model

has good expense control, and this situation represents a rare chance event. (2) The company has lost control over this expense and should find the cause. If no investigation is made, the risk is that some real change might have occurred, and the company will fall behind. If the environment is investigated, the risk is that the investigation will uncover nothing and be a waste of time and effort.

The behaviour of successive observations even within the upper and lower control limits should be watched. Note in Figure 4.2 that the level of the expense-to-sales ratio rose steadily from the ninth period onward. The probability of encountering six successive increases in what should be independent events is only 1 in 64.[38] This unusual pattern should have led to an investigation sometime before the fifteenth observation.

FINANCIAL ANALYSIS The expense-to-sales ratios should be analyzed in an overall financial framework to determine how and where the company is making its money. Marketers are increasingly using financial analysis to find profitable strategies beyond sales building.

Management uses financial analysis to identify the factors that affect the company's *rate of return on net worth*.[39] The main factors are shown in Figure 4.3, along with illustrative numbers for a large chain-store retailer. The retailer is earning a 12.5 percent return on net worth. The return on net worth is the product of two ratios, the company's *return on assets* and its *financial leverage*. To improve its return on net worth, the company must increase its ratio of net profits to its assets or

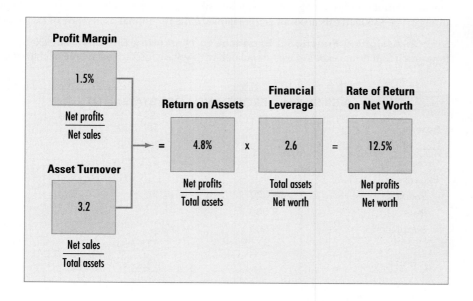

FIGURE 4.3

Financial Model of Return on Net Worth

increase the ratio of its assets to its net worth. The company should analyze the composition of its assets (i.e., cash, accounts receivable, inventory, and plant and equipment) and see if it can improve its asset management.

The return on assets is the product of two ratios, the *profit margin* and the *asset turnover*. The profit margin in Figure 4.3 seems low, whereas the asset turnover is more normal for retailing. The marketing executive can seek to improve performance in two ways: (1) Increase the profit margin by increasing sales or cutting costs; and (2) increase the asset turnover by increasing sales or reducing assets (e.g., inventory, receivables) that are held against a given level of sales.[40]

Profitability Analysis

Companies can benefit from deeper financial analysis. Companies should measure the profitability of their products, territories, customer groups, segments, trade channels, and order sizes. This information can help management determine whether any products or marketing activities should be expanded, reduced, or eliminated. The results can often be surprising. Here are some disconcerting findings from a bank profitability study:

> We have found that anywhere from 20 to 40 percent of an individual institution's products are unprofitable, and up to 60 percent of their accounts generate losses. Our research has shown that, in most firms, more than half of all customer relationships are not profitable, and 30 to 40 percent are only marginally so. It is frequently a mere 10 to 15 percent of a firm's relationships that generate the bulk of its profits. Our profitability research into the branch system of a regional bank produced some surprising results . . . 30 percent of the bank's branches were unprofitable.[41]

MARKETING-PROFITABILITY ANALYSIS   We will illustrate the steps in marketing-profitability analysis with the following example:

The marketing vice-president of a lawnmower company wants to determine the profitability of selling its lawnmower through three types of retail channels: hardware stores, garden supply shops, and department stores. The company's profit-and-loss statement is shown in Table 4.6.

Step 1: Identifying Functional Expenses   Assume that the expenses listed in Table 4.6 are incurred to sell the product, advertise it, pack and deliver it, and bill and collect for it. The first task is to measure how much of each expense was incurred in each activity.

Suppose that most of the salary expense went to sales representatives and the rest went to an advertising manager, packing and delivery help, and an office accountant. Let the breakdown of the $9300 be $5100, $1200, $1400, and $1600, respectively. Table 4.7 shows the allocation of the salary expense to these four activities.

Table 4.7 also shows the rent account of $3000 allocated to the four activities. Because the sales reps work away from the office, none of the building's rent expense is assigned to selling. Most of the expenses for floor space and rented equipment are for packing and delivery. The supplies account covers promotional materials, packing materials, fuel purchases for delivery, and home office stationery. The $3500 in this account is reassigned to the functional uses made of the supplies.

Step 2: Assigning Functional Expenses to Marketing Entities   The next task is to measure how much functional expense was associated with selling through each type of channel. Consider the

TABLE 4.6	A SIMPLIFIED PROFIT-AND-LOSS STATEMENT	
Sales		$60 000
Cost of goods sold		39 000
Gross margin		$21 000
Expenses		
Salaries	$9 300	
Rent	3 000	
Supplies	3 500	
		15 800
Net profit		$5 200

TABLE 4.7	MAPPING NATURAL EXPENSES INTO FUNCTIONAL EXPENSES				
Natural Accounts	Total	Selling	Advertising	Packing and Delivery	Billing and Collecting
Salaries	$9 300	$5 100	$1 200	$1 400	$1 600
Rent	3 000	—	400	2 000	600
Supplies	3 500	400	1 500	1 400	200
	$15 800	$5 500	$3 100	$4 800	$2 400

selling effort. The selling effort is indicated by the number of sales made in each channel. This number is found in the selling column of Table 4.8. Altogether, 275 sales calls were made during the period. Because the total selling expense amounted to $5500 (see Table 4.8), the selling expense per call averaged $20.

Advertising expense can be allocated according to the number of ads addressed to different channels. Because there were 100 ads altogether, the average ad cost $31.

The packing and delivery expense is allocated according to the number of orders placed by each type of channel. This same basis was used for allocating billing and collection expense.

Step 3: Preparing a Profit-and-Loss Statement for Each Marketing Entity A profit-and-loss statement can now be prepared for each type of channel (see Table 4.9). Because hardware stores accounted for half of total sales ($30 000 out of $60 000), this channel is charged with half the cost of goods sold ($19 500 out of $39 000). This leaves a gross margin from hardware stores of $10 500. From this must be deducted the proportions of the functional expenses hardware stores consumed.

TABLE 4.8	BASES FOR ALLOCATING FUNCTIONAL EXPENSES TO CHANNELS			
Channel Type	Selling	Advertising	Packing and Delivery	Billing and Collecting
Hardware	200	50	50	50
Garden supply	65	20	21	21
Department stores	10	30	9	9
	275	100	80	80
Functional expense	$5500	$3100	$4800	$2400
÷ No. of Units	275	100	80	80
Equals	$ 20	$ 31	$ 60	$ 30

TABLE 4.9	PROFIT-AND-LOSS STATEMENTS FOR CHANNELS			
	Hardware	Garden Supply	Dept. Stores	Whole Company
Sales	$30 000	$10 000	$20 000	$60 000
Cost of goods sold	19 500	6 500	13 000	39 000
Gross margin	$10 500	$ 3 500	$ 7 000	$21 000
Expenses				
Selling ($20 per call)	$ 4 000	$ 1 300	$ 200	$ 5 500
Advertising ($31 per advertisement)	1 550	620	930	3 100
Packing and delivery ($60 per order)	3 000	1 260	540	4 800
Billing ($30 per order)	1 500	630	270	2 400
Total Expenses	$10 050	$ 3 810	$ 1 940	$ 15 800
Net profit or loss	$ 450	$ (310)	$ 5 060	$ 5 200

According to Table 4.8, hardware stores received 200 out of 275 total sales calls. At an imputed value of $20 a call, hardware stores have to be charged with a $4000 selling expense. Table 4.8 also shows that hardware stores were the target of 50 ads. At $31 an ad, the hardware stores are charged with $1550 of advertising. The same reasoning applies in computing the share of the other functional expenses to charge to hardware stores. The result is that hardware stores gave rise to $10 050 of the total expenses. Subtracting this from the gross margin, the profit of selling through hardware stores is only $450.

This analysis is repeated for the other channels. The company is losing money in selling through garden supply shops and makes virtually all of its profits through department stores. Notice that gross sales is not a reliable indicator of the net profits for each channel.

DETERMINING CORRECTIVE ACTION It would be naïve to conclude that the company should drop garden supply shops and possibly hardware stores so that it can concentrate on department stores. The following questions need to be answered first:

- To what extent do buyers buy on the basis of type of retail outlet versus brand?
- What are the trends with respect to the importance of these three channels?
- How good are the company marketing strategies directed at the three channels?

On the basis of the answers, marketing management can evaluate five alternatives:

1. Establish a special charge for handling smaller orders.
2. Give more promotional aid to garden supply shops and hardware stores.
3. Reduce the number of sales calls and the amount of advertising going to garden supply shops and hardware stores.
4. Do not abandon any channel entirely, but only the weakest retail units in each channel.
5. Do nothing.

In general, marketing-profitability analysis indicates the relative profitability of different channels, products, territories, or other marketing entities. It does not prove that the best course of action is to drop the unprofitable marketing entities, nor does it capture the likely profit improvement if these marginal marketing entities are dropped.

DIRECT VERSUS FULL COSTING Like all information tools, marketing-profitability analysis can lead or mislead marketing executives, depending on how well they understand its methods and limitations. The lawnmower company showed some arbitrariness in its choice of bases for allocating the functional expenses to its marketing entities. "Number of sales calls" was used to allocate selling expenses, when in principle "number of sales working hours" is a more accurate indicator of cost. The former base was used because it involves less record keeping and computation.

Far more serious is another judgmental element affecting profitability analysis. The issue is whether to allocate full costs or only direct and traceable costs in evaluating a marketing entity's performance. The lawnmower company sidestepped this problem by assuming only simple costs that fit in with marketing activities, but the question cannot be avoided in real-world analyses of profitability. Three types of costs have to be distinguished:

1. *Direct costs.* These are costs that can be assigned directly to the proper marketing entities. Sales commissions are a direct cost in a profitability analysis of sales territories, sales representatives, or customers. Advertising expenditures are a direct cost in a profitability analysis of products to the extent that each advertisement promotes only one product. Other direct costs for specific purposes are sales-force salaries and travelling expenses.

2. *Traceable common costs.* These are costs that can be assigned only indirectly, but on a plausible basis, to the marketing entities. In the example, rent was analyzed this way.

3. *Nontraceable common costs.* These are common costs whose allocation to the marketing entities is highly arbitrary. To allocate "corporate image" expenditures equally to all products would be arbitrary, because all products do not benefit equally. To allocate them proportionately to the sales of the various products would be arbitrary because relative product sales reflect many factors besides corporate image making. Other examples are top management salaries, taxes, interest, and other overhead.

No one disputes including direct costs in marketing cost analysis. There is a small amount of controversy about including traceable common costs, which lump together costs that would change with the scale of marketing activity and costs that would not change. If the lawnmower company drops garden supply shops, it would probably continue to pay the same rent. In this event, its profits would not rise immediately by the amount of the present loss in selling to garden supply shops ($310).

The major controversy concerns whether the nontraceable common costs should be allocated to the marketing entities. Such allocation is called the *full-cost approach*, and its advocates argue that all costs must ultimately be imputed in order to determine true profitability. However, this argument confuses the use of accounting for financial reporting with its use for managerial decision making. Full costing has three major weaknesses:

1. The relative profitability of different marketing entities can shift radically when one arbitrary way to allocate nontraceable common costs is replaced by another.

2. The arbitrariness demoralizes managers, who feel that their performance is judged adversely.

3. The inclusion of nontraceable common costs could weaken efforts at real cost control.

Operating management is most effective in controlling direct costs and traceable common costs. Arbitrary assignments of nontraceable common costs can lead managers to spend their time fighting arbitrary cost allocations rather than managing controllable costs well.

Companies are showing a growing interest in using marketing-profitability analysis or its broader version, activity-based cost accounting (ABC), to quantify the true profitability of different activities.[42] To improve profitability, managers can then examine ways to reduce the resources required to perform various activities, or make the resources more productive or acquire them at lower cost. Alternatively, management may raise prices on products that consume heavy amounts of support resources. The contribution of ABC is to refocus management's attention away from using only labour or material standard costs to allocate full cost, and toward capturing the actual costs of supporting individual products, customers, and other entities.

Marketing Mix Modelling

Marketing accountability also means that marketers can more precisely estimate the effects of different marketing investments. *Marketing-mix models* analyze data from a variety of sources, such as retailer scanner data, company shipment data, pricing, and media and promotion spending data, to understand more precisely the effects of specific marketing activities. To deepen understanding, multivariate analyses are conducted to sort through how each marketing element influences marketing outcomes of interest such as brand sales or market share.[43]

Especially popular with packaged goods marketers such as Procter & Gamble, Clorox, and Colgate, the findings from marketing-mix modelling are used to allocate or reallocate expenditures. Analyses explore which part of ad budgets are wasted, what optimal spending levels are, and what minimum investment levels should be.[44] Although marketing-mix modelling helps to isolate effects, it is less effective at assessing how different marketing elements work in combination.

Forecasting and Demand Measurement

One major reason for undertaking marketing research is to identify market opportunities. Once the research is complete, the company must measure and forecast the size, growth, and profit potential of each market opportunity. Sales forecasts are used by finance to raise the needed cash for investment and operations; by the manufacturing department to establish capacity and output levels; by purchasing to acquire the right amount of supplies; and by human resources to hire the needed number of workers. Marketing is responsible for preparing the sales forecasts. If its forecast is far off the mark, the company will be saddled with excess inventory or have inadequate inventory. Sales forecasts are based on estimates of demand. Managers need to define what they mean by market demand. Here is a good example of the importance of defining the market correctly:

Coca-Cola

When Roberto Goizueta became CEO of Coca-Cola, many people thought that Coke's sales were maxed out. Goizueta, however, reframed the view of Coke's market share. He noted that Coca-Cola accounted for only about 3 percent of the nearly 2 litres of fluid that each of the world's people drank on average every day. "The enemy is coffee, milk, tea, water," he told his people at Coke, and he ushered in a huge period of growth.

An ad for a Clorox product, Gladware. Clorox is one of the companies that uses marketing-mix modelling to test the effectiveness of its advertising.

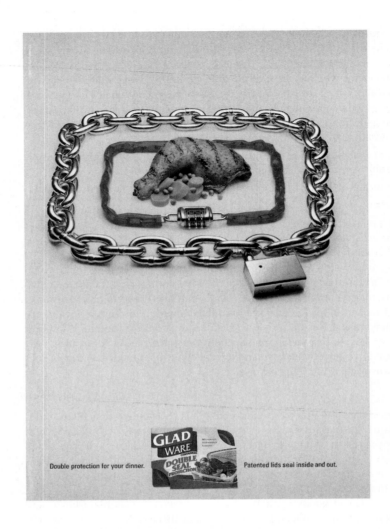

The Measures of Market Demand

Companies can prepare as many as 90 different types of demand estimates (see Figure 4.4). Demand can be measured for six different product levels, five different space levels, and three different time levels.

FIGURE 4.4

Ninety Types of Demand Measurement (6 × 5 × 3)

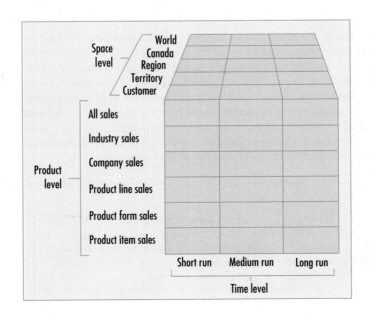

Each demand measure serves a specific purpose. A company might forecast short-run demand for a particular product for the purpose of ordering raw materials, planning production, and borrowing cash. It might forecast regional demand for its major product line to decide whether to set up regional distribution.

Forecasts also depend on which type of market is being considered. The size of a market hinges on the number of buyers who might exist for a particular market offer. But there are many productive ways to break down the market:

- The **potential market** is the set of consumers who profess a sufficient level of interest in a market offer. However, consumer interest is not enough to define a market. Potential consumers must have enough income and must have access to the product offer.

- The **available market** is the set of consumers who have interest, income, and access to a particular offer. For some market offers, the company or government may restrict sales to certain groups. For example, a particular province might ban motorcycle sales to anyone under 21 years of age. The eligible adults constitute the *qualified available market*—the set of consumers who have interest, income, access, and qualifications for the particular market offer.

- The **target market** is the part of the qualified available market the company decides to pursue. The company might decide to concentrate its marketing and distribution effort on the East Coast. The company will end up selling to a certain number of buyers in its target market.

- The **penetrated market** is the set of consumers who are buying the company's product.

These definitions are a useful tool for market planning. If the company is not satisfied with its current sales, it can take a number of actions. It can try to attract a larger percentage of buyers from its target market. It can lower the qualifications of potential buyers. It can expand its available market by opening distribution elsewhere or lowering its price; or it can reposition itself in the minds of its customers. Consider the case of the Women's Television Network.

The New W

WTN, a cable channel owned by Toronto-based Corus Entertainment, thought it had a winning concept—a serious TV channel that talks about women's issues 24/7. However, the channel's audience remained small. WTN drew only 52 000 viewers, who spent less than an hour a week watching the programming. Unhappy with these numbers, WTN revised its goal: to become the number-one specialty service for females mainly in the 25- to 40-year-old age group. To accomplish this aim, it started by doing extensive research: 500 phone interviews, and seven focus groups. The research findings suggested that women watch TV for many of the same reasons men do—to be entertained. Thus, WTN repositioned its offerings and renamed the channel "W." It then did a third study to ensure that the new brand resonated with the new, younger target. TV, radio, print, and Web advertising were used to communicate the image of the repositioned channel to its new audience.[45]

A Vocabulary for Demand Measurement

The major concepts in demand measurement are market demand and company demand. Within each, we distinguish among a demand function, a sales forecast, and a potential.

MARKET DEMAND   As we have seen, the marketer's first step in evaluating marketing opportunities is to estimate total market demand. **Market demand** for a product is the total volume that would be bought by a defined customer group in a defined geographical area in a defined time period in a defined marketing environment under a defined marketing program.

Market demand is not a fixed number, but rather a function of the stated conditions. For this reason, it can be called the *market demand function*. The dependence of total market demand on underlying conditions is illustrated in Figure 4.5(a). The horizontal axis shows different possible levels of industry marketing expenditure in a given time period. The vertical axis shows the resulting demand level. The curve represents the estimated market demand associated with varying levels of industry marketing expenditure. The analysis can be further refined if marketers consider responses to marketing expenditures under different economic conditions, such as prosperity or recession, as illustrated in Figure 4.5(b).

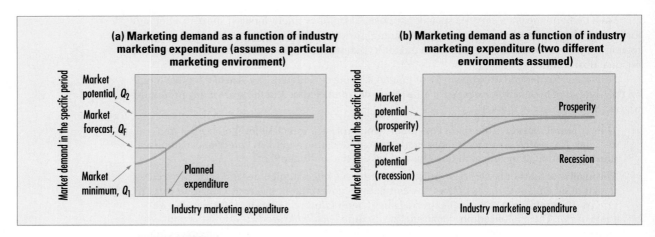

FIGURE 4.5

Market Demand Functions

Some base sales (called the *market minimum*, labelled Q_1 in the figure) would take place without any demand-stimulating expenditures. Higher levels of industry marketing expenditures would yield higher levels of demand, first at an increasing rate, then at a decreasing rate. Marketing expenditures beyond a certain level would not stimulate much further demand, thus suggesting an upper limit to market demand called the *market potential* (labelled Q_2 in the figure).

The distance between the market minimum and the market potential shows the overall *marketing sensitivity of demand*. We can think of two extreme types of markets, the expansible and the nonexpansible. An *expansible market*, such as the market for racquetball playing, is very much affected in its total size by the level of industry marketing expenditures. In terms of Figure 4.5(a), the distance between Q_1 and Q_2 is relatively large. A *nonexpansible market*—for example, the market for opera—is not much affected by the level of marketing expenditures; the distance between Q_1 and Q_2 is relatively small. Organizations selling in a nonexpansible market must accept the market's size (the level of *primary demand* for the product class) and direct their efforts to winning a larger **market share** for their product (the level of selective demand for the company's product).

It pays to compare the current level of market demand to the potential demand level. The result is called the **market penetration index**. A low market penetration index indicates substantial growth potential for all the firms. A high market penetration index suggests that there will be increased costs in attracting the few remaining prospects. Generally, price competition increases and margins fall when the market penetration index is already high.

A company should also compare its current market share to its potential market share. The result is called the company's **share penetration index**. A low share penetration index indicates that the company can greatly expand its share. The underlying factors holding it back could be many: low brand awareness, low brand availability, benefit deficiencies, or too high a price. A firm should calculate the share penetration increases that would occur with investments to remove each deficiency, to see which investments would produce the greatest improvement in share penetration.[46]

It is important to remember that the market demand function is not a picture of market demand over time. Rather, the curve shows alternative current forecasts of market demand associated with alternative possible levels of industry marketing effort in the current period.

MARKET FORECAST   Only one level of industry marketing expenditure will actually occur. The market demand corresponding to this level is called the **market forecast**.

MARKET POTENTIAL   The market forecast shows expected market demand, not maximum market demand. For the latter, we have to visualize the level of market demand resulting from a "very high" level of industry marketing expenditure, where further increases in marketing effort would have little effect in stimulating further demand. **Market potential** is the limit approached by market demand as industry marketing expenditures approach infinity for a given marketing environment.

The phrase "for a given market environment" is crucial. Consider the market potential for automobiles in a period of recession versus a period of prosperity. The market potential is higher during

Canada has the second-highest cable TV penetration of any country in the world, surpassed only by Belgium, which, unlike Canada, has the advantage of a small geographic area and very high population density.[48]

prosperity. The dependence of market potential on the environment is illustrated in Figure 4.5(b). Market analysts distinguish between the position of the market demand function and movement along it. Companies cannot do anything about the position of the market demand function, which is determined by the marketing environment. However, companies influence their particular location on the function when they decide how much to spend on marketing.

Companies interested in market potential have a special interest in the **product penetration percentage**, which is the percentage of ownership or use of a product or service in a population. For example, a recent Ipsos-Reid poll revealed how Canadians feel about fixed rate versus floating rate mortgages. The survey found that 68 percent of those who own a home and carry a mortgage are in a fixed interest rate product, while only 22 percent of homeowners hold a flexible, variable rate mortgage.[47]

COMPANY DEMAND   We are now ready to define company demand: **Company demand** is the company's estimated share of market demand at alternative levels of company marketing effort in a given time period. The company's share of market demand depends on how its goods, services, prices, communications, and so on are perceived relative to the competitors'. If other things are equal, the company's market share would depend on the size and effectiveness of its market expenditures relative to competitors. Marketing model builders have developed sales-response functions to measure how a company's sales are affected by its marketing expenditure level, marketing mix, and marketing effectiveness.[49]

COMPANY SALES FORECAST   Once marketers have estimated company demand, their next task is to choose a level of marketing effort. The chosen level will produce an expected level of sales. The **company sales forecast** is the expected level of company sales based on a chosen marketing plan and an assumed marketing environment.

The company sales forecast is represented graphically with company sales on the vertical axis and company marketing effort on the horizontal axis, as in Figure 4.5. Too often the sequential relationship between the company forecast and the company marketing plan is confused. One frequently hears that the company should develop its marketing plan on the basis of its sales forecast. This forecast-to-plan sequence is valid if "forecast" means an estimate of national economic activity or if company demand is nonexpansible. The sequence is not valid, however, where market demand is expansible or where "forecast" means an estimate of company sales. The company sales forecast does not establish a basis for deciding what to spend on marketing. On the contrary, the sales forecast is the result of an assumed marketing expenditure plan.

Two other concepts are worth mentioning in relation to the company sales forecast. A **sales quota** is the sales goal set for a product line, company division, or sales representative. It is primarily a managerial device for defining and stimulating sales effort. Management sets sales quotas on the basis of the company sales forecast and the psychology of stimulating its achievement. Generally, sales quotas are set slightly higher than estimated sales to stretch the sales force's effort.

A **sales budget** is a conservative estimate of the expected volume of sales and is used primarily for making current purchasing, production, and cash flow decisions. The sales budget is based on the sales forecast and the need to avoid excessive risk. Sales budgets are generally set slightly lower than the sales forecast.

COMPANY SALES POTENTIAL Company sales potential is the sales limit approached by company demand as company marketing effort increases relative to that of competitors. The absolute limit of company demand is, of course, the market potential. The two would be equal if the company got 100 percent of the market. In most cases, company sales potential is less than the market potential, even when company marketing expenditures increase considerably, relative to competitors. The reason is that each competitor has a hard core of loyal buyers who are not very responsive to other companies' efforts to woo them.

Estimating Current Demand

We are now ready to examine practical methods for estimating current market demand. Marketing executives want to estimate total market potential, area market potential, and total industry sales and market shares.

TOTAL MARKET POTENTIAL Total market potential is the maximum amount of sales that might be available to all the firms in an industry during a given period, under a given level of industry marketing effort and environmental conditions. A common way to estimate total market potential is as follows: Estimate the potential number of buyers times the average quantity purchased by a buyer times the price.

If 12 million Canadians buy books each year, and the average book buyer buys three books a year, and the average price of a book is $20, then the total market potential for books is $720 million (12 million $\times$ 3 $\times$ $20). The most difficult component to estimate is the number of buyers for the specific product or market. One can always start with the total population in the nation, say, 32 million people. The next step is to eliminate groups that obviously would not buy the product. Let us assume that illiterate people and children under 12 do not buy books, and they constitute 20 percent of the population.

This means that only 80 percent of the population, or approximately 25.6 million people, would be in the suspect pool. We might do further research and find that people of low income and low education do not read books, and they constitute over 30 percent of the suspect pool. Eliminating them, we arrive at a prospect pool of approximately 17.9 million book buyers. We would use this number of potential buyers to calculate total market potential.

A variation on this method is the *chain-ratio method*. It involves multiplying a base number by several adjusting percentages. Suppose a brewery is interested in estimating the market potential for a new light beer. An estimate can be made by the following calculation:

> Demand for the new light beer = Population $\times$ personal discretionary income per capita $\times$ average percentage of discretionary income spent on food $\times$ average percentage of amount spent on food that is spent on beverages $\times$ average percentage of amount spent on beverages that is spent on alcoholic beverages $\times$ average percentage of amount spent on alcoholic beverages that is spent on beer $\times$ expected percentage of amount spent on beer that will be spent on light beer.

AREA MARKET POTENTIAL Companies face the problem of selecting the best territories and allocating their marketing budget optimally among these territories. Therefore, they need to estimate the market potential of different cities, provinces, regions, and nations. Two major methods of assessing area market potential are available: the market-buildup method, which is used primarily by business marketers, and the multiple-factor index method, which is used primarily by consumer marketers.

Market-Buildup Method The **market-buildup method** calls for identifying all the potential buyers in each market and estimating their potential purchases. This method produces accurate results if we have a list of all potential buyers and a good estimate of what each will buy. Unfortunately, this information is not always easy to gather.

Consider a machine-tool company that wants to estimate the area market potential for its wood lathe in the Montreal area. Its first step is to identify all potential buyers of wood lathes in the area. The buyers consist primarily of manufacturing establishments that have to shape or ream wood as part of their operation, so the company could compile a list from a directory of all manufacturing establishments in the Montreal area. Then it could estimate the number of lathes each industry might purchase based on the number of lathes per thousand employees or per $1 million of sales in that industry.

An efficient method of estimating area market potentials makes use of the *North American Industry Classification System (NAICS)*, developed by the U.S., Canadian, and Mexican governments.[50] The NAICS classifies all manufacturing into 20 major industry sectors. Each sector is further broken into a six-digit, hierarchical structure as follows (illustrated with paging).

51	Industry Sector (Information)
513	Industry Subsector (Broadcasting and telecommunications)
5133	Industry Group (Telecommunications)
51332	Industry (Wireless telecommunications carriers, except satellite)
513321	Industry (Paging) North America

For each six-digit NAICS number, a company can purchase CD-ROMs of business directories that provide complete company profiles of millions of establishments, subclassified by location, number of employees, annual sales, and net worth.

To use the NAICS, the manufacturer of pagers must first determine the six-digit NAICS codes that represent products whose manufacturers are likely to require pagers. To get a full picture of all six-digit NAICS industries that might use pagers, the company can (1) determine past customers' NAICS codes; (2) go through the NAICS manual and check off all the six-digit industries that might have an interest in pagers; (3) mail questionnaires to a wide range of companies inquiring about their interest in pagers.

The company's next task is to determine an appropriate base for estimating the number of pagers that will be used in each industry. Suppose customer industry sales are the most appropriate base. Once the company estimates the rate of pager ownership relative to the customer industry's sales, it can compute the market potential.

Multiple-Factor Index Method Like business marketers, consumer companies also have to estimate area market potentials, but the customers of consumer companies are too numerous to be listed. The method most commonly used in consumer markets is a straightforward index method. A drug manufacturer, for example, might assume that the market potential for drugs is directly related to population size. If the province of British Columbia has 13.04 percent of the Canadian population, the company might assume that B.C. will be a market for 13.04 percent of total drugs sold in Canada.

A single factor, however, is rarely a complete indicator of sales opportunity. Regional drug sales are also influenced by per capita income and the number of physicians per 10 000 people. Thus it makes sense to develop a multiple-factor index, with each factor assigned a specific weight. The numbers are the weights attached to each variable. For example, suppose B.C. has 12.79 percent of the Canadian disposable personal income, 11.71 percent of Canadian retail sales, and 13.04 percent of Canadian population, and the respective weights are 0.5, 0.3, and 0.2. The buying-power index for B.C. would be 12.52 [0.5(12.79) + 0.3(11.71) + 0.2(13.04)]. Thus 12.52 percent of the nation's drug sales might be expected to take place in B.C.

The weights used in the buying-power index are somewhat arbitrary. Other weights can be assigned if appropriate. Furthermore, a manufacturer would want to adjust the market potential for additional factors, such as competitors' presence in that market, local promotional costs, seasonal factors, and local market idiosyncrasies.

Many companies compute other area indexes as a guide to allocating marketing resources. Suppose the drug company is reviewing the six cities listed in Table 4.10. The first two columns show its percentage of brand and category sales in these six cities. The third column shows the **brand development index (BDI)**, which is the index of brand sales to category sales. Montreal, for example, has a BDI of 114 because the brand is relatively more developed than the category in Montreal. Toronto has a BDI of 65, which means that the brand in Toronto is relatively underdeveloped. Normally, the lower the BDI, the higher the market opportunity, in that there is room to grow the brand. However, other marketers would argue the opposite, that marketing funds should go into the brand's strongest markets—where it might be important to reinforce loyalty or more easily capture additional brand share.[51]

After the company decides on the city-by-city allocation of its budget, it can refine each city allocation down to census tracts or postal code centres. *Census tracts* are small, locally defined statistical areas in metropolitan areas and some other counties. They generally have stable boundaries and a population of about 4000. Postal code centres are a little larger than neighbourhoods. Data on population size, median family income, and other characteristics are available for these geographical units. Marketers have found these data extremely useful for identifying high-potential retail areas within large cities or for buying mailing lists to use in direct-mail campaigns (see Chapter 6).

TABLE 4.10	CALCULATING THE BRAND DEVELOPMENT INDEX		
	(a) % of Brand Sales	(b) % of Category Sales	BDI (a ÷ b) × 100
Montreal	3.09	2.71	114
Toronto	6.74	10.41	65
Vancouver	3.49	3.85	91
Halifax	0.97	0.81	120
Winnipeg	1.13	0.81	140
Calgary	3.12	3.00	104

INDUSTRY SALES AND MARKET SHARES Besides estimating total potential and area potential, a company needs to know the actual industry sales taking place in its market. This means identifying competitors and estimating their sales.

The industry trade association will often collect and publish total industry sales, although it usually does not list individual company sales separately. With this information, each company can evaluate its performance against the whole industry. Suppose a company's sales are increasing by 5 percent a year, and industry sales are increasing by 10 percent. This company is actually losing its relative standing in the industry.

Another way to estimate sales is to buy reports from a marketing research firm that audits total sales and brand sales. Nielsen Media Research audits retail sales in various product categories in supermarkets and drugstores and sells this information to interested companies. These audits can give a company valuable information about its total product-category sales as well as brand sales. It can compare its performance to the total industry or any particular competitor to see whether it is gaining or losing share.

Business-goods marketers typically have a harder time estimating industry sales and market shares. Business marketers have no Nielsens to rely on. Distributors typically will not supply information about how much of the competitors' products they are selling. Business-goods marketers, therefore, operate with less knowledge of their market-share results.

Estimating Future Demand

Very few products or services lend themselves to easy forecasting; those that do generally involve a product whose absolute level or trend is fairly constant and where competition is nonexistent (public utilities) or stable (pure oligopolies). In most markets, total demand and company demand are not stable. Good forecasting becomes a key factor in company success. The more unstable the demand is, the more critical forecast accuracy is, and the more elaborate forecasting procedure is.

Companies commonly use a three-stage procedure to prepare a sales forecast. They prepare a macroeconomic forecast first, followed by an industry forecast, followed by a company sales forecast. The macroeconomic forecast calls for projecting inflation, unemployment, interest rates, consumer spending, business investment, government expenditures, net exports, and other variables. The end result is a forecast of gross national product, which is then used, along with other environmental indicators, to forecast industry sales. The company derives its sales forecast by assuming that it will win a certain market share.

How do firms develop their forecasts? Firms may do it internally or buy forecasts from outside sources such as marketing research firms, which develop a forecast by interviewing customers, distributors, and other knowledgeable parties. Specialized forecasting firms produce long-range forecasts of particular macroenvironmental components, such as population, natural resources, and technology. Some examples are Global Insight (a merger of Data Resources and Wharton Econometric Forecasting Associates), Forrester Research, and the Gartner Group. The Economic Services Group of the Conference Board of Canada specializes in developing economic and forecasting models for Canadian companies. Canada's banks also perform economic forecasts, many of which are placed online. (For example, see TD Bank's Economic Group forecast at **www.td.com/economics.**)

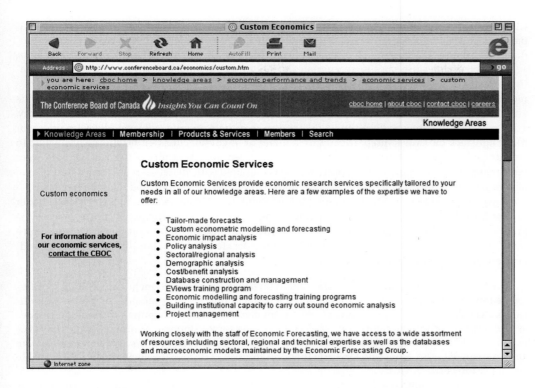

The Conference Board of Canada, Economic Services Branch, specializes in developing economic and forecasting models for Canadian companies.

All forecasts are built on one of three information bases: what people say, what people do, or what people have done. The first basis—what people say—involves surveying the opinions of buyers or those close to them, such as salespeople or outside experts. It includes three methods: surveys of buyers' intentions, composites of sales force opinions, and expert opinion. Building a forecast on what people do involves another method—putting the product into a test market to measure buyer response. The final basis—what people have done—involves analyzing records of past buying behaviour or using time-series analysis or statistical demand analysis.

SURVEY OF BUYERS' INTENTIONS   **Forecasting** is the art of anticipating what buyers are likely to do under a given set of conditions. Because buyer behaviour is so important, buyers should be surveyed. For major consumer durables (for example, major appliances), several research organizations conduct periodic surveys of consumer buying intentions. These organizations ask questions like the following:

Do you intend to buy an automobile within the next six months?

0.00	0.20	0.40	0.60	0.80	1.00
No chance	Slight possibility	Fair possibility	Good possibility	High possibility	Certain

This is called a **purchase probability scale**. The various surveys also inquire into consumers' present and future personal finances and their expectations about the economy. The various bits of information are then combined into a consumer confidence (Conference Board) or consumer sentiment measure (Survey Research Center of the University of Michigan). Consumer durable-goods producers subscribe to these indexes in the hope of anticipating major shifts in buying intentions so they can adjust production and marketing plans accordingly.

For business buying, research firms can carry out buyer-intention surveys regarding plant, equipment, and materials. Their estimates tend to fall within a 10 percent error band of the actual outcomes. Buyer-intention surveys are particularly useful in estimating demand for industrial products, consumer durables, product purchases where advanced planning is required, and new products. The value of a buyer-intention survey increases to the extent that the cost of reaching buyers is small, the buyers are few, they have clear intentions, they implement their intentions, and they willingly disclose their intentions.

COMPOSITE OF SALES FORCE OPINIONS When buyer interviewing is impractical, the company may ask its sales representatives to estimate their future sales. Each sales representative estimates how much each current and prospective customer will buy of each of the company's products.

Few companies use sales force estimates without making some adjustments. Sales representatives might be pessimistic or optimistic, or they might go from one extreme to another because of a recent setback or success. Furthermore, they are often unaware of larger economic developments and do not know how their company's marketing plans will influence future sales in their territory. They might deliberately underestimate demand so that the company will set a low sales quota, or they might lack the time to prepare careful estimates or might not consider the effort worthwhile. To encourage better estimating, the company could offer certain aids or incentives. For example, sales reps might receive a record of their past forecasts compared with actual sales and also a description of company assumptions on the business outlook, competitor behaviour, and marketing plans.

Involving the sales force in forecasting brings a number of benefits. Sales reps might have better insight into developing trends than any other single group. After participating in the forecasting process, reps might have greater confidence in their sales quotas and more incentive to achieve them. Also, a "grassroots" forecasting procedure provides detailed estimates broken down by product, territory, customer, and sales rep.

EXPERT OPINION Companies can also obtain forecasts from experts, including dealers, distributors, suppliers, marketing consultants, and trade associations. Large appliance companies periodically survey dealers for their forecasts of short-term demand, as do car companies. Dealer estimates are subject to the same strengths and weaknesses as sales force estimates. Many companies buy economic and industry forecasts from well-known economic-forecasting firms. These specialists are able to prepare better economic forecasts than the company because they have more data available and more forecasting expertise.

Occasionally, companies will invite a group of experts to prepare a forecast. The experts exchange views and produce a group estimate (*group-discussion method*); or the experts supply their estimates individually, and an analyst combines them into a single estimate (*pooling of individual estimates*). Alternatively, the experts supply individual estimates and assumptions that are reviewed by the company, and are then revised. Further rounds of estimating and refining follow (this is the Delphi method).[52]

PAST-SALES ANALYSIS Sales forecasts can be developed on the basis of past sales. *Time-series analysis* consists of breaking down past time series into four components (trend, cycle, seasonal, and erratic) and projecting these components into the future. *Exponential smoothing* consists of projecting the next period's sales by combining an average of past sales and the most recent sales, giving more weight to the latter. *Statistical demand analysis* consists of measuring the impact level of each of a set of causal factors (e.g., income, marketing expenditures, price) on the sales level. Finally, *econometric analysis* consists of building sets of equations that describe a system, and proceeding to fit the parameters statistically.

MARKET-TEST METHOD When buyers do not plan their purchases carefully or experts are not available or reliable, a direct-market test is desirable. A direct-market test is especially desirable in forecasting new-product sales or established product sales in a new distribution channel or territory. (We discuss market testing in detail in Chapter 12.)

SUMMARY

1. Companies can conduct their own marketing research or hire other companies to do it for them. Good marketing research is characterized by the scientific method, creativity, multiple research methods, accurate model building, cost-benefit analysis, healthy skepticism, and an ethical focus.

2. The marketing research process consists of defining the problem and research objective, developing the research plan, collecting the information, analyzing the information, presenting the findings to management, and making the decision.

3. In conducting research, firms must decide whether to collect their own data or use data that already exist. They must also decide which research approach (observational, focus-group, survey, behavioural data, or experimental) and which research instruments (questionnaire or mechanical instruments) to use. In addition, they must decide on a sampling plan and contact methods.

4. Analysis should ensure that the company achieves the sales, profits, and other goals established in its annual plan. The main tools are sales analysis, market-share analysis, marketing expense-to-sales analysis, and financial analysis of the marketing plan.

5. Profitability analysis seeks to measure and control the profitability of various products, territories, customer groups, trade channels, and order sizes. An important part of controlling for profitability is assigning costs and generating profit-and-loss statements.

6. There are two types of demand: market demand and company demand. To estimate current demand, companies attempt to determine total market potential, area market potential, industry sales, and market share. To estimate future demand, companies survey buyers' intentions, solicit their sales force's input, gather expert opinions, or engage in market testing. Mathematical models, advanced statistical techniques, and computerized data collection procedures are essential to all types of demand and sales forecasting.

APPLICATIONS

Marketing Debate: What Is the Best Type of Marketing Research?

Many market researchers have their favourite research approaches or techniques, although different researchers often have different preferences. Some researchers maintain that the only way to really learn about consumers or brands is through in-depth, qualitative research. Others contend that the only legitimate and defensible form of marketing research involves quantitative measures.

Take a position: Marketing research should be quantitative versus Marketing research should be qualitative.

Marketing Discussion

When was the last time you participated in a survey? How helpful do you think was the information you provided? How could the research have been done differently to make it more effective?

Marketing Spotlight: Sony

Sony started as a radio repair shop, founded by Masuru Ikura and Akio Morita after World War II. The company began its long history of producing compact consumer electronics in 1957, when it introduced the world's first pocket-sized all-transistor radio. The company's name, Sony, was taken from *sonus*, the Latin word for "sound." Sony went on to invent a series of transistor-based TVs and increasingly smaller audio-

cassette recorders. In 1979, the Sony Walkman introduced the world to a new way of listening to music in public. Sony became a world leader in consumer electronics and was the first Japanese company to have its shares traded on the New York Stock Exchange.

In the late 1980s, Sony began expanding into media, purchasing a U.S. record company (CBS Records for US$22 billion in 1988) and a major Hollywood studio (Columbia Pictures for US$4.9 billion in 1989). The purchases made Sony a major force in the entertainment industry.

The importance of marketing at Sony started with Akio Morita, who said that for a company to be successful, it must have three kinds of creativity: creativity to make inventions, creativity in product planning and production, and creativity in marketing.

Creativity in marketing at Sony means not just clever ads, but deep insight into its customers. For example, Sony knows its PlayStation customers like to find clues and to decode things. So Sony's ads for PlayStation 2, like "Signs," feature a young man walking the streets of a city where he encounters various signs foreshadowing the events. Mannequins appear in a store window, arms outstretched, and point enigmatically to something that's about to happen. "The lead character is almost in the midst of his own role-playing game. He needs to follow clues to save the heroine," said Andrew House, Sony's executive vice president of marketing. In the ads, "we were essentially trying to tap into a range of emotions that we think we deliver in the games—intrigue, foreboding, excitement, panic, relief and achievement at the end."

Sony's marketing also includes careful measurement of each campaign's effectiveness. For example, Sony runs 30-second commercials for its PlayStation as part of the previews in more than 1800 theatres and on 8000 movie screens. The ads appear before such films as *The Cat in the Hat.* Sony Computer Entertainment America has been running movie ads for six years. "Cinema advertising has been very effective for us," said Ami Blaire, director of product marketing. "The reason why we have committed to cinema every year is the tremendous unaided recall shown by our own research and Communicus-commissioned ad tracking."

Another example of measurement is Sony's GenY youth marketing efforts. "The online program promoting the NetMD, ATRAC CD Walkman and Cybershot U30 ran July 1 through September 30, 2003, and we found that more than 70 percent of the clickthroughs were spurred by rich media ads via Eyeblaster, versus static banners," said Serge Del

Grosso, Sony Electronics' director of media and Internet strategy.

In fact, Sony has even developed a direct marketing solution that it sells to other companies who want to measure marketing effectiveness. The product, called eBridge™, allows marketers to use video, measure the effectiveness of the campaign, and gain insight into the target audience, all in one package.

Sony expects that the next big breakthrough will not come from a single new electronic device. Rather, Sony president Kunitake Ando says that the future lies in making a whole range of devices more useful by linking them in a networked home-entertainment system. Sony believes that its clout in consumer electronics, combined with its media content, will allow it to steer that convergence in a way that suits it. Whether the future of convergence resides in TVs or PCs or devices, US$62 billion Sony makes every one of them—with a strong brand name that gives them an extra push off retail shelves around the world.

DISCUSSION QUESTIONS

1. What have been the key success factors for Sony?

2. Where is Sony vulnerable? What should it watch out for?

3. What recommendations would you make to senior marketing executives going forward? What should the company be sure to do with its marketing?

Sources: John Teresko, "ASIA: Yesterday's Fast Followers Today's Global Leaders," *Industry Week*, February 2004, pp. 22–28; Gregory Solman, "Sony's Got Game on Movie, TV Screens," *ADWEEK*, November 26, 2003; "Sony Launches Holiday Ad Blitz," *Technology Advertising & Branding Report*, December 1, 2003; Tobi Elkin, "Sony Rolls Cinematic PS2 Push," *Advertising Age*, September 2, 2002, p. 4; "Digital Player: Serge Del Grosso," *Advertising Age*, October 27, 2003, p. 44; "The Complete Home Entertainer?" *The Economist*, March 1, 2003; **www.sony.com**.

CONNECTING WITH CUSTOMERS

IN THIS CHAPTER, WE WILL ADDRESS THE FOLLOWING QUESTIONS:

- What are customer value, satisfaction, and loyalty, and how can companies deliver them?

- What is the lifetime value of customers?

- How can companies both attract and retain customers?

- How can companies cultivate strong customer relationships?

- How can companies deliver total quality?

- What is database marketing?

CHAPTER 5

Creating Customer Value, Satisfaction, and Loyalty

PROFILE: CANADIAN MARKETING EXCELLENCE

You would be hard pressed to find a Canadian who has not shopped at Canadian Tire. It may be even harder to find someone who has never held a bill of Canadian Tire "money" in his or her hand and wondered what to purchase with it. However, you may be hard pressed to find a Canadian who can understand exactly how Canadian Tire has been so successful over the years, particularly now that it faces one of the most aggressive competitive environments with the entry and expansion of major U.S. retailers such as Home Depot and Wal-Mart into its space. But not only has Canadian Tire been able to stand its ground successfully, it has been pursuing one of the most extensive store renewal and redevelopment programs in Canadian history.

Canadian Tire grew out of a Toronto garage bought by brothers J. W. and A. J. Billes for $1800 in 1922. In Canadian Tire's early days, it fought off auto manufacturers angry about the store's cut-rate prices on car parts. In the 1950s, Canadian Tire took on gas retailers with a chain of eponymous gas bars. When the oil companies cut off its supply, then-CEO A. J. Billes bought nearly 230 million litres from the Soviet Union—at the height of the Cold War.

Canadian Tire's strategy has been built on creating customer value by doing things just a little bit differently. It has a very unique product mix, including automotive parts, sports and leisure products, and house wares, which has been said to defy all logic by industry watcher Rob Gerlsbeck: "It's so bizarre a store concept that it has never been replicated anywhere else, even in the U.S." While competitors like Home Depot are becoming very successful in Canada, Canadian Tire remains the undisputed champion in categories like house wares and hardware. It's estimated that Canadian Tire sells one of every three bicycles purchased in Canada, one of every four tires, and one of every two airbeds. It's also a leader in the sales of boating and camping gear, and sells 100 million metres of fishing line each year.

In addition, the company implemented what has become arguably the most successful loyalty program in Canadian history with Canadian Tire "money." First introduced at gas bars in 1958, Canadian Tire "money" makes its way into places all over Canada, but particularly into automobile glove compartments. Today, there is a reported $30 million in Canadian Tire "money" floating in the marketplace, driving customers to come back.

The company is also extremely focused on remaining competitive by upgrading facilities, making strategic acquisitions, and tackling customer service issues. The company has been continuing to pursue an aggressive store renewal program—by the end of 2005, 75 percent of Canadian Tire stores will be less than ten years old. In 2003, the company opened four of its new Concept 20/20 stores that offer everything found in a normal Canadian Tire store in a newer, increasingly shopper-friendly retail design. The design includes less warehousing and more merchandising. In 2001, the company completed its acquisition of Mark's Work Wearhouse clothing chain, an ambitious expansion strategy. Also in 2001, the company launched its E-learning program—an electronic education tool for the employees of the independently operated stores to address customer service complaints that Canadian Tire employees were often unable to answer questions about products on the shelves. Not only is the training program credited with helping to get customer satisfaction levels back on track, but it has also had a hand in boosting sales.

Some statistics indicate just how important Canadian Tire has become to the Canadian retail marketplace: nine out of ten adult Canadians shop at Canadian Tire at least twice a year; 40 percent of Canadians shop at Canadian Tire every week; and 85 percent of the Canadian population lives within a 15-minute drive of a Canadian Tire store.

Perhaps it is due to its history and brand in the Canadian marketplace, perhaps it is due to its unique combination of products, or perhaps it is the ubiquity of the Canadian Tire dollar bill, but one thing is clear: Canadian Tire continues to deliver value to Canadians.

Sources: Canadian Tire, **www.canadiantire.ca**, (viewed July 9, 2004); Andy Holloway, "The Countdown Continues," *Canadian Business Online*, **www.canadianbusiness.com**, September 15, 2003 (viewed July 9, 2004); Zena Olijnyk and Laura Bogomolny, "The Best Managers in Canada," *Canadian Business Online*, **www.canadianbusiness.com**, April 26, 2004 (viewed July 9, 2004); Sara Minogue, "Blurring the Boundaries: Will Retail Expansion Confuse Consumers? Analysts Don't Think So," *Strategy Magazine Online*, **www.strategymag.com**, June 30, 2003, p. 13 (viewed July 9, 2004); Peter Diekmeyer, "Hardware Heats Up: Rona Looks to Double Market Share While Réno Dépôt Goes on the Block," *Strategy Magazine Online*, **www.strategymag.com**, April 7, 2003 (viewed July 9, 2004); Chris Powell, "On a Roll," *Marketing Magazine Online*, **www.marketingmag.ca**, July 1, 2002 (viewed July 9, 2004).

Today, companies face their toughest competition ever. Moving from a product and sales philosophy to a marketing philosophy, however, gives a company a better chance of outperforming its competition. And the cornerstone of a well-conceived marketing orientation is strong customer relationships. Marketers must connect with customers—informing, engaging, and maybe even energizing them in the process. John Chambers, CEO of Cisco Systems, put it well: "Make your customer the center of your culture." Customer-centred companies are adept at building customers, not just products; they are skilled in market engineering, not just product engineering.

As the Canadian Tire experience shows, successful marketers are the ones that deliver value to their customers. In this chapter, we spell out in detail how companies can go about winning customers and beating competitors. The answer lies largely in doing a better job of meeting or exceeding customer expectations.

Building Customer Value, Satisfaction, and Loyalty

Managers who believe the customer is the company's only true "profit centre" consider the traditional organization chart in Figure 5.1(a)—a pyramid with the president at the top, management in the middle, and front-line people and customers at the bottom—obsolete. Successful marketing companies invert the chart (Figure 5.1b). At the top are customers; next in importance are front-line people who meet, serve, and satisfy customers; under them are the middle managers, whose job is to support the front-line people so they can serve customers well; and at the base is top management,

FIGURE 5.1

Traditional Organization versus Modern Customer-Oriented Organization

whose job is to hire and support good middle managers. We have added customers along the sides of Figure 5.1(b) to indicate that managers at every level must be personally involved in knowing, meeting, and serving customers.

Some companies have been founded with the customer-on-top business model and have had customer advocacy as their strategy—and competitive advantage—all along. Online auction giant eBay Inc. epitomizes this New World Order:

eBay

In 2005, eBay's Web site boasted that it serves more than 157 million registered users worldwide, that it helps people sell goods in more than 50 000 categories, and that each and every day it hosts millions of auctions worldwide, with over 1 million new items joining the "for sale" list every 24 hours. Consumer trust is the key element of eBay's success, enabling the company to support commerce between millions of anonymous buyers and sellers. To establish trust, eBay tracks and publishes the reputations of both buyers and sellers on the basis of feedback from each transaction, and eBay's millions of passionate users have come to demand a voice in all major decisions the company makes. Listening, adapting, and enabling are what eBay sees as its main roles. This is clear in one of eBay's most cherished institutions: the Voice of the Customer program. Every few months, eBay brings in as many as a dozen sellers and buyers and asks them questions about how they work and what else eBay needs to do. At least twice a week the company holds hour-long teleconferences to poll users on almost every new feature or policy. The result is that users (eBay's customers) feel like owners, and they have taken the initiative to expand the company into ever-new territory.[1]

With the rise of digital technologies like the Internet, today's increasingly informed consumers expect companies to do more than connect with them, more than satisfy them, and even more than delight them. For instance, customers now have a quick and easy means of doing comparison-shopping through sites like Biz.rate, Shopping.com, and Pricegrabber.com. The Internet also facilitates communication between customers. Web sites like Epinions.com and Amazon.ca enable customers to share information about their experiences using various products and services.

Customer Perceived Value

Consumers are more educated and informed than ever, and they have the tools to verify companies' claims and seek out superior alternatives.[2] How then do they ultimately make choices? Customers tend to be value-maximizers, within the bounds of search costs and limited knowledge, mobility, and income. Customers estimate which offer will deliver the most perceived value and act on it

FIGURE 5.2

Determinants of Customer-
Delivered Value

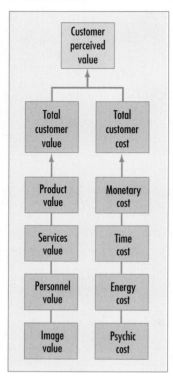

(Figure 5.2). Whether or not the offer lives up to expectation affects customer satisfaction and the probability that the customer will purchase the product again.

Customer perceived value (CPV) is the difference between the prospective customer's evaluation of all the benefits and all the costs of an offering and the perceived alternatives. **Total customer value** is the perceived monetary value of the bundle of economic, functional, and psychological benefits customers expect from a given market offering. **Total customer cost** is the bundle of costs customers expect to incur in evaluating, obtaining, using, and disposing of the given market offering, including monetary, time, energy, and psychic costs.

Customer perceived value is thus based on the difference between what the customer gets and what he or she gives for different possible choices. The customer gets benefits and assumes costs. The marketer can increase the value of the customer offering by some combination of raising functional or emotional benefits and/or reducing one or more of the various types of costs. The customer who is choosing between two value offerings, V1 and V2, will examine the ratio V1:V2 and favour V1 if the ratio is larger than one, favour V2 if the ratio is smaller than one, and will be indifferent if the ratio equals one.

APPLYING VALUE CONCEPTS An example will help here. Suppose the buyer for a large construction company wants to buy a tractor from Caterpillar or Komatsu. The competing salespeople carefully describe their respective offers. The buyer wants to use the tractor in residential construction work. He would like the tractor to deliver certain levels of reliability, durability, performance, and resale value. He evaluates the tractors and decides that Caterpillar has a higher product value based on perceptions of those attributes. He also perceives differences in the accompanying services—delivery, training, and maintenance—and decides that Caterpillar provides better service and more knowledgeable and responsive personnel. Finally, he places higher value on Caterpillar's corporate image. He adds up all the values from these four sources—product, services, personnel, and image—and perceives Caterpillar as delivering greater customer value.

Does he buy the Caterpillar tractor? Not necessarily. He also examines his total cost of transacting with Caterpillar versus Komatsu, which consists of more than the money. As Adam Smith observed over two centuries ago, "The real price of anything is the toil and trouble of acquiring it." Total customer cost includes the buyer's time, energy, and psychic costs. The buyer evaluates these elements together with the monetary cost to form a total customer cost. Then the buyer considers whether Caterpillar's total customer cost is too high in relation to the total customer value Caterpillar delivers. If it is, the buyer might choose the Komatsu tractor. The buyer will choose whichever source he thinks delivers the highest perceived customer value.

Now let us use this decision-making theory to help Caterpillar succeed in selling to this buyer. Caterpillar can improve its offer in three ways. First, it can increase total customer value by improving product, services, personnel, and/or image benefits. Second, it can reduce the buyer's nonmonetary costs by reducing the time, energy, and psychic costs. Third, it can reduce its product's monetary cost to the buyer.

Suppose Caterpillar concludes that the buyer sees its offer as worth $20 000. Further, suppose Caterpillar's cost of producing the tractor is $14 000. This means that Caterpillar's offer potentially generates $6000 over the company's cost, so Caterpillar needs to charge a price between $14 000 and $20 000. If it charges less than $14 000, it won't cover its costs; if it charges more than $20 000, it will price itself out of the market.

The price Caterpillar charges will determine how much value will be delivered to the buyer and how much will flow to Caterpillar. For example, if Caterpillar charges $19 000, it is creating $1000 of customer perceived value and keeping $5000 for itself. The lower Caterpillar sets its price, the higher the customer perceived value and, therefore, the higher the customer's incentive to purchase. To win the sale, Caterpillar must offer more customer perceived value than Komatsu does.[3]

CHOICES AND IMPLICATIONS Some marketers might argue that the process we have described is too rational. Suppose the customer chose the Komatsu tractor. How can we explain this choice? Here are three possibilities:

1. *The buyer might be under orders to buy at the lowest price.* The Caterpillar salesperson's task is to convince the buyer's manager that buying on price alone will result in lower long-term profits.

2. *The buyer will retire before the company realizes that the Komatsu tractor is more expensive to operate.* The buyer will look good in the short run; he is maximizing personal benefit. The

Caterpillar sells tractors like this one not just on the product's attributes, but also on the value of the services, personnel, and image the company offers.

Caterpillar salesperson's task is to convince other people in the customer company that Caterpillar delivers greater customer value.

3. *The buyer enjoys a long-term friendship with the Komatsu salesperson.* In this case, Caterpillar's salesperson needs to show the buyer that the Komatsu tractor will draw complaints from the tractor operators when they discover its high fuel cost and need for frequent repairs.

The point of these examples is clear: Buyers operate under various constraints and occasionally make choices that give more weight to their personal benefit than to the company's benefit.

Customer perceived value is a useful framework that applies to many situations and yields rich insights. Here are its implications: First, the seller must assess the total customer value and total customer cost associated with each competitor's offer in order to know how his or her offer rates in the buyer's mind. Second, the seller who is at a customer perceived value disadvantage has two alternatives: to increase total customer value or to decrease total customer cost. The former calls for strengthening or augmenting the offer's product, services, personnel, and image benefits. The latter calls for reducing the buyer's costs by reducing the price, simplifying the ordering and delivery process, or absorbing some buyer risk by offering a warranty.[4]

DELIVERING HIGH CUSTOMER VALUE   Consumers have varying degrees of loyalty to specific brands, stores, and companies. Oliver defines **loyalty** as "A deeply held commitment to re-buy or re-patronize a preferred product or service in the future despite situational influences and marketing efforts having the potential to cause switching behavior."[5]

The key to generating high customer loyalty is to deliver high customer value. According to Michael Lanning, in his *Delivering Profitable Value*, a company must design a competitively superior value proposition aimed at a specific market segment, backed by a superior value-delivery system.[6]

The **value proposition** consists of the whole cluster of benefits the company promises to deliver; it is more than the core positioning of the offering. For example, Volvo's core positioning has been "safety," but the buyer is promised more than just a safe car; other benefits include a long-lasting car, good service, and a long warranty period. Basically, the value proposition is a statement about the resulting experience customers will gain from the company's market offering and from their relationship with the supplier. The brand must represent a promise about the total experience customers can expect. Whether the promise is kept depends on the company's ability to manage its value-delivery system. The **value-delivery system** includes all the experiences the customer will have on the way to obtaining and using the offering.

British Airways

British Airways and American Airlines may use the same kind of aircraft to fly executives first class between New York and London, but British Airways (BA) beats American Airlines by meeting customers' needs for convenience and rest at every step of the journey. BA's value-delivery system includes a separate first-class express check-in and security clearance, plus a pre-flight express meal service in the first-class lounge so that time-pressed executives can maximize sleep time on the plane without the distraction of in-flight meals. BA was the first to install seats that recline into perfectly flat beds in its first-class section, and in the United Kingdom a fast-track customs area speeds busy executives on their way.[7]

A similar theme is emphasized by Simon Knox and Stan Maklan in their *Competing on Value*.[8] Too many companies create a value gap by failing to align brand value with customer value. Brand marketers try to distinguish their brand from others by a slogan ("washes whiter") or a unique selling proposition ("A Mars a day helps you work, rest, and play"), or by augmenting the basic offering with added services ("Our hotel will provide a computer upon request"). Yet, they are less successful in delivering distinctive customer value, primarily because their marketing people focus on the brand image and not enough on actual product or service performance. Whether customers will actually receive the promised value proposition will depend on the marketer's ability to influence various core business processes. Knox and Maklan want company marketers to spend as much time influencing the company's core processes as they do designing the brand profile. Here is an example of a company that is a master at delivering customer value.

Superquinn

Superquinn is Ireland's largest supermarket chain and its founder, Feargal Quinn, is Ireland's master marketer. A greeter is posted at the store entrance to welcome and help customers and even offer coffee, and to provide umbrellas in case of rain and carryout service to customers' cars. Department managers post themselves in the aisles to interact with customers and answer questions. There is a high-quality salad bar, fresh bread baked every four hours, and indications of when produce arrived, including the farmers' pictures. Superquinn operates a child-care centre. It offers a loyalty program that gives points for the amount purchased and also for discovering anything wrong with the store, such as dented cans or bad tomatoes. The loyalty card is recognized by a dozen other firms (a bank, gas station, etc.) who give points for purchasing at their establishments. Because everything is done to exceed normal customer expectations, Superquinn stores enjoy an almost cult following.[9]

Total Customer Satisfaction

Whether the buyer is satisfied after purchase depends on the offer's performance in relation to the buyer's expectations. In general, **satisfaction** is a person's feelings of pleasure or disappointment resulting from comparing a product's perceived performance (or outcome) to his or her expectations. If the performance falls short of expectations, the customer is dissatisfied. If the performance matches the expectations, the customer is satisfied. If the performance exceeds expectations, the customer is highly satisfied or delighted.[10]

Although the customer-centred firm seeks to create high customer satisfaction, that is not its ultimate goal. If the company increases customer satisfaction by lowering its price or increasing its services, the result may be lower profits. The company might be able to increase its profitability by means other than increased satisfaction (for example, by improving manufacturing processes or investing more in R&D). Also, the company has many stakeholders, including employees, dealers, suppliers, and shareholders. Spending more to increase customer satisfaction might divert funds from increasing the satisfaction of other "partners." Ultimately, the company must divide its total resources such that it is able to deliver a high level of customer satisfaction while also delivering acceptable levels of satisfaction to the other stakeholders.

CUSTOMER EXPECTATIONS   How do buyers form their expectations? From past buying experience, friends' and associates' advice, and marketers' and competitors' information and promises. If

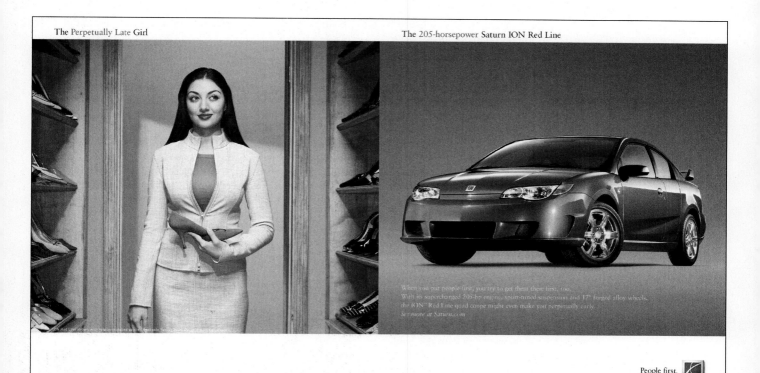

The Perpetually Late Girl

The 205-horsepower **Saturn ION Red Line**

People first.

This Saturn Ion ad looks like a lot of other car ads. But buying a Saturn has unique advantages: no haggling over price, a 30-day money-back guarantee, and salespeople on salary, not commission.

marketers raise expectations too high, the buyer is likely to be disappointed. However, if the company sets expectations too low, it won't attract enough buyers (although it will satisfy those who do buy).[11] Some of today's most successful companies are raising expectations and delivering performances to match. When General Motors launched the Saturn car division, it changed the whole buyer–seller relationship with a new deal for car buyers: There would be a fixed price (none of the traditional haggling); a 30-day guarantee or money back; and salespeople on salary, not on commission (none of the traditional hard sell).[12] Look at what high satisfaction can do.

JetBlue

JetBlue Airways, founded in New York in 1999, significantly raised customer expectations of low-fare carriers. With its brand new Airbus jets, comfy leather seats, live satellite TV, free wireless Internet access, and a consumer-friendly policy of never bumping a passenger, it has inspired lots of low-fare/high-service copycats. Like pioneer Southwest, where JetBlue's CEO David Neeleman tried out his wings, JetBlue finds employees who know how to keep customers coming back. He asks each person he hires to follow a few corporate commandments known as the Values, including safety, caring, integrity, fun, and passion. Even CEO Neeleman and the pilots get on their hands and knees to pick trash out from between seats and scrub the restrooms to prep planes for the next trip. The pitch-in prepping keeps turnaround time down, another reason more and more customers come to JetBlue. The proof is in the numbers: While almost every other airline is drowning in red ink, JetBlue is in the black. Since Canada's discount airline WestJet became a high flyer by mimicking airlines south of the border, it will be interesting to see if it copies some of JetBlue's most recent innovations.[13]

A customer's decision to be loyal or to defect is the sum of many small encounters with the company. Consulting firm Forum Corporation says that in order for all these small encounters to add up to customer loyalty, companies need to create a "branded customer experience." See what TD

Canada Trust did to ensure ongoing customer satisfaction during one of the largest mergers in Canadian banking history.

TD Canada Trust

Mergers between two firms often drive customer satisfaction ratings to an all-time low. In fact, research has shown that during bank mergers, customers often flee at rates as high as 10 percent, since neither bank's customers like the products or services offered by the new entity. No one would have been surprised if this occurred in 2001 when Toronto Dominion Bank (TD) acquired Canada Trust—the big surprise was that customers did not make tracks!

Canada Trust was known for its high levels of customer service, while TD was valued for its extensive product offerings. To do the impossible and retain customers, TD Canada Trust knew it had to keep the best parts of both companies. Instead of beginning by marketing its new brand identity, TD Canada Trust started with an internal marketing campaign. "Our driving philosophy has always been, 'What does the customer want?' This knowledge is then translated into building favourable customer experiences," says Chuck Hounsell, senior VP, e-bank, TD Canada Trust. Each of the 1300 branches and the 19 000 employees received information packages outlining the conversion and stressing the need to make customers feel that they belonged in the new entity. The employee evaluation process was also changed to reward the creation of customer satisfaction. As one executive noted, "Employee marketing is where it starts." Continuous measurement was another key to success. Each and every day, the bank called 1000 customers to inquire about their same-day experience with the bank.

The efforts certainly paid off. Not only did TD Canada Trust gain market share, it ranked number one in customer satisfaction according to the annual survey conducted by Toronto's Market Facts.[14]

Measuring Satisfaction

Many companies are systematically measuring customer satisfaction and the factors shaping it. For example, IBM tracks how satisfied customers are with each IBM salesperson they encounter, and makes this a factor in each salesperson's compensation.

A company would be wise to measure customer satisfaction regularly because one key to customer retention is customer satisfaction. A highly satisfied customer generally stays loyal longer, buys

During its 2001 merger, TD Canada Trust did the impossible—it kept customer satisfaction high.

more as the company introduces new products and upgrades existing products, talks favourably about the company and its products, pays less attention to competing brands and is less sensitive to price, offers product or service ideas to the company, and costs less to serve than new customers because transactions are routine.

The link between customer satisfaction and customer loyalty, however, is not proportional. Suppose customer satisfaction is rated on a scale from one to five. At a very low level of customer satisfaction (level one), customers are likely to abandon the company and even bad-mouth it. At levels two to four, customers are fairly satisfied but still find it easy to switch when a better offer comes along. At level five, the customer is very likely to repurchase and even spread good word of mouth about the company. High satisfaction or delight creates an emotional bond with the brand or company, not just a rational preference. Xerox's senior management found out that its "completely satisfied" customers are six times more likely to repurchase Xerox products over the following 18 months than its "very satisfied" customers.[15]

When customers rate their satisfaction with an element of the company's performance—say, delivery—the company needs to recognize that customers vary in how they define good delivery. It could mean early delivery, on-time delivery, order completeness, and so on. The company must also realize that two customers can report being "highly satisfied" for different reasons. One may be easily satisfied most of the time and the other might be hard to please but was pleased on this occasion.[16]

A number of methods exist to measure customer satisfaction. *Periodic surveys* can track customer satisfaction directly. Respondents can also be asked additional questions to measure repurchase intention and the likelihood or willingness to recommend the company and brand to others. Paramount attributes the success of its five theme parks to the thousands of Web-based guest surveys it sends to customers who have agreed to be contacted. In 2003, the company conducted more than 55 Web-based surveys and netted 100 000 individual responses that described guest satisfaction on topics including rides, dining, shopping, games, and shows.[17]

Companies can monitor the *customer loss rate* and contact customers who have stopped buying or who have switched to another supplier to learn why this happened. Finally, companies can hire *mystery shoppers* to pose as potential buyers and report on strong and weak points experienced in buying the company's and competitors' products. Managers themselves can enter company and competitor sales situations where they are unknown and experience firsthand the treatment they receive, or phone their own company with questions and complaints to see how the calls are handled.

For customer satisfaction surveys, it's important that companies ask the right questions. Frederick Reichheld suggests that perhaps only one question really matters: "Would you recommend this product or service to a friend?" He maintains that marketing departments typically focus surveys on the areas they can control, such as brand image, pricing, and product features. According to Reichheld, a customer's willingness to recommend to a friend results from how well the customer is treated by front-line employees, which in turn is determined by all the functional areas that contribute to a customer's experience.[18]

In addition to tracking customer value expectations and satisfaction, companies need to monitor their competitors' performance in these areas. One company was pleased to find that 80 percent of its customers said they were satisfied. Then the CEO found out that its leading competitor had a 90 percent customer satisfaction score. He was further dismayed when he learned that this competitor was aiming for a 95 percent satisfaction score.

For customer-centred companies, customer satisfaction is both a goal and a marketing tool. Companies need to be especially concerned today with their customer satisfaction level because the Internet provides a tool for consumers to spread bad word of mouth—as well as good word of mouth—to the rest of the world. On Web sites like troublebenz.com and lemonmb.com, angry Mercedes-Benz owners have been airing their complaints on everything from faulty key fobs and leaky sunroofs to balky electronics that leave drivers and their passengers stranded.[19]

Companies that do achieve high customer-satisfaction ratings make sure their target market knows it. When J. D. Power began to rate national home mortgage leaders, Countrywide was quick to advertise its number-one ranking in customer satisfaction. Dell Computer's meteoric growth in the computer systems industry can be partly attributed to achieving and advertising its number-one rank in customer satisfaction.

A survey performed by *Canadian Business* magazine found that some of the best and worst customer satisfaction levels were found within the same industries, illustrating just how effective customer satisfaction can be as tool for differentiating against competitors. In financial services, credit unions were found to have 82 percent satisfaction, while the range of satisfaction for the big five

A Countrywide ad touts its #1 Customer Satisfaction rating from J. D. Power and Associates. Ratings like these are important to a customer-centred company, because word of mouth, good and bad, spreads so quickly on the Internet.

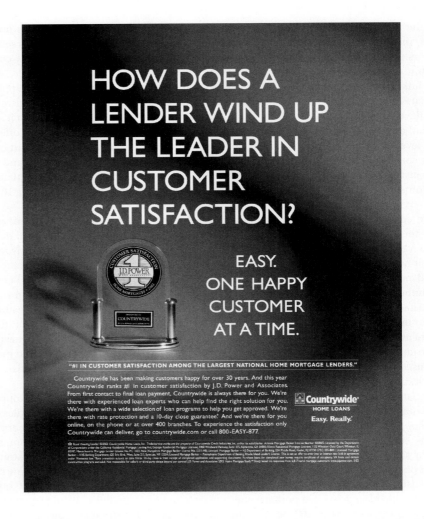

banks was between 38 and 47 percent. The biggest gap was in the Canadian airline industry, where Air Canada fetched a rating of 16 percent satisfaction (the lowest in the survey, scoring even lower than the Canada Customs and Revenue Agency), while WestJet came in at 89 percent (the highest rating in the survey).[20]

Product and Service Quality

Satisfaction will also depend on product and service quality. What exactly is quality? Various experts have defined it as "fitness for use," "conformance to requirements," "freedom from variation," and so on.[21] We will use the American Society for Quality Control's definition: **Quality** is the totality of features and characteristics of a product or service that bear on its ability to satisfy stated or implied needs.[22] This is clearly a customer-centred definition. We can say that the seller has delivered quality whenever the seller's product or service meets or exceeds the customers' expectations. A company that satisfies most of its customers' needs most of the time is called a quality company, but it is important to distinguish between *conformance* quality and *performance* quality (or grade). A Lexus provides higher performance quality than a Hyundai: The Lexus rides smoother, goes faster, and lasts longer. Yet both a Lexus and a Hyundai can be said to deliver the same conformance quality if all the units are built to their design specifications (i.e., they produce the horsepower the engineers specified for the car, they consume the stated amount of fuel per kilometre, etc.).

Total quality is the key to value creation and customer satisfaction and, as such, is the responsibility of every functional department in an organization. This idea was expressed well by Daniel Beckham:

Marketers who don't learn the language of quality improvement, manufacturing, and operations will become as obsolete as buggy whips. The days of functional marketing are gone. We can no longer afford to think of ourselves as market researchers, advertising people, direct marketers, strategists—we have to think of ourselves as customer satisfiers—customer advocates focused on whole processes.[23]

Marketing managers have two responsibilities in a quality-centred company. First, they must participate in formulating strategies and policies to help the company win through total quality excellence. Second, they must deliver marketing quality alongside production quality. Each marketing activity—marketing research, sales training, advertising, customer service, and so on—must be performed to high standards.

Total Quality Management

The quest to maximize customer satisfaction led some firms to adopt total quality management principles. **Total quality management (TQM)** is an organization-wide approach to continuously improving the quality of all the organization's processes, products, and services.

According to GE's former chairman, John F. Welch Jr., "Quality is our best assurance of customer allegiance, our strongest defense against foreign competition, and the only path to sustained growth and earnings."[24] The drive to produce goods that are superior in world markets has led some countries—and groups of countries—to recognize or award prizes to companies that exemplify the best quality practices (e.g., the Deming Prize in Japan, the Malcolm Baldridge National Quality Award in the United States, the European Quality Award, and the K. C. Irving Quality Award in Canada).

Product and service quality, customer satisfaction, and company profitability are intimately connected. Higher levels of quality result in higher levels of customer satisfaction, which support higher prices and (often) lower costs. Studies have shown a high correlation between relative product quality and company profitability.[25]

In practising TQM, however, some firms ran into implementation problems as they became overly focused—perhaps even obsessed—with processes and *how* they were doing business. They lost sight of the needs and wants of customers and *why* they were doing business. In some cases, companies were able to achieve benchmarks against top quality standards, but only by incurring prohibitive increases in costs. For example, scientific equipment maker Varian embraced TQM principles but found itself so rushed to meet production schedules and deadlines that managers now feel it may not have been that important to their customers to begin with.

In a reaction to this somewhat myopic behaviour, some companies now concentrate their efforts on "return on quality" or ROQ. ROQ adherents advocate improving quality only on those dimensions that produce tangible customer benefits, lower costs, or increased sales. This bottom-line orientation forces companies to make sure that the quality of the product offerings is in fact the quality consumers actually want.[26]

Rust, Moorman, and Dickson studied managers seeking to increase their financial returns from quality improvements.[27] They found that firms that adopted primarily a revenue expansion emphasis (externally focusing on growing demand through catering to and increasing consumers' preferences for quality) performed better as compared to firms that adopted primarily a cost reduction emphasis (internally focusing on improving the efficiency of internal processes) or firms that attempted to adopt both emphases simultaneously.

Marketers play several roles in helping their companies define and deliver high-quality goods and services to target customers. First, they bear the major responsibility for correctly identifying the customers' needs and requirements. Second, they must communicate customer expectations properly to product designers. Third, they must make sure that customers' orders are filled correctly and on time. Fourth, they must check that customers have received proper instructions, training, and technical assistance in the use of the product. Fifth, they must stay in touch with customers after the sale to ensure that they are satisfied and remain satisfied. Sixth, they must gather customer ideas for product and service improvements and convey them to the appropriate departments. When marketers do all this, they are making substantial contributions to total quality management and customer satisfaction, as well as to customer and company profitability.

Maximizing Customer Lifetime Value

Ultimately, marketing is the art of attracting and keeping profitable customers. According to James V. Putten of American Express, the best customers outspend others by ratios of 16 to 1 in retailing, 13 to 1 in the restaurant business, 12 to 1 in the airline business, and 5 to 1 in the hotel and motel industry.[28] Yet every company loses money on some of its customers. The well-known 20–80 rule says that the top 20 percent of the customers may generate as much as 80 percent of the company's profits. Sherden suggested amending the rule to read 20-80-30, to reflect the idea that the top 20 percent of customers generate 80 percent of the company's profits, half of which are lost serving the bottom 30 percent of unprofitable customers.[29] The implication is that a company could improve its profits by "firing" its worst customers.

Furthermore, it is not necessarily the company's largest customers who yield the most profit. The largest customers demand considerable service and receive the deepest discounts. The smallest customers pay full price and receive minimal service, but the costs of transacting with small customers reduce their profitability. The midsize customers receive good service and pay nearly full price and are often the most profitable. This fact helps explain why many large firms are now invading the middle market. Major air express carriers, for instance, are finding that it does not pay to ignore small and midsize international shippers. Programs geared toward smaller customers provide a network of drop boxes, which allow for substantial discounts over letters and packages picked up at the shipper's place of business. United Parcel Service (UPS) conducts seminars to instruct exporters in the finer points of shipping overseas.[30]

Customer Profitability

What makes a customer profitable? A **profitable customer** is a person, household, or company that over time yields a revenue stream that exceeds by an acceptable amount the company's cost stream of attracting, selling, and servicing that customer. Note that the emphasis is on the lifetime stream of revenue and cost, not on the profit from a particular transaction.[31] Customer profitability can be assessed individually, by market segment, or by channel.

Although many companies measure customer satisfaction, most companies fail to measure individual customer profitability. Banks claim that this is a difficult task because a customer uses different banking services and the transactions are logged in different departments. However, banks that have succeeded in linking customer transactions have been appalled by the number of unprofitable customers in their customer base. Some banks report losing money on over 45 percent of their retail customers. There are only two solutions to handling unprofitable customers: raise fees or reduce service support.[32]

CUSTOMER PROFITABILITY ANALYSIS   A useful type of profitability analysis is shown in Figure 5.3.[33] Customers are arrayed along the columns and products along the rows. Each cell contains a symbol for the profitability of selling that product to that customer. Customer 1 is very profitable; he buys three profit-making products (P_1, P_2, and P_4). Customer 2 yields a picture of mixed profitability; she buys one profitable product and one unprofitable product. Customer 3 is a losing customer because he buys one profitable product and two unprofitable products.

What can the company do about customers 2 and 3? (1) It can raise the price of its less profitable products or eliminate them, or (2) it can try to sell them its profit-making products. Unprofitable customers who defect should not concern the company. In fact, the company should encourage these customers to switch to competitors.

FIGURE 5.3

Customer–Product Profitability
Analysis

Products	Customers			
	C_1	C_2	C_3	
P_1	+	+	+	Highly profitable product
P_2	+			Profitable product
P_3		−	−	Losing product
P_4	+		−	Mixed-bag product
	High-profit customer	Mixed-bag customer	Losing customer	

Customer profitability analysis (CPA) is best conducted with the tools of an accounting technique called activity-based costing (ABC). The company estimates all revenue coming from the customer, less all costs. The costs should include not only the cost of making and distributing the goods and services, but also such costs as taking phone calls from the customer, travelling to visit the customer, entertainment, and gifts—all the company's resources that went into serving that customer. When this is done for each customer, it is possible to classify customers into different profit tiers: platinum customers (most profitable), gold customers (profitable), iron customers (low profitability but desirable), and lead customers (unprofitable and undesirable).

The company's job is to move iron customers into the gold tier and gold customers into the platinum tier, while dropping the lead customers or making them profitable by raising their prices or lowering the cost of serving them. More generally, marketers must segment customers into those worth pursuing versus those potentially less lucrative customers that should receive less attention, if any at all.

Dhar and Glazer make an interesting analogy between the individuals that make up the firm's customer portfolio and the stocks that make up an investment portfolio.[34] Just as with the latter, it is important to calculate the beta, or risk–reward value, for each customer and diversify the customer portfolio accordingly. From their perspective, firms should assemble portfolios of negatively correlated individuals so that the financial contributions of one offset the deficits of another to maximize the portfolio's risk-adjusted lifetime value.

RBC Investments

Ultimately, "what we want to understand is what value propositions make sense to which customers," says Jay Slade, manager of client intelligence and analysis at RBC Investments in Toronto. RBC has discovered through customer profitability analysis that some clients are very experienced investors and therefore do not require an advisor. While it would make sense for these customers to be using RBC's self-directed brokerage, that is not always the case. RBC has found through dissecting its customer information that its clients are not always aligned against the appropriate products and services. To protect the long-term retention and lifetime profitability of its clients, it sometimes makes sense to tell a customer he or she is not using the right service, even if that service generates more revenue in the short term. According to Slade, RBC's return on investment from this kind of customer analysis has been "in the millions of dollars—probably the tens of millions."[35]

COMPETITIVE ADVANTAGE Companies must not only be able to create high absolute value, but also high value relative to competitors at a sufficiently low cost. **Competitive advantage** is a company's ability to perform in one or more ways that competitors cannot or will not match. Michael Porter urged companies to build a sustainable competitive advantage.[36] But few competitive advantages are sustainable. At best, they may be leverageable. A *leverageable advantage* is one that a company can use as a springboard to new advantages, much as Microsoft has leveraged its operating system to Microsoft Office and then to networking applications. In general, a company that hopes to endure must be in the business of continuously inventing new advantages.

Any competitive advantage must be seen by customers as a *customer advantage*. For example, if a company delivers faster than its competitors, this will not be a customer advantage if customers do not value speed. Companies must focus on building customer advantages. Then they will deliver high customer value and satisfaction, which leads to high repeat purchases and ultimately to high company profitability.

Measuring Customer Lifetime Value

The case for maximizing long-term customer profitability is captured in the concept of customer lifetime value. **Customer lifetime value (CLV)** describes the net present value of the stream of future profits expected over the customer's lifetime purchases. The company must subtract from the expected revenues the expected costs of attracting, selling, and servicing that customer, applying the appropriate discount rate (e.g., 10–20 percent, depending on cost of capital and risk attitudes). Various CLV estimates have been made for different products and services:

- Carl Sewell, in *Customers for Life* (with Paul Brown), estimated that a customer entering his car dealership for the first time represents a potential lifetime value of over US$300 000.[37] If the

A GM customer shops the showroom at Hoskins Chevrolet in Elk Grove Village, Illinois. What GM wants is to satisfy him so he comes back to Hoskins and GM each time he needs a car.

satisfied customer brings in other customers, the figure would be higher. Similarly, General Motors estimates its lifetime customers to be worth US$276 000 on average. These six-figure values are a graphic illustration of the importance of keeping the customer satisfied for the life of the automobile to better the chances of a repeat purchase.[38]

- Even though tacos may cost less than a dollar each, executives at Taco Bell have determined that a repeat customer is worth as much as US$11 000. By sharing such estimates of customer lifetime value with its employees, Taco Bell's managers help employees understand the value of keeping customers satisfied.[39]

- Mark Grainer, former chairman of the Technical Assistance Research Programs Institute (TARP), estimated that a loyal supermarket customer is worth US$3800 annually.[40]

We can work out an example of estimating CLV. Suppose a company analyzes its new-customer acquisition cost:

- Cost of average sales call (including salary, commission, benefits, and expenses): $300
- Average number of sales calls to convert an average prospect into a customer: 4
- Cost of attracting a new customer: $1200

This is an underestimate because we are omitting the cost of advertising and promotion, plus the fact that only a fraction of all pursued prospects end up being converted into customers.

Now suppose the company estimates average customer lifetime value as follows:

- Annual customer revenue: $500
- Average number of loyal years: 20
- Company profit margin: 0.10
- Customer lifetime value: $1000

This company is spending more to attract new customers than they are worth. Unless the company can sign up customers with fewer sales calls, spend less per sales call, stimulate higher new-customer annual spending, retain customers longer, or sell them higher-profit products, it is headed for bankruptcy. Of course, in addition to an average customer estimate, a company needs a way of estimating CLV for each individual customer to decide how much to invest in each customer.

CLV calculations provide a formal quantitative framework for planning customer investment and helps marketers to adopt a long-term perspective. One challenge in applying CLV concepts, however, is to arrive at reliable cost and revenue estimates. Marketers who use CLV concepts must also be careful to not forget the importance of short-term, brand-building marketing activities that will help to increase customer loyalty.

Customer Equity

Canadian marketing consultant Ian Gordon defines relationship marketing as:

> The ongoing process of identifying and creating new value with individual customers and then sharing the benefits from this over a lifetime of association. It involves the understanding, focusing and management of ongoing collaboration between suppliers and selected customers for mutual value creation and sharing through interdependence and organizational alignment.[41]

Toronto-based Bayer Canada, for example, works with Canadians firms to help them assess how they are spending their health-care dollars within their employer benefit programs and finds ways to save them money.

The aim of customer relationship management (CRM) is to produce high customer equity. **Customer equity** is the total of the discounted lifetime values of all of the firm's customers.[42] Clearly, the more loyal the customers, the higher the customer equity. Rust, Zeithaml, and Lemon distinguish three drivers of customer equity: value equity, brand equity, and relationship equity:[43]

- *Value equity* is the customer's perceptions of benefits relative to costs. The sub-drivers of value equity are quality, price, and convenience. These sub-drivers are industry specific. An airline passenger, for example, might define quality as seat width; a hotel guest might define quality as check-in speed. Value equity makes the biggest contribution to customer equity when products are differentiated and when they are more complex and need to be evaluated. Value equity especially drives customer equity in business markets.

- *Brand equity* is the customer's subjective and intangible assessment of the brand, above and beyond its objectively perceived value. The sub-drivers of brand equity are customer brand awareness, customer attitude toward the brand, and customer perception of brand ethics. Companies use advertising, public relations, and other communication tools to affect these sub-drivers. Brand equity is more important than the other drivers of customer equity where products are less differentiated and have more emotional impact. We consider brand equity in detail in Chapter 7.

- *Relationship equity* is the customer's tendency to stick with the brand, above and beyond objective and subjective assessments of its worth. Sub-drivers of relationship equity include loyalty programs, special recognition and treatment programs, community-building programs, and knowledge-building programs. Relationship equity is especially important where personal relationships count for a lot and where customers tend to continue with suppliers out of habit or inertia.

This formulation integrates *value management, brand management,* and *relationship management* within a customer-centred focus. Companies can decide which driver(s) to strengthen for the best payoff. The Bank of Montreal, for example, has been busy analyzing the 100 million transactions that take place through its multiple channels each month to better understand customer attitudes and behaviour so that it can build better relationships with its customers.

Customer equity represents a promising approach to marketing management. "Marketing Insight: Progress and Priorities in Customer Equity Management" highlights some recent academic thinking on the subject. Note too that customer equity notions can be extended. Mohan Sawhney defines the **relational equity** of the firm as the cumulative value of the firm's network of relationships with its customers, partners, suppliers, employees, and investors.[44] Relational equity depends on the company's ability to attract and retain talent, customers, investors, and partners.

Cultivating Customer Relationships

Maximizing customer value means cultivating long-term customer relationships. In past centuries, producers customized their offerings to each customer: The tailor fitted a suit and a cobbler made shoes for each individual. The Industrial Revolution ushered in an era of mass production. To maximize economies of scale, companies made standard goods in advance of orders and left it to individuals to fit into whatever was available. Producers moved from *built-to-order* marketing to *built-to-stock* marketing.

Companies are moving away from wasteful mass marketing to more precision marketing designed to build strong customer relationships.[45] Today's economy is supported by information businesses. Information has the advantages of being easy to differentiate, customize, personalize, and dispatch over networks at incredible speed.

Progress and Priorities in Customer Equity Management

Customer equity has roots in many different marketing concepts—direct marketing and database marketing, service quality, relationship marketing, and brand equity. Its unique focus, however, is on understanding the value of the customer to the firm and how to manage the customer as a strategic asset to increase overall firm value for shareholders.

Customer equity can be seen as the expected lifetime value of a firm's existing customer base plus the expected future lifetime value of newly acquired customers. This basic CLV model can be modified to incorporate several other dimensions, such as individual customer risk, the social effects of word of mouth, and competitive and environmental effects that can dampen customer retention rates.

A special issue of the *Journal of Service Research* devoted to articles on the topic of customer equity included contributions by top academics working on that topic. The papers covered a wide range of issues, among them how to implement customer equity management:

1. *Assemble individual-level, industry-wide consumer data.* Pooled customer information by all industry competitors can provide insight into crucial considerations such as an individual's share of requirements. The benefits of broad industry cooperation can offset the costs from the loss of company-specific knowledge.

2. *Track marketing's effect on the balance sheet, not just the income statement.* Accounting principles are needed that recognize the customer asset. The challenge is that CLV calculations depend on assumptions about a host of factors, such as the future income stream from a customer, appropriate cost allocations to a customer, discount factors, and the expected economic life of a customer.

3. *Model future revenues appropriately.* Decisions about the timing and probability of revenue flows have important implications.

4. *Maximize (don't just measure) CLV.* Marketers must implement marketing initiatives to maximize the value of the customer franchise (e.g., loyalty programs, customer reactivations, and cross-selling).

5. *Align the organization with customer management activities.* For example, some catalogue retailers or credit card companies commonly separate the prospect acquisition team from a customer conversion team from those responsible for ongoing customer retention and servicing. Another team may even be assigned to work on reactivation of dormant accounts.

6. *Respect the sensitivity of customer information.* Consider decentralizing customer information storage and having data reside with the consumer, on personal computers or smart cards. Also, allow consumers the right to audit and contest the accuracy of their profiles.

7. *Develop CRM from an efficiency tool into a service improvement tool.* The most successful CRM implementations re-evaluate and refine all customer-facing business processes; develop and motivate all service and support personnel; and select and tailor appropriate technologies.

Source: Special Issue on Customer Equity Management, *Journal of Services Research*, 5, no. 1 (August 2002).

As companies have grown proficient at gathering information about individual customers and business partners (suppliers, distributors, retailers), and as their factories are designed more flexibly, they have increased their ability to individualize market offerings, messages, and media. **Mass customization** is the ability of a company to meet each customer's requirements—to prepare on a mass basis individually designed products, services, programs, and communications.[46] While Levi's and Lands' End were among the first clothing manufacturers to introduce custom jeans, now there are many players in the mass customization market. Consider what Rogers Wireless has been up to.

Rogers Wireless

In creating its current cell phone packages, Rogers Wireless, of Toronto, has been using a much more personalized approach in recent years. In addition to being able to select specific airtime packages, Rogers' customers can personalize their phone by downloading RealTrax or Polyphonic ring tunes, Celebrity Voicemail, Graphics, and Java games. In part, customization has played a role in the cell phone industry, becoming the "fastest growing consumer product in history," John Boynton, vice-president of consumer marketing, says. In addition, Boyton believes that customization has a significant impact on increasing customer loyalty and retention, which he believes is achieved by staying with consumers throughout major life changes. For example, if a teenager buys a cell phone, he or she is likely to want a different experience during university, and then again upon getting married. As a result, Rogers Wireless tracks usage patterns with specific focus on date-of-birth information so it can anticipate a major lifestyle change.[47]

Rogers Wireless has been employing a mass customization strategy by creating downloadable ring tunes for its customers.

Customer Relationship Management (CRM)

In addition to working with partners—called **partner relationship management (PRM)**—many companies are intent on developing stronger bonds with their customers—called **customer relationship management (CRM)**. This is the process of managing detailed information about individual customers and carefully managing all customer "touch points" to maximize customer loyalty. A *customer touch point* is any occasion on which a customer encounters the brand and product—from actual experience to personal or mass communications to casual observation. For a hotel, the touch points include reservations, check-in and checkout, frequent-stay programs, room service, business services, exercise facilities, laundry service, restaurants, and bars. For instance, the Four Seasons relies on personal touches, such as a staff that always addresses guests by name, high-powered employees who understand the needs of sophisticated business travellers, and at least one best-in-region facility, such as a premier restaurant or spa.[48]

Customer relationship management enables companies to provide excellent real-time customer service through the effective use of individual account information. Based on what they know about each valued customer, companies can customize market offerings, services, programs, messages, and media. CRM is important because a major driver of company profitability is the aggregate value of the company's customer base.[49] A pioneer in the application of CRM techniques is Fairmont Hotels.

Fairmont Hotels

Canada's Fairmont Hotels (the Royal York, Hotel Vancouver, and Chateau Frontenac to name a few members of the worldwide chain) are the masters when it comes to using customer information to tailor offerings and build relationship equity. Platinum members of the Fairmont's Presidents Club (high-value customers who stay at Fairmont hotels more than 25 nights per year) receive regular newsletters and exclusive promotional offers such as free room nights in highly desirable locations such as Bermuda. They are given $50 discounts off dinners in the hotels they frequent most often. They will be welcomed when they check in with words like "Welcome back, Dr. Cunningham." Room preferences are carefully recorded so returning guests will always get their favourite room made up with the pillow type they prefer and the newspaper they want. They get free room upgrades, in-room delivery of a welcome fruit basket, free high-speed Internet connections, shoeshines, and local phone calls. One guest was given a card when she visited a Fairmont hotel on her birthday. Despite the premium prices, it's no wonder these guests keep coming back again and again.[50]

Fairmont hotels use customer information to build relationship equity.

Some of the groundwork for customer relationship management was laid by Don Peppers and Martha Rogers in a series of books.[51] Peppers and Rogers outline a four-step framework for one-to-one marketing that can be adapted to CRM marketing as follows:

- *Identify your prospects and customers.* Do not go after everyone. Build, maintain, and mine a rich customer database with information derived from all the channels and customer touch points.

- *Differentiate customers in terms of (1) their needs and (2) their value to your company.* Spend proportionately more effort on the most valuable customers (MVCs). Apply activity based costing and calculate customer lifetime value. Estimate net present value of all future profits coming from purchases, margin levels, and referrals, less customer-specific servicing costs.

- *Interact with individual customers to improve your knowledge about their individual needs and to build stronger relationships.* Formulate customized offerings that are communicated in a personalized way.

- *Customize products, services, and messages to each customer.* Facilitate customer/company interaction through the company contact centre and Web site.

Table 5.1 lists the main differences between mass marketing and one-to-one marketing.

A key driver of shareholder value is the aggregate value of the customer base. Winning companies improve the value of their customer base by excelling at strategies such as the following:

- *Reducing the rate of customer defection.* Whole Foods Market, the world's largest retailer of natural and organic foods (with stores in Toronto and Oakville, Ontario), woos customers with a commitment to marketing the best foods and a team concept for employees. Selecting and training employees to be knowledgeable and friendly increases the likelihood that the inevitable shopping questions from customers will be answered satisfactorily.

- *Increasing the longevity of the customer relationship.* The more involved a customer is with the company, the more likely he or she is to stick around. Some companies treat their customers as partners—especially in business-to-business markets—soliciting their help in the design of new products or improving their customer service. Instant Web Companies (IWCO), a direct-mail printer, launched a monthly Customer Spotlight program where guest companies provide an overview of their business and direct-mail programs and comment on IWCO practices, products, and services. IWCO's staff not only gains exposure to customers, but also develops a

TABLE 5.1	MASS MARKETING VERSUS ONE-TO-ONE MARKETING
Mass Marketing	**One-to-One Marketing**
Average customer	Individual customer
Customer anonymity	Customer profile
Standard product	Customized market offering
Mass production	Customized production
Mass distribution	Individualized distribution
Mass advertising	Individualized message
Mass promotion	Individualized incentives
One-way message	Two-way messages
Economies of scale	Economies of scope
Share of market	Share of customer
All customers	Profitable customers
Customer attraction	Customer retention

Source: Adapted from Don Peppers and Martha Rogers, *The One-to-One Future* (New York: Doubleday/Currency, 1993). See their Web site **www.1to1.com**.

broader perspective on customers' business and marketing objectives and how to add value and identify options that help meet their customers' goals.[52]

- *Enhancing the growth potential of each customer through "share-of-wallet," cross-selling, and up-selling.*[53] Harley-Davidson, Inc., capped off its 100th anniversary year by announcing record sales and a 21 percent rise in profits. Harley has enjoyed 18 consecutive years of growth. Harley-Davidson sells more than motorcycles and riding supplements (such as gloves, leather jackets, helmets, and sunglasses). Harley dealerships sell more than 3000 items of clothing—some even have their own fitting rooms. Licensed goods sold by others range from the predictable (shot glasses, cue balls, and Zippo cigarette lighters) to the more surprising items (cologne, dolls, and cell phones). The 2003 100th-anniversary model year also saw strong sales of apparel and collectibles tied to the anniversary.

- *Making low-profit customers more profitable or terminating them.* To avoid the direct need for termination, unprofitable customers can be made to buy more or in larger quantities, forgo certain features or services, or pay higher amounts or fees. Banks, phone companies, and travel agencies are all charging for once-free services to ensure minimum customer revenue levels.

- *Focusing disproportionate effort on high-value customers.* The most valuable customers can be treated in a special way. Thoughtful gestures such as birthday greetings, small gifts, or invitations to special sports or arts events can send a strong signal to the customer.

Attracting, Retaining, and Growing Customers

Customers are becoming harder to please. They are smarter, more price conscious, more demanding, less forgiving, and they are approached by many more competitors with equal or better offers. The challenge, according to Jeffrey Gitomer, is not necessarily to produce satisfied customers; several competitors can do this. The challenge is to produce delighted and loyal customers.[54]

Companies seeking to expand their profits and sales have to spend considerable time and resources searching for new customers. To generate leads, the company develops ads and places them in media that will reach new prospects; it sends direct mail and makes phone calls to possible new prospects; its salespeople participate in trade shows where they might find new leads; it purchases names from list brokers; and so on. All this activity produces a list of suspects. *Suspects* are people or organizations who might conceivably have an interest in buying the company's product or service, but may not have the means or real intention to buy. The next task is to identify which suspects are really good *prospects*—customers with the motivation, ability, and opportunity to make a purchase—by interviewing them, checking on their financial standing, and so on. Then it is time to send out the salespeople.

Marketing Memo

How to Handle Customer Complaints

No matter how perfectly designed and implemented a marketing program is, mistakes will happen. Given the potential downside of an unhappy customer, it is critical that the negative experience be dealt with properly. As with any marketing crisis large or small, swiftness and sincerity are the key watchwords. Customers must feel an immediate sense that the company truly cares. Beyond that, the following procedures can help to recover customer goodwill:

1. Set up a 7-day, 24-hour toll-free "hotline" (by phone, fax, or e-mail) to receive and act on customer complaints.

2. Contact the complaining customer as quickly as possible. The slower the company is to respond, the more dissatisfaction may grow and lead to negative word of mouth.

3. Accept responsibility for the customer's disappointment; don't blame the customer.

4. Use customer service people who are empathic.

5. Resolve the complaint swiftly and to the customer's satisfaction. Some complaining customers are not looking for compensation so much as a sign that the company cares.

Source: Philip Kotler, *Kotler on Marketing* (New York, NY: The Free Press, 1999), pp. 21–22.

It is not enough, however, to attract new customers; the company must keep them and increase their business. Too many companies suffer from high **customer churn**—high customer defection. It is like adding water to a leaking bucket. Cellular carriers, for example, are plagued with "spinners," customers who switch carriers at least three times a year looking for the best deal. Many lose 25 percent of their subscribers each year at an estimated cost of US$2 billion to US$4 billion. Unfortunately, much marketing theory and practice centres on the art of attracting new customers, rather than on retaining and cultivating existing ones. The emphasis traditionally has been on making sales rather than building relationships; on pre-selling and selling rather than caring for the customer afterward.

There are two main ways to strengthen customer retention. One is to erect high switching barriers. Customers are less inclined to switch to another supplier when this would involve high capital costs, high search costs, or the loss of loyal-customer discounts. The better approach is to deliver high customer satisfaction. This makes it harder for competitors to offer lower prices or inducements to switch.

Some companies think they are getting a sense of customer satisfaction by tallying complaints, but 96 percent of dissatisfied customers don't complain; they just stop buying.[55] The best thing a company can do is to make it easy for the customer to complain. Suggestion forms, toll-free numbers, Web sites, and e-mail addresses allow for quick, two-way communication. The 3M Company claims that over two-thirds of its product-improvement ideas come from listening to customer complaints.

Listening is not enough, however. The company must respond quickly and constructively to any complaint (see "Marketing Memo: How to Handle Customer Complaints"):

> Of the customers who register a complaint, between 54 and 70% will do business again with the organization if their complaint is resolved. The figure goes up to a staggering 95% if the customer feels that the complaint was resolved quickly. Customers who have complained to an organization and had their complaints satisfactorily resolved tell an average of five people about the good treatment they received.[56]

Dell Computer Corp. quickly yanked its corporate PC tech support out of India and to a domestic call centre when its U.S.-based customers complained about the quality of help they received: rigid, "by the book" technicians who wasted their time wading through fixes they already tried, problems with poor phone connections, and strongly accented English that was hard to understand.[57]

More companies now recognize the importance of satisfying and retaining customers. Satisfied customers constitute the company's *customer relationship capital*. If the company were to be sold, the acquiring company would have to pay not only for the plant and equipment and the brand name, but also for the delivered *customer base*, the number and value of the customers who would do business with the new firm. Here are some interesting facts bearing on customer retention:[58]

1. Acquiring new customers can cost five times more than the costs involved in satisfying and retaining current customers. It requires a great deal of effort to induce satisfied customers to switch away from their current suppliers.

2. The average company loses 10 percent of its customers each year.

3. A 5 percent reduction in the customer defection rate can increase profits by 25 percent to 85 percent, depending on the industry.

4. The customer profit rate tends to increase over the life of the retained customer.

Figure 5.4 shows the main steps in the process of attracting and keeping customers. The starting point is everyone who might conceivably buy the product or service (*suspects*). From these the company determines the most likely *prospects*, which it hopes to convert into *first-time customers*, and then into *repeat customers*, and then into *clients*—people whom the company treats very specially and knowledgeably. The next challenge is to turn clients into *members* by starting a membership program that offers benefits to customers who join, and then into *advocates*, customers who enthusiastically recommend the company and its products and services to others. The ultimate challenge is to turn advocates into *partners*.

Markets can be characterized by their long-term buying dynamics and how easily and often customers can enter and leave.[59]

1. *Permanent capture markets*. Once a customer, always a customer (e.g., nursing homes and trust funds).

2. *Simple retention markets*. Customers can permanently be lost after each period (e.g., telecom, cable, financial services, other services, subscriptions).

3. *Customer migration markets*. Customers can leave and come back (e.g., catalogues, consumer products, retail, and airlines).

Some customers inevitably become inactive or drop out. The challenge is to reactivate dissatisfied customers through win-back strategies. It is often easier to re-attract ex-customers (because the company knows their names and histories) than to find new ones. The key is to analyze the causes of customer defection through exit interviews and lost customer surveys. The aim is to win back only those customers who have strong profit potential.

Building Loyalty

How much should a company invest in building loyalty so that the costs do not exceed the gains? We need to distinguish five different levels of investment in customer relationship building:

1. *Basic marketing*. The salesperson simply sells the product.

2. *Reactive marketing*. The salesperson sells the product and encourages the customer to call if he or she has questions, comments, or complaints.

3. *Accountable marketing*. The salesperson phones the customer to check whether the product is meeting expectations. The salesperson also asks the customer for any product or service improvement suggestions and any specific disappointments.

4. *Proactive marketing*. The salesperson contacts the customer from time to time with suggestions about improved product uses or new products.

5. *Partnership marketing*. The company works continuously with its large customers to help improve their performance. (General Electric, for example, has stationed engineers at large utilities to help them produce more power.)

Most companies practise only basic marketing when their markets contain many customers and their unit profit margins are small. Whirlpool is not going to phone each washing machine buyer to express appreciation. It may set up a customer hotline. In markets with few customers and high profit margins, most sellers will move toward partnership marketing. Boeing, for example, works closely with American Airlines to design airplanes that fully satisfy American's requirements. As Figure 5.5 shows, the likely level of relationship marketing depends on the number of customers and the profit margin level.

An increasingly essential ingredient for the best relationship marketing today is the right technology. Table 5.2 highlights five imperatives of CRM and where technology fits in. GE Plastics could not target its e-mail effectively to different customers if it were not for advances in database software. Dell Computer could not customize computer ordering for its global corporate customers without advances in Web technology. Companies are using e-mail, Web sites, call centres, databases, and database software to foster continuous contact between company and customer. Here is how one company used technology to build customer value:

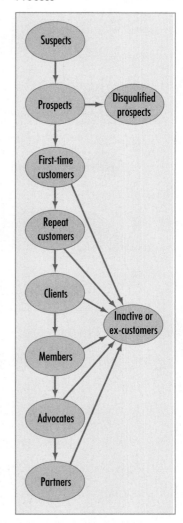

FIGURE 5.4

The Customer Development Process

Source: See Jill Griffin, *Customer Loyalty: How to Earn It, How to Keep It* (New York: Lexington Books, 1995), p. 36. Also see Murray Raphel and Neil Raphel, *Up the Loyalty Ladder: Turning Sometime Customers into Full-Time Advocates of Your Business* (New York: HarperBusiness, 1995).

FIGURE 5.5

Levels of Relationship
Marketing

	High Margin	Medium Margin	Low Margin
Many customers/ distributors	Accountable	Reactive	Basic or reactive
Medium number of customers/ distributors	Proactive	Accountable	Reactive
Few customers/ distributors	Partnership	Proactive	Accountable

Grocery Gateway

Grocery Gateway, the online grocery company in Toronto, practises this type of marketing regularly. Receiving surprise gifts via e-mail is a common occurrence for Grocery Gateway customers. The company's marketing policy is to send coupons at customer milestones, such as their 25th or 50th online order, rewarding them with electronic coupons that are redeemable online when they make their next grocery purchase. Sometimes customers will even receive a gift basket full of Grocery Gateway products, customized according to past purchases. The crucial point for Grocery Gateway is that the customer doesn't know what triggers the reward. "There are two mind-sets about marketing," says director of marketing Scott Robinson. "One is fostering an expectation and delivering on it. Then there's the unexpected customer appreciation tactics. We do both. It's a bizarre way of saying thanks a lot for your business, and we really value it."[60]

At the same time, online companies need to make sure their attempts to create relationships with customers don't backfire, as when customers are bombarded by computer-generated recommendations that consistently miss the mark. Buy a lot of baby gifts on Amazon, and your personalized recommendations suddenly don't look so personal. E-tailers need to recognize the limitations of online personalization at the same time that they work harder to find technology and processes that really work.[61]

Online grocer Grocery Gateway provides customers with free gifts at key milestones to build loyalty.

TABLE 5.2	BREAKING DOWN CUSTOMER RELATIONSHIP MANAGEMENT: WHAT CUSTOMER RELATIONSHIP MANAGEMENT REALLY COMPRISES			
CRM Imperative				
Acquiring the right customer	Crafting the right value proposition	Instituting the best processes	Motivating employees	Learning to retain customers
You Get It When . . .				
■ You've identified your most valuable customers. ■ You've calculated your share of their wallet for your goods and services.	■ You've studied what products or services your customers need today and will need tomorrow. ■ You've surveyed what products or services your competitors offer today and will offer tomorrow. ■ You've spotted what products or services you should be offering.	■ You've researched the best way to deliver your products or services to customers, including the alliances you need to strike, the technologies you need to invest in, and the service capabilities you need to develop or acquire.	■ You know what tools your employees need to foster customer relationships. ■ You've identified the HR systems you need to institute in order to boost employee loyalty.	■ You've learned why customers defect and how to win them back. ■ You've analyzed what your competitors are doing to win your high-value customers. ■ Your senior management monitors customer-defection metrics.
CRM Technology Can Help . . .				
■ Analyze customer revenue and cost data to identify current and future high-value customers. ■ Target your direct-marketing efforts better.	■ Capture relevant product and service behaviour data. ■ Create new distribution channels. ■ Develop new pricing models. ■ Build communities.	■ Process transactions faster. ■ Provide better information to the front line. ■ Manage logistics and the supply chain more efficiently. ■ Catalyze collaborative commerce.	■ Align incentives and metrics. ■ Deploy knowledge management systems.	■ Track customer-defection and retention levels. ■ Track customer-service satisfaction levels.

Source: Darrel K. Rigby, Frederick F. Reichheld, and Phil Schefter, *Harvard Business Review* (February 2002): 106.

Companies are also recognizing the importance of the personal component to CRM and what happens once customers make actual contact. As Stanford's business guru Jeffrey Pfeffer puts it, "The best companies build cultures in which front-line people are empowered to do what's needed to take care of the customer." He cites examples of firms like SAS, the Scandinavian airline, which engineered a turnaround in part based on the insight that a customer's impressions of a company are formed through a myriad of small interactions—checking in, boarding the plane, eating a meal, and so on.[62]

Reducing Customer Defection

There are five main steps a company can take to reduce the defection rate.

First, the company must define and measure its retention rate. For a magazine, the renewal rate is a good measure of retention. For a university or college, it could be the first- to second-year retention rate, or the class graduation rate.

Second, the company must distinguish the causes of customer attrition and identify those that can be managed better. (See "Marketing Memo: Asking Questions When Customers Leave.") The Forum Corporation analyzed the customers lost by 14 major companies for reasons other than leaving the region or going out of business: 15 percent switched because they found a better product;

Marketing Memo

Asking Questions When Customers Leave

To create effective retention programs, marketing managers need to identify customer defection patterns. This analysis should start with internal records, such as sales logs, pricing records, and customer survey results. The next step is extending defection research to outside sources, such as benchmarking studies and statistics from trade associations. Some key questions to ask:

1. Do customers defect at different rates during the year?

2. Does retention vary by office, region, sales representative, or distributor?

3. What is the relationship between retention rates and changes in prices?

4. What happens to lost customers, and where do they usually go?

5. What are the retention norms for your industry?

6. Which company in your industry retains customers the longest?

Source: Reprinted from William A. Sherden, "When Customers Leave," *Small Business Reports* (November 1994): 45.

another 15 percent found a cheaper product; and 70 percent left because of poor or little attention from the supplier. Not much can be done about customers who leave the region or go out of business, but much can be done about those who leave because of poor service, shoddy products, or high prices.[63]

Third, the company needs to estimate how much profit it loses when it loses customers. In the case of an individual customer, the lost profit is equal to the customer's lifetime value—that is, the present value of the profit stream that the company would have realized if the customer had not defected prematurely—based on some of the calculations outlined above.

Fourth, the company needs to figure out how much it would cost to reduce the defection rate. As long as the cost is less than the lost profit, the company should spend the money. And finally, nothing beats listening to customers. Some companies have created an ongoing mechanism that keeps senior managers permanently plugged in to front-line customer feedback. MBNA, the credit-card giant, asks every executive to listen in on telephone conversations in the customer service area or customer recovery units. Deere & Company, which makes John Deere tractors and has a superb record of customer loyalty—nearly 98 percent annual retention in some product areas—uses retired employees to interview defectors and customers.[64]

Forming Strong Customer Bonds

"Marketing Memo: Building Strong Customer Bonds" offers some tips in connecting with customers. Berry and Parasuraman have identified three retention-building approaches:[65] adding financial benefits, adding social benefits, and adding structural ties.

ADDING FINANCIAL BENEFITS Two financial benefits that companies can offer are frequency programs and club marketing programs. **Frequency programs (FPs)** are designed to provide rewards to customers who buy frequently and in substantial amounts.[66] Frequency marketing is an acknowledgment of the fact that 20 percent of a company's customers might account for 80 percent of its business. Frequency programs are seen as a way to build long-term loyalty with these customers, potentially creating cross-selling opportunities in the process.

American Airlines was one of the first companies to pioneer a frequency program in the early 1980s, when it decided to offer free mileage credit to its customers. Hotels next adopted FPs, with Marriott taking the lead with its Honored Guest Program, followed by car rental firms. Then credit-card companies began to offer points based on card usage level.

In Canada alone there are many widely recognized reward programs, such as the Zellers "club card"; the Shoppers Optimum card, which allows users to accumulate points to apply toward free goods at Shoppers Drug Mart; the CIBC Aerogold Visa, which allows users to

Marketing Memo

Building Strong Customer Bonds

Companies that want to form strong customer bonds need to attend to the following basics:

- Get cross-departmental participation in planning and managing the customer satisfaction and retention process.

- Integrate the "Voice of the Customer" to capture their stated and unstated needs or requirements in all business decisions.

- Create superior products, services, and experiences for the target market.

- Organize and make accessible a database of information on individual customer needs, preferences, contacts, purchase frequency, and satisfaction.

- Make it easy for customers to reach appropriate company personnel and express their needs, perceptions, and complaints.

- Run award programs recognizing outstanding employees.

accumulate Aeroplan points for Air Canada and Star Alliance flights; the President's Choice Financial Master Card, which allows users to accumulate points to purchase groceries at Loblaws stores; and the HBC Rewards card, which allows users to accumulate points with purchases from the Bay and others. The list goes on and on. According to a 2002 Ipsos-Reid survey, of all Canadian adult credit card holders (80 percent of all adults), 68 percent belong to at least one retail store reward program, and between 40 and 60 percent of such users have at some point redeemed their points for rewards. And according to J. C. Williams Group, the average Canadian belongs to 4.5 different loyalty programs.[67]

Typically, the first company to introduce an FP gains the most benefit, especially if competitors are slow to respond. After competitors respond, FPs can become a financial burden to all the offering companies, but some companies are more efficient and creative in managing an FP. For example, airlines run tiered loyalty programs in which they offer different levels of rewards to different travellers (e.g., Aeroplan Prestige, Aeroplan Elite, Aeroplan Super-Elite). They may offer one frequent-flyer mile for every mile flown to occasional travellers and two frequent-flyer miles for every mile flown to top customers.

Many companies have created club membership programs. Club membership can be open to everyone who purchases a product or service, or it can be limited to an affinity group or to those willing to pay a small fee. Although open clubs are good for building a database or snagging customers from competitors, limited membership clubs are more powerful long-term loyalty builders. Fees and membership conditions prevent those with only a fleeting interest in a company's products from joining. These clubs attract and keep those customers who are responsible for the largest portion of business. Some highly successful clubs include the following:

Apple

Apple encourages owners of its computers to form local Apple-user groups. By 2001, there were over 600 groups ranging in size from fewer than 25 members to over 1000 members. Today, you can find user groups in almost every country around the world. The user groups provide Apple owners with opportunities to learn more about their computers, share ideas, and get product discounts. They sponsor special activities and events and perform community service. A visit to Apple's Web site will help a customer find a nearby user group.[68]

Harley-Davidson

The world-famous motorcycle company sponsors the Harley Owners Group (H.O.G.), which now numbers 650 000 members in over 1200 chapters. The first-time buyer of a Harley-Davidson motorcycle gets a free one-year membership. H.O.G. benefits include a magazine called *Hog Tales*, a touring handbook, emergency road service, a specially designed insurance program, theft reward service, discount hotel rates, and a Fly & Ride program enabling members to rent Harleys while on vacation. The company also maintains an extensive Web site devoted to H.O.G., which includes information on club chapters, events, and a special members-only section.[69]

ADDING SOCIAL BENEFITS Company personnel work on cementing social bonds with customers by individualizing and personalizing customer relationships. In essence, thoughtful companies turn their customers into clients. Donnelly, Berry, and Thompson draw this distinction:

> Customers may be nameless to the institution; clients cannot be nameless. Customers are served as part of the mass or as part of larger segments; clients are served on an individual basis. Customers are served by anyone who happens to be available; clients are served by the professional assigned to them.[70]

E-commerce companies looking to attract and retain customers are discovering that personalization goes beyond creating customized information.[71] For example, the Lands' End Live Web site offers visitors the opportunity to talk with a customer service representative. Nordstrom takes a similar approach with its Web site to ensure that online buyers are as satisfied with the company's cus-

Member of the Westsachsen, Germany, chapter of an H.O.G. club at a gathering in Hamburg to celebrate Harley-Davidson's 100th anniversary. Harley-Davidson uses its Web site to run one of the most successful club membership programs.

tomer service as the in-store visitors; and, with the click of a button, Eddie Bauer's e-commerce site connects shoppers to customer service representatives with a text-based chat feature.

A 2001 survey of 3500 Web shoppers found that 77 percent of online shoppers have at least once selected an item for purchase but failed to complete the transaction.[72] Jupiter Media Metrix has reported that two-thirds of Web shoppers abandon shopping carts.[73] Worse, only 1.8 percent of visits to online retailers lead to sales, compared with 5 percent of visits to department stores. Analysts attribute this behaviour partly to a general absence of interactive customer service in e-commerce. Customers looking for help are often sent to a text help file rather than a live sales representative.

Veseys

Prince Edward Island–based Veseys has over 60 years of experience providing goods, services, and advice to Canadian gardeners. To ensure that its customers will receive seeds and plants that will flourish in Canada's harsh conditions and short growing season, Veseys' flower and vegetable seed varieties undergo extensive trial gardening at the Veseys Research Farm. Today's operation has long outgrown the one room of his home Arthur Vesey used to start his seed business. Now customers can order products through its catalogues by calling its toll-free number or by ordering from its Web site. Veseys works to personalize its Web offerings by showing photos of the service team that stands behind the company's products and by clearly posting contact information where customers can reach a Veseys service person should they need a more personal touch.[74]

Not all customer service features involve live personnel. Both Macys.com and gap.com offer pre-recorded customer service information. Gap's Web site includes a "zoom" feature, which shoppers can use to get a close look at every detail of a garment, from elastic waistbands to fabric prints. Lands' End Live allows customers to "try on" clothes online using virtual models based on measurements supplied by customers.

ADDING STRUCTURAL TIES   The company may supply customers with special equipment or computer links that help customers manage orders, payroll, and inventory. A good example is McKesson Corporation, a leading pharmaceutical wholesaler, which invested millions of dollars in EDI capabilities to help independent pharmacies manage inventory, order-entry processes, and shelf space. Another example is Milliken & Company, which provides proprietary software programs, marketing research, sales training, and sales leads to loyal customers.

Lester Wunderman, an astute observer of contemporary marketing, thinks talk about "loyalizing" customers misses the point.[75] People can be loyal to country, family, and beliefs, but less so to their toothpaste, soap, or even beer. The marketer's aim should be to increase the consumer's *proclivity to repurchase* the company's brand. Here are his suggestions for creating structural ties with the customer:

1. *Create long-term contracts.* A newspaper subscription replaces the need to buy a newspaper each day. A 20-year mortgage replaces the need to re-borrow the money each year. A home heating oil agreement assures continuous delivery without renewing the order.

2. *Charge a lower price to consumers who buy larger supplies.* Offer lower prices to people who agree to be supplied regularly with a certain brand of toothpaste, detergent, or beer.

3. *Turn the product into a long-term service.* DaimlerChrysler is considering selling miles of reliable transportation instead of cars, with the consumer able to order different cars at different times, such as a station wagon for shopping and a convertible for the weekend. Gaines, the dog food company, could offer a Pet Care service that includes kennels, insurance, and veterinary care along with food.

Customer Databases and Database Marketing

Marketers must know their customers. And in order to know the customer, the company must collect information, store it in a database, and do database marketing. A **customer database** is an organized collection of comprehensive information about individual customers or prospects that is current, accessible, and actionable for such marketing purposes as lead generation, lead qualification, sale of a product or service, or maintenance of customer relationships. **Database marketing** is the process of building, maintaining, and using customer databases and other databases (products, suppliers, resellers) for the purpose of contacting, transacting, and building customer relationships.

Customer Databases

As the former chief marketing officer of Amazon liked to point out, when you walk through the door of a department store, the retailer has no idea who you are. When you log on to Amazon, however, you are greeted by name, presented a customized set of product purchase suggestions based on your past purchase choices, and offered an accompanying series of frank customer reviews. As you log off the site, you are also asked permission to be e-mailed special offers.[76]

Many companies confuse a customer mailing list with a customer database. A **customer mailing list** is simply a set of names, addresses, and telephone numbers. A customer database contains much more information, accumulated through customer transactions, registration information, telephone queries, cookies, and every customer contact.

Ideally, a customer database contains the consumer's past purchases, demographics (age, income, family members, birthdays), psychographics (activities, interests, and opinions), mediagraphics (preferred media), and other useful information. The catalogue company Fingerhut possesses some 1400 pieces of information about each of the 30 million households in its massive customer database. And the Royal Bank of Canada has individual data on its 9 million customers and is able to model the lifetime value of individual customers, their potential interest in different offerings, and their vulnerability to attrition.

Ideally, a **business database** would contain business customers' past purchases; past volumes, prices, and profits; buyer team member names (and ages, birthdays, hobbies, and favourite foods); status of current contracts; an estimate of the supplier's share of the customer's business; competitive suppliers; assessment of competitive strengths and weaknesses in selling and servicing the account; and relevant buying practices, patterns, and policies. For example, a Latin American unit of the Swiss pharmaceutical firm Novartis keeps data on 100 000 of Argentina's farmers, knows their crop protection chemical purchases, groups them by value, and treats each group differently.

Figure 5.6 displays a method for selectively gaining greater share of a customer's business, based on the presumption that the firm has gained a deep understanding of the customer.

Data Warehouses and Datamining[77]

Savvy companies are capturing information every time a customer comes into contact with any of its departments. Touch points include a customer purchase, a customer-requested service call, an online query, or a mail-in rebate card. Banks and credit-card companies, telephone companies, catalogue marketers, and many other companies have a great deal of information about their customers, including not only addresses and phone numbers, but also their transactions and enhanced data on age, family size, income, and other demographic information.

FIGURE 5.6

Increasing Customer Share of
Requirements

Source: James C. Anderson and
James A. Narus, *MIT Sloan
Management Review* (Spring 2003):
45.

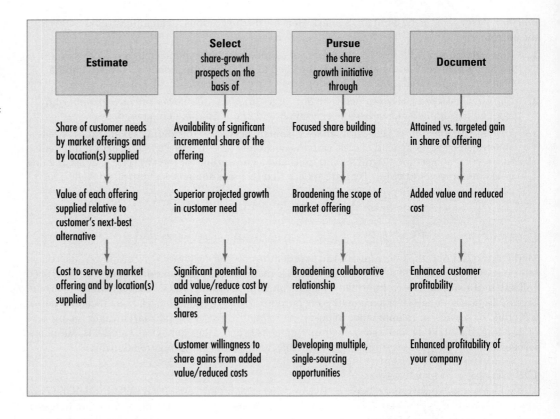

These data are collected by the company's contact centre and organized into a **data warehouse**. Company personnel can capture, query, and analyze the data. Inferences can be drawn about an individual customer's needs and responses. Telemarketers can respond to customer inquiries based on a total picture of the customer relationship.

Through **datamining**, marketing statisticians can extract useful information about individuals, trends, and segments from the mass of data. Datamining involves the use of sophisticated statistical and mathematical techniques such as cluster analysis, automatic interaction detection, predictive modelling, and neural networking.[78] Some observers believe that a proprietary database can provide a company with a significant competitive advantage. As such, a company that wants to learn the most from its database needs to engage the services of a person or company skilled in datamining. (See Figure 5.7 for examples of companies that use datamining.)

USING THE DATABASE   In general, companies can use their databases in five ways:

1. *To identify prospects.* Many companies generate sales leads by advertising their product or service. The ads generally contain a response feature, such as a business reply card or toll-free phone number. The database is built from these responses. The company sorts through the database to identify the best prospects, and then contacts them by mail, phone, or personal call in an attempt to convert them into customers.

2. *To decide which customers should receive a particular offer.* Companies are interested in selling, up-selling, and cross-selling their products and services. Companies set up criteria describing the ideal target customer for a particular offer. Then they search their customer databases for those who most closely resemble the ideal type.

3. *To deepen customer loyalty.* Companies can build interest and enthusiasm by remembering customer preferences, and by sending appropriate gifts, discount coupons, and interesting reading material.

4. *To reactivate customer purchases.* Companies can install automatic mailing programs (automatic marketing) that send out birthday or anniversary cards, Christmas shopping reminders, or off-season promotions. The database can help the company make attractive or timely offers.

Foster Parents Plan of Canada Toronto-based Foster Parents Plan of Canada (FPP) recently began combining market research with information from its own database to help it predict whether a foster parent will continue his or her support of the organization. Having this information not only allows the nonprofit organization to better understand the financial risks it faces, it also enables it to take the appropriate actions to try to retain donors. To build predictive profiles that differentiate between committed versus uncommitted people required analysis of a large sample of over 5000 people. The analysis, however, revealed key predictors of commitment and allowed FPP to tag people in its database accordingly.

Royal Caribbean Royal Caribbean uses its database to offer spur-of-the-moment cruise packages to fill all the berths on its ships. It focuses on retired people and single people because they are more able to make quick commitments. Fewer empty berths mean maximized profits for the cruise line.

Mars Mars is a market leader not only in candy, but also in pet food. In Germany, Mars has compiled the names of virtually every cat-owning German family by contacting veterinarians and also advertising a free booklet titled "How to Take Care of Your Cat." Those who request the booklet fill out a questionnaire, so Mars knows the cat's name, age, and birthday. Mars now sends a birthday card to each cat each year, along with a new-cat-food sample or money-saving coupons for Mars brands. Do the cat owners appreciate this? You bet!

American Express It is no wonder that, at its secret location in Phoenix, security guards watch over American Express's 500 billion bytes of data on how its customers have used the company's 35 million green, gold, and platinum charge cards. Amex uses the database to include precisely targeted offers in its monthly mailing of millions of customer bills.

Qwest Twice a year Qwest sifts through its customer list looking for customers that have the potential to be more profitable. The company's database contains as many as 200 observations about each customer's calling patterns. By looking at demographic profiles, plus the mix of local versus long-distance calls or whether a consumer has voice mail, Qwest can estimate potential spending. Next, the company determines how much of the customer's likely telecom budget is already coming its way. Armed with that knowledge, Qwest sets a cut-off point for how much to spend marketing to this customer.

FIGURE 5.7

Examples of Database Marketing

5. *To avoid serious customer mistakes.* A major bank confessed to a number of mistakes that it had made by not using its customer database well. In one case, the bank charged a customer a penalty for late payment on his mortgage, failing to note that he headed a company that was a major depositor in this bank. He quit the bank. In a second case, two different staff members of the bank phoned the same mortgage customer offering a home equity loan at different prices. Neither knew that the other had made the call. In a third case, a bank gave a premium customer only standard service in another country.

The Downside of Database Marketing and CRM

Four problems can deter a firm from effectively using CRM. The first is that building and maintaining a customer database requires a large investment in computer hardware, database software, analytical programs, communication links, and skilled personnel. It is difficult to collect the right data, especially to capture all the occasions of company interaction with individual customers. Building a customer database would not be worthwhile in the following cases: (1) where the product is a once-in-a-lifetime purchase (e.g., a grand piano), (2) where customers show little loyalty to a brand (i.e., there is lots of customer churn), (3) where the unit sale is very small (e.g., a chocolate bar), and (4) where the cost of gathering information is too high.

The second problem is the difficulty of getting everyone in the company to be customer-oriented and to use the available information. Employees find it far easier to carry on traditional transaction marketing than to practise customer relationship marketing. Effective database marketing requires managing and training employees as well as dealers and suppliers.

The third problem is that not all customers want a relationship with the company, and they may resent knowing that the company has collected that much personal information about them. Marketers must be concerned about customer attitudes toward privacy and security. American Express, long regarded as a leader on privacy issues, does not sell information on specific customer transactions. However, American Express found itself the target of consumer outrage when it announced a partnership with KnowledgeBase Marketing, Inc., that would have made data on 175 million people available to any merchant who accepts American Express cards. American Express killed the partnership. AOL, also targeted by privacy advocates, junked a plan to sell subscribers' telephone numbers.

Online companies would be smart to explain their privacy policies and to give consumers the right not to have their information stored in a database. RBC Financial Group, Canada's largest financial institution, has been a forerunner in this regard; it implemented a privacy code in 1987.

Around the world, privacy legislation has gone in a number of different directions. European countries, for example, do not look favourably upon database marketing. In 1995, the European Union issued a Directive on the Protection of Personal Data that lays down strict guidelines about what information can be collected and how it can be used and transferred. Predictably, the United States and Canada have responded to the privacy issue very differently. While the United States opted for industry self-regulation, Canadian federal and provincial governments believed more controls were needed. Until recently, Quebec was the only province with legislation dealing with the privacy of personal information. Then, on January 1, 2001, the Personal Information Protection and Electronic Documents Act came into effect and companies had until January 1, 2004, to comply (see the Privacy Commissioner of Canada Web site at **www.privcom.gc.ca**). The act is based on four key principles:

- *Consumer knowledge and consent.* Consumers must know that information about them is being gathered and they must provide consent before firms can collect, use, or disclose consumers' personal information.

- *Limitations.* Firms can only collect and use information appropriate to the transaction being undertaken. For example, if a firm needs to mail you something, it can ask for your home address, but it may not request additional information unrelated to this task.

- *Accuracy.* Firms must be sure that the information they gather is recorded accurately. Firms must appoint a privacy officer to be responsible for this task. For example, to comply with this portion of the legislation, Peter Cullen was designated as the corporate privacy officer at the Royal Bank of Canada.

- *Right to access.* Finally, individuals have the right to know what information is being held about them. They can also demand that errors in their personal information be corrected and they may request that their personal information be withdrawn from a firm's database.

A fourth problem is that the assumptions behind CRM may not always hold true.[79] For example, it may not be the case that it costs less to serve more loyal customers. High-volume customers often know their value to a company and can leverage it to extract premium service and/or price discounts. Loyal customers may expect and demand more from the firm and resent any attempt by the firm to receive full or higher prices. They may also be jealous of attention lavished on other customers. When eBay began to chase big corporate customers such as IBM, Disney, and Sears, some small mom-and-pop businesses who helped to build the brand felt abandoned.[80] Loyal customers may not necessarily be the best ambassadors for the brand. One study found that customers who scored high on behavioural loyalty and bought a lot of a company's products were less active word-of-mouth marketers to others than customers who scored high on attitudinal loyalty and expressed greater commitment to the firm.

Thus, the benefits of database marketing do not come without heavy costs, not only in collecting the original customer data, but also in maintaining them and mining them. Yet, when it works, a data warehouse yields more than it costs. A 1996 study by DWI estimated that the average return on investment for a data warehouse over the course of three years is more than 400 percent, but the data have to be in good condition, and the discovered relationships must be valid. Consider the following case where database marketing went awry:

British Columbia Telecom

This company decided to invite 100 of its best customers to a Vancouver Grizzlies basketball game and selected customers who were heavy 900-number users. The invitations were already at the printer when the marketing staff discovered that heavy 900-number users included sex-line enthusiasts. They quickly added other criteria to search for a revised list of guests. It turns out that database marketing is not for everyone.

Database marketing is most frequently used by business marketers and service providers (hotels, banks, airlines, and insurance, credit card, and telephone companies) that normally and easily collect a lot of customer data. Other types of companies that are in the best position to invest in

This Enterprise Rent-A-Car ad focuses on CRM: "There's a place where the number one priority is you."

CRM are companies that do a lot of cross-selling and up-selling (e.g., GE and Amazon) or companies whose customers have highly differentiated needs and are of highly differentiated value to the company. It is used less often by packaged-goods retailers and consumer packaged-goods companies, though some companies (Kraft, Quaker Oats, Ralston Purina, and Nabisco) have built databases for certain brands. Businesses where the CLV is low, who have high churn, and where there is no direct contact between the seller and ultimate buyer may not benefit as much from CRM. Some businesses cited as CRM successes include Enterprise Rent-A-Car, Fidelity Investments, Lexus, and Capital One.[81]

Deloitte Consulting reported in 1999 that 70 percent of firms found little or no improvement through CRM implementation. The reasons are many: The system was poorly designed, it became too expensive, users didn't make much use of it or report much benefit, and collaborators ignored the system. One set of business commentators suggested the following as the four main perils of CRM:[82]

1.   Implementing CRM before creating a customer strategy.

2.   Rolling out CRM before changing organization to match.

3.   Assuming more CRM technology is better.

4.   Stalking, not wooing, customers.

All this points to the need for each company to determine how much to invest in building and using database marketing to conduct its customer relationships. "Marketing Insight: Succeeding at CRM" provides some best practice guidelines.

MARKETING INSIGHT

Succeeding at CRM

Based on a comprehensive survey of leading companies, Wharton's George Day concludes that superior CRM performance comes from integrating three components of the customer-relating capability: an organizational orientation that makes customer retention a priority and gives employees wide latitude to satisfy customers; information about relationships, including the quality of relevant customer data and the systems for sharing this information across the firm; and configuration, the alignment of the organization toward building customer relationships, achieved through incentives, metrics, organization structure, and accountabilities.

Configuration was the factor that most separated good firms from bad firms. Day observed that relatively few businesses in the survey emphasized customer satisfaction and retention in their incentives. An exception was Siebel Systems, which tied 50 percent of management's incentive compensation and 25 percent of salespeople's compensation to measures of customer satisfaction. The real payoff, he notes, is when all the elements of a configuration—metrics, incentives, and structures—are properly aligned, citing General Electric Aircraft Engine Business Group's attempts to improve service for their jet engine customers. A study of customer needs led GE to assign a corporate vice-president to each of the top 50 customers, putting leaders of their quality program on site with customers, using the Internet to personalize delivery of parts, and incorporating customer service metrics into employee evaluation criteria.

Day also found that information was less important than orientation and configuration in distinguishing leaders from followers. He concluded that big investments in CRM technology were yielding negligible competitive advantages. He also concluded that one of the reasons many CRM failures occur is that companies concentrate on customer contact processes without making corresponding changes in internal structures and systems. His recommendation? Change the configuration before installing CRM: "Our survey results confirm that a superior customer relating capability has everything to do with how a business builds and manages its organization and not much to do with the CRM tools and technologies it employs."

Sources: George S. Day, "Creating a Superior Customer-Relating Capability," *Sloan Management Review*, 44, no. 3 (2003): 77–82; George S. Day, "Creating a Superior Customer-Relating Capability," *MSI Report No. 03-101*, Marketing Science Institute, Cambridge, MA; "Why Some Companies Succeed at CRM (and Many Fail)," *Knowledge at Wharton*, **http://knowledge.wharton.upenn.edu**, January 15, 2003.

SUMMARY

1. Customers are value-maximizers. They form an expectation of value and act on it. Buyers will buy from the firm that they perceive to offer the highest customer-delivered value, defined as the difference between total customer value and total customer cost.

2. A buyer's satisfaction is a function of the product's perceived performance and the buyer's expectations. Recognizing that high satisfaction leads to high customer loyalty, many companies today are aiming for TCS—total customer satisfaction. For such companies, customer satisfaction is both a goal and a marketing tool.

3. Losing profitable customers can dramatically affect a firm's profits. The cost of attracting a new customer is estimated to be five times the cost of keeping a current customer happy. The key to retaining customers is relationship marketing.

4. Quality is the totality of features and characteristics of a product or service that bear on its ability to satisfy stated or implied needs. Today's companies have no choice but to implement total quality management programs if they are to remain solvent and profitable.

5. Marketing managers have two responsibilities in a quality-centred company. First, they must participate in formulating strategies and policies designed to help the company win through total quality excellence. Second, they must deliver marketing quality alongside production quality.

6. Companies are also becoming skilled in customer relationship management (CRM), which focuses on meeting the individual needs of valued customers. The skill requires building a customer database and doing data-mining to detect trends, segments, and individual needs.

APPLICATIONS

Marketing Debate: Online versus Offline Privacy?

As more and more firms practise relationship marketing and develop customer databases, privacy issues are emerging as an important topic. Consumers and public interest groups are scrutinizing—and sometimes criticizing—the privacy policies of firms. Concerns are also being raised about potential theft of online credit-card information or other potentially sensitive or confidential financial information. Others maintain that the online privacy fears are unfounded and that security issues are every bit as much a concern in the offline world. They argue that the opportunity to steal information exists virtually everywhere and that it is up to the consumer to protect his or her interests.

Take a position: (1) Privacy is a bigger issue in the online world than the offline world versus Privacy is no different online than offline. (2) Consumers on the whole receive more benefit than risk from marketers knowing their personal information.

Marketing Discussion

Consider the lifetime value of customers (CLV). Choose a business and show how you would go about developing a quantitative formulation that captures the concept. How would organizations change if they totally embraced the customer equity concept and maximized CLV?

Marketing Spotlight: Dell

"We have a tremendously clear business model," says Michael Dell. "There's no confusion about what the value proposition is, what the company offers, and why it's great for customers." Dell is now the number-one computer systems company.

Dell is extremely responsive. Buyers go on Dell's Web site and design their own computer. They give their payment authorization, which means that Dell receives the money in advance and can use the funds to pay for the supplies needed to build the computer. Because its computers are built-to-order, Dell carries an industry-leading four days of inventory. It takes delivery of components just minutes before they are needed. At its Austin, Texas, factories, a Dell System can in some cases be built, have the software installed, be tested, and be packed in eight hours. Dell's costs are lower, allowing it to price its computers lower than competitors' prices if it wishes.

Yet speed is only one part of the Dell equation. Service is the other. In fact, it was through veering away from its successful business model that Dell discovered the importance of customer service. In 1993, the company began trying to sell to retailers, mainly because everyone else was. Customers were disgruntled because of poor retail service. Dell ultimately abandoned the retail channel.

Most important, Michael Dell decided that "there would be more things we'd have to do besides build a PC." He knew his company had two kinds of customers, corporate and consumer. Whereas the consumer would buy mainly because of price, the corporate buyer needed a carefully developed relationship. Like most successful companies, Dell put the most resources into building relationships with its most profitable customers.

Corporate customers make up about 80 percent of Dell's business, and the company manages its corporate accounts with a top-notch sales team. Dell also installs custom software and keeps track of business customers' inventory for them. Through the use of Premier Dell.com, customized customer Web pages at the Dell site, the company has created a 24-hour order-entry system. Big customers can click on the site to see all kinds of information about their preferences and needs. The site can be accessed worldwide by any company subsidiary; and employees, not just purchasing agents, can use the Premier Dell.com to purchase computers according to an automated policy. "It's the ultimate network," Michael Dell says, "and a fabulous way for us to interact with our customers."

The normal practice of companies is to "build to stock." This is a guessing game that companies often lose by building too much or too little. In the auto industry, cars will sit unsold in dealers' lots for 60 days, tying up working capital. Why have auto and other companies not moved from the inefficient "build to stock" model of production to Dell's "build to order" model? Auto manufacturers have invited Michael Dell to speak to them on several occasions. The consensus seems to be that Dell works with 50 main suppliers to put together a $1000 PC, but a car manufacturer may have to work with 900 suppliers to put together a $20 000 car. In addition to the technical challenge, the auto industry faces dealer and legislative hurdles.

DISCUSSION QUESTIONS

1. What have been the key success factors for Dell?

2. Where is Dell vulnerable? What should it watch out for?

3. What recommendations would you make to senior marketing executives going forward? What should they be sure to do with its marketing?

Sources: Michele Marchetti, "Dell Computer," *Sales & Marketing Management* (October 1997): 50–53; Evan Ramstad, "Dell Fights PC Wars by Emphasizing Customer Service—Focus Wins Big Clients and Gives IBM and Compaq a Run for Their Money," *Wall Street Journal*, August 15, 1997, p. B4; Saroja Girishankar, "Dell's Site Has Business in Crosshairs," *Internetweek*, April 13, 1998, p. 1; "The Internetweek Interview—Michael Dell, Chairman and CEO, Dell Computer," *Internetweek*, April 13, 1998, p. 8; Dale Buss, "Custom Cars Stuck in Gridlock," *The Industry Standard*, October 23, 2000, pp. 90–97; "A Revolution of One," *The Economist*, April 14, 2001; Betsy Morris, "Can Michael Dell Escape the Box?" *Fortune*, October 16, 2000; Gary McWilliams, "Dell Computer Has a Midlife Crisis," *Wall Street Journal*, August 31, 2000; "Dell Increases Its Market Share as PC Sales Slow," *New York Times*, January 22, 2001; Leah Beth Ward, "Dell Sales Overtake Compaq," *Dallas Morning News*, January 24, 2000.

6

- How do consumer characteristics influence buying behaviour?

- What major psychological processes influence consumer responses to the marketing program?

- How do consumers make purchasing decisions?

- How do marketers analyze consumer decision making?

6

CHAPTER 6

Analyzing Consumer Markets

PROFILE: CANADIAN MARKETING EXCELLENCE

BMW Group Canada, based in Whitby, Ontario, is responsible for the distribution of BMW luxury performance automobiles, sports activity vehicles, motorcycles, and the 2003 North American Car of the Year—the MINI. The company itself and its network of 36 independent BMW retail centres, 17 independent BMW motorcycle retailers, and 17 MINI retailers work tirelessly to build strong relationships with current and potential customers. Strong marketing programs designed to build and sustain relationships, along with the firm's ability to create exciting, high-performance products, are at the core of BMW Group's considerable success. In January 2005, BMW Group Canada reported a 6.6 percent increase in sales from a year earlier. This is its fourteenth consecutive year of increasing sales.

The new president of BMW Canada, Lindsay Duffield, has a passion not just for BMWs, but also for marketing. He's been credited with turning BMW's Canadian subsidiary into a force to be reckoned with, not just in the Canadian automotive market, but also within the international firm itself. BMW is one of those companies where the CEO is also the CBO—the chief branding officer. Each and every day he tries to exemplify the values that run through the minds of all BMW drivers: passion and joy. In fact, "joy" is the core of all BMW's global marketing efforts. Each subsidiary takes that single word and then interprets it for all communications within its individual market. In the United States, joy translates into "The Ultimate Driving Machine." In Canada, it becomes "The Ultimate Driving Experience."

BMW dominates the luxury segment in Canada, which represents 8.1 percent of the total passenger vehicle market. Although BMW Group Canada's sales have been increasing, it still accounts for only 1.4 percent of the total Canadian automotive market. The company has lofty ambitions and BMW Canada wants to become the same force it is in some other international marketplaces. In South Africa, for example, the firm commands 10 percent of the market.

One way to achieve this goal is to tailor the selection of BMW products specifically to the needs of the Canadian marketplace. The company will put more emphasis on products like its X5 sports activity vehicle. "We do not call them SUVs, [and] we don't use the word 'truck.' We are building the ultimate driving machine, definitely not a truck." Moreover, Canadians can go to the company's Web site and quickly discover how they can tailor a BMW vehicle specifically to their own needs and passions.

The next element of BMW Canada's strategy was to revamp the dealer network. In the automotive industry, a successful market presence depends, to a large degree, on the quality of the retail outlets. Not only did the new president want to bring each of the dealerships in line with BMW's sales goals, he knew it was essential that every retailer reflect the style and the attitude that characterizes BMW worldwide. BMW dealerships, whether in uptown Toronto or downtown Sydney, Australia, are expected to have a distinct corporate identity created by using strong shades of grey, silver, and white, extensive use of glass, and lots of natural light. This blend of design elements creates a modern air aligned with BMW's culture. But Canadian dealers hadn't kept up with this image-building effort, and investments of more than $150 million had to be made to transform Canadian dealerships into the experience-creating venues that were essential to the building of the BMW brand.

BMW prides itself in being innovative not only when it comes to the development of new vehicles, but also when it comes to marketing and building customer experiences. Customer insight and innovation are essential since BMW has more limited marketing resources than the huge players that dominate the North American automotive industry. Thus, in recent years, BMW has used an increasing number of nontraditional, but highly effective, communication techniques. For example, it orchestrated a high-profile product placement in the James Bond film *GoldenEye*. In 2000, it created BMWFilms, which the company distributed through the Internet (see www.bmwfilms.com). In each of the series of eight films, different models of cars share the starring role with a "driver" who is the central character in the films. The films were a hit with a younger demographic of potential consumers. As one of millions of visitors to the site noted, "What a great way to market a great line of automobiles. I have been captivated by not only the films but also the vehicles."

BMW Canada also knows that timing is important when it comes to customer relationship building and maintenance. The company is a master at approaching consumers at the point when they are ready to buy. Kelly Lam, manager of customer relationship marketing, says the company targets "hand-raisers"—customers who express interest in a particular BMW product—and then approaches them with information and/or offers via direct mail or e-mail. "The last thing we want to do is mass market to everybody," says Lam.

One way BMW Group Canada finds prospective customers is by setting up information kiosks at events such as Formula One racing or the Rogers AT&T Cup tennis tournament, which had a booth showing off the new X3 vehicle. The kiosks allow prospective customers to leave their personal information so that, with their permission, BMW can follow up with paced informational campaigns aimed specifically at the customers' expressed interests. Lam adds that these campaigns are not just for prospective customers, but for current customers as well, in order to encourage loyalty and ongoing interest in new product introductions.

Finally, to further improve customers' experience with BMW, the company launched its Fascination Driver Training in Canada in 2003. As a world leader in automotive safety and driver education, BMW now offers Canadian drivers a series of courses and the unique opportunity to learn from highly qualified BMW instructors, whether they own a BMW or other make of vehicle. Through all of these integrated efforts, BMW Group Canada is hoping that more and more Canadians will get behind the wheel of a new 7-series, X5, or Z4.

When customers pull away from the retailer's lot and step on the throttle, Lindsay Duffield and his colleagues know they'll never again have to ask what "joy" is.

Sources: Paul Ferriss, "BMW's Ultimate Driver," *Marketing Magazine*, September 15, 2003; Kristen Vinakmens, "Timing Is Everything," *Strategy Magazine*, September 8, 2003; BMW Group Canada, **www.bmw.ca** (viewed October 15, 2004); Youngme Moon, "BMWFilms," Harvard Business School case #9-502-046, December 19, 2002; "BMW Group Canada achieves all-time best January sales," BMW Press Release, February 4, 2005.

The aim of marketing is to meet and satisfy target customers' needs and wants better than competitors. **Consumer behaviour** is the study of how individuals, groups, and organizations select, buy, use, and dispose of goods, services, ideas, or experiences to satisfy their needs and wants. Studying consumers provides clues for improving or introducing products or services, setting prices, devising channels, crafting messages, and developing other marketing activities. Marketers are always looking for emerging trends that suggest new marketing opportunities. The metrosexual is one:

> In the summer of 2003, some marketing pundits proclaimed the existence of a new male market—the "metrosexual"—which was defined as straight urban men who enjoy such things as shopping and using grooming products and services. English soccer star David Beckham, with his carefully crafted fashion look, has been touted as the quintessential metrosexual icon. He's not afraid to wear either nail polish or sarongs (off the field, that is). One researcher estimated that 30 to 35 percent of young North American men exhibited metrosexual tendencies, as evidenced in part by their purchase of products such as skin-care cream and fragrances. Another study found "an emerging wave of men who chafe against the restrictions of traditional male roles and do what they want, buy what they want, enjoy what they want—regardless of whether some people might consider them unmanly." The emergence of this market has been a boon for men's grooming products, fuelling the success of brands such as Unilever's Axe, a fragrant all-over body spray, The Body Shop's "For Men" line, and U.K. drugstore chain Boots' newly opened Men's Zones.[1]

Successful marketing requires that companies fully connect with their customers. Adopting a holistic marketing orientation means understanding consumers—gaining a 360-degree view of both their daily lives and the changes that occur during their lifetimes. Gaining a thorough, in-depth consumer understanding helps to make sure that the right products are marketed to the right consumers in the right way. This chapter explores individual consumer buying dynamics; the next chapter explores the buying dynamics of business buyers.

British soccer star David Beckham is as well known for his style as he is for his playing.

What Influences Consumer Behaviour?

Marketers must fully understand both the theory and reality of consumer behaviour. Table 6.1 includes some interesting facts about Canadian consumption expenditures, and "Marketing Insight: A Maturing Market" describes the maturing marketplace in Canada and potential implications for marketing.

A consumer's buying behaviour is influenced by cultural, social, and personal factors. Cultural factors exert the broadest and deepest influence.

Cultural Factors

Culture, subculture, and social class are particularly important influences on consumer buying behaviour. **Culture** is the fundamental determinant of a person's wants and behaviour. The growing child acquires a set of values, perceptions, preferences, and behaviours through his or her family and other key institutions. A child growing up in Canada is exposed to the following values: respect for diversity, respect for basic human rights and individual freedoms (e.g., freedom of speech, freedom of religion, and the right to be equal before and under the law), love of the outdoors and nature, achievement and success, activity, efficiency and practicality, progress, material comfort and external comfort, humanitarianism, and youthfulness.[2]

The culturally based, shared understanding of certain symbols can provide marketers with powerful communication tools. Savvy marketers are using such Canadian icons as the Canadian flag, Canadian wildlife, and Mounties to help tie their products to the sense of pride many Canadians take in their country and its products. Companies such as Roots, Petro Canada, Molson, Tim Hortons, and Air Canada follow this practice.[3]

Each culture consists of smaller **subcultures** that provide more specific identification and socialization for their members. Subcultures include nationalities, religions, racial groups, and geographic regions. When subcultures grow large and affluent enough, companies often design specialized marketing programs to serve them. *Multicultural marketing* grew out of careful marketing research,

TABLE 6.1	CANADIAN CONSUMPTION STATISTICS
Based on an estimated 11.7 million Canadian households, total average annual expenditures were reported to be $60 090 in 2002, broken down into the following categories:	
Personal income taxes	$12 025
Shelter	11 204
Transportation	8 431
Food	6 684
Eating out (estimated at 30%)	1 951
Recreation	3 537
Personal insurance payments and pension contributions	3 415
Household operation	2 783
Clothing	2 450
Household furnishings and equipment	1 793
Health care	1 590
Tobacco products and alcoholic beverages	1 478
Gifts of money and contributions	1 444
Education	926
Miscellaneous	901
Personal care	829
Games of chance (net amount)	313
Reading materials and other printed matter	285

Source: Statistics Canada, "Average Household Expenditures, Provinces and Territories," 2001 Census Data, CANSIM Table 203-0001, last modified January 27, 2004 (viewed online, www.statscan.ca, July 14, 2004).

MARKETING INSIGHT

A Maturing Market

The median age in Canada is higher than ever before (median age is defined as the point where exactly one-half of the population is older, and the other half is younger). The most recent census data (2001) on age and sex shows the median age of Canada's population as 37.6 years, an increase of 2.3 years from 35.3 in 1996. This was the biggest census-to-census increase in a century. To see how rapidly the Canadian population has aged, it is interesting to note that the median age in Canada in 1966 (the year when the last of the baby boomers was born) was 25.4 years. Today, Canada's working-age population is dominated by older individuals, but there are regional variations. Nova Scotia and Quebec have the oldest populations. Each has a median age of 38.8 years. Alberta is the youngest with a median age of 35.0.

The greying of Canada means that companies will have to do more than pay lip service to the idea of marketing to older people. Yet, businesses are not suddenly going to lose all interest in the 18- to 34-year-old demographic. Instead, companies will have to learn to establish brands that attract older consumers without alienating younger ones. One example: a recent Pepsi commercial features a teenage boy in the middle of a mosh pit at a rock concert. He turns around to discover his father rocking nearby. People aren't considered over the hill at 50 any more. Smart marketers will capitalize on this knowledge and create the image of an ageless society where people define themselves more by the activities they're involved in than by their age. For instance, university students can be 20, 30, or 60 years old.

Sources: Alison Stein Wellner, "The Next 25 Years," *American Demographics* (April 2003): 24–27; Statistics Canada, "Profile of the Canadian Population by Age and Sex: Canada Ages," Detailed analysis of the 2001 Census population data released July 16, 2002.

which revealed that different ethnic and demographic niches did not always respond favourably to mass-market advertising. Companies have capitalized on well-thought-out multicultural marketing strategies in recent years (see "Marketing Insight: Marketing to Quebec and French-Canadian Consumers"). Consider the tactics Western Union used to attract Toronto's Caribbean community:

Western Union

One of Western Union's major strategies is to target communities who find it important to keep in touch with people from their native countries. Such people may use Western Union to wire money back to family members. Toronto's Caribbean community and people of Caribbean origin who visit Toronto for the Caribana Festival presented Western Union with such an opportunity. It's not surprising, therefore, that Western Union has been an official sponsor of the event for many years. Since it is a Caribbean tradition to use a little towel, handkerchief, or scrap of cloth to wave to music, Western Union printed yellow and black handkerchiefs with its logo and gave them away to people to wave during the parade and other festivities. The idea gave Western Union an extremely high profile at the event and helped the company communicate its product message effectively with this community.[4]

Virtually all human societies exhibit *social stratification*. Stratification sometimes takes the form of a caste system where the members of different castes are reared for certain roles and cannot change their caste membership. More frequently, it takes the form of **social classes**, relatively homogeneous and enduring divisions in a society, which are hierarchically ordered and whose members share similar values, interests, and behaviour.

Social classes have several characteristics. First, those within each class tend to behave more alike than persons from two different social classes. Social classes differ in dress, speech patterns, recreational preferences, and many other characteristics. Second, persons are perceived as occupying inferior or superior positions according to social class. Third, social class is indicated by a cluster of variables—for example, occupation, income, wealth, education, and value orientation—rather than by any single variable. Fourth, individuals can move up or down the social-class ladder during their lifetimes. The extent of this mobility varies according to how rigid the social stratification is in a given society.

Marketing to Quebec and French-Canadian Consumers

Quebec has long prided itself on being a "distinct society." Marketers must be aware of Quebec's uniqueness if they are to be successful in the province. Quebec is characterized by unique laws, a different mix of indigenous and national businesses and industries, and distinct attitudes and values when compared to the rest of Canada. According to the most recent census data (2001), almost 6 million (or 81 percent) of the 7 125 580 people who make up Quebec's population claim French as their mother tongue. In contrast, roughly 600 000 claim English as their native language, and 700 000 have another language as their native tongue.

Known for their "joie de vivre," the majority of Quebec's population (52 percent, or 3.7 million people) lived in the Montreal area in 2001. Montreal has a large number of high-tech industries. As well as being the second largest metropolitan area in Canada (behind Toronto and leading Vancouver), Montreal is also the second largest French-speaking city in the world. One must not assume that the population of the Montreal region is homogeneous and made up only of French Canadians, however. Bilingualism is very common, and like other large Canadian cities, the population is diverse as a result of immigration, though Montreal does not receive as many immigrants as Toronto or Vancouver.

To protect its French culture and affirm the province's French-speaking identity, successive Quebec governments have passed legislation to ensure the use of French in the various areas of public life. Education in the province is also mostly in French, although it is also available in English.

Marketers who want to appeal to Quebec consumers need to do more than communicate in French using dictionary translations of words. Take a recent successful campaign by the Bank of Montreal that used the tagline "Profitez." You wouldn't fully understand the campaign if you only used a dictionary-based interpretation of the word. You'd find translations that said Profitez means "Profit from," "To profit," "To earn," or "Something profitable." However, for Quebec consumers the meaning is more nuanced. They translate it as "Make the most of it," "Enjoy," or "Take advantage," and the expression is strongly associated with the enjoyment of life—meanings that make the campaign more powerful and rich. Language and the meanings derived from it are very cultural and context-based. Furthermore, research has revealed differences in the activities, interests, opinions, and consumption habits of French-Canadian versus English-Canadian consumers. French Canadians value their European roots, their rich and diverse cultural venues, gourmet food, and fine wines. As a result, Montreal is known as one of the trendiest centres in the world. French-Canadian women are more family oriented and fashion conscious than women in the rest of Canada.

Research conducted by S. C. Johnson revealed that even attitudes toward cleaning vary between English and French Canada. While English Canadians just want to get the job done and see cleaning as a necessary evil, people in Quebec get a sense of pride and accomplishment after they clean. Using this research, S. C. Johnson designed a highly successful campaign for its cleaning products that centred on the distinctly Québécois custom of the July 1 moving day—the date on which people tend to move from one apartment to another because leases in Quebec traditionally expire on June 30.

Such differences are partly derived from culture; their Latin roots may make French Canadians more emotional and impulsive. Demographic and socioeconomic differences also exist: education and income are both lower in Quebec than in Ontario. The legal environment is also different for marketers in Quebec. Besides strict language laws, there are stronger restrictions on advertising to children, for example. To be successful in French Canada, marketers must develop appeals that take these differences into account. For example, while many marketers are using national symbols to appeal to their customers, Quebec's separatist sentiments make this practice unwise.

Quebec also has a distinct business and retail climate. Lavo Group, for example, is a packaged goods manufacturer whose products rival those of Procter & Gamble and Colgate in the province. Many Québécois buy such Lavo products as La Parisienne laundry detergent and fabric softener instead of Tide and Downy, Hertel liquid cleanser instead of Mr. Clean, and Old Dutch powder cleanser instead of Comet. The financial services industry is also very different in Quebec from the rest of Canada. Two players that are almost nonexistent in English Canada, the Mouvement Desjardins (the federation of Quebec credit unions) and the National Bank, account for more than 60 percent of the province's financial services marketplace. Both organizations utilize integrated and Quebec-specific communications campaigns.

Quebec-based hardware chains Réno-Depot and RONA have many loyal customers in the province. When Home Depot entered Quebec in 2000, it had to compete with these companies—a completely different set of competitors from what it had confronted in the rest of Canada. To help Home Depot gain acceptance, Montreal-based Cossette Communications developed an advertising campaign that appealed to Québécois' unique sense of humour. Rather than creating ads with rational appeals that proclaimed Home Depot's high-quality service, Cossette conducted qualitative research to uncover examples of realistic and believable bad shopping experiences of Quebec consumers. The campaign that resulted from this research features one commercial that shows a clerk literally running away from a client. In another commercial, a group of clerks chant, "It is not my department" despite customers' looks of dismay. The campaign not only created awareness of Home Depot, but was listed among Montrealers' favourite commercials in a recent survey.

For a long time, Quebec lagged behind the rest of Canada in terms of Internet adoption and usage. Today, however, more than 60 percent of Quebec adults are online. There are a growing number of French sites and online services such as La Toile du Québec (www.toile.qc.ca), InfiniT (www.infinit.com), and PetitMonde (www.petitmonde.qc.ca), as well as the French versions of popular portals like Sympatico, Yahoo!, and MSN. Marketers have been quick to leverage this new interconnectivity. Volkswagen, Avon, L'Oréal, and La Senza are some of the Quebec-based companies that have jumped on the bandwagon. Not only are they building French versions of their company Web sites, they have intensified their e-mail marketing campaigns in the province. The race is on to build databases to further this effort. Sympatico.ca, for example, has an opt-in e-mail database of 700 000 French Canadians, comprising adults aged 25 to 49, most with families.

If marketers respect Quebec's unique laws with regard to contests and sweepstakes, they can utilize these tools to help build their databases. Sympatico.ca experienced phenomenal results when it ran a contest to meet Bryan Adams in Scotland. People had to register online and Sympatico amassed 20 000 new Quebec subscribers as a result of this campaign. As their marketing manager noted, "French-speaking people love to play. And because they love to play, they tend to give their personal information freely—and by that I mean their postal code, age, and gender." Marketers have to tread softly, however. Quebecers still like to be wooed, especially when it comes to developing a one-to-one relationship. People from Quebec prefer more face-to-face interactions and personal contact than do people from the rest of the country.

Marketers must also be aware that Quebec has its own icons and unique media personalities. For example, Bell Canada's long-running Monsieur B campaign, which originated in 1992, is almost unknown in the rest of Canada. However, it has approached legendary status in the province, the way other advertising icons like the Green Giant, Aunt Jemima, and the lonely Maytag repairman have done in the rest of Canada. Jean-François Richard, vice-president of marketing communications at Bell in Montreal, notes, "I don't know of any creative platform (anywhere) that has lasted so long and generated such results for so long for any advertiser!"

Because of all these differences, many advertisers develop unique campaigns designed just for the Quebec marketplace. Take the case of Pepsi, for example. Five different young actors are featured in the spots. They walk around wearing T-shirts with the letters that spell the word Pepsi, while celebrating such cultural expressions as poutine and the fact that Quebecers say "icit," not "ici." Other firms, like Calgary-based Telus Mobility, use standardized themes, but heavily tailor them to better communicate with the Quebec audience. Says Anne-Marie LaBerge, director of communications (Quebec), for Telus Mobility, "We have one brand, and we don't create a separate campaign for Quebec. . . . We take the national campaign and work with Taxi to adapt it. The message is the same and we give it a Quebec flavour." Other organizations, such as the communications firm Bos, believe that while Quebec is different in many respects, firms can save a lot of money by looking for similarities that resonate across Canadian marketplaces. This is the approach Bos took to developing a new campaign for the Weather Network. Bos developed a common "creative platform" for the new advertising, but realized that the media used to communicate the sponsor's message had to be different. In particular, TV was used as the core medium in English Canada, while radio was chosen to reach Quebec viewers.

Sources: Samson Okalow, "Vive la Difference: Does That Mean I Have to Have a Separate Campaign?" *Strategy Magazine*, October 15, 2004; Nicolette Flemming, "The True Meaning of 'Profitez'," *Marketing Magazine*, June 10, 2002, p. 31; Samson Okalow, "Quebec Success: Weather Network and Dairy Farmers of Canada Hit the Right Formula," *Strategy Magazine*, October 15, 2004, p. 32; Bernadette Johnson, "E-mail Marketing Begins to Flourish in La Belle Province," *Strategy: The Canadian Marketing Report*, May 20, 2002, p. D10; Helena Katz, "Johnson Sharpens Its Quebec Strategy," *Marketing Magazine*, October 12, 1998, p. 3; Shawna Steinberg, "Only in English Canada, You Say?," *Marketing Magazine*, November 12, 1998, p. 10; Danny Kucharsky, "Monsieur B's Family," *Marketing Magazine Online*, **www.marketingmag.ca**, June 11, 2001; Nathalie Fortier, "Building Success: How Cossette Poked Fun at Bad Customer Service to Give Home Depot a Firm Foundation in Quebec," *Marketing Magazine Online*, **www.marketingmag.ca**, September 24, 2001; Tracey Arial, "Taking Aim at the Giants," *Marketing Magazine Online*, **www.marketingmag.ca**, June 11, 2001; Government of Quebec, **www.gouv.qc.ca** (viewed June 5, 2002).

The Bank of Montreal's "Profitez" tagline conveyed to Quebecers meanings associated with the enjoyment of life.

Social classes show distinct product and brand preferences in many areas, including clothing, home furnishings, leisure activities, and automobiles. Social classes differ in media preferences, with upper-class consumers often preferring magazines and books and lower-class consumers often preferring television. Even within a media category such as TV, upper-class consumers tend to prefer news and drama, and lower-class consumers tend to prefer soap operas and sports programs. There are also language differences among the social classes. Advertising copy and dialogue must ring true to the targeted social class.

Regionalism

Canada is an increasingly regional country and the way people think, act, and buy varies greatly from one region to the next. The sheer size of the country and its varied geographic features and climate have certainly shaped regional character and personality. For example, Atlantic Canada is largely defined by its proximity to and historical relationship with the sea. Equally, the isolation imposed by the mountain barrier, along with the abundance and grandeur of British Columbia's natural environment, shaped the outlook of that region's residents. Immigration has also had a differential effect on the different regions within Canada. The economy of each region furthers these differences. The fate of regions linked to the rise and decline of such tradable commodities as fish, timber, wheat, minerals, or petroleum have affected the mindsets and buying behaviour of people living within Canada's different regions. In particular, regional inequalities that resulted from this kind of resource economy contributed to the rise of regional grievances, stereotypes, and dependencies that became part of each region's identity. However, many analysts today disagree with the view that regional disparities in outlook and behaviour are a simple byproduct of economics and geography. Instead they argue that these marked regional differences result from social relationships. In particular, disparities in political power have driven increased regionalism. The emergence of a new social class in Quebec—a new middle class of educated francophone professionals whose aspirations were blocked by the lack of opportunities for their skills within the old Quebec, with its backward state, its outdated, Church-administered social programs, and its Anglo-dominated business sector—is credited with giving birth to this trend. However, Quebec is not alone. In Alberta, a more regional identity has also emerged as the province has striven to be more politically assertive and pro-business. It also focuses on a set of issues centred on energy and taxation policies that are quite different from those at the top of the political agenda in the other provinces.[5]

Social Factors

In addition to cultural factors, a consumer's behaviour is influenced by such social factors as reference groups, family, and social roles and statuses.

REFERENCE GROUPS A person's **reference groups** consist of all the groups that have a direct (face-to-face) or indirect influence on his or her attitudes or behaviour. Groups having a direct influence on a person are called **membership groups**. Some membership groups are **primary groups**, such as family, friends, neighbours, and co-workers, those with whom the person interacts fairly continuously and informally. People also belong to **secondary groups**, such as religious, professional, and trade-union groups, which tend to be more formal and require less continuous interaction.

People are significantly influenced by their reference groups in at least three ways. Reference groups expose an individual to new behaviours and lifestyles, they influence attitudes and self-concept; and they create pressures for conformity that may affect actual product and brand choices. People are also influenced by groups to which they do not belong. **Aspirational groups** are those a person hopes to join; **dissociative groups** are those whose values or behaviour an individual rejects. Teens, for example, often wish to dissociate themselves from their parents.

Manufacturers of products and brands where group influence is strong must determine how to reach and influence opinion leaders in these reference groups. An **opinion leader** is the person in informal, product-related communications who offers advice or information about a specific product or product category, such as which of several brands is best or how a particular product may be used.[6] Marketers try to reach opinion leaders by identifying demographic and psychographic characteristics associated with opinion leadership, identifying the media read by opinion leaders, and directing messages at opinion leaders.

Nestlé

Prior to the launch of its KitKat Kubes, a variant of the popular KitKat brand, Nestlé hired an agency to create a buzz among opinion leaders in the 16- to 25-year-old market. A database of about 20 000 people were sent text messages and then this database was whittled down to 100 opinion leaders by a phone questionnaire. The opinion leaders were then sent a large box of KitKat Kubes. As one project manager at Nestlé Rowntree said: "It only takes 50 people to make a craze." But of course, it has to be the right 50 people.[7]

In Japan, high-school girls have often been credited with creating the buzz that makes products such as Shiseido's cosmetics Neuve nail polish a big hit.[8]

FAMILY   The family is the most important consumer-buying organization in society, and family members constitute the most influential primary reference group.[9] We can distinguish between two families in the buyer's life. The **family of orientation** consists of parents and siblings. From parents a person acquires an orientation toward religion, politics, and economics and a sense of personal ambition, self-worth, and love.[10] Even if the buyer no longer interacts very much with his or her parents, their influence on behaviour can be significant. In countries where parents live with grown children, their influence can be substantial. A more direct influence on everyday buying behaviour is the **family of procreation**—namely, one's spouse and children.

Marketers are interested in the roles and relative influence of family members in the purchase of a large variety of products and services. In North America, husband–wife involvement has traditionally varied widely by product category. The wife has usually acted as the family's main purchasing agent, especially for food, sundries, and staple-clothing items, while husbands were targeted for more infrequent, big-ticket items such as electronics and cars. Now traditional purchasing roles are changing, and marketers would be wise to see both men and women as possible targets. For example, in 1978 only 10 percent of males were classified as primary shoppers, but in 1998 the figure had risen to 17 percent. *Canadian Grocer* magazine estimates that 25 to 30 percent of men now grocery-shop. Some males are forced into the role of shopper by demographic and lifestyle changes such as late marriage and high divorce rates, but most take on the role as a result of being part of a time-pressed, two-income household.[11]

With expensive products and services like cars, vacations, or housing, the vast majority of husbands and wives engage in more joint decision making.[12] Given women's increasing wealth and income-generating ability, financial service firms such as Citigroup, Charles Schwab, and Merrill Lynch have expanded their efforts to attract women investors and business owners.[13] Upscale leisure activities are also being targeted more and more at women. For example, the golf club at the Whistler resort in British Columbia offers women-only golf lessons. And marketers are realizing that men aren't the main buyers of high-tech gizmos and gadgets these days. Women actually buy more technology than men do, but consumer electronics stores have been slow to catch on to this fact. Some savvy electronics stores are starting to heed women's complaints of being ignored, patronized, or offended by salespeople. RadioShack Corp., a 7000-store chain, began actively recruiting female store managers so that now a woman manages about one out of every seven stores.[14]

Nevertheless, men and women may respond differently to marketing messages.[15] One study showed that women valued connections and relationships with family and friends and placed a high priority on people. Men, on the other hand, related more to competition and placed a high priority on action. Marketers are taking more direct aim at women with new products such as Quaker's

Marketers are focusing more closely on women and their needs: This Dutch Boy "Twist and Pour" ad, which features a new, easy-to-use paint container, is targeted specifically at women.

Nutrition for Women cereals and Crest Rejuvenating Effects toothpaste. Gillette Co. researched psychological issues specific to women and came out with an ergonomically designed razor, Venus, that fit more easily in a woman's hand. Sherwin-Williams recently designed a Dutch Boy easy-to-use "Twist and Pour" paint can targeted specifically at women.

The Royal Bank is another institution that has aggressively pursued the women's market.

Royal Bank

You won't hear anyone in the Royal Bank's branches referring to women's business plans as "nice little hobbies," as old-fashioned bankers once did. In one of its largest educational initiatives ever undertaken, the Royal Bank hired a specialist to train its 1400 business account managers about the importance of women's markets and about gender-sensitive communication. To attract female business owners, it sponsored a magazine supplement titled Canada's 100 Top Women Entrepreneurs and launched the bi-annual newsletter *Champions—Break-throughs and Resources for Women Entrepreneurs*. It also provides special services for businesswomen on the Internet. There is no doubt that its efforts have paid off. The Royal Bank's market share climbed to 21 percent, well ahead of its nearest competitor, TD Canada Trust, with 18.3 percent of the marketplace according to independent consultants.[16]

Another shift in buying patterns is an increase in the amount of money spent and the direct and indirect influence wielded by children and teens.[17] Direct influence describes children's "pester power"—their hints, requests, and demands (e.g., "I want to go to McDonald's"). Research by

Toronto-based Corus Entertainment indicates that kids currently influence some $20 million in household spending in Canada each year and have memorized between 300 and 400 brand names by age ten. The study also suggests that time-pressed, guilt-ridden parents respond favourably to 75 percent of kids' requests. It's not surprising, therefore, that industry spending on advertising to children has exploded in the past decade, increasing from a mere $100 million in 1990 to more than $2 billion by the year 2000.[18] Indirect influence means that parents know the brands, product choices, and preferences of their children without hints or outright requests. One research study showed that teenagers were playing a more active role than before in helping parents choose a car, audio/video equipment, or a vacation spot.[19]

Shaw Communications

Shaw@Home, the Internet service provider arm of Shaw Communications, ran an advertising campaign urging children to educate their parents on high-speed Internet access. Shaw posted ad banners on Web sites frequented by 12- to 17-year-olds where the services offered would be more easily accessed with high-speed Internet access (typically download sites such as Shockwave.com, MuchMusic.com, billboard.com, getmusic.com, or imdb.com). The banners posted on these sites (seen only by those in B.C., Alberta, Saskatchewan, and Manitoba) advertised free installation and one month of free Shaw high-speed Internet service. In one ad (part of the offline components of the campaign), a picture of a young child is accompanied by the message: "Sure I'll slow down. When I'm 15. Until then, I'll need a faster connection."[20]

Marketers use every possible channel of communication to reach kids, especially such popular media as Nickelodeon, the Cartoon Network, and the Disney Channel on TV, and magazines such as *Nickelodeon*, *Sports Illustrated for Kids*, and *Disney Adventures*. Corus Entertainment offers Canadian advertisers a host of products they can use to reach young consumers, including YTV, Teletoon, and Discovery Kids.

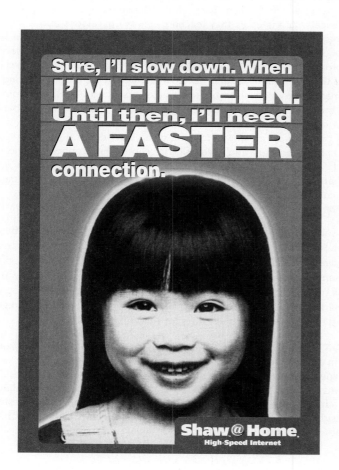

Shaw Communications advertised high-speed Internet to children knowing that they carry significant influence with parents.

YTV

YTV prides itself on being Canada's leading youth network. Its programs, aimed at audiences from 2 to 17 years of age and their families, are viewed by over 8.2 million Canadian households. The network broadcasts 17 of the top 20 children's shows in Canada. It segments its programming by time of day. It has a daytime preschool block, *The Zone* is Canada's number-one after-school block, and *Vortex* is a Saturday-morning animation-fest. Evenings, which are dedicated to tweens, teens, and family viewing, feature a line-up of drama, comedy, and animation shows. YTV's offerings go far beyond television: It has bragging rights as the number-one Canadian kids' Web site; it has its own travelling road show, *Weird on Wheels*; and it publishes *YTV Whoa!*, a magazine. YTV also takes its role as a responsible children's programmer to heart. It is a founding member of Canadian Cable in the Classroom, it encourages media literacy awareness through *TV & Me*, and it has partnered with the Kids Help Phone.[21]

The Lizzie McGuire juggernaut demonstrates how powerful television can be in reaching children, and marketers are using television to target children at younger ages than ever before. By the time children are around two years old, they can often recognize characters, logos, and specific brands. Marketers are tapping into that audience with product tie-ins, placed at a child's eye level, on just about everything—from Scooby Doo vitamins to Elmo juice and cookies.[22]

The Canadian Marketing Association makes it clear that special care must be taken by marketers when seeking to target the children's market. However, marketing to children is not new. Take the case of Le Mouvement des Caisses Desjardins, the huge Quebec banking cooperative:

Le Mouvement des Caisses Desjardins

The Mouvement Desjardins has had a program directed at children since 1901, and while they would not have used the word "marketing," their efforts have resulted in one of the most effective programs in Canada. Through the Caisse scolaire program, schools are provided with educational materials that teachers can use in lessons about money management. Students are given the opportunity to practise their skills and save by operating "mini" bank accounts, complete with their own bankbook but free from any service charges. In 2001 the program had close to 200 000 account holders between the ages of 6 and 11. It is estimated that 2.5 million students have participated in the program during its 100-year history, and many have gone on to be loyal customers as adults. Furthermore, since withdrawals from these accounts had to be co-signed by the child's parent, the bank effectively reached other family members too.

How has the program continued to exist, given Quebec's statutory restrictions against marketing to children or displaying advertising in schools? Francophone financial institutions were granted the right to educate kids about savings in Quebec schools under a 1908 statute. Furthermore, the program has such a venerable history and is so much a part of francophone culture that it hasn't been subject to intense scrutiny.[23]

Today companies are also likely to use the Internet to show products to children and solicit marketing information from them (consider, for example, the Shaw Communications example). Millions of kids under the age of 17 are online. Marketers have jumped online with them, offering freebies in exchange for personal information. Many have come under fire for this practice and for not clearly differentiating ads from games or entertainment. The Canadian Marketing Association has taken a strong stand on marketing to children on the Internet. For its guidelines, see "Marketing Memo: What Every Marketer Needs to Know—Internet Ethics for Targeting Kids."

ROLES AND STATUSES A person participates in many groups—family, clubs, organizations. The person's position in each group can be defined in terms of role and status. A **role** consists of the activities a person is expected to perform. Each role carries a **status**. A senior vice-president of marketing has more status than a sales manager, and a sales manager has more status than an office clerk. People choose products that reflect and communicate their role and actual or desired status in society. Company presidents often drive Mercedes, wear expensive suits, and drink Chivas Regal scotch. Marketers must be aware of the status-symbol potential of products and brands.

Personal Factors

A buyer's decisions are also influenced by personal characteristics. These include the buyer's age and stage in the life cycle, occupation and economic circumstances, personality and self-concept, and lifestyle and values. Because many of these characteristics have a very direct impact on consumer behaviour, it is important for marketers to follow them closely.

AGE AND STAGE IN THE LIFE CYCLE

People buy different goods and services over a lifetime. Taste in food, clothes, furniture, and recreation is often age related. Consumption is also shaped by the *family life cycle* and the number, age, and gender of people in the household at any point in time. North American households are increasingly fragmented—the traditional family of four with a husband, wife, and two kids makes up a much smaller percentage of total households than it once did. In addition, *psychological* life-cycle stages may matter. Adults experience certain "passages" or "transformations" as they go through life.[24]

Marketers should also consider *critical life events or transitions*—marriage, childbirth, illness, relocation, divorce, career change, widowhood—as giving rise to new needs. These should alert service providers—banks, lawyers, and marriage, employment, and bereavement counsellors—to ways they can help.[25]

OCCUPATION AND ECONOMIC CIRCUMSTANCES

Occupation may also influence consumption patterns, but caution has to be used not to make stereotypical decisions. A blue-collar worker will buy work clothes, work shoes, and lunchboxes, but may also belong to the local yacht club. A company president will buy dress suits and air travel, but may also play in the local men's hockey league. Marketers try to identify the occupational groups that have above-average interest in their products and services. A company can even tailor its products for certain occupational groups: Computer software companies, for example, design different products for brand managers, engineers, lawyers, and physicians.

Product choice is greatly affected by economic circumstances: spendable income (level, stability, and time pattern), savings and assets (including the percentage that is liquid), debts, borrowing power, and attitudes toward spending and saving. Luxury goods makers such as Gucci, Prada, and Burberry can be vulnerable to an economic downturn. If economic indicators point to a recession, marketers can take

Marketing Memo

What Every Marketer Needs to Know— Internet Ethics for Targeting Kids

The Canadian Marketing Association determined that marketing to children on the World Wide Web posed unique challenges for information-based marketers. As a result, it amended its code of ethics, and the provisions that affect marketing to children online came into effect on April 1, 1999. A child is defined as a person who has not reached his or her 13th birthday. The new code notes the vulnerability of children to marketing claims and imposes a special responsibility on marketers when they market to this group. The main provisions are outlined below:

- *Consent.* All marketing interactions directed to children, including collection, transfer, and requests for personal information, require the express consent of the child's parent or guardian. As defined in the Canadian Standards Association (CSA) Model Code for the Protection of Personal Information, express consent "is given explicitly, either orally or in writing."

- *Contests, games, or sweepstakes directed to children.* Marketers may collect personal information from children for the purposes of contests, games, or sweepstakes without obtaining the parent or guardian's express consent, only if the marketer:
  - Collects a minimal amount of personal information, sufficient only to determine the winner(s);
  - Deals only with the winner(s)' parent or guardian and does not contact the winner(s);
  - Does not retain the personal information following the conclusion of the contest or sweepstakes;
  - Makes no use of the personal information, other than to determine the contest or sweepstakes winner(s); and
  - Does not transfer or make available the personal information to any other individual or organization.

- *Credulity.* Marketing to children shall not exploit children's credulity, lack of experience, or sense of loyalty.

- *Age-appropriate language.* Marketers shall use age-appropriate language in marketing to children. Offers shall be presented in simple language, easily understood by children.

- *Commercial transactions.* Marketers shall not accept an order from a child without a parent or guardian's express consent. Marketers shall not pressure children to urge their parents or guardians to purchase a product or service.

In addition to the new provisions in its code of ethics, the Canadian Marketing Association provides tips to parents to help them protect their children while they are online.

Source: Canadian Marketing Association, **www.the-cma.org** (viewed June 8, 2002).

steps to redesign, reposition, and reprice their products or introduce or increase the emphasis on discount brands so that they can continue to offer value to target customers.

PERSONALITY AND SELF-CONCEPT   Each person has personality characteristics that influence his or her buying behaviour. By **personality**, we mean a set of distinguishing human psychological traits that lead to relatively consistent and enduring responses to environmental stimuli. Personality is often described in terms of such traits as self-confidence, dominance, autonomy, deference, sociability, defensiveness, and adaptability.[26] Personality can be a useful variable in analyzing consumer brand choices. The idea is that brands also have personalities, and consumers are likely to choose brands whose personalities match their own. We define **brand personality** as the specific mix of human traits that may be attributed to a particular brand.

Stanford's Jennifer Aaker conducted research into brand personalities and identified the following five traits:[27]

1. Sincerity (down-to-earth, honest, wholesome, and cheerful)

2. Excitement (daring, spirited, imaginative, and up to date)

3. Competence (reliable, intelligent, and successful)

4. Sophistication (upper-class and charming)

5. Ruggedness (outdoorsy and tough)

She proceeded to analyze some well-known brands and found that a number of them tended to be strong on one particular trait: Levi's with "ruggedness"; MTV with "excitement"; CNN with "competence"; and Campbell's with "sincerity." The implication is that these brands will attract persons who are high on the same personality traits. A brand personality may have several attributes: Levi's suggests a personality that is also youthful, rebellious, and authentic. The company utilizes product features, services, and image making to transmit the product's personality.

Consumers often choose and use brands that have a brand personality consistent with their own *actual self-concept* (how one views oneself), although in some cases the match may be based on consumer's *ideal self-concept* (how one would like to view oneself) or even *others' self-concept* (how one thinks others see one) rather than actual self-image.[28] These effects may also be more pronounced for publicly consumed products as compared to privately consumed goods.[29] On the other hand, consumers who are high "self-monitors"—that is, sensitive to how others see them—are more likely to choose brands whose personalities fit the consumption situation.[30]

A Levi's ad expresses the brand personality: youthful, rebellious, and authentic.

LIFESTYLE AND VALUES People from the same subculture, social class, and occupation may lead quite different lifestyles. A **lifestyle** is a person's pattern of living in the world as expressed in activities, interests, and opinions. Lifestyle portrays the "whole person" interacting with his or her environment. Marketers search for relationships between their products and lifestyle groups. For example, a computer manufacturer might find that most computer buyers are achievement-oriented. The marketer may then aim the brand more clearly at the achiever lifestyle. Marketers are always uncovering new trends in consumer lifestyles. Here's an example of one of the latest lifestyle trends businesses are currently targeting:

LOHAS

Consumers who worry about the environment, want products to be produced in a sustainable way, and spend money to advance their personal development and potential have been named "LOHAS." The name is an acronym standing for *lifestyles of health and sustainability*. The market for LOHAS products encompasses things like organic foods, energy-efficient appliances and sonar panels, alternative medicine, yoga tapes, and eco-tourism. Rather than looking at discrete product categories like cars or organic foods, it is more important to look at the common factors linking these product groups—for example, at cars, energy, and household products that are perceived as better for the environment and society. Companies like Loblaws serve this emerging segment by offering alternative products such as its line of organic foods.[31]

Lifestyles are shaped partly by whether consumers are *money-constrained* or *time-constrained*. Companies aiming to serve money-constrained consumers will create lower-cost products and services. By appealing to the money-constrained, Wal-Mart has become the largest company in the world. Its "everyday low prices" have wrung tens of billions of dollars out of the retail supply chain, passing the larger part of savings along to shoppers with rock-bottom bargain prices.[32]

Consumers who experience time famine are prone to **multitasking**, that is, doing two or more things at the same time. They will phone or eat while driving, or bicycle to work to get exercise. They will also pay others to perform tasks because time is more important than money. They may prefer bagels to breakfast cereals because they are quicker. Companies aiming to serve them will create convenient products and services for this group. Much of the wireless revolution is fuelled by the multitasking trend. Waterloo, Ontario–based Research in Motion (RIM) is widely regarded as an industry leader in wireless solutions and personal digital assistant handheld devices that provide seamless access to time-sensitive information including e-mail, phone, SMS messaging, Internet, and intranet-based applications.

In some categories, notably food processing, companies targeting time-constrained consumers need to be aware that these very same consumers seek the illusion that they are not operating within time constraints. The food processing industry has a name for those who seek both convenience and some involvement in the cooking process: the "convenience involvement segment."[33]

Hamburger Helper

Launched in 1971 in response to tough economic times, the inexpensive pasta-and-powdered mix Hamburger Helper was designed to quickly and inexpensively stretch a pound of meat into a family meal. With an estimated 44 percent of evening meals prepared in under 30 minutes and strong competition from fast-food drive-through windows, restaurant deliveries, and precooked grocery store dishes, Hamburger Helper's days of prosperity might seem numbered. Market researchers found, however, that some consumers do not necessarily want the fastest microwavable meal solution possible—they also want to feel good about how they prepare a meal. In fact, on average, they would prefer to use at least one pot or pan and 15 minutes of time. To remain attractive to the segment who want to spend less time in the kitchen without totally abandoning their traditional roles as family meal-makers, marketers of Hamburger Helper are always introducing new flavours to tap into the latest consumer taste trends.[34]

Consumer decisions are also influenced by **core values**, the belief systems that underlie consumer attitudes and behaviours. Core values go much deeper than behaviour or attitude, and determine, at a basic level, people's choices and desires over the long term. Marketers who target consumers on the basis of their values believe that by appealing to people's inner selves, it is possible to influence their outer selves—their purchase behaviour.

Key Psychological Processes

The starting point for understanding consumer behaviour is the stimulus-response model shown in Figure 6.1. A set of psychological processes combines with environmental stimuli and certain consumer characteristics, ultimately resulting in purchase decisions. The marketer's task is to understand what happens in the consumer's consciousness between the arrival of the outside marketing stimuli and the ultimate purchase decisions. Four key psychological processes—motivation, perception, learning, and memory—fundamentally influence consumer responses to the various marketing stimuli.

Motivation: Freud, Maslow, Herzberg

A person has many needs at any given time. Some needs are *biogenic*; they arise from physiological states of tension such as hunger, thirst, or discomfort. Other needs are *psychogenic*; they arise from psychological states of tension such as the need for recognition, esteem, or belonging. A need becomes a motive when it is aroused to a sufficient level of intensity. A **motive** is a need that is sufficiently pressing to drive the person to act.

Three of the best-known theories of human motivation—those of Sigmund Freud, Abraham Maslow, and Frederick Herzberg—carry quite different implications for consumer analysis and marketing strategy.

FREUD'S THEORY Sigmund Freud assumed that the psychological forces shaping people's behaviour are largely unconscious, and that a person cannot fully understand his or her own motivations. When a person examines specific brands, he or she will react not only to their stated capabilities, but also to other, less conscious cues. Shape, size, weight, material, colour, and brand name can all trigger certain associations and emotions. A technique called *laddering* can be used to trace a person's motivations from the stated instrumental ones to the more terminal ones. Then the marketer can decide at what level to develop the message and appeal.[35]

Motivation researchers often collect "in-depth interviews" with a few dozen consumers to uncover deeper motives triggered by a product. They use various *projective techniques* such as word association, sentence completion, picture interpretation, and role playing. Many of these techniques were pioneered by Ernest Dichter, a Viennese psychologist who settled in the United States.[36]

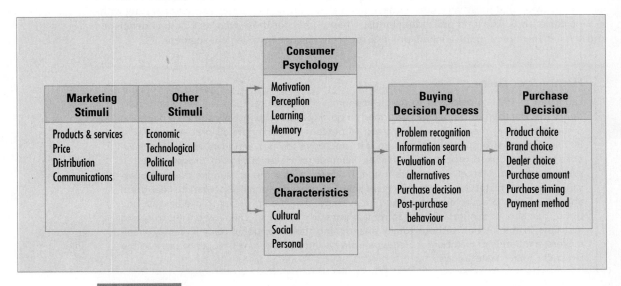

FIGURE 6.1

Model of Consumer Behaviour

Today motivational researchers continue the tradition of Freudian interpretation. Jan Callebaut identifies different motives a product can satisfy. For example, whisky can meet the need for social relaxation, status, or fun. Different whisky brands need to be motivationally positioned in one of these three appeals.[37] Another motivation researcher, Clotaire Rapaille, works on breaking the "code" behind a lot of product behaviour. Research analyzing paper towels, according to Rapaille, revealed that its appeal to mothers is in how cleanliness plays into their instinctive desire to have their genes survive. "You are not just cleaning the table. You are saving the whole family," asserts the researcher.[38]

MASLOW'S THEORY   Abraham Maslow sought to explain why people are driven by particular needs at particular times.[39] Why does one person spend considerable time and energy on personal safety and another on pursuing the high opinion of others? Maslow's answer is that human needs are arranged in a hierarchy, from the most pressing to the least pressing. In order of importance, they are physiological needs, safety needs, social needs, esteem needs, and self-actualization needs (see Figure 6.2). People will try to satisfy their most important needs first. When a person succeeds in satisfying an important need, he or she will then try to satisfy the next-most-important need. For example, a starving man (need 1) will not take an interest in the latest happenings in the art world (need 5), nor in how he is viewed by others (need 3 or 4), nor even in whether he is breathing clean air (need 2); but when he has enough food and water, the next-most-important need will become salient.

Maslow's theory helps marketers understand how various products fit into the plans, goals, and lives of consumers.

HERZBERG'S THEORY Frederick Herzberg developed a two-factor theory that distinguishes *dissatisfiers* (factors that cause dissatisfaction) and *satisfiers* (factors that cause satisfaction).[40] The absence of dissatisfiers is not enough; satisfiers must be present to motivate a purchase. For example, a computer that does not come with a warranty would be a dissatisfier. Yet the presence of a product warranty would not act as a satisfier or motivator of a purchase, because it is not a source of intrinsic satisfaction. Ease of use would be a satisfier.

Herzberg's theory has two implications. First, sellers should do their best to avoid dissatisfiers (e.g., a poor training manual or a poor service policy). Although these things will not sell a product, they might easily unsell it. Second, the seller should identify the major satisfiers or motivators of purchase in the market and then supply them. These satisfiers will make the major difference as to which brand the customer buys.

Perception

A motivated person is ready to act. How the motivated person actually acts is influenced by his or her view or perception of the situation. **Perception** is the process by which an individual selects, organizes, and interprets information inputs to create a meaningful picture of the world.[41] Perception depends not only on the physical stimuli, but also on the stimuli's relation to the surrounding field and on conditions within the individual. The key point is that perceptions can vary widely among individuals exposed to the same reality. One person might perceive a fast-talking salesperson as aggressive and insincere; another, as intelligent and helpful. Each will respond differently to the salesperson.

In marketing, perceptions are more important than the reality, as it is perceptions that will affect consumers' actual behaviour. People can emerge

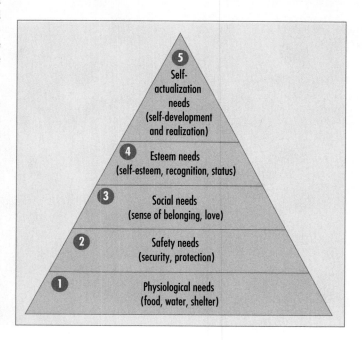

FIGURE 6.2

Maslow's Hierarchy of Needs

Source: *Motivation and Personality*, 2nd ed., by A. H. Maslow, 1970. Reprinted by permission of Prentice Hall, Inc., Upper Saddle River, New Jersey.

with different perceptions of the same object because of three perceptual processes: selective attention, selective distortion, and selective retention.

SELECTIVE ATTENTION It has been estimated that the average person may be exposed to over 1500 ads or brand communications a day. Because a person cannot possibly attend to all of these, most stimuli will be screened out—a process called **selective attention**. Selective attention means that marketers have to work hard to attract consumers' notice. The real challenge is to explain which stimuli people will notice. Here are some findings:

1. *People are more likely to notice stimuli that relate to a current need.* A person who is motivated to buy a computer will notice computer ads; he or she will be less likely to notice DVD ads.

2. *People are more likely to notice stimuli that they anticipate.* You are more likely to notice computers than radios in a computer store because you do not expect the store to carry radios.

3. *People are more likely to notice stimuli whose deviations are large in relation to the normal size of the stimuli.* You are more likely to notice an ad offering $100 off the list price of a computer than one offering $5 off.

Although people screen out much of the surrounding stimuli, they are influenced by unexpected stimuli, such as sudden offers in the mail, over the phone, or from a salesperson. Marketers may attempt to promote their offers intrusively to bypass selective attention filters.

SELECTIVE DISTORTION Even noticed stimuli do not always come across in the way the senders intended. **Selective distortion** is the tendency to interpret information in a way that will fit our preconceptions. Consumers will often distort information to be consistent with prior brand and product beliefs.[42]

A stark demonstration of the power of consumer brand beliefs is the typical result of product sampling tests. In "blind" taste tests, one group of consumers samples a product without knowing which brand it is, whereas another group of consumers samples the product knowing which brand it is. Invariably, differences arise in the opinions of the two groups despite the fact that the two groups are *literally consuming exactly the same product*!

When consumers report different opinions between branded and unbranded versions of identical products, it must be the case that their brand and product beliefs, created by whatever means (e.g., past experiences, marketing activity for the brand, etc.), have somehow changed their product perceptions. Examples of branded differences can be found with virtually every type of product. For example, one study found that consumers were equally split in their preference for Diet Coke versus

A Pepsi Challenge taste test in New York's Central Park. Companies like Pepsi often do taste tests of their products against other branded products to see if brand really makes a difference in customer preferences.

Diet Pepsi when tasting both on a blind basis.[43] When tasting the branded versions, however, consumers preferred Diet Coke by 65 percent and Diet Pepsi by only 23 percent (with the remainder seeing no difference).

Selective distortion can work to the advantage of marketers with strong brands when consumers distort neutral or ambiguous brand information to make it more positive. In other words, beer may seem to taste better, a car may seem to drive more smoothly, the wait in a bank line may seem shorter, and so on, depending on the particular brands involved.

SELECTIVE RETENTION People will fail to register much information to which they are exposed in memory, but will tend to retain information that supports their attitudes and beliefs. Because of **selective retention**, we are likely to remember good points about a product we like and forget good points about competing products. Selective retention again works to the advantage of strong brands. It also explains why marketers need to use repetition in sending messages to their target market—to make sure their message is not overlooked.

SUBLIMINAL PERCEPTION The selective perception mechanisms require active engagement and thought by consumers. A topic that has fascinated armchair marketers for ages is **subliminal perception**. The argument is that marketers embed covert, subliminal messages in ads or packages. Consumers are not consciously aware of these messages, yet they affect their behaviour. Although it is clear many subtle subconscious effects can exist with consumer processing,[44] no evidence supports the notion that marketers can systematically control consumers at that level.[45]

Learning

When people act, they learn. **Learning** involves changes in an individual's behaviour arising from experience. Most human behaviour is learned. Learning theorists believe that learning is produced through the interplay of drives, stimuli, cues, responses, and reinforcement.

A **drive** is a strong internal stimulus impelling action. **Cues** are minor stimuli that determine when, where, and how a person responds. Suppose you buy a Dell computer. If your experience is rewarding, your response to computers and Dell will be positively reinforced. Later on, when you want to buy a printer, you may assume that because Dell makes good computers, Dell also makes good printers. In other words, you *generalize* your response to similar stimuli. A countertendency to generalization is discrimination. **Discrimination** means that the person has learned to recognize differences in sets of similar stimuli and can adjust responses accordingly.

Learning theory teaches marketers that they can build demand for a product by associating it with strong drives, using motivating cues, and providing positive reinforcement. A new company can enter the market by appealing to the same drives that competitors use and by providing similar cue configurations, because buyers are more likely to transfer loyalty to similar brands (generalization); or the company might design its brand to appeal to a different set of drives and offer strong cue inducements to switch (discrimination).

Memory

All the information and experiences individuals encounter as they go through life can end up in their long-term memory. Cognitive psychologists distinguish between **short-term memory (STM)**—a temporary repository of information—and **long-term memory (LTM)**—a more permanent repository.

Most widely accepted views of long-term memory structure involve some kind of associative model formulation.[46] For example, the **associative network memory model** views LTM as consisting of a set of nodes and links. *Nodes* are stored information connected by *links* that vary in strength. Any type of information can be stored in the memory network, including information that is verbal, visual, abstract, or contextual. A spreading activation process from node to node determines the extent of retrieval and what information can actually be recalled in any given situation. When a node becomes activated because external information is being encoded (e.g., when a person reads or hears a word or phrase) or internal information is retrieved from LTM (e.g., when a person thinks about some concept), other nodes are also activated if they are sufficiently strongly associated with that node.

Consistent with the associative network memory model, consumer brand knowledge in memory can be conceptualized as consisting of a brand node in memory with a variety of linked associations. The strength and organization of these associations will be important determinants of the information that can be recalled about the brand. **Brand associations** consist of all brand-related thoughts, feelings, perceptions, images, experiences, beliefs, attitudes, and so on that become linked to the brand node.

Marketing can be seen as making sure that consumers have the right types of product and service experiences such that the right brand knowledge structures are created and maintained in memory.

Godiva Chocolatier

Godiva Chocolatier's success is based on the appeal of emotional brand associations. In 1994, when the recession slowed sales of super-premium goods, such as chocolates that sold for as much as $45 a pound, Godiva underwent a marketing makeover in its retail stores. The idea was to define, through store design, what the experience of eating chocolate felt like—sensual, indulgent, even sinful. In its multi-million-dollar redesign Godiva created elegant Art Noveau–style stores with bleached wood floors and wood and glass display cases. Customers were able to sample chocolates and find price lists instead of having to ask the salesperson the prices (which they might have found embarrassing). As redesigned "test" stores began to post significantly higher sales, Godiva rolled out the whole redesign and now the brand's associations of luxurious indulgence and sensuality have become ingrained in consumer's minds.[47]

Companies such as Procter & Gamble like to create mental maps of consumers that depict brand associations that are likely to be triggered in a marketing setting, and their relative strength, favourability, and uniqueness to consumers. Figure 6.3 displays a very simple mental map highlighting brand beliefs for a hypothetical consumer for the Dole brand.

MEMORY PROCESSES: ENCODING **Memory encoding** refers to how and where information gets into memory. Memory encoding can be characterized according to the amount or quantity of processing that information receives at encoding (i.e., how much a person thinks about the information) and the nature or quality of processing that information receives at encoding (i.e., the manner in which a person thinks about the information). The quantity and quality of processing will be an important determinant of the strength of an association.[48]

FIGURE 6.3

Hypothetical Dole Mental Map

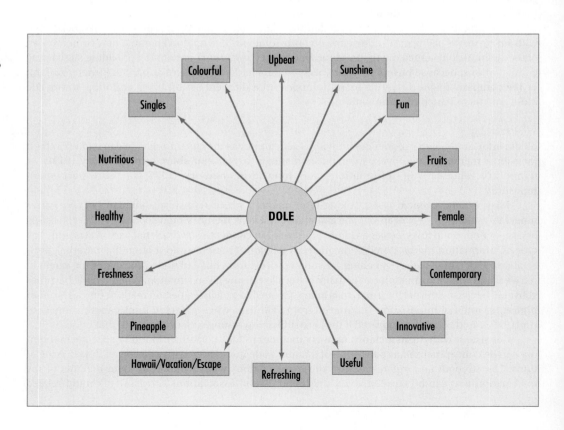

In general, the more attention placed on the meaning of information during encoding, the stronger the resulting associations in memory will be.[49] When a consumer actively thinks about and "elaborates" on the significance of product or service information, stronger associations are created in memory. Another key determinant of the strength of a newly formed association will be the content, organization, and strength of existing brand associations in memory. It will be easier for consumers to create an association to new information when extensive, relevant knowledge structures already exist in memory. One reason why personal experiences create such strong brand associations is that information about the product is likely to be related to existing knowledge.

Consider the brand associations that might be created by a new TV ad campaign employing a popular Canadian sports figure designed to create a new benefit association for a well-known brand. For example, consider the case when Olympic speed skater and gold-medallist Catriona Lemay Doan appeared in a commercial for Nestlé PowerBar. Viewers might process the ad in very different ways:

1. Some consumers may barely notice the ads so that the amount of processing devoted to the ads is extremely low, resulting in weak to nonexistent brand associations.

2. The ads may catch the attention of other consumers, resulting in sufficient processing, but these consumers may devote most of the time during the ads thinking about the Olympics and wondering how they can get their children to this level of athletic excellence.

3. Another group of consumers may not only notice the ads but may think of how they had a wrong impression of PowerBars. The ad may cause them to think in a "different" way about the product. For example, women may have perceived that this is a "men's only" product and may now realize it is also aimed at their needs.

In addition to congruency or consistency with existing knowledge, the ease with which new information can be integrated into established knowledge structures clearly depends on the nature of that information, in terms of characteristics such as simplicity, vividness, and concreteness.

Repeated exposures to information provide greater opportunity for processing and thus the potential for stronger associations. Recent advertising research in a field setting, however, suggests that qualitative considerations and the manner or style of consumer processing engendered by an ad are generally more important than the cumulative total of ad exposures.[50] In other words, high levels of repetition for an un-involving, unpersuasive ad is unlikely to have as much sales impact as lower levels of repetition for an involving, persuasive ad.

MEMORY PROCESSES: RETRIEVAL **Memory retrieval** refers to how information gets out of memory. According to the associative network memory model, the strength of a brand association increases both the likelihood that that information will be accessible and the ease with which it can be recalled by "spreading activation." Successful recall of brand information by consumers does not depend only on the initial strength of that information in memory. Three factors are particularly important.

First, the presence of *other* product information in memory can produce interference effects. It may cause the information to be either overlooked or confused. One challenge in a category crowded with many competitors—such as airlines, financial services, and insurance companies—is that consumers may mix up brands.

Second, the time since exposure to information at encoding affects the strength of a new association—the longer the time delay, the weaker the association. The time elapsed since the last exposure opportunity, however, has been shown generally to produce only gradual decay. Cognitive psychologists believe that memory is extremely durable, so that once information becomes stored in memory, its strength of association decays very slowly.[51]

Third, information may be "available" in memory (i.e., potentially recallable) but may not be "accessible" (i.e., unable to be recalled) without the proper retrieval cues or reminders. The particular associations for a brand that "come to mind" depend on the context in which the brand is considered. The more cues linked to a piece of information, however, the greater the likelihood that the information can be recalled. The effectiveness of retrieval cues is one reason why marketing *inside* a supermarket or any retail store is so critical—in terms of the actual product packaging, the use of in-store mini-billboard displays, and so on. The information they contain and the reminders they provide of advertising or other information already conveyed outside the store will be prime determinants of consumer decision making.

The Buying Decision Process: The Five-Stage Model

FIGURE 6.4

Five-Stage Model of the Consumer Buying Process

These basic psychological processes play an important role in understanding how consumers actually make their buying decisions. Marketers must understand every facet of consumer behaviour. Table 6.2 provides a list of some key consumer behaviour questions in terms of "who, what, when, where, how, and why." Smart companies try to fully understand the customers' buying decision process—all their experiences in learning, choosing, using, and even disposing of a product.[52]

Honda engineers took videos of shoppers loading groceries into car trunks to observe their frustrations and generate possible design solutions. Intuit, the maker of Quicken financial software, watched first-time buyers try to learn Quicken to sense their problems in learning how to use the product. Bissel developed its Steam n' Clean vacuum cleaner based on the product trial experiences of a local PTA group near its corporate headquarters. The result was a name change, colour-coded attachments, and an infomercial highlighting its special features.[53]

Marketing scholars have developed a "stage model" of the buying decision process (see Figure 6.4). The consumer passes through five stages: problem recognition, information search, evaluation of alternatives, purchase decision, and post-purchase behaviour. Clearly, the buying process starts long before the actual purchase and has consequences long afterward.[54]

But consumers do not always pass through all five stages in buying a product. They may skip or reverse some stages. A woman buying her regular brand of toothpaste goes directly from the need for toothpaste to the purchase decision, skipping information search and evaluation. The model in Figure 6.4 provides a good frame of reference, however, because it captures the full range of considerations that arise when a consumer faces a highly involving new purchase.[55]

Problem Recognition

The buying process starts when the buyer recognizes a problem or need. The need can be triggered by internal or external stimuli. With an internal stimulus, one of the person's normal needs—hunger, thirst, sex—rises to a threshold level and becomes a drive; or a need can be aroused by an external stimulus. A person may admire a neighbour's new car or see a television ad for a Hawaiian vacation, which triggers thoughts about the possibility of making a purchase. A believer in "retail theatre," Krispy Kreme lights a neon "HOT NOW" sign to get attention—and purchase interest—each time a new batch of doughnuts is baked.

Marketers need to identify the circumstances that trigger a particular need by gathering information from a number of consumers. They can then develop marketing strategies that trigger consumer interest. This is particularly important with discretionary purchases such as luxury goods,

TABLE 6.2	UNDERSTANDING CONSUMER BEHAVIOUR

- Who buys our product or service?
- Who makes the decision to buy the product?
- Who influences the decision to buy the product?
- How is the purchase decision made? Who assumes what role?
- What does the customer buy? What needs must be satisfied?
- Why do customers buy a particular brand?
- Where do they go or look to buy the product or service?
- When do they buy? Any seasonality factors?
- How is our product perceived by customers?
- What are customers' attitudes toward our product?
- What social factors might influence the purchase decision?
- Do customers' lifestyles influence their decisions?
- How do personal or demographic factors influence the purchase decision?

Source: Based on list from George Belch and Michael Belch, *Advertising and Communication Management*, 6th ed. (Homewood, IL: Irwin, 2003).

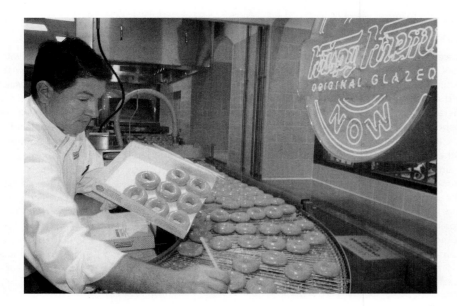

Triggering need: The "HOT NOW" sign is lit at this new Krispy Kreme store at Harrod's in London to signal the arrival of a batch of freshly baked doughnuts.

vacation packages, and entertainment options. Consumer motivation may need to be increased so that a potential purchase is even given serious consideration.

Information Search

An aroused consumer will be inclined to search for more information. We can distinguish between two levels of arousal. The milder search state is called *heightened attention*. At this level a person simply becomes more receptive to information about a product. At the next level, the person may enter an *active information search*: looking for reading material, phoning friends, going online, and visiting stores to learn about the product.

Of key interest to the marketer are the major information sources to which the consumer will turn and the relative influence each will have on the subsequent purchase decision. These information sources fall into four groups:

- *Personal.* Family, friends, neighbours, acquaintances.
- *Commercial.* Advertising, Web sites, salespersons, dealers, packaging, displays.
- *Public.* Mass media, consumer-rating organizations.
- *Experiential.* Handling, examining, using the product.

The relative amount and influence of these sources vary with the product category and the buyer's characteristics. Generally speaking, the consumer receives the most information about a product from commercial sources—that is, marketer-dominated sources. However, the most effective information often comes from personal sources or public sources that are independent authorities. More than 40 percent of all car shoppers consult *Consumer Reports*, making it the biggest single source of information.[56] Each information source performs a different function in influencing the buying decision. Commercial information normally performs an information function, whereas personal sources perform a legitimizing or evaluation function. For example, physicians often learn of new drugs from commercial sources but turn to other doctors for evaluations.

The Internet has changed information search. Today's marketplace is made up of traditional consumers (who do not shop online), cyber-consumers (who mostly shop online), and hybrid consumers (who do both).[57] Most consumers are hybrid: They shop in grocery stores but occasionally order from Grocery Gateway; they shop for books in Chapters and Indigo bookstores but also sometimes order books from Chapters.Indigo.ca. People still like to squeeze the tomatoes, touch the fabric, smell the perfume, and interact with salespeople. They are motivated by more than shopping efficiency. Most companies will need a presence both offline and online to cater to these hybrid consumers.

National Post

Since the beginning of mass consumption of the Internet, newspapers have wrestled with how to balance online and offline content. In particular, they are concerned with how to ensure that online offerings do not cannibalize newspaper sales. Pricing is also a big issue, and newspapers that have gone online have struggled to increase revenues, wondering if there should be a subscription fee to access online content. Different newspapers have responded in different ways. Some, such as *The Wall Street Journal*, only allow people who pay a subscription fee for their physical newspapers to have access to their online content. Others are using a two-tier system where some or all of the news stories are free, but premium services such as archives, sports, and financial news require a fee. In 2004, CanWest introduced a combined subscription/pay model for its ten city dailies and the *National Post*. The model has four tiers: (1) breaking news free for all Web surfers; (2) newspaper's content and access to archives to offline CanWest newspaper subscribers; (3) a PDF-format electronic edition of the newspaper delivered to subscribers via e-mail by 5:00 A.M. for a fee (targeted at travelling Canadians, including business professionals and snowbirds, and a younger online demographic); and (4) a multimedia product that includes streaming video and audio for a subscription fee. Only the future will tell whether the strategy will be successful.[58]

Through gathering information, the consumer learns about competing brands and their features. The first box in Figure 6.5 shows the *total set* of brands available to the consumer. The individual consumer will come to know only a subset of these brands (*awareness set*). Some brands will meet initial buying criteria (*consideration set*). As the consumer gathers more information, only a few will remain as strong contenders (*choice set*). The consumer makes a final choice from this set.[59]

Figure 6.5 makes it clear that a company must strategize to get its brand into the prospect's awareness set, consideration set, and choice set. Food companies might work with supermarkets, for instance, in changing the way they display products. If a store owner arranges yogurt first by brand (like Dannon and Yoplait) and then by flavour within each brand, consumers will tend to select their flavours from the same brand. However, if the products had been displayed with all the strawberry yogurts together, then all the vanilla yogurts, and so forth, consumers would probably choose which flavours they wanted first, and then choose which brand name they would most like for that particular flavour. Australian supermarkets arrange meats by the way they might be cooked, and stores use more descriptive labels, like "a 10-minute herbed beef roast." The result is that Australians buy a greater variety of meats than North Americans, who choose from meats laid out by animal type—beef, chicken, pork, and so on.[60]

The company must also identify the other brands in the consumer's choice set so that it can plan the appropriate competitive appeals. In addition, the company should identify the consumer's information sources and evaluate their relative importance. Consumers should be asked how they first heard about the brand, what information came later, and the relative importance of the different sources. The answers will help the company prepare effective communications for the target market.

FIGURE 6.5

Successive Sets Involved in Consumer Decision Making

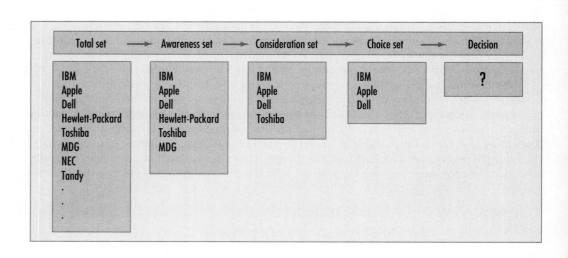

Evaluation of Alternatives

How does the consumer process competitive brand information and make a final value judgment? No single process is used by all consumers or by one consumer in all buying situations. There are several processes, the most current models of which see the process as cognitively oriented. That is, they see the consumer as forming judgments largely on a conscious and rational basis.

Some basic concepts will help us understand consumer evaluation processes: First, the consumer is trying to satisfy a need. Second, the consumer is looking for certain benefits from the product solution. Third, the consumer sees each product as a bundle of attributes with varying abilities for delivering the benefits sought to satisfy this need. The attributes of interest to buyers vary by product—for example:

1. *Cameras.* Picture sharpness, camera speeds, camera size, price.

2. *Hotels.* Location, cleanliness, atmosphere, price.

3. *Mouthwash.* Colour, effectiveness, germ-killing capacity, price, taste/flavour.

4. *Tires.* Safety, tread life, ride quality, price.

Consumers will pay the most attention to attributes that deliver the sought-after benefits. The market for a product can often be segmented according to attributes that are important to different consumer groups.

BELIEFS AND ATTITUDES Evaluations often reflect beliefs and attitudes. Through experience and learning, people acquire beliefs and attitudes. These in turn influence buying behaviour. A **belief** is a descriptive thought that a person holds about something. People's beliefs about the attributes and benefits of a product or brand influence their buying decisions. Just as important as beliefs are attitudes. An **attitude** is a person's enduring favourable or unfavourable evaluation, emotional feeling, and action tendencies toward some object or idea.[61] People have attitudes toward almost everything: religion, politics, clothes, music, and food.

Attitudes put people into a frame of mind: liking or disliking an object, moving toward or away from it. Attitudes lead people to behave in a fairly consistent way toward similar objects. Because attitudes economize on energy and thought, they can be very difficult to change. A company is well advised to fit its product into existing attitudes rather than to try to change attitudes. Of course, there are exceptions, where the cost of trying to change attitudes might pay off, especially if you are trying to market a controversial product or idea.

Council for Biotechnology Information (CBI)

The Council for Biotechnology Information began a new transit shelter campaign in Toronto to coincide with the BIO 2002 conference. The advertising was aimed at the 15 000 visitors expected to attend the conference, as well as at city residents. A series of three ads posed "teaser questions" and referred viewers to the council's Web site (www.whybiotech.com) to find answers. The copy read, "How can a canola plant save energy?" "How does Canada regulate biotech corn?" and "How can a cotton plant resist pests?" Since biotechnology is controversial and since it's neither a brand nor a product, generating awareness and encouraging people to get accurate information has been the focus of the council's advertising and communications efforts.[62]

EXPECTANCY-VALUE MODEL The consumer arrives at attitudes (judgments, preferences) toward various brands through an attribute evaluation procedure.[63] He or she develops a set of beliefs about where each brand stands on each attribute. The **expectancy-value model** of attitude formation posits that consumers evaluate products and services by combining their brand beliefs—the positives and negatives—according to importance.

Suppose Linda Brown has narrowed her choice set to four laptop computers (A, B, C, D). Assume that she is interested in four attributes: memory capacity, graphics capability, size and weight, and price. Table 6.3 shows her beliefs about how each brand rates on the four attributes. If one computer dominated the others on all the criteria, we could predict that Linda would choose it. But, as is often the case, her choice set consists of brands that vary in their appeal. If Linda wants the best memory capacity, she should buy A; if she wants the best graphics capability, she should buy B; and so on.

Changing attitudes is difficult, but with good information, such as that presented by the Biotechnology Council's Web site, it can be accomplished.

Computer	Attribute			
	Memory Capacity	**Graphics Capability**	**Size and Weight**	**Price**
A	10	8	6	4
B	8	9	8	3
C	6	8	10	5
D	4	3	7	8

TABLE 6.3   A CONSUMER'S BRAND BELIEFS ABOUT COMPUTERS

Note: Each attribute is rated from 0 to 10, where 10 represents the highest level on that attribute. Price, however, is indexed in a reverse manner, with a 10 representing the lowest price, because a consumer prefers a low price to a high price.

Most buyers consider several attributes in their purchase decision. If we knew the weights that Linda Brown attaches to the four attributes, we could more reliably predict her computer choice. Suppose Linda assigned 40 percent of the importance to the computer's memory capacity, 30 percent to graphics capability, 20 percent to size and weight, and 10 percent to price. To find Linda's perceived value for each computer, according to the expectancy-value model, we multiply her weights by her beliefs about each computer's attributes. This computation leads to the following perceived values:

Computer A = 0.4(10) + 0.3(8) + 0.2(6) + 0.1(4) = 8.0
Computer B = 0.4(8) + 0.3(9) + 0.2(8) + 0.1(3) = 7.8
Computer C = 0.4(6) + 0.3(8) + 0.2(10) + 0.1(5) = 7.3
Computer D = 0.4(4) + 0.3(3) + 0.2(7) + 0.1(8) = 4.7

An expectancy-model formulation would predict that Linda will favour computer A, which (at 8.0) has the highest perceived value.[64]

Suppose most computer buyers form their preferences the same way. Knowing this, a computer manufacturer can do a number of things to influence buyer decisions. The marketer of computer B, for example, could apply the following strategies to stimulate greater interest in brand B:

- *Redesign the computer.* This technique is called real repositioning.
- *Alter beliefs about the brand.* Attempting to alter beliefs about the brand is called psychological repositioning.
- *Alter beliefs about competitors' brands.* This strategy, called competitive depositioning, makes sense when buyers mistakenly believe a competitor's brand has more quality than it actually has.
- *Alter the importance weights.* The marketer could try to persuade buyers to attach more importance to the attributes in which the brand excels.
- *Call attention to neglected attributes.* The marketer could draw buyers' attention to neglected attributes, such as styling or processing speed.
- *Shift the buyer's ideals.* The marketer could try to persuade buyers to change their ideal levels for one or more attributes.[65]

"Marketing Memo: Applying Customer Value Analysis" describes a cost–benefit technique that provides additional insight into consumer decision making in a competitive setting.

Purchase Decisions

In the evaluation stage, the consumer forms preferences among the brands in the choice set. The consumer may also form an intention to buy the most preferred brand. In executing a purchase intention, the consumer may make up to five sub-decisions: *brand* (brand A), *dealer* (dealer 2), *quantity* (one computer), *timing* (weekend), and *payment method* (credit card). Purchases of everyday products involve fewer decisions and less deliberation. For example, in buying sugar, a consumer gives little thought to vendor or payment method.

In some cases, consumers may decide not to formally evaluate each and every brand; in other cases, intervening factors may affect the final decision.

NONCOMPENSATORY MODELS OF CONSUMER CHOICE The expectancy-value model is a compensatory model in that perceived good things for a product can help to overcome perceived bad things. But consumers may not want to invest so much time and energy to evaluate brands. They often take "mental shortcuts" that involve various simplifying *choice heuristics.*

With **noncompensatory models** of consumer choice, positive and negative attribute considerations do not necessarily net out. Evaluating attributes more in isolation makes decision making easier for a consumer, but also increases the likelihood that the person would have made a different choice if he or she had deliberated in greater detail. We highlight three such choice heuristics here:

1. With the **conjunctive heuristic**, the consumer sets a minimum acceptable cutoff level for each attribute and chooses the first alternative that meets the minimum standard for all attributes. For example, if Linda Brown decided that all attributes had to be rated at least a 7, she would choose computer B.

2. With the **lexicographic heuristic**, the consumer chooses the best brand on the basis of its perceived most important attribute. With this decision rule, Linda Brown would choose computer C.

3. With the **elimination-by-aspects heuristic**, the consumer compares brands on an attribute selected probabilistically—where the probability of choosing an attribute is positively related to its importance—and brands are eliminated if they do not meet minimum acceptable cutoff levels.

Characteristics of the person (e.g., brand or product knowledge), the purchase decision task and setting (e.g., number and similarity of brand choices and time pressure involved), and social context (e.g., need for justification to a peer or boss) all may affect if and how choice heuristics are used.[66]

Consumers do not necessarily adopt only one type of choice rule in making purchase decisions. In some cases, they adopt a phased decision strategy that combines two or more decision rules. For example, they might use a noncompensatory decision rule such as the conjunctive heuristic to reduce the number of brand choices to a more manageable number and then evaluate the remaining brands. Understanding if and how consumers screen brands can be critical. One reason for the runaway success of the Intel Inside campaign in the 1990s was that it made the brand the first cutoff for many consumers—they would only buy a PC which had an Intel microprocessor. PC makers such as IBM and Dell had no choice but to support Intel's marketing efforts.

Marketing Memo

Applying Customer Value Analysis

A useful technique to gain consumer insight is customer value analysis. *Customer value analysis* assumes that customers choose between competitive brand offerings on the basis of which delivers the most customer value. Customer value is given by:

Customer value = Customer benefits – Customer costs

Customer benefits include *product benefits, service benefits, personnel benefits*, and *image benefits*. Assume customers can judge the relative benefit level or worth of different brands. Suppose a customer is considering three brands, A, B, and C, and judges the customer benefits to be worth $150, $140, and $135, respectively. If the customer costs are the same, the customer would clearly choose brand A.

However, the costs are rarely the same. In addition to *purchase price*, costs include *acquisition costs, usage costs, maintenance costs, ownership costs*, and *disposal costs*. Often a customer will buy a more expensive brand because that particular brand will impose lower costs of the other kinds. Consider Table 6.4. A, the highest-priced brand, also involves a lower total cost than lower-priced brands B and C. Clearly, supplier A has done a good job of reducing customers' other costs. Now we can compare the customer value of the three brands:

TABLE 6.4	CUSTOMER COSTS OF THREE BRANDS		
	A	**B**	**C**
Price	$100	$90	$ 80
Acquisition costs	15	25	30
Usage costs	4	7	10
Maintenance costs	2	3	7
Ownership costs	3	3	5
Disposal costs	6	5	8
Total Cost	$130	$135	$140

Customer value of A = $150 – $130 = $20
Customer value of B = $140 – $135 = $5
Customer value of C = $135 – $140 = –$5

The customer will prefer brand A both because the benefit level is higher and the customer costs are lower, but this does not have to be the case. Suppose A decided to charge $120 instead of $100 to take advantage of its higher perceived benefit level. Then A's customer cost would have been $150 instead of $130 and just offset its higher perceived benefit. Brand A, because of its greed, would lose the sale to brand B.

Very often, managers conduct a **customer value analysis** to reveal the company's strengths and weaknesses relative to various competitors. The major steps in such an analysis are:

1. *Identify the major attributes customers value.* Customers are asked what attributes and performance levels they look for in choosing a product and vendors.

2. *Assess the quantitative importance of the different attributes.* Customers are asked to rate the importance of the different attributes. If the customers diverge too much in their ratings, they should be clustered into different segments.

3. *Assess the company's and competitors' performances on the different customer values against their rated importance.* Customers describe where they see the company's and competitors' performances on each attribute.

4. *Examine how customers in a specific segment rate the company's performance against a specific major competitor on an attribute-by-attribute basis.* If the company's offer exceeds the competitor's offer on all important attributes, the company can charge a higher price (thereby earning higher profits), or it can charge the same price and gain more market share.

5. *Monitor customer values over time.* The company must periodically redo its studies of customer values and competitors' standings as the economy, technology, and features change.

INTERVENING FACTORS Even if consumers form brand evaluations, two general factors can intervene between the purchase intention and the purchase decision (Figure 6.6).[67] The first factor is the *attitudes of others*. The extent to which another person's attitude reduces the preference for an alternative depends on two things: (1) the intensity of the other person's negative attitude toward the consumer's preferred alternative and (2) the consumer's motivation to comply with the other person's

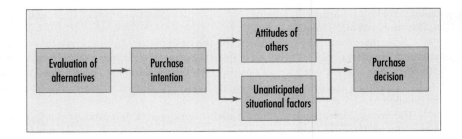

FIGURE 6.6

Steps between Evaluation of Alternatives and a Purchase Decision

wishes.[68] The more intense the other person's negativism and the closer the other person is to the consumer, the more the consumer will adjust his or her purchase intention. The converse is also true: A buyer's preference for a brand will increase if someone he or she respects favours the same brand strongly.

Related to the attitudes of others is the role played by infomediaries who publish their evaluations. Examples include *Consumer Reports*, which provides unbiased expert reviews of all types of products and services; J. D. Powers, which provides consumer-based ratings of cars, financial services, and travel products and services; professional movie, book, and music reviewers; customer reviews of books and music in Chapters.Indigo.ca; and the increasing number of chat rooms where people discuss goods, services, and companies. Consumers are undoubtedly influenced by these evaluations, as evidenced by the success of a small-budget movie like *My Big Fat Greek Wedding* by Canadian actor and screen-writer Nia Vardalos which received a slew of favourable reviews by moviegoers on many Web sites.

The second factor is *unanticipated situational factors* that may erupt to change the purchase intention. Linda Brown might lose her job, some other purchase might become more urgent, or a store salesperson may turn her off. Preferences and even purchase intentions are not completely reliable predictors of purchase behaviour.

A consumer's decision to modify, postpone, or avoid a purchase decision is heavily influenced by *perceived risk*.[69] There are many different types of risks that consumers may perceive in buying and consuming a product:

1. *Functional risk*—the product does not perform up to expectations.
2. *Physical risk*—the product poses a threat to the physical well-being or health of the user or others.
3. *Financial risk*—the product is not worth the price paid.
4. *Social risk*—the product results in embarrassment from others.
5. *Psychological risk*—the product affects the mental well-being of the user.
6. *Time risk*—the failure of the product results in an opportunity cost of finding another satisfactory product.

The amount of perceived risk varies with the amount of money at stake, the amount of attribute uncertainty, and the amount of consumer self-confidence. Consumers develop routines for reducing risk, such as decision avoidance, information gathering from friends, and preference for national brand names and warranties. Marketers must understand the factors that provoke a feeling of risk in consumers and provide information and support to reduce perceived risk.

Post-purchase Behaviour

After the purchase, the consumer might experience dissonance that stems from noticing certain disquieting features or hearing favourable things about other brands, and will be alert to information that supports his or her decision. Marketing communications should supply beliefs and evaluations that reinforce the consumer's choice and help him or her feel good about the brand.

The marketer's job therefore does not end with the purchase. Marketers must monitor post-purchase satisfaction, post-purchase actions, and post-purchase product uses.

POST-PURCHASE SATISFACTION What determines customer satisfaction with a purchase? Satisfaction is a function of the closeness between expectations and the product's perceived performance.[70] If performance falls short of expectations, the consumer is *disappointed*; if it meets expectations, the consumer is *satisfied*; if it exceeds expectations, the consumer is *delighted*. These feelings make a difference in whether the customer buys the product again and talks favourably or unfavourably about it to others.

Consumers form their expectations on the basis of messages received from sellers, friends, and other information sources. The larger the gap between expectations and performance, the greater the dissatisfaction. Here the consumer's coping style comes into play. Some consumers magnify the gap when the product is not perfect, and they are highly dissatisfied; others minimize the gap and are less dissatisfied.[71]

The importance of post-purchase satisfaction suggests that product claims must truthfully represent the product's likely performance. Some sellers might even understate performance levels so that consumers experience higher-than-expected satisfaction with the product.

POST-PURCHASE ACTIONS   Satisfaction or dissatisfaction with the product will influence subsequent behaviour. If the consumer is satisfied, he or she will exhibit a higher probability of purchasing the product again. For example, data on automobile brand choice show a high correlation between being highly satisfied with the last brand bought and intention to buy the brand again. One survey showed that 75 percent of Toyota buyers were highly satisfied and about 75 percent intended to buy a Toyota again; 35 percent of Chevrolet buyers were highly satisfied and about 35 percent intended to buy a Chevrolet again. The satisfied customer will also tend to say good things about the brand to others. Marketers say: "Our best advertisement is a satisfied customer."[72]

Dissatisfied consumers may abandon or return the product. They may seek information that confirms its high value. They may take public action by complaining to the company, going to a lawyer, or complaining to other groups (such as business, private, or government agencies). Private actions include making a decision to stop buying the product (*exit option*) or warning friends (*voice option*).[73] In all these cases, the seller has done a poor job of satisfying the customer.[74]

Chapter 3 described CRM programs designed to build long-term brand loyalty. Post-purchase communications to buyers have been shown to result in fewer product returns and order cancellations.[75] Computer companies, for example, can send a letter to new owners congratulating them on having selected a fine computer. They can place ads showing satisfied brand owners. They can solicit customer suggestions for improvements and list the location of available services. They can write intelligible instruction booklets. They can send owners a magazine containing articles describing new computer applications. In addition, they can provide good channels for speedy redress of customer grievances.

POST-PURCHASE USE AND DISPOSAL Marketers should also monitor how buyers use and dispose of the product (Figure 6.7). A key driver of sales frequency is product consumption rate—the more quickly buyers consume a product, the sooner they may be back in the market to repurchase it.

One potential opportunity to increase frequency of product use is when consumer's perceptions of their usage differ from the reality. Consumers may fail to replace products with relatively short life spans in a timely manner because of a tendency to underestimate product life.[76] One strategy to speed up replacement is to tie the act of replacing the product to a certain holiday, event, or time of year.

FIGURE 6.7

How Customers Use or Dispose of Products

Source: From Jacob Jacoby, Carol K. Berning, and Thomas Dietvorst, "What about Disposition?" *Journal of Marketing* (July 1977): 23. Reprinted with permission of the American Marketing Association.

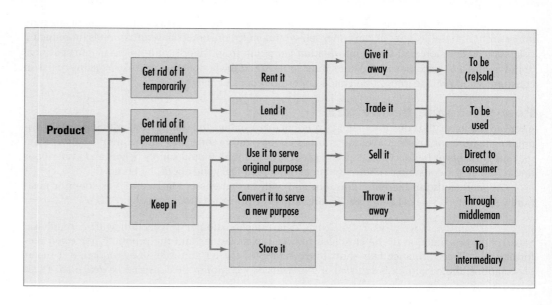

For example, several brands have run promotions tied in with the springtime switch to daylight savings time (e.g., Oral-B toothbrushes). Another strategy might be to provide consumers with better information as to either (1) when the product was first used or would need to be replaced or (2) the current level of performance. For example, batteries offer built-in gauges that show how much power they have left; toothbrushes have colour indicators on their bristles to indicate when they are too worn; and so on. Perhaps the simplest way to increase usage is when actual usage of a product is less than optimal or recommended. In this case, consumers must be persuaded of the merits of more regular usage, and potential hurdles to increased usage must be overcome.

If consumers throw the product away, the marketer needs to know how they dispose of it, especially if it can damage the environment (as in the case with batteries, beverage containers, and disposable diapers). Increased public awareness of recycling and ecological concerns as well as consumer complaints about having to throw away beautiful bottles led French perfume maker Rochas to think about introducing a refillable fragrance line.

Other Theories of Consumer Decision-Making

The consumer decision process may not always develop in a carefully planned fashion. It is important to understand other theories and approaches to how consumers make decisions and when they might apply.

Level of Consumer Involvement

The expectancy-value model assumes a high level of involvement on the part of the consumer. **Consumer involvement** can be defined in terms of the level of engagement and active processing undertaken by the consumer in responding to a marketing stimulus (e.g., from viewing an ad or evaluating a product or service).

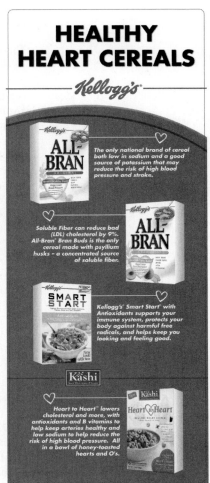

ELABORATION LIKELIHOOD MODEL   An influential model of attitude formation and change, Richard Petty and John Cacioppo's *elaboration likelihood model*, describes how consumers make evaluations in both low- and high-involvement circumstances.[77] There are two means of persuasion with their model: the central route, where attitude formation or change involves much thought and is based on a diligent, rational consideration of the most important product or service information; and the peripheral route, where attitude formation or change involves comparatively much less thought and is a consequence of the association of a brand with either positive or negative peripheral cues. Examples of peripheral cues for consumers might be a celebrity endorsement, a credible source, or any object that engendered positive feelings.

Consumers follow the central route only if they possess sufficient *motivation, ability,* and *opportunity*. In other words, consumers must want to evaluate a brand in detail, must have the necessary brand and product or service knowledge in memory, and must be given sufficient time and the proper setting to actually do so. If any one of those three factors are lacking, consumers will tend to follow the peripheral route and consider less central, more extrinsic factors in their decisions.

LOW-INVOLVEMENT MARKETING STRATEGIES Many products are bought under conditions of low involvement and the absence of significant brand differences. Consider salt. Consumers have little involvement in this product category. They go to the store and reach for the brand. If they keep reaching for the same brand, it is out of habit, not strong brand loyalty. There is good evidence that consumers have low involvement with most low-cost, frequently purchased products.

Marketers use four techniques to try to convert a low-involvement product into one of higher involvement. First, they can link the product to some involving issue, as when Crest toothpaste is linked to avoiding cavities. Second, they can link the product to some involving personal situation—for example, fruit juices began to include vitamins and calcium to fortify their drinks. Third, they might design advertising to trigger strong emotions related to personal values or ego defence, as when cereal makers began to advertise their heart-healthy nature to adults and the importance of living a long time to enjoy family life. Fourth, they might add an important feature—for example, when GE light bulbs introduced "Soft White" versions. These strategies at best raise consumer involvement from a low to a moderate level; they do not necessarily propel the consumer into highly involved buying behaviour.

Converting a low-involvement product to a higher-involvement product: Kellogg's now advertises its products as "healthy heart cereals" to make consumers aware that which cereal you eat matters.

If, regardless of what the marketer can do, consumers have low involvement with a purchase decision, they are likely to follow the peripheral route. Marketers must pay special attention to giving consumers one or more positive cues that they can use to justify their brand choice. Brand familiarity can be important if consumers decide to just buy the brand about which they have heard or seen the most. Frequent ad repetition, visible sponsorships, and vigorous PR are all ways to enhance brand familiarity. Other peripheral cues can also be used. A beloved celebrity endorser, attractive packaging, or an appealing promotion all might tip the balance in favour of the brand.[78]

VARIETY-SEEKING BUYING BEHAVIOUR Some buying situations are characterized by low involvement but significant brand differences. Here consumers often do a lot of brand switching. Think about cookies. The consumer has some beliefs about cookies, chooses a brand of cookies without much evaluation, and evaluates the product during consumption. Next time, the consumer may reach for another brand out of a wish for a different taste. Brand switching occurs for the sake of variety rather than dissatisfaction.

The market leader and the minor brands in this product category have different marketing strategies. The market leader will try to encourage habitual buying behaviour by dominating the shelf space with a variety of related but different product versions, avoiding out-of-stock conditions, and sponsoring frequent reminder advertising. Challenger firms will encourage variety seeking by offering lower prices, deals, coupons, free samples, and advertising that tries to break the consumer's purchase and consumption cycle and presents reasons for trying something new.

Decision Heuristics and Biases

As the low involvement and noncompensatory model discussions suggest, consumers do not always process information or make decisions in a deliberate, rational manner. Behavioural decision theory is a thriving area in consumer research. Behavioural decision theorists have identified many different heuristics and biases in everyday consumer decision making. **Heuristics** are rules of thumb or mental shortcuts in the decision process.

Heuristics can come into play when consumers forecast the likelihood of future outcomes or events.[79]

1. The **availability heuristic**: Consumers base their predictions on the quickness and ease with which a particular example of an outcome comes to mind. If an example comes to mind too easily, consumers might overestimate the likelihood of the outcome or event happening. For example, a recent product failure may lead a consumer to inflate the likelihood of a future product failure and make him or her more inclined to purchase a product warranty.

2. The **representativeness heuristic**: Consumers base their predictions on how representative or similar the outcome is to other examples. One reason why package appearances may be so similar for different brands in the same product category is that they want to be seen as representative of the category as a whole.

3. The **anchoring and adjustment heuristic**: Consumers arrive at an initial judgment and then make adjustments off that first impression based on additional information. For services marketers, it is critical to make a strong first impression to establish a favourable anchor so that subsequent experiences are interpreted in a more favourable light.

Note that marketing managers also may use heuristics and be subject to biases in their decision making. "Marketing Memo: Decision Traps" reveals ten common mistakes managers make in their decisions.

Mental Accounting

Researchers have found that consumers use mental accounting when they handle their money.[80] **Mental accounting** refers to the manner by which consumers code, categorize, and evaluate financial outcomes of choices. Formally, it has been defined in terms of "The tendency to categorize funds or items of value even though there is no logical basis for the categorization, e.g., individuals often segregate their savings into separate accounts to meet different goals even though funds from any of the accounts can be applied to any of the goals."[81]

For example, assume you spend $50 to buy a ticket to see a concert.[82] As you arrive at the show, you realize you've lost your ticket. You may be unsure about purchasing another ticket for $50. Assume, on the other hand, that you realized you had lost $50 on the way to buy the ticket. You might be much more likely to go ahead and buy the ticket anyway. Although the amount lost in each case was the same—$50—the reactions were very different. In the first case, you may have mentally allocated $50 for going to a concert. Buying another ticket would therefore exceed your mental concert budget. In the second case, the money that was lost did not belong to any account, so the mental concert budget had not yet been exceeded.

According to Richard Thaler, mental accounting is based on a set of key core principles:

1. Consumers tend to *segregate gains*. When a seller has a product with more than one positive dimension, it is desirable to have each dimension evaluated separately. Listing multiple benefits of a large industrial product, for example, can make the sum of the parts seem greater than the whole.

2. Consumers tend to *integrate losses*. Marketers have a distinct advantage in selling something if its cost can be added to another large purchase. House buyers are more inclined to view additional expenditures favourably given the high price of buying a house.

3. Consumers tend to *integrate smaller losses with larger gains*. The "cancellation" principle might explain why withholding taxes taken from monthly paycheques are less aversive than large lump-sum tax payments—they are more likely to be absorbed by the larger pay amount.

4. Consumers tend to *segregate small gains from large losses*. The "silver lining" principle might explain the popularity of rebates on big-ticket purchases such as cars.

The principles of mental accounting are derived in part from prospect theory. **Prospect theory** maintains that consumers frame decision alternatives in terms of gains and losses according to a value function. Consumers are generally loss averse. Consumers tend to overweight very low probabilities and underweight very high probabilities.

Profiling the Customer Buying Decision Process

How can marketers learn about the stages in the buying process for their product? They can think about how they themselves would act (*introspective method*). They can interview a small number of recent purchasers, asking

Marketing Memo

Decision Traps

In *Decision Traps*, Jay Russo and Paul Schoemaker reveal the ten most common mistakes managers make in their decisions.

1. *Plunging in.* Beginning to gather information and reach conclusions without taking a few minutes to think about the crux of the issue you're facing or to think through how you believe decisions like this one should be made.

2. *Frame blindness.* Setting out to solve the wrong problem because you've created a mental framework for your decision, with little thought, that causes you to overlook the best options or lose sight of important objectives.

3. *Lack of frame control.* Failing to consciously define the problem in more ways than one or being unduly influenced by the frames of others.

4. *Overconfidence in your judgment.* Failing to collect key factual information because you are too sure of your assumptions and opinions.

5. *Shortsighted shortcuts.* Relying inappropriately on "rules of thumb" such as implicitly trusting the most readily available information or anchoring too much on convenient facts.

6. *Shooting from the hip.* Believing you can keep straight in your head all the information you've discovered, and therefore "winging it" rather than following a systematic procedure when making the final choice.

7. *Group failure.* Assuming that with many smart people involved, good choices will follow automatically, and therefore failing to manage the group decision-making process.

8. *Fooling yourself about feedback.* Failing to interpret the evidence from past outcomes for what it really says, either because you are protecting your ego or because you are tricked by hindsight effects.

9. *Not keeping track.* Assuming that experience will make its lessons available automatically, and therefore failing to keep systematic records to track the results of your decisions and failing to analyze these results in ways that reveal their key lessons.

10. *Failure to audit your decision process.* Failing to create an organized approach to understanding your own decision making, so you remain constantly exposed to all the other nine decision traps.

Sources: J. Edward Russo and Paul J. H. Schoemaker, *Decision Traps: Ten Barriers to Brilliant Decision-Making and How to Overcome Them* (New York: Doubleday, 1990); see also J. Edward Russo and Paul J. H. Schoemaker, *Winning Decisions: Getting It Right the First Time* (New York: Doubleday, 2001).

them to recall the events leading to their purchase (*retrospective method*). They can locate consumers who plan to buy the product and ask them to think out loud about going through the buying process (*prospective method*); or they can ask consumers to describe the ideal way to buy the product (*prescriptive method*). Each method yields a picture of the steps in the process.

Trying to understand the customer's behaviour in connection with a product has been called mapping the customer's *consumption system*,[83] *customer activity cycle*,[84] or *customer scenario*.[85] This can be done for such activity clusters as doing laundry, preparing for a wedding, or buying a car. Buying a car, for example, involves a whole cluster of activities, including choosing the car, financing the purchase, buying insurance, buying accessories, and so on.

SUMMARY

1. Consumer behaviour is influenced by three factors: cultural (culture, subculture, and social class); social (reference groups, family, and social roles and statuses); and personal (age, stage in the life cycle, occupation, economic circumstances, lifestyle, personality, and self-concept). Research into all these factors can provide marketers with clues to reach and serve consumers more effectively.

2. Four main psychological processes affect consumer behaviour: motivation, perception, learning, and memory.

3. To understand how consumers actually make buying decisions, marketers must identify the person who makes the decision to buy the product, the person who actually buys the product, and the people who influence the decision to buy the product.

4. The typical buying process consists of the following sequence of events: problem recognition, information search, evaluation of alternatives, purchase decision, and post-purchase behaviour. The marketer's job is to understand behaviour at each stage. The attitudes of others, unanticipated situational factors, and perceived risk may all affect the decision to buy, as will consumers' levels of post-purchase satisfaction and post-purchase actions on the part of the company.

APPLICATIONS

Marketing Debate: Is Target Marketing Ever Bad?

As marketers increasingly develop marketing programs tailored to certain target market segments, some critics have denounced these efforts as exploitative. For example, the preponderance of billboards advertising lotteries, alcohol, video gaming machines, and other vices in low-income areas is seen as taking advantage of a vulnerable market segment. Critics can be especially harsh in evaluating marketing programs that target minority groups, claiming that they often employ clichéd stereotypes and inappropriate depictions. Others counter with the point of view that targeting and positioning is critical to marketing and that these marketing programs are an attempt to be relevant to a certain consumer group.

Take a position: Targeting minorities is exploitative versus Targeting minorities is a sound business practice.

Marketing Discussion: What Are Your Mental Accounts?

What mental accounts do you have in your mind about purchasing products or services? Do you have any rules you employ in spending money? Are they different from what other people do? Do you follow Thaler's four principles in reacting to gains and losses?

Marketing Spotlight: Disney

The Walt Disney Company, a US$27 billion-a-year global entertainment giant, recognizes what its customers value in the Disney brand: a fun experience and homespun entertainment based on old-fashioned family values. Disney responds to these consumer preferences by leveraging the brand across different consumer markets. Say a family goes to see a Disney movie together. They have a great time. They want to continue the experience. Disney Consumer Products, a division of the Walt Disney Company, lets them do just that through product lines aimed at specific age groups.

Take the 2004 *Home on the Range* movie. In addition to the movie, Disney created an accompanying soundtrack album, a line of toys and kids' clothing featuring the heroine, a theme park attraction, and a series of books. Similarly, Disney's 2003 *Pirates of the Caribbean* had a theme park ride, merchandising program, video game, TV series, and comic books. Disney's strategy is to build consumer segments around each of its characters, from classics like Mickey Mouse and Snow White to new hits like Kim Possible. Each brand is created for a special age group and distribution channel. Baby Mickey & Co. and Disney Babies both target infants, but the former is sold through department stores and specialty gift stores whereas the latter is a lower-priced option sold through mass-market channels. Disney's Mickey's Stuff for Kids targets boys and girls, while Mickey Unlimited targets teens and adults.

On TV, the Disney Channel is the top primetime destination for kids 6 to 14, and Playhouse Disney is Disney's preschool programming targeting kids 2 to 6. Other products, like Disney's co-branded Visa card, target adults. Cardholders earn one Disney "dollar" for every $100 charged to the card, and then redeem the earnings for Disney merchandise or services, including Disney's theme parks and resorts, Disney Stores, Walt Disney Studios, and Disney stage productions. Disney is even in Home Depot, with a line of licensed kids-room paint colours with paint swatches in the signature mouse-and-ears shape.

Disney also has licensed food products with character brand tie-ins. For example, Disney Yo-Pals Yogurt features Winnie the Pooh and Friends. The yogurt cups are aimed at preschoolers and have an illustrated short story under each lid that encourages reading and discovery. Keebler Disney Holiday Magic Middles are vanilla sandwich cookies that have an individual image of Mickey, Donald Duck, and Goofy imprinted in each cookie.

The integration of all the consumer product lines can be seen with Disney's *Kim Possible* TV program. The series follows the action-adventures of a typical high-school girl who, in her spare time, saves the world from evil villains. The top-rated cable program has spawned a variety of merchandise offered by the seven Disney Consumer Products division. The merchandise includes:

- Disney Hardlines—stationery, lunchboxes, food products, room decor.
- Disney Softlines—sportswear, sleepwear, daywear, accessories.
- Disney Toys—action figures, wigglers, beanbags, plush, fashion dolls, poseables.
- Disney Publishing—diaries, junior novels, comic books.
- Walt Disney Records—*Kim Possible* soundtrack.
- Buena Vista Home Entertainment—DVD/video.
- Buena Vista Games—GameBoy Advance.

"The success of *Kim Possible* is driven by action-packed storylines which translate well into merchandise in many categories," said Andy Mooney, chairman, Disney Consumer Products Worldwide. Rich Ross, president of entertainment, Disney Channel, added: "Today's kids want a deeper experience with their favorite television characters, like Kim Possible. This line of products extends our viewers' experience with Kim, Rufus, Ron and other show characters, allowing [kids] to touch, see and live the *Kim Possible* experience."

Walt Disney created Mickey Mouse in 1928 (Walt wanted to call his creation Mortimer until his wife convinced him Mickey Mouse was better). Disney's first feature-length musical animation, *Snow White and the Seven Dwarfs*, debuted in 1937. Today, the pervasiveness of Disney product offerings is staggering—all in all, there are over 3 billion entertainment-based impressions of Mickey Mouse received by children every year. But as Walt Disney said: "I only hope that we don't lose sight of one thing—that it was all started by a mouse."

DISCUSSION QUESTIONS

1. What have been the key success factors for Disney?

2. Where is Disney vulnerable? What should it watch out for?

3. What recommendations would you make to the company's senior marketing executives going forward? What should they be sure to do with its marketing?

Sources: Bruce Orwall and Emily Nelson, "Disney's Kingdom: 80 Years of Culture," *Wall Street Journal*, February 13, 2004; "Mouse Hunt," *Fortune*, January 12, 2004; "Keebler Disney Holiday Magic Middles," *Product Alert*, January 26, 2004; Reil Hoards, "Yogurt Finds a New Groove," *Frozen Food Age* (July 2003): 1; *Movers and Shakers* (New York: Basic Books, 2003); Kelly Shermach, "Co-branding Marches on with New Alliances," *Potentials* (July 2003): 7; Megan Larson, "Disney Channel Grows Tween Scene," *MediaWeek*, August 11, 2003, p. 4; www.disney.com.

7

- What is the business market, and how does it differ from the consumer market?

- What buying situations do organizational buyers face?

- Who participates in the business-to-business buying process?

- How do business buyers make their decisions?

- How can companies build strong relationships with business customers?

- How do institutional buyers and government agencies do their buying?

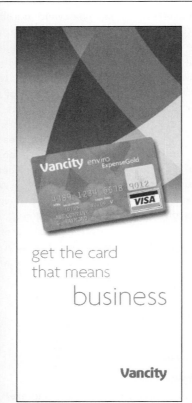

get the card that means **business**

Vancity

get the card that makes good business sense

Vancity's ExpenseGold VISA® is the perfect card for all your business, travel and entertainment expenses. And the 21-day interest-free grace period allows cash flow flexibility every business needs. It's accepted worldwide and comes with great VISA features you can use at home or on the road.

You can get up to three supplementary ExpenseGold VISA cards at no additional cost. Each card carries both the name of your business and the cardholder's name.

Becoming an ExpenseGold VISA cardholder is easier than you think. Approval is based on your personal credit history.

taking care of business is rewarding
Earn My VISA Rewards Plus points at a rate of one point for each dollar you spend. They're easily redeemable online at myvisarewardsplus.com for great merchandise, travel, financial products or charitable donations.

Get 2,500 bonus points when you become an ExpenseGold VISA cardholder and an additional 3,500 bonus points when you renew your card each year.

And you'll also be helping the environment because a minimum of 5% of Vancity VISA profits go to supporting local environmental projects through the enviroFund.™

Apply today for your ExpenseGold VISA card at your Vancity branch to get your 2,500 bonus points.

For more information, call 1.800.611.8472 or visit vancity.com/mybusiness

Vancity

™Vancity EnviroFund is a Trademark of Vancouver City Savings Credit Union.
®VISA Int./Vancity, Licensed User.
Process chlorine-free, 100% postconsumer recycled fibre. Printed with non-toxic vegetable based inks.

CHAPTER 7

Analyzing Business Markets

PROFILE: CANADIAN MARKETING EXCELLENCE

Founded in 1946 to provide financial services to the people of British Columbia, Vancity is now Canada's largest credit union, reporting $10.5 billion in assets, 310 000 members, and 43 branches throughout Greater Vancouver, the Fraser Valley, and Victoria. The once-small credit union has become a major player in B.C.'s financial services marketplace.

Vancity is a unique business. As a credit union, it is owned by its members, who are also its customers. This creates an organizational structure based almost entirely on service and accountability. Furthermore, Vancity is a socially minded and community-focused company, releasing an annual accountability report following a social audit process (in addition to the more familiar annual reporting process). In 2003 alone, Vancity was ranked one of *Maclean's* magazines' "Top 100 Employers," it was recognized as part of an elite group of Power Smart Certified companies for energy efficiency leadership by B.C. Hydro, it launched Canada's first low-interest loan for hybrid vehicles, and it was given an Innovation Award from Credit Union Central of B.C. for its lesbian and gay marketing campaign. While this socially based mission and operating philosophy has had a great deal to do with Vancity's success in the hypercompetitive world of banking and financial services, it has been crucial for Vancity to deploy excellent marketing tactics to continue to grow and succeed. One of the ways Vancity has done so is through its business-to-business marketing initiatives.

In the late 1990s, Vancity had only 12 000 to 15 000 small and medium-size business customers; in 2004 the company reported an estimated 25 000 business customers, representing approximately 10 percent of the credit union's entire customer base. This phenomenal growth in the business-to-business segment is considered notable given that marketing to business owners is considered far more difficult than reaching individual consumers in the retail segment.

Vancity began targeting the business market through several different touch points: print ads in publications such as *Business in Vancouver*, e-mail and direct mail, and sponsorships, such as the Vancouver Board of Trade. Yet the key to Vancity's business segment marketing strategy is products tailored specifically to that segment. For example, in 2004, Vancity launched a direct-mail campaign aimed at 2800 business owners for a new Vancity Expense Gold Visa. Not only could small businesses charge their business purchases to the cards, it also offered the business owners personal reward benefits. The cards, therefore, featured both a customer's business and personal name on the card. The strategy with the product was to appeal to the business side of each owner while also addressing his or her consumer sensibility. Vancity also invested in its service personnel, increasing its business client staff to 80 people. To target potential customers, business account managers were trained to give in-person or e-mail presentations tailored specifically to various businesses.

"We aim to build strong relationships with members who we define as high-value. For high-value clients, account managers contact them quarterly, even monthly. They will uncover what needs the customer is looking for, as well as anticipate what products they might need in the future," said Kevin Zakus, vice-president, business services.

These efforts were met with considerable success according to Zakus: "In terms of deposits and loans, we have tripled our business with them over the last seven years." Through the creation of relevant and innovative products, and well-crafted marketing tactics, Vancity has substantially increased the amount of business it does with this segment and ultimately created more value for its members in the process.

Sources: Vancity, **www.vancity.com** (viewed July 26, 2004); Vancity, *2003 Annual Report*; Chris Daniels, "Taking Care of B2B," *Marketing Magazine Online*, **www.marketingmag.com**, June 28, 2004 (viewed July 26, 2004).

Business organizations do not only sell. They also buy vast quantities of raw materials, manufactured components, plant and equipment, supplies, and business services. There are over 14 million buying organizations in North America alone. To create and capture value, sellers need to understand these organizations' needs, resources, policies, and buying procedures.

SAP

German software company SAP has become a leading seller to the business market by specializing in software to automate business functions, such as finance and factory management. It owns over half the market. SAP's leadership strategy is to focus carefully on what customers want, and show them how SAP's software applications can improve profits, raise revenue, or reduce costs. Partly through acquisitions, SAP offers IT customers one-stop shopping to standardize business processes.[1]

Some of the world's most valuable brands belong to business marketers: Magna International, Research in Motion, Caterpillar, DuPont, FedEx, GE, Alcan, IBM, Intel, and Bombardier. Much of basic marketing also applies to business marketers. They need to embrace holistic marketing principles, such as building strong relationships with their customers, just like any marketer. Consider the case of Dofasco. It is Canada's most successful steel producer and one of North America's most progressive and profitable steel-makers. And it has achieved its success not only by providing high-quality flat-rolled and tubular steel to customers throughout North America, but also by practising a customer-focused "Solutions in Steel"™ strategy. This breakthrough strategy has transformed Dofasco from a manufacturer of steel to the producer of innovative, value-added steel products designed to solve the immediate and future needs of its customers. But there are some unique considerations in selling to other businesses.[2] In this chapter, we will highlight some of the crucial differences for marketing in business markets.

What Is Organizational Buying?

Webster and Wind define **organizational buying** as the decision-making process by which formal organizations establish the need for purchased products and services and identify, evaluate, and choose among alternative brands and suppliers.[3]

The Business Market versus the Consumer Market

The **business market** consists of all the organizations that acquire goods and services used in the production of other goods or services that are sold, rented, or supplied to others. The major industries making up the business market are agriculture, forestry, and fisheries; mining; manufacturing; construction; transportation; communication; public utilities; banking, finance, and insurance; distribution; and services.

More dollars and items are involved in sales to business buyers than to consumers. Consider the process of producing and selling a simple pair of shoes. Hide dealers must sell hides to tanners, who sell leather to shoe manufacturers, who sell shoes to wholesalers, who sell shoes to retailers, who finally sell them to consumers. Each party in the supply chain also has to buy many other goods and services.

Business markets have several characteristics that contrast sharply with those of consumer markets:

- *Fewer, larger buyers.* The business marketer normally deals with far fewer, much larger buyers than the consumer marketer does. The fate of Goodyear Tire Company and other automotive part suppliers depends on getting contracts from a few major automakers. A few large buyers do most of the purchasing in such industries as aircraft engines and defence weapons. Although it should be noted that as a slowing economy has put a stranglehold on large corporations' purchasing departments, the small and midsize business market is offering new opportunities for suppliers.[4] See "Marketing Memo: Guidelines for Selling to Small Business" for more on how to access this promising new business-to-business (B2B) market.

- *Close supplier–customer relationship.* Because of the smaller customer base and the importance and power of the larger customers, suppliers are frequently expected to customize their offerings to individual business customer needs. Business buyers often select suppliers who also buy from them. An example would be a paper manufacturer that buys chemicals from a chemical company that buys a considerable amount of its paper.

- *Professional purchasing.* Business goods are often purchased by trained purchasing agents, who must follow their organi-

Marketing Memo

Guidelines for Selling to Small Business

- *Don't lump small and midsize business together.* There's a big gap between $1 million in revenue and $50 million or between a start-up with ten employees and a more mature business with 100. IBM customizes its small and midsize business portal (www.ibm.com/businesscenter/us) with call-me or text-chat buttons that are connected to products for different market segments.

- *Don't waste their time.* That means no cold calls, entertaining sales shows, or sales pitches over long boozy lunches.

- *Do keep it simple.* This could be a corollary to "don't waste their time." Simplicity means one point of contact with a supplier for all service problems or one single bill for all services and products. AT&T Corporation, which serves 3.9 million businesses with fewer than 100 employees, bundles data management, networking, and other abilities into convenient single packages for this market.

- *Do use the Internet.* In its research on buying patterns of small business owners, Hewlett-Packard found that these time-strapped decision makers prefer to buy, or at least research, products and services online. To that end, HP has designed a site targeted to small and midsize businesses and pulls business owners to the site through extensive advertising, direct mail, e-mail campaigns, catalogues, and events. IBM prospects via eBay by selling refurbished or phased-out equipment on its new B2B site. About 80 percent of IBM's equipment is sold to small businesses that are new to IBM—half of which have agreed to receive calls with other offers.

- *Don't forget about direct contact.* Even if a small business owner's first point of contact is via the Internet, you still need to offer phone or face time. Sprint connects with small businesses through its Sprint Experience Centers. Located in major metropolitan areas, these centres bring Sprint's products to life and serve as a place where Sprint reps or dealer reps can invite prospects and let them interact with the technologies.

- *Do provide support after the sale.* Small businesses want partners, not pitchmen. When the DeWitt Company, a 100-employee landscaping products business, purchased a large piece of machinery from Moeller, a German company, the company's president paid DeWitt's CEO a personal visit and stayed until the machine was up and running properly.

- *Do your homework.* The realities of small or midsize business management are different from those at a large corporation. Microsoft created a small fictional executive research firm, Southridge, and baseball-style trading cards of its key decision makers in order to help Microsoft employees tie sales strategies to small business realities.

Sources: Based on Barnaby J. Feder, "When Goliath Comes Knocking on David's Door," *New York Times*, May 6, 2003, p. G13; Jay Greene, "Small Biz: Microsoft's Next Big Thing?" *Business Week*, April 21, 2003, pp. 72–73; Jennifer Gilbert, "Small but Mighty," *Sales & Marketing Management*, January 2004, pp. 30–35; Verne Kopytoff, "Businesses Click on eBay," *San Francisco Chronicle*, July 28, 2003, p. E1.

zation's purchasing policies, constraints, and requirements. Many of the buying instruments—for example, requests for quotations, proposals, and purchase contracts—are not typically found in consumer buying. Professional buyers spend their careers learning how to buy better. Many belong to the Purchasing Managers Association of Canada (PMAC), which seeks to improve professional buyers' effectiveness and status. This means that business marketers have to provide greater technical data about their product and its advantages over competitors' products.

- *Several buying influences.* More people typically influence business buying decisions. Buying committees consisting of technical experts and even senior management are common in the purchase of major goods. Business marketers have to send well-trained sales representatives and sales teams to deal with the well-trained buyers.

- *Multiple sales calls.* Because more people are involved in the selling process, it takes multiple sales calls to win most business orders, and some sales cycles can take years. A study by McGraw-Hill found that it takes four to four and a half calls to close an average industrial sale. In the case of capital equipment sales for large projects, it may take multiple attempts to fund a project, and the sales cycle—between quoting a job and delivering the product—is often measured in years.[5]

- *Derived demand.* The demand for business goods is ultimately derived from the demand for consumer goods. For this reason, the business marketer must closely monitor the buying patterns of ultimate consumers. For instance, the Big Three automakers have been driving the boom in demand for steel-bar products. Much of that demand is derived from consumers' continued love affair with minivans and other light trucks, which consume far more steel than cars. Business buyers must also pay close attention to current and expected economic factors, such as the level of production, investment, consumer spending, and the interest rate. In a recession, business buyers reduce their investment in plant, equipment, and inventories. Business marketers can do little to stimulate total demand in this environment. They can only fight harder to increase or maintain their share of demand.

- *Inelastic demand.* The total demand for many business goods and services is inelastic—that is, not much affected by price changes. Shoe manufacturers are not going to buy much more leather if the price of leather falls, nor will they buy much less leather if the price rises, unless they can find satisfactory substitutes. Demand is especially inelastic in the short run because producers cannot make quick changes in production methods. Demand is also inelastic for business goods that represent a small percentage of the item's total cost, such as shoelaces.

- *Fluctuating demand.* The demand for business goods and services tends to be more volatile than the demand for consumer goods and services. A given percentage increase in consumer demand can lead to a much larger percentage increase in the demand for plant and equipment necessary to produce the additional output. Economists refer to this as the *acceleration effect.* Sometimes a rise of only 10 percent in consumer demand can cause as much as a 200 percent rise in business demand for products in the next period; a 10 percent fall in consumer demand may cause a complete collapse in business demand.

- *Geographically concentrated buyers.* About 58 percent of all Canadian businesses are located in Ontario and Quebec, concentrated in the metropolitan areas between Windsor and Quebec City. Thirty-five percent of Canada's businesses are in the Western provinces, and 6 percent are located in the Atlantic provinces.[6] The provinces of Ontario and Quebec are home to the country's auto industry, and Canada's high-tech firms are clustered in Ottawa, Montreal, and Toronto. The petroleum industry calls Calgary and Edmonton home, while New Brunswick attracts the telemarketing industry and is the location of many companies' call centres. Most agricultural output comes from relatively few provinces.

- *Direct purchasing.* Business buyers often buy directly from manufacturers rather than through intermediaries, especially items that are technically complex or expensive (such as mainframes or aircraft).

Buying Situations

The business buyer faces many decisions in making a purchase. The number of decisions depends on the buying situation: complexity of the problem being solved, newness of the buying requirement, number of people involved, and time required. Patrick Robinson and others distinguish three types of buying situations: the straight rebuy, modified rebuy, and new task.[7]

STRAIGHT REBUY The purchasing department reorders on a routine basis (e.g., office supplies, bulk chemicals) and chooses from suppliers on an "approved list." The suppliers make an effort to maintain product and service quality and often propose automatic reordering systems to save time. "Out-suppliers" attempt to offer something new or to exploit dissatisfaction with a current supplier. Out-suppliers try to get a small order and then enlarge their purchase share over time.

MODIFIED REBUY The buyer wants to modify product specifications, prices, delivery requirements, or other terms. The modified rebuy usually involves additional participants on both sides. The in-suppliers become nervous and have to protect the account. The out-suppliers see an opportunity to propose a better offer to gain some business.

NEW TASK A purchaser buys a product or service for the first time (e.g., office building, new security system). The greater the cost or risk, the larger the number of participants and the greater their information gathering—and therefore the longer the time to reach a decision.[8]

The business buyer makes the fewest decisions in the straight rebuy situation and the most in the new-task situation. Over time, new-buy situations become straight rebuys and routine purchase behaviour. New-task buying passes through several stages: awareness, interest, evaluation, trial, and adoption.[9] The effectiveness of communication tools varies at each stage. Mass media are most important during the initial awareness stage; salespeople have their greatest impact at the interest stage; and technical sources are the most important during the evaluation stage.

In the new-task situation, the buyer has to determine product specifications, price limits, delivery terms and times, service terms, payment terms, order quantities, acceptable suppliers, and the selected supplier. Different participants influence each decision, and the order in which these decisions are made varies. This situation is the marketer's greatest opportunity and challenge. Because of the complicated selling involved, many companies use a *missionary sales force* consisting of their most effective salespeople. The brand promise and the manufacturer's brand name recognition will be important in establishing trust and the customer's willingness to consider change. The marketer also tries to reach as many key participants as possible and provide helpful information and assistance.

Once a customer is acquired, in-suppliers are continually seeking ways to add value to their market offer to facilitate rebuys. Often they do this by giving customers customized solutions:

Magna International

One of the most diversified automotive parts suppliers in the world, Magna International, based in Aurora, Ontario, supplies automobile parts to DaimlerChrysler, BMW, Volkswagen, Ford, GM, and others. Magna has a history and culture of offering innovation and customization as a key supplier in the automobile industry. For example, in 2003 it developed an automated after-market roof rack for the Hummer H2 and exterior lighting systems featured on the Aston Martin. Magna has pioneered sophisticated vehicle interior integration—the first fully integrated vehicle interior was the 2002 Cadillac CTS (for which General Motors won the "Interior of the Year" award at Detroit's 2003 Auto Interiors Show). Working collaboratively with its clients, Magna is involved all the way from the vehicle design stage to developing after-market solutions, at each stage developing custom products and solutions that fortify those very relationships even further. In 2003, Magna reported over $15 billion in worldwide sales and a 22 percent cumulative average growth rate from 1993.[10]

Customers considering dropping six or seven figures on one transaction for big-ticket goods and services want all the information they can get. One way to entice new buyers is to create a customer reference program in which satisfied existing customers act in concert with the company's sales and marketing department by agreeing to serve as references. Companies that have such programs include Siebel Systems, PeopleSoft, and Sun Microsystems.

Specialized B2B marketers such as Magna International provide customized solutions for their customers. Magna developed an automated roof rack specifically designed for the Hummer H2.

PeopleSoft

When PeopleSoft merged with J. D. Edwards in 2004, it became the world's second largest provider of enterprise application software. It has over 12 000 employees worldwide, and has Canadian offices in Vancouver, Edmonton, Calgary, Toronto, Ottawa, and Montreal. The company invites customers with a story that's "relevant to new customers" to join its reference program and specify the level at which they would like to participate. Customers might agree to take phone calls from potential customers, host a site visit, or simply lend their names or blurbs to press releases and other copy. PeopleSoft knows that hearing other customers' stories is crucial for prospective buyers. The company evaluates the benefit of those customer references by tracking sales generated in the earlier stages of the prospect's contact with the program. For a seven-month period in 2002–2003, the reference program helped generate more than US$35 million in software licensing fees.

Systems Buying and Selling

Many business buyers prefer to buy a total solution to a problem from one seller. Called *systems buying*, this practice originated with government purchases of major weapons and communications systems. The government would solicit bids from *prime contractors*, who assembled the package or system. The contractor who was awarded the contract would be responsible for bidding out and assembling the system's subcomponents from *second-tier contractors*. The prime contractor would thus provide a turnkey solution, so-called because the buyer simply had to turn one key to get the job done.

Ford

Ford has transformed itself from being mainly a car manufacturer to being mainly a car assembler. Ford relies primarily on a few major systems suppliers to provide seating systems, braking systems, door systems, and other major assemblies. In designing a new automobile, Ford works closely with (say) its seat manufacturer and creates a *black box specification* of the basic seat dimensions and performance that it needs, and then waits for the seat supplier to propose the most cost-effective design. When they agree, the seat supplier subcontracts with parts suppliers to produce and deliver the needed components.

Ford assembly line in action: Worker assembling autos at Ford Motor Company's St. Thomas auto plant in Ontario.

Sellers have increasingly recognized that buyers like to purchase in this way, and many have adopted systems selling as a marketing tool. One variant of systems selling is *systems contracting*, where a single supplier provides the buyer with his or her entire requirement of MRO (maintenance, repair, operating) supplies. During the contract period, the supplier manages the customer's inventory. For example, Shell Oil manages the oil inventory of many of its business customers and knows when it requires replenishment. The customer benefits from reduced procurement and management costs and from price protection over the term of the contract. The seller benefits from lower operating costs because of a steady demand and reduced paperwork.

Systems selling is a key industrial marketing strategy in bidding to build large-scale industrial projects, such as dams, steel factories, irrigation systems, sanitation systems, pipelines, utilities, and even new towns. Project engineering firms must compete on price, quality, reliability, and other attributes to win contracts. Consider the following example.

Japan and Indonesia

The Indonesian government requested bids to build a cement factory near Jakarta. A U.S. firm made a proposal that included choosing the site, designing the cement factory, hiring the construction crews, assembling the materials and equipment, and turning over the finished factory to the Indonesian government. A Japanese firm, in outlining its proposal, included all of these services, plus hiring and training the workers to run the factory, exporting the cement through its trading companies, and using the cement to build roads and new office buildings in Jakarta. Although the Japanese proposal involved more money, it won the contract. Clearly, the Japanese viewed the problem not just as one of building a cement factory (the narrow view of systems selling) but as one of contributing to Indonesia's economic development. They took the broadest view of the customer's needs. This is true systems selling.

Participants in the Business Buying Process

Who buys the trillions of dollars' worth of goods and services needed by business organizations? Purchasing agents are influential in straight-rebuy and modified-rebuy situations, whereas other department personnel are more influential in new-buy situations. Engineering personnel usually have a major influence in selecting product components, and purchasing agents dominate in selecting suppliers.[11]

The Buying Centre

Webster and Wind call the decision-making unit of a buying organization *the buying centre*. It is composed of "all those individuals and groups who participate in the purchasing decision-making process, who share some common goals and the risks arising from the decisions."[12] The buying centre includes all members of the organization who play any of seven roles in the purchase decision process:[13]

1. *Initiators.* Those who request that something be purchased. They may be users or others in the organization.

2. *Users.* Those who will use the product or service. In many cases, the users initiate the buying proposal and help define the product requirements.

3. *Influencers.* People who influence the buying decision. They often help define specifications and also provide information for evaluating alternatives. Technical personnel are particularly important influencers.

4. *Deciders.* People who decide on product requirements or on suppliers.

5. *Approvers.* People who authorize the proposed actions of deciders or buyers.

6. *Buyers.* People who have formal authority to select the supplier and arrange the purchase terms. Buyers may help shape product specifications, but they play their major role in selecting vendors and negotiating. In more complex purchases, the buyers might include high-level managers.

7. *Gatekeepers.* People who have the power to prevent sellers or information from reaching members of the buying centre. For example, purchasing agents, receptionists, and telephone operators may prevent salespersons from contacting users or deciders.

Several individuals can occupy a given role (e.g., there may be many users or influencers), and the individual may occupy multiple roles.[14] A purchasing manager, for example, often occupies simultaneously the roles of buyer, influencer, and gatekeeper: he or she can determine which sales reps can call on other people in the organization, what budget and other constraints to place on the purchase, and which firm will actually get the business, even though others (deciders) might select two or more potential vendors who can meet the company's requirements.

The typical buying centre has a minimum of five or six members and often dozens. The buying centre may include people outside the target customer organization, such as government officials, consultants, technical advisors, and other members of the marketing channel.

Buying Centre Influences

Buying centres usually include several participants with differing interests, authority, status, and persuasiveness. Each member of the buying centre is likely to give priority to very different decision criteria. For example, engineering personnel may be concerned primarily with maximizing the actual performance of the product; production personnel may be concerned mainly with ease of use and reliability of supply; financial personnel may focus on the economics of the purchase; purchasing may be concerned with operating and replacement costs; union officials may emphasize safety issues, and so on.

Business buyers also respond to many influences when they make their decisions. Each buyer has personal motivations, perceptions, and preferences, which are influenced by the buyer's age, income, education, job position, personality, attitudes toward risk, and culture. Buyers definitely exhibit different buying styles. There are "keep-it-simple" buyers, "own-expert" buyers, "want-the-best" buyers, and "want-everything-done" buyers. Some younger, highly educated buyers are computer experts who conduct rigorous analyses of competitive proposals before choosing a supplier. Other buyers are "toughies" from the old school and pit the competing sellers against one another.

Webster cautions that ultimately, individuals, not organizations, make purchasing decisions.[15] Individuals are motivated by their own needs and perceptions in an attempt to maximize the rewards (pay, advancement, recognition, and feelings of achievement) offered by the organization. Personal needs "motivate" the behaviour of individuals, but organizational needs "legitimize" the buying decision process and its outcomes. People are not buying "products." They are buying solutions to two problems: the organization's economic and strategic problem and their own personal "problem" of obtaining individual achievement and reward. In this sense, industrial buying decisions are both "rational" and "emotional," as they serve both the organization's and the individual's needs.[16]

Buying Centre Targeting

To target their efforts properly, business marketers have to figure out: Who are the major decision participants? What decisions do they influence? What is their level of influence? What evaluation criteria do they use? Consider the following example:

A company sells nonwoven disposable surgical gowns to hospitals. The hospital personnel who participate in this buying decision include the vice-president of purchasing, the operating-room administrator, and the surgeons. The vice-president of purchasing analyzes whether the hospital should buy disposable gowns or reusable gowns. If the findings favour disposable gowns, then the operating-room administrator compares various competitors' products and prices and makes a choice. This administrator considers absorbency, antiseptic quality, design, and cost, and normally buys the brand that meets the functional requirements at the lowest cost. Surgeons influence the decision retroactively by reporting their satisfaction with the particular brand.

The business marketer is not likely to know exactly what kind of group dynamics take place during the decision process, although whatever information he or she can discover about personalities and interpersonal factors is useful.

Small sellers concentrate on reaching the *key buying influencers*. Larger sellers go for *multilevel in-depth selling* to reach as many participants as possible. Their salespeople virtually "live" with high-volume customers. Companies will have to rely more heavily on their communications program to reach hidden buying influences and keep current customers informed.[17]

Canadian National Railway Company

In April 2004, CN undertook a major reorganization of its sales organization, principally by separating it from the marketing function and creating a whole new sales department, complete with a new vice-president of sales. Under the new structure, the sales department effectively has two tiers: national accounts and regional accounts. National account sales are managed across customer product lines, while regional account sales are managed across geographical boundaries. This structure allows CN to establish clear objectives for its sales organization and prioritize more important accounts. For example, a national sales manager in the forest products division can focus exclusively on developing and cultivating relationships with large national forestry products producers, whereas a regional sales manager for the Alberta region will focus on smaller accounts within that geography, in any particular industry requiring rail-transport services. By having separately managed national accounts, CN can dedicate significant resources to understanding and delivering on customer needs for high-value, national clients.[18]

Business marketers must periodically review their assumptions about buying centre participants. For years, Kodak sold X-ray film to hospital lab technicians. Kodak research indicated that professional administrators were increasingly making purchasing decisions. As a result, Kodak revised its marketing strategy and developed new advertising to reach out to these decision makers.

In defining target segments, four types of business customers can often be identified, with corresponding marketing implications:

1. *Price-oriented customers* (transactional selling). Price is everything.

2. *Solution-oriented customers* (consultative selling). They want low prices but will respond to arguments about lower total cost or more dependable supply or service.

3. *Gold-standard customers* (quality selling). They want the best performance in terms of product quality, assistance, reliable delivery, and so on.

4. *Strategic-value customers* (enterprise selling). They want a fairly permanent sole-supplier relationship with your company.

Major business marketers like the Canadian National Railway Company have developed unique sales force structures to ensure customer needs are met appropriately.

Some companies are willing to handle price-oriented buyers by setting a lower price, but establishing restrictive conditions: (1) limiting the quantity that can be purchased; (2) no refunds; (3) no adjustments; and (4) no services.[19]

■ *Cardinal Health* set up a bonus dollars scheme at one time and gave points according to how much the business customer purchased. The points could be turned in for extra goods or free consulting.

■ *GE* is installing diagnostic sensors in its airline engines and railroad engines. It is now compensated for hours of flight or railroad travel.

■ *IBM* is now more of a service company aided by products than a product company aided by services. It may offer to sell computer power on demand (like video on demand) as an alternative to selling computers.

Risk and gain sharing can be used to offset requested price reductions from customers. For example, say Medline, a hospital supplier, signs an agreement with Highland Park Hospital promising $350 000 in savings over the first 18 months in exchange for a tenfold increase of the hospitals' share of supplies. If Medline achieves less than this promised savings, it will make up the difference. If Medline achieves substantially more than this promise, it participates in the extra savings. To make such arrangements work, the supplier must be willing to assist the customer in building a historical database, reaching an agreement for measuring benefits and costs, and devising a dispute resolution mechanism.

Solution selling can also alleviate price pressure and comes in different forms. Here are three examples:[20]

■ *Solutions to enhance customer revenues.* Hendrix Voeders used its sales consultants to help farmers deliver an incremental animal weight gain of 5 to 10 percent over competitors.

■ *Solutions to decrease customer risks.* ICI Explosives formulated a safer way to ship explosives for quarries.

■ *Solutions to reduce customer costs.* W. W. Grainger employees work at large customer facilities to reduce materials-management costs.

The Purchasing/Procurement Process

Every organization has specific purchasing objectives, policies, procedures, organizational structures, and systems. In principle, business buyers seek to obtain the highest benefit package (economic, technical, service, and social) in relation to a market offering's costs. A business buyer's incentive to purchase will be greater in proportion to the ratio of perceived benefits to costs. The marketer's task is to construct a profitable offering that delivers superior customer value to the target buyers.

Purchasing Orientations

In the past, purchasing departments occupied a low position in the management hierarchy, in spite of often managing more than half the company's costs. Recent competitive pressures have led many companies to upgrade their purchasing departments and elevate administrators to vice-presidential rank. Today's purchasing departments are staffed with MBAs who aspire to be CEOs—like Thomas Stallkamp, Chrysler's former executive vice-president of procurement and supply, who cut costs and streamlined the automaker's manufacturing processes.[21]

These new, more strategically oriented purchasing departments have a mission to seek the best value from fewer and better suppliers. Some multinationals have even elevated them to "strategic supply departments" with responsibility for global sourcing and partnering. At Caterpillar, for example, purchasing, inventory control, production scheduling, and traffic have been combined into one department. Lockheed Martin is another firm that has improved its business buying practices.

Lockheed Martin

At defence contractor Lockheed Martin, which spends US$13.2 billion annually, a Strategic Sourcing Solutions Group was created to centralize the company's purchasing functions across divisions and consolidate redundancies. The group is comprised of 52 employees with cross-functional experience, and their mission is "to be an integrated, leading-edge team that provides industry-recognized supply chain intelligence and innovative sourcing strategies, while fully optimizing customer value." As an example of the group's strategic focus, Lockheed Martin found it was spending roughly 25 to 40 percent more than it should on machining. A machining council was assigned to look into driving down the number of suppliers and consolidating among the preferred ones. The supply base was reduced by a combination of driving more business to preferred suppliers, increasing the frequency of negotiating, and introducing reverse auctions where appropriate.[22]

The upgrading of purchasing means that business marketers must upgrade their sales personnel to match the higher calibre of the business buyers. Formally, we can distinguish three company purchasing orientations:[23]

- *Buying orientation.* The purchaser's focus is short-term and tactical. Buyers are rewarded on their ability to obtain the lowest price from suppliers for the given level of quality and availability. Buyers use two tactics: *commoditization*, where they imply that the product is a commodity and care only about price; and *multisourcing*, where they use several sources and make them compete for shares of the company's purchases.

- *Procurement orientation.* Here buyers simultaneously seek quality improvements and cost reductions. Buyers develop collaborative relationships with major suppliers and seek savings through better management of acquisition, conversion, and disposal costs. They encourage early supplier involvement in materials handling, inventory levels, just-in-time management, and even product design. They negotiate long-term contracts with major suppliers to ensure the timely flow of materials. They work closely with their manufacturing group on materials requirement planning (MRP) to make sure supplies arrive on time.

- *Supply chain management orientation.* Here purchasing's role is further broadened to become a more strategic, value-adding operation. Purchasing executives at the firm work with marketing and other company executives to build a seamless supply chain management system, from the purchase of raw materials to the on-time arrival of finished goods to the end users.

Types of Purchasing Processes

Marketers need to understand how business purchasing departments work. These departments purchase many types of products, and the purchasing process will vary depending on the types of products involved. Peter Kraljic distinguished four product-related purchasing processes:[24]

1. *Routine products.* These products have low value and cost to the customer and involve little risk (e.g., office supplies). Customers will seek the lowest price and emphasize routine ordering. Suppliers will offer to standardize and consolidate orders with blanket contracts and facilities management.

2. *Leverage products.* These products have high value and cost to the customer but involve little risk of supply (e.g., engine pistons) because many companies make them. The supplier knows that the customer will compare market offerings and costs, and it needs to show that its offering minimizes the customer's total cost.

3. *Strategic products.* These products have high value and cost to the customer and also involve high risk (e.g., mainframe computers). The customer will want a well-known and trusted supplier and be willing to pay more than the average price. The supplier should seek strategic alliances that take the form of early supplier involvement, co-development programs, and co-investment.

4. *Bottleneck products.* These products have low value and cost to the customer but they involve some risk (e.g., spare parts). The customer will want a supplier who can guarantee a steady supply of reliable products. The supplier should propose standard parts and offer a tracking system, delivery on demand, and a help desk.

Purchasing Organization and Administration

Most purchasing professionals describe their jobs as more strategic, technical, team-oriented, and involving more responsibility than ever before. "Purchasing is doing more cross-functional work than it did in the past," says David Duprey, a buyer for Anaren Microwave, Inc. Sixty-one percent of buyers surveyed said the buying group was more involved in new-product design and development than it was five years ago; and more than half of the buyers participate in cross-functional teams, with suppliers well represented.[25]

In multidivisional companies, most purchasing is carried out by separate divisions. Some companies, however, have started to centralize purchasing. Headquarters identifies materials purchased by several divisions and buys them centrally, thereby gaining more purchasing clout. The individual divisions can buy from another source if they can get a better deal, but in general, centralized purchasing produces substantial savings. For the business marketer, this development means dealing with fewer and higher-level buyers and using a national account sales group to deal with large corporate buyers.

At the same time, companies are decentralizing some purchasing operations by empowering employees to purchase small-ticket items such as special binders, coffeemakers, or Christmas trees. This has come about through the availability of corporate purchasing cards issued by credit-card organizations. Companies distribute the cards to foremen, clerks, and secretaries; the cards incorporate codes that set credit limits and restrict where they can be used. National Semiconductor's purchasing chief has noted that the cards have cut processing costs from US$30 an order to a few cents. The additional benefit is that buyers and suppliers now spend less time on paperwork.

Stages in the Buying Process

At this point we are ready to describe the general stages in the business buying decision process. Robinson and Associates have identified eight stages and called them *buyphases*.[26] The stages are shown in Table 7.1. This model is called the *buygrid* framework.

Table 7.1 describes the buying stages involved in a new-task buying situation. In modified-rebuy or straight-rebuy situations, some stages are compressed or bypassed. For example, in a straight-rebuy situation, the buyer normally has a favourite supplier or a ranked list of suppliers. Thus the supplier search and proposal solicitation stages would be skipped.

The eight-stage buyphase model describes the major steps in the business buying process. Tracing out a buyflow map can provide many clues to the business marketer. A buyflow map for the purchase of a packaging machine in Japan is shown in Figure 7.1. The numbers within the icons are defined at the right. The italicized numbers between icons show the flow of events. Over 20 people in the purchasing company were involved, including the production manager and staff, new-product committee, company laboratory, marketing department, and the department for market develop-

TABLE 7.1	BUYGRID FRAMEWORK: MAJOR STAGES (BUYPHASES) OF THE INDUSTRIAL BUYING PROCESS IN BUYCLASSES			
			BUYCLASSES	
		New Task	Modified Rebuy	Straight Rebuy
BUYPHASES	1. Problem recognition	Yes	Maybe	No
	2. General need description	Yes	Maybe	No
	3. Product specification	Yes	Yes	Yes
	4. Supplier search	Yes	Maybe	No
	5. Proposal solicitation	Yes	Maybe	No
	6. Supplier selection	Yes	Maybe	No
	7. Order-routine specification	Yes	Maybe	No
	8. Performance review	Yes	Yes	Yes

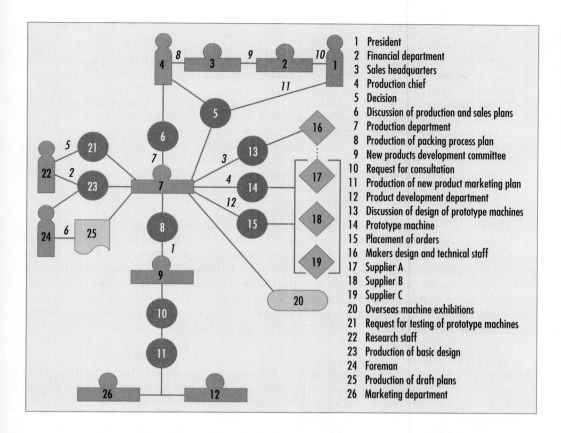

FIGURE 7.1

Organizational Buying Behaviour in Japan: Packaging Machine Purchasing Process

Source: "Japanese Firms Use Unique Buying Behavior," *The Japan Economic Journal*, December 23, 1980, p. 29. Reprinted by permission.

1   President
2   Financial department
3   Sales headquarters
4   Production chief
5   Decision
6   Discussion of production and sales plans
7   Production department
8   Production of packing process plan
9   New products development committee
10 Request for consultation
11 Production of new product marketing plan
12 Product development department
13 Discussion of design of prototype machines
14 Prototype machine
15 Placement of orders
16 Makers design and technical staff
17 Supplier A
18 Supplier B
19 Supplier C
20 Overseas machine exhibitions
21 Request for testing of prototype machines
22 Research staff
23 Production of basic design
24 Foreman
25 Production of draft plans
26 Marketing department

ment. The entire decision-making process took 121 days. There are important considerations in each of the eight stages.

Problem Recognition

The buying process begins when someone in the company recognizes a problem or need that can be met by acquiring a good or service. The recognition can be triggered by internal or external stimuli. Internally, some common events lead to problem recognition. The company decides to develop a new product and needs new equipment and materials. A machine breaks down and requires new parts. Purchased material turns out to be unsatisfactory, and the company searches for another supplier. A purchasing manager senses an opportunity to obtain lower prices or better quality. Externally, the buyer may get new ideas at a trade show, see an ad, or receive a call from a sales representative who offers a better product or a lower price. Business marketers can stimulate problem recognition by direct mail, telemarketing, and calling on prospects.

General Need Description and Product Specification

Next, the buyer determines the needed item's general characteristics and required quantity. For standard items, this is simple. For complex items, the buyer will work with others—engineers, users—to define characteristics like reliability, durability, or price. Business marketers can help by describing how their products meet or even exceed the buyer's needs. While many people believe that only feature/function-based messaging appeals to today's sophisticated purchasers, Ceridian Canada has discovered that powerful B2B brand messages with an emotional dimension can also help to win over business clients.

Ceridian Canada Ltd.

Ceridian Canada Ltd., headquartered in Winnipeg, Manitoba, provides payroll management and related services to large and small businesses across Canada. It is the country's leading payroll services provider, with offices from coast to coast, serving 40 000 businesses and paying more than 2.6 million Canadians. In 2002, Ceridian launched a new multifaceted campaign based on the platform "The freedom to succeed." The advertisements are full of images associated with success and freedom, but they also provide information on cost savings and employee satisfaction. "This brand strategy allows Ceridian to communicate the benefits of their services at an emotional level, aligning their product with core audience goals such as success, creativity, freedom, focus, and confidence," said Rick Denomme, the CEO of Ceridian's marketing and communications agency, HBS.[27]

The buying organization now develops the item's technical specifications. Often, the company will assign a product-value-analysis engineering team to the project. *Product value analysis* (PVA) is an approach to cost reduction in which components are studied to determine if they can be redesigned or standardized or made by cheaper methods of production. The PVA team will examine the high-cost components in a given product. The team will also identify overdesigned components that last longer than the product itself. Tightly written specifications will allow the buyer to refuse components that are too expensive or that fail to meet specified standards. Suppliers can use product value analysis as a tool for positioning themselves to win an account.

Supplier Search

The buyer next tries to identify the most appropriate suppliers through trade directories, contacts with other companies, trade advertisements, and trade shows. Business marketers also put products, prices, and other information on the Internet.[28] While B2B electronic commerce has not delivered on its early promise, it still far outstrips B2C (business-to-consumer) commerce. In 2004, according to Industry Canada, 81.6 percent of Canadian businesses used the Internet (compared to 63.4 percent in the year 2000). However, only 7.0 percent used this technology to sell goods or services. Nonetheless, businesses spent about $19.8 billion on online transactions with other businesses in 2004. By comparison, consumers spent only $8.5 billion on goods and services online in 2004. The total value of Canadian e-commerce sales in 2004 was estimated at $28.3 billion.[29] The move to Internet purchasing has far-reaching implications for suppliers and will change the shape of purchasing for years to come. (See "Marketing Insight: The Business-to-Business Cyberbuying Bazaar.")

Ceridian Canada's "freedom to succeed" campaign has hit home with its business clients on both an emotional and rational level.

The Business-to-Business (B2B) Cyberbuying Bazaar

With the growth of consumer online shopping, it is easy to lose sight of one of the most significant trends in e-commerce: the growth of business-to-business e-procurement. In addition to posting their own Web pages on the Internet, companies have established intranets for employees to communicate with one another, and extranets to link a company's communications and data with regular suppliers and distributors.

So far, most of the products businesses are buying electronically are MRO materials (maintenance, repair, and operations) and travel and entertainment services. MRO materials make up 30 percent of business purchases, and the transaction costs for order processing are high, which means there is a huge incentive to streamline the process. Here are some examples: Los Angeles County purchases everything from chickens to condoms over the Internet. National Semiconductor has automated almost all of the company's 3500 monthly requisitions to buy materials ranging from the sterile booties worn in its fabrication plants to state-of-the-art software. GE buys not only general operating supplies, but also industrial supplies online. Now that GE Information Services (GEIS) has opened its buying site to other companies, the company is well on its way to creating a vast electronic clearinghouse. Hundreds of thousands of firms will exchange trillions of dollars of industrial inputs—with GEIS running the show.

Many bricks-and-mortar companies have expanded their online presence by building their business-to-business operations and targeting small businesses (those employing fewer than 50 people), which account for 94.6 percent of all Canadian businesses.[30] The companies that now purchase over the Internet are utilizing electronic marketplaces that are popping up in several forms:

- *Catalogue sites*. Companies can order thousands of items through electronic catalogues distributed by e-procurement software, such as Grainger's.

- *Vertical markets*. Companies buying industrial goods such as plastics, steel, or chemicals, or services such as logistics or media, can go to specialized Web sites (called e-hubs). For example, Plastics.com allows thousands of plastics buyers to search for the best prices from the thousands of plastics sellers.

- *"Pure play" auction sites*. These are online marketplaces such as eBay and Freemarkets.com that could not have been realized without the Internet and for which no business model existed before their formation. Freemarkets.com provides online auctions for buyers and sellers of industrial parts, raw materials, commodities, and services in over 50 product categories and has facilitated over US$40 billion worth of commerce since 1995.

- *Spot (or exchange) markets*. On spot electronic markets, prices change by the minute. ChemConnect.com is an exchange for buyers and sellers of bulk chemicals such as benzene and is a B2B success in an arena littered with failed online exchanges. First to market, it is now the biggest online exchange for chemical trading, with volume of US$8.8 billion in 2002. Customers like Vanguard Petroleum Corp. conduct about 15 percent of their spot purchases and sales of natural-gas liquids on ChemConnect's commodities trading site.

- *Private exchanges*. Hewlett-Packard, IBM, and Wal-Mart operate private exchanges to link with specially invited groups of suppliers and partners over the Web.

- *Barter markets*. In these markets, participants offer to trade goods or services.

- *Buying alliances*. Several companies buying the same goods join together to form purchasing consortia and gain deeper discounts on volume purchases (Transora, Covisint).

Online business buying offers several advantages: It shaves transaction costs for both buyers and suppliers, reduces time between order and delivery, consolidates purchasing systems, and forges more intimate relationships between partners and buyers. On the downside, it may help to erode supplier–buyer loyalty and create potential security problems. Businesses also face a technological dilemma because no single system yet dominates.

Sources: Robert Yoegel, "The Evolution of B-to-B Selling on the 'Net,'" *Target Marketing* (August 1998): 34; Andy Reinhardt, "Extranets: Log On, Link Up, Save Big," *Business Week*, June 22, 1998, p. 134; "To Byte the Hand that Feeds," *The Economist*, June 17, 1998, pp. 61–62; John Evan Frook, "Buying Behemoth—By Shifting $5B in Spending to Extranets, GE Could Ignite a Development Frenzy," *Internetweek*, August 17, 1998, p. 1; Nicole Harris, "'Private Exchanges' May Allow B-to-B Commerce to Thrive After All," *Wall Street Journal*, March 16, 2001, pp. B1, B4; Olga Kharif, "B2B, Take 2," *Business Week*, November 25, 2003; George S. Day, Adam J. Fein, and Gregg Ruppersberger, "Shakeouts in Digital Markets: Lessons from B2B Exchanges," *California Management Review*, 45, no. 2 (Winter 2003): 131–151; Julia Angwin, "Top Online Chemical Exchange Is Unlikely Success Story," *Wall Street Journal*, January 8, 2004, p. A15.

E-Procurement

Web sites are organized around two types of e-hubs: *vertical hubs* centred on industries (plastics, steel, chemicals, paper) and *functional hubs* (logistics, media buying, advertising, energy management). In addition to using these Web sites, companies can do e-procurement in other ways:

- *Direct extranet links to major suppliers.* A company can set up extranet links to its major suppliers. For example, it can set up a direct e-procurement account at Dell or Office Depot, and its employees can make their purchases this way.

- *Buying alliances.* Coca-Cola, Sara Lee, Kraft, PepsiCo, Gillette, P&G, and several other companies joined forces to form a buying alliance called Transora to use their combined leverage to obtain lower prices for raw materials. Transora members also share data on less expensive ways to ship products and track inventory. Several auto companies (GM, Ford, DaimlerChrysler) formed Covisint for the same reason. They believe they can save as much as US$1200 per car.

- *Company buying sites.* Bombardier Aerospace posts lists of approved suppliers, its quality specifications, and requests for proposals (RFPs) on the suppliers' section of its Web site (**www.bombardier.com**).

Moving into e-procurement involves more than acquiring software; it requires changing purchasing strategy and structure. However, the benefits are many: Aggregating purchasing across multiple departments gains larger, centrally negotiated volume discounts. There is less buying of substandard goods from outside the approved list of suppliers, and a smaller purchasing staff is required.

Owens Corning

In 2001, the Owens Corning purchasing organization set a goal of wiping out 80 percent of its paper invoices by the end of 2004. The strategic objectives underlying this goal were cost reduction, supply chain visibility, business process integration, and a common standardized process for all suppliers. To accomplish these objectives, Owens Corning signed on with Advanced Data Exchange (ADX), an outsourced provider of EDI and XML, which takes whatever suppliers have to work with and effectively translates it into a usable electronic format for Owens Corning. The electronic invoicing initiative worked with the company's use of e-auctions. Starting in 2004, all suppliers participating in e-auctions will be told that as part of online auction bids they must agree to exchange invoices and purchase orders electronically if they are awarded the contract. With a US$3 billion annual spending budget, Owens Corning has the kind of clout to ensure suppliers get online.[31]

The supplier's task is to get listed in major online catalogues or services, develop a strong advertising and promotion program, and build a good reputation in the marketplace. This often means creating a well-designed and easy-to-use Web site.

Hewlett-Packard

In 2003, Hewlett-Packard Co. was named number one in *BtoB* magazine's annual ranking of the top B-to-B Web sites. The site (www.hp.com) was launched after HP's merger with Compaq Computer and has 2.5 million pages and roughly 1900 site areas. The challenge for HP was to integrate this enormous amount of information and present it coherently. Upon entering the site, users can click directly into their customer segment and search for information by product or by solution or click into a product category. The site allows companies to create customized catalogues for frequently purchased products, set up automatic approval routing for orders, and conduct end-to-end transaction processing. To further build relationships with customers, HP.com features Flash demos that show how to use the site, e-newsletters, live chats with sales reps, online classes, and real-time customer support. HP's Web efforts are paying off big—roughly 55 percent of the company's total sales come from the Web site.[32]

Suppliers who lack the required production capacity or suffer from a poor reputation will be rejected. Those who qualify may be visited by the buyer's agents, who will examine the suppliers' manufacturing facilities and meet their personnel. After evaluating each company, the buyer will end up with a short list of qualified suppliers. Many professional buyers have forced suppliers to change their marketing to increase their likelihood of making the cut.

Cutler-Hammer

Pittsburgh-based Cutler-Hammer supplies circuit breakers, motor starters, and other electrical equipment to industrial manufacturers such as Ford Motor Company. In response to the growing complexity and proliferation of its products, C-H developed "pods" of salespeople focused on a particular geographic region, industry, or market concentration. Each person brings a degree of expertise about a product or service. Now the salespeople can leverage the knowledge of co-workers to sell to increasingly sophisticated buying teams instead of working in isolation.[33]

Proposal Solicitation

The buyer invites qualified suppliers to submit proposals. If the item is complex or expensive, the buyer will require a detailed written proposal from each qualified supplier. After evaluating the proposals, the buyer will invite a few suppliers to make formal presentations.

Business marketers must be skilled in researching, writing, and presenting proposals. Written proposals should be marketing documents that describe value and benefits in customer terms. Oral presentations should inspire confidence, and position the company's capabilities and resources so that they stand out from the competition.

Consider the hurdles that Xerox has set up in qualifying suppliers:

Xerox

Xerox qualifies only suppliers who meet the ISO 9000 quality standards, but to win the company's top award—certification status—a supplier must first complete the Xerox Multinational Supplier Quality Survey. The survey requires the supplier to issue a quality assurance manual, to adhere to continuous improvement principles, and to demonstrate effective systems implementation. Once qualified, a supplier must participate in Xerox's Continuous Supplier Involvement process: The two companies work together to create specifications for quality, cost, delivery times, and process capability. The final step toward certification requires a supplier to undergo additional, rigorous quality training and an evaluation based on the same criteria as the Malcolm Baldridge National Quality Award. Not surprisingly, only 176 suppliers worldwide have achieved the 95 percent rating required for certification as a Xerox supplier.[34]

Supplier Selection

Before selecting a supplier, the buying centre will specify desired supplier attributes and indicate their relative importance. To rate and identify the most attractive suppliers, buying centres often use a supplier-evaluation model such as the one shown in Table 7.2.

Business marketers need to do a better job of understanding how business buyers arrive at their valuations.[35] Anderson, Jain, and Chintagunta conducted a study of the main methods business marketers use to assess customer value and found eight different *customer value assessment (CVA)* methods. Companies tended to use the simpler methods, although the more sophisticated ones promise to produce a more accurate picture of customer perceived value. (See "Marketing Memo: Methods of Assessing Customer Value.")

The choice and importance of different attributes varies with the type of buying situation.[36] Delivery reliability, price, and supplier reputation are important for routine-order products. For procedural-problem products, such as a copying machine, the three most important attributes are technical service, supplier flexibility, and product reliability. For political-problem products that stir rivalries in the organization (such as the choice of a computer system), the most important attributes are price, supplier reputation, product reliability, service reliability, and supplier flexibility.

TABLE 7.2	AN EXAMPLE OF VENDOR ANALYSIS				
Attributes			**Rating Scale**		
	Importance Weights	Poor (1)	Fair (2)	Good (3)	Excellent (4)
Price	0.30				x
Supplier reputation	0.20			x	
Product reliability	0.30				x
Service reliability	0.10		x		
Supplier flexibility	0.10			x	
Total score: 0.30(4) + 0.20(3) + 0.30(4) + 0.10(2) + 0.10(3) = 3.5					

The buying centre may attempt to negotiate with preferred suppliers for better prices and terms before making the final selection. Despite moves toward strategic sourcing, partnering, and participation in cross-functional teams, buyers still spend a large chunk of their time haggling with suppliers on price. In 1998, 92 percent of buyers responding to a *Purchasing* magazine survey cited negotiating price as one of their top responsibilities. Nearly as many respondents said price remains a key criterion they use to select suppliers.[37]

Marketers can counter the request for a lower price in a number of ways. They may be able to show evidence that the "total cost of ownership"—that is, the "life-cycle cost" of using their product—is lower than that of competitors' products. They can also cite the value of the services the buyer now receives, especially if those services are superior to those offered by competitors.

Other approaches may also be used to counter intense price pressure. Consider the following example.

Lincoln Electric

Lincoln Electric has a decades-long tradition of working with its customers to reduce costs through its Guaranteed Cost Reduction Program. When a customer insists that a Lincoln distributor lower prices to match Lincoln's competitors, the company and the particular distributor may guarantee that, during the coming year, they will find cost reductions in the customer's plant that meet or exceed the price difference between Lincoln's products and the competition's. If an independent audit at the end of the year does not reveal the promised cost savings, Lincoln Electric and the distributor compensate the customer for the difference. In all the years the program has been in existence, Lincoln has had to write a cheque only once or twice.[38]

As part of the buyer selection process, buying centres must decide how many suppliers to use. Companies are increasingly reducing the number of suppliers. Ford, Motorola, and Honeywell have cut the number of suppliers by anywhere from 20 to 80 percent. These companies want their chosen suppliers to be responsible for a larger component system; they want them to achieve continuous quality and performance improvement while at the same time lowering the supply price each year by a given percentage. These companies expect their suppliers to work closely with them during product development, and they value their suggestions. There is even a trend toward single sourcing.

Companies that use multiple sources often cite the threat of a labour strike as the biggest deterrent to single sourcing. Another reason companies may be reluctant to use a single source is they fear they will become too comfortable in the relationship and lose their competitive edge.

Order-Routine Specification

After selecting suppliers, the buyer negotiates the final order, listing the technical specifications, the quantity needed, the expected time of delivery, return policies, warranties, and so on. Many industrial buyers lease heavy equipment like machinery and trucks. The lessee gains a number of advantages: conserving capital, getting the latest products, receiving better service, and some tax advantages. The lessor often ends up with a larger net income and the chance to sell to customers who could not afford outright purchase.

In the case of maintenance, repair, and operating items, buyers are moving toward blanket contracts rather than periodic purchase orders. A blanket contract establishes a long-term relationship in which the supplier promises to resupply the buyer as needed, at agreed-upon prices, over a specified period of time. Because the stock is held by the seller, blanket contracts are sometimes called *stockless purchase plans*. The buyer's computer automatically sends an order to the seller when stock is needed. This system locks suppliers in tighter with the buyer and makes it difficult for out-suppliers to break in unless the buyer becomes dissatisfied with the in-supplier's prices, quality, or service.

Companies that fear a shortage of key materials are willing to buy and hold large inventories. They will sign long-term contracts with suppliers to ensure a steady flow of materials. For example, General Motors wants to buy from fewer suppliers who are willing to locate close to its plants and produce high-quality components. In addition, business marketers are using the Internet to set up extranets with important customers to facilitate and lower the cost of transactions. The customers enter orders directly on the computer, and these orders are automatically transmitted to the supplier. Some companies go further and shift the ordering responsibility to their suppliers in systems called *vendor-managed inventory*. These suppliers are privy to the customer's inventory levels and take responsibility to replenish it automatically through *continuous replenishment programs*.

Marketing Memo

Methods of Assessing Customer Value

1. *Internal engineering assessment.* Company engineers use laboratory tests to estimate the product's performance characteristics. Weakness: Ignores the fact that in different applications, the product will have different economic value.

2. *Field value-in-use assessment.* Customers are interviewed about cost elements associated with using the new-product offering compared to an incumbent product. The task is to assess how much each element is worth to the buyer.

3. *Focus-group value assessment.* Customers in a focus group are asked what value they would put on potential market offerings.

4. *Direct survey questions.* Customers are asked to place a direct dollar value on one or more changes in the market offering.

5. *Conjoint analysis.* Customers are asked to rank their preference for alternative market offerings or concepts. Statistical analysis is used to estimate the implicit value placed on each attribute.

6. *Benchmarks.* Customers are shown a "benchmark" offering and then a new market offering. They are asked how much more they would pay for the new offering or how much less they would pay if certain features were removed from the benchmark offering.

7. *Compositional approach.* Customers are asked to attach a monetary value to each of three alternative levels of a given attribute. This is repeated for other attributes. The values are then added together for any offer configuration.

8. *Importance ratings.* Customers are asked to rate the importance of different attributes and the supplier firms' performance on these attributes.

Source: James C. Anderson, Dipak C. Jain, and Pradeep K. Chintagunta, "A Customer Value Assessment in Business Markets: A State-of-Practice Study," *Journal of Business-to-Business Marketing*, 1, no. 1 (1993): 3–29.

"OTIFNE" is a term that summarizes three desirable outcomes of a B2B transaction:

- OT—deliver on time
- IF—in full
- NE—no error

All three matter. If a supplier achieves on-time compliance of only 80 percent, in-full compliance of 90 percent, and no error compliance of 70 percent, overall performance computes at $80\% \times 90\% \times 70\%$—only 50%!

Performance Review

The buyer periodically reviews the performance of the chosen supplier(s). Three methods are commonly used. The buyer may contact the end users and ask for their evaluations; the buyer may rate the supplier on several criteria using a weighted score method; or the buyer might aggregate the cost of poor performance to come up with adjusted costs of purchase, including price. The performance review may lead the buyer to continue, modify, or end a supplier relationship.

Many companies have set up incentive systems to reward purchasing managers for good buying performance, in much the same way that sales personnel receive bonuses for good selling performance. These systems are leading purchasing managers to increase pressure on sellers for the best terms.

Managing Business-to-Business Customer Relationships

To improve effectiveness and efficiency, business suppliers and customers are exploring different ways to manage their relationships. Closer relationships are driven in part by trends related to supply chain management, early supplier involvement, purchasing alliances, and so on.[39] Cultivating the right relationships with business is paramount with any holistic marketing program.

The Benefits of Vertical Coordination

Much research has advocated greater vertical coordination between buying partners and sellers so that they transcend mere transactions to engage in activities that create more value for both parties. Building trust between parties is often seen as one prerequisite to healthy long-term relationships.[40] "Marketing Insight: Establishing Corporate Trust and Credibility" identifies some key dimensions of those concepts. Consider the mutual benefits from the following arrangement.

Motoman Inc. and Stillwater Technologies

Motoman Inc., a leading supplier of industry robotic systems, and Stillwater Technologies, a contract tooling and machinery company and a key supplier to Motoman, are tightly integrated. Not only do they occupy office and manufacturing space in the same facility, but their telephone and computer systems are linked, and they share a common lobby, conference room, and employee cafeteria. Philip V. Morrison, chairman and CEO of Motoman, says it is like "a joint venture without the paperwork." Short delivery distances are just one benefit of the unusual partnership. Also key is the fact that employees of both companies have ready access to one another and can share ideas on improving quality and reducing costs. This close relationship has opened the door to new opportunities. Both companies had been doing work for Honda Motor Company, and Honda suggested that they work together on systems projects. The integration makes the two bigger than they are individually.[41]

One historical study of four very different business-to-business relationships found that several factors, by affecting partner interdependence and/or environmental uncertainty, influenced the development of a relationship between business partners.[42] The relationship between advertising agencies and clients illustrates these findings:

- *In the relationship formation stage, one partner experienced substantial market growth.* Manufacturers capitalizing on mass-production techniques developed national brands, which increased the importance and amount of mass-media advertising.

- *There was sufficient information asymmetry that the clients would generate more profits from a partnership with the agency than they would if they attempted to perform the agency's function themselves.* Advertising agencies had specialized knowledge that their clients would have had difficulty obtaining.

- *At least one partner had high barriers to entry that would prevent the other partner from entering the business.* Advertising agencies could not easily become national manufacturers, and for years, manufacturers were not eligible to receive media commissions.

- *Dependence asymmetry existed such that one partner was more able to control or influence the other's conduct.* Advertising agencies had control over media access.

- *One partner benefited from economies of scale related to the relationship.* Ad agencies gained by providing the same market information to multiple clients.

Cannon and Perreault found that buyer–supplier relationships differed according to four factors: availability of alternatives; importance of supply; complexity of supply; and supply market dynamism. Based on these four factors, they classified buyer–supplier relationships into eight different categories:[43]

1. *Basic buying and selling*—relatively simple, routine exchanges with moderately high levels of cooperation and information exchange.

2. *Bare bones*—similar to basic buying and selling but more adaptation by the seller and less cooperation and information exchange.

MARKETING INSIGHT

Establishing Corporate Trust and Credibility

Strong bonds and relationships between firms depend on their perceived credibility. *Corporate credibility* refers to the extent to which customers believe that a firm can design and deliver goods and services that satisfy their needs and wants. Corporate credibility relates to the reputation that a firm has achieved in the marketplace and is the foundation for a strong relationship. It is difficult for a firm to develop strong ties with another firm unless it is seen as highly credible.

Corporate credibility, in turn, depends on three factors:

- *Corporate expertise*—the extent to which a company is seen as able to make and sell products or conduct services.

- *Corporate trustworthiness*—the extent to which a company is seen as motivated to be honest, dependable, and sensitive to customer needs.

- *Corporate likability*—the extent to which a company is seen as likable, attractive, prestigious, dynamic, and so on.

In other words, a credible firm is seen as being good at what it does, keeps its customers' best interests in mind, and is enjoyable to work with.

Trust is a particularly important determinant of credibility and a firm's relationships with other firms. Trust is reflected in the willingness and confidence of a firm to rely on a business partner. A number of interpersonal and interorganizational factors affect trust in a business-to-business relationship, such as the perceived competence, integrity, honesty, and benevolence of the firm. Trust will be affected by personal interactions between employees of a firm as well as opinions about the company as a whole, and perceptions of trust will evolve with more experience with a company.

Trust can be especially tricky in online settings, and firms often impose more stringent requirements on their online business partners. Business buyers worry that they won't get products of the right quality delivered to the right place at the right time. Sellers worry about getting paid on time—or at all—and how much credit they should expend. Some firms, such as transportation and supply chain management company Ryder System, are using tools such as automated credit-checking applications and online trust services to help determine the credibility of trading partners.

Sources: Robert M. Morgan and Shelby D. Hunt, "The Commitment-Trust Theory of Relationship Marketing," *Journal of Marketing*, 58, no. 3 (1994): 20–38; Christine Moorman, Rohit Deshpande, and Gerald Zaltman, "Factors Affecting Trust in Market Research Relationships," *Journal of Marketing*, 57 (January 1993): 81–101; Kevin Lane Keller and David A. Aaker, "Corporate-Level Marketing: The Impact of Credibility on a Company's Brand Extensions," *Corporate Reputation Review*, 1 (August 1998): 356–378; Bob Violino, "Building B2B Trust," *Computerworld*, June 17, 2002, p. 32; Richard E. Plank, David A. Reid, and Ellen Bolman Pullins, "Perceived Trust in Business-to-Business Sales: A New Measure," *Journal of Personal Selling and Sales Management*, 19, no. 3 (Summer 1999): 61–72.

3. *Contractual transaction*—generally low levels of trust, cooperation, and interaction; exchange is defined by formal contract.

4. *Customer supply*—traditional custom supply situation where competition rather than cooperation is the dominant form of governance.

5. *Cooperative systems*—although coupled closely in operational ways, neither party demonstrates structural commitment through legal means or adaptation approaches.

6. *Collaborative*—much trust and commitment leading to true partnership.

7. *Mutually adaptive*—much relationship-specific adaptation for buyer and seller, but without necessarily strong trust or cooperation.

8. *Customer is king*—although bonded by a close, cooperative relationship, the seller adapts to meet the customer's needs without expecting much adaptation or change on the part of the customer in exchange.

Some firms find that their needs can be satisfied with fairly basic supplier performance. They do not want or require a close relationship with a supplier. Alternatively, some suppliers may not find it worth their while to invest in customers with limited growth potential. One study found that the closest relationships between customer and suppliers arose when the supply was important to the customer and when there were procurement obstacles such as complex purchase requirements and few alternative suppliers.[44] Another study suggested that greater vertical coordination between buyer and seller through information exchange and planning is usually necessary only when high environmental uncertainty exists and specific investments are modest.[45]

Business Relationships: Risks and Opportunism

Buvik and John note that in establishing a customer–supplier relationship, there is tension between safeguarding and adaptation. Vertical coordination can facilitate stronger customer–seller ties but at the same time may increase the risk to the customer's and supplier's specific investments. *Specific investments* are those expenditures tailored to a particular company and value chain partner (e.g., investments in company-specific training, equipment, and operating procedures or systems).[46] Specific investments help firms grow profits and achieve their positioning.[47] For example, Xerox worked closely with its suppliers to develop customized processes and components that reduced its copier-manufacturing costs by 30 to 40 percent. In return, suppliers received sales and volume guarantees, an enhanced understanding of their customer needs, and a strong position with Xerox for future sales.[48]

Specific investments, however, also entail considerable risk to both customer and supplier. Transaction theory from economics maintains that because these investments are partially sunk, they lock in the firms that make the investments to a particular relationship. Sensitive cost and process information may need to be exchanged. A buyer may be vulnerable to hold-up because of switching costs; a supplier may be more vulnerable to hold-up in future contracts because of dedicated assets and/or expropriation of technology/knowledge. In terms of the latter risk, consider the following example.[49]

An automobile component manufacturer wins a contract to supply an under-hood component to an original equipment manufacturer. A one-year, sole-source contract safeguards the supplier's OEM-specific investments in a dedicated production line. However, the supplier may also be obliged to work (noncontractually) as a partner with the OEM's internal engineering staff (using linked computing facilities) to exchange detailed engineering information and coordinate frequent design and manufacturing changes over the term of the contract. These interactions could reduce costs and/or increase quality by improving the firm's responsiveness to marketplace changes. Such interactions could also potentially magnify the threat to the supplier's intellectual property.

When buyers cannot easily monitor supplier performance, the supplier might shirk or cheat and not deliver the expected value. *Opportunism* can be thought of as "some form of cheating or under-supply relative to an implicit or explicit contract."[50] It may involve blatant self-interest and deliberate misrepresentation that violates contractual agreements. In creating the 1996 version of the Ford Taurus, Ford Corporation chose to outsource the whole process to one supplier, Lear Corporation. Lear committed to a contract that, for various reasons, it knew it was unable to fulfill. According to Ford, Lear missed deadlines, failed to meet weight and price objectives, and furnished parts that did not work.[51] A more passive form of opportunism might involve a refusal or unwillingness to adapt to changing circumstances.

Opportunism is a concern because firms must devote resources to control and monitoring that otherwise could be allocated to more productive purposes. Contracts may become inadequate to govern supplier transactions when supplier opportunism becomes difficult to detect; as firms make specific investments in assets that cannot be used elsewhere; and as contingencies are harder to anticipate. Customers and suppliers are more likely to form a joint venture (versus a simple contract) when the supplier's degree of asset specificity is high, monitoring the supplier's behaviour is difficult, and the supplier has a poor reputation.[52] When a supplier has a good reputation, for example, it is more likely to avoid opportunism to protect this valuable intangible asset.

The presence of a significant future time horizon and/or strong solidarity norms so that customers and suppliers are willing to strive for joint benefits can cause a shift in the effect of specific investments, from expropriation (increased opportunism on the receiver's part) to bonding (reduced opportunism).[53]

Institutional and Government Markets

Our discussion has concentrated largely on the buying behaviour of profit-seeking companies. Much of what we have said also applies to the buying practices of institutional and government organizations. However, we want to highlight certain special features of these markets.

The **institutional market** consists of schools, hospitals, nursing homes, prisons, and other institutions that must provide goods and services to people in their care. Many of these organizations are characterized by low budgets and captive clienteles. For example, hospitals have to decide what quality of food to buy for patients. The buying objective here is not profit, because the food is provided as part of the total service package; nor is cost minimization the sole objective, because poor food will cause patients to complain and hurt the hospital's reputation. The hospital purchasing agent has to search for institutional-food vendors whose quality meets or exceeds a certain minimum standard and whose prices are low. In fact, many food vendors set up a separate division to sell to institutional buyers because of these buyers' special needs and characteristics. Heinz produces, packages, and prices its ketchup differently to meet the requirements of hospitals, colleges, and prisons.

Governments—federal, provincial, and municipal—are major purchasers of goods and services. The Canadian government buys approximately $13 billion worth of goods and services every year from thousands of suppliers. There are over 85 departments, agencies, Crown corporations, and special operating agencies. Public Works and Government Services Canada (PWGSC) is the government's largest purchasing organization, averaging 33 000 contracts and totalling $10 billion annually. While PWGSC buys goods for most departments of the federal government, the departments buy most services themselves.[54]

Government organizations typically require suppliers to submit bids, and normally they award the contract to the lowest bidder. In some cases, the government unit will make allowance for the supplier's superior quality or reputation for completing contracts on time. Governments will also buy on a negotiated contract basis, primarily in the case of complex projects involving major R&D costs and risks and in cases where there is little competition. Government organizations tend to favour domestic suppliers. A major complaint of multinationals operating in Europe was that each country showed favouritism toward its nationals in spite of superior offers available from foreign firms. The European Union is removing this bias.

Like consumer and business buyers, government buyers are affected by environmental, organizational, interpersonal, and individual factors. One unique aspect of government buying is that it is carefully watched by outside publics, from Parliament to various private groups interested in how the government spends taxpayers' money. Because their spending decisions are subject to public review, government organizations require considerable documentation from suppliers, who often complain about excessive paperwork, bureaucracy, regulations, decision-making delays, and frequent shifts in procurement personnel.

Many firms complain about selling to governments because of the red tape they perceive to be involved in making a sale. Federal, provincial, and municipal governments are now posting a great deal of information online to help businesses better understand their purchasing processes, supplier selection criteria, and sales opportunities. For example, on the federal government's Contracts Canada site (**http://contractscanada.gc.ca**), you can find a wealth of information with only a click of the mouse on such buttons as "The Basics of Selling to Government" or "Electronic Tendering Service," which posts opportunities to bid to supply government services. You can also access information about how to become a registered government supplier. The Canadian Business Service Centres (**www.cbsc.org**) is another site established by the government to help Canadian businesses. The site is a goldmine of information on topics as varied as training, importing, and taxation. It features online workshops for small businesses as well as a comprehensive database of government services and programs. The federal government also issues a weekly bulletin, *Government Business Opportunities*, to alert prospective suppliers to the government's plans to purchase products or services.

If anyone knows how to market to business and government clients, it is Bombardier, with its more than 50 years of experience serving the military in both Canada and the United States.

Bombardier

Bombardier is a leading rail transportation and aerospace equipment manufacturer that markets products to both governments and private firms around the world. In fact, Bombardier earns more than 95 percent of its revenues from markets outside Canada. It has sold aircraft to China and transportation systems to Romania. In April 2003, Bombardier won its biggest ever transportation supply contract worth $7.9 billion for the London Underground in the United Kingdom. Since government clients are very cost-sensitive, Bombardier locates facilities near its clients' operations. This not only increases responsiveness and flexibility, it also ensures cost-effective service delivery while respecting the tight security requirements of its military clients.[55]

There are a number of reasons many companies that sell to the government have not used a marketing orientation. The government's procurement policies have traditionally emphasized price, leading suppliers to invest considerable effort in bringing costs down. Where product characteristics are carefully specified, product differentiation is not a marketing factor; nor are advertising and personal selling of much consequence in winning bids. Some companies have pursued government business by establishing separate government marketing departments.

Companies such as Dell Canada, Kodak, and Goodyear anticipate government needs and projects, participate in the product specification phase, gather competitive intelligence, prepare bids carefully, and produce strong communications to describe and enhance their companies' reputations.

SUMMARY

1. Organizational buying is the decision-making process by which formal organizations establish the need for purchased products and services, then identify, evaluate, and choose among alternative brands and suppliers. The business market consists of all the organizations that acquire goods and services used in the production of other products or services that are sold, rented, or supplied to others.

2. Compared to consumer markets, business markets generally have fewer and larger buyers, a closer customer–supplier relationship, and more geographically concentrated buyers. Demand in the business market is derived from demand in the consumer market and fluctuates with the business cycle. Nonetheless, the total demand for many business goods and services is quite price-inelastic. Business marketers need to be aware of the role of professional purchasers and their influencers, the need for multiple sales calls, and the importance of direct purchasing, reciprocity, and leasing.

3. The buying centre is the decision-making unit of a buying organization. It consists of initiators, users, influencers, deciders, approvers, buyers, and gatekeepers.

To influence these parties, marketers must be aware of environmental, organizational, interpersonal, and individual factors.

4. The buying process consists of eight stages called buyphases: (1) problem recognition, (2) general need description, (3) product specification, (4) supplier search, (5) proposal solicitation, (6) supplier selection, (7) order-routine specification, and (8) performance review.

5. Business marketers must form strong bonds and relationships with their customers and provide them added value. Some customers, however, may prefer more of a transactional relationship.

6. The institutional market consists of schools, hospitals, nursing homes, prisons, and other institutions that provide goods and services to people in their care. Buyers for government organizations tend to require a great deal of paperwork from their vendors and to favour open bidding and domestic companies. Suppliers must be prepared to adapt their offers to the special needs and procedures found in institutional and government markets.

APPLICATIONS

Marketing Debate: How Different Is Business-to-Business Marketing?

Many business-to-business marketing executives lament the challenges of business-to-business marketing, maintaining that many traditional marketing concepts and principles do not apply. For a number of reasons, they assert that selling products and services to a company is fundamentally different from selling to individuals. Others disagree, claiming that marketing theory is still valid and only involves some adaptation in the marketing tactics.

Take a position: Business-to-business marketing requires a special, unique set of marketing concepts and principles versus Business-to-business marketing is really not that different and the basic marketing concepts and principles apply.

Marketing Discussion

Consider some of the consumer behaviour topics from Chapter 6. How might you apply them to business-to-business settings? For example, how might noncompensatory models of choice work?

Marketing Spotlight: General Electric

GE is an amazingly large company made up of 11 major divisions that operate in areas as diverse as home appliances, jet engines, security systems, wind turbines, and financial services. The company is so large (2003 revenues of US$134 billion) that even if each of its 11 business units were ranked separately, all would appear on the *Fortune 500* list. If GE were its own country, it would be one of the 50 largest and would rank ahead of Finland, Israel, and Ireland.

GE became the acknowledged pioneer in business-to-business marketing in the 1950s and 1960s. Back then, GE's tagline was "Live better electrically." As the company diversified its product lines, it created new campaigns, including "Progress for people" and "We bring good things to life."

In 2003, the company faced a new challenge: how to promote its brand globally with a unified message. GE launched a major new campaign, "Imagination at work," which earned it the 2003 B2B Best Award for a top integrated campaign. The purpose of the campaign was not simply to create warm feelings for the company, but to achieve real business results. The campaign promoted GE's B2B units such as GE Aircraft Engines, GE Medical Systems, and GE Plastics. The goal was to unify these divisions under the GE brand while giving them a voice. The new campaign highlights the breadth of GE's product offerings.

GE spends some US$150 million on corporate advertising—a large sum, but a sum that gains efficiencies by focusing on the core GE brand. The challenge with creating a unified message was that each GE business had to fit with that brand image. GE chose "Imagination at Work" because it portrayed the innovation inherent in all its wide-ranging products.

The new integrated campaign got results. "Research indicates GE is now being associated with attributes such as being high-tech, leading-edge, innovative, contemporary and creative," said Judy Hu, GE's general manager for global advertising and branding. Just as encouraging, market research found that respondents still associate GE with some of its traditional attributes, such as being trustworthy and reliable.

"We believe 'Imagination at Work' has proven to be a strong global message for us," said GE's chief marketing officer Beth Comstock. "Our goal is to be more present around the world and more consistent. To do it more broadly and faster. Going forward, you'll see medical and health care as the face of GE."

While the campaign unites all the GE business units, GE's success rests on its ability to understand the business market and the business buying process. GE puts itself in the shoes of its business customers. Consider, for example, GE's approach to pricing its aircraft engines. One would expect GE to charge a particular price for a particular engine type. But GE is aware that for the customer, purchasing an aircraft engine is a multimillion-dollar expenditure (US$21 million for each large engine). And the expenditure doesn't end with the purchase of the engine—customers (airlines) face substantial maintenance costs to meet aviation guidelines and ensure the reliability of engines. So in 1999, GE pioneered a new pricing option. The concept, called "Power by the Hour," gives its customers an opportunity to pay a fixed fee each time they run the engine. In return, GE performs all of the maintenance and guarantees the reliability of the engine. GE gives its customers a lower cost of ownership of the GE aircraft engine.

Business buyers value this option because it shifts risk away from them. In times of uncertain air travel, buying new jet engines for new airliners is a major financial risk. "Power by the Hour" lets the airlines pay only when they use the engine. Moreover, airlines do not have to worry about unexpected high maintenance costs. Buyers are assured a low, predictable cost of ownership through the preset pricing.

This kind of B2B savvy has helped GE cement its top position in the *Financial Times* World's Most Respected Companies survey. Chief executives from 20 countries have given GE the top spot in the survey for six years.

GE's understanding of the business markets, its way of doing business, and its brand marketing have kept GE's brand equity growing. Indeed, GE's brand equity was valued at US$53.6 billion by Corebrand in the fourth quarter 2003.

"The GE brand is what connects us all and makes us so much better than the parts," chief marketing officer Comstock said.

DISCUSSION QUESTIONS

1. What have been the key success factors for GE?
2. Where is GE vulnerable? What should it watch out for?
3. What recommendations would you make to GE's senior marketing executives going forward? What should they be sure to do with its marketing?

Sources: Michael Skapinker, "Brand Strength Proves Its Worth," *Financial Times*," January 20, 2004; Sean Callahan, "Exclusive: Microsoft, GE Top Brand Equity Study," *BtoB*, January 19, 2004; "Marketer of the Year Special Report," *BtoB*, December 8, 2003, pp. 16, 22; "More Imagination," *Delaney Report*, October 20, 2003, p. 1; Sean Callahan, "BtoB Q&A: New GE CMO Taps 'Imagination,'" *BtoB*, August 11, 2003; www.ge.com.

8

IN THIS CHAPTER, WE WILL ADDRESS THE FOLLOWING QUESTIONS:

- What are the different levels of market segmentation?

- How can a company divide a market into segments?

- How should a company choose the most attractive target markets?

- What are the requirements for effective segmentation?

CHAPTER 8

Identifying Market Segments and Targets

PROFILE: CANADIAN MARKETING EXCELLENCE

lululemon athletica is a yoga-inspired apparel company. It was founded in 1998 by Chip Wilson in response to the rapid increase in the participation of women in sports and especially yoga. Until that point, men had dominated sports and were the focus of the sporting goods manufacturers. As a result, women were using male sports equipment and wearing men's athletic clothing in smaller sizes.

While attending yoga classes, Chip not only realized the benefits of yoga for people in all sports, but he also saw the need for a technical line of women-specific product. Inspired by Vancouver, a city recognized for its health and athletic culture, he decided to focus his mission on "providing components for people to live a longer, healthier and more fun life."

To create the most functional and well-designed apparel possible, the company started by having their design room surrounded by a retail store. This allowed the designers to receive instant feedback on the product. In addition, they had local yoga instructors in the community test their products and provide feedback on performance. Instructors loved the clothing and in turn began recommending it to participants in their classes.

lululemon's products focus on being physically functional, with technical athletic qualities, while ensuring that they are flattering at the same time. The company continues to encourage customer feedback on everything from product development to store layout. Store staff are passionate about the brand and are highly knowledgeable about the product.

lululemon's products are costly to produce and as a result are priced at a premium: a pair of lululemon pants retails for about $90. This does not, however, seem to be inhibiting growth or success. Since 1998, lululemon has opened stores across Canada, the United States, and internationally in Tokyo and Melbourne. The company plans to continue its rapid growth, reinforcing the importance of consumer feedback, relationship building, and clear market segmentation.

Sources: lululemon website, **www.lululemon.ca**, viewed August 12, 2004; Kristen Vinakmens, "lululemon: Building the brand from the ground—yoga mat—up," *Strategy Magazine Online*, **www.strategymag.com**, January 13, 2003 (viewed August 12, 2004); Michelle Halpern, "Cute, but Scary," *Marketing Magazine Online*, **www.marketingmag.ca**, August 09, 2004 (viewed August 12, 2004).

Markets are not homogeneous. A company cannot connect with all customers in large, broad, or diverse markets. Consumers vary on many dimensions and often can be grouped according to one or more characteristics. A company needs to identify which market segments it can serve effectively. Such decisions require a keen understanding of consumer behaviour and careful strategic thinking. Marketers sometimes mistakenly chase after the same market segment as many other firms and overlook other, potentially more lucrative segments.

To compete more effectively, many companies are now embracing target marketing. Instead of scattering their marketing effort (a "shotgun" approach), they focus on those consumers they have the greatest chance of satisfying (a "rifle" approach).

Effective target marketing requires that marketers:

1. Identify and profile distinct groups of buyers who differ in their needs and preferences (market segmentation).

2. Select one or more market segments to enter (market targeting).

3. For each target segment, establish and communicate the distinctive benefit(s) of the company's market offering (market positioning).

This chapter will focus on the first two steps. Chapters 9 and 10 discuss brand and market positioning.

Levels of Market Segmentation

The starting point for discussing segmentation is **mass marketing**. In mass marketing, the seller engages in the mass production, mass distribution, and mass promotion of one product for all buyers. Henry Ford epitomized this strategy when he offered the Model-T Ford in one colour, black. Coca-Cola also practised mass marketing when it sold only one kind of Coke in one size bottle.

The argument for mass marketing is that it creates the largest potential market, which leads to the lowest costs, which in turn can lead to lower prices or higher margins. However, many critics point to the increasing splintering of the market, which makes mass marketing more difficult. The proliferation of advertising media and distribution channels is making it difficult and increasingly expensive to reach a mass audience. Some claim that mass marketing is dying. Most companies are turning to *micro-marketing* at one of four levels: segments, niches, local areas, and individuals.

Segment Marketing

A market segment consists of a group of customers who share a similar set of needs and wants. Thus we distinguish between car buyers who are primarily seeking low-cost basic transportation from those seeking a luxurious driving experience from those seeking driving thrills and performance. We must be careful not to confuse a *segment* and a *sector*. A car company might say that it will target young, middle-income car buyers. The problem is that young, middle-income car buyers will differ about what they want in a car. Some will want a low-cost car and others will want an expensive car. Young, middle-income car buyers are a sector, not a segment.

The marketer does not create the segments; the marketer's task is to identify the segments and decide which one(s) to target. Segment marketing offers key benefits over mass marketing. The company can presumably better design, price, communicate, and deliver the product or service to satisfy the target market. The company also can fine-tune the marketing program and activities to better reflect competitors' marketing.

However, even a segment is partly a fiction, in that not everyone wants exactly the same thing. Anderson and Narus have urged marketers to present flexible market offerings to all members of a segment.[1]

A **flexible market offering** consists of two parts: a *naked solution* containing the product and service elements that all segment members value, and *discretionary options* that some segment members value. Each option might carry an additional charge. For example, Delta Airlines offers all economy passengers a seat, food, and soft drinks. It charges economy passengers extra for alcoholic beverages and earphones. Siemens Electrical Apparatus Division sells metal-clad boxes to small manufacturers whose price includes free delivery and a warranty, but also offers installation, tests, and communication peripherals as extra-cost options.

FIGURE 8.1

Basic Market-Preference Patterns

(a) Homogeneous preferences

Creaminess

Sweetness

(b) Diffused preferences

Creaminess

Sweetness

(c) Clustered preferences

Creaminess

Sweetness

Market segments can be defined in many different ways. One way to carve up a market is to identify *preference segments*. Suppose ice cream buyers are asked how much they value sweetness and creaminess as two product attributes. Three different patterns can emerge:

1. *Homogeneous preferences.* Figure 8.1(a) shows a market where all the consumers have roughly the same preferences. The market shows no natural segments. We would predict that existing brands would be similar and cluster around the middle of the scale in both sweetness and creaminess.

2. *Diffused preferences.* At the other extreme, consumer preferences may be scattered throughout the space (Figure 8.1[b]), indicating that consumers vary greatly in their preferences. The first brand to enter the market is likely to position itself to appeal to the most people. A second competitor could locate next to the first brand and fight for market share, or it could locate in a corner to attract a customer group that was not satisfied with the centre brand. If several brands are in the market, they are likely to position themselves throughout the space and show real differences to match differences in consumer preference.

3. *Clustered preferences.* The market might reveal distinct preference clusters, called *natural market segments* (Figure 8.1[c]). The first firm in this market has three options. It might position in the centre, hoping to appeal to all groups. It might position in the largest market segment (*concentrated marketing*). It might develop several brands, each positioned in a different segment. If the first firm developed only one brand, competitors would enter and introduce brands in the other segments.

Later in the chapter, we will consider various ways to segment and compete in a market.

Niche Marketing

A niche is a more narrowly defined customer group seeking a distinctive mix of benefits. Marketers usually identify niches by dividing a segment into subsegments. For example, Progressive, a U.S. auto insurer, sells "nonstandard" auto insurance to risky drivers with a record of auto accidents or drunkenness, charging a high price for coverage and making a lot of money in the process.

An attractive niche is characterized as follows: The customers in the niche have a distinct set of needs; they will pay a premium to the firm that best satisfies their needs; the niche is not likely to attract other competitors; the nicher gains certain economies through specialization; and the niche has size, profit, and growth potential. Whereas segments are fairly large and normally attract several competitors, niches are fairly small and normally attract only one or two.

Enterprise

Enterprise Rent-A-Car has challenged Hertz's supremacy in the rental car market by tailoring its marketing program to a relatively neglected target market.[2] While Hertz, Avis, Alamo, and others specialize in airport rental cars for business and leisure travellers, Enterprise has attacked the low-budget, insurance-replacement market by primarily renting to customers whose cars have been wrecked or stolen. Enterprise charges low rental rates by avoiding expensive airport and downtown locations, by only opening for daylight hours, and by holding on to its fleet of cars for a longer period of time before replacing them. Enterprise also distinguishes itself, in part, by offering to pick up customers. Enterprise has a limited advertising budget, relying more on a grassroots marketing push based on referrals from insurance agents and adjusters, car dealers, body shops, and garages. By creating points of difference of low cost and convenience in an overlooked niche market, Enterprise has been highly profitable.

Larger companies, such as IBM, have lost pieces of their market to nichers: this confrontation has been labelled "guerrillas against gorillas."[3] Some large companies have even turned to niche marketing. Hallmark commands a 55 percent share of the US$7.8 billion global greeting-card market by rigorously segmenting its greeting-card business. In addition to popular sub-branded card lines like the humorous Shoebox Greetings, Hallmark has introduced lines targeting specific market segments. Fresh Ink targets 18- to 39-year-old women, Hallmark En Espanol targets Hispanic card givers, and Out of the Blue targets those who want inexpensive cards that can be sent for no reason.[4]

Marketers can aim at local niches or niches in the worldwide marketplace. The latter is where Toronto's Brunico Communications plays.

Brunico Communications

Entrepreneur Jim Shenkman founded Brunico Communications in 1986 around a single product—a trade publication called *Playback*, aimed at Canadian film and TV producers and broadcasters. Three years later, he launched *Strategy*. He believed there was an unmet need in the marketplace, since rival *Marketing Magazine* appealed more to those in marketing service companies than to client marketers. It wasn't long before the power of these concepts was proven, and today Brunico publishes five trade magazines that appeal to different niche markets. Three have an international readership and over half the company's revenues come from outside of the country. *RealScreen* has become the leading publication in the world for documentary filmmakers and broadcasters, while *KidScreen* is the world leader for producers, broadcasters, and consumer marketers interested in reaching children through entertainment. In the mid-1990s, Jim realized that his brands were so strong that he could leverage them into events. Brunico, therefore, now annually produces 25 marketing and entertainment-industry conferences in Canada and the United States. The RealScreen Summit in Washington, D.C., is the largest of these, drawing over 700 professionals from around the globe.

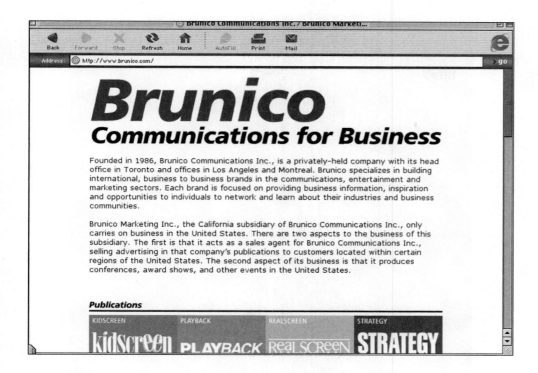

Toronto's Brunico Communications has discovered the power of niche marketing with its KidScreen, RealScreen, Playback, and Strategy brands.

Niche marketers presumably understand their customers' needs so well that the customers willingly pay a premium. Tom's of Maine all-natural personal care products sometimes commands a 30 percent premium on its toothpaste because its unique, environmentally friendly products and charitable donation programs appeal to consumers who have been turned off by big businesses.[5] As marketing efficiency increases, niches that were seemingly too small may become more profitable.[6]

In the world of pharmaceuticals, biotech company Genentech stands out for developing drugs that target tiny niche markets instead of going after blockbusters like Pfizer's Lipitor or Merck's Zocor, cholesterol medications that rack up billions of dollars in sales:

Genentech

Genentech pursues "targeted therapies," drugs aimed at relatively small subsets of patients. The drugs produce the same kind of dramatic benefit doctors get when they identify the specific type of bacteria causing an infection and slam it with the right antibiotic. A few years ago, the company launched the first highly targeted therapy—Herceptin, a breast-cancer drug that is prescribed only to the 25 percent or so of patients whose tumours harbour a particular genetic quirk—and it hasn't looked back. Genentech's targeted therapies make economic sense because Genentech is small, doesn't need to sell billions of dollars of drugs each year to support an army of sales reps or marketing executives, and can charge premium prices because its anti-cancer drugs really work. Genentech's revenues were US$2.7 billion in 2002, up 24 percent from 2001.[7]

Globalization has facilitated niche marketing. For example, the German economy has more than 300 000 small and midsize companies (known as *the Mittelstand*). Many enjoy over 50 percent market share in well-defined global niches. Hermann Simon dubbed these global niche leaders "hidden champions."[8] Here are some examples:

- Tetra Food supplies 80 percent of the food for feeding tropical fish.
- Hohner has 85 percent of the world harmonica market.
- Becher has 50 percent of the world's oversized umbrella market.
- Steiner Optical has 80 percent of the world's military field glasses market.

Niche marketer Tom's of Maine makes environmentally friendly products and participates in a number of environmental action programs, like the Tom's of Maine National Rivers Awareness Program™.

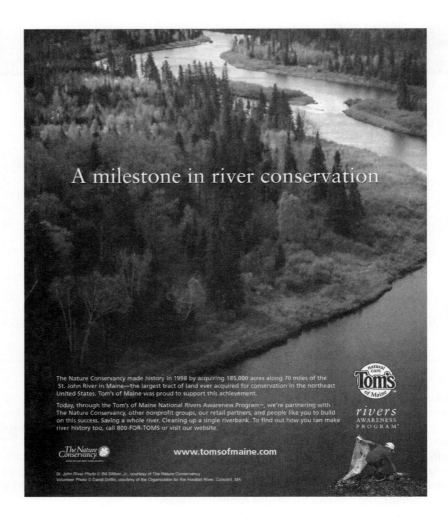

These hidden champions tend to be found in stable markets, are typically family owned or closely held, and are long-lived. They are dedicated to their customers and offer superior performance, responsive service, and punctual delivery (rather than low price) as well as customer intimacy. Senior management emphasizes continuous innovation and stays in direct and regular contact with top customers.

The low cost of setting up shop on the Internet has also led to many small business start-ups aimed at niches. The recipe for Internet niching success: Choose a hard-to-find product that customers do not need to see and touch. This "Webpreneur" followed the recipe with astonishing results:[9]

Ostrichesonline.com

Whereas Internet giants like Amazon.com have yet to realize a profit, Steve Warrington is earning a six-figure income selling ostriches—and every product derived from them—online (www.ostrichesonline.com). Since the site was launched for next to nothing in 1996, Warrington's business has sold to over 20 000 clients in over 125 countries from a catalogue of more than 17 500 ostrich-related products. Visitors to the site can buy ostrich meat, feathers, leather jackets, videos, eggshells, and subscribe to a newsletter devoted to ostriches.[10]

Local Marketing

Target marketing is leading to marketing programs tailored to the needs and wants of local customer groups (trading areas, neighbourhoods, even individual stores). Canada's credit unions provide different mixes of banking services in their branches, depending on neighbourhood demographics.

Kraft helps supermarket chains identify the cheese assortment and shelf positioning that will optimize cheese sales in low-, middle-, and high-income stores, and in different ethnic neighbourhoods.

Ford Canada

The Oakville, Ontario–based arm of the global automobile manufacturer Ford Motor Company regularly practises local marketing to sell its vehicles. While some campaigns can be leveraged across international boundaries to leverage economies of scale, more often than not, many campaigns must be tailored to the Canadian context. When it comes to creating a marketing campaign for a particular vehicle, Ford Canada examines the U.S. campaign to determine if it will resonate with Canadian consumers. If it does not, the company will invest in local creative content. For example, in putting together advertising for the flagship pick-up truck, the Ford F-150, it decided that the planned U.S. execution was too "American." In particular, the advertising depicted characters driving on an obviously American landscape that was not expected to resonate with a Canadian audience. As a result, the Canadian subsidiary launched the Rethink Truck campaign, featuring voiceovers by Canadian actor Kiefer Sutherland. It positions Ford Trucks as loaded with DVD players, luxurious interiors, leather seats, burled wood, nice instrument panels, and room for three adults in the back. It turned out to be one of Ford's most successful integrated launches ever.[11]

Local marketing reflects a growing trend called grassroots marketing. Marketing activities concentrate on getting as close and personally relevant to individual customers as possible. Much of Nike's initial success has been attributed to the ability to engage target consumers through grassroots marketing such as sponsorship of local school teams, expert-conducted clinics, and provision of shoes, clothing, and equipment.

A large part of local, grassroots marketing is experiential marketing, which promotes a product or service not just by communicating its features and benefits, but by also connecting it with unique and interesting experiences. One marketing commentator describes experiential marketing this way: "The idea is not to sell something, but to demonstrate how a brand can enrich a customer's life."[12] "Marketing Insight: Experiential Marketing" describes the concept of customer experience management.

Holiday Inn Hotels and Resorts is trying to recharge its faded brand image through experiential marketing aimed not only at creating new customer experiences, but also at getting customers to kindle nostalgia for their own childhood experiences with the brand:

Holiday Inn Hotels and Resorts

The chain that defined the overnight roadside experience is trying to push itself back into North Americans' consciousness. The marketing push is geared at evoking the good old days when their popularity was reflected in stolen towels—the chain still claims to lose 560 000 towels annually. So in 2003 Holiday Inn designated August 28 as "National Towel Amnesty Day." Extending through Labour Day weekend, each Holiday Inn distributed 50 limited-edition towels that read, "100 percent cotton, 100 percent guilt-free, 100 percent yours." In addition, the chain created an Internet site at www.holiday-inn.com/towels where visitors could share towel stories. For each story collected, $1 was donated to a charity benefiting children with life-threatening diseases who wish to visit central Florida attractions. By getting customers involved in swapping stories, the hotel chain hopes to play up the emotional connection many still have with its simple, dependable white-bread image.[13]

Pine and Gilmore, who are pioneers on the topic, have argued that we are on the threshold of the "Experience Economy," a new economic era in which all businesses must orchestrate memorable events for their customers.[14] They assert:

- If you charge for stuff, then you are in the *commodity business*.
- If you charge for tangible things, then you are in the *goods business*.
- If you charge for the activities you perform, then you are in the *service business*.

Experiential Marketing

Through several books and papers, Columbia University's Bernd Schmitt has developed the concept of *customer experience management (CEM)*—the process of strategically managing a customer's entire experience with a product or company. According to Schmitt, brands can help to create five different types of experiences: (1) sense, (2) feel, (3) think, (4) act, and (5) relate. In each case, Schmitt distinguishes between hard-wired and acquired experiential response levels. He maintains that marketers can provide experiences for customers through a set of experience providers:

1. *Communications*—advertising, public relations, annual reports, brochures, newsletters, and "magalogs."

2. *Visual/verbal identity*—names, logos, signage, and transportation vehicles.

3. *Product presence*—product design, packaging, and point-of-sale displays.

4. *Co-branding*—event marketing and sponsorships, alliances and partnerships, licensing, and product placement in movies or TV.

5. *Environments*—retail and public spaces, trade booths, corporate buildings, office interiors, and factories.

6. *Web sites and electronic media*—corporate sites, product or service sites, CD-ROMs, automated e-mails, online advertising, and intranets.

7. *People*—salespeople, customer service representatives, technical support or repair providers, company spokespersons, and CEOs and other executives.

The CEM framework is made up of five basic steps:

1. *Analyzing the experiential world of the customer*—gaining insights into the sociocultural context of consumers or the business context of business customers.

2. *Building the experiential platform*—developing a strategy that includes the positioning for the kind of experience the brand stands for ("what"), the value proposition of what relevant experience to deliver ("why"), and the overall implementation theme that will be communicated ("how").

3. *Designing the brand experience*—implementing their experiential platform in the look and feel of logos and signage, packaging, and retail spaces, in advertising, collaterals, and online.

4. *Structuring the customer interface*—implementing the experiential platform in the dynamic and interactive interfaces including face-to-face, in stores, during sales visits, at the check-in desk of a hotel, or the e-commerce engine of a Web site.

5. *Engaging in continuous innovation*—implementing the experiential platform in new product development, creative marketing events for customers, and fine-tuning the experience at every point of contact.

Schmitt cites Pret A Manger, the U.K.-based sandwich company, as an example of a company that provides an attractive brand experience, customer interface, and ongoing innovation: "The Pret A Manger brand is about great tasting, handmade, natural products served by amazing people who are passionate about their work. The sandwiches and stores look appealing and attractive. The company hires only 5% of those who apply and only after they have worked for a day in the shop. This process ensures good fit and good teamwork." He also offers Singapore Airlines, Starbucks, and Amazon.com as outstanding providers of customer experiences.

Sources: **www.exgroup.com**; Bernd Schmitt, *Customer Experience Management: A Revolutionary Approach to Connecting with Your Customers* (New York: John Wiley and Sons, 2003); Bernd Schmitt, David L. Rogers, and Karen Vrotsos, *There's No Business That's Not Show Business: Marketing in an Experience Culture* (Upper Saddle River, NJ: Prentice Hall, 2003); Bernd Schmitt, *Experiential Marketing: How to Get Companies to Sense, Feel, Think, Act, and Relate to Your Company and Brands* (New York: Free Press, 1999); Bernd Schmitt and Alex Simonson, *Marketing Aesthetics: The Strategic Management of Brands, Identity and Image* (New York: Free Press, 1997).

■ If you charge for the time customers spend with you, then and only then are you in the *experience* business.

Citing examples from a range of companies from Disney to AOL, they maintain that salable experiences come in four varieties: entertainment, education, aesthetic, and escapist. VANS, which pioneered slip-on sneakers for skateboarding, has succeeded in that market with an offbeat marketing mix of events, sponsorships, and even a documentary film, all celebrating the skateboard

Pro skateboarders Darrell Stanton and Scott Kane in a VANS ad. Both Stanton and Kane are part of a VANS-sponsored team.

culture.[15] The centrepiece of the marketing campaign is elaborate skateboard parks at malls. VANS' CEO Gary Schoenfeld proclaims, "Our vision is not to hit our target audience over the head with our ads, but to integrate ourselves into the places they are most likely to be."

Those who favour localized marketing see national advertising as wasteful because it is too "arm's length" and fails to address local needs. Those against local marketing argue that it drives up manufacturing and marketing costs by reducing economies of scale. Logistical problems are magnified. A brand's overall image might be diluted if the product and message are different in different localities.

Customerization

The ultimate level of segmentation leads to "segments of one," "customized marketing," or "one-to-one marketing."[16]

Today customers are taking more individual initiative in determining what and how to buy. They log onto the Internet; look up information and evaluations of product or service offers; dialogue with suppliers, users, and product critics; and in many cases, design the product they want. More online companies today are offering customers a Choiceboard, an interactive online system that allows individual customers to design their own products and services by choosing from a menu of attributes, components, prices, and delivery options. The customer's selections send signals to the supplier's manufacturing system that set in motion the wheels of procurement, assembly, and delivery.[17]

Wind and Rangaswamy see the Choiceboard as a movement toward "customerizing" the firm.[18] **Customerization** combines operationally driven mass customization with customized marketing in a way that empowers consumers to design the product and service offering of their choice. The firm no longer requires prior information about the customer, nor does the firm need to own manufacturing. The firm provides a platform and tools and "rents" out to customers the means to design their own products. A company is customerized when it is able to respond to individual customers by customizing its goods, services, and messages on a one-to-one basis.[19]

Each business unit will have to decide whether it would gain more by designing its business system to create offerings for *segments* or for *individuals*. Companies that favour segmentation see it as more efficient, as requiring less customer information, and as permitting more standardization of market offerings. Those who favour individual marketing claim that segments are a fiction, that individuals within so-called segments differ greatly, and that marketers can achieve much more precision and effectiveness by addressing individual needs.

Customization is certainly not for every company: It may be very difficult to implement for complex products such as automobiles. Customization can raise the cost of goods by more than the customer is willing to pay. Some customers do not know what they want until they see actual

FIGURE 8.2

Examples of Marketing Customization

Sources: "Creating Greater Customer Value May Require a Lot of Changes," *Organizational Dynamics* (Summer 1998): 26; Erick Schonfeld, "The Customized, Digitized, Have-It-Your-Way Economy," *Fortune*, September 28, 1998, pp. 115–124; Jim Barlow, "Individualizing Mass Production," *Houston Chronicle*, April 13, 1997, p. E1; Sarah Schafer, "Have It Your Way," *Inc.*, November 18, 1997, pp. 56–64; Jim Christie, "Mass Customization: The New Assembly Line?" *Investor's Daily*, February 25, 2000.

Acumins

Internet-based vitamin company Acumins blends vitamins, herbs, and minerals according to a customer's instructions, compressing up to 95 ingredients into three to five "personalized pills." The Acumins premise is simple and attractive: Why swallow dozens of pills when you can take three pills with dozens of ingredients of your choosing?

Paris Miki

The Japanese company Paris Miki, one of the largest eyeglass retailers in the world, uses a design tool that takes a digital picture of the customer's face. The customer describes the style he or she wants—sports, elegant, traditional—and the system displays alternatives on the computerized photograph. After selecting the frame, the customer also chooses nosepieces, hinges, and arms. The glasses are ready within an hour.

DeBeers

With DeBeers' Design Your Own Ring program, customers can design their own diamond rings by choosing from any of 189 unique combinations of centre stone and side stone shapes and weights and band metal, as well as connect with a local jeweller who can help them buy it.

Andersen Windows

Andersen Windows of Bayport, Minnesota, a leading window and patio door manufacturer, has developed an interactive computer version of its catalogues for distributors and retailers that is linked directly to the factory. With the system, now in 650 showrooms, salespeople can help customers customize each window, check the design for structural soundness, and generate a price quote. From there Andersen went on to develop a "batch of one" manufacturing process in which every window and door part is made to order, thus reducing its finished parts inventory (a major cost to the company).

ChemStation

Based in Dayton, Ohio, ChemStation offers customized soap formulas to its industrial customers, who range from car washes to the U.S. Air Force. What cleans a car will not clean an airplane or equipment in a mine shaft. Salespeople visit customer sites to gather information. All the data from the company's chemical lab and its field studies are kept in a central database called Tank Management System (TMS). TMS is linked directly to both the lab and the company's 40 plants across the United States, where computer-operated machines mix each customer's special formula.

products. Customers cannot cancel the order after the company has started to work on the product. The product may be hard to repair and have little sales value. In spite of this, customization has worked well for some products. Figure 8.2 shows examples of companies that employ customization.

Segmenting Consumer Markets

Two broad groups of variables are used to segment consumer markets. Some researchers try to form segments by looking at descriptive characteristics: geographic, demographic, and psychographic. Then they examine whether these customer segments exhibit different needs or product responses. For example, they might examine the differing attitudes of "professionals," "blue collars," and other groups toward, say, "safety" as a car benefit.

Other researchers try to form segments by looking at "behavioural" considerations, such as consumer responses to benefits, use occasions, or brands. Once the segments are formed, the researcher sees whether different characteristics are associated with each consumer-response segment. For example, the researcher might examine whether people who want "quality" rather than "low price" in buying an automobile differ in their geographic, demographic, and psychographic makeup.

Regardless of which type of segmentation scheme is employed, the key is that the marketing program can be profitably adjusted to recognize customer differences. The major segmentation variables—geographic, demographic, psychographic, and behavioural segmentation—are summarized in Table 8.1.

Geographic Segmentation

Geographic segmentation calls for dividing the market into different geographical units such as nations, provinces, regions, counties, cities, or neighbourhoods. The company can operate in one or a few areas, or operate in all but pay attention to local variations. For example, Hilton Hotels customizes rooms and lobbies according to location. Hotels in Central Canada are sleeker and more cosmopolitan. Western hotels are more rustic. Major retailers such as Wal-Mart, Sears, Roebuck & Co., and Kmart all allow local managers to stock products that suit the local community.[20]

TABLE 8.1	MAJOR SEGMENTATION VARIABLES FOR CONSUMER MARKETS
Geographic	
Region	Atlantic Provinces, Quebec, Central Provinces, Western Provinces, Northern Territories
City or metro size	Under 5000; 5000–20 000; 20 000–50 000; 50 000–100 000; 100 000–250 000; 250 000–500 000; 500 000–1 000 000; 1 000 000–4 000 000; 4 000 000 or over
Density	Urban, suburban, rural
Climate	Far north, near north, mountain, maritime
Demographic	
Age	Under 6, 6–11, 12–19, 20–34, 35–49, 50–64, 65+
Family size	1–2, 3–4, 5+
Family life cycle	Young, single; young, married, no children; young, married, youngest child under 6; young, married, youngest child 6 or over; older, married, with children; older, married, no children under 18; older, single; other
Gender	Male, female
Income	Under $10 000; $10 000–$15 000; $15 000–$20 000; $20 000–$30 000; $30 000–$50 000; $50 000–$100 000; $100 000 and over
Occupation	Professional and technical; managers, officials, and proprietors; clerical sales; craftspeople; forepersons; operatives; farmers; retired; students; homemakers; unemployed
Education	Grade school or less; some high school; high school graduate; some community college; community college graduate, some university, university graduate, graduate degree
Religion	Catholic, Protestant, Jewish, Muslim, Hindu, other
Race	White, Black, Asian, Native Canadian
Generation	Baby boomers, Generation Xers
Nationality	English, French, German, Italian, Japanese, Middle Eastern
Social class	Lower lowers, upper lowers, working class, middle class, upper middles, lower uppers, upper uppers
Psychographic	
Lifestyle	Culture-oriented, sports-oriented, outdoor-oriented
Personality	Compulsive, gregarious, authoritarian, ambitious
Behavioural	
Occasions	Regular occasion, special occasion
Benefits	Quality, service, economy, speed
User status	Nonuser, ex-user, potential user, first-time user, regular user
Usage rate	Light user, medium user, heavy user
Loyalty status	None, medium, strong, absolute
Readiness stage	Unaware, aware, informed, interested, desirous, intending to buy
Attitude toward product	Enthusiastic, positive, indifferent, negative, hostile

The Globe and Mail

One of only two national daily newspapers in Canada, *The Globe and Mail* strives to provide a national and international flavour to its newspaper content. However, in 2003 the *Globe* began an effort to target the Toronto market more aggressively by beefing up its Toronto news coverage with the launch of a new Toronto section. This section is expanded on weekends and is featured as a stand-alone section. The intention is to more effectively reach Toronto's influential and discerning readership in a cluttered and intensely competitive market—one that is more inundated with media than any other part of Canada.[21]

More and more, regional marketing means marketing right down to a specific neighbourhood.[22] Many companies use mapping software to show the geographic locations of their customers. The software may show a retailer that most of his customers are within only a 10-kilometre radius of his store, and further concentrated within a certain area. By mapping the densest areas, the retailer can resort to *customer cloning*, assuming that the best prospects live where most of his customers come from.

Some approaches combine geographic data with demographic data to yield even richer descriptions of consumers and neighbourhoods. Claritas, Inc., has developed a geoclustering approach called PRIZM (Potential Rating Index by Zip Markets) that classifies over half a million residential U.S. neighbourhoods into 15 distinct groups and 66 distinct lifestyle segments called PRIZM Clusters.[23] The groupings take into consideration 39 factors in 5 broad categories: (1) education and affluence, (2) family life cycle, (3) urbanization, (4) race and ethnicity, and (5) mobility. The inhabitants in a cluster tend to lead similar lives, drive similar cars, have similar jobs, and read similar magazines. Here is an example of a PRIZM cluster:[24]

> *Young Digerati*: Couples or single-headed households, most of them with kids, who have decided to stay in urban centres rather than flee to the suburbs. This sector includes a high proportion of affluent, tech-savvy 20-somethings, who tend to hold master's degrees and live in fashionable neighbourhoods on the urban fringe. They are staking out territory in once-forgotten neighbourhoods in large cosmopolitan cities.

Marketers can use PRIZM to answer such questions as these: Which geographic areas contain our most valuable customers? How deeply have we already penetrated these segments? Which distribution channels and promotional media work best in reaching our target clusters in each area? Geoclustering captures the increasing diversity of the population. Upscale sportswear retailer Eddie Bauer has used geoclustering information to better locate stores and serve customers. Based on a successful pilot with *Veggie Tales* concerts, Clear Channel Communications is using geoclustering information to send targeted e-mails to prospects for national tours in all entertainment venues.[25] Marketing to micro-segments has become accessible even to small organizations as database costs decline, PCs proliferate, software becomes easier to use, data integration increases, and the Internet grows.[26]

Demographic Segmentation

In demographic segmentation, the market is divided into groups on the basis of variables such as age, family size, family life cycle, gender, income, occupation, education, religion, race, generation, nationality, and social class. There are several reasons for the popularity of demographic variables to distinguish customer groups. One reason is that consumer needs, wants, and usage rates and product and brand preferences are often associated with demographic variables. Another is that demographic variables are easier to measure. Even when the target market is described in nondemographic terms (say, a personality type), the link back to demographic characteristics is needed in order to estimate the size of the market and the media that should be used to reach it efficiently.

Canadian Foundation for AIDS Research (CANFAR)

Since sexual awareness and activity begins in teenage years, CANFAR (www.canfar.com) directs its Have a Heart campaign at this demographic. The annual initiative targets students in middle schools, high schools, community colleges, and universities in Canada. Its aim is to educate students about HIV/AIDS prevention and raise funds for research. Poly-bagged "Heart o'Grams," containing an HIV/AIDS pamphlet, an AIDS ribbon, tattoo, or pin, scratch and win cards, and a Nestlé chocolate bar, are sold as Valentine's Day gifts. CANFAR also chose age-relevant communication tools to promote the program—posters, bathroom ads, direct mail, and a Web page.[27]

Here is how certain demographic variables have been used to segment markets.

AGE AND LIFE-CYCLE STAGE Consumer wants and abilities change with age. Toothpaste brands such as Crest and Colgate offer three main lines of products to target kids, adults, and older consumers. Age segmentation can be even more refined. Pampers divides its market into prenatal, newborn (0–1 month), infant (2–5 months), cruiser (6–12 months), toddler (13–18 months), explorer (19–23 months), and preschooler (24 months+).

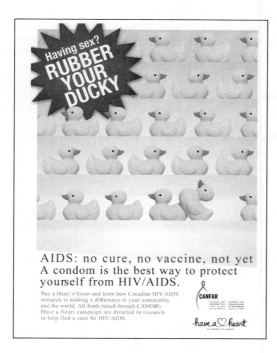

CANFAR's "Have a Heart" campaign targets students from elementary school to university to educate and eventually raise funds for AIDS research.

Nevertheless, age and life cycle can be tricky variables.[28] In some cases, the target market for products may be the psychologically young. For example, Honda tried to target 21-year-olds with its boxy Element, which company officials described as a "dorm room on wheels." So many baby boomers were attracted to the car's ads depicting sexy college kids partying near the car at a beach, however, that the average age of buyers turned out to be 42! Nostalgia can also play a role. Chrysler had a young target market in mind for the PT Cruiser, but found that lots of older consumers were reminded of hot rods from their youth. Toyota has been more successful with its younger pitch for Scion.[29]

Scion

Named for wealthy offspring, Scion is an attempt by Toyota to attract the Gen Y audience, which might see Toyota as their parents' brand. The Scion has a hip look and feel—and an industrial strength stereo—and is sold in chrome and black showrooms tucked inside Toyota dealerships. Priced at under US$15 000 and sold on a fixed price basis (no haggling), the marketing strategy is to go underground and link the brand to up-and-coming entertainment and events, allowing the youthful target to "discover" the brand.

LIFE STAGE Persons in the same part of the life cycle may differ in their life stage. **Life stage** defines a person's major concern, such as going through a divorce, going into a second marriage, taking care of an older parent, deciding to cohabit with another person, deciding to buy a new home, and so on. These life stages present opportunities for marketers who can help people cope with their major concerns.

Newlyweds

Marketers know that marriage often means that two sets of shopping habits and brand preferences have to be blended into one. Companies such as Procter & Gamble, Clorox, and Colgate-Palmolive include their products in "Newlywed Kits" that are distributed when couples apply for their marriage licence. J. C. Penney has identified "Starting Outs" as one of its two major customer groups. Marketers pay companies a premium for name lists to assist their direct marketing because, as one marketer noted, newlywed names "are like gold."[30]

GENDER Men and women tend to have different attitudinal and behavioural orientations, based partly on genetic makeup and partly on socialization. For example, women tend to be more communal-minded and men tend to be more self-expressive and goal-directed; women tend to take in more of the data in their immediate environment; men tend to focus on the part of the environment that helps them achieve a goal. A research study examining how men and women shop found that men often need to be invited to touch a product, while women are likely to pick it up without prompting. Men often like to read product information; women may relate to a product on a more personal level.[31]

Gender differentiation has long been applied in clothing, hairstyling, cosmetics, and magazines. Avon has built a US$6 billion-plus business selling beauty products to women. Some products have been positioned as more masculine or feminine. Gillette's Venus is the most successful female shaving line ever, with over 70 percent of the market, and has appropriate product design, packaging, and advertising cues to reinforce a female image; Camel emphasizes men and surrounds the brand with more masculine, rugged cues.

Women are said to be a consumer group that controls over 80 percent of consumer dollars spent in North America. It is no wonder that some companies are working very hard to find ways to communicate—or more importantly, connect—with female consumers. Here is just a sampling of companies likely to reap significant benefits:

RBC Financial Group

Canada's largest financial institution invested four years and significant dollars into creating a "gender intelligent sales force" to train 1500 account managers how to meet the needs of women. Only one year after the training was complete, RBC witnessed a 10-point jump in market share and a 29 percent increase in customer satisfaction levels of women entrepreneurs.

Toyota Canada

Toyota recently reinvented its sales process. Appropriately called "Access," the principal goal of the new process is to meet the needs of women consumers. After conducting an audit of its sales training program, Toyota discovered that making the process more women-friendly actually increased the program's effectiveness overall. As a result, Toyota reported substantial gains in its customer satisfaction numbers.

Holiday Inn Toronto

The hotel located in downtown Toronto created a program for women business travellers called Stay Assured. It focused on gender-intelligent benefits like safety and witnessed a 400 percent increase of traffic.

Maytag Canada

Although Burlington, Ontario–based Maytag has long targeted women, its recent co-branding effort with lingerie retailer La Vie en Rose resulted in a 25 percent sales increase of the firm's new Neptune dryer. Brand manager Scott Rider knew he needed a "reason why" women should buy the new cabinet-like dryer. With increases in appliance reliability, replacement rates for dryers were low. The "reason why" came when Scott's research showed that most women wouldn't dare put their expensive underwear in traditional dryers. The co-branding effort brought home the point that with the Neptune dryer, women could now toss even their finest lingerie into the high-end drying cabinet.[32]

INCOME Income segmentation is a long-standing practice in such product and service categories as automobiles, clothing, cosmetics, travel, and financial services.

BMO InvestorLine

To attract wealthy executives and encourage them to buy investment products during a recent RRSP season, BMO scored with its online Ultimate Golf Getaway contest. Contestants had to play a virtual round of golf to qualify for the chance to win golf vacations. The goal of the innovative campaign was to increase market share by retaining existing clients and acquiring new ones. BMO shunned traditional methods in striving toward this goal. "We wanted to have advertising that was more distinct and more interactive," says Kelly Harper, senior marketing manager for BMO InvestorLine. Their agency, Tribal, developed a Flash-based golf game that challenged players to sink a putt or drive down the fairway while learning about InvestorLine products. The promotion was targeted toward affluent males aged 40 to 55. They fell into two segments: life-goal planners (a group that wants to exercise more control over their portfolios), and serious investors (men who are concerned with frequent trading). The campaign was a huge success. Participation in the promotion increased 165 percent over what was achieved in previous years, and 15 percent of the people who took part in the promotion opened up new accounts with InvestorLine.[33]

However, income does not always predict the best customers for a given product. Blue-collar workers were among the first purchasers of colour television sets; it was cheaper for them to buy these sets than to go to movies and restaurants.

Increasingly, companies are finding that their markets are "hourglass-shaped" as middle-market consumers migrate toward more premium products.[34] When Whirlpool launched a pricey Duet washer line, sales doubled those forecasted even in a weak economy, due primarily to middle-class shoppers who traded up. Michael Silverstein, a senior vice president and director for the Boston Consulting Group, and former BCG partner Neil Fiske have been studying this phenomenon, which they call "trading up." Their new book, *Trading Up: The New American Luxury*, documents their investigation into the forces driving the trend and points out companies that have cracked the code for success in this market:[35]

Panera Bread

While lunch at Panera's bakery cafés costs twice as much as at Burger King, customers don't mind paying because the cafés deliver all three benefits that Silverstein and Fiske say are common to successful new-luxury goods: *technical benefits* (how a product is engineered), *functional benefits* (the experience it provides the customer), and *emotional benefits* (how it makes the customer feel). Getting a smoked turkey breast with chipotle mayonnaise on Asiago cheese focaccia and a chai latte in a pleasing café atmosphere is the kind of satisfying experience "trading-up" customers crave. And being able to deliver that experience quickly and relatively inexpensively has spurred the growth of Panera and others in the so-called "fast casual" dining segment.

According to Silverstein and Fiske, companies that make a concerted effort to reinvent their product and come up with something genuinely better will find a huge potential market. In the United States, the trading-up universe generally begins with households earning at least US$50 000. Due to the higher cost of living in Canada, people must earn more than this figure to trade up. Of course, if companies miss out on this new market, they risk being "trapped in the middle" and seeing their market share steadily decline. General Motors was caught in the middle, between highly engineered German imports in the luxury market and high-value Japanese and Korean models in the economy class.[36]

GENERATION Each generation is profoundly influenced by the times in which it grows up—the music, movies, politics, and defining events of that period. Demographers call these groups *cohorts*. Members of a cohort share the same major cultural, political, and economic experiences. They have similar outlooks and values. Marketers often advertise to a cohort group by using the icons and images prominent in their experiences. "Marketing Insight: A Guide to Generation Y" provides insight into one key age cohort.

Yet, while distinctions can be made between different cohorts, generational cohorts also influence each other. For instance, because so many members of Generation Y—"Echo Boomers"—are living with their boomer parents, the parents are being influenced and exhibiting what demographers are calling a "boom-boom effect." The same products that appeal to 21-year-olds are appealing to youth-obsessed baby boomers. Boomer parents are watching MTV's *The Osbournes*, the reality show based on heavy-metal rocker Ozzy Osbourne and his family, right alongside their children.

Meredith, Schewe, and Karlovich developed a framework called the Lifestage Analytic Matrix, which combines information on cohorts, life stages, physiographics, emotional effects, and socioeconomics in analyzing a segment or individual.[37] For example, two individuals from the same cohort may differ in their *life stages* (having a divorce, getting remarried), *physiographics* (coping with hair loss, menopause, arthritis, or osteoporosis), *emotional effects* (nostalgia for the past, wanting experiences instead of things), or *socioeconomics* (losing a job, receiving an inheritance). The authors believe this analysis will lead to more efficient targeting and messages.

SOCIAL CLASS   Social class has a strong influence on preference in cars, clothing, home furnishings, leisure activities, reading habits, and retailers. Many companies design products and services for specific social classes. The tastes of social classes change with the years. The 1990s were about greed and ostentation for the upper classes. Affluent tastes now run more conservatively, although luxury goods makers such as Coach, Tiffany, Burberry, TAG Heuer, and Louis Vuitton still successfully sell to those seeking the good life.[38]

MARKETING INSIGHT

A Guide to Generation Y

Generation Y is the term most commonly applied to North Americans born between 1977 and 1999. Today's teenagers are part of this group. According to Statistics Canada, in 2005 there were 4.2 million people between the ages of 10 and 19. The highest numbers live in Ontario and the West. They are a diverse group. All tend to be focused on fashion and music, but they split into various subcultures: hip hops, ravers, skaters, clubbers, mods, preppies, Goths, the R&B set, punks, jocks, and more. Each subculture has an attitude of its own, says Insignia Marketing Research of Toronto: "Hip hop culture focuses on individual strength; preppies are clean-cut; and skaters are cool, sometimes rough, their culture revolving around a sport." Even though peer pressure is a significant influence on their choices, they loathe being branded as followers.

Generation Y is also marked by racial diversity, and they may be the first truly "colour-blind" generation. They are also very comfortable with technology and are big users of both cell phones and the Internet. They value content that is designed just for them and want Web sites that are refreshed frequently.

The following are traits often ascribed to Generation Y:

- Optimism and big expectations for the future
- An obsession with achievement
- Technological savvy
- Greater acceptance of racial and ethnic differences
- Media savvy
- Busy schedules
- Higher levels of stress
- A heightened ability to multitask
- A strong sense of community and teamwork
- A wish to make money, but a need to give back
- Emphasis on immediate gratification
- Suspicion of advertising

Sources: Jo Marney, "They've Gotta Have It," *Marketing Magazine Online*, **www.marketingmag.ca**, October 18, 1999 (viewed October 23, 2002); J. M. Lawrence, "Trends: X-ed Out: Gen Y Takes Over," *Boston Herald*, February 2, 1999, p. 243; and Martha Irvine, "Labels Don't Fit Us, Gen Y Insists," *Denver Post*, April 19, 2001, p. A9. Statistics Canada Table "Population by sex and age group," 27 October, 2005 **http://www40.statcan.ca/l01/cst01/demo10a.htm**

Psychographic Segmentation

Psychographics is the science of using psychology and demographics to better understand consumers. In *psychographic segmentation*, buyers are divided into different groups on the basis of lifestyle or personality or values. People within the same demographic group can exhibit very different psychographic profiles.

One of the most popular commercially available classification systems based on psychographic measurements is SRI Consulting Business Intelligence's (SRIC-BI) VALS™ framework. VALS classifies all adults into eight primary groups based on personality traits and key demographics. The segmentation system is based on responses to a questionnaire featuring four demographic and 35 attitudinal questions. The VALS system is continually updated with new data from more than 80 000 surveys per year (see Figure 8.3).[39]

The major tendencies of the four groups with high resources are:

1. *Innovators.* Successful, sophisticated, active, "take-charge" people with high self-esteem. Purchases often reflect cultivated tastes for relatively upscale, niche-oriented products and services.

2. *Thinkers.* Mature, satisfied, and reflective people who are motivated by ideals and value order, knowledge, and responsibility. Favour durability, functionality, and value in products.

3. *Achievers.* Successful career- and work-oriented people who value consensus and stability. Favour established, prestige products that demonstrate success to their peers.

4. *Experiencers.* Young, enthusiastic, impulsive people who seek variety and excitement. Spend a comparatively high proportion of income on fashion, entertainment, and socializing.

The major tendencies of the four groups with lower resources are:

1. *Believers.* Conservative, conventional, and traditional people with concrete beliefs. Favour familiar products and are loyal to established brands.

2. *Strivers.* Trendy and fun-loving people who seek approval of others but are resource-constrained. Favour stylish products that emulate the purchases of those with greater material wealth.

3. *Makers.* Practical, self-sufficient, traditional, and family-oriented people who focus on their work and home context. Favour basic products with a practical or functional purpose.

4. *Strugglers.* Elderly, resigned, passive people who are concerned about change. Loyal to their favourite brands.

You can find out which VALS type you are by going to SRIC-BI's Web site (**www.sric-bi.com**).

Lifestyle segmentation schemes are by no means universal. The Japanese version of VALS divides society into ten segments on the basis of two key consumer attributes: life orientation (traditional ways, occupations, innovation, and self-expression) and attitudes to social change (sustaining, pragmatic, adapting, and innovating).

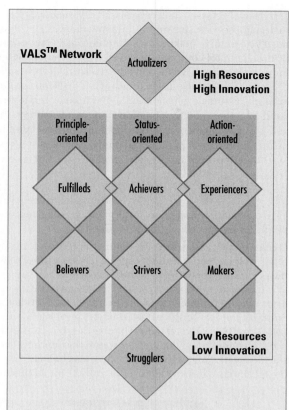

FIGURE 8.3

The VALS Segmentation System: An Eight-Part Typology

Source: © 2004 by SRI Consulting Business Intelligence. All rights reserved. Printed by permission.

Behavioural Segmentation

In behavioural segmentation, buyers are divided into groups on the basis of their knowledge of, attitude toward, use of, or response to a product.

DECISION ROLES It is easy to identify the buyer for many products. In North America, men normally choose their shaving equipment, and women choose their pantyhose; but even here marketers must be careful in making their targeting decisions, because buying roles change. When ICI, the giant British chemical company, discovered that women made 60 percent of the decisions on the brand of household paint, it decided to advertise its DuLux brand to women.

People play five roles in a buying decision: *initiator, influencer, decider, buyer,* and *user.* For example, assume a wife initiates a purchase by requesting a new treadmill for her birthday. The husband may then seek information from many sources, including his best friend who has a treadmill and is a key influencer in what models to consider. After presenting the alternative choices to his wife, he then purchases her preferred model which, as it turns out, ends up being used by the entire family. Different people are playing different roles, but all are crucial in the decision process and ultimate consumer satisfaction.

BEHAVIOURAL VARIABLES Many marketers believe that behavioural variables—occasions, benefits, user status, usage rate, loyalty status, buyer-readiness stage, and attitude—are the best starting points for constructing market segments.

Occasions Occasions can be defined in terms of the time of day, week, month, year or in terms of other well-defined temporal aspects of a consumer's life. Buyers can be distinguished according to the occasions when they develop a need, purchase a product, or use a product. For example, air travel is triggered by occasions related to business, vacation, or family. Occasion segmentation can help firms expand product usage. For example, the Florida Citrus Growers ran an ad campaign—"Orange juice. It's not just for breakfast anymore"—to expand its usage to other parts of the day. During the 1960s and 1970s, Ocean Spray Cranberries, Inc., was essentially a single-purpose, single-usage product: Consumption of cranberries was almost entirely confined to the serving of cranberry sauce as a side dish with Thanksgiving and Christmas holiday dinners. After a pesticide scare one Thanksgiving drastically cut sales and almost put growers out of business, the cooperative embarked on a program

Once cranberries were used only for holiday dinner at Thanksgiving and Christmas. Ocean Spray cranberry-based juice drinks have given the company a year-round market for its product.

The First Great Temptation

The Second Great Temptation

Ocean Spray will give you a dime off just to tempt you to try a bottle of Cranapple. The crazy-mixed-up drink that's not quite apple. Not quite cranberry. We took the forbidden fruit. Added a jolt of cranberries. And came up with a fruit drink that some people swear is made in paradise. Give new Ocean Spray Cranapple a try. We'll bet you a dime you won't be able to resist it.

NEW Ocean spray CRANAPPLE CRANBERRY-APPLE DRINK

to diversify and create a year-round market by producing cranberry-based juice drinks and other products.[40]

Marketers also can try to extend activities associated with certain holidays to other times of the year. For instance, while Christmas, Mother's Day, and Valentine's Day are the three major gift-giving holidays, these and other holidays account for just over half of the gifters' budgets. That leaves the rest available throughout the year for occasion-driven gift-giving: birthdays, weddings, anniversaries, housewarming, and new babies.[41]

Benefits Buyers can be classified according to the benefits they seek. Even car drivers who want to stop for gas may seek different benefits. Through its research, Mobil identified five different benefit segments and their sizes:

1. *Road warriors*—premium products and quality service (16 percent)
2. *Generation F*—fast fuel, fast service, and fast food (27 percent)
3. *True blues*—branded products and reliable service (16 percent)
4. *Home bodies*—convenience (21 percent)
5. *Price shoppers*—low price (20 percent)

Surprisingly, although gasoline is largely a commodity, price shoppers constituted only 20 percent of the buyers. Mobil decided to focus on the less price-sensitive segments and rolled out *Friendly Serve*: cleaner property, bathrooms, better lighting, well-stocked stores, and friendlier personnel. Although Mobil charged US$0.02 per gallon more than its competitors, sales increased by 20 to 25 percent.[42]

User Status Markets can be segmented into nonusers, ex-users, potential users, first-time users, and regular users of a product. Blood banks cannot rely only on regular donors to supply blood; they must also recruit new first-time donors and contact ex-donors. Each will require a different marketing strategy. Included in the potential user group are consumers who will become users in connection with some life stage or life event. Mothers-to-be are potential users who will turn into heavy users. Producers of infant products and services learn their names and shower them with products and ads to capture a share of their future purchases. Market-share leaders tend to focus on attracting potential users because they have the most to gain. Smaller firms focus on trying to attract current users away from the market leader.

Usage Rate Markets can be segmented into light, medium, and heavy product users. Heavy users are often a small percentage of the market but account for a high percentage of total consumption. For example, heavy beer drinkers account for 87 percent of the beer consumed—almost seven times as much as the light beer drinkers. Marketers would rather attract one heavy user than several light users. A potential problem, however, is that heavy users are often either extremely loyal to one brand, or never stay loyal to a brand and are always looking for the lowest price.

Buyer-Readiness Stage A market consists of people in different stages of readiness to buy a product. Some are unaware of the product, some are aware, some are informed, some are interested, some desire the product, and some intend to buy. The relative numbers make a big difference in designing the marketing program. Suppose a health agency wants to encourage women to have an annual Pap test to detect possible cervical cancer. At the beginning, most women may be unaware of the Pap test. The marketing effort should go into awareness-building advertising using a simple message. Later, the advertising should dramatize the benefits of the Pap test and the risks of not taking it. A special offer of a free health examination might motivate women to actually sign up for the test.

Loyalty Status Buyers can be divided into four groups according to brand loyalty status:

1. *Hard-core loyals*—Consumers who buy only one brand all the time.
2. *Split loyals*—Consumers who are loyal to two or three brands.
3. *Shifting loyals*—Consumers who shift loyalty from one brand to another.
4. *Switchers*—Consumers who show no loyalty to any brand.[43]

A company can learn a great deal by analyzing the degrees of brand loyalty: (1) By studying its hard-core loyals, the company can identify its products' strengths. (2) By studying its split loyals, the company can pinpoint which brands are most competitive with its own. (3) By looking at customers who are shifting away from its brand, the company can learn about its marketing weaknesses and attempt to correct them.

Companies selling in a market dominated by switchers may have to rely more on price-cutting. If mistreated, customers can turn to another firm to satisfy their needs. One caution: What appear to

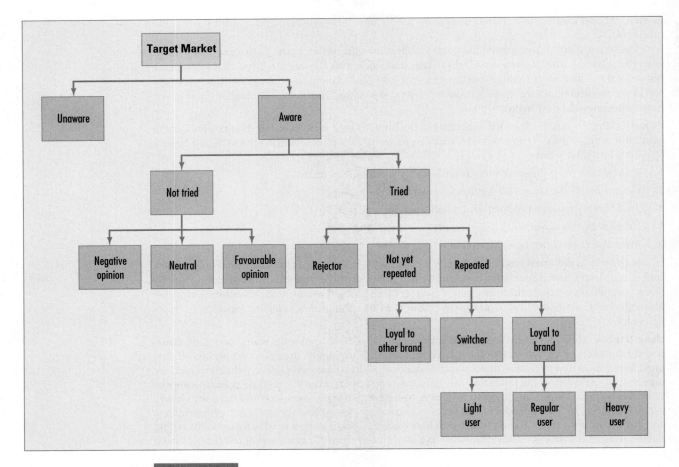

FIGURE 8.4

Behavioural Segmentation Breakdown

be brand-loyal purchase patterns may reflect habit, indifference, a low price, a high switching cost, or the nonavailability of other brands.

Attitude Five attitude groups can be found in a market: enthusiastic, positive, indifferent, negative, and hostile. Door-to-door workers in a political campaign use voter attitude to determine how much time to spend with that voter. They thank enthusiastic voters and remind them to vote; they reinforce those who are positively disposed; they try to win the votes of indifferent voters; they spend no time trying to change the attitudes of negative and hostile voters.

Combining different behavioural bases can help to provide a more comprehensive and cohesive view of a market and its segments. Figure 8.4 depicts one possible way to break down a target market by various behavioural segmentation bases.

THE CONVERSION MODEL The Conversion Model has been developed to measure the strength of the psychological commitment between brands and consumers and their openness to change.[44] To determine the ease with which a consumer can be converted to another choice, the model assesses commitment based on factors such as consumer attitudes toward and satisfaction with current brand choices in a category and the importance of the decision to select a brand in the category.[45]

The model segments *users* of a brand into four groups based on strength of commitment, from low to high, as follows:

1. *Convertible*—users who are most likely to defect.

2. *Shallow*—consumers who are uncommitted to the brand and could switch; some are actively considering alternatives.

3. *Average*—consumers who are also committed to the brand they are using, but not as strongly; they are unlikely to switch brands in the short term.

4. *Entrenched*—consumers who are strongly committed to the brand they are currently using; they are highly unlikely to switch brands in the foreseeable future.

The model also classifies *nonusers* of a brand into four other groups based on their "balance of disposition" and openness to trying the brand, from low to high, as follows:

1. *Strongly unavailable*—nonusers who are unlikely to switch to the brand; their preference lies strongly with their current brands.

2. *Weakly unavailable*—nonusers who are not available to the brand because their preference lies with their current brand, although not strongly.

3. *Ambivalent*—nonusers who are as attracted to the brand as they are to their current brands.

4. *Available*—nonusers of the brand who are most likely to be acquired in the short run.

In an application of the Conversion Model, Lloyds TSB bank discovered that the profitability of their clients who had been identified as "least committed" had fallen by 14 percent in a 12-month period, whereas those that were "most committed" had increased by 9 percent. Those who were "committed" were 20 percent more likely to increase the number of products they held during the 12-month period. As a result, the bank took action to attract and retain high-value committed customers, resulting in increased profitability.

Bases for Segmenting Business Markets

Business markets can be segmented with some of the same variables used in consumer market segmentation, such as geography, benefits sought, and usage rate, but business marketers also use other variables. Bonoma and Shapiro proposed segmenting the business market with the variables shown in Table 8.2. The demographic variables are the most important, followed by the operating variables—down to the personal characteristics of the buyer.

The table lists major questions that business marketers should ask in determining which segments and customers to serve. A rubber-tire company should first decide which industries it wants to serve. It can sell tires to manufacturers of automobiles, trucks, farm tractors, forklift trucks, or aircraft. Within a chosen target industry, a company can further segment by company size. The company might set up separate operations for selling to large and small customers. Consider how Dell is organized.

Dell

Dell is divided into two direct sales divisions: One sells to consumers and small businesses; another manages the company's corporate accounts. Three key segments are included under the corporate accounts umbrella: the enterprise group (*Fortune* 500 companies), large corporate accounts (multinational companies in what would be the *Fortune* 501 to 2000 range), and preferred accounts (medium businesses with 200 to 2000 employees).

Marketing to Small Businesses

Small businesses, in particular, have become a Holy Grail for business marketers.[46] In Canada, small businesses are responsible for roughly 25 percent of the gross domestic product according to Industry Canada.[47] Here is an example of a consumer-focused company that also is striving to serve small businesses.

Costco Wholesale Corp. (Vancouver)

Big box stores such as Costco have been strictly a suburban phenomenon, but this is beginning to change. Big players such as Home Depot, Rona, Future Shop and, of course, Costco have started to cozy up to the urban market. Principally, this shift is all about expanding their access to a broader set of market segments—and one of the largest of these segments is small business. Costco Wholesale Corp. is working toward unveiling a 147 000 square foot store in the vicinity of GM Place in downtown Vancouver. One of its objectives is to get closer to small businesses such as convenience stores. In order to do this, it is using a distinct approach. For example, Costco plans to give this location its own marketing group that will be responsible for building relationships and integrating with the business community.[48]

TABLE 8.2	MAJOR SEGMENTATION VARIABLES FOR BUSINESS MARKETS

Demographic

1. *Industry:* Which industries should we serve?

2. *Company size:* What size companies should we serve?

3. *Location:* What geographical areas should we serve?

Operating Variables

4. *Technology:* What customer technologies should we focus on?

5. *User or nonuser status:* Should we serve heavy users, medium users, light users, or nonusers?

6. *Customer capabilities:* Should we serve customers needing many or few services?

Purchasing Approaches

7. *Purchasing-function organization:* Should we serve companies with highly centralized or decentralized purchasing organizations?

8. *Power structure:* Should we serve companies that are engineering dominated, financially dominated, and so on?

9. *Nature of existing relationships:* Should we serve companies with which we have strong relationships or simply go after the most desirable companies?

10. *General purchase policies:* Should we serve companies that prefer leasing? Service contracts? Systems purchases? Sealed bidding?

11. *Purchasing criteria:* Should we serve companies that are seeking quality? Service? Price?

Situational Factors

12. *Urgency:* Should we serve companies that need quick and sudden delivery or service?

13. *Specific application:* Should we focus on certain applications of our product rather than all applications?

14. *Size of order:* Should we focus on large or small orders?

Personal Characteristics

15. *Buyer–seller similarity:* Should we serve companies whose people and values are similar to ours?

16. *Attitudes toward risk:* Should we serve risk-taking or risk-avoiding customers?

17. *Loyalty:* Should we serve companies that show high loyalty to their suppliers?

Source: Adapted from Thomas V. Bonoma and Benson P. Shapiro, *Segmenting the Industrial Market* (Lexington, MA: Lexington Books, 1983).

Within a given target industry and customer size, a company can segment by purchase criteria. For example, government laboratories need low prices and service contracts for scientific equipment; university laboratories need equipment that requires little service; and industrial laboratories need equipment that is highly reliable and accurate.

Sequential Segmentation

Business marketers generally identify segments through a sequential process. Consider an aluminum company: The company first undertook macro-segmentation. It looked at which end-use market to serve: automobile, residential, or beverage containers. It chose the residential market, and needed to determine the most attractive product application: semi-finished material, building components, or aluminum mobile homes. Deciding to focus on building components, it considered the best customer size and chose large customers. The second stage consisted of micro-segmentation. The company distinguished among customers buying on price, service, or quality. Because the aluminum company had a high-service profile, it decided to concentrate on the service-motivated segment of the market.

Business buyers seek different benefit bundles based on their stage in the purchase decision process:[49]

1. *First-time prospects*—Customers who have not yet purchased but want to buy from a vendor who understands their business, who explains things well, and whom they can trust.

2. *Novices*—Customers who are starting their purchasing relationship want easy-to-read manuals, hot lines, a high level of training, and knowledgeable sales reps.

3. *Sophisticates*—Established customers want speed in maintenance and repair, product customization, and high technical support.

These segments may also have different channel preferences. First-time prospects would prefer to deal with a company salesperson instead of a catalogue or direct-mail channel, because the latter provides too little information. Sophisticates, on the other hand, may want to conduct more of their buying over electronic channels.

One proposed segmentation scheme classifies business buyers into three groups, each warranting a different type of selling:[50]

- *Price-oriented customers (transactional selling).* They want value through lowest price.

- *Solution-oriented customers (consultative selling).* They want value through more benefits and advice.

- *Strategic-value customers (enterprise selling).* They want value through the supplier co-investing and participating in the customer's business.

The authors cite several cases of mismanagement by companies that did not understand the business buyer:

- A packaging manufacturer decided to upgrade and rename sales reps as packaging consultants at a cost of US$10 million, but 90 percent of its customers bought transactionally. The company failed and was acquired by a major competitor who reintroduced a transactional selling effort.

- A consulting firm replaced its long-term consultants with salespeople to sell quick consulting projects. They acquired many new clients but lost most of their old clients who wanted consultative selling.

- A container manufacturer selling consultatively to a major food company was asked to join in some risk and gain sharing involving co-development of radically new packaging approaches. It refused and lost the account.

Market Targeting

Once the firm has identified its market-segment opportunities, it has to decide how many and which ones to target. Marketers are increasingly combining several variables in an effort to identify smaller, better-defined target groups. Thus, a bank may not only identify a group of wealthy retired adults, but within that group distinguish several segments depending on current income, assets, savings, and risk preferences. This has led some market researchers to advocate a *needs-based market segmentation approach*. Roger Best proposed the seven-step approach shown in Table 8.3.

Effective Segmentation Criteria

Not all segmentation schemes are useful. For example, table salt buyers could be divided into blond and brunette customers, but hair colour is undoubtedly irrelevant to the purchase of salt. Furthermore, if all salt buyers buy the same amount of salt each month, believe all salt is the same, and would pay only one price for salt, this market would be minimally segmentable from a marketing point of view.

To be useful, market segments must rate favourably on five key criteria:

- *Measurable.* The size, purchasing power, and characteristics of the segments can be measured.

- *Substantial.* The segments are large and profitable enough to serve. A segment should be the largest possible homogeneous group worth going after with a tailored marketing program. It would not pay, for example, for an automobile manufacturer to develop cars for people who are 120 cm tall.

- *Accessible.* The segments can be effectively reached and served.

Single-segment concentration

	M₁	M₂	M₃
P₁			
P₂			
P₃			

Selective specialization

	M₁	M₂	M₃
P₁			
P₂			
P₃			

Product specialization

	M₁	M₂	M₃
P₁			
P₂			
P₃			

Market specialization

	M₁	M₂	M₃
P₁			
P₂			
P₃			

Full market coverage

	M₁	M₂	M₃
P₁			
P₂			
P₃			

P = Product   M = Market

FIGURE 8.5

Five Patterns of Target Market Selection

Source: Adapted from Derek F. Abell, *Defining the Business: The Starting Point of Strategic Planning* (Upper Saddle River, NJ: Prentice Hall, 1980), pp. 192–196.

TABLE 8.3	STEPS IN THE SEGMENTATION PROCESS	
1.	Needs-Based Segmentation	Group customers into segments based on similar needs and benefits sought by customer in solving a particular consumption problem.
2.	Segment Identification	For each needs-based segment, determine which demographics, lifestyles, and usage behaviours make the segment distinct and identifiable (actionable).
3.	Segment Attractiveness	Using predetermined segment attractiveness criteria (such as market growth, competitive intensity, and market access), determine the overall attractiveness of each segment.
4.	Segment Profitability	Determine segment profitability.
5.	Segment Positioning	For each segment, create a "value proposition" and product-price positioning strategy based on that segment's unique customer needs and characteristics.
6.	Segment "Acid Test"	Create "segment storyboards" to test the attractiveness of each segment's positioning strategy.
7.	Marketing-Mix Strategy	Expand segment positioning strategy to include all aspects of the marketing mix: product, price, promotion, and place.

Source: Adapted from Robert J. Best, *Market-Based Management* (Upper Saddle River, NJ: Prentice Hall, 2000).

■ *Differentiable.* The segments are conceptually distinguishable and respond differently to different marketing-mix elements and programs. If married and unmarried women respond similarly to a sale on perfume, they do not constitute separate segments.

■ *Actionable.* Effective programs can be formulated for attracting and serving the segments.

Evaluating and Selecting the Market Segments

In evaluating different market segments, the firm must look at two factors: the segment's overall attractiveness and the company's objectives and resources. How well does a potential segment score on the five criteria? Does a potential segment have characteristics that make it generally attractive, such as size, growth, profitability, scale economies, and low risk? Does investing in the segment make sense given the firm's objectives, competencies, and resources? Some attractive segments may not mesh with the company's long-run objectives, or the company may lack one or more necessary competencies to offer superior value.

After evaluating different segments, the company can consider five patterns of target market selection, as shown in Figure 8.5.

SINGLE-SEGMENT CONCENTRATION Volkswagen concentrates on the small-car market and Porsche on the sports car market. Through concentrated marketing, the firm gains a strong knowledge of the segment's needs and achieves a strong market presence. Furthermore, the firm enjoys operating economies through specializing its production, distribution, and promotion. If it captures segment leadership, the firm can earn a high return on its investment.

However, there are risks. A particular market segment can turn sour or a competitor may invade the segment: When digital camera technology took off, Polaroid's earnings fell sharply. For these reasons, many companies prefer to operate in more than one segment. If selecting more than one segment to serve, the company should pay close attention to segment interrelationships on the cost, performance, and technology side. A company carrying fixed costs (sales force, store outlets) can add products to absorb and share some costs. The sales force will sell additional products, and a fast-food outlet will offer additional menu items. Economies of scope can be just as important as economies of scale.

Companies can try to operate in super-segments rather than in isolated segments. A **super-segment** is a set of segments sharing some exploitable similarity. For example, many symphony orchestras target people who have broad cultural interests, rather than only those who regularly attend concerts.

SELECTIVE SPECIALIZATION   The firm selects a number of segments, each objectively attractive and appropriate. There may be little or no synergy among the segments, but each promises to be a moneymaker. This multi-segment strategy has the advantage of diversifying the firm's risk. When Procter & Gamble launched Crest Whitestrips, initial target segments included newly engaged women and brides-to-be as well as gay males.

PRODUCT SPECIALIZATION   The firm makes a certain product that it sells to several different market segments. An example would be a microscope manufacturer who sells to university, government, and commercial laboratories. The firm makes different microscopes for the different customer groups and builds a strong reputation in the specific product area. The downside risk is that the product may be supplanted by an entirely new technology.

MARKET SPECIALIZATION   The firm concentrates on serving many needs of a particular customer group. An example would be a firm that sells an assortment of products only to university laboratories. The firm gains a strong reputation in serving this customer group and becomes a channel for additional products the customer group can use. The downside risk is that the customer group may suffer budget cuts or shrink in size.

FULL MARKET COVERAGE   The firm attempts to serve all customer groups with all the products they might need. Only very large firms such as IBM (computer market), General Motors (vehicle market), and Coca-Cola (nonalcoholic beverage market) can undertake a full market coverage strategy. Large firms can cover a whole market in two broad ways: through undifferentiated marketing or differentiated marketing.

In *undifferentiated marketing*, the firm ignores segment differences and goes after the whole market with one offer. It designs a product and a marketing program that will appeal to the broadest number of buyers. It relies on mass distribution and advertising. It aims to endow the product with a superior image. Undifferentiated marketing is "the marketing counterpart to standardization and mass production in manufacturing."[51] The narrow product line keeps down costs of research and development, production, inventory, transportation, marketing research, advertising, and product management. The undifferentiated advertising program keeps down advertising costs. Presumably, the company can turn its lower costs into lower prices to win the price-sensitive segment of the market.

In *differentiated marketing*, the firm operates in several market segments and designs different products for each segment. Cosmetics firm Estée Lauder markets brands that appeal to women (and men) of different tastes: The flagship brand, the original Estée Lauder, appeals to older consumers; Clinique caters to middle-aged women; M.A.C. to youthful hipsters; Aveda to aromatherapy enthusiasts; and Origins to eco-conscious consumers who want cosmetics made from natural ingredients.[52]

Loblaws

Loblaws offers everything from private-label brands for discount shoppers to its upscale President's Choice brands. It has recently added financial service products and a new line of organic products as it constantly strives to fill more and more diverse customer needs.

MANAGING MULTIPLE SEGMENTS   The best way to manage multiple segments is to appoint segment managers with sufficient authority and responsibility for building the segment's business. At the same time, segment managers should not be so focused as to resist cooperating with other groups in the company. Consider the following situation.

Baxter

Baxter operates several divisions selling different products and services to hospitals. Each division sends out its own invoices. Some hospitals complain about receiving as many as seven different Baxter invoices each month. Baxter's marketers finally convinced the separate divisions to send the invoices to headquarters so that Baxter could send one invoice a month to each of its customers.

DIFFERENTIATED MARKETING COSTS Differentiated marketing typically creates more total sales than undifferentiated marketing. However, it also increases the costs of doing business. The following costs are likely to be higher:

■ *Product modification costs.* Modifying a product to meet different market-segment requirements usually involves R&D, engineering, and special tooling costs.

■ *Manufacturing costs.* It is usually more expensive to produce 10 units of 10 different products than 100 units of one product. The longer the production set-up time and the smaller the sales volume of each product, the more expensive the product becomes. However, if each model is sold in sufficiently large volume, the higher set-up costs may be quite small per unit.

■ *Administrative costs.* The company has to develop separate marketing plans for each market segment. This requires extra marketing research, forecasting, sales analysis, promotion, planning, and channel management.

■ *Inventory costs.* It is more costly to manage inventories containing many products.

■ *Promotion costs.* The company has to reach different market segments with different promotion programs. The result is increased promotion-planning costs and media costs.

Because differentiated marketing leads to both higher sales and higher costs, nothing general can be said regarding this strategy's profitability. Companies should be cautious about oversegmenting their market. If this happens, they may want to turn to *countersegmentation* to broaden the customer base. For example, Johnson & Johnson broadened its target market for its baby shampoo to include adults. Smith Kline Beecham launched its Aquafresh toothpaste to attract three benefit segments simultaneously: those seeking fresh breath, whiter teeth, and cavity protection.

Additional Considerations

Three other considerations must be taken into account in evaluating and selecting segments: segment-by-segment invasion plans, updating segmentation schemes, and ethical choice of market targets.

SEGMENT-BY-SEGMENT INVASION PLANS A company would be wise to enter one segment at a time. Competitors must not know to what segment(s) the firm will move next. Segment-by-segment invasion plans are illustrated in Figure 8.6. Three firms, A, B, and C, have specialized in adapting computer systems to the needs of airlines, railroads, and trucking companies. Company A meets all the computer needs of airlines. Company B sells large computer systems to all three transportation sectors. Company C sells personal computers to trucking companies.

Where should company C move next? Arrows have been added to the chart to show the planned sequence of segment invasions. Company C will next offer mid-sized computers to trucking companies. Then, to allay company B's concern about losing some large computer business with trucking companies, C's next move will be to sell personal computers to railroads. Later, C will offer mid-sized computers to railroads. Finally, it may launch a full-scale attack on company B's large computer position in trucking companies. Of course, C's hidden planned moves are provisional in that much depends on competitors' segment moves and responses.

FIGURE 8.6

Segment-by-Segment Invasion Plan

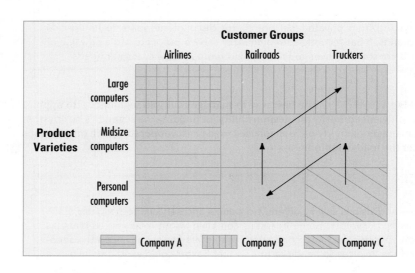

Unfortunately, too many companies fail to develop a long-term invasion plan. PepsiCo is an exception. It first attacked Coca-Cola in the grocery market, then in the vending-machine market, then in the fast-food market, and so on. Japanese firms also plot their invasion sequence. They first gain a foothold in a market, and then enter new segments with products. Toyota began by introducing small cars (Tercel, Corolla), then expanded into midsize cars (Camry, Avalon), and finally into luxury cars (Lexus).

A company's invasion plans can be thwarted when it confronts blocked markets. The invader must then figure out a way to break in. The problem of entering blocked markets calls for a mega-marketing approach. **Megamarketing** is the strategic coordination of economic, psychological, political, and public-relations skills to gain the cooperation of a number of parties in order to enter or operate in a given market. Pepsi used megamarketing to enter the Indian market.

PepsiCo

After Coca-Cola left India, Pepsi worked with an Indian business group to gain government approval for its entry, over the objections of domestic soft-drink companies and anti-multinational legislators. Pepsi offered to help India export some agricultural products in a volume that would more than cover the cost of importing soft-drink concentrate. Pepsi also promised to help rural areas in their economic development. It further offered to transfer food-processing, packaging, and water-treatment technology to India. Pepsi's bundle of benefits won the support of various Indian interest groups.

Once in, a multinational must be on its best behaviour. This calls for well-thought-out *civic positioning*.

Hewlett-Packard

Hewlett-Packard positions itself as a company implementing "e-inclusion"—the attempt to help bring the benefits of technology to the poor. Toward that end, HP has begun a three-year project designed to create jobs, improve education, and provide better access to government services in the Indian state of Kuppam. Working with the local government, as well as a branch of HP Labs based in India, the company is helping provide the rural poor with access to government records, schools, health information, crop prices, and so forth. HP's hope is to stimulate small tech-based businesses. Not only does this build goodwill and the HP brand in India, but it will also help the company discover new, profitable lines of business.[53]

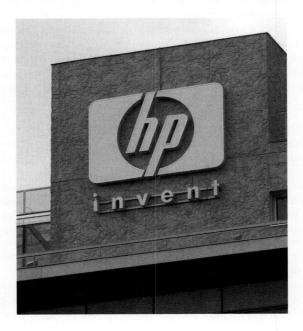

As a company implementing "e-inclusion," Hewlett-Packard is working to improve the lives of low-income people.

A Pepsi ad from India. To enter the Indian market, Pepsi used megamarketing: With the aid of an Indian business group, it offered a package of benefits that gained it acceptance.

UPDATING SEGMENTATION SCHEMES Market segmentation analysis must be done periodically because segments change. At one time the personal computer industry segmented its products purely on speed and power. Later, PC marketers recognized an emerging "Soho" market, named for "small office and home office." Mail-order companies such as Dell and Gateway appealed to this market's requirement for high performance coupled with low price and user-friendliness. Shortly thereafter, PC makers began to see Soho as comprised of smaller segments. "Small-office needs might be very different from home-office needs," says one Dell executive.[54]

One way to discover new segments is to investigate the hierarchy of attributes consumers examine in choosing a brand if they use phased decision strategies. This process is called **market partitioning**. Years ago, most car buyers first decided on the manufacturer and then on one of its car divisions (*brand-dominant hierarchy*). A buyer might favour General Motors cars and, within this set, Pontiac. Today, many buyers decide first on the nation from which they want to buy a car (*nation-dominant hierarchy*). Buyers may first decide they want to buy a Japanese car, then Toyota, and then the Corolla model of Toyota. Companies must monitor potential shifts in consumers' hierarchy of attributes and adjust to changing priorities.

The hierarchy of attributes can reveal customer segments. Buyers who first decide on price are price dominant; those who first decide on the type of car (e.g., sports, passenger, station wagon) are type dominant; those who first decide on the car brand are brand dominant. Those who are type/price/brand dominant make up a segment; those who are quality/service/type dominant make up another segment. Each segment may have distinct demographics, psychographics, and mediagraphics.[55]

ETHICAL CHOICE OF MARKET TARGETS Market targeting sometimes generates public controversy.[56] The public is concerned when marketers take unfair advantage of vulnerable groups (such as children) or disadvantaged groups (such as inner-city poor people), or promote potentially harmful products. The cereal industry has been heavily criticized for marketing efforts directed toward children. Critics worry that high-powered appeals presented through the mouths of lovable animated characters will overwhelm children's defences and lead them to want sugared cereals or poorly balanced breakfasts. Toy marketers have been similarly criticized. McDonald's and other chains have drawn criticism for pitching their high-fat, salt-laden fare to low-income, inner-city residents. Internal documents from R. J. Reynolds and Brown & Williamson Tobacco Corporation (marketer of the Kool brand) have revealed the extent to which these companies targeted black youths aged 16 to 25, particularly with their menthol brands.[57]

Not all attempts to target children, minorities, or other special segments draw criticism. Those in charge of multicultural marketing at Scotiabank in Toronto make Chinese clients more comfortable through the use of ancient traditional symbols like the Wisdom Sacks used in a promotion dur-

Socially responsible marketing: Colgate Junior Toothpaste ads promote special features designed to get children to brush more often.

ing the Year of the Dragon celebration.[58] Colgate-Palmolive's Colgate Junior toothpaste has special features designed to get children to brush longer and more often. Other companies are responding to the special needs of minority segments. Thus the issue is not who is targeted, but rather, how and for what. Socially responsible marketing calls for targeting that serves not only the company's interests, but also the interests of those targeted.

This is the case being made by many companies marketing to preschoolers. With the number of youngsters attending some kind of organized child-care, the potential market—including both kids and parents—is too great to pass up. So in addition to stocking the usual standards like art easels, gerbil cages, and blocks, preschools are likely to have Care Bear worksheets, Pizza Hut reading programs, and Nickelodeon magazines.

Nickelodeon, Pizza Hut, Ford Motor Corp.

U.S. cable TV station Nickelodeon was one of the first companies to capitalize on the preschool market when it launched *Nick Jr.* family magazine in 1999. It distributes half of the magazine's 1 million copies to preschools for free and makes no bones about the fact that it is trying to sell parents on Nickelodeon shows and licensed products. In contrast, other corporations insist that their preschool products are designed purely to meet a social need. Pizza Hut is one. Its preschool program offers each student a certificate for a personal pizza if his or her teacher spends at least 60 minutes a week reading to the class for four consecutive weeks. In 2002 1.6 million preschoolers in 33 800 child-care facilities participated. Likewise, automaker Ford says it sends posters to 100 000 preschools, child-care centres, and kindergarten classes to encourage children ages two to five to think about safety. The poster is an alphabet of safety tips with, not surprisingly, A for automobile (but no F for Ford).

Teachers and parents are divided in their feelings about the ethics of this increasing preschool marketing push. Some feel that preschoolers are incredibly susceptible to advertising and that schools' endorsements of products make children believe the product is good for them—no matter what it is. Yet, many preschools and daycare centres operating on tight budgets welcome the free resources.[59]

When it comes to advertising to children, the Concerned Children's Advertisers (CCA) is a non-profit organization supported by over 20 Canadian companies (including Corus Entertainment Inc., CTV Television Inc., Frito Lay Canada, and General Mills Canada Corp.) that work together to establish children's advertising policies and the delivery of socially responsible programs for Canadian youth. The group's kid-friendly television commercials are seen daily across the country. Themes of the ads range from managing peer pressure and building self-esteem to media literacy.[60]

SUMMARY

1. Target marketing involves three activities: market segmentation, market targeting, and market positioning.

2. Markets can be targeted at four levels: segments, niches, local areas, and individuals. Market segments are large identifiable groups within a market. A niche is a more narrowly defined group. Marketers appeal to local markets through grassroots marketing for trading areas, neighbourhoods, and even individual stores.

3. More companies now practise individual and mass customization. The future is likely to see more self-marketing, a form of individual marketing in which individual consumers take the initiative in designing products and brands.

4. There are two bases for segmenting consumer markets: consumer characteristics and consumer responses. The major segmentation variables for consumer markets are geographic, demographic, psychographic, and behavioural. These variables can be used singly or in combination.

5. Business marketers use all these variables along with operating variables, purchasing approaches, and situational factors.

6. To be useful, market segments must be measurable, substantial, accessible, differentiable, and actionable.

7. A firm has to evaluate the various segments and decide how many and which ones to target: a single segment, several segments, a specific product, a specific market, or the full market. If it serves the full market, it must choose between differentiated and undifferentiated marketing. Firms must also monitor segment relationships, and seek economies of scope and the potential for marketing to super-segments. They should develop segment-by-segment invasion plans.

8. Marketers must choose target markets in a socially responsible manner.

APPLICATIONS

Marketing Debate: Is Mass Marketing Dead?

With marketers increasingly adopting more and more refined market segmentation schemes—fuelled by the Internet and other customization efforts—some critics claim that mass marketing is dead. Others counter that there will always be room for large brands that employ marketing programs targeting the mass market.

Take a position: Mass marketing is dead versus Mass marketing is still a viable way to build a profitable brand.

Marketing Discussion: Descriptive versus Behavioural Market Segmentation Schemes

Think of various product categories. How would you classify yourself in terms of the various segmentation schemes? How would marketing be more or less effective for you depending on the segment involved? How would you contrast demographic versus behavioural segment schemes? Which ones do you think would be most effective for marketers trying to sell to you?

Marketing Spotlight: HSBC

HSBC is known as the "world's local bank." Originally the Hong Kong and Shanghai Banking Corporation Limited, HSBC was established in 1865 to finance the growing trade between China and the United Kingdom. HSBC is now the second largest bank in the world, serving 100 million customers through 9500 branches in 79 countries. Its 170 Canadian offices offer day-to-day banking, lending, and investment services. The company is organized by business line (personal financial services, consumer finance, commercial banking, corporate investment banking and markets, and private banking), as well as by geographic segment (Asia-Pacific, U.K./Eurozone, North America/NAFTA, South America, and the Middle East).

Despite operating in 79 different countries, the bank works hard to maintain a local feel and local knowledge in each area. HSBC's fundamental operating strategy is to remain close to its customers. As HSBC chairman Sir John Bond said in November 2003, "Our position as the world's local bank enables us to approach each country uniquely, blending local knowledge with a world-wide operating platform."

For example, consider HSBC's local marketing efforts in New York City. To prove to jaded New Yorkers that the London-based financial behemoth was the "world's local bank," HSBC held a "New York City's Most Knowledgeable Cabbie" contest. The winning cabbie got paid to drive full-time for HSBC for the year, and HSBC customers won, too. Any customer showing an HSBC bankcard, chequebook, or bank statement could get a free ride in the HSBC-branded Bankcab. The campaign demonstrated HSBC's local knowledge. "In order to make New Yorkers believe you're local, you have to act local," said Renegade Marketing Group's CEO Drew Neisser.

Across the world in Hong Kong, HSBC undertook a different campaign. In the region hit hard by the severe acute respiratory syndrome (SARS) outbreak, HSBC launched a program to revitalize the local economy. HSBC "plowed back interest payments" to customers who worked in industries most affected by SARS (cinemas, hotels, restaurants, and travel agencies). The program eased its customers' financial burden. The bank also boosted Hong Kong's commercial sector by offering discounts and rebates for customers who use an HSBC credit card when shopping and dining out. More than 1500 local merchants participated in the promotion.

In addition to local marketing, HSBC does niche marketing. For example, HSBC found a little-known product area that was growing at 125 percent a year—pet insurance. In December 2003 it announced that it would distribute pet insurance through its HSBC Insurance agency, making the insurance available to its depositors.

HSBC also segments demographically. In the United States, the bank will target the immigrant population, particularly Hispanics, now that the bank has acquired Bital in Mexico, where many migrants to the United States deposit money.

Overall, the bank has been consciously pulling together its worldwide businesses under a single global brand with the "world's local bank" slogan. The aim is to link its international size with close relationships in each of the countries in which it operates. The company spends US$600 million annually on global marketing and will likely consolidate and use fewer ad agencies. HSBC will decide who gets the account by giving each agency a "brand-strategy exercise." Agencies will be vying for the account by improving on HSBC's number-37 global brand ranking.

DISCUSSION QUESTIONS

1. What have been the key success factors for HSBC?

2. Where is HSBC vulnerable? What should it watch out for?

3. What recommendations would you make to senior marketing executives going forward? What should HBSC be sure to do with its marketing?

Sources: Deborah Orr, "New Ledger," *Forbes*, March 1, 2004 p. 72; "HSBC's Global Marketing Head Explains Review Decision," *ADWEEK*, January 19, 2004; "Now Your Customers Can Afford to Take Fido to the Vet," *Bank Marketing*, December 2003, p. 47; Kenneth Hein, "HSBC Bank Rides the Coattails of Chatty Cabbies," *Brandweek*, December 1, 2003, p. 30; Sir John Bond and Stephen Green, "HSBC Strategic Overview," presentation to investors, November 27, 2003; "Lafferty Retail Banking Awards 2003," *Retail Banker International*, November 27, 2003, pp. 4–5; "Ideas that Work," *Bank Marketing* (November 2003): 10; "HSBC Enters the Global Branding Big League," *Bank Marketing International* (August 2003): 1–2; Normandy Madden, "HSBC Rolls Out Post-SARS Effort," *Advertising Age*, June 16, 2003, p. 12; **www.hsbc.com**.

4 PART FOUR

BUILDING STRONG BRANDS

- What is a brand and how does branding work?

- What is brand equity?

- How is brand equity built, measured, and managed?

- What are the important decisions in developing a branding strategy?

CHAPTER 9

Creating Brand Equity

PROFILE: CANADIAN MARKETING EXCELLENCE

Imagine this challenge. Take a product, one among many in a commodity-like marketplace, a product aimed at consumers aged 55 and over, and make it cool. Impossible, you say. Well, that is exactly the challenge that SISU Inc. and its agency faced when marketing vitamins and supplements. They rebranded, repackaged, and remarketed the products, and created a lot of buzz as they worked to increase awareness and sales.

Burnaby, B.C.–based SISU Inc. was founded by pharmacist Harlan Lahti, owner of Finlandia Pharmacy. He was convinced that, through research and education, people could stay healthy longer and recover from illness more rapidly if they prudently used well-formulated vitamins and supplements. Harlan's goal was to create and produce formulas that would meet the exacting standards of the Canadian government, exceed the requirements of physicians, and—most importantly—provide discerning consumers with the very best supplements possible.

The company name, SISU, was drawn from Lahti's Finnish roots (*sisu* is Finnish for fortitude). The people of Finland learned to survive and prosper in a rugged northern environment by developing extraordinary inner strength, courage, stamina, and stubborn determination. The name SISU was chosen because the products were designed to bring out the "sisu" in all those who take assertive, determined control of their health. As Lahti notes, "We package sisu in every bottle."

By the time the rebranding project began, SISU had grown into a national brand (the fifth largest in Canada, with sales of $17 million). Despite the fact that the company's name was synonymous with innovation and uncompromising quality, the brand was a mess of inconsistent packaging, colours, images, and motifs on its more than 150 products.

Gord Gilles, the director of sales and marketing, was in charge of the project. He knew that he would have to draw on his wealth of experience to take on this challenge (he'd worked at Kraft Canada as a sales rep and a trade marketer on key accounts, he'd managed Nestlé's Koala Beverages sales and marketing team, and he had been director of sales and then head of marketing at Johnson & Johnson's Lifescan).

Gilles began by conducting a series of focus groups in which he showed consumers photographs of the products on actual shelves. "Every time we showed the photo—and we did this with nine different groups—the whole group sat back and went 'eeww.' It gave us a really good hint that it was time for a change." Now in a market where consumers tend to be older and retailers are powerful, change cannot be undertaken lightly—it involves a big risk.

After the initial research was completed, Gilles mapped out SISU's new strategy. He wanted to retain the equity the brand had built up over its history, in particular the Scandinavian cachet behind the name. While almost 42 percent of Canadians take vitamins, Gilles wanted to target a new group, the 25-to-55-year-old female demographic.

Gord Gilles hired Grey Worldwide Northwest of Vancouver to help him revamp the brand. The members of the agency were thrilled since Gilles gave them licence to change everything but the name.

The creative team gave the brand a clean, stripped-down look through new packaging, labelling, and logos. Bottles are sleek grey with vivid cobalt blue lettering. Two 15-second TV spots were developed titled "Yoga" and "Jump-rope." They are unusual ads—"Yoga," for example, features a stark white background and an orange blob that transforms into a yoga-like figure (you can view these advertisements by going to the company Web site at www.sisuhealth.com/en). As one analyst noted, "Clearly, this ain't grandma's vitamins." The ads ran nationally for eight weeks. To help keep customers informed, the TV spots were supported by a print campaign that ran in health magazines.

Consumer marketing was only half the challenge, however. SISU's 20-person sales team had to be motivated so that they could re-educate retailers about the products. Their strategy was "sell the science" rather than simply pushing products at them. No opportunity was missed to communicate with this target. "Every time a bill went out the door, a piece of communication went with it explaining 'here's the new label, here's how you talk to consumers about it,' " says Gilles. In addition, shelf talkers were placed in the stores and recommenders (in-store staff) were sent to health food stores to advise customers. The results of all these efforts didn't constitute a pill that was hard for the company to swallow—brand awareness has jumped by 33 percent and sales are up by almost 5 percent.

Sources: SISU Inc., **www.sisuhealth.com/en** (viewed October 23, 2004); Natalia Williams, "Extreme Makeover," *Strategy Magazine*, September 17, 2004, p. 16.

Perhaps the most distinctive skill of professional marketers is their ability to create, maintain, enhance, and protect brands. Branding has become a marketing priority. Successful brands such as Starbucks, Sony, and Nike command a price premium and elicit much loyalty. New brands such as Allstream (formerly AT&T Canada), Accenture, Cake Beauty, Tango, Lululemon, and eBay capture the imagination of consumers and the financial community alike. Marketers of successful twenty-first-century brands must excel at the strategic brand management process. **Strategic brand management** involves the design and implementation of marketing activities and programs to build, measure, and manage brands to maximize their value. The strategic brand management process involves four main steps:

■ Identifying and establishing brand positioning.
■ Planning and implementing brand marketing.
■ Measuring and interpreting brand performance.
■ Growing and sustaining brand value.

Chapter 10 deals with brand positioning. The remaining topics are discussed in this chapter. Chapter 11 reviews important concepts dealing with competition.

What Is Brand Equity?

The American Marketing Association defines a **brand** as "a name, term, sign, symbol, or design, or a combination of them, intended to identify the goods or services of one seller or group of sellers and to differentiate them from those of competitors." A brand is thus a product or service that adds dimensions that differentiate it in some way from other products or services designed to satisfy the same need. These differences may be functional, rational, or tangible—related to product performance of the brand. They may also be more symbolic, emotional, or intangible—related to what the brand represents.

Branding has been around for centuries as a means to distinguish the goods of one producer from those of another.[1] The earliest signs of branding in Europe were the medieval guilds' requirement that craftspeople put trademarks on their products to protect themselves and consumers against inferior quality. In the fine arts, branding began with artists signing their works. Brands today play a number of important roles that improve consumers' lives and enhance the financial value of firms.

The Role of Brands

Brands identify the source or maker of a product and allow consumers—either individuals or organizations—to assign responsibility to a particular manufacturer or distributor. Consumers may evaluate the identical product differently depending on how it is branded. Consumers learn about brands through past experiences with the product and its marketing program. They find out which brands satisfy their needs and which ones do not. As consumers' lives become more complicated, rushed, and time-starved, the ability of a brand to simplify decision making and reduce risk is invaluable.[2]

Brands also perform valuable functions for firms.[3] First, they simplify product handling or tracing. Brands help to organize inventory and accounting records. A brand also offers the firm legal protection for unique features or aspects of the product.[4] The brand name can be protected through registered trademarks, manufacturing processes can be protected through patents, and packaging can be protected through copyrights and designs. These intellectual property rights ensure that the firm can safely invest in the brand and reap the benefits of a valuable asset.

Brands can signal a certain level of quality so that satisfied buyers can easily choose the product again.[5] Brand loyalty provides predictability and security of demand for the firm and creates barriers to entry that make it difficult for other firms to enter the market. Loyalty also can translate into a willingness to pay a higher price—often 20 to 25 percent more.[6] Although competitors may easily duplicate manufacturing processes and product designs, they cannot easily match lasting impressions in the minds of individuals and organizations from years of marketing activity and product experience. In this sense, branding can be seen as a powerful means to secure a competitive advantage.[7]

To firms, brands thus represent enormously valuable pieces of legal property that can influence consumer behaviour, be bought and sold, and provide the security of sustained future revenues to their owner.[8] Large earning multiples have been paid for brands in mergers or acquisitions, starting with the boom years of the mid-1980s. The price premium is often justified on the basis of assumptions of the extra profits that could be extracted and sustained from the brands, as well as the tremendous difficulty and expense of creating similar brands from scratch. The financial industry believes that strong brands result in better earnings and profit performance for firms, which, in turn, create greater value for shareholders. Much of the recent interest in brands from senior management has been a result of these bottom-line financial considerations. "Marketing Memo: The Brand Report Card" lists ten key characteristics based on a review of the world's strongest brands.[9]

The Scope of Branding

How then do you "brand" a product? Although firms provide the impetus to brand creation through marketing programs and other activities, ultimately a brand is something that resides in the minds of consumers. A brand is a perceptual entity that is rooted in reality but reflects the perceptions and perhaps even the idiosyncrasies of consumers.

Branding is endowing products and services with the power of a brand. Branding is all about creating differences. To brand a product, it is necessary to teach consumers "who" the product is—by giving it a name and using other brand elements to help identify it—as well as "what" the product does and "why" consumers should care. Branding involves creating mental structures and helping consumers organize their knowledge about products and services in a way that clarifies their decision making and, in the process, provides value to the firm.

Marketing Memo

The Brand Report Card

The world's strongest brands share ten attributes:

1. *The brand excels at delivering the benefits consumers truly desire.* Do you focus relentlessly on maximizing customers' product and service experiences?

2. *The brand stays relevant.* Are you in touch with your customers' tastes, current market conditions, and trends?

3. *The pricing strategy is based on consumer perceptions of value.* Have you optimized price, cost, and quality to meet or exceed customer expectations?

4. *The brand is properly positioned.* Have you established necessary and competitive points of parity with competitors? Have you established desirable and deliverable points of difference?

5. *The brand is consistent.* Are you sure that your marketing programs are not sending conflicting messages?

6. *The brand portfolio and hierarchy makes sense.* Can the corporate brand create a seamless umbrella for all the brands in the portfolio? Do you have a brand hierarchy that is well thought out and well understood?

7. *The brand makes use of and coordinates a full repertoire of marketing activities to build equity.* Have you capitalized on the unique capabilities of each communication option while ensuring that the meaning of the brand is consistently represented?

8. *The brand's managers understand what the brand means to consumers.* Do you know what customers like and do not like about your brand? Have you created detailed, research-driven portraits of your target customers?

9. *The brand is given proper, sustained support.* Are the successes or failures of marketing programs fully understood before they are changed? Is the brand given sufficient R&D support?

10. *The company monitors sources of brand equity.* Have you created a brand charter that defines the meaning and equity of the brand and how it should be treated? Have you assigned explicit responsibility for monitoring and preserving brand equity?

Source: Adapted from Kevin Lane Keller, "The Brand Report Card," *Harvard Business Review*, January 1, 2000, pp. 147–157.

For branding strategies to be successful and brand value to be created, consumers must be convinced that there are meaningful differences among brands in the product or service category. The key to branding is that consumers must not think that all brands in the category are the same.

Brand differences often are related to attributes or benefits of the product itself. Gillette, Merck, Sony, 3M, and others have been leaders in their product categories for decades due, in part, to continual innovation. Other brands create competitive advantages through non–product-related means. Coca-Cola, Calvin Klein, Gucci, Tommy Hilfiger, Marlboro, and others have become leaders in their product categories by understanding consumer motivations and desires and creating relevant and appealing images around their products.

Branding can be applied virtually anywhere a consumer has a choice. It is possible to brand a physical good (Campbell's soup, Dove soap, or Molson's Canadian beer), a service (Air Canada, Bank of Nova Scotia, or Great West Life medical insurance), a store (Foot Locker specialty store, or Sobey's supermarket), a person (Margaret Atwood, Shania Twain, or Wayne Gretzky), a place (the city of Sydney, province of Newfoundland, or country of Spain), an organization (UNICEF, Canadian Automobile Association, or CARE), or an idea (abortion rights, free trade, or freedom of speech).

Defining Brand Equity

Brand equity is the added value endowed to goods and services. This value may be reflected in how consumers think, feel, and act with respect to the brand, as well as the prices, market share, and profitability that the brand commands for the firm. Brand equity is an important intangible asset to the firm that has psychological and financial value.

Marketers and researchers use various perspectives to study brand equity.[10] Customer-based approaches view brand equity from the perspective of the consumer—either an individual or an organization.[11] The premise of customer-based brand equity models is that the power of a brand lies in what customers have seen, read, heard, learned, thought, and felt about the brand over time. In other words, the power of a brand lies in the minds of existing or potential customers and what they have experienced directly and indirectly about the brand.[12]

Customer-based brand equity can be defined as the differential effect that brand knowledge has on consumer response to the marketing of that brand.[13] A brand is said to have positive customer-based brand equity when consumers react more favourably to a product and the way it is marketed when the brand is identified as compared to when it is not. A brand is said to have negative customer-based brand equity if consumers react less favourably to marketing activity for the brand under the same circumstances.

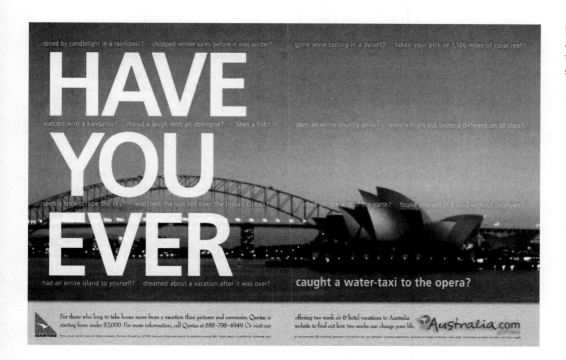

Branding a place: ad for Australia tourism focusing on the city of Sydney with its signature opera house.

There are three key ingredients to this definition. First, brand equity arises from differences in consumer response. If no differences occur, then the brand-name product can essentially be classified as a commodity or generic version of the product. Competition would then probably be based on price.

Second, these differences in response are a result of consumers' knowledge about the brand. **Brand knowledge** consists of all the thoughts, feelings, images, experiences, beliefs, and so on that become associated with the brand. In particular, brands must create strong, favourable, and unique brand associations with customers, as has been the case with Volvo (*safety*), Hallmark (*caring*), and Harley-Davidson (*adventure*). Third, the differential response by consumers that makes up the brand equity is reflected in perceptions, preferences, and behaviour related to all aspects of the marketing of a brand. Table 9.1 summarizes some of these key benefits of brand equity.

The challenge for marketers in building a strong brand is therefore ensuring that customers have the right type of experiences with goods and services and their marketing programs to create the desired brand knowledge structures for the brand.

TABLE 9.1	MARKETING ADVANTAGES OF STRONG BRANDS

- Improved perceptions of product performance
- Greater loyalty
- Less vulnerability to competitive marketing actions
- Less vulnerability to marketing crises
- Larger margins
- More inelastic consumer response to price increases
- More elastic consumer response to price decreases
- Greater trade cooperation and support
- Increased marketing communications effectiveness
- Possible licensing opportunities
- Additional brand extension opportunities

Apple Computer

Apple Computer is recognized as a master at building a strong brand that resonates with customers across generations and national boundaries. Named "2003 Marketer of the Year" by *Advertising Age* magazine, Apple achieves incredible brand loyalty largely by delivering on its mission as defined by CEO Steven Jobs: "To create great things that change people's lives." Apple is famous for the innovative advertising that brings this mission alive for consumers. In 2001, for example, Markham, Ontario–based Apple Canada promoted its newest iMac computer by putting huge murals on the 1500 square metres of exterior wall space of a building facing the busy Toronto Gardiner Expressway. But advertising isn't its only tool. Some of its biggest buzz campaigns don't even originate with the company: In a trendy club in Manhattan, two DJs host Tuesday night "Open iPod DJ Parties." Yet, the company doesn't rely on customers to do its marketing. Apple spent US$293 million to create 73 retail stores to fuel excitement for the brand, including a store in New York's SoHo that drew over 14 million visitors in 2003. The rationale behind the move to retail is that the more people who can see and touch Apple products—and see what Apple can do for them—the more likely Apple is to increase its market share, which is still a tiny slice of the PC market.[14]

Consumer knowledge is what drives the differences that manifest themselves in brand equity. In an abstract sense, brand equity can be seen as providing marketers with a vital strategic "bridge" from their past to their future.

Brand Equity as a Bridge

From the perspective of brand equity, all the marketing dollars spent each year on goods and services should be thought of as investments in consumer brand knowledge. The *quality* of the investment in brand building is the critical factor, not necessarily the *quantity*, beyond some minimal threshold amount.

It is actually possible to "overspend" on brand building if money is not spent wisely. In the beverage category, brands such as Labatt Blue and 7Up saw sales decline in the early 1990s despite sizable marketing support, arguably because of poorly targeted and delivered marketing campaigns. And there are numerous examples of brands that amass a great deal of brand equity by spending on marketing activities that create valuable, enduring memory traces in consumers' minds. Despite being outspent by such beverage brand giants as Coca-Cola and Pepsi, the B.C. Dairy Foundation used its Cold Crew street teams (subtly branded teams of young, sexy, urban girls and guys who create buzz around milk at major teen-targeted events such as the Kelowna Regatta) in the summer of 2003 to generate lots of conversation and to do something seemingly impossible—make milk (a safe, uncool beverage) hip and sexy with teens. Along with television and print advertising based on the slogan "Don't take your body for granted," the campaign was brought to life in an irreverent way by posing the question, "What would life be like without a body?"[15]

At the same time, the brand knowledge created by these marketing investments dictates appropriate future directions for the brand. Consumers will decide, based on what they think and feel about the brand, where (and how) they believe the brand should go and grant permission (or not) to any marketing action or program. New products such as Crystal Pepsi, Levi's Tailored Classic suits, Fruit of the Loom laundry detergent, and Roots Air failed because consumers found them inappropriate.

A brand is essentially a marketer's promise to deliver predictable product or service performance. A **brand promise** is the marketer's vision of what the brand must be and do for consumers. At the end of the day, the true value and future prospects of a brand rest with consumers, their knowledge about the brand, and their likely response to marketing activity as a result of this knowledge. Understanding consumer brand knowledge—all the different things that become linked to the brand in the minds of consumers—is thus of paramount importance because it is the foundation of brand equity.

Virgin, the brainchild of England's flamboyant Richard Branson, vividly illustrates the power enjoyed and responsibility assumed by a strong brand.[16]

Virgin

Starting with Virgin Music, Branson's Virgin Group Ltd. now spans three continents and 200 businesses, including Virgin Atlantic Airways, Virgin Mobile (cell phones), its online and physical Virgin Megastores, Virgin Energy, Virgin Rail, Virgin Direct (insurance, mortgages, and investment funds), and Virgin Hotels. Clearly, Branson can create interest in almost any business he wants by simply attaching the name "Virgin" to it. Virgin Mobile exemplifies this strategy. Branson supplies the brand, a small initial investment, and takes a majority control while big-name partners come up with the cash. Some marketing and financial critics point out that he is diluting the brand, that it covers too many businesses. Branson has had some fumbles: Virgin Cola, Virgin Cosmetics, and Virgin Vodka have all but disappeared. But Branson replies: "We have a strategy of using the credibility of our brand to challenge the dominant players in a range of industries where we believe the consumer is not getting value for money. . . . If the consumer benefits, I see no reason why we should be frightened about launching new products." One of Branson's newest ventures? He's jumping into the fiercely competitive discount airline business in the United States with Virgin USA in 2005.

Brand Equity Models

Although there is agreement about basic principles, a number of models of brand equity offer some different perspectives. Here we briefly highlight four of the more established ones.

BRAND ASSET VALUATOR   Advertising agency Young and Rubicam (Y&R) developed a model of brand equity called Brand Asset Valuator (BAV). Based on research with almost 200 000 consumers in 40 countries, BAV provides comparative measures of the brand equity of thousands of brands across hundreds of different categories. There are four key components—or pillars—of brand equity according to BAV:

- *Differentiation* measures the degree to which a brand is seen as different from others.
- *Relevance* measures the breadth of a brand's appeal.
- *Esteem* measures how well a brand is regarded and respected.
- *Knowledge* measures how familiar and intimate consumers are with a brand.

Differentiation and Relevance combine to determine *Brand Strength*. These two pillars point to the brand's future value, rather than just reflecting its past. Esteem and Knowledge together create *Brand Stature*, which is more of a "report card" on past performance.

Examining the relationships among these four dimensions—a brand's "pillar pattern"—reveals much about its current and future status. Brand Strength and Brand Stature can be combined to form a power grid that depicts the stages in the cycle of brand development—each with its characteristic pillar patterns—in successive quadrants (see Figure 9.1). New brands, just after they are launched, show low levels on all four pillars. Strong new brands tend to show higher levels of Differentiation than Relevance, while both Esteem and Knowledge are lower still. Leadership brands show high levels on all four pillars. Finally, declining brands show high Knowledge—evidence of past performance—relative to a lower level of Esteem, and even lower Relevance and Differentiation.

AAKER MODEL   Former UC-Berkeley marketing professor David Aaker views brand equity as a set of five categories of brand assets and liabilities linked to a brand that add to or subtract from the value provided by a product or service to a firm and/or to that firm's customers. These categories of brand assets are (1) brand loyalty, (2) brand awareness, (3) perceived quality, (4) brand associations, and (5) other proprietary assets such as patents, trademarks, and channel relationships.

According to Aaker, a particularly important concept for building brand equity is *brand identity*—the unique set of brand associations that represent what the brand stands for and promises to customers.[17] Aaker sees brand identity as consisting of twelve dimensions organized around four perspectives: *brand-as-product* (product scope, product attributes, quality/value, uses, users, country of origin); *brand-as-organization* (organizational attributes, local versus global); *brand-as-person* (brand personality, brand–customer relationships); and *brand-as-symbol* (visual imagery/metaphors and brand heritage).

Aaker also conceptualizes brand identity as including a core and an extended identity. The core identity—the central, timeless essence of the brand—is most likely to remain constant as the brand

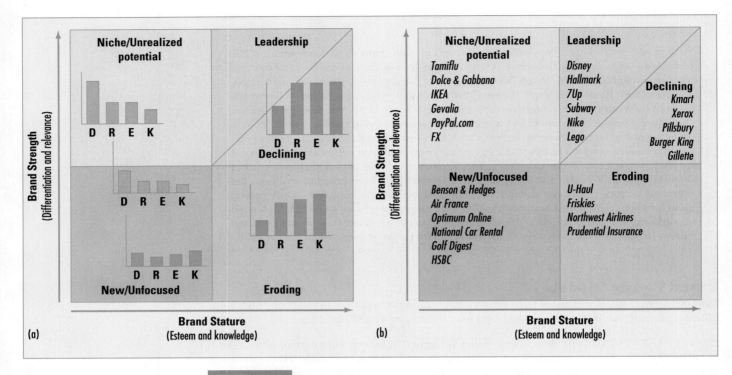

FIGURE 9.1

BAV Power Grid

travels to new markets and products. The extended identity includes various brand identity elements, organized into cohesive and meaningful groups. Applying this approach to General Motors Canada might yield the following:

- *Core identity.* A world-class car company known for its technical expertise.
- *Extended identity.* An Oshawa-based company willing to utilize its expertise to further the cause of Canadian sport. This extension of brand identity might have arisen because of GM Canada's 2004 offer of its state-of-the-art wind tunnel at the GM Aerodynamics Laboratory to the Canadian men's downhill ski team. Said Don Johnson, general director of sales, service, and marketing of GM Canada: "We hope the learning from this training session will propel these athletes to greater success on the World Cup circuit this year."[18]

BRANDZ Marketing research consultants Millward Brown and WPP have developed the BRANDZ model of brand strength, at the heart of which is the BrandDynamics pyramid. According to this model, brand building involves a sequential series of steps, where each step is contingent upon successfully accomplishing the previous step. The objectives at each step, in ascending order, are as follows:

- *Presence.* Do I know about it?
- *Relevance.* Does it offer me something?
- *Performance.* Can it deliver?
- *Advantage.* Does it offer something better than others?
- *Bonding.* Nothing else beats it.

Research has shown that bonded consumers, those at the top level of the pyramid, build stronger relationships with the brand and spend more of their category expenditures on the brand than those at lower levels of the pyramid. More consumers, however, will be found at the lower levels. The challenge for marketers is to develop activities and programs that help consumers move up the pyramid.

BRAND RESONANCE   The brand resonance model also views brand building as an ascending, sequential series of steps, from bottom to top: (1) ensuring identification of the brand with customers and an association of the brand in customers' minds with a specific product class or customer need; (2) firmly establishing the totality of brand meaning in the minds of customers by strategically linking a host of tangible and intangible brand associations; (3) eliciting the proper customer responses in terms of brand-related judgment and feelings; and (4) converting brand response to create an intense, active loyalty relationship between customers and the brand.

According to this model, enacting the four steps involves establishing six "brand building blocks" with customers. These brand building blocks can be assembled in terms of a brand pyramid, as illustrated in Figure 9.2. The model emphasizes the duality of brands—the rational route to brand building is the left-hand side of the pyramid, whereas the emotional route is the right-hand side.[19]

MasterCard is an example of a brand with duality, as it emphasizes both the rational advantage to the credit card, through its acceptance at establishments worldwide, and the emotional advantage through its award-winning "priceless" advertising campaign, which shows people buying items to reach a certain goal. The goal itself—a feeling, an accomplishment, or other intangible—is "priceless" ("There are some things money can't buy. For everything else, there's MasterCard").

Creating significant brand equity involves reaching the top or pinnacle of the brand pyramid and will occur only if the right building blocks are put into place.

- *Brand salience* relates to how often and easily the brand is evoked under various purchase or consumption situations.
- *Brand performance* relates to how the product or service meets customers' functional needs.
- *Brand imagery* deals with the extrinsic properties of the product or service, including the ways in which the brand attempts to meet customers' psychological or social needs.
- *Brand judgments* focus on customers' own personal opinions and evaluations.
- *Brand feelings* are customers' emotional responses and reactions with respect to the brand.
- *Brand resonance* refers to the nature of the relationship that customers have with the brand and the extent to which customers feel that they are "in sync" with the brand.

Resonance is characterized in terms of the intensity or depth of the psychological bond customers have with the brand, as well as the level of activity engendered by this loyalty. Examples of brands with high resonance include Harley-Davidson, Apple, and eBay.

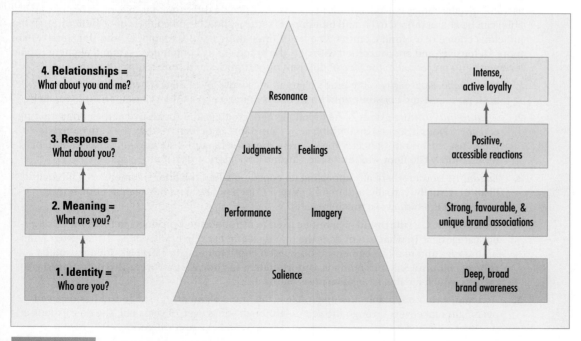

FIGURE 9.2

Brand Resonance Pyramid

Building Brand Equity

Marketers build brand equity by creating the right brand knowledge structures with the right consumers. This process depends on *all* brand-related contacts—whether marketer-initiated or not. From a marketing management perspective, however, there are three main sets of *brand equity drivers*:

1. *The initial choices for the brand elements or identities making up the brand (e.g., brand names, URLs, logos, symbols, characters, spokespeople, slogans, jingles, packages, and signage).* Old Spice uses bright red packaging and its familiar ocean schooner to reinforce its nautical theme while also launching deodorant and antiperspirant extensions, adding the High Endurance and Red Zone brand names.[20]

2. *The product and service and all accompanying marketing activities and supporting marketing programs.* Joe Boxer made its name selling colourful underwear with its signature yellow smiley face, Mr. Licky, in a hip, fun way. The company spent almost zero on advertising; clever stunts and events garnered publicity and word of mouth. An exclusive deal with Kmart has generated strong retail support.[21]

3. *Other associations indirectly transferred to the brand by linking it to some other entity (e.g., a person, place, or thing).* Subaru used the rugged Australian Outback and actor Paul Hogan of *Crocodile Dundee* movie fame in ads to help craft the brand image of the Subaru Outback line of cars and sports utility wagons.

Choosing Brand Elements

Brand elements are those trademarkable devices that serve to identify and differentiate the brand. Most strong brands employ multiple brand elements. Nike has the distinctive "swoosh" logo, the empowering "Just Do It" slogan, and the mythological "Nike" name based on the winged goddess of victory.

Brand elements can be chosen to build as much brand equity as possible. The test of the brand-building ability of these elements is what consumers would think or feel about the product *if* they only knew about the brand element. A brand element that provides a positive contribution to brand equity, for example, would be one where consumers assumed or inferred certain valued associations or responses. Based on its name alone, a consumer might expect ColorStay lipsticks to be long-lasting and SnackWell to be healthful snack foods.

BRAND ELEMENT CHOICE CRITERIA   There are six criteria in choosing brand elements (as well as more specific choice considerations in each case). The first three (memorable, meaningful, and likable) can be characterized as "brand building" in terms of how brand equity can be built through the judicious choice of a brand element. The latter three (protectable, adaptable, and transferable) are more "defensive" and are concerned with how the brand equity contained in a brand element can be leveraged and preserved in the face of different opportunities and constraints.

1. *Memorable.* How easily is the brand element recalled? How easily recognized? Is this true at both purchase and consumption? Short brand names such as Tide, Crest, and Puffs can help.

2. *Meaningful.* To what extent is the brand element credible and suggestive of the corresponding category? Does it suggest something about a product ingredient or the type of person who might use the brand? Consider the inherent meaning in names such as Motomaster auto batteries, Mop & Glo floor wax, and Lean Cuisine low-calorie frozen entrées.

3. *Likability.* How aesthetically appealing do consumers find the brand element? Is it inherently likable—visually, verbally, and in other ways? Concrete brand names such as Sunkist, Mr. Clean, and Firebird evoke much imagery.

4. *Transferable.* Can the brand element be used to introduce new products in the same or different categories? To what extent does the brand element add to brand equity across geographic boundaries and market segments? Volkswagen chose to name its new SUV Touareg, after a tribe of colourful Saharan nomads. Unfortunately, historically they were also notorious slave owners, which created a negative press backlash.[22]

5. *Adaptable.* How adaptable and updatable is the brand element? Betty Crocker has received over eight makeovers through the years—although she is over 75 years old, she doesn't look a day over 35!

6. *Protectable.* How legally protectable is the brand element? How competitively protectable? Can it be easily copied? It is important that names that become synonymous with product categories—such as Kleenex, Kitty Litter, Jell-O, Scotch Tape, Xerox, and Rollerblade—retain their trademark rights and not become generic.

THE
Great-West Life
ASSURANCE G⚷ COMPANY

Insurance firms such as
Great-West Life use symbols
of security, such as a key, to
brand themselves.

DEVELOPING BRAND ELEMENTS In creating a brand, marketers have many choices of brand elements to identify their products. Before, companies chose brand names by generating a list of possible names, debating their merits, eliminating all but a few, testing them with target consumers, and making a final choice.[23] Today, many companies hire a marketing research firm to develop and test names. These companies use human brainstorming sessions and vast computer databases, catalogued by association, sounds, and other qualities. Name-research procedures include *association tests* (What images come to mind?), *learning tests* (How easily is the name pronounced?), *memory tests* (How well is the name remembered?), and *preference tests* (Which names are preferred?). Of course, the firm must also conduct searches to make sure the chosen name has not already been registered.

Brand elements can play a number of brand-building roles. If consumers do not examine much information in making their product decisions, brand elements should be easily recognized and recalled and inherently descriptive and persuasive. Memorable or meaningful brand elements can reduce the burden on marketing communications to build awareness and link brand associations. The different associations that arise from the likability and appeal of brand elements may also play a critical role in the equity of a brand. The Keebler elves reinforce home-style baking quality and a sense of magic and fun for that line of cookies. The Molson Canadian Rant campaign featuring Joe Canadian used your average Canadian 20- or 30-something guy—arguably the beer industry's most coveted and competitive target market—to link what it means to be Canadian with that brand.

Brand names are not the only important brand element. Often, the less concrete brand benefits are, the more important it is that they capture the brand's intangible characteristics. Many financial services and insurance firms use symbols of strength (the Rock of Gibraltar for Prudential and the Lion for RBC Financial Group), security (the key for Great-West Life), or some combination of the two (the castle for Fortis).

A powerful—but sometimes overlooked—brand element is slogans. Like brand names, slogans are an extremely efficient means to build brand equity. Slogans can function as useful "hooks" or "handles" to help consumers grasp what the brand is and what makes it special. They are an indispensable means of summarizing and translating the intent of a marketing program. Think of the inherent brand meaning in slogans such as "Like a Good Neighbor, State Farm Is There," "Like a Rock" (GM trucks), and "Home Hardware, Help Is Close to Home."

Avis Group Holdings Inc.

A classic case of a company using a slogan to build brand equity is that of Avis's "We Try Harder" ad campaign. In 1963, when the campaign was developed, Avis was losing money and widely considered the number-two car rental company next to market leader Hertz. When account executives from DDB ad agency met with Avis managers, they asked: "What can you do that we can say you do better than your competitors?" An Avis manager replied, "We try harder because we have to." Someone at DDB wrote this down and it became the heart of the campaign. Avis was hesitant to air the campaign because of its blunt, break-the-rules honesty, but also because the company had to deliver on that promise. Yet, by creating buy-in on "We Try Harder" from all Avis employees, especially its front-line employees at the rental desks, the company was able to create a company culture and brand image out of an advertising slogan.[24]

Designing Holistic Marketing Activities

Although the judicious choice of brand elements and secondary associations can make important contributions to building brand equity, the primary input comes from the product or service and supporting marketing activities.

Brands are not built by advertising. Customers come to know a brand through a range of contacts and touch points: personal observation and use, word of mouth, interactions with company personnel, online or telephone experiences, and payment transactions. A **brand contact** can be defined as any information-bearing experience a customer or prospect has with the brand, the product category, or the market that relates to the marketer's product or service.[25] Any of these experiences can be positive or negative. The company must put as much effort into managing these experiences as it does in producing its ads.[26]

The strategy and tactics behind marketing programs have changed dramatically in recent years.[27] Marketers are creating brand contacts and building brand equity through many avenues, such as clubs and consumer communities, trade shows, event marketing, sponsorship, factory visits, public relations and press releases, and social cause marketing. To market its cereals, General Mills supplemented traditional advertising and promotion with, among other things, a family-themed entertainment-based retail destination, Cereal Adventure, inside Minneapolis's Mall of America, one of the world's largest shopping malls.[28] Chupa Chups has developed an extensive marketing program.

Chupa Chups

Who says lollipops are just for kids? Not Spanish Chupa Chups, the world's largest maker of lollipops. In order to extend the Chupa Chups brand beyond children, Chupa Chups is taking a truly holistic approach, which includes savvy—and totally free—product placement, fresh marketing ideas, and even its own line of retail boutiques. An internal task force, dubbed 4C for Chupa Chups Corporate Communications, is charged with raising brand awareness among fashion-conscious and media-saturated teens and youth. One example: When he learned that the coach of Barcelona's soccer team was struggling to quit smoking, a 4C sports fan sent him a complimentary box of Chupa Chups. For the rest of the season, the coach was rarely seen on the sidelines without a lollipop in his mouth. Chupa Chups sales in soccer-crazed Catalonia doubled that year. The company also gains visibility at high-profile awards ceremonies. When A-list stars come out at such events as the Venice Film Festival or the Grammys, a scantily clad "Chupa Chick" in a lollipop-studded bra top is there to greet them. So far Chupa's "celebrity suckers"—those caught on camera sucking a Chupa Chups—include Jerry Seinfeld, Elton John, Georgio Armani, Sheryl Crow, and Magic Johnson. Once Chupa Chups has caught teens' attention via these "nonendorser endorsers," they can point them to Chupa Chups packed in makeup kits or to clothing, eyewear, motorcycle helmets, and other items bearing the brand name.[29]

Regardless of the particular tools or approaches they choose, holistic marketers emphasize three important new themes in designing brand-building marketing programs: personalization, integration, and internalization.

PERSONALIZATION The rapid expansion of the Internet has created opportunities to personalize marketing.[30] Marketers are increasingly abandoning the mass-market practices that built brand powerhouses in the 1950s, 1960s, and 1970s for new approaches that are in fact a throwback to marketing practices from a century ago, when merchants literally knew their customers by name. To adapt to the increased consumer desire for personalization, marketers have embraced concepts such as experiential marketing, one-to-one marketing, and permission marketing. Chapter 5 summarized some of these concepts; "Marketing Insight: Applying Permission Marketing" highlights key principles of that particular approach.

From a branding point of view, these concepts are about getting consumers more actively involved with a brand by creating an intense, active relationship. *Personalizing marketing* is about making sure that the brand and its marketing are as relevant as possible to as many customers as possible—a challenge given that no two customers are ever identical.

MARKETING INSIGHT

Applying Permission Marketing

Permission marketing, the practice of marketing to consumers only after gaining their express permission, is a tool companies can use to break through clutter and build customer loyalty. With the help of large databases and advanced software, companies can store gigabytes of customer data and send targeted, personalized marketing messages to customers.

Seth Godin, a pioneer in the technique, estimates that individuals receive about 3000 marketing messages daily. He maintains that marketers can no longer use "interruption marketing" via mass media campaigns. Marketers can develop stronger consumer relationships by respecting consumers' wishes and sending messages only when they express a willingness to become more involved with the brand. According to Godin, effective permission marketing works because it is "anticipated, personal, and relevant."

Godin identifies five steps to effective permission marketing:

1. Offer the prospect an incentive to volunteer (e.g., free sample, sales promotion, or contest).
2. Offer the interested prospect a curriculum over time that teaches the consumer about the product or service.
3. Reinforce the incentive to guarantee that the prospect maintains the permission.
4. Offer additional incentives to get more permission from the consumer.
5. Over time, leverage the permission to change consumer behaviour toward profits.

Permission marketing does have drawbacks. One is that it presumes consumers to some extent "know what they want." But in many cases, consumers have undefined, ambiguous, or conflicting preferences. In applying permission marketing, consumers may need to be given assistance in forming and conveying their preferences. "Participatory marketing" may be a more appropriate concept because marketers and consumers need to work together to find out how the firm can best satisfy consumers.

Sources: Seth Godin, *Permission Marketing: Turning Strangers into Friends, and Friends into Customers* (New York: Simon & Schuster, 1999); Susan Fournier, Susan Dobscha, and David Mick, "Preventing the Premature Death of Relationship Marketing," *Harvard Business Review* (January–February 1998): 42–51.

Jones Soda

Peter van Stolk founded Jones Soda on the premise that Gen Y consumers would be more accepting of a new soft-drink brand if they felt they discovered it themselves. Jones Soda initially was sold only in shops that sell surfboards, snowboards, and skateboards. The Jones Soda Web site encourages fans to send in personal photos for possible use on Jones Soda labels. Although only maybe 40 or so are picked annually from the tens of thousands of entries, the approach helps to create relevance and an emotional connection.[31]

INTEGRATION One implication of these new marketing approaches is that the traditional "marketing mix" concept and the notion of the "four Ps" may not adequately describe modern marketing programs. **Integrating marketing** is about mixing and matching marketing activities to maximize their individual and collective effects.[32] As part of integrated marketing, marketers need a variety of different marketing activities that reinforce the brand promise. Olive Garden has become the second largest casual dining restaurant chain in the United States, with US$2 billion in sales and over 500 restaurants, in part through a fully integrated marketing program.

Olive Garden

The Olive Garden brand promise is "the idealized Italian family meal" characterized by "fresh, simple delicious Italian food," "complimented by a great glass of wine," "welcomed by people who treat you like family," "in a comfortable home-like setting." To live up to that brand promise, Olive Garden sends select managers and servers on cultural immersion trips to Italy; it launched the Culinary Institute of Tuscany in Italy to inspire new dishes; it conducts wine training workshops for employees and in-restaurant wine sampling for customers; and it remodelled restaurants to give them a Tuscan farmhouse look. Communications include in-store, employee, and mass-media messages that all reinforce the brand promise and ad slogan, "When You're Here, You're Family."[33]

The Olive Garden's integrated marketing program includes sending managers and servers to Italy on cultural immersion trips. Part of the trip is training classes at the Olive Garden's Culinary Institute of Tuscany. In this photo, they are learning about pasta.

Integration is especially critical with marketing communications. From the perspective of brand building, all communication options should be evaluated in terms of ability to affect brand equity. Each communication option can be judged in terms of the effectiveness and efficiency with which it affects brand awareness and with which it creates, maintains, or strengthens brand image. **Brand awareness** is consumers' ability to identify the brand under different conditions, as reflected by their brand recognition or recall performance. **Brand image** is the perceptions and beliefs held by consumers, as reflected in the associations held in consumer memory.

As we discuss in Chapter 17, different communication options have different strengths and can accomplish different objectives. It is important to employ a mix of different communication options, each of which plays a specific role in building or maintaining brand equity. Although Michelin may invest in R&D and engage in advertising, promotions, and other communications to reinforce the tires' "safety" association, it may also choose to sponsor events to make sure Michelin is seen as contemporary and up to date. The marketing communication program should be put together so that the whole is greater than the sum of the parts. In other words, as much as possible, there should be a match among certain communication options so that the effects of any one option are enhanced by the presence of another.

INTERNALIZATION Marketers must now "walk the walk" to deliver the brand promise. They must adopt an *internal* perspective to consider what steps to take to be sure employees and marketing partners appreciate and understand basic branding notions, and how they can help—or hurt—brand equity.[34] **Internal branding** is activities and processes that help to inform and inspire employees.[35] An up-to-date, deep understanding of the brand and its promise by all employees is critical for service companies and retailers.

Brand bonding occurs when customers experience the company as delivering on its brand promise. All of the customers' contacts with company employees and company communications must be positive. *The brand promise will not be delivered unless everyone in the company lives the brand.* One of the most potent influences on brand perception is the experience customers have with company personnel.

AIM Trimark Investments

Money management firm AIM Trimark engaged its employees in a major internal marketing effort to ensure that every member of the organization understood, bought into, and was capable of articulating its brand. To do this, the company went through a very comprehensive process that involved all the company employees in crafting a company mission and a set of defining principles. These ideas were tested and retested through a series of focus groups and employee feedback programs. After the process was complete, the company created a set of tools and programs that would ensure that the values of the brand would last beyond this process. They included an award-winning electronic newsletter, which now maintains a 90 percent readership rate among employees; employee videos for all-employee meetings, which told real stories of employees "living" the brand; and workspace materials that reflected the brand and its values, including mouse pads, wall plaques, and coffee mugs. The program worked—AIM Trimark was named company of the year at the 2003 Canadian Investment Awards and *Advisor's Edge* magazine recognized AIM Trimark as having the best customer service and best communications in 2003.[36]

Companies need to engage in continual open dialogue with employees. Some firms have pushed "B2E" (business-to-employee) programs through corporate intranets and other means. Disney is so successful at internal branding and having employees support its brand that it even teaches seminars at the Disney Institute on the "Disney Style" to employees from other companies.

Holistic marketers must go even further and train and encourage distributors and dealers to serve their customers well. Poorly trained dealers can ruin the best efforts to build a strong brand image.

Leveraging Secondary Associations

The third and final way to build brand equity is, in effect, to "borrow" it. That is, brand associations may themselves be linked to other entities that have their own associations, creating "secondary" brand associations. In other words, brand equity may be created by linking the brand to other information in memory that conveys meaning to consumers (see Figure 9.3 on the next page).

The brand may be linked to certain source factors, such as the company (through branding strategies), countries or other geographical regions (through identification of product origin), and channels of distribution (through channel strategy), as well as to other brands (through ingredient or co-branding), characters (through licensing), spokespeople (through endorsements), sporting or cultural events (through sponsorship), or some other third-party sources (through awards or reviews).

For example, assume Burton—makers of snowboards as well as ski boots, bindings, clothing, and outerwear—decided to introduce a new surfboard called "The Dominator." Burton has over a third of the snowboard market by closely aligning itself with top professional riders and creating a strong amateur snowboarder community. In creating the marketing program to support the new Dominator surfboard, Burton could attempt to leverage secondary brand knowledge in a number of different ways:

- Burton could leverage associations to the corporate brand by "sub-branding" the product, calling it "Dominator by Burton." Consumers' evaluations of the new product would be influenced by how they felt about Burton and how they felt that such knowledge predicted the quality of a Burton surfboard.

- Burton could try to rely on its rural New England origins, but such a geographical location would seem to have little relevance to surfing.

- Burton could also try to sell through popular surf shops in the hope that its credibility would "rub off" on the Dominator brand.

- Burton could attempt to co-brand by identifying a strong ingredient brand for its foam or fibreglass materials (as Wilson did by incorporating Goodyear tire rubber on the soles of its ProStaff Classic tennis shoes).

FIGURE 9.3

Secondary Sources of Brand
Knowledge

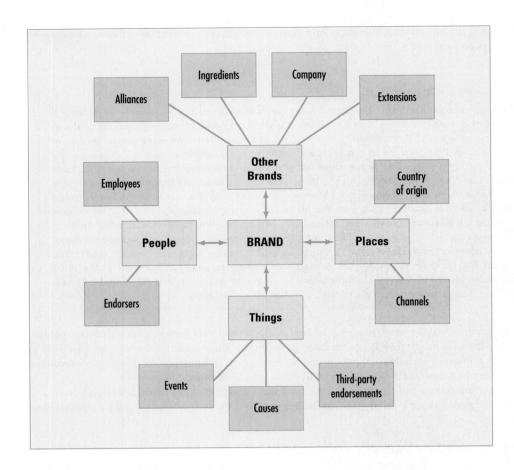

- Burton could attempt to find one or more top professional surfers to endorse the surfboard or choose to become a sponsor of a surfing competition or even the entire Association of Surfing Professionals (ASP) World Tour.
- Burton could attempt to secure and publicize favourable ratings from third-party sources like *Surfer* or *Surfing* magazine.

Thus, independent of the associations created by the surfboard itself, its brand name, or any other aspects of the marketing program, Burton may be able to build equity by linking the brand to these other entities.

Measuring Brand Equity

Given that the power of a brand resides in the minds of consumers and how it changes their response to marketing, there are two basic approaches to measuring brand equity. An *indirect* approach assesses potential sources of brand equity by identifying and tracking consumer brand knowledge structures. A *direct* approach assesses the actual impact of brand knowledge on consumer response to different aspects of the marketing. "Marketing Insight: The Brand Value Chain" shows how the two measurement approaches can be linked.

The two general approaches are complementary, and marketers can employ both. In other words, for brand equity to perform a useful strategic function and guide marketing decisions, it is important for marketers to fully understand (1) the sources of brand equity and how they affect outcomes of interest, as well as (2) how these sources and outcomes change, if at all, over time. Brand audits are important for the former; brand tracking is important for the latter.

MARKETING INSIGHT

The Brand Value Chain

The **brand value chain** is a structured approach to assessing the sources and outcomes of brand equity and the manner in which marketing activities create brand value. The brand value chain is based on several basic premises.

The brand value creation process begins when the firm invests in a marketing program targeting actual or potential customers. Any marketing program investment that can be attributed to brand value development, either intentional or not, falls into this category—product research, development, and design; trade or intermediary support; and marketing communications.

The marketing activity associated with the program affects the customer "mindset" with respect to the brand. The issue is, in what ways have customers been changed as a result of the marketing program? This mindset, across a broad group of customers, then results in certain outcomes for the brand in terms of how it performs in the marketplace. This is the collective impact of individual customer actions regarding how much and when they purchase, the price that they pay, and so on. Finally, the investment community considers market performance and other factors such as replacement cost and purchase price in acquisitions to arrive at an assessment of shareholder value in general and the value of a brand in particular.

The model also assumes that a number of linking factors intervene between these stages and determine the extent to which value created at one stage transfers to the next stage. Three sets of multipliers moderate the transfer between the marketing program and the subsequent three value stages—the program multiplier, the customer multiplier, and the market multiplier. The *program multiplier* determines the ability of the marketing program to affect the customer mindset and is a function of the quality of the program investment. The *customer multiplier* determines the extent to which value created in the minds of customers affects market performance. This result depends on contextual factors external to the customer. Three such factors are competitive superiority (how effective is the quantity and quality of the marketing investment of other competing brands), channel and other intermediary support (how much brand reinforcement and selling effort is being put forth by various marketing partners), and customer size and profile (how many and what types of customers, profitable or not, are attracted to the brand). The *market multiplier* determines the extent to which the value shown by the market performance of a brand is manifested in shareholder value. It depends, in part, on the actions of financial analysts and investors.

Sources: Kevin Lane Keller and Don Lehmann, "How Do Brands Create Value," *Marketing Management* (May/June 2003): 27–31. See also Rajendra K. Srivastava, Tasadduq A. Shervani, and Liam Fahey, "Market-Based Assets and Shareholder Value," *Journal of Marketing*, 62, no. 1 (1998): 2–18; M. J. Epstein and R. A. Westbrook, "Linking Actions to Profits in Strategic Decision Making," *MIT Sloan Management Review* (Spring 2001): 39–49. In terms of related empirical insights, see Manoj K. Agrawal and Vithala Rao, "An Empirical Comparison of Consumer-Based Measures of Brand Equity," *Marketing Letters*, 7, no. 3 (1996): 237–247; Walfried Lassar, Banwari Mittal, and Arun Sharma, "Measuring Customer-Based Brand Equity," *Journal of Consumer Marketing*, 12, no. 4 (1995): 11–19.

Brand Audits

To better understand their brands, marketers often need to conduct brand audits. A **brand audit** is a consumer-focused exercise that involves a series of procedures to assess the health of the brand, uncover its sources of brand equity, and suggest ways to improve and leverage its equity.

The brand audit can be used to set strategic direction for the brand. Are the current sources of brand equity satisfactory? Do certain brand associations need to be strengthened? Does the brand lack uniqueness? What brand opportunities exist and what potential challenges exist for brand equity? As a result of this strategic analysis, the marketer can develop a marketing program to maximize long-term brand equity.

Marketers should conduct a brand audit whenever they consider important shifts in strategic direction. With newspapers experiencing declining circulation as more people rely on radio, TV, and the Internet for their news, some publishers are now commissioning brand audits and attempting to redesign newspapers to be contemporary, relevant, and interesting to readers. Conducting brand audits on a regular basis (e.g., annually) allows marketers to keep their fingers on the pulse of their brands so that they can manage them more proactively and responsively. Audits are particularly useful background for managers as they set up their marketing plans.

Brand audits can have profound implications for strategic direction and brands' resulting performance.[37]

Polaroid

The results of a brand audit in Western Europe led Polaroid to decide to try to change its conventional photography image there to emphasize the "fun side" of its cameras. Polaroid gave one group of consumers 35 mm cameras and another group Polaroid cameras. Both groups went to a wedding and were told to shoot a roll of film. The 35 mm photos were typical wedding fare—posed and proper. The Polaroid photos were completely different—spontaneous and spirited. Those consumers with the Polaroids began to tell stories of the amusing antics that happened when the camera appeared. Polaroid learned from this research that its cameras could be a social stimulant and catalyst, bringing fun into people's lives, a theme that was picked up in advertising and that suggested new distribution strategies.

A brand audit requires understanding sources of brand equity from the perspective of both the firm and the consumer.[38] From the perspective of the firm, it is necessary to understand exactly what products and services are currently being offered to consumers and how they are being marketed and branded. From the perspective of the consumer, it is necessary to dig deeply into the minds of consumers and uncover the true meaning of brands and products. Brand audits consist of two steps: the brand inventory and the brand exploratory.

BRAND INVENTORY The purpose of the brand inventory is to provide a current, comprehensive profile of how all the goods and services sold by a company are marketed and branded. Profiling each product or service requires identifying all associated brand elements as well as the supporting marketing program. This information should be accurate, comprehensive, and timely and summarized in both visual and verbal form. As part of the brand inventory, it is also advisable to profile competitive brands, in as much detail as possible, in terms of their branding and marketing efforts.

The brand inventory helps to suggest what consumers' current perceptions *may* be based on. Although the brand inventory is primarily a descriptive exercise, some useful analysis can be conducted too. For example, marketers can assess the consistency of all the different goods or services sharing a brand name. Are the different brand elements used in a consistent way or are there many different variations and versions—perhaps for no obvious reason—depending on geographical market, market segment, and so forth? Similarly, are the supporting marketing programs logical and consistent across related brands?

BRAND EXPLORATORY The *brand exploratory* is research activity conducted to understand what consumers think and feel about the brand and its corresponding product category to identify sources of brand equity.

Several preliminary activities are useful for the brand exploratory. A number of prior research studies may be relevant. It is also useful to interview company personnel to gain an understanding of their beliefs about consumer perceptions. The diversity of opinion that typically emerges from these internal interviews serves several functions: it increases the likelihood that useful insights or ideas will be generated, and it also points out any internal inconsistencies or misconceptions.

Although these preliminary activities may yield useful findings and suggest certain hypotheses, they are often incomplete. Additional research is often required to better understand how customers shop for and use products and services and what they think of various brands. To allow a broad range of issues to be covered and to permit certain issues to be pursued in greater depth, the brand exploratory often employs qualitative research techniques, such as word associations, projective techniques, visualization, brand personification, and laddering (see Chapter 4).

Many firms are now using ethnography to supplement traditional focus groups. They study consumers in their everyday habitats at home, at work, at play, or shopping. Based on ethnographic research, Duracell, for example, learned that people had trouble removing a tab from its hearing aid batteries. The result was the introduction of a new product, Easy Tab. Whirlpool learned that people didn't want to wait for their dishwashers to fill up before running the machine, so its Kitchen Aid unit introduced a smaller version called Briva.

Standard Life

Montreal-based Standard Life conducted a brand audit in 2002 in which it discovered that the company's most prominent strength was in the dedication and values its employees adhered to and exhibited. As a result, it concluded that the best way to exhibit the company brand was through employee testimonials. The company crafted a television campaign featuring four spots, two in each language, with the tagline "Keeping our word is standard." In one of the French ads, the employees say such things as "I'll do what I said I'll do," "I don't do things halfway," and "I'll be tolerant with you." The campaign also includes a print component, with inserts running in business publications, including *Report on Business* magazine, *Time*, *Maclean's*, *L'Actualité*, *Affaires Plus*, and *MoneySense*.[39]

Brand Tracking

Tracking studies collect information from consumers on a routine basis over time. Tracking studies typically employ quantitative measures to provide marketers with current information as to how their brands and marketing programs are performing on the basis of a number of key dimensions. Tracking studies are a means of understanding where, how much, and in what ways brand value is being created.

These studies perform an important function for managers by providing consistent baseline information to facilitate day-to-day decision making. As more varied marketing activity surrounds the brand, it becomes difficult and expensive to research each individual marketing action. Tracking studies provide valuable diagnostic insights into the collective effects of a host of marketing activities. Regardless of how few or many changes are made in the marketing program over time, it is important to monitor the health of the brand and its equity so that proper adjustments can be made.

Brand Valuation

Brand equity needs to be distinguished from **brand valuation**, which is the job of estimating the total financial value of the brand. Certain companies base their growth on acquiring and building rich brand portfolios. Nestlé has acquired Rowntree (U.K.), Carnation (U.S.), Stouffer (U.S.), Buitoni-Perugina (Italy), and Perrier (France), making it the world's largest food company.

Table 9.2 displays the world's most valuable brands in 2003 according to one ranking.[40] With these well-known companies, brand value is typically over one-half of the total company market capitalization. John Stuart, co-founder of Quaker Oats, said: "If this business were split up, I would give you the land and bricks and mortar, and I would take the brands and trade marks, and I would fare better than you." North American companies do not list brand equity on their balance sheets because of the arbitrariness of the estimate. However, brand equity is given a value by some companies in the United Kingdom, Hong Kong, and Australia. "Marketing Insight: What Is a Brand Worth?" reviews one popular valuation approach, based in part on the price premium the brand commands times the extra volume it moves over an average brand.[41]

TABLE 9.2	THE WORLD'S TEN MOST VALUABLE BRANDS	
Rank	Brand	2003 Brand Value (US$ Billions)
1	Coca-Cola	$70.45
2	Microsoft	$65.17
3	IBM	$51.77
4	GE	$42.34
5	Intel	$31.11
6	Nokia	$29.44
7	Disney	$28.44
8	McDonald's	$24.60
9	Marlboro	$22.18
10	Mercedes	$21.37

What Is a Brand Worth?

According to top brand valuation firm Interbrand, brand valuation is based on an assessment of what the value is today of the earnings or cash flow the brand can be expected to generate in the future. To estimate brand value, it is necessary to (1) identify the true earnings that can be attributed strictly to the brand and (2) capitalize the earnings by applying a multiple to historic earnings as a discount rate to future cash flow.

Brand Earnings

Interbrand maintains that not all of a brand's profitability can necessarily be applied to the valuation of that brand. A brand may essentially be a commodity or derive much of its profitability from non–brand-related considerations (like its distribution system). Elements of profitability that do not result from the brand's identity must therefore be excluded. Because the valuation may be adversely affected by using a single year's profit, Interbrand uses a three-year weighted average of historical profit.

Brand earnings are calculated by subtracting a number of items from brand sales: (1) costs of brand sales, (2) marketing costs, (3) variable and fixed overheads, including depreciation and central overhead allocation, (4) remuneration of capital charge (a 5 to 10 percent rental charge on the replacement value of the capital employed in the line of production), and (5) taxation.

Brand Strength

To adjust these earnings, Interbrand conducts an in-depth assessment of brand strength. The assessment involves a detailed review of the brand, its positioning, the market in which it operates, competition, past performance, future plans, and risks to the brand. Interbrand administers a detailed questionnaire to collect the information from managers and customers. It also examines annual reports and other printed materials, and even conducts inspection visits to distributors and retail outlets.

Brand strength is a composite of seven weighted factors, each of which is scored according to established guidelines (see the list below). The resulting total, known as the *brand strength score*, is expressed as a percentage. This score is converted to an earnings multiple to be used against the brand-related profits. Certain adjustments are made to create a weighted average of post-tax brand profitability against which the brand multiplier is applied. Interbrand makes the comparison between the reciprocal of these multipliers and typical discount rates (or interest rates): A so-called perfect brand with a brand strength score of 100 would have a discount rate of 5 percent (1 over 20), which would be the typical return on a fairly low-risk investment; a weaker brand with a lower multiplier would have a higher discount rate to reflect the greater risk.

Interbrand Brand Strength Formula (Weights in Parentheses)

1. *Leadership* (25%). The brand's ability to influence its market and be a dominant force with a strong market share such that it can set price points, command distribution, and resist competitive invasions. A brand that leads its market or market sector is a more stable and valuable property than a brand lower down the order.

2. *Stability* (15%). The ability of the brand to survive over a long period of time based on consumer loyalty and past history. Long-established brands that have become part of the "fabric" of their markets are particularly valuable.

3. *Market* (10%). The brand's trading environment in terms of growth prospects, volatility, and barriers to entry. Brands in markets such as foods, drinks, and publishing are intrinsically more valuable than brands in, for example, high-tech or clothing areas, as the latter markets are more vulnerable to technological or fashion changes.

4. *Geographic spread* (25%). The ability of the brand to cross geographic and cultural borders. Brands that are international are inherently more valuable than national or regional brands due in part to their economies of scale.

5. *Trend* (10%). The ongoing direction and ability of the brand to remain contemporary and relevant to consumers.

6. *Support* (10%). The amount and consistency of marketing and communication activity. Those brand names that have received consistent investment and focused support must be regarded as more valuable than those

that have not. While the amount spent in supporting a brand is important, the quality of this support is equally significant.

7. *Protection* (5%). The brand owner's legal titles. A registered trademark is a statutory monopoly in a name, device, or in a combination of these two. Other protection may exist in common law, at least in certain countries. The strength and breadth of the brand's protection is critical in assessing its worth.

Sources: Michael Birkin, "Assessing Brand Value," in *Brand Power*, edited by Paul Sobart (New York: Macmillan); Simon Mottram, "The Power of the Brand," ARF Brand Equity Conference, February 15–16, 1994; John Murphy, *Brand Valuation* (London: Hutchinson Business Books, 1989); Jean-Noel Kapferer, *Strategic Brand Management* (London: Kogan Page Limited, 1992); Noel Penrose and Martin Moorhouse, "The Valuation of Brands," *Trademark World*, no. 17 (February 1989); Tom Blackett, "The Role of Brand Valuation in Marketing Strategy," *Marketing Research Today*, 17, no. 4 (November 1989): 245–248.

Managing Brand Equity

Effective brand management requires a long-term view of marketing decisions. Because consumer responses to marketing activity depend on what they know and remember about a brand, short-term marketing actions, by changing brand knowledge, necessarily increase or decrease the success of future marketing actions. Additionally, a long-term view results in proactive strategies designed to maintain and enhance customer-based brand equity over time in the face of external changes in the marketing environment and internal changes in a firm's marketing goals and programs.

Brand Reinforcement

As the company's major enduring asset, a brand needs to be carefully managed so that its value does not depreciate. Many brand leaders of 70 years ago are still today's brand leaders: Kodak, Canadian Tire, Coca-Cola, Heinz, and Campbell Soup, but only by constantly striving to improve their goods, services, and marketing. "Marketing Memo: Twenty-First-Century Branding" offers some contemporary perspectives on enduring brand leadership.

Brand equity is reinforced by marketing actions that consistently convey the meaning of the brand to consumers in terms of (1) what products the brand represents; what core benefits it supplies; and what needs it satisfies; as well as (2) how the brand makes those products superior and which strong, favourable, and unique brand associations should exist in the minds of consumers. Nivea, one of Europe's strongest brands, has expanded its meaning from a skin cream brand to a skin care and personal care brand through carefully designed and implemented brand extensions reinforcing the Nivea brand promise of "mild," "gentle," and "caring" in a broader arena.

Reinforcing brand equity requires innovation and relevance throughout the marketing program. Marketers must introduce new products and conduct new marketing activities that truly satisfy their target market. The brand must always be moving forward—but moving forward in the right direction. Marketing must always find new and compelling offerings and ways to market them. Brands that fail to do so—such as Kmart, Levi-Strauss, Eaton's, Oldsmobile, and Polaroid—find that their market leadership dwindles or even disappears.

Kellogg

After experiencing falling market share and profits through the 1990s, Kellogg was able to re-establish market leadership in the cereal business by getting consumers to pay more for their high-profit brands. The secret? Adding new features to old favourites such as Special K Red Berries cereal with freeze-dried berries, offered at nearly double the price of Raisin Bran cereal, or adding toys and computer CDs inside boxes of kids' cereals.[42]

An important consideration in reinforcing brands is the consistency of the marketing support the brand receives, in terms of both amount and kind. Consistency does not mean uniformity and no changes: Many tactical changes may be necessary to maintain the strategic thrust and direction of the brand. Unless there is some change in the marketing environment, however, there is little need to

Campbell's Soup continually updates its marketing and its ads: This ad for its new "Soup at Hand" product features Bucky Lasek, a top pro skateboarder.

Marketing Memo

Twenty-First-Century Branding

As one of the most successful marketers of the last 15 years, Scott Bedbury played a key role in the rise of both Nike and Starbucks. In his insightful book, *A New Brand World,* he offers the following branding principles:

1. *Relying on brand awareness has become marketing fool's gold*—Smart brands are more concerned with brand relevance and brand resonance.

2. *You have to know it before you can grow it*—Most brands don't know who they are, where they've been, and where they're going.

3. *Always remember the Spandex rule of brand expansion*—Just because you can doesn't mean you should.

4. *Great brands establish enduring customer relationships*—They have more to do with emotions and trust than with footwear cushioning or the way a coffee bean is roasted.

5. *Everything matters*—Even your restroom.

6. *All brands need good parents*—Unfortunately most brands come from troubled homes.

7. *Big is no excuse for being bad*—Truly great brands use their superhuman powers for good and place people and principles before profits.

8. *Relevance, simplicity, and humanity*—Rather than technology—will distinguish brands in the future.

Source: Scott Bedbury, *A New Brand World* (New York: Viking Press, 2002).

deviate from a successful positioning. In such cases, sources of brand equity should be vigorously preserved and defended.

Volvo

In an attempt to woo a different audience, Volvo drifted away from its heritage of safety in the late 1990s to push driving fun, speed, and performance. Purchased by Ford in 1999, the company dropped its ReVOLVOlution-themed ad campaign for the brand and went back to its roots in an attempt to revive sagging sales. Volvo's positioning was updated, however, to convey "active safety" and transcend the brand's boxy, sturdy, "passive safety" image. With product introductions that maximized safety but that still encompassed style, performance, and luxury, Volvo's sales set records in 2003.[43]

In managing brand equity, it is important to recognize the trade-offs between those marketing activities that fortify the brand and reinforce its meaning and those that attempt to leverage or borrow from existing brand equity to reap some financial benefit.[44] At some point, failure to reinforce the brand will diminish brand awareness and weaken brand image.

Home Depot

Since Home Depot opened its first store in 1978 in Atlanta, the company has emphasized exemplary customer service. Its sales staff is trained to offer on-the-spot lessons in tile laying, electrical installations, and other projects; they are experienced tradespersons—plumbers, electricians, and carpenters. In recent years, however, there were customer complaints about clutter in the aisles and salespeople stocking items instead of providing service. Starting in 2001, Home Depot gave its stores a makeover called Service Performance Improvement (SPI). SPI limits restocking to off-peak hours and prohibits forklifts in store aisles during the day. The program resulted in up to a 70 percent increase in employee interactions with customers. Before SPI was introduced, employees spent as little as 40 percent of their time with customers.

Brand Revitalization

Changes in consumer tastes and preferences, the emergence of new competitors or new technology, or any new development in the marketing environment could potentially affect the fortunes of a brand. In virtually every product category, there are examples of once prominent and admired brands—such as Smith Corona, Zenith, and Canadian Airlines—that have fallen on hard times or, in some cases, disappeared.[45] Nevertheless, a number of these brands have managed to make impressive comebacks in recent years, as marketers have breathed new life into their customer franchises. Brands such as RCA, Breck, Dr. Scholls, and Fanta have all seen their brand fortunes successfully turned around to varying degrees.

Reversing a fading brand's fortunes requires either that brands "return to their roots" and lost sources of brand equity be restored or that new sources of brand equity be established. Regardless of which approach is taken, brands on the comeback trail have to make more "revolutionary" changes than the "evolutionary" changes.

Often, the first place to look in turning around the fortunes of a brand is to understand what the sources of brand equity were to begin with. Are positive associations losing their strength or uniqueness? Have negative associations become linked to the brand? Decisions must then be made as to whether or not to retain the same positioning or create a new positioning and, if so, which positioning to adopt. Sometimes the positioning is still appropriate, and it's the actual marketing program that is the source of the problem because it is failing to deliver on the brand promise. In those instances, a "back to basics" strategy may make sense, as was the case with Harley-Davidson.

Harley-Davidson

Founded in 1903 in Milwaukee, Wisconsin, Harley-Davidson has twice narrowly escaped bankruptcy but is today one of the most-recognized motor vehicle brands in the world. In dire financial straits in the 1980s, it desperately licensed its name for such ill-advised ventures as Harley-Davidson cigarettes and wine coolers. Although consumers loved the brand, sales were depressed by product quality problems. Harley's return to greatness began by improving manufacturing processes. Harley also developed a strong brand community in the form of an owners club, called the Harley Owners Group (HOG), which sponsors bike rallies, charity rides, and other motorcycle events. Harley-Davidson has continued to promote its brand with grassroots marketing efforts and finds itself in the enviable position of having consumer demand exceed what it can supply.

In other cases, however, the old positioning is just no longer viable and a "reinvention" strategy is necessary. Mountain Dew completely overhauled its brand image to become a soft drink powerhouse. As its history reveals, it is often easiest to revive a brand that is still around but has more or less been forgotten.

Mountain Dew

Introduced in 1969, Pepsi initially marketed Mountain Dew with the countrified tagline "Yahoo Mountain Dew! It'll tickle your innards." By the 1990s, the brand was languishing on store shelves despite an attempt to evolve the image with outdoor action scenes. To turn the brand around, Mountain Dew updated the packaging and launched ads featuring a group of anonymous young males—the "Dew Dudes"—participating in extreme sports such as bungee jumping, skydiving, and snowboarding while consuming Mountain Dew. The brand slogan became "Do the Dew." The brand's successful pursuit of young soda drinkers led to Mountain Dew challenging Diet Coke to become the number-three selling soft drink in terms of market share by 2000.

There is obviously a continuum involved with revitalization strategies, with pure "back to basics" at one end and pure "reinvention" at the other end. Many revitalizations combine elements of both strategies. To refresh old sources of brand equity or create new sources, two main approaches are possible:

1. Expand the depth and/or breadth of brand awareness by improving consumer recall and recognition of the brand during purchase or consumption settings.

2. Improve the strength, favourability, and uniqueness of brand associations making up the brand image. This approach may involve programs directed at existing or new brand associations.

Brand revitalizations of almost any kind start with the product. General Motors' turnaround with its fading Cadillac brand was fuelled by new model designs that redefined the Cadillac look and styling, such as with the CTS sedan, XLR roadster, and ESV sport utility vehicle.[46]

Brand Crisis

Marketing managers must assume that at some point in time, some kind of brand crisis will arise. Diverse brands such as Jack in the Box restaurants, Firestone tires, Exxon oil, Suzuki Samurai sport utility vehicles, and Martha Stewart have all experienced a serious, potentially crippling brand crisis. In general, the more that brand equity and a strong corporate image have been established—especially with respect to corporate credibility and trustworthiness—the more likely it is that the firm can weather the storm. Careful preparation and a well-managed crisis management program, however, are also critical. The most famous example is Johnson & Johnson's nearly flawless handling of the Tylenol product-tampering incident. In the fall of 1982, seven people in Chicago died after ingesting cyanide-laced Extra-Strength Tylenol capsules. Although it was quickly determined that someone tampered with the capsules after they had left J&J's manufacturing facilities, Johnson & Johnson's top management put customer safety first, and alerted consumers via the media not to consume any type of Tylenol product.[47] As this case illustrates, the key to managing a crisis is that consumers see the response by the firm as both *swift* and *sincere*.

In terms of swiftness, the longer it takes a firm to respond to a marketing crisis, the more likely it is that consumers can form negative impressions as a result of unfavourable media coverage or word of mouth. Perhaps even worse, consumers may find out that they do not really like the brand that much after all and permanently switch to alternative brands or products.

Perrier

Perrier was forced to halt production worldwide and recall all of its existing bottles in February 1994 when traces of benzene, a known carcinogen, were found in excessive quantities in the bottled water. Over the course of the next few weeks, several explanations were offered as to how the contamination occurred, creating confusion and skepticism. Perhaps even more damaging, the product itself was off the shelves until May 1994. Despite an expensive re-launch featuring ads and promotions, the brand struggled to regain lost market share, and a full year later found sales less than half of what they once had been. Part of the problem was that during the time the product was unavailable, consumers and retailers found satisfactory substitutes. With its key "purity" association tarnished—the brand had been advertised as the "Earth's First Soft Drink" and "It's Perfect. It's Perrier"—the brand had no other compelling points of difference over its competitors.[48] Eventually, the company was taken over by Nestlé SA.

Second, swift actions must also come across as sincere. The more sincere the response by the firm—in terms of public acknowledgment of the severity of the impact on consumers and a willingness of the firm to take whatever steps are necessary and feasible to solve the crisis—the less likely it is that consumers will form negative attributions.

Gerber

Although Gerber had established a strong image of trust with consumers, baby food is a product category characterized by an extremely high level of involvement and need for reassurance. When consumers reported finding shards of glass in some jars of its baby food, Gerber tried to reassure the public that there were no problems in its manufacturing plants. But the company adamantly refused to have its baby food withdrawn from food stores. Some consumers clearly found Gerber's response unsatisfactory: Its market share slumped from 66 percent to 52 percent within a couple of months. As one company official admits, "Not pulling our baby food off the shelf gave the appearance that we aren't a caring company."[49]

Devising a Branding Strategy

The **branding strategy** for a firm reflects the number and nature of common and distinctive brand elements applied to the different products sold by the firm. In other words, devising a branding strategy involves deciding the nature of new and existing brand elements to be applied to new and existing products.

Deciding how to brand new products is especially critical. When a firm introduces a new product, it has three main choices:

1. It can develop new brand elements for the new product.
2. It can apply some of its existing brand elements.
3. It can use a combination of new and existing brand elements.

When a firm uses an established brand to introduce a new product, it is called a **brand extension**. When a new brand is combined with an existing brand, the brand extension can also be called a **sub-brand**, as with Hershey Kisses candy, Adobe Acrobat software, the Toyota Camry automobile, and the CIBC Aerogold Visa. An existing brand that gives birth to a brand extension is referred to as the **parent brand**. If the parent brand is already associated with multiple products through brand extensions, then it may also be called a **family brand**.

Brand extensions can be broadly classified into two general categories:[50] In a **line extension**, the parent brand is used to brand a new product that targets a new market segment within a product category currently served by the parent brand (e.g., through new flavours, forms, colours, added ingredients, and package sizes). Dannon has introduced several types of Dannon yogurt line extensions through the years—Fruit on the Bottom, Natural Flavors, Fruit Blends, and Whipped. In a **category extension**, the parent brand is used to enter a different product category from that currently served by the parent brand (e.g., Swiss Army watches). Honda has used its company name to cover such different products as automobiles, motorcycles, snowblowers, lawnmowers, marine engines, and snowmobiles. This allows Honda to advertise that it can fit "six Hondas in a two-car garage."

A **brand line** consists of all products—original as well as line and category extensions—sold under a particular brand. A **brand mix** (or brand assortment) is the set of all brand lines that a particular seller makes available to buyers. Many companies are now introducing **branded variants**, which are specific brand lines supplied to specific retailers or distribution channels. They result from the pressure retailers put on manufacturers to provide distinctive offerings. A camera company may supply its low-end cameras to mass merchandisers while limiting its higher-priced items to specialty camera shops. Valentino may design and supply different lines of suits and jackets to different department stores.[51]

A **licensed product** is one whose brand name has been licensed to other manufacturers who actually make the product. Corporations have seized on licensing to push the company name and image across a wide range of products—from bedding to shoes—making it a US$35 billion business.[52] Jeep's licensing program added up to US$400 million in global sales in 2002 and included everything from strollers (built for a father's longer arms) to apparel (with Teflon in the denim)—as long as they fit the brand's positioning of "Life Without Limits."[53]

Branding Decision: To Brand or Not to Brand?

The first branding strategy decision is whether to develop a brand name for a product. Today, branding is such a strong force that hardly anything goes unbranded. So-called commodities do not have to remain commodities. A *commodity* is a product presumably so basic that it cannot be physically differentiated in the minds of consumers. Over the years, a number of products that at one time were seen as essentially commodities have become highly differentiated as strong brands have emerged in the category.[54] Some notable examples (with brand pioneers in parentheses) are coffee (Maxwell House), bath soap (Ivory), flour (Gold Medal), beer (Budweiser), oatmeal (Quaker), pickles (Vlasic), bananas (Chiquita), pineapples (Dole), and even salt (Morton).

Assuming a firm decides to brand its products or services, it must then choose which brand names to use. Four general strategies are often used:

1. *Individual names.* This policy is followed by General Mills (Bisquick, Gold Medal flour, Nature Valley granola bars, Old El Paso Mexican foods, Pop Secret popcorn, Wheaties cereal, and Yoplait yogurt). A major advantage of an individual-names strategy is that the company does not tie its reputation to the product's. If the product fails or appears to have low quality, the company's name or image is not hurt. Companies often use different brand names for different quality lines within the same product class. For example, when Air Canada experimented with low-cost fares, it introduced its Tango and Zip services.

2. *Blanket family names.* This policy is followed by Heinz and General Electric. A blanket family name also has advantages. Development cost is less because there is no need for "name" research or heavy advertising expenditures to create brand-name recognition. Furthermore, sales of the new product are likely to be strong if the manufacturer's name is good. Campbell's

introduces new soups under its brand name with extreme simplicity and achieves instant recognition.

3. *Separate family names for all products.* This policy is followed by Sears (Kenmore for appliances, Craftsman for tools, and Homart for major home installations). If a company produces quite different products, it is not desirable to use one blanket family name.

4. *Corporate name combined with individual product names.* This sub-branding policy is followed by Kellogg (Kellogg's Rice Krispies, Kellogg's Raisin Bran, and Kellogg's Corn Flakes), as well as Honda, Sony, and Hewlett-Packard. The company name legitimizes, and the individual name individualizes, the new product.

The first two strategies are sometimes referred to as a "house of brands" and a "branded house," respectively, and can be seen as representing two ends of a brand relationship continuum, with the latter two strategies as being in between and combinations of the two. Although firms rarely adopt a pure example of any of the four strategies, deciding which general strategy to emphasize depends on several factors, as evidenced by Table 9.3.

Two key components of virtually any branding strategy are brand extensions and brand portfolios.

TABLE 9.3	SELECTING A BRAND RELATIONSHIP SPECTRUM POSITION
Toward a Branded House	**Toward a House of Brands**
Does the parent brand contribute to the offering by adding . . .	Is there a compelling need for a separate brand because it will . . .
■ Associations enhancing the value proposition?	■ Create and own an association?
■ Credibility through organizational associations?	■ Represent a new, different offering?
■ Visibility?	■ Retain/capture a customer/brand bond?
■ Communication efficiencies?	■ Deal with channel conflict?
Will the master brand be strengthened by associating with the new offering?	Will the business support a new brand name?

Source: Adapted from David A. Aaker and Erich Joachimsthaler, *Brand Leadership* (New York: Free Press, 2000), Figure 4-6, p. 120.

Brand Extensions

Recognizing that one of their most valuable assets is their brands, many firms have decided to leverage that asset by introducing a host of new products under some of their strongest brand names. Most new products are in fact line extensions—typically 80 to 90 percent in any one year. Moreover, many of the most successful new products, as rated by various sources, are extensions (e.g., Microsoft Xbox video game system, Apple iPod digital music player, and Nokia 6800 cell phone). Nevertheless, many new products are introduced each year as new brands (e.g., Bulls-Eye barbeque sauce, TiVo digital video recorders, and Mini automobile).

ADVANTAGES OF BRAND EXTENSIONS Two main advantages of brand extensions are that they can facilitate new product acceptance, as well as provide positive feedback to the parent brand and company.

New Product Success Brand extensions improve the odds of new product success in a number of ways. With a brand extension, consumers can make inferences and form expectations as to the likely composition and performance of a new product based on what they already know about the parent brand itself and the extent to which they feel this information is relevant to the new product.[55] For example, when Sony introduced Vaio, a new personal computer tailored for multimedia applications, consumers may have been more likely to feel comfortable with its anticipated performance because of their experience with and knowledge of other Sony products.

By setting up positive expectations, extensions reduce risk.[56] Because of the potentially increased consumer demand resulting from introducing a new product as an extension, it also may be easier to convince retailers to stock and promote a brand extension. From a marketing communications perspective, an introductory campaign for an extension does not have to create awareness of both the brand and the new product but instead can concentrate on the new product itself.[57]

Extensions can thus result in reduced costs of the introductory launch campaign, important given that establishing a new brand name in the North American marketplace for a mass-consumer-packaged good can cost over $100 million! They also can avoid the difficulty—and expense—of coming up with a new name. Extensions allow for packaging and labelling efficiencies. Similar or virtually identical packages and labels for extensions can result in lower production costs and, if coordinated properly, more prominence in the retail store by creating a "billboard" effect. For example, Michelina's offers a variety of frozen entrées with identical orange packaging that increases their visibility when they are stocked together in the freezer. By offering consumers a portfolio of brand variants within a product category, consumers who need a change—because of boredom, satiation, or whatever—can switch to a different product type without having to leave the brand family.

Dove

The ubiquitous personal care brand Dove is sold by Unilever Canada, and includes a variety of personal care products such as shampoos and conditioners, skin lotions, antiperspirants, and so forth. Given the amount of brand switching and the large number of brands kept in inventory by consumers with personal care products in general—and shampoos in particular—the ability of Dove to offer a full product line is a competitive advantage. By continually extending its line, Dove keeps up with any new market trend or shift in consumer demand. In 2004, Dove launched its newest line extension—Dove Daily Hydrating Cleansing Cloths—which won the Dove team one of the inaugural Best New Product awards in 2004 that recognized 16 new products as the best innovations in food, personal care, and household brands in Canada.[58]

Positive Feedback Effects Besides facilitating acceptance of new products, brand extensions can also provide feedback benefits.[59] They can help to clarify the meaning of a brand and its core brand values or improve consumer perceptions of the credibility of the company behind the extension.

Dove's ability to a provide a full line of personal care products is a competitive advantage, and it keeps up with new market trends by continually extending its line.

Thus, through brand extensions, Crayola means "colourful crafts for kids," Aunt Jemima means "breakfast foods," and Weight Watchers means "weight loss and maintenance."

Line extensions can renew interest and liking for the brand and benefit the parent brand by expanding market coverage. Kimberly-Clark's Kleenex unit has a goal of getting facial tissue in every room of the home. This philosophy has led to a wide variety of Kleenex facial tissues and packaging, including scented, ultra-soft, and lotion-impregnated tissues; boxes with drawings of dinosaurs and dogs for children's rooms or colourful, stylish designs to match room décor; and a "man-sized" box with tissues 50 percent larger than regular Kleenex. One benefit of a successful extension is that it may also serve as the basis for subsequent extensions. During the 1970s and 1980s, Billabong established its brand credibility with the young surfing community as a designer and producer of quality surf apparel. This success permitted it to extend into other youth-oriented areas, such as snowboarding and skateboarding.

DISADVANTAGES OF BRAND EXTENSIONS On the downside, line extensions may cause the brand name to not be as strongly identified with any one product.[60] Ries and Trout call this the "line-extension trap."[61] By linking its brand to mainstream food products such as mashed potatoes, dried milk, soups, and beverages, Cadbury ran the risk of losing its more specific meaning as a chocolates and candy brand.[62] **Brand dilution** occurs when consumers no longer associate a brand with a specific product or highly similar products and start thinking less of the brand.

If a firm launches extensions consumers deem inappropriate, they may question the integrity and competence of the brand. Different varieties of line extensions may confuse and perhaps even frustrate consumers: Which version of the product is the "right one" for them? As a result, they may reject new extensions for "tried and true" favourites or all-purpose versions. Retailers have to reject many new products and brands because they do not have the shelf or display space for them.

The worst possible scenario with an extension is that not only does it fail, but it harms the parent brand image in the process. Fortunately, such events are rare. "Marketing failures," where insufficient consumers were attracted to a brand, are typically much less damaging than "product failures," where the brand fundamentally fails to live up to its promise. Even then, product failures dilute brand equity only when the extension is seen as very similar to the parent brand. The Audi 5000 car suffered from a tidal wave of negative publicity and word of mouth in the mid-1980s when it was alleged to have a "sudden acceleration" problem. The adverse publicity also spilled over to the 4000 model. But the Quattro was relatively more insulated from negative repercussions, because it was distanced from the 5000 by its more distinct branding and advertising strategy.[63]

Even if sales of a brand extension are high and meet targets, it is possible that this revenue may have resulted from consumers switching to the extension from existing product offerings of the parent brand—in effect *cannibalizing* the parent brand. Intrabrand shifts in sales may not necessarily be so undesirable, as they can be thought of as a form of *pre-emptive cannibalization*. In other words, consumers might have switched to a competing brand instead of the line extension if it had not been introduced into the category. Tide laundry detergent maintains the same market share now compared to 50 years ago because of the sales contributions of the various line extensions (scented and unscented powder, tablet, liquid, and other forms).

One easily overlooked disadvantage to brand extensions is that by introducing a new product as a brand extension, the firm forgoes the chance to create a new brand with its own unique image and equity. Consider the advantages to Disney of having introduced more adult-oriented Touchstone films; to Levi's of having introduced casual Dockers pants; and to Black and Decker of having introduced high-end Dewalt power tools.

SUCCESS CHARACTERISTICS A potential new product extension for a brand must be judged by how effectively it leverages existing brand equity from the parent brand to the new product, as well as how effectively the extension, in turn, contributes to the equity of the parent brand.[64] Crest White-strips leveraged the strong reputation of Crest and dental care to provide reassurance in the teeth-whitening arena, while also reinforcing its dental authority image. The most important consideration with extensions is that there is "fit" in the minds of the consumer. Consumers may see a basis of fit for an extension in many ways—common physical attributes, usage situations, or user types.

One major mistake in evaluating extension opportunities is failing to take *all* of consumers' brand knowledge structures into account. Often marketers mistakenly focus on one or perhaps a few brand associations as a potential basis of fit and ignore other, possibly more important, associations in the process.

Crest Whitestrips leverages the strong reputation of Crest in dental care.

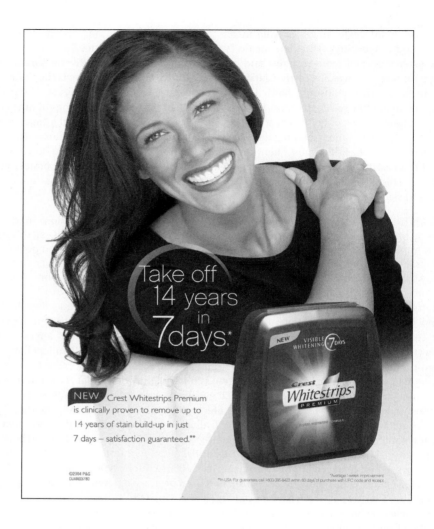

Bic

The French company Societé Bic, by emphasizing inexpensive, disposable products, was able to create markets for nonrefillable ballpoint pens in the late 1950s; disposable cigarette lighters in the early 1970s; and disposable razors in the early 1980s. It unsuccessfully tried the same strategy in marketing Bic perfumes in the United States and Europe in 1989. The perfumes—two for women ("Nuit" and "Jour") and two for men ("Bic for Men" and "Bic Sport for Men")—were packaged in quarter-ounce glass spray bottles that looked like fat cigarette lighters and sold for about $5 each. The products were displayed on racks at checkout counters throughout Bic's extensive distribution channels. At the time, a Bic spokeswoman described the new products as extensions of the Bic heritage—"high quality at affordable prices, convenient to purchase, and convenient to use." The brand extension was launched with a US$20 million advertising and promotion campaign containing images of stylish people enjoying themselves with the perfume and using the tagline "Paris in Your Pocket." Nevertheless, Bic was unable to overcome its lack of cachet and negative image associations, and the extension was a failure.[65]

"Marketing Memo: Research Insights on Brand Extensions" outlines a number of academic research findings on brand extensions.

Brand Portfolios

All brands have boundaries—a brand can only be stretched so far. Multiple brands are often necessary to pursue multiple market segments. Any one brand is not viewed equally favourably by all the different market segments that the firm would like to target. Some other reasons for introducing multiple brands in a category include:[66]

1. To increase shelf presence and retailer dependence in the store.

2. To attract consumers seeking variety who may otherwise have switched to another brand.

3. To increase internal competition within the firm.

4. To yield economies of scale in advertising, sales, merchandising, and physical distribution.

The **brand portfolio** is the set of all brands and brand lines a particular firm offers for sale to buyers in a particular category. Different brands may be designed and marketed to appeal to different market segments.

The Gap

Founded in 1969 and named after the "generation gap," retail clothing manufacturer the Gap grew by selling colourful Gap-branded clothing positioned as casual, functional, and "basic with attitude." The Gap expanded beyond its flagship stores through acquisitions and extensions. GapKids is a highly successful extension introduced in 1986. The Gap brought Banana Republic and its unique travel and safari-themed stores and catalogues in 1983, and reformulated the clothing to reflect more urban tastes. In March 1994, the Gap introduced Old Navy stores to sell Gap-like men's, women's, and children's apparel at lower prices in large warehouse-style outlets.

A brand portfolio must be judged by its ability to maximize brand equity. The optimal brand portfolio is one where each brand maximizes equity in combination with all other brands in the portfolio. In designing the optimal brand portfolio, marketers generally need to trade off market coverage and these other considerations with costs and profitability. A portfolio is too big if profits can be increased by dropping brands; a portfolio is not big enough if profits can be increased by adding brands. In general, the basic principle in designing a brand portfolio is to *maximize market coverage*, so that no potential customers are being ignored, but to *minimize brand overlap*, so that brands are not competing to gain customer approval. Each brand should be clearly differentiated and appeal to a sizable enough marketing segment to justify its marketing and production costs.[67]

Brand portfolios need to be carefully monitored over time to identify weak brands and kill unprofitable ones.[68]

Electrolux

In the late 1990s, consumer durables manufacturer Electrolux offered a range of professional food service equipment in Western Europe. By 1996, the company had 15 brands in the professional food service equipment market, but only one, Zanussi, was sold in more than one country in Europe. By moving from a segmentation scheme based on price—low, medium, and high—to one based on consumer needs—from basic solutions to prestige gourmet—Electrolux was able to go from 15 local brands to four pan-European brands. The resulting economies of scale and scope helped turn Electrolux's fortunes around, so that even though Electrolux deleted many brands, its professional kitchenware division's sales never dwindled and it was finally able to turn a profit in 2001.

Brand lines with poorly differentiated brands are likely to be characterized by much cannibalization and require pruning.[69] Kellogg's Eggo waffles come in 16 flavours. Investors can choose among 8000 mutual funds. Students can choose among hundreds of business schools. For the seller, this may spell hypercompetition. For the buyer, this may spell too much choice.

Besides these considerations, there are a number of specific roles brands can play as part of a brand portfolio.

Marketing Memo

Research Insights on Brand Extensions

Academics have studied brand extensions closely. Here is a summary of some of their key research findings.

- Successful brand extensions occur when the parent brand is seen as having favourable associations and there is a perception of fit between the parent brand and the extension product.
- There are many bases of fit: product-related attributes and benefits, as well as non–product-related attributes and benefits related to common usage situations or user types.
- Depending on consumer knowledge of the categories, perceptions of fit may be based on technical or manufacturing commonalties or more surface considerations such as necessary or situational complementarity.
- High-quality brands stretch farther than average-quality brands, although both types of brands have boundaries.
- A brand that is seen as prototypical of a product category can be difficult to extend outside the category.
- Concrete attribute associations tend to be more difficult to extend than abstract benefit associations.
- Consumers may transfer associations that are positive in the original product class but become negative in the extension context.
- Consumers may infer negative associations about an extension, perhaps even based on other inferred positive associations.
- It can be difficult to extend into a product class that is seen as easy to make.
- A successful extension can not only contribute to the parent brand image but also enable a brand to be extended even farther.
- An unsuccessful extension hurts the parent brand only when there is a strong basis of fit between the two.
- An unsuccessful extension does not prevent a firm from "backtracking" and introducing a more similar extension.
- Vertical extensions can be difficult and often require sub-branding strategies.
- The most effective advertising strategy for an extension emphasizes information about the extension (rather than reminders about the parent brand).

Source: Kevin Lane Keller, *Strategic Brand Management*, 2nd ed. (Upper Saddle River, NJ: Prentice-Hall, 2003).

FLANKERS Flanker or "fighter" brands are positioned with respect to competitors' brands so that more important (and more profitable) *flagship brands* can retain their desired positioning. Procter & Gamble markets Luvs diapers in a way to flank the more premium positioned Pampers. In designing these fighter brands, marketers must walk a fine line. Fighter brands must not be so attractive that they take sales away from their higher-priced comparison brands or referents. At the same time, if fighter brands are seen as connected to other brands in the portfolio in any way (e.g., by virtue of a common branding strategy), then fighter brands must not be designed so cheaply that they reflect poorly on these other brands.

CASH COWS Some brands may be kept around despite dwindling sales because they still manage to hold on to a sufficient number of customers and maintain their profitability with virtually no marketing support. These "cash cow" brands can be effectively "milked" by capitalizing on their reservoir of existing brand equity. For example, despite the fact that technological advances have moved much of its market to the newer Mach III brand of razors, Gillette still sells the older Trac II, Atra, and Sensor brands. Because withdrawing these brands may not necessarily result in customers switching to another Gillette brand, it may be more profitable for Gillette to keep them in its brand portfolio for razor blades.

LOW-END ENTRY-LEVEL The role of a relatively low-priced brand in the brand portfolio often may be as a means of attracting customers to the brand franchise. Retailers like to feature these "traffic builders" because they are able to "trade up" customers to a higher-priced brand. For example, BMW introduced certain models into its 3-series automobiles in part as a means of bringing new customers into the brand franchise with the hope of later "moving them up" to higher-priced models when they later decided to trade in their cars.

HIGH-END PRESTIGE The role of a relatively high-priced brand in the brand family often is to add prestige and credibility to the entire portfolio. For example, one analyst argued that the real value to Chevrolet of its Corvette high-performance sports car was in "its ability to lure curious customers into showrooms and at the same time help improve the image of other Chevrolet cars. It does not mean a hell of a lot for GM profitability, but there is no question that it is a traffic builder."[70] Corvette's technological image and prestige was meant to cast a halo over the entire Chevrolet line.

SUMMARY

1. A brand is a name, term, sign, symbol, or design, or some combination of these elements, intended to identify the goods and services of one seller or group of sellers and to differentiate them from those of competitors. The different components of a brand—brand names, logos, symbols, package designs, and so on—are brand elements.

2. Brands offer a number of benefits to customers and the firms. Brands are valuable intangible assets that need to be managed carefully. The key to branding is that consumers perceive differences among brands in a product category.

3. Brand equity should be defined in terms of marketing effects uniquely attributable to a brand. That is, brand equity relates to the fact that different outcomes result in the marketing of a product or service because of its brand, as compared to the results if that same product or service was not identified by that brand.

4. Building brand equity depends on three main factors: (1) The initial choices for the brand elements or identities making up the brand; (2) The way the brand is integrated into the supporting marketing program; and (3) The associations indirectly transferred to the brand by linking the brand to some other entity (e.g., the company, country of origin, channel of distribution, or another brand).

5. Brand equity needs to be measured in order to be managed well. Brand audits are in-depth examinations of the health of a brand and can be used to set strategic direction for the brand. Tracking studies involve information collected from consumers on a routine basis over time and provide valuable tactical insights into the short-term effectiveness of marketing programs and activities. Brand audits measure "where the brand has been," and tracking studies measure "where the brand is at now" and whether marketing programs are having the intended effects.

6. A branding strategy for a firm identifies which brand elements a firm chooses to apply across the various products it sells. In a brand extension, a firm uses an established brand name to introduce a new product. Potential extensions must be judged by how effectively they leverage existing brand equity to a new product, as well as how effectively the extension, in turn, contributes to the equity of the existing parent brand.

7. Brands can play a number of different roles within the brand portfolio. Brands may expand coverage, provide protection, extend an image, or fulfill a variety of other roles for the firm. Each brand name product must have a well-defined positioning. In that way, brands can maximize coverage and minimize overlap and thus optimize the portfolio.

APPLICATIONS

Marketing Debate: Are Line Extensions Good or Bad?

Some critics vigorously denounce the practice of brand extensions, as they feel that too often companies lose focus and consumers become confused. Other experts maintain that brand extensions are a critical growth strategy and source of revenue for the firm.

Take a position: Line extensions can endanger brands versus Line extensions are an important brand growth strategy.

Marketing Discussion

How can you relate the different models of brand equity presented in the chapter? How are they similar? How are they different? Can you construct a brand equity model that incorporates the best aspects of each model?

Marketing Spotlight: Procter & Gamble

Procter & Gamble (P&G) is one of the most skilled marketers of consumer packaged goods. It markets the leading brand in 19 of the 39 categories in which it competes. Its average market share is close to 25 percent. Its market leadership rests on several principles:

- *Customer knowledge.* P&G studies its customers—both final consumers and the trade—through continuous marketing research and intelligence gathering. It prints its toll-free 800 number on every product.

- *Long-term outlook.* P&G takes the time to analyze each opportunity carefully and prepare the best product, and then commits itself to making this product a success. It struggled with Pringles potato chips for almost a decade before achieving market success.

- *Product innovation.* P&G is an active product innovator, devoting US$1.7 billion (4 percent of sales) to research and development, an impressively high amount for a packaged-goods company. Part of its innovation process is developing brands that offer new consumer benefits. Recent examples include Febreze, an odour-eliminating fabric spray; Dryel, a product that allows consumers to clean and freshen "dry clean only" clothes at home; and Swiffer, a new cleaning system that more effectively removes dust, dirt, and hair from floors and other hard surfaces.

- *Quality strategy.* P&G designs products of above-average quality and continuously improves them. When P&G announces "new and improved," it means it. Recent examples include Tide and Ariel compact detergents that remove stains and sanitize laundry while protecting original fabric colours; and Pampers Rash Guard, the only diaper designed to treat and prevent diaper rash.

- *Line-extension strategy.* P&G produces its brands in several sizes and forms. This strategy gains more shelf space and prevents competitors from moving in to satisfy unmet market needs.

- *Brand-extension strategy.* P&G often uses its strong brand names to launch new products. The Ivory brand has been extended from a soap to include a liquid soap, a dishwashing detergent, and a shampoo. Old Spice was successfully extended from men's fragrances to deodorant. Launching a new product under a strong existing brand name gives the new brand instant recognition and credibility with much less advertising outlay.

- *Multibrand strategy.* P&G markets several brands in the same product category. Each brand meets a different consumer want and competes against specific competitors' brands. Each brand manager competes for company resources. More recently, P&G has begun to reduce its vast array of products, sizes, flavours, and varieties to bring down costs.

- *Heavy advertising and media pioneer.* P&G is the United States' second largest consumer-packaged-goods advertiser, spending over US$3 billion a year on advertising. A pioneer in using the power of television to create strong consumer awareness and preference, P&G is now taking a leading role in building its brand on the Web.

- *Aggressive sales force:* In 1998, P&G's sales force was named one of the top 25 sales forces by *Sales & Marketing Management* magazine. A key to P&G's success is the close ties its sales force forms with retailers, notably Wal-Mart. The 150-person team that serves the retail giant works closely with Wal-Mart to improve both the products that go to the stores and the process by which they get there.

- *Effective sales promotion.* P&G's sales-promotion department counsels its brand managers on the most effective promotions to achieve particular objectives. The department develops an expert sense of these deals' effectiveness under varying circumstances. At the same time, P&G tries to minimize the use of sales promotion and move toward "everyday low prices."

- *Competitive toughness.* P&G carries a big stick when it comes to aggressors. It is willing to spend large sums of money to outpromote new competitive brands and prevent them from gaining a foothold.

- *Manufacturing efficiency and cost cutting.* P&G's reputation as a great marketing company is matched by its excellence as a manufacturing company. P&G spends large sums developing and improving production operations to keep its costs among the lowest in the industry; and P&G has recently begun slashing its costs even further, allowing it to reduce the premium prices at which some of its goods sell.

- *Brand-management system.* P&G originated the brand-management system, in which one executive is responsible for each brand. The system has been copied by many competitors but frequently without P&G's success. Recently, P&G modified its general management structure so that each brand category is now run by a category manager with volume and profit responsibility. Although this new organization does not replace the brand-management system, it helps to sharpen strategic focus on key consumer needs and competition in the category.

Thus P&G's market leadership is not based on doing one thing well, but on the successful orchestration of myriad factors that contribute to market leadership.

DISCUSSION QUESTIONS

1. What have been the key success factors for Procter & Gamble?

2. Where is Procter & Gamble vulnerable? What should it watch out for?

3. What recommendations would you make to their senior marketing executives going forward? What should they be sure to do with their marketing?

Sources: Melanie Wells, "Kid Nabbing," *Forbes*, February 2, 2004, p. 84; *P&G Fact Sheet*, August 2003; "Chairman's Address," *Annual Shareholder Meeting*, October 14, 2003; Ed Tazzia, "What's Entertaining?" *Brandweek*, November 17, 2003, p. 40; Noreen O'Leary, "The New and Improved P&G," *Brandweek*, November 17, 2003, p. 44; **www.pg.com**.

10

- How can a firm choose and communicate an effective positioning in the market?

- How are brands differentiated?

- What marketing strategies are appropriate at each stage of the product life cycle?

- What are the implications of market evolution for marketing strategies?

CHAPTER 10

Crafting the Brand Positioning

PROFILE: CANADIAN MARKETING EXCELLENCE

If you visit the Canadian Tourism Commission (CTC) Web site (www.travelcanada.ca), you will find vast amounts of information tailored to specific target audiences. There's everything from survey results aimed at tourism operators and researchers to travel information for people from different countries. If you are Australian, for example, you can quickly find everything from information on how long you can stay in the country without a visa to where you can enjoy a ski vacation. The main role of the organization, however, is to position Canada to the world as a four-season travel destination. Even more importantly, the CTC is tasked with positioning Canada in the minds of both business travellers and tourists and creating a brand for the country that will communicate to the world what Canada is all about, what it has to offer, and how Canada differs from other travel destinations. In other words, Canada's competition for travel and tourism dollars is, effectively, every other country on the globe.

The CTC is a Crown corporation of the federal government, and it works in partnership with the country's tourism industries. Positioning Canada as an exciting and rewarding destination is an important task. Just consider these figures. Canada's tourism industry is made up of almost 190 000 enterprises. These businesses operate in communities large and small, in every province and territory. In 2004, they employed 615 300 Canadians directly, and a million more Canadians rely on the industry indirectly for their livelihood. In 2004 Canada attracted almost 39 million nonresident travellers. In addition, the industry serves Canadians travelling within the country. These travellers spent a whopping $57.5 billion in Canada in 2004 alone. While Canadians account for some two-thirds of tourism spending, the amount spent here by foreign travellers also makes tourism an important export industry. The Canadian tourism industry ranks 12th in the world in terms of revenues generated and it is 10th in the world in terms of the numbers of visitors the country attracts.

Despite this record of success, the CTC faces some daunting challenges as it works to build the Canadian industry. Tourism is still feeling the aftershocks of the terrorist attacks in September 2001, the 2003 SARS outbreak, the war in Iraq, avian flu, and—the most recent challenge—a 25 percent surge in the Canadian dollar relative to the American greenback. These hurdles have resulted in the number of international visitors to Canada dropping sharply. Revenues fell by $920 million between

2002 and 2003. While spending by Canadians travelling within the country rose 3.3 percent, reaching $35 billion, the gain was not sufficient to offset the sharp decline in visits from international travellers.

It's not surprising, therefore, that tourism marketers are in crisis-management mode. Repositioning was needed since many believed that Canada's image was tired and clichéd—RCMP, beavers, hockey players, and a great natural landscape—which would come as no surprise to Canadians who struggle to communicate the Canadian identity abroad beyond those iconic symbols. As Randy Williams, president of the Toronto-based Tourism Industry Association of Canada, notes, "[A branding] exercise hadn't taken place for a number of years, and it's now timely to do that. The world has changed a lot in the last couple of years so it's timely that Canada looks at the way it brands itself and its positioning statements."

For example, it is not widely known—either at home or abroad—that Canada has some of the most multicultural and cosmopolitan cities in the world. Doing a little self-examination, the CTC realized that it might have been partially responsible for perpetuating a stereotypical image of Canada. Its last brand positioning exercise, undertaken in 1999 to 2000, was based on the tagline "Discover Our True Nature." The CTC now believes that people didn't understand the double meaning behind this tagline. While it was meant to convey things about our wonderful landscapes, the CTC also hoped people would see Canada as a way of rediscovering something about themselves. However, the slogan and campaign didn't work as hoped. This time, says Jean B. Chrétien, the CTC's senior vice-president of marketing and sales, they wanted to do it right. "We decided to . . . consult customers around the world to see if what we're going to come up with really means something to them."

Addressing these challenges led the CTC to begin to think more strategically about how to better position Canada as a global tourist and business destination. Working with the Toronto Office of DDB Canada over a seven-month period, the CTC conducted extensive research to examine perceptions about Canada, including interviews with over 400 Canadian travel professionals and 18 consumer focus groups conducted in six countries—Canada, the United States, the United Kingdom, Germany, Japan, and Mexico. The result was "Brand Canada"—a simple, compelling message that does not define Canada, but positions it as an ideal destination for travellers seeking their own unique individual experience: "Travellers both domestic and abroad won't be guided or told what to think, feel and experience—they will be empowered to make this experience their own. At the same time, quietly proud Canadians will be motivated to raise their voice and become Canadian ambassadors from coast to coast to coast and abroad." The tagline "Canada. Keep Exploring" will evoke emotion and inspire travellers to create their own adventures. Michele McKenzie, president and CEO of the CTC, says, "Canada is a catalyst for self-expression where destinations turn into one-of-a-kind experiences."

While positioning Canadian travel to residents will be a priority, the bulk of the CTC's efforts will be aimed at the United States, Europe, and Asia. The long-term goal of the CTC is to increase revenues from its 11 core markets by $7.5 billion, or close to 23 percent, over the next five years.

Sources: Canadian Tourism Commission Web site, **www.canadiantourism.com** (viewed August 20, 2004); "Canada's Clichéd Image Inspires a New Initiative: Canadian Tourism Commission Announces Brand Vision for Canada," CTC News Release, May 11, 2005; Rebecca Harris, "Seeking a New Destination," *Marketing Magazine Online*, **www.marketingmag.ca**, August 23, 2004 (viewed August 20, 2004); Lisa D'Innocenzo, "How Can Marketers Deal with the Lofty Loonie?" *Strategy Magazine Online*, **www.strategymag.com**, February 23, 2004 (viewed August 20, 2004); "Welcome to the Tourism Industry Association of Canada," **www.tiac-aitc.ca/english/welcome.asp** (viewed February 7, 2005).

No company can win if its products and offerings resemble every other product and offering. Organizations must pursue relevant positioning and differentiation. As part of the strategic brand management process, each organization and offering must represent a distinctive big idea in the mind of the target market.

As the CTC's challenges with positioning Canada demonstrate, even when an organization (in this case, a country) succeeds in distinguishing itself, it may not be all that effective at driving the desired outcome. As the CTC is doing with Canada, companies normally reformulate their marketing strategies and offerings several times. Economic conditions change, competitors launch new assaults, and products pass through new stages of buyer interest and requirements. Marketers must develop strategies for each stage in the product's life cycle. The goal is to extend the product's life and profitability, keeping in mind that products do not last forever. This chapter explores specific ways a company can effectively position and differentiate its offerings to achieve a competitive advantage throughout the life cycle of a product or an offering.

Developing and Communicating a Positioning Strategy

All marketing strategy is built on STP—*segmentation*, *targeting*, and *positioning*. A company discovers different needs and groups in the marketplace, targets those needs and groups that it can satisfy in a superior way, and then positions its offering so that the target market recognizes the company's distinctive offering and image. If a company does a poor job of positioning, the market will be confused. This happened when National Car Company and Alamo Rent-a-Car were combined by their former parent, ANC Rental Corp.

National Car Rental and Alamo Rent-a-Car

Premium brand National traditionally catered to business travellers, whereas Alamo Rent-a-Car got 90 percent of its business from leisure travellers. After the two merged, the dual Alamo/National logos were plastered on everything from airport shuttle buses to workers' polo shirts. Customers of both Alamo and National had problems distinguishing between the brands, even though National's cars typically rented for 10 to 20 percent more than Alamo's. After all, the customers had to stand in the same line behind the same airport counter, receive service from the same rental agents, ride the same shuttle buses, and drive cars from the same fleet. National was most hurt by the lack of differentiation at these key touch points, and its market share fell 5 to 10 percent.[1]

If a company does an excellent job of positioning, then it can work out the rest of its marketing planning and differentiation from its positioning strategy. We define positioning as follows: **Positioning** is the act of designing the company's offering and image to occupy a distinctive place in the mind of the target market. The goal is to locate the brand in the minds of consumers to maximize the potential benefit to the firm. A good brand positioning helps guide marketing strategy by clarifying the brand's essence, what goals it helps the consumer achieve, and how it does so in a unique way. The result of positioning is the successful creation of a customer-focused value proposition, a cogent reason why the target market should buy the product. Table 10.1 shows how three companies—Butterball, Volvo, and Domino's—defined their value proposition given their target customers, benefits, and prices.

The word *positioning* was popularized by two advertising executives, Al Ries and Jack Trout. They see positioning as a creative exercise done with an existing product:

> Positioning starts with a product. A piece of merchandise, a service, a company, an institution, or even a person. . . . But positioning is not what you do to a product. Positioning is what you do to the mind of the prospect. That is, you position the product in the mind of the prospect.[2]

"Marketing Insight: Value Disciplines Positioning" offers another point of view about positioning. According to virtually all approaches, positioning requires that similarities and differences between brands be defined and communicated. Specifically, deciding on a positioning requires

TABLE 10.1	EXAMPLES OF VALUE PROPOSITIONS, DEMAND STATES, AND MARKETING TASKS			
Company and Product	**Target Customers**	**Benefits**	**Price**	**Value Proposition**
Butterball (turkey)	Inexperienced or time-pressured cooks	Juicy turkey guaranteed	20% premium	Risk- and hassle-free cooking for anyone lacking time or confidence in preparing a weekday or holiday meal
Volvo (station wagon)	Safety-conscious "upscale" families	Durability and safety	20% premium	The safest, most durable wagon in which your family can ride
Domino's (pizza)	Convenience-minded pizza lovers	Delivery speed and good quality	15% premium	A good pizza, delivered to your door within 30 minutes of ordering, at a moderate price

MARKETING INSIGHT

Value Disciplines Positioning

Two consultants, Michael Treacy and Fred Wiersema, proposed a positioning framework called *value disciplines*. Within its industry, a firm could aspire to be the *product leader,* the *operationally excellent firm*, or the *customer intimate firm*. This framework is based on the notion that in every market there is a mix of three types of customers. Some customers favour the firm that is on the technological frontier (product leadership), other customers want highly reliable performance (operational excellence), and still others want high responsiveness in meeting their individual needs (customer intimacy).

A firm cannot normally be best in all three ways, or even in two ways. Each value discipline requires different managerial mind-sets and investments that often conflict. Thus McDonald's excels at operational excellence, but could not afford to slow down its service to prepare hamburgers differently for each customer. Nor could McDonald's lead in new products because each addition would disrupt the smooth functioning of normal operations. Even within a large company, such as GE, each division might follow a different value discipline: GE's major appliance division pursues operational excellence, its engineered plastics division pursues customer intimacy, and its jet engine division pursues product leadership.

Treacy and Wiersema propose that a business should follow four rules for success:

1. Become the best at one of the three value disciplines.

2. Achieve an adequate performance level in the other two disciplines.

3. Keep improving one's superior position in the chosen discipline so as not to lose out to a competitor.

4. Keep becoming more adequate in the other two disciplines, because competitors keep raising customers' expectations.

Sources: Michael Treacy and Fred Wiersema, *The Disciplines of Market Leaders* (Reading, MA: Addison-Wesley, 1994).

determining a frame of reference by identifying the target market and the competition, and identifying the ideal points-of-parity and points-of-difference brand associations.

Competitive Frame of Reference

A starting point in defining a competitive frame of reference for a brand positioning is to determine **category membership**—the products or sets of products with which a brand competes and which function as close substitutes. As we discuss in Chapter 11, competitive analysis will consider a whole host of factors—including the resources, capabilities, and likely intentions of various other firms—in choosing those markets where consumers can be profitably serviced.

Target market decisions are often a key determinant of the competitive frame of reference. Deciding to target a certain type of consumer can define the nature of competition because certain firms have decided to target that segment in the past (or plan to do so in the future), or consumers in that segment already may look to certain brands in their purchase decisions. Determining the proper competitive frame of reference requires understanding consumer behaviour and the consideration sets consumers use in making brand choices. In the United Kingdom, for example, the Automobile Association has positioned itself as the fourth "emergency service"—along with police, fire, and ambulance—to convey greater credibility and urgency. And look at how Maple Leaf Foods has positioned itself:

Maple Leaf Foods

The meat industry in Canada and around the world has been challenged by issues ranging from mad cow disease to allegations of uninspected meat. Maple Leaf Foods responded to these issues by incorporating consumer concerns into core brand positioning efforts. It all started in the early 1990s, when the *Maple Leaf Prime™ Chicken* brand was launched as part of the company's vision to transform into a highly innovative food processor and packaged-goods manufacturer. Maple Leaf Foods was the first manufacturer to introduce a branded product in the meat counter and also pioneered air-chilled chicken, a processing technology that was new to the Canadian market. In 2001, the company developed *Maple Leaf Prime™ Naturally**, Canada's leading brand of value-added chicken, fed all-vegetable grain feed containing no animal by-products. This product was developed to respond to consumers who wanted an added level of confidence in the food they purchase. In 2002, Maple Leaf Foods launched an overarching new corporate positioning and brand promise behind all Maple Leaf products: "We Take Care." The Maple Leaf brand commitment provides consumers with the highest level of food safety assurance. This gives consumers greater confidence and assurance around taste delivery, family appeal, and, ultimately, the safety of Maple Leaf products.

*Canada's Leading Brand of Chicken.

Points-of-Parity and Points-of-Difference

Once the competitive frame of reference for positioning has been fixed by defining the customer target market and nature of competition, marketers can define the appropriate points-of-difference and points-of-parity associations.[4]

POINTS-OF-DIFFERENCE   Points-of-difference (PODs) are attributes or benefits consumers strongly associate with a brand, positively evaluate, and believe that they could not find to the same extent with a competitive brand. Strong, favourable, and unique brand associations that make up PODs may be based on virtually any type of attribute or benefit. Examples are FedEx (*guaranteed overnight delivery*), Nike (*performance*), and Lexus (*quality*).

Creating strong, favourable, and unique associations as PODs is a real challenge, but essential in terms of competitive brand positioning. Consider the success of IKEA.

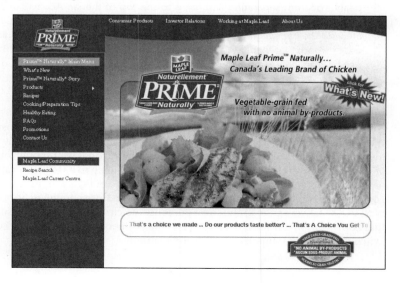

Maple Leaf Foods' Prime brand positioning has been effective in boosting consumer confidence around its food safety.

IKEA

Swedish retailer IKEA took a luxury product—home furnishings and furniture—and made it a reasonably priced alternative for the mass market. IKEA supports its low prices by having customers self-serve, deliver, and assemble the products themselves. IKEA also gains a POD through its product offerings. As one commentator noted, "IKEA built its reputation on the notion that Sweden produces good, safe, well-built things for the masses. It has some of the most innovative designs at the lowest cost out there." It also operates an excellent restaurant in each store (rare among furniture stores); offers child-care services while the parents shop; offers a membership program entitling members to special discounts on their purchases beyond the normal low price; and mails out millions of catalogues featuring the latest furniture.[5]

POINTS-OF-PARITY Points-of-parity (POPs), on the other hand, are associations that are not necessarily unique to the brand but may in fact be shared with other brands. These types of associations come in two basic forms: category and competitive.

Category POPs are associations consumers view as essential to be a legitimate and credible offering within a certain product or service category. In other words, they represent necessary—but not necessarily sufficient—conditions for brand choice. Consumers might not consider a travel agency truly a travel agency unless it is able to make air and hotel reservations, provide advice about leisure packages, and offer various ticket payment and delivery options. Category POPs may change over time due to technological advances, legal developments, or consumer trends, but they are the "greens fees" to play the marketing game.

Competitive POPs are associations designed to negate competitors' PODs. If, in the eyes of consumers, the brand association designed to be the competitor's POD is as strong for a brand as for competitors *and* the brand is able to establish another association as strong, favourable, and unique as part of its POD, then the brand should be in a superior competitive position. In other words, if a brand can "break even" in those areas where the competitors are trying to find an advantage *and* can achieve advantages in other areas, the brand should be in a strong—and perhaps unbeatable—competitive position. While other luxury goods makers slumped in 2000, Coach saw its sales zoom ahead by adding style and fashion to its legendary rugged bags and briefcases.[6] As another example, see what J. M. Smucker did with Adams Natural Peanut Butter:

Adams Natural Peanut Butter

In 2000, Toronto's J. M. Smucker acquired the Adams brand natural peanut butter, with the intention of growing it in a market already dominated by well-established players such as Kraft and Skippy. As part of this objective, the company created a new campaign focused on a key POD between natural peanut butter and stabilized peanut butters (such as Kraft and Skippy). Stabilized peanut butters contain sugar and hydrogenated oil, which prevents the natural peanut oil from separating and rising to the top of the jar. Adams's strategy was to use this difference as a means to communicate the natural quality of the product. One billboard created for the campaign was made out of rough-hewn wood with a headline, also constructed out of wood, that reads: "Like Adams peanut butter, this billboard is 100% natural." The campaign launched in Vancouver and Victoria, Adams's two best-established markets.[7]

POPS VERSUS PODS To achieve a POP on a particular attribute or benefit, a sufficient number of consumers must believe that the brand is "good enough" on that dimension. There is a "zone" or "range of tolerance or acceptance" with POPs. The brand does not literally have to be seen as equal to competitors, but consumers must feel that the brand does well enough on that particular attribute or benefit. If consumers feel that way, they may be willing to base their evaluations and decisions on other factors potentially more favourable to the brand. A light beer presumably would never taste as good as a full-strength beer, but it would have to taste close enough to be able to effectively compete. With PODs, however, the brand must demonstrate clear superiority. Consumers must be convinced that Louis Vuitton has the most stylish handbags, Energizer is the longest-lasting battery, and Merrill Lynch offers the best financial advice and planning.

Often, the key to positioning is not so much in achieving a POD as in achieving POPs!

Visa versus American Express

Visa's POD in the credit card category is that it is the most widely available card, which underscores the category's main benefit of convenience. American Express, on the other hand, has built the equity of its brand by highlighting the prestige associated with the use of its card. Having established their PODs, Visa and American Express now compete by attempting to blunt each other's advantage to create POPs. Visa offers gold and platinum cards to enhance the prestige of its brand and advertises "It's Everywhere You Want to Be" in settings that reinforce exclusivity and acceptability. American Express has substantially increased the number of vendors that accept its cards and created other value enhancements through its "Make Life Rewarding" program.

Establishing Category Membership

Target customers are aware that Maybelline is a leading brand of cosmetics, Cheerios is a leading brand of cereal, Accenture is a leading consulting firm, and so on. Often, however, marketers must inform consumers of a brand's category membership. Perhaps the most obvious situation is the introduction of new products, especially when the category membership is not apparent. This uncertainty can be a special problem for high-tech products. There are also situations where consumers know a brand's category membership, but may not be convinced that the brand is a valid member of the category. For example, consumers may be aware that Hewlett Packard produces digital cameras, but they may not be certain whether Hewlett-Packard cameras are in the same class with Sony, Olympus, Kodak, and Nikon. In this instance, HP might find it useful to reinforce category membership.

Brands are sometimes affiliated with categories in which they do not hold membership. This approach is one way to highlight a brand's POD, providing that consumers know the brand's actual membership. With this approach, however, it is important that consumers understand what the brand stands for, and not just what it is *not*. It is important not to be trapped between categories. The Konica e-mini M digital camera and MP3 player was marketed as the "four-in-one entertainment solution" but suffered from functional deficiencies in each of its product applications and languished in the marketplace.[8]

The preferred approach to positioning is to inform consumers of a brand's membership before stating its POD. Presumably, consumers need to know what a product is and what function it serves before deciding whether it dominates the brands against which it competes. For new products, initial advertising often concentrates on creating brand awareness and subsequent advertising attempts to craft the brand image.

Occasionally, a company will try to straddle two frames of reference:

BMW

When BMW first made a strong competitive push into the North American market in the early 1980s, it positioned the brand as being the only automobile that offered both luxury *and* performance. At that time, American luxury cars were seen by many as lacking performance, and American performance cars were seen as lacking luxury. By relying on the design of its cars, its German heritage, and other aspects of a well-conceived marketing program, BMW was able to simultaneously achieve (1) a POD on luxury and a POP on performance with respect to performance cars, and (2) a POD on performance and a POP on luxury with respect to luxury cars. The clever slogan "The Ultimate Driving Machine" effectively captured the newly created umbrella category—luxury performance cars.

While a straddle positioning often is attractive as a means of reconciling potentially conflicting consumer goals, it also carries an extra burden. If the POPs and PODs with respect to both categories are not credible, the brand may not be viewed as a legitimate player in either category. Many early PDAs that unsuccessfully tried to straddle categories ranging from pagers to laptop computers provide a vivid illustration of this risk.

There are three main ways to convey a brand's category membership:

1. *Announcing category benefits.* To reassure consumers that a brand will deliver on the fundamental reason for using a category, benefits are frequently used to announce category membership. Thus, industrial tools might claim to have durability and antacids might announce their efficacy. A brownie mix might attain membership in the baked desserts category by claiming the benefit of great taste and support this benefit claim by possessing high-quality ingredients (performance) or by showing users delighting in its consumption (imagery).

2. *Comparing to exemplars.* Well-known, noteworthy brands in a category can also be used to specify category membership. When Tommy Hilfiger was an unknown, advertising announced his membership as a great American designer by associating him with Geoffrey Beene, Stanley Blacker, Calvin Klein, and Perry Ellis, who were recognized members of that category.

3. *Relying on the product descriptor.* The product descriptor that follows the brand name is often a concise means of conveying category origin. Ford Motor Co. invested more than US$1 billion on a radical new 2004 model named the X-Trainer, which combines the attributes of an SUV, a minivan, and a station wagon. To communicate its unique position—and to avoid association with its Explorer and Country Squire models—the vehicle is designated a "sports wagon."[9]

Choosing POPs and PODs

Points-of-parity are driven by the needs of category membership (to create category POPs) and the necessity of negating competitors' PODs (to create competitive POPs). In choosing points-of-difference, two important considerations are that consumers find the POD desirable and that the firm has the capabilities to deliver on the POD.

There are three key consumer desirability criteria for PODs:

1. *Relevance.* Target consumers must find the POD personally relevant and important. The Westin Stamford hotel in Singapore advertised that it was the world's tallest hotel, but a hotel's height is not important to many tourists.

2. *Distinctiveness.* Target consumers must find the POD distinctive and superior. When entering a category where there are established brands, the challenge is to find a viable basis for differentiation. Splenda sugar substitute overtook Equal and Sweet 'n Low to become the leader in its category in 2003 by differentiating itself on its authenticity as a product derived from sugar, without any of the associated drawbacks.[10]

3. *Believability.* Target consumers must find the POD believable and credible. A brand must offer a compelling reason for choosing it over the other options. Mountain Dew may argue that it is more energizing than other soft drinks and support this claim by noting that it has a higher level of caffeine. Chanel No. 5 perfume may claim to be the quintessential elegant French perfume and support this claim by noting the long association between Chanel and haute couture.

There are three key deliverability criteria:

1. *Feasibility.* The firm must be able to actually create the POD. The product design and marketing offering must support the desired association. Does communicating the desired association involve real changes to the product itself, or just perceptual ones as to how the consumer thinks of the product or brand? It is obviously easier to convince consumers of some fact about the brand that they were unaware of and may have overlooked than to make changes in the product *and* convince consumers of these changes. General Motors has had to work to overcome public perceptions that Cadillac is not a youthful, contemporary brand.

2. *Communicability.* It is very difficult to create an association that is not consistent with existing consumer knowledge or that consumers, for whatever reason, have trouble believing. Consumers must be given a compelling reason and understandable rationale as to why the brand can deliver the desired benefit. What factual, verifiable evidence or "proof points" can be given as support so that consumers will actually believe in the brand and its desired associations? Substantiators often come in the form of patented, branded ingredients, such as Nivea Wrinkle Control Crème with Q10 co-enzyme or Herbal Essences hair conditioner with Hawafena.

3. *Sustainability.* Is the positioning pre-emptive, defensible, and difficult to attack? Can the favourability of a brand association be reinforced and strengthened over time? If yes, the positioning is likely to be enduring. Sustainability will depend on internal commitment and use of resources as well as external market forces. It is generally easier for market leaders such as

Gillette, Intel, and Microsoft, whose positioning is based in part on demonstrable product performance, to sustain their positioning than it is for market leaders such as Gucci, Prada, and Hermes, whose positioning is based on fashion and is thus subject to the whims of a more fickle market.

Marketers must decide at which level(s) to anchor the brand's points-of-differences. At the lowest level are the *brand attributes*, at the next level are the *brand's benefits*, and at the top are the *brand's values*. Thus marketers of Dove soap can talk about its attribute of one-quarter cleansing cream; or its benefit of softer skin; or its value of being more attractive. Attributes are typically the least desirable level to position. First, the buyer is more interested in benefits. Second, competitors can easily copy attributes. Third, the current attributes may become less desirable.

Research has shown, however, that brands can sometimes be successfully differentiated on seemingly irrelevant attributes *if* consumers infer the proper benefit. Procter & Gamble differentiates its Folger's instant coffee by its "flaked coffee crystals" created through a "unique patented process." In reality, the coffee particle's shape is irrelevant because the crystal immediately dissolves in the hot water. Saying that a brand of coffee is "mountain grown" is irrelevant because most coffee is mountain grown. "Marketing Memo: Writing a Positioning Statement" outlines how positioning can be expressed formally.

Marketing Memo

Writing a Positioning Statement

To communicate a company or brand positioning, marketing plans often include a *positioning statement*. The statement should follow the form: To *(target group and need)* our *(Brand)* is *(concept)* that *(point-of-difference)*. For example: "To *busy professionals who need to stay organized, Palm Pilot* is *an electronic organizer* that *allows you to back up files on your PC more easily and reliably than competitive products.*" Sometimes the positioning statement is more detailed:

> *Mountain Dew:* To young, active soft-drink consumers who have little time for sleep, Mountain Dew is the soft drink that gives you more energy than any other brand because it has the highest level of caffeine. With Mountain Dew, you can stay alert and keep going even when you haven't been able to get a good night's sleep.

Note that the positioning first states the product's membership in a category (e.g., Mountain Dew is a soft drink) and then shows its point-of-difference from other members of the group (e.g., has more caffeine). The product's membership in the category suggests the points-of-parity that it might have with other products in the category, but the case for the product rests on its points-of-difference. Sometimes the marketer will put the product in a surprisingly different category before indicating the points-of-difference.

Sources: Bobby J. Calder and Steven J. Reagan, "Brand Design," in *Kellogg on Marketing,* edited by Dawn Iacobucci (New York: John Wiley & Sons, 2001), p. 61; Alice M. Tybout and Brian Sternthal, "Brand Positioning," in *Kellogg on Marketing,* edited by Dawn Iacobucci (New York: John Wiley & Sons, 2001), p. 54.

Creating POPs and PODs

One common difficulty in creating a strong competitive brand positioning is that many of the attributes or benefits that make up the POPs and PODs are negatively correlated. If consumers rate the brand highly on one particular attribute or benefit, they also rate it poorly on another important attribute. For example, it might be difficult to position a brand as "inexpensive" and at the same time assert that it is "of the highest quality." Table 10.2 displays some other examples of negatively correlated attributes and benefits. Moreover, individual attributes and benefits often have positive *and* negative aspects. For example, consider a long-lived brand that is seen as having a great deal of heritage. Heritage could suggest experience, wisdom, and expertise. On the other hand, it could also easily be seen as a negative: it might imply being old-fashioned and not up to date.

TABLE 10.2	EXAMPLES OF NEGATIVELY CORRELATED ATTRIBUTES & BENEFITS	
Low Price vs. High Quality		Powerful vs. Safe
Taste vs. Low Calories		Strong vs. Refined
Nutritious vs. Good Tasting		Ubiquitous vs. Exclusive
Efficacious vs. Mild		Varied vs. Simple

Moores Clothing for Men

Men's clothing retailer Moores is a company that must balance a negatively correlated POD and POP as a suit retailer that is positioned as the cheaper alternative, while still maintaining quality (a difficult task when you are selling men's suits—hardly a budget purchase). The company ran into problems when it launched a campaign that diluted this principle POD (quality business attire at reasonable prices). The company made the mistake of launching a campaign that featured television spots such as "Garden Parties," which gave the company a more upscale positioning similar to Harry Rosen's, which targeted upscale fashion-conscious yuppies. Moores' success had been built on helping the everyday guy who doesn't like to shop find a suit that won't break the bank. Moores discovered very quickly that the strategy was too high-class and, as a result, its sales began to decline. The company then quickly decided to return to a positioning that had brought it much success in the past— "Well-dressed. Well-priced. Well-made" (originally launched in 1999)—targeting the average guy on the street, with a house and a mortgage, two kids, and a dog.[11]

Unfortunately, consumers typically want to maximize *both* attributes and benefits. Much of the art and science of marketing is dealing with trade-offs, and positioning is no different. The best approach clearly is to develop a product or service that performs well on both dimensions. BMW was able to establish its "luxury and performance" straddle positioning due in large part to product design and the fact that the car was seen as both luxurious and high-performance. Gore-Tex was able to overcome the seemingly conflicting product image of "breathable" and "waterproof" through technological advances. There are additional ways to address the problem of negatively correlated POPs and PODs.

PRESENT SEPARATELY An expensive but sometimes effective approach to address negatively correlated attributes and benefits is to launch two different marketing campaigns, each one devoted to a different brand attribute or benefit. These campaigns may run together at one point in time or sequentially over time. Head & Shoulders shampoo met success in Europe with a dual campaign where one campaign emphasized its dandruff removal efficacy while another emphasized the appearance and beauty of hair after its use. The hope is that consumers will be less critical when judging the POP and POD benefits in isolation. The downside with such an approach is that you need two strong campaigns. Moreover, if marketers do not address the negative correlation head-on, consumers may not develop the desired positive associations.

LEVERAGE EQUITY OF ANOTHER ENTITY Brands can potentially link themselves to any kind of entity that possesses the right kind of equity as a means to establish an attribute or benefit as a POP or POD. Branded ingredients may also lend some credibility to a questionable attribute in consumers' minds. Borrowing equity, however, is not riskless. Personal computer manufacturers such as IBM and Compaq found that the Intel Inside co-op advertising program, which gave Intel exposure in the PC makers' ad, resulted in consumers seeking Intel-based computers.

REDEFINE THE RELATIONSHIP Another potentially powerful but often difficult way to address the negative relationship between attributes and benefits is to convince consumers that, in fact, the relationship is positive. This redefinition can be accomplished by providing consumers a different perspective and suggesting that they may be overlooking or ignoring certain considerations.

Apple Computers

When Apple Computers launched MacIntosh, its key POD was "user friendly." Many consumers valued ease of use, especially those who bought personal computers for the home. One drawback with a "user friendly" association was that customers who bought personal computers for business applications thought that if a personal computer was easy to use, then it must not be very powerful. Recognizing this potential problem, Apple ran a clever ad campaign with the tagline "The Power to Be Your Best." The strategy behind the ads was that because Apple was easy to use, people in fact did just that—they used it!—a simple but important indication of "power." In other words, the most powerful computers were ones people actually used.

Weighing only 2.9 pounds, the Mac mini offers users the ability to "live the digital life in stylish simplicity." (www.apple.com/macmini)

Differentiation Strategies

To avoid the commodity trap, marketers must start with the belief that you can differentiate anything. (See "Marketing Memo: How to Derive Fresh Consumer Insights to Differentiate Products and Services.") Brands can be differentiated on the basis of many variables. WestJet has differentiated itself in several different ways.

WestJet

This Calgary-based airline (modelled on Dallas-based Southwest Airlines) carved its niche in short-haul flights with low prices, reliable service, and an off-the-wall sense of humour. To differentiate itself from other Canadian airlines, which it saw as look-alikes, it did not compete head-on for the coveted business traveller market to ensure profitability. Rather, it began specializing in serving what it calls the VFR market (people visiting friends and relatives). It saw its main competitor as the family car and realized that if it could offer lower fares, people would choose to fly rather than drive to visit friends and relatives. WestJet keeps costs low by offering only basic in-flight service (no meals, no movies) and rapid turnaround at the gates to keep the planes in the air.[12]

The obvious means of differentiation, and often the most compelling ones to consumers, relate to aspects of the product and service. Swatch offers colourful, fashionable watches. Subway differentiates itself in terms of healthy sandwiches as an alternative to fast food. Method built a US$10 million business in a year by creating a line of nontoxic household cleaning products with bright colours and sleek designs totally unique to the category.[13] In competitive markets, however, firms may need to go beyond these. Among the other dimensions a company can use to differentiate its market offering are personnel, channel, and image. This section highlights these three different differentiation strategies.

Product Differentiation

As Chapter 12 describes, brands can be differentiated on the basis of a number of different product or service dimensions: product form, features, performance, conformance, durability, reliability, reparability, style, and design, as well as such service dimensions as ordering ease, delivery, installa-

Marketing Memo

How to Derive Fresh Consumer Insights to Differentiate Products and Services

In "Discovering New Points of Differentiation," Ian C. MacMillan and Rita Gunther McGrath argue that if companies examine customers' entire experience with a product or service—the consumption chain—they can uncover opportunities to position their offerings in ways that neither they nor their competitors thought possible. MacMillan and McGrath list a set of questions marketers can use to help them identify new, consumer-based points of differentiation:

- How do people become aware of their need for your product and service?
- How do consumers find your offering?
- How do consumers make their final selection?
- How do consumers order and purchase your product or service?
- What happens when your product or service is delivered?
- How is your product installed?
- How is your product or service paid for?
- How is your product stored?
- How is your product moved around?
- What is the consumer really using your product for?
- What do consumers need help with when they use your product?
- What about returns or exchanges?
- How is your product repaired or serviced?
- What happens when your product is disposed of or no longer used?

Source: Ian C. MacMillan and Rita Gunther McGrath, "Discovering New Points of Differentiation," *Harvard Business Review* (July–August 1997): 133–145.

tion, customer training, customer consulting, and maintenance and repair.

Besides these specific concerns, one more general positioning for brands is as "best quality." How important is a high-quality product positioning? The Strategic Planning Institute studied the impact of higher relative product quality and found a significantly positive correlation between relative product quality and return on investment (ROI).[14] High-quality business units earned more because premium quality allowed them to charge a premium price; they benefited from more repeat purchase, consumer loyalty, and positive word of mouth; and the costs of delivering more quality were not much higher than for business units producing low quality.

Quality will depend on actual product performance, but it is also communicated by choosing physical signs and cues. Here are some examples:

- A lawnmower manufacturer that claims its lawnmower is "powerful" has given it a noisy motor because buyers think noisy lawnmowers are more powerful.
- A truck manufacturer undercoats the chassis not because it needs undercoating but because undercoating suggests concern for quality.
- A car manufacturer makes sure its car doors make a solid sound when they slam shut because many buyers slam the doors in the showroom to test how well the car is built.
- Ritz Carlton hotels signal high quality by training employees to answer calls within three rings, to answer with a genuine "smile" in their voices, and to be extremely knowledgeable about all hotel services.

Quality is also communicated through other marketing elements. A high price usually signals premium quality. Quality image is also affected by packaging, distribution, advertising, and promotion. Here are some cases where a brand's quality image was hurt:

- A well-known frozen-food brand lost its prestige image by being on sale too often.
- A premium beer's image was hurt when it switched from bottles to cans.
- A highly regarded television receiver lost its quality image when mass-merchandise outlets began to carry it.

A manufacturer's reputation also contributes to the perception of quality. Certain companies are sticklers for quality—for example, consumers expect Nestlé and IBM products to be well made. Smart companies communicate quality to buyers and guarantee "customer satisfaction or your money back."

Personnel Differentiation

Companies can gain a strong competitive advantage through having better-trained people. Singapore Airlines enjoys an excellent reputation in large part because of its flight attendants. McDonald's people are courteous, IBM people are professional, and Disney people are upbeat. The sales forces of such companies as General Electric, Cisco, and Pfizer enjoy an excellent reputation.[15] Better-trained personnel exhibit six characteristics:

- *Competence*—they possess the required skill and knowledge.
- *Courtesy*—they are friendly, respectful, and considerate.
- *Credibility*—they are trustworthy.
- *Reliability*—they perform the service consistently and accurately.
- *Responsiveness*—they respond quickly to customers' requests and problems.
- *Communication*—they make an effort to understand the customer and communicate clearly.[16]

Retailers, large and small, are likely to use their front-line employees as a means of differentiating and positioning their brand. This is certainly true of Capital City Savings and Credit Union:

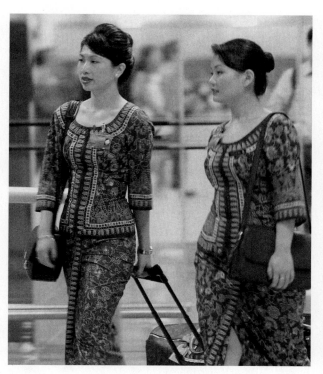

Becoming a Singapore Airlines flight attendant is not easy: Company requirements are strict. But Singapore Airlines has a worldwide reputation for excellent service, built largely on the customer relations skills of its flight attendants.

Capital City Savings and Credit Union

Capital City Savings and Credit Union Limited, located in Edmonton, traces its roots back to 1938 when it began business with a simple promise—to serve its members. Throughout its history, the credit union has excelled at providing its members financial health, giving community support, and being sure it had a well-cared-for staff in addition to its fully competitive products and services. It trains its staff to provide specialized services to meet a growing set of needs, well beyond those offered by traditional banks. Take its new auto specialist, Shawn Bazin. Before credit union members shop for a new or used car they can seek advice from Shawn, who will help them save money on financing or negotiate a fair price. Shawn can show them, for example, why zero percent financing isn't always the best deal. Talking to Shawn is a free service and it is only one of the value-added services Capital City's front-line employees provide for their members. Given this level of customer care, it's not surprising that Capital City was one of the 2003 winners of Canada's 50 Best Managed Companies.[17]

Channel Differentiation

Companies can achieve competitive advantage through the way they design their distribution channels' *coverage*, *expertise*, and *performance*. Caterpillar's success in the construction-equipment industry is based partly on superior channel development. Its dealers are found in more locations than competitors' dealers, and they are typically better trained and perform more reliably. Dell in computers and Avon in cosmetics distinguish themselves by developing and managing high-quality direct-marketing channels. Back in 1946, pet food was cheap, not too nutritious, and sold exclusively in supermarkets and the occasional feed store. Dayton, Ohio–based Iams found success selling premium pet food through regional veterinarians, breeders, and pet stores.

Apollo Group Inc.

Apollo Group Inc. has turned conventional higher education on its head by launching an online university geared toward the neglected market of working adults. University of Phoenix Online is one of Apollo's most successful ventures, with 50 000 students, and 2004's enrollment surged by 70 percent over the previous year. In 1989, it began offering working Canadians the chance to earn a degree, and many of Canada's traditional universities are paying attention since this competitor offers reasonable pricing in addition to convenience.[18]

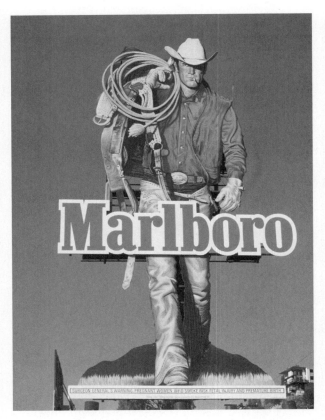

Image differentiation: The world-famous "Marlboro Man" image is instantly recognizable on billboards and in print ads.

Image Differentiation

Buyers respond differently to company and brand images. The primary way to account for Marlboro's extraordinary worldwide market share (around 30 percent) is that Marlboro's "macho cowboy" image has struck a responsive chord with much of the cigarette-smoking public. Wine and liquor companies also work hard to develop distinctive images for their brands.

Identity and image need to be distinguished. *Identity* is the way a company aims to identify or position itself or its product. *Image* is the way the public perceives the company or its products. An effective identity does three things: It establishes the product's character and value proposition, it conveys this character in a distinctive way, and it delivers emotional power beyond a mental image. For the identity to work, it must be conveyed through every available communication vehicle and brand contact. It should be diffused in ads, annual reports, brochures, catalogues, packaging, company stationery, and business cards. If "IBM means service," this message must be expressed in symbols, colours and slogans, atmosphere, events, and employee behaviour.

Even a seller's physical space can be a powerful image generator. Hyatt Regency hotels developed a distinctive image through its atrium lobbies. Companies can create a strong image by inviting prospects and customers to visit their headquarters and factories. Boeing, Ben & Jerry's, Hershey's, Saturn, and Crayola all sponsor excellent company tours that draw millions of visitors a year.[19] Companies such as Hallmark and Kohler have built corporate museums at their headquarters that display their history and the drama of producing and marketing their products. Many tourists who make their way through Toronto visit the Bata Shoe Museum on Bloor Street to get a peek at over 10 000 pairs of shoes ranging from Chinese bound-foot shoes and ancient Egyptian sandals to chestnut-crushing clogs and Elton John's platforms. The museum, originally built simply to house and make public the incredible collection of shoes that the Bata family had amassed, also serves to promote the Bata brand in a very unique and differentiated manner.[20]

"Marketing Memo: Exceeding Customer Expectations" describes one systematic approach to developing a differentiated customer-oriented offering.

Product Life-Cycle Marketing Strategies

A company's positioning and differentiation strategy must change as the product, market, and competitors change over the *product life cycle* (PLC). To say that a product has a life cycle is to assert four things:

1. Products have a limited life.

2. Product sales pass through distinct stages, each posing different challenges, opportunities, and problems to the seller.

3. Profits rise and fall at different stages of the product life cycle.

4. Products require different marketing, financial, manufacturing, purchasing, and human resource strategies in each life-cycle stage.

Product Life Cycles

Most product life-cycle curves are portrayed as bell-shaped (see Figure 10.1). This curve is typically divided into four stages: introduction, growth, maturity, and decline.[21]

1. *Introduction.* A period of slow sales growth as the product is introduced in the market. Profits are nonexistent because of the heavy expenses of product introduction.

2. *Growth.* A period of rapid market acceptance and substantial profit improvement.

3. *Maturity.* A slowdown in sales growth because the product has achieved acceptance by most potential buyers. Profits stabilize or decline because of increased competition.

4. *Decline.* Sales show a downward drift and profits erode.

The PLC concept can be used to analyze a product category (liquor), a product form (white liquor), a product (vodka), or a brand (Smirnoff). Not all products exhibit a bell-shaped PLC.[22] Three common alternative patterns are shown in Figure 10.2.

Figure 10.2(a) shows a *growth-slump-maturity pattern*, often characteristic of small kitchen appliances such as handheld mixers and bread makers. Sales grow rapidly when the product is first introduced and then fall to a "petrified" level that is sustained by late adopters buying the product for the first time and early adopters replacing the product.

The *cycle-recycle pattern* in Figure 10.2(b) often describes the sales of new drugs. The pharmaceutical company aggressively promotes its new drug, and this produces the first cycle. Later, sales start declining and the company gives the drug another promotion push, which produces a second cycle (usually of smaller magnitude and duration).[23]

Another common pattern is the *scalloped PLC* in Figure 10.2(c). Here sales pass through a succession of life cycles based on the discovery of new-product characteristics, uses, or users. Nylon's sales, for example, show a scalloped pattern because of the many new uses—parachutes, hosiery, shirts, carpeting, boat sails, automobile tires—that continue to be discovered over time.[24]

Style, Fashion, and Fad Life Cycles

We need to distinguish three special categories of product life cycles—styles, fashions, and fads (Figure 10.3). A style is a basic and distinctive mode of expression appearing in a field of human endeavour. Styles appear in homes (colonial, ranch, Cape Cod); clothing (formal, casual, funky); and art (realistic, surrealistic, abstract). A style can last for generations, and go in and out of vogue. A fashion is a currently accepted or popular style in a given field. Fashions pass through four stages: distinctiveness, emulation, mass fashion, and decline.[25]

The length of a fashion cycle is hard to predict. One point of view is that fashions end because they represent a purchase compromise, and consumers start looking for missing attributes.[26] For example, as automobiles become smaller, they become less comfortable, and then a growing number of buyers start wanting larger cars. Furthermore, too many consumers adopt the fashion, thus turning others away. Another observation is that the length of a particular fashion cycle depends on the extent to which the fashion

Marketing Memo

Exceeding Customer Expectations

Crego and Schiffrin have proposed that customer-centred organizations should study what customers value and then prepare an offering that exceeds their expectations. They see this as a three-step process:

1. *Defining the customer value model.* The company first lists all the product and service factors that might influence the target customers' perception of value.

2. *Building the customer value hierarchy.* The company now assigns each factor to one of four groups: basic, expected, desired, and unanticipated. Consider the set of factors at a fine restaurant:

   - *Basic.* The food is edible and delivered in a timely fashion. (If this is all the restaurant does right, the customer would normally not be satisfied.)

   - *Expected.* There is good china and tableware, a linen tablecloth and napkin, flowers, discreet service, and well-prepared food. (These factors make the offering acceptable, but not exceptional.)

   - *Desired.* The restaurant is pleasant and quiet, and the food is especially good and interesting.

   - *Unanticipated.* The restaurant serves a complimentary sorbet between the courses and places candy on the table after the last course is served.

3. *Deciding on the customer value package.* Now the company chooses that combination of tangible and intangible items, experiences, and outcomes designed to outperform competitors and win the customers' delight and loyalty.

Sources: Edwin T. Crego Jr. and Peter D. Schiffrin, *Customer Centered Reengineering* (Homewood, IL: Irwin, 1995).

FIGURE 10.1

Sales and Profit Life Cycles

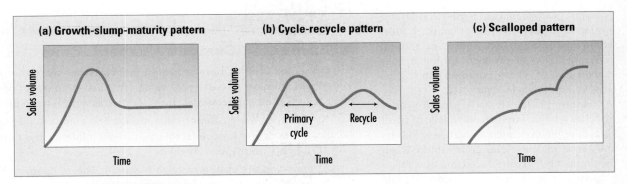

FIGURE 10.2

Common Product Life-Cycle Patterns

FIGURE 10.3

Style, Fashion, and Fad Life Cycles

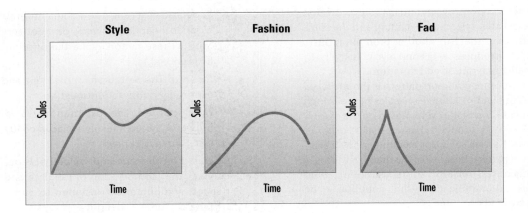

meets a genuine need, is consistent with other trends in the society, satisfies societal norms and values, and does not exceed technological limits as it develops.[27]

Fads are fashions that come quickly into public view, are adopted with great zeal, peak early, and decline very fast. Their acceptance cycle is short, and they tend to attract only a limited following of those who are searching for excitement or want to distinguish themselves from others. Fads do not survive because they do not normally satisfy a strong need. The marketing winners are those who recognize fads early and leverage them into products with staying power. Here is a success story of a company that managed to extend a fad's life span:

Trivial Pursuit

Since its debut at the International Toy Fair in 1982, Trivial Pursuit (developed by two Canadian entrepreneurs) has sold 65 million copies in 18 languages in 32 countries, and it remains one of the best-selling adult games. Parker Brothers has kept the product's popularity going by making a new game with updated questions every year. It also keeps creating offshoots—travel packs, a children's version, Trivial Pursuit Genus IV, and an interactive CD-ROM from Virgin Entertainment Interactive. The game has its own Web site (www. trivialpursuit.com), which received 100 000 visitors in its initial two-month test period. If you are having trouble making dinner conversation on a date—no problem: NTN Entertainment Network has put Trivial Pursuit in about 3000 restaurants.[28]

Marketing Strategies: Introduction Stage and the Pioneer Advantage

Because it takes time to roll out a new product, work out the technical problems, fill dealer pipelines, and gain consumer acceptance, sales growth tends to be slow at this stage.[29] Sales of expensive new products such as high-definition TV are slowed by additional factors such as product complexity and fewer potential buyers.

Profits are negative or low in the introduction stage. Promotional expenditures are at their highest ratio to sales because of the need to (1) inform potential consumers, (2) induce product trial, and (3) secure distribution in retail outlets.[30] Firms focus on those buyers who are the readiest to buy, usually higher-income groups. Prices tend to be high because costs are high.

Companies that plan to introduce a new product must decide when to enter the market. To be first can be rewarding, but risky and expensive. To come in later makes sense if the firm can bring superior technology, quality, or brand strength.

Speeding up innovation time is essential in an age of shortening product life cycles. Being early can pay off. One study found that products that came out six months late—but on budget—earned an average of 33 percent less profit in their first five years; products that came out on time but 50 percent over budget cut their profits by only 4 percent.

Most studies indicate that the market pioneer gains the most advantage. Companies like Campbell, Coca-Cola, Hallmark, and Amazon.com developed sustained market dominance.[31] Carpenter and Nakamoto found that 19 out of 25 companies who were market leaders in 1923 were still the market leaders in 1983, 60 years later.[32] Robinson and Min found that in a sample of industrial goods businesses, 66 percent of pioneers survived at least ten years, versus 48 percent of the early followers.[33]

What are the sources of the pioneer's advantage?[34] Early users will recall the pioneer's brand name if the product satisfies them. The pioneer's brand also establishes the attributes the product class should possess. The pioneer's brand normally aims at the middle of the market and so captures more users. Customer inertia also plays a role, and there are producer advantages: economies of scale, technological leadership, patents, ownership of scarce assets, and other barriers to entry. Pioneers can have more effective marketing spending and enjoy higher rates of consumer repeat purchases. An alert pioneer can maintain its leadership indefinitely by pursuing various strategies.[35]

The pioneer advantage, however, is not inevitable.[36] Look at the fate of Bowmar (hand calculators), Apple's Newton (personal digital assistant), Netscape (Web browser), Reynolds (ballpoint pens), and Osborne (portable computers), market pioneers who were overtaken by later entrants. Steven Schnaars studied 28 industries where the imitators surpassed the innovators.[37] He found several weaknesses among the failing pioneers, including new products that were too crude, were improperly positioned, or appeared before there was strong demand; product-development costs that exhausted the innovator's resources; a lack of resources to compete against entering larger firms; and managerial incompetence or unhealthy complacency. Successful imitators thrived by offering lower prices, improving the product more continuously, or using brute market power to overtake the pioneer. None of the companies that now dominate in the manufacture of personal computers— including Dell, Gateway, and Compaq—were first movers.[38]

Golder and Tellis raise further doubts about the pioneer advantage.[39] They distinguish between an *inventor* (first to develop patents in a new-product category), a *product pioneer* (first to develop a working model), and a *market pioneer* (first to sell in the new-product category). They also include nonsurviving pioneers in their sample. They conclude that although pioneers may still have an advantage, a larger number of market pioneers fail than has been reported and a larger number of early market leaders (though not pioneers) succeed. Examples of later entrants overtaking market pioneers are IBM over Sperry in mainframe computers, Matsushita over Sony in VCRs, and GE over EMI in CAT scan equipment. In a more recent study, Tellis and Golder identify the following five factors as underpinning long-term market leadership: vision of a mass market, persistence, relentless innovation, financial commitment, and asset leverage.[40]

The pioneer should visualize the various product markets it could initially enter, knowing that it cannot enter all of them at once. Suppose market-segmentation analysis reveals the product market segments shown in Figure 10.4. The pioneer should analyze the profit potential of each product market singly and in combination and decide on a market expansion path. Thus the pioneer in Figure 10.4 plans first to enter product market P_1M_1, then move the product into a second market (P_1M_2), then surprise the competition by developing a second product for the second market (P_2M_2),

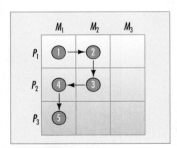

FIGURE 10.4

Long-Range Product-Market Expansion Strategy
(P_1 = Product 1; M_1 = Market 1)

then take the second product back into the first market (P_2M_1), and then launch a third product for the first market (P_3M_1). If this game plan works, the pioneer firm will own a good part of the first two segments and serve them with two or three products.

Marketing Strategies: Growth Stage

The growth stage is marked by a rapid climb in sales. Early adopters like the product, and additional consumers start buying it. New competitors enter, attracted by the opportunities. They introduce new product features and expand distribution.

Prices remain where they are or fall slightly, depending on how fast demand increases. Companies maintain their promotional expenditures at the same or at a slightly increased level to meet competition and to continue to educate the market. Sales rise much faster than promotional expenditures, causing a welcome decline in the promotion–sales ratio. Profits increase during this stage as promotion costs are spread over a larger volume and unit manufacturing costs fall faster than price declines, owing to the producer learning effect. Firms have to watch for a change from an accelerating to a decelerating rate of growth in order to prepare new strategies.

During this stage, the firm uses several strategies to sustain rapid market growth:

- It improves product quality and adds new product features and improved styling.
- It adds new models and flanker products (i.e., products of different sizes, flavours, and so forth that protect the main product).
- It enters new market segments.
- It increases its distribution coverage and enters new distribution channels.
- It shifts from product-awareness advertising to product-preference advertising.
- It lowers prices to attract the next layer of price-sensitive buyers.

These market expansion strategies strengthen the firm's competitive position. Consider how Yahoo! has fuelled growth.

Yahoo!

Founded in 1994 by Web-surfing Stanford University grad students, Yahoo! has become the number-one place to be on the Web, averaging 120 million visitors in a month. The company grew into more than just a search engine; it became a portal, offering a full-blown package of information and services, from e-mail to online shopping malls. Yahoo!'s revenues, which exceeded US$1.3 billion in 2003, come from a number of sources—banner ads, paid search, subscriptions for services such as personals, and a broadband partnership with SBC Communications. Yahoo!'s US$1.6 billion acquisition of Overture Services, a key paid search competitor of Google, helped strengthen its claim as a one-stop shop for advertisers. Yahoo! also continued to grow globally with strong emphasis on Europe and Asia.[41]

A firm in the growth stage faces a trade-off between high market share and high current profit. By spending money on product improvement, promotion, and distribution, it can capture a dominant position. It forgoes maximum current profit in the hope of making even greater profits in the next stage.

Marketing Strategies: Maturity Stage

At some point, the rate of sales growth will slow, and the product will enter a stage of relative maturity. This stage normally lasts longer than the previous stages and poses big challenges to marketing management. *Most products are in the maturity stage of the life cycle, and most marketing managers cope with the problem of marketing the mature product.*

The maturity stage divides into three phases: growth, stable, and decaying maturity. In the first phase, the sales growth rate starts to decline. There are no new distribution channels to fill. In the second phase, sales flatten on a per capita basis because of market saturation. Most potential consumers have tried the product, and future sales are governed by population growth and replacement demand. In the third phase, decaying maturity, the absolute level of sales starts to decline, and customers begin switching to other products.

The sales slowdown creates overcapacity in the industry, which leads to intensified competition. Competitors scramble to find niches. They engage in frequent markdowns. They increase advertising

Sustaining rapid market growth by adding new models and flanker products: the Snapple product line.

and trade and consumer promotion. They increase R&D budgets to develop product improvements and line extensions. They make deals to supply private brands. A shakeout begins, and weaker competitors withdraw. The industry eventually consists of well-entrenched competitors whose basic drive is to gain or maintain market share.

Dominating the industry are a few giant firms—perhaps a quality leader, a service leader, and a cost leader—that serve the whole market and make their profits mainly through high volume and lower costs. Surrounding these dominant firms is a multitude of market nichers, including market specialists, product specialists, and customizing firms. The issue facing a firm in a mature market is whether to struggle to become one of the "big three" and achieve profits through high volume and low cost or to pursue a niching strategy and achieve profits through low volume and a high margin.

Some companies abandon weaker products and concentrate on more profitable products and on new products. Yet they may be ignoring the high potential many mature markets and old products still have. Industries widely thought to be mature—autos, motorcycles, television, watches, cameras—were proved otherwise by the Japanese, who found ways to offer new value to customers. Seemingly moribund brands like RCA, Jell-O, and Ovaltine have achieved sales revivals through the exercise of marketing imagination.[42] The rebirth of the Mini after its acquisition by BMW is a case study in reviving an old, nearly forgotten brand.

Mini

The Mini began its public life in the UK in 1959. It was designed simply to be an affordable car that could seat four adults and still be small enough to cope with the increasing numbers of cars on the road. It became wildly popular in the 1960s when it was transformed from a "housewives' shopping car" to the must-have fashion accessory as it achieved international stardom on the rally scene. Nonetheless, the 1970 to 1990 period was a dark one for the brand and it came close to dying completely. BMW purchased the company in 2001 and saved the brand, taking it back to its roots, but incorporating new performance and safety features. Since the Mini hadn't been sold in Canada for almost 20 years, BMW Canada needed breakthrough advertising to revitalize the brand. It partnered with Taxi Advertising. It wasn't long until the Mini was winning awards—both for its engineering and its advertising—and BMW Canada began racking up sales.[43]

MARKET MODIFICATION   The company might try to expand the market for its mature brand by working with the two factors that make up sales volume:

Volume = number of brand users × usage rate per user

It can try to expand the number of brand users by *converting nonusers*. The key to the growth of airfreight service is the constant search for new users to whom air carriers can demonstrate the benefits of using airfreight rather than ground transportation.

Dental Floss

Despite the fact that the Academy of General Dentistry touts brushing and flossing as the best methods for fighting tooth decay, only 24 percent of households use floss. Several oral care marketers see this as a golden opportunity to convert the floss-averse. Aquafresh, owned by GlaxoSmithKline, has created Aquafresh Floss 'N' Cap which combines toothpaste and floss with a cap that doubles as a built-in floss dispenser. Johnson & Johnson, the market leader in this category, has developed a special handheld flosser called the Reach Access Daily Flosser. Glide, newly acquired by Procter & Gamble and the most recommended brand by dentists, perhaps has the easiest job convincing people to floss; the company got a boost when hygiene-obsessed Jerry Seinfeld used Glide on his hugely popular TV show.[44]

It can also try to expand the number of brand users by *entering new market segments*. When Goodyear decided to sell its tires via Wal-Mart, Sears, and Discount Tire, it boosted market share from 14 percent to 16 percent in the first year.[45] In recent years Alliance Atlantis has shifted the market segments that it targets:[46]

Alliance Atlantis Broadcasting (Life Network)

Alliance Atlantis Broadcasting Group has controlling interest in five established Canadian specialty television channels (including Showcase, Life Network, History Television, HGTV Canada, and Food Network Canada, as well as seven Canadian digital channels). Each channel has its own unique strategic brand, so that Alliance Atlantis can offer targeted programming to a varied audience as well as offer advertising choices to its commercial clients. Recently, the company began shifting the target demographic of its Life Network channel through a rebranding and repositioning effort, which effectively involved substantial changes in programming. When the Life Network was first launched in 1995, it was skewed toward a female demographic aged 25 to 54 with its "how-to" programming focused on crafts, decorating, and cooking. Since 2000, Life began featuring more real-life and youthful programs, such as *Matchmaker*, *Temptation Island*, and *America's Top Model*, in an attempt to lure women aged 18 to 49. More importantly, the company wanted to distance the Life Network from HGTV (Home and Garden Television) because it found the networks were attracting a similar audience. This was a problem because Alliance Atlantis wanted to offer a broad base of audiences to its advertisers. To support its repositioning effort Alliance Atlantis also redesigned the network's logo, since the original logo, with its primary colours, was deemed "too soft." The new logo is circular with deep purple and hot pink hues, carrying the tagline "real." The strategy has been successful, with 17 percent more viewers from the target demographic are tuning their dials to the new Life.[47]

As part of a major repositioning effort, the Life Network changed its logo to have a sassier appeal.

A third way to expand the number of brand users is *winning competitors' customers.* Examples of this approach abound. Marketers of Puffs facial tissues are always wooing Kleenex customers. Volume can also be increased by convincing current users to increase their brand usage: (1) *Use the product on more occasions.* Serve Campbell's soup for a snack. Use Heinz vinegar to clean windows. Take Kodak pictures of your pets. (2) *Use more of the product on each occasion.* Drink a larger glass of orange juice. (3) *Use the product in new ways.* Use Tums antacid as a calcium supplement.[48]

PRODUCT MODIFICATION   Managers also try to stimulate sales by modifying the product's characteristics through quality improvement, feature improvement, or style improvement.

Quality improvement aims at increasing the product's functional performance. A manufacturer can often overtake its competition by launching a "new and improved" product. Grocery manufacturers call this a "plus launch" and promote a new additive or advertise something as "stronger," "bigger," or "better." This strategy is effective to the extent that the quality is improved, buyers accept the claim of improved quality, and a sufficient number of buyers will pay for higher quality. In the case of the canned coffee industry, manufacturers are using "freshness" to better position their brands in the face of fierce competition from premium rivals, such as store brands where customers grind their own beans in the store. Kraft's Maxwell House will tout coffee sold in its new Fresh Seal packaging and P&G's Folger's ads will show how its AromaSeal canisters—plastic, peel-top, resealable, and easy-grip packages—will make their ground beans fresher.[49]

However, customers are not always willing to accept an "improved" product, as the classic tale of New Coke illustrates:

Coca-Cola

Battered by competition from the sweeter Pepsi-Cola, Coca-Cola decided in 1985 to replace its old formula with a sweeter variation, dubbed the New Coke. Coca-Cola spent US$4 million on market research. Blind taste tests showed that Coke drinkers preferred the new, sweeter formula, but the launch of New Coke provoked a huge uproar. Market researchers had measured the taste but had failed to measure the emotional attachment consumers had to Coca-Cola. There were angry letters, formal protests, and even lawsuit threats to force the retention of "The Real Thing." Ten weeks later, the company withdrew New Coke and reintroduced its century-old formula as "Classic Coke," giving the old formula even stronger status in the marketplace.

Feature improvement aims at adding new features (e.g., size, weight, materials, additives, accessories) that expand the product's performance, versatility, safety, or convenience. In 1998, after years of research and development, Vlasic created a cucumber 10 times larger than the traditional pickle cucumber. The chips, sold as "Hamburger Stackers," are large enough to cover the entire surface of a hamburger and are stacked a dozen high in jars.[50]

Pfizer also embarked on feature improvement for its Listerine brand:

Pfizer Inc.

"Obviously it's very difficult for people to walk down the street with a bottle of Listerine, take a swig and spit it out," says Dermot Boden, vice-president for global oral care at Pfizer Inc., which owns the Listerine brand. This is the rationale behind Cool Mint Listerine's PocketPak, oral care strips that dissolve instantly in the mouth, allowing for oral care on the go. Six years in the making, this new convenient form of Listerine not only enabled the brand to reach younger consumers, but also generated a hefty US$120 million in less than a year after its release.[51]

This strategy has several advantages. New features build the company's image as an innovator and win the loyalty of market segments that value these features. They provide an opportunity for free publicity and they generate sales force and distributor enthusiasm. The chief disadvantage is that feature improvements are easily imitated; unless there is a permanent gain from being first, the feature improvement might not pay off in the long run.[52]

Style improvement aims at increasing the product's aesthetic appeal. The periodic introduction of new car models is largely about style competition, as is the introduction of new packaging for

Feature improvement: Vlasic Hamburger Stackers.

consumer products. A style strategy might give the product a unique market identity. Yet style competition has problems. First, it is difficult to predict whether people—and which people—will like a new style. Second, a style change usually requires discontinuing the old style, and the company risks losing customers.

MARKETING PROGRAM MODIFICATION Product managers might also try to stimulate sales by modifying other marketing program elements. They should ask the following questions:

- *Prices.* Would a price cut attract new buyers? If so, should the list price be lowered, or should prices be lowered through price specials, volume or early-purchase discounts, freight cost absorption, or easier credit terms? Or would it be better to raise the price to signal higher quality?

- *Distribution.* Can the company obtain more product support and display in existing outlets? Can more outlets be penetrated? Can the company introduce the product into new distribution channels?

- *Advertising.* Should advertising expenditures be increased? Should the message or copy be changed? Should the media mix be changed? Should the timing, frequency, or size of ads be changed?

- *Sales promotion.* Should the company step up sales promotion—trade deals, cents-off coupons, rebates, warranties, gifts, and contests?

- *Personal selling.* Should the number or quality of salespeople be increased? Should the basis for sales force specialization be changed? Should sales territories be revised? Should sales force incentives be revised? Can sales-call planning be improved?

- *Services.* Can the company speed up delivery? Can it extend more technical assistance to customers? Can it extend more credit?

Marketers often debate which tools are most effective in the mature stage. For example, would the company gain more by increasing its advertising or its sales-promotion budget? Sales promotion has more impact at this stage because consumers have reached an equilibrium in their buying habits and preferences, and psychological persuasion (advertising) is not as effective as financial persuasion (sales-promotion deals). Many consumer-packaged-goods companies now spend over 60 percent of their total promotion budget on sales promotion to support mature products. Other marketers argue that brands should be managed as capital assets and supported by advertising. Advertising expenditures should be treated as a capital investment. Brand managers use sales promotion because its effects are quicker and more visible to their superiors; but excessive sales-promotion activity can hurt the brand's image and long-run profit performance.

Marketing Strategies: Decline Stage

Sales decline for a number of reasons, including technological advances, shifts in consumer tastes, and increased domestic and foreign competition. All lead to overcapacity, increased price-cutting, and profit erosion. The decline might be slow, as in the case of sewing machines; or rapid, as in the case of the 5.25 floppy disks. Sales may plunge to zero, or they may petrify at a low level.

As sales and profits decline, some firms withdraw from the market. Those remaining may reduce the number of products they offer. They may withdraw from smaller market segments and weaker trade channels, and they may cut their promotion budgets and reduce prices further. Unfortunately, most companies have not developed a policy for handling aging products.

Unless strong reasons for retention exist, carrying a weak product is very costly to the firm—and not just by the amount of uncovered overhead and profit: There are many hidden costs. Weak products often consume a disproportionate amount of management's time; require frequent price and inventory adjustments; generally involve short production runs in spite of expensive set-up times; require both advertising and sales force attention that might be better used to make the healthy products more profitable; and can cast a shadow on the company's image. The biggest cost might well lie in the future. Failing to eliminate weak products delays the aggressive search for replacement products. The weak products create a lopsided product mix, long on yesterday's breadwinners and short on tomorrow's.

In handling aging products, a company faces a number of tasks and decisions. The first task is to establish a system for identifying weak products. Many companies appoint a product-review committee with representatives from marketing, R&D, manufacturing, and finance. The controller's office supplies data for each product showing trends in market size, market share, prices, costs, and profits. A computer program then analyzes this information. The managers responsible for dubious products fill out rating forms showing where they think sales and profits will go, with and without any changes in marketing strategy. The product-review committee makes a recommendation for each product— leave it alone, modify its marketing strategy, or drop it.[53]

Some firms abandon declining markets earlier than others. Much depends on the presence and height of exit barriers in the industry.[54] The lower the exit barriers, the easier it is for firms to leave the industry, and the more tempting it is for the remaining firms to stay and attract the withdrawing firms' customers. For example, Procter & Gamble stayed in the declining liquid-soap business and improved its profits as others withdrew.

In a study of company strategies in declining industries, five strategies are available to the firm:

1. Increasing the firm's investment (to dominate the market or strengthen its competitive position).

2. Maintaining the firm's investment level until the uncertainties about the industry are resolved.

3. Decreasing the firm's investment level selectively, by dropping unprofitable customer groups while simultaneously strengthening the firm's investment in lucrative niches.

4. Harvesting ("milking") the firm's investment to recover cash quickly.

5. Divesting the business quickly by disposing of its assets as advantageously as possible.[55]

The appropriate strategy depends on the industry's relative attractiveness and the company's competitive strength in that industry. A company that is in an unattractive industry but possesses competitive strength should consider shrinking selectively. A company that is in an attractive industry and has competitive strength should consider strengthening its investment. Look what Quaker Oats has done with oatmeal.

Quaker Oats

After being banished to the cupboard for years, instant oatmeal has staged a comeback with campaigns emphasizing health (for all) and fun (for kids) as oatmeal sales shot up in the late 1990s. Quaker Oats, which owns almost two-thirds of the category, capitalized on the opportunity to target kids by infusing fun with nutrition through new oatmeal products such as Sea Adventures and Dinosaur Eggs.[56]

If the company were choosing between harvesting and divesting, its strategies would be quite different. *Harvesting* calls for gradually reducing a product or business's costs while trying to maintain sales. The first step is to cut R&D costs and plant and equipment investment. The company might also reduce product quality, sales force size, marginal services, and advertising expenditures. It would try to cut these costs without letting customers, competitors, and employees know what is happening. Harvesting is an ethically ambivalent strategy, and it is also difficult to execute. Yet many mature products warrant this strategy. Harvesting can substantially increase the company's current cash flow.[57]

Companies that successfully restage or rejuvenate a mature product often do so by adding value to the original product. Consider the experience of Pitney Bowes, the dominant producer of postage meters.

Pitney Bowes

In 1996, critics, and even Pitney Bowes insiders, predicted that faxes would kill regular mail, on which Pitney's business relies. Then they predicted that e-mail would kill faxes and that all these technological advances combined would kill Pitney's profits. As it happens, the surge in direct mail and Internet-related bills has generated more mail, not less, but the Internet also enabled new companies such as e-Stamps and stamps.com to enter Pitney's territory by offering a way to download stamps over the Internet. Pitney recast itself as a messaging company—its slogan became "Engineering the Flow of Communication." It developed software products that let customers track incoming materials and outgoing products, convert bills and print files to fax or e-mail, and track when a document has been acted upon. Pitney also provides electronic billing services for e-commerce companies and even added an electronic-stamp business to compete with the stamp start-ups. Pitney's view: The Internet is not the enemy; rather, it is a vehicle for becoming a broad-based messaging company.[58]

When a company decides to drop a product, it faces further decisions. If the product has strong distribution and residual goodwill, the company can probably sell it to another firm. If the company can't find any buyers, it must decide whether to liquidate the brand quickly or slowly. It must also decide on how much inventory and service to maintain for past customers.

The Product Life-Cycle Concept: Critique

The PLC concept helps marketers interpret product and market dynamics. It can be used for planning and control, although it is useful as a forecasting tool. PLC theory has its share of critics. They claim that life-cycle patterns are too variable in shape and duration. Critics charge that marketers can seldom tell what stage the product is in. A product may appear to be mature when actually it has reached a plateau prior to another upsurge. They charge that the PLC pattern is the result of marketing strategies rather than an inevitable course that sales must follow:

> Suppose a brand is acceptable to consumers but has a few bad years because of other factors—for instance, poor advertising, delisting by a major chain, or entry of a "me-too" competitive product backed by massive sampling. Instead of thinking in terms of corrective measures, management begins to feel that its brand has entered a declining stage. It therefore withdraws funds from the promotion budget to finance R&D on new items. The next year the brand does even worse, panic increases. Clearly, the PLC is a dependent variable which is determined by marketing actions; it is not an independent variable to which companies should adapt their marketing programs.[59]

Table 10.3 summarizes the characteristics, marketing objectives, and marketing strategies of the four stages of the PLC.

TABLE 10.3	SUMMARY OF PRODUCT LIFE-CYCLE CHARACTERISTICS, OBJECTIVES, AND STRATEGIES			
	Introduction	**Growth**	**Maturity**	**Decline**
Characteristics				
Sales	Low sales	Rapidly rising sales	Peak sales	Declining sales
Costs	High cost per customer	Average cost per customer	Low cost per customer	Low cost per customer
Profits	Negative	Rising profits	High profits	Declining profits
Customers	Innovators	Early adopters	Middle majority	Laggards
Competitors	Few	Growing number	Stable number beginning to decline	Declining number
Marketing Objectives				
	Create product awareness and trial	Maximize market share	Maximize profit while defending market share	Reduce expenditure and milk the brand
Strategies				
Product	Offer a basic product	Offer product extensions, service, warranty	Diversify brands and items models	Phase out weak
Price	Charge cost-plus	Price to penetrate market	Price to match or best competitors'	Cut price
Distribution	Build selective distribution	Build intensive distribution	Build more intensive distribution	Go selective: phase out unprofitable outlets
Advertising	Build product awareness among early adopters and dealers	Build awareness and interest in the mass market	Stress brand differences and benefits	Reduce to level needed to retain hard-core loyals
Sales Promotion	Use heavy sales promotion to entice trial	Reduce to take advantage of heavy consumer demand	Increase to encourage brand switching	Reduce to minimal level

Sources: Chester R. Wasson, *Dynamic Competitive Strategy and Product Life Cycles* (Austin, TX: Austin Press, 1978); John A. Weber, "Planning Corporate Growth with Inverted Product Life Cycles," *Long Range Planning* (October 1976): 12–29; Peter Doyle, "The Realities of the Product Life Cycle," *Quarterly Review of Marketing* (Summer 1976).

Market Evolution

Because the PLC focuses on what is happening to a particular product or brand rather than on what is happening to the overall market, it yields a product-oriented picture rather than a market-oriented picture. Firms need to visualize a *market's* evolutionary path as it is affected by new needs, competitors, technology, channels, and other developments.[60]

In the course of a product's or brand's existence, its positioning must change to keep pace with market developments. Consider the case of LEGO:

LEGO Group

LEGO Group, the Danish toy company, enjoyed a 72 percent global market share of the construction toy market; but children were spending more of their spare time with video games, computers, and television and less time with traditional toys. Lego recognized the need to change or expand its market space. It redefined its market space as "family edutainment," which included toys, education, interactive technology, software, computers, and consumer electronics. All involved exercising the mind and having fun. Part of LEGO Group's plan is to capture an increasing share of customer spending as children become young adults and then parents.

Like products, markets evolve through four stages: emergence, growth, maturity, and decline.

EMERGENCE Before a market materializes, it exists as a latent market. For example, for centuries people have wanted faster means of calculation. The market satisfied this need with abacuses, slide rules, and large adding machines. Suppose an entrepreneur recognizes this need and imagines a

An ad to the trade for the LEGO 2004 product line. LEGO is redefining its market space as "family edutainment," not just children's construction toys.

FIGURE 10.5

Market-Fragmentation and
Market-Consolidation
Strategies

(a) Market-fragmentation Stage

(b) Market-consolidation Stage

technological solution in the form of a small, handheld electronic calculator. He now has to determine the product attributes, including physical size and number of mathematical functions. Because he is market-oriented, he interviews potential buyers and finds that target customers vary greatly in their preferences. Some want a four-function calculator (adding, subtracting, multiplying, and dividing) and others want more functions (calculating percentages, square roots, and logs). Some want a small hand calculator and others want a large one. This type of market, in which buyer preferences scatter evenly, is called a *diffused-preference market.*

The entrepreneur's problem is to design an optimal product for this market. He or she has three options:

1. The new product can be designed to meet the preferences of one of the corners of the market (*a single-niche strategy*).

2. Two or more products can be simultaneously launched to capture two or more parts of the market (*a multiple-niche strategy*).

3. The new product can be designed for the middle of the market (*a mass-market strategy).*

For small firms, a single-niche market strategy makes the most sense. A small firm does not have the resources for capturing and holding the mass market. A large firm might go after the mass market by designing a product that is medium in size and number of functions. Assume that the pioneer firm is large and designs its product for the mass market. On launching the product, the *emergence* stage begins.[61]

GROWTH If the new product sells well, new firms will enter the market, ushering in a *market-growth stage.* Where will a second firm enter the market, assuming that the first firm established itself in the centre? If the second firm is small, it is likely to avoid head-on competition with the pioneer and to launch its brand in one of the market corners. If the second firm is large, it might launch its brand in the centre against the pioneer. The two firms can easily end up sharing the mass market. Or a large second firm can implement a multiple-niche strategy and surround and box in the pioneer.

MATURITY Eventually, the competitors cover and serve all the major market segments and the market enters the *maturity stage.* In fact, they go further and invade each other's segments, reducing everyone's profits in the process. As market growth slows down, the market splits into finer segments and high *market fragmentation* occurs. This situation is illustrated in Figure 10.5(a), where the letters represent different companies supplying various segments. Note that two segments are unserved because they are too small to yield a profit.

Market fragmentation is often followed by a *market consolidation* caused by the emergence of a new attribute that has strong appeal. This situation is illustrated in Figure 10.5(b) and the expansive size of the X territory. However, even a consolidated market condition will not last. Other companies will copy a successful brand, and the market will eventually splinter again. Mature markets swing between fragmentation and consolidation. The fragmentation is brought about by competition, and the consolidation is brought about by innovation. Consider the evolution of the paper-towel market:

Paper Towels

Originally, homemakers used cotton and linen dishcloths and towels in their kitchens. A paper company, looking for new markets, developed paper towels. This development crystallized a latent market. Other manufacturers entered the market. The number of brands grew and created market fragmentation. Industry overcapacity led manufacturers to search for new features. One manufacturer, hearing consumers complain that paper towels were not absorbent, introduced "absorbent" towels and increased its market share. This market consolidation did not last long because competitors came out with their own versions of absorbent paper towels. The market fragmented again. Then another manufacturer introduced a "superstrength" towel. It was soon copied. Another manufacturer introduced a "lint-free" paper towel, which was subsequently copied. Thus paper towels evolved from a single product to one with various absorbencies, strengths, and applications. Market evolution was driven by the forces of innovation and competition.

DECLINE Eventually, demand for the present products will begin to decrease, and the market will enter the *decline stage.* Either society's total need level declines or a new technology replaces the old. For example, shifts in tradition and a trend toward cremation have caused casket makers and funeral homes to reconsider how to conduct their business.[62]

SUMMARY

1. Deciding on positioning requires determining a frame of reference—by identifying the target market and the nature of the competition—and the ideal points-of-parity and points-of-difference brand associations. Determining the proper competitive frame of reference depends on understanding consumer behaviour and the considerations consumers use in making brand choices.

2. Points-of-difference are those associations unique to the brand that are also strongly held and favourably evaluated by consumers. Points-of-parity are those associations not necessarily unique to the brand but perhaps shared with other brands. Category point-of-parity associations are associations consumers view as being necessary to a legitimate and credible product offering within a certain category. Competitive point-of-parity associations are those associations designed to negate competitors' points-of-difference.

3. The key to competitive advantage is product differentiation. A market offering can be differentiated along five dimensions: product (form, features, performance quality, conformance quality, durability, reliability, reparability, style, design); services (order ease, delivery, installation, customer training, customer consulting, maintenance and repair, miscellaneous services); personnel; channel; or image (symbols, media, atmosphere, and events).

4. Because economic conditions change and competitive activity varies, companies normally find it necessary to reformulate their marketing strategy several times during a product's life cycle. Technologies, product forms, and brands also exhibit life cycles with distinct stages. The general sequence of stages in any life cycle is introduction, growth, maturity, and decline. The majority of products today are in the maturity stage.

5. Each stage of the product life cycle calls for different marketing strategies. The introduction stage is marked by slow growth and minimal profits. If successful, the product enters a growth stage marked by rapid sales growth and increasing profits. There follows a maturity stage in which sales growth slows and profits stabilize. Finally, the product enters a decline stage. The company's task is to identify the truly weak products; develop a strategy for each one; and phase out weak products in a way that minimizes the hardship to company profits, employees, and customers.

6. Like products, markets evolve through four stages: emergence, growth, maturity, and decline.

APPLICATIONS

Marketing Debate: Do Brands Have Finite Lives?

Often, after a brand begins to slip in the marketplace or disappears altogether, commentators observe, "all brands have their day." Their rationale is that all brands, in some sense, have a finite life and cannot be expected to be leaders forever. Other experts, however, contend that brands can live forever, and their long-term success depends on the skill and insight of the marketers involved.

Take a position: Brands cannot be expected to last forever versus There is no reason for a brand to ever become obsolete.

Marketing Discussion

Identify other negatively correlated attributes and benefits not included in Table 10.2 (page 317). What strategies do firms use to try to position themselves on the basis of pairs of attributes and benefits?

Marketing Spotlight: Krispy Kreme

Krispy Kreme makes 2.7 billion doughnuts a year. But it took more than fresh hot doughnuts to earn Krispy Kreme the title of "hottest brand in America" in 2003. Krispy Kreme's stock price quadrupled in the three years following its IPO in 2000, and the entire chain now generates US$1 billion in annual revenues across more than 300 outlets.

How did Krispy Kreme turn doughnuts into dollars? Careful brand positioning and local marketing tell the story. "We have a humble brand and product," says Krispy Kreme CEO Scott Livengood. "It's not flashy." The company is not new—it was founded in 1937—and part of its brand image is an old-fashioned feel. The plain red, green, and white colours and retro graphics evoke the squeaky-clean *Happy Days* of the 1950s, as do the Formica-filled, kid-friendly shops. "We want every customer experience to be associated with good times and warm memories," Livengood says.

The company's brand image also rests on its fresh, hot doughnuts—a freshness that's measured in hours. In a world of processed, prepackaged food, nothing beats a fresh hot doughnut. The company's marketing is grassroots local. Krispy Kreme has no traditional media advertising budget. Rather, local "community marketing managers" enlist the aid of local groups and charities. For example, the company helps charities raise money by selling them doughnuts at half price, which they can resell at full price. Local bake sales become a promotional tool for Krispy Kreme.

Another tactic is giving away free doughnuts to TV, news-papers, and radio stations before entering a market. Krispy Kreme scored a publicity coup in 1996 when it opened its first store in New York City. The company delivered boxes of doughnuts to the *Today Show*, garnering millions of dollars worth of exposure for the price of a few doughnuts. Even the day of the IPO relied on the buzz from free Krispy Kreme doughnuts on the floor of the stock exchange.

Each local outlet is an emissary for the brand, and Krispy Kreme's signature Doughnut Theater defines the brand image. A multi-sensory experience, Doughnut Theater occurs several times a day at each shop. When the store flicks on its "Hot Doughnuts Now" sign, the performance is about to begin. A large plate glass wall lets customers watch the whole process.

The Doughnut Theater experience works on three levels. On a direct level, the performance entertains customers and draws them into the doughnut-making experience. On an indirect level, it shows that the products are freshly made in a clean environment. On a subliminal level, as CEO Livengood describes it, "The movement of the products on the convey-or through our proofbox has this relaxing, almost mesmeriz-ing effect. The only other thing like it is standing on the oceanfront and watching the tide come in. It has that same consistent, relaxing motion that is really positive to people." People flock to the store to see wave after wave of doughnuts emerge hot and deliciously fresh. They happily stand in long lines around newly opened outlets to get the aroma of the doughnuts being made, the sight of the vanilla glaze water-fall, and the warmth of the hot doughnut that "just melts in your mouth and tastes so good," Livengood says.

Doughnut Theater is a bit of show business that draws customers into the baking experience and makes them feel like they are a part of the process. Another aspect of show business is product placements on hit shows like the *Sopranos* and *Will & Grace* and movies like *Bruce Almighty*. Finally, international expansion is fuelled by celebrities like Dick Clark, Hank Aaron, and Jimmy Buffet, who clamoured for Krispy Kreme franchises of their own. Krispy Kreme doesn't just grant franchise rights to anyone.

Krispy Kreme makes 65 percent of its revenue selling doughnuts directly to the public through its 106 company-owned stores. Another 31 percent comes from selling flour mix, doughnut-making machines, and doughnut supplies to its 186 franchised stores. The final 4 percent of revenue comes from franchisee licences and fees.

Krispy Kreme is now expanding and selling doughnuts through convenience stores. Will this hurt the brand? Stan Parker, Krispy Kreme's senior vice-president of marketing, says it won't because the company continues to emphasize freshness. It replenishes the packaged doughnuts daily from the local Krispy Kreme store and removes any unsold pack-ages. The doughnuts' presence in convenience stores will help remind people of the taste of a fresh, *hot* Krispy Kreme doughnut, and that brings them back into a Krispy Kreme shop.

The success of Krispy Kreme has been a wake-up call for competitor Dunkin' Doughnuts, which had become compla-cent. The one-two punch of Krispy Kreme in doughnuts and Starbucks in coffee led Dunkin' Doughnuts to revamp its menu and its stores, neither of which had changed in years. Rather than innovating, Dunkin' Doughnuts looked at what customers were already eating elsewhere. It brought in basic products like bagels, low-fat muffins, and breakfast sandwich-es. Dunkin Doughnuts still dwarfs Krispy Kreme in size, but it must work to find new ways of creating excitement that builds customer pride. Because one thing is sure: Krispy Kreme refuses to be dull.

DISCUSSION QUESTIONS

1. What have been the key success factors for Krispy Kreme?

2. Where is Krispy Kreme vulnerable? What should it watch out for?

3. What recommendations would you make to senior marketing executives going forward? What should they be sure to do with its marketing?

Sources: Andy Serwer, "The Hole Story: How Krispy Kreme Became the Hottest Brand in America," *Fortune*, July 7, 2003, pp. 52–62; "How to Create 'Spontaneous' Media Events," *Business 2.0*, December 2003; Barbara Grondin Francella, "Krispy Kreme Is Sweet on C-Stores," *Convenience Store News*, October 12, 2003, p. 70; "Profile: Ethical Sweetener—Charlotte Taylor, Community Marketing Manager, Krispy Kreme,"*Marketing*, September 11, 2003, p. 18; Dan Malovany, "Kreme de la Kreme," *Snack Food & Wholesale Bakery*, February 2002; Kirk Kazanjian and Amy Joyner, *Making Dough: The 12 Secret Ingredients of Krispy Kreme's Sweet Success* (New York: John Wiley & Sons, 2003); Daniel McGinn, "Oh, Sweet Revenge: Dunkin' Donuts Faces Two High-End Rivals," *Newsweek*, September 29, 2003, p. 34; **www.krispykreme.com**.

11

IN THIS CHAPTER, WE WILL ADDRESS THE FOLLOWING QUESTIONS:

- How do marketers identify primary competitors?

- How should we analyze competitors' strategies, objectives, strengths, and weaknesses?

- How can market leaders expand the total market and defend market share?

- How should market challengers attack market leaders?

- How can market followers or nichers compete effectively?

11

CHAPTER 11

Dealing with Competition

PROFILE: CANADIAN MARKETING EXCELLENCE

Poor firms ignore their competitors, average firms copy their competitors, and winning firms lead their competitors. One of Canada's most admired companies, Montreal-based Bombardier, is certainly one of those firms that lead the pack. Its focus on leadership is captured in its mission statement:

> Our mission is to be the world's leading manufacturer of planes and trains. We are committed to providing superior value and service to our customers and sustained profitability to our shareholders by investing in our people and products. We lead through innovation and outstanding product safety, efficiency and performance. Our standards are high. We define excellence—and we deliver.

Bombardier is the leading manufacturer of transportation solutions, headquartered in Montreal. It manufactures transportation equipment from regional aircraft and business jets to rail transportation equipment. It operates on five continents, with high concentration in North America and Europe, and employ just under 60 000 people. Its revenues for the fiscal year ending on January 31, 2005 were $U.S. 15.8 billion. More than 95 percent of its revenues come from markets outside of Canada. Bombardier attributes its success to its customer orientation, its skill at keeping abreast of market trends, and its ability to provide, in a timely manner, top-quality products and services at the best price/quality ratio.

Bombardier distinguishes itself by technical and administrative innovation and high productivity. It prides itself in its tenacity, achieving world leadership by taking a series of small steps. Its culture is both entrepreneurial and innovative. Bombardier works to apply best management practices, including Six Sigma, a quality methodology developed in 1984 at Motorola's Government Electronics Group that provides a basis for all employees to improve product quality and reduce costs.

Bombardier also takes pride in its record of social responsibility. It is committed to being a good corporate citizen in all the communities in which it operates. Through its J. Armand Bombardier Foundation, to which it allocates 3 percent of its profits annually, Bombardier donated $8 million in 2004 and $5.5 million in 2005 to organizations in various areas, with a priority placed on higher education.

Bombardier's history can be traced back to 1942 when the company was founded by J. Armand Bombardier to manufacture what is now commonly known as the snowmobile or—Bombardier's brand—the Ski-Doo. Eventually, this business became the recreational products division of a much more diversified portfolio of products, including rail transportation and transit systems, as well as regional and business aircraft manufacturing. In 1974 Bombardier ventured into the business of transportation with a major contract to manufacture rolling stock for Montreal's subway system. In December 1986 the company acquired Canadair, a leading Canadian aircraft manufacturer, marking the start of a new chapter for the company. Bombardier's transportation division went on to become the world's leader in rail transportation and equipment manufacturing, with the acquisition of DaimlerChrysler's Rail Systems GmbH (Adtranz) in 2001. Its Aerospace group was also very successful, holding a near monopoly position until 1996.

It was then that Bombardier's Aerospace group began to encounter severe turbulence in the form of intense competition from its Brazilian rival Embraer. In just two years, Bombardier lost almost half its market share as it faced severe price competition from its rival. Embraer began selling its regional jets $3 million cheaper than Bombardier. Moreover, Embraer offered would-be purchasers financing deals that cut another $4.5 million off the list price. How was Embraer able to do this? Bombardier claimed that export subsidies provided by the Brazilian government under its Pro-ex program radically reduced the aerospace manufacturer's cost of borrowing money.

Not being a firm to run from a fight, Bombardier enlisted the help of the Canadian government and took the dispute to the World Trade Commission. Embraer and the Brazilian government countered these claims with accusations of their own about Canadian subsidies. Even though the World Trade Commission ruled in 1999 that the Brazilian program was illegal, the battle continues between the two manufacturers and their government allies. As one Canadian analyst notes, "The stakes are too important for Canada, Brazil—and for the United States and Europe for that matter—to leave their aerospace companies by the wayside." Bombardier must keep an eagle eye on its competitors' every move to counter their attacks with marketing and product excellence.

The slowdown in the airline industry resulting from the September 11, 2001, terrorist attacks continues to depress Bombardier's aerospace business. Between 2003 to 2005, it was forced to lay off staff and cut production. In 2003 Bombardier also sold off some of its business divisions, including its recreational products division, so that it could focus more on its core transportation businesses. Because the company was under increasing fire for receiving federal aerospace loans, it spent $300 000 on a two-week national advertising campaign to tell Canadians about the importance and role of the company. The ads read: "Bombardier creates value for our country. Get to know us better." One ad notes that Bombardier earned 94 percent of its revenue outside Canada, yet employs more than a third of its workers here. Despite these challenges, the company continues to be a global leader. It has new orders coming in, like the $2 million one from Qantas Airways. Its Skyjet service division, the premier service for booking private business jets, reported that the 2004 holiday season reached a seven-year high both in the volume of trips and revenue. Thus, if the firm can maintain a technological and service quality lead over its competitors, it will surely find sunnier skies ahead.

Sources: Bombardier Web site, **www.bombardier.com** (viewed February 10, 2005); Bombardier 2004 Annual Report (viewed September 10, 2004); Bombardier Press Releases, "Bombardier Charts the Course for Growth," Montreal, June 04, 2002 (viewed June 7, 2002), "Bombardier Aerospace Implements Measures to Meet Market Challenges," Montreal, September 27, 2002 (viewed October 18, 2002), and "Bombardier Wins Rail Transportation Contracts in Europe and South America for a Total Value of $54 Million," Montreal, October 17, 2002 (viewed October 18, 2002); Bertrand Marotte,

"Bombardier Slashes Work Force," *The Globe and Mail*, September 28, 2002, p. B1; Bombardier 2001 Annual Report; Mehrdad Baghai, Stephen Coley, and David White, "Bombardier-Embraer Dogfight Heats Up," *The Globe and Mail*, February 19, 1999, pp. B1, B6; Konrad Yakabuski, "Bombardier Soars on Jet Orders, but Turbulence May Loom Ahead," *The Globe and Mail*, February 22, 1999, pp. B1, B5; Andrea Zoe Aster, "Bombardier Ads Take Aim at Critics," *Marketing Magazine*, February 3, 2003.

Building strong brands requires a keen understanding of competition, and competition grows more intense every year. New competition is coming from all directions—from global competitors eager to grow sales in new markets, from online competitors seeking cost-efficient ways to expand distribution, from private label and store brands designed to provide low-price alternatives, and from brand extensions from strong mega-brands leveraging their strengths to move into new categories. To effectively devise and implement the best possible brand positioning strategies, companies must pay keen attention to their competitors.[1] Markets have become too competitive to just focus on the consumer alone. This chapter examines the role competition plays and how marketers can best manage their brands, depending on their market position.

Competitive Forces

Michael Porter has identified five forces that determine the intrinsic long-run attractiveness of a market or market segment: industry competitors, potential entrants, substitutes, buyers, and suppliers. His model is shown in Figure 11.1. The threats these forces pose are as follows:

1. *Threat of intense segment rivalry.* A segment is unattractive if it already contains numerous, strong, or aggressive competitors. It is even more unattractive if it is stable or declining, if plant capacity additions are done in large increments, if fixed costs are high, if exit barriers are high, or if competitors have high stakes in staying in the segment. These conditions will lead to frequent price wars, advertising battles, and new-product introductions, and will make it expensive to compete. The cellular phone market has seen fierce competition due to segment rivalry.

2. *Threat of new entrants.* A segment's attractiveness varies with the height of its entry and exit barriers.[2] The most attractive segment is one in which entry barriers are high and exit barriers are low. Few new firms can enter the industry, and poor-performing firms can easily exit. When both entry and exit barriers are high, profit potential is high, but firms face more risk because poorer-performing firms stay in and fight it out. When both entry and exit barriers are low, firms easily enter and leave the industry, and the returns are stable and low. The worst case is when entry barriers are low and exit barriers are high: Here firms enter during good times but find it hard to leave during bad times. The result is chronic overcapacity and depressed earnings for all. The airline industry has low entry barriers but high exit barriers, leaving all the companies struggling during economic downturns.

3. *Threat of substitute products.* A segment is unattractive when there are actual or potential substitutes for the product. Substitutes place a limit on prices and on profits. The company has to monitor price trends closely. If technology advances or competition increases in these substitute industries, prices and profits in the segment are likely to fall. Greyhound buses and Via trains have seen profitability threatened by the rise of air travel.

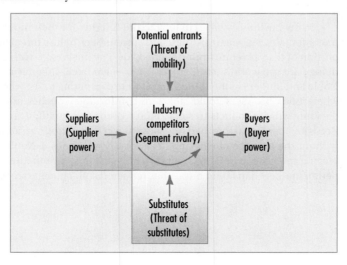

FIGURE 11.1

Five Forces Determining Segment Structural Attractiveness

Source: Reprinted with the permission of the Free Press, an imprint of Simon & Schuster, from Michael E. Porter, *Competitive Advantage: Creating and Sustaining Superior Performance.* Copyright 1985 by Michael E. Porter.

4. *Threat of buyers' growing bargaining power.* A segment is unattractive if buyers possess strong or growing bargaining power. The rise of retail giants such as Wal-Mart has led some analysts to conclude that the potential profitability of packaged good companies will become curtailed. Buyers' bargaining power grows when they become more concentrated or organized, when the product represents a significant fraction of the buyers' costs, when the product is undifferentiated, when the buyers' switching costs are low, when buyers are price sensitive because of low profits, or when buyers can integrate upstream. To protect themselves, sellers might select buyers who have the least power to negotiate or switch suppliers. A better defence consists of developing superior offers that strong buyers cannot refuse.

5. *Threat of suppliers' growing bargaining power.* A segment is unattractive if the company's suppliers are able to raise prices or reduce quantity supplied. Oil companies such as BP, Chevron-Texaco, ExxonMobil, Imperial Oil, Petro-Canada, and Shell are at the mercy of the amount of oil reserves and the actions of oil-supplying cartels like OPEC. Suppliers tend to be powerful when they are concentrated or organized, when there are few substitutes, when the supplied product is an important input, when the costs of switching suppliers are high, and when the suppliers can integrate downstream. The best defences are to build win–win relations with suppliers or use multiple supply sources.

Identifying Competitors

It would seem a simple task for a company to identify its competitors. PepsiCo knows that Coca-Cola's Dasani is the major bottled water competitor for its Aquafina brand; RBC Financial Group knows that TD Canada Trust is a major banking competitor; and Expedia.ca knows that a major online competitor is Travelocity.ca. However, the range of a company's actual and potential competitors can be much broader. And a company is more likely to be hurt by emerging competitors or new technologies than by current competitors. This certainly has been true for Toys R Us and other major toy retailers:

Toys R Us

Pricing pressure from Wal-Mart and Target discounters and even electronics vendors such as Best Buy and Future Shop has pummelled the toy chains and sent some of them into bankruptcy. During the 2004 holiday season, Wal-Mart made its most aggressive move yet into the toy business, drastically reducing prices and undercutting Toys R Us by 20 percent. With their bare-bones prices, the discounters have higher sales, more locations, and the flexibility, if necessary, to break even or even lose money in areas such as toys while falling back on other product revenue. In response, some chains, such as the venerable FAO Schwartz (with its famous New York City store facing Central Park), were forced to temporarily close their doors while they totally refocused their product line on upscale, hard-to-find items. Toys R Us has been forced to close 182 of its freestanding North American Kids R Us stores as well as its Imaginarium chain.[3]

Many businesses failed to look to the Internet for their most formidable competitors. Web sites that offer jobs, real estate listings, and automobiles online threaten newspapers, which derive a huge portion of their revenue from classified ads. The businesses with the most to fear from Internet technology are the world's middlemen. A few years back, Chapter and Indigo in Canada and Barnes & Noble and Borders in the United States were competing to see who could build the most mega-stores, where book browsers could sink into comfortable couches and sip cappuccino. While they were deciding which products to stock, Jeffrey Bezos was building an online empire called Amazon.com. Bezos's cyber-bookstore had the advantage of offering an almost unlimited selection of books without the expense of stocking inventory. Now Barnes & Noble, Borders, and Chapters Indigo are playing catch-up in building their own online stores. "Competitor myopia"—a focus on current competitors rather than latent ones—has rendered some businesses extinct:[4]

Encyclopaedia Britannica

In 1996, 230-year-old Encyclopaedia Britannica dismissed its entire home sales force after the arrival of its US$5-per-month subscription Internet site made the idea of owning a 32-volume set of books for US$1250 less appealing to parents. Britannica decided to create an online site after realizing that computer-savvy kids most often sought information online or on CD-ROMs such as Microsoft's Encarta, which sold for US$50. What really smarts is that Britannica had the opportunity to partner with Microsoft in providing content for Encarta but refused. Britannica now sells print sets and offers online access to premium subscribers on its Web site.[5]

We can examine competition from both an industry and a marketing point of view.[6]

Industry Concept of Competition

What exactly is an industry? An **industry** is a group of firms that offer a product or class of products that are close substitutes for one another. Industries are classified according to number of sellers; degree of product differentiation; presence or absence of entry, mobility, and exit barriers; cost structure; degree of vertical integration; and degree of globalization.

NUMBER OF SELLERS AND DEGREE OF DIFFERENTIATION   The starting point for describing an industry is to specify the number of sellers and whether the product is homogeneous or highly differentiated. These characteristics give rise to four industry structure types:

1. *Pure monopoly.* Only one firm provides a certain product or service in a certain country or area (a local water or cable company). An unregulated monopolist might charge a high price, do little or no advertising, and offer minimal service. If partial substitutes are available and there is some danger of competition, the monopolist might invest in more service and technology. A regulated monopolist is required to charge a lower price and provide more service as a matter of public interest.

2. *Oligopoly.* A small number of (usually) large firms produce products that range from highly differentiated to standardized. *Pure oligopoly* consists of a few companies producing essentially the same commodity (oil, steel). Such companies would find it hard to charge anything more than the going price. If competitors match on price and services, the only way to gain a competitive advantage is through lower costs. *Differentiated oligopoly* consists of a few companies producing products (autos, cameras) partially differentiated along lines of quality, features, styling, or services. Each competitor may seek leadership in one of these major attributes, attract the customers favouring that attribute, and charge a price premium for that attribute.

3. *Monopolistic competition.* Many competitors are able to differentiate their offers in whole or in part (restaurants, beauty shops). Competitors focus on market segments where they can meet customer needs in a superior way and command a price premium.

4. *Pure competition.* Many competitors offer the same product and service (stock market, commodity market). Because there is no basis for differentiation, competitors' prices will be the same. No competitor will advertise unless advertising can create psychological differentiation (cigarettes, beer), in which case it would be more proper to describe the industry as monopolistically competitive.

An industry's competitive structure can change over time. For instance, the media industry has continued to consolidate, turning from monopolistic competition into a differentiated oligopoly:

Media Industry

For more than a decade, the media business has been steadily consolidating to the point that media empires can now vertically integrate content with distribution. In the United States, there are four principal media empires that have combined studios that produce programming, with cable and broadcasting units that distribute content. In Canada, the media industry is slightly less consolidated, but the same vertical integration model has been applied. BCE Inc., principally a telecommunications company (Bell Canada, Bell Mobility, etc.), acquired the CTV television network and the *Globe and Mail* and formed Bell Globemedia. Alliance Atlantis, which began as a film production and distribution company, now owns a successful combination of specialty television networks (e.g., Showcase, Life Network) and rights to major U.S. television shows, such as *CSI*. CanWest Global Communications is Canada's largest newspaper empire, and it also owns major Canadian networks such as Global Television and specialty television stations such as Prime TV. Rogers began as a radio broadcasting company, and then grew into Canada's pre-eminent cable provider. It also competes in the telecommunications marketplace, and it owns other major media assets such as *Maclean's* magazine. Consumer advocates are concerned about the effects of dwindling competition. The effects of this consolidation are most obvious in the film industry, where small independent films with unique content struggle for production and distribution funding, given that large media conglomerates favour blockbuster films that are more certain to ensure profitability for shareholders.[7]

ENTRY, MOBILITY, AND EXIT BARRIERS Industries differ greatly in ease of entry. It is easy to open a new restaurant but difficult to enter the aircraft industry. Major *entry barriers* include high capital requirements; economies of scale; patents and licensing requirements; scarce locations, raw materials, or distributors; and reputation requirements. Even after a firm enters an industry, it might face *mobility barriers* when it tries to enter more attractive market segments.

Corel Corporation

Corel, the Ottawa-based software company, built a worldwide reputation and global customer following with its innovative computer graphics program, CorelDRAW, first introduced in the Spring of 1989. In 1996, the company branched out, acquiring WordPerfect and entering the highly competitive office productivity market dominated by Microsoft. Playing in the same markets with larger competitors has never daunted the feisty software company. In 2004, it further refined its focus to concentrate on consumers and the small business marketplace with a number of products tailored specifically to the needs of these markets. And the marketplace has responded, giving Corel's WordPerfect Office, CorelDRAW Graphics Suite, Corel Painter, and the Paint Shop family of digital imaging software a number of international awards. WordPerfect Office has been praised as an affordably priced word processing, spreadsheet, and slideshow combination that introduced friendly formatting and built-in PDF output. Says David Dobson, CEO of Corel Corporation, "Corel's mission is to be the global leader in providing high quality, affordable, and easy-to-use software products and services that help people improve their productivity and extend their creativity at work and at home."[8]

Firms often face *exit barriers*, such as legal or moral obligations to customers, creditors, and employees; government restrictions; low asset salvage value due to overspecialization or obsolescence; lack of alternative opportunities; high vertical integration; and emotional barriers.[9] Many firms stay in an industry as long as they cover their variable costs and some or all of their fixed costs. Their continued presence, however, dampens profits for everyone. Even if some firms do not want to exit the industry, they might decrease their size. Companies can try to reduce shrinkage barriers to help ailing competitors get smaller gracefully.[10]

COST STRUCTURE Each industry has a certain cost burden that shapes much of its strategic conduct. For example, steel-making involves heavy manufacturing and raw-material costs; toy manufacturing involves heavy distribution and marketing costs. Firms strive to reduce their largest costs.

Corel aims to be a global leader in the marketplace, offering high quality, affordability, and easy-to-use software.

The integrated steel company with the most cost-efficient plant will have a great advantage over other integrated steel companies; but even it has higher costs than the new steel mini-mills.

DEGREE OF VERTICAL INTEGRATION   Companies find it advantageous to integrate backward or forward (**vertical integration**). Major oil producers carry on oil exploration, oil drilling, oil refining, chemical manufacture, and service-station operation. Vertical integration often lowers costs, and the company gains a larger share of the value-added stream. In addition, vertically integrated firms can manipulate prices and costs in different parts of the value chain to earn profits where taxes are lowest. There can be disadvantages, such as high costs in certain parts of the value chain and a lack of flexibility. Companies are increasingly questioning how vertical they should be. Many are outsourcing more activities, especially those that can be done better and more cheaply by specialist firms.

DEGREE OF GLOBALIZATION   Some industries are highly local (such as lawn care); others are global (such as oil, aircraft engines, cameras). Companies in global industries need to compete on a global basis if they are to achieve economies of scale and keep up with the latest advances in technology.[11]

Market Concept of Competition

Using the market approach, competitors are companies that satisfy the same customer need. For example, a customer who buys a word-processing package really wants "writing ability"—a need that can also be satisfied by pencils, pens, or typewriters. Marketers must overcome "marketing myopia" and stop defining competition in traditional category terms.[12] Coca-Cola, focused on its soft-drink business, missed seeing the market for coffee bars and fresh-fruit juice bars that eventually impinged on its soft-drink business.

The market concept of competition reveals a broader set of actual and potential competitors. Rayport and Jaworski suggest profiling a company's direct and indirect competitors by mapping the buyer's steps in obtaining and using the product. Figure 11.2 illustrates their *competitor map* of Eastman Kodak in the film business. In the centre is a listing of consumer activities: buying a camera, buying film, taking pictures, and so on. The first outer ring lists Kodak's main competitors with respect to each consumer activity: Olympus for buying a camera, Fuji for purchasing film, and so on. The second outer ring lists indirect competitors—HP, Intel, cameraworks.com—who in Kodak's case are increasingly becoming direct competitors. This type of analysis highlights both the opportunities and the challenges a company faces.[13]

Shell Oil is a vertically integrated firm that is also today becoming an environmentally friendly firm. This ad is one of a series in a campaign to spotlight Shell's sustainable development program.

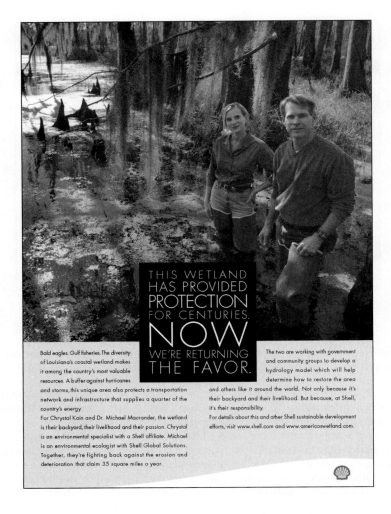

THIS WETLAND HAS PROVIDED **PROTECTION** FOR CENTURIES. **NOW** WE'RE RETURNING THE FAVOR.

Bald eagles. Gulf fisheries. The diversity of Louisiana's coastal wetland makes it among the country's most valuable resources. A buffer against hurricanes and storms, this unique area also protects a transportation network and infrastructure that supplies a quarter of the country's energy.

For Chrystal Kain and Dr. Michael Macrander, the wetland is their backyard, their livelihood and their passion. Chrystal is an environmental specialist with a Shell affiliate. Michael is an environmental ecologist with Shell Global Solutions. Together, they're fighting back against the erosion and deterioration that claim 35 square miles a year.

The two are working with government and community groups to develop a hydrology model which will help determine how to restore the area and others like it around the world. Not only because it's their backyard and their livelihood. But because, at Shell, it's their responsibility.

For details about this and other Shell sustainable development efforts, visit www.shell.com and www.americaswetland.com.

FIGURE 11.2

Competitor Map—Eastman Kodak

Source: Adapted from Jeffrey F. Rayport and Bernard J. Jaworski, *e-Commerce* (New York: McGraw-Hill, 2001), p. 53.

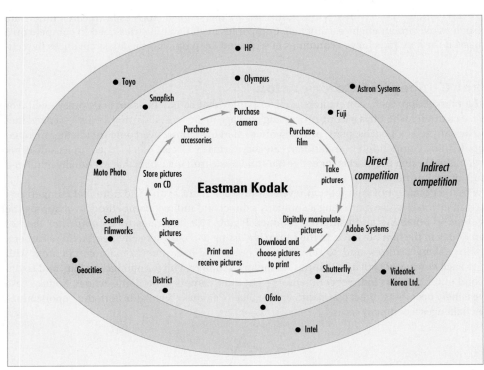

Analyzing Competitors

Once a company identifies its primary competitors, it must ascertain their strategies, objectives, and strengths and weaknesses.

Strategies

A group of firms following the same strategy in a given target market is called a **strategic group**.[14] Suppose a company wants to enter the major appliance industry. What is its strategic group? It develops the chart shown in Figure 11.3 and discovers four strategic groups based on product quality and level of vertical integration. Group A has one competitor (Maytag), group B has three (General Electric, Whirlpool, and Sears), group C has four, and group D has two. Important insights emerge from this exercise. First, the height of the entry barriers differs for each group. Second, if the company successfully enters a group, the members of that group become its key competitors.

Objectives

Once a company has identified its main competitors and their strategies, it must ask: What is each competitor seeking in the marketplace? What drives each competitor's behaviour? Many factors shape a competitor's objectives, including size, history, current management, and financial situation. If the competitor is a division of a larger company, it is important to know whether the parent company is running it for growth, profits, or milking it.[15]

One useful initial assumption is that competitors strive to maximize profits. However, companies differ in the emphasis they put on short-term versus long-term profits. Many Canadian and U.S. firms have been criticized for operating on a short-run model, largely because current performance is judged by shareholders who might lose confidence, sell their stock, and cause the company's cost of capital to rise. Japanese firms operate largely on a market-share-maximization model. They receive much of their funds from banks at a lower interest rate and in the past have readily accepted lower profits. An alternative assumption is that each competitor pursues some mix of objectives: current profitability, market-share growth, cash flow, technological leadership, or service leadership.

Finally, a company must monitor competitors' expansion plans. Figure 11.4 shows a product-market battlefield map for the personal computer industry. Dell, which started out as a strong force in selling personal computers to individual users, is now a major force in the commercial and industrial market. Other incumbents may try to set up mobility barriers to Dell's further expansion.

Strengths and Weaknesses

A company needs to gather information on each competitor's strengths and weaknesses. Table 11.1 shows the results of a company survey that asked customers to rate its three competitors, A, B, and C, on five attributes. Competitor A turns out to be well known and respected for producing high-quality products sold by a good sales force. Competitor A is poor at providing product availability and technical assistance. Competitor B is good across the board and excellent in product availability and sales force. Competitor C rates poor to fair on most attributes. This suggests that the company could attack Competitor A on product availability and technical assistance and Competitor C on almost anything, but should not attack B, which has no glaring weaknesses.

FIGURE 11.3

Strategic Groups in the Major Appliance Industry

FIGURE 11.4

A Competitor's Expansion Plans

TABLE 11.1	CUSTOMERS' RATINGS OF COMPETITORS ON KEY SUCCESS FACTORS				
	Customer Awareness	Product Quality	Product Availability	Technical Assistance	Selling Staff
Competitor A	E	E	P	P	G
Competitor B	G	G	E	G	E
Competitor C	F	P	G	F	F

Note: E = excellent, G = good, F = fair, P = poor.

In general, a company should monitor three variables when analyzing competitors:

1. *Share of market.* The competitor's share of the target market.
2. *Share of mind.* The percentage of customers who named the competitor in responding to the statement "Name the first company that comes to mind in this industry."
3. *Share of heart.* The percentage of customers who named the competitor in responding to the statement "Name the company from which you would prefer to buy the product."

There is an interesting relationship among these three measures. Table 11.2 shows the numbers for these three measures for the three competitors listed in Table 11.1. Competitor A enjoys the highest market share but is slipping. Its mind share and heart share are also slipping, probably because it is not providing good product availability and technical assistance. Competitor B is steadily gaining market share, probably due to strategies that are increasing its mind share and heart share. Competitor C seems to be stuck at a low level of market share, mind share, and heart share, probably because of its poor product and marketing attributes. We could generalize as follows: *Companies that make steady gains in mind share and heart share will inevitably make gains in market share and profitability.*

To improve market share, many companies benchmark their most successful competitors as well as world-class performers. The technique and its benefits are described in "Marketing Memo: Benchmarking to Improve Competitive Performance."

Selecting Competitors

After the company has conducted customer value analysis and examined competitors carefully, it can focus its attack on one of the following classes of competitors: strong versus weak, close versus distant, and "good" versus "bad."

■ *Strong versus weak.* Most companies aim their shots at weak competitors, because this requires fewer resources per share point gained. Yet, the firm should also compete with strong competitors to keep up with the best. Even strong competitors have some weaknesses.

■ *Close versus distant.* Most companies compete with competitors who resemble them the most. Chevrolet competes with Ford, not with Ferrari. Yet companies should also recognize distant competitors. Coca-Cola states that its number-one competitor is tap water, not Pepsi. U.S. Steel worries more about plastic and aluminum than about Bethlehem Steel; museums now worry about theme parks and malls.

TABLE 11.2	MARKET SHARE, MIND SHARE, AND HEART SHARE								
	Market Share			Mind Share			Heart Share		
	2000	2001	2002	2000	2001	2002	2000	2001	2002
Competitor A	50%	47%	44%	60%	58%	54%	45%	42%	39%
Competitor B	30	34	37	30	31	35	44	47	53
Competitor C	20	19	19	10	11	11	11	11	8

- *"Good" versus "bad."* Every industry contains "good" and "bad" competitors. A company should support its good competitors and attack its bad competitors. Good competitors play by the industry's rules; they make realistic assumptions about the industry's growth potential; they set prices in reasonable relation to costs; they favour a healthy industry; they limit themselves to a portion or segment of the industry; they motivate others to lower costs or improve differentiation; and they accept the general level of their share and profits. Bad competitors try to buy share rather than earn it; they take large risks; they invest in overcapacity; and they upset industrial equilibrium.

Competitive Strategies for Market Leaders

We can gain further insight by classifying firms by the roles they play in the target market: leader, challenger, follower, or nicher. Suppose a market is occupied by the firms shown in Figure 11.5. Forty percent of the market is in the hands of a *market leader;* another 30 percent is in the hands of a *market challenger;* another 20 percent is in the hands of a *market follower,* a firm that is willing to maintain its market share and not rock the boat. The remaining 10 percent is in the hands of *market nichers,* firms that serve small market segments not being served by larger firms.

Many industries contain one firm that is the acknowledged market leader. This firm has the largest market share in the relevant product market, and usually leads the other firms in price changes, new-product introductions, distribution coverage, and promotional intensity. Some well-known market leaders are Microsoft (computer software), Intel (microprocessors), Bombardier (aerospace and rail transport), Future Shop and Best Buy (retail electronics), McDonald's (fast food), Gillette (razor blades), RBC Financial Group (financial services), and Visa (credit cards).

Ries and Trout argue that well-known products generally hold a distinctive position in consumers' minds. Nevertheless, unless a dominant firm enjoys a legal monopoly, its life is not altogether easy. It must maintain constant vigilance. A product innovation may come along and hurt the leader (e.g., Nokia's and Ericsson's digital cell phones took over from Motorola's analogue models). The leader might spend conservatively whereas a challenger spends liberally (consider Zellers' loss of its discount retail dominance to Wal-Mart). The leader might misjudge its competition and find itself left behind (as Sears did when it underestimated Kmart and later Wal-Mart). The dominant firm might look old-fashioned against new and peppier rivals (Pepsi has attempted to take share from Coke by portraying itself as the more youthful brand). The dominant firm's costs might rise excessively and hurt its profits, or a discount competitor can undercut prices. "Marketing Insight: When Your Competitor Delivers More for Less" describes how leaders can respond to an aggressive competitive price discounter.

Marketing Memo

Benchmarking to Improve Competitive Performance

Benchmarking is the art of learning from companies that perform certain tasks better than other companies. There can be as much as a tenfold difference in the quality, speed, and cost performance of a world-class company and an average company. The aim of benchmarking is to copy or improve on "best practices," either within an industry or across industries. Benchmarking involves seven steps:

1. Determine which functions to benchmark.
2. Identify the key performance variables to measure.
3. Identify the best-in-class companies.
4. Measure performance of best-in-class companies.
5. Measure the company's performance.
6. Specify programs and actions to close the gap.
7. Implement and monitor results.

How can companies identify best-practice companies? A good starting point is asking customers, suppliers, and distributors whom they rate as doing the best job.

Sources: Robert C. Camp, *Benchmarking: The Search for Industry-Best Practices That Lead to Superior Performance* (White Plains, NY: Quality Resources, 1989); Michael J. Spendolini, *The Benchmarking Book* (New York: Amacom, 1992); Stanley Brown, "Don't Innovate—Imitate!" *Sales & Marketing Management* (January 1995): 24–25; Tom Stemerg, "Spies Like Us," *Inc.* (August 1998): 45–49. See also **www.benchmarking.org**; Michael Hope, "Contrast and Compare," *Marketing*, August 28, 1997, pp. 11–13; Robert Hiebeler, Thomas B. Kelly, and Charles Ketteman, *Best Practices: Building Your Business with Customer-Focused Solutions* (New York: Arthur Andersen/Simon & Schuster, 1998).

FIGURE 11.5

Hypothetical Market Structure

MARKETING INSIGHT

When Your Competitor Delivers More for Less

Companies offering the powerful combination of low prices and high quality are capturing the hearts and wallets of consumers in Europe and North America, where more than half of the population now shops weekly at mass merchants like Wal-Mart and Costco, up from 25 percent in 1996. These and similar value players, such as Aldi, Zellers, Dell, E*Trade Financial, WestJet, Dollar Store, and Winners, are transforming the way consumers of nearly every age and income purchase groceries, apparel, airline tickets, financial services, and computers.

The market share gains of value-based players give their higher-priced rivals definite cause for alarm. After years of near-exclusive sway over all but the most discount-minded consumers, many mainstream companies now face steep cost disadvantages and lack the product and service superiority that once set them apart from low-priced competitors. Today, as value-driven companies in a growing number of industries move from competing solely on price to catching up on attributes such as quality, service, and convenience, traditional players rightly feel threatened.

To compete with value-based rivals, mainstream companies must reconsider the perennial routes to business success: keeping costs in line, finding sources of differentiation, and managing prices effectively. Succeeding in value-based markets requires infusing these timeless strategies with greater intensity and focus and then executing them flawlessly. Differentiation, for example, becomes less about the abstract goal of rising above competitive clutter and more about identifying opportunities left open by the value players' business models. Effective pricing means waging a transaction-by-transaction perception battle to win over consumers predisposed to believe that value-oriented competitors are always cheaper.

Competitive outcomes will be determined, as always, on the ground—in product aisles, merchandising displays, process rethinks, and pricing stickers. When it comes to value-based competition, traditional players can't afford to drop a stitch. Value-driven competitors have changed the expectations of consumers about the trade-off between quality and price. This shift is gathering momentum, placing a new premium on—and adding new twists to—the old imperatives of differentiation and execution.

Differentiation

To counter value-based players, it will be necessary to focus on areas where their business models give other companies room to manoeuvre. Instead of trying to compete with Wal-Mart and other value retailers on price, for example, Shoppers Drug Mart (which includes Pharmaprix stores in Quebec) emphasizes convenience, a growing selection of high-end products, and the promise that consumers can trust its expert advice whether they are buying pharmaceutical products or cosmetics. It has expanded rapidly—it now has 925 stores from coast to coast—so that its stores would be ubiquitous. It generally locates in malls with easy parking. It overhauled its in-store layouts by renovating and expanding existing locations and building new format stores that are as large as 14 000 square feet. It has worked to increase the value it offers customers through its Optimum Loyalty program, which it launched in 2000. By the end of 2004, it had become one of the most successful loyalty programs in Canada, boasting over 8 million members. Finally, while pharmacy sales are still Shoppers' mainstay, it is adding many prestige products from giftware to high-end cosmetics and fragrances.

Execution

Value-based markets also place a premium on execution, particularly in prices and costs. Kmart's disastrous experience trying to compete head-on with Wal-Mart highlights the difficulty of challenging value leaders on their own terms. Matching or even beating a value player's prices—as Kmart briefly did—won't necessarily win the battle of consumer perceptions against companies with reputations for the lowest prices. Value players tend to price frequently purchased, easy-to-compare products and services aggressively and to make up for lost margins by charging more for higher-end offerings. Focused advertising to showcase "special buys" and the use of simple, prominent signage enable retailers to get credit for the value they offer and will probably become an ever more visible feature of the competitive landscape.

Ultimately, of course, the ability to offer even selectively competitive prices depends on keeping costs in line. Continual improvement is necessary, suggesting an increasing role, in a variety of industries, for Toyota's lean-manufacturing methods, which aim to reduce costs and improve quality constantly and simultaneously. In financial services, for example, banks have used lean techniques to speed cheque processing and mortgage approvals and to improve call-centre performance. Lean operations will probably emerge in more industries. Companies have no choice—those that fail to take out costs constantly may perish.

Source: Robert J. Frank, Jeffrey P. George, and Laxman Narasimhan, "When Your Competitor Delivers More for Less," *McKinsey Quarterly* (Winter 2004): 48–59; Angela Kryhul, "Shoppers' Prestige Play" *Marketing Magazine*, January 19, 2004; Chris Daniels, "Vendor Bender," *Marketing Magazine*, April 05, 2004; Shoppers Drug Mart Web site: **www.shoppersdrugmart.ca/english/corporate_information/about_us/index.html** (viewed August 24, 2005).

See what the Fairmont Hotels & Resorts are doing to extend their leadership in the North American marketplace worldwide.

Fairmont Hotels & Resorts

Headquartered in Toronto, Fairmont is the largest luxury hotel management company in North America. It has a worldwide reputation for excellence. Fairmont takes pride in the fact that it earns the loyalty of each guest by exceeding his or her expectations. As it continues to grow globally, it promises that "one thing will remain constant—any hotel under the Fairmont flag will do more than just sell rooms, for we are in the business of creating extraordinary guest experiences in extraordinary places." Fairmont leads in more than just market share—it also has an outstanding reputation for community involvement, innovative social programs, and environmental stewardship.[16]

Remaining number one calls for action on three fronts. First, the firm must find ways to expand total market demand. Second, the firm must protect its current market share through good defensive and offensive actions. Third, the firm can try to increase its market share, even if market size remains constant.

Expanding the Total Market

The dominant firm normally gains the most when the total market expands. If people increase their consumption of ketchup, Heinz stands to gain the most because it sells the majority of ketchup. If Heinz can convince more people to use ketchup, or to use ketchup with more meals, or to use more ketchup on each occasion, Heinz will benefit considerably. In general, the market leader should look for new customers or more usage from existing customers.

NEW CUSTOMERS   Every product class has the potential of attracting buyers who are unaware of the product or who are resisting it because of price or lack of certain features. A company can search for new users among three groups: those who might use it but do not *(market-penetration strategy)*, those who have never used it *(new-market segment strategy)*, or those who live elsewhere *(geographical-expansion strategy)*.

Starbucks Coffee is one of the best-known brands in the world. Starbucks is able to sell a cup of coffee for $3 while the store next door can only get $1. And if you want the popular café latte, it's $4. At the end of 2004, Starbucks had 8569 stores—4293 stores in the United States, 372 in Canada, and 3904 in 32 other countries. Its annual revenue topped US$5.3 billion. Its corporate Web site gives a peek into its multi-pronged approach to growth:[17]

> Starbucks purchases and roasts high-quality whole bean coffees and sells them along with fresh, rich-brewed, Italian-style espresso beverages, a variety of pastries and confections, and coffee-related accessories and equipment—primarily through its company-operated retail stores. In addition, Starbucks sells whole bean coffees through a specialty sales group and supermarkets. Additionally, Starbucks produces and sells bottled Frappuccino® coffee drink and a line of premium ice creams through its joint venture partnerships and offers a line of innovative premium teas produced by its wholly owned subsidiary, Tazo Tea Company. The company's objective is to establish Starbucks as the most recognized and respected brand in the world. To achieve this goal, the company plans to continue to rapidly expand its retail operations, grow its specialty sales and other operations, and selectively pursue opportunities to leverage the Starbucks brand through the introduction of new products and the development of new distribution channels.

MORE USAGE   Usage can be increased by increasing the *level or quantity* of consumption or increasing the *frequency* of consumption.

Increasing the amount of consumption can sometimes be done through packaging or product design. Larger package sizes have been shown to increase the amount of product that consumers use at one time.[18] Usage of "impulse" consumption products such as soft drinks and snacks increases when the product is made more available.

Increasing frequency of use, on the other hand, involves identifying additional opportunities to use the brand in the same basic way or identifying completely new and different ways to use the brand. In some cases, the product may be seen as useful only in certain places and at certain times, especially if it has strong brand associations with particular usage situations or user types.

To generate additional usage opportunities, a marketing program can communicate the appropriateness and advantages of using the brand more frequently in new or existing situations and/or remind consumers to actually use the brand as close as possible to those situations. The wine industry launched a number of initiatives in the late 1990s to attract Gen Xers and convince them that wine was a "casual, everyday libation to be drunk like bottled water, beer or soda."[19]

Another potential opportunity to increase frequency of use is when consumers' perceptions of their usage differs from the reality of their usage. For many products with relatively short life spans, consumers may fail to replace the product in a timely manner because of a tendency to underestimate the length of productive usage.[20] One strategy to speed up product replacement is to tie the act of replacing the product to a certain holiday, event, or time of year. Another strategy might be to provide consumers with better information as to either (1) when the product was first used or would need to be replaced or (2) the current level of product performance. Each Gillette Mach3 cartridge features a blue stripe that slowly fades with repeated use. After about a dozen shaves, it fades away, signalling the user to move on to the next cartridge.

The second approach is to identify completely new and different applications. For example, food product companies have long advertised new recipes that use their branded products in entirely different ways. Given that the average North American eats dry breakfast cereal three mornings a week, cereal manufacturers would gain if they could promote cereal eating on other occasions—perhaps as a snack.

Arm & Hammer

After discovering that consumers used Arm & Hammer baking soda brand as a refrigerator deodorant, a heavy promotion campaign was launched focusing on this single use. After succeeding in getting a substantial portion of North American homes to place an open box of baking soda in the refrigerator, the brand was then extended into a variety of new product categories, such as toothpaste, antiperspirant, and laundry detergent.

Product development can spur new uses. Chewing gum manufacturers are exploring ways to make "nutracuetical" products as a cheap, effective delivery mechanism for medicine. The majority of Adams chewing gums (number two in the world) claim health benefits. Aquafresh and Arm & Hammer are two dental gums that have achieved some success.[21]

Defending Market Share

While trying to expand total market size, the dominant firm must continuously defend its current business. The leader is like a large elephant being attacked by a swarm of bees. Tropicana must constantly guard against Minute Maid orange juice; Duracell against Energizer batteries; Hertz against Avis rental cars; Kodak against Fuji film.[22] Sometimes the competitor is domestic; sometimes it is foreign.

What can the market leader do to defend its terrain? The most constructive response is *continuous innovation*. The leader leads the industry in developing new product and customer services, distribution effectiveness, and cost cutting. It keeps increasing its competitive strength and value to customers.

Consider how Caterpillar has become dominant in the construction-equipment industry despite charging a premium price and being challenged by a number of able competitors, including John Deere, J. I. Case, Komatsu, and Hitachi. Several policies combine to explain Caterpillar's success:[23]

- *Premium performance.* Caterpillar produces high-quality equipment known for its reliability and durability—key buyer considerations in the choice of heavy industrial equipment.
- *Extensive and efficient dealership system.* Caterpillar maintains the largest number of independent construction-equipment dealers in the industry, all of whom carry a complete line of Caterpillar equipment.
- *Superior service.* Caterpillar has built a worldwide parts and service system second to none in the industry.

- *Full-line strategy.* Caterpillar produces a full line of construction equipment to enable customers to do one-stop buying.

- *Good financing.* Caterpillar provides a wide range of financial terms for customers who buy its equipment.

In satisfying customer needs, a distinction can be drawn between responsive marketing, anticipative marketing, and creative marketing. A *responsive* marketer finds a stated need and fills it. An *anticipative* marketer looks ahead into what needs customers may have in the near future. A *creative* marketer discovers and produces solutions customers did not ask for but to which they enthusiastically respond.

Sony exemplifies creative marketing. It has introduced many successful new products that customers never asked for or even thought were possible: Walkmans, VCRs, video cameras, CDs. Sony is a *market-driving firm,* not just a market-driven firm.

Akio Morita and an early Walkman. Morita refused to abandon his idea for a portable cassette player, saying that Sony doesn't serve markets—Sony creates markets. And he was certainly right: By the twentieth anniversary of the Walkman, Sony had sold over 250 million units.

Akio Morita, its founder, once proclaimed that Sony doesn't serve markets; Sony creates markets.[24] The Walkman is a classic example. In the late 1970s Akio Morita was working on a pet project that would revolutionize the way people listened to music: a portable cassette player he called the Walkman. Engineers at the company insisted there was little demand for such a product, but Morita refused to part with his vision. By the twentieth anniversary of the Walkman, Sony had sold over 250 million in nearly 100 different models.[25]

Consider the cellular phone market and how Cantel AT&T thought about defending its market share:

Cantel AT&T

"Churn" is jargon for customer turnover in the wireless phone industry—and according to analysts, it has become endemic. Turnover is a major problem when the cost of acquiring customers is high. In this industry, customer acquisition costs are in the range of $600 per customer. Yet Canada's four major cellular companies may lose up to one-quarter of their customers every year. Churn is a self-inflicted problem in this industry. All the players have encouraged turnover with an onslaught of promotions and special offers aimed at new customers, while taking existing customers for granted. But this is starting to change.

Consider the example of Cantel AT&T (now Rogers Wireless Communications). In 1999 it analyzed its customer base and discovered that 8 percent of its customers equalled more than 25 percent of its revenue. However, to its horror, Cantel also discovered that these people were the most dissatisfied and most likely to switch providers. Cantel's most valuable customers just didn't feel appreciated. Moreover, they perceived that new customers were being treated better than they were. Cantel rushed to solve the problem. It developed its "Inner Circle" program designed especially for its high-value customers. It gave them a dedicated hotline and advance notification of new product launches. It sent out surveys asking for feedback on problems and made every effort to solve them. Every respondent received a bounce-back mailer that was customized to his or her needs and concerns, along with an unexpected gift—a subscription to a magazine of the respondent's choice. The program helped Cantel reduce churn by 22 percent, which significantly improved its revenue and helped it learn an important lesson about maintaining customer loyalty.[26]

Even when it does not launch offensives, the market leader must not leave any major flanks exposed. It must consider carefully which terrains are important to defend, even at a loss, and which can be surrendered.[27] The aim of defensive strategy is to reduce the probability of attack, divert attacks to less threatening areas, and lessen their intensity. The defender's speed of response can make an important difference in the profit consequences. A dominant firm can use the six defence strategies summarized in Figure 11.6.[28]

FIGURE 11.6

Six Types of Defence Strategies

POSITION DEFENCE Position defence involves occupying the most desirable market space in the mind of the consumer, making the brand almost impregnable, like Tide laundry detergent with cleaning, Crest toothpaste with cavity prevention, and Pampers diapers with dryness.

FLANK DEFENCE Although position defence is important, the market leader should also erect outposts to protect a weak front or possibly serve as an invasion base for counterattack. When Heublein's brand Smirnoff, which had 23 percent of the U.S. vodka market, was attacked by low-priced competitor Wolfschmidt, Heublein actually *raised* the price and put the increased revenue into advertising. At the same time, Heublein introduced another brand, Relska, to compete with Wolfschmidt and still another, Popov, to sell for less than Wolfschmidt. This strategy effectively bracketed Wolfschmidt and protected Smirnoff's flanks.

PRE-EMPTIVE DEFENCE A more aggressive manoeuvre is to attack *before* the enemy starts its offence. A company can launch a pre-emptive defence in several ways. It can wage guerrilla action across the market—hitting one competitor here, another there—and keep everyone off balance; or it can try to achieve a grand market envelopment. Bank of America's 13 000 ATMs and 4500 branches around the United States now provide steep competition to local and regional banks. It can send out market signals to dissuade competitors from attacking.[29] It can introduce a stream of new products, making sure to precede them with *pre-announcements*—deliberate communications regarding future actions.[30] Pre-announcements can signal to competitors that they will have to fight to gain market share.[31] If Microsoft announces new product development plans, smaller firms may choose to concentrate their development efforts in other directions to avoid head-to-head competition. Some high-tech firms have even been accused of engaging in "vaporware"—pre-announcing products that miss delivery dates or are not even ever introduced.[32]

COUNTEROFFENSIVE DEFENCE When attacked, most market leaders will respond with a counterattack. Counterattacks can take many forms. In a *counteroffensive*, the leader can meet the attacker frontally or hit its flank or launch a pincer movement. An effective counterattack is to invade the attacker's main territory so that it will have to pull back to defend the territory. After FedEx watched UPS successfully invade its airborne delivery system, FedEx invested heavily in ground delivery service through a series of acquisitions to challenge UPS on its home turf.[33] When WestJet decided to establish operations at Pearson International Airport in Toronto and attack Air Canada head-on, Air Canada was quick to respond. It launched its own discount airline and began operations on WestJet's home turf in western Canada. Another common form of counteroffensive is the exercise of economic or political clout. The leader may try to crush a competitor by subsidizing lower prices for the vulnerable product with revenue from its more profitable products; or the leader may prematurely announce that a product upgrade will be available, to prevent customers from buying the competitor's product; or the leader may lobby legislators to take political action to inhibit or cripple the competition.

MOBILE DEFENCE In mobile defence, the leader stretches its domain over new territories that can serve as future centres for defence and offence through market broadening and market diversification. *Market broadening* involves shifting focus from the current product to the underlying generic need. The company gets involved in R&D across the whole range of technology associated with that need. Thus "petroleum" companies sought to recast themselves into "energy" companies. Implicitly, this change demanded that they dip their research fingers into the oil, coal, nuclear, hydroelectric, and chemical industries. *Market diversification* involves shifting into unrelated industries. When U.S. tobacco companies like Reynolds and Philip Morris acknowledged the growing curbs on cigarette smoking, they were not content with position defence or even with looking for cigarette substitutes. Instead they moved quickly into new industries, such as beer, liquor, soft drinks, and frozen foods.

CONTRACTION DEFENCE   Large companies sometimes recognize that they can no longer defend all of their territory. The best course of action then appears to be *planned contraction* (also called *strategic withdrawal*): giving up weaker territories and reassigning resources to stronger territories. Bombardier did this recently when it made the historic decision to spin off its recreational products division (maker of the famed Ski-Doo and Sea-Doo products) to focus more closely on aerospace and rail transport.

Expanding Market Share

Market leaders can improve their profitability by increasing their market share. In many markets, one share point is worth tens of millions of dollars. No wonder normal competition has turned into marketing warfare.

Gaining increased share in the served market, however, does not automatically produce higher profits—especially for labour-intensive service companies that may not experience many economies of scale. Much depends on the company's strategy.

Because the cost of buying higher market share may far exceed its revenue value, a company should consider four factors before pursuing increased market share:

- The possibility of provoking antitrust action, such as recently occurred with investigations of Microsoft and Intel. Jealous competitors are likely to cry "monopoly" if a dominant firm makes further inroads. This rise in risk would diminish the attractiveness of pushing market-share gains too far.

- Economic cost. Figure 11.7 shows that profitability might fall with further market-share gains after some level. In the illustration, the firm's *optimal market share* is 50 percent. The cost of gaining further market share might exceed the value. The "holdout" customers may dislike the company, be loyal to competitive suppliers, have unique needs, or prefer dealing with smaller suppliers. The cost of legal work, public relations, and lobbying rises with market share. Pushing for higher market share is less justified when there are few scale or experience economies, unattractive market segments exist, buyers want multiple sources of supply, and exit barriers are high. Some market leaders have even increased profitability by selectively decreasing market share in weaker areas.[34]

- Pursuing the wrong marketing-mix strategy. Kim Campbell's infamous campaign ad during the 1993 election campaign poking fun at Jean Chrétien's trademark facial droop (a medical condition from which he suffers), while highly distinctive, contributed to the rapid and steep decline in support for Progressive Conservative Party—they ultimately lost the election to a huge Liberal majority.[35] Companies successfully gaining share typically outperform competitors in three areas: new-product activity, relative product quality, and marketing expenditures.[36] Companies that cut prices more deeply than competitors typically do not achieve significant gains, as enough rivals meet the price cuts and others offer other values so that buyers do not switch. Competitive rivalry and price cutting have been shown to be most intense in industries with high fixed costs, high inventory costs, and stagnant primary demand, such as steel, auto, paper, and chemicals.[37]

- The effect of increased market share on actual and perceived quality.[38] Too many customers can put a strain on the firm's resources, hurting product value and service delivery. America Online experienced growing pains when its customer base expanded, resulting in system outages and access problems. Consumers may also infer that "bigger is not better" and assume that growth will lead to a deterioration of quality. If "exclusivity" is a key brand benefit, existing customers may resent additional new customers.

FIGURE 11.7

The Concept of Optimal Market Share

Other Competitive Strategies

Firms that occupy second, third, and lower ranks in an industry are often called runner-up, or trailing firms. Some, such as Colgate, Ford, Avis, and PepsiCo, are quite large in their own right. These firms can adopt one of two postures. They can attack the leader and other competitors in an aggressive bid for further market share (market challengers), or they can play ball and not "rock the boat" (market followers).

Market-Challenger Strategies

Many market challengers have gained ground or even overtaken the leader. Toyota today produces more cars than General Motors and British Airways flies more international passengers than the former leader, Pan Am, did in its heyday. Airbus delivers more aircraft than Boeing.

Boeing and Airbus

When it closed the books on December 31, 2004, Airbus, the company that began in 1970 as an unwieldy confederation of European aerospace firms, had replaced 90-year-old Boeing as the world's largest manufacturer of commercial aircraft. What happened? Challenger Airbus began with a clean slate. It created an innovative new product line equipped with modern features—the massive A380 designed to carry 555 passengers at only 2.5 cents per seat mile. In contrast, Boeing had an arcane production system developed in World War II and couldn't match Airbus's advances without redesigning aircraft at prohibitive costs. Once the manufacturing marvel of the world, Boeing fell behind in both technology and manufacturing efficiency during the 1990s. "A new player that's aggressive and focused will almost always gain ground on an established player," says Dean Headley, co-author of a national airline quality report. And in the aircraft business, when it can take nearly a decade to go from design to launch, lost ground can be incredibly difficult to regain.[39]

Challengers like Airbus set high aspirations, leveraging their resources while the market leader often runs the business as usual. That why the CEO of Airbus, Noel Foregard, vows to keep what he calls the "mentality of a challenger." Now let's examine the competitive attack strategies available to market challengers.

DEFINING THE STRATEGIC OBJECTIVE AND OPPONENT(S) A market challenger must first define its strategic objective. Most aim to increase market share. The challenger must decide whom to attack:

- *It can attack the market leader.* This is a high-risk but potentially high-payoff strategy and makes good sense if the leader is not serving the market well. The alternative strategy is to out-innovate the leader across the whole segment. Xerox wrested the copy market from 3M by developing a better copying process. Later, Canon grabbed a large chunk of Xerox's market by introducing desk copiers.
- *It can attack firms of its own size that are not doing the job and are underfinanced.* These firms have aging products, are charging excessive prices, or are not satisfying customers in other ways.
- *It can attack small local and regional firms.* Several major banks grew to their present size by gobbling up smaller regional banks, or "guppies."

If the attacking company goes after the market leader, its objective might be to gain a certain share. Labatt is under no illusion that it can topple Molson in the domestic beer market—it is simply seeking a larger share. If the attacking company goes after a small local company, its objective might be to drive that company out of existence.

CHOOSING A GENERAL ATTACK STRATEGY Given clear opponents and objectives, what attack options are available? We can distinguish among five attack strategies: frontal, flank, encirclement, bypass, and guerrilla attacks.

Frontal Attack In a pure *frontal attack*, the attacker matches its opponent's product, advertising, price, and distribution. The principle of force says that the side with the greater manpower (resources) will win. A modified frontal attack, such as cutting price vis-à-vis the opponent's, can work if the market leader does not retaliate and if the competitor convinces the market that its product is equal to the leader's. Helene Curtis is a master at convincing the market that its brands—such as Suave and Finesse—are equal in quality but a better value than higher-priced brands.

Flank Attack An enemy's weak spots are natural targets. A *flank attack* can be directed along two strategic dimensions—geographic and segmental. In a geographic attack, the challenger spots areas where the opponent is underperforming. For example, some of IBM's former mainframe rivals, such as Honeywell, chose to set up strong sales branches in medium- and smaller-sized cities that were relatively neglected by IBM. The other flanking strategy is to serve uncovered market needs, as Japanese automakers did when they developed more fuel-efficient cars.

A flanking strategy is another name for identifying shifts in market segments that are causing gaps to develop, and then rushing in to fill the gaps and develop them into strong segments.

Harvey's

Mississauga, Ontario–based Cara Operations recently launched a flanking strategy for its Harvey's restaurants, which is a market challenger in the highly competitive fast-food marketplace dominated by big names such as McDonald's, Wendy's, and Burger King. While most of its competitors are jumping on the healthier food bandwagon, adding new salads and other healthy options to their menu, Harvey's wants to occupy a different space. The company believes that healthy food is not what built their business. At the core of Harvey's historical positioning is a better hamburger prepared in a better way. As a result, Cara is going to continue to focus on a clear and defined target—"the guys who just want to chow down on a good burger"—by creating new products such as the Big Harv. The ultimate goal for Harvey's, which has 339 locations and usually finds itself the number-four or number-five player in the category, is to gain enough market share to move up the ranks.[40]

Flanking is in the best tradition of modern marketing, which holds that the purpose of marketing is to discover needs and satisfy them. Flank attacks are particularly attractive to a challenger with fewer resources than its opponent and are much more likely to be successful than frontal attacks.

Encirclement Attack The encirclement manoeuvre is an attempt to capture a wide slice of the enemy's territory through a "blitz." It involves launching a grand offensive on several fronts. Encirclement makes sense when the challenger commands superior resources and believes a swift encirclement will break the opponent's will. In making a stand against archrival Microsoft, Sun Microsystems licensed its Java software to hundreds of companies and millions of software developers for all sorts of consumer devices. As consumer-electronics products began to go digital, Java started appearing in a wide range of gadgets.

Bypass Attack The most indirect assault strategy is the *bypass*. It means bypassing the enemy and attacking easier markets to broaden one's resource base. This strategy offers three lines of approach: diversifying into unrelated products, diversifying into new geographical markets, and leapfrogging into new technologies to supplant existing products. Pepsi used a bypass strategy against Coke by purchasing (1) orange juice giant Tropicana for US$3.3 billion in 1998, which owned almost twice the market share of Coca-Cola's Minute Maid, and (2) Quaker Oats for US$14 billion in 2000. (Quaker owns Gatorade sports drink, which boasts a huge market share lead over Pepsi's Powerade.)[41]

Technological leapfrogging is a bypass strategy practised in high-tech industries. The challenger patiently researches and develops the next technology and launches an attack, shifting the battleground to its territory, where it has an advantage. Nintendo's successful attack in the video-game market was precisely about wresting market share by introducing a superior technology and redefining the "competitive space." Then Sega/Genesis did the same with more advanced technology, and now Sony's Playstation has grabbed the technological lead to gain almost 60 percent of the video-game market.[42] Challenger Google used technological leapfrogging to overtake Yahoo! and become the market leader in search engines. Now another company is using the same tactic to try to become the "Google" of e-mail:

Stata Labs

If Raymie Stata, co-founder of Stata Labs, has his way you will "bloomba" your e-mail in the same way that you "google" a company name or product on the Internet. He created his Bloomba e-mail management system in response to flaws in Microsoft's Outlook, which is used by 50 percent of office workers. Stata feels that people waste precious time adapting to what he sees as a counterintuitive e-mail management system. Rather than using folders or other complicated filing systems, Bloomba features a powerful search function that indexes all of your messages—even attachments—and lets you search for them in seconds. While it has yet to overtake Microsoft's Outlook, business journalists are hailing Bloomba's technology as the wave of the future for serious e-mail communicators.[43]

A Gatorade ad with the soccer star Mia Hamm. In a bypass strategy against Coca-Cola, Pepsi bought the Quaker Oats Company, owner of Gatorade Thirst Quenchers, which has a much larger share of the sports drink market than Coca-Cola's Powerade.

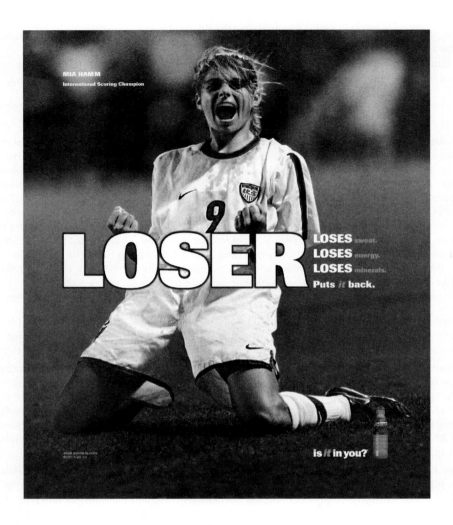

Guerrilla Warfare Guerrilla warfare consists of waging small, intermittent attacks to harass and demoralize the opponent and eventually secure permanent footholds. The guerrilla challenger uses both conventional and unconventional means of attack. These include selective price cuts, intense promotional blitzes, and occasional legal action. Princeton Review successfully challenged Kaplan Educational Centers, the largest test-preparation business in the United States, through e-mail horror stories about Kaplan and brash ads—"Stanley's a wimp," or "Friends don't let friends take Kaplan"—while always touting the Princeton Review's smaller, livelier classes.

Normally, guerrilla warfare is practised by a smaller firm against a larger one. The smaller firm launches a barrage of attacks in random corners of the larger opponent's market in a manner calculated to weaken the opponent's market power. Military dogma holds that a continual stream of minor attacks usually creates more cumulative impact, disorganization, and confusion in the enemy than a few major attacks. A guerrilla campaign can be expensive, although admittedly less expensive than a frontal, encirclement, or flank attack. Guerrilla warfare is more a preparation for war than a war itself. Ultimately, it must be backed by a stronger attack if the challenger hopes to beat the opponent.

CHOOSING A SPECIFIC ATTACK STRATEGY The challenger must go beyond the five broad strategies and develop more specific strategies:

- *Price discount.* The challenger can offer a comparable product at a lower price. This is the strategy of discount retailers. Three conditions must be fulfilled. First, the challenger must convince buyers that its product and service are comparable to the leader's. Second, buyers must be price sensitive. Third, the market leader must refuse to cut its price in spite of the competitor's attack.

- *Lower-price goods.* The challenger can offer an average- or lower-quality product at a much lower price. For example, Loblaws is featuring a laundry detergent in packages that closely mimic Tide's, but the President's Choice brand detergent is sold at prices approximately one-third lower. Shelf displays challenge consumers to compare the prices. Firms that establish themselves through a lower-price strategy, however, can be attacked by firms whose prices are even lower.

- *Value-priced goods and services.* In recent years companies ranging from retailers such as Target and airlines such as WestJet have been combining low prices and high quality to snag market share from market leaders. In the United Kingdom, premium retailers like Boots and Sainsbury are now scrambling to meet intensifying price—and quality—competition from ASDA and Tesco.[44]

- *Prestige goods.* A market challenger can launch a higher-quality product and charge a higher price than the leader. Mercedes gained on Cadillac in the U.S. market by offering a car of higher quality at a higher price.

- *Product proliferation.* The challenger can attack the leader by launching a larger product variety, thus giving buyers more choice. Baskin-Robbins achieved its growth in the ice cream business by promoting more flavours—31—than its larger competitors.

- *Product innovation.* The challenger can pursue product innovation. 3M typically enters new markets by introducing a product improvement or breakthrough.

- *Improved services.* The challenger can offer new or better services to customers. Avis's famous attack on Hertz, "We're only second. We try harder," was based on promising and delivering cleaner cars and faster service than Hertz.

- *Distribution innovation.* A challenger might develop a new channel of distribution. Avon became a major cosmetics company by perfecting door-to-door selling instead of battling other cosmetic firms in conventional stores.

- *Manufacturing-cost reduction.* The challenger might achieve lower manufacturing costs than its competitors through more efficient purchasing, lower labour costs, and more modern production equipment.

- *Intensive advertising promotion.* Some challengers attack the leader by increasing expenditures on advertising and promotion. Substantial promotional spending, however, is usually not a sensible strategy unless the challenger's product or advertising message is superior. Humour, for example, is the key factor that 62 percent of Canadians believe makes beer commercials appealing. Molson has won this battle hands down. Its 2002 "I AM Canadian" campaign is still one of the most easily recalled beer campaigns. When it was first run, it created a 27 percent awareness level, outperforming Labatt's "Free Your Time" campaign, with its 16 percent awareness level.[45]

A challenger's success depends on combining several strategies to improve its position over time.

Samsung

Korean consumer electronics giant Samsung has used many of the challenger strategies to take on Japanese manufacturers and begin outselling them across a wide range of products. Like many other Asian companies, Samsung used to stress volume and market domination rather than profitability. Yet during the Asian financial crisis of the late 1990s, when other Korean *chaobols* collapsed beneath a mountain of debt, Samsung took a different tack. It cut costs and placed new emphasis on manufacturing flexibility, which allows its consumer electronics goods to go from project phase to store shelves within six months. It also began a serious focus on innovation, using technological leapfrogging to produce state-of-the-art mobile telephone handsets that are big sellers not only across Asia but also in Europe and North America.[46]

"Marketing Memo: Making Smaller Better" provides some additional tips for challenger brands.

Market-Follower Strategies

In the 1960s, Theodore Levitt wrote an article entitled "Innovative Imitation," in which he argued that a strategy of *product imitation* might be as profitable as a strategy of *product innovation*.[47] The innovator bears the expense of developing the new product, getting it into distribution, and informing and educating the market. The reward for all this work and risk is normally market leadership. However, another firm can come along and copy or improve on the new product. Although it probably will not overtake the leader, the follower can achieve high profits because it did not bear any of the innovation expense.

S&S Cycle

S&S Cycle is the biggest supplier of complete engines and major motor parts to more than 15 companies that build several thousand Harley-like cruiser bikes each year. These cloners charge as much as US$30 000 for their customized creations. S&S has built its name by improving on Harley-Davidson's handiwork. Its customers are often would-be Harley buyers frustrated by long waiting lines at the dealers. Other customers simply want the incredibly powerful S&S engines. S&S stays abreast of its evolving market by ordering a new Harley bike every year and taking apart the engine to see what it can improve upon.[48]

Many companies prefer to follow rather than challenge the market leader. Patterns of "conscious parallelism" are common in capital-intensive, homogeneous-product industries, such as steel, fertilizers, and chemicals. The opportunities for product differentiation and image differentiation are low; service quality is often comparable; and price sensitivity runs high. The mood in these industries is against short-run grabs for market share because that strategy only provokes retaliation. Most firms decide against stealing one another's customers. Instead, they present similar offers to buyers, usually by copying the leader. Market shares show high stability.

This is not to say that market followers lack strategies. A market follower must know how to hold current customers and win a fair share of new customers. Each follower tries to bring distinctive advantages to its target market—location, services, financing. Because the follower is often a major target of attack by challengers, it must keep its manufacturing costs low and its product quality and services high. It must also enter new markets as they open up. The follower has to define a growth path, but one that does not invite competitive retaliation. Four broad strategies can be distinguished:

1. *Counterfeiter.* The counterfeiter duplicates the leader's product and package and sells it on the black market or through disreputable dealers. Music record firms, Apple Computer, and Rolex have been plagued with the counterfeiter problem, especially in Asia.

2. *Cloner.* The cloner emulates the leader's products, name, and packaging, with slight variations. For example, Ralcorp Holding Inc. sells imitations of name-brand cereals in look-alike boxes. Its Tasteeos, Fruit Rings, and Corn Flakes sell for about $1 a box less than the leading name brands.

3. *Imitator.* The imitator copies some things from the leader but maintains differentiation in terms of packaging, advertising, pricing, or

Marketing Memo

Making Smaller Better

Adam Morgan offers eight suggestions for how small brands can better compete:

1. *Break with your immediate past.* Don't be afraid to ask "dumb" questions to challenge convention and view your brand differently.

2. *Build a "lighthouse identity."* Establish values and communicate who and why you are (e.g., Apple).

3. *Assume thought leadership of the category.* Break convention in terms of representation (what you say about yourself), where you say it (medium), and experience (what you do beyond talk).

4. *Create symbols of re-evaluation.* A rocket uses half of its fuel in the first mile to break loose from the gravitational pull—you may need to polarize people.

5. *Sacrifice.* Focus your target, message, reach and frequency, distribution, and line extensions, and recognize that less can be more.

6. *Overcommit.* Although you may do fewer things, do "big" things when you do them.

7. *Use publicity and advertising to enter popular culture.* Unconventional communications can get people talking.

8. *Be idea-centred, not consumer-centred.* Sustain challenger momentum by not losing sight of what the brand is about and can be and redefine marketing support and the centre of the company to reflect this vision.

Source: Adam Morgan, *Eating the Big Fish: How Challenger Brands Can Compete Against Brand Leaders* (New York: John Wiley Sons, 1999).

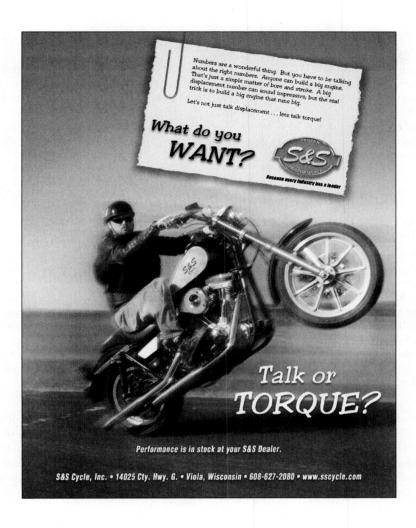

Market follower strategies: S&S Cycle supplies engines and parts to companies that build Harley-Davidson clones. S&S has a reputation for building powerful engines that improve on the Harley product.

location. The leader does not mind the imitator as long as the imitator does not attack the leader aggressively. Fernandez Pujals grew up in Fort Lauderdale, Florida, and took Domino's home delivery idea to Spain, where he borrowed US$80 000 to open his first store in Madrid. His TelePizza chain now operates almost 1000 stores in Europe and Latin America.

4. *Adapter*. The adapter takes the leader's products and adapts or improves them. The adapter may choose to sell to different markets, but often the adapter grows into the future challenger, as many Japanese firms have done after adapting and improving products developed elsewhere.

What does a follower earn? Normally, less than the leader. For example, a study of food-processing companies showed the largest firm averaging a 16 percent return on investment; the number-two firm, 6 percent; the number-three firm, –1 percent, and the number-four firm, –6 percent. In this case, only the top two firms have profits. No wonder Jack Welch, former CEO of GE, told his business units that each must reach the number-one or -two position in its market or else! Followership is often not a rewarding path.

Market-Nicher Strategies

An alternative to being a follower in a large market is to be a leader in a small market, or niche. Smaller firms normally avoid competing with larger firms by targeting small markets of little or no interest to the larger firms. Here is an example:

Logitech International

Logitech has become a US$1.3 billion global success story by making every variation of computer mouse imaginable. The company turns out mice for left- and right-handed people, cordless mice that use radio waves, mice shaped like real mice for children, and 3-D mice that let the user appear to move behind screen objects. It sells to OEMs as well as via its own brand at retail. Its global dominance in the mouse category enabled the company to expand into other computer peripherals, such as PC Headsets, PC gaming peripherals, and Webcams.[49]

Even large, profitable firms use niching strategies for some of their business units or companies.

The Beer Industry

Microbrewers' specialty beers—such as Banks beer from the Hart Brewing Co. Ltd. of Ottawa or Hemp Cream Ale from B.C.'s Bowen Island Brewing Company—were the only markets showing any growth potential in the late 1990s. Today, they account for approximately 5 percent of the country's beer sales. Growth in this segment has prompted Canada's two mega-brewers—Labatt and Molson—to launch their own specialty beers. Responding to the "low-carb" craze, Labatt launched a new beer, Labatt Sterling, in bottles at the end of 2003. Labatt's director of public affairs believes they hit gold with the product since it was a low-carb option that didn't compromise on taste. The company couldn't keep the beer in stock when it was first introduced, and it proved so popular that Labatt offered it in draught form beginning in 2004.

Firms with low shares of the total market can be highly profitable through smart niching. A. T. Cross niched itself in the high-price writing instruments market with its famous gold and silver items. Family-run Tire Rack sells 2 million specialty tires a year though the Internet, telephone, and mail from its South Bend, Indiana, location.[50] Such companies tend to offer high value, charge a premium price, achieve lower manufacturing costs, and shape a strong corporate culture and vision. New Balance is a classic example of a small company that has successfully used market-nicher strategies to establish a strong market position.

Running Room

New niche retailers such as the Running Room are following a market-niche strategy to compete against much bigger retailers that have large and difficult-to-manage product lines. Running Room, as the name suggests, is a store for runners. It carries everything from shoes and running clothing to specialty watches. Launched in Edmonton in 1984, the company now has 57 stores across Canada and three in the United States. The retailer practises strategies such as streamlining running shoes by breaking them down by type of shoe rather than by supplier, and then custom-fitting each customer. It also runs its own clinics—from "Learn to Run" to "Triathlon"—which are staffed by people who have graduated from the programs and are runners themselves. It has a bi-monthly magazine featuring stories and tips from other runners that is mailed out to a 150 000-strong database. The niche retailer has typically achieved 20 percent growth in sales, year over year.[51]

In a study of hundreds of business units, the Strategic Planning Institute found that the return on investment averaged 27 percent in smaller markets, but only 11 percent in larger markets.[52] Why is niching so profitable? The main reason is that the market nicher ends up knowing the target customers so well that it meets their needs better than other firms selling to this niche casually. As a result, the nicher can charge a substantial price over costs. The nicher achieves *high margin*, whereas the mass marketer achieves *high volume*.

Nichers have three tasks: creating niches, expanding niches, and protecting niches. Niching carries a major risk in that the market niche might dry up or be attacked. The company is then stuck with highly specialized resources that may not have high-value alternative uses.

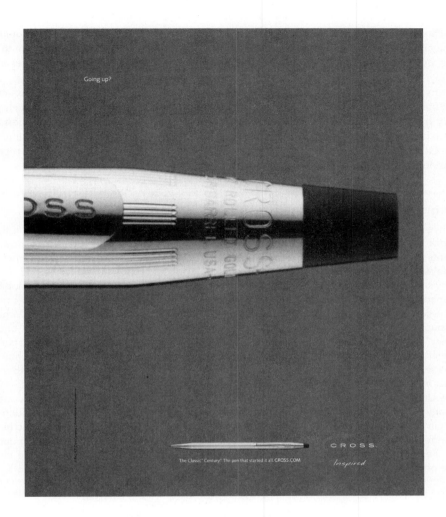

Market nicher strategies: A.T. Cross's famous gold and silver pens are in the high-priced writing instruments niche.

Zippo

With smoking on a steady decline, Zippo Manufacturing is finding the market for its iconic metal cigarette lighter drying up. Zippo marketers now find themselves needing to diversify and to broaden their focus to "selling flame." With a goal of reducing reliance on tobacco-related products to 50 percent of revenue by 2010, the company introduced a long, slender multipurpose lighter for candles, grills, and fireplaces in 2001, explored licensing arrangements with suppliers of flame-related outdoor products, and diversified its operations by acquiring Case Cutlery, a knife-maker.[53]

The Running Room practises a market-niche strategy targeting the runner retail segment.

Because niches can weaken, the firm must continually create new ones. The firm should "stick to its niching" but not necessarily to its niche. That is why *multiple niching* is preferable to *single niching*. By developing strength in two or more niches, the company increases its chances for survival.

Firms entering a market should aim at a niche initially rather than the whole market. (See "Marketing Memo: Strategies for Entering Markets Held by Incumbent Firms.") The cell-phone industry has experienced phenomenal growth but is now experiencing fierce competition as the numbers of new potential users dwindle. Through innovative partnerships and marketing, Virgin Mobile Canada has successfully tapped into one of the few remaining high growth segments, Generation Y customers entering the market.[54]

Virgin Mobile Canada

While Virgin is a big player in music, air travel, and other industries, it is the new kid on the block in the wireless business. Yet, rather than launching a frontal attack on major incumbents in the industry, the Virgin Group and Bell Mobility (Canada's largest retail and wholesale wireless provider) in March 2004 announced plans to launch mobile voice and data services aimed at the youth segment through a jointly owned company, Virgin Mobile Canada. The new company will focus on introducing Virgin's unique style of wireless communications to younger Canadian consumers. Sir Richard Branson, chairman of the Virgin Group, commented, "Canada represents a great opportunity for our mobile phone business. We plan to deliver transparent value for money and great customer service." The partnership is a win–win enterprise for both players. Bell, with its somewhat staid "old school" image, will benefit from Virgin's trend-setting style. Virgin, in return, will have access to the best infrastructure network and coverage in Canada. Virgin hopes to build on its success in the United Kingdom. It launched its services in Britain in November 1999 and now, with nearly 4 million customers, it is the fastest-growing mobile phone company in the country. Virgin Mobile offers one of the simplest prepaid plans around, with no contracts and no hidden fees. The company touts cool features such as a "rescue ring" to escape a boring date or the voice of Isaac Hayes or Grandpa Munster for the greeting. And, to emphasize that the phone plan has "nothing to hide," Virgin runs provocative ads featuring nude actors.[55]

Balancing Customer and Competitor Orientations

We have stressed the importance of a company's positioning itself competitively as a market leader, challenger, follower, or nicher. Yet a company must not spend all its time focusing on competitors.

Competitor-Centred Companies

A *competitor-centred company* sets its course as follows:

Situation

- Competitor W is going all out to crush us in Winnipeg.
- Competitor X is improving its distribution coverage in Saskatoon and hurting our sales.
- Competitor Y has cut its price in Montreal, and we lost three share points.
- Competitor Z has introduced a new service feature in Victoria, and we are losing sales.

Reactions

- We will withdraw from the Winnipeg market because we cannot afford to fight this battle.
- We will increase our advertising expenditure in Saskatoon.
- We will meet competitor Y's price cut in Montreal.
- We will increase our sales-promotion budget in Victoria.

This kind of planning has some pluses and minuses. On the positive side, the company develops a fighter orientation. It trains its marketers to be on constant alert, to watch for weaknesses in its competitors' and its own position. On the negative side, the company is too reactive. Rather than formulating and executing a consistent, customer-oriented strategy, it determines its moves based on its competitors' moves. It does not move toward its own goals. It does not know where it will end up, because so much depends on what its competitors do.

Customer-Centred Companies

A *customer-centred company* focuses more on customer developments in formulating its strategies:

Situation

- The total market is growing at 4 percent annually.
- The quality-sensitive segment is growing at 8 percent annually.
- The deal-prone customer segment is also growing fast, but these customers do not stay with any supplier very long.
- A growing number of customers have expressed an interest in a 24-hour hotline, which no one in the industry offers.

Reactions

- We will focus more effort on reaching and satisfying the quality segment of the market. We will buy better components, improve quality control, and shift our advertising theme to quality.
- We will avoid cutting prices and making deals because we do not want the kind of customer that buys this way.
- We will install a 24-hour hotline if it looks promising.

Clearly, the customer-centred company is in a better position to identify new opportunities and set a course that promises to deliver long-run profits. By monitoring customer needs, it can decide which customer groups and emerging needs are the most important to serve, given its resources and objectives. Jeff Bezos, founder of Amazon.com, strongly favours a customer-centred orientation: "Amazon.com's mantra has been that we were going to obsess over our customer and not our competitors. We watch our competitors, learn from them, see the things that they were doing good for customers and copy those things as much as we can. But we were never going to obsess over them."[56]

Marketing Memo

Strategies for Entering Markets Held by Incumbent Firms

Carpenter and Nakamoto examined strategies for launching a new product into a market dominated by one brand, such as Jell-O or FedEx. (These brands, which include many market pioneers, are particularly difficult to attack because many are the standard against which others are judged.) They identified four strategies that have good profit potential in this situation:

1. *Differentiation*. Positioning away from the dominant brand with a comparable or premium price and heavy advertising spending to establish the new brand as a credible alternative. Example: Honda's motorcycle challenges Harley-Davidson.

2. *Challenger*. Positioning close to the dominant brand with heavy advertising spending and comparable or premium price to challenge the dominant brand as the category standard. Example: Pepsi competing against Coke.

3. *Niche*. Positioning away from the dominant brand with a high price and a low advertising budget to exploit a profitable niche. Example: Tom's of Maine all-natural toothpaste competing against Crest.

4. *Premium*. Positioning near the dominant brand with little advertising spending but a premium price to move "up market" relative to the dominant brand. Examples: Godiva chocolate and Häagen-Dazs ice cream competing against standard brands.

Sources: Gregory S. Carpenter and Kent Nakamoto, "Competitive Strategies for Late Entry into a Market with a Dominant Brand," *Management Science* (October 1990): 1268–1278; Gregory S. Carpenter and Kent Nakamoto, "The Impact of Consumer Preference Formation on Marketing Objectives and Competitive Second Mover Strategies," *Journal of Consumer Psychology*, 5, no. 4 (1996): 325–358. Venkatesh Shankar, Gregory Carpenter, and Lakshman Krishnamurthi, "Late Mover Advantage: How Innovative Late Entrants Outsell Pioneers," *Journal of Marketing Research*, 35 (February 1998): 54–70.

SUMMARY

1. To prepare an effective marketing strategy, a company must study competitors as well as actual and potential customers. Companies need to identify competitors' strategies, objectives, strengths, and weaknesses.

2. A company's closest competitors are those seeking to satisfy the same customers and needs and making similar offers. A company should also pay attention to latent competitors, who may offer new or other ways to satisfy the same needs. A company should identify competitors by using both industry and market-based analyses.

3. A market leader has the largest market share in the relevant product market. To remain dominant, the leader looks for ways to expand total market demand, attempts to protect its current market share, and perhaps tries to increase its market share.

4. A market challenger attacks the market leader and other competitors in an aggressive bid for more market share. Challengers can choose from five types of general attack; challengers must also choose specific attack strategies.

5. A market follower is a runner-up firm that is willing to maintain its market share and not rock the boat. A follower can play the role of counterfeiter, cloner, imitator, or adapter.

6. A market nicher serves small market segments not being served by larger firms. The key to nichemanship is specialization. Nichers develop offerings to fully meet a certain group of customer's needs, commanding a premium price in the process.

7. As important as a competitive orientation is in today's global markets, companies should not overdo the emphasis on competitors. They should maintain a good balance of consumer and competitor monitoring.

APPLICATIONS

Marketing Debate: How Do You Attack a Category Leader?

Attacking a leader is always difficult. Some strategists recommend attacking a leader head-on by targeting its strengths. Other strategists disagree and recommend flanking and attempting to avoid the leader's strengths.

Take a position: The best way to challenge a leader is to attack its strengths versus The best way to attack a leader is to avoid a head-on assault and to adopt a flanking strategy.

Marketing Discussion

Pick an industry. Classify firms according to the four different roles they might play: leader, challenger, follower, and nicher. How would you characterize the nature of competition? Do the firms follow the principles described in the chapter?

Marketing Spotlight: Accenture

Accenture started life as the consulting arm of accounting firm Arthur Andersen. Over the years, the consultants progressively changed their name to build their brand image. They started as the Administrative Accounting Group and then became the Management Information Consulting Division. In 1989, Andersen Consulting separated from Arthur Andersen in order to position itself against its IT services competitors. At the time, Andersen Consulting was already doing US$1 billion a year in business, but it wasn't known in the information technology world and was mistakenly associated with accounting. The new spin-off needed to promote its name as an innovator in IT consulting and separate itself from its accounting heritage.

The IT consulting marketplace was crowded with competitors ranging from nuts-and-bolts hardware/software providers like IBM to leading strategy firms like McKinsey and the Boston Consulting Group. To make a name for itself, Andersen Consulting launched the first large-scale advertising campaign in the professional services area. By the end of the decade, it was the world's largest management and technology consulting organization. It employs over 100 000 people in 48 countries. Together with its affiliates, Accenture has over 4700 employees in Canada.

In 2000, following arbitration against its former parent, Anderson Consulting was granted its full independence from Arthur Andersen—but at the price of giving up the Andersen name. Andersen Consulting had three months to find, implement, and introduce the world to a new corporate name. This effort would become one of the largest and most successful re-branding campaigns in corporate history.

A consultant from the Oslo office coined the Accenture name because it rhymed with "adventure" and connoted an "accent on the future." The name emerged as the winner because it was catchy and distinctive and embodied bold growth and innovation. It retained the "Ac" of the original Andersen Consulting name (echoing the Ac.com Web site), which would help the firm retain some of the brand equity held in its original name. The Accenture name campaign of 2001 delivered results. It built awareness of the firm's breadth and depth of services. The effect of the advertising campaign was to increase by 350 percent the number of firms considering purchasing Accenture's services.

In 2002, Accenture launched the "Innovation Delivered" campaign to distinguish itself from the competition. Competitors in the IT arena, such as IBM and EDS, lacked broader business consulting expertise and weren't seen as knowledgeable in business strategy and processes. They tended to approach firms from the IT level, not the C-level (CEO, CFO, CIO). Competitors in the business consulting arena like McKinsey, in contrast, had brand strength associated with strategic thinking. They were seen as thought leaders, but not as collaborative partners who would roll up their shirt-sleeves and implement the ideas they suggested.

Accenture saw its differentiator as the ability to provide both innovative ideas—ideas grounded in business processes as well as IT—and the ability to execute those innovative ideas. Ian Watmore, Accenture's U.K. chief, explained the need to have both strategy and execution: "Unless you can provide both transformational consulting and outsourcing capability, you're not going to win. Clients expect both. That's why we've grown our outsourcing capabilities, and that's why companies like IBM and EDS are trying to get transforma-

tional capabilities." IBM did exactly that, purchasing PriceWaterhouseCooper's consulting arm, thereby becoming a much more formidable competitor to Accenture.

Accenture surveyed senior executives from different industries and countries and confirmed that executives saw the inability to execute and deliver on ideas as the number-one barrier to success. With its "Innovation Delivered" campaign, Accenture positioned itself as the firm that would bring results and put plans into action: "From innovation to execution, Accenture helps accelerate your vision." The award-winning campaign delivered a high return on investment. For example, the firm estimates its ROI for U.K. marketing activities was 215 percent.

In 2002, the climate changed. After the dot-com crash and the economic downturn, innovation was no longer enough. Executives wanted bottom-line results. Accenture launched its "High Performance Delivered" campaign with Tiger Woods as the spokesperson. Accenture's continued success is demonstrated in its revenues (US$11.8 billion in 2003) and its number-52 ranking on *Business Week*'s top 100 brands.

DISCUSSION QUESTIONS

1. What have been the key success factors for Accenture?

2. Where is Accenture vulnerable? What should it watch out for?

3. What recommendations would you make to senior marketing executives going forward? What should the company be sure to do with its marketing?

Sources: "Lessons Learned from Top Firms' Marketing Blunders," *Management Consultant International* (December 2003): 1; Sean Callahan, "Tiger Tees Off in New Accenture Campaign," *B to B*, October 13, 2003, p. 3; "Inside Accenture's Biggest UK Client," *Management Consultant International* (October 2003): 1–3; "Accenture Re-Branding Wins UK Plaudits," *Management Consultant International* (October 2002): 5; "Accenture's Results Highlight Weakness of Consulting Market," *Management Consultant International* (October 2003): 8–10; **www.accenture.com**.

SHAPING THE MARKET OFFERINGS

IN THIS CHAPTER, WE WILL ADDRESS THE FOLLOWING QUESTIONS:

- What are the characteristics of products and how can they be classified?

- How can companies differentiate products?

- How can a company build and manage its product mix and product lines?

- How can companies combine products to create strong co-brands or ingredient brands?

- How can companies use packaging, labelling, warranties, and guarantees as marketing tools?

CHAPTER 12

Setting Product Strategy

PROFILE: CANADIAN MARKETING EXCELLENCE

Rumba Games Inc. has become a leader in the creation, manufacture, and distribution of innovative, award-winning board games for all ages, even though the company was only launched in 1999 with a single game—Countdown, an educational children's game. The Mississauga, Ontario–based company was founded by Jean-Paul Teskey.

While it is a relatively new kid on the block, the company's been winning awards, attracting international press attention, and winning accolades from both parents and toy-testing organizations because of its dedication to superior quality in design and game play. It's not surprising it's been raising a few eyebrows. The company grew an astounding 1907 percent between the years 2000 and 2002 alone. As *Marketing Magazine* recently wrote, "If you studied Jean-Paul Teskey's face whenever someone breaks out a board game, you might notice his eyebrows rise and the beginnings of a devilish smile. It would probably be the same look you'd find on Donald Trump's face if you asked him to play Monopoly. Teskey has a lot to smile about." The company generated almost $4 million in sales in 2004, and it is projected to have sales close to $7 million in 2005. It's not surprising that Rumba was third on the list of Canada's fastest-growing companies, according to a recent *Profit* magazine ranking.

Earning this ranking in an industry that seemed ready to die just a few years ago is amazing, but the industry has been making a determined comeback. In Canada, the sector accounts for about $100 million in retail sales, while the worldwide market is projected to be US$2.4 billion. Growth in the industry was spawned by the cocooning trend of the 1990s and the terrorist attacks of September 2001, which made more people just want to stay at home and have fun with their families. Rumba is certainly poised to win a significant share of this substantial market.

Rumba has a portfolio of well-known game titles, but it continues to innovate. Here are just some of the products it launched in 2004: Read'em, an educational word-building card game; Guesstimation, a guessing game presenting astounding facts and figures; Sound Effects, a CD guessing game; and Trivia by the Pound. Read'em is typical of the insight about gaming that has made Rumba so successful. It is a family game that combines the skill of word-building with the thrill of poker. The object is to win chips from other players by creating the best hand—or by bluffing your opponents into thinking you have. Players spell the best word possible with five cards, and then they can choose to "stay" or trade in some cards in an attempt to spell a better word. In a recent press release, Rumba Games president Jean-Paul Teskey said, "The reward is not money but the fun and fast pace of the game, combined with a valuable learning experience."

Rumba's core product line features such well-loved game titles as Survivor: The Game, and Urban Myth. Survivor: The Game (which targets people eight years and up) was licensed from CBS Consumer Products. The design of the game lets people mimic the hit TV show. Players form two tribes and compete in a series of creative "immunity" challenges using objects that can be found around the home—anything from juggling oranges to singing the theme song from *The Love Boat*. If a team loses too many, they must go to tribal council and vote a tribe member "off the couch." Urban Myth (designed for players over the age of 12) challenges players to discern whether stories they've heard through the grapevine are true or pure myth. For example, "Did Marilyn Monroe have 11 toes?" Or "Are there really alligators in the sewers of New York City?"

It is difficult to build a strong market presence with only a narrow line of products. Thus, to accelerate its growth, Rumba negotiated an exclusive sales and distribution agreement with Cadaco to market its product line in Canada. Cadaco, founded in 1935, is one of the United States' oldest independent family-owned game and toy companies, and it has the world's largest line of magic products that it markets under the Marshall Brodien™ brand name. The partnership promises to be win–win, as noted by John Lindsay, president of Cadaco: "Rumba's knowledge, experience and relationships with customers will provide Cadaco with an enhanced presence in this important market."

Having a great product line is only a very small part of winning the battle for market share. Getting a new game into the hands of retailers isn't an easy task. Competition for shelf space is intense. Thus, Teskey has had to be as creative about his marketing to potential distributors as he was about his games. He was afraid that if he just shipped prospective retailers a sample game, they wouldn't even open the box. But if he could involve them in the game and its premise, their curiosity might make them explore the product further. Thus, Teskey tailored game cards to target particular customers. For example, when generating interest for Urban Myth, Teskey sent buyers in New York cards about giant alligators living in the city's sewer system. Teskey also realized early on that nontraditional retailers would be more open to selling games than the well-established channels where competition was intense. Thus, he came up with the novel idea of selling his games through bookstores, believing that "cerebral" games like Urban Myth would be a perfect complement to book retailers' traditional products. The game is now distributed at Chapters and Indigo stores in Canada, and through Books-a-Million and Barnes & Noble in the United States.

Grocery store chain Loblaws was another seemingly unlikely retailer approached by Teskey. He was one of the first game producers to realize that the grocery store was no longer just selling food—it was diversifying into hobby areas such as gardening. So he kept calling Loblaws' management until they agreed to meet with him. It wasn't long before his proposition won them over. Rumba now also sells its games online through Amazon.com and through the Grand River Toy Company, a Canadian catalogue seller.

Finally comes the task of promoting the product line. Board game marketers rarely use traditional advertising. Instead, they rely on word-of-mouth driven by buzz-generating promotions designed to get people talking about and trying the games. In fact, if a game marketer can't find a hook upon which to build a promotional plan, it may doom the product to the garbage can. Rumba Games is no exception. Take Survivor: The Game. There's no doubt that part of its success results from its association with the top-rated reality show and its millions of fans. Promoting the game was merely a matter of taking former *Survivor* contestants on whirlwind media tours that attracted not only the press, but also throngs of fans. And the tactic has worked. Since its launch in the fall of 2003, Rumba has sold over 125 000 units. For Rumba products not based on hot TV properties, Teskey says the key is matching the promotional medium to the product. Urban Myth, a deductive reasoning game, for example, gets better results when promoted during morning radio programs, when hosts can take more time describing the game as part of giveaway contests. While Rumba is still dwarfed when compared to industry giants like Milton Bradley, which owns titles like Trivial Pursuit, Monopoly, and Scrabble, Rumba has certainly shown it can cut a mean figure on the road to success.

Sources: Paul-Mark Rondon, "Game Boys," *Marketing Magazine*, February 14, 2005; "Cadaco Brings Its Award-Winning Products to Canada Through New Distribution Agreement with Rumba Games," Cadaco Toys press release, **www.cadaco.com/press/press-canadianmarket.html** (viewed February 16, 2005); Erik Arneson, "Read'em from Rumba Games," Board Games Blog, September 2, 2004, **http://boardgames.about.com/b/a/108735.htm**; Allan Britnell, "Cracking the Mega-stores," *PROFIT-X*, September 25, 2003.

Rumba's success story underscores the importance of the first and most important element of the marketing mix: the product. All the advertising and promotion in the world will not make consumers buy a game for themselves or their children if they don't trust its quality.

Marketing planning begins with formulating an offering to meet target customers' needs or wants. The customer will judge the offering by three basic elements: product features and quality, services mix and quality, and price (see Figure 12.1). In this chapter, we examine product; in Chapter 13, services; and in Chapter 14, prices. All three elements must be meshed into a competitively attractive offering.

Product Characteristics and Classifications

Many people think that a product is a tangible offering, but a product can be more than that. A **product** is anything that can be offered to a market to satisfy a want or need. Products that are marketed include physical goods, services, experiences, events, persons, places, properties, organizations, information, and ideas.

Product Levels: The Customer Value Hierarchy

In planning its market offering, the marketer needs to address five product levels (see Figure 12.2).[1] Each level adds more customer value, and the five constitute a **customer value hierarchy**. The fundamental level is the **core benefit**: the service or benefit the customer is really buying. A hotel guest is buying "rest and sleep." The purchaser of a drill is buying "holes." Marketers must see themselves as benefit providers.

At the second level, the marketer has to turn the core benefit into a **basic product**. Thus a hotel room includes a bed, bathroom, towels, desk, dresser, and closet.

At the third level, the marketer prepares an **expected product**, a set of attributes and conditions buyers normally expect when they purchase this product. Hotel guests expect a clean bed, fresh towels, working lamps, and a relative degree of quiet. Because

FIGURE 12.1

Components of the Marketing Offering

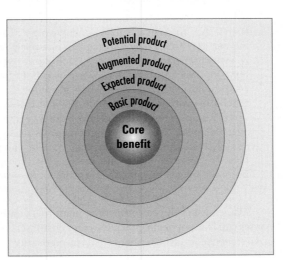

FIGURE 12.2

Five Product Levels

most hotels can meet this minimum expectation, the traveller normally will settle for whichever hotel is most convenient or least expensive.

At the fourth level, the marketer prepares an **augmented product** that exceeds customer expectations. In developed countries, brand positioning and competition take place at this level. In developing countries and emerging markets such as China and India, however, competition takes place mostly at the expected product level.

Differentiation arises on the basis of product augmentation. Product augmentation also leads the marketer to look at the user's total **consumption system**: the way the user performs the tasks of getting and using products and related services.[2] As Levitt observed long ago:

> The new competition is not between what companies produce in their factories, but between what they add to their factory output in the form of packaging, services, advertising, customer advice, financing, delivery arrangements, warehousing, and other things that people value.[3]

Some things should be noted about product-augmentation strategy. First, each augmentation adds cost. Second, augmented benefits soon become expected benefits and necessary points-of-parity. Today's hotel guests expect cable or satellite television with a remote control and high-speed Internet access or two phone lines. This means competitors will have to search for still other features and benefits. Third, as companies raise the price of their augmented product, some competitors offer a "stripped-down" version at a much lower price. Thus, alongside the growth of fine hotels like Fairmont and Ritz Carlton, we see the emergence of lower-cost hotels and motels like Motel 6 and Comfort Inn, which cater to clients who simply want the basic product.

Jamestown Container Co.

What could be harder to differentiate than corrugated cardboard? Yet, Jamestown Container Company, the lead supplier of corrugated products for companies such as 3M, has formed strategic partnerships with area manufacturers to provide every part of the shipping system. It not only provides boxes, but also offers tape, shrink-wrap, and everything else needed either to display or to ship a customer's final product. "It's a combination for survival," says the company's CEO. "More customers want to call one place for everything. We have to keep reinventing ourselves and form these kinds of relationships to remain competitive."[4]

At the fifth level stands the **potential product**, which encompasses all the possible augmentations and transformations the product or offering might undergo in the future. Here is where companies search for new ways to satisfy customers and distinguish their offer. For instance, in an era when customers are demanding ever-faster Internet and wireless connections, Verizon is investing its capital in creating a raft of potential products:

Verizon

Rather than be seen as a follower in the highly competitive telecom industry, Verizon is pushing fast into totally new territory. For one thing, Verizon is rolling out fibre-optic connections to every home and business in 29 U.S. states over the next 10 to 15 years. This will allow the lightning-fast transmission of everything from traditional phone service to HDTV. The company is no less aggressive when it comes to wireless technology. Verizon has covered Manhattan with more than 1000 Wi-Fi hotspots that let any Verizon broadband subscriber use a laptop to tap into the Net wirelessly when near a Verizon pay phone. The company is also deploying 3G, a third-generation wireless service that lets customers make super-speedy Net connections from their mobile phones. In short, the company is investing billions in services customers don't even know they want yet, but which—Verizon is betting—will set the standard for the entire industry.[5]

Also consider the customization platforms new e-commerce sites are offering, from which companies can learn by seeing what different customers prefer. Proctor & Gamble, for example, has developed Reflect.com, which offers customized beauty products created interactively on the Web site.

Product Classifications

Marketers have traditionally classified products on the basis of characteristics: durability, tangibility, and use (consumer or industrial). Each product type has an appropriate marketing-mix strategy.[6]

DURABILITY AND TANGIBILITY Products can be classified into three groups, according to durability and tangibility:

1. *Nondurable goods* are tangible goods normally consumed in one or a few uses, like beer and soap. Because these goods are consumed quickly and purchased frequently, the appropriate strategy is to make them available in many locations, charge only a small markup, and advertise heavily to induce trial and build preference.

2. *Durable goods* are tangible goods that normally survive many uses: refrigerators, machine tools, and clothing. Durable products normally require more personal selling and service, command a higher margin, and require more seller guarantees.

3. *Services* are intangible, inseparable, variable, and perishable products. As a result, they normally require more quality control, supplier credibility, and adaptability. Examples include haircuts, legal advice, and appliance repairs.

CONSUMER-GOODS CLASSIFICATION The vast array of goods consumers buy can be classified on the basis of shopping habits. We can distinguish among convenience, shopping, specialty, and unsought goods.

The consumer usually purchases **convenience goods** frequently, immediately, and with a minimum of effort. Examples include tobacco products, soaps, and newspapers. Convenience goods can be further divided. *Staples* are goods consumers purchase on a regular basis. A buyer might routinely purchase Heinz ketchup, Crest toothpaste, and Ritz crackers. *Impulse goods* are purchased without any planning or search effort. Candy bars and magazines are impulse goods. *Emergency goods* are purchased when a need is urgent—umbrellas during a rainstorm, boots and shovels during the first winter snowstorm. Manufacturers of impulse and emergency goods will place them in those outlets where consumers are likely to experience an urge or compelling need to make a purchase.

Shopping goods are goods that the consumer, in the process of selection and purchase, characteristically compares on such bases as suitability, quality, price, and style. Examples include furniture, clothing, used cars, and major appliances. Shopping goods can be further divided. *Homogeneous shopping goods* are similar in quality but different enough in price to justify shopping comparisons. *Heterogeneous shopping goods* differ in product features and services that may be more important than price. The seller of heterogeneous shopping goods carries a wide assortment to satisfy individual tastes and must have well-trained salespeople to inform and advise customers.

Specialty goods have unique characteristics or brand identification for which a sufficient number of buyers are willing to make a special purchasing effort. Examples include cars, stereo components, photographic equipment, and men's suits. A Mercedes is a specialty good because interested buyers will travel far to buy one. Specialty goods do not involve making comparisons; buyers invest time only to reach dealers carrying the wanted products. Dealers do not need convenient locations, although they must let prospective buyers know their locations.

Unsought goods are those the consumer does not know about or does not normally think of buying, like smoke detectors. The classic examples of known but unsought goods are life insurance, cemetery plots, gravestones, and encyclopedias. Unsought goods require advertising and personal-selling support.

INDUSTRIAL-GOODS CLASSIFICATION Industrial goods can be classified in terms of how they enter the production process and their relative costliness. We can distinguish three groups of industrial goods: materials and parts, capital items, and supplies and business services.

Materials and parts are goods that enter the manufacturer's product completely. They fall into two classes: raw materials and manufactured materials and parts. *Raw materials* fall into two major groups: *farm products* (e.g., wheat, cotton, livestock, fruits, and vegetables) and *natural products* (e.g., fish, lumber, crude petroleum, and iron ore). Farm products are supplied by many producers, who turn them over to marketing intermediaries, who provide assembly, grading, storage, transportation, and selling services. Their perishable and seasonal nature gives rise to special marketing practices. Their commodity character results in relatively little advertising and promotional activity, with some exceptions. At times, commodity groups will launch campaigns to promote their product—potatoes, cheese, and beef. Some producers brand their product—Dole salads, Mott's apples, and Chiquita bananas.

A Beef Council ad, part of the "Beef, It's What's for Dinner" campaign of TV and print ads designed to promote beef as a good food.

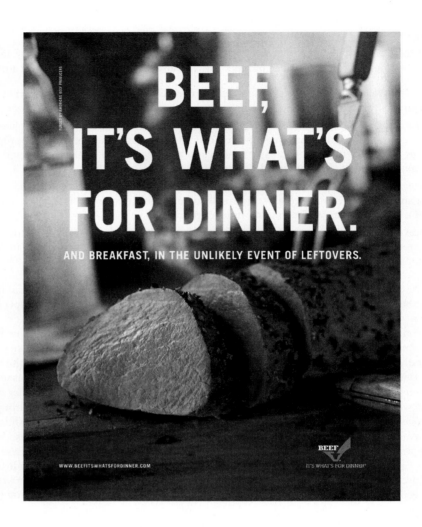

Natural products are limited in supply. They usually have great bulk and low unit value and must be moved from producer to user. Fewer and larger producers often market them directly to industrial users. Because the users depend on these materials, long-term supply contracts are common. The homogeneity of natural materials limits the amount of demand-creation activity. Price and delivery reliability are the major factors influencing the selection of suppliers.

Manufactured materials and parts fall into two categories: component materials (iron, yarn, cement, wires) and component parts (small motors, tires, castings). *Component material*s are usually fabricated further—pig iron is made into steel, and yarn is woven into cloth. The standardized nature of component materials usually means that price and supplier reliability are key purchase factors. *Component parts* enter the finished product with no further change in form, as when small motors are put into vacuum cleaners, and tires are put on automobiles. Most manufactured materials and parts are sold directly to industrial users. Price and service are major marketing considerations, and branding and advertising tend to be less important.

Capital items are long-lasting goods that facilitate developing or managing the finished product. They include two groups: installations and equipment. *Installations* consist of buildings (factories, offices) and heavy equipment (generators, drill presses, mainframe computers, elevators). Installations are major purchases. They are usually bought directly from the producer, with the typical sale preceded by a long negotiation period. The producer's sales force includes technical personnel. Producers have to be willing to design to specification and to supply post-sale services. Advertising is much less important than personal selling.

Equipment comprises portable factory equipment and tools (hand tools, lift trucks) and office equipment (personal computers, desks). These types of equipment do not become part of a finished product. They have a shorter life than installations but a longer life than operating supplies. Although some equipment manufacturers sell direct, more often they use intermediaries, because the market is geographically dispersed, the buyers are numerous, and the orders are small. Quality, features, price, and service are major considerations. The sales force tends to be more important than advertising, although the latter can be used effectively.

Supplies and business services are short-term goods and services that facilitate developing or managing the finished product. Supplies are of two kinds: *maintenance and repair items* (paint, nails, brooms), and *operating supplies* (lubricants, coal, writing paper, pencils). Together, they go under the name of MRO goods. Supplies are the equivalent of convenience goods; they are usually purchased with minimum effort on a straight rebuy basis. They are normally marketed through intermediaries because of their low unit value and the great number and geographic dispersion of customers. Price and service are important considerations, because suppliers are standardized and brand preference is not high.

Business services include *maintenance and repair services* (window cleaning, copier repair) and *business advisory services* (legal, management consulting, advertising). Maintenance and repair services are usually supplied under contract by small producers or are available from the manufacturers of the original equipment. Business advisory services are usually purchased on the basis of the supplier's reputation and staff. Ceridian Canada, for example, is the country's leading payroll management company. It provides payroll and human resource management services to 38 500 Canadian businesses of all sizes, in virtually every industry. See how another business service company built a position as a world leader.

CHC Helicopter Corporation

St. John's, Newfoundland–based CHC is the world's leading offshore helicopter services company, with a combined fleet of more than 300 light, medium, and heavy helicopters operating in 30 countries. It employs approximately 3500 people worldwide. CHC's core business is providing safe, reliable, efficient helicopter services to the world's offshore oil and gas companies. Approximately two-thirds of CHC's revenue is generated by offshore helicopter services. The remainder comes from other services such as air ambulance, search and rescue, onshore work, and repair and overhaul. An example of an operation that it carried out in September 2003 was the rescue of two fishermen who had spent 25 hours clinging to their semi-submerged fishing vessel in the Irish Sea.

CHC's most recent marketing challenge was to develop a brand profile that would enable it to be instantly recognized and valued in all its markets around the world. "In the helicopter industry, branding has never been seen as important," explains Sylvain Allard, CHC's president. "You're not dealing with the public—you're not selling hamburgers—you're a service company. We saw an opportunity to do it first."

Many business-to-business firms neglect branding. The helicopter-service industry was one where companies believed that customers knew, almost by osmosis, the different service offerings, levels of quality, and prices available. But CHC believed developing a brand position was essential to strengthen its image with customers, to integrate the employees of a larger company it had recently acquired into its culture, and to explain its value to potential shareholders, most of whom had little knowledge of the helicopter-service industry.

CHC's efforts were highly successful, due to strategic insight about the value it provides and innovative advertising. The campaign featured expansive photographs taken from the vantage point of a helicopter passenger. The copy drove home the company's role in the oil-and-gas industry: for example, one ad stated, "162 miles offshore. 140 workers. 2 weeks on. 2 weeks off. One way home."[7]

Differentiation

To be branded, products must be differentiated. Physical products vary in their potential for differentiation. At one extreme, we find products that allow little variation: chicken, aspirin, and steel. Yet even here, some differentiation is possible: Perdue chickens, Bayer aspirin, and India's Tata Steel have carved out distinct identities in their categories. Procter & Gamble makes Tide, Cheer, and Gain laundry detergents, each with a separate brand identity. At the other extreme are products capable of high differentiation, such as automobiles, commercial buildings, and furniture. Here the seller faces an

Canadian helicopter service company CHC has become a world leader through branding and service quality.

abundance of design parameters, including form, features, performance quality, conformance quality, durability, reliability, reparability, and style.[8]

Marketers are always looking for new dimensions of differentiation. Otis Elevator Company has upped the ante in its category by making its elevators smarter:

Otis Elevator Company

At a typical bank of elevators in an office building lobby, you press the "up" button and take the first elevator that comes, with no idea how many stops there will be until you get to your floor. Now Otis has developed a "smart" elevator. You key in your floor on a centralized panel. The panel tells you which elevator is going to take you to your floor. Your elevator takes you right to your floor and races back to the lobby. With this simple change, Otis has managed to turn every elevator into an express. This remarkable differentiator means a speedier ride and less groaning and sighing by riders, but it also has big benefits for builders. Buildings need fewer elevators for a given density of people, so builders can use the extra space for people rather than people conveyers.[9]

Product Differentiation

FORM Many products can be differentiated in **form**—the size, shape, or physical structure of a product. Consider the many possible forms taken by products such as aspirin. Although aspirin is essentially a commodity, it can be differentiated by dosage size, shape, colour, coating, or action time.

FEATURES Most products can be offered with varying **features** that supplement its basic function. A company can identify and select appropriate new features by surveying recent buyers and then calculating *customer value* versus *company cost* for each potential feature. The company should also consider how many people want each feature, how long it would take to introduce each feature, and whether competitors could easily copy the feature. Companies must also think in terms of feature bundles or packages. Auto companies often manufacture cars at several "trim levels." This lowers manufacturing and inventory costs. Each company must decide whether to offer feature customization at a higher cost or a few standard packages at a lower cost.

PERFORMANCE QUALITY   Most products are established at one of four performance levels: low, average, high, or superior. **Performance quality** is the level at which the product's primary characteristics operate. Firms should not necessarily design the highest performance level possible. The manufacturer must design a performance level appropriate to the target market and competitors' performance levels. A company must also manage performance quality through time. Continuously improving the product can produce high returns and market share. Lowering quality in an attempt to cut costs often has dire consequences. Schlitz, the number-two beer brand in the United States in the 1960s and 1970s, was driven into the dust because management adopted a financially motivated strategy to increase its short-term profits and curry favour with shareholders. Purdy's Chocolates would never consider such a tactic:

RC Purdy's Chocolates Ltd.

Since its birth in Vancouver almost 100 years ago, one thing has remained constant at Purdy's—a commitment to quality and tradition. "We take pride in using only the finest quality, purest, freshest ingredients—just as Mr. Purdy did all those years ago," says Charles Flavelle, chairman of the firm and chief taster. To live up to this commitment, Purdy's searches the world for the highest-quality ingredients—chocolate from Belgium, ginger from Australia, cashews from India, and the freshest dairy products from British Columbia's Fraser Valley. Purdy's markets through its 47 retail outlets in western Canada, its new Ontario outlets, and through its Web site (www.purdys.com) for the rest of Canada and the United States. No matter what the outlet, Purdy's service quality matches its product quality. Customers are always guaranteed to have a sweet experience with Purdy's![10]

In fact, quality is becoming an increasingly important parameter for differentiation as companies adopt a value model and provide higher quality for less money, whereas other firms, like Harry Rosen, charge premium prices as it raises the quality bar higher.

CONFORMANCE QUALITY   Buyers expect products to have a high **conformance quality**, which is the degree to which all the produced units are identical and meet the promised specifications. Suppose a Porsche 944 is designed to accelerate to 100 kilometres per hour within 10 seconds. If every Porsche 944 coming off the assembly line does this, the model is said to have high conformance quality. The problem with low conformance quality is that the product will disappoint some buyers.

DURABILITY   **Durability**, a measure of the product's expected operating life under natural or stressful conditions, is a valued attribute for certain products. Buyers will generally pay more for vehicles and kitchen appliances that have a reputation for being long lasting. However, this rule is subject to some qualifications. The extra price must not be excessive. Furthermore, the product must not be subject to rapid technological obsolescence, as is the case with personal computers and video cameras.

RELIABILITY   Buyers normally will pay a premium for more reliable products. **Reliability** is a measure of the probability that a product will not malfunction or fail within a specified time period. Maytag, which manufactures major home appliances, has an outstanding reputation for creating reliable appliances.

REPARABILITY   **Reparability** is a measure of the ease of fixing a product when it malfunctions or fails. Ideal reparability would exist if users could fix the product themselves with little cost in money or time. Some products include a diagnostic feature that allows service people to correct a problem over the telephone or advise the user how to correct it. Many computer hardware and software companies offer technical support over the phone, or by fax or e-mail. Cisco put together a Knowledge Base of Frequently Asked Questions (FAQs) on its Web site, which it estimates handles about 80 percent of the roughly 4 million monthly requests for information, saving the company US$250 million annually. Each new call and solution goes to a tech writer who adds the solution to the FAQs, thus reducing the number of future phone calls.[11]

STYLE **Style** describes the product's look and feel to the buyer. Car buyers pay a premium for Jaguars because of their extraordinary look. Aesthetics plays a key role in such brands as Absolut vodka, Apple computers, Montblanc pens, Godiva chocolates, and Harley-Davidson motorcycles.[12] Style has the advantage of creating distinctiveness that is difficult to copy. On the negative side, strong style does not always mean high performance. A car may look sensational but spend a lot of time in the repair shop.

Design: The Integrative Force

As competition intensifies, design offers a potent way to differentiate and position a company's products and services.[13] In increasingly fast-paced markets, price and technology are not enough. Design is the factor that will often give a company its competitive edge. **Design** is the totality of features that affect how a product looks and functions in terms of customer requirements.

Design is particularly important in making and marketing retail services, apparel, packaged goods, and durable equipment. All the qualities we have discussed are design parameters. The designer has to figure out how much to invest in form, feature development, performance, conformance, durability, reliability, reparability, and style. To the company, a well-designed product is one that is easy to manufacture and distribute. To the customer, a well-designed product is one that is pleasant to look at and easy to open, install, use, repair, and dispose of. The designer has to take all these factors into account.

The arguments for good design are particularly compelling for smaller consumer products companies and start-ups that don't have big advertising dollars. That's how one small brewery got noticed:

Steam Whistle Brewing Co. uses product design and a distinctive packing style to differentiate its product from competitors.

Steam Whistle Brewing Co.

Product design is an essential part of Toronto-based Steam Whistle Brewing Co.'s marketing strategy. Since Molson and Labatt signed a standard bottle agreement in 1992, micro-breweries have been able to use bottle design to differentiate themselves from the big guys. So when Steam Whistle was founded in 1998, it thought long and hard about the packaging style that it chose. The company decided to create a product with a 40s and 50s classic style using a distinctive green glass bottle. The bottles are decorated with a painted label (as opposed to the stickers you see on larger brewery beer), and are fully reusable with a nontwist top. The bottles are custom-made with a unique shape and 30 percent more glass than any other beer bottle on the market. This allows Steam Whistle to recycle its bottles considerably more than the average bottle—giving the company both differentiated packaging and an economic benefit as well. Steam Whistle also has a unique "suitcase" box design with graphics that pay homage to the simplicity of brand marketing in the 40s and 50s. Further marketing efforts have ranged from using 1950s vintage vehicles as travelling billboards to focusing on event sponsorship to build brand buzz as the company sets out to achieve its goal—to create "Canada's Premium Pilsner."[14]

Certain countries are winning on design: Italian design in apparel and furniture; Scandinavian design for functionality, aesthetics, and environmental consciousness. Braun, a German division of Gillette, has elevated design to a high art in its electric shavers, coffeemakers, hair dryers, and food processors. The company's design department enjoys equal status with engineering and manufacturing. The Danish firm Bang & Olufsen has received many kudos for the design of its stereos, TV equipment, and telephones. "Marketing Insight: Design as a Powerful Marketing Tool" describes some successes and failures in design.

Design as a Powerful Marketing Tool

Manufacturers, service providers, and retailers seek new designs to create differentiation and establish a more complete connection with consumers. Holistic marketers recognize the emotional power of design and the importance to consumers of how things look and feel. Design is now more fully integrated into the marketing management process. For example:

- After seeing some of their brands lose share to competitors with stronger designs and aesthetics, Procter & Gamble appointed a *chief design officer* in 2001 and now hands out an A. G. Lafley Design award each fall. Lafley, P&G's CEO, is credited with pushing for more products to involve design at the front end—not as an afterthought. These products, such as Crest Whitestrips, Olay Daily Facials, and the whole line of Swiffer Quick Clean products, have generated more trials, more repurchases, and more sales.

- Sweden's IKEA has become one of the top furniture retailers in the world in part through its ability to design and manufacture inexpensive furniture that doesn't seem cheap. Another Scandinavian company, Finland's Nokia, is credited with taking a little black blob with tiny buttons and turning it into an object of desire. Nokia was the first to introduce user-changeable covers for cell phones, the first to have elliptical-shaped, soft and friendly forms, and the first with big screens. In the early 1990s, Nokia controlled only 12 percent of the global market for cell phones. Today, it is the world leader in handsets, with 38 percent of the market.

With an increasingly visually oriented culture, translating brand meaning and positioning through design is critical. "In a crowded marketplace," writes Virginia Postrel in *The Substance of Style*, "Aesthetics is often the only way to make a product stand out." Design can shift consumer perceptions to make brand experiences more rewarding. Consider the lengths Boeing went to make its 777 airplane seem roomier and more comfortable. Raised centre bins, side luggage bins, divider panels, gently arched ceilings, and raised seats make the aircraft interior seem bigger. As one design engineer noted, "If we do our jobs, people don't realize what we have done. They just say they feel more comfortable."

Designers sometimes put a human face—literally—on their products. The Porsche Boxster's bulges and curves can be seen as suggestive of muscle; the Apple iMac was thought by one designer to be "a head stuck to body via a long skinny arm"; and Microsoft's optical mouse can be seen as an outstretched hand. When Frog Design set out to make a Disney cordless phone for kids, it wanted the design to live up to the famed Disney imagery. After exhaustive study, Frog defined the composite elements of a Disney character and applied it to the phone. The eyes were interpreted in terms of the LCD screen and were made as big as possible; the torso was interpreted in terms of the housing of the phone and was S-shaped, with a roundness in the top front and bottom back; and the feet were interpreted in terms of the base and charger stand, which used built-up plastic to emulate a sock pushed up around an ankle.

A bad design can also ruin a product's prospects. Sony's e-Villa Internet appliance was intended to allow consumers to have Internet access from their kitchen. But at nearly 15 kilograms and 40 centimetres, the mammoth product was so awkward and heavy that the owner's manual recommended customers use their legs, not their back, to pick it up. The product was eventually withdrawn after three months.

Sources: A. G. Lafley, "Delivering Delight," *Fast Company*, June 2004, p. 51; Frank Nuovo, "A Call for Fashion," *Fast Company*, June 2004, p. 52; Bobbie Gossage, "Strategies: Designing Success," *Inc. Magazine*, May 2004, pp. 27–29; Jim Hopkins, "When the Devil Is in the Design," *USA Today*, December 31, 2001, p. 3B; J. Lynn Lunsford and Daniel Michaels, "Masters of Illusion," *Wall Street Journal*, November 25, 2002, pp. B1, B5; Jerome Kathman, "Building Leadership Brands By Design," *Brandweek*, December 1, 2003, p. 20; Bob Parks, "Deconstructing Cute," *Business 2.0* (December 2002/January 2003): 47–50; Lisa Margonelli, "How Ikea Designs Its Sexy Price Tags," *Business 2.0* (October 2002): 106–112.

Services Differentiation

When the physical product cannot easily be differentiated, the key to competitive success may lie in adding valued services and improving their quality. The main service differentiators are ordering ease, delivery, installation, customer training, customer consulting, and maintenance and repair.

ORDERING EASE **Ordering ease** refers to how easy it is for the customer to place an order with the company. Baxter Healthcare has eased the ordering process by supplying hospitals with computer terminals through which they send orders directly to Baxter. Many banks now provide home banking software to help customers get information and do transactions more efficiently. Consumers are now able to order and receive groceries without going to the supermarket through services such as Grocery Gateway.

DELIVERY **Delivery** refers to how well the product or service is delivered to the customer. It includes speed, accuracy, and care attending the delivery process. Today's customers have grown to expect delivery speed: pizza delivered in one-half hour, film developed in one hour, eyeglasses made in one hour, cars lubricated in 15 minutes. Levi Strauss, Benetton, and The Limited have adopted computerized *quick response systems* (QRS) that link the information systems of their suppliers, manufacturing plants, distribution centres, and retailing outlets. Cemex, a giant cement company based in Mexico, has transformed the cement business by promising to deliver concrete faster than pizza. Cemex equips every truck with a *global positioning system* (GPS) so that its real-time location is known and full information is available to drivers and dispatchers. Cemex is able to promise that if your load is more than 10 minutes late, you get a 20 percent discount.[15]

INSTALLATION **Installation** refers to the work done to make a product operational in its planned location. Buyers of heavy equipment expect good installation service. Differentiating at this point in the consumption chain is particularly important for companies with complex products. Ease of installation becomes a true selling point, especially when the target market is technology novices. For customers wishing to connect to the Internet using a high-speed digital subscriber line (DSL), Pacific Bell developed installation kits that included an interactive software set-up program so customers could complete their DSL set-up in less than an hour.[16]

CUSTOMER TRAINING **Customer training** refers to training the customer's employees to use the vendor's equipment properly and efficiently. General Electric not only sells and installs expensive X-ray equipment in hospitals; it also gives extensive training to users of this equipment. McDonald's requires its new franchisees to attend Hamburger University in Oak Brook, Illinois, for two weeks, to learn how to manage the franchise properly.

CUSTOMER CONSULTING **Customer consulting** refers to data, information systems, and advice services that the seller offers to buyers.

A group of franchisees learning the business at McDonald's Hamburger University in Oak Brook, Illinois.

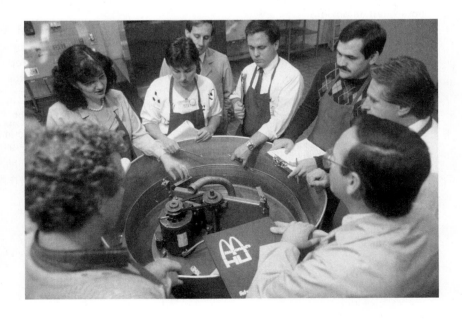

Herman Miller Inc.

Herman Miller, a large office furniture company, has partnered with a California firm to show corporate clients how to get the full benefits out of its furnishings. The firm, Future Industrial Technologies, specializes in workplace ergonomics training. Working through Herman Miller's dealership network, customers can arrange two-hour training sessions for small groups of employees. The sessions are run by some of the 1200 physical therapists, occupational therapists, registered nurses, and chiropractors that work under contract to Future Industrial Technologies. While customer ergonomics training results in only modest revenue gains for Herman Miller, the company feels that teaching healthy work habits creates higher levels of satisfaction for customers and sets Herman Miller products apart.[17]

Canada's largest drug store group, Shoppers Drug Mart, takes pride in its consultation initiatives:

Shoppers Drug Mart

Shoppers Drug Mart/Pharmaprix was founded in 1962 by Toronto pharmacist Murray Koffler. Koffler had an idea that revolutionized the retail drug industry. He believed that it was possible to build a national organization of pharmacies without sacrificing the personalized service of local community pharmacists, who knew their customers well and depended on this intimacy to ensure a successful relationship. Today, the dream is a reality. Shoppers Drug Mart (Pharmaprix in Quebec) is Canada's largest retail drug store group and one of the most recognized names in Canadian retailing, with over 825 stores serving Canadians' health-care needs. It takes pride in its Healthwatch program, through which Shoppers' pharmacists still provide personal advice to customers and consult with them on their health-related issues. Shoppers also publishes a series of award-winning brochures to further inform consumers about topics of special interest, such as children's safety. Finally, its Web site provides a wealth of information on health issues (see www.shoppersdrugmart.ca).[18]

MAINTENANCE AND REPAIR   **Maintenance and repair** describes the service program for helping customers keep purchased products in good working order. Hewlett-Packard offers online technical support, or "e-support," for its customers. In the event of a service problem, customers can use various online tools to find a solution. Those aware of the specific problem can search an online database for fixes; those unaware can use diagnostic software that finds the problem and searches the online database for an automatic fix. Customers can also seek online help from a technician.[19]

Best Buy

As consolidation and competitive pricing among electronics retailers continues, companies are increasingly looking for new ways to stand out in the crowd. That's why Best Buy contracted with the Geek Squad, a small residential computer services company in its home market of Minnesota, to revamp the chain's in-store computer repair services. Previously, PCs were sent to regional repair facilities, a process that was time consuming and ultimately contributed to a high degree of consumer dissatisfaction. Now about half of all repairs are made in Best Buy stores. But the real differentiator is the Geek Squad's ability to make house calls (at a higher fee). Geek Squad house calls are called a "Beetle Roll" because of the squad's signature fleet of hip VW Beetles. Geek Squad employees even dress differently for house calls—wearing a distinctive "geek" look as opposed to the traditional Best Buy blue they wear at the in-store service centres.[20]

Product and Brand Relationships

Each product can be related to other products.

The Product Hierarchy

The product hierarchy stretches from basic needs to particular items that satisfy those needs. We can identify six levels of the product hierarchy (using life insurance as an example):

1. *Need family*—The core need that underlies the existence of a product family. Example: security.

2. *Product family*—All the product classes that can satisfy a core need with reasonable effectiveness. Example: savings and income.

3. *Product class*—A group of products within the product family recognized as having a certain functional coherence. Also known as product category. Example: financial instruments.

4. *Product line*—A group of products within a product class that are closely related because they perform a similar function, are sold to the same customer groups, are marketed through the same outlets or channels, or fall within given price ranges. A product line may be composed of different brands or a single family brand or individual brand that has been line extended. Example: life insurance.

5. *Product type*—A group of items within a product line that share one of several possible forms of the product. Example: term life.

6. *Item (also called stock-keeping unit or product variant)*—A distinct unit within a brand or product line distinguishable by size, price, appearance, or some other attribute. Example: Prudential renewable term life insurance.

Product Systems and Mixes

A **product system** is a group of diverse but related items that function in a compatible manner. For example, palmOne handheld and smartphone product lines come with attachable products including headsets, cameras, keyboards, presentation projectors, e-books, MP3 players, and voice recorders. A **product mix** (also called a **product assortment**) is the set of all products and items a particular seller offers for sale. A product mix consists of various product lines. In General Electric's Consumer Appliance Division, there are product-line managers for refrigerators, stoves, and washing machines. NEC's (Japan) product mix consists of communication products and computer products. Michelin has three product lines: tires, maps, and restaurant-rating services. At Queen's University, there are separate academic deans for the Faculty of Applied Science, the Faculty of Arts and Science, the Faculty of Education, the Faculty of Health Sciences, the Faculty of Law, the School of Business, and the School of Physical and Health Sciences.

A company's product mix has a certain width, length, depth, and consistency. These concepts are illustrated in Table 12.1 for selected Procter & Gamble consumer products.

- The *depth* of a product mix refers to how many different product lines the company carries. Table 12.1 shows a product-mix width of five lines. (In fact, P&G produces many additional lines.)

- The *length* of a product mix refers to the total number of items in the mix. In Table 12.1, it is 20. We can also talk about the average length of a line. This is obtained by dividing the total length (here 20) by the number of lines (here five), for an average product length of four.

- The width of a product mix refers to how many variants are offered of each product in the line. If Tide comes in two scents (Mountain Spring and Regular), two formulations (liquid and powder), and two additives (with or without bleach), Tide has a depth of eight as there are eight distinct variants. The average depth of P&G's product mix can be calculated by averaging the number of variants within the brand groups.

- The *consistency* of the product mix refers to how closely related the various product lines are in end use, production requirements, distribution channels, or some other way. P&G's product lines are consistent insofar as they are consumer goods that go through the same distribution channels. The lines are less consistent insofar as they perform different functions for the buyers.

These four product-mix dimensions permit the company to expand its business in four ways. It can add new product lines, thus widening its product mix. It can lengthen each product line. It can add more product variants to each product and deepen its product mix. Finally, a company can pursue more product-line consistency. To make these product and brand decisions, it is useful to conduct product-line analysis.

Product-Line Analysis

In offering a product line, companies normally develop a basic platform and modules that can be added to meet different customer requirements. Car manufacturers build their cars around a basic platform. Homebuilders show a model home to which additional features can be added. This modular approach enables the company to offer variety while lowering production costs.

Product-line managers need to know the sales and profits of each item in their line in order to determine which items to build, maintain, harvest, or divest.[21] They also need to understand each product line's market profile.

SALES AND PROFITS   Figure 12.3 shows a sales and profit report for a five-item product line. The first item accounts for 50 percent of total sales and 30 percent of total profits. The first two items account for 80 percent of total sales and 60 percent of total profits. If these two items were suddenly hurt by a competitor, the line's sales and profitability could collapse. These items must be carefully monitored and protected. At the other end, the last item delivers only 5 percent of the product line's sales and profits. The product-line manager may consider dropping this item unless it has strong growth potential.

Every company's product portfolio contains products with different margins. Supermarkets make almost no margin on bread and milk; reasonable margins on canned and frozen foods; and even better margins on flowers, ethnic food lines, and freshly baked goods. A local telephone company makes different margins on its core telephone service, call waiting, caller ID, and voice mail.

A company can classify its products into four types that yield different gross margins, depending on sales volume and promotion. To illustrate with personal computers:

The palmOne Zire 31 hand-held. Owners can select from more than 20 000 available applications and use the expansion slot to add more memory, applications, or MP3 tunes.

- *Core product.* Basic computers that produce high sales volume and are heavily promoted but with low margins because they are viewed as undifferentiated commodities.

- *Staples.* Items with lower sales volume and no promotion, such as faster CPUs or bigger memories. These yield a somewhat higher margin.

- *Specialties.* Items with lower sales volume but which might be highly promoted, such as digital movie-making equipment; or might generate income for services, such as personal delivery, installation, or on-site training.

TABLE 12.1	PRODUCT-MIX WIDTH AND PRODUCT-LINE LENGTH FOR PROCTER & GAMBLE PRODUCTS (INCLUDING DATES OF INTRODUCTION)				
			Product-Mix Width		
	Detergents	**Toothpaste**	**Bar Soap**	**Disposable Diapers**	**Paper Products**
	Ivory Snow (1930)	Gleem (1952)	Ivory (1879)	Pampers (1961)	Charmin (1928)
	Dreft (1933)	Crest (1955)	Camay (1926)	Luvs (1976)	Puffs (1960)
PRODUCT	Tide (1946)		Zest (1952)		Bounty (1965)
LINE	Cheer (1950)		Safeguard (1963)		
LENGTH	Dash (1954)		Oil of Olay (1993)		
	Bold (1965)				
	Gain (1966)				
	Era (1972)				

FIGURE 12.3

Product-Item Contributions to
a Product Line's Total Sales
and Profits

- *Convenience items.* Peripheral items that sell in high volume but receive less promotion, such as computer monitors, printers, upscale video or sound cards, and software. Consumers tend to buy them where they buy the original equipment because it is more convenient than making further shopping trips. These items can carry higher margins.

The main point is that companies should recognize that these items differ in their potential for being priced higher or advertised more as ways to increase their sales, margins, or both.[22]

MARKET PROFILE   The product-line manager must review how the line is positioned against competitors' lines.[23] Consider paper company X with a paperboard product line. Two paperboard attributes are weight and finish quality. Paper weight is usually offered at standard levels of 90, 120, 150, and 180 weight. Finish quality is offered at low, medium, and high levels. Figure 12.4 shows the location of the various product-line items of company X and four competitors, A, B, C, and D. Competitor A sells two product items in the extra-high weight class ranging from medium to low finish quality. Competitor B sells four items that vary in weight and finish quality. Competitor C sells three items in which the greater the weight, the greater the finish quality. Competitor D sells three items, all lightweight but varying in finish quality. Company X offers three items that vary in weight and finish quality.

The product map shows which competitors' items are competing against company X's items. For example, company X's low-weight, medium-quality paper competes against competitor D's and B's papers, but its high-weight, medium-quality paper has no direct competitor. The map also reveals possible locations for new items. No manufacturer offers a high-weight, low-quality paper. If company X estimates a strong unmet demand and can produce and price this paper at low cost, it could consider adding this item to its line.

FIGURE 12.4

Product Map for Paper-
Product Line

Source: Benson P. Shapiro,
*Industrial Product Policy: Managing
the Existing Product Line*
(Cambridge, MA: Marketing
Science Institute Report No.
77-110).

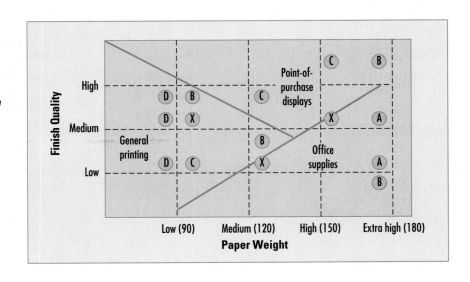

Another benefit of product mapping is that it identifies market segments. Figure 12.4 shows the types of paper, by weight and quality, preferred by the general printing industry, the point-of-purchase display industry, and the office-supply industry. The map shows that company X is well positioned to serve the needs of the general printing industry but is less effective in serving the other two industries.

Product-line analysis provides information for two key decision areas—product-line length and product-mix pricing.

Product-Line Length

Company objectives influence product-line length. One objective is to create a product line to induce up-selling: Thus BMW would like to move customers up from the 3 series to the 5 to 7 series. A different objective is to create a product line that facilitates cross-selling: Hewlett-Packard sells printers as well as computers. Still another objective is to create a product line that protects against economic ups and downs; Electrolux offers white goods such as refrigerators, dishwashers, and vacuum cleaners under different brand names in the discount, middle market, and premium segments, in part in case the economy moves up or down.[24] Companies seeking high market share and market growth will generally carry longer product lines. Companies that emphasize high profitability will carry shorter lines consisting of carefully chosen items.

Product lines tend to lengthen over time. Excess manufacturing capacity puts pressure on the product-line manager to develop new items. The sales force and distributors also pressure the company for a more complete product line to satisfy customers. But as items are added, costs rise: design and engineering costs, inventory-carrying costs, manufacturing-changeover costs, order-processing costs, transportation costs, and new-item promotional costs. Eventually, someone calls a halt: Top management may stop development because of insufficient funds or manufacturing capacity. The controller may call for a study of money-losing items. A pattern of product-line growth followed by massive pruning may repeat itself many times.

A company lengthens its product line in two ways: by line stretching and line filling.

LINE STRETCHING   Every company's product line covers a certain part of the total possible range. For example, BMW automobiles are located in the upper price range of the automobile market. **Line stretching** occurs when a company lengthens its product line beyond its current range. The company can stretch its line down-market, up-market, or both ways.

Down-Market Stretch   A company positioned in the middle market may want to introduce a lower-priced line for any of three reasons:

1. The company may notice strong growth opportunities as mass retailers such as Wal-Mart, Best Buy, and others attract a growing number of shoppers who want value-priced goods.

2. The company may wish to tie up lower-end competitors who might otherwise try to move up-market. If the company has been attacked by a low-end competitor, it often decides to counter-attack by entering the low end of the market.

3. The company may find that the middle market is stagnating or declining.

A company faces a number of naming choices in deciding to move down-market. Sony, for example, faced three choices:

1. Use the name Sony on all of its offerings. (Sony did this.)

2. Introduce lower-priced offerings using a sub-brand name, such as Sony Value Line. Other companies have done this, such as Gillette with Gillette Good News and Ramada Limited. The risks are that the Sony name loses some of its quality image and that some Sony buyers might switch to the lower-priced offerings.

3. Introduce the lower-priced offerings under a different name, without mentioning Sony; but Sony would have to spend a lot of money to build up the new brand name, and the mass merchants may not even accept a brand that lacks the Sony name.

Moving down-market carries risks. Kodak introduced Kodak Funtime film to counter lower-priced brands, but it did not price Kodak Funtime low enough to match the lower-priced film. It also found some of its regular customers buying Funtime, so it was cannibalizing its core brand. It withdrew the product. On the other hand, Mercedes successfully introduced its C-Class cars at US$30 000 without injuring its ability to sell other Mercedes cars for US$100 000 and up. John Deere introduced a lower-priced line of lawn tractors called Sabre from John Deere while still selling its more expensive tractors under the John Deere name. Air Canada has been notorious for doing this with line extensions such as Tango and Zip (which are now no longer operational) to compete with the discount airliners such as WestJet, JetsGo, and others.

Up-Market Stretch Companies may wish to enter the high end of the market for more growth, higher margins, or simply to position themselves as full-line manufacturers. Many markets have spawned surprising upscale segments: Starbucks in coffee, Häagen-Dazs in ice cream, and Evian in bottled water. The leading Japanese auto companies have each introduced an upscale automobile—Toyota's Lexus, Nissan's Infiniti, and Honda's Acura. Note that they invented entirely new names rather than using or including their own names.

Other companies have included their own name in moving up-market. Gallo introduced Gallo of Sonoma (priced at US$10 to US$30 a bottle) to compete in the premium wine segment, using the founder's grandchildren as spokespeople in an intensive push and pull campaign. With a hip, young, and fun image, case sales volume tripled to 680 000 in 1999. General Electric introduced the GE Profile brand for its large appliance offerings in the upscale market.[25] Some brands have used modifiers to signal a noticeable, although presumably not dramatic, quality improvement, such as Ultra Dry Pampers, Extra Strength Tylenol, or PowerPro Dustbuster Plus.

Two-Way Stretch Companies serving the middle market might decide to stretch their line in both directions. Texas Instruments (TI) introduced its first calculators in the medium-price-medium-quality end of the market. Gradually, it added calculators at the lower end, taking market share away from Bowmar, and at the higher end to compete with Hewlett-Packard. This two-way stretch won TI early market leadership in the hand-calculator market.

Holiday Inn Worldwide also has performed a two-way stretch of its hotel product line. The hotel chain broke its domestic hotels into five separate chains to tap into five different benefit segments—the upscale Crowne Plaza, the traditional Holiday Inn, the budget Holiday Inn Express, and the business-oriented Holiday Inn Select and Holiday Inn Suites & Rooms. Different branded chains received different marketing programs and emphasis. Holiday Inn Express has been advertised with the

A print ad for Gallo of Sonoma showing members of the younger generation of the Gallo family, with the tagline "New Generation. World Class."

humorous "Stay Smart" advertising campaign showing the brilliant feats that ordinary people could attempt after staying at the chain. By basing the development of these brands on distinct consumer targets with unique needs, Holiday Inn is able to ensure against overlap between brands.

LINE FILLING   A product line can also be lengthened by adding more items within the present range. There are several motives for *line filling*: reaching for incremental profits, trying to satisfy dealers who complain about lost sales because of missing items in the line, trying to utilize excess capacity, trying to be the leading full-line company, and trying to plug holes to keep out competitors.

BMW AG

In four years BMW has morphed from a one-brand, five-model carmaker into a three-brand, ten-model powerhouse. Not only has the carmaker expanded BMW's product range downward with Mini Coopers and its compact 1-series models, but it has also built it upward with Rolls-Royce while filling the gaps in between with its X3 Sports Activity Vehicle and a 6-series coupe. The company has used line filling successfully to boost its appeal to the wannabe-rich, the rich, and the super-rich, all without departing from its pure premium positioning.[26]

Line filling is overdone if it results in self-cannibalization and customer confusion. The company needs to differentiate each item in the consumer's mind. Each item should possess a *just-noticeable difference*. According to Weber's law, customers are more attuned to relative than to absolute difference.[27] They will perceive the difference between boards 20 and 30 centimetres long and boards 2 and 3 metres long but not between boards 2.9 and 3 metres long. The company should also check that the proposed item meets a market need and is not being added simply to satisfy an internal need. The Edsel automobile, on which Ford lost US$350 million, met Ford's internal positioning needs for a car between its Ford and Lincoln lines but not the market's needs.

LINE MODERNIZATION, FEATURING, AND PRUNING   Product lines need to be modernized. A company's machine tools might have a 1970s look and lose out to newer-styled competitors' lines. The issue is whether to overhaul the line piecemeal or all at once. A piecemeal approach allows the company to see how customers and dealers take to the new style. It is also less draining on the company's cash flow, but it allows competitors to see changes and to start redesigning their own lines.

In rapidly changing product markets, modernization is continuous. Companies plan improvements to encourage customer migration to higher-valued, higher-priced items. Microprocessor companies such as Intel and AMD, and software companies such as Microsoft and Oracle, continually introduce more advanced versions of their products. A major issue is timing improvements so they do not appear too early (damaging sales of the current line) or too late (after the competition has established a strong reputation for more advanced equipment).

The product-line manager typically selects one or a few items in the line to feature. Sears will announce a special low-priced washing machine to attract customers. At other times, managers will feature a high-end item to lend prestige to the product line. Sometimes a company finds one end of its line selling well and the other end selling poorly. The company may try to boost demand for the slower sellers, especially if they are produced in a factory that is idled by lack of demand; but it could be counterargued that the company should promote items that sell well rather than try to prop up weak items.

Product-line managers must periodically review the line for deadwood that is depressing profits. "Marketing Insight: Rationalizing Brand Portfolios for Growth" describes some developments with that strategy. The weak items can be identified through sales and cost analysis. A chemical company cut down its line from 217 to the 93 products with the largest volume, the largest contribution to profits, and the greatest long-term potential. Pruning is also done when the company is short of production capacity. Companies typically shorten their product lines in periods of tight demand and lengthen their lines in periods of slow demand.

Product-Mix Pricing

Chapter 14 describes pricing concepts, strategies, and tactics in detail, but it is useful to consider some basic product-mix pricing issues here. Price-setting logic must be modified when the product is part of a product mix. In this case, the firm searches for a set of prices that maximizes profits on the

Rationalizing Brand Portfolios for Growth[28]

In 1999, Unilever owned more than 1600 distinct brands. Some of Unilever's famed brands include Lipton tea, Snuggle fabric softener, Ragu pasta sauces, Bird-Eye frozen foods, Close-Up toothpaste, Calvin Klein fragrances, and Dove personal care products. But more than 90 percent of its profits came from just 400 brands. That year, the company announced its "Path to Growth" program designed to get the most value from its brand portfolio by eliminating three-quarters of its brands by 2003. The company intended to retain global brands such as Lipton, as well as regional brands and "local jewels" such as Persil, the leading detergent in the United Kingdom. Unilever co-chairman Niall FitzGerald likened the brand reduction to weeding a garden so that "the light and air get in to the blooms which are likely to grow the best."

Unilever is not alone. Multi-brand companies all over the world are attempting to optimize their brand portfolios. In many cases, this has led to a greater focus on core brand growth, to concentrating energy and resources on the biggest and most established brands. Hasbro has designated a set of core toy brands, including GI Joe, Transformers, and My Little Pony, to emphasize in its marketing. Procter & Gamble's "back to basics strategy" concentrates on its 12 US$1 billion-plus brands, such as Tide, Crest, Pampers, and Pringles.

At the same time, firms have to be careful to avoid overreliance on existing brands at the expense of any new brands. Kraft spent the early part of the 2000s introducing one line extension after another of its established brands such as Oreo cookies, Chips Ahoy, and Jell-O. Some extensions failed. A Chips Ahoy extension, Gooey Warm n' Chewy, turned out to be tricky to heat and too pricey. Extension proliferation meant that the company missed out on important health and nutrition trends in the marketplace. Stagnant sales led to the ousting of co-CEO Betsy Holden in December 2003.

Sources: "A Chat with Unilever's Niall FitzGerald," *BusinessWeek Online*, August 2, 2001; Nirmalya Kumar, "Kill a Brand, Keep a Customer," *Harvard Business Review*, December 2003, pp. 86–95; Sarah Ellison, "Kraft's Stale Strategy," *Wall Street Journal*, December 18, 2003, pp. B1, B6; Brad Stone, "Back to Basics," *Newsweek*, August 4, 2003, pp. 42–44.

---

total mix. Pricing is difficult because the various products have demand and cost interrelationships and are subject to different degrees of competition. We can distinguish six situations involving product-mix pricing: product-line pricing, optional-feature pricing, captive-product pricing, two-part pricing, byproduct pricing, and product-bundling pricing.

PRODUCT-LINE PRICING Companies normally develop product lines rather than single products and introduce price steps.

> **Intel**
>
> Intel has segmented its product line into microprocessors aimed at specific markets, such as cheap PCs, mid-tier "performance" PCs, and powerful servers. This strategy let Intel balance thin profits from chips like the Celeron—new models of which sell for as little as US$150 and go into low-priced PCs—with cash cows like the Itanium workstation and server chips, which cost up to US$4200 each. The company's most profitable chips are the Pentium 4 chips, priced between US$300 and US$600, depending on processor speed.[29]

In many lines of trade, sellers use well-established price points for the products in their line. A men's clothing store might carry men's suits at three price levels: $200, $400, and $600. Customers will associate low-, average-, and high-quality suits with the three price points. The seller's task is to establish perceived-quality differences that justify the price differences.

OPTIONAL-FEATURE PRICING Many companies offer optional products, features, and services along with their main product. The automobile buyer can order electric window controls, defoggers, light dimmers, and an extended warranty. Pricing is a sticky problem, because companies must decide which items to include in the standard price and which to offer as options. For many years, auto companies advertised a stripped-down model for $10 000 to pull people into showrooms. The

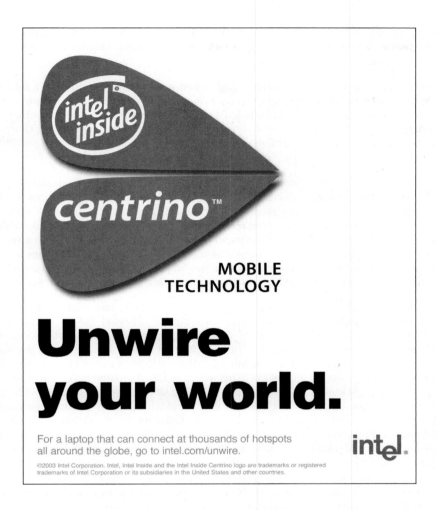

©2003 Intel Corporation. Intel, Intel Inside and the Intel Inside Centrino logo are trademarks or registered trademarks of Intel Corporation or its subsidiaries in the United States and other countries.

Print ad for Intel® Centrino™, part of Intel's product line of microprocessors segmented by market. Centrino mobile technology is a set of notebook technologies designed specifically for wireless notebook PCs and for the top of the market.

economy model was stripped of so many features that most buyers left the showroom spending $13 000.

Restaurants face a similar pricing problem. Customers can often order liquor in addition to the meal. Many restaurants price their liquor high and their food low. The food revenue covers costs, and the liquor produces the profit. This explains why servers often press hard to get customers to order drinks. Other restaurants price their liquor low and food high to draw in a drinking crowd.

CAPTIVE-PRODUCT PRICING   Some products require the use of ancillary, or **captive, products**. Manufacturers of razors and cameras often price them low and set high markups on razor blades and film, respectively. Rogers Wireless and Bell Mobility may give a cellular phone free if the person commits to buying two years of phone service.

Hewlett-Packard

In 1996, Hewlett-Packard (HP) began drastically cutting prices on its printers, by as much as 60 percent in some cases. HP could afford to make such dramatic cuts because customers typically spend twice as much on replacement ink cartridges, toner, and specialty paper than on the actual printer over the life of the product. As the price of printers dropped, printer sales rose, as did the number of aftermarket sales. HP now owns about 40 percent of the worldwide printer business. Its inkjet supplies carry 35 percent profit margins and generated US$2.2 billion in operating profits in 2002—over 70 percent of the company's total.[30]

There is a danger in pricing the captive product too high in the aftermarket. Caterpillar, for example, makes high profits in the aftermarket by pricing its parts and service high. This practice has given rise to "pirates," who counterfeit the parts and sell them to "shady tree" mechanics who install them, sometimes without passing on the cost savings to customers. Meanwhile, Caterpillar loses sales.[31]

TWO-PART PRICING Service firms often engage in **two-part pricing**, consisting of a fixed fee plus a variable usage fee. Telephone users pay a minimum monthly fee plus charges for calls beyond a certain area. Amusement parks charge an admission fee plus fees for rides over a certain minimum. The service firm faces a problem similar to captive-product pricing—namely, how much to charge for the basic service and how much for the variable usage. The fixed fee should be low enough to induce purchase of the service; the profit can then be made on the usage fees.

BYPRODUCT PRICING The production of certain goods—meats, petroleum products, and other chemicals—often results in byproducts. If the byproducts have value to a customer group, they should be priced on their value. Any income earned on the byproducts will make it easier for the company to charge a lower price on its main product if competition forces it to do so. Australia's CSR was originally named Colonial Sugar Refinery and its early reputation was formed as a sugar company. The company began to sell byproducts of its sugar cane: waste sugar cane fibre was used to manufacture wallboard. By the mid-1990s, through product development and acquisition, CSR had become one of the top ten companies in Australia selling building and construction materials.

PRODUCT-BUNDLING PRICING Sellers often bundle products and features. **Pure bundling** occurs when a firm only offers its products as a bundle. Michael Ovitz's company, Artists Management Group, will sign up a "hot" actor if the film company will also accept other talents that Ovitz represents (directors, writers, scripts). This is a form of *tied-in sales*. In **mixed bundling**, the seller offers goods both individually and in bundles. When offering a mixed bundle, the seller normally charges less for the bundle than if the items were purchased separately. An auto manufacturer might offer an option package at less than the cost of buying all the options separately. A theatre company will price a season subscription at less than the cost of buying all the performances separately. Because customers may not have planned to buy all the components, the savings on the price bundle must be substantial enough to induce them to buy the bundle.[32]

Some customers will want less than the whole bundle. Suppose a medical equipment supplier's offer includes free delivery and training. A particular customer might ask to forgo the free delivery and training in exchange for a lower price. The customer is asking the seller to "unbundle" or "rebundle" its offer. If a supplier saves $100 by not supplying delivery and reduces the customer's price by $80, the supplier has kept the customer happy while increasing its profit by $20.

Studies have shown that as promotional activity increases on individual items in the bundle, buyers perceive less saving on the bundle and are less apt to pay for the bundle. This research has offered the following three suggested guidelines for correctly implementing a bundling strategy:[33]

- Don't promote individual products in a package as frequently and cheaply as the bundle. The bundle price should be much lower than the sum of individual products or the consumer will not perceive its attractiveness.

- Limit promotions to a single item in the mix if you still want to promote individual products. Another option: alternate promotions, one after another, in order to avoid conflicting promotions.

- If you decide to offer large rebates on individual products, it must be the absolute exception and done with discretion. Otherwise, the consumer uses the price of individual products as an external reference for the bundle, which then loses value.

Co-Branding and Ingredient Branding

CO-BRANDING Products are often combined with products from other companies in various ways. A rising phenomenon is the emergence of **co-branding**—also called dual branding or brand bundling—in which two or more well-known existing brands are combined into a joint product and/or marketed together in some fashion.[34] One form of co-branding is *same-company co-branding*, as when General Mills advertises Trix and Yoplait yogurt. Still another form is *retail co-branding*, where two retail establishments use the same location as a way to optimize both space and profits. There is *multiple-sponsor co-branding*, as in the case of Taligent, a technological alliance of Apple, IBM, and Motorola, or the recent efforts by Subway to offer its products by co-branding them with the famous Atkins diet.[35] Finally, there is *co-branding* by linking the products or services of two independent firms, as in the case of General Electric and Hitachi light bulbs in Japan or the 2005 union between RBC Royal Bank and Starbucks and their new Starbucks Duetto** Visa* card. Consider Rogers Cable and Yahoo!'s decision to co-brand a new product:

Rogers Cable and Yahoo!

Two big names in Internet services, Rogers and Yahoo!, decided to co-brand a new integrated broadband service called Rogers Yahoo! Hi-Speed Internet. The product combines speed with popular broadband services, including security services (e.g., e-mail, anti-virus, and parental control technology); Rogers Yahoo! Mail, which allows customers to create up to eight secondary e-mail accounts; and Yahoo! Photos, which offers unlimited storage for digital photos. In addition, entertainment-driven features give customers access to music videos and commercial-free radio across North America. Subscribers can also customize home pages, as well as their tool bar.[36]

The main advantage to co-branding is that a product may be convincingly positioned by virtue of the multiple brands involved. Co-branding can generate greater sales from the existing target market as well as open additional opportunities with new consumers and channels. Co-branding also can reduce the cost of product introduction because two well-known images are combined, accelerating potential adoption. And co-branding may be a valuable means to learn about consumers and how other companies approach them. Companies within the automotive industry have reaped all of these benefits of co-branding.

The potential disadvantages of co-branding are the risks and lack of control from becoming aligned with another brand in the minds of consumers. Consumer expectations about the level of involvement and commitment with co-brands are likely to be high, so unsatisfactory performance could have negative repercussions for the brands involved. If the other brand has entered into a number of co-branding arrangements, there may be a risk that overexposure will dilute the transfer of any association. It may also result in a lack of focus on existing brands.

A necessary condition for co-branding success is that the two brands separately have brand equity—adequate brand awareness and a sufficiently positive brand image. The most important requirement is that there is a logical fit between the two brands such that the combined brand or marketing activity maximizes the advantages of the individual brands while minimizing the disadvantages. Research studies show that consumers are more apt to perceive co-brands favourably if the two brands are complementary rather than similar:[37]

Co-branding: The Royal Bank and Starbucks joined forces to offer the new Duetto Visa card that allows coffee lovers to earn 1 percent back in Duetto dollars that they can use at their favourite Starbucks.

Godiva & Slim-Fast

Godiva (fine chocolate) rates high on taste and richness, whereas Slim-Fast (weight-loss products) rates favourably on calorie content and value. A hypothetical cake-mix extension of either brand alone was judged by sample consumers to be similar to the parent brand. For instance, Godiva cake mix was judged to be good tasting but high on calories, whereas Slim-Fast cake mix was perceived to be low on both calories and taste. In contrast, co-brands such as Slim-Fast cake mix by Godiva or Godiva cake mix by Slim-Fast were judged to possess the desirable attributes of *both* brands.

**Trademarks or registered trademarks of Starbucks Coffee Company. Used under license.
*Visa Int./Royal Bank of Canada and Starbucks Coffee Company, Lic. Users.

Besides these strategic considerations, co-branding ventures must be entered into and executed carefully. There must be the right kind of fit in values, capabilities, and goals, in addition to an appropriate balance of brand equity. There must be detailed plans to legalize contracts, make financial arrangements, and coordinate marketing programs. As one executive at Nabisco put it, "Giving away your brand is a lot like giving away your child—you want to make sure everything is perfect." The financial arrangement between brands may vary, although one common approach involves a licensing fee and royalty from the brand more involved in the production process.

Brand alliances involve a number of decisions.[38] What capabilities do you not have? What resource constraints are you faced with (people, time, money, etc.)? What growth goals or revenue needs do you have? In assessing a joint branding opportunity, a number of questions need to be asked. Is it a profitable business venture? How does it help to maintain or strengthen brand equity? Is there any possible risk of dilution of brand equity? Does it offer any extrinsic advantages (e.g., learning opportunities)?

INGREDIENT BRANDING **Ingredient branding** is a special case of co-branding. It involves creating brand equity for materials, components, or parts that are necessarily contained within other branded products. Some successful ingredient brands include Dolby noise reduction, Gore-Tex water-resistant fibres, and Scotchgard fabrics. Some popular ingredient-branded products are Betty Crocker baking mixes with Hershey's chocolate syrup, Lunchables lunch combinations with Taco Bell tacos, and Lay's potato chips made with KC Masterpiece barbecue sauce.

An interesting take on ingredient branding is "self-branding" in which companies advertise and even trademark their own branded ingredients. For instance, Westin Hotels advertises its "Heavenly Bed" and "Heavenly Shower," and Tide announces that it contains the scent of "Everfresh" bath soap, an ingredient it developed. Life Savers cough lozenges contain its own "Clear Cold" cough liquid. If you can do it well, it makes much more sense to self-brand ingredients because you have more control and can develop the ingredient to suit your purposes.[39]

Ingredient brands attempt to create sufficient awareness and preference for their product such that consumers will not buy a "host" product that does not contain the ingredient. DuPont has achieved success marketing its products as ingredient brands.

DuPont

Over the years, DuPont has introduced a number of innovative products, such as Corian® solid surface material, for use in markets ranging from apparel to aerospace. Many of these products, such as Lycra® and Stainmaster® fabrics, Teflon® coating, and Kevlar® fibre, became household names as ingredient brands in consumer products manufactured by other companies. Several recent ingredient brands include Supro® isolated soy proteins used in food products and RiboPrinter® genetic fingerprinting technology.[40]

Many manufacturers make components or materials that enter into final branded products, but whose individual identity normally gets lost. One of the few component branders who have succeeded in building a separate identity is Intel. Intel's consumer-directed brand campaign convinced many personal computer buyers to buy only computer brands with "Intel Inside." As a result, major PC manufacturers such as Dell and Compaq purchase their chips from Intel at a premium price rather than buy equivalent chips from an unknown supplier. Most component manufacturers, however, would find it difficult to create a successful ingredient brand. "Marketing Memo: Making Ingredient Branding Work" outlines the characteristics of successful ingredient branding.

Packaging, Labelling, Warranties, and Guarantees

Most physical products have to be packaged and labelled. Some packages—such as the Coke bottle and the L'eggs container—are world famous. Many marketers have called packaging a fifth P, along with price, product, place, and promotion. Most marketers, however, treat packaging and labelling as an element of product strategy. Warranties and guarantees can also be an important part of the product strategy, and often appear on the package.

Packaging

We define **packaging** as all the activities of designing and producing the container for a product. Packages might include up to three levels of material. Paco Rabanne cologne is in a bottle (*primary package*) that is in a

Marketing Memo

Making Ingredient Branding Work

What are the requirements for success for ingredient branding?

1. Consumers must perceive that the ingredient matters to the performance and success of the end product. Ideally, this intrinsic value is easily visible or experienced.

2. Consumers must be convinced that not all ingredient brands are the same and that the ingredient is superior.

3. A distinctive symbol or logo must clearly signal to consumers that the host product contains the ingredient. Ideally, the symbol or logo would function like a "seal" and would be simple and versatile and credibly communicate quality and confidence.

4. A coordinated "pull" and "push" program must help consumers understand the importance and advantages of the branded ingredient. Channel members must offer full support. Often this will involve consumer advertising and promotions and—sometimes in collaboration with manufacturers—retail merchandising and promotion programs.

Sources: Kevin Lane Keller, *Strategic Brand Management*, 2nd ed. (Upper Saddle River, NJ: Prentice-Hall, 2003); Paul F. Nunes, Stephen F. Dull, and Patrick D. Lynch, "When Two Brands Are Better Than One," *Outlook*, no.1 (2003): 14–23.

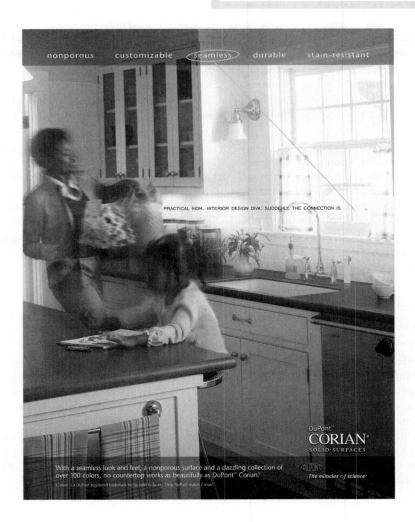

A DuPont ad for its Corian® solid-surface material, used here in a familiar household application as a kitchen countertop.

cardboard box (*secondary package*) that is in a corrugated box (*shipping package*) containing six dozen boxes of Paco Rabanne.

Well-designed packages can create convenience and promotional value. We must include packaging as a styling weapon, especially in food products, cosmetics, toiletries, and small consumer appliances. The package is the buyer's first encounter with the product and is capable of turning the buyer on or off. For Arizona Iced Tea, packaging is definitely a turn-on.[41]

Arizona Iced Tea

Arizona Iced Tea marketer Ferolito, Vultaggio, & Sons has gained success by taking a rather straightforward drink—tea—and putting it into unusual bottles with elaborate designs. The wide-mouthed, long-necked bottles have been trendsetters in the New Age beverage category, and customers often buy the tea just for the bottle. Because consumers are known to hang on to their empties or convert them into lamps and other household objects, the company uses unique bottle shapes for its line extensions. It uses a ridged grip design on Arizona Rx Elixirs, miniature jugs for Arizona Iced Coffees, and a pint-sized deep-blue urn for Blue Luna Café Latte.[42]

Various factors have contributed to the growing use of packaging as a marketing tool:

■ *Self-service.* An increasing number of products are sold on a self-service basis. In an average supermarket, which stocks 15 000 items, the typical shopper passes by some 300 items per minute. Given that 53 percent of all purchases are made on impulse, the effective package must perform many of the sales tasks: attract attention, describe the product's features, create consumer confidence, and make a favourable overall impression. A good example is the book publishing industry, where customers often quite literally choose a book by its cover: The number-one classics publisher Penguin Books Ltd. is repackaging most of its titles and spending US$500 000 to promote them under the banner "Classic Books, Fresh Looks." Sales have increased 400 percent for Dorothy Parker's *Complete Stories*, 50 percent for a new translation of *Don Quixote*, and 43 percent for *Pride and Prejudice*.[43]

■ *Consumer affluence.* Rising consumer affluence means consumers are willing to pay a little more for the convenience, appearance, dependability, and prestige of better packages.

■ *Company and brand image.* Packages contribute to instant recognition of the company or brand.

■ *Innovation opportunity.* Innovative packaging can bring large benefits to consumers and profits to producers. Companies are incorporating unique materials and features such as resealable spouts and openings. Heinz's unique, colourful EZ Squirt ketchup revitalized that brand's sales. Dutch Boy developed the award-winning Twist & Pour paint container, an easy-to-carry, easy-to-open, easy-to-pour-and-close paint jug. Not only did the new packaging increase sales, it also gave Dutch Boy more distribution at higher retail prices.[44]

Developing an effective package requires a number of decisions. From the perspective of both the firm and consumers, packaging must achieve a number of objectives:[45]

1. Identify the brand.

2. Convey descriptive and persuasive information.

3. Facilitate product transportation and protection.

4. Assist at-home storage.

5. Aid product consumption.

To achieve the marketing objectives for the brand and satisfy the desires of consumers, the aesthetic and functional components of packaging must be chosen correctly. Aesthetic considerations relate to a package's size and shape, material, colour, text, and graphics. Colour must be carefully chosen: Blue is cool and serene, red is active and lively, yellow is medicinal and weak, pastel colours are feminine, and dark colours are masculine. Functionally, structural design is crucial. For example, packaging innovations with food products over the years have resulted in packages becoming resealable, tamper-proof, and more convenient to use (easy-to-hold, easy-to-open, or squeezable). Changes in canning have made vegetables crunchier, and special wraps have extended the life of refrigerated food.[46]

The various packaging elements must be harmonized. The packaging elements must also be harmonized with decisions on pricing, advertising, and other parts of the marketing program. Packaging changes can have immediate impact on sales. For example, sales of the Heath candy bar increased 25 percent after its wrapper was redone.

After packaging is designed, it must be tested. *Engineering tests* are conducted to ensure that the package stands up under normal conditions; *visual tests*, to ensure that the script is legible and the colours harmonious; *dealer tests*, to ensure that dealers find the packages attractive and easy to handle; and *consumer tests*, to ensure favourable consumer response.

Developing effective packaging may cost several hundred thousand dollars and take several months to complete. Companies must pay attention to growing environmental and safety concerns about packaging. Shortages of paper, aluminum, and other materials suggest that marketers should try to reduce packaging. Many packages end up as broken bottles and crumpled cans littering the streets and countryside. Packaging creates a major problem for solid waste disposal, requiring huge amounts of labour and energy. Fortunately, many companies have gone "green."

Tetra Pak

Tetra Pak, a major Swedish multinational, provides an example of the power of innovative packaging and customer thinking. Tetra Pak invented an "aseptic" package that enables milk, fruit juice, and other perishable liquid foods to be distributed without refrigeration. So dairies can distribute milk over a wider area without investing in refrigerated trucks and facilities. Supermarkets can carry Tetra Pak packaged products on ordinary shelves, allowing them to save expensive refrigerator space. Tetra's motto is "the package should save more than it costs." Tetra Pak advertises the benefits of its packaging to consumers directly and even initiates recycling programs to save the environment. Its new American headquarters in Vernon Hills, Illinois, was built using recycled materials and other environmentally sensitive building products and techniques. Tetra Pak Canada is located in Richmond Hill, Ontario.[47]

Labelling

Sellers must label products. The label may be a simple tag attached to the product or an elaborately designed graphic that is part of the package. The label might carry only the brand name or a great deal of information. Even if the seller prefers a simple label, the law may require additional information.

Labels perform several functions. First, the label *identifies* the product or brand—for instance, the name Sunkist stamped on oranges. The label might also *grade* the product; canned peaches are grade labelled A, B, and C. The label might *describe* the product: who made it, where it was made, when it was made, what it contains, how it is to be used, and how to use it safely. Finally, the label might *promote* the product through attractive graphics. New technology allows for 360-degree

Ivory soap labels through the years: the label in 1892, and the three-bar package in 2003.

shrink-wrapped labels to surround containers with bright graphics and accommodate more on-pack product information, replacing paper labels glued on to cans and bottles.[48]

Labels eventually become outmoded and need freshening up. The label on Ivory soap has been redone at least 18 times since the 1890s, with gradual changes in the size and design of the letters. The label for Milk-Bone dog biscuits was redesigned to emphasize the key visual elements that emerged from consumer research—the dog, the biscuit, and the bone shape—and helped to stem a sales slide for the brand.[49] Companies with labels that have become icons need to tread very carefully when initiating a redesign:

Campbell Soup Company

The Campbell Soup Company has estimated that the average shopper sees its familiar red-and-white can 76 times a year, creating the equivalent of millions of dollars worth of advertising. Its label is such an icon that pop artist Andy Warhol immortalized it in one of his silk screens in the 1960s. The original Campbell's Soup label—with its scripted name and signature red-and-white—was designed in 1898, and the company did not redesign it until more than a century later, in 1999. With the goal of making the label more contemporary and making it easier for customers to find individual soups, Campbell made the famous script logo smaller and featured a photo of a steaming bowl of the soup flavour inside. In addition to the new graphic, the company put nutritional information on the packaging, serving suggestions, quick dinner ideas, and coloured bands that identify the six subgroups of condensed soup—creams, broths, and so on.[50]

There is a long history of legal concerns surrounding labels, as well as packaging. In Canada, it is mandatory that labels have three elements: They must identify the product, give the quantity being sold, and state the name and place of business of the producer. There are numerous other regulations affecting labelling practices that vary depending on the type of product being sold. Details can be found on the Government of Canada's Competition Bureau Web site (**http://cb-bc.gc.ca/epic/internet/incb-bc.nsf/en/cp01007e.html**). Consumerists have lobbied for additional labelling laws to require *open dating* (to describe product freshness), *unit pricing* (to state the product cost in standard measurement units), *grade labelling* (to rate the quality level), and *percentage labelling* (to show the percentage of each important ingredient).

Warranties and Guarantees

All sellers are legally responsible for fulfilling a buyer's normal or reasonable expectations. Warranties are formal statements of expected product performance by the manufacturer. Products under warranty can be returned to the manufacturer or designated repair centre for repair, replacement, or refund. Warranties, whether expressed or implied, are legally enforceable.

Mitsubishi Motors North America

To counter consumer perceptions that Mitsubishi lags behind competitors when it comes to quality, the company has begun offering a new ten-year, 100 000-mile (161 000-kilometre) Powertrain warranty. This warranty, which is retroactive on all 2004 vehicles, replaces its seven-year, 60 000-mile (97 000-kilometre) warranty. Mitsubishi hopes that the new longer-term warranty will signal to consumers that the company has confidence in the quality and reliability of its vehicles.[51]

Many sellers offer either general guarantees or specific guarantees.[52] A company such as Procter & Gamble promises general or complete satisfaction without being more specific—"If you are not satisfied for any reason, return for replacement, exchange, or refund." Other companies offer specific guarantees and in some cases, extraordinary guarantees:

- General Motors' Saturn car division will accept the return of a new car within 30 days if the buyer is not satisfied.
- Hampton Inn motels guarantee a restful night or the customer does not have to pay.

- A. T. Cross guarantees its Cross pens and pencils for life. The customer mails the pen to A. T. Cross (mailing envelopes are provided at stores selling Cross writing instruments), and the pen is repaired or replaced at no charge.

- FedEx won its place in the minds and hearts of mailers by promising next-day delivery "absolutely, positively by 10:30 A.M."

- BBBK, a pest extermination company, offers the following guarantee: (1) no payment until all pests are eradicated; (2) if the effort fails, the customer receives a full refund to pay the next exterminator; (3) if guests on the client's premises spot a pest, BBBK will pay for the guest's room and send an apology letter; and (4) if the client's facility is closed down, BBBK will pay all fines, lost profits, and US$5000.

Guarantees reduce the buyer's perceived risk. They suggest that the product is of high quality and that the company and its service performance are dependable. All this enables the company to charge a higher price than a competitor who is not offering an equivalent guarantee.

Guarantees are most effective in two situations. The first is where the company or the product is not well known. For example, a company might sell a liquid claiming to remove the toughest spots. A "money-back guarantee if not satisfied" would provide buyers with some confidence in purchasing the product. The second situation is where the product's quality is superior to the competition. The company can gain by guaranteeing superior performance, knowing that competitors cannot match its guarantee.

SUMMARY

1. Product is the first and most important element of the marketing mix. Product strategy calls for making coordinated decisions on product mixes, product lines, brands, and packaging and labelling.

2. In planning its market offering, the marketer needs to think through the five levels of the product: the core benefit, the basic product, the expected product, the augmented product, and the potential product, which encompasses all the augmentations and transformations the product might ultimately undergo.

3. Products can be classified in several ways. In terms of durability and reliability, products can be nondurable goods, durable goods, or services. In the consumer-goods category, products are convenience goods (staples, impulse goods, emergency goods), shopping goods (homogeneous and heterogeneous), specialty goods, or unsought goods. In the industrial-goods category, products fall into one of three categories: materials and parts (raw materials and manufactured materials and parts), capital items (installations and equipment), or supplies and business services (operating supplies, maintenance and repair items, maintenance and repair services, and business advisory services).

4. Brands can be differentiated on the basis of a number of different product or service dimensions: product form, features, performance, conformance, durability, reliability, reparability, style, and design, as well as such service dimensions as ordering ease, delivery, installa-tion, customer training, customer consulting, and maintenance and repair.

5. Most companies sell more than one product. A product mix can be classified according to width, length, depth, and consistency. These four dimensions are the tools for developing the company's marketing strategy and deciding which product lines to grow, maintain, harvest, and divest. To analyze a product line and decide how many resources should be invested in that line, product-line managers need to look at sales and profits and market profile.

6. A company can change the product component of its marketing mix by lengthening its product via line stretching (down-market, up-market, or both) or line filling, by modernizing its products, by featuring certain products, and by pruning its products to eliminate the least profitable.

7. Brands are often sold or marketed jointly with other brands. Ingredient brands and co-brands can add value, assuming they have equity and are perceived as fitting appropriately.

8. Physical products have to be packaged and labelled. Well-designed packages can create convenience value for customers and promotional value for producers. In effect, they can act as "five-second commercials" for the product. Warranties and guarantees can offer further assurance to consumers.

APPLICATIONS

Marketing Debate: Are Line Extensions Good or Bad?

The "form versus function" debate applies in many arenas, including marketing. Some marketers believe that product performance is the end-all and be-all. Other marketers maintain that the looks, feel, and other design elements of products are what really make the difference.

Take a position: Product functionality is the key to brand success versus Product design is the key to brand success.

Marketing Discussion

Consider the different means of differentiating products and services. Which ones have the most impact on your choices? Why? Can you think of certain brands that excel on a number of these different means of differentiation?

Marketing Spotlight: Toyota

Toyota may have gotten its start in automaking by being a fast follower, but it is now the innovator. In 1936, Toyota admitted following Chrysler's landmark Airflow and patterning its engine after a 1933 Chevrolet engine. But by 2000, when it introduced the first hybrid electric-gasoline car, the Prius, Toyota was the leader. In 2002, when the second-generation Prius hit showrooms, dealers received 10 000 orders before the car was even available; GM followed with an announcement that it would enter the hybrid market with models of its own.

Toyota's strategy for the Prius was to build an environmentally friendly car that reduced the footprint on the environment by reducing energy consumption, greenhouse gas emission rates, and smog emission rates. Toyota president Fujio Cho sees environmental performance as essential to the future of cars.

Introducing such leading-edge products presents marketing challenges. For example, the marketing messages must educate consumers that the Prius doesn't need to be plugged in, as an electric car does. The marketing messages must also communicate the value of fuel efficiency, not just for fuel savings for customers, but for the environment as well. "Every gallon of gas burned releases 20 pounds of carbon dioxide into the atmosphere. The general public still lags in appreciating the global warming significance of that," said Dave Hermance, executive engineer for environmental engineering, at Toyota's Technical Center in Los Angeles.

Toyota offers a full line of cars for the North American market, from family sedans to sport utility vehicles to trucks to minivans. Toyota also has products for different price points, from lower-cost Scions to mid-priced Camrys to the luxury Lexus. Designing these different products means listening to different customers, building the cars they want, and then crafting the marketing to reinforce each make's image. For example, Toyota spent four years carefully listening to teens before launching the Scion for first-time car buyers. It learned, for instance, that Scion's target age group of 16- to 21-year-olds wanted personalization. To meet that preference, Toyota will build the car mono-spec at the factory and let customers at dealerships choose from over 40 customization elements, from stereo components to wheels and even floor mats. Toyota markets the Scion at music events and will have showrooms where "young people feel comfortable hanging out and not a place where they just go stare at a car," said Scion vice president Jim Letz.

In contrast, Toyota's marketing strategy for the Lexus line focuses on perfection. The tagline for the global strategy is "Passionate Pursuit of Perfection." Dealerships offer white-glove treatment. Toyota markets Lexus globally and understands that different regions define perfection differently. In the United States, for example, perfection and luxury mean comfort, size, and dependability. In Europe, luxury means attention to detail and brand heritage. Therefore, although the core of Lexus marketing is similar (a consistent Lexus visual vocabulary, logo, font, and overall communication), the advertising varies by country.

A big reason behind Toyota's success is its manufacturing. Toyota's combination of manufacturing speed and flexibility is world class. Its plants can make as many as eight different models at the same time, which brings Toyota huge increases in productivity and market responsiveness. Toyota is in the midst of integrating its assembly plants around the world into a single giant network. The plants will customize cars for local markets as well as be able to shift production quickly to satisfy any surges in demand from markets worldwide. With a manufacturing network, Toyota can build a wide variety of models much more inexpensively. That means Toyota will be able to fill market niches as they emerge without having to build whole new assembly operations. "If there's a market or market segment where they aren't present, they go there," said Tatsuo Yoshida, auto analyst at Deutsche Securities Ltd. And with consumers increasingly fickle about what they want in a car, such market agility gives Toyota a huge competitive edge.

Toyota's sales rose in every region of the world in 2003, and the company earned US$146 billion. It edged past Ford Motor Co. to become the world's second-largest carmaker, and its market cap of US$110 billion is more than that of GM, Ford, and DaimlerChrysler combined. Toyota is now eyeing the top spot, with a goal of surpassing GM as the world's largest carmaker by 2010.

DISCUSSION QUESTIONS

1. What have been the key success factors for Toyota?

2. Where is Toyota vulnerable? What should marketers watch out for?

3. What recommendations would you make to senior marketing executives going forward? What should they be sure to do with the company's marketing?

Sources: Stuart F. Brown, "Toyota's Global Body Shop," *Fortune*, February 9, 2004, p. 120; James B. Treece, "Ford Down; Toyota Aims for No. 1," *Automotive News*, February 2, 2004, p. 1; Karl Greenberg, "Automakers Drive Sales with Internet Advances," *Brandweek*, February 2, 2004, p. 16; Brian Bemner and Chester Dawson, "Can Anything Stop Toyota?" *BusinessWeek*, November 17, 2003, pp. 114–122; "Toyota Selects Attik for Youth Creative Strategy," *Marketing*, July 18, 2002; "Toyota Looks to Drive Generation Y Sales for Scion with Personalization," *Brandweek*, July 15, 2002, p. 14; John Teresko, "ASIA: Yesterday's Fast Followers Today's Global Leaders," *Industry Week* (February 2004): 22–29; "Lexus Considers Global Marketing," *Automotive News*, January 26, 2004, p. 17; **www.toyota.com**.

13

IN THIS CHAPTER, WE WILL ADDRESS THE FOLLOWING QUESTIONS:

- How are services defined and classified, and how do they differ from goods?

- How are services marketed?

- How can service quality be improved?

- How do services marketers create strong brands?

- How can goods-producing companies improve customer support services?

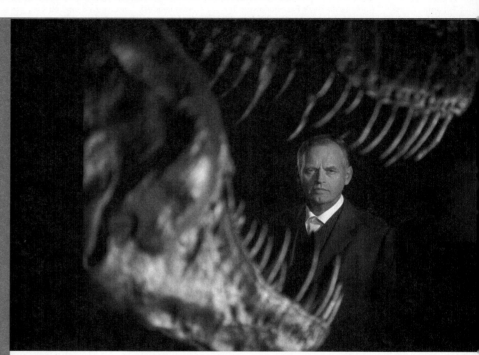

CHAPTER 13

Designing and Managing Services

PROFILE: CANADIAN MARKETING EXCELLENCE

Look any Canadian earnestly in the eye and spout the phrase "Save your money!" and that person will instantly think of ING Direct Canada. This is quite a feat given that the online bank has only been operating in Canada for the last eight years. While ING has operated in Canada since the 1950s, the launch of the new branchless bank in 1997 presented a significant marketing challenge. Would a financial services company with no physical offices be trusted by Canadians as a place to deposit their hard-earned money?

The new venture hired a young, upstart advertising agency to help ING win the hearts, minds, and wallets of Canadians. Garneau Würstlin Philp Brand Engineering of Toronto (which later became known as GWP Brand Engineering) was barely three months old when representatives of International Nederlanden Groep NV, the parent firm of ING Direct, came calling. The new bank wanted to target 20- to 55-year-olds earning more than $50 000 annually, and it needed a memorable way of portraying its services and building credibility. Not an easy task for a Dutch financial institution that would only exist as a voice on the other end of the telephone.

While Canadians had long socked their money away in the big six banks, valuing them for their safety and stability, research told GWP that Canadians had a "love–hate relationship with the big banks." Canadians "hate it when they're turned down for mortgages and they hate being nailed by all the little service charges," said GWP president Bruce Philp. Thus the agency had to walk a fine balance. If it was too aggressive and slammed the big institutions, the new campaign would incite an advertising war and unsettle potential customers. In the end, the campaign simply said, "If you are not happy with your bank, shop around for the best value for each financial product you can get."

It helped that ING had a distinct service and price advantage. As York University professor Alan Middleton stresses, "We know the most important thing for a new service, brand or product is that it's seen as relevantly different. Relevant to what the target group needs, and different from the rest." Since ING Direct had no physical branches, its overhead was low, allowing the bank to pay higher rates of interest on savings and to levy fewer service charges. ING Direct's 4 percent interest rate and promise of no service charges or fees and no minimum deposit requirements was a substantially better offer than the service charges and 0.15 to 0.35 percent daily interest savings rates offered by the big banks.

GWP also wanted to be sure that the new ads for ING Direct looked nothing like the "typical stuff" embraced by the big six banks. Said a GWP spokesperson, "We weren't going to do the standard claptrap like, 'We're going to be there by your side.'"

The ING Direct television campaign was launched in the prime-time viewing period during the evening of April 28, 1997. The TV spots were supported by the now-famous orange billboards. Just as they do today, the first spot featured Danish actor Frederik DeGroot (who today has become a Canadian celebrity and sex symbol). In his now famous no-nonsense way, he laid out ING Direct's value proposition. "Out here you have real power," he said in the ad, while walking along a busy downtown corridor. "People compete for your business. If you are not happy, you go across the street." Unlike the fact-filled, product-based ads of its competitors, this plain-talking message aimed to connect emotionally with Canadians' frustrations.

The advertising team held their breath to see if the strategy worked. They waited in an office just above ING's call centre and they collectively cheered as the phones immediately began to ring off the wall. "Simplicity is the key to everything we do," said Jim Kelly, vice-president of marketing for ING Direct. "It is the cornerstone for all our marketing" and the cornerstone of all the products and services the bank offers today.

When ING Direct first moved into the Canadian market, it offered only savings accounts. Today, it has worked to expand its offerings, always keeping the theme of simplicity top of mind. Recently, ING Direct looked at its mortgage business with an eye to improving the customer experience by simplifying and shortening the process. It also wanted to get rid of all the paper and help its own internal staff do their jobs more effectively. It employed advanced information processing technology, named the Mortgage Application Processing Solution (MAPS), to accomplish these aims. The new system allowed ING Direct to integrate all of its client-related information into its customer relationship management system. The new system helped position the bank to grow rapidly without increasing its costs. And even more important, it helped the bank accomplish its overriding goal of providing superior value to its clients along with an exceptional service experience. The initiative was a huge success and ING Direct increased its conversion rates (the rate of inquiries to those clients who actually entered into a mortgage agreement) by 50 percent in six months. As Brenda Rideout, the bank's chief information officer, explains, "Our customers tell us we have taken a lot of the stress out of buying a home by getting answers back to them so quickly. At the same time, because we spend less time processing paperwork, we can spend more time providing people with the services and support they need to make good financial decisions." In recognition of its success, ING Direct was named one of the Canadian Information Productivity Award winners in 2004.

ING Direct has certainly proven itself to be the little Canadian bank that could. Its parent, ING Direct (Global), was voted "world's leading direct bank" in the Lafferty International Retail Banking Awards of 2003, and has been recognized as one of the top-20 financial services organizations in the world. In 2005, ING Direct Canada provided financial services to almost 1 million customers and it held over $14 billion in assets.

The move into Canada in many ways was a test market for loftier ambitions. ING Direct is now eyeing markets south of the border. It's selected the same Toronto ad agency to lead its U.S. offensive. However, the same communication strategy may not work to market ING Direct's services in this new market. GWP president Bruce Philp notes, "The assumption we made in Canada eight years ago was that we were not dealing with an empowered customer when dealing with financial services, and we were going to empower them. In the States, we do have an empowered consumer." Moreover, in the United States, financial services ads are more intellectual, and an emotional appeal may not have as much power. It will be interesting to see how this new services marketing effort unfolds.

Sources: David Menzies, "How to Launch a Bank, *Marketing Magazine*, December 1, 1997; Patti Summerfield, "Big Five Banks Set Sights on Financial Upstarts," *Strategy Magazine*, July 30, 2001, p. 2; John Gray, "Top Client, Financial Services: Simplicity the Crux of ING Proposition," *Strategy Magazine*, August 2, 1999, p. B5; "ING Direct Lowers Mortgage Rates Again," ING Direct press release, Toronto, March 25, 2004; C.I.P.A. 2004 Award Winners, ING Direct Canada, **www.cipa.com/award_winners/winners_04/INGDirectCnd.html** (viewed March 11, 2005); Keith Mcarthur, "Are Americans Ready to Save Their Money?" *Globe and Mail*, February 22, 2005, p. B1.

Service businesses increasingly fuel the world economy. Because understanding the special nature of services and what that means to marketers is critical, in this chapter we systematically analyze services and how to market them most effectively.

The Nature of Services

One of the megatrends of recent years has been the phenomenal growth of services. In Canada, the services sector accounts for 69 percent of the GDP, while goods-producing industries account for 31 percent (of which manufacturing accounts for only 17 percent). Service industries in Canada grow faster than both goods-producing industries and the economy as a whole. Service industries in Canada grew 4.0 percent between 1997 and 2003, goods-producing industries grew 3.0 percent, and overall GDP grew 3.6 percent. Some service sectors grew even more, such as wholesale trade and information and cultural services, which grew at rates between 6 and 7 percent.[1]

Similarly, the services sector is a much larger employer than the goods-producing sector. In July 2004, the services sector of the Canadian economy employed almost 12 million Canadians, compared to the 4 million people working in the goods-producing sector. The largest number of employers—132 000—come from the retail trade industry.[2]

Service Industries Are Everywhere

The *government sector*, with its courts, employment services, hospitals, loan agencies, military services, police and fire departments, postal service, regulatory agencies, and schools, is in the service business. The *private nonprofit sector*, with its museums, charities, churches, universities, colleges, foundations, and hospitals, is in the service business. A good part of the *business sector*, with its airlines, banks, hotels, insurance companies, law firms, management consulting firms, motion-picture companies, plumbing-repair companies, and real estate firms, is in the service business. Many workers in the *manufacturing sector*, such as computer operators, accountants, and legal staff, are really service providers. In fact, they make up a "service factory" providing services to the "goods factory." And those in the *retail sector*, such as cashiers, clerks, salespeople, and customer service representatives, are also providing a service.

We define a service as follows: A **service** is any act or performance that one party can offer to another that is essentially intangible and does not result in the ownership of anything. Its production may or may not be tied to a physical product.

Manufacturers, distributors, and retailers can provide value-added services or simply excellent customer service to differentiate themselves.

OnStar

General Motors has gone a step further with its OnStar service, which helps customers with related tasks including emergency services dispatch, stolen vehicle location, roadside assistance, remote diagnostics, and route support. Every month OnStar unlocks about 28 000 car doors, dispatches 13 000 roadside assistance vehicles, and locates 700 lost vehicles. While the first year of OnStar is free to GM car owners, it now claims renewal rates as high as 80 percent at annual subscription fees ranging from US$200 to more than US$800. By 2005, OnStar is projected to bring in more than US$2 billion for GM.[3]

Many pure service firms are now using the Internet to reach customers. A little surfing on the Web will turn up a large number of virtual service providers. Here are some that dispense online advice:

Dot-com Providers

Log on to Health Canada's Web site (www.hc-sc.gc.ca/english/iyh/index.html) if you have a medical problem—the site posts a wealth of information. Are you a small business that needs legal advice? Go to www.canadalegal.com. The site was named by *Small Business Canada Magazine* as an outstanding resource for Canadian firms. If you need adult or child counselling, click on http://adultandchildcounsel.uswestdex.com and talk with Bailey Molineaux or Bill Evans about marital and family therapy, children's problems, or job stress. If you want a psychic reading, click on www.psychicrealm.com. Canadian investors can even get advice online—go to adviceforinvestors.com at www.fin-info.com.

Categories of Service Mix

A company's offerings often include some services. The service component can be a minor or a major part of the total offering. Five categories of offerings can be distinguished:

1. *Pure tangible good.* The offering consists primarily of a tangible good such as soap, toothpaste, or salt. No services accompany the product.

2. *Tangible good with accompanying services.* The offering consists of a tangible good accompanied by one or more services. Levitt observes that "the more technologically sophisticated the generic product (e.g., cars and computers), the more dependent are its sales on the quality and availability of its accompanying customer services (e.g., display rooms, delivery, repairs and maintenance, application aids, operator training, installation advice, warranty fulfillment). In this sense, General Motors is probably more service intensive than manufacturing intensive. Without its services, its sales would shrivel."[4]

3. *Hybrid.* The offering consists of equal parts of goods and services. For example, people patronize restaurants for both food and service.

4. *Major service with accompanying minor goods and services.* The offering consists of a major service along with additional services or supporting goods. For example, airline passengers buy transportation. The trip includes some tangibles, such as food and drinks, a ticket stub, and an airline magazine. The service requires a capital-intensive good—an airplane—for its realization, but the primary item is a service.

5. *Pure service.* The offering consists primarily of a service. Examples include baby-sitting, psychotherapy, and massage.

Because of this varying goods-to-service mix, it is difficult to generalize about services without further distinctions. Here are some additional distinctions that can be helpful:

- Services vary as to whether they are *equipment-based* (automated car washes, vending machines) or *people-based* (window washing, accounting services). People-based services vary by whether they are provided by unskilled, skilled, or professional workers.

- Service companies can choose among different *processes* to deliver their service. Restaurants have developed such different formats as cafeteria-style, fast-food, buffet, and candlelight service.

- Some services require the *client's presence* and some do not. Brain surgery involves the client's presence, a car repair does not. If the client must be present, the service provider has to be considerate of his or her needs. Thus beauty salon operators will invest in décor, play background music, and engage in light conversation with the client.

- Services differ as to whether they meet a *personal need* (personal services) or a *business need* (business services). Service providers typically develop different marketing programs for personal and business markets.

- Service providers differ in their *objectives* (profit or nonprofit) and *ownership* (private or public). These two characteristics, when crossed, produce four quite different types of organizations. The marketing programs of a private investor hospital such as the Shouldice Hernia

Centre in Thornhill, Ontario, will differ from those of a public hospital or a veterans' hospital such as Ste. Anne's Hospital in Sainte-Anne-de-Bellevue, Quebec.[5]

The nature of the service mix also has implications for how consumers evaluate quality. For some services, customers cannot judge the technical quality even after they have received the service. Figure 13.1 shows various products and services according to difficulty of evaluation.[6] At the left are goods high in *search qualities*—that is, characteristics the buyer can evaluate before purchase. In the middle are goods and services high in *experience qualities*—characteristics the buyer can evaluate after purchase. At the right are goods and services high in *credence qualities*—characteristics the buyer normally finds hard to evaluate even after consumption.[7]

Because services are generally high in experience and credence qualities, there is more risk in purchase. This has several consequences. First, service consumers generally rely on word of mouth rather than advertising. Second, they rely heavily on price, personnel, and physical cues to judge quality. Third, they are highly loyal to service providers who satisfy them. Fourth, because of the switching costs involved, much consumer inertia can exist. It can be challenging to entice a customer away from a competitor. Avis's slogan, "we try harder," was a call to action to new and existing customers alike.

Distinctive Characteristics of Services

Services have four distinctive characteristics that greatly affect the design of marketing programs: *intangibility, inseparability, variability,* and *perishability.*

INTANGIBILITY Unlike physical products, services cannot be seen, tasted, felt, heard, or smelled before they are bought. The person getting a face-lift cannot see the results before the purchase, and the patient in the psychiatrist's office cannot know the exact outcome.

To reduce uncertainty, buyers will look for evidence of quality. They will draw inferences about quality from the place, people, equipment, communication material, symbols, and price that they see. Therefore, the service provider's task is to "manage the evidence," to "tangibilize the intangible."[8] Whereas product marketers are challenged to add abstract ideas, service marketers are challenged to add physical evidence and imagery to abstract offers.

Service companies can try to demonstrate their service quality through *physical evidence* and *presentation.*[9] A hotel will develop a look and style of dealing with customers that realizes its intended customer value proposition, whether it is cleanliness, speed, or some other benefit. Suppose a bank wants to position itself as the "fast" bank. It could make this positioning strategy tangible through a number of marketing tools:

1. *Place.* The exterior and interior should have clean lines. The layout of the desks and the traffic flow should be planned carefully. Waiting lines should not get overly long.

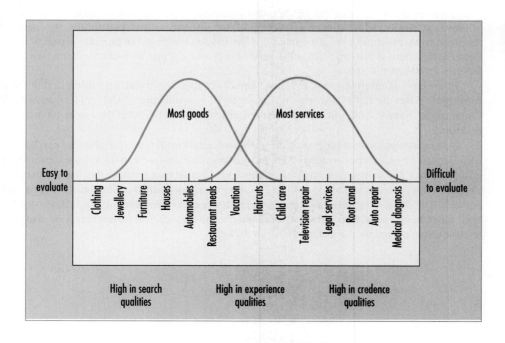

FIGURE 13.1

Continuum of Evaluation for Different Types of Products

2. *People.* Personnel should be busy. There should be a sufficient number of employees to manage the workload.

3. *Equipment.* Computers, copying machines, and desks should be and look "state of the art."

4. *Communication material.* Printed materials—text and photos—should suggest efficiency and speed.

5. *Symbols.* The name and symbol should suggest fast service.

6. *Price.* The bank could advertise that it will deposit $5 in the account of any customer who waits in line for more than five minutes.

Service marketers must be able to transform intangible services into concrete benefits. To aid in "tangibilizing the intangible," Carbone and Haeckel propose a set of concepts under the name *customer experience engineering.*[10] Companies must first develop a clear picture of what they want the customer's perception of an experience to be and then design a consistent set of *performance and context clues* to support that experience. In the case of a bank, whether the teller dispensed the right amount of cash is a performance clue; a context clue is whether the teller was properly dressed. The context clues in a bank are delivered by people (*humanics*) and things (*mechanics*). The company assembles the clues in an *experience blueprint*, a pictorial representation of the various clues. To the extent possible, the clues should address all five senses. The Disney Company is a master at developing *experience blueprints* in its theme parks. See how the Yukon government likewise uses experience marketing to gain insight and publicity for the territory:

The Yukon

With mining on the wane, tourism is the biggest hope for Yukon's economy. However, it isn't exactly a top-of-mind destination for most people, who are unaware of its attractions or daunted because of its remote location. Officials wondered what could be done to overcome this problem, especially with a limited budget. The answer—invite a small group of influential marketers from Canada, the United States, and Europe to the Yukon and let them experience it firsthand so that they could not only offer marketing insights but also spread the word about the wonders of the Yukon. The group was taken snowmobiling down the frozen Yukon River, snowshoeing, and dogsledding. They gambled in Klondike-era clothing, drank champagne at the Arctic Circle, and flew over stunning mountains. As one participant noted, "Having such a magnificent experience, we came away full of excitement and were able to translate that into sound ideas about how they can go about getting a lot of people to go there."[11]

INSEPARABILITY   Services are typically produced and consumed simultaneously. This is not true of physical goods, which are manufactured, put into inventory, distributed through multiple resellers, and consumed later. If a person renders the service, then the provider is part of the service. Because the client is also present as the service is produced, provider–client interaction is a special feature of services marketing.

In the case of entertainment and professional services, buyers are very interested in the specific provider. It is not the same concert if the Tragically Hip are indisposed and replaced by Anne Murray. When clients have strong provider preferences, price is raised to ration the preferred provider's limited time.

Several strategies exist for getting around this limitation. The service provider can learn to work with larger groups. Psychotherapists have moved from one-on-one therapy to small-group therapy to groups of over 300 people in a large hotel ballroom. The service provider can learn to work faster—the psychotherapist can spend 30 minutes with each patient instead of 50 minutes and can see more patients. The service organization can train more service providers and build up client confidence, as H&R Block has done with its network of trained tax consultants. Creative artists have also developed techniques to overcome the limits of inseparability.

Cirque du Soleil

Cirque du Soleil, the world-renowned Quebec-based company, produces spectacular resident and touring stage productions using basic circus elements combined with innovative visual and musical effects and stunning staging. It got its start in 1984 as a troupe of street performers known as "Le Club des Talons Hauts" (the high-heels club). Guy Laliberté, founding president and CEO, began as a musician and fire-breather. In 1984, 73 people worked for Cirque du Soleil. Today, the organization has over 3000 employees worldwide and is one of Canada's leading exports. In 2004, the company had five touring shows playing in cities all over the world and permanent show sites like Disney World and Las Vegas. Every night its custom-built Las Vegas theatres draw roughly 10 000 people willing to pay between US$60 and US$150 apiece.

"Cirque du Soleil put an entirely new face on entertainment in Las Vegas," says Bobby Baldwin, a top executive with the MGM/Mirage hotel chain. From 1984 to 1989, Cirque played to an average of 270 000 people a year. In 2003 alone, nearly 7 000 000 people saw a Cirque du Soleil show. To increase its audience even further, it recently created *Solstrom*, a television production of its famous shows, that aired for 13 weeks on CBC television.[12]

VARIABILITY   Because they depend on who provides them and when and where they are provided, services are highly variable. Some doctors have excellent bedside manner; others are less patient with their patients. Some surgeons are very successful in performing a certain operation; others are not. Service buyers are aware of this variability and often talk to others before selecting a service provider. Here are three steps service firms can take to increase quality control:

1. *Invest in good hiring and training procedures.* Recruiting the right employees and providing them with excellent training is crucial, regardless of whether employees are highly skilled professionals or low-skilled workers. Ideally, employees should exhibit competence, a caring attitude, responsiveness, initiative, problem-solving ability, and goodwill. Canada Post, for example, has its own Learning Institute that offers employees opportunities for learning and growth. It provides diagnostic testing so that employees can assess their current skills, as well

Cirque du Soleil founders overcame the challenge of service inseparability by growing the company into an international touring company, by having permanent shows, and through television productions.

as programs through which they can improve their job specific skills. If employees wish to further their training and education by taking evening or weekend courses outside normal working hours, Canada Post will reimburse tuition costs for courses that relate to the person's professional development. Some organizations even create their own university equivalent programs for employees. The Credit Union Institute of Canada, for example, offers a series of courses for Credit Union employees whereby they can earn professional designations.

2. *Standardize the service-performance process throughout the organization.* This is done by preparing a *service blueprint* that depicts events and processes in a flowchart, with the objective of recognizing potential fail points. Figure 13.2 shows a service blueprint for a nationwide floral-delivery organization.[13] The customer's experience is limited to dialling the phone, making choices, and placing an order. Behind the scenes, the floral organization gathers the flowers, places them in a vase, delivers them, and collects payment. Any one of these activities can be done well or poorly.

3. *Monitor customer satisfaction.* Employ suggestion and complaint systems, customer surveys, and comparison shopping. General Electric sends out 700 000 response cards a year asking households to rate its service people's performance. Citibank checks continuously on measures of ART (accuracy, responsiveness, and timeliness). Firms can also develop customer information databases and systems to permit more personalized, customized service.[14]

PERISHABILITY   Services cannot be stored. Perishability is not a problem when demand is steady. When demand fluctuates, service firms have problems. For example, public transportation companies have to own much more equipment because of rush-hour demand than if demand were even throughout the day. Some doctors charge patients for missed appointments because the service value exists only at that point.

Several strategies can produce a better match between demand and supply in a service business.[15] On the demand side:

■ *Differential pricing* will shift some demand from peak to off-peak periods. Examples include low early-evening movie prices and weekend discount prices for car rentals.

■ *Nonpeak demand* can be cultivated. McDonald's pushes breakfast service, and hotels promote mini-vacation weekends.

■ *Complementary* services can be developed to provide alternatives to waiting customers, such as cocktail lounges in restaurants and automatic teller machines in banks.

■ *Reservation systems* are a way to manage the demand level. Airlines, hotels, and physicians employ them extensively.

On the supply side:

■ *Part-time employees* can be hired to serve peak demand. Universities and colleges add part-time teachers when enrollment goes up, and restaurants call in part-time servers when needed.

■ *Peak-time efficiency* routines can be introduced. Employees perform only essential tasks during peak periods. Paramedics assist physicians during busy periods.

FIGURE 13.2

A Service-Performance-Process Map: Nationwide Floral Delivery

Source: Adapted from G. Lynn Shostack, "Service Positioning Through Structural Change," *Journal of Marketing* (January 1987): 39. Reprinted with permission of the American Marketing Association.

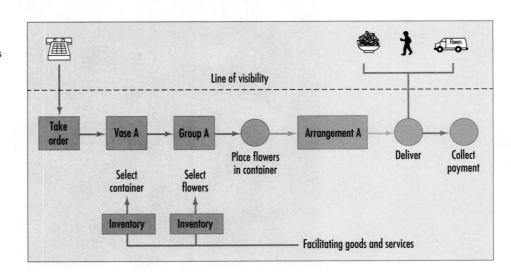

- *Increased consumer participation* can be encouraged. Consumers fill out their own medical records or bag their own groceries.
- *Shared* services can be developed. Several hospitals can share medical-equipment purchases.
- *Facilities for future expansion* can be developed. An amusement park buys surrounding land for later development.

Many airlines, hotels, and resorts have e-mail alerts to self-selected segments of their customer base that offer special short-term discounts and promotions. Club Med uses early to midweek e-mails to people in its database to pitch unsold weekend packages, typically 30 to 40 percent off the standard package price.[16] After 40 years of making people stand in line at its theme parks, Disney instituted Fastpass, which allows visitors to reserve a spot in line and eliminate the wait. When polled, it turns out that 95 percent of visitors like the change. Disney's vice-president Dale Stafford told a reporter, "We have been teaching people how to stand in line since 1955, and now we are telling them they don't have to. Of all the things we can do and all the marvels we can create with the attractions, this is something that will have a profound effect on the entire industry."[17]

Marketing Strategies for Service Firms

At one time, service firms lagged behind manufacturing firms in their use of marketing because they were small, or they were professional businesses that did not use marketing, or they faced large demand or little competition. This has certainly changed. "Marketing Memo: A Services Marketing Checklist" outlines the questions top service marketing organizations should be asking.

A Shifting Customer Relationship

Not all companies, however, have invested in providing superior service, at least not to all customers. Customers have often complained about inaccurate information; unresponsive, rude, or poorly trained personnel; and long wait times. Customer service complaints are on the rise, even though many complaints never actually reach a live human being. Here are some statistics that should give service companies and customer service departments pause:[18]

- *On the phone.* Some 80 percent of companies haven't figured out how to get customers the assistance they need.
- *Online.* Forrester Research estimates that 35 percent of all e-mail inquiries to companies don't get a response within seven days and about 25 percent don't get a response at all.
- *Interactive Voice Response.* While many of the largest companies have installed call-routing software called Interactive Voice Response Systems, more than 90 percent of financial services consumers say they don't like them.

In former times, service companies held out a welcoming hand to all customers, but these companies now have so much data on individuals that they are able to classify their customers into profit tiers. So service is not uniformly bad for all customers. Airlines, hotels, and banks all pamper good customers. Big spenders get special discounts, promotional offers, and lots of special service. The rest of their customers get higher fees, stripped-down service, and at best a voice message to answer inquiries.

Financial services giants have installed special software that tells them—in an instant—when a lucrative customer is on the phone. Such systems immediately send the call ahead of dozens—even hundreds—of other callers who must wait while the big spender gets special attention.[19] Charles Schwab's best customers get their calls answered in 15 seconds; other customers can wait 10 minutes or more. Sears sends a repairperson to its best customers within two hours; other customers wait four hours.

This shift from a customer service democracy to a meritocracy is also a response to lower profit margins resulting from customers becoming more price-driven and less loyal. Companies are now

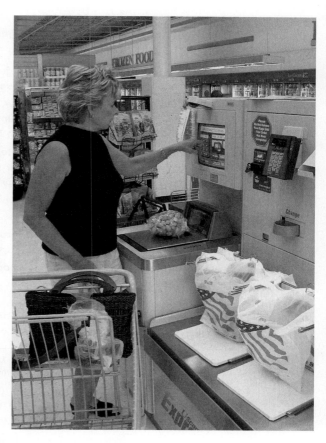

A shopper uses the automatic express checkout to pay for and bag purchases herself. These computerized checkout systems allow the shopper to pay with a credit card, a debit card, or cash.

Marketing Memo

A Services Marketing Checklist

Customers' expectations are the true standards for judging service quality. Berry and Parasuraman propose that marketing managers ask the following questions as they seek to manage and exceed expectations:

1. *Do we strive to present a realistic picture of our service to customers?* Do we always check the accuracy of our promotional messages? Is there regular communication between employees who serve customers and those who make promises to customers? Do we assess the impact on customer expectations of cues such as price?

2. *Is performing the service right the first time a top priority?* Are our employees trained and rewarded for delivering error-free service? Do we regularly evaluate our service designs to identify and correct potential flaws?

3. *Do we communicate effectively with customers?* Do we periodically contact customers to ascertain their needs and let them know we appreciate their business? Do we train and require employees to demonstrate to customers that we care about and value them?

4. *Do we surprise customers during the service process?* Are our employees aware that the service delivery process is our prime opportunity to exceed customers' expectations? Do we take specific steps to encourage excellence?

5. *Do our employees regard service problems as opportunities to impress customers?* Do we prepare and encourage employees to excel in the service recovery process? Do we reward them for providing exceptional recovery service?

6. *Do we continuously evaluate and improve our performance against customers' expectations?* Do we perform consistently above the adequate service level? Do we capitalize on opportunities to exceed the desired service level?

Source: Excerpted from Leonard L. Berry and A. Parasuraman, *Marketing Services: Competing Through Quality* (New York: The Free Press, 1991), pp. 72–73. Also see Leonard L. Berry, *On Great Service: A Framework for Action* (New York: The Free Press, 1995), and his *Discovering the Soul of Service* (New York: The Free Press, 1999).

driven to seek ways to squeeze more profit out of the different customer tiers. Firms have decided to raise fees and lower service to customers who barely pay their way, and to coddle big spenders to retain their patronage as long as possible.

Companies that provide differentiated levels of service, however, must be careful about claiming superior service—the customers who receive poor treatment will bad-mouth the company and injure its reputation. Delivering services that maximize both customer satisfaction and company profitability can be challenging. Consider Air Canada's incredibly difficult struggle:

Air Canada

Many factors will determine whether or not Air Canada can emerge from under the cloud of bankruptcy protection it filed for in 2004. Halfway through 2005, Air Canada was still reporting operating losses, but the skies are starting to look sunnier for the troubled airline. In July 2005, it reported its 16th consecutive month of improved load factors (load factors reflect how close to full capacity an airline's flights are). As with all service offerings, inventory cannot be stored, so selling as many seats on its flights as possible is important. As Montie Brewer, president and CEO of Air Canada, exclaimed, "This achievement reflects in great part our ability to better match capacity to demand. Our performance in the Canadian market remains particularly strong—an indication of a healthy market and growing consumer preference for Air Canada's product offering." To keep growing its revenues, Air Canada has been adding new routes in both domestic and international markets. For example, in 2005, it launched its first nonstop service between eastern Canada and Beijing. To attract even more customers in Canada and around the world, Air Canada developed new advertising, which features Céline Dion and its now-famous tagline "You and I were meant to fly!" Air Canada's customer service, recently lamented by many travellers, has also experienced a significant turnaround. In June 2005, the airline was ranked as Best Airline in North America in a worldwide survey of more than 12 million air travellers. Star Alliance, of which Air Canada is a founding member, was ranked as Best Airline Alliance. With these improvements, Air Canada is hopeful that it will soon return to profitability.[20]

There are also shifts that favour the customer in the client relationship. Customers are becoming more sophisticated about buying product support services and are pressing for "services unbundling." They want separate prices for each service element and the right to select the elements they want. Customers also increasingly dislike having to deal with a multitude of service providers handling different types of equipment. Some third-party service organizations now service a greater range of equipment.[21]

Most important, the Internet has empowered customers by letting them vent their rage about bad service—or reward good service—and have their comments beamed around the world with a mouse click. See "Marketing Insight: Voice Mail Hell" for a look at some ways in which the scales are tipping in the customer's favour and why service industries better take heed.

MARKETING INSIGHT

Voice Mail Hell

As anyone who has ever spent 15 minutes in interactive voice mail "hell" knows, customer rage is a fact of twenty-first-century life. While we have ever more products that are supposed to make our lives more convenient, there are ever more companies we need to deal with to install and set up those products or fix a problem when they fail. In the past, we used to interact with a human; now we are more likely to interact with a prerecorded voice message or a remote "online technical help" centre. The result: more customer rage than ever. In fact, Virginia-based Customer Care Alliance, in a survey of 1094 households, has concluded that companies are driving their customers crazy.

Of the 45 percent of households that reported at least one "serious problem" with a product or service in the past year, more than two-thirds of those customers experienced "rage" over the way the incident was handled. Sixteen percent of respondents said they wanted "revenge" on the company, and 3 percent took legal action.

Rising frustration levels come at a price for companies. Angry customers can damage a brand or company with bad word of mouth. Ninety percent of angry customers reported that they shared their story with a friend. Now, they can share their stories with strangers via the Internet. "The Internet is word of mouth on steroids," Pete Blackshaw likes to say, and he should know. Blackshaw is chief marketing and customer satisfaction officer for Intelliseek, a company that has made a profit by allowing consumers to rant—or rave—on its Planetfeedback.com site. With a few clicks on the Planetfeedback site, shoppers can send an e-mail, complaint, compliment, suggestion, or question directly to a company, with the option to post comments publicly at the site as well.

That's what Beth Heckel, a Colorado preschool aide, did after she received a series of threatening letters from CD club Columbia House, a full six years after her daughter's membership expired. Heckel couldn't get a response from the company by phone or mail and was on the verge of sending in the disputed US$40 just to salvage her credit rating. When Heckel sent her complaint to Columbia House via Planetfeedback.com, she got an e-mail conceding the company's error and the letters stopped. The likelihood of finally getting some action—or just the satisfaction of venting publicly—is why consumers sent 67 000 e-mails to 15 000 companies via Planetfeedback in 2003 alone. Sue MacDonald, an Intelliseek spokesperson, said: "About 80 percent of the companies respond to the complaints, some within an hour."

More important than simply responding to a disgruntled customer, however, is preventing dissatisfaction from occurring in the future. Ironically, Blackshaw says, "a company will spend hundreds of dollars per customer to attract people to its business, but far less to keep that customer once he or she has been acquired." That may mean simply taking the time to nurture customer relationships and give customers attention from an actual living, breathing human being. Columbia Records claims it is now spending US$10 million to improve its call centre, and customers who phone the company can now "opt out" to reach an operator at any point in their calls.

Sources: Jane Spencer, "Cases of Customer Rage Mount As Bad Service Prompts Venting," *Wall Street Journal*, September 17, 2003, p. D4; Judi Ketteler, "Grumbling Groundswell," *Cincinnati Business Courier*, September 8, 2003; Richard Halicks, "You Can Count on Customer Disservice," *The Atlanta Journal Constitution*, June 29, 2003, p. D4; Michelle Slatella, "Toll-Free Apology Soothes Savage Beast," *New York Times*, February 12, 2004, p. G4; Bruce Horovitz, "Whatever Happened to Customer Service?," *USA Today*, September 26, 2003, p. A1.

Holistic Marketing for Services

Because service encounters are complex interactions affected by multiple elements, adopting a holistic marketing perspective is especially important. The service outcome, and whether or not people will remain loyal to a service provider, is influenced by a host of variables. Keaveney identified more than 800 critical behaviours that cause customers to switch services.[22] These behaviours can be placed into one of eight categories (see Table 13.1).

Holistic marketing for services requires external, internal, and interactive marketing (see Figure 13.3).[23] *External marketing* describes the normal work of preparing, pricing, distributing, and promoting the service to customers. *Internal marketing* describes training and motivating employees to serve customers well. Berry has argued that the most important contribution the marketing department can make is to be "exceptionally clever in getting everyone else in the organization to practice marketing."[24]

TABLE 13.1	FACTORS LEADING TO CUSTOMER SWITCHING BEHAVIOUR	
Pricing		**Response to Service Failure**
■ High Price		■ Negative Response
■ Price Increases		■ No Response
■ Unfair Pricing		■ Reluctant Response
■ Deceptive Pricing		**Competition**
Inconvenience		■ Found Better Service
■ Location/Hours		**Ethical Problems**
■ Wait for Appointment		■ Cheat
■ Wait for Service		■ Hard Sell
Core Service Failures		■ Unsafe
■ Service Mistakes		■ Conflict of Interest
■ Billing Errors		**Involuntary Switching**
■ Service Catastrophe		■ Customer Moved
Service Encounter Failures		■ Provider Closed
■ Uncaring		
■ Impolite		
■ Unresponsive		
■ Unknowledgeable		

Source: Susan M. Keaveney, "Customer Switching Behavior in Service Industries: An Exploratory Study," *Journal of Marketing* (April 1995): 71–82.

FIGURE 13.3

Three Types of Marketing
Service Industries

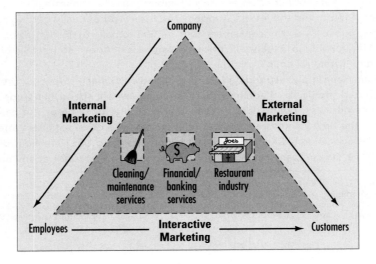

Singapore Airlines (SIA)

Singapore Airlines is consistently recognized as the world's "best" airline, in large part due to its stellar efforts at internal marketing. SIA strives to create a "wow effect" and regularly surprise its customers. It does this by listening intensely and constantly identifying opportunities generated by customer feedback. Some examples of this are SIA's new lighter, more nutritious fare and its in-flight e-mail service. SIA places a high emphasis on training. Its latest initiative, called "Transforming Customer Service (TCS)," involves staff in five key operational areas: cabin crew, engineering, ground services, flight operations, and sales support. The TCS culture is embedded in all management training, companywide. TCS also uses a 40-30-30 rule in its holistic approach to people, processes, and products: 40 percent of resources go to training and invigorating staff, 30 percent is spent on reviewing process and procedures, and the last 30 percent on creating new product and service ideas.[25]

Interactive marketing describes the employees' skill in serving the client. Clients judge service not only by its *technical quality* (e.g., was the surgery successful?) but also by its *functional quality* (e.g., did the surgeon show concern and inspire confidence?).[26] Technology has great power to make service workers more productive.[27] Respiratory therapists at the University of California at San Diego Medical Center now carry miniature computers in their coat pockets so that they can call up patient records on handheld computers and therefore spend more time working directly with patients.

Companies must avoid pushing productivity so hard, however, that they reduce perceived quality. Some methods lead to too much standardization. Service providers must deliver "high-touch" as well as "high-tech."[28] Consider Via Rail.

VIA Rail

As the Canadian transportation industry becomes increasingly competitive, many believe train travel will disappear. VIA Rail has responded by increasing services, especially for first-class business travellers, who are now offered computer plug-ins, a choice of meals, and free alcoholic beverages. It is also tailoring its advertising to different segments of the market. For vacationers, it doesn't offer travel, it offers "experiences." Like many companies, VIA is using the Web to offer secondary service features that were never possible before. People can go to www.viarail.ca and instantly download schedules, gather information about activities and tourist attractions across the country, join its "Preference" loyalty program, and make travel reservations.

Managing Service Quality

The service quality of a firm is tested at each service encounter. If retail clerks are bored, cannot answer simple questions, or are visiting with each other while customers are waiting, customers will think twice about doing business again with that seller.

Customer Expectations

Customers form service expectations from many sources, such as past experiences, word of mouth, and advertising. In general, customers compare the *perceived service* with the *expected service*.[29] If the perceived service falls below the expected service, customers are disappointed. If the perceived service meets or exceeds their expectations, they are apt to use the provider again. Successful companies add benefits to their offering that not only *satisfy* customers but also surprise and *delight* them. Delighting customers is a matter of exceeding expectations.

Ritz-Carlton Hotels

Ritz-Carlton Hotels' legendary service starts with 100 hours of training annually for every employee. The company empowers employees to make decisions and spend money to solve customer-service issues. Guestrooms are exhaustively reviewed every 90 days and guaranteed to be defect free, check-in time has been cut in half, and special programs created for family travellers and weddings. It's perhaps no surprise that Ritz-Carlton was the first two-time winner of the Malcolm Baldrige National Quality Award.[30]

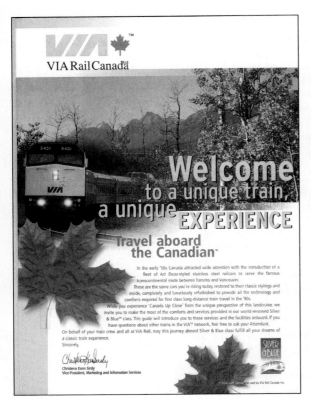

Via Rail promises an "experience," not just rail transportation.

Parasuraman, Zeithaml, and Berry formulated a service-quality model that highlights the main requirements for delivering high service quality.[31] The model, shown in Figure 13.4, identifies five gaps that cause unsuccessful delivery:

1. *Gap between consumer expectation and management perception.* Management does not always correctly perceive what customers want. Hospital administrators may think that patients want better food, but patients may be more concerned with nurse responsiveness.

2. *Gap between management perception and service-quality specification.* Management might correctly perceive customers' wants but not set a performance standard. Hospital administrators may tell the nurses to give "fast" service without specifying it in minutes.

3. *Gap between service-quality specifications and service delivery.* Personnel might be poorly trained, or incapable or unwilling to meet the standard; or they may be held to conflicting standards, such as taking time to listen to customers and serving them fast.

4. *Gap between service delivery and external communications.* Consumer expectations are affected by statements made by company representatives and ads. If a hospital brochure shows a beautiful room, but the patient arrives and finds the room to be cheap and tacky looking, external communications have distorted the customer's expectations.

5. *Gap between perceived service and expected service.* This gap occurs when the consumer misperceives the service quality. The physician may keep visiting the patient to show care, but the patient may interpret this as an indication that something really is wrong.

Based on this service-quality model, these researchers identified the following five determinants of service quality, in order of importance.[32]

1. *Reliability*—The ability to perform the promised service dependably and accurately.

2. *Responsiveness*—The willingness to help customers and to provide prompt service.

3. *Assurance*—The knowledge and courtesy of employees and their ability to convey trust and confidence.

4. *Empathy*—The provision of caring, individualized attention to customers.

5. *Tangibles*—The appearance of physical facilities, equipment, personnel, and communication materials.

Based on these five factors, the researchers developed the 21-item SERVQUAL scale (see Table 13.2).[33] They also note that there is a *zone of tolerance* or range where consumer perceptions on a service dimension would be deemed satisfactory, anchored by the minimum level consumers would be willing to accept and the level that customers believe can and should be delivered. "Marketing Insight: The Role of Expectations in Service Quality Perceptions" describes important recent research on services marketing. "Marketing Memo: Assessing E-Service Quality" reviews models of online service quality.

Best Practices of Service Quality Management

Various studies have shown that well-managed service companies share the following common practices: a strategic concept, a history of top-management commitment to quality, high standards, self-service technologies, systems for monitoring service performance and customer complaints, and an emphasis on employee satisfaction. "Marketing Memo: Recommendations for Improving Service Quality" also offers a comprehensive set of guidelines for service marketers. Vidéotron, a Quebec-based cable provider, is learning this slowly but surely.

FIGURE 13.4

Service-Quality Model

Sources: A. Parasuraman, Valarie A. Zeithaml, and Leonard L. Berry, "A Conceptual Model of Service Quality and Its Implications for Future Research," *Journal of Marketing* (Fall 1985): 44. This model is more fully discussed or elaborated in Valarie A. Zeithaml and Mary Jo Bitner, *Services Marketing* (New York: McGraw-Hill, 1996), ch 2.

TABLE 13.2	SERVQUAL ATTRIBUTES

Reliability

- Providing service as promised
- Dependability in handling customers' service problems
- Performing services right the first time
- Providing services at the promised time
- Maintaining error-free records

Responsiveness

- Keeping customer informed as to when services will be performed
- Prompt service to customers
- Willingness to help customers
- Readiness to respond to customers' requests

Assurance

- Employees who instill confidence in customers
- Making customers feel safe in their transactions
- Employees who are consistently courteous
- Employees who have the knowledge to answer customer questions

Empathy

- Giving customers individual attention
- Employees who deal with customers in a caring fashion
- Having the customer's best interests at heart
- Employees who understand the needs of their customers
- Convenient business hours

Tangibles

- Modern equipment
- Visually appealing facilities
- Employees who have a neat, professional appearance
- Visually appealing materials associated with the service

The Role of Expectations in Service Quality Perceptions

The Parasuraman, Ziethaml, and Berry service-quality model highlights some of the gaps that cause unsuccessful service delivery. Subsequent research has extended the model to incorporate additional considerations. Boulding, Kalra, Staelin, and Zeithaml have developed a dynamic process model of service quality. The model is based on the premise that customer perceptions and expectations of service quality change over time, but at any one point in time are a function of prior expectations of what *will* and what *should* happen during the service encounter, as well as the *actual* service delivered during the last contact. The researcher's empirically tested model contends that the two different types of expectations have opposing effects on perceptions of service quality.

1. *Increasing* customer expectations of what the firm *will* deliver can lead to improved perceptions of overall service quality.

2. *Decreasing* customer expectations of what the firm *should* deliver can lead to improved perceptions of overall service quality.

Much work has validated the role of expectations in consumers' interpretations and evaluations of the service encounter and the relationship they adopt with a firm over time. Consumers are often forward-looking with respect to their decision to keep or switch from a service relationship. Any marketing activity that affects current or expected future usage can help to solidify a service relationship.

With continuously provided services, such as public utilities, health care, financial services, computing services, insurance, and other professional, membership, or subscription services, customers have been observed to mentally calculate their *payment equity*—the perceived fairness of the level of economic benefits derived from service usage in relation to the level of economic costs. Payment costs typically consist of some combination of an initial payment such as a membership fee or retainer; a fixed, periodic fee such as a monthly service charge; and a variable fee such as usage-based charges. Payment benefits depend on current payment and usage levels. The perceived fairness of the exchange determines service satisfaction and future usage. In other words, it is as if customers ask themselves, "Am I using this service enough, given what I pay for it?" Customers may be satisfied even with low usage *if* that is their expectation.

There can be a dark side to long-term service relationships. For example, with an ad agency, the client may feel that over time, the agency loses objectivity and becomes stale in its thinking or begins to take advantage of the relationship.

Sources: William Boulding, Ajay Kalra, Richard Staelin, and Valarie A. Zeithaml, "A Dynamic Model of Service Quality: From Expectations to Behavioral Intentions," *Journal of Marketing Research*, 30 (February), 1993, pp. 7–27; Katherine N. Lemon, Tiffany Barnett White, and Russell S. Winer, "Dynamic Customer Relationship Management: Incorporating Future Considerations into the Service Retention Decision," *Journal of Marketing*, 6 (January 2002): 1–14; Ruth N. Bolton and Katherine N. Lemon, "A Dynamic Model of Customers' Usage of Services: Usage as an Antecedent and Consequence of Satisfaction," *Journal of Marketing*, 36 (May 1999): 171–186; Kent Grayson and Tim Ambler, "The Dark Side of Long-Term Relationships in Marketing Services," *Journal of Marketing Research*, 36 (February 1999): 132–141.

Vidéotron

As is often the case with monopolies, Quebec cable provider Vidéotron was not very sensitive to customer needs and did not do much with regard to customer service. In fact, the company admits it did not hesitate to translate inefficiencies in its business into rate increases for its customers. If anyone called its customer service line, he or she may have simply been ignored. And, if the call was answered, there was little certainty that the problem would be effectively solved. All this has changed with the arrival of new and aggressive competition from the satellite providers. Vidéotron invested heavily in improving its service model. For example, it stopped investing in repair trucks that often sat unused in parking lots and re-invested these funds into its customer service organization. Now 98 percent of all phone calls are answered—80 percent of them within 20 seconds or less. While the company still suffers from its past mistakes, its investments are beginning to pay off. In fact, in early December of 2003, a Washington-based customer respect group performed a survey in Canada which found that Vidéotron and Rogers were the only Canadian telecommunications companies to score a perfect 10 in getting back to customers.[34]

Marketing Memo

Assessing E-Service Quality

Zeithaml, Parasuraman, and Malhotra define online service quality as the extent to which a Web site facilitates efficient and effective shopping, purchasing, and delivery. They identified 11 dimensions of perceived e-service quality: access, ease of navigation, efficiency, flexibility, reliability, personalization, security/privacy, responsiveness, assurance/trust, site aesthetics, and price knowledge. Some of these service-quality dimensions were the same online as offline, but some specific underlying attributes were different. Different dimensions emerged with e-service quality too. They also found that empathy didn't seem to be as important online, unless there were service problems. Core dimensions of regular service quality were efficiency, fulfillment, reliability, and privacy; core dimensions of service recovery were responsiveness, compensation, and real-time access to help.

Wolfinbarger and Gilly developed a reduced scale of online service quality with four key dimensions: reliability/fulfillment, Web site design, security/privacy, and customer service. The researchers interpret their study findings to suggest that the most basic building blocks of a "compelling online experience" are reliability and outstanding Web site functionality in terms of time savings, easy transactions, good selection, in-depth information, and the "right level" of personalization. Their 14-item scale is displayed here:

Reliability/Fulfillment

The product that came was represented accurately by the Web site.
You get what you ordered from this Web site.
The product is delivered by the time promised by the company.

Web Site Design

This Web site provides in-depth information.
The site doesn't waste my time.
It is quick and easy to complete a transaction at this Web site.
The level of personalization at this site is about right, not too much or too little.
This Web site has good selection.

Security/Privacy

I feel that my privacy is protected at this site.
I feel safe in my transactions with this Web site.
This Web site has adequate security transactions.

Customer Service

The company is willing and ready to respond to customer needs.
When you have a problem, the Web site shows a sincere interest in solving it.
Inquiries are answered promptly.

Sources: Valarie A. Zeithaml, A. Parsu Parasuraman, and Arvind Malhorta, "A Conceptual Framework for Understanding e-Service Quality: Implications for Future Research and Managerial Practice," Marketing Science Institute Working Paper, Report No. 00-115, 2000; Mary Wolfingarger and Mary C. Gilly, ".comQ: Dimensionalizing, Measuring, and Predicting Quality of the E-tail Experience," Marketing Science Institute Working Paper, Report No. 02-100, 2002.

STRATEGIC CONCEPT Top service companies are "customer obsessed." They have a clear sense of their target customers and their needs. They have developed a distinctive strategy for satisfying these needs. While most brokerage firms chase after an older, wealthy customer base, online broker E*Trade targets 24- to 37-year-old Gen Xers who are technologically savvy and self-sufficient but largely ignored by other firms. As CEO Christos Cotsakos observes, "There's this whole generation that's very computer literate, that's building wealth and looking for solutions that aren't like their grandfathers'. If we can identify with this new class of individuals and provide them with the best value, we think we can own that space."[35]

TOP-MANAGEMENT COMMITMENT Companies such as Marriott, Disney, Canadian Tire, and credit unions in Canada have a thorough commitment to service quality. Their managements look not only at financial performance on a monthly basis, but also at service performance. Ray Kroc of McDonald's insisted on continually measuring each McDonald's outlet on its conformance to QSCV: quality, service, cleanliness, and value. Some companies insert a reminder along with employees'

Marketing Memo

Recommendations for Improving Service Quality

Parasuraman, Berry, and Zeithaml, who are academic research pioneers on services, offer ten lessons that they maintain are essential for improving service quality across service industries:

1. *Listening.* Understand what customers really want through continuous learning about the expectations and perceptions of customers and noncustomers (e.g., by means of a service-quality information system).

2. *Reliability.* Reliability is the single most important dimension of service quality and must be a service priority.

3. *Basic service.* Service companies must deliver the basics and do what they are supposed to do—keep promises, use common sense, listen to customers, keep customers informed, and be determined to deliver value to customers.

4. *Service design.* Develop a holistic view of the service while managing its many details.

5. *Recovery.* To satisfy customers who encounter a service problem, service companies should encourage customers to complain (and make it easy for them to do so), respond quickly and personally, and develop a problem resolution system.

6. *Surprising customers.* Although reliability is the most important dimension in meeting customers' service expectations, process dimensions (e.g., assurance, responsiveness, and empathy) are most important in exceeding customer expectations—for example, by surprising customers with uncommon swiftness, grace, courtesy, competence, commitment, and understanding.

7. *Fair play.* Service companies must make special efforts to be fair and to demonstrate fairness to customers and employees.

8. *Teamwork.* Teamwork is what enables large organizations to deliver service with care and attentiveness by improving employee motivation and capabilities.

9. *Employee research.* Conduct research with employees to reveal why service problems occur and what companies must do to solve problems.

10. *Servant leadership.* Quality service comes from inspired leadership throughout the organization; from excellent service-system design; from the effective use of information and technology; and from a slow-to-change, invisible, all-powerful, internal force called corporate culture.

Sources: Leonard L. Berry, A. Parasuraman, and Valarie A. Zeithaml, "Ten Lessons for Improving Service Quality," *MSI Reports Working Paper Series, No. 03-001,* 2003 (Cambridge, MA: Marketing Science Institute), pp. 61–82.

---

paycheques: "Brought to you by the customer." Sam Walton of Wal-Mart required the following employee pledge: "I solemnly swear and declare that every customer that comes within 10 feet of me, I will smile, look them in the eye, and greet them, so help me Sam."

HIGH STANDARDS The best service providers set high service-quality standards. In 1961 the Royal Bank was the first financial institution in Canada to install a computer. Since that time it has leveraged technology to help its people provide superior service anywhere, at any time. The standards must be set *appropriately* high. A 98 percent accuracy standard may sound good, but it would result in FedEx losing 64 000 packages a day; six misspelled words on each page of a book; and unsafe drinking water eight days a year. One can distinguish between companies offering "merely good" service and those offering "breakthrough" service, aimed at being 100 percent defect-free.[36]

A service company can differentiate itself by designing a better and faster delivery system. There are three levels of differentiation.[37] The first is *reliability:* Some suppliers are more reliable in their on-time delivery, order completeness, and order-cycle time. The second is *resilience:* Some suppliers are better at handling emergencies, product recalls, and answering inquiries. The third is *innovativeness:* Some suppliers create better information systems, introduce bar coding and mixed pallets, and in other ways help the customer.

Many distribution experts say that a company's money would be better spent on improving delivery performance than on advertising. They say that superior service performance is a more effective differentiator than image expenditures. Furthermore, it is harder for a competitor to duplicate a superior distribution system than to copy an advertising campaign.

Chapters.ca

There are few firms in Canada that have elicited such mixed reactions as Chapters.ca. Launched with much ballyhoo and heavy advertising, Chapters got many Canadians clicking instead of going to their local bookstore. Claims were made about its ruthless tactics, which drove many small booksellers out of business. It was the darling of investors, however, even though its original e-business model showed that every dollar of sales cost $1.12 to produce. It wasn't until after its acquisition by Indigo in 2001 that it started to turn itself around. But in 2002 Chapters.Indigo.ca had a significant new challenge to face. Amazon.ca came to town and many book buyers hoped they would now be able to access the parent firm's extensive inventory without the hassle of getting books through customs, paying high shipping costs, or converting prices set in U.S. dollars. Amazon.ca was the company's fifth international Web site (it had already set up shop in the United Kingdom, Japan, France, and Germany). However, as one journalist found out, the new site had some problems getting out of the starting gate. He ordered the same books from the new Canadian site and from the U.S.-based parent, only to find that books still came faster and more reliably from the United States. Such problems angered consumers and gave Chapters.Indigo.ca breathing space.[38]

SELF-SERVICE TECHNOLOGIES (SSTS) As is the case with products, consumers value convenience in services.[39] Many person-to-person service interactions are being replaced by self-service technologies.[40] To the traditional vending machines, we can add Automated Teller Machines (ATMs), self-pumping at gas stations, self-check-out at hotels, self-ticket purchasing on the Internet, and self-customization of products on the Internet. Loblaws, for example, has recently added new scanners to its supermarkets so that Canadian shoppers can scan their own groceries, pack, and pay for them without waiting for a cashier.

Not all SSTs improve service quality, but they have the potential of making service transactions more accurate, convenient, and faster. Every company needs to think about improving its service using SSTs. Companies would be smart to enable customers to call the company when they need more information than the SST provides. Online hotel reservation Web sites often include a "Call Me" button. If the customer clicks on it, a service rep will immediately phone the person to answer a question. Even banks miss an opportunity to use their ATMs. A customer might draw money from the ATM and see the message: "Call 1-800-123-4567 to earn more interest"; but the customer goes home and forgets to call. The ATM's message could have been: "You have $6000 over the required balance."

Imagine an auto insurance company wanting to improve its claim service and assistance. Normally, a driver involved in an accident has to wait for a claims adjuster to show up, assess the damage, and offer a settlement. The insurance company's Web site could include step-by-step guidelines telling the insured person what to do. It would list the kinds of documents needed by the police and by the hospital; suggest the names of reliable medical and legal professionals; and list reputable car rental firms and repair shops in the customer's area. Claim forms would be filled out on the Web site. The claims adjuster, when he or she visits the driver, can use a handheld mobile computing device and digital camera to photograph the damage, send a streaming video back to headquarters, get approval, and print out a cheque for car repair on the spot.

When initiating self-service technologies, some companies have found that the biggest obstacle is not the technology itself, but convincing customers to use it. "Marketing Memo: Getting Self-Service Kiosks off the Ground" offers some tips.

MONITORING SYSTEMS Top firms audit service performance, both their own and competitors, on a regular basis. They collect *voice of the customer (VOC) measurements* to probe customer satisfiers and dissatisfiers. They use comparison shopping, ghost shopping, customer surveys, suggestion and complaint forms, service-audit teams, and letters to the president. The First Chicago Bank employs a weekly Performance Measurement Program charting its performance on a large number of customer-sensitive issues. Figure 13.5 shows a typical chart that tracks speed in answering customer service phone inquiries. The bank will take action whenever performance falls below the minimum acceptable level. It also raises its performance goal over time.

Mystery shopping—the use of undercover shoppers who are paid to report back to the company—is now big business: US$500 000 million worldwide. Fast food chains, big-box stores, gas stations, and even large government agencies are using mystery shoppers to pinpoint and fix customer service problems.

Marketing Memo

Getting Self-Service Kiosks off the Ground

With air travellers already skittish about security-imposed delays, the idea that a self-service kiosk will malfunction with no one around to help can make them avoid self-service altogether, even if they have to wait longer. Delta Air Lines has been successful in getting customers to use its self-service kiosks by employing a number of tactics.

1. *Advertise the advantages.* Delta initiated a major ad campaign to make customers aware of self-service's advantages. Ads saying "Experience Waitlessness" and "Delta Air Lines" with "Lines" crossed out appeared all over New York City. Once at the airport, customers in check-in lines are approached by customer reps who direct them to the kiosks.

2. *Be there to help.* First-time users, in particular, need handholding, so a live employee should be available to show them the ropes and to help if a machine malfunctions. If people have a good experience the first time, they will become kiosk converts.

3. *Maintain the machines.* Machines break down, particularly in a rugged, heavy-use environment like an airport. Delta tries to prevent self-service kiosk breakdowns rather than having to put up an "out of order" sign.

Source: John McCormick, "Roadblock: The Customer; Airlines, Railroads, Grocery Stores and Hotels Racing to Deploy Self-Service Check-In Devices Have Discovered Two Things," *Baseline*, April 1, 2003.

Services can be judged on *customer importance* and *company performance*. *Importance-performance analysis* is used to rate the various elements of the service bundle and identify what actions are required. Table 13.3 shows how customers rated 14 service elements (attributes) of an automobile dealer's service department on importance and performance. For example, "Job done right the first time" (attribute 1) received a mean importance rating of 3.83 and a mean performance rating of 2.63, indicating that customers felt it was highly important but not performed well.

The ratings of the 14 elements are displayed in Figure 13.6 and divided into four sections. Quadrant A shows important service elements that are not being performed at the desired levels; they include elements 1, 2, and 9. The dealer should concentrate on improving the service department's performance on these elements. Quadrant B shows important service elements that are being performed well; the company needs to maintain the high performance. Quadrant C shows minor service elements that are being delivered in a mediocre way but do not need any attention. Quadrant D shows that a minor service element, "Send out maintenance notices," is being performed in an excellent manner. Perhaps the company should spend less on sending out maintenance notices and use the savings to improve performance on important elements. The analysis can be enhanced by checking on the competitors' performance levels on each element.[41]

SATISFYING CUSTOMER COMPLAINTS Studies of customer dissatisfaction show that customers are dissatisfied with their purchases about 25 percent of the time but that only about 5 percent complain. The other 95 percent either feel complaining is not worth the effort, or they do not know how or to whom to complain.

Of the 5 percent who complain, only about 50 percent report a satisfactory problem resolution. Yet the need to resolve a customer problem in a satisfactory manner is critical. On average, a satisfied customer tells three people about a good product experience. The average dissatisfied customer gripes to 11 people. If each of them tells still other people, the number of people exposed to bad word of mouth may grow exponentially.

Customers whose complaints are satisfactorily resolved often become more company-loyal than customers who were never dissatisfied.[42] About 34 percent of customers who register major complaints will buy again from the company if their complaint is resolved, and this number rises to 52

FIGURE 13.5

Tracking Customer Service Performance

TABLE 13.3	CUSTOMER IMPORTANCE AND PERFORMANCE RATINGS FOR AN AUTO DEALERSHIP		
Attribute Number	Attribute Description	Mean Importance Rating[a]	Mean Performance Rating[b]
1	Job done right the first time	3.83	2.63
2	Fast action on complaints	3.63	2.73
3	Prompt warranty work	3.60	3.15
4	Able to do any job needed	3.56	3.00
5	Service available when needed	3.41	3.05
6	Courteous and friendly service	3.41	3.29
7	Car ready when promised	3.38	3.03
8	Perform only necessary work	3.37	3.11
9	Low prices on service	3.29	2.00
10	Clean up after service work	3.27	3.02
11	Convenient to home	2.52	2.25
12	Convenient to work	2.43	2.49
13	Courtesy buses and cars	2.37	2.35
14	Send out maintenance notices	2.05	3.33

[a]Ratings obtained from a four-point scale of "extremely important" (4), "important" (3), "slightly important" (2), and "not important" (1).

[b]Ratings obtained from a four-point scale of "excellent" (4), "good" (3), "fair" (2), and "poor" (1). A "no basis for judgment" category was also provided.

percent for minor complaints. If the complaint is resolved quickly, between 52 percent (major complaints) and 95 percent (minor complaints) will buy again from the company.[43]

Every complaint is a gift if handled well. Companies that encourage disappointed customers to complain—and also empower employees to remedy the situation on the spot—have been shown to achieve higher revenues and greater profits than companies that do not have a systematic approach for addressing service failures.[44] Pizza Hut prints its toll-free number on all pizza boxes. When a customer complains, Pizza Hut sends voice mail to the store manager, who must call the customer within 48 hours and resolve the complaint. Hyatt Hotels gets high marks on many of these criteria.

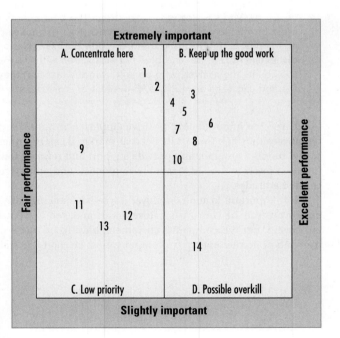

FIGURE 13.6

Importance-Performance Analysis

Hyatt Hotels

Hyatt Hotels excels at answering complaints in an extraordinarily short time. One business customer, for example, checked into the Denver Hyatt but did not like his room. He turned on the television and was greeted by a screen with the Hyatt customer survey. Using the TV remote, he punched in his evaluations. To his surprise and delight, within five minutes of receiving the electronic communication, the hotel manager called him to say that because the hotel was entirely booked and the room could not be changed, the guest could expect a hospitality gift for his inconvenience.[45]

Research has shown that customers evaluate complaint incidents in terms of the outcomes they receive, the procedures used to arrive at those outcomes, and the nature of the interpersonal treatment during the process.[46]

Getting front-line employees to adopt *extra-role behaviours*—to advocate the interests and image of the firm to consumers, to take initiative, and to practise conscientious behaviour in dealing with customers—can be a critical asset in handling complaints.[47] Companies also are increasing the quality of their *call centres* and their *customer service representatives* (CSRs). Handling phone calls more efficiently can improve service, reduce complaints, and extend customer longevity.

SATISFYING EMPLOYEES AS WELL AS CUSTOMERS   Excellent service companies know that positive employee attitudes will promote stronger customer loyalty. Sears found a high correlation between customer satisfaction, employee satisfaction, and store profitability. In companies such as Hallmark, John Deere, and Toronto-based Four Seasons Hotels, employees exhibit real pride in their companies. Consider the crucial role of employees with Re/Max:[48]

Re/Max

Re/Max has actually made its real estate brokers and franchisees the prime focus of its marketing. As one industry observer noted, "Agents perceive that Re/Max is the place where top agents work. That message is very clear and it's a powerful one to people in the business." Re/Max's philosophy is to attract the best agents who in turn attract the best and most profitable customers—an approach that has led Re/Max agents to the highest average annual commissions in the real estate business. National consumer advertising and the distinctive red, white, and blue hot air balloon with the Re/Max logo are funded in part by the agents themselves, who benefit from the fact that they are compensated largely by flat fee and can keep as much as 95 percent of a given commission.

Given the importance of positive employee attitudes, service companies must attract the best employees they can find. They need to market a career rather than just a job. They must design a sound training program and provide support and rewards for good performance. They can use the intranet, internal newsletters, daily reminders, and employee roundtables to reinforce customer-centred attitudes.

It is important to audit employee job satisfaction regularly. Karl Albrecht observed that unhappy employees can be "terrorists." Rosenbluth and Peters went so far as to say that the company's employees, not the company's customers, have to be made number one if the company hopes to truly satisfy its customers.[49] A company must be careful in training its employees to be friendly:

Outstanding Agents.
Outstanding Results.

RE/MAX agents average more
experience and more sales than
other real estate agents.

That's good news for you and
your family – whether you're
hoping to buy or looking to sell.

www.remax.com

RE/MAX Community
555-1212

Each RE/MAX® real estate office is
independently owned and operated.

Agents are the focus of
Re/Max marketing, as this
print ad shows. Advertising
like this is paid for in part by
the agents themselves.

Safeway Stores

In the 1990s, supermarket chain Safeway instituted "Superior Service," an unusually aggressive program to build employee friendliness toward customers. Among the rules: Make eye contact with all customers, smile, greet each other, offer samples of products, make suggestions about other possible items to purchase. To ensure compliance, "mystery shoppers" secretly graded workers. Those who received poor grades were sent to a training program. Although surveys showed that customers were pleased with the program, many employees admitted to being stressed out and several quit in protest over the plan. "It's so artificial, it's unreal," said one second-generation Safeway employee who quit her job as cashier after 20 years with the chain, partly out of frustration with the Superior Service program. Several female employees even filed sexual harassment suits against Safeway, charging that the forced smiles were misinterpreted and led to unwelcome advances from male customers.[50]

Managing Service Brands

Some of the world's strongest brands are services—consider financial service leaders such as the Royal Bank of Canada, Visa, TD Canada Trust, HSBC, and Goldman Sachs. As with any brand, service brands must be skillful at differentiating themselves and developing appropriate brand strategies.

Differentiating Services

Service marketers frequently complain about the difficulty of differentiating their services. The deregulation of several major service industries—communications, transportation, energy, banking—has resulted in intense price competition. To the extent that customers view a service as fairly homogeneous, they care less about the provider than the price. Consider how Research in Motion (RIM) has differentiated its BlackBerry handheld device and service:

BlackBerry

Waterloo, Ontario–based Research in Motion is responsible for the market-leading wireless handheld product and service widely known as the BlackBerry. BlackBerry is heralded as the best wireless handheld service and brand worldwide as professionals around the globe continue to adopt the product/service at an astonishing rate. The service has been successful because it is the fastest and most secure delivery system (unlike its competitors, RIM does not rely on the public Internet). Furthermore, the company is unique in its provision of a complete, integrated system—the mobile device itself, the operating software, and the software required to integrate the device with desktop PCs and corporate servers. In September 2005, RIM announced that it surged past the three-million subscriber milestone, adding one million subscribers in the previous six months. This represents more than the global market for handheld e-mail devices.[51]

Service offerings, however, can be differentiated in many ways. The offering can include innovative features. What the customer expects is called the *primary service package*. Vanguard, a major U.S. mutual fund company, has a unique client ownership structure that lowers costs and permits better fund returns. Strongly differentiated from many competitors, the brand grew through word-of-mouth, PR, and viral marketing.[52]

The provider can add *secondary service features* to the package. In the airline industry, various carriers have introduced such secondary service features as movies, merchandise for sale, air-to-ground telephone service, and frequent-flier award programs. Marriott is setting up hotel rooms for high-tech travellers who need accommodations that will support computers, fax machines, and e-mail. Many companies are using the Web to offer secondary service features that were never possible before:

Pizza Pizza

Toronto-based Pizza Pizza developed a sophisticated online pizza ordering system that is complete with all the benefits of ordering pizza in the traditional manner—except you don't need the phone. First you register for a free account with a username and password and create your profile. In your profile you include your address and telephone number information so that orders can be delivered to your door without having to provide your address each time you want to order. You can also include directions on how to get to the house (e.g., through the backyard) and confirm the closest Pizza Pizza location to your home to ensure speedy delivery or convenient pick-up. Then you are ready to order. The site lists all available pizza products, specials and, of course, toppings. You can even do half-and-half pizzas without any extra trouble. The site keeps track of what you order on a main screen so that you can go back and change any order before you are ready to submit.[53]

Conversely, other service providers are adding a human element to combat competition from online businesses. This is happening in many large drugstores. As in-store pharmacies see competition from low-cost online mail-order drugstores, they are playing up the presence of on-site healthcare professionals. For instance, Brooks Pharmacy is establishing "RX Care Centers" in many of its remodelled stores. There are private consulting rooms where pharmacists can speak at length with patients about complicated prescription benefit plans, potentially dangerous drug interactions, and embarrassing subjects like urinary incontinence. CVS is giving its pharmacists more time to speak to customers by investing in machines that count pills and fill pill bottles, a time-consuming and tedious task for most pharmacists.[54]

Sometimes the company achieves differentiation through the sheer range of its service offerings and the success of its cross-selling efforts. The major challenge is that most service offerings and innovations are easily copied. Still, the company that regularly introduces innovations will gain a succession of temporary advantages over competitors.

Pizza Pizza's online ordering system allows customers to order a pizza in virtually the same manner as they would over the phone.

Schneider National

Schneider National is the world's largest long-haul truckload freight carrier, with more than 40 000 bright orange trailers on the roads. Although the core benefit is to move freight from one location to another, Don Schneider is in the *customer solutions* business. His company is expert at providing a cost-minimizing trailer for each load. He offers service guarantees backed by monetary incentives for meeting tight schedules. He runs driver-training programs to improve driver performance. Dispatchers are assigned to large customers. Schneider was the first to introduce a computerized tracking system in each truck. Even painting the trucks orange was part of the branding strategy. If further innovations come into this industry, they will probably come from Schneider.

Developing Brand Strategies for Services

Developing brand strategies for a service brand requires special attention to choosing brand elements, establishing image dimensions, and devising the branding strategy. Once service firms lagged behind manufacturing firms in their use of marketing because they were small or professional businesses that did not use marketing, or they faced large demand or little competition, but this situation has certainly changed. Consider the case of one legal firm:

Fraser Milner Casgrain LLP

Fraser Milner Casgrain (FMC) debuted its first-ever advertising campaign in 2001. It is one of Canada's leading legal firms, with offices in Vancouver, Calgary, Edmonton, Toronto, Ottawa, and Montreal. It faced the same issue many legal firms are wrestling with today—how to distinguish itself in an increasingly competitive environment. Legal service providers were slow to utilize marketing and advertising. For much of their history, provincial law societies forbade such practices, but those rules have loosened over the years.

Basing its campaign on sound research, FMC decided to use its own clients as its spokespeople. Print ads were run in national newspapers featuring testimonials from large clients such as Petro-Canada and small technology firms such as Jive Media Technologies. The testimonials were a highly credible means of demonstrating how FMC's lawyers helped solve each company's business issues. As FMC's director of marketing and communications noted, "If you're not telling your target audience how it will benefit from using you, the message is lost."[55]

The RBC Financial Group has one of the best-recognized brand symbols in Canada.

CHOOSING BRAND ELEMENTS The intangibility of services has implications for the choice of brand elements. Because service decisions and arrangements are often made away from the actual service location itself (e.g., at home or at work), brand recall becomes critically important. In such cases, an easy-to-remember brand name is critical.

Other brand elements—logos, symbols, characters, and slogans—can also "pick up the slack" and complement the brand name to build brand awareness and brand image. These other brand elements often attempt to make the service and some of its key benefits more tangible, concrete, and real (e.g., the "lion" of RBC).

Because a physical product does not exist, the physical facilities of the service provider—its primary and secondary signage, environmental design and reception area, apparel, collateral material, and so on—are especially important. All aspects of the service delivery process can be branded, which is why UPS has developed such strong equity with the brown colour of its trucks.

ESTABLISHING IMAGE DIMENSIONS Organizational associations—such as perceptions about the people who make up the organization and who provide the service—are likely to be particularly important brand associations that may affect evaluations of service quality directly or indirectly. One particularly important association is company credibility and perceived expertise, trustworthiness, and likability.

Service firms must therefore design marketing communication and information programs so that consumers learn more about the brand than the information they get from service encounters alone. These programs may involve marketing communications, which may be particularly effective at helping the firm to develop the proper brand personality. Consider the Calgary restaurant Sugo:

Sugo

This Calgary restaurant wanted to break through the advertising clutter and create a stir, grab some press coverage, and differentiate itself from other Italian eateries. Just saying that it is a great place to eat and one where the chef comes out to chat with the clientele wasn't going to accomplish this task. Sugo wanted to convey that it is a cutting-edge, New York–style restaurant whose food and ambience are so good as to be addictive. With the help of creative agency Push, it developed just such a campaign. Its print ads are simple, making its point by building on symbols associated with other addictive substances. One ad shows a syringe; another shows lines of white substance on a plate. Head chef Angelo Contrada remarked, "I don't care if it is controversial. People who have eaten here know what we're about."[56]

Sugo's controversial advertising created buzz that differentiated the restaurant from its competitors.

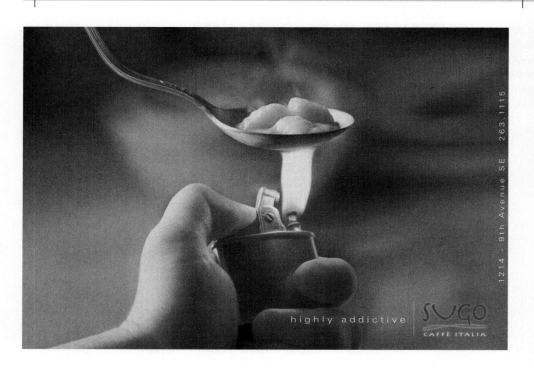

DEVISING BRANDING STRATEGY Finally, services also must consider developing a brand hierarchy and brand portfolio that permits positioning and targeting of different market segments. Classes of service can be branded vertically on the basis of price and quality. Vertical extensions often require sub-branding strategies where the corporate name is combined with an individual brand name or modifier. In the hotel and airlines industry, brand lines and portfolios have been created by brand extension and introductions. For example, Air Canada brands its business class service as Executive First Class, its frequent flier program as Aeroplan, and its in-flight magazine as *enRoute*. Hilton Hotels has a portfolio of brands that includes Hilton Garden Inns to target budget-conscious business travellers and compete with the popular Courtyard by Marriott chain, as well as DoubleTree, Embassy Suites, Homewood Suites, and Hampton Inn. Cirque du Soleil has adopted a very strict branding strategy.[57]

Cirque du Soleil

Cirque du Soleil has a very unique product and thus chooses a corresponding branding strategy to reflect that. Each production is loosely tied together with a theme such as "a tribute to the nomadic soul" (*Varekai*) or "a phantasmagoria of urban life" (*Saltimbanco*). Given that most theatrical productions fail, the fact that all of Cirque du Soleil's productions have succeeded and that the firm nets $100 million a year is impressive. Part of its success results from a company culture that encourages creativity and innovation and carefully safeguards the brand. Each production is created in-house (roughly one a year) and is totally unique—there are no duplicate touring companies.

Managing Product Support Services

Thus far we have focused on service industries. No less important are product-based industries that must provide a service bundle. Manufacturers of equipment—small appliances, office machines, tractors, mainframes, airplanes—all have to provide *product support services*. Product support service is becoming a major battleground for competitive advantage. Chapter 12 described how products could be augmented with key service differentiators—ordering ease, delivery, installation, customer training, customer consulting, and maintenance and repair. Some equipment companies, such as Caterpillar Tractor and John Deere, make over 50 percent of their profits from these services. In the global marketplace, companies that make a good product but provide poor local service support are seriously disadvantaged. Firms that provide high-quality service outperform their less service-oriented competitors.

Identifying and Satisfying Customer Needs

The company must define customer needs carefully in designing a service support program. Customers have three specific worries:[58]

- They worry about reliability and *failure frequency*. A farmer may tolerate a combine that will break down once a year, but not two or three times a year.
- They worry about *downtime*. The longer the downtime, the higher the cost. The customer counts on the seller's *service dependability*—the seller's ability to fix the machine quickly, or at least provide a loaner.[59]
- They worry about *out-of-pocket costs*. How much does the customer have to spend on regular maintenance and repair costs?

A buyer takes all these factors into consideration in choosing a vendor. The buyer tries to estimate the **life-cycle cost**, which is the product's purchase cost plus the discounted cost of maintenance and repair less the discounted salvage value. Buyers ask for hard data in choosing among vendors.

The importance of reliability, service dependability, and maintenance vary. A one-computer office will need higher product reliability and faster repair service than an office where other computers are available if one breaks down. An airline needs 100 percent reliability in the air. Where reliability is important, manufacturers or service providers can offer guarantees to promote sales.

To provide the best support, a manufacturer must identify the services customers value most and their relative importance. In the case of expensive equipment, manufacturers offer *facilitating services* such as installation, staff training, maintenance and repair services, and financing. They may also add *value-augmenting services*. Herman Miller, a major office furniture company, offers the Herman Miller promise to buyers: (1) five-year product warranties; (2) quality audits after project installation; (3) guaranteed move-in dates; (4) trade-in allowances on systems products.

A manufacturer can offer and charge for product support services in different ways. One specialty organic-chemical company provides a standard offering plus a basic level of services. If the customer wants additional services, it can pay extra or increase its annual purchases to a higher level, in which case additional services would be included. As another alternative, many companies offer *service contracts* (also called *extended warranties*), in which sellers agree to provide free maintenance and repair services for a specified period of time at a specified contract price. Service contracts often have variable lengths and different deductibles so that customers can choose the service level they want beyond the basic service package.

Companies need to plan product design and service-mix decisions in tandem. Design and quality-assurance managers should be part of the new-product development team. Good product design will reduce the amount of subsequent servicing. The Canon home copier uses a disposable toner cartridge that greatly reduces the need for service calls. Kodak and 3M designed equipment allowing the user to "plug in" to a central diagnostic facility that performs tests, locates the trouble, and fixes the equipment over the telephone lines. Companies are adding modularity and disposability to facilitate self-servicing.

Post-Sale Service Strategy

The quality of customer service departments varies greatly. At one extreme are departments that simply transfer customer calls to the appropriate person or department for action, with little follow-up. At the other extreme are departments eager to receive customer requests, suggestions, and even complaints and handle them expeditiously.

In providing service, most companies progress through a series of stages. Manufacturers usually start out by running their own parts-and-service department. They want to stay close to the equipment and know its problems. They also find it expensive and time-consuming to train others, and discover that they can make good money running the parts-and-service business. As long as they are the only supplier of the needed parts, they can charge a premium price. In fact, many equipment manufacturers price their equipment low and compensate by charging high prices for parts and service. (This explains why competitors manufacture the same or similar parts and sell them to customers or intermediaries for less.)

Over time, manufacturers switch more maintenance and repair service to authorized distributors and dealers. These intermediaries are closer to customers, operate in more locations, and can offer quicker service. Manufacturers still make a profit on the parts but leave the servicing profit to intermediaries. Still later, independent service firms emerge. Over 40 percent of auto-service work is now done outside franchised automobile dealerships by independent garages and chains such as Midas Muffler, Sears, and Canadian Tire. Independent service organizations handle mainframes, telecommunications equipment, and a variety of other equipment lines. They typically offer a lower price or faster service than the manufacturer or authorized intermediaries.

Customer service choices are expanding rapidly, however, and this is holding down prices and profits on service. Equipment manufacturers increasingly have to figure out how to make money on their equipment, independent of service contracts. Some new car warranties now cover 160 000 kilometres before servicing. The increase in disposable or never-fail equipment makes customers less inclined to pay from 2 percent to 10 percent of the purchase price every year for a service. Some large customers handle their own maintenance and repair. A company with several hundred personal computers, printers, and related equipment might find it cheaper to have its own service personnel on-site. These companies typically press the manufacturer for a lower price, because they are providing their own services.

SUMMARY

1. A service is any act or performance that one party can offer to another that is essentially intangible and does not result in the ownership of anything. It may or may not be tied to a physical product.

2. Services are intangible, inseparable, variable, and perishable. Each characteristic poses challenges and requires certain strategies. Marketers must find ways to give tangibility to intangibles; to increase the productivity of service providers; to increase and standardize the quality of the service provided; and to match the supply of services with market demand.

3. Service industries lagged behind manufacturing firms in adopting and using marketing concepts and tools, but this situation has now changed. Service marketing must be done holistically: it calls not only for external marketing but also for internal marketing to motivate employees and interactive marketing to emphasize the importance of both "high-tech" and "high-touch."

4. Customers' expectations play a critical role in their service experiences and evaluations. Companies must manage service quality by understanding the effects of each service encounter.

5. Top service companies excel at the following practices: a strategic concept, a history of top-management commitment to quality, high standards, self-service technologies, systems for monitoring service performance and customer complaints, and an emphasis on employee satisfaction.

6. To brand a service organization effectively, the company must differentiate its brand through primary and secondary service features and develop appropriate brand strategies. Effective branding programs for services often employ multiple brand elements. They also develop brand hierarchies and portfolios and establish image dimensions to reinforce or complement service offerings.

7. Even product-based companies must provide post-purchase service. To provide the best support, a manufacturer must identify the services customers value most and their relative importance. The service mix includes both pre-sale services (facilitating and value-augmenting services) and post-sale services (customer service departments, repair and maintenance services).

APPLICATIONS

Marketing Debate: Is Service Marketing Different from Product Marketing?

Some services marketers vehemently maintain that services marketing is fundamentally different from product marketing and that different skills are involved. Some traditional product marketers disagree, saying "good marketing is good marketing."

Take a position: Product and services marketing are fundamentally different versus Product and services marketing are highly related.

Marketing Discussion

Colleges, universities, and other educational institutions can be classified as service organizations. How can you apply the marketing principles developed in this chapter to your school? Do you have any advice as to how it could become a better service marketer?

Marketing Spotlight: Southwest Airlines

Southwest Airlines entered the U.S. airline industry in 1971 with little money but lots of personality. Marketing itself as the LUV airline, the company featured a bright red heart as its first logo. In the 1970s, flight attendants in red-orange hot pants served Love Bites (peanuts) and Love Potions (drinks).

With little money for advertising in the early days, Southwest relied on its outrageous antics to generate word-of-mouth advertising.

Later ads showcased Southwest's low fares, frequent flights, on-time arrivals, and top safety record. Throughout all the advertising, the spirit of fun pervades. For example, one TV spot showed a small bag of peanuts with the words, "This is what our meals look like at Southwest Airlines . . . It's also what our fares look like." Southwest used ads with humour to poke fun at itself and to convey its personality.

Southwest's fun spirit attracts customers and employees alike. Although Southwest doesn't take itself seriously, it does take its work seriously. Southwest's strategy is to be the low-cost carrier. Indeed, the strategy takes on epic proportions. An internal slogan, "It's not just a job, it's a crusade" embodies the company mission to open up the skies, to give ordinary people a chance to fly by keeping costs so low that it competes with ground transportation like cars and buses. Employees see themselves as protecting "small businesses and senior citizens who count on us for low fares."

Southwest can offer low fares because it streamlines operations. For example, Southwest only flies one type of aircraft, Boeing 737s, which have all been fitted with identical flight instruments. This saves time and money by simplifying training: pilots, flight attendants, and mechanics only need to know procedures for a single model of Boeing 737. Management can substitute aircraft, reschedule flight crews, or transfer mechanics quickly. The tactic also saves money through lower spare parts inventories and better deals when acquiring new planes.

Southwest also bucks the traditional hub-and-spoke system and offers only point-to-point service. Southwest intentionally chooses to fly to smaller airports that have lower gate fees and less congestion, which speeds aircraft turnaround. Southwest's 15- to 20-minute turnaround time (from flight landing to departure) is half the industry average, giving Southwest better asset utilization (flying more flights and more passengers per plane per day). Southwest knows that if the plane and crew aren't in the air, the company isn't making money.

Southwest grows by entering new markets that are overpriced and underserved by current airlines. The company feels it can bring fares down by one-third to one-half whenever it enters a new market. Southwest grows the market in every city it serves by making flying affordable to people who previously could not afford to fly.

Even though Southwest is a low-cost airline, it has pioneered many additional services and programs, such as same-day freight service, senior discounts, Fun Fares, and Fun Packs. Despite Southwest's reputation for low fares and no-frills service, the company wins the hearts of customers. Southwest has been ranked the number-one U.S. airline in terms of customer service for 12 years in a row, yet the average price of a Southwest flight is US$87. Southwest has been ranked by *Fortune* magazine as the U.S.'s most admired airline since 1997, the third most-admired corporation in 2004, and as one of the top-five best places to work in the United States. Southwest's financial results also shine: The company has been profitable for 31 straight years. Following the terrorist attacks in September 2001, Southwest was the only U.S. airline to report profits every quarter since the tragedy, and was one of the few airlines to have no layoffs amid a travel slump created by a slow economy and the threat of terrorism.

Although the hot pants are long gone, the LUVing spirit remains at the heart of Southwest. The company's stock symbol on the NYSE is LUV and red hearts can be found everywhere across the company. These symbols embody the Southwest spirit of employees "caring about themselves, each other and Southwest's customers," states an employee booklet. "Our fares can be matched; our airplanes and routes can be copied. But we pride ourselves on our customer service," said Sherry Phelps, director of corporate employment. That's why Southwest looks for and hires people who generate enthusiasm. In fact, having a sense of humour is a selection criteria Southwest uses for hiring. As one employee explained, "We can train you to do any job, but we can't give you the right spirit."

Southwest is so confident of its culture and its employees that in 2004 it allowed itself to be the subject of a reality TV show called *Airline*. It's not worried about competitors copying the company. "What we do is very simple, but it's not simplistic," said president and COO Colleen Barrett. "We really do everything with passion."

DISCUSSION QUESTIONS

1. What are the key success factors for Southwest Airlines? Why do you think the founders of WestJet used Southwest as a model when starting their airline?

2. Where is Southwest Airlines vulnerable? What should it watch out for?

3. What recommendations would you make to the company's senior marketing executives moving forward? What should they be sure to do with its marketing?

Sources: Andy Serwer, "Southwest Airlines: The Hottest Thing in the Sky," *Fortune*, March 8, 2004; Colleen Barrett, "Fasten Your Seat Belts," *Adweek*, January 26, 2004, p. 17; Kevin Freiberg and Jackie Freiberg, *Nuts! Southwest Airlines's Crazy Recipe for Business and Personal Success* (Austin, TX: Bard, 1996); "Southwest May Not Be No. 1, but It Sure Looks Like the Leader," *Airline Financial News*, November 24, 2003; Eva Kaplan-Leiserson, "Strategic Service," *Training and Development* (November 2003): 14–16; Micheline Maynard, "In Philadelphia, Southwest Is Trying the Front Door," *The New York Times*, January 31, 2004, p. B1; **www.southwest.com**.

IN THIS CHAPTER, WE WILL ADDRESS THE FOLLOWING QUESTIONS:

- How do consumers process and evaluate prices?

- How should a company set prices initially for products or services?

- How should a company adapt prices to meet varying circumstances and opportunities?

- When should a company initiate a price change?

- How should a company respond to a competitor's price change?

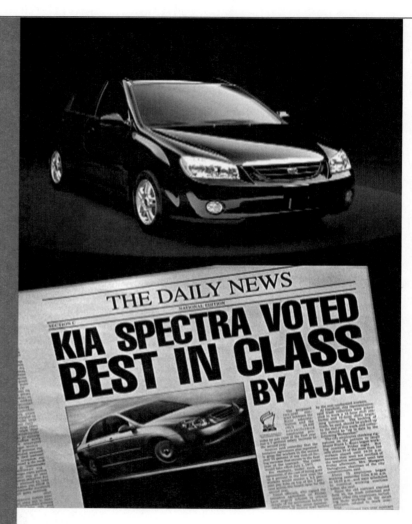

14

CHAPTER 14

Developing Pricing Strategies and Programs

PROFILE: CANADIAN MARKETING EXCELLENCE

Philip Kotler admonishes: Sell value, not price. This could be the mantra of Kia Canada, a subsidiary of Hyundai Motor Co. of South Korea. During its 1999 launch year, its goals were simple—to have 24 dealers in place, and build as high a brand awareness as possible in each market as a retail presence was established. Of course, the question of how to reach these goals and "sell value" became a pivotal one for Kia.

Over the next two years, Kia's answer was to use comparative pricing; its new "Extra Care" warranty; an innovative brand-building strategy using the slogan "It's about time everyone had a well made car"; and breakthrough, humorous advertising and promotions. Kia firmly believes that driving should be fun, as its self-description shows:

> So we've built a sturdy yet stylish reputation that just gets stronger with every new car we introduce. And we've also developed a bit of an attitude. Not arrogance, mind you. But a radical point of view that says cars should be both well made and priced well below the competitive models in their class. Oh yes, and they should be fun to drive, although fun is a tough factor to quantify. But we figure we'd measure somewhere about 9.7 on a funometer.

Kia competes unashamedly on price and doesn't pull any punches about comparing itself to key competitors. Its Web site (www.kia.ca) features a price calculator that allows viewers to immediately determine the price of the vehicle they select in addition to financing and leasing rates. The Rio, Kia's lowest-priced vehicle, with a base price of $12 995, is compared to the Toyota Echo, the Honda Accent, and the Daewoo Lanso on price, mechanical features, warranty, safety, and convenience.

Since price competition in the automotive industry is predicted to increase, Kia knew that it couldn't build awareness or its brand on price alone. Kia targets young single adults (especially female purchasers) and young families. Buying a car is a high-risk purchase for most consumers, especially young buyers with little experience. Thus, developing brand credibility and a clear value proposition for both corporate name and the individual brands was also critical to Kia's success.

Building brand awareness certainly isn't cheap. Analysts estimated that the advertising budget for Kia's launch was between $5 million and $10 million, and its expenditures on advertising have grown each year as it competes for a larger share of the Canadian market. Brand building is a multifaceted effort. Mass-media advertising is just one of the keys to reaching Kia's target markets. So Kia utilized TV, radio, and print advertising, along with event sponsorship, in its campaigns. The TV spots made no bones about comparing the Sephia's price to those of its nearest competitors, the Honda Civic and Toyota Corolla.

Kia's famous "swamp tour" ad for the Sportage SUV was one of its most successful ads. A couple is shown taking a journey through the swamplands of Louisiana with a "good old boy." Kia knew the ad was a hit when people walked up to its car show booth to yell out, "Ay-ee!" The popularity of the spot inspired Kia to build a small licensing program around it. Its line of swamp-tour merchandise and clothing has proved exceptionally popular.

Kia also uses events to leverage its brand. It took its Sephia model on a 200 000 km endurance test from coast to coast to prove its durability, and a Kia Sportage successfully completed the Paris–Dakar–Cairo 2000 Rally.

Has Kia's unconventional, price-based, attitude-laden marketing strategy paid off? Judge for yourself. Kia Canada had to establish a dealer network from scratch, and has gone from zero dealerships in 1999 to 150 dealerships stretching right across the country by 2004. In 2005, a global research firm named Kia the fastest-growing automaker in the world. The Automotive Journalists Association of Canada named one of its nine car models, the sporty Kia Spectra Sedan, the "Best New Economy Car" for 2005 (you can view Kia's ad announcing this award at www.performancekia.ca/atkia/index.asp). Its Sorento, a stylishly rugged SUV that was launched in the summer of 2002 at prices ranging from $29 000 to about $37 000, was named "Best in Class" in the compact SUV segment by Motor Trend's *Truck Trend* magazine in the May/June 2004 issue. Although Kia holds less than two percent of the Canadian passenger vehicle market, it's safe to say that Kia has added some spark to the staid automobile industry!

Sources: Kia Canada Web site, **www.kia.ca** (viewed March 11, 2005); Ralph Luciw, Vice President, Public Relations, Griffin Bacal Volny, e-mail to author, July 4, 2002; Laura Pratt, "Offbeat Approach Fuels Kia Brand Build," *Strategy: The Canadian Marketing Report*, March 26, 2001; Patti Summerfield, "Kia Plays the Value Card in Adapted Creative," *Strategy: The Canadian Marketing Report*, August 16, 1999, p. 6; Lesley Daw, "Korea's Time," *Marketing*, September 13, 1998, pp. 17–18; Patti Summerfield, "Budget Korean Cars Daewoo, Kia to Hit Canadian Streets," *Strategy: The Canadian Marketing Report*, February 15, 1999, p. 4; Patti Summerfield, "Kia Picks Griffin Bacal Volny for Canadian Launch," *Strategy: The Canadian Marketing Report*, March 29, 1999, p. 2; "Kia Ads Showcase Safety," *Marketing Magazine Online*, **www.marketingmag.ca**, September 3, 2001; and "Kia Shifts $30M Biz to Publicist," *Marketing Magazine Online*, **www.marketingmag.ca**, February 11, 2002.

Price is the one element of the marketing mix that produces revenue; the other elements produce costs. Prices are perhaps the easiest element of the marketing program to adjust; product features, channels, and even promotion take more time. Price also communicates to the market the company's intended value positioning of its product or brand. A well-designed and marketed product can command a price premium and reap big profits. Consider Whirlpool.

Whirlpool

Washers and dryers traditionally were seen as utilitarian products that could never justify a high price. In 2001, Whirlpool introduced the Duet, a front-loading washer-dryer combo that retailed at US$2300—nearly four times the price of comparative models. How did Whirlpool do it? The Duet was a truly unique offering that promised "performance and efficiency without compromise." Its huge capacities could wash and dry big loads, yet it used much less water and electricity than competitors. It also washed all types of clothing—from silks and lace to sleeping bags and comforters. Duet also could claim an emotional benefit for users— bigger loads meant fewer loads and therefore more time and freedom to do other things.[1]

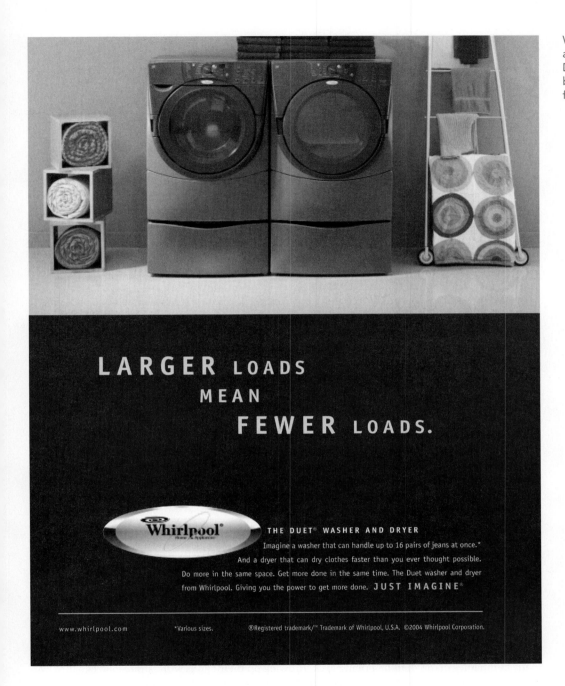

Whirlpool was able to charge a premium price for its new Duet washer and dryer because of the unique benefits offered to consumers.

The Duet pricing plan was the result of a broader shift in Whirlpool's pricing strategy to reduce the frequency of costly and potentially confusing discounts. It wanted to find the optimal prices for its products. Many marketers, however, neglect their pricing strategies—one survey found that managers spent less than 10 percent of their time on pricing.[2]

Pricing decisions are clearly complex and difficult. Holistic marketers must take into account many factors in making pricing decisions—the company, the customers, the competition, and the marketing environment. Pricing decisions must be consistent with the firm's marketing strategy and its target markets and brand positionings.

In this chapter, we provide concepts and tools to facilitate the setting of initial prices and adjusting prices over time and markets.

Understanding Pricing

Price is not just a number on a tag or an item:

> Price is all around us. You pay rent for your apartment, tuition for your education, and a fee to your physician or dentist. The airline, railway, taxi, and bus companies charge you a fare; the local utilities call their price a rate; and the local bank charges you interest for the money you borrow. . . . The company that insures your car charges you a premium. The guest lecturer charges an honorarium. Clubs or societies to which you belong may make a special assessment to pay unusual expenses. Your regular lawyer may ask for a retainer to cover her services. The "price" of an executive is a salary, the price of a salesperson may be a commission, and the price of a worker is a wage. Finally, although economists would disagree, many of us feel that income taxes are the price we pay for the privilege of making money.[3]

Throughout most of history, prices were set by negotiation between buyers and sellers. "Bargaining" is still a sport in some areas. Setting one price for all buyers is a relatively modern idea that arose with the development of large-scale retailing at the end of the nineteenth century. F. W. Woolworth, Tiffany and Co., John Wanamaker, and others advertised a "strictly one-price policy," because they carried so many items and supervised so many employees.

Today the Internet is partially reversing the fixed pricing trend. Computer technology is making it easier for sellers to use software that monitors customers' movements over the Web and allows them to customize offers and prices. New software applications are also allowing buyers to compare prices instantaneously through online robotic shoppers or "shopbots." As one industry observer noted, "We are moving toward a very sophisticated economy. It's kind of an arms race between merchant technology and consumer technology."[4] (See "Marketing Insight: The Internet and Pricing Effects on Sellers and Buyers.")

Traditionally, price has operated as the major determinant of buyer choice. This is still the case in poorer nations, among poorer groups, and with commodity-type products. Although nonprice factors have become more important in recent decades, price still remains one of the most important elements determining market share and profitability. Consumers and purchasing agents have more access to price information and price discounters. Consumers put pressure on retailers to lower their prices. Retailers put pressure on manufacturers to lower their prices. The result is a marketplace characterized by heavy discounting and sales promotion.

How Companies Price

Companies do their pricing in a variety of ways. In small companies, prices are often set by the boss. In large companies, pricing is handled by division and product-line managers. Even here, top management sets general pricing objectives and policies and often approves the prices proposed by lower levels of management. In industries where pricing is a key factor (aerospace, railroads, oil companies), companies will often establish a pricing department to set or assist others in determining appropriate prices. This department reports to the marketing department, finance department, or top management. Others who exert an influence on pricing include sales managers, production managers, finance managers, and accountants.

Executives complain that pricing is a big headache—and one that is getting worse by the day. Many companies do not handle pricing well, throwing up their hands with "strategies" like this: "We determine our costs and take our industry's traditional margins." Other common mistakes are: Price is not revised often enough to capitalize on market changes; price is set independent of the rest of the marketing mix rather than as an intrinsic element of market-positioning strategy; and price is not varied enough for different product items, market segments, distribution channels, and purchase occasions.

Others have a different attitude: They use price as a key strategic tool. Consider what Quiznos Canada is doing:

MARKETING INSIGHT

The Internet and Pricing Effects on Sellers and Buyers

E-commerce has been arguably the Web's hottest application. Yet the Internet is more than simply a new "marketspace." Internet-based technologies are actually changing the rules of the market. Here is a short list of how the Internet allows sellers to discriminate between buyers and buyers to discriminate between sellers.

Buyers can:

- *Get instant price comparisons from thousands of vendors.* One site, PriceScan.com, lures thousands of visitors a day, most of them corporate buyers. Intelligent shopping agents ("bots") take price comparison a step further and seek out products, prices, and reviews from as many as 2000 merchants. Whether they use "bots" or not, consumers now regularly check online prices, compare them with those in their local stores, and may well take a peek at what customers in other countries are paying and order from overseas. Consumers also may unbundle product information from the transaction themselves. For instance, someone might use the Internet to research digital cameras, but visit an electronics store for a hands-on demonstration, then walk out of the store without buying, go home to use a search engine to find the lowest price, and buy a camera online.

- *Name their price and have it met.* On Priceline.com, the customer states the price he or she wants to pay for an airline ticket, hotel, or rental car and Priceline checks whether any seller is willing to meet that price. Consumers can fix their own prices, and sellers can use it too: Airlines can fill in demand for empty seats, and hotels welcome the chance to sell vacant rooms. Volume-aggregating sites combine the orders of many customers and press the supplier for a deeper discount.

- *Get products for free.* Open Source, the free software movement that started with Linux, will erode margins for just about any company doing software. Open-source software is popping up everywhere. It's in PCs and cell phones and set-top boxes. It's in servers that power the world's Web sites, such as Google and Amazon, and in giant corporate and government systems. The biggest challenge confronting Microsoft, Oracle, IBM, and virtually every other major software program is now: How do you compete with programs that people can get for free?

Sellers can:

- *Monitor customer behaviour and tailor offers to individuals.* Although shopping agent software and price comparison Web sites provide published prices, consumers may be missing out on the special deals they can get with the help of new technologies. GE Lighting, which gets 55 000 pricing requests a year, has Web programs that evaluate 300 factors that go into a pricing quote, such as past sales data and discounts, so that it can reduce processing time from up to 30 days to 6 hours.

- *Give certain customers access to special prices.* CDNOW, an online vendor of music albums, e-mails certain buyers a special Web site address with lower prices. Unless you know the secret address, you pay full price. Business marketers are already using extranets to get a precise handle on inventory, costs, and demand at any given moment in order to adjust prices instantly.

Both buyers and sellers can:

- *Negotiate prices in online auctions and exchanges.* Want to sell hundreds of excess and slightly worn widgets? Post a sale on eBay. Want to purchase vintage baseball cards at a bargain price? Go to www.baseballplanet.com.

Sources: Amy E. Cortese, "Good-Bye to Fixed Pricing?" *BusinessWeek*, May 4, 1998, pp. 71–84; Michael Menduno, "Priced to Perfection," *Business 2.0*, March 6, 2001, pp. 40–42; Faith Keenan, "The Price Is Really Right," *BusinessWeek*, March 31, 2003, pp. 61–67; Paul Markillie, "A Perfect Market: A Survey of E-Commerce," *The Economist*, May 15, 2004, pp. 3–20; David Kirpatrick, "How the Open-Source World Plans to Smack Down Microsoft, and Oracle, and . . . ," *Fortune*, February 23, 2004, pp. 92–100. For a discussion of some of the academic issues involved, see Florian Zettelmeyer, "Expanding to the Internet: Pricing and Communication Strategies When Firms Compete on Multiple Channels," *Journal of Marketing Research*, 37 (August 2000): 292–308; John G. Lynch Jr. and Dan Ariely, "Wine Online: Search Costs Affect Competition on Price, Quality, and Distribution," *Marketing Science* (Winter 2000): 83–103; Rajiv Lal and Miklos Sarvary, "When and How Is the Internet Likely to Decrease Price Competition?" *Marketing Science*, 18, no. 4 (1999): 485–503.

Quiznos Canada

In 2004, following the market obsession with low-carbohydrate diets, Quiznos decided to launch a new low-carb menu. Calling it the "largest low-carb menu in Canada," it boasts a line-up of sandwiches made with soy flatbread. However, due to uncertainty about low-carb food advertising regulations, Quiznos decided to use price as a key strategic tool for getting customers to sample its new offerings, and used a pair of radio spots that advertised a small sandwich for $2.99 (a discount of $2.50) to drive customers to the stores. However, once inside the restaurant, customers will be exposed to new point-of-sale displays highlighting the low-carb sandwiches. In addition, Quiznos distributed 6 million direct mailings nationally (excluding Quebec), featuring a photograph of one of its new low-carb sandwiches and including a coupon offer—"buy one low-carb sandwich, get the second free."[5]

The importance of pricing for profitability was demonstrated in a 1992 study by McKinsey & Company. Examining 2400 companies, McKinsey concluded that a 1 percent improvement in price created an improvement in operating profit of 11.1 percent. By contrast, 1 percent improvements in variable cost, volume, and fixed cost produced profit improvements, respectively, of only 7.8 percent, 3.3 percent, and 2.3 percent.

Effectively designing and implementing pricing strategies requires a thorough understanding of consumer pricing psychology and a systematic approach to setting, adapting, and changing prices.

Consumer Psychology and Pricing

Many economists assume that consumers are "price takers" and accept prices at "face value" or as given. Marketers recognize that consumers often actively process price information, interpreting prices in terms of their knowledge from prior purchasing experience, formal communications (advertising, sales calls, and brochures), informal communications (friends, colleagues, or family members), and point-of-purchase or online resources.[6] Purchase decisions are based on how consumers perceive prices and what they consider to be the current actual price—*not* the marketer's stated price. They may have a lower price threshold below which prices may signal inferior or unacceptable quality, as well as an upper price threshold above which prices are prohibitive and seen as not worth the money.

Understanding how consumers arrive at their perceptions of prices is an important marketing priority. Here we consider three key topics—reference prices, price-quality inferences, and price endings.

REFERENCE PRICES   Prior research has shown that although consumers may have fairly good knowledge of the range of prices involved, surprisingly few can recall specific prices of products accurately.[7] When examining products, however, consumers often employ **reference prices**. In considering an observed price, consumers often compare it to an internal reference price (pricing information from memory) or an external frame of reference (such as a posted "regular retail price").[8]

All types of reference prices are possible (see Table 14.1). Sellers often attempt to manipulate reference prices. For example, a seller can situate its product among expensive products to imply that it

TABLE 14.1	POSSIBLE CONSUMER REFERENCE PRICES

- "Fair Price" (what the product should cost)
- Typical Price
- Last Price Paid
- Upper-Bound Price (reservation price or what most consumers would pay)
- Lower-Bound Price (lower threshold price or the least consumers would pay)
- Competitor Prices
- Expected Future Price
- Usual Discounted Price

Source: Russell S. Winer, "Behavioral Perspectives on Pricing: Buyer's Subjective Perceptions of Price Revisited," in *Issues in Pricing: Theory and Research*, edited by Timothy Devinney (Lexington, MA: Lexington Books, 1988), pp. 35–57.

belongs in the same class. Department stores will display women's apparel in separate departments differentiated by price; dresses found in the more expensive department are assumed to be of better quality.

Reference-price thinking is also encouraged by stating a high manufacturer's suggested price, or by indicating that the product was priced much higher originally, or by pointing to a competitor's high price.[9]

Consumer Electronics

On JVC's Web site, the manufacturer's suggested retail price often bears no relationship to what you would be charged by a retailer for the same item. For instance, for a model of mini-digital video camcorder that doubles as a digital still camera, JVC suggests a retail price of US$1099.95, but Circuit City was selling it for US$799.99 and Amazon.com for US$699.99. Compared with other consumer items, from clothing to cars to furniture to toothbrushes, the gap between the prices routinely quoted by manufacturer and retailer in consumer electronics is large. "The simplest thing to say is that we have trained the consumer electronics buyer to think he is getting 20 or 30 or 40 percent off," said Robert Atkins, a vice-president at Mercer Management Consulting. A product manager for Olympus America, primarily known for its cameras, defends the practice by saying that the high manufacturer's suggested retail price is a psychological tool, a reference price that makes people see they are getting something of value for less than top price. Regardless of how inflated—and how perplexing—manufacturers' suggested retail prices are, everyone usually winds up happy. Manufacturers, like JVC or Olympus, get their sales. Retailers get buyers to think they are getting a bargain, and consumers get gadgets they want at prices they think are good.[10]

Clever marketers try to frame the price to signal the best value possible. For example, a relatively more expensive item can be seen as less expensive by breaking the price down into smaller units. A $500 annual membership may be seen as more expensive than "under $50 a month" even if the totals are the same.[11]

When consumers evoke one or more of these frames of reference, their perceived price can vary from the stated price.[12] Research on reference prices has found that "unpleasant surprises"—when perceived price is lower than the stated price—can have a greater impact on purchase likelihood than pleasant surprises.[13]

PRICE-QUALITY INFERENCES Many consumers use price as an indicator of quality. Image pricing is especially effective with ego-sensitive products such as perfumes and expensive cars. A $100 bottle of perfume might contain $10 worth of scent, but gift givers pay $100 to communicate their high regard for the receiver.

Price and quality perceptions of cars interact.[14] Higher-priced cars are perceived to possess high quality. Higher-quality cars are likewise perceived to be higher priced than they actually are. Table 14.2 shows how consumer perceptions about cars can differ from reality. When alternative information about true quality is available, price becomes a less significant indicator of quality. When this information is not available, price acts as a signal of quality.

Centrum Vitamins

In branding Centrum Performance vitamins, Kevin Brady, president of Anderson DDB in Toronto (responsible for advertising Wyeth Consumer Healthcare's Centrum brand of vitamins), believes wholeheartedly in the notion of creating a price-quality difference between Centrum brands and private-label competitors such as Shoppers Drug Mart's Life brand products. He believes that Centrum has its own brand personality. It has unique vitamin content, comes from a quality manufacturer, and has a longstanding heritage as a leadership brand. The combination of these elements contributes to consumer acceptance of Centrum's higher price relative to alternatives. Maintaining the importance of these benefits in the minds of consumers is crucial given the constant risk of commoditization that faces a consumer packaged good such as vitamins.[15]

TABLE 14.2	CONSUMER PERCEPTIONS VERSUS REALITY FOR CARS

Wall Street firm Morgan Stanley used J. D. Power and Associates 2003 Vehicle Dependability Study, which tracks reliability over three years, and CNW Market Research's Perceived Quality Survey to find out which car brands were potentially over- and undervalued.

Overvalued: Brands whose perceived quality exceeds actual quality by percentage

Land Rover	75.3%
Kia	66.6%
Volkswagen	58.3%
Volvo	36.0%
Mercedes	34.2%

Undervalued: Brands whose actual quality exceeds perceived quality by percentage

Mercury	42.3%
Infiniti	34.1%
Buick	29.7%
Lincoln	25.3%
Chrysler	20.8%

Source: David Kiley, "U.S. Automakers Get a Bum Rap," *USA Today*, January 15, 2004, p. B5.

Some brands adopt scarcity as a means to signify quality and justify premium pricing. Some automakers have bucked the massive discounting craze that shook the industry and are producing smaller batches of new models, creating a buzz around them, and using the demand to raise the sticker price.[16] Waiting lists, once reserved for limited-edition cars like Ferraris, are becoming more common for mass-market models, including Volkswagen and Acura SUVs and Toyota and Honda minivans.

As the Beanie Baby craze demonstrated, scarcity combined with strong demand can lead to high market prices. Here is another example:

Tequila Shortage

Some people may remember the sudden and dramatic increase in the price of a standard bottle of tequila in Canada in 2000. Tequila is made from the Blue Agave, which takes nearly 12 years to mature and can only be made from Blue Agave crops harvested from around the village of Tequila according to the strict regulations of the Mexican government. Not only is there the Tequila Regulatory Council, which monitors distilleries and approves the authenticity of the spirit, but tequila is also regulated by NAFTA: "Canada and the United States shall not permit the sale of any product as Tequila, unless it has been manufactured in Mexico in accordance with the laws and regulations of Mexico governing the manufacturer of Tequila." In the late 1990s, a deadly virus attacked Mexico's Agave plants and decimated the crops, resulting in yields that were insufficient to keep up with the growing worldwide demand for tequila. The disease's impact on retail prices was dramatic. In Ontario, prices jumped a whopping 60 percent (shooting up from $40 to $60 per bottle). The price increase was explained by printed notices at stores about the worldwide tequila shortage. Tequila began to occupy the same price category as other premium alcoholic beverages such as single-malt whiskeys and cognacs.[17]

PRICE CUES Consumer perceptions of prices are also affected by alternative pricing strategies. Many sellers believe that prices should end in an odd number. Many customers see a stereo amplifier priced at $299 instead of $300 as a price in the $200 range rather than $300 range. Research has shown that consumers tend to process prices in a "left-to-right" manner rather than by rounding.[18] Price encoding in this fashion is important if there is a mental price break at the higher, rounded price. Another explanation for "9" endings is that they convey the notion of a discount or bargain, suggesting that if a company wants a high-price image, it should avoid the odd-ending tactic.[19] One study even showed that demand actually increased one-third by *raising* the price of a dress from $34 to $39, but demand was unchanged when prices increased from $34 to $44.[20]

Prices that end with "0" and "5" are also common in the marketplace, as they are thought to be easier for consumers to process and retrieve from memory.[21] "Sale" signs next to prices have been shown to spur demand, but only if not overused: Total category sales are highest when some, but not all, items in a category have sale signs; past a certain point, use of additional sale signs will cause total category sales to fall.[22] "Marketing Memo: When to Use Price Cues" provides some guidelines.

Marketing Memo

When to Use Price Cues

Pricing cues, such as sale signs and prices that end in 9, become less effective the more they are employed. Anderson and Simester maintain that they must be used judiciously on those items where consumers' price knowledge may be poor. They cite the following examples:

1. Customers purchase the item infrequently.

2. Customers are new.

3. Product designs vary over time.

4. Prices vary seasonally.

5. Quality or sizes vary across stores.

Source: Eric Anderson and Duncan Simester, "Mind Your Pricing Cues," *Harvard Business Review* (September 2003): 96–103.

Setting the Price

A firm must set a price for the first time when it develops a new product, when it introduces its regular product into a new distribution channel or geographical area, and when it enters bids on new contract work. The firm must decide where to position its product on quality and price. In some markets, like the auto market, as many as eight *price points* or price tiers and levels can be found:

Segment	Example
Ultimate	Rolls-Royce
Gold Standard	Mercedes-Benz
Luxury	Audi
Special Needs	Volvo
Middle	Buick
Ease/Convenience	Ford Escort
Me Too, but Cheaper	Hyundai
Price Alone	Kia

Most markets have three to five price points or tiers. Marriott Hotels is good at developing different brands for different price points: Marriott Vacation Club—Vacation Villas (highest price), Marriott Marquis (high price), Marriott (high-medium price), Renaissance (medium-high price), Courtyard (medium price), Towne Place Suites (medium-low price), and Fairfield Inn (low price).

Consumers often rank brands according to price tiers in a category.[23] For example, Figure 14.1 shows the three price tiers that resulted from a study of the ice cream market.[24] In that market, as the figure shows, there is also a relationship between price and quality. Within any tier, as the figure shows, there is a range of acceptable prices, called *price bands*. The price bands provide managers with some indication of the flexibility and breadth they can adopt in pricing their brands within a particular price tier.

The firm has to consider many factors in setting its pricing policy.[25] We will describe a six-step procedure: (1) selecting the pricing objective; (2) determining demand; (3) estimating costs; (4) analyzing competitors' costs, prices, and offers; (5) selecting a pricing method; and (6) selecting the final price.

Step 1: Selecting the Pricing Objective

The company first decides where it wants to position its market offering. The clearer a firm's objectives, the easier it is to set price. A company can pursue any of five major objectives through pricing: survival, maximum current profit, maximum market share, maximum market skimming, or product-quality leadership.

FIGURE 14.1

Price Tiers in the Ice Cream
Market

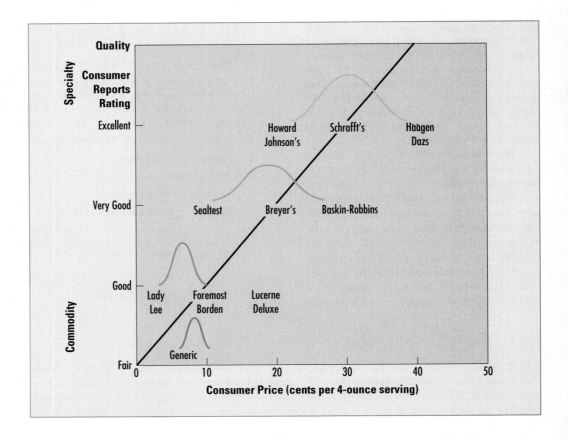

SURVIVAL Companies pursue *survival* as their major objective if they are plagued with overcapacity, intense competition, or changing consumer wants. As long as prices cover variable costs and some fixed costs, the company stays in business. Survival is a short-run objective; in the long run, the firm must learn how to add value or face extinction.

MAXIMUM CURRENT PROFIT Many companies try to set a price that will *maximize current profits*. They estimate the demand and costs associated with alternative prices and choose the price that produces maximum current profit, cash flow, or rate of return on investment. This strategy assumes that the firm has knowledge of its demand and cost functions; in reality, these are difficult to estimate. In emphasizing current performance, the company may sacrifice long-run performance by ignoring the effects of other marketing-mix variables, competitors' reactions, and legal restraints on price.

MAXIMUM MARKET SHARE Some companies want to *maximize their market share.* They believe that a higher sales volume will lead to lower unit costs and higher long-run profit. They set the lowest price, assuming the market is price-sensitive. Texas Instruments (TI) has practised this **market-penetration pricing**. TI would build a large plant, set its price as low as possible, win a large market share, experience falling costs, and cut its price further as costs fall.

The following conditions favour setting a low price: (1) The market is highly price-sensitive, and a low price stimulates market growth; (2) production and distribution costs fall with accumulated production experience; and (3) a low price discourages actual and potential competition.

MAXIMUM MARKET SKIMMING Companies unveiling a new technology favour setting high prices to *maximize market skimming*. Sony is a frequent practitioner of **market-skimming pricing**, where prices start high and are slowly lowered over time. When Sony introduced the world's first high-definition television (HDTV) to the Japanese market in 1990, it was priced at US$43 000. So that Sony could "skim" the maximum amount of revenue from the various segments of the market, the price dropped steadily through the years—a 28-inch HDTV cost just over US$6000 in 1993 and a 40-inch HDTV cost about US$2000 in 2001.[26]

Market skimming makes sense under the following conditions: (1) A sufficient number of buyers have a high current demand; (2) the unit costs of producing a small volume are not so high that they cancel the advantage of charging what the traffic will bear; (3) the high initial price does not attract more competitors to the market; (4) the high price communicates the image of a superior product.

PRODUCT-QUALITY LEADERSHIP A company might aim to be the *product-quality leader* in the market. Many brands strive to be "affordable luxuries"—products or services characterized by high levels of perceived quality, taste, and status, with a price just high enough to not be out of consumer's reach. Brands such as Starbucks coffee, Aveda shampoo, Victoria's Secret lingerie, BMW cars, and Viking ranges are able to position themselves as quality leaders in their category, combining quality, luxury, and premium prices with an intensely loyal customer base.[27] Grey Goose and Absolut carved out a super-premium niche in the essentially odourless, colourless, and tasteless vodka category through clever on-premise and off-premise marketing that made the brands seem hip and exclusive.[28]

OTHER OBJECTIVES Nonprofit and public organizations may have other pricing objectives. A university aims for *partial cost recovery*, knowing that it must rely on private gifts and public grants to cover the remaining costs. A nonprofit theatre company may price its productions to fill the maximum number of theatre seats. A social service agency may set a service price geared to client income.

Whatever the specific objective, businesses that use price as a strategic tool will profit more than those who simply let costs or the market determine their pricing.

Step 2: Determining Demand

Each price will lead to a different level of demand and therefore have a different impact on a company's marketing objectives. The relation between alternative prices and the resulting current demand is captured in a demand curve (see Figure 14.2). In the normal case, demand and price are inversely related: the higher the price, the lower the demand. In the case of prestige goods, the demand curve sometimes slopes upward. A perfume company raised its price and sold more perfume rather than less! Some consumers take the higher price to signify a better product. However, if the price is too high, the level of demand may fall.

PRICE SENSITIVITY The demand curve shows the market's probable purchase quantity at alternative prices. It sums the reactions of many individuals who have different price sensitivities. The first step in estimating demand is to understand what affects price sensitivity. Generally speaking, customers are most price-sensitive to products that cost a lot or are bought frequently. They are less price-sensitive to low-cost items or items they buy infrequently. They are also less price-sensitive when price is only a small part of the total cost of obtaining, operating, and servicing the product over its lifetime. A seller can charge a higher price than competitors and still get the business if the company can convince the customer that it offers the lowest *total cost of ownership* (TCO).

Companies, of course, prefer customers who are less price-sensitive. Table 14.3 lists some characteristics that are associated with decreased price sensitivity. On the other hand, the Internet has the potential to increase customers' price sensitivity. In buying a specific book online, for example, a customer can compare the prices offered by over two dozen online bookstores by just clicking mySimon.com. These prices can differ by as much as 20 percent.

FIGURE 14.2

Inelastic and Elastic Demand

TABLE 14.3	FACTORS LEADING TO LESS PRICE SENSITIVITY

- The product is more distinctive.
- Buyers are less aware of substitutes.
- Buyers cannot easily compare the quality of substitutes.
- The expenditure is a smaller part of the buyer's total income.
- The expenditure is small compared to the total cost of the end product.
- Part of the cost is borne by another party.
- The product is used in conjunction with assets previously bought.
- The product is assumed to have more quality, prestige, or exclusiveness.
- Buyers cannot store the product.

Source: Thomas T. Nagle and Reed K. Holden, *The Strategy and Tactics of Pricing*, 3rd ed. (Upper Saddle River, NJ: Prentice Hall, 2001), ch 4.

Although the Internet increases the opportunity for price-sensitive buyers to find and favour lower-price sites, many buyers may not be that price-sensitive. McKinsey conducted a study and found that 89 percent of a sample of Internet customers visited only one book site, 84 percent visited only one toy site, and 81 percent visited only one music site, which indicates that there is less price-comparison shopping taking place on the Internet than is possible.

Companies need to understand the price sensitivity of their customers and prospects and the trade-offs people are willing to make between price and product characteristics. Targeting only price-sensitive consumers may in fact be "leaving money on the table."

ESTIMATING DEMAND CURVES Most companies make some attempt to measure their demand curves using several different methods:

- *Statistical analysis* of past prices, quantities sold, and other factors can reveal their relationships. The data can be longitudinal (over time) or cross-sectional (different locations at the same time). Building the appropriate model and fitting the data with the proper statistical techniques calls for considerable skill.

- *Price experiments* can be conducted. Bennett and Wilkinson systematically varied the prices of several products sold in a discount store and observed the results.[29] An alternative approach is to charge different prices in similar territories to see how sales are affected. Still another approach is to use the Internet. An e-business could test the impact of a 5 percent price increase by quoting a higher price to every fortieth visitor to compare the purchase response. However, it must do this carefully and not alienate customers, as happened when Amazon price-tested discounts of 30 percent, 35 percent, and 40 percent for DVD buyers, only to find that those receiving the 30 percent discount were upset.[30]

- *Surveys* can explore how many units consumers would buy at different proposed prices, although there is always the chance that they might understate their purchase intentions at higher prices to discourage the company from setting higher prices.[31]

In measuring the price–demand relationship, the market researcher must control for various factors that will influence demand. The competitor's response will make a difference. Also, if the company changes other marketing-mix factors besides price, the effect of the price change itself will be hard to isolate. Nagle presents an excellent summary of the various methods for estimating price sensitivity and demand.[32]

PRICE ELASTICITY OF DEMAND Marketers need to know how responsive, or elastic, demand would be to a change in price. Consider the two demand curves in Figure 14.2. With demand curve (a), a price increase from $10 to $15 leads to a relatively small decline in demand from 105 to 100. With demand curve (b), the same price increase leads to a substantial drop in demand from 150 to 50. If demand hardly changes with a small change in price, we say the demand is *inelastic*. If demand changes considerably, demand is *elastic*. The higher the elasticity, the greater the volume growth resulting from a 1 percent price reduction.

Demand is likely to be less elastic under the following conditions: (1) There are few or no substitutes or competitors; (2) buyers do not readily notice the higher price; (3) buyers are slow to change their buying habits; (4) buyers think the higher prices are justified. If demand is elastic, sellers will consider lowering the price. A lower price will produce more total revenue. This makes sense as long as the costs of producing and selling more units do not increase disproportionately.[33]

The following case illustrates the effects of not considering the needs of customers for whom demand is most elastic:

Public Transit

Understanding different consumer price elasticities should be an important facet of public transit pricing. To encourage increased use, many transit authorities and companies, like Ottawa-Carleton Transit and Ontario's regional GO Transit, offer riders weekly or monthly passes instead of making them purchase single-ride tickets. These passes strongly appeal to daily commuters who receive a significant benefit from the discounted fare. However, since these people are price inelastic, the transit authorities may be leaving money on the table. In fact, the demand curve of many commuters is perfectly inelastic; no matter what happens to the fare, people without alternative means of transportation must get to work and get back home. Other commuters have a more elastic demand curve. These are people who have cars or who can walk to work. Shoppers and casual users who use transit for special events may be the most price elastic of all. Given these varying price sensitivities, transit authorities could improve their revenues by reversing their pricing strategies. However, this is rarely done, since transit is seen as a public service and a means of reducing pollution by getting cars off the roads.[34]

Price elasticity depends on the magnitude and direction of the contemplated price change. It may be negligible with a small price change and substantial with a large price change. It may differ for a price cut versus a price increase, and there may be a *price indifference band* within which price changes have little or no effect. A McKinsey pricing study estimated that the price indifference band can range as large as 17 percent for mouthwash, 13 percent for batteries, 9 percent for small appliances, and 2 percent for term deposits.

Finally, long-run price elasticity may differ from short-run elasticity. Buyers may continue to buy from a current supplier after a price increase, but they may eventually switch suppliers. Here demand is more elastic in the long run than in the short run, or the reverse may happen: Buyers may drop a supplier after being notified of a price increase but return later. The distinction between short-run and long-run elasticity means that sellers will not know the total effect of a price change until time passes.

Step 3: Estimating Costs

Demand sets a ceiling on the price the company can charge for its product. Costs set the floor. The company wants to charge a price that covers its cost of producing, distributing, and selling the product, including a fair return for its effort and risk. Yet, when companies price products to cover full costs, the net result is not always profitability. See "Marketing Memo: Three Myths about Pricing Strategy" for more on common pricing strategy errors.

TYPES OF COSTS AND LEVELS OF PRODUCTION   A company's costs take two forms, fixed and variable. **Fixed costs** (also known as **overhead**) are costs that do not vary with production or sales revenue. A company must pay bills each month for rent, heat, interest, salaries, and so on, regardless of output.

Variable costs vary directly with the level of production. For example, each hand calculator produced by Texas Instruments involves a cost of plastic, microprocessor chips, packaging, and the like. These costs tend to be constant per unit produced. They are called variable because their total varies with the number of units produced.

Total costs consist of the sum of the fixed and variable costs for any given level of production. **Average cost** is the cost per unit at that level of production; it is equal to total costs divided by production. Management wants to charge a price that will at least cover the total production costs at a given level of production.

Marketing Memo

Three Myths about Pricing Strategy

According to George E. Cressman, Jr., senior pricer at Strategic Pricing Group, marketers nurture three major myths about pricing strategy:

- *Pricing our products to cover full costs will make us profitable.* Marketers often do not realize the value they actually do provide but think in terms of product features. They frequently treat the service elements in a product offering as sales incentives rather than value-enhancing augmentations for which they can charge. Says Cressman, "When we price to cover costs, there is an underlying assumption that customers value us for our costs. Then the logical conclusions would be that we should increase costs so we can increase price, and customers will love us even more!" Marketers should instead determine how many customers will ascribe how much value to their offerings, then ask, "Given our cost structure, what volume changes are necessary to make price changes profitable?"

- *Pricing our products to grow market share will make us profitable.* Cressman reminds marketers that share is determined by value delivery at competitive advantage, not just price cuts. Therefore, "The correct question is not: 'What level of price will enable us to achieve our sales and market share objectives?' but 'What shares of the market can we most profitably serve?'"

- *Pricing our products to meet customer demands will make us profitable.* Cutting prices to keep customers or beat competitive offers encourages customers to demand price concessions and trains salespeople to offer them. "When you're tempted to ask what customers will pay," says Cressman, "don't ask them. You know you won't like the answer." Instead, marketers should ask, "What prices can we convince customers are supported by the value of our products and services?" and "How can we better segment the market to reflect differences in value delivered to different types of customers?" Create different levels of value and price options for different market segments and their respective value needs. And to finesse a price cut, provide a reduced-priced option. "That makes the demand for a price concession the customer's problem, for it must then choose which benefits to forgo."

Source: Adapted from Bob Donath, "Dispel Major Myths About Pricing," *Marketing News*, February 3, 2003, p. 10.

To price intelligently, management needs to know how its costs vary with different levels of production. Take the case in which a company such as TI has built a fixed-size plant to produce 1000 hand calculators a day. The cost per unit is high if few units are produced per day. As production approaches 1000 units per day, the average cost falls because the fixed costs are spread over more units. Short-run average cost increases after 1000 units, because the plant becomes inefficient: Workers have to line up for machines, machines break down more often, and workers get in each other's way (see Figure 14.3[a]).

If TI believes it can sell 2000 units per day, it should consider building a larger plant. The plant will use more efficient machinery and work arrangements, and the unit cost of producing 2000 units per day will be less than the unit cost of producing 1000 units per day. This is shown in the long-run average cost curve (LRAC) in Figure 14.3(b). In fact, a 3000-capacity plant would be even more efficient according to Figure 14.3(b), but a 4000-daily production plant would be less efficient because of increasing diseconomies of scale: There are too many workers to manage, and paperwork slows things down. Figure 14.3(b) indicates that a 3000-daily production plant is the optimal size if demand is strong enough to support this level of production.

ACCUMULATED PRODUCTION Suppose TI runs a plant that produces 3000 hand calculators per day. As TI gains experience producing hand calculators, its methods improve. Workers learn shortcuts, materials flow more smoothly, and procurement costs fall. The result, as Figure 14.4 shows, is that average cost falls with accumulated production experience. Thus the average cost of producing the first 100 000 hand calculators is $10 per calculator. When the company has produced the first 200 000 calculators, the average cost has fallen to $9. After its accumulated production experience doubles again to 400 000, the average cost is $8. This decline in the average cost with accumulated production experience is called the **experience curve** or **learning curve.**

Now suppose three firms compete in this industry, TI, A, and B. TI is the lowest-cost producer at $8, having produced 400 000 units in the past. If all three firms sell the calculator for $10, TI makes $2 profit per unit, A makes $1 per unit, and B breaks even. The smart move for TI would be to lower its price to $9. This will drive B out of the market, and even A may consider leaving. TI will pick up the business that would have gone to B (and possibly A). Furthermore, price-sensitive customers will enter the market at the lower price. As production increases beyond 400 000 units, TI's costs will drop still further and faster and more than restore its profits, even at a price of $9. TI has used this aggressive pricing strategy repeatedly to gain market share and drive others out of the industry.

Experience-curve pricing nevertheless carries major risks. Aggressive pricing might give the product a cheap image. The strategy also assumes that competitors are weak followers. It leads the company into building more plants to meet demand, while a competitor innovates a lower-cost technology. The market leader is now stuck with the old technology.

Most experience-curve pricing has focused on manufacturing costs, but all costs, including marketing costs, can be improved on. If three firms are each investing a large sum of money in telemarketing, the firm that has used it the longest might achieve the lowest costs. This firm can charge a little less for its product and still earn the same return, all other costs being equal.[35]

ACTIVITY-BASED COST ACCOUNTING Today's companies try to adapt their offers and terms to different buyers. A manufacturer, for example, will negotiate different terms with different retail chains. One retailer may want daily delivery (to keep inventory lower) while another may accept twice-a-week delivery in order to get a lower price. The manufacturer's costs will differ with each chain, and so will its profits. To estimate the real profitability of dealing with different retailers, the manufacturer needs to use **activity-based cost (ABC) accounting** instead of standard cost accounting.[36]

ABC accounting tries to identify the real costs associated with serving each customer. It allocates indirect costs like clerical costs, office expenses, supplies, and so on, to the activities that use them, rather than in some proportion to direct costs. Both variable and overhead costs are tagged back to each customer. Companies that fail to measure their costs correctly are not measuring their profit correctly and are likely to misallocate their marketing effort. The key to effectively employing ABC is to define and judge "activities" properly. One proposed time-based solution calculates the cost of one minute of overhead and then decides how much of this cost each activity uses.[37]

TARGET COSTING Costs change with production scale and experience. They can also change as a result of a concentrated effort by designers, engineers, and purchasing agents to reduce them through **target costing**.[38] Market research is used to establish a new product's desired functions and the price at which the product will sell, given its appeal and competitors' prices. Deducting the desired profit margin from this price leaves the target cost that must be achieved. Each cost element—design, engineering, manufacturing, sales—must be examined, and different ways to bring down costs must be considered. The objective is to bring the final cost projections into the target cost range. If this is not possible, it may be necessary to stop developing the product because it could not sell for the target price and make the target profit.

To hit price and margin targets, marketers of 9 Lives brand of cat food employed target costing to bring their price down to "four cans for a dollar" via a reshaped package and redesigned manufacturing processes. Even with lower prices, profits for the brand doubled.

Step 4: Analyzing Competitors' Costs, Prices, and Offers

Within the range of possible prices determined by market demand and company costs, the firm must take competitors' costs, prices, and possible price reactions into account. The firm should first consider the nearest competitor's price. If the firm's offer contains features not offered by the nearest competitor, its worth to the customer should be evaluated and added to the competitor's price. If the competitor's offer contains some features not offered by the firm, its worth to the customer should be evaluated and subtracted from the firm's price. Now the firm can decide whether it can charge more, the same, or less than the competitor. But competitors can change their prices in reaction to the price set by the firm, as we'll see later in the chapter.

FIGURE 14.3

Cost per Unit at Different Levels of Production per Period

(a) Cost behaviour in a fixed-size plant

(b) Cost behaviour over different-size plants

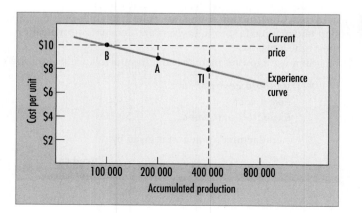

FIGURE 14.4

Cost per Unit as a Function of Accumulated Production: The Experience Curve

The redesigned 9 Lives®
four-pack package.

FIGURE 14.5

The Three Cs Model for Price
Setting

High Price
(No possible demand at this price)
Ceiling price
Customers' assessment of unique product features
Orienting point
Competitors' prices and prices of substitutes
Costs
Floor price
Low Price
(No possible profit at this price)

Sprint Canada

Bell Canada is unquestionably the dominant player when it comes to both local and long-distance phone service. Other players, such as Rogers Communications, that entered the market after government deregulation of the industry moved early to build share with regard to Internet access services. Thus, when late mover Sprint Canada entered the marketplace, it attacked the entrenched players with competitive pricing. In 2002, Sprint launched a campaign using the tagline "There's a new kid in town," showcasing Sprint's RightPlan, which offered a 10 percent discount across its local phone service, long-distance, and Internet access communication platforms. Hoping to provide consumers with real benefits, Sprint placed price at the core of its message.[39]

Step 5: Selecting a Pricing Method

Given the three Cs—the customers' demand schedule, the cost function, and competitors' prices—the company is now ready to select a price. Figure 14.5 summarizes the three major considerations in price setting. Costs set a floor to the price. Competitors' prices and the price of substitutes provide an orienting point. Customers' assessment of unique features establishes the price ceiling.

Companies select a pricing method that includes one or more of these three considerations. We will examine six price-setting methods: markup pricing, target-return pricing, perceived-value pricing, value pricing, going-rate pricing, and auction-type pricing.

MARKUP PRICING The most elementary pricing method is to add a standard **markup** to the product's cost. Construction companies submit job bids by estimating the total project cost and adding a standard markup for profit. Lawyers and accountants typically price by adding a standard markup on their time and costs.

Suppose a toaster manufacturer has the following costs and sales expectations:

Variable cost per unit	$10
Fixed cost	$300 000
Expected unit sales	50 000

The manufacturer's unit cost is given by:

$$\text{Unit cost} = \text{variable cost} + \frac{\text{fixed cost}}{\text{unit sales}} = \$10 + \frac{\$300\,000}{50\,000} = \$16$$

Now assume the manufacturer wants to earn a 20 percent markup on sales. The manufacturer's markup price is given by:

$$\text{Markup price} = \frac{\text{unit cost}}{(1 - \text{desired return on sales})} = \frac{\$16}{1 - 0.2} = \$20$$

The manufacturer would charge dealers $20 per toaster and make a profit of $4 per unit. The dealers in turn will mark up the toaster. If dealers want to earn 50 percent on their selling price, they will mark up the toaster to $40. This is equivalent to a cost markup of 100 percent. Markups are generally higher on seasonal items (to cover the risk of not selling), specialty items, slower-moving items, items with high storage and handling costs, and demand-inelastic items, such as prescription drugs.

Does the use of standard markups make logical sense? Generally, no. Any pricing method that ignores current demand, perceived value, and competition is not likely to lead to the optimal price. Markup pricing works only if the marked-up price actually brings in the expected level of sales.

Companies introducing a new product often price it high, hoping to recover their costs as rapidly as possible. But this strategy could be fatal if a competitor is pricing low. This happened to Philips, the Dutch electronics manufacturer, in pricing its videodisc players. Philips wanted to make a profit on each player. Japanese competitors priced low and succeeded in building their market share rapidly, which in turn pushed down their costs substantially.

Still, markup pricing remains popular. First, sellers can determine costs much more easily than they can estimate demand. By tying the price to cost, sellers simplify the pricing task. Second, where all firms in the industry use this pricing method, prices tend to be similar. Price competition is therefore minimized. Third, many people feel that cost-plus pricing is fairer to both buyers and sellers. Sellers do not take advantage of buyers when the latter's demand becomes acute, and sellers earn a fair return on investment.

TARGET-RETURN PRICING   In **target-return pricing**, the firm determines the price that would yield its target rate of return on investment (ROI). Target pricing is used by General Motors, which prices its automobiles to achieve a 15 to 20 percent ROI. This method is also used by public utilities, which need to make a fair return on investment.

Suppose the toaster manufacturer has invested $1 million in the business and wants to set a price to earn a 20 percent ROI, specifically $200 000. The target-return price is given by the following formula:

$$\text{Target-return price} = \text{unit cost} + \frac{\text{desired return} \times \text{invested capital}}{\text{unit sales}}$$

$$= \$16 + \frac{0.20 \times \$1\ 000\ 000}{50\ 000} = \$20$$

The manufacturer will realize this 20 percent ROI provided its costs and estimated sales turn out to be accurate. But what if sales do not reach 50,000 units? The manufacturer can prepare a break-even chart to learn what would happen at other sales levels (see Figure 14.6). Fixed costs are $300 000 regardless of sales volume. Variable costs, not shown in the figure, rise with volume. Total costs equal the sum of fixed costs and variable costs. The total revenue curve starts at zero and rises with each unit sold.

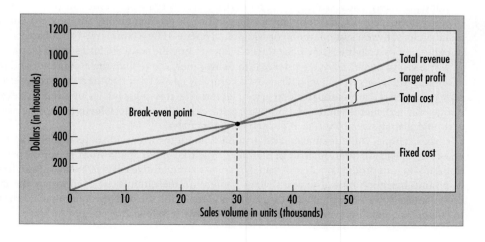

FIGURE 14.6

Break-Even Chart for Determining Target-Return Price and Break-Even Volume

The total revenue and total cost curves cross at 30 000 units. This is the break-even volume. It can be verified by the following formula:

$$\text{Break-even volume} = \frac{\text{fixed cost}}{(\text{price} - \text{variable cost})} = \frac{\$300\ 000}{\$20 - \$10} = 30\ 000$$

The manufacturer, of course, is hoping that the market will buy 50 000 units at $20, in which case it earns $200 000 on its $1 million investment, but much depends on price elasticity and competitors' prices. Unfortunately, target-return pricing tends to ignore these considerations. The manufacturer needs to consider different prices and estimate their probable impacts on sales volume and profits. The manufacturer should also search for ways to lower its fixed or variable costs, because lower costs will decrease its required break-even volume.

PERCEIVED-VALUE PRICING An increasing number of companies base their price on the customer's **perceived value**. They must deliver the value promised by their value proposition, and the customer must perceive this value. They use the other marketing-mix elements, such as advertising and sales force, to communicate and enhance perceived value in buyers' minds.[40]

Perceived value is made up of several elements, such as the buyer's image of the product performance, the channel deliverables, the warranty quality, customer support, and softer attributes such as the supplier's reputation, trustworthiness, and esteem. Furthermore, each potential customer places different weights on these different elements, with the result that some will be *price buyers*, others will be *value buyers*, and still others will be *loyal buyers*. Companies need different strategies for these three groups. For price buyers, companies need to offer stripped-down products and reduced services. For value buyers, companies must keep innovating new value and aggressively reaffirming their value. For loyal buyers, companies must invest in relationship building and customer intimacy.

Caterpillar uses perceived value to set prices on its construction equipment. It might price its tractor at $100 000, although a similar competitor's tractor might be priced at $90 000. When a prospective customer asks a Caterpillar dealer why he should pay $10 000 more for the Caterpillar tractor, the dealer answers:

$ 90 000	is the tractor's price if it is only equivalent to the competitor's tractor
$ 7 000	is the price premium for Caterpillar's superior durability
$ 6 000	is the price premium for Caterpillar's superior reliability
$ 5 000	is the price premium for Caterpillar's superior service
$ 2 000	is the price premium for Caterpillar's longer warranty on parts
$110 000	is the normal price to cover Caterpillar's superior value
– $ 10 000	discount
$100 000	final price

The Caterpillar dealer is able to indicate why Caterpillar's tractor delivers more value than the competitor's. Although the customer is asked to pay a $10 000 premium, he is actually getting $20 000 extra value! He chooses the Caterpillar tractor because he is convinced that its lifetime operating costs will be lower.

Yet even when a company claims that its offering delivers more total value, not all customers will respond positively. There is always a segment of buyers who care only about the price. There are other buyers who suspect that the company is exaggerating its product quality and services. One company installed its software system in one or two plants operated by a company. The substantial and well-documented cost savings convinced the customer to buy the software for its other plants.

The key to perceived-value pricing is to deliver more value than the competitor and to demonstrate this to prospective buyers. Basically, a company needs to understand the customer's decision-making process. The company can try to determine the value of its offering in several ways: managerial judgments within the company, value of similar products, focus groups, surveys, experimentation, analysis of historical data, and conjoint analysis.[41]

For example, DuPont educated its customers about the true value of its higher-grade polyethylene resin called Alathon. Instead of claiming only that pipes made from it were 5 percent more durable, DuPont produced a detailed analysis of the comparative costs of installing and maintaining in-ground irrigation pipe. The real savings came from the diminished need to pay the labour and crop damage costs associated with digging up and replacing the underground pipe. DuPont was able to charge 7 percent more and still see its sales double the following year.

VALUE PRICING In recent years, several companies have adopted **value pricing**: they win loyal customers by charging a fairly low price for a high-quality offering. Among the best practitioners of value pricing are IKEA and Southwest Airlines.

In the early 1990s, Procter & Gamble created quite a stir when it reduced prices on supermarket staples such as Pampers and Luvs diapers, liquid Tide detergent, and Folger's coffee to value price them. In the past, a brand-loyal family had to pay what amounted to a US$725 premium for a year's worth of P&G products versus private-label or low-priced brands. To offer value prices, P&G underwent a major overhaul. It redesigned the way it developed, manufactured, distributed, priced, marketed, and sold products to deliver better value at every point in the supply chain.[42]

Value pricing is not a matter of simply setting lower prices; it is a matter of re-engineering the company's operations to become a low-cost producer without sacrificing quality, and lowering prices significantly to attract a large number of value-conscious customers.

An important type of value pricing is **everyday low pricing (EDLP)**, which takes place at the retail level. A retailer who holds to an EDLP pricing policy charges a constant low price with little or no price promotions and special sales. These constant prices eliminate week-to-week price uncertainty and can be contrasted to the "high-low" pricing of promotion-oriented competitors. In **high-low pricing**, the retailer charges higher prices on an everyday basis but then runs frequent promotions in which prices are temporarily lowered below the EDLP level.[43] The two different pricing strategies have been shown to affect consumer price judgments—deep discounts (EDLP) can lead to lower perceived prices by consumers over time than frequent, shallow discounts (high-low), even if the actual averages are the same.[44]

In recent years, high-low pricing has given way to EDLP at such widely different venues as General Motors' Saturn car dealerships and upscale department stores such as Nordstrom; but the king of EDLP is surely Wal-Mart, which practically defined the term. Except for a few sale items every month, Wal-Mart promises everyday low prices on major brands. "It's not a short-term strategy," says one Wal-Mart executive. "You have to be willing to make a commitment to it, and you have to be able to operate with lower ratios of expense than everybody else."

Some retailers have even based their entire marketing strategy around what could be called *extreme* everyday low pricing. Partly fuelled by an economic downturn, even once unfashionable "dollar stores" are gaining in popularity. Consider the Bay's recent and enduring focus on value:

Shoppers at Wal-Mart get EDLP—everyday low pricing—on major brands.

The Bay

The Hudson Bay Company, which owns and operates more than 500 outlets (under the banners the Bay, Zellers, and Home Outfitters, is Canada's largest department store retailer. In 2002, the Bay dropped its "Shopping is good" slogan after a three-year run and launched a new positioning strategy grounded in the notion of value. The tagline "More than you came for" was introduced to emphasize affordability and value. The shift in strategy resulted from the company's belief that customers understood that the Bay could deliver style, but did not associate the brand with affordability. To promote its message, the Bay ran television ads with women talking about all the good value they find at the Bay. The Bay also introduced a number of more moderately priced products in addition to its private-label brands.[45]

The most important reason retailers adopt EDLP is that constant sales and promotions are costly and have eroded consumer confidence in the credibility of everyday shelf prices. Consumers also have less time and patience for such time-honoured traditions as watching for supermarket specials and clipping coupons. Yet, there is no denying that promotions create excitement and draw shoppers. For this reason, EDLP is not a guarantee of success. As supermarkets face heightened competition from their counterparts and from alternative channels, many find that the key to drawing shoppers is using a combination of high-low and everyday low pricing strategies, with increased advertising and promotions.[46]

GOING-RATE PRICING   In **going-rate pricing**, the firm bases its price largely on competitors' prices. The firm might charge the same, more, or less than major competitor(s). In oligopolistic industries that sell a commodity such as steel, paper, or fertilizer, firms normally charge the same price. The smaller firms "follow the leader," changing their prices when the market leader's prices change rather than when their own demand or costs change. Some firms may charge a slight premium or slight discount, but they preserve the amount of difference. Thus minor gasoline retailers usually charge a bit less per litre than the major oil companies, without letting the difference increase or decrease.

Going-rate pricing is quite popular. Where costs are difficult to measure or competitive response is uncertain, firms feel that the going price is a good solution because it is thought to reflect the industry's collective wisdom.

AUCTION-TYPE PRICING   Auction-type pricing is growing more popular, especially with the growth of the Internet. There are over 2000 electronic marketplaces selling everything from pigs to used vehicles to cargo to chemicals. One major use of auctions is to dispose of excess inventories or used goods. Companies need to be aware of the three major types of auctions and their separate pricing procedures:

- *English auctions (ascending bids).* One seller and many buyers. On sites such as Yahoo! and eBay, the seller puts up an item and bidders raise the offer price until the top price is reached. English auctions are being used today for selling antiques, cattle, real estate, and used equipment and vehicles. After seeing ticket brokers and scalpers reap millions by charging what the market would bear, Ticketmaster Corp. began auctioning the best seats to concerts in late 2003 through its Web site, ticketmaster.com.[47]

- *Dutch auctions (descending bids).* One seller and many buyers, or one buyer and many sellers. In the first kind, an auctioneer announces a high price for a product and then slowly decreases the price until a bidder accepts the price. In the other, the buyer announces something that he or she wants to buy and then potential sellers compete to get the sale by offering the lowest price. Each seller sees what the last bid is and decides whether to go lower. FreeMarkets.com helped Royal Mail Group plc, the United Kingdom's public mail service company, save approximately 2.5 million pounds in part via an auction where 25 airlines bid for its international freight business.[48]

- *Sealed-bid auctions.* Would-be suppliers can submit only one bid and cannot know the other bids. Governments often use this method to procure supplies. A supplier will not bid below its cost but cannot bid too high for fear of losing the job. The net effect of these two pulls can be described in terms of the bid's *expected profit*. Using expected profit for setting price makes sense for the seller that makes many bids. The seller who bids only occasionally or who needs a particular contract badly will not find it advantageous to use expected profit. This criterion does not distinguish between a $1000 profit with a 0.10 probability and a $125 profit with a 0.80 probability. Yet the firm that wants to keep production going would prefer the second contract to the first.

Step 6: Selecting the Final Price

Pricing methods narrow the range from which the company must select its final price. In selecting that price, the company must consider additional factors, including the impact of other marketing activities, company pricing policies, gain-and-risk-sharing pricing, and the impact of price on other parties.

IMPACT OF OTHER MARKETING ACTIVITIES   The final price must take into account the brand's quality and advertising relative to the competition. In a classic study, Farris and Reibstein examined the relationships among relative price, relative quality, and relative advertising for 227 consumer businesses, and found the following:

- Brands with average relative quality but high relative advertising budgets were able to charge premium prices. Consumers apparently were willing to pay higher prices for known products than for unknown products.

- Brands with high relative quality and high relative advertising obtained the highest prices. Conversely, brands with low quality and low advertising charged the lowest prices.

- The positive relationship between high prices and high advertising held most strongly in the later stages of the product life cycle for market leaders.[49]

These findings suggest that price is not as important as quality and other benefits in the market offering. One study asked consumers to rate the importance of price and other attributes in using online retailing. Only 19 percent cared about price; far more cared about customer support (65 percent), on-time delivery (58 percent), and product shipping and handling (49 percent).[50]

COMPANY PRICING POLICIES The price must be consistent with company pricing policies. At the same time, companies are not averse to establishing pricing penalties under certain circumstances.[51]

Airlines charge fees to those who change their reservations on discount tickets. Banks charge fees for too many withdrawals in a month or for early withdrawal of a term deposit. Car rental companies charge penalties for no shows for specialty vehicles. Although these policies are often justifiable, they must be used judiciously so as not to unnecessarily alienate customers. (See "Marketing Insight: Stealth Price Increases.")

Many companies set up a pricing department to develop policies and establish or approve decisions. The aim is to ensure that salespeople quote prices that are reasonable to customers and profitable to the company. Dell Computer has developed innovative pricing techniques.

MARKETING INSIGHT

Stealth Price Increases

With consumers stubbornly resisting higher prices, companies are trying to figure out how to increase revenue without really raising prices. Increasingly, the solution has been through the addition of fees for what had once been free features. Although some consumers abhor "nickel-and-dime" pricing strategies, small additional charges can add up to a substantial source of revenue for North American firms.

The numbers can be staggering. Fees for consumers who pay bills online, bounce cheques, or use automated teller machines bring banks an estimated $30 billion annually. Retailers Target and Best Buy charge a 15 percent "restocking fee" for returning electronic products. Credit card late payments—up by 11 percent in 2003—exceed $10 billion in total. The telecommunications industry in general has been aggressive at adding fees for set-up, change of service, service termination, directory assistance, regulatory assessment, number portability, and cable hookup and equipment, costing consumers billions of dollars. By charging its long-distance customers a new 99 cents monthly "regulatory assessment fee," AT&T could bring in as much as $475 million.

This explosion of fees has a number of implications. Given that list prices stay fixed, they may result in inflation being understated. They also make it harder for consumers to compare competitive offerings. Although various citizen groups have been formed to pressure companies to roll back some of these fees, they don't always get a sympathetic ear from federal, provincial, and municipal governments who have been guilty of their own array of fees, fines, and penalties to raise necessary revenue.

Companies justify the extra fees as the only fair and viable way to cover expenses without losing customers. Many argue that it makes sense to charge a premium for added services that cost more to provide, rather than charge all customers the same amount regardless of whether or not they use the extra service. Breaking out charges and fees according to the services involved is seen as a way to keep the basic costs low. Companies also use fees as a means to weed out unprofitable customers or change their behaviour. Air Canada, for example, recently decreased its free baggage allowance. Passengers can now only take two bags weighing up to 50 pounds (23 kg). The previous allowance was 70 pounds (32 kg). If bags are overweight, passengers must pay an excess baggage fee of $35 for travel within North America and $60 for all international travel for bags weighing 50 to 70 pounds (23 to 32 kg).

Ultimately, the viability of extra fees will be decided in the marketplace and by the willingness of consumers to vote with their wallets and pay the fees or vote with their feet and move on.

Source: Adapted from Michael Arndt, "Fees! Fees! Fees!" *BusinessWeek*, September 29, 2003, pp. 99–104; "The Price Is Wrong," *The Economist*, May 25, 2002, pp. 59–60.

Dell

Dell uses a high-tech "cost-forecasting" system that enables it to scale its selling prices[52] based on consumer demand and the company's own costs. The company instituted this flexible pricing model in 2001 to maximize its margins during the economic slowdown. Dell managers get cost information from suppliers, which they then combine with knowledge about profit targets, delivery dates, and competition to set prices for business segments. On any given day, the same computer might sell at different prices depending on whether the purchaser is a government, small business, or home PC buyer. The cost-forecasting system may help to explain why Dell survived the 2001 high-tech meltdown. According to International Data Corporation, Dell held first place in the Canadian PC marketplace in 2004.[53]

GAIN-AND-RISK-SHARING PRICING Buyers may resist accepting a seller's proposal because of a high perceived level of risk. The seller has the option of offering to absorb part or all of the risk if he or she does not deliver the full promised value. Baxter Healthcare, for example, offered to develop an information management system that would save a hospital several million dollars over an eight-year period. When the hospital balked, Baxter offered to guarantee the savings. When Queen's School of Business launched its first private MBA program, it guaranteed students their salaries would increase or their tuition would be refunded. An increasing number of companies, especially business marketers who promise great savings with their equipment, may have to stand ready to guarantee the promised savings, and possibly participate in them if the gains are much greater than expected.

IMPACT OF PRICE ON OTHER PARTIES Management must also consider the reactions of other parties to the contemplated price.[54] How will distributors and dealers feel about it? If they do not make enough profit, they may not choose to bring the product to market. Will the sales force be willing to sell at that price? How will competitors react? Will suppliers raise their prices when they see the company's price? Will the government intervene and prevent this price from being charged?

While Wal-Mart's relentless drive to squeeze out costs and lower prices has benefited consumers, the downward price pressure is taking a big toll on suppliers such as Vlasic.[55]

Vlasic

In the late 1990s, when Wal-Mart offered giant gallon-sized jars of Vlasic pickles for only US$2.97, customers were overjoyed—even though they couldn't possibly eat them fast enough. Yet, what was lauded as a "statement item" for Wal-Mart—the kind of item that trumpets the company's commitment to low prices—reshaped every aspect of Vlasic's pickle business, and with devastating results. Here's the math: Vlasic's gallon jar of pickles went into every one of Wal-Mart's 3000 stores for US$2.97. At that price, Vlasic and Wal-Mart were making only a penny or two a jar. Yet, by selling 80 jars a week in every store, you're talking 240 000 jars every week. Quickly, the gallon jar started cannibalizing Vlasic's non-Wal-Mart business, since the company had to struggle to get enough pickles to fill the jars. The gallon jar chewed up the profit margins of its Wal-Mart account, which grew to 30 percent of Vlasic's business. While the sheer volume of pickles going out of Vlasic's plants gave Vlasic strong sales numbers, strong growth numbers, and a vaunted place in the world of pickles at Wal-Mart, the company's profits shrivelled. Eventually, Vlasic was able to get the price to just over half the original size jar for US$2.97.

Marketers need to know the laws regulating pricing. The Competition Act states that sellers must set prices without talking to competitors: price-fixing is illegal. Many federal and provincial statutes protect consumers against deceptive pricing practices. For example, it is illegal for a company to set artificially high "regular" prices, and then announce a "sale" at prices close to previous everyday prices.

Adapting the Price

Companies usually do not set a single price, but rather a pricing structure that reflects variations in geographical demand and costs, market-segment requirements, purchase timing, order levels, delivery frequency, guarantees, service contracts, and other factors. As a result of discounts, allowances, and promotional support, a company rarely realizes the same profit from each unit of a product that it sells. Here we will examine several price-adaptation strategies: geographical pricing, price discounts and allowances, promotional pricing, and differentiated pricing.

Geographical Pricing (Cash, Countertrade, Barter)

Geographical pricing involves the company in deciding how to price its products to different customers in different locations and countries.

Procter & Gamble

China is P&G's sixth largest market, yet two-thirds of China's population earns less than US$25 per month. So in 2003, P&G developed a tiered pricing initiative to help compete against cheaper local brands while still protecting the value of its global brands. P&G introduced a 320-gram bag of Tide Clean White for US$0.23, compared with US$0.33 for 350 grams of Tide Triple Action. The Clean White version doesn't offer such benefits as stain removal and fragrance, but it costs less to make and, according to P&G, outperforms every other brand at that price level.[56]

Should the company charge higher prices to distant customers to cover the higher shipping costs or a lower price to win additional business? How should exchange rates and the strength of different currencies be accounted for? A weak U.S. dollar in the summer of 2003 allowed some U.S. companies to mark up prices and still match more expensive imports. During this time, Dow Chemical was able to achieve price increases of almost 15 percent for 2003.[57]

Another issue is how to get paid. This issue is critical when buyers lack sufficient hard currency to pay for their purchases. Many buyers want to offer other items in payment, a practice known as **countertrade**. Companies are often forced to engage in countertrade if they want the business. Countertrade may account for 15 to 25 percent of world trade and takes several forms:[58] barter, compensation deals, buyback agreements, and offset.

- *Barter.* The direct exchange of goods, with no money and no third party involved. In 1993, Eminence S.A., one of France's major clothing makers, launched a five-year deal to barter US$25 million worth of underwear and sportswear to customers in eastern Europe, in exchange for a variety of goods and services, including global transportation and advertising space in eastern European magazines.

- *Compensation deal.* The seller receives some percentage of the payment in cash and the rest in products. A British aircraft manufacturer sold planes to Brazil for 70 percent cash and the rest in coffee.

- *Buyback arrangement.* The seller sells a plant, equipment, or technology to another country and agrees to accept as partial payment products manufactured with the supplied equipment. A U.S. chemical company built a plant for an Indian company and accepted partial payment in cash and the remainder in chemicals manufactured at the plant.

- *Offset.* The seller receives full payment in cash but agrees to spend a substantial amount of the money in that country within a stated time period. For example, PepsiCo sells its cola syrup to Russia for rubles and agrees to buy Russian vodka at a certain rate for sale in the United States.

Price Discounts and Allowances

Most companies will adjust their list price and give discounts and allowances for early payment, volume purchases, and off-season buying (see Table 14.4).[59] Companies must do this carefully or find that their profits are much less than planned.[60]

Discount pricing has become the modus operandi of a surprising number of companies offering both products and services. Some product categories tend to self-destruct by always being on sale. Salespeople, in particular, are quick to give discounts in order to close a sale. But word can get around

TABLE 14.4	PRICE DISCOUNTS AND ALLOWANCES
Cash Discount:	A price reduction to buyers who pay bills promptly. A typical example is "2/10, net 30," which means that payment is due within 30 days and that the buyer can deduct 2 percent by paying the bill within 10 days.
Quantity Discount:	A price reduction to those who buy large volumes. A typical example is "$10 per unit for less than 100 units; $9 per unit for 100 or more units." Quantity discounts must be offered equally to all customers and must not exceed the cost savings to the seller. They can be offered on each order placed or on the number of units ordered over a given period.
Functional Discount:	Discount (also called *trade discount*) offered by a manufacturer to trade-channel members if they will perform certain functions, such as selling, storing, and record-keeping. Manufacturers must offer the same functional discounts within each channel.
Seasonal Discount:	A price reduction to those who buy merchandise or services out of season. Hotels, motels, and airlines offer seasonal discounts in slow selling periods.
Allowance:	An extra payment designed to gain reseller participation in special programs. *Trade-in allowances* are granted for turning in an old item when buying a new one. *Promotional allowances* reward dealers for participating in advertising and sales support programs.

fast that the company's list price is "soft," and discounting becomes the norm. The discounts undermine the value perceptions of the offerings.

Some companies in an overcapacity situation are tempted to give discounts or even begin to supply a retailer with a store brand version of their product at a deep discount. Because the store brand is priced lower, however, it may start making inroads on the manufacturer's brand. Manufacturers should stop to consider the implications of supplying product at a discount to retailers because they may end up losing long-run profits in an effort to meet short-run volume goals.

When automakers get rebate-happy, the market just sits back and waits for a deal. When Ford was able to buck that trend, it achieved positive results.

Ford

In 2003, at a time when other auto companies were emphasizing rebates and 0 percent loans, Ford Motor Company actually raised average prices through "smart pricing." The company analyzed sales data from dealerships to predict which prices and incentives would be the most effective for different models in different markets. More marketing funds were allocated to high-margin but slow-selling models, such as the F-150 truck, as well as to push lucrative options and extras. Ford offered only a US$1000 rebate on the popular Escape small sport-utility vehicle, but US$3000 on the slower-selling Explorer model.[61] Ford actually increased market share during this time and estimated that smart pricing contributed one-third of its profit.

Kevin Clancy, chairman of Copernicus, a major marketing research and consulting firm, found that only between 15 and 35 percent of buyers in most categories are price-sensitive. People with higher incomes and higher product involvement willingly pay more for features, customer service, quality, added convenience, and the brand name. So it can be a mistake for a strong, distinctive brand to plunge into price discounting to respond to low-price attacks.[62]

At the same time, discounting can be a useful tool if the company can gain concessions in return, such as when the customer agrees to sign a three-year contract, is willing to order electronically, thus saving the company money, or agrees to buy in truckload quantities.

Sales management needs to monitor the proportion of customers who are receiving discounts, the average discount, and the particular salespeople who are overrelying on discounting. Higher levels of management should conduct a **net price analysis** to arrive at the "real price" of their offering.

The real price is affected not only by discounts, but by many other expenses (see the section "Promotional Pricing" below) that reduce the realized price: Suppose the company's list price is $3000. The average discount is $300. The company's promotional spending averages $450 (15 percent of the list price). Co-op advertising money of $150 is given to retailers to back the product. The company's net price is $2100, not $3000.

Promotional Pricing

Companies can use several pricing techniques to stimulate early purchase:

- *Loss-leader pricing.* Supermarkets and department stores often drop the price on well-known brands to stimulate additional store traffic. This pays if the revenue on the additional sales compensates for the lower margins on the loss-leader items. Manufacturers of loss-leader brands typically object because this practice can dilute the brand image and bring complaints from retailers who charge the list price. Manufacturers have tried to restrain intermediaries from loss-leader pricing through lobbying for retail-price-maintenance laws, but these laws have been revoked.

- *Special-event pricing.* Sellers will establish special prices in certain seasons to draw in more customers. Every August, for example, there are back-to-school sales.

- *Cash rebates.* Auto companies and other consumer-goods companies offer cash rebates to encourage purchase of the manufacturers' products within a specified time period. Rebates can help clear inventories without cutting the stated list price.

- *Low-interest financing.* Instead of cutting its price, the company can offer customers low-interest financing. Automakers have even announced no-interest financing to attract customers.

- *Longer payment terms.* Sellers, especially mortgage banks and auto companies, stretch loans over longer periods and thus lower the monthly payments. Consumers often worry less about the cost (i.e., the interest rate) of a loan and more about whether they can afford the monthly payment.

- *Warranties and service contracts.* Companies can promote sales by adding a free or low-cost warranty or service contract.

- *Psychological discounting.* This strategy involves setting an artificially high price and then offering the product at substantial savings; for example, "Was $359, now $299." Some unscrupulous retailers advertise these types of prices and then try to switch people to higher-priced items by stating the advertised item is sold out. Called "bait and switch," this is illegal under Canada's Competition Act. Retailers must offer rain cheques if no stock of the sale item is currently available.

Promotional-pricing strategies are often a zero-sum game. If they work, competitors copy them and they lose their effectiveness. If they do not work, they waste money that could have been put into other marketing tools, such as building up product quality and service or strengthening product image through advertising.

Differentiated Pricing

Companies often adjust their basic price to accommodate differences in customers, products, locations, and so on. **Price discrimination** occurs when a company sells a product or service at two or more prices that do not reflect a proportional difference in costs. In first-degree price discrimination, the seller charges a separate price to each customer depending on the intensity of his or her demand. In second-degree price discrimination, the seller charges less to buyers who buy a larger volume. In third-degree price discrimination, the seller charges different amounts to different classes of buyers, as in the following cases:

- *Customer-segment pricing.* Different customer groups are charged different prices for the same product or service. For example, museums often charge a lower admission fee to students and senior citizens.

- *Product-form pricing.* Different versions of the product are priced differently but not proportionately to their respective costs. Evian prices a 1.5-litre bottle of its mineral water at $2.00. It takes the same water and packages 50 mL in a moisturizer spray for $6.00. Through product-form pricing, Evian manages to charge $6.00 for 50 mL in one form, and about $0.07 for 50 mL in another.

- *Image pricing.* Some companies price the same product at two different levels based on image differences. A perfume manufacturer can put the perfume in one bottle, give it a name and image, and price it at $10 for 10 mL. It can put the same perfume in another bottle with a different name and image and price it at $30 for 10 mL.

- *Channel pricing.* Coca-Cola carries a different price depending on whether it is purchased in a fine restaurant, a fast-food restaurant, or a vending machine.

- *Location pricing.* The same product is priced differently at different locations even though the cost of offering it at each location is the same. A theatre varies its seat prices according to audience preferences for different locations.

- *Time pricing.* Prices are varied by season, day, or hour. Public utilities vary energy rates to commercial users by time of day and weekend versus weekday. Restaurants charge less to "early bird" customers. Hotels charge less on weekends.

The airline and hospitality industries use yield management systems and **yield pricing**, by which they offer discounted but limited early purchases, higher-priced late purchases, and the lowest rates on unsold inventory just before it expires.[63] Airlines charge different fares to passengers on the same flight, depending on the seating class; the time of day (morning or night coach); the day of the week (workday or weekend); the season; the person's company, past business, or status (youth, military, senior citizen); and so on. That's why on a flight from Toronto to Vancouver you might have paid $300 and be sitting across from someone who has paid $800. Take Continental Airlines: It launches 2000 flights a day and each flight has between 10 and 20 prices. Continental starts booking flights 330 days in advance, and every flying day is different from every other flying day. At any given moment the market has more than 7 million prices. And in a system that tracks the difference in prices and the price of competitors' offerings, airlines change thousands of prices a day! It's a system designed to punish procrastinators by charging them the highest possible prices.

The phenomenon of offering different pricing schedules to different consumers and dynamically adjusting prices is exploding.[64] See "Marketing Insight: Smart Pricing Takes Off" for more on how companies are using software packages that provide real-time controlled tests of actual consumer response to different pricing schedules.

Most consumers are probably not even aware of the degree to which they are the targets of discriminatory pricing. For instance, catalogue retailers like Victoria's Secret routinely send out catalogues that sell identical goods except at different prices. Consumers who live in a more free-spending region may see only the higher prices. Office-product superstore Staples also sends out office supply catalogues with different prices.

Some forms of price discrimination (in which sellers offer different price terms to different people within the same trade group) are illegal. However, price discrimination is legal if the seller can prove that its costs are different when selling different volumes or different qualities of the same product to different retailers. Predatory pricing—selling below cost with the intention of destroying competition—is unlawful.[65] Air Canada has been accused of predatory pricing on a number of occasions by competitors such as former airline Canada 3000, CanJet, and WestJet. Even if legal, some differentiated pricing may meet with a hostile reaction. Coca-Cola considered raising its vending machine soda prices on hot days using wireless technology, and lowering the price on cold days. Customers so disliked the idea that Coke abandoned it.

MARKETING INSIGHT

Smart Pricing Takes Off

Stelios Haji-Ioannou has made a fortune with easyJet, the eight-year-old airline that offers dynamically priced discount fares. In a nutshell, passengers pay less for a seat the earlier they buy. Stelios, as he's universally known, has applied the same yield management formula with varying degrees of success to car rentals, credit cards, and even Internet cafés. Now he's taking the concept to the movies. In 2003 he launched easyCinema, a 2000-seat 10-screen complex outside London, England. It is founded on the premise that 80 percent of cinema seats never see a bottom. At easyCinema tickets start at about 30 cents and rise with demand, rewarding patrons who book in advance or enjoy off-peak screenings. But the same system that netted a fortune for easyJet is facing hurdles: Britain's big movie distributors don't like getting a lump sum from Stelios rather than creaming off a high percentage of box-office revenue in the first weeks of a film's run (the least revenue-producing for Stelios). Still Stelios isn't giving up, and under the umbrella of easyGroup, the entrepreneur also plans to launch a cruise ship (easyCruise), a hotel chain (easyDorm), and even fast food (easyPizza)!

Stelios's easyGroup leads the field in what has been alternately called revenue management or yield management—pricing a perishable resource in accordance with demand from multiple customer segments to maximize revenue or profit. Prices are adjusted dynamically as a function of inventory level and time left in the selling season. Yet, "dynamic pricing" (or "smart pricing" or "scientific pricing") is not only the province of those with perishable inventory, such as the airline and hospitality industries. With the advent of Internet technology, there has been an explosion of information about customers and their preferences. Combine this capacity with businesses' pressing needs and you can see why we are entering a new era of pricing. In a sluggish economy, companies haven't been able to raise prices for years. Like easyGroup, they are taking a page from the airlines, which have been using revenue management techniques for 25 years.

The new dynamic pricing systems, produced by SAP and start-ups like DemandTec and ProfitLogic Inc., sift through massive databases available on a corporate intranet. These databases include up-to-date information about orders, promotions, product revenue, and stock levels in warehouses. Early adopters using Web-based pricing tools include Best Buy, Ford Motor Co., and Home Depot. Here are two success stories:

Casual Male

A retail chain offering clothing to big and tall men, Casual Male analyzed sales data to determine exactly how to "slice and dice" markets to offer the right prices at the right time. Using two years worth of sales data on 40 000 items, from ties to sweaters, in 410 stores, the company is able to estimate when and how much to cut prices. Pricing could reflect the fact that people in cooler regions stopped buying bathing suits in July, while demand stayed strong in some markets through August, and never really stopped in the southern United States. As a result of more flexible and responsive pricing, gross margins rose 25 percent in 2002.

DHL Worldwide Express Inc.

DHL used to have one-price-fits-all list prices for shipping packages, and when potential customers called for rates, DHL scared them off by asking for more than FedEx or UPS. With Web pricing tools, DHL tested the market by offering cold callers different prices to see how low prices could go and still make a profit. In the end, DHL wound up changing hundreds of prices. There were plenty of surprises. Most prices did go down, but the company didn't have to match the competition. In fact, by lowering prices a bit, DHL's ad hoc business not only stabilized but grew. For instance, of those people who called to get a quote, 17 percent actually shipped orders prior to the pricing overhaul. The new prices have increased the ratio to nearly 25 percent.

Constant price variation, however, can be tricky where consumer relationships are concerned. Research shows it tends to work best in situations where there's no bond between the buyer and the seller. One way to make it work is to offer customers a unique bundle of products and services to meet their needs precisely, making it harder for them to make price comparisons. This tactic is being used to sell software, which is vulnerable to price wars because the cost of producing more copies is near zero. Application service providers are "renting" their software and support by the month instead of selling an unlimited-use licence.

The tactic most companies favour, however, is to market perfect pricing as a reward for good behaviour rather than as a penalty. For instance, shipping company APL, Inc., rewards customers who can better predict how much cargo space they'll need with cheaper rates for booking early. Customers are getting savvier about how to avoid buyer's remorse. They are changing their buying behaviour to accommodate the new realities of dynamic pricing—where prices vary frequently by channels, products, customers, and time.

Sources: Ajit Kambil, "Are You Leaving Money on the Table?" *The Journal of Business Strategy* (January/February 2002): 40–43; Peter Coy, "The Power of Smart Pricing," *Business Week*, April 10, 2000, pp. 160–164; Charles Fishman, "Which Price Is Right?" *Fast Company* (March 2003): 92–102; Mark Ritson, "Stelios Shows There's an 'Easy' Way to a Smart Pricing Strategy," *Marketing*, April 10, 2003, p. 16; Ian Wylie, "In Movieland, Not So Easy," *Fast Company* (October 2003): 35; Bob Tedeschi, "E-Commerce Report," *New York Times*, September 2, 2002, p. C5; Faith Keenan, "The Price Is Really Right," *Business Week*, March 31, 2003, pp. 62–67. For a review of recent and seminal work linking pricing decisions with operational insights, see Moritz Fleischmann, Joseph M. Hall, and David F. Pyke, "Research Brief: Smart Pricing," *MIT Sloan Management Review* (Winter 2004): 9–13.

Initiating and Responding to Price Changes

Companies often face situations where they may need to cut or raise prices.

Initiating Price Cuts

Several circumstances might lead a firm to cut prices. One is excess plant capacity: The firm needs additional business and cannot generate it through increased sales effort, product improvement, or other measures. It may resort to aggressive pricing, but in initiating a price cut, the company may trigger a price war. McDonald's Restaurants of Canada is a case in point.

McDonald's Canada

In January 2002, McDonald's began testing its "McValue" menu, moving away from its recent brand-building strategy to one of price promotion. One analyst noted, "In Ontario, McDonald's new 'McMenu' test reportedly offers a McChicken, Big Xtra burger, Filet-O-Fish, or Egg McMuffin for 98 cents if consumers also purchase fries and a drink." McDonald's share price had been dropping steadily, and the move was seen as a means of driving short-term results to halt its stock price erosion. The price promotions were not a hit with stock analysts, however. As one pointedly noted, "When you begin to crave the temporary boost afforded by price promotions, it can ultimately erode the overall health of your brand. As soon as consumers begin choosing you primarily on price, other values they previously associated with your brand begin to diminish." It's not surprising, then, that McDonalds backed away from this tactic. In 2004 and 2005, it introduced its "Balanced Lifestyle Initiative," complete with new offerings like Deli Sandwiches and tips on living a more active life.[66]

Companies sometimes initiate price cuts in a *drive to dominate the market through lower costs.* Either the company starts with lower costs than its competitors or it initiates price cuts in the hope of gaining market share and lower costs. A price-cutting strategy involves possible traps:

- *Low-quality trap.* Consumers will assume that the quality is low.
- *Fragile-market-share trap.* A low price buys market share but not market loyalty. The same customers will shift to any lower-priced firm that comes along.
- *Shallow-pockets trap.* The higher-priced competitors may cut their prices and may have longer staying power because of deeper cash reserves.

Initiating Price Increases

A successful price increase can raise profits considerably. For example, if the company's profit margin is 3 percent of sales, a 1 percent price increase will increase profits by 33 percent if sales volume is unaffected. This situation is illustrated in Table 14.5. The assumption is that a company charged $10 and sold 100 units and had costs of $970, leaving a profit of $30, or 3 percent on sales. By raising its price by 10 cents (1 percent price increase), it boosted its profits by 33 percent, assuming the same sales volume.

A major circumstance provoking price increases is *cost inflation.* Rising costs unmatched by productivity gains squeeze profit margins and lead companies to regular rounds of price increases. Companies often raise their prices by more than the cost increase, in anticipation of further inflation or government price controls, in a practice called *anticipatory pricing.*

TABLE 14.5	PROFITS BEFORE AND AFTER A PRICE INCREASE	
	Before	**After**
Price	$ 10	$10.10 (a 1 percent price increase)
Units sold	100	100
Revenue	$1000	$1010
Costs	−970	2970
Profit	$ 30	$ 40 (a 33.3 percent profit increase)

Another factor leading to price increases is *overdemand*. When a company cannot supply all of its customers, it can raise its prices, ration supplies to customers, or both. The price can be increased in the following ways. Each has a different impact on buyers.

- *Delayed quotation pricing.* The company does not set a final price until the product is finished or delivered. This pricing is prevalent in industries with long production lead times, such as industrial construction and heavy equipment.

- *Escalator clauses.* The company requires the customer to pay today's price and all or part of any inflation increase that takes place before delivery. An escalator clause bases price increases on some specified price index. Escalator clauses are found in contracts for major industrial projects, like aircraft construction and bridge building.

- *Unbundling.* The company maintains its price but removes or prices separately one or more elements that were part of the former offer, such as free delivery or installation. Car companies sometimes add anti-lock brakes and passenger-side airbags as supplementary extras to their vehicles.

- *Reduction of discounts.* The company instructs its sales force not to offer its normal cash and quantity discounts.

A company needs to decide whether to raise its price sharply on a one-time basis or to raise it by small amounts several times. Generally, consumers prefer small price increases on a regular basis to sudden, sharp increases.

In passing price increases on to customers, the company must avoid looking like a price gouger.[67] Companies also need to think of who will bear the brunt of increased prices. Customer memories are long, and they can turn against companies they perceive as price gougers. Price hikes without corresponding investments in the value of the brand increase vulnerability to lower-priced competition. Consumers may be willing to "trade down" because they no longer can justify to themselves that the higher-priced brand is worth it. This happened to Kraft.

Kraft Foods Inc.

Early in 2003, Kraft responded to increasing commodity costs for coffee and cheese by raising its own prices. The move widened the gap between Kraft's brand-name items and its generic competitors, many of which held the line on price increases. Recession-weary consumers flocked to the cheaper choices. As sales fell, Kraft back-pedalled, rolling back many prices and flooding the market with new coupons and promotions. It was a costly misstep. Kraft, which typically spends about US$900 million a year on marketing, spent an extra US$200 million to lure back lost customers. Analysts and other observers questioned whether the company would have been better off boosting margins through additional cost-cutting, including reduced ad spending.[68]

Several techniques help consumers avoid sticker shock and a hostile reaction when prices rise: One is that a sense of fairness must surround any price increase, and customers must be given advance notice so they can do forward buying or shop around. Sharp price increases need to be explained in understandable terms. Making low-visibility price moves first is also a good technique: Eliminating discounts, increasing minimum order sizes, and curtailing production of low-margin products are some examples; and contracts or bids for long-term projects should contain escalator clauses based on such factors as increases in recognized national price indexes.[69] "Marketing Memo: Marketing Strategies to Avoid Raising Prices" describes other means by which companies can respond to higher costs or overdemand without raising prices.

Reactions to Price Changes

Any price change can provoke a response from customers, competitors, distributors, suppliers, and even government.

CUSTOMER REACTIONS   Customers often question the motivation behind price changes.[70] A price cut can be interpreted in different ways: The item is about to be replaced by a new model; the item is faulty and is not selling well; the firm is in financial trouble; the price will come down even further; the quality has been reduced. A price increase, which would normally deter sales, may carry some positive meanings to customers: The item is "hot" and represents an unusually good value.

COMPETITOR REACTIONS Competitors are most likely to react when the number of firms is small, the product is homogeneous, and buyers are highly informed. Competitor reactions can be a special problem when they have a strong value proposition.

Zantac versus Tagamet

Pharmaceutical company Glaxo introduced its ulcer medication Zantac to attack market incumbent Tagamet. The conventional wisdom was that, as the "second one in," Glaxo should price Zantac 10 percent below Tagamet. CEO Paul Girolam knew that Zantac was superior to Tagamet in terms of fewer drug interactions and side effects and more convenient dosing. Glaxo introduced Zantac at a significant price premium over Tagamet and still gained the market-leader position.[71]

How can a firm anticipate a competitor's reactions? One way is to assume that the competitor reacts in a set way to price changes. The other is to assume that the competitor treats each price change as a fresh challenge and reacts according to self-interest at the time. Now the company will need to research the competitor's current financial situation, recent sales, customer loyalty, and corporate objectives. If the competitor has a market-share objective, it is likely to match the price change.[72] If it has a profit-maximization objective, it may react by increasing the advertising budget or improving product quality.

The problem is complicated because the competitor can put different interpretations on a price cut: that the company is trying to steal the market, that the company is doing poorly and trying to boost its sales, or that the company wants the whole industry to reduce prices to stimulate total demand.

Responding to Competitors' Price Changes

How should a firm respond to a price cut initiated by a competitor? In markets characterized by high product homogeneity, the firm should search for ways to enhance its augmented product. If it cannot find any, it will have to meet the price reduction. If the competitor raises its price in a homogeneous product market, other firms might not match it unless the increase will benefit the industry as a whole. Then the leader will have to roll back the increase.

Marketing Memo

Marketing Strategies to Avoid Raising Prices

Given strong consumer resistance to price hikes, marketers go to great lengths to find alternative approaches that will allow them avoid increasing prices when they otherwise would have done so. Here are a few popular ones:

- Shrinking the amount of product instead of raising the price. (Hershey Foods maintained its chocolate bar price but trimmed its size. Nestlé maintained its size but raised the price.)
- Substituting less expensive materials or ingredients. (Many candy companies substituted synthetic chocolate for real chocolate to fight price increases in cocoa.)
- Reducing or removing product features. (Sears engineered down a number of its appliances so they could be priced competitively with those sold in discount stores.)
- Removing or reducing product services, such as installation or free delivery.
- Using less expensive packaging material or larger package sizes.
- Reducing the number of sizes and models offered.
- Creating new economy brands. (Jewel food stores introduced 170 generic items selling at 10 percent to 30 percent less than national brands.)

In nonhomogeneous product markets, a firm has more latitude. It needs to consider the following issues: (1) Why did the competitor change the price? To steal the market, to utilize excess capacity, to meet changing cost conditions, or to lead an industry-wide price change? (2) Does the competitor plan to make the price change temporary or permanent? (3) What will happen to the company's market share and profits if it does not respond? Are other companies going to respond? (4) What are the competitor's and other firms' responses likely to be to each possible reaction?

Market leaders frequently face aggressive price-cutting by smaller firms trying to build market share. Using price, Fuji attacks Kodak, Schick attacks Gillette, and AMD attacks Intel. Brand leaders also face lower-priced private-store brands. The brand leader can respond in several ways:

- *Maintain price.* The leader might maintain its price and profit margin, believing that (1) it would lose too much profit if it reduced its price, (2) it would not lose much market share, and (3) it could regain market share when necessary. However, the argument against price maintenance

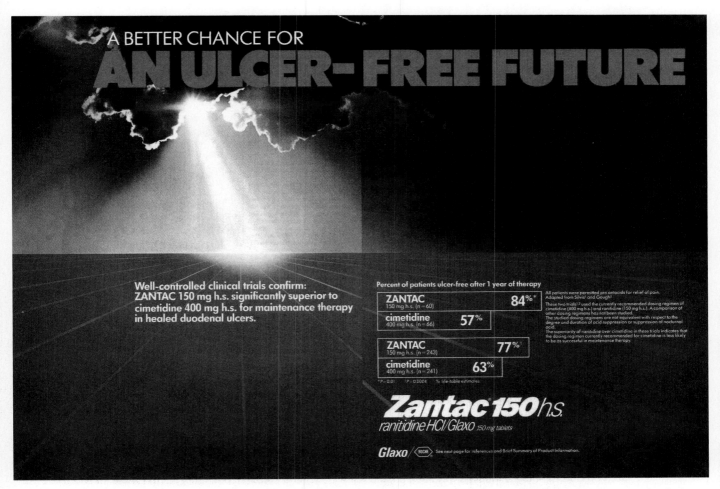

Print ad for Zantac, which took market leadership from competitor Tagamet despite being introduced at a price premium.

is that the attacker gets more confident, the leader's sales force gets demoralized, and the leader loses more share than expected. The leader panics, lowers price to regain share, and finds that regaining its market position is more difficult than expected.

- *Maintain price and add value.* The leader could improve its product, services, and communications. The firm may find it cheaper to maintain price and spend money to improve perceived quality than to cut price and operate at a lower margin.

- *Reduce price.* The leader might drop its price to match the competitor's price. It might do so because (1) its costs fall with volume, (2) it would lose market share because the market is price-sensitive, and (3) it would be hard to rebuild market share once it is lost. This action will cut profits in the short run.

- *Increase price and improve quality.* The leader might raise its price and introduce new brands to bracket the attacking brand.

- *Launch a low-price fighter line.* It might add lower-priced items to the line or create a separate, lower-priced brand.

The best response varies with the situation. The company has to consider the product's stage in the life cycle, its importance in the company's portfolio, the competitor's intentions and resources, the market's price and quality sensitivity, the behaviour of costs with volume, and the company's alternative opportunities.

An extended analysis of alternatives may not be feasible when the attack occurs. The company may have to react decisively within hours or days. It would make better sense to anticipate possible competitors' price changes and to prepare contingent responses. Figure 14.7 shows a *price-reaction program* to be used if a competitor cuts prices. Reaction programs for meeting price changes find their greatest application in industries where price changes occur with some frequency and where it is important to react quickly—for example, in the meatpacking, lumber, and oil industries.

FIGURE 14.7

Price-Reaction Program for Meeting a Competitor's Price Cut

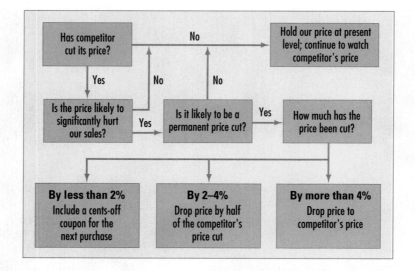

SUMMARY

1. Despite the increased role of nonprice factors in modern marketing, price remains a critical element of the marketing mix. Price is the only one of the four Ps that produces revenue; the others produce costs.

2. In setting pricing policy, a company follows a six-step procedure. It selects its pricing objective. It estimates the demand curve, the probable quantities it will sell at each possible price. It estimates how its costs vary at different levels of output, at different levels of accumulated production experience, and for differentiated marketing offers. It examines competitors' costs, prices, and offers. It selects a pricing method. It selects the final price.

3. Companies do not usually set a single price, but rather a pricing structure that reflects variations in geographical demand and costs, market-segment requirements, purchase timing, order levels, and other factors. Several price-adaptation strategies are available: (1) geographical pricing; (2) price discounts and allowances; (3) promotional pricing; and (4) discriminatory pricing.

4. After developing pricing strategies, firms often face situations in which they need to change prices. A price decrease might be brought about by excess plant capacity, declining market share, a desire to dominate the market through lower costs, or economic recession. A price increase might be brought about by cost inflation or overdemand. Companies must carefully manage customer perceptions in raising prices.

5. Companies must anticipate competitor price changes and prepare contingent responses. A number of possible responses are possible in terms of maintaining or changing price or quality.

6. The firm facing a competitor's price change must try to understand the competitor's intent and the likely duration of the change. Strategy often depends on whether a firm is producing homogeneous or nonhomogeneous products. Market leaders attacked by lower-priced competitors can choose to maintain price, raise the perceived quality of their product, reduce price, increase price and improve quality, or launch a low-priced fighter line.

APPLICATIONS

Marketing Debate: Is the Right Price a Fair Price?

Prices are often set to satisfy demand or to reflect the premium that consumers are willing to pay for a product or service. Some critics shudder, however, at the thought of $2 bottles of water, $150 running shoes, and $500 concert tickets.

Take a position: Prices should reflect the value that consumers are willing to pay versus Prices should primarily just reflect the cost involved in making a product or service.

Marketing Discussion

Think of the various pricing methods described in the chapter—markup pricing, target-return pricing, perceived value pricing, value pricing, going rate pricing, and auction-type pricing. As a consumer, which method do you personally prefer to deal with? Why? If the average price were to stay the same, which would you prefer: (1) for firms to set one price and not deviate or (2) to employ slightly higher prices most of the year, but slightly lower discounted prices or specials for certain occasions.

Marketing Spotlight: eBay

Pierre Omidayar, a French-Iranian immigrant to the United States, created eBay as a way to help his girlfriend sell and trade her Pez candy dispenser collection. Soon the site grew into a broader auction site where consumers could auction collectibles like baseball cards and Barbie dolls. The momentum continued, with sellers posting new and unusual items and customers coming to eBay looking for everyday products from used furniture to new digital cameras. Small businesses discovered that eBay was an efficient way to reach consumers and other businesses. Large companies saw eBay as an opportunity to sell bulk lots of unsold inventory. By helping buyers get the best price for their items and by letting customers decide the price they want to pay for products, eBay had created a pricing revolution.

By 2003, eBay was transacting US$23 billion in worldwide sales in 23 merchandise categories. The site has 62 million registered users and receives 43 million unique visitors a month. Yet, eBay itself doesn't buy any inventory or own the products on its site. It earns its money by collecting a fee for the auction listing, plus a commission when the sale is completed. With eBay's expansion into other categories, collectibles now make up only 13 percent of eBay sales. eBay is constantly creating new categories of merchandise for buyers and businesses, like used restaurant equipment (pots, pans, cappuccino makers).

For example, after noticing that someone was auctioning a real Ferrari in the toy car segment of eBay, eBay created a new category: used cars. Traditionally, used cars were sold locally, but eBay Motors created a used-car marketplace that is now one of eBay's largest segments. Given the reputation of used-car salespeople, how could anyone trust a seemingly anonymous car seller in a distant location? eBay Motors created the following trust-building elements in its used-car brokerage operations:

- Online reputation ratings of buyers and sellers
- Escrow service for holding funds until the car is delivered
- Fraud-protection warranty of up to US$20 000
- Network of available third-party inspectors

The majority of car listings on eBay are from dealers. It sounds surprising, but in fact dealers get a bargain: for US$40, a dealer can reach an international audience. In contrast, dealers spend upward of US$500 to get one local customer to buy one car, according to the National Automotive Dealers Association. Thus, eBay is an amazingly efficient distribution channel for dealers. The dealers also get a better price because more people look at the car online, which increases the chance of finding someone who really wants that car. In any given month (such as April 2003), 8 million customers come to the eBay Motors site. Each auction gets an average of seven to eight bids.

And the company doesn't just deal in collectibles and cars. eBay is positioning itself to be a global giant: part international swap meet, part clearinghouse for the world's manufacturers and retailers. For instance, it is trying to get its PayPal electronic payment system established worldwide and it is beefing up its U.S. site by adding new categories and big partners like Sears, Sharper Image, and IBM, all of which unload excess inventory over eBay.

Although eBay began as an auction site, it evolved to also offer a fixed-price "buy it now" option to buyers who didn't want to wait for an auction and were willing to pay the price set by the seller. For years, buyers and sellers used eBay as an informal guide to market value. eBay became the de facto arbiter of price. A consumer or businessperson who wanted to know the going price for anything from a copier to a new DVD player checked on eBay. Companies with a new product design who wanted to test its consumer appeal and pricing could try it out on eBay. In late 2003, eBay began selling sales price data on thousands of goods auctioned on the site. PGA.com, for example, uses eBay's data to set market values for more than 2000 models of used golf clubs.

The pricing revolution gives customers control. Customers choose the price they want to pay. At the same time, the efficiency and wide reach of the site lets sellers make good margins. eBay charges a listing fee and a commission that ranges from 1 to 5 percent. Merchants report profit margins of 40 percent. Of the thousands of Internet auction sites, eBay is the largest and was profitable from the get-go. It expects to hit US$3 billion in revenue by the end of 2004 and netted US$422 million in 2003. In the next two years, eBay's revenues should soar to over US$4 billion in annual sales, coming mainly from the fees it collects on more than US$40 billion worth of merchandise that it sells over its site. Not bad for a company that doesn't actually sell anything.

DISCUSSION QUESTIONS

1. What are the key success factors for eBay?

2. Where is eBay vulnerable? What should it watch out for?

3. What recommendations would you make to senior marketing executives moving forward? What should they be sure to do with the company's marketing?

Sources: Betsy Streisand, "Make New Sales, but Keep the Old," *U.S. News & World Report*, February 16, 2004, p. 40; "Booting Online," *The Economist*, January 24, 2004, p. 30; David Kirkpatrick, "Why 'Bottom Up' Is On Its Way Up," *Fortune*, January 26, 2004; "Simon Rothman," *Fast Company* (May 2003): 68; Patricia Seybold, *The Customer Revolution* (New York: Crown Business, 2001); Chris Taylor, "Getting a Little Wild on the Net," *Time*, December 1, 2003, p. 7; Adam Lashinsky, "There's No Stopping eBay," *Fortune*, February 23, 2004, p. 78.

6

DELIVERING VALUE

IN THIS CHAPTER, WE WILL ADDRESS THE FOLLOWING QUESTIONS:

- What is a marketing channel system and value network?

- What work do marketing channels perform?

- How should channels be designed?

- What decisions do companies face in managing their channels?

- How should companies integrate channels and manage channel conflict?

- What is the future for e-commerce?

CHAPTER 15

Designing and Managing Marketing Channels and Value Networks

PROFILE: CANADIAN MARKETING EXCELLENCE

Developing new channels and creating real value is not easy. Furthermore, creating a strong revenue-generating e-business model is even more difficult. In fact, as the burst of the dot-com bubble illustrated, setting up a successful e-business requires just as much patience, investment, and diligence as does a traditional business. Longueuil, Quebec–based e-business Mediagrif Interactive Technologies Inc., however, has joined the ranks of eBay and Amazon in successfully forging into this new and challenging territory.

Effectively an eBay for business, Mediagrif helps buyers and sellers interact. Today it prides itself on being a world-leading operator of e-business networks and a provider of complete e-business solutions. It provides the technology behind online marketplaces, where industry buyers and suppliers can connect to do business. Some analysts refer to it as an online business-to-business brokerage. The company's e-business networks allow buyers and sellers within specific industries to source, purchase, or sell products and to exchange information over the Internet. The company operates 12 networks, including the Broker Forum, Power Source On-Line, Telecom Finders, Polygon, and Global Wine & Spirits. It also owns and operates the MERX e-tendering service, the official distributor of tender documents for the Canadian federal government, and is a leading provider of government bid aggregation services and e-procurement services in the United States. Customer service is provided 24 hours a day, in more than 20 languages. It serves over 33 000 customers in 60 countries. Mediagrif was founded in 1996, and since then has grown to over 400 employees, with revenues of $48 million in 2004.

When Mediagrif began operations, founder Denis Gadbois used his experience as a former IT executive to identify an opportunity for an online computer-parts network, the Broker Forum. It proved to be a smart place to start, since tech-savvy people were already using the Internet to look for deals on computer parts. The company also attributed much of its success to its pricing strategy, which charges users a membership fee rather than a commission on sales. While the company understood that both methods could generate sufficient revenue, it felt that a commission-based service would generate less interest.

To help maintain the brisk pace of sales, the firm also worked hard to know its customers. It scrutinized the activity on the Web site very carefully, rooting out members who had not accessed the site for an extended period, and then asked them for feedback, with the aim of better understanding what was driving customers both to and from the site. Such information became an important asset, helping Mediagrif attain a membership renewal rate consistently between 70 and 80 percent.

After a series of acquisitions and partnerships to develop new networks, the company went public in 2000 and broadened its networks beyond computer parts: It launched Telecom Finders for selling used telecommunications parts; B2B Vertical Markets Inc., an electronic-banking joint venture with the Royal Bank; a partnership with the Société des alcools du Québec (SAQ); Global Wine & Spirits, a virtual marketplace that allows buyers and sellers to exchange information; Medical Equipment Finders; Viewtrak, which collects animal-breeding and production data; Truck Parts Locator; Carrus Technologies, which deals with automotive parts; and its most recent purchase, the Merx platform, an electronic tendering service for public-sector contracts (acquired from BMO Financial Group in December 2002). Most recently, the company announced that it would enter the diamond and jewellery industry with the acquisition of PolyGroup Ltd. in 2004.

With strong profits and very distinct expertise in building e-business networks, Mediagrif has created value for a large number of customers with distinctly different needs through its ever-growing Internet channels. The company's success is mirrored in its financial statements. Revenue has been growing at astounding rates: by 37.6 percent in 2003, by 48.7 percent in 2004, and by 46.3 percent in 2005. Mediagrif, which has been racking up awards in recognition of its success, was twice selected as one of Canada's 50 best-managed companies, and was honoured at the 2004 Deloitte & Touche Canadian Technology Fast 50 awards, ranking 16th in Canada and third in Quebec.

Sources: Raizel Robin, "Net Gains," *Canadian Business Magazine Online*, **www.canadianbusiness.com**, October 27, 2003 (viewed October 6, 2004); Mediagrif Web site, **www.mediagrif.com** (viewed October 6, 2004); GlobeInvestor Web site, **www.theglobeandmail.com** (viewed October 6, 2004).

Successful value creation needs successful value delivery. Holistic marketers are increasingly taking a value network view of their businesses. Instead of limiting their focus to their immediate suppliers, distributors, and customers, they are examining the whole supply chain that links raw materials, components, and manufactured goods and shows how they move toward the final consumers. Companies are looking at their suppliers' suppliers upstream and at their distributors' customers downstream. They are looking at customer segments and how company resources can best be organized to meet needs. Failure to coordinate the value network properly can have dire consequences, as discount chain Kmart discovered. Unable to match Wal-Mart's everyday low prices and plagued by a terrible replenishment system, which resulted in numerous hot sellers being out of stock, Kmart filed for bankruptcy in 2002.[1]

Companies today must build and manage a continuously evolving value network. In this chapter, we consider strategic and tactical issues with marketing channels and value networks. We will examine marketing channel issues from the perspective of retailers, wholesalers, and physical-distribution agencies in Chapter 16.

Marketing Channels and Value Networks

Most producers do not sell their goods directly to the final users; between them stands a set of intermediaries performing a variety of functions. These intermediaries constitute a marketing channel (also called a trade channel or distribution channel). Formally, **marketing channels** are sets of inter-dependent organizations involved in the process of making a product or service available for use or consumption. They are the set of pathways a product or service follows after production, culminating in purchase and use by the final end user.[2]

Some intermediaries—such as wholesalers and retailers—buy, take title to, and resell the merchandise; they are called *merchants*. Others—brokers, manufacturers' representatives, sales agents—search for customers and may negotiate on the producer's behalf but do not take title to the goods; they are called *agents*. Still others—transportation companies, independent warehouses, banks, advertising agencies—assist in the distribution process but neither take title to goods nor negotiate purchases or sales; they are called *facilitators*.

The Importance of Channels

A **marketing channel system** is the particular set of marketing channels employed by a firm. Decisions about the marketing channel system are among the most critical facing management. In North America, channel members collectively earn margins that account for 30 to 50 percent of the ultimate selling price. In contrast, advertising typically accounts for less than 5 to 7 percent of the final price.[3] Marketing channels also represent a substantial opportunity cost. Converting potential buyers into profitable orders is one of the chief roles of marketing channels. Marketing channels must not just *serve* markets—they must also *make* markets.[4]

The channels chosen affect all other marketing decisions. The company's pricing depends on whether it uses mass merchandisers or high-quality boutiques. The firm's sales force and advertising decisions depend on how much training and motivation dealers need. In addition, channel decisions involve relatively long-term commitments to other firms as well as a set of policies and procedures. When an automaker signs up independent dealers to sell its automobiles, the automaker cannot buy them out the next day and replace them with company-owned outlets.[5]

In managing its intermediaries, the firm must decide how much effort to devote to push versus pull marketing. A **push strategy** involves the manufacturer using its sales force and trade promotion money to induce intermediaries to carry, promote, and sell the product to end users. Push strategy is appropriate where there is low brand loyalty in a category, brand choice is made in the store, the product is an impulse item, and product benefits are well understood. A **pull strategy** involves the manufacturer using advertising and promotion to induce consumers to ask intermediaries for the product, thus inducing the intermediaries to order it. Pull strategy is appropriate when there is high brand loyalty and high involvement in the category, when people perceive differences between brands, and when people choose the brand before they go to the store. Top marketing companies such as Nike, Intel, and Coca-Cola skillfully employ both push and pull strategies. As the following case illustrates, a pull campaign can be very extensive:

Men with Brooms

The Canadian film *Men with Brooms* hoped to sweep consumers off their feet when it launched in March 2002. And it put up in excess of $1 million to accomplish this task, an unusually large budget for a Canadian film. Says Frank Mendicino, vice-president of marketing, motion pictures distribution at Alliance Atlantis, "It's a great Canadian film and it deserved a lot of push and a lot of aggressive marketing" to both Canadian and American audiences. Alliance advertised heavily during the 2002 Olympic hockey series, which drew over 10 million viewers. In addition to TV ads, Alliance used movie theatre banners and posters, teasers and trailers before *The Lord of the Rings*, a cross-country press junket with a private jet, a 15-song soundtrack, and an e-mail campaign through the Canadian Curling Association to pull people into the theatres.[6]

Channel Development

A new firm typically starts as a local operation selling in a limited market, using existing intermediaries. The number of such intermediaries is apt to be limited: a few manufacturers' sales agents, a few wholesalers, several established retailers, a few trucking companies, and a few warehouses. Deciding on the best channels might not be a problem. The problem might be to convince the available intermediaries to handle the firm's line.

If the firm is successful, it might branch into new markets and use different channels in different markets. In smaller markets, the firm might sell directly to retailers; in larger markets, it might sell through distributors. In rural areas, it might work with general-goods merchants; in urban areas, with limited-line merchants. In one part of the country, it might grant exclusive franchises; in another, it might sell through all outlets willing to handle the merchandise. In one country it might use international sales agents; in another, it might partner with a local firm.[7] In short, the channel system evolves in response to local opportunities and conditions.

Today's successful companies are also multiplying the number of "go-to-market" or **hybrid** channels in any one market area:

- IBM uses its sales force to sell to large accounts, outbound telemarketing to sell to medium-sized accounts, direct mail with an inbound number for small accounts, retailers to sell to still smaller accounts, and the Internet to sell specialty items.

- TD Canada Trust enables its customers to do transactions in its branches, through ABMs, over the phone, or on the Internet.

- Staples markets through its traditional retail channel, a direct-response Internet site, virtual malls, and thousands of links on affiliated sites.

Companies that manage hybrid channels must make sure these channels work well together and match each target customer's preferred ways of doing business. Customers expect *channel integration,* characterized by the following features:

- The ability to order a product online and pick it up at a convenient retail location.
- The ability to return an online-ordered product to a nearby store of the retailer.
- The right to receive discounts based on total online and offline purchases.

"Marketing Memo: Multi-Channel Shopping Checklist" offers some concrete advice on channel integration. Here are a couple of examples of how retailers are managing their hybrid channels in order to make the online experience resemble parts of the offline experience:

La Senza

In order to address the reservations of shoppers who miss the tactile aspect of shopping for clothing in person, Montreal-based lingerie retailer La Senza launched a live Webcast of a holiday fashion show in November 2003. Following a model first tried by U.S.-based Victoria's Secret, the company broadcast a runway event featuring models wearing La Senza's silk and satin underwear. The Webcast was e-mailed to 200 000 La Senza subscribers.

Danier Leather

Toronto-based Danier Leather has developed an e-commerce site (www.danier.com) that uses Webcam software to view merchandise at the company's Toronto flagship store. In order to approximate the offline experience, a live chat option allows visitors to connect directly with store staff. For example, customers can ask staff to try on a jacket or other items for size. Since shopping for leather is as much about the feel of a jacket or pant as it is about the look of the product, the Danier site also features a "touch-and-smell" button, which enables customers to request leather swatches free of charge. The company has been impressed by the customer response; many show up at the store with printed pages from the Web site. In addition, both in-store and online sales are growing at double-digit rates.[8]

Different consumers, however, have different needs during the purchase process. Nunes and Cespedes argue that in many markets, buyers fall into one of four categories:[9]

1. *Habitual shoppers* purchase from the same places in the same manner over time.
2. *High-value deal seekers* know their needs and "channel surf" a great deal before buying at the lowest possible price.

3. *Variety-loving shoppers* gather information in many channels, take advantage of high-touch services, and then buy in their favourite channel, regardless of price.

4. *High-involvement shoppers* gather information in all channels, make their purchase in a low-cost channel, but take advantage of customer support from a high-touch channel.

The same consumer may choose to use different channels for different functions in making a purchase. A consumer may choose to browse through a catalogue before visiting a store or take a test drive at a dealer before ordering a car online.

Consumers may seek different types of channels depending on the particular types of goods involved. Some consumers are willing to "trade up" to retailers offering higher-end goods such as TAG Heuer watches or Callaway golf clubs; these same consumers are also willing to "trade down" to discount retailers to buy private-label paper towels, detergent, or vitamins.[10]

Value Networks

A supply chain view of a firm sees markets as destination points and amounts to a linear view of the flow. The company should first think of the target market, however, and then design the supply chain backward from that point. This view has been called **demand chain planning**. Northwestern University's Don Schultz says: "A demand chain management approach doesn't just push things through the system. It emphasizes what solutions consumers are looking for, not what products we are trying to sell them." Schultz has suggested that the traditional marketing "four Ps" be replaced by a new acronym, SIVA, which stands for solutions, information, value, and access.[11]

Marketing Memo

Multi-Channel Shopping Checklist

During the 2003 back-to-school season, the e-tailing group, an e-commerce consulting firm in Chicago, sent mystery shoppers to visit retail locations of 16 e-tailers to test their claims of an integrated shopping experience in the online/retail returns process. Overall, the study found that 44 percent of in-store returns of merchandise purchased online required a store manager to override the retail system in order to accept the return. In response to this and several other inadequacies revealed by the study, the e-tailing group created a "Best of Breed Multi-Channel Shopping Checklist" to help marketers better integrate online and offline channels:

- Train all store associates on processes for online merchandise returns.

- List your company's 800 number on the Web home page, and be sure your customer service hours of operation are easily accessible.

- Provide an information centre that is easy to navigate and includes contact information, FAQs, guarantees, return policies, and tips for first-time customers.

- Implement a store locator feature that includes store locations, hours, and events.

- Make store pickup for purchases an option and include real-time inventory levels, where applicable.

- Post the store's weekly circular online for a more complete multi-channel experience.

- Offer gift certificates that can be redeemed online and offline.

- Send e-mail notifications of the order, shipping, and return credit; include a reminder of the returns process in notifications as well as a link to your store locator.

- Supply all pertinent/compatible information for store return of merchandise on the packing slip or invoice.

Source: Excerpted from Hallie Mummert, "Multi-Channel Marketers Earn a 'C+' on Returns," *Target Marketing* (October 2003): 158.

An even broader view sees a company at the centre of a **value network**—a system of partnerships and alliances that a firm creates to source, augment, and deliver its offerings. A value network includes a firm's suppliers, its suppliers' suppliers, its immediate customers, and their end customers. The value network includes valued relations with others such as university researchers and government approval agencies.

A company needs to orchestrate these parties to enable it to deliver superior value to the target market. Palm, the leading manufacturer of handheld devices, is a whole community of suppliers and assemblers of semiconductor components, plastic cases, LCD displays, and accessories; of offline and online resellers; and of 275 000 developers who have created over 21 000 software programs and 100 hardware add-ons for the Palm operating systems for handheld computers and smartphones.

Demand chain planning yields several insights. First, the company can estimate whether more money is made upstream or downstream, in case it might want to integrate backward or forward. Second, the company is more aware of disturbances anywhere in the supply chain that might cause costs, prices, or supplies to change suddenly. Third, companies can go online with their business partners to carry on faster and more accurate communications, transactions, and payments to reduce costs, speed up information, and increase accuracy. With the advent of the Internet, companies are forming more numerous and complex relationships with other firms. For example, Ford not only manages numerous supply chains, but also sponsors or transacts on many B2B Web sites and exchanges as needs arise.

Managing this value network has required companies to make increasing investments in information technology (IT) and software. They have invited such software firms as SAP and Oracle to design comprehensive *enterprise resource planning* (ERP) systems to manage cash flow, manufacturing, human resources, purchasing, and other major functions within a unified framework. They hope to break up department silos and carry out core business processes more seamlessly. In most cases, however, companies are still a long way from truly comprehensive ERP systems.

Marketers, for their part, have traditionally focused on the side of the value network that looks toward the customer. In the future, they will increasingly participate in and influence their companies' upstream activities and become network managers, not only product and customer managers.

The Role of Marketing Channels

Why would a producer delegate some of the selling job to intermediaries? Delegation means relinquishing some control over how and to whom the products are sold. Producers do gain several advantages by using intermediaries:

- *Many producers lack the financial resources to carry out direct marketing.* For example, General Motors sells its cars through more than 8000 dealer outlets in North America alone. Even General Motors would be hard-pressed to raise the cash to buy out its dealers.

- *Producers who do establish their own channels can often earn a greater return by increasing investment in their main business.* If a company earns a 20 percent rate of return on manufacturing and a 10 percent return on retailing, it does not make sense to do its own retailing.

- *In some cases direct marketing simply is not feasible.* The William Wrigley Jr. Company would not find it practical to establish small retail gum shops throughout the world or to sell gum by mail order. It would have to sell gum along with many other small products and would end up in the drugstore and grocery store business. Wrigley finds it easier to work through the extensive network of privately owned distribution organizations.

Intermediaries normally achieve superior efficiency in making goods widely available and accessible to target markets. Through their contacts, experience, specialization, and scale of operation, intermediaries usually offer the firm more than it can achieve on its own. According to Stern and his colleagues:

> Intermediaries smooth the flow of goods and services. . . . This procedure is necessary in order to bridge the discrepancy between the assortment of goods and services generated by the producer and the assortment demanded by the consumer. The discrepancy results from the fact that manufacturers typically produce a large quantity of a limited variety of goods, whereas consumers usually desire only a limited quantity of a wide variety of goods.[12]

Figure 15.1 shows one major source of cost savings using intermediaries. Part (a) shows three producers, each using direct marketing to reach three customers. This system requires nine different contacts. Part (b) shows the three producers working through one distributor, who contacts the three customers. This system requires only six contacts. In this way, intermediaries reduce the number of contacts and the work.

Channel Functions and Flows

A marketing channel performs the work of moving goods from producers to consumers. It overcomes the time, place, and possession gaps that separate goods and services from those who need or want them. Members of the marketing channel perform a number of key functions (see Table 15.1).

Some functions (physical, title, promotion) constitute a *forward flow* of activity from the company to the customer; other functions (ordering and payment) constitute a *backward flow* from customers to the company. Still others (information, negotiation, finance, and risk taking) occur in both directions. Five flows are illustrated in Figure 15.2 for the marketing of forklift trucks. If these flows were superimposed in one diagram, the tremendous complexity of even simple marketing channels would be apparent. A manufacturer selling a physical product and services might require three channels: a *sales channel*, a *delivery channel*, and a *service channel*. To sell its Bowflex fitness equipment, the Nautilus Group has used television infomercials, the telephone, and the Internet as sales chan-

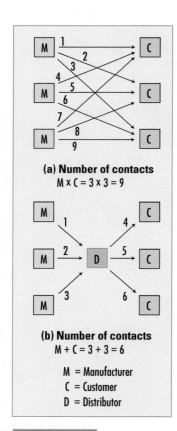

(a) Number of contacts
M x C = 3 x 3 = 9

(b) Number of contacts
M + C = 3 + 3 = 6

M = Manufacturer
C = Customer
D = Distributor

FIGURE 15.1

How a Distributor Increases Efficiency

TABLE 15.1	CHANNEL MEMBER FUNCTIONS

- Gather information about potential and current customers, competitors, and other actors and forces in the marketing environment.
- Develop and disseminate persuasive communications to stimulate purchasing.
- Reach agreements on price and other terms so that transfer of ownership or possession can be effected.
- Place orders with manufacturers.
- Acquire the funds to finance inventories at different levels in the marketing channel.
- Assume risks connected with carrying out channel work.
- Provide for the successive storage and movement of physical products.
- Provide for buyers' payment of their bills through banks and other financial institutions.
- Oversee actual transfer of ownership from one organization or person to another.

nels; UPS ground service as the delivery channel; and local repair people as the service channel. When sales failed to meet goals, Nautilus added retail stores to its sales channels in 2003. When a competitor infringed on the Bowflex patent by placing an imitation product into retail stores, Nautilus began selling Bowflex home gyms through the retail channel.

The question is not *whether* various channel functions need to be performed—they must be—but rather, *who* is to perform them. All channel functions have three things in common: They use up scarce resources; they can often be performed better through specialization; and they can be shifted among channel members. When the manufacturer shifts some functions to intermediaries, the producer's costs and prices are lower, but the intermediary must add a charge to cover its work. If the intermediaries are more efficient than the manufacturer, prices to consumers should be lower. If consumers perform some functions themselves, they should enjoy even lower prices.

Marketing functions, then, are more basic than the institutions that perform them at any given time. Changes in channel institutions largely reflect the discovery of more efficient ways to combine or separate the economic functions that provide assortments of goods to target customers.

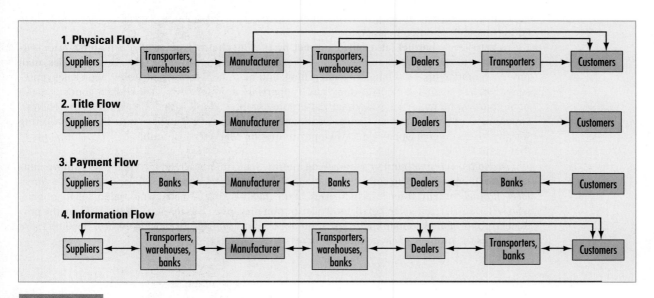

FIGURE 15.2

Five Marketing Flows in the Marketing Channel for Forklift Trucks

Sales channel for Bowflex fitness equipment: a print ad with a coupon and an 800 number for phone calls.

Channel Levels

The producer and the final customer are part of every channel. We will use the number of intermediary levels to designate the length of a channel. Figure 15.3(a) illustrates several consumer-goods marketing channels of different lengths.

A **zero-level channel** (also called a **direct-marketing channel**) consists of a manufacturer selling directly to the final customer. The major examples are door-to-door sales, home parties, mail order, telemarketing, TV selling, Internet selling, and manufacturer-owned stores. Avon sales representatives sell cosmetics door-to-door; and Tupperware representatives sell kitchen goods through home parties. Many charities and activist groups, such as World Vision Canada, the United Way, Greenpeace, and the Canadian Cancer Society, also rely on direct channels to raise funds. "Marketing Insight: M-Commerce Opens Up New Opportunities for Marketers" describes new developments in that area.

A *one-level channel* contains one selling intermediary, such as a retailer. A *two-level channel* contains two intermediaries. In consumer markets, these are typically a wholesaler and a retailer. A *three-level channel* contains three intermediaries. In the meatpacking industry, wholesalers sell to jobbers, who sell to small retailers. In Japan, food distribution may involve as many as six levels. From the producer's point of view, obtaining information about end users and exercising control become more difficult as the number of channel levels increases.

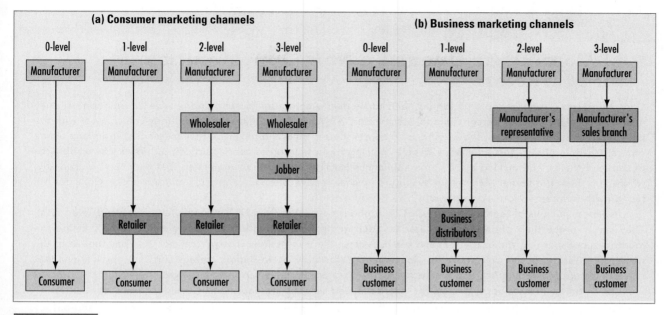

FIGURE 15.3

Consumer and Industrial Marketing Channels

The Promotional Products Industry

You may be surprised to learn that there is a $2.1 billion industry in Canada devoted to the selling of promotional items to businesses. It even has its own trade association, the Promotional Products Association of Canada. And, if research predictions made by Professor Michel Laroche of Concordia University are borne out, the industry will continue to grow. Firms buy hundreds of promotional products as incentives or rewards for employees, as advertising gimmicks, or as gifts to thank customers.

The promotional products business is a complex, multi-tiered industry, comprised of over 3700 distributors and more than 1000 suppliers. Suppliers may be large multinationals like 3M, which has a whole department exclusively devoted to manufacturing promotional products, or smaller firms like Toronto-based Justwhiteshirts.com. Suppliers spend a lot on R&D to keep abreast of the latest technological advances so they can offer the most innovative products and services. The distributors are a diverse group of agencies, business-people, and entrepreneurs. They are known for their creativity and imagination. However, as more marketers begin to purchase their promotional products directly from manufacturers via the Internet, distributors will be forced to provide added value to their clients. More and more are helping marketers determine and achieve clear objectives for their promotions, custom design various promotional products, implement distribution plans, and measure results.[13]

Figure 15.3(b) shows channels commonly used in industrial marketing. An industrial-goods manufacturer can use its sales force to sell directly to industrial customers; or it can sell to industrial distributors, who sell to the industrial customers; or it can sell through manufacturer's representatives or its own sales branches directly to industrial customers, or indirectly to industrial customers through industrial distributors. Zero-, one-, and two-level marketing channels are quite common.

Channels normally describe a forward movement of products from source to user. One can also talk about *reverse-flow channels*. They are important in the following cases: (1) to reuse products or containers (such as refillable chemical-carrying drums); (2) to refurbish products (such as circuit boards or computers) for resale; (3) to recycle products (such as paper); and (4) to dispose of products and packaging (waste products). Several intermediaries play a role in reverse-flow channels, including manufacturers' redemption centres, community groups, and traditional intermediaries such as soft-drink intermediaries, trash-collection specialists, recycling centres, trash-recycling brokers, and central-processing warehousing.[14]

MARKETING INSIGHT

M-Commerce Opens Up New Opportunities for Marketers

Consumers and businesspeople no longer need to be near a computer to send and receive information. All they need is a cellular phone or personal digital assistant (PDA). While they are on the move, they can connect with the Internet to check stock prices, the weather, and sports scores; send and receive e-mail messages; and place online orders. A whole field called *telematics* involves placing wireless Internet-connected computers in the dashboards of cars and trucks, and making more home appliances (such as computers) wireless so that they can be used anywhere in or near the home. Many see a big future in what is now called *m-commerce* (m for mobile). Consider the fast growth of Internet-connected phones.

In Japan, millions of teenagers carry DoCoMo phones available from NTT (Nippon Telephone and Telegraph). They can also use their phone to order goods. Each month, the subscriber receives a bill from NTT listing the monthly subscriber fee, the usage fee, and the cost of all the transactions. The person can then pay the bill at the nearest 7-11 store. In the United States, Conversagent (formerly ActiveBuddy) creates software applications that connect Instant Messaging users to marketer-created data using conversational language.

The potential market opportunities for location-based services are enormous. Consider some possibilities:

- Getting a Coke by pointing and clicking the phone at a vending machine. The bottle drops down and an appropriate amount is deducted from the owner's bank account.
- Using the phone to search for a nearby restaurant that meets the customer's entered criteria.
- Watching stock prices while sitting in the restaurant and deciding to place a purchase order.
- Clicking the phone to pay the bill for the meal; the cellular phone replaces the credit card.
- Coming home and clicking a combination of keys on the phone to open the door.

Some see positive benefits, such as locating people making emergency 911 calls or checking on the whereabouts of one's children late at night. Others worry about privacy issues. What if an employer learns that an employee is being treated for AIDS at a local clinic, or a wife finds out her husband is out clubbing? Like so many new technologies, location-based services have potential for good or harm, and ultimately will warrant public scrutiny and regulation.

Sources: Douglas Lamont, *Conquering the Wireless World: The Age of M-Commerce* (New York: Wiley, 2001); Marc Weingarten, "The Medium Is the Instant Message," *Business 2.0* (February 2002): 98–99.

Dell Canada

The question of how to dispose of obsolete computer equipment is becoming a major issue. According to Environment Canada, by 2005 the amount of disposed computers and peripherals will exceed 67 000 tonnes. Computers contain a lot of potentially harmful waste. There are an estimated 4740 tonnes of lead in personal computers and televisions thrown away each year in Canada, in addition to the 4.5 tonnes of cadmium and 1.1 tonnes of mercury. The problem may accelerate as replacement cycles are getting shorter for desktop PCs among Canadian households. Dell, the Canadian market leader, has started to take action to address this problem, offering its customers a free recycling program for home computers.[15]

Service Sector Channels

Marketing channels are not limited to the distribution of physical goods. Producers of services and ideas also face the problem of making their output available and accessible to target populations. Schools develop "educational-dissemination systems" and hospitals develop "health-delivery systems." In Canada, these institutions must figure out agencies and locations for reaching a population spread out over a wide geographic area.

Citizens Bank, a virtual bank, was formed by Vancity Credit Union so that it could offer services nationally.

Marketing channels also keep changing in "person" marketing. Before 1940, professional comedians could reach audiences through vaudeville houses, special events, nightclubs, radio, movies, carnivals, and theatres. Vaudeville houses have vanished and been replaced by comedy clubs and cable television stations. Politicians also must choose a mix of channels—mass media, rallies, coffee hours, spot TV ads, direct mail, billboards, faxes, e-mail, Web sites—for delivering their messages to voters.[16]

As Internet and other technology advances, service industries such as banking, insurance, travel, and stock buying and selling are taking place through new channels. For example, ING Direct and Citizens Bank (formed by the Vancity Credit Union as a means of creating a national bank) don't use physical branches. All transactions are done via the telephone or over the Internet.

Reaching the right customers was a key factor in one of the biggest financial services mergers in the world:

Citicorp

Distribution strategy and the blend of different customer segment targets was a stated objective of the US$70 billion merger between Citicorp and Travelers Group. Citicorp was one of the world's biggest banks, while Travelers focused on insurance, mutual funds, and investment banking businesses. One of the major stated goals of the merger was the ability of each organization to cross-sell the other's products to its customers and to exploit the two organizations' distribution channels to maximize the penetration of the merged companies' products throughout the world.[17]

Channel-Design Decisions

Designing a marketing channel system involves analyzing customer needs, establishing channel objectives, identifying major channel alternatives, and evaluating major channel alternatives.

Analyzing Customers' Desired Service Output Levels

In designing the marketing channel, the marketer must understand the service output levels desired by target customers. Channels produce five service outputs:

1. *Lot size.* The number of units the channel permits a typical customer to purchase on one occasion. In buying cars for its fleet, Hertz prefers a channel from which it can buy a large lot size; a household wants a channel that permits buying a lot size of one.

2. *Waiting and delivery time.* The average time customers of that channel wait for receipt of the goods. Customers increasingly prefer faster and faster delivery channels.

3. *Spatial convenience.* The degree to which the marketing channel makes it easy for customers to purchase the product. Chevrolet, for example, offers greater spatial convenience than Cadillac, because there are more Chevrolet dealers. Chevrolet's greater market decentralization helps customers save on transportation and search costs in buying and repairing an automobile.

4. *Product variety.* The assortment breadth provided by the marketing channel. Normally, customers prefer a greater assortment because more choices increase the chance of finding what they need.

5. *Service backup.* The add-on services (credit, delivery, installation, repairs) provided by the channel. The greater the service backup, the greater the work provided by the channel.[18]

The marketing-channel designer knows that providing greater service outputs means increased channel costs and higher prices for customers. Different customers have different service needs. The success of discount stores indicates that many consumers are willing to accept smaller service outputs if they can save money.

Establishing Objectives and Constraints

Channel objectives should be stated in terms of targeted service output levels. Under competitive conditions, channel institutions should arrange their functional tasks to minimize total channel costs and still provide desired levels of service outputs.[19] Usually, planners can identify several market segments that want different service levels. Effective planning requires determining which market segments to serve and the best channels for each.

Channel objectives vary with product characteristics. Perishable products require more direct marketing. Bulky products, such as building materials, require channels that minimize the shipping distance and the amount of handling. Nonstandard products, such as custom-built machinery and specialized business forms, are sold directly by company sales representatives. Products requiring installation or maintenance services, such as heating and cooling systems, are usually sold and maintained by the company or by franchised dealers. High-unit-value products such as generators and turbines are often sold through a company sales force rather than intermediaries.

Channel design must take into account the strengths and weaknesses of different types of intermediaries. For example, manufacturers' reps are able to contact customers at a low cost per customer because the total cost is shared by several clients, but the selling effort per customer is less intense than if company sales reps did the selling. Channel design is also influenced by competitors' channels.

Channel design must adapt to the larger environment. When economic conditions are depressed, producers want to move their goods to market using shorter channels and without services that add to the final price of the goods. Legal regulations and restrictions also affect channel design. Canadian regulators look unfavourably on channel arrangements that may tend to substantially lessen competition or create a monopoly.

Identifying Major Channel Alternatives

Companies can choose from a wide variety of channels for reaching customers—from sales forces to agents, distributors, dealers, direct mail, telemarketing, and the Internet. Each channel has unique strengths as well as weaknesses. Sales forces can handle complex products and transactions, but they are expensive. The Internet is much less expensive, but it cannot handle complex products. Distributors can create sales, but the company loses direct contact with customers.

The problem is further complicated by the fact that most companies now use a mix of channels. Each channel hopefully reaches a different segment of buyers and delivers the right products to each at the least cost. When this does not happen, there is usually channel conflict and excessive cost.

A channel alternative is described by three elements: the types of available business intermediaries, the number of intermediaries needed, and the terms and responsibilities of each channel member.

TYPES OF INTERMEDIARIES A firm needs to identify the types of intermediaries available to carry on its channel work. For example, a test-equipment manufacturer developed an audio device for detecting poor mechanical connections in machines with moving parts. Company executives felt this product would sell in all industries where electric, combustion, or steam engines were used, such as aviation, automobiles, railroads, food canning, construction, and oil. The sales force was small. The problem was how to reach these diverse industries effectively. The following alternatives were identified:

- Expand the company's direct sales force. Assign sales representatives to contact all prospects in an area, or develop separate sales forces for the different industries.
- Hire manufacturers' agents in different regions or end-use industries to sell the new equipment.
- Find distributors in the different regions or end-use industries that will buy and carry the device. Give them exclusive distribution, adequate margins, product training, and promotional support.

Table 15.2 lists channel alternatives identified by a consumer electronics company that produces cellular car phones.

Companies should search for innovative marketing channels. Medion sold 600 000 PCs in Europe, mostly via major one- or two-week "burst promotions" at Aldi's supermarkets.[20] Columbia House has successfully merchandised music albums through the mail.

Sometimes a company chooses an unconventional channel because of the difficulty or cost of working with the dominant channel. The advantage is that the company will encounter less competition during the initial move into this channel. After trying to sell its inexpensive Timex watches through regular jewellery stores, the U.S. Time Company placed its watches in fast-growing mass-merchandise outlets. To increase familiarity and demand for its Clodhoppers candy, Winnipeg-based Kraves Candy Co. made a deal with Air Canada to give out its candy to passengers.

NUMBER OF INTERMEDIARIES Companies have to decide on the number of intermediaries to use at each channel level. Three strategies are available: exclusive distribution, selective distribution, and intensive distribution.

Exclusive distribution means severely limiting the number of intermediaries. It is used when the producer wants to maintain control over the service level and outputs offered by the resellers. Often it involves *exclusive dealing* arrangements. By granting exclusive distribution, the producer hopes to obtain more dedicated and knowledgeable selling. It requires greater partnership between seller and reseller and is used in the distribution of new automobiles, some major appliances, and some women's apparel brands. When legendary Italian designer label Gucci found its image severely tarnished by overexposure from licensing and discount stores, Gucci decided to end contracts with third-party suppliers, control its distribution, and open its own stores to bring back some of the lustre.[21] Exclusive deals between suppliers and retailers are becoming a mainstay for specialists looking for an edge in a business world that is increasingly driven by price:[22]

- Disney Consumer Products and Wal-Mart signed a landmark pact in 2003 giving Wal-Mart a six-month exclusive on sales of toys and merchandise from Disney's new *Kim Possible* franchise.
- When Scholastic Entertainment relaunched its *Clifford the Big Red Dog* kids' franchise after leaving it neglected for years, the company used exclusive deals with Target and J. C. Penny to

TABLE 15.2	CHANNEL ALTERNATIVES FOR A CELLULAR CAR PHONE MAKER

- The company could sell its car phones to automobile manufacturers to be installed as original equipment.
- The company could sell its car phones to auto dealers.
- The company could sell its car phones to retail automotive-equipment dealers through a direct sales force or through distributors.
- The company could sell its car phones to car phone specialist dealers through a direct sales force or dealers.
- The company could sell its car phones through mail-order catalogues.
- The company could sell its car phones through mass merchandisers such as Best Buy or Circuit City.

enjoy a comfort zone it wouldn't have had if the product had been launched across several channels.

■ Toronto-based Moontaxi is leading the way in legal digital music distribution, having signed a deal in 2002 to be the exclusive online distributor of Universal Canada's entire record collection, including the Tragically Hip and Eminem.[23]

Selective distribution involves the use of more than a few but less than all of the intermediaries who are willing to carry a particular product. It is used by established companies and by new companies seeking distributors. The company does not have to worry about too many outlets; it can gain adequate market coverage with more control and less cost than intensive distribution. Disney is a good example of selective distribution:

Disney

Disney sells its videos through five main channels: movie rental stores like Blockbuster; the company's proprietary retail stores, called Disney Stores; retail stores like Best Buy; online retailers like Amazon.com and Disney's own online Disney Stores; and the Disney catalogue and other catalogue sellers. These varied channels afford Disney maximum market coverage, and enable the company to offer its videos at a number of price points.[24]

Intensive distribution consists of the manufacturer placing the goods or services in as many outlets as possible. This strategy is generally used for items such as tobacco products, soap, snack foods, and gum, products for which the consumer requires a great deal of location convenience.

Manufacturers are constantly tempted to move from exclusive or selective distribution to more intensive distribution to increase coverage and sales. This strategy may help in the short term, but often hurts long-term performance. Intensive distribution increases product and service availability but may also result in retailers competing aggressively. If price wars ensue, retailer profitability may also decline, potentially dampening retailer interest in supporting the product. It may also harm brand equity, as the Calvin Klein experience illustrates:

Calvin Klein

In May 2000, designer Calvin Klein sued Linda Wachner, CEO of Warnaco Group Inc., for selling his jeans to cut-rate mass-market outlets without his permission. Warnaco, which has the licence to make and distribute the jeans, was accused by Calvin Klein of making lower-quality jeans for these outlets, and therefore hurting his image. The suit was settled out of court in January 2001, and both sides said they "look forward to expanding jeans wear sales consistent with the image and prestige of Calvin Klein products." Warnaco would limit distributing jeans wear products to department and specialty stores.

TERMS AND RESPONSIBILITIES OF CHANNEL MEMBERS The producer must determine the rights and responsibilities of participating channel members. Each channel member must be treated respectfully and given the opportunity to be profitable.[25] The main elements in the "trade-relations mix" are price policies, conditions of sale, territorial rights, and specific services to be performed by each party.

Price policy calls for the producer to establish a price list and schedule of discounts and allowances that intermediaries see as equitable and sufficient.

Conditions of sale refers to payment terms and producer guarantees. Most producers grant cash discounts to distributors for early payment. Producers might also guarantee distributors against defective merchandise or price declines. A guarantee against price declines gives distributors an incentive to buy larger quantities.

Distributors' territorial rights define the distributors' territories and the terms under which the producer will enfranchise other distributors. Distributors normally expect to receive full credit for all sales in their territory, whether or not they did the selling.

Mutual services and responsibilities must be carefully spelled out, especially in franchised and exclusive-agency channels. McDonald's provides franchisees with a building, promotional support, a record-keeping system, training, and general administrative and technical assistance. In turn, franchisees are expected to satisfy company standards regarding physical facilities, cooperate with new promotional programs, furnish requested information, and buy supplies from specified vendors.

Evaluating the Major Alternatives

Each channel alternative needs to be evaluated against economic, control, and adaptive criteria.

ECONOMIC CRITERIA   Each channel alternative will produce a different level of sales and costs. Figure 15.4 shows how six different sales channels stack up in terms of the value added per sale and the cost per transaction. For example, in selling industrial products costing between $3000 and $8000, the cost per transaction has been estimated as $780 (field sales), $310 (distributors), $80 (telesales), and $15 (Internet). Banks claim that in selling retail banking services, the cost per transaction is $3 (teller), $0.75 (ABM), and $0.15 (Internet). Clearly, sellers would try to replace high-cost channels with low-cost channels when the value added per sale was sufficient. The lower-cost channels tend to be low-touch channels. This is not important in ordering commodity items, but buyers who are shopping for more complex products may prefer high-touch channels such as salespeople.

When sellers discover a convenient lower-cost channel, they try to get their customers to use it. The company may reward customers for switching. Many airlines initially gave bonus frequent flier mileage awards when customers booked reservations online. Other companies may raise the fees on customers using their higher-cost channels to get them to switch. Companies that are successful in switching their customers to lower-cost channels, assuming no loss of sales or deterioration in service quality, will gain a **channel advantage**.[26]

As an example of an economic analysis of channel choices, consider the following situation:

A Montreal furniture manufacturer wants to sell its line to retailers on the West Coast. The manufacturer is trying to decide between two alternatives: One calls for hiring 10 new sales representatives who would operate out of a sales office in Vancouver. They would receive a base salary plus commissions. The other alternative would be to use a Vancouver-based manufacturers' sales agency that has extensive contacts with retailers. The agency has 30 sales representatives, who would receive a commission based on their sales.

The first step is to determine whether a company sales force or a sales agency will produce more sales. Most marketing managers believe that a company sales force will sell more. They concentrate on the company's products; they are better trained to sell those products; they are more aggressive because their future depends on the company's success; and they are more successful because many customers prefer to deal directly with the company. However, the sales agency could conceivably sell more. First, the agency has 30 representatives, not just 10. This sales force might be just as aggressive as a direct sales force, depending on the commission level. Some customers prefer dealing with agents who represent several manufacturers rather than with salespersons from one company; and the agency has extensive contacts and marketplace knowledge, whereas a company sales force would need to build these from scratch.

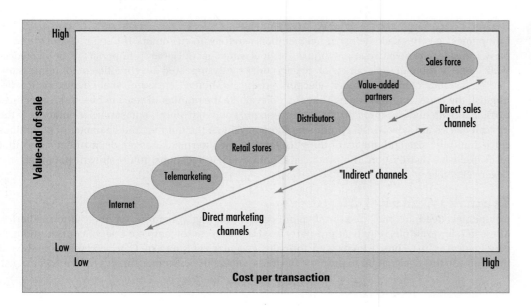

FIGURE 15.4

The Value-Adds versus Costs of Different Channels

Source: Oxford Associates, adapted from Dr. Rowland T. Moriarty, Cubex Corp.

FIGURE 15.5

Break-Even Cost Chart for the Choice Between a Company Sales Force and a Manufacturer's Sales Agency

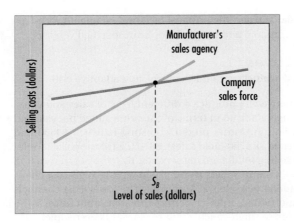

The next step is to estimate the costs of selling different volumes through each channel. The cost schedules are shown in Figure 15.5. The fixed costs of engaging a sales agency are lower than those of establishing a company sales office, but costs rise faster through an agency because sales agents get a larger commission than company salespeople. The final step is comparing sales and costs. As Figure 15.5 shows, there is one sales level (S_B) at which selling costs are the same for the two channels. The sales agency is thus the better channel for any sales volume below S_B, and the company sales branch is better at any volume above S_B. Given this information, it is not surprising that sales agents tend to be used by smaller firms, or by large firms in smaller territories where the volume is low.

CONTROL AND ADAPTIVE CRITERIA Using a sales agency poses a control problem. A sales agency is an independent firm seeking to maximize its profits. Agents may concentrate on the customers who buy the most, not necessarily those who buy the manufacturer's goods. Furthermore, agents might not master the technical details of the company's product or handle its promotion materials effectively.

To develop a channel, members must make some degree of commitment to each other for a specified period of time. Yet these commitments invariably lead to a decrease in the producer's ability to respond to a changing marketplace. In rapidly changing, volatile, or uncertain product markets, the producer needs channel structures and policies that provide high adaptability.

Channel-Management Decisions

After a company has chosen a channel alternative, individual intermediaries must be selected, trained, motivated, and evaluated. Channel arrangements must be modified over time.

Selecting Channel Members

Companies need to select their channel members carefully. To customers, the channels are the company. Consider the negative impression customers would get of Harvey's, Imperial Oil, or Mercedes-Benz if one or more of their outlets or dealers consistently appeared dirty, inefficient, or unpleasant.

To facilitate channel member selection, producers should determine what characteristics distinguish the better intermediaries. They should evaluate the number of years in business, other lines carried, growth and profit record, financial strength, cooperativeness, and service reputation. If the intermediaries are sales agents, producers should evaluate the number and character of other lines carried and the size and quality of the sales force. If the intermediaries are department stores that want exclusive distribution, the producer should evaluate locations, future growth potential, and type of clientele.

Training Channel Members

Companies need to plan and implement careful training programs for their intermediaries. Microsoft, for example, requires third-party service engineers to complete a set of courses and take certification exams. Those who pass are formally recognized as Microsoft Certified Professionals, and they can use this designation to promote business. Others use customer surveys rather than exams.

Kyocera Mita Corporation

Kyocera Mita was born after a 2000 merger between Kyocera, who had global leadership in printer technology, and Mita, with its strength in copiers. Today, it is one of the world's largest manufacturers of office information equipment, including network-ready printers and digital copiers. In 2003, it commissioned J. D. Power and Associates to develop a program to survey Kyocera Mita dealers' customers and certify those dealers that met or exceeded benchmarks for sales and service customer satisfaction. Certification is based on customer satisfaction with an office equipment dealer's product knowledge, expertise in machine operation, ability to advise customers about their specific needs, and timely delivery of the equipment. "The J. D. Power and Associates certification recognizes Kyocera Mita Total Solution Provider dealers for outstanding customer experience, and allows them to differentiate within the dealer marketplace, helping to contribute to increased customer traffic and higher sales," said Michael Pietrunti, vice-president of marketing at Kyocera Mita America. "This certification positions dealers as industry-wide leaders in customer satisfaction."[27]

Motivating Channel Members

A company needs to view its intermediaries in the same way it views its end users. It needs to determine intermediaries' needs and construct a channel positioning such that its channel offering is tailored to provide superior value to these intermediaries.

Stimulating channel members to top performance starts with understanding their needs and wants. The company should provide training programs, market research programs, and other capability-building programs to improve intermediaries' performance. The company must constantly communicate its view that the intermediaries are partners in a joint effort to satisfy end users of the product.

Producers vary greatly in skill in managing distributors. **Channel power** can be defined as the ability to alter channel members' behaviour so that they take actions they would not have taken otherwise.[28] Manufacturers can draw on the following types of power to elicit cooperation:

- *Coercive power.* A manufacturer threatens to withdraw a resource or terminate a relationship if intermediaries fail to cooperate. This power can be effective, but its exercise produces resentment and can generate conflict and lead the intermediaries to organize countervailing power.

- *Reward power.* The manufacturer offers intermediaries an extra benefit for performing specific acts or functions. Reward power typically produces better results than coercive power, but can be overrated. The intermediaries may come to expect a reward every time the manufacturer wants a certain behaviour to occur.

- *Legitimate power.* The manufacturer requests a behaviour that is warranted under the contract. As long as the intermediaries view the manufacturer as a legitimate leader, legitimate power works.

- *Expert power.* The manufacturer has special knowledge that the intermediaries value. Once the expertise is passed on to the intermediaries, however, this power weakens. The manufacturer must continue to develop new expertise so that the intermediaries will want to continue cooperating.

- *Referent power.* The manufacturer is so highly respected that intermediaries are proud to be associated with it. Companies such as IBM, Caterpillar, and Hewlett-Packard have high referent power.[29]

Coercive and reward power are objectively observable; legitimate, expert, and referent power are more subjective and dependent on the ability and willingness of parties to recognize them.

Most producers see gaining intermediaries' cooperation as a huge challenge.[30] They often use positive motivators, such as higher margins, special deals, premiums, cooperative advertising allowances, display allowances, and sales contests. At times they will apply negative sanctions, such as threatening to reduce margins, slow down delivery, or terminate the relationship. The weakness of this approach is that the producer is using crude, stimulus-response thinking.

More sophisticated companies try to forge a long-term partnership with distributors. The manufacturer clearly communicates what it wants from its distributors in the way of market coverage, inventory levels, marketing development, account solicitation, technical advice and services, and marketing information. The manufacturer seeks distributor agreement with these policies and may introduce a compensation plan for adhering to the policies. Here are three examples of successful partner-building practices:

- Timken Corporation (roller bearings) has its sales reps make multilevel calls on its distributors.
- DuPont has a distributor marketing steering committee that meets regularly.
- Rust-Oleum introduces a menu of marketing programs each quarter; distributors choose the programs that fit their needs.

Evaluating Channel Members

Producers must periodically evaluate intermediaries' performance against such standards as sales-quota attainment, average inventory levels, customer delivery time, treatment of damaged and lost goods, and cooperation in promotional and training programs. A producer will occasionally discover that it is paying too much to particular intermediaries for what they are actually doing. One manufacturer that was compensating a distributor for holding inventories found that the inventories were actually held in a public warehouse at its expense. Producers should set up functional discounts in which they pay specified amounts for the trade channel's performance of each agreed-upon service. Underperformers need to be counselled, retrained, motivated, or terminated.

Modifying Channel Arrangements

A producer must periodically review and modify its channel arrangements. Modification becomes necessary when the distribution channel is not working as planned, consumer buying patterns change, the market expands, new competition arises, innovative distribution channels emerge, and the product moves into later stages in the product life cycle. Consider Apple:

Apple

Apple is pursuing a number of different channel strategies to better reach its customers. In the United States, it has opened more than 75 retail locations since 2001. The stores sell Apple products exclusively and target tech-savvy customers with in-store product presentations and workshops, a full line of Apple products, software, and accessories, and a "Genius Bar" staffed by an Apple specialist. In Canada, with its more geographically dispersed population, it's relying more on the Internet and traditional retailers. Canadians can now purchase the complete range of Apple hardware and software products directly from Apple over the Internet and take advantage of Apple's unique configure-to-order capabilities when configuring and ordering products (see www.apple.com/canadastore). Customers can click on the Resource Locator tool to find an Authorized Apple Reseller to purchase Apple products for the home, school, or business.[31]

The children's corner in an Apple retail store. Apple stores are designed to be a complete technology experience for the customer, who has access to every Apple product, to in-store presentations and workshops, and to expert advice.

No marketing channel will remain effective over the whole product life cycle. Early buyers might be willing to pay for high value-added channels, but later buyers will switch to lower-cost channels. Small office copiers were first sold by manufacturers' direct sales forces, later through office equipment dealers, still later through mass merchandisers, and now by mail-order firms and Internet marketers.

In competitive markets with low entry barriers, the optimal channel structure will inevitably change over time. The change could involve adding or dropping individual channel members, adding or dropping particular market channels, or developing a totally new way to sell goods.

Adding or dropping individual channel members requires an incremental analysis. What would the firm's profits look like with and without this intermediary? An automobile manufacturer's decision to drop a dealer requires subtracting the dealer's sales and estimating the possible sales loss or gain to the manufacturer's other dealers.

Sometimes a producer considers dropping all intermediaries whose sales are below a certain amount. Consider Navistar:

Navistar

Navistar's operating company, International Truck and Engine Corporation, noted at one time that 5 percent of its dealers were selling fewer than three or four trucks a year. It cost the company more to service these dealers than their sales were worth, but dropping these dealers could have repercussions on the system as a whole. The unit costs of producing trucks would be higher, because the overhead would be spread over fewer trucks; some employees and equipment would be idled; some business in these markets would go to competitors; and other dealers might become insecure. Other factors include nonrepresentation in smaller markets, long-time loyal customers not being serviced appropriately, and overall fewer dealers with technical knowledge to serve the current customer base. All these factors must be taken into account.

The most difficult decision involves revising the overall channel strategy.[32] Distribution channels clearly become outmoded, and a gap arises between the existing distribution system and the ideal system that would satisfy target customers' needs and desires (see "Marketing Memo: Designing a Customer-Driven Distribution System"). Examples abound: Avon's door-to-door system for selling cosmetics had to be modified as more women entered the workforce, IBM's exclusive reliance on a field sales force had to be modified with the introduction of low-priced personal computers, and banks are closing more and more branches, especially in small towns.

A Navistar truck, one of the many models the company produces and sells through a network of dealerships that have the technical expertise and local contacts to keep Navistar in markets both large and small.

Marketing Memo

Designing a Customer-Driven Distribution System

Stern and Sturdivant have outlined an excellent framework, called Customer-Driven Distribution System Design, for moving a poorly functioning distribution system closer to a customer's ideal system. Companies have to reduce the gaps between the service outputs that target customers desire, those the existing channel system delivers, and those management thinks are feasible within the existing constraints. Six steps are involved:

1. Research target customers' value perceptions, needs, and desires regarding channel service outputs.

2. Examine the performance of the company's and competitors' existing distribution systems in relation to customer desires.

3. Find service output gaps that need corrective action.

4. Identify major constraints that will limit possible corrective actions.

5. Design a "management-bounded" channel solution.

6. Implement the reconfigured distribution system.

Source: Anne T. Coughlan, Erin Anderson, Louis W. Stern, and Adel I. El-Ansary, *Marketing Channels*, 6th ed. (Upper Saddle River, NJ: Prentice Hall, 2001).

Channel Integration and Systems

Distribution channels do not stand still. New wholesaling and retailing institutions emerge, and new channel systems evolve. We will look at the recent growth of vertical, horizontal, and multi-channel marketing systems; the next section examines how these systems cooperate, conflict, and compete.

Vertical Marketing Systems

One of the most significant recent channel developments is the rise of vertical marketing systems. A **conventional marketing channel** comprises an independent producer, wholesaler(s), and retailer(s). Each is a separate business seeking to maximize its own profits, even if this goal reduces profit for the system as a whole. No channel member has complete or substantial control over other members.

A **vertical marketing system (VMS)**, by contrast, comprises the producer, wholesaler(s), and retailer(s) acting as a unified system. One channel member, the *channel captain*, owns the others or franchises them or has so much power that they all cooperate. The channel captain can be the producer, the wholesaler, or the retailer. Notable producer channel captains are Coca-Cola with soft drinks, Gillette with shaving, and Procter & Gamble with detergents.

VMSs arose as a result of strong channel members' attempts to control channel behaviour and eliminate the conflict that results when independent members pursue their own objectives. VMSs achieve economies through size, bargaining power, and elimination of duplicated services. They have become the dominant mode of distribution in the North American consumer marketplace, serving between 70 and 80 percent of the total market. There are three types of VMS: corporate, administered, and contractual.

CORPORATE VMS A *corporate VMS* combines successive stages of production and distribution under single ownership. For example, Sears obtains over 50 percent of the goods it sells from companies that it partly or wholly owns. Sherwin-Williams makes paint but also owns and operates 2000 retail outlets. Both Canadian Tire and Loblaws sell their own brand of products (Mastercraft and President's Choice respectively) through their stores.

ADMINISTERED VMS An *administered VMS* coordinates successive stages of production and distribution through the size and power of one of the members. Manufacturers of a dominant brand are able to secure strong trade cooperation and support from resellers. Thus Kodak, Gillette, and Campbell Soup are able to command high levels of cooperation from their resellers in connection with displays, shelf space, promotions, and price policies.

The most advanced supply-distributor arrangement for administered VMS involves **distribution programming**, which can be defined as building a planned, professionally managed, vertical marketing system that meets the needs of both manufacturer and distributors. The manufacturer establishes a department within the company called *distributor-relations planning*. Its job is to identify distributor needs and build up merchandising programs to help each distributor operate as efficiently as possible. This department and the distributors jointly plan merchandising goals, inventory levels, space and visual merchandising plans, sales-training requirements, and advertising and promotion plans. The aim is to convert the distributors from thinking that they make their money primarily on the buying side (through tough negotiation with the manufacturer) to seeing that they make their money on the selling side (by being part of a sophisticated vertical marketing system). Kraft and Procter & Gamble are two companies with excellent distributor-relations planning.

CONTRACTUAL VMS   A *contractual VMS* consists of independent firms at different levels of production and distribution integrating their programs on a contractual basis to obtain more economies or sales impact than they could achieve alone. Johnston and Lawrence call them "value-adding partnerships" (VAPs).[33] Contractual VMSs now constitute one of the most significant developments in the economy. They are of three types:

1. *Wholesaler-sponsored voluntary chains.* Wholesalers organize voluntary chains of independent retailers to help them compete with large chain organizations. The wholesaler develops a program in which independent retailers standardize their selling practices and achieve buying economies that enable the group to compete effectively with chain organizations.

2. *Retailer cooperatives.* Retailers take the initiative and organize a new business entity to carry on wholesaling and possibly some production. Members concentrate their purchases through the retailer co-op and plan their advertising jointly. Profits are passed back to members in proportion to their purchases. Nonmember retailers can also buy through the co-op but do not share in the profits.

3. *Franchise organizations.* A channel member called a *franchisor* might link several successive stages in the production-distribution process. Franchising has been the fastest-growing retailing development in recent years. Although the basic idea is an old one, some forms of franchising are quite new.

The traditional system is the *manufacturer-sponsored retailer franchise.* Ford, for example, licenses dealers to sell its cars. The dealers are independent businesspeople who agree to meet specified conditions of sales and services. Another is the *manufacturer-sponsored wholesaler franchise.* Coca-Cola, for example, licenses bottlers (wholesalers) in various markets who buy its syrup concentrate and then carbonate, bottle, and sell it to retailers in local markets. A newer system is the *service-firm-sponsored retailer franchise.* A service firm organizes a whole system for bringing its service efficiently to consumers. Examples are found in the auto rental business (Hertz, Avis), fast-food-service business (McDonald's, Burger King), and motel business (Howard Johnson, Ramada Inn).

THE NEW COMPETITION IN RETAILING   Many independent retailers that have not joined VMSs have developed specialty stores that serve special market segments. The result is a polarization in retailing between large vertical marketing organizations and independent specialty stores, which creates a problem for manufacturers. They are strongly tied to independent intermediaries, but must eventually realign themselves with the high-growth vertical marketing systems on less attractive terms. Furthermore, vertical marketing systems constantly threaten to bypass large manufacturers and set up their own manufacturing. *The new competition in retailing is no longer between independent business units but between whole systems of centrally programmed networks (corporate, administered, and contractual) competing against one another to achieve the best cost economies and customer response.*

Horizontal Marketing Systems

Another channel development is the **horizontal marketing system**, in which two or more unrelated companies put together resources or programs to exploit an emerging marketing opportunity. Many supermarket chains have arrangements with local banks to offer in-store banking. Each company lacks the capital, know-how, production, or marketing resources to venture alone, or it is afraid of the risk. The companies might work with each other on a temporary or permanent basis or create a joint venture company. H&R Block, Inc., for example, entered into an agreement with GEICO insurance to provide car insurance information to Block customers. Customers now can contact GEICO through a special toll-free number.

Multi-Channel Marketing Systems

Once, many companies sold to a single market through a single channel. Today, with the proliferation of customer segments and channel possibilities, more companies have adopted multi-channel marketing. **Multi-channel marketing** occurs when a single firm uses two or more marketing channels to reach one or more customer segments.

Consider some of the new channel opportunities that daily newspaper companies in Canada are using:

Paid Daily Newspapers

The Canadian daily newspaper industry has changed significantly in recent years. With the massive proliferation of other media and growing information flow as a result of the digital revolution, the mass readership of daily newspapers (such as the *Toronto Star*, *Globe and Mail*, and *National Post*) delivered right to people's doorsteps continues to decline. Gone are the days when everybody relied on daily newspapers as the source of news and information. As a result, daily newspaper publishers are continuing to look for new channels to deliver readers to advertisers. They have responded in several ways: (1) They have developed online offerings to deliver a younger, Internet-savvy audience to advertisers; (2) they have acquired and/or built community newspaper products to deliver the family market to advertisers (particularly through sophisticated flyer products); and (3) they have built free daily commuter papers available at bus stops and subway platforms to deliver the time-starved urban professional audience to advertisers (e.g., *Metro Today* and *24 Hours* in Toronto, the *Metro* in Montreal). Looking for new channels (and developing the corresponding new products) to access different demographics has been and will continue to be imperative for traditional daily newspaper companies in Canada.[34]

By adding more channels, companies can gain three important benefits. The first is increased market coverage. The second is lower channel cost—selling by phone rather than personal visits to small customers. The third is more customized selling—adding a technical sales force to sell more complex equipment. The gains from adding new channels come at a price, however. New channels typically introduce conflict and control problems. Two or more channels may end up competing for the same customers. The new channels may be more independent and make cooperation more difficult.

PLANNING CHANNEL ARCHITECTURE   Clearly, companies need to think through their channel architecture. Moriarty and Moran propose using the hybrid grid shown in Figure 15.6 to plan the channel architecture.[35] The grid shows several marketing channels (rows) and several demand-generation tasks (columns). The grid illustrates why using only one channel is not efficient. Consider using only a direct sales force. A salesperson would have to find leads, qualify them, presell, close the sale, provide service, and manage account growth. It would be more efficient for the company to perform the earlier tasks, leaving the salesperson to invest his or her costly time primarily to close the sale. The company's marketing department would generate leads through telemarketing, direct mail, advertising, and trade shows. The leads would be sorted into hot, warm, and cool by using qualifying techniques such as checking whether a lead wants a sales call and has adequate purchasing power. The department would also run a preselling campaign informing prospects about the company's products through advertising, direct mail, and telemarketing. The salesperson comes to the prospect when the prospect is ready to talk business. This multi-channel architecture optimizes coverage, customization, and control while minimizing cost and conflict.

Companies should use different channels for selling to different-size customers. A company can use its direct sales force to sell to large customers, telemarketing to sell to midsize customers, and distributors to sell to small customers; but these gains can be compromised by an increased level of conflict over who has account ownership. For example, territory-based sales representatives may want credit for all sales in their territories, regardless of the marketing channel used.

Multi-channel marketers also need to decide how much of their product to offer in each of the channels. There are many different approaches to take—compare the following two providers of outdoor and sporting gear:[36]

SportChek

A member of the Forzani Group, SportChek owns more than 100 SportChek stores across the country where you can buy anything from hockey gear to exercise clothing. The company also has a powerful Web site, but it sees it as an information tool for its customers, noting that "Sportchek.ca is here to help you research footwear, athletic and casual clothing and sports equipment for your in-store purchases." People who register on the site can also receive regular newsletters featuring articles on sports and new products as well as exclusive offers, events, and promotions.

Demand-Generation Tasks

		Lead Generation	Qualifying Sales	Presales	Close of Sale	Postsales Service	Account Management
	Internet						
	National Account Management						
	Direct Sales						
	Telemarketing						
	Direct Mail						
	Retail Stores						
	Distributors						
	Dealers and Value-Added Resellers						
	Advertising						

Marketing Channels and Methods — VENDOR ... CUSTOMER

FIGURE 15.6

The Hybrid Grid

Source: Rowland T. Moriarty and Ursula Moran, "Marketing Hybrid Marketing Systems," *Harvard Business Review* (November–December 1990): 150.

Mountain Equipment Co-op (MEC)

MEC has ten retail outlets located in major cities across Canada. It also has a call centre that accepts orders from members by mail, phone, or fax. It features a partial line of its products on its Web site. Not only can Canadians and Americans order from this site, it also allows people in many other countries to order MEC gear. The site provides information on shipping times and relevant import duties around the world. No matter what the delivery channel, MEC prides itself on the quality of its products and the service it provides.

Conflict, Cooperation, and Competition

No matter how well channels are designed and managed, there will be some conflict, if for no other reason than that the interests of independent business entities do not always coincide. **Channel conflict** is generated when one channel member's actions prevent the channel from achieving its goal. **Channel coordination** occurs when channel members are brought together to advance the goals of the channel, as opposed to their own potentially incompatible goals.[37] Here we examine three questions: What types of conflict arise in channels? What causes channel conflict? What can be done to resolve conflict situations?

Types of Conflict and Competition

Suppose a manufacturer sets up a vertical channel consisting of wholesalers and retailers. The manufacturer hopes for channel cooperation that will produce greater profits for each channel member. Yet vertical, horizontal, and multi-channel conflict can occur.

Vertical channel conflict means conflict between different levels within the same channel. General Motors came into conflict with its dealers in trying to enforce policies on service, pricing, and advertising. Coca-Cola came into conflict with bottlers who also agreed to bottle Dr. Pepper.

Horizontal channel conflict involves conflict between members at the same level within the channel. Some Ford car dealers in Chicago complained about other Chicago Ford dealers advertising and pricing too aggressively. Some Pizza Inn franchisees complained about other Pizza Inn franchisees cheating on ingredients, providing poor service, and hurting the overall Pizza Inn image.

Multi-channel conflict exists when the manufacturer has established two or more channels that sell to the same market. Multi-channel conflict is likely to be especially intense when the members of one channel get a lower price (based on larger volume purchases) or work with a lower margin. When Goodyear began selling its popular tire brands through Sears, Wal-Mart, and Discount Tire, it angered its independent dealers. It eventually placated them by offering exclusive tire models that would not be sold in other retail outlets. Such a strategy does not always work. When Pacific Cycles purchased Schwinn, it decided to supplement the brand's higher-end 2700-dealer network with some of its own channels where it sold its own mid-tier bikes through large retail chains such as Toys "R" Us, Target, and Wal-Mart. Even though Pacific Cycles offered exclusive models to the existing Schwinn network, over 1700 dealers pedalled away. A key question was whether the sales gains from the big retail chains would offset the loss from the dealer defections.[38]

Causes of Channel Conflict

It is important to identify the causes of channel conflict. Some are easy to resolve, others are not.

One major cause is *goal incompatibility*. For example, the manufacturer may want to achieve rapid market penetration through a low-price policy. Dealers, in contrast, may prefer to work with high margins and pursue short-run profitability. Sometimes conflict arises from *unclear roles and rights*. HP may sell personal computers to large accounts through its own sales force, but its licensed dealers may also be trying to sell to large accounts. Territory boundaries and credit for sales often produce conflict.

Conflict can also stem from *differences in perception*. The manufacturer may be optimistic about the short-term economic outlook and want dealers to carry higher inventory. Dealers may be pessimistic. In the beverage category, it is not uncommon for disputes to arise between manufacturers and their distributors about the optimal advertising strategy. Conflict might also arise because of the intermediaries' *dependence* on the manufacturer. The fortunes of exclusive dealers, such as auto dealers, are profoundly affected by the manufacturer's product and pricing decisions. This situation creates a high potential for conflict.

Managing Channel Conflict

As companies add channels to grow sales, they run the risk of creating channel conflict. Some channel conflict can be constructive and lead to better adaptation to a changing environment, but too much is dysfunctional. The challenge is not to eliminate conflict but to manage it better. Here's an example of how one B2B company added a potentially conflicting e-commerce channel and still managed to build trust—not stir up conflict—with its distributors:[39]

AB Dick

Printing equipment manufacturer AB Dick was on the verge of bypassing an important distributor channel for a direct e-commerce channel. Instead, the company developed a tiered dealer model and formed strategic supply chain partnerships with influential distributors. AB Dick would deal directly via the Web with all customers in a particular dealer's territory for sales of supplies. The dealer would act as the distribution point, bill and collect from the customer, maintain the relationship in terms of high-end equipment sales, earn incremental margins from the online sales of supplies (even though the transaction would be direct from AB Dick to the end user), and remain the local contact for equipment sales. According to AB Dick's vice president of technology, the dealers were happy because they picked up margin on business they never had, but they also picked up collections, freight, transportation, and labour. AB Dick benefited from reduced costs per online transaction and incremental sales. It had to balance the efficiencies and convenience of direct online ordering for its end users with the need to maintain its dealers as local points-of-distribution and customer contact.

There are several mechanisms for effective conflict management.[40] One is the adoption of superordinate goals. Channel members come to an agreement on the fundamental goal they are jointly seeking, whether it is survival, market share, high quality, or customer satisfaction. They usually do this when the channel faces an outside threat, such as a more efficient competing channel, an adverse piece of legislation, or a shift in consumer desires.

A useful step is to exchange persons between two or more channel levels. General Motors executives might agree to work for a short time in some dealerships, and some dealership owners might work in GM's dealer policy department. Hopefully, the participants will grow to appreciate the other's point of view.

Co-optation is an effort by one organization to win the support of the leaders of another organization by including them in advisory councils, boards of directors, and the like. As long as the initiating organization treats the leaders seriously and listens to their opinions, co-optation can reduce conflict, but the initiating organization may have to compromise its policies and plans to win their support.

Much can be accomplished by encouraging joint membership in and between trade associations. For example, there is good cooperation between the Grocery Manufacturers of America and the Food Marketing Institute, which represents most of the U.S. food chains; this cooperation led to the development of the universal product code (UPC). Presumably, the associations can consider issues between food manufacturers and retailers and resolve them in an orderly way.

When conflict is chronic or acute, the parties may have to resort to diplomacy, mediation, or arbitration. *Diplomacy* takes place when each side sends a person or group to meet with its counterpart to resolve the conflict. *Mediation* means resorting to a neutral third party who is skilled in conciliating the two parties' interests. *Arbitration* occurs when the two parties agree to present their arguments to one or more arbitrators and accept the arbitration decision. Sometimes, when none of these methods proves effective, a company or a channel partner may choose to file a lawsuit. Levi Strauss and U.K. retailer Tesco became locked in a legal battle beginning in 1999.

Levi's

Levi's filed a suit with the European Court of Justice against Tesco claiming the retailer's selling of low-priced Levi's jeans imported from outside Britain "undermines the product experience." Tesco had offered genuine Levis at roughly half the price of other U.K. retailers. Levi's also objected to the fact that its jeans appear in the same stores that sell produce and other food items. After much legal wrangling, the courts decided in favour of Levi's in November 2001. Levi's subsequently decided to introduce a much less expensive value line of Signature jeans that could be sold in Asda supermarkets in the United Kingdom, as well as in Wal-Mart in the United States.[41]

Legal and Ethical Issues in Channel Relations

For the most part, companies are legally free to develop whatever channel arrangements suit them. Canada's Competition Act regulates the nature of competition between wholesalers and retailers, since they are viewed under the law as direct competitors. One of the aims of the act is to ensure a competitive marketplace that benefits both the business and the customers. It also places legal restrictions on some specialized distribution practices such as pyramid selling (also called multi-level marketing plans). In particular, it prohibits schemes that have mandatory participation fees, purchase requirements as a condition of participation, inventory loading, or insufficient buy-back guarantees. New provisions have also been put in place to govern fraudulent telemarketing practices. Here we briefly consider the legality of some other practices, including exclusive dealing, tying agreements, and dealers' rights.

Many producers like to develop exclusive channels for their products. A strategy in which the seller allows only certain outlets to carry its products is called **exclusive distribution**. When the seller requires that these dealers not handle competitors' products, this is called **exclusive dealing**. Both parties benefit from exclusive arrangements: The seller obtains more loyal and dependable outlets, and the dealers obtain a steady source of supply of special products and stronger seller support. Exclusive arrangements are legal as long as they do not substantially lessen competition or tend to create a monopoly, and as long as both parties enter into the agreement voluntarily.

Producers of a strong brand sometimes sell it to dealers only if they will take some or all of the rest of the line. This practice is called full-line forcing. Such **tying agreements** are not necessarily illegal, unless they substantially lessen competition.

Producers are free to select their dealers, but their right to terminate dealers is somewhat restricted. In general, sellers can drop dealers "for cause," but they cannot drop dealers if, for example, the dealers refuse to cooperate in a doubtful legal arrangement, such as exclusive dealing or tying agreements.

E-Commerce Marketing Practices

E-business describes the use of electronic means and platforms to conduct a company's business.[42] Mediagrif, the organization described at the outset of this chapter, is entirely an e-business. **E-commerce** means that the company or site offers to transact or facilitate the selling of products and services online. E-commerce has given rise in turn to e-purchasing and e-marketing. **E-purchasing** means companies decide to purchase goods, services, and information from various online suppliers. Smart e-purchasing has already saved companies millions of dollars. **E-marketing** describes company efforts to inform, communicate, promote, and sell its products and services over the Internet. The *e* prefix is also used in terms such as e-finance, e-learning, and e-service. But as someone observed, the *e* will eventually be dropped when most business practice is online.

We can distinguish between **pure-online** companies (referred to by some as *pure-click* companies), those that launched a Web site without any previous existence as a firm (e.g., ING Direct), and hybrid companies (sometimes referred to as *brick-and-click* companies), existing companies that added an online site for information and/or e-commerce.

Pure-Online Companies

There are several kinds of pure-online companies: search engines, Internet service providers (ISPs), commerce sites, transaction sites, content sites, and enabler sites. Commerce sites sell all types of goods and services, notably books, music, toys, insurance, stocks, clothes, financial services, and so on. Among the most prominent commerce sites are eBay and Expedia.

The Internet is most useful for goods and services when the shopper seeks greater ordering convenience (e.g., books and music) or lower cost (e.g., stock trading or news reading). It is also useful when buyers need information about product features and prices (e.g., automobiles or computers). The Internet is less useful for products that must be touched or examined in advance. But even this has exceptions. People can order furniture from EthanAllen.com, major appliances from Sears.com, and expensive computers from Dell or Gateway without trying them in advance.

THE DOT-COM BUBBLE Pure-online Web businesses reached astronomical capitalization levels in the late 1990s, in some cases far exceeding the capitalization of major companies such as United Airlines or Pepsi-Cola. They were considered a major threat to traditional businesses until the investing frenzy collapsed in 2000. "Marketing Insight: Burst of the Dot-Com Bubble" describes the decline in dot-com fortunes. As much as the Internet boom was overhyped, its demise may have also been

MARKETING INSIGHT

Burst of the Dot-Com Bubble

Although the Internet ushered in a new era, many businesses did not capitalize on the initial opportunities and made a host of errors. Dot-coms failed for a variety of reasons: Many rushed into the market without proper research or planning. They had poorly designed Web sites with problems of complexity, poor navigation, and downtime. They lacked adequate infrastructures for shipping on time and for answering customer inquiries. They believed that the first company entering a category would win category leadership. These companies wanted to exploit network economies, namely the fact that the value of a network to each of its members is proportional to the number of other users (Metcalfe's Law). Some just rushed into the market in the hope of launching an initial public offering (IPO) while the market was hot.

Many dot-coms did not build a sound business model that would deliver eventual profits. The ease of entry of competitors and the ease of customers switching Web sites in search of better prices forced them to accept margin-killing low prices. To acquire customers, dot-coms spent large amounts on mass marketing and offline advertising. They relied on spin and buzz instead of target marketing and word-of-mouth marketing, and they devoted too much effort to acquiring customers instead of building loyal and more frequent users among current customers. They did not understand customer behaviour when it came to online surfing and purchasing.

Bottom line: Building an effective online business requires much of the same hard work, careful planning, and patience as does a traditional business.

Source: Adapted from Timothy J. Mullaney, The "E-Biz Surprise," *BusinessWeek*, May 12, 2003, pp. 60–68.

TABLE 15.3	E-BUSINESS PERCEPTION VERSUS REALITY
Perception	**Reality**
Profitable Internet companies are rare.	About 40 percent of 200-plus public Net companies made a fourth-quarter profit in 2003.
Companies ditched Web efforts amid the tech recession.	Spending on e-business projects has risen every year since the bust, now comprising 27 percent of all tech spending.
Broadband has not gained traction.	Broadband users represented 53.6 percent of the online population in Canada in 2003. (U.S. broadband users accounted for 33.8 percent of the online population.)
The productivity gain from e-business turned out to be modest.	Productivity growth doubled as the Net proliferated, but most of the acceleration was in industries that use tech a lot, such as autos.
Online advertising died.	The popularity of banner ads gave way to ads tied to search results, boosting North American online advertising to US$10.2 billion in 2005, or just over 5 percent share of total ad spending.
IPO investors in e-tailors lost lots of money.	An investment of $1000 in every e-tail IPO, good or bad, would have increased about 35 percent.
B2B e-commerce never really happened.	Although hundreds of B2B exchanges failed, an estimated US$3.9 trillion worth of e-commerce was conducted worldwide in 2003.
Web-era productivity gains are confined to tech companies.	More than 80 percent of post-1995 acceleration is in nontech industries.

Sources: Timothy J. Mullaney, "The E-Biz Surprise," *BusinessWeek*, May 12, 2003, pp. 60–68; Chris Daniels, "Broadband Wins on the Web," *Marketing Magazine Online*, **www.marketingmag.ca**, March 18, 2003 (viewed October 6, 2004); "Forecast: 2005 Online Ad Spend Will Rise 30%,"**www.adxchange.com/**.

greatly exaggerated, as Canadian tech giants Nortel and JDS Uniphase are still able to find markets for their networking technologies. Table 15.3 displays some common misperceptions about the current state of e-business and e-commerce.

BUSINESS-TO-BUSINESS E-COMMERCE Although the popular press has given the most attention to business-to-consumer (B2C) Web sites, even more activity is being conducted on business-to-business (B2B) sites. The B2B sites are changing the supplier–customer relationship in profound ways. Firms are using B2B auction sites, spot exchanges, online product catalogues, barter sites, and other online resources to obtain better prices. In 2002, LendingTree brokered 1.5 million loans on behalf of 170 lenders. Retail loans are an ideal commodity to trade online: Loans are highly standardized, the lending industry is fragmented, and large volumes of transactions allow small profit margins to add up.[43]

The impact of B2B sites is to make markets more efficient. In the past, buyers had to exert a lot of effort to gather information on worldwide suppliers. With the Internet, buyers have easy access to a great deal of information. They can get information from (1) supplier Web sites, (2) *infomediaries*, third parties that add value by aggregating information about alternatives; (3) *market makers*, third parties that create markets linking buyers and sellers, and (4) *customer communities*, which are Web sites where buyers can swap stories about suppliers' products and services.[44]

The net impact of these mechanisms is to make prices more transparent. In the case of undifferentiated products, price pressure will increase. In the case of highly differentiated products, buyers will gain a better picture of their true value. Suppliers of superior products will be able to offset price transparency with value transparency; suppliers of undifferentiated products will have to drive down their costs in order to compete.

Hybrid Companies

Many brick-and-mortar companies have agonized over whether to add an online e-commerce channel. Many companies moved quickly to open Web sites describing their businesses but resisted adding e-commerce to their sites. They felt that selling their products or services online would produce channel conflict—they would be competing with their offline retailers, agents, or own stores.[45]

Compaq feared, for example, that its retailers would drop its line of computers if Compaq offered to sell the same computers directly online. Merrill Lynch hesitated to introduce online stock trading to compete with E*TRADE, TD Waterhouse, and other online brokerages, fearing that its own brokers would rebel. Even the store-based bookseller Chapters (now Chapters Indigo) delayed opening an online site to challenge Amazon. All eventually succumbed after seeing how much business was rushing to its online competitors.

Yet adding an e-commerce channel creates the threat of a backlash from retailers, brokers, agents, and other intermediaries. The question is how to sell both through intermediaries and online. There are at least three strategies for trying to gain acceptance from intermediaries: (1) Offer different brands or products on the Internet; (2) offer the offline partners higher commissions to cushion the negative impact on sales; and (3) take orders on the Web site but have retailers deliver and collect payment. Harley-Davidson treaded carefully before going online:

Harley-Davidson

Given that Harley sells more than US$500 million worth of parts and accessories to its loyal followers, an online venture was an obvious next step to generate even more revenue. Harley needed to be careful, however, to avoid the wrath of 650 dealers who benefited from the high margins on those sales. Harley's solution was to send customers seeking to buy accessories online to the company's Web site. Before they can buy anything, they are prompted to select a participating Harley-Davidson dealer. When the customer places the order, it is transmitted to the selected dealer for fulfillment, ensuring that the dealer still remains the focal point of the customer experience. Dealers, in turn, had to agree to a number of standards, such as checking for orders twice a day and shipping orders promptly. The Web site now gets more than 1 million visitors a month.[46]

Some pure or predominantly online companies have invested in brick-and-mortar sites. Dell introduced kiosks into big-name chains such as Sears to better target consumers and allow product trial. Dell was rebuffed by some retailers, such as Best Buy, who viewed the company as a competitor.[47]

Companies who have an established presence and have built a reputation for customer service must set up and operate their e-commerce Web sites carefully. Consider what Future Shop has done:

Future Shop

Attempting to create a similar experience between both online and offline shopping, Future Shop added a "Learn More" option with links to product reviews and buyer guides for the company's products. For example, it offers a "Freezer Buying Guide" that helps customers select the right model and size of freezer—tailoring options to particular families. "Ask the expert" provides reviews of the latest products, such as the Apple iPod. An interactive flyer on the site replicates those that are found in-store and visitors can check product availability with the click of a mouse. So far, Future Shop's e-commerce strategy has been successful. In 2004, online visits increased by 50 percent and orders increased by more than 100 percent over those received in 2003.[48]

Ultimately, companies may need to decide whether to drop some or all of their retailer outlets and go direct. Banks, however, have found that despite the convenience of online services, some customers still prefer to conduct certain transactions at the bank itself—80 percent of new chequing and savings accounts are still opened in physical bank branches.[49] Not everyone, however, has embraced the Internet as a channel. Consider Stihl:

Stihl

Stihl manufactures handheld outdoor power equipment. All Stihl products are branded under one name and Stihl does not do private labels for other companies. Stihl is best known for chain saws, but has expanded into string trimmers, blowers, hedge trimmers, and cut-off machines. It distributes products through a network of geographically exclusive distribution points, and then through a network of independent servicing dealers. Stihl is one of the few outdoor power equipment companies that do not sell their products through mass merchants, catalogues, or the Internet.[50]

Stihl Canada's Web site includes links to dealerships as well as other helpful information.

SUMMARY

1. Most producers do not sell their goods directly to final users. Between producers and final users stands one or more marketing channels, a host of marketing intermediaries performing a variety of functions.

2. Marketing-channel decisions are among the most critical decisions facing management. The company's chosen channel(s) profoundly affect all other marketing decisions.

3. Companies use intermediaries when they lack the financial resources to carry out direct marketing, when direct marketing is not feasible, and when they can earn more by doing so. The most important functions performed by intermediaries are information, promotion, negotiation, ordering, financing, risk taking, physical possession, payment, and title.

4. Manufacturers have many alternatives for reaching a market. They can sell direct or use one-, two-, or three-level channels. Deciding which type(s) of channel to use calls for analyzing customer needs, establishing channel objectives, and identifying and evaluating the major alternatives, including the types and numbers of intermediaries involved in the channel.

5. Effective channel management calls for selecting intermediaries and training and motivating them. The goal is to build a long-term partnership that will be profitable for all channel members.

6. Marketing channels are characterized by continuous and sometimes dramatic change. Three of the most important trends are the growth of vertical marketing systems, horizontal marketing systems, and multi-channel marketing systems.

7. All marketing channels have the potential for conflict and competition resulting from such sources as goal incompatibility, poorly defined roles and rights, perceptual differences, and interdependent relationships. Companies can manage conflict by striving for superordinate goals, exchanging people among two or more channel levels, co-opting the support of leaders in different parts of the channel, and encouraging joint membership in and between trade associations.

8. Channel arrangements are up to the company, but there are certain legal and ethical issues to be considered with regard to practices such as exclusive dealing or territories, tying agreements, and dealers' rights.

9. E-commerce has grown in importance as companies have adopted "brick-and-click" channel systems. Channel integration must recognize the distinctive strengths of online and offline selling and maximize their joint contributions.

APPLICATIONS

Marketing Debate: Does It Matter Where You Are Sold?

Some marketers feel that the image of the particular channel in which they sell their products does not matter—all that matters is that the right customers shop there and the product is displayed in the right way. Others maintain that channel images—such as a retail store—can be critical and must be consistent with the image of the product.

Take a position: Channel images do not really affect the brand images of the products they sell that much versus Channel images must be consistent with the brand image.

Marketing Discussion

Think of your favourite retailers. How have they integrated their channel system? How would you like their channels to be integrated? Do you use multiple channels from them? Why?

Marketing Spotlight: Amazon

Amazon started as the "world's largest bookstore" in July 1995. It was a virtual bookstore that physically owned no books. Many detractors wondered if the online channel was right for books. Without browsing, as in a retail store, how could book buyers decide whether they might like a book? Without a friendly, knowledgeable staff, how could book buyers find the right books? The only positive side of the new channel seemed to be that Amazon would be able to offer a vastly broader selection of titles than could be found in most local bookstores.

Amazon took steps to replicate the features of a physical bookstore in its online channel. First, it replicated the "friendly, knowledgeable staff" advice through reader book reviews. Anyone can write a review of a book on Amazon, and these reviews help customers pick books. A built-in ranking system lets browsers rank which reviews are helpful and which are not. Some reviewers even enjoy a kind of fame, writing hundreds of reviews over the years and garnering loyal followers who gladly buy books based on their comments.

Second, Amazon replicated the serendipity of browsing by offering a personalized recommendation service. Amazon realized that if one person is buying the same book as a second person bought, the two people probably share similar interests and outlooks. Thus, the first person might also be interested in other books that the second person bought. Amazon's personal recommendation service aggregates data on buying patterns to infer recommendations of who might like which book. The result is a list next to every book saying, "People who bought this book also bought the following books...." This invites people to browse Amazon's virtual shelves.

Amazon is also tackling the last downside of the virtual channel. The company started offering peeks into books' contents, index, and beginning pages. In 2003, Amazon pushed the virtual channel even further, introducing a "search inside the book" feature that lets customers search the entire text of 120 000 books—about as many titles as are in a Barnes & Noble bookstore. The service is free, although customers must register and have a credit card on file with Amazon. Customers type in a word, name, or phrase, and they get a list of the book pages in which those words appear. Customers can view an image of the page and two pages on either side of it, but they cannot print the results.

The Internet channel lets Amazon do promotions that a physical bookstore could not do. For example, during the 2003 holiday season, Amazon held a star-studded promotion: each day, a celebrated actor, author, director, musician, or media personality offered a piece of exclusive online content to Amazon.com shoppers free of charge. For example, Michael J. Fox and Jack Black exhibited original artwork. Musicians like Bruce Springsteen gave a sneak peek of an upcoming concert video and special "behind the scenes" content.

Amazon's goal with the promotion was to delight customers and to drive traffic and increase sales. So, the celebrities also recommended one to three of their favourite products that were available on Amazon.com. They could recommend their own CDs or movies, or they could choose something that they enjoyed owning themselves. "Having the participants recommend products was a great way to introduce shoppers to items they could buy for the holidays—but it also allowed them to get some insight into the celebrities. It was a very impactful promotion," said Amazon spokesperson Emily Glassman.

By keeping the schedule of "appearances" secret, Amazon gave customers an incentive to come to the site daily to see who would be making the next appearance. The promotion, along with the extended product offering and free shipping for orders over US$25, gave Amazon its busiest holiday season ever. More than 2.1 million units were ordered in a single day—24 items per second.

Amazon doesn't have a retail presence, and therefore doesn't need to worry about pricing differences between online and retail stores. Retailers who try to operate both channels run the risk of channel conflict—turf wars between the online and physical retail channels over sharing costs (e.g., marketing), price competition (if the online channel undercuts the physical channel), and sharing profits (e.g., when a consumer near a physical store buys online).

Go to many Amazon pages and you will find used copies of the book for sale alongside new copies. These used books are actually sold by independent used booksellers, not by Amazon. Why does Amazon cannibalize its own new book sales with sales of used books that it does not even own? The key is that the transaction fees and profits for a used book are not similar to the profits from new book sales. Amazon's own new book sales give it higher revenues than helping someone else sell a used copy, but the new book sales also have much higher costs. In the end, helping others to sell used books brings in both more profits and more customers to Amazon's site.

Amazon doesn't fear the retail channel. In fact, it gets revenue by helping traditional brick-and-mortar retailers like Target.com and Nordstrom and Toys "R" Us enter the online world. Not only does Amazon get a service fee for opening the online site, it also gets a cut of the sales sold through the online channel, which helped increase Amazon's overall sales revenue by 33 percent in 2003. For Amazon, the channel is not about buying wholesale and selling retail—it is about creating a retail service channel that connects sellers to consumers.

DISCUSSION QUESTIONS

1. What have been the key success factors for Amazon?

2. Where is Amazon vulnerable? What should it watch out for?

3. What recommendations would you make to its senior marketing executives going forward? What should the company be sure to do with its marketing?

Sources: Elizabeth West, "Who's Next?" *Potentials* (February 2004): 7–8; Nikki Swartz, "Amazon.com's Text Search Revolution," *Information Management Journal* (January–February 2004): 18–19; Chris Taylor, "Smart Library," *Time*, November 17, 2003, p. 68; Cynthia L. Webb, "Amazon's Lump of Coal?" Washingtonpost.com, October 22, 2003.

16

- What major types of marketing intermediaries occupy this sector?

- What marketing decisions do these marketing intermediaries make?

- What are the major trends with marketing intermediaries?

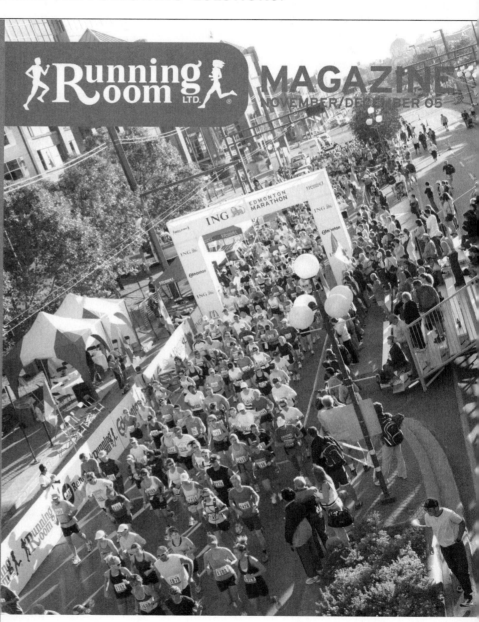

CHAPTER 16

Managing Retailing, Wholesaling, and Logistics

PROFILE: CANADIAN MARKETING EXCELLENCE

No Canadian retail concept has a more inspiring beginning than the Running Room Ltd., founded by John Stanton. When participating in a three-kilometre "fun run" with his sons, he found to his dismay that he could only run the distance between two streetlights. He was so embarrassed by his lack of fitness that he started running at night. It wasn't long before he discovered the benefits of fitness. He also discovered, however, that running alone at night wasn't much fun. That was when the light went on that he needed a group to keep himself motivated. When such a group proved hard to find, John started to dream, and he envisioned opening a store that could help people get good running advice and products while also serving as a place where runners and walkers could meet and form a community to run together.

Stanton soon turned the dream into reality. He opened his first Running Room location in 1984 in Edmonton in an old house shared with a hairdressing shop. Today, Running Room stores can be found in 63 locations in Canada and the United States. Runners who join the stores' community are often inspired by John, who has now run over 55 marathons, hundreds of road races, and numerous triathlons, including the Canadian Ironman and the Hawaiian World Championship Ironman competition. He is also the author of two Canadian best-selling books on running and spends much of his time motivating people to improve their lives through fitness.

In 2004 the Running Room Ltd. was honoured with the "Innovative Retailer of the Year" award (mid-size category) by the Retail Council of Canada. It was cited for its innovative approach to employee training and its obsession with product knowledge and community-centric activities that have undoubtedly contributed to the retailer's ongoing success. As Janet Brisebois, president of the Retail Council, noted when announcing the award, the Running Room has shunned fad techniques like shock advertising and proven that innovative thinking in a very focused and wholesome business can be a winning combination.

The Running Room is all about people and building relationships among them—the customers and the in-store team. It is a store for runners, managed by runners. The staff knows that buying running shoes, for novices and experts alike, is often an overwhelming process. Thus, not only can the highly knowledgeable staff provide expert advice, the in-store displays make browsing for shoes a less daunting experience. Shoes are classified by type rather than by supplier, as is the case in other sports stores. In-store staff also work hard to custom-fit each customer.

To get people involved in fitness, the Running Room offers clinics—from "Learn to Run" to "Triathlon." Clinic instructors teach the basics as well as the benefits of better nutrition and fitness. Each clinic is led by a graduate of the program who shows participants how to make progress. Over 40 000 people a year participate in the various clinics, which cost $75 for each ten-week program.

Through such clinics and the sponsorship of running-related events in its communities, the Running Room maintains close relationships with its customers. As John Stanton notes, "If you are building and supporting and involved in the community, by definition, you're involved with your customer." For example, to commemorate the firm's 20th anniversary in July 2004, thousands of people gathered at Running Rooms across North America to take the "20-Minute Challenge." Challenge organizers wanted to encourage more people to get off the couch and take a first step toward becoming fit for life. People of all fitness levels were encouraged to bring as many friends and family members as possible to walk or run for up to 20 minutes. Participants also received a free commemorative red running cap to serve as a symbol of their commitment to their own personal fitness.

Keeping in touch with the customer is the touchstone of the Running Room chain. When staff members run with their customers, they know what they are thinking and feeling at the end of a run. It's this real-time learning that gets translated back into the product selection and service the customers receive at the store.

The Running Room's clinics are advertised in all the stores on a big sandwich board as well as in community newspapers. The company also publishes its own bi-monthly magazine, which offers stories and tips by runners. The magazine has over 127 000 subscribers, and with its "pass-along" readership, it is read by more than half a million people. Advertisers can buy space in the magazine to feature their products or sporting events.

Small, niche retailers like the Running Room have effectively tapped into consumers' desire to be treated as individuals. "We have watched an exodus from department stores and seen the specialty store channel grow," says David Howell, vice-president at Toronto-based market researcher NPD Group. While department store sales declined by 6 percent between 1999 and 2003, specialty retailers saw their dollar share of the market jump from 41.3 percent to 43.5 percent. David Howell goes on to note, "Due to time constraints, customers want service. They're not only looking for value—they're looking for attention."

Building communities of runners and maintaining close relationships has helped the Running Room reach the finish line before its many competitors. Year in, year out, the niche chain typically achieves 20 percent growth in sales.

Sources: Kristen Vinakmens, "Small but Mighty," *Strategy Magazine*, December 15, 2003, p. 1; "Running Room Ltd.: 20-Minute Challenge Aims to Get Canadians Moving," *Business Wire*, June 25, 2004; Running Room Web site, **www.runningroom.com**; Retail Council of Canada, "2004 Award Winners," **www.retailcouncil.ca/media/press/pr20040531.asp**.

In the previous chapter, we examined marketing intermediaries from the viewpoint of manufacturers who wanted to build and manage marketing channels. In this chapter, we view these intermediaries—retailers, wholesalers, and logistical organizations—as requiring and forging their own marketing strategies. Intermediaries must strive for marketing excellence like any company or suffer the consequences. Some intermediaries dominate the manufacturers who deal with them. Many use strategic planning, advanced information systems, and sophisticated marketing tools. They measure performance more on a return-on-investment basis than on a profit-margin basis. They segment their markets, improve their market targeting and positioning, and aggressively pursue market expansion and diversification strategies. In this chapter, we consider marketing excellence in retailing, wholesaling, and logistics.

Retailing

Retailing includes all the activities involved in selling goods or services directly to final consumers for personal, nonbusiness use. A **retailer** or **retail store** is any business enterprise whose sales volume comes primarily from retailing.

Any organization selling to final consumers—whether it is a manufacturer, wholesaler, or retailer—is doing retailing. It does not matter *how* the goods or services are sold (by person, mail, telephone, vending machine, or Internet) or *where* they are sold (in a store, on the street, or in the consumer's home).

Types of Retailers

Consumers today can shop for goods and services in a wide variety of retail organizations. There are store retailers, nonstore retailers, and retail organizations. Perhaps the best-known type of retailer is the department store. Japanese department stores such as Takashimaya and Mitsukoshi attract millions of shoppers each year. These stores feature art galleries, restaurants, cooking classes, and children's playgrounds.

Retail-store types pass through stages of growth and decline that can be described as the *retail life cycle*.[1] A type emerges, enjoys a period of accelerated growth, reaches maturity, and then declines. Department stores took 80 years to reach maturity, whereas warehouse retail outlets reached maturity in 10 years. One of the biggest trends in Canadian retailing is the consolidation of retailing in many areas. In particular is the growing dominance of chain stores in grocery retailing. By 2002, the big grocery and convenience outlet chains (e.g., Loblaws, Sobeys, A&P, and members of the Couche Tarde family of convenience stores) attained a 60.7 percent market share compared to the 57.85 achieved in the previous year.[2] The most important retail-store types are described in Table 16.1.

LEVELS OF SERVICE The *wheel-of-retailing* hypothesis explains one reason that new store types emerge.[3] Conventional retail stores typically increase their services and raise their prices to cover the costs. These higher costs provide an opportunity for new store forms to offer lower prices and less

TABLE 16.1	MAJOR RETAILER TYPES

Specialty store: Narrow product line. *Examples:* Footlocker, Tall Girl, The Body Shop.

Department store: Several product lines. *Examples:* Sears, The Bay.

Supermarket: Large, low-cost, low-margin, high-volume, self-service store designed to meet total needs for food and household products. *Examples:* Loblaws, Sobeys, Provigo.

Convenience store: Small store in residential area, often open 24/7, limited line of high-turnover convenience products plus takeout. *Examples:* 7-Eleven, Mac's Milk.

Discount store: Standard or specialty merchandise; low-price, low-margin, high-volume stores. *Examples:* Wal-Mart, Kmart, Future Shop.

Off-price retailer: Leftover goods, overruns, irregular merchandise sold at less than retail. *Example:* Winners.

Superstore: Huge selling space, routinely purchased food and household items, plus services (laundry, shoe repair, dry cleaning, cheque cashing). Category killer (deep assortment in one category) such as Petsmart, Staples, Home Depot, Canadian Tire; combination store such as Jewel, Osco; hypermarket (huge stores that combine supermarket, discount, and warehouse retailing), such as Carrefour in France, Pyrca in Spain, and Meijer's in the Netherlands.

Catalogue showroom: Broad selection of high-markup, fast-moving, brand-name goods sold by catalogue at discount. Customers pick up merchandise at the store. *Example:* Service Merchandise.

service. New store types meet widely different consumer preferences for service levels and specific services.

Retailers can position themselves as offering one of four levels of service:

1. *Self-service*. Self-service is the cornerstone of all discount operations. Many customers are willing to carry out their own locate-compare-select process to save money.

2. *Self-selection*. Customers find their own goods, although they can ask for assistance.

3. *Limited service*. These retailers carry more shopping goods, and customers need more information and assistance. The stores also offer services (such as credit and merchandise-return privileges).

4. *Full service*. Salespeople are ready to assist in every phase of the locate-compare-select process. Customers who like to be waited on prefer this type of store. The high staffing cost, along with the higher proportion of specialty goods and slower-moving items and the many services, results in high-cost retailing.

By combining these different service levels with different assortment breadths, we can distinguish the four broad positioning strategies available to retailers, as shown in Figure 16.1:

1. *Holt Renfrew*. Stores that feature a broad product assortment and high value added. Stores in this quadrant pay close attention to store design, product quality, service, and image. Their profit margin is high, and if they are fortunate enough to have high volume, they will be very profitable.

2. *Birks*. Stores that feature a narrow product assortment and high value added. Such stores cultivate an exclusive image and tend to operate on a high margin and low volume.

3. *Sunglass Hut*. Stores that feature a narrow line and low value added. Such stores keep their costs and prices low by centralizing buying, merchandising, advertising, and distribution.

4. *Zellers*. Stores that feature a broad line and low value added. They focus on keeping prices low so that they have an image of being a place for good buys. They make up for low margin by high volume.

Although the overwhelming bulk (97 percent) of goods and services is sold through stores, *nonstore retailing* has been growing much faster than store retailing. Nonstore retailing falls into four major categories: direct selling, direct marketing (which includes telemarketing and Internet selling), automatic vending, and buying services:

1. *Direct selling* (also called *multi-level selling, network marketing*) is a $1.6 billion industry in Canada according to the Direct Sellers Association. Well-known in one-to-one selling are Avon, Cutco Knives, Electrolux, Tupperware, and Mary Kay Cosmetics. A salesperson goes to the home of a host who has invited friends; the salesperson demonstrates the products and takes orders. Pioneered by Amway, the multi-level (network) marketing sales system consists of recruiting independent businesspeople who act as distributors. The distributor's compensation includes a percentage of sales of those the distributor recruits as well as earnings on direct sales to customers. These direct selling firms, now finding fewer consumers at home, are developing multi-distribution strategies.

FIGURE 16.1

Retail Positioning Map

Source: Adapted from William T. Gregor and Eileen M. Friars, *Money Merchandising: Retail Revolution in Consumer Financial Service* (Cambridge, MA: The MAC Group, 1982).

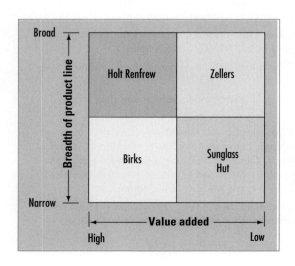

2. *Direct marketing* has roots in direct mail and catalogue marketing (e.g., Tilley Endurables, Mountain Equipment Co-op); it includes *telemarketing* (e.g., 1-800-FLOWERS), *television direct-response marketing* (e.g., The Shopping Channel), and *electronic shopping* (e.g., Chapters.Indigo.ca, Dell.ca). Of these, electronic shopping experienced a major take-off in the late 1990s as consumers flocked to dot-com sites to buy books, music, toys, electronics, and other products.

3. *Automatic vending* is used for a variety of merchandise, including impulse goods like cigarettes, soft drinks, coffee, candy, newspapers, magazines, and other products like hosiery, cosmetics, hot food, condoms, and paperbacks. Vending machines are found in factories, offices, large retail stores, gasoline stations, hotels, restaurants, and many other places. They offer 24-hour selling, self-service, and merchandise that is always fresh. Japan has the most vending machines per person—Coca-Cola has over 1 million there, and annual vending sales of US$50 billion (twice that of the United States). These reliable, high-tech machines allow consumers to buy products ranging from blue jeans to expensive lunches.[4]

4. *Buying service* is a storeless retailer serving a specific clientele—usually employees of large organizations—who are entitled to buy from a list of retailers that have agreed to give discounts in return for membership.

CORPORATE RETAILING   Although many retail stores are independently owned, an increasing number are part of some form of **corporate retailing**. Corporate retail organizations achieve economies of scale, greater purchasing power, wider brand recognition, and better-trained employees. The major types of corporate retailing—corporate chain stores, voluntary chains, retailer cooperatives, franchises, and merchandising conglomerates—are described in Table 16.2. Franchising is described in detail in "Marketing Insight: Franchise Fever."

New Models for Success

In the past, retailers held customers by offering convenient location, special or unique assortments of goods, greater or better services than competitors, and store credit cards. All of this has changed. Today, national brands such as Ralph Lauren Polo, Calvin Klein, and Levi's are found in department stores, in their own shops, in merchandise outlets, and in off-price discount stores. In their drive for volume, national-brand manufacturers have placed their branded goods everywhere. The result is that retail-store assortments have grown more alike.

Service differentiation also has eroded. Many department stores have trimmed services, and many discounters have increased services. Customers have become smarter shoppers. They do not

TABLE 16.2	MAJOR TYPES OF CORPORATE RETAIL ORGANIZATIONS

Corporate chain store: Two or more outlets owned and controlled, employing central buying and merchandising, and selling similar lines of merchandise. *Examples:* The Gap, Club Monaco, and Pottery Barn.

Voluntary chain: A wholesaler-sponsored group of independent retailers engaged in bulk buying and common merchandising. *Example:* Independent Grocers Alliance (IGA).

Retailer cooperative: Independent retailers using a central buying organization and joint promotion efforts. *Examples:* Associated Grocers, ACE Hardware.

Consumer cooperative: A retail firm owned by its customers. Members contribute money to open their own store, vote on its policies, elect a group to manage it, and receive dividends.

Franchise organization: Contractual association between a franchiser and franchisees, popular in a number of product and service areas. *Examples:* Canadian Tire, Harvey's, Subway, Pizza Hut, Mr. Lube, 7-Eleven.

Merchandising conglomerate: A corporation that combines several diversified retailing lines and forms under central ownership, with some integration of distribution and management. *Examples:* Allied Domeq PLC with Dunkin' Donuts and Baskin-Robbins, plus a number of British retailers and a wine and spirits group.

MARKETING INSIGHT

Franchise Fever

There are over 1300 franchisors in Canada responsible for over 75 000 actual franchise units (e.g., store fronts), employing approximately 3.4 percent of all Canadians (over 1 million people). They are grouped into 44 different industry sectors. The restaurant category alone accounts for over 18 000 franchise units (almost half of which are fast food). In fact, statistically speaking, a new franchise opens very two hours every day, 365 days a year in Canada. This figure should not come as a surprise in a society where it is nearly impossible to stroll down a city block or drive on a suburban thoroughfare without seeing a McDonald's, Mr. Lube, a Magicuts, or a 7-Eleven.

In a franchising system, individual *franchisees* are a tightly knit group of enterprises whose systematic operations are planned, directed, and controlled by the operation's innovator, called a *franchisor*. Franchises are distinguished by three characteristics:

1. The franchisor owns a trade or service mark and licenses it to franchisees in return for royalty payments.

2. The franchisee pays for the right to be part of the system. Start-up costs include rental and lease equipment and fixtures, and usually a regular licence fee. In Canada, the average start-up investment fee for franchises is just over $160 000. The average annual franchise fee is just over $23 000.

3. The franchisor provides its franchisees with a system for doing business. McDonald's requires franchisees to attend "Hamburger University" in Oak Brook, Illinois, for three weeks to learn how to manage the business. Franchisees must follow certain procedures in buying materials.

Franchising is mutually beneficial to both franchisor and franchisee. Among the benefits reaped by franchisors are the motivation and hard work of employees who are entrepreneurs rather than "hired hands," the franchisees' familiarity with local communities and conditions, and the enormous purchasing power of the franchisor. Franchisees benefit from buying into a business with a well-known and accepted brand name. They find it easier to borrow money from financial institutions, and they receive support in areas ranging from marketing and advertising to site selection and staffing.

Franchisees do walk a line between being independent and loyal to the franchisor. Their independence can allow them more flexibility. When Mike Roper opened his first Quiznos Sub franchise south of Chicago in the fall of 2000, the restaurant industry was about to collapse into its longest slump in nearly 30 years. Yet, his sales leapt 40 percent in his store's second year, far exceeding his projection of only 4 percent growth. Whenever business slows, he pretends it is "grand-opening day" again, with coupons and cookie giveaways to draw more traffic. "When you have your own money on the line, you act a little differently," he says. "You tend to be a little more aggressive on the day to day."

The franchise explosion in recent years, however, has increasingly saturated the market. To sustain growth, firms are looking overseas (McDonald's has over 30 000 restaurants in 119 countries) or in nontraditional site locations. Franchises are opening in airports, sports stadiums, college campuses, hospitals, gambling casinos, theme parks, convention halls, and even riverboats.

Sources: Francon Canada Web site, **www.francon.com** (viewed October 18, 2004); Norman D. Axelrad and Robert E. Weigand, "Franchising—A Marriage of System Members," in *Marketing Managers Handbook,* 3rd ed., edited by Sidney Levy, George Frerichs, and Howard Gordon (Chicago: Dartnell, 1994), pp. 919–934; Meg Whittemore, "New Directions in Franchising," *Nation's Business* (January 1995): 45–52; "Trouble in Franchise Nation," *Fortune,* March 6, 1995, pp. 115–129; Carol Steinberg, "Millionaire Franchisees," *Success* (March 1995): 65–69; Richard Gibson, "Even 'Copycat' Businesses Require Creativity and Flexibility," *Wall Street Journal Online,* March 2004; **www.entrepreneur.com**.

want to pay more for identical brands, especially when service differences have diminished; nor do they need credit from a particular store, because bank credit cards are almost universally accepted.

In the face of increased competition from discount houses and specialty stores, department stores are waging a comeback war. In addition to locations in the centres of cities, many have branches in suburban shopping centres, where parking is plentiful and family incomes are higher. Bloomingdale's opened a store in downtown SoHo to attract young, well-heeled New Yorkers who would rarely venture up to their flagship midtown store.[5] To better compete, other department stores update merchandise more frequently, remodel their stores, introduce their own brands, and experiment with mail-order and online marketing, and telemarketing.[6]

Wall poster ads for Bloomingdale's new SoHo store in New York.

Two models for department store success seem to be emerging:[7]

- *Strong retail brand approach.* In this type of department store, typified by Marks and Spencer in the United Kingdom and Kohl's in the United States, in-house brands feature strongly and managers take an active role in choosing inventory. Kohl's and Marks and Spencer are more interested in promoting themselves as brands than promoting any particular brand within them. While these stores tend to have high operating costs, they usually command high margins if their in-house brands are both fashionable and popular.

- *The showcase store.* Typified by Galeries Lafayette in Paris and Selfridges in London, the showcase store not only sells other people's brands but often gets the vendors of those brands to take responsibility for stock, staff, and even the selling space. The vendors then hand over a percentage of the sales to the store's owner. This translates into lower gross margins for the department store but also lower operating costs. The showcase store needs to keep droves of customers coming in, and that means it needs to be an entertainment destination in its own right. Galeries Lafayette's flagship Paris store recently offered free lessons from professional striptease artists to promote the opening of its huge new lingerie department.

Supermarkets have opened larger stores, carried a larger number and variety of items, and upgraded facilities. Supermarkets have also increased their promotional budgets and moved heavily into private brands. Others have sought to create stronger differentiation.

Whole Foods Market

In 157 stores located in Canada, the United States, and Great Britain, Whole Foods creates celebrations of food. The markets are bright and well staffed, and food displays are bountiful and seductive. Whole Foods is the largest organic and natural foods grocer in North America and offers lots of information about its food. If you want to know, for instance, whether the chicken in the display case lived a happy, free-roaming life, you get a 16-page booklet and an invitation to visit the farm where it was raised. If you can't find the information you need, you have only to ask a well-trained and knowledgeable employee. Whole Foods' approach is working, especially for consumers who view organic and artisanal food as an affordable luxury. Between 2000 and 2003, Whole Foods beat Wal-Mart in both overall and comparable-store, year-to-year sales growth.[8]

Marketing Decisions

We will examine retailers' marketing decisions in the areas of target market, product assortment and procurement, services and store atmosphere, price, communication, and location. (See also "Marketing Memo: Helping Stores to Sell.")

TARGET MARKET   A retailer's most important decision concerns the target market. Until the target market is defined and profiled, the retailer cannot make consistent decisions on product assortment, store décor, advertising messages and media, price, and service levels. Zellers, for example, targets two main groups: moms (with children under the age of 12) who want relief from the challenges of shopping for the family, and Canadians who are looking for great value without compromising quality or style. Both groups have an average household income of $50 000.[9] Some retailers define their target market more narrowly:

The North West Company

Headquartered in Winnipeg, this venerable retailer can trace its roots back to the 1700s. Today its 181 outlets are the lifeline of many remote communities from British Columbia to Labrador. As *Canadian Business* notes, "If the key to success in retail is to know your customer, then North West is on top of its game." Its mostly Aboriginal customers can obtain everything from fresh vegetables to traditional foods to financial services. Despite facing some of the most challenging obstacles faced by any Canadian retailer—vast distances, extreme cold—the firm continues to rack up profits to the tune of $0.57 per share. (Compare this to the $0.02 returns posted in the same period by the Hudson Bay Company.) Moreover, since one of the firm's largest shareholders is a consortium of Aboriginal groups, much of this profit goes back to the First Nations.[10]

Marketing Memo

Helping Stores to Sell

In the pursuit of higher sales volume, retailers are studying their store environments for ways to improve the shopper experience. Paco Underhill, managing director of the retail consultant Envirosell Inc., offers the following advice for fine-tuning retail space in order to keep shoppers spending:

- *Attract shoppers and keep them in the store.* The amount of time shoppers spend in a store is perhaps the single most important factor in determining how much they will buy.
- *Honour the "transition zone."* On entering a store, people need to slow down and sort out the stimuli, which means that shoppers will likely be moving too fast to respond positively to signs, merchandise, or sales clerks in the zone they cross before making that transition. Make sure there are clear sight lines.
- *Don't make them hunt.* Put the most popular products up front to reward busy shoppers and encourage leisurely shoppers to look more. At Staples, ink cartridges are one of the first products shoppers encounter after entering.
- *Make merchandise available to the reach and touch.* It is hard to overemphasize the importance of customers' hands. A store can offer the finest, cheapest, sexiest goods, but if the shopper cannot reach or pick them up, much of their appeal can be lost.
- *Men do not ask questions.* Men always move faster than women do through store's aisles. In many settings, it is hard to get them to look at anything they had not intended to buy. Men also do not like asking where things are. If a man cannot find the section he is looking for, he will wheel about once or twice, then leave the store without ever asking for help.
- *Women need space.* A shopper, especially a woman, is far less likely to buy an item if her derriere is brushed, even lightly, by another customer when she is looking at a display. Keeping aisles wide and clear is crucial.
- *Make checkout easy.* Be sure to have the right high-margin goods near cash registers to satisfy impulse shoppers. And people love to buy candy when they check out—so satisfy their sweet tooth.

Sources: Paco Underhill, *Why We Buy: The Science of Shopping* (New York: Simon & Schuster, 1999); Keith Hammonds, "How We Sell," *Fast Company* (November 1999): 294; Paul Keegan, "The Architect of Happy Customers," *Business 2.0* (August 2002): 85–87; Bob Parks, "5 Rules of Great Design," *Business 2.0* (March 2003): 47–49.

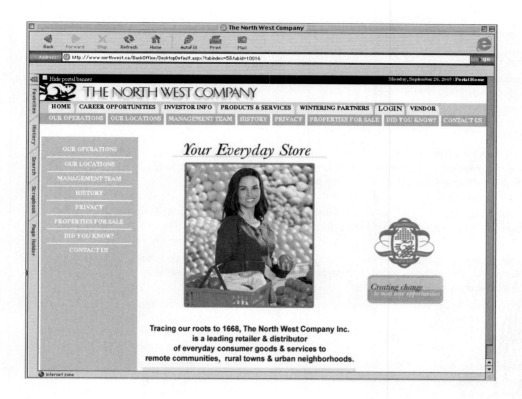

Knowing the needs of its precisely defined target market has led the North West Company to success.

Today, retailers are slicing the market into finer and finer segments and introducing new lines of stores to provide a more relevant set of offerings to exploit niche markets.[11]

PRODUCT ASSORTMENT   The retailer's product assortment must match the target market's shopping expectations. The retailer has to decide on product-assortment *breadth* and *depth*. A restaurant can offer a narrow and shallow assortment (small lunch counters), a narrow and deep assortment (delicatessen), a broad and shallow assortment (cafeteria), or a broad and deep assortment (large restaurant). Table 16.3 provides an illustration of how Borders developed category assortment within a section of its stores.

Consider the assortment strategies of these Canadian retailers:

- *Mountain Equipment Co-op.* A narrow yet deep assortment of outdoor clothing and equipment for hiking, camping, cycling, climbing, and canoeing.

- *Loblaws.* A shallow and broad assortment of food, cleaning products, health-care products, and even house wares.

- *Pita Pit.* A narrow and shallow assortment of pitas that come in only a few basic varieties (e.g., chicken, souvlaki, B.L.T., falafel).

- *Pet Value.* A narrow and deep selection of pet food and pet supplies.

The real challenge begins after defining the store's product assortment, and that is to develop a product-differentiation strategy. Here are some possibilities:

- *Feature exclusive national brands that are not available at competing retailers.* Thus the Bay might get exclusive rights to carry the dresses of a well-known international designer.

- *Feature mostly private branded merchandise.* Benetton and the Gap design most of the clothes carried in their stores. Many supermarket and drug chains carry private branded merchandise.

- *Feature blockbuster distinctive merchandise events.* Pier 1 Imports will run month-long shows featuring the goods of another country, such as India or China, throughout the store.

- *Feature surprise or ever-changing merchandise.* Benetton changes some portion of its merchandise every month so that customers will want to drop in frequently. Winners offers surprise assortments of distress merchandise (goods the owner must sell immediately because it needs cash), overstocks, and closeouts.

TABLE 16.3	RETAIL CATEGORY MANAGEMENT	
Step	**What It Means**	**How Borders Applied It**
1. Define the category.	Decide where you draw the line between product categories. For example, do your customers view alcohol and soft drinks as one beverage category, or should you manage them separately?	Named the cookbook section "Food and Cooking" because consumers expected to see books on nutrition there as well.
2. Figure out its role.	Determine how the category fits into the whole store. For example, "destination" categories lure folks in, so they get maximum marketing push, while "fill-ins" carry a minimal assortment.	Decided to make "Food and Cooking" a destination category.
3. Assess performance.	Analyze sales data from ACNielsen, Information Resources Inc., and others. Identify opportunities.	Learned that cookbooks sell faster than expected during holidays. Responded by creating gift promotions.
4. Set goals.	Agree on the category's objectives, including sales, profit, and average-transaction targets, as well as customer satisfaction levels.	Aimed to grow cookbook sales faster than the store average and to grab market share from competition.
5. Choose the audience.	Sharpen your focus within the category for maximum effect.	Decided to go after repeat buyers. "Since 30% of shoppers buy 70% of the cookbooks sold, we are aiming at the enthusiast," says Borders chief marketing officer Mike Spinozzi.
6. Figure out tactics.	Decide the best product selection, promotion merchandising, and pricing to achieve the category's goals.	Gave more prominent display to books by celebrity chiefs like Mario Batali. Created a more approachable product selection by reducing the number of titles on certain subjects.
7. Implement the plan.	Set the timetable and execute the tactics.	Introduced changes to its cooking sections as of November 2002.

Source: Andrew Raskin, "Who's Minding the Store," *Business 2.0* (February 2003): 73.

- *Feature the latest or newest merchandise first.* Hot Topic sells hip clothing and hard-to-find pop culture merchandise to teens, catching trends to launch new products in six to eight weeks, literally months before traditional competitors using off-shore suppliers.[12]
- *Offer merchandise customizing services.* Harrod's of London will make custom-tailored suits, shirts, and ties for customers, in addition to ready-made menswear.
- *Offer a highly targeted assortment.* Lane Bryant carries goods for the larger woman. Brookstone offers unusual tools and gadgets for the person who wants to shop in an "adult toy store."[13]

Merchandise may vary by geographical market. In 2003, electronics superstore Best Buy reviewed each of its 25 000 SKUs to adjust its merchandise according to income level and buying habits of shoppers.[14]

PROCUREMENT After deciding on the product-assortment strategy, the retailer must establish merchandise sources, policies, and practices. In the corporate headquarters of a supermarket chain, specialist buyers (sometimes called *merchandise managers*) are responsible for developing brand assortments and listening to salespersons' presentations. In some chains, buyers have the authority to accept or reject new items. In other chains, they are limited to screening "obvious rejects" and "obvious accepts"; they bring other items to the buying committee for approval. Even when an item is accepted by a chain-store buying committee, individual stores in the chain may not carry it. About one-third of the items must be stocked and about two-thirds are stocked at the discretion of each store manager.

Manufacturers face a major challenge trying to get new items onto store shelves. They offer supermarkets between 150 and 250 new items each week, of which store buyers reject over 70 percent. Manufacturers need to know the acceptance criteria used by buyers, buying committees, and store managers. ACNielsen Company interviewed store managers and found that they are most influ-

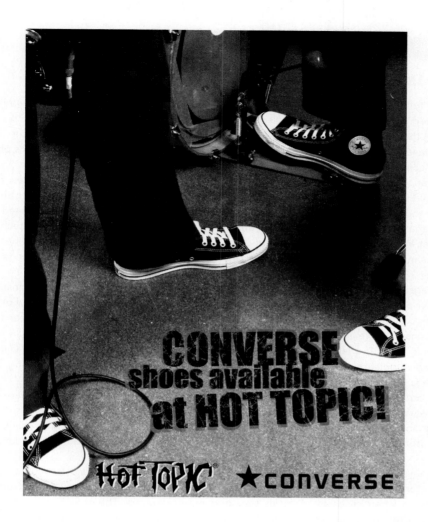

Print ad for Hot Topic and Converse shoes: Hot Topic features the merchandise teens want, usually before the competition does.

enced (in order of importance) by strong evidence of consumer acceptance, a well-designed advertising and sales-promotion plan, and generous financial incentives to the trade.

Retailers are rapidly improving their skills in demand forecasting, merchandise selection, stock control, space allocation, and display. They are using computers to track inventory, compute economic order quantities, order goods, and analyze dollars spent on vendors and products. Supermarket chains are using scanner data to manage their merchandise mix on a store-by-store basis, and soon all stores will probably be using "smart tags" to track goods, in real time, as they move from factories to supermarkets to shopping baskets. Smart tags are based on inexpensive versions of Radio Frequency Identification (RFID) tracking technology. RFID systems are made up of readers and smart tags—microchips attached to antennas. When a tag nears a reader, it broadcasts the information in the chip. Smart tags contain unique numbers to identify products and to provide a means to look up detailed additional information stored in the computer. For more on the possible uses—and abuses—of this technology, see "Marketing Insight: Making Labels Smarter."

When retailers do study the economics of buying and selling individual products, they typically find that a third of their space is being tied up by products that do not make an economic profit (above the cost of capital) for the store. Another third of the space is typically allocated to product categories that have break-even economics. And the final third of space actually creates more than 100 percent of the economic profit. Yet, most retailers are unaware of which third of their products is generating the profit.[15]

Stores are using **direct product profitability (DPP)** to measure a product's handling costs (receiving, moving to storage, paperwork, selecting, checking, loading, and space cost) from the time it reaches the warehouse until a customer buys it in the retail store. Resellers who have adopted DPP learn to their surprise that the gross margin on a product often bears little relation to the direct product profit. Some high-volume products may have such high handling costs that they are less

MARKETING INSIGHT

Making Labels Smarter

In April 2004, several pallets of toilet paper arrived at Wal-Mart's Sanger, Texas, distribution centre. This seemingly mundane event actually heralded a revolution in retailing technology. With a small electronic tag affixed to each crate of Kimberly Clark goods, the toilet tissue announced its own arrival to the distribution centre at the same time that a computer checked that the crates were the exact same ones that rumbled out of Kimberly Clark's plant. If any crates were missing, the computer would issue an alert.

Radio Frequency Identification (RFID) or "smart" tags have been around for decades. Wal-Mart's widespread adoption of them, however, could make them as common as bar codes. For just as the pallets of tissue paper, shampoo, and other goods were announcing their own arrival in Wal-Mart's distribution centre, Wal-Mart stunned the retailing world by announcing that it expects—no, demands—that its top 100 suppliers implement RFID technology by January 2005. And what Wal-Mart demands, suppliers *do*. If Wal-Mart's suppliers meet the deadline, the mega-retailer stands to save as much as US$8 billion a year. Here's just a snapshot of how RFID will change the business landscape.

A key rationale for RFID tags is that retailers can alert manufacturers before shelves go bare, and consumer goods manufacturers can further perfect their supply chain so that they don't produce or distribute too few or too many goods. Gillette maintains that retailers and consumer goods firms lose around US$30 billion a year from being out of stock on crucial items. Gillette is using smart tags to let store owners know that they need to reorder more stock, as well as to provide alerts if a large decrease from a shelf may be the result of shoplifting. Gillette also is using smart tags to improve logistics and shipping from factories versus traditional bar code scanning. IBM consultants assert that smart tags can shrink inventories by 5 to 25 percent.

RFID technology has the potential to transform our relationship to the objects around us and the relationship of objects to each other. For instance, your clothes might soon be able to tell your washing machine what settings to use. Frozen dinners may be able to tell the microwave what setting to use. "RFID could help give inanimate objects the power to sense, reason, communicate and even act," says Glover Ferguson, chief scientist for consulting firm Accenture.

The ability to link product IDs with databases containing the life histories and whereabouts of products makes RFID useful for preventing counterfeiting and even ensuring food and drug safety. A food company could program a system to alert plant managers when cases of meat sit too long unrefrigerated. The U.S. Food and Drug Administration is already pushing for the widespread tagging of medicines to keep counterfeit pharmaceuticals from entering the market. Some retailers are using RFID to prevent shoplifting.

Although a potential boon to marketers, smart tags raise issues of consumer privacy. Take the example of tagged medications. Electronic readers in office buildings might detect the type of medication carried by employees—an invasion of privacy. Or what about RFID-enabled customer loyalty cards that encode all sorts of personal and financial data? Already more than 40 public-interest groups have called for strict public-notification rules, the right to demand deactivation of the tag when people leave stores, and overall limits on the technology's use until privacy concerns have been better addressed. Privacy advocates have ample time to organize. So far the price of RFID technology is too prohibitive to tag individual items. At a price of between 25 and 50 cents per tag, it is not yet worth it to put them on every can of soda or tube of toothpaste.

Sources: Christine Y. Chen, "Wal-Mart Drives a New Tech Boom," *Fortune*, June 28, 2004, p. 202; Rana Foroohar, "The Future of Shopping," *Newsweek*, June 7, 2004, p. 74; Jonathan Krim, "Embedding Their Hopes in RFID: Tagging Technology Promises Efficiency but Raises Privacy Issue," *The Washington Post*, June 23, 2004, p. E01; Barbara Rose, "Smart-Tag Wave About to Wash over Retailing," *Chicago Tribune*, April 18, 2004, p. 5; "The Best Thing Since Bar Code," *The Economist*, February 8, 2003, pp. 57–58.

profitable and deserve less shelf space than low-volume products. Clearly, vendors are facing increasingly sophisticated retailers.

To better differentiate themselves and generate consumer interest, some luxury retailers are attempting to make their stores and merchandise more varied. Burberry's sells antique cufflinks and made-to-measure Scottish kilts only in London and customized trench coats only in New York.[16]

Many people are familiar with Costco's enduring procurement strategy:

Costco

The bulk store Costco, with its 64 Canadian locations, has a unique procurement strategy that is driven almost exclusively on price and value. The company stocks products where they can provide the lowest price with the most to offer, and they sell in bulk. For example, one week they may stock a Panasonic stereo with certain features. If they find a Sony stereo of similar quality offering equal or better features at a better price, they will stock the Sony, once the Panasonics are out of stock. They are not product or brand loyal. For consumers, what this means is that they cannot expect to see the same products, or even the same brands, between Costco shopping excursions, but what they can expect is good value at reasonable prices.[17]

SERVICES AND STORE ATMOSPHERE   The services mix is a key tool for differentiating one store from another. Retailers must decide on the *services mix* to offer customers:

- Pre-purchase services include accepting telephone and mail orders, advertising, window and interior display, fitting rooms, shopping hours, fashion shows, trade-ins.
- Post-purchase services include shipping and delivery, gift-wrapping, adjustments and returns, alterations and tailoring, installations, engraving.
- Ancillary services include general information, cheque cashing, parking, restaurants, repairs, interior decorating, credit, washrooms, baby-attendant service.

Retailers also need to consider differentiating based on unerringly reliable customer service. Pressed by discounters and by shoppers who are increasingly blasé about brands, retailers are rediscovering the usefulness of customer service as a point of differentiation, whether it is face-to-face, across phone lines, or even via a technological innovation:

- The Gap's clerks are getting twice as much training as in the past and are encouraged to help customers plan outfits, which could mean more items rung up at the register.
- Wal-Mart has installed self-checkout lanes in some stores to speed harried customers through the final stage of shopping.
- Grocery stores have started zeroing in on customers and asking what they want to see in the store. Loblaws has done just that and has expanded its organic and natural food selection as a result.

Consider the case of Rona:

Rona

Rona, the Montreal-based home improvement chain, is the largest Canadian distributor and retailer of hardware, home renovation, and gardening products. It operates a network of some 530 franchised, affiliated, and corporate stores of various sizes and formats. It has 63 big box stores, 291 traditional stores, and 174 specialized stores. Says Michael Brossard, the national marketing director, "The flexibility of our network is our strength—we don't have a cookie cutter approach. We know from our studies that big box isn't for everyone, so we have a multifaceted network." Building relationships is also a key facet in Rona's strategy, especially for 80 small specialized Rona Hardware shops, most of which are located in Quebec. Plans are in place to expand the concept to Ontario and western Canada. The shops are located in densely populated areas with a high percentage of apartment buildings. The smaller format allows Rona merchants to offer personalized service, something that isn't always possible at a huge big box store, which could see 2000 customers on the weekend. "For a customer who has an immediate problem, local convenience is what they need, so all the core items are available in the small-format store." The mixed format strategy is certainly paying off. Rona has doubled its profits in recent years and sales have jumped almost 19 percent.[18]

Whatever retailers do to enhance customer service, they will have to keep women in mind. Approximately 85 percent of everything sold in North America is bought or influenced by a woman, and women are fed up with the decline in customer service. They are finding every possible way to get around the system, from ordering online to resisting fake sales or just doing without.[19] See "Marketing Memo: What Women Want from Customer Service," for guidelines on making the shopping experience more rewarding for women—and for your bottom line.

Atmosphere is another element in the store arsenal. Every store has a physical layout that makes it hard or easy to move around. Every store has a "look." The store must embody a planned atmosphere that suits the target market and draws consumers toward purchase. Supermarkets have found that varying the tempo of music affects the average time spent in the store and the average expenditures. Retailers are now adding fragrances to stimulate certain moods in shoppers. London's Heathrow Airport sprays the scent of pine needles because it stimulates the sense of holidays and weekend walks. Automobile dealers will spray a "leather" scent in second-hand cars to make them smell "new."[20]

West Edmonton Mall

With more than 800 shops and over 110 restaurants, the West Edmonton Mall bills itself as the world's largest entertainment and shopping complex, a place filled with excitement and adventure. It boasts seven world-class attractions—the world's largest indoor amusement park, the world's largest wave pool, Deep Sea Adventure (the world's largest indoor lake that offers submarine rides), an 18-hole mini golf course, an Ice Palace, Dolphin Lagoon, and Sea Life Caverns. There are also various nightclubs, restaurants, theatres, a Las Vegas–style Casino, a 3-D IMAX theatre, Playdium, and a live dinner theatre. Occasionally, shoppers are able to watch the Edmonton Oilers hockey team practise on the mall's skating rink. It even offers "doggie daycare" so people don't leave their pets shut in hot vehicles. Large numbers of tourists flock to Edmonton from distant locations just to visit the mall and stay at the adjacent luxury hotel, which is integral to their experience. You can take a virtual video tour by visiting www.westedmall.com.[21]

STORE ACTIVITIES AND EXPERIENCES The growth of e-commerce has forced traditional brick-and-mortar retailers to respond. In addition to their natural advantages, such as products that shoppers can actually see, touch, and test, real-life customer service, and no delivery lag time for small or medium-sized purchases, they also provide a shopping experience as a strong differentiator.[22]

To entice Internet-savvy consumers to visit their stores, real-life retailers are developing new services and promotions. The change in strategy can be noticed in practices as simple as calling each shopper a "guest" (as many stores are beginning to do) or as grandiose as building an indoor amusement park, much like West Edmonton Mall.

For example, REI applies the principle of "experiential retailing" in selling outdoor gear and clothing products: Consumers are able to test climbing equipment on 7-metre or even 20-metre walls in the store and can test Gore-Tex raincoats by going under a simulated rain shower.[23] Victoria's Secret stores work on the concept of "retail theatre": Customers feel they are in a romance novel, with lush music and faint floral scents in the background.

There has been a marked rise in establishments that provide a place for people to congregate, such as cafés, juice bars, bookshops, and brew pubs. Canadians have now come to expect a Starbucks coffee when shopping at Chapters. Similarly, at Metro Credit Union's Toronto flagship store, customers can sit and have a coffee while they peruse banking products. IKEA stores offer a supervised playroom, pushchairs, baby-care rooms, children's rooms, food-warming facilities, and children's meals.

Retailers are also creating in-store entertainment in the hope of attracting customers who want fun and excitement. In the United Kingdom, Selfridges is the champion of the showcase business model and the retail theme park. Selfridges also carves out areas within stores for outside manufacturers to control and display their brands as they see fit. Selfridges encourages these vendors to create vibrant, exciting areas that not only look very different, but also do different things. As the retailer strives to get "a younger centre of gravity," Selfridges' sales have increased 10.6 percent from 2002 to 2003.

Even manufacturers such as Maytag are realizing the power of adding retail theatre to their brand and have created showcase stores. At the grand opening of Maytag's Costa Mesa, California, store, customers were invited to "Bake cookies, clean your dishes. Take our washer for a spin. Stop in and test-drive your new appliance today." Test-driving appliances is not just an opening-day gig for

Maytag, but an everyday occurrence. Customers sit and eat pastries in Maytag's well-appointed kitchens and then see how clean the dishwasher can get their plates. They bring in their dirty laundry to try out a Maytag stackable washer/dryer while their children watch cartoons on TV.[24]

Super-regional malls are anchoring themselves with unique and interesting shops, rather than the brand-name department stores and national retailers that fill most traditional malls. Says Laurence C. Siegel, chairman and CEO at Mills Corp., "There are no Macy's at our centers. We want to create destination retail." The Sony Style store, where Sony entertainment and electronics products are displayed in environments that encourage customers to test them, is an example of a mega-mall store.

PRICE DECISION Prices are a key positioning factor and must be decided in relation to the target market, the product-and-service assortment mix, and the competition. All retailers would like to achieve high volumes and high gross margins. They would like high *Turns × Earns*, but the two usually do not go together. Most retailers fall into the *high-markup*, *lower-volume* group (fine specialty stores) or the *low-markup*, *higher-volume* group (mass merchandisers and discount stores). Within each of these groups are further gradations. Thus, at the West Edmonton Mall you can find two very different types of jewellery stores: Almaz "for the discriminating shopper" and Claire's for the "coolest chains, the hottest hairwear, and awesome accessories."

Retailers must also pay attention to pricing tactics. Most retailers will put low prices on

---

Marketing Memo

What Women Want from Customer Service

1. *Start at the end: speed up the checkout.* Don't tempt a woman to walk out by wasting her time. Whole Foods guarantees a maximum four-minute wait at its supermarkets. National Car Rental has eliminated waiting in line by allowing customers to reserve their vehicles online. So think a minute: What are you doing for your "big order" customers while the "10 item" dabblers whisk right through the turnstile?

2. *Make the experience worth having.* Figure out a way to teach anyone who's stationed near a store entrance the basic skills of saying "hello" and knowing the store layout. Wal-Mart and Old Navy have permanent greeters. If you can't afford extra people, ensure that the nicer staff work near the front door.

3. *Assign patrolling customer-care watchdogs on the sales floor.* Many women answer, "May I help you?" with "Just looking." She probably is. But watch when her head jerks up suddenly and her eyes scan the horizon looking for assistance. She is ready for help and she wants it NOW. It's the moment of truth, and if you miss it, you lose.

4. *Know who you are.* There's a reason that retailers like Chico's, The Limited, and Kohl's have been able to consistently turn in good numbers. Not only are their brands integrated (merchandise, environment, service, and pricing), but they also cater to the expectations of the customers who want them. Too many retailers covet "new" customers (read younger, thinner, hipper, richer), and ignore their core shoppers. Be proud of who you are—and love the one you're with.

Source: Adapted from Mary Lou Quinlan, "Women Aren't Buying It," *Brandweek*, June 2, 2003, pp. 20–22.

---

some items to serve as traffic builders or loss leaders. They will run storewide sales. They will plan markdowns on slower-moving merchandise. Shoe retailers, for example, expect to sell 50 percent of their shoes at the normal markup, 25 percent at a 40 percent markup, and the remaining 25 percent at cost.

As Chapter 14 notes, some retailers such as Wal-Mart have abandoned "sales pricing" in favour of everyday low pricing (EDLP). EDLP could lead to lower advertising costs, greater pricing stability, a stronger image of fairness and reliability, and higher retail profits. Research has shown that supermarket chains practising EDLP can be more profitable than those practising Hi-Lo sales pricing, but only in certain circumstances.[25]

COMMUNICATION DECISION   Retailers use a wide range of communication tools to generate traffic and purchases. They place ads, run special sales, issue money-saving coupons, and run frequent-shopper reward programs, in-store food sampling, and coupons on shelves or at checkout points. Each retailer must use communications that support and reinforce its image positioning. Fine stores will place tasteful full-page ads in magazines such as *Vogue, Vanity Fair,* or *Harper's*. They will carefully train salespeople to greet customers, interpret their needs, and handle complaints. Off-price retailers will arrange their merchandise to promote the idea of bargains and large savings, while conserving on service and sales assistance. Some retailers, like the LCBO, have even developed their own unique publications to better communicate their key messages:

The Liquor Control Board of Ontario (LCBO)

The LCBO is the mainstay retail destination for purchasing wine and spirits in Ontario. In fact, the organization has a monopoly on the sale of spirits in that province (while wine can also be purchased in some small shops, and beer can also be purchased at the Beer Store). While often criticized for its policies and spending priorities (as a government-owned organization and near monopoly), it has some unique communication tools that it has developed to generate additional traffic through the store. For example, the company has developed a "magalogue" (a unique combination of a magazine and catalogue) called *Food and Drink*. Customers can pick up a free copy of *Food and Drink* at LCBO stores when it is issued periodically throughout the year (generally around seasonal changes). The magalogue focuses on recipes, décor, music, and other lifestyle content. The LCBO has also set up kitchens in many of its stores that pick up on promotional themes and allow patrons to sample recommended foods and alcoholic beverages.[26]

LOCATION DECISION Retailers are accustomed to saying that the three keys to success are "location, location, and location." Department-store chains, oil companies, and fast-food franchisers exercise great care in selecting locations. The problem breaks down into selecting regions of the country in which to open outlets, then particular cities, and then particular sites. For example, even though the Forzani Group (which operates its stores under the banners SportChek, Sport Mart, and Coast Mountain Sports) has 16.4 percent overall market share in Canada, that share is not evenly spread across the provinces and there may be room for further penetration in certain provinces. The company's provincial market share in British Columbia, Alberta, and Quebec is greater than 20 percent, whereas in Saskatchewan, Manitoba, Ontario, and the Maritime provinces the company's provincial market share is less than 15 percent. This may provide guidance for where there is additional opportunity (all else being equal).[27]

Retailers can locate their stores in the central business district, a regional shopping centre, a community shopping centre, a shopping strip, or within a larger store:

- *General business districts.* This is the oldest and most heavily trafficked city area, often known as "downtown." Store and office rents are normally high. Most downtown areas were hit by a flight to the suburbs in the 1960s, resulting in deteriorated retailing facilities; but in the 1990s, a minor renaissance of interest in downtown apartments, stores, and restaurants began in many cities.

- *Regional shopping centres.* These are large suburban malls containing 40 to 200 stores. They usually draw customers from a 10- to 30-kilometre radius. Typically, malls featured one or two nationally known anchor stores, such as the Bay or Sears, and a great number of smaller stores, many under franchise operation. The department store's role, however, is increasingly taken over by a combination of big box stores such as the Shoe Company, Future Shop, Old Navy, Home Depot, and Staples.[28] Malls are attractive because of generous parking, one-stop shopping, restaurants, and recreational facilities. Successful malls charge high rents and may get a share of stores' sales.

- *Community shopping centres.* These are smaller malls with one anchor store and between 20 and 40 smaller stores.

- *Strip malls* (also called shopping strips). These contain a cluster of stores, usually housed in one long building, serving a neighbourhood's needs for groceries, hardware, laundry, shoe repair, and dry cleaning. They usually serve people within a five- to ten-minute driving range.

- *A location within a larger store.* Certain well-known retailers—Swiss Chalet, Starbucks, Tim Hortons—locate new, smaller units as concession space within larger stores or operations, such as airports, schools, or department stores.

In view of the relationship between high traffic and high rents, retailers must decide on the most advantageous locations for their outlets. They can use a variety of methods to assess locations, including traffic counts, surveys of consumer shopping habits, and analysis of competitive locations.[29] Several models for site location have also been formulated.[30]

Retailers can assess a particular store's sales effectiveness by looking at four indicators: (1) number of people passing by on an average day; (2) percentage who enter the store; (3) percentage of those entering who buy; and (4) average amount spent per sale.

Trends in Retailing

At this point, we can summarize the main developments retailers and manufacturers need to take into account in planning competitive strategies:

1. *New retail forms and combinations.* Some supermarkets include bank branches. Bookstores feature coffee shops. Gas stations include food stores. Loblaws supermarkets have added fitness clubs to their stores. Shopping malls and bus and train stations have peddler's carts in their aisles. Retailers are also experimenting with limited-time-only stores called "pop-ups" that let retailers promote brands, reach seasonal shoppers for a few weeks in busy areas, and create buzz. When U.S.-based Target launched its line of clothes designed by Isaac Mizrahi, it set up a temporary Target store at Rockefeller Center in New York City, which sold only the Mizrahi line.[31]

2. *Growth of intertype competition.* Different types of stores—discount stores, catalogue showrooms, department stores—all compete for the same consumers by carrying the same type of merchandise. Retailers that have helped shoppers to be economically cautious and to simplify their increasingly busy and complicated lives and that provide an emotional connection are the winners in the new retailing landscape of the twenty-first century. The biggest winners: supercentres, dollar stores, warehouse clubs, and the Internet.[32]

3. *Competition between store-based and non–store-based retailing.* Consumers now receive sales offers through direct mail letters and catalogues, and over television, computers, and telephones. These non–store-based retailers are taking business away from store-based retailers. Some store-based retailers initially saw online retailing as a definite threat. Home Depot shocked its top vendors (Black & Decker, Stanley Tools, etc.) by issuing a memo implying that if they started to sell online, Home Depot might drop them as suppliers. Now Home Depot is finding it advantageous to work with online retailers. Wal-Mart recently joined with America Online (AOL) so that AOL will provide a low-cost Internet access service that carries the Wal-Mart brand, and Wal-Mart will promote the service and AOL in its stores and through TV advertising. Stores such as Canadian Tire and Mountain Equipment Co-op have developed their own Web sites, and some online retailers are finding it advantageous to own or manage physical outlets, either retail stores or warehouses.

4. *Growth of giant retailers.* Through their superior information systems, logistical systems, and buying power, giant retailers are able to deliver good service and immense volumes of product at appealing prices to masses of consumers. They are crowding out smaller manufacturers who cannot deliver enough quantity and even dictating to the most powerful manufacturers what to make, how to price and promote, when and how to ship, and even how to improve production and management. Manufacturers need these accounts; otherwise they would lose 10 to 30 percent of the market. Some giant retailers are *category killers* that concentrate on one product category, such as toys (Toys "R" Us), home improvement (Home Depot), or office supplies (Staples). Others are *supercentres* that combine grocery items with a huge selection of nonfood merchandise (Wal-Mart).[33]

5. *Decline of middle-market retailers.* Increasingly, the retail market can be characterized as being hourglass or dog-bone shaped: Growth seems to be centred at the top (with luxury offerings from retailers like Holt Renfrew and Harry Rosen) or at the bottom (with discount pricing for outlets like Winners and Old Navy). Opportunities are scarcer in the middle where retailers such as Sears and the Bay have struggled. Supermarkets, department stores, and drugstores are most at risk or on the brink—since 2000, fewer consumers have shopped these channels weekly, as newer, more relevant places have come to serve their needs.[34] As discount retailers improve their quality and image, consumers have been willing to trade down. Thirty percent of Zellers' sales now come from its store brands like Truly and Cherokee.[35] To better compete, Sears adjusted its merchandise, service, and prices in an attempt to provide a more compelling alternative to discounters and department stores.[36]

6. *Growing investment in technology.* Retailers are using computers to produce better forecasts, control inventory costs, order electronically from suppliers, send e-mail between stores, and even sell to customers within stores. They are adopting checkout scanning systems,[37] electronic funds transfer, electronic data interchange,[38] in-store television, store traffic radar systems,[39] and improved merchandise-handling systems.

7. *Global presence of major retailers.* Retailers with unique formats and strong brand positioning (McDonald's, The Limited, Gap, and Toys "R" Us) now have a global presence.[40] Wal-Mart operates over 700 stores abroad. Among overseas-based global retailers in North America are

Britain's Marks and Spencer, Italy's Benetton, Spain's Zara, Sweden's IKEA home furnishings stores, and Japan's Yaohan supermarkets.[41]

Private Labels

A growing trend and major marketing decision for retailers concerns private labels. A **private label brand** (also called reseller, store, house, or distributor brand) is one retailers and wholesalers develop. Retailers such as Benetton, The Body Shop, and Marks & Spencer carry mostly own-brand merchandise. In Britain, the largest food chains, Sainsbury and Tesco, sell 50 and 45 percent store-label goods, respectively. In Canada, the President's Choice private label brand sold at Loblaws carries enormous market strength.

Some experts believe that 50 percent is the natural limit for carrying private brands because (1) consumers prefer certain national brands, and (2) many product categories are not feasible or attractive on a private-brand basis.

Indeed, private brands are rapidly gaining ascendance in a way that has manufacturers of name brands running scared. Consider the following:[42]

- Wal-Mart's Ol Roy dog food has surpassed Nestlé's venerable Purina brand as the top-selling dog chow.
- One in every two ceiling fans sold is from Home Depot and most of those are its own Hampton Bay brand.
- *Consumer Reports* rated Winn-Dixie supermarket's chocolate ice cream ahead of brand name Breyers.
- Private label sales at Loblaws make up 30 percent of its sales (compared to the national average of 20 percent for other private labels).

Private labels can be found in many categories. When they found the computer selections on their shelves shrinking, big electronics retailers such as Best Buy and Radio Shack launched their own house-brand PCs.[43] Consider the following example of Bluenotes, which illustrates the power a private label brand can have:

Bluenotes

In 2000, Toronto-based retailer Thrifty's, then owned by Canadian retail giant Dylex, was sold to American Eagle Outfitters. At the time, Thrifty's sold a popular private-label brand of jeans called Bluenotes, in addition to national brands such as Levi's. When American Eagle purchased the company, one of the first major decisions was to rename the struggling retail store. It decided to rename the store after its most popular item, and what it had come to be known for—Bluenotes denim. Four years later, there are still some Thrifty's stores kicking around, but the company plans to have all 111 retail outlets under the Bluenotes name very soon. The popularity of the Bluenotes stores and brand was demonstrated in a recent survey conducted by Toronto-based youth marketing firm Youthography. The results listed Bluenotes as the store in which the greatest number of 13- to 19-year-olds frequently shop. Clearly private label brands are a driving force in retail![44]

House Brands

Why do intermediaries bother to sponsor their own brands? First, they are more profitable. Intermediaries search for manufacturers with excess capacity who will produce the private label at a low cost. Other costs, such as research and development, advertising, sales promotion, and physical distribution, are also much lower. This means that the private brander can charge a lower price and yet make a higher profit margin. Second, retailers develop exclusive store brands to differentiate themselves from competitors. Many consumers develop a preference for store brands in certain categories.

Loblaws

Since 1984, when its President's Choice line of foods made its debut, it has been difficult to say "private label" without Loblaws and President's Choice coming instantly to mind. Toronto-based Loblaws' Decadent Chocolate Chip Cookie quickly became a Canadian leader and showed how innovative store brands could compete effectively with national brands by matching or even exceeding their quality. A finely tuned brand strategy involving its premium President's Choice line and no-frills, yellow-labelled No Name line has helped differentiate its stores and build Loblaws into a powerhouse in Canada and the United States. The President's Choice line of products has become so successful that Loblaws is licensing it to noncompetitive retailers in other countries, thus turning a local store brand into—believe it or not—a global brand. Today, private label sales make up 30 percent of Loblaws' total sales, compared with a Canadian average of 20 percent.[45]

That's how store brands were "born." Today, more and more chains, like Shoppers Drug Mart with its Life brand, are looking to distinguish themselves in a crowded retail field with a brand that is available nowhere else. In some cases, there has even been a return to "no branding" of certain staple consumer goods and pharmaceuticals. Carrefours, the originator of the French hypermarket, introduced a line of "no brands" or generics in its stores in the early 1970s. **Generics** are unbranded, plainly packaged, less expensive versions of common products such as spaghetti, paper towels, and canned peaches. They offer standard or lower quality at a price that may be as much as 20 percent to 40 percent lower than nationally advertised brands and 10 percent to 20 percent lower than retailer private label brands. The lower price of generics is made possible by lower-quality ingredients, lower-cost labelling and packaging, and minimal advertising.

The Private Label Threat

In the confrontation between manufacturers' and private brands, retailers have many advantages and increasing market power. Because shelf space is scarce, many supermarkets now charge a *slotting fee* for accepting a new brand, to cover the cost of listing and stocking it. Retailers also charge for special display space and in-store advertising space. They typically give more prominent display to their own brands and make sure they are well stocked. Retailers are now building better quality into their store brands.

Shoppers Drug Mart has captured a piece of the personal care product market by selling its own brand of products, which cannot be purchased at any other store.

The growing power of store brands is not the only factor weakening national brands. Consumers are more price-sensitive. They are noting better quality as competing manufacturers and national retailers copy and duplicate the qualities of the best brands. The continuous barrage of coupons and price specials has trained a generation of shoppers to buy on price. The fact that companies have reduced advertising to 30 percent of their total promotion budget has weakened their brand equity. The endless stream of brand extensions and line extensions has blurred brand identity and led to a confusing amount of product proliferation.

Manufacturers have reacted to the private label threat, in part, by spending substantial amounts of money on consumer-directed advertising and promotion to maintain strong brand preference. The prices have to be somewhat higher to cover the higher promotion cost. At the same time, mass distributors pressure manufacturers to put more promotional money into trade allowances and deals if they want adequate shelf space. Once manufacturers start giving in, they have less to spend on advertising and consumer promotion, and their brand leadership spirals down. This is the national brand manufacturers' dilemma.

To maintain their power, leading brand marketers should invest in heavy and continuous R&D to bring out new brands, line extensions, features, and quality improvements. They must sustain a strong "pull" advertising program to maintain high consumer brand recognition and preference. They must find ways to partner with major mass distributors in a joint search for logistical economies and competitive strategies that produce savings. It is imperative to cut all unnecessary costs to have more competitive prices. National brands may command a price premium, but not one that exceeds the value perceptions of consumers.[46] Here is an example of what leading brand marketers must do:

Heinz

H. J. Heinz has retained market leadership in the ketchup category by combining a distinctive, slightly sweet-tasting product; a carefully monitored price gap with competitors; and aggressive packaging, product development, and promotional efforts (e.g., squeezable, "no drips" bottles, flavoured and coloured [Blastin' Green] ketchup, and hipper advertising).

Wholesaling

Wholesaling includes all the activities involved in selling goods or services to those who buy for resale or business use. Wholesaling excludes manufacturers and farmers because they are engaged primarily in production, and it excludes retailers. Wholesalers (also called *distributors*) differ from retailers in a number of ways. First, wholesalers pay less attention to promotion, atmosphere, and location because they are dealing with business customers rather than final consumers. Second,

Company-supplied photo for the introduction of three new colours of Heinz EZ Squirt: children and parents don't have a clue as to what's inside until they squirt it or draw with it on their favourite foods. The colours: Passion Pink, Awesome Orange, and Totally Teal.

wholesale transactions are usually larger than retail transactions, and wholesalers usually cover a larger trade area than retailers. Third, the government deals with wholesalers and retailers differently in terms of legal regulations and taxes.

Why are wholesalers used at all? Why do manufacturers not sell directly to retailers or final consumers? For answers to these questions, consider the case of Canadian film distributors:

Canadian Film Distribution Industry

The Canadian film distribution industry, which includes both motion picture and videotape distribution, is sandwiched between the production companies that produce the films and the theatres that show films or the retailers that distribute video products. The film distributors take on many important functions far beyond just being an intermediary. Distributors are responsible for much of the marketing activity for films, including formulating and implementing promotional and advertising strategies, developing key liaisons with the media, production of all promotional materials (publicity shots, stills, artwork, press kits), providing advice to producers so that the marketability of the film will be enhanced, and providing financing for productions through advances and buying of rights.[47]

In general, wholesalers are used when they are more efficient in performing one or more of the following functions:

- *Selling and promoting.* Wholesalers' sales forces help manufacturers reach many small business customers at a relatively low cost. Wholesalers have more contacts, and often buyers trust wholesalers more than they trust a distant manufacturer.
- *Buying and assortment building.* Wholesalers are able to select items and build the assortments their customers need, saving the customers considerable work.
- *Bulk breaking.* Wholesalers achieve savings for their customers through buying in large carload lots and breaking the bulk into smaller units.
- *Warehousing.* Wholesalers hold inventories, thereby reducing inventory costs and risks to suppliers and customers.
- *Transportation.* Wholesalers can often provide quicker delivery to buyers because they are closer to the buyers.
- *Financing.* Wholesalers finance customers by granting credit, and finance suppliers by ordering early and paying bills on time.
- *Risk bearing.* Wholesalers absorb some risk by taking title and bearing the cost of theft, damage, spoilage, and obsolescence.
- *Market information.* Wholesalers supply information to suppliers and customers regarding competitors' activities, new products, price developments, and so on.
- *Management services and counselling.* Wholesalers often help retailers improve their operations by training sales clerks, helping with store layouts and displays, and setting up accounting and inventory-control systems. They may help industrial customers by offering training and technical services.

The Growth and Types of Wholesaling

Wholesaling has grown in recent years.[48] A number of factors explain this: the growth of larger factories located some distance from the principal buyers; production in advance of orders rather than in response to specific orders; an increase in the number of levels of intermediate producers and users; and the increasing need for adapting products to the needs of intermediate and final users in terms of quantities, packages, and forms. The major types of wholesalers are described in Table 16.4.

Wholesaler Marketing Decisions

Wholesaler-distributors have faced mounting pressures in recent years from new sources of competition, demanding customers, new technologies, and more direct-buying programs by large industrial, institutional, and retail buyers. They have had to develop appropriate strategic responses. One major drive has been to increase asset productivity by managing their inventories and receivables better. They also have had to improve their strategic decisions on target markets, product assortment and services, price, promotion, and place.

TABLE 16.4	MAJOR WHOLESALER TYPES

Merchant wholesalers: Independently owned businesses that take title to the merchandise they handle. They are full-service and limited-service jobbers, distributors, and mill supply houses.

Full-service wholesalers: Carry stock, maintain a sales force, offer credit, make deliveries, and provide management assistance. Wholesale merchants sell primarily to retailers: some carry several merchandise lines, some carry one or two lines, others carry only part of a line. Industrial distributors sell to manufacturers and also provide services like credit and delivery.

Limited-service wholesalers: *Cash and carry wholesalers* sell a limited line of fast-moving goods to small retailers for cash. *Truck wholesalers* sell and deliver a limited line of semi-perishable goods to supermarkets, grocery stores, hospitals, restaurants, and hotels. *Drop shippers* serve bulk industries such as coal, lumber, and heavy equipment. They assume title and risk from the time an order is accepted to its delivery. *Rack jobbers* serve grocery retailers in nonfood items. Delivery people set up displays, price goods, and keep inventory records; they retain title to goods and bill retailers only for goods sold to end of year. *Producers' cooperatives* assemble farm produce to sell in local markets. *Mail-order wholesalers* send catalogues to retail, industrial, and institutional customers; orders are filled and sent by mail, rail, plane, or truck.

Brokers and agents: Facilitate buying and selling, on commission of 2 to 6 percent of the selling price; limited functions; generally specialize by product line or customer type. *Brokers* bring buyers and sellers together and assist in negotiation; paid by the party hiring them. Food brokers, real estate brokers, insurance brokers. *Agents* represent buyers or sellers on a more permanent basis. Most manufacturers' agents are small businesses, with a few skilled salespeople: selling agents have contractual authority to sell a manufacturer's entire output; purchasing agents make purchases for buyers and often receive, inspect, warehouse, and ship merchandise; commission merchants take physical possession of products and negotiate sales.

Manufacturers' and retailers' branches and offices: Wholesaling operations conducted by sellers or buyers themselves rather than through independent wholesalers. Separate branches and offices are dedicated to sales or purchasing. Many retailers set up purchasing offices in major market centres.

Specialized wholesalers: Agricultural assemblers (buy the agricultural output of many farms), petroleum bulk plants and terminals (consolidate the output of many wells), and auction companies (auction cars, equipment, etc. to dealers and other businesses).

TARGET MARKET Wholesalers need to define their target markets. They can choose a target group of customers by size (only large retailers), type of customer (convenience food stores only), need for service (customers who need credit), or other criteria. Within the target group, they can identify the most profitable customers and design stronger offers to build better relationships with them. They can propose automatic reordering systems, set up management-training and advisory systems, and even sponsor a voluntary chain. They can discourage less profitable customers by requiring larger orders or adding surcharges to smaller ones.

PRODUCT ASSORTMENT AND SERVICES The wholesalers' "product" is their assortment. Wholesalers are under great pressure to carry a full line and maintain sufficient stock for immediate delivery, but the costs of carrying huge inventories can kill profits. Wholesalers today are re-examining how many lines to carry and are choosing to carry only the more profitable ones. They are also examining which services count most in building strong customer relationships and which ones should be dropped or charged for. The key is to find a distinct mix of services valued by their customers.

PRICE DECISION Wholesalers usually mark up the cost of goods by a conventional percentage, say 20 percent, to cover their expenses. Expenses may run 17 percent of the gross margin, leaving a profit margin of approximately 3 percent. In grocery wholesaling, the average profit margin is often less than 2 percent. Wholesalers are beginning to experiment with new approaches to pricing. They might cut their margin on some lines in order to win important new customers. They will ask suppliers for a special price break when they can turn it into an opportunity to increase the supplier's sales.

PROMOTION DECISION   Wholesalers rely primarily on their sales force to achieve promotional objectives. Even here, most wholesalers see selling as a single salesperson talking to a single customer, instead of a team effort to sell, build, and service major accounts. Wholesalers would benefit from adopting some of the image-making techniques used by retailers. They need to develop an overall promotion strategy involving trade advertising, sales promotion, and publicity. They also need to make greater use of supplier promotion materials and programs.

PLACE DECISION   In the past, wholesalers were typically located in low-rent, low-tax areas and put little money into their physical setting and offices. Often the materials-handling systems and order-processing systems lagged behind the available technologies. Today, progressive wholesalers have been improving materials-handling procedures and costs by developing *automated warehouses* and improving their supply capabilities through advanced information systems. Here is an example:[49]

McKesson

McKesson Corporation is a leading health-care services company providing pharmaceutical and medical-surgical supply management, information solutions, pharmacy automation, and sales and marketing services to the health-care industry. The company has unmatched depth, breadth, and reach, delivering unique cost-saving and quality-improvement solutions to pharmacies, hospitals, physicians, extended care sites, payor sites, and pharmaceutical and medical-surgical manufacturers. McKesson maintains a strong presence on the Internet through its Web site (www.mckesson.com). The site offers access to information about the company, its people, products, and services. McKesson customers can use the Web site to access the company's health-care software applications as well as order and track pharmaceutical and medical-surgical products.[50]

TRENDS IN WHOLESALING   Manufacturers always have the option of bypassing wholesalers or replacing inefficient wholesalers with better ones. Manufacturers' major complaints against wholesalers are as follows: They do not aggressively promote the manufacturer's product line, and act more like order takers; they do not carry enough inventory and therefore fail to fill customers' orders fast enough; they do not supply the manufacturer with up-to-date market, customer, and competitive information; they do not attract high-calibre managers and bring down their own costs; and they charge too much for their services.

It even appeared that wholesalers were headed for a significant decline as large manufacturers and retailers moved aggressively into direct buying programs. Savvy wholesalers rallied to the challenge and began to re-engineer their businesses. The most successful wholesaler-distributors adapted their services to meet their suppliers' and target customers' changing needs. They recognized that they had to add value to the channel. They also had to reduce their operating costs by investing in more advanced materials-handling technology, information systems, and the Internet.

Macdonalds Consolidated

Calgary-based food wholesaler and distributor Macdonalds Consolidated owned by Canada Safeway offers its retailers considerable value. Principally, the company boasts strong buying power resulting in significant price advantages for its independent retail customers. However, it has also managed to explore other ways to both retain and grow existing accounts, in addition to acquiring new ones. For example, Macdonalds negotiated the exclusive right to offer Air Miles B2B to independent retailers. Like the consumer version of Air Miles, retailers accumulate points based upon purchases. They also offer a flexible weekly flyer program that comes in either a four-page or an eight-page format, depending on the individual retailer's needs. The four-page flyer appeals to smaller businesses that may not have fresh meat, produce, or deli sections, while the eight-page version is for full-size, full-service grocery retailers. Regardless of whether the customer is on the four- or eight-page program, the individual store's banner is clearly printed across the bottom of the front page. The company also offers consumer promotions programs that feature big-ticket draws for prizes such as a Ford F150 truck or a Harley-Davidson motorcycle.[51]

Narus and Anderson interviewed leading industrial distributors and identified four ways they strengthened their relationships with manufacturers:

1. They sought a clear agreement with their manufacturers about their expected functions in the marketing channel.

2. They gained insight into the manufacturers' requirements by visiting their plants and attending manufacturer association conventions and trade shows.

3. They fulfilled their commitments to the manufacturer by meeting the volume targets, paying bills promptly, and feeding back customer information to their manufacturers.

4. They identified and offered value-added services to help their suppliers.[52]

The wholesaling industry remains vulnerable to one of the most enduring trends—fierce resistance to price increases and the winnowing out of suppliers based on cost and quality. The trend toward vertical integration, in which manufacturers try to control or own their intermediaries, is still strong. "Marketing Memo: Strategies of High-Performance Wholesaler-Distributors" outlines some of the strategies used by successful wholesale organizations.

Market Logistics

Physical distribution starts at the factory. Managers choose a set of warehouses (stocking points) and transportation carriers that will deliver the goods to final destinations in the desired time or at the lowest total cost. Physical distribution has now been expanded into the broader concept of **supply chain management (SCM)**. Supply chain management starts before physical distribution: It involves procuring the right inputs (raw materials, components, and capital equipment); converting them efficiently into finished products; and dispatching them to the final destinations. An even broader perspective calls for studying how the company's suppliers themselves obtain their inputs. The supply chain perspective can help a company identify superior suppliers and distributors and help them improve productivity, which ultimately brings down the company's costs.

Market logistics involves planning the infrastructure to meet demand, then implementing and controlling the physical flows of materials and final goods from points of origin to points of use, to meet customer requirements at a profit.

Market logistics planning has four steps:[53]

1. Deciding on the company's value proposition to its customers. (What on-time delivery standard should be offered? What levels should be attained in ordering and billing accuracy?)

2. Deciding on the best channel design and network strategy for reaching the customers. (Should the company serve customers directly or through intermediaries? What products to source from which manufacturing facilities? How many warehouses to maintain and where should they be located?)

3. Developing operational excellence in sales forecasting, warehouse management, transportation management, and materials management.

4. Implementing the solution with the best information systems, equipment, policies, and procedures.

Market logistics leads to an examination of the most efficient way to deliver value:

■ A software company normally sees its challenge as producing and packaging software disks and manuals, then shipping them to wholesalers—who ship them to retailers, who sell them to customers. Customers bring the software package to home or office and download the software onto a hard drive. Market logistics would look at two superior delivery systems. The first involves ordering the software to be downloaded onto the customer's hard drive. The second system allows software to be loaded onto a computer by the computer manufacturer. Both solutions eliminate the need for printing, packaging, shipping, and stocking millions of disks and manuals. The same solutions are available for distributing music, newspapers, video games, films, and other products that deliver voice, text, data, or images.

■ The IKEA Retailers, franchisees of the world-famous IKEA concept for retail sale of furniture and home furnishings, are able to sell good-quality furniture and home furnishings at 20 percent less than competitors. The cost savings stem from several sources: (1) The IKEA Retailers buy in such large volume that they get lower prices; (2) the furniture and home furnishings are designed in "knockdown" form and shipped flat at a much lower transportation cost; (3) the customer drives the furniture home, which saves delivery cost; (4) the customer assembles the furniture. The IKEA concept works on a low markup and high volume.

The IKEA concept works on a low markup and high volume, allowing them to sell quality furniture and home furnishings for less than their competitors can.

Integrated Logistics Systems

The market logistics task calls for **integrated logistics systems (ILS)**, involving materials management, material flow systems, and physical distribution, abetted by information technology (IT). Third-party suppliers, such as FedEx Logistics Services or Ryder Integrated Logistics, often participate in designing or managing these systems. Volvo, working with FedEx, set up a warehouse in Memphis, Tennessee, with a complete stock of truck parts. A dealer, needing a part in an emergency, phones a toll-free number, and the part is flown out the same day and delivered that night either at the airport or at the dealer's office or even at the roadside repair site.

Information systems play a critical role in managing market logistics, especially computers, point-of-sale terminals, uniform product bar codes, satellite tracking, electronic data interchange (EDI), and electronic funds transfer (EFT). These developments have shortened the order-cycle time, reduced clerical labour, reduced the error rate in documents, and provided improved control of operations. They have enabled companies to make promises such as "The product will be at dock 25 at 10:00 A.M. tomorrow," and control this promise through information.

Market logistics involves several activities. The first is sales forecasting, on the basis of which the company schedules distribution, production, and inventory levels. Production

Marketing Memo

Strategies for High-Performance Wholesaler-Distributors

Lusch, Zizzo, and Kenderine studied 136 wholesalers in North America and concluded that the progressive ones are renewing themselves in five ways:

1. *Strengthening core operations.* Wholesalers develop such expertise in distributing their particular product line that manufacturers and retailers cannot duplicate the efficiency.

2. *Expanding into global markets.* Wholesalers, especially in the chemical, electronics, and computer fields, have been expanding globally.

3. *Doing more with less.* Wholesalers have been investing heavily in technology, including bar coding and scanning, fully automated warehouses, electronic data interchange (EDI), and advanced information technology.

4. *Committing to TQM.* Progressive wholesalers are moving toward managing processes to improve outcomes as perceived by customers, including performing quality assessment of suppliers' products and thereby adding value. As wholesalers move toward zero-defect customer service, manufacturers and retailers see this trend as contributing to their own capacity to satisfy customers.

5. *Marketing support philosophy.* Wholesalers recognize that their role is not simply to represent the suppliers' interests, or their customers' interests, but to support both by acting as a valued member of the marketing value chain.

Sources: Robert F. Lusch, Deborah Zizzo, and James M. Kenderine, "Strategic Renewal in Distribution," *Marketing Management 2*, no. 2 (1993): 20–29. Also see their *Foundations of Wholesaling—A Strategic and Financial Chart Book, Distribution Research Program* (Norman, OK: College of Business Administration, University of Oklahoma, 1996).

plans indicate the materials the purchasing department must order. These materials arrive through inbound transportation, enter the receiving area, and are stored in raw-material inventory. Raw materials are converted into finished goods. Finished-goods inventory is the link between customer orders and manufacturing activity. Customers' orders draw down the finished-goods inventory level, and manufacturing activity builds it up. Finished goods flow off the assembly line and pass through packaging, in-plant warehousing, shipping-room processing, outbound transportation, field warehousing, and customer delivery and servicing.

Management has become concerned about the total cost of market logistics, which can amount to 30 to 40 percent of the product's cost. The U.S. grocery industry alone thinks it can decrease its annual operating costs by 10 percent, or US$30 billion, by revamping its market logistics. A typical box of breakfast cereal takes 104 days to get from factory to supermarket, chugging through a labyrinth of wholesalers, distributors, brokers, and consolidators.[54] With inefficiencies like these, it is no wonder that experts call market logistics "the last frontier for cost economies." Lower market-logistics costs will permit lower prices, yield higher profit margins, or both. Even though the cost of market logistics can be high, a well-planned program can be a potent tool in competitive marketing. Companies can attract additional customers by offering better service, faster cycle time, or lower prices through market-logistics improvements.

Market-Logistics Objectives

Many companies state their market-logistics objective as "getting the right goods to the right places at the right time for the least cost." Unfortunately, this objective provides little practical guidance. No system can simultaneously maximize customer service and minimize distribution cost. Maximum customer service implies large inventories, premium transportation, and multiple warehouses, all of which raise market-logistics costs.

A company cannot achieve market-logistics efficiency by asking each market-logistics manager to minimize his or her own logistics costs. Market-logistics costs interact and are often negatively related. For example:

- The traffic manager favours rail shipment over air shipment because rail costs less. However, because the railroads are slower, rail shipment ties up working capital longer, delays customer payment, and might cause customers to buy from competitors who offer faster service.

- The shipping department uses cheap containers to minimize shipping costs. Cheaper containers lead to a higher rate of damaged goods and customer ill will.

- The inventory manager favours low inventories. This increases stockouts, back orders, paperwork, special production runs, and high-cost fast-freight shipments.

Given that market-logistics activities involve strong trade-offs, decisions must be made on a total system basis. The starting point is to study what customers require and what competitors are offering. Customers are interested in on-time delivery, supplier willingness to meet emergency needs, careful handling of merchandise, and supplier willingness to take back defective goods and resupply them quickly.

The company must then research the relative importance of these service outputs. For example, service-repair time is very important to buyers of copying equipment. Xerox developed a service-delivery standard that "can put a disabled machine anywhere in the continental United States back into operation within three hours after receiving the service request." It then designed a service division of personnel, parts, and locations to deliver on this promise.

The company must also consider competitors' service standards. It will normally want to match or exceed the competitors' service level, but the objective is to maximize profits, not sales. The company has to look at the costs of providing higher levels of service. Some companies offer less service and charge a lower price; other companies offer more service and charge a premium price.

The company ultimately has to establish some promise to the market. Coca-Cola wants to "put Coke within an arm's length of desire." Some companies define standards for each service factor. One appliance manufacturer has established the following service standards: to deliver at least 95 percent of the dealer's orders within seven days of order receipt, to fill the dealer's orders with 99 percent accuracy, to answer dealer inquiries on order status within three hours, and to ensure that damage to merchandise in transit does not exceed 1 percent.

Given the market-logistics objectives, the company must design a system that will minimize the cost of achieving these objectives. Each possible market-logistics system will lead to the following cost:

$$M = T + FW + VW + S$$

where M = total market-logistics cost of proposed system
T = total freight cost of proposed system
FW = total fixed warehouse cost of proposed system
VW = total variable warehouse costs (including inventory) of proposed system
S = total cost of lost sales due to average delivery delay under proposed system

Choosing a market-logistics system calls for examining the total cost *(M)* associated with different proposed systems and selecting the system that minimizes it. If it is hard to measure S, the company should aim to minimize $T + FW + VW$ for a target level of customer service.

Market-Logistics Decisions

Four major decisions must be made with regard to market logistics: (1) How should orders be handled? (order processing); (2) Where should stocks be located? (warehousing); (3) How much stock should be held? (inventory); and (4) How should goods be shipped? (transportation).

ORDER PROCESSING   Most companies today are trying to shorten the *order-to-payment cycle*—that is, the elapsed time between an order's receipt, delivery, and payment. This cycle involves many steps, including order transmission by the salesperson, order entry and customer credit check, inventory and production scheduling, order and invoice shipment, and receipt of payment. The longer this cycle takes, the lower the customer's satisfaction and the lower the company's profits. Salespeople may be slow in sending in orders and use inefficient communications; these orders may pile up on the desk of order processors while they wait for credit department approval and inventory availability information from the warehouse.

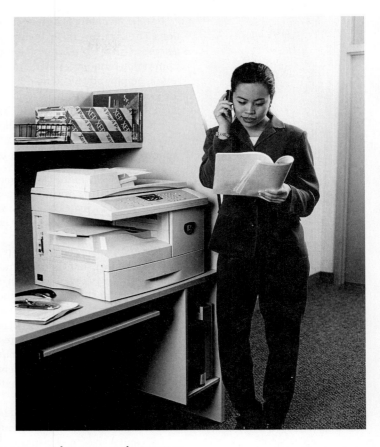

Xerox serviceperson checking with the home office on a repair call. Xerox's service standard is to put a disabled machine back in operation within three hours after receiving a call.

Companies need to prepare criteria for the Perfect Order. Suppose the customer expects on-time delivery, order completeness, picking accuracy, and billing accuracy. Suppose the supplier has a 70 percent chance of delivering all four of these perfectly on any order. Then the probability that the supplier will fulfill perfect orders five times in a row to that customer would be $0.70^5 = 0.168$. The customer's series of disappointments is likely to lead him or her to drop this supplier. A 70 percent standard is not good enough.

Companies are making progress, however. For example, General Electric operates an information system that checks the customer's credit standing upon receipt of an order, and determines whether and where the items are in stock. The computer issues an order to ship, bills the customer, updates the inventory records, sends a production order for new stock, and relays the message back to the sales representative that the customer's order is on its way—all in less than 15 seconds.

WAREHOUSING   Every company has to store finished goods until they are sold, because production and consumption cycles rarely match. The storage function helps to smooth discrepancies between production and quantities desired by the market. The company must decide on the number of inventory stocking locations. Consumer packaged-goods companies have been reducing their number of stocking locations from 10–15 to about 5–7; and pharmaceutical and medical distributors have cut their stocking locations from 90 to about 45. On the one hand, more stocking locations means that goods can be delivered to customers more quickly, but it also means higher warehousing and inventory costs. To reduce warehousing and inventory duplication costs, the company might centralize its inventory in one place and use fast transportation to fulfill orders. After National Semiconductor shut down its six storage warehouses and set up a central distribution warehouse in Singapore, its standard delivery time decreased by 47 percent, its distribution costs fell 2.5 percent, and its sales increased 34 percent.[55]

Some inventory is kept at or near the plant, and the rest is located in warehouses in other locations. The company might own private warehouses and also rent space in public warehouses. *Storage warehouses* store goods for moderate-to-long periods of time. *Distribution warehouses* receive goods from various company plants and suppliers and move them out as soon as possible. *Automated warehouses* employ advanced materials-handling systems under the control of a central computer. When the Helene Curtis Company replaced its six antiquated warehouses with a new US$32 million facility, it cut its distribution costs by 40 percent.[56]

Some warehouses are now taking on activities formerly done in the plant. These include assembly, packaging, and constructing promotional displays. "Postponing" finalization of the offering can achieve savings in costs and finer matching of offerings to demand.

INVENTORY   Inventory levels represent a major cost. Salespeople would like their companies to carry enough stock to fill all customer orders immediately. However, this is not cost-effective. *Inventory cost increases at an accelerating rate as the customer service level approaches 100 percent.* Management needs to know how much sales and profits would increase as a result of carrying larger inventories and promising faster order fulfillment times, and then make a decision.

Inventory decision making involves knowing when to order and how much to order. As inventory draws down, management must know at what stock level to place a new order. This stock level is called the *order (reorder) point*. An order point of 20 means reordering when the stock falls to 20 units. The order point should balance the risks of stockout against the costs of overstock. The other decision is how much to order. The larger the quantity ordered, the less frequently an order has to be placed. The company needs to balance order-processing costs and inventory-carrying costs. *Order-processing costs* for a manufacturer consist of *set-up costs* and *running costs* (operating costs when production is running) for the item. If set-up costs are low, the manufacturer can produce the item often, and the average cost per item is stable and equal to the running costs. If set-up costs are high, however, the manufacturer can reduce the average cost per unit by producing a long run and carrying more inventory.

Order-processing costs must be compared with *inventory-carrying costs*. The larger the average stock carried, the higher the inventory-carrying costs. These carrying costs include storage charges, cost of capital, taxes and insurance, and depreciation and obsolescence. Carrying costs might run as high as 30 percent of inventory value. This means that marketing managers who want their companies to carry larger inventories need to show that the larger inventories would produce incremental gross profit to exceed incremental carrying costs.

The optimal order quantity can be determined by observing how order-processing costs and inventory-carrying costs sum up at different order levels. Figure 16.2 shows that the order-processing cost per unit decreases with the number of units ordered because the order costs are spread over more units. Inventory-carrying charges per unit increase with the number of units ordered because each unit remains longer in inventory. The two cost curves are summed vertically into a total-cost curve. The lowest point on the total-cost curve is projected down on the horizontal axis to find the optimal order quantity Q^*.[57]

FIGURE 16.2

Determining Optimal Order Quantity

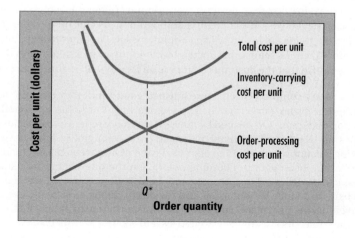

Companies are reducing their inventory costs by treating inventory items differently. They are positioning inventory items according to risk and opportunity. They distinguish between bottleneck items (high risk, low opportunity), critical items (high risk, high opportunity), commodities (low risk, high opportunity), and nuisance items (low risk, low opportunity).[58] They are also keeping slow-moving items in a central location while carrying fast-moving items in warehouses closer to customers.

The ultimate answer to carrying *near-zero inventory* is to build for order, not for stock. Sony calls it SOMA, "sell-one, make-one." Dell, for example, gets the customer to order a computer and pay for it in advance. Then Dell uses the customer's money to pay suppliers to ship the necessary components. As long as customers do not need the item immediately, everyone can save money.

Some retailers are using eBay to unload excess inventory. At least half a dozen big chains have set up "eBay Stores," Web pages devoted to their merchandise. They use the pages to auction off an assortment of items ranging from overstock goods to returned, reconditioned, or slightly damaged products. By cutting out the traditional liquidator intermediary, retailers can make 60 to 80 cents on the dollar as opposed to 10 cents on the dollar. Among those who have hung out their eBay shingles are Sears and Best Buy.[59]

TRANSPORTATION Marketers need to be concerned with transportation decisions. Transportation choices will affect product pricing, on-time delivery performance, and the condition of the goods when they arrive, all of which affects customer satisfaction.

In shipping goods to its warehouses, dealers, and customers, the company can choose among five transportation modes: rail, air, truck, waterway, and pipeline. Shippers consider such criteria as speed, frequency, dependability, capability, availability, traceability, and cost. For speed, air, rail, and truck are the prime contenders. If the goal is low cost, then it is water and pipeline.

Shippers are increasingly combining two or more transportation modes, thanks to containerization. **Containerization** consists of putting the goods in boxes or trailers that are easy to transfer between two transportation modes. *Piggyback* describes the use of rail and trucks; *fishyback*, water and trucks; *trainship*, water and rail; and *airtruck*, air and trucks. Each coordinated mode offers specific advantages. For example, piggyback is cheaper than trucking alone, yet provides flexibility and convenience.

In deciding on transportation modes, shippers can choose from private, contract, and common carriers. If the shipper owns its own truck or air fleet, the shipper becomes a *private carrier*. A *contract carrier* is an independent organization selling transportation services to others on a contract basis. A *common carrier* provides services between predetermined points on a scheduled basis and is available to all shippers at standard rates.

Today billions of dollars are being invested to develop "last-mile delivery systems" to bring products to homes within a short delivery period. Domino's Pizza organized its franchised stores to be in locations where it could promise to deliver hot pizzas to homes within one-half hour. Consumers

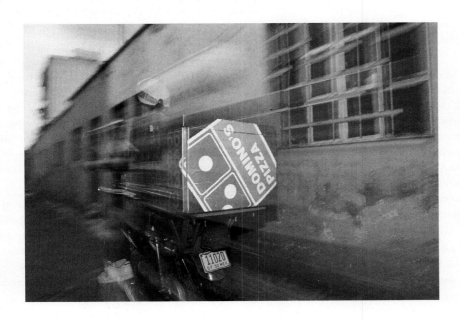

Mexico City: Domino's deliveryperson speeds hot pizza to waiting customers.

may soon think twice about whether they should exert themselves to travel to stores to get their food, videos, or clothes or simply ask the stores to bring it to them in about the same amount of time.

Organizational Lessons

Experience with market logistics has taught executives three major lessons:

1. Companies should appoint a senior vice-president of logistics to be the single point of contact for all logistical elements. This executive should be accountable for logistical performance on both cost and customer-satisfaction criteria.

2. The senior vice-president of logistics should hold periodic meetings (weekly, biweekly) with sales and operations people to review inventory, operating costs, and customer service and satisfaction, as well as to consider market conditions and whether changes should be made in production schedules.

3. New software and systems are the key to achieving competitively superior logistics performance in the future.

Market-logistics strategies must be derived from business strategies, rather than solely from cost considerations. The logistics system must be information-intensive and establish electronic links among all the significant parties. Finally, the company should set its logistics goals to match or exceed competitors' service standards and should involve members of all relevant teams in the planning process.

What happens if a firm's market logistics are not set up properly? Kodak launched a national advertising campaign for a new instant camera before it had delivered enough cameras to the stores. Customers found that it was not available and bought Polaroid cameras instead.

Today's stronger demands for logistical support from large customers will increase suppliers' costs. Customers want more frequent deliveries so that they do not have to carry as much inventory. They want shorter order-cycle times, which means that suppliers will have to carry high in-stock availability. Customers often want direct store delivery rather than shipments to distribution centres. They want mixed pallets rather than separate pallets. They want tighter promised delivery times. They may want custom packaging, price tagging, and display building.

Suppliers cannot say no to many of these requests, but at least they can set up different logistical programs with different service levels and customer charges. Smart companies will adjust their offerings to each major customer's requirements. The company's trade group will set up *differentiated distribution* by offering different bundled service programs for different customers.

SUMMARY

1. Retailing includes all the activities involved in selling goods or services directly to final consumers for personal, nonbusiness use. Retailers can be understood in terms of store retailing, nonstore retailing, and retail organizations.

2. Like products, retail-store types pass through stages of growth and decline. As existing stores offer more services to remain competitive, costs and prices go up, which opens the door to new retail forms that offer a mix of merchandise and services at lower prices. The major types of retail stores are specialty stores; department stores; supermarkets; convenience stores; discount stores; off-price retailers (factory outlets, independent off-price retailers, and warehouse clubs); superstores (combination stores and supermarkets); and catalogue showrooms.

3. Although most goods and services are sold through stores, nonstore retailing has been growing. The major types of nonstore retailing are direct selling (one-to-one

selling, one-to-many-party selling, and multi-level network marketing); direct marketing (which includes e-commerce and Internet retailing); automatic vending; and buying services.

4. Although many retail stores are independently owned, an increasing number are falling under some form of corporate retailing. Retail organizations achieve many economies of scale, such as greater purchasing power, wider brand recognition, and better-trained employees. The major types of corporate retailing are corporate chain stores, voluntary chains, retailer cooperatives, consumer cooperatives, franchise organizations, and merchandising conglomerates.

5. Like all marketers, retailers must prepare marketing plans that include decisions on target markets, product assortment and procurement, services and store atmosphere, price, promotion, and place. These decisions must take into account major trends, such as the growth of private labels, new retail forms and combina-

tions, growth of intertype retail competition, competition between store-based and non–store-based retailing, growth of giant retailers, decline of middle-market retailers, growing investment in technology, and global presence of major retailers.

6. Wholesaling includes all the activities involved in selling goods or services to those who buy for resale or business use. Wholesalers can perform functions better and more cost-effectively than the manufacturer can. These functions include selling and promoting, buying and assortment building, bulk breaking, warehousing, transportation, financing, risk bearing, dissemination of market information, and provision of management services and consulting.

7. There are four types of wholesalers: merchant wholesalers; brokers and agents; manufacturers' and retailers'

sales branches, sales offices, and purchasing offices; and miscellaneous wholesalers such as agricultural assemblers and auction companies.

8. Like retailers, wholesalers must decide on target markets, product assortment and services, price, promotion, and place. The most successful wholesalers are those who adapt their services to meet suppliers' and target customers' needs.

9. Producers of physical products and services must decide on market logistics—the best way to store and move goods and services to market destinations, to coordinate the activities of suppliers, purchasing agents, manufacturers, marketers, channel members, and customers. Major gains in logistical efficiency have come from advances in information technology.

APPLICATIONS

Marketing Debate: Should National Brand Manufacturers Also Supply Private Label Brands?

One controversial move by some marketers of major brands is to supply private label makers. For example, Ralston-Purina, Borden, ConAgra, and Heinz have all admitted to supplying products—sometimes lower in quality—to be used for private labels. Other marketers, however, criticize this "if you can't beat them, join them" strategy, maintaining that these actions, if revealed, may create confusion or even reinforce a perception by consumers that all brands in a category are essentially the same.

Take a position: Manufacturers should feel free to sell private labels as a source of revenue versus National manufacturers should never get involved with private labels.

Marketing Discussion

Think of your favourite stores. What do they do that encourages your loyalty? What do you like about the in-store experience?

Marketing Spotlight: Wal-Mart

Wal-Mart Stores, Inc., is the largest retailer in the world, with sales of US$303.8 billion in 2004, 1.5 million employees, and 4300 facilities. Wal-Mart Canada was founded in March of 1994 when it acquired 122 Woolco stores. The Wal-Mart Canada home office is located in Mississauga, Ontario, and it is in charge of administering the 235 stores and six Sam's Clubs that employ more than 60 000 Canadians. Each week around the world, over 100 million customers visit a Wal-Mart store. Sam Walton founded the company in 1962 with a simple goal: offer low prices to everyone. His notions of hard work and thrift continue to permeate Wal-Mart today,

although he died in 1992. Employees see their jobs as a mission "to lower the world's cost of living." Wal-Mart's philosophy is to enable people of average means to buy more of the same products that were previously available only to rich folks. The company works hard at being efficient and using its buying clout to extract lower prices from suppliers and then pass those savings on to customers.

Wal-Mart succeeds in the competitive retail market for several reasons. First, its low prices, vast selection, and superior service keep the customers coming in the door. But one of Wal-Mart's biggest strengths is not even inside the store. Wal-Mart's unrivalled logistics ensure that it can keep prices low while keeping the right goods on the shelves. As the world's biggest retailer, Wal-Mart's logistics demands are considerable. The company must coordinate with more than 85 000 suppliers, manage billions in inventory in its warehouses, and bring that inventory to its retail shelves.

To streamline these tasks, Wal-Mart set up a "hub-and-spoke" network of massive distribution centres (DC). Strategically spaced across the countries in which it operates, no store location is more than a day's drive away from a DC. For example, its massive distribution centre in Brockville, Ontario, services many of its Ontario and Quebec outlets. Wal-Mart is known as "the king of store logistics" for its ability to effectively manage such a vast network.

Sam Walton was something of a visionary when it came to logistics. He had the foresight to realize, as early as the 1960s, that his goals for company growth required advanced information systems to manage high volumes of merchandise. The key to low-cost retail is knowing what goods would sell and in what quantities—ensuring that store shelves never have too much or too little of any item. In 1966, Walton hired the top graduate of an IBM school and assigned him the task of computerizing Wal-Mart's operations. As a result of this forward-looking move, Wal-Mart grew to be the icon of just-in-time inventory control and sophisticated logistics. By 1998, Wal-Mart's computer database was second only to the U.S. Pentagon's in terms of capacity.

Wal-Mart's logistics success is astounding considering its size: over 100 million items per day must get to the right store at the right time. To accomplish this goal, Wal-Mart developed several IT systems that work together. It all begins at the cash register or point-of-sale (POS) terminal. Every time an item is scanned, the information is relayed to headquarters via satellite data links. Using up-to-the-minute sales information, Wal-Mart's Inventory Management System calculates the rate of sales, factors in seasonal and promotional factors, and automatically places replenishment orders to distribution centres and vendor partners.

Wal-Mart uses its information systems for more than just logistics. Suppliers can use its voluminous POS databases to analyze customers' regional buying habits. For example, Proctor & Gamble learned that liquid Tide sells better in the U.S. North and Northeast while Tide powder sells better in the South and Southwest. P&G uses information such as this to tailor its product availability to specific local regions. This means that it delivers different Tide products to different Wal-Mart locations based on local customer preferences. Wal-Marts may look the same on the outside, but the company uses its information systems and logistics to customize the offerings inside each store to suit regional demand.

Wal-Mart continues to grow. If Wal-Mart maintains the average growth rate of the past decade, it could become the world's first trillion-dollar company.

DISCUSSION QUESTIONS

1. What have been the key success factors for Wal-Mart?

2. Where is Wal-Mart vulnerable? What should it watch out for?

3. What recommendations would you make to senior marketing executives going forward? What should the company be sure to do with its marketing?

Sources: Jerry Useem, "Should We Admire Wal-Mart?" *Fortune*, March 8, 2004, pp. 118–121; Perry A. Trunick, "Wal-Mart Sells Its Suppliers on RFID," *Logistics Today* (December 2003): pp. 1–3; *Wal-Mart Case Study*, 1997 Innovation Collection. Smithsonian/Computerworld Awards; Jim Collins, "Bigger, Getter, Faster," *Fast Company* (June 2003): 74–78; *Wal-Mart Fact Sheet*, February 2004; **www.walmart.com**; **www.walmartcanada.ca/Canada-About_Walmart.html**.

COMMUNICATING VALUE

IN THIS CHAPTER, WE WILL ADDRESS THE FOLLOWING QUESTIONS:

- What is the role of marketing communications?

- How does marketing communications work?

- What are the major steps in developing effective communications?

- What is the communications mix and how should it be set?

- What is an integrated marketing communications program?

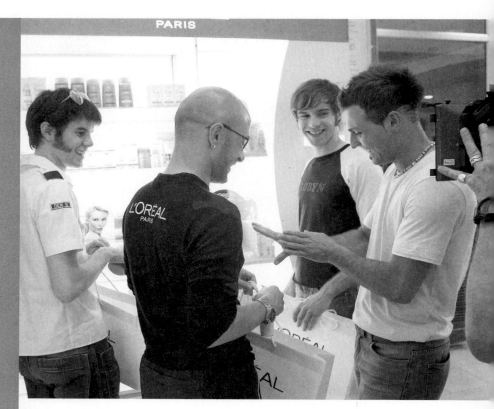

17

CHAPTER 17

Designing and Managing Integrated Marketing Communications

PROFILE: CANADIAN MARKETING EXCELLENCE

With 19 different brands of cosmetics sold across Canada, including such diverse brands as Ombrelle sun protection, Ralph Lauren fragrances, and Plénitude skin care, L'Oréal Canada is a marketer renowned for its integrated marketing communications strategies. Its parent, L'Oréal Paris, prides itself on its use of avant-garde technology and anticipating consumers' needs and bringing them the most effective products at the best price. Its success has been based on a single-minded philosophy— innovate—both in terms of its products and marketing initiatives.

While L'Oréal Canada, founded in 1958, is a subsidiary of the world's largest cosmetic company, its international parent is a firm believer in allowing its subsidiaries to create unique local marketing campaigns. As a result, L'Oréal Canada focuses on creating distinctly Canadian campaigns to communicate with people across the country.

This is a company that also puts its money behind such talk. Take the case of its five-year-old brand Garnier: "There is an increased belief that marketing is driving sales," says Scott Moon, director of marketing at Garnier. "From that respect the CEO and head of corporate finance are letting us increase marketing spend year after year." For 2005 Garnier's marketing and ad spending is up another 30 percent.

Creating an integrated strategy for brands, which range from those that are definitely up-market to those that are more economically priced, is no easy feat. L'Oréal Canada works very hard to create a culture of success in the world of brand management and marketing communications. The company invests heavily in nurturing its internal and external relationships. For example, L'Oréal worked hard to convince many retailers such as London Drugs, Shoppers Drug Mart, and Jean Coutu to open beauty concept stores in an effort to capture the youth market. To be sure it is on the right track with this market, L'Oréal Canada hires young people and empowers them to be independently creative and an integral part of the brand management team.

What really sets L'Oréal Canada apart is its ability to capture markets using incredibly creative, fully integrated, intelligent messaging and savvy associations. Consider the campaigns it developed for International Women's Day, *Star Académie*, and *Canadian Idol*.

In the province of Quebec, L'Oréal had developed a well-known association with International Women's Day. In 2002, however, the company wanted to use the event as a national platform. To accomplish this aim, L'Oréal partnered with CanWest Global to develop a series of vignettes and editorials by high-profile Canadian women speaking about International Women's Day. The Global television network showcased the vignettes for three weeks leading up to the March 2002 event in its top 10 shows strategically selected to reach women of all ages, but with a special focus on younger women. Programs included *The Grammy Awards*, *Survivor*, and *Everybody Loves Raymond*. The campaign also matched the vignettes to each program's environment. For example, the vignette featuring the president of Sony Music Canada aired during the Grammies.

Other components of the campaign included a 40-page keepsake magazine; an exclusive sponsorship of a commercial-free vintage French movie on Prime Television; ads in the *National Post's Financial Post* section featuring some selected dailies; special creative on Canada.com with links to the L'Oréal Web site; and an ad in the inaugural issue of *Fashion Post*.

The company's campaign goals were to raise awareness among English-speaking women (especially younger women) and to link the company to International Women's Day. The campaign was intended to reinforce the company's own positioning strategy focused on giving women confidence and stature. The campaign was certainly win–win for both the company and the event. Awareness of International Women's Day rose from 73 percent to 85 percent. Moreover, the greatest gain in awareness was among women aged 18 to 34. Awareness of L'Oréal's association with the event increased 111 percent among all women and 150 percent among women 18 to 34.

In the winter of 2003, L'Oréal signed its more economically priced line of Maybelline products on as a major sponsor of the highly successful reality show *Star Académie* (the *Canadian Idol* of Quebec). Maybelline needed a significant boost in Quebec and the show paid off in spades. At the conclusion of the series, more than 3 million Quebecers (or more than 40 percent of the population) were watching. By early March, Montrealers aged 18 to 64 were listing Maybelline as the second most frequently recalled brand in marketing research tests of unaided recall. The Quebec business magazine *Commerce* estimated the economic return for Maybelline was three times its *Star Académie* ad spend.

Could L'Oréal Canada repeat its success with *Star Académie* in English Canada? Launching one of the largest mass-media efforts it ever engaged in, L'Oréal Canada signed on with *Canadian Idol*, recognizing it as one of the most attractive television communications opportunities—particularly for a younger demographic—in Canada. Its award-winning campaign consisted of 30-second advertisements run during the show, opening and closing billboards, a major presence on the *Canadian Idol* Web site, and on-air sponsorship announcements during the show. The most crucial piece of the campaign, however, was product placements in several of the show's segments. For example, the company featured a segment for L'Oréal's EasyColor interactive application—which invited visitors to the L'Oréal Paris Web site to upload pictures of themselves and create new looks. The segment generated significant Web traffic to the site. The campaign also integrated the *Canadian Idol* relationship at the retail level, with a contest and special displays at Shoppers Drug Mart.

The effort was a roaring success. Sales growth for the brand exceeded the campaign goal and increased sales by more than 30 percent during the *Idol* promotion. It also increased brand awareness among younger women. At Shoppers locations, sales of L'Oréal's products increased by 20 percent, while sales of products featured during *Canadian Idol* shows increased by 85 percent. The campaign was so successful that it won L'Oréal *Marketing Magazine's* 2003 Marketer of the Year award for excellence in integrated marketing communications. There's no doubt that innovation in marketing communications can be just as rewarding as product innovation.

Sources: Danny Kucharsky, "Because You're Worth It, L'Oréal," *Marketing Magazine*, February 9, 2004; Natalia Williams, "Shiny Happy Marketers!" 1st Annual Report on the Canadian Marketing Sector, *Strategy Magazine*, March 8, 2005; Media Innovation Awards Issue, "Mixed Media Under $1 Million," *Marketing Magazine Online*, **www.marketingmag.ca**, November 11, 2002 (viewed October 23, 2004); Danny Kucharsky, "Highlighting a Canadian Approach," *Marketing Magazine Online*, December 8, 2003 (viewed October 23, 2004); L'Oréal Canada's Web site, **www.lorealparis.ca**.

Marketing communications can have a huge payoff. This chapter describes how communications work and what marketing communications can do for a company. It also addresses how holistic marketers combine and integrate marketing communications. Chapter 18 examines the different forms of mass (nonpersonal) communications (advertising, sales promotion, events and experiences, and public relations and publicity); Chapter 19 examines the different forms of personal communications (direct marketing, including e-commerce and personal selling).

The Role of Marketing Communications

Marketing communications are the means by which firms attempt to inform, persuade, and remind consumers—directly or indirectly—about the products and brands that they sell. In a sense, marketing communications represent the "voice" of the brand and are a means by which it can establish a dialogue and build relationships with consumers.

Marketing communications perform many functions for consumers. Consumers can be told or shown how and why a product is used, by what kind of person, and where and when; consumers can learn about who makes the product and what the company and brand stand for; and consumers can be given an incentive or reward for trial or usage. Marketing communications allow companies to link their brands to other people, places, events, brands, experiences, feelings, and things. Marketing communications can contribute to brand equity by establishing the brand in memory and crafting a brand image.

Marketing Communications and Brand Equity

Although advertising is often a central element of a marketing communications program, it is usually not the only one—or even the most important one—in terms of building brand equity. The **marketing communications mix** consists of six major modes of communication:[1]

1. *Advertising.* Any paid form of nonpersonal presentation and promotion of ideas, goods, or services by an identified sponsor.

2. *Sales promotion.* A variety of short-term incentives to encourage trial or purchase of a product or service.

3. *Events and experiences.* Company-sponsored activities and programs designed to create daily or special brand-related interactions.

4. *Public relations and publicity.* A variety of programs designed to promote or protect a company's image or its individual products.

5. *Direct marketing.* Use of mail, telephone, fax, e-mail, or Internet to communicate directly with or solicit response or dialogue from specific customers and prospects.

6. *Personal selling.* Face-to-face interaction with one or more prospective purchasers for the purpose of making presentations, answering questions, and procuring orders.

Table 17.1 lists numerous communication platforms. Company communication goes beyond those specific platforms. The product's styling and price, the shape and colour of the package, the salesperson's manner and dress, the store décor, the company's stationery—all communicate something to buyers. Every *brand contact* delivers an impression that can strengthen or weaken a customer's view of the company.

As Figure 17.1 shows, marketing communication activities contribute to brand equity in many ways: by creating awareness of the brand; linking the right associations to the brand image in consumers' memory; eliciting positive brand judgments or feelings; and/or facilitating a stronger consumer–brand connection.

One implication of the concept of brand equity is that the manner in which brand associations are formed does not matter. In other words, if a consumer has an equally strong, favourable, and unique brand associations between Subaru and the concepts "outdoors," "active," and "rugged" because of exposure to a TV ad that shows the car driving over rugged terrain at different times of the year or because of the fact that Subaru sponsors ski, kayak, and mountain bike events, the impact in terms of brand equity should be identical.

But these marketing communication activities must be integrated to deliver a consistent message and achieve the strategic positioning. The starting point in planning marketing communications is an audit of all the potential interactions that customers in the target market may have with the brand and the company. For example, someone interested in purchasing a new computer might talk to others, see television ads, read articles, look for information on the Internet, and look at computers in a store. Marketers need to assess which experiences and impressions will have the most influence at each stage of the buying process. This understanding will help them allocate communications dollars more efficiently and design and implement the right communication programs.

Kleenex Soft Pack

To launch its new Kleenex Soft Pack product, Kimberly-Clark budgeted 75 percent of its overall advertising dollars to television, 23 percent for print, and 2 percent online to build awareness and drive trial. Online ads were found to help reach an audience that TV might have overlooked, and online and magazine ads were found to be the most effective mix for brand awareness.[2]

| **TABLE 17.1** | **COMMON COMMUNICATION PLATFORMS** |

Advertising	Sales Promotion	Events/Experiences	Public Relations	Personal Selling	Direct Marketing
Print and broadcast ads	Contests, games, sweepstakes, lotteries	Sports	Press kits	Sales presentations	Catalogues
Packaging–outer	Premiums and gifts	Entertainment	Speeches	Sales meetings	Mailings
Packaging inserts	Sampling	Festivals	Seminars	Incentive programs	Telemarketing
Motion pictures	Fairs and trade shows	Arts	Annual reports	Samples	Electronic shopping
Brochures and booklets	Exhibits	Causes	Charitable donations	Fairs and trade shows	TV shopping
Posters and leaflets	Demonstrations	Factory tours	Publications		Fax mail
Directories	Coupons	Company museums	Community relations		E-mail
Reprints of ads	Rebates	Street activities	Lobbying		Voice mail
Billboards	Low-interest financing		Identity media		
Display signs	Entertainment		Company magazine		
Point-of-purchase displays	Trade-in allowances				
Audiovisual material	Continuity programs				
Symbols and logos	Tie-ins				
Videotapes					

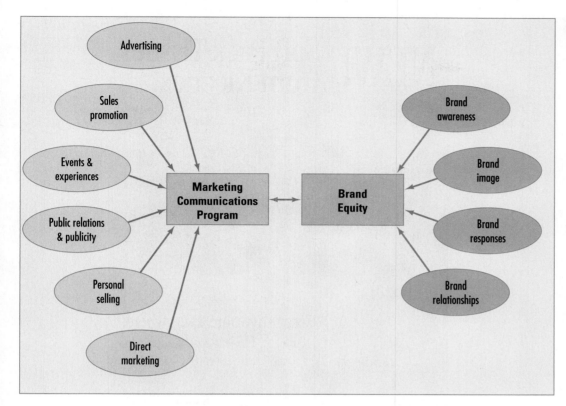

FIGURE 17.1

Integrating Marketing
Communications to Build
Brand Equity

Armed with these insights, marketers can judge marketing communications according to its ability to build brand equity and drive brand sales. For example, how well does a proposed ad campaign contribute to awareness or to creating, maintaining, or strengthening brand associations? Does a sponsorship cause consumers to have more favourable brand judgments and feelings? To what extent does a promotion encourage consumers to buy more of a product? At what price premium?

From the perspective of building brand equity, marketers should evaluate *all* the different possible communication options according to effectiveness criteria (how well does it work) as well as efficiency considerations (how much does it cost). This broad view of brand-building activities is especially relevant when marketers are considering strategies to improve brand awareness.

Brand awareness is a function of the number of brand-related exposures and experiences accumulated by the consumer.[3] *Anything* that causes the consumer to notice and pay attention to the brand can increase brand awareness, at least in terms of brand recognition. The visibility of the brand typically found with sponsorships suggests that these activities may be especially valuable for enhancing brand recognition. To enhance brand recall, however, more intense and elaborate processing may be necessary so that stronger brand links to the product category or consumer needs are established to improve memory performance.

Similarly, because brand associations, responses, and relationships can be created in many different ways, *all* possible marketing communication options should be considered to create the desired brand image and knowledge.

For the launch of Kleenex®
Soft Pack Tissues, print
advertising was combined
with a coupon, a common
sales promotion tool.

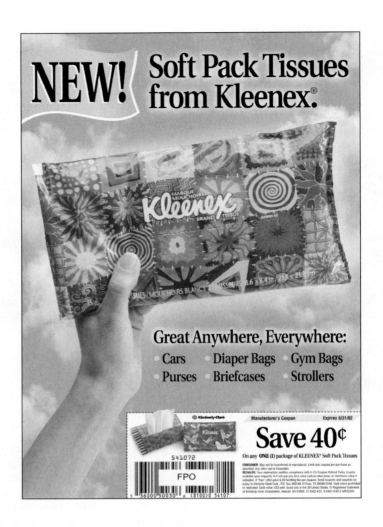

Boston Symphony Orchestra Inc.

With classical music audiences dwindling to a small core of older and more affluent con-
certgoers, the famous Boston Symphony Orchestra (BSO) knew that it had to revamp its
advertising to reach new audiences through a variety of communication channels. Prior to
1998, BSO rarely relied on the Internet. But then, through a carefully coordinated series of
market research efforts that included detailed surveys and focus groups, it discovered that
while there was little difference between older and younger audiences when it came to
product interest, there was a big gap in terms of media preferences. The older concert-
goers were more avid readers of both books and magazines while younger people were
more involved with the Internet and electronic media. BSO developed an integrated campaign that combined direct mail, e-mail marketing, customized online infomercials, and taxi-
top ads. As a result, the BSO increased online revenues from tickets and other sales to
US$3.7 million in fiscal year 2002, up from US$320 000 in fiscal year 1997. Total sales
reached US$19 million in 2002, up from US$16.7 million in 1997.[4]

The Communication Process Models

Marketers should understand the fundamental elements of effective communication. Two models
are useful: a macro model and a micro model.

MACRO MODEL OF THE COMMUNICATION PROCESS Figure 17.2 shows a macro communication model with nine elements. Two represent the major parties in a communication—sender
and receiver. Two represent the major communication tools—message and media. Four represent

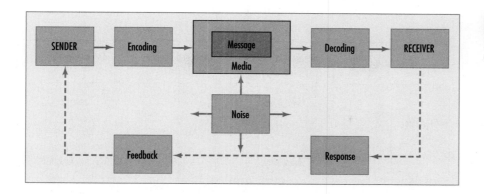

FIGURE 17.2

Elements in the
Communications Process

major communication functions—*encoding, decoding, response,* and *feedback.* The last element in the system is *noise* (random and competing messages that may interfere with the intended communication).[5]

The model emphasizes the key factors in effective communication. Senders must know what audiences they want to reach and what responses they want to get. They must encode their messages so that the target audience can decode them. They must transmit the message through media that reach the target audience and develop feedback channels to monitor the responses. The more the sender's field of experience overlaps with that of the receiver, the more effective the message is likely to be.

Note that selective attention, distortion, and retention processes—concepts first introduced in Chapter 6—may be operating during communication, as follows:

1. *Selective attention.* People are bombarded by about 1500 commercial messages a day, which explains why advertisers sometimes go to great lengths to grab audience attention through fear, music, sex appeal, or bold headlines promising something, such as "How to Make a Million." Ad clutter is also a major obstacle to gaining attention—noneditorial or programming content ranges from 25 to 33 percent for TV and radio to over 50 percent for magazines and newspapers.

2. *Selective distortion.* Receivers will hear what fits into their belief systems. As a result, receivers often add things to the message that are not there (amplification) and do not notice other things that are there (levelling). The task is to strive for simplicity, clarity, interest, and repetition to get the main points across.

3. *Selective retention.* People will retain in long-term memory only a small fraction of the messages that reach them. If the receiver's initial attitude toward the object is positive and he or she rehearses support arguments, the message is likely to be accepted and have high recall. If the initial attitude is negative and the person rehearses counterarguments, the message is likely to be rejected but to stay in long-term memory. Because persuasion requires the receiver's rehearsal of his or her own thoughts, much of what is called persuasion is actually self-persuasion.[6]

MICRO MODEL OF CONSUMER RESPONSES Micro models of marketing communications concentrate on consumer's specific responses to communications. Figure 17.3 summarizes four classic *response hierarchy models.*

All these models assume that the buyer passes through a cognitive, affective, and behavioural stage, in that order. This "learn-feel-do" sequence is appropriate when the audience has high involvement with a product category perceived to have high differentiation, as in purchasing an automobile or house. An alternative sequence, "do-feel-learn," is relevant when the audience has high involvement but perceives little or no differentiation within the product category, as in purchasing an airline ticket or personal computer. A third sequence, "learn-do-feel," is relevant when the audience has low involvement and perceives little differentiation within the product category, as in purchasing salt or batteries. By choosing the right sequence, the marketer can do a better job of planning communications.[7]

Here we will assume that the buyer has high involvement with the product category and perceives high differentiation within the category. We will illustrate the *hierarchy-of-effects model* (in the second column of Figure 17.3) in the context of a marketing communication campaign for a small Saskatchewan university named Assinboia:

FIGURE 17.3

Response Hierarchy Models

Sources: [a]E. K. Strong. *The Psychology of Selling* (New York: McGraw-Hill. 1925), p. 9; [b]Robert J. Lavidge and Gary A. Steiner, "A Model for Predictive Measurements of Advertising Effectiveness," *Journal of Marketing* (October 1961): 61; [c]Everett M. Rogers, *Diffusion of Innovation* (New York: The Free Press, 1962), pp. 79–86; [d]various sources.

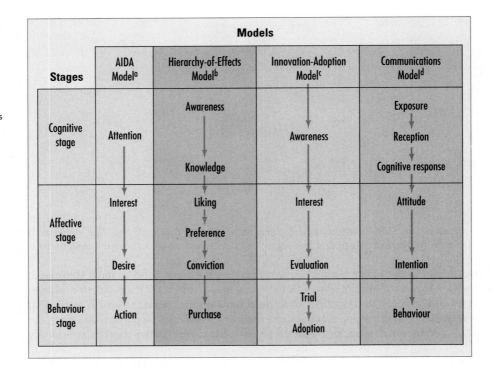

- *Awareness.* If most of the target audience is unaware of the object, the communicator's task is to build awareness. Suppose Assinboia seeks applicants from Alberta but has no name recognition there. Suppose there are 30 000 students in grade 11 and 12 in Alberta who may potentially be interested in Assinboia University. The university might set the objective of making 70 percent of these students aware of Assinboia's name within one year.

- *Knowledge.* The target audience might have brand awareness but not know much more. Assinboia may want its target audience to know that it is a private four-year university with excellent programs in English, foreign languages, and history. It needs to learn how many people in the target audience have little, some, or much knowledge about Assinboia. If knowledge is weak, Assinboia may decide to select brand knowledge as its communication objective.

- *Liking.* If target members know the brand, how do they feel about it? If the audience looks unfavourably on Assinboia University, the communicator has to find out why. If the unfavourable view is based on real problems, Assinboia will have to fix its problems and then communicate its renewed quality. Good public relations calls for "good deeds followed by good words."

- *Preference.* The target audience might like the product but not prefer it to others. In this case, the communicator must try to build consumer preference by comparing quality, value, performance, and other features to likely competitors.

- *Conviction.* A target audience might prefer a particular product but not develop a conviction about buying it. The communicator's job is to build conviction and purchase intent among students interested in Assinboia University.

- *Purchase.* Finally, some members of the target audience might have conviction but may not quite get around to making the purchase. The communicator must lead these consumers to take the final step, perhaps by offering the product at a low price, offering a premium, or letting consumers try it out. Assinboia might invite selected high school students to visit the campus and attend some classes, or it might offer partial scholarships to deserving students.

To show how fragile the whole communication process is, assume that the probability of *each* of the six steps being successfully accomplished is 50 percent. The laws of probability suggest that the probability of *all* six steps occurring successfully, assuming they are independent events, would be $0.5 \times 0.5 \times 0.5 \times 0.5 \times 0.5 \times 0.5$, which equals 1.5625 percent. If the probability of each step occurring, on average, was a more moderate 10 percent, then the joint probability of all six events occurring would be 0.0001—in other words, only 1 in 10 000!

To increase the odds for a successful marketing communications campaign, marketers must attempt to increase the likelihood that *each* step occurs. For example, from an advertising standpoint, the ideal ad campaign would ensure that:

1. The right consumer is exposed to the right message at the right place and at the right time.
2. The ad causes the consumer to pay attention to the ad but does not distract from the intended message.
3. The ad properly reflects the consumer's level of understanding about the product and the brand.
4. The ad correctly positions the brand in terms of desirable and deliverable points-of-difference and points-of-parity.
5. The ad motivates consumers to consider purchase of the brand.
6. The ad creates strong brand associations with all of these stored communication effects so that they can have an effect when consumers are considering making a purchase.

Developing Effective Communications

Figure 17.4 shows the eight steps in developing effective communications. We begin with the basics: identifying the target audience, determining the objectives, designing the communications, selecting the channels, and establishing the budget.

Identify the Target Audience

The process must start with a clear target audience in mind: potential buyers of the company's products, current users, deciders, or influencers; individuals, groups, particular publics, or the general public. The target audience is a critical influence on the communicator's decisions on what to say, how to say it, when to say it, where to say it, and to whom to say it.

The target audience can potentially be profiled in terms of any of the market segments identified in Chapter 8. It is often useful to define target audience in terms of usage and loyalty. Is the target new to the category or a current user? Is the target loyal to the brand, loyal to a competitor, or someone who switches between brands? If the target is a brand user, is he or she a heavy or light user? Communication strategy will differ depending on the usage and loyalty involved. *Image analysis* can be conducted to profile the target audience in terms of brand knowledge to provide further insight.

A major part of audience analysis is assessing the current image of the company, its products, and its competitors. **Image** is the set of beliefs, ideas, and impressions a person holds regarding an object. People's attitudes and actions toward an object are highly conditioned by that object's image.

The first step is to measure the target audience's knowledge of the object, using the *familiarity scale:*

Never Heard of	Heard of Only	Know a Little Bit	Know a Fair Amount	Know Very Well

If most respondents circle only the first two categories, the challenge is to build greater awareness.

Respondents who are familiar with the product can be asked how they feel toward it using the *favourability scale:*

Very Unfavourable	Somewhat Unfavourable	Indifferent	Somewhat Favourable	Very Favourable

If most respondents check the first two categories, then the organization must overcome a negative image problem.

The two scales can be combined to develop insight into the nature of the communication challenge. Suppose area residents are asked about their familiarity with and attitudes toward four local hospitals, A, B, C, and D. Their responses are averaged and shown in Figure 17.5. Hospital A has the most positive image: Most people know it and like it. Hospital B is less familiar to most people, but those who know it like it. Hospital C is viewed negatively by those who know it, but (fortunately for the hospital) not too many people know it. Hospital D is seen as a poor hospital, and everyone knows it!

Each hospital faces a different communication task. Hospital A must work at maintaining its good reputation and high awareness. Hospital B must gain the attention of more people. Hospital C

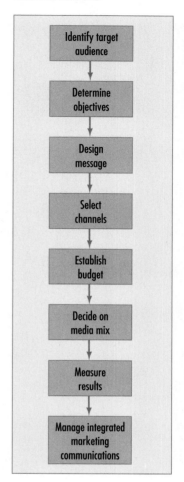

FIGURE 17.4

Steps in Developing Effective Communications

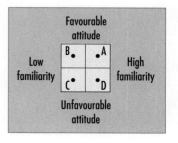

FIGURE 17.5

Familiarity–Favourability Analysis

must find out why people dislike it and take steps to improve its quality while keeping a low profile. Hospital D should lower its profile, improve its quality, and then seek public attention.

Images are "sticky"; they persist long after the organization has changed. Image persistence is explained by the fact that once people have a certain image, they perceive what is consistent with that image. It will take highly disconfirming information to raise doubts and open their minds, especially when people do not have continuous or new firsthand experiences with the changed object.

Häagen Dazs

In recent years, the premium ice cream maker has battled an onslaught of new premium brands while hampered by the image it acquired back in the 1980s. The brand hired ad agency Goodby, Silverstein and Partners to peel off Häagen Dazs's sticky image with a new campaign. "The name brought up cheesy luxury and [people] thought of the snobby hedonism of the '80s, like the guy in the ascot leaning against the Bentley," said Goodby's associate creative director Albert Kelly. Goodby developed a campaign that focused on the product's high quality, especially the quality of its ingredients. Two spots, "Strawberry" and "Vanilla," show strawberry fields and vanilla plants with the tagline "Häagen Dazs. Made Like No Other," in contrast to previous advertising that focused on luxury with lines such as "Pure Pleasure" and "Just Perfect."[8]

Determine the Communication Objectives

As we showed with Assinboia University, communication objectives can be set at any level of the hierarchy-of-effects model. Rossiter and Percy identify four possible objectives, as follows:[9]

1. *Category need.* Establishing a product or service category as necessary to remove or satisfy a perceived discrepancy between a current motivational state and a desired emotional state. A new-to-the-world product such as electric cars would always begin with a communication objective of establishing category need.

2. *Brand awareness.* Ability to identify (recognize or recall) the brand within the category, in sufficient detail to make a purchase. Recognition is easier to achieve than recall—consumers are more likely to recognize Stouffer's distinctive orange packages than recall the brand if asked to think of a brand of frozen entrées. Brand recall is important outside the store; brand recognition is important inside the store. Brand awareness provides a foundation for brand equity.

3. *Brand attitude.* Evaluation of the brand with respect to its perceived ability to meet a currently relevant need. Relevant brand needs may be negatively oriented (problem removal, problem avoidance, incomplete satisfaction, normal depletion) or positively oriented (sensory gratification, intellectual stimulation, or social approval). Household cleaning products often use problem-solution; food products, on the other hand, often use sensory-oriented ads emphasizing appetite appeal.

4. *Brand purchase intention.* Self-instructions to purchase the brand or to take purchase-related action. Promotional offers in the form of coupons or two-for-one deals encourage consumers to make a mental commitment to buy a product. But many consumers do not have an expressed category need and may not be in the market when exposed to an ad, making intentions less likely to be formed. For example, in any given week, only about 20 percent of adults may be planning to buy detergent; only 2 percent may be planning to buy a carpet cleaner; and only 0.25 percent may be planning to buy a car.

The most effective communications often can achieve multiple objectives. For example, Geico advertises that a 15-minute phone call can result in a 15 percent reduction on auto insurance, combining both brand attitude and a call to action to build brand purchase intentions.

Design the Communication

Formulating the communication to achieve the desired response will require solving three problems: what to say (message strategy), how to say it (creative strategy), and who should say it (message source).

MESSAGE STRATEGY In determining message strategy, management searches for appeals, themes, or ideas that will tie into the brand positioning and help to establish points-of-parity or points-of-difference. Some of these may be related directly to product or service performance (the quality, economy, or value of the brand) whereas others may be related to more extrinsic considerations (the brand as being contemporary, popular, or traditional).

John Maloney saw buyers as expecting one of four types of reward from a product: rational, sensory, social, or ego satisfaction.[10] Buyers might visualize these rewards from results-of-use experience, product-in-use experience, or incidental-to-use experience. Crossing the four types of rewards with the three types of experience generates 12 types of messages. For example, the appeal "gets clothes cleaner" is a rational-reward promise following results-of-use experience. The phrase "real beer taste in a great light beer" is a sensory-reward promise connected with product-in-use experience.

It is widely believed that industrial buyers are most responsive to performance messages. They are knowledgeable about the product, trained to recognize value, and accountable to others for their choices. Consumers, when they buy certain big-ticket items, also tend to gather information and estimate benefits.

CREATIVE STRATEGY Communication effectiveness depends on how a message is being expressed as well as the content of the message itself. An ineffective communication may mean that the wrong message was used or the right message was just being expressed poorly. *Creative strategies* are how marketers translate their messages into a specific communication. Creative strategies can be broadly classified as involving either "informational" or "transformational" appeals.[11] These two general categories each encompass several different specific creative approaches.

Informational Appeals An *informational appeal* elaborates on product or service attributes or benefits. Examples in advertising are problem-solution ads (Claritin gives you all-day allergy relief without drowsiness), product demonstration ads (Glad Press'n Seal sealable plastic wrap doesn't just cling, it seals), product comparison ads (Sprint offers cheaper Internet and phone services than Bell), and testimonials from unknown or celebrity endorsers (Céline Dion singing for Air Canada). Informational appeals assume very rational processing of the communication on the part of the consumer. Logic and reason rule.

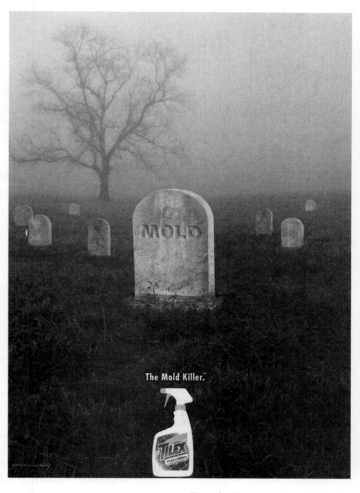

Developing creative strategy: This ad for Tilex, a household product, focuses on problem-solution—Tilex is called "The Mold Killer."™

Hovland's research at Yale has shed much light on informational appeals and their relation to such issues as conclusion drawing, one- versus two-sided arguments, and order of argument presentation. Some early experiments supported stating conclusions for the audience. Subsequent research, however, indicates that the best ads ask questions and allow readers and viewers to form their own conclusions.[12] If Honda had hammered away that the Element was for young people, this strong definition might have blocked older age groups from buying it. Some stimulus ambiguity can lead to a broader market definition and more spontaneous purchases.

You would think that one-sided presentations that praise a product would be more effective than two-sided arguments that also mention shortcomings. Yet two-sided messages may be more appropriate, especially when negative associations must be overcome. Heinz ran the message "Heinz Ketchup is slow good" and Listerine ran the message "Listerine tastes bad twice a day."[13] Two-sided messages are more effective with more educated audiences and those who are initially opposed.[14]

Finally, the order in which arguments are presented is important.[15] In the case of a one-sided message, presenting the strongest argument first has the advantage of arousing attention and interest. This is important in media where the audience often does not attend to the whole message. With a captive audience, a climactic presentation might be more effective. In the case of a two-sided message, if the audience is initially opposed, the communicator might start with the other side's argument and conclude with his or her strongest argument.[16]

Transformational Appeals A *transformational appeal* elaborates on a non–product-related benefit or image. It might depict what kind of person uses a brand (VW advertises to active, youthful people with their "Drivers Wanted" campaign) or what kind of experience results from using the brand (The Bay's "More than you came for"). Transformational appeals often attempt to stir up emotions that will motivate purchase. This is the route Clairol took to revive a moribund brand from the 1970s.

Clairol Herbal Essences

"Yes, Yes, Yes," actresses exclaim as they simulate sexual ecstasy while washing their hair and enjoying what the tagline dubs "A Truly Organic Experience." Some women find the ad's coy double entendre demeaning. Procter & Gamble, which acquired Clairol in 2002, credits the ad with bringing the near-dead brand back to life. Herbal Essences became one of the fastest-growing brands in the world, climbing in sales from zero to US$700 million in seven years. In explaining its success, the agency creator, The Kaplan Thaler Group, maintains "emotion is the lightning rod, the trigger to making a purchase."[17]

Communicators use negative appeals such as fear, guilt, and shame to get people to do things (brush their teeth, have an annual health check-up) or stop doing things (smoking, alcohol abuse, overeating). Fear appeals work best when they are not too strong. Furthermore, fear appeals work better when source credibility is high and when the communication promises to relieve, in a believable and efficient way, the fear it arouses.[18] Messages are most persuasive when they are moderately discrepant with what the audience believes. Messages that state only what the audience already believes at best only reinforce beliefs, and if the messages are too discrepant, they will be counterargued and disbelieved. Consider what the B.C. poultry industry did to allay fear during an industry crisis:

Four Feathers Group

When avian influenza ("bird flu") was discovered on a Fraser Valley, B.C., poultry farm in February 2004, local farmers immediately recognized the threat to their $1-billion-a-year industry. Strains of the virus had infected many and killed 20 people in Asia and Europe. Other, less dangerous strains had led to the slaughter of millions of birds and forced countries worldwide to ban poultry imports. As a result, when avian flu arrived in the Fraser Valley, four B.C. poultry producer organizations, known as the Four Feathers Group, worked with the Wilcox group, a Vancouver-based PR firm, to help them respond to the crisis. Three key messages formed the basis of the campaign: (1) reassure consumers that poultry products were safe to eat; (2) emphasize that the strain of avian influenza in B.C. posed little risk to human health; and (3) raise awareness of the steps poultry producers were taking to combat the disease under the lead of the federal government's Canadian Food Inspection Agency. The joint public relations effort lasted more than four months and helped place the local industry at the forefront of Canadian consciousness. Despite being hit hard by the crisis during the four-month period, public health concerns were largely allayed and consumers continued to eat Fraser Valley poultry products and maintain their confidence in the food supply due to consistent messaging and commitment to the campaign.[19]

Communicators also use positive emotional appeals such as humour, love, pride, and joy. Motivational or "borrowed interest" devices—such as the presence of cute babies, frisky puppies, popular music, or provocative sex appeals—are often employed to attract consumer attention and raise their involvement with an ad.

Borrowed interest techniques are thought to be necessary in the tough new media environment characterized by low-involvement consumer processing and much competing ad and programming clutter. In 2003, British singer Sting, who in the 1980s had refused to allow the song "Don't Stand So Close to Me" to be used in a deodorant ad, made a lucrative deal with Ford Motor Company as part of the company's efforts to reach consumers aged 35 and over. In an ad for Jaguar, he was shown being driven around in the car while his latest single, "Desert Rose," played in the background.[20]

Although these borrowed interest approaches can attract attention and create more liking and belief in the sponsor, they may also detract from comprehension, wear out their welcome fast, and overshadow the product.[21] Attention-getting tactics are often *too* effective and distract from brand or product claims. Thus, one challenge in arriving at the best creative strategy is figuring out how to "break through the clutter" to attract the attention of consumers—but still be able to deliver the intended message.

The magic to advertising is to bring concepts on a piece of paper to life in the minds of the consumer target. In a print ad, the communicator has to decide on headline, copy, illustration, and colour. For a radio message, the communicator has to choose words, voice qualities, and vocalizations. The "sound" of an announcer promoting a used automobile has to be different from one promoting a new Cadillac. If the message is to be carried on television or in person, all these elements plus body language (nonverbal clues) have to be planned. Presenters have to pay attention to facial expressions, gestures, dress, posture, and hairstyle. If the message is carried by the product or its packaging, the communicator has to pay attention to colour, texture, scent, size, and shape.

Every detail matters. Think how the ad taglines listed on the right were able to bring to life the brand themes listed on the left.

Brand Theme	Ad Tagline
Our hamburgers are bigger.	Where's the Beef? (Wendy's restaurants)
We make good coffee.	Always got time for Tim Hortons (Tim Hortons)
No hard sell, just a good car.	Drivers Wanted (Volkswagen automobiles)
We don't rent as many cars, so we have to do more for our customers.	We Try Harder (Avis auto rental)
Your local, friendly hardware store.	Home of the handyman (Home Hardware)

MESSAGE SOURCE   Many communications do not use a source beyond the company itself. Others use known or unknown people. Messages delivered by attractive or popular sources can potentially achieve higher attention and recall, which is why advertisers often use celebrities as spokespeople. Celebrities are likely to be effective when they personify a key product attribute. Catherine Deneuve's beauty did this for Chanel No. 5 perfume, and Paul Hogan's Aussie ruggedness did this for the Subaru Outback wagon. On the other hand, using James Garner and Cybill Shepherd to sell beef backfired: Garner subsequently had quintuple bypass surgery, and Shepherd proclaimed she was a vegetarian.

What is important is the spokesperson's credibility. What factors underlie source credibility? The three most often identified are expertise, trustworthiness, and likability.[22] *Expertise* is the specialized knowledge the communicator possesses to back the claim. *Trustworthiness* is related to how objective and honest the source is perceived to be. Friends are trusted more than strangers or salespeople, and people who are not paid to endorse a product are viewed as more trustworthy than people who are paid.[23] *Likability* describes the source's attractiveness. Qualities like candour, humour, and naturalness make a source more likable.

The most highly credible source would be a person who scores high on all three dimensions. Pharmaceutical companies want doctors to testify about product benefits because doctors have high credibility. Anti-drug crusaders will use ex–drug addicts because they have higher credibility. Before his death, Dave Thomas, who had folksy appeal and inherent credibility, did over 800 Wendy's commercials in his trademark red tie and short-sleeve shirt. Roots used Canadian Olympic athletes in its campaigns wearing the Roots-designed Olympic uniforms, and the Hudson Bay Company hopes to win the same accolades now that it has won the Olympic account.

A well-chosen celebrity endorsement can catapult even the most unlikely product to stardom.

Salton and George Foreman

Salton was a little-known manufacturer of oddball appliances that gained temporary fame in the 1950s with its Salton Hot Tray, a must-have item for every bridal registry at the time. In the early 1990s, the company came up with an indoor grill that seemed destined for obscurity until two-time heavyweight champ George Foreman chose to not only endorse it, but partner with the company to sell it. Foreman and his Lean, Mean, Fat-Reducing Grilling Machine proved a match made in hamburger heaven. Foreman, now presented as a lovable lug, was renowned for his love of cheeseburgers. A year after the launch, he went on the home shopping channel QVC to sell the grills. The camera caught him in an unscripted moment while presenters were chatting, leaving George with nothing to do except look at the sizzling burgers. He took a roll, grabbed one, started eating, and the phone lines began to buzz. Foreman has helped Salton sell more than 40 million grilling machines since the mid-1990s, and because he gets a share of the proceeds, he has earned more than he did as a boxer—over US$150 million. While the overall housewares industry expands only 7 percent annually, Salton has grown more than 46 percent a year since 1995.[24]

"Marketing Insight: Celebrity Endorsements as a Strategy" focuses on the use of testimonials.

If a person has a positive attitude toward a source and a message, or a negative attitude toward both, a state of *congruity* is said to exist. What happens if the person holds one attitude toward the source and the opposite toward the message? Suppose a consumer hears a likable celebrity praise a brand that she dislikes? Osgood and Tannenbaum say that *attitude change will take place in the direction of increasing the amount of congruity between the two evaluations.*[25] The consumer will end up respecting the celebrity somewhat less or respecting the brand somewhat more. If she encounters the same celebrity praising other disliked brands, she will eventually develop a negative view of the celebrity and maintain her negative attitudes toward the brands. The **principle of congruity** implies

MARKETING INSIGHT

Celebrity Endorsements as a Strategy

A well-chosen celebrity can draw attention to a product or brand, as when Sarah, Duchess of York—better known as Fergie—showed how she slimmed down thanks to Weight Watchers; or, the celebrity's mystique can transfer to the brand—Bill Cosby entertains a group of kids while eating a bowl of Jell-O.

The choice of the celebrity is critical. The celebrity should have high recognition, high positive affect, and high appropriateness to the product. Britney Spears has high recognition but negative affect among many groups. Robin Williams has high recognition and high positive affect but might not be appropriate for advertising a World Peace Conference. Tom Hanks, Meryl Streep, and Oprah Winfrey could successfully advertise a large number of products because they have extremely high ratings for familiarity and likability (known as the Q factor in the entertainment industry).

Celebrities show up everywhere. In the hotly contested male-impotence drug category, pharmaceutical marketers have turned to celebrities to gain product attention and relevance. Initially advertised by retired politician Bob Dole, Pfizer turned to 40-year-old baseball slugger Rafael Palmeiro and 45-year-old NASCAR driver Mark Martin to give its market leader drug, Viagra, a younger appeal. Competitor Levitra turned to famed football coach Iron Mike Ditka to assure its audience of its speed and quality. Only number-three brand Cialis eschewed celebrity endorsers, spending US$100 million to run ads showing couples in romantic settings.

Athletes are commonly employed to endorse athletic products, beverages, and apparel. One of the premier athletic endorsers is cyclist Lance Armstrong, who battled and beat testicular cancer on his way to winning seven consecutive Tour de France championships. He endorses a number of bicycle and sports products companies, including Trek, PowerBar, and Nike. Armstrong's improbable "against all odds" success story enabled him to win endorsement contracts from companies unaffiliated with sports, such as Bristol-Myers Squibb pharmaceuticals, Coca-Cola, Subaru, and the U.S. Postal Service. The total amount he earned from endorsements in 2003 topped US$10 million.

Celebrities can play a more strategic role for their brands, not only endorsing a product but also helping design, position, and sell merchandise and services. Since signing Tiger Woods in 1996, Nike has seen its share of the golf ball market jump from 1 to 6 percent. Woods has played a key role in developing a series of golf products and apparel that Nike has periodically altered to reflect his changing personality and design tastes.

Using celebrities poses certain risks. The celebrity might hold out for a larger fee at contract renewal time or withdraw. Just as can happen with movies and records, celebrity campaigns can sometimes be an expensive flop. Even though Céline Dion was locked into a three-year, US$14 million deal, Chrysler chose to discontinue her ads when they deemed them ineffective. Similarly, Pepsi chose to drop star endorsers Britney Spears and Beyoncé Knowles, whose personalities may have been too overpowering for the brand, to focus on promoting occasions that go well with drinking Pepsi.

The celebrity might lose popularity or, even worse, get caught in a scandal or embarrassing situation. After NBA legend Magic Johnson went public with his HIV diagnosis and his extramarital affairs in 1991, his ads were pulled from the air and his endorsement deals were not renewed. McDonald's chose not to renew a US$12 million annual contract with basketball star Kobe Bryant after accusations of rape.

Sources: Irving Rein, Philip Kotler, and Martin Scoller, *The Making and Marketing of Professionals into Celebrities* (Chicago: NTC Business Books, 1997); Greg Johnson, "Woods' Cautious Approach to the Green," *Los Angeles Times*, July 26, 2000, p. A1; Bruce Horovitz, "Armstrong Rolls to Market Gold," *USA Today*, May 4, 2000, p. 1B; Theresa Howard, "Pepsi Takes Some Fizz off Vanilla Rival," *USA Today*, November 16, 2003; Keith Naughton, "The Soft Sell," *Newsweek*, February 2, 2004, pp. 46–47; Betsy Cummings, "Star Power," *Sales and Marketing Management*, April 2001, pp. 52–59.

that communicators can use their good image to reduce some negative feelings toward a brand but in the process might lose some esteem with the audience.

Multinational companies wrestle with a number of challenges in developing global communications programs: They must decide whether the product is appropriate for a country. They must make sure the market segment they address is both legal and customary. They must decide if the style of the ad is acceptable, and they must decide whether ads should be created at headquarters or locally.[26]

1. *Product.* Many products are restricted or forbidden in certain parts of the world. Beer, wine, and spirits cannot be advertised or sold in Muslim countries. Tobacco products are subject to strict regulation in many countries.

2. *Market segment.* North American toy makers were surprised to learn that in many countries (Norway and Sweden, for example) no TV ads may be directed at children under 12. Sweden lobbied hard to extend that ban to all EU member countries in 2001 but failed. To play it safe, McDonald's advertises itself as a family restaurant in Sweden.

3. *Style.* Comparative ads, while acceptable and even common in Canada and the United States, are less commonly used in the United Kingdom, unacceptable in Japan, and illegal in India and Brazil. PepsiCo had a comparative taste test ad in Japan that was refused by many TV stations and eventually led to a lawsuit.

4. *Local or global.* Today, more and more multinational companies are attempting to build a global brand image by using the same advertising in all markets. When Daimler AG and Chrysler merged to become the world's fifth-largest automaker, they ran a three-week ad campaign in more than 100 countries consisting of a 12-page magazine insert, 9 newspaper spreads, and a 24-page brochure that was sent to business, government, and union leaders and to the news media. The campaign's tagline was "Expect the extraordinary," and it featured people from both companies working together.

Companies that sell their products to different cultures or in different countries must be prepared to vary their messages. In advertising its hair-care products in different countries, Helene Curtis adjusts its messages. Middle-class British women wash their hair frequently, whereas the opposite is true among Spanish women. Japanese women avoid overwashing their hair for fear of removing protective oils. Consider how Bell Canada communicated with the Asian community to advertise its satellite television service, Bell ExpressVu:

Bell ExpressVu

Bell ExpressVu launched a print campaign targeted at the large Canadian South Asian community to promote the fact that Bell ExpressVu carries the Asian Television Network, a 24-hour service offering programs in English, Hindi, Punjabi, Tamil, Urdu, and other South Asian languages. The company did not have the budget to launch separate campaigns for all the subtargets in this group. As a result, Toronto-based Vickers & Benson Advertising decided that the solution was to write the copy in English, given that it is spoken throughout the subcontinent. However, they used copywriters that were themselves of Asian descent and employed what is commonly referred to as "Indian English"—the variant of the language typically spoken in South Asian countries. The copy read: "Big big news for all cousin brothers and sisters. We are maha proud to inform you that you are now able to get Asian Television Network full day, full night" and "First dish, then dishum dishum" which meant "First you buy your satellite dish, then the action begins." Furthermore, they used visual cues that reinforced a connection with Asian countries such as an auto-rickshaw and a piece of sari fabric. Finally, to allay the risk that readers might mistake the ads as mockery, they included the line "The writers of this advertisement are coming from exactly the same native place as you and, like you, are very homesick also."[27]

Select the Communication Channels

Selecting efficient channels to carry the message becomes more difficult as channels of communication become more fragmented and cluttered. Think of the challenges in the pharmaceutical industry: Sales reps "detail" doctors every day, hoping to get five minutes of a busy doctor's time. Some 40 percent of calls do not even result in seeing the doctor, which makes sales calling extremely expensive.

The industry has had to expand its battery of communication channels to include ads in medical journals, direct mail (including audio and videotapes), free samples, and even telemarketing. Pharmaceutical companies sponsor clinical conferences at which they pay physicians to spend a weekend listening to leading physicians extol certain drugs in the morning, followed by an afternoon of golf or tennis.

All of these channels are used in the hope of building physician preference for their branded therapeutic agent. Pharmaceutical companies are also using new technologies to reach doctors through handheld devices, online services, and videoconferencing equipment.[28]

Communication channels may be personal and nonpersonal. Within each are many subchannels.

PERSONAL COMMUNICATION CHANNELS **Personal communication channels** involve two or more persons communicating directly face-to-face, person-to-audience, over the telephone, or through e-mail. Instant messaging and independent sites to collect consumer reviews are another means of growing importance in recent years. Personal communication channels derive their effectiveness through individualized presentation and feedback.

A further distinction can be drawn among advocate, expert, and social communication channels. *Advocate channels* consist of company salespeople contacting buyers in the target market. *Expert channels* consist of independent experts making statements to target buyers. *Social channels* consist of neighbours, friends, family members, and associates talking to target buyers. In a study of 7000 consumers in seven European countries, 60 percent said they were influenced to use a new brand by family and friends.[29]

A study by Burson-Marsteller and Roper Starch Worldwide found that one influential person's word of mouth tends to affect the buying attitudes of two other people, on average. That circle of influence, however, jumps to eight online. There is considerable consumer-to-consumer communication on the Web on a whole range of subjects. Online visitors increasingly create product information, not just consume it. They join Internet interest groups to share information, so that "word of Web" is joining "word of mouth" as an important buying influence. Words about good companies travel fast; words about bad companies travel even faster. As one marketer noted, "You don't need to reach 2 million people to let them know about a new product—you just need to reach the right 2000 people in the right way and they will help you reach 2 million."[30]

Personal influence carries especially great weight in two situations. One is with products that are expensive, risky, or purchased infrequently. The other is where the product suggests something about the user's status or taste. People often ask others for a recommendation for a doctor, plumber, hotel, lawyer, accountant, architect, insurance agent, interior decorator, or financial consultant. If we have confidence in the recommendation, we normally act on the referral. In such cases, the recommender has potentially benefited the service provider as well as the service seeker. Service providers clearly have a strong interest in building referral sources.

Communication researchers are moving toward a social-structure view of interpersonal communication.[31] They see society as consisting of *cliques,* small groups whose members interact frequently. Clique members are similar, and their closeness facilitates effective communication but also insulates the clique from new ideas. The challenge is to create more openness so that cliques exchange information with others in the society. This openness is helped by people who function as liaisons and bridges. A *liaison* is a person who connects two or more cliques without belonging to either. A *bridge* is a person who belongs to one clique and is linked to a person in another clique.

Many companies are becoming acutely aware of the power of *word of mouth* or *buzz.* (See "Marketing Insight: Buzz Marketing.") Products and brands such as Converse sneakers, Krispy Kreme doughnuts, and the blockbuster movie *The Passion of The Christ* were built through buzz.[32] Companies such as Body Shop, Starbucks, Palm Pilot, and Amazon were essentially built by word of mouth, with very little advertising. In some cases, positive word of mouth happens in a natural way.

Buzz Marketing

Marketers' growing interest in word of mouth, buzz, and viral marketing has led to a number of new concepts and ideas. Here are three sets of such insights.

Renée Dye: The 5 Myths of Buzz

Research conducted by Renée Dye, a strategy expert with McKinsey, suggests that buzz evolves according to basic principles. Dye contends that companies seeking to take advantage of buzz must first overcome five misconceptions about marketing contagion. Here are "The 5 Myths of Buzz":

1. *Only outrageous or edgy products are buzz-worthy.* The most unlikely products, like prescription drugs, can generate tremendous buzz.

2. *Buzz just happens.* Buzz is increasingly the result of shrewd marketing tactics in which companies seed a vanguard group, ration supplies, use celebrities to generate buzz, leverage the power of lists, and initiate grassroots marketing.

3. *The best buzz-starters are your best customers.* Often, a counterculture has a greater ability to start buzz.

4. *To profit from buzz, you must act first and fast.* Copycat companies can reap substantial profits if they know when to jump in—and when not to.

5. *The media and advertising are needed to create buzz.* When used either too early or too much, the media and advertising can squelch buzz before it ignites.

Michael Cafferky: Word-of-Mouth Marketing Tips

Marketing author Michael Cafferky's Word-of-Mouth Marketing Tips Web site offers many suggestions on how to build a network of referral sources. Here are five:

1. *Involve your customers in the process of making or delivering your product or service.*

2. *Solicit testimonials from your customers.* Use a response form that asks for feedback—and permission to quote it.

3. *Tell true stories to your customers.* Stories are the central vehicle for spreading reputations because they communicate on an emotional level.

4. *Educate your best customers.* You can pick any topic that is relevant to your best customers and have them become the source of credible, up-to-date information on that topic.

5. *Offer fast complaint handling.* A speedy response is vital to preventing negative word of mouth from starting, because negative feelings about a product or service may linger for years.

Malcolm Gladwell: The Law of the Few, Stickiness, and the Power of Context

Malcolm Gladwell claims that three factors work to ignite public interest in an idea. He calls the first "The Law of the Few." Three types of people help spread an idea like an epidemic. First are *Mavens*, people who are knowledgeable about big and small things. Second are *Connectors*, people who know and communicate with a great number of other people. Third are *Salesmen*, those who possess great natural persuasive power.

Any idea that catches the interest of Mavens, Connectors, and Salesmen is likely to be broadcast far and wide. A second factor is "stickiness." An idea must be expressed so that it motivates people to act. Otherwise "The Law of the Few" will not lead to a self-sustaining epidemic. A third factor, the Power of Context, will control whether those spreading an idea are able to organize groups and communities around it.

Sources: Renée Dye, "The Buzz on Buzz," *Harvard Business Review* (November–December 2000): 139; Scott R. Herriott, "Identifying and Developing Referral Channels," *Management Decision* 30, no. 1 (1992): 4–9; Peter H. Riengen and Jerome B. Kernan, "Analysis of Referral Networks in Marketing: Methods and Illustration," *Journal of Marketing Research* (November 1986): 37–78; Jerry R. Wilson, *Word of Mouth Marketing* (New York: John Wiley, 1991); Cafferky's Free Word-of-Mouth Marketing Tips, 1999, **www.geocities.com/wallstreet/6246**. Also see Emanuel Rosen, *The Anatomy of Buzz* (New York: Doubleday, 2000); Malcolm Gladwell, *The Tipping Point: How Little Things Can Make a Big Difference* (Boston: Little, Brown & Company, 2000).

Campbell's Soup Company

When Campbell's launched its Gardennay soup brand in western Canada, it formulated a word-of-mouth campaign for the uniquely Canadian product. The product was armed with several differentiators, such as its box packaging and healthy attributes. However, the core message that Campbell's wanted to communicate surrounded taste (the soup is cooked briefly before being packaged in an aseptic box designed to preserve the soup's taste, freshness, and texture). The company believed that this differentiator was not easily communicated because it was rooted in the package. As a result, Campbell's found an estimated 200 women who were considered trendsetters and gave each of them 24 cartons of Gardennay. The women were selected based on social connectedness and influence among their peers. They were encouraged to try the product, share it with friends, and offer feedback. While Campbell's has not abandoned traditional communications strategies, it believed word of mouth was particularly useful for this product.[33]

In most cases, "buzz" is managed.[34] Agencies have been created solely to help clients create buzz (e.g., Buzz Agent is a company that has assembled an army of volunteers who talk up products in return for a sample products—and who promote only those they like to ensure honesty). Companies can take several steps to stimulate personal influence channels to work on their behalf:

- *Identify influential individuals and companies and devote extra effort to them.* In technology, influencers might be large corporate customers, industry analysts and journalists, selected policy makers, and a sampling of early adopters.[35]

- *Create opinion leaders by supplying certain people with the product on attractive terms.* Pepsi liberally sampled its Mountain Dew spin-off, Code Red, and also encouraged its core 13-to-19-year-old target audience to stumble on the new flavour in such places as vending machines at malls. As one executive noted, "We allowed these teen influencers to be advocates for the brand. They launched it in their own little world."[36]

- *Work through community influentials such as local disk jockeys, class presidents, and presidents of women's organizations.* When Ford introduced the Focus, it handed out the cars to DJs and trendy people so they would be seen around town in them. Ford also identified 100 influential young consumers in five key marketing regions and also gave them cars to drive around.[37]

The Campbell's Soup Company used a word-of-mouth campaign to launch its Gardennay brand in western Canada.

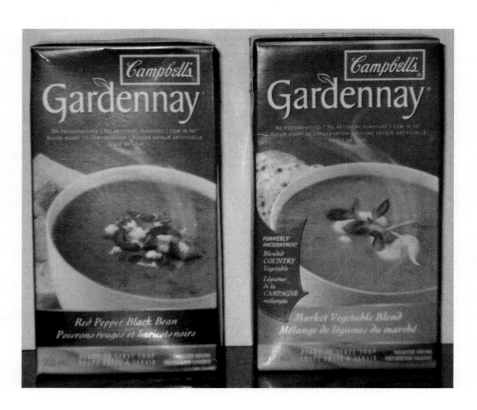

- *Use influential or believable people in testimonial advertising.* Accenture, American Express, Nike, and Buick use golf mega-star Tiger Woods as an endorser to talk up the virtues of their respective companies and products.

- *Develop advertising that has high "conversation value,"* or better yet, incorporate buzz-worthy features into your product design: Some ads have a slogan that becomes part of the cultural vernacular, such as Molson's "I AM Canadian."

- *Develop word-of-mouth referral channels to build business.* Professionals will often encourage clients to recommend their services. Weight Watchers found that word-of-mouth referrals from a relationship with someone in the program had a huge impact on its business.[38]

- *Establish an electronic forum.* Toyota owners who use the Internet can hold online discussions to share experiences.

- *Use viral marketing.* Internet marketers are using **viral marketing** as form of word of mouth, or word of mouse, to draw attention to their sites.[39] Viral marketing involves passing on company-developed products, services, or information from user to user. As a classic example, Hotmail, an Internet service provider, offered a free e-mail account to anyone who signed up. Each e-mail sent by a Hotmail subscriber included the simple tag at the bottom of each message: "Get your free private e-mail at **http://www.hotmail.com**." Users were in effect advertising Hotmail to others. Hotmail spent less than US$500 000 on marketing and within 18 months attracted 12 million subscribers.

One team of viral marketing experts caution that while influencers or "alphas" start trends, they are often too introspective and socially alienated to spread them. They advise marketers to cultivate "bees," hyper-devoted customers who are not just satisfied knowing about the next trend but who live to spread the word.[40] Here's how one company cultivated bees and harvested "honey" in the form of millions of media impressions and huge sales:

InZone Brands Inc.

With a minuscule budget, InZone Brands relied at first on the power of licensing and packaging to create brand awareness for its BellyWashers, beverages for kids packaged in fun-looking bottles decorated with cartoon characters. It then set out to develop buzz by harnessing the most powerful force in kids' marketing: peer-to-peer influence. The company launched a Kids Board, a national panel that acts as a mini business unit with the company. Every year, the company selects 15 extremely devoted customers and sponsors their community service projects. In turn, the kids help InZone come up with new product ideas and, more important, build grassroots fervour. In 2003 alone, board members have organized 40 community service projects involving 60 000 kids, all under the BellyWashers banner. The program is estimated to have generated 4 million media impressions. The buzz generated by BellyWashers' fanatical customers and collectors has sent the products flying off the shelves at Toys "R" Us and Wal-Mart. Word of mouth also created a vibrant aftermarket, with first-edition BellyWashers getting high bids on eBay.[41]

Marketers must be careful in reaching out to consumers. Consumers also can resent personal communications if unsolicited. A 2003 survey found that roughly 80 percent of the sample of consumers were very annoyed by pop-up ads, spam, and telemarketing.[42]

NONPERSONAL COMMUNICATION CHANNELS Nonpersonal channels are communications directed to more than one person and include media, sales promotions, events, and publicity:

- *Media* consist of print media (newspapers and magazines), broadcast media (radio and television), network media (telephone, cable, satellite, wireless), electronic media (audiotape, videotape, videodisk, CD-ROM, Web page), and display media (billboards, signs, posters). Most nonpersonal messages come through paid media. Ownership of media in Canada is converging. See how Microsoft leveraged this trend:

Microsoft Canada

The ownership of media is starting to converge. Keeping this in mind is essential when marketers plan to create efficient and effective national campaigns. Microsoft leveraged this convergence in a campaign called "Agility." The objective of the campaign was to increase awareness and understanding of Microsoft Canada's capabilities at providing business-critical technology solutions. It was aimed at business decision makers in medium- and large-sized Canadian companies. As with previous campaigns, television, print, and radio advertising were used. However, to attract the attention of corporate decision makers, a 12-part weekly editorial series called "Canadian Competitiveness" was also commissioned. Microsoft paid to have this sponsored material carried in both CanWest Global Communications and Rogers Communications platforms such as CanWest's *National Post*, *Vancouver Sun*, *Edmonton Journal*, *Ottawa Citizen*, and *Calgary Herald* newspapers, and Rogers-owned *Canadian Business* magazine, *Maclean's*, and radio stations 680News in Toronto and News1130 in Vancouver. The last element, called "Case Study," a monthly profile of excellence in Canadian corporate practice, was placed in the *National Post Business Magazine*. Anne McKeon, senior communications officer of Microsoft Canada, noted, "We needed an innovative advertising approach to effectively reach senior executives."[43]

- *Sales promotions* consist of consumer promotions (such as samples, coupons, and premiums); trade promotions (such as advertising and display allowances); and business and sales-force promotions (contests for sales reps).

- *Events and experiences* include sports, arts, entertainment, and cause events, as well as less formal activities that create novel brand interactions with consumers.

- *Public relations* include communications directed internally to employees of the company or externally to consumers, other firms, the government, and media.

Much of the recent growth of nonpersonal channels has been with events and experiences. A company can build its brand image through creating or sponsoring events. Event marketers who once favoured sports events are now using other venues such as art museums, zoos, or ice shows to entertain clients and employees. IBM sponsors Cirque du Soleil performances; Bell Canada is an active sponsor of the Olympics; Harley-Davidson sponsors annual motorcycle rallies; and Perrier sponsors sports and other events.

Companies are searching for better ways to quantify the benefits of sponsorship and are demanding greater accountability from event owners and organizers. Companies can also create events designed to surprise the public and create a buzz. Many amount to guerrilla marketing tactics. Here are some examples:

- Driver 2, a new car-chase video game, arranged for a convoy of 20 car wrecks with smoke pouring from their engines to crawl through Manhattan and Los Angeles to attract attention to the new game.

- Ask Jeeves, the Internet search engine, sent 35 actors in British butlers' outfits to guide visitors to their seats and answer tennis trivia questions at the U.S. Open tennis tournament.

- Kibu.com pays hundreds of school girls to do "peer marketing" by hanging around with their peers, handing out free lip gloss, and talking up Kibu's cosmetic site.[44]

The increased use of attention-getting events is a response to the fragmentation of media: Consumers can turn to hundreds of cable channels, thousands of magazine titles, and millions of Internet pages. Events can create attention, although whether they have a lasting effect on brand awareness, knowledge, or preference will vary considerably, depending on the quality of the product, the event itself, and its execution.

INTEGRATION OF COMMUNICATION CHANNELS Although personal communication is often more effective than mass communication, mass media might be the major means of stimulating personal communication. Mass communications affect personal attitudes and behaviour through a two-step process. Ideas often flow from radio, television, and print to opinion leaders and from these to the less media-involved population groups. This two-step flow has several implications. First, the influence of mass media on public opinion is not as direct, powerful, and automatic as supposed. It is mediated by opinion leaders, people whose opinions are sought or who carry their opinions to others. Second, the two-step flow challenges the notion that consumption styles are primarily influenced by a "trickle-down" or "trickle-up" effect from mass media. People interact primarily within their own social groups and acquire ideas from opinion leaders in their groups. Third, two-step communication suggests that mass communicators should direct messages specifically to opinion leaders and let them carry the message to others.

Finally, any discussion about the effectiveness of mass communication has to take into account the dramatic changes that have eroded the effectiveness of the mass media. For a look at the forces with which advertisers must contend today, see "Marketing Insight: "Hitting the Bull's Eye in a Post–Mass-Market World."

MARKETING INSIGHT

Hitting the Bull's Eye in a Post–Mass-Market World

In 1960, Procter & Gamble could reach 80 percent of American women with one 30-second Tide commercial aired simultaneously on only three TV networks: NBC, ABC, and CBS. Today, the same ad would have to run on 100 channels to achieve this marketing feat, and even then it would run an increasing risk of being "zapped" by consumers armed with Personal Video Recorders such as TiVo or Replay TV. In fact, a recent study by the Yankee Group, "The Death of the 30-Second Commercial," calculated that by 2007 some US$5.5 billion spent on TV advertising will be wasted.

Two forces are to blame for the demise of what used to be the most powerful means of hitting the consumer marketing bull's eye. One is the fragmentation of North American audiences and, with the advent of digital technology and the Internet, the media now used to reach them. Prime time ratings and circulations have been on the downslide since the 1970s. What's new is the proliferation of media and entertainment options—from hundreds of cable TV and radio stations and thousands of magazines and webzines to uncountable Web sites, blogs, video games, and cell phone screens. Consumers not only have more choice of which medium to use, they also have choice over whether and how they want to receive commercial content.

And that's part of the second force leaching oomph out of the 30-second spot. Digital television and the new personal video recorders (PVRs) allow consumers to eliminate commercials with the push of a fast forward button. The Yankee Group estimates that PVRs will be in almost 25 million homes or 20 percent of U.S. households by 2008. In 2004, Rogers Cable reported that 729 000 Canadian households were equipped with digital set-top boxes. A Decima survey in the same year found that only 13 percent of Canadian analogue cable television subscribers said they would switch to digital television service.

The Internet is even more of a threat. In 2004, according to TNS Canadian Facts' continuous tracking study of Canadian Internet usage, "the proportion of Canadian households online has remained stable (73 percent compared to 72 percent in 2003), while e-commerce has increased, with 34 percent of online Canadians having purchased something in the past year."

So advertisers are adding a variety of new communication tools to their IMC kits, many of which are further blurring the line between advertising and entertainment. Participants on CBS's *Survivor* series subsisted on Frito-Lay's Doritos, Pepsi Cola's Mountain Dew, or Anheuser Busch's Budweiser beer. Firms are also using exclusive TV sponsorships. Fox's series *24* premiered with a single sponsor, the Ford-150 truck. Instead of ads breaking up the show, a three-minute short film—very similar in style to the series and featuring the truck—ran both before and after the show. In addition, the main character drove a Ford Explorer. Other advertisers are just going beyond TV. Nike Europe has amassed a worldwide player base for the online soccer games it launched in the past three years.

Sources: Noreen O'Leary, "The 30-Second Spot Is Dead, Long Live the 30-Second Spot," *Adweek*, November 17, 2003, pp. 12–21; Anthony Bianco, "The Vanishing Mass Market," *Business Week*, July 12, 2004, pp. 60–68; Susan Thea Posnock, "It Can Control Madison Avenue," *American Demographics*, February 2004, pp. 28–33; Jennifer Pendleton, "Multi TASKERS," *Advertising Age*, March 29, 2004, pp. S1, S8; Hank Kim, "Madison Ave. Melds Pitches and Content," *Advertising Age*, October 7, 2002, pp. 1, 14; Christopher Reynolds, "Game Over," *American Demographics*, February 2004, pp. 34–38; Decima Research, "The Digital Domain: Canadian Consumer Research Study," Media Release, September 15, 2004; **http://media.corporate-ir.net/.../TOR/RCI.B.TO/reports/RCI%20Fact%20Sheet% 20Q3%2004%20Nov%202004%20Update.pdf**; "Internet Penetration Remains Stable; E-Commerce Up," *Marketnews*, August 16, 2005, **http://marketnews.ca/news_detail.asp?nid=965**.

Establish the Total Marketing Communications Budget

One of the most difficult marketing decisions is determining how much to spend on promotion. John Wanamaker, the department-store magnate, once said, "I know that half of my advertising is wasted, but I don't know which half."

Industries and companies vary considerably in how much they spend on promotion. Expenditures might be 30 to 50 percent of sales in the cosmetics industry and 5 to 10 percent in the industrial-equipment industry. Within a given industry, there are low- and high-spending companies.

How do companies decide on the promotion budget? We will describe four common methods: the affordable method, percentage-of-sales method, competitive-parity method, and objective-and-task method.

AFFORDABLE METHOD Many companies set the promotion budget at what they think the company can afford. The affordable method completely ignores the role of promotion as an investment and the immediate impact of promotion on sales volume. It leads to an uncertain annual budget, which makes long-range planning difficult.

PERCENTAGE-OF-SALES METHOD Many companies set promotion expenditures at a specified percentage of sales (either current or anticipated) or of the sales price. Automobile companies typically budget a fixed percentage for promotion based on the planned car price. Oil companies set the appropriation at a fraction of a cent for each litre of gasoline sold under their own label.

Supporters of the percentage-of-sales method see a number of advantages. First, promotion expenditures will vary with what the company can "afford." This satisfies financial managers, who believe that expenses should be closely related to the movement of corporate sales over the business cycle. Second, it encourages management to think of the relationship among promotion cost, selling price, and profit per unit. Third, it encourages stability when competing firms spend approximately the same percentage of their sales on promotion.

In spite of these advantages, the percentage-of-sales method has little to justify it. It views sales as the determiner of promotion rather than as the result. It leads to a budget set by the availability of funds rather than by market opportunities. It discourages experimentation with countercyclical promotion or aggressive spending. Dependence on year-to-year sales fluctuations interferes with long-range planning. There is no logical basis for choosing the specific percentage, except what has been done in the past or what competitors are doing. Finally, it does not encourage building the promotion budget by determining what each product and territory deserves.

COMPETITIVE-PARITY METHOD Some companies set their promotion budget to achieve share-of-voice parity with competitors. Two arguments are made in support of the competitive-parity method. One is that competitors' expenditures represent the collective wisdom of the industry. The other is that maintaining competitive parity prevents promotion wars. Neither argument is valid. There are no grounds for believing that competitors know better. Company reputations, resources, opportunities, and objectives differ so much that promotion budgets are hardly a guide. Furthermore, there is no evidence that budgets based on competitive parity discourage promotional wars.

OBJECTIVE-AND-TASK METHOD The objective-and-task method calls upon marketers to develop promotion budgets by defining specific objectives, determining the tasks that must be performed to achieve these objectives, and estimating the costs of performing these tasks. The sum of these costs is the proposed promotion budget.

For example, suppose Cadbury Schweppes wants to introduce a new natural energy drink called Sunburst for the casual athlete.[45]

1. *Establish the market-share goal.* The company estimates 50 million potential users and sets a target of attracting 8 percent of the market—that is, 4 million users.

2. *Determine the percentage of the market that should be reached by advertising.* The advertiser hopes to reach 80 percent (40 million prospects) with the advertising message.

3. *Determine the percentage of aware prospects that should be persuaded to try the brand.* The advertiser would be pleased if 25 percent of aware prospects (10 million) tried Sunburst. This is because it estimates that 40 percent of all triers, or 4 million people, would become loyal users. This is the market goal.

4. *Determine the number of advertising impressions per 1 percent trial rate.* The advertiser estimates that 40 advertising impressions (exposures) for every 1 percent of the population would bring about a 25 percent trial rate.

5. *Determine the number of gross rating points that would have to be purchased.* A gross rating point is one exposure to 1 percent of the target population. Because the company wants to achieve 40 exposures to 80 percent of the population, it will want to buy 3200 gross rating points.

6. *Determine the necessary advertising budget on the basis of the average cost of buying a gross rating point.* To expose 1 percent of the target population to one impression costs an average of $3277. Therefore, 3200 gross rating points would cost $10 486 400 (= $3277 × 3200) in the introductory year.

The objective-and-task method has the advantage of requiring management to spell out its assumptions about the relationship among dollars spent, exposure levels, trial rates, and regular usage.

A major question is how much weight marketing communications should receive in relation to alternatives such as product improvement, lower prices, or better service. The answer depends on where the company's products are in their life cycles, whether they are commodities or highly differentiable products, whether they are routinely needed or have to be "sold," and other considerations. Marketing communication budgets tend to be higher when there is low channel support, much change in the marketing program over time, many hard-to-reach customers, more complex customer decision making, differentiated products and nonhomogeneous customer needs, and frequent product purchases in small quantities.[46]

In theory, the total communications budget should be established so that the marginal profit from the last communication dollar just equals the marginal profit from the last dollar in the best noncommunication use. Implementing this principle, however, is not easy.

Deciding on the Marketing Communications Mix

Companies must allocate the marketing communications budget over the six major modes of communication—advertising, sales promotion, public relations and publicity, events and experiences, sales force, and direct marketing. Within the same industry, companies can differ considerably in their media and channel choices. Avon concentrates its promotional funds on personal selling, whereas Revlon spends heavily on advertising. Electrolux spends heavily on a door-to-door sales force, whereas Hoover relies more on advertising. Consider some of the unique issues facing the Canadian pharmaceuticals industry:

Novartis

Based in Dorval, Quebec, the pharmaceutical company Novartis has to make some interesting choices about its marketing communications strategy for the company's Diovan drug, which treats high blood pressure. The company's American counterparts employed a campaign consisting of newspaper ads, television, physician communication, and a Web site (http://healthybp.com). However, because of strict Canadian regulations about direct-to-consumer advertising of prescription pharmaceuticals (ads can only feature information about high blood pressure and the need to treat it, but cannot mention the Diovan brand itself), Novartis has spent the majority of its advertising dollars on reaching out to physicians. The communications budget supports the sponsorship of golf tournaments, guest lectures at medical forums, and having sales reps work with the communications departments at hospitals or medical associations. Novartis aims at offering doctors credible scientific resources to understand the drug. However, the biggest issue with respect to Diovan has been lack of patient understanding. Misperceptions result in patients ceasing use too early to realize the benefits of the drug. To overcome this problem, the company plans to allocate an increasing portion of its budget to empower and educate patients, which will require careful regulatory and ethical considerations.[47]

Companies are always searching for ways to gain efficiency by replacing one promotional tool with others. Many companies are replacing some field sales activity with ads, direct mail, and telemarketing. One auto dealer dismissed his five salespeople and cut his prices, and sales exploded. Companies are shifting advertising funds into sales promotion. The substitutability among promotional tools explains why marketing functions need to be coordinated. For example, a new Web site and a coordinated TV ad campaign targeting the greater Los Angeles area sparked record sales for Hawaii's Aloha Airlines, selling over US$1 million tickets on one day. The TV ads were designed to create awareness for Aloha and drive traffic to the Web site, where the sale would be closed.[48]

Characteristics of the Marketing Communications Mix

Each communication tool has its own unique characteristics and costs.

ADVERTISING Advertising can be used to build up a long-term image for a product (Coca-Cola ads) or trigger quick sales (a Sears ad for a weekend sale). Advertising can efficiently reach geographically dispersed buyers. Certain forms of advertising (TV) can require a large budget, whereas other forms (newspaper) do not. Just the presence of advertising might have an effect on sales: Consumers might believe that a heavily advertised brand must offer "good value."[49] Because of the many forms and uses of advertising, it is difficult to make generalizations.[50] Yet the following qualities can be noted:

1. *Pervasiveness.* Advertising permits the seller to repeat a message many times. It also allows the buyer to receive and compare the messages of various competitors. Large-scale advertising says something positive about the seller's size, power, and success.

2. *Amplified expressiveness.* Advertising provides opportunities for dramatizing the company and its products through the artful use of print, sound, and colour.

3. *Impersonality.* The audience does not feel obligated to pay attention or respond to advertising. Advertising is a monologue in front of, not a dialogue with, the audience.

SALES PROMOTION Companies use sales-promotion tools—coupons, contests, premiums, and the like—to draw a stronger and quicker buyer response. Sales promotion can be used for short-run effects such as to highlight product offers and boost sagging sales. Sales-promotion tools offer three distinctive benefits:

1. *Communication.* They gain attention and may lead the consumer to the product.

2. *Incentive.* They incorporate some concession, inducement, or contribution that gives value to the consumer.

3. *Invitation.* They include a distinct invitation to engage in the transaction now.

PUBLIC RELATIONS AND PUBLICITY Marketers tend to underuse public relations, yet a well-thought-out program coordinated with the other promotion-mix elements can be extremely effective. At a recent conference, Wende Knapp, head of public relations for Xerox Canada, and Andrew Berthoff, senior vice-president of Environics Communications, stressed the power of PR:[51]

Xerox Canada

When charged with the task of building a brand, many marketing managers assume that a major investment in advertising is required. But advertising is not necessarily the right or the only solution. In fact, many strong brands like Xerox have been created through a blend of marketing components such as media and public relations. With increased pressure to "think global" and "act local" on a shrinking budget, public relations may be the secret weapon in the integrated marketing communications arsenal. Knapp and Berthoff believe that public relations return a huge value on investment and provide a cost-effective alternative to advertising. It can generate third-party endorsement by independent media sources, enhance corporate/brand credibility, and enable organizations to reach their customers through a variety of contact points—media coverage, special events, conferences, industry networking, and targeted sponsorships. It also allows firms to establish relationships with customers and partners, creating less commercial—and more compelling—communication.

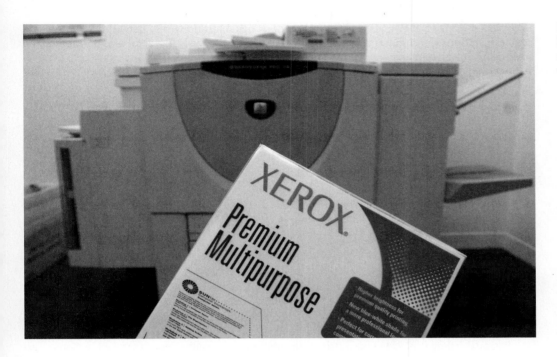

Strong brands like Xerox have been created through a blend of marketing components.

The appeal of public relations and publicity is based on three distinctive qualities:

1. *High credibility.* News stories and features are more authentic and credible to readers than ads.
2. *Ability to catch buyers off guard.* Public relations can reach prospects who prefer to avoid sales-people and advertisements.
3. *Dramatization.* Public relations have the potential for dramatizing a company or product.

EVENTS AND EXPERIENCES There are many advantages to events and experiences:

1. *Relevant.* A well-chosen event or experience can be seen as highly relevant as the consumer gets personally involved.
2. *Involving.* Given its live, real-time quality, consumers can find events and experiences more actively engaging.
3. *Implicit.* Events are more of an indirect "soft-sell."

DIRECT MARKETING The many forms of direct marketing—direct mail, telemarketing, Internet marketing—share three distinctive characteristics. Direct marketing is:

1. *Customized.* The message can be prepared to appeal to the addressed individual.
2. *Up to date.* A message can be prepared very quickly.
3. *Interactive.* The message can be changed depending on the person's response.

PERSONAL SELLING Personal selling is the most effective tool at later stages of the buying process, particularly in building up buyer preference, conviction, and action. Personal selling has three distinctive qualities:

1. *Personal interaction.* Personal selling involves an immediate and interactive relationship between two or more persons. Each party is able to observe the other's reactions.
2. *Cultivation.* Personal selling permits all kinds of relationships to spring up, ranging from a matter-of-fact selling relationship to a deep personal friendship.
3. *Response.* Personal selling makes the buyer feel under some obligation for having listened to the sales talk.

Factors in Setting the Marketing Communications Mix

Companies must consider several factors in developing their communications mix: type of product market, consumer readiness to make a purchase, and stage in the product life cycle. Also important is the company's market rank.

TYPE OF PRODUCT MARKET Communications mix allocations vary between consumer and business markets. Consumer marketers tend to spend comparatively more on sales promotion and advertising; business marketers tend to spend comparatively more on personal selling. In general, personal selling is used more with complex, expensive, and risky goods and in markets with fewer and larger sellers (hence, business markets).

Although advertising is used less than sales calls in business markets, it still plays a significant role:

- Advertising can provide an introduction to the company and its products.
- If the product has new features, advertising can explain them.
- Reminder advertising is more economical than sales calls.
- Advertisements offering brochures and carrying the company's phone number are an effective way to generate leads for sales representatives.
- Sales representatives can use tear sheets of the company's ads to legitimize their company and products.
- Advertising can remind customers of how to use the product and reassure them about their purchase.

A number of studies have underscored advertising's role in business markets. Advertising combined with personal selling can increase sales over what would have resulted if there had been no advertising.[52] Corporate advertising can improve a company's reputation and improve the sales force's chances of getting a favourable first hearing and early adoption of the product.[53]

Personal selling can also make a strong contribution in consumer-goods marketing. Some consumer marketers use the sales force mainly to collect weekly orders from dealers and to see that sufficient stock is on the shelf. Yet an effectively trained company sales force can make four important contributions:

1. *Increased stock position.* Sales reps can persuade dealers to take more stock and devote more shelf space to the company's brand.
2. *Enthusiasm building.* Sales reps can build dealer enthusiasm by dramatizing planned advertising and sales-promotion backup.
3. *Missionary selling.* Sales reps can sign up more dealers.
4. *Key account management.* Sales reps can take responsibility for growing business with the most important accounts.

BUYER-READINESS STAGE Communication tools vary in cost-effectiveness at different stages of buyer readiness. Figure 17.6 shows the relative cost-effectiveness of four communication tools. Advertising and publicity play the most important roles in the awareness-building stage. Customer comprehension is primarily affected by advertising and personal selling. Customer conviction is influenced mostly by personal selling. Closing the sale is influenced mostly by personal selling and sales promotion. Reordering is also affected mostly by personal selling and sales promotion, and somewhat by reminder advertising.

FIGURE 17.6

Cost-Effectiveness of Three Different Communication Tools at Different Buyer-Readiness Stages

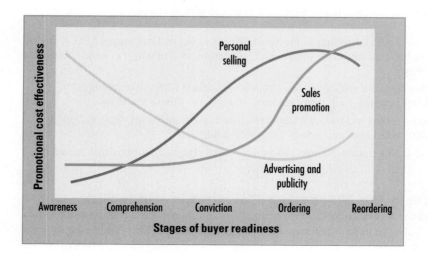

PRODUCT LIFE-CYCLE STAGE Communication tools also vary in cost-effectiveness at different stages of the product life cycle. In the introduction stage, advertising and publicity have the highest cost-effectiveness, followed by personal selling to gain distribution coverage and sales promotion to induce trial. In the growth stage, demand has its own momentum through word of mouth. In the maturity stage, sales promotion, advertising, and personal selling all grow more important, in that order. In the decline stage, sales promotion continues to be strong, advertising and publicity are reduced, and salespeople give the product only minimal attention. Consider this intriguing example of a promotion mix used in the growth stage of a service life cycle:

Tourism Newfoundland and Labrador

Newfoundland and Labrador tourism marketers know that there is no such thing as an accidental tourist when it comes to someone visiting their province. People must make a deliberate choice to visit there. As a result, the province has been aggressive in promoting the unique benefits of a trip there. Using print advertising and its Web page, it demonstrates what is unique and different about Newfoundland culture, history, lifestyle, nature, and scenery. These promotional tools alone aren't enough to guarantee a thriving tourism industry, however. New infrastructure had to be built to make travel to and within the province easier. Thus the province expanded its airport and improved its roadways. It encouraged the building of hotels, golf courses, and spas. It created events, such as the 500th anniversary of the Cabot landing, to draw people from around the world. The province's efforts have met with resounding success, and Newfoundland and Labrador has become Canada's fastest-growing tourism destination, with an increase in visitation of 37 percent.[54]

Measuring Communication Results

Senior managers want to know the *outcomes* and *revenues* resulting from their communications investments. Too often, however, their communications directors supply only *outputs* and *expenses*: press clipping counts, numbers of ads placed, media costs. In fairness, the communications directors try to translate outputs into intermediate outputs such as reach and frequency, recall and recognition scores, persuasion changes, and cost-per-thousand calculations. Ultimately, behaviour-change measures capture the real payoff.

After implementing the communication plan, the communications director must measure its impact on the target audience. Members of the target audience are asked whether they recognize or recall the message, how many times they saw it, what points they recall, how they felt about the

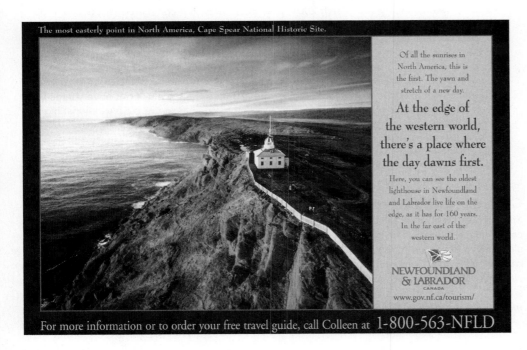

Integrated marketing communications were critical in boosting tourism in Newfoundland and Labrador.

FIGURE 17.7

Current Consumer States for Two Brands

message, and their previous and current attitudes toward the product and the company. The communicator should also collect behavioural measures of audience response, such as how many people bought the product, liked it, and talked to others about it.

Figure 17.7 provides an example of good feedback measurement. We find that 80 percent of the consumers in the total market are aware of brand A, 60 percent have tried it, and only 20 percent who have tried it are satisfied. This indicates that the communications program is effective in creating awareness, but the product fails to meet consumer expectations. In contrast, only 40 percent of the consumers in the total market are aware of brand B, and only 30 percent have tried it, but 80 percent of those who have tried it are satisfied. In this case, the communications program needs to be strengthened to take advantage of the brand's power.

Managing the Integrated Marketing Communications Process

As defined by the American Association of Advertising Agencies, **integrated marketing communications (IMC)** is a concept of marketing communications planning that recognizes the added value of a comprehensive plan. Such a plan evaluates the strategic roles of a variety of communications disciplines—for example, general advertising, direct response, sales promotion, and public relations—and combines these disciplines to provide clarity, consistency, and maximum impact through the seamless integration of messages.

Unfortunately, many companies still rely on one or two communication tools. This practice persists in spite of the fragmenting of mass markets into a multitude of mini markets, each requiring its own approach; the proliferation of new types of media; and the growing sophistication of consumers. The wide range of communication tools, messages, and audiences makes it imperative that companies move toward integrated marketing communications. Companies must adopt a "360 degree view" of consumers to fully understand all the different ways that communications can affect consumer behaviour in their daily lives.

Here is a successful example of an integrated marketing communication program:

Accenture

Forced to change its company name from Andersen Consulting after an arbitrator's decision, Accenture developed a rebranding campaign that utilized a fully integrated communications program. By January 2001, television, print, Internet, and poster ads featuring the Accenture name appeared in each of 48 different countries where the company did business. Between January and March 2001, over 6000 television commercial spots and 1000 print ads were run in global markets. In Australia, the company placed a "cover wrap" on the magazine *Business Review Weekly* and advertising on bus stops and park benches in Sydney's business district. The company placed large-scale outdoor ads in Milan's Oberdan Square and coated 10 taxis in London with Accenture signage. The January 2001 Accenture World Match Play Championship allowed the company to run some 300 commercials in its international markets and 100 commercials in the United States, plus print advertisements in major newspapers, business periodicals, and golf magazines in the U.S. Additional high-profile global advertising sponsorship opportunities included the Formula 1 Racing Series, several European skiing events, the Six Nations Rugby tournament, the Asian PGA tour, the World Soccer Dream Match in Japan, and the Italian Football Championship.

Coordinating Media

Media coordination can occur across and within media types. Personal and nonpersonal communication channels should be combined to achieve maximum impact. Imagine a marketer using a single tool in a "one-shot" effort to reach and sell a prospect. An example of a *single-vehicle, single-stage campaign* is a one-time mailing offering a cookware item. A *single-vehicle, multiple-stage campaign* would involve successive mailings to the same prospect. Magazine publishers, for example, send about four renewal notices to a household before giving up. A more powerful approach is the *multiple-vehicle, multiple-stage campaign*. Consider the following sequence:

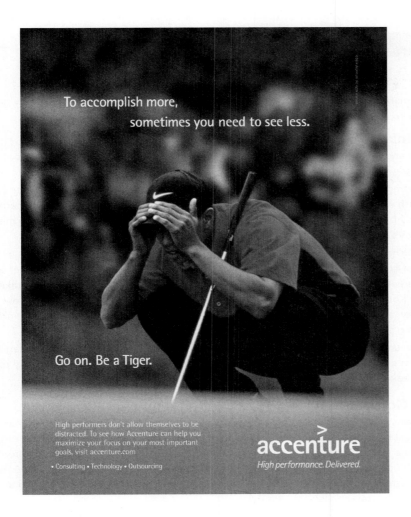

One of a series of Tiger Woods ads that are part of the Accenture rebranding campaign.

News campaign about a new product → Paid ad with a response mechanism → Direct mail → Outbound telemarketing → Face-to-face sales call → Ongoing communication.

Multiple media deployed within a tightly defined time frame can increase message reach and impact. For a Citibank campaign to market home equity loans, instead of using only "mail plus an 800 number," Citibank used "mail plus coupon plus 800 number plus outbound telemarketing plus print advertising." Although the second campaign was more expensive, it resulted in a 15 percent increase in the number of new accounts compared with direct mail alone.[55]

Research has also shown that promotions can be more effective when combined with advertising.[56] The awareness and attitudes created by advertising campaigns can improve the success of more direct sales pitches. "Marketing Insight: Coordinating Media to Build Brand Equity" describes how to leverage television advertising in other media.

Many companies are coordinating their online and offline communication activities. About a third of advertisers who bought television advertising for the 2002–2003 season bought ad space on the station's Web sites.[60] Listing URL Web addresses in ads (especially print) and on packages allows people to more fully explore a company's products, find store locations, and get more product or service information. Dannon makes it a priority to drive traffic to its Dannon Yogurt homepage so that the company can benefit from the twin paybacks of (1) forging direct relationships with customers and (2) building a database of its best customers whose loyalty can be strengthened with more targeted coupon and direct mail promotional efforts.[61]

Pepsi has been highly successful in linking its online and offline efforts. In 2001, Pepsi and Yahoo! joined forces for an online promotion that increased sales 5 percent at a cost of about one-fifth of the previous mail-in promotion. During the promotion, Pepsi displayed the portal's logo on 1.5 billion cans while Yahoo! created a co-branded PepsiStuff.com e-commerce site where visitors

MARKETING INSIGHT

Coordinating Media to Build Brand Equity

To develop effective integrated marketing communications programs, marketers sometimes must explicitly tie marketing communications together to create or enhance brand equity.

Problem: Weak Brand Links

To build brand equity, communication effects created by advertising must be linked to the brand. Often, such links are difficult to create because of:

- *Competitive clutter.* Competing ads in the product category can create "interference" and consumer confusion as to which ad goes with which brand.[57] When Eveready launched a clever ad campaign for Energizer batteries featuring a pink toy bunny that kept on "going . . . and going . . . and going," 40 percent mistakenly attributed it to Eveready's main competitor, Duracell.

- *Ad content and structure.* Although "borrowed interest" tactics may grab consumers' attention, the resulting processing may *not* create strong brand associations. When the popular actor James Garner was advertising for Polaroid, marketing research surveys routinely noted that interview respondents mistakenly attributed his promotion to Kodak, its chief competitor. Delaying brand identification or providing few brand mentions in an ad may raise processing intensity but result in attention directed away from thinking about the brand, contributing to weak brand links.[58]

- *Consumer involvement.* Consumers may not have any inherent interest in the product or service category or may lack knowledge of the specific brand. The resulting decrease in consumer motivation and ability to process also translates to weaker brand links.[59]

Solution: Strengthening Communication Effects

Advertising may "work" in the sense that communication effects are stored in memory. Yet advertising may "fail" in the sense that these communication effects are *not* accessible when consumers make critical brand-related decisions. To address this problem, one common tactic is to make the brand name and package information prominent in the ad. Unfortunately, although consumers are better able to recall the advertised brand with this tactic, there is less other information about the brand to actually recall. Three potentially more effective strategies are brand signatures, ad retrieval cues, and media interactions:

- *Brand signatures.* The *brand signature* is the manner by which the brand is identified at the conclusion of a TV or radio ad or displayed within a print ad. An effective brand signature provides a seamless connection to the ad as a whole. For example, the famous "Got milk?" campaign always displayed that tagline or slogan in a manner fitting the ad (e.g., in flames for the "yuppie in hell" ad or in primary school print for the "school lunchroom bully" ad).

- *Ad retrieval cues.* An *advertising retrieval cue* is a key visual, a catchy slogan, or any unique advertising element that serves as an effective reminder to consumers. Eveready featured a picture of the pink bunny character on the packages for energizer batteries to reduce confusion with Duracell. Ad retrieval cues can be placed in the store (on the package or as part of a shelf-talker or some other point-of-purchase device), combined with a promotion (an FSI coupon), included as part of a yellow pages directory listing, or embedded in any marketing communication option where recall of communication effects can be advantageous.

- *Media interactions.* Print and radio reinforcement of TV ads—where the video and audio components of a TV ad serve as the basis for other types of ads—can be an effective means to leverage existing communication effects from TV ad exposure and more strongly link them to the brand. A potentially useful, although rarely employed, media strategy is to run explicitly linked print or radio ads *prior* to the accompanying TV ad. The print and radio ads increase consumer motivation to process the more "complete" TV ad.

Source: Kevin Lane Keller, *Strategic Brand Management*, 2nd edition (Upper Saddle River, NJ: Prentice-Hall, 2002).

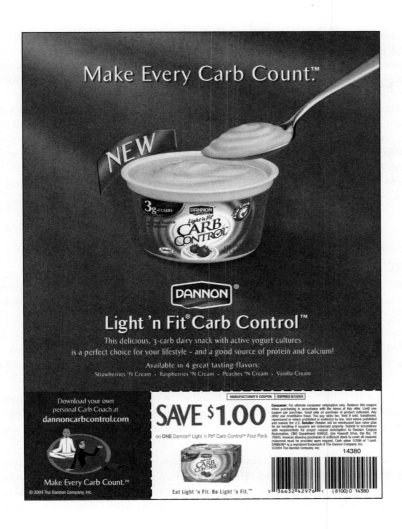

This Dannon print ad includes a Web address as well as a coupon, to drive readers and customers to the Dannon Web site as well as to buy the product.

could redeem points from bottle caps for prizes ranging from electronic goods to concert tickets.[62] When Dutch financial services firm ING Group launched its brand in North America, TV and print ads were paired with online ads. In one campaign on financial news sites, all the "ings" in the news text turned orange—matching ING's corporate colours.[63]

Even if consumers do not order online, they can use Web sites in ways that drive them into stores to buy. Future Shop's Web site can be seen as a research tool for consumers, as surveys revealed that 40 percent of their customers looked online first before coming into the store.[64]

Implementing IMC

Integrated marketing communications has been slow to take hold for several reasons. Large companies often employ several communications specialists to work with their brand managers who may know comparatively little about the other communication tools. Further complicating matters is that many global companies use a large number of ad agencies located in different countries and serving different divisions, resulting in uncoordinated communications and image diffusion.

Today, however, a few large agencies have substantially improved their integrated offerings. To facilitate one-stop shopping, major ad agencies have acquired promotion agencies, public relations firms, package-design consultancies, Web site developers, and direct-mail houses. Many international clients have opted to put a substantial portion of their communications work through one agency. An example is IBM turning all of its advertising over to Ogilvy to attain uniform branding. The result is integrated and more effective marketing communications and a much lower total communications cost.

Integrated marketing communications can produce stronger message consistency and greater sales impact. It forces management to think about every way the customer comes in contact with the company, how the company communicates its positioning, the relative importance of each vehicle, and timing issues. It gives someone the responsibility—where none existed before—to unify the company's brand images and messages as they come through thousands of company activities. IMC should improve the company's ability to reach the right customers with the right messages at the right time and in the right place.[65] "Marketing Memo: How Integrated Is Your IMC Program?" provides some guidelines.

IMC advocates describe it as a way of looking at the whole marketing process instead of focusing on individual parts of it. Companies such as Motorola, Xerox, and Hewlett-Packard are bringing together advertising, direct marketing, public relations, and employee communications experts into "supercouncils" that meet a few times each year for training and improved communications among them. Procter & Gamble recently revised its communications planning by requiring that each new program be formulated jointly, with its ad agency sitting together with P&G's public relations agencies, direct-marketing units, promotion-merchandising firms, and Internet operations.

Marketing Memo

How Integrated Is Your IMC Program?

In assessing the collective impact of an IMC program, the overriding goal is to create the most effective and efficient communication program possible. The following six criteria can be used to help determine whether communications are truly integrated:

- *Coverage*. Coverage is the proportion of the audience that is reached by each communication option employed, as well as how much overlap exists among communication options. In other words, to what extent do different communication options reach the designated target market and the same or different consumers making up that market?

- *Contribution*. Contribution is the inherent ability of a marketing communication to create the desired response and communication effects from consumers in the absence of exposure to any other communication option. How much does a communication affect consumer processing and build awareness, enhance image, elicit responses, and induce sales?

- *Commonality*. Commonality is the extent to which *common* associations are reinforced across communication options—that is, the extent to which information conveyed by different communication options share meaning. The consistency and cohesiveness of the brand image is important because it determines how easily existing associations and responses can be recalled and how easily additional associations and responses can become linked to the brand in memory.

- *Complementarity*. Communication options are often more effective when used in tandem. Complementarity relates to the extent to which *different* associations and linkages are emphasized across communication options. Different brand associations may be most effectively established by capitalizing on those marketing communication options best suited to eliciting a particular consumer response or establishing a particular type of brand association. As part of the highly successful "Drivers Wanted" campaign, Volkswagen has used television to introduce a storyline that it continued and embellished on its Web site.

- *Versatility*. With any integrated communication program, when consumers are exposed to a particular marketing communication, some consumers will have already been exposed to other marketing communications for the brand, whereas other consumers will not have had any prior exposure. Versatility refers to the extent that a marketing communication option is robust and "works" for different groups of consumers. The ability of a marketing communication to work at "two levels"—effectively communicating to consumers who have or have *not* seen other communications—is critically important.

- *Cost*. Evaluations of marketing communications on all of these criteria must be weighed against their cost to arrive at the most effective *and* efficient communications program.

Source: Kevin Lane Keller, *Strategic Brand Management*, 2nd ed. (Upper Saddle River, NJ: Prentice-Hall, 2003).

SUMMARY

1. Modern marketing calls for more than developing a good product, pricing it attractively, and making it accessible to target customers. Companies must also communicate with present and potential stakeholders, and with the general public.

2. The marketing communications mix consists of six major modes of communication: advertising, sales promotion, public relations and publicity, events and experiences, direct marketing, and personal selling.

3. The communication process consists of nine elements: sender, receiver, message, media, encoding, decoding, response, feedback, and noise. To get their messages through, marketers must encode their messages in a way that takes into account how the target audience usually decodes messages. They must also transmit the message through efficient media that reach the target audience and develop feedback channels to monitor response to the message. Consumer response to a communication can often be modelled in terms of a response hierarchy and "learn-feel-do" sequence.

4. Developing effective communications involves eight steps: (1) identify the target audience, (2) determine the communications objectives, (3) design the communication, (4) select the communication channels, (5) establish the total communications budget, (6) decide on the communications mix, (7) measure the communications results, and (8) manage the integrated marketing communications process.

5. In identifying the target audience, the marketer needs to close any gap that exists between current public perception and the image sought. Communications objectives may involve category need, brand awareness,

brand attitude, or brand purchase intention. Formulating the communication requires solving three problems: what to say (message strategy), how to say it (creative strategy), and who should say it (message source). Communications channels may be personal (advocate, expert, and social channels) or nonpersonal (media, atmospheres, and events). The objective-and-task method of setting the promotion budget, which calls upon marketers to develop their budgets by defining specific objectives, is the most desirable.

6. In deciding on the marketing communications mix, marketers must examine the distinct advantages and costs of each communication tool and the company's market rank. They must also consider the type of product market in which they are selling, how ready consumers are to make a purchase, and the product's stage in the product life cycle. Measuring the marketing communications mix's effectiveness involves asking members of the target audience whether they recognize or recall the communication, how many times they saw it, what points they recall, how they felt about the communication, and their previous and current attitudes toward the product and the company.

7. Managing and coordinating the entire communications process calls for integrated marketing communications (IMC): marketing communications planning that recognizes the added value of a comprehensive plan that evaluates the strategic roles of a variety of communications disciplines and combines these disciplines to provide clarity, consistency, and maximum impact through the seamless integration of discrete messages.

APPLICATIONS

Marketing Debate: What Is the Biggest Obstacle to Integrating Marketing Communications?

Although integrated marketing communications is a frequently espoused goal, truly integrated programs have been hard to come by. Some critics maintain the problem is an organizational one—the agencies have not done a good job of putting together all the different teams and organizations involved with a communications campaign. Others maintain that the biggest problem is the lack of managerial guidelines for evaluating IMC programs. How does a manager know when his or her IMC program is satisfactorily integrated?

Take a position: The biggest obstacle to effective IMC programs is a lack of agency coordination across communica-

tion units versus The biggest obstacle to effective IMC programs is a lack of understanding as to how to optimally design and evaluate such programs.

Marketing Discussion

Pick a brand and go to the Web site. Locate as many forms of communications as you can find. Conduct an informal communications audit. What do you notice? How consistent are the different communications?

Marketing Spotlight: Intel

Intel makes the microprocessors that are found in 80 percent of the world's personal computers. In the early days, Intel microprocessors were known simply by their engineering numbers, such as "80386" or "80486." Intel positioned its chips as the most advanced. The trouble was, as Intel soon learned, numbers can't be trademarked. Competitors came out with their own "486" chips, and Intel had no way to distinguish itself from the competition. Worse, Intel's products were hidden from consumers, buried deep inside PCs. With a hidden, untrademarked product, Intel had a hard time convincing consumers to pay more for its high-performance products.

Intel's response was a marketing campaign that created history. The company chose a trademarkable name (Pentium) and launched a marketing campaign to build awareness of the Intel brand. The "Intel Inside" campaign was Intel's effort to get its name outside of the PC and into the minds of consumers.

Intel used an innovative cooperative scheme to extend the reach of its campaign. Intel would help computer makers, who used Intel processors, to advertise their PCs if the makers also included the Intel logo in their ads. Intel also gave computer manufacturers a rebate on Intel processors if they agreed to place an "Intel Inside" sticker on the outside of their PCs and laptops.

Simultaneously with the cooperative ads, Intel began its own ad program to familiarize consumers with the Intel name. The "Intel Inside" campaign changed Intel's image from a microprocessor maker to a quality standard-bearer. The ads that included the Intel Inside logo were designed to create confidence in the consumer's mind that purchasing a personal computer with an Intel microprocessor was both a safe and technologically sound choice. Between 1990 and 1993, Intel invested over US$500 million in advertising and promotional programs designed to build Intel's brand equity. By 1993, *Financial World* estimated the Intel brand to be worth US$17.8 billion.

Intel continues its integrated campaigns to this day. For example, when launching its Centrino mobile platform, Intel began with TV ads that aired in 12 other countries. These ads include the animated logo and now familiar five-note brand signature melody. Print, online, and outdoor advertising followed shortly thereafter. Print ads ran in magazines and featured ads that targeted that magazine. For instance, an ad appearing in a sports magazine showed the logo in the centre of a tennis racquet with the tagline "High performance laptop. No strings attached."

Simultaneously, Intel held a "One Unwired Day" event that took place in major U.S. cities such as New York, Chicago, San Francisco, and Seattle. In addition to allowing free trial Wi-Fi access, each city held festival events that included live music, product demonstrations, and prize giveaways. The company also set up free access demonstration sites (with wireless Centrino-powered laptops) in areas frequented by road warriors, such as San Francisco's airport.

To boost interest in mobile computing, the company partnered with Zagat Survey to produce a mini-guide inserted into *The New Yorker* that identified more than 50 "Wi-Fi Hotspots"—namely restaurants and hotels—in the "One Wired Day" cities. Finally, Intel ran online ads on such Web sites as CNET.com and Weather.com. Yahoo! created a Wi-Fi Center Web site co-sponsored by Intel and featuring Centrino advertising.

The "Unwired" campaign was another Intel success of marketing integration. The US$300 million total media effort for the Centrino mobile platform helped generate US$2 billion in revenue for Intel during the first nine months of the campaign. Among marketers, Intel won the Innovation award in the Business Superbrands Awards 2003.

Going forward, Intel CEO Craig Barrett said the company will aggressively target opportunities outside of its traditional revenue stream in PCs. The company will be moving beyond "Intel Inside" to "Intel Everywhere"—Intel chips in every type of digital device possible, from cell phones to flat-panel TVs to portable video players and wireless home networks, even medical diagnostic gear. The company is targeting ten new product areas for its chips. If the new markets take off, they'll increase demand for PCs and services, bringing new revenues for Intel's core products even if its own new products do not succeed in these markets. In 2005, former marketer Paul Otellini will succeed Craig Barrett as CEO and take the helm of this US$34 billion company.

DISCUSSION QUESTIONS

1. What have been the key success factors for Intel?

2. Where is Intel vulnerable? What should it watch out for?

3. What recommendations would you make to senior marketing executives going forward? What should the company be sure to do with its marketing?

Sources: Cliff Edwards, "Intel Everywhere?" *Business Week*, March 8, 2004, pp. 56–63; Scott Van Camp, "ReadMe.1st," *Brandweek*, February 23, 2004, pp. 17–18; "How to Become a Superbrand," *Marketing*, January 8, 2004, p. 15; Roger Slavens, "Pam Pollace, VP-Director, Corporate Marketing Group, Intel Corp.," *B to B*, December 8, 2003, p. 19; Kenneth Hein, "Study: New Brand Names Not Making Their Mark," *Brandweek*, December 8, 2003, pp. 12–13; Heather Clancy, "Intel Thinking Outside the Box," *Computer Reseller News*, November 24, 2003, p. 14; Cynthia L. Webb, "A Chip Off the Old Recovery?" **Washingtonpost.com**, October 15, 2003; "Intel Launches Second Phase of Centrino Ads," *Technology Advertising & Branding Report*, October 6, 2003; David Kirkpatrick, "At Intel, Speed Isn't Everything," *Fortune*, February 9, 2004, p. 34.

IN THIS CHAPTER, WE WILL ADDRESS THE FOLLOWING QUESTIONS:

- What steps are involved in developing an advertising program?

- How should sales promotion decisions be made?

- What are the guidelines for effective brand-building events and experiences?

- How can companies exploit the potential of public relations and publicity?

Relax, it's just a game.

HOCKEY CANADA

hockeycanad

18

CHAPTER 18

Managing Mass Communications: Advertising, Sales Promotions, Events, and Public Relations

PROFILE: CANADIAN MARKETING EXCELLENCE

In 2005 some new records were set. For the eighth consecutive year, national marketing communications agency DDB Canada (formerly Palmer Jarvis DDB) was recognized as Canada's most creative agency at the 2005 Marketing Awards. The agency won 33 awards, or a fifth of the night's total, including eight Golds, at Canada's most prestigious advertising award show. The company also continued a winning streak started in 1997 at the "Olympics of Advertising," the Cannes International Advertising Festival, and again won more Lions than any other Canadian agency. At the Canadian Marketing Association (CMA) Awards, DDB Canada won the "Best of the Best" awards in 2003 and 2004 for a PSA campaign for Hockey Canada, and the Ontario Provincial Election "Engage-the-Vote" campaign, which encouraged youth to vote. Using print, radio, TV, and in-rink ads with the tagline "What if kids pressured us the way we pressure them? Relax. It's just a game," the Hockey Canada campaign became one of the most talked about in Canadian history, generating over 1000 documented news stories across Canada, the U.K., and U.S.A., including the BBC, ABC, CNN, and the Oprah Winfrey Show.

These records would be unbelievable if you didn't know DDB Canada's philosophy, culture, and the passion its people pour into their work. Its culture, founded on creativity and humanity, inspires powerful creative collaboration across borders, across disciplines and with clients, generating better ideas and better results. The personality of its people is characterized by unashamed passion for what they do, by determination and persistence in the pursuit of excellence in all they do, and by having fun together as they do it. Since its inception, the agency has produced a winning creative culture that has survived the ever-changing marketing landscape and has continued to recruit and groom many of the industry's top creative talents.

The agency was founded in Vancouver by marketing icon Frank Palmer in 1969, and was originally known as Palmer Jarvis Advertising. It expanded operations in 1980, merging with another agency in Edmonton to better service the mid-west region. In 1997, Palmer Jarvis merged with DDB Worldwide, a like-minded agency, to form Palmer Jarvis DDB (PJ DDB). The merger gave the agency a strong beachhead in Toronto to expand operations, and rekindled the DDB brand in Canada. Seven years later, as part of a global re-branding initiative by DDB Worldwide, Palmer Jarvis DDB was renamed DDB Canada. Today, the agency has offices in Vancouver, Edmonton, and Toronto and is ranked among the top three communications companies in Canada.

DDB Canada has helped numerous clients reach their business goals by providing creative marketing solutions that deliver results. Today, select clients of the agency include Imperial Oil, the Canadian Tourism Commission, Johnson & Johnson, Energizer Canada, Subaru Canada, TELUS, Hockey Canada, the BC Dairy Foundation, and Mountain Equipment Co-op.

DDB Canada, however, is far more than an advertising agency. Over the years, it has acquired other specialized communication companies, creating a total communications company offering best-in-class integrated services. These services include: DDB Kidthink (youth marketing); DDB Public Relations; Karacters Design Group (corporate identity and branding); Rapp Collins Worldwide (direct response and customer relationship marketing); and Tribal DDB Canada (digital and interactive marketing). What's more, DDB Canada has the insight and know-how to weave all these marketing services together so clients can communicate in a meaningful fashion and in many mediums with their target audiences.

Sources: DDB Canada Web site, **www.ddbcanada.com**; Rebecca Harris, "CMA Awards 2004, *Marketing Magazine*, November 22, 2004; "Creative Report Card," *Strategy: The Canadian Marketing Report*, December 17, 2001, p. 9; "Palmer Jarvis DDB: Strategy's Agency of the Year," *Strategy: The Canadian Marketing Report*, December 4, 2000, p. 1; Stan Sutter, "PJ DDB Rules," *Marketing Magazine*, April 1, 2002, p. 22; Jason MacDonald, "PJ DDB Tops at Marketing Awards," *Marketing Magazine Online*, **www.marketingmag.ca**, April 1, 2002; John Heinzl, "Palmer Jarvis Wins Tourism Commission's Ad Business," *The Globe and Mail*, November 26, 2002, p. B7; Michelle Warren, "Palmer Jarvis Name Drops," *Marketing Magazine*, January 19, 2004.

At an annual Association of Advertising Agencies conference in 1994, Procter & Gamble CEO Ed Atrzt shook up the advertising world by proclaiming that marketers needed to develop and embrace new media. Ten years later, at that same conference, P&G CMO Jim Stengel gave a status report on how well he felt marketers have fared.[1] Stengel pointed out that although new media were now abundant, marketers and agencies were not using or measuring them sufficiently. In 1994, 90 percent of P&G's global ad spending was on TV, but one of its most successful brand launches in history, for Prilosec OTC in 2003, allocated only about one-quarter of its spending to TV. Here is some of what Jim Stengel said:

> There must be—and is—life beyond the 30-second spot. But our systems still revolve around that. Today's marketing world is broken. . . . We are still too dependent on marketing tactics that are not in touch with today's consumers. . . . All marketing should be permission marketing. All marketing should be so appealing that consumers want us in their lives. . . . The traditional marketing model is obsolete. Holistic marketing is driving our business.

Procter & Gamble is not alone. Marketers of all kinds are trying to come to grips with how to best use mass media in the new communication environment. In this chapter, we examine the nature and use of four mass communication tools—advertising, sales promotion, events and experiences, and public relations and publicity.

Developing and Managing an Advertising Program

Advertising is any paid form of nonpersonal presentation and promotion of ideas, goods, or services by an identified sponsor. Ads can be a cost-effective way to disseminate messages, whether to build a brand preference or to educate people.

Organizations handle advertising in different ways. In small companies, advertising is handled by someone in the sales or marketing department, who works with an advertising agency. A large company will often set up its own department, whose manager reports to the vice-president of marketing. The department's job is to propose a budget, develop strategy, approve ads and campaigns, and handle direct-mail advertising, dealer displays, and other forms of advertising.

Most companies use an outside agency, such as DDB Canada, to help create advertising campaigns and to select and purchase media. Today, advertising agencies are redefining themselves as *communication companies* that assist clients to improve their overall communication effectiveness by offering strategic and practical advice on many forms of communication.[2]

In developing an advertising program, marketing managers must always start by identifying the target market and buyer motives. Then they can make the five major decisions, known as "the five Ms": *Mission*: What are the advertising objectives? *Money*: How much can be spent? *Message*: What message should be sent? *Media*: What media should be used? *Measurement*: How should the results be evaluated? These decisions are summarized in Figure 18.1 and described in the following sections.

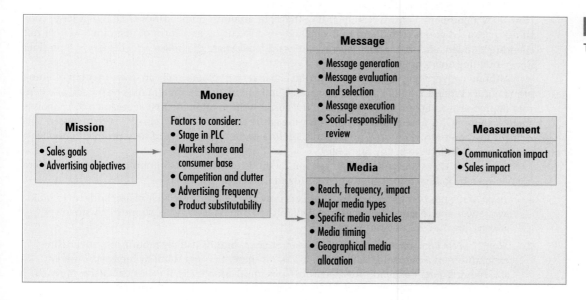

FIGURE 18.1

The Five Ms of Advertising

Setting the Objectives

The advertising objectives must flow from prior decisions on target market, brand positioning, and the marketing program.

An **advertising goal** (or **objective**) is a specific communication task and achievement level to be accomplished with a specific audience in a specific period of time:[3]

> To increase among 30 million homemakers who own automatic washers the number who identify brand X as a low-sudsing detergent and who are persuaded that it gets clothes cleaner from 10 percent to 40 percent in one year.

Advertising objectives can be classified according to whether their aim is to inform, persuade, remind, or reinforce. They aim at different stages in the *hierarchy of effects* discussed in Chapter 17.

■ *Informative advertising* aims to create brand awareness and knowledge of new products or new features of existing products. One of the all-time most memorable ads starred Australian rugby player Jacko for Energizer batteries. He was shown dressed as a battery, bursting into an early morning subway car, repeatedly shouting out the brand name to the commuters. Unfortunately, people remembered the name—but hated the ad! Brand awareness cannot come at the expense of brand attitudes.

- *Persuasive advertising* aims to create liking, preference, conviction, and purchase of a product or service. Chivas Regal attempts to persuade consumers that it delivers more taste and status than other brands of Scotch whiskey. Some persuasive advertising uses comparative advertising, which makes an explicit comparison of the attributes of two or more brands.[4] For years, VISA has run a successful ad campaign called "It's Everywhere You Want to Be" that showcases desirable locations and events that don't accept the American Express card. Comparative advertising works best when it elicits cognitive and affective motivations simultaneously.[5]

- *Reminder advertising* aims to stimulate repeat purchase of products and services. Expensive, four-colour Coca-Cola ads in magazines are intended to remind people to purchase Coca-Cola.

- *Reinforcement advertising* aims to convince current purchasers that they made the right choice. Automobile ads often depict satisfied customers enjoying special features of their new car.

The advertising objective should emerge from a thorough analysis of the current marketing situation. If the product class is mature, the company is the market leader, and brand usage is low, the proper objective should be to stimulate more usage. If the product class is new, the company is not the market leader, but the brand is superior to the leader, then the proper objective is to convince the market of the brand's superiority.

Deciding on the Advertising Budget

How does a company know if it is spending the right amount? Some critics charge that large consumer packaged-goods firms tend to overspend on advertising as a form of insurance against not spending enough, and that industrial companies underestimate the power of company and product image building and tend to underspend.[6]

Although advertising is treated as a current expense, part of it is really an investment in building brand equity. When $5 million is spent on capital equipment, the equipment may be treated as a five-year depreciable asset and only one-fifth of the cost is written off in the first year. When $5 million is spent on advertising to launch a new product, the entire cost must be written off in the first year. This reduces the company's reported profit and therefore limits the number of new-product launches a company can undertake in any one year.

In Chapter 17, we described some general methods to estimate communication budgets. Here are five specific factors to consider when setting the advertising budget:[7]

1. *Stage in the product life cycle*. New products typically receive large advertising budgets to build awareness and to gain consumer trial. Established brands usually are supported with lower advertising budgets as a ratio to sales.[8]

2. *Market share and consumer base*. High-market-share brands usually require less advertising expenditure as a percentage of sales to maintain share. To build share by increasing market size requires larger expenditures. On a cost-per-impression basis, it is less expensive to reach consumers of a widely used brand than to reach consumers of low-share brands.

3. *Competition and clutter*. In a market with a large number of competitors and high advertising spending, a brand must advertise more heavily to be heard. Even simple clutter from advertisements not directly competitive to the brand creates a need for heavier advertising.

4. *Advertising frequency*. The number of repetitions needed to put across the brand's message to consumers has an important impact on the advertising budget.

5. *Product substitutability*. Brands in less well-differentiated or commodity-like product classes (beer, soft drinks, banks, and airlines) require heavy advertising to establish a differential image. Advertising is also important when a brand can offer unique physical benefits or features.

In one study of budget allocation, Low and Mohr found that managers allocate less to advertising: As brands move to the more mature phase of the product life cycle, when a brand is well-differentiated from the competition, when managers are rewarded on short-term results, as retailers gain more power, and when managers have less experience with the company.[9]

Developing the Advertising Campaign

In designing and evaluating an ad campaign, it is important to distinguish the *message strategy* or positioning of an ad (what the ad attempts to convey about the brand) from its *creative strategy* (how the ad expresses the brand claims). So designing effective advertising campaigns is both an art and a science. To develop a message strategy, advertisers go through three steps: message generation and evaluation, creative development and execution, and social responsibility review.

MESSAGE GENERATION AND EVALUATION It is important to generate fresh insights and avoid using the same appeals and positions as others. Many of today's automobile ads have a sameness about them—a car driving at high speed on a curved mountain road or across a desert. The result is that only a weak link is established between the brand and the message.

A good ad normally focuses on one or two core selling propositions. As part of refining the brand positioning, the advertiser should conduct market research to determine which appeal works best with its target audience. Once they find an effective appeal, advertisers should prepare a *creative brief*, typically covering one or two pages. It is an elaboration of the *positioning statement* (see Chapter 9) and includes key message, target audience, communication objectives (to do, to know, to believe), key brand benefits, supports for the brand promise, and media. All the team members working on the campaign need to agree on the creative brief before investing in costly ads.

How many alternative ad themes should the advertiser create before making a choice? The more ads created, the higher the probability of finding an excellent one. Under a commission system, an agency may not like to go to the expense of creating and pretesting many ads. Fortunately, the expense of creating rough ads is rapidly falling due to computers. An ad agency's creative department can compose many alternative ads in a short time by drawing from computer files containing still and video images.

CREATIVE DEVELOPMENT AND EXECUTION The ad's impact depends not only on what is said, but often more important, on how it is said. Message execution can be decisive. In preparing an ad campaign, the advertiser can prepare a *copy strategy statement* describing the objective, content, support, and tone of the desired ad. Here is the strategy statement for a Pillsbury product called 1869 Brand Biscuits:

Pillsbury

The advertising *objective* is to convince biscuit users they can buy a canned biscuit that is as good as homemade—Pillsbury's 1869 Brand Biscuits. The *content* consists of emphasizing the following product characteristics: They look like, have the same texture as, and taste like homemade biscuits. *Support* for the "good as homemade" promise will be twofold: (1) 1869 Brand Biscuits are made from a special kind of flour used to make homemade biscuits but never before used in making canned biscuits, and (2) the use of traditional biscuit recipes. The tone of the advertising will be a news announcement, tempered by a warm, reflective mood emanating from a look back at traditional baking quality.

Every advertising medium has specific advantages and disadvantages. Here, we review television, radio, and print advertising media.

Television Ads Television is generally acknowledged as the most powerful advertising medium and reaches a broad spectrum of consumers. The wide reach translates to low cost per exposure. From a brand-building perspective, TV advertising has two particularly important strengths. First, it can be an effective means of vividly demonstrating product attributes and persuasively explaining their corresponding consumer benefits. Second, TV advertising can be a compelling means for dramatically portraying user and usage imagery, brand personality, and other brand intangibles.

Television advertising also has its drawbacks. Because of the fleeting nature of the message and the potentially distracting creative elements often found in a TV ad, product-related messages and the brand itself can be overlooked. Moreover, the large number of ads and nonprogramming material on television creates clutter that makes it easy for consumers to ignore or forget ads. Another important disadvantage is the high cost of production and placement. Even though the price of TV advertising has skyrocketed, the share of the prime-time audience for the major networks has steadily declined. By any number of measures, the effectiveness of any one ad, on average, has diminished. For example, Video Storyboards reported that the number of viewers who said that they paid attention to TV ads dropped significantly in the last decade.

Nevertheless, properly designed and executed TV ads can improve brand equity and affect sales and profits. Over the years, one of the most consistently successful TV advertisers has been Apple. The "1984" ad for the introduction of the Macintosh personal computer—portraying a stark Orwellian future with a feature film look—ran only once on TV but is one of the best-known ads ever. In the years that followed, Apple advertising successfully created awareness and image for a series of products, most recently with its acclaimed "Think Different" campaign. Recently, Apple's iPod ads have created quite a buzz with bright colours and silhouettes of people dancing to the digital music streaming from their iPod. One spot even includes Bono from U2! Even with the decline in audiences for the TV advertisement, a well-done TV commercial can still be a powerful marketing tool.

Rona Inc.

Boucherville, Quebec–based Rona Inc. has shown how to use television advertising effectively. Its successful TV spots made a substantial impression as a central force in the marketing efforts that won Rona *Strategy Magazine*'s 2004 Marketer of the Year in the home improvement category. As part of a major company effort to grow the business in English Canada, Rona launched the "how-to" campaign. Created by Montreal-based agency BCP, the spots featured a variety of everyday people put into humorous situations requiring renovation skills. Rona promises them they can help "make it happen." The spots are also notable for featuring women equally with men. This was critical since research showed traffic by gender at Rona stores is about 50–50. The success of the campaign can be seen in the numbers. Having run for three years, Rona has generated a 10-point gain in awareness in English Canada. The spots are all part of Rona's growth strategy: at 540 stores now, the company plans to grow to 700 stores and $7 billion in annual sales by 2007.[10]

Print Ads Print media offers a stark contrast to broadcast media. Because of its self-paced nature, magazines and newspapers can provide much detailed product information and can also effectively communicate user and usage imagery. At the same time, the static nature of the visual images in print media makes it difficult to provide dynamic presentations or demonstrations. Another disadvantage is that it can be a fairly passive medium.

In general, the two main print media—magazines and newspapers—have many of the same advantages and disadvantages. Although newspapers are timely and pervasive, magazines are typically more effective at building user and usage imagery. Daily newspapers are read by roughly three-fourths of the population and tend to be used a lot for local—especially retailer—advertising. Although advertisers have some flexibility in designing and placing newspaper ads, poor reproduction quality and short shelf life can diminish their impact.

Format elements such as ad size, colour, and illustration also affect a print ad's impact. A minor rearrangement of mechanical elements can improve attention-getting power. Larger ads gain more attention, though not necessarily by as much as their difference in cost. Four-colour illustrations increase ad effectiveness and ad cost. New electronic eye movement studies show that consumers can be led through an ad by strategic placement of dominant elements.

Researchers studying print advertisements report that the *picture, headline,* and *copy* are important, in that order. The picture must be strong enough to draw attention. Then the headline must reinforce the picture and lead the person to read the copy. The copy itself must be engaging and the advertised brand's name must be sufficiently prominent. Even then, a really outstanding ad will be noted by less than 50 percent of the exposed audience. About 30 percent might recall the headline's main point; about 25 percent might remember the advertiser's name; and less than 10 percent will read most of the body copy. Ordinary ads do not achieve even these results.

Given how consumers process print ads, some clear managerial implications emerge, as summarized in "Marketing Memo: Print Ad Evaluation Criteria." One print ad campaign that successfully carved out a brand image is Absolut vodka:

Absolut Vodka

Vodka is generally viewed as a commodity product, yet the amount of brand preference and loyalty in the vodka market is astonishing. Most of this preference and loyalty is attributed to brand image. When the Swedish brand Absolut entered the North American market in 1979, the company sold a disappointing 7000 cases. By 1991, sales had soared to over 2 million cases. Absolut became the largest-selling imported vodka, with 65 percent of the market, thanks in large part to its marketing strategy. Absolut has aimed for sophisticated, upwardly mobile, affluent drinkers. The vodka comes in a distinctive clear bottle that is used as the centrepiece of every ad. Well-known artists—including Warhol, Haring, and Scharf—have designed Absolut ads, and the bottle image always fits with the caption in a clever way.[11]

Radio Ads Radio is a pervasive medium: Canadians who listen to the radio listen, on average, over 19 hours a week.[12] Perhaps radio's main advantage is flexibility—stations are very targeted, ads are relatively inexpensive to produce and place, and short closings allow for quick response. Radio is a particularly effective medium in the morning; it can also let companies achieve a balance between broad and localized market coverage.

The obvious disadvantages of radio are the lack of visual images and the relatively passive nature of the consumer processing that results.[13] Nevertheless, radio ads can be extremely creative. Some see the lack of visual images as a plus because they feel the clever use of music, sound, and other creative devices can tap into the listener's imagination to create powerfully relevant and liked images. Here is an example:

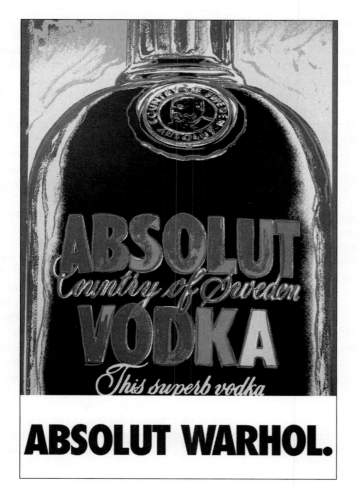

Absolut Warhol, the Absolut print ad by Andy Warhol.

Black's

Markham, Ontario–based Black's Photo has always used radio in select markets to support its print and in-store efforts, particularly to increase reach and frequency beyond the company's flyer distribution. In the last decade, however, Black's has faced a major threat to its business with the entry of large retailers such as Shoppers Drug Mart and Wal-Mart into the photo-finishing market. As a result, Black's has had to do some major brand building to differentiate itself and to sell digital hardware while also positioning itself as the expert in digital photography. The result was the "I know Black's knows" radio campaign created by Toronto-based Brazil Communications for the holiday season in 2002. The results of the campaign were profound. In-store sales associates were seeing customers walking into the stores reciting back to the staff that "I know Black's knows." The numbers were talking too. Sales rose 11.4 percent from November 2002 to December 2003 and its market share for digital cameras grew 1 percent for Christmas 2002 and 2003.[14]

SOCIAL RESPONSIBILITY REVIEW Advertisers and their agencies must be sure advertising does not overstep social and legal norms. Public policy makers have developed a substantial body of laws and regulations to govern advertising.

Two bodies oversee Canadian practices: the Canadian Radio-television and Telecommunications Commission (CRTC) (**www.crtc.gc.ca**) and Advertising Standards Canada (ASC), formerly the Canadian Advertising Foundation (**www.adstandards.com**). The mission of the CRTC is to find a balance between public- and private-sector interests. It governs ownership of broadcasting outlets, licences, and programming content, and it handles complaints about programming and advertising. It works closely with the ASC, which is a national industry association committed to assuring integrity and viability of advertising through industry self-regulation.

Advertising Standards Canada administers the Canadian Code of Advertising Standards, which was first published in 1963. The Code includes dictates that advertisements must not present inaccurate or deceptive claims, that advertisements must not omit relevant information, and that advertising claims must be supportable. The commercial intent of an advertisement must be obvious to the viewer or reader. Furthermore, advertisements must not include deceptive price claims or discounts, or unrealistic price comparisons. Advertising to children is subject to a special code, the Broadcast Code for Advertising to Children. (It should also be noted that Quebec prohibits advertising to children.) The ASC carefully considers and responds to all written consumer complaints submitted to them about advertising that does not comply with the Code, and it produces an Advertising Complaints Report.

Marketing Memo

Print Ad Evaluation Criteria

In judging the effectiveness of a print ad, in addition to considering the communication strategy (target market, communication objectives, and message and creative strategy) the following questions should be answered affirmatively concerning the executional elements:

1. Is the message clear at a glance? Can you quickly tell what the advertisement is all about?
2. Is the benefit in the headline?
3. Does the illustration support the headline?
4. Does the first line of the copy support or explain the headline and illustration?
5. Is the ad easy to read and follow?
6. Is the product easily identified?
7. Is the brand or sponsor clearly identified?

Source: Philip Ward Burton and Scott C. Purvis, *Which Ad Pulled Best*, 9th ed. (Lincolnwood IL: NTC Business Books, 2002).

In addition to the work performed by Canada's two official watchdogs, other groups, such as the Media Awareness Network (**www.media-awareness.ca**), keep their eye on Canadian advertising practices.

To be socially responsible, advertisers must be careful not to offend the general public as well as any ethnic groups, racial minorities, or special-interest groups.[15] Ads for Calvin Klein apparel have often been accused of crossing the lines of decency, with ads featuring the waifish model Kate Moss that came under attack from Boycott Anorexic Marketing, and ads featuring pubescent models—some reportedly as young as 15—in provocative poses, which resulted in a massive letter-writing campaign from the American Family Association.[16]

Every year, nonprofit trade group Advertising Women of New York singles out TV and print ads that they feel portray particularly good or bad images of women. In 2004, Sirius Satellite Radio won the TV Grand Ugly award for its "Car Wash" ad, which featured Pam Anderson in a wet tank top using her entire body to clean a young man's car. Print Grand Ugly went to a Sony Playstation ad that featured a woman giving birth to the head of a grown man. The TV Grand Good ad went to a MasterCard commercial in which a woman opens a jar of pickles after her weakling husband fails the test.[17]

Men's groups, however, are speaking up too. A Canadian commercial showed a woman eyeing a young male sales clerk as he loaded her groceries into the back of her Ford Focus. She then pushed him in along with the groceries and drove off. Advertising Standards Canada received nine complaints from men's rights groups, asserting that the ad promoted abduction and would not be condoned if the sexes of the characters were reversed. Ford Canada withdrew the commercial.

Some companies have begun to build ad campaigns on a platform of social responsibility.

Ethical Funds

When people buy shares in Vancouver-based Ethical Funds, they know that fund managers will not invest in corporations involved in the production of military weapons, tobacco, or nuclear power; those that have unfair employment practices or poor environmental records; or those that support reactionary political regimes. A tough-talking advertising campaign for Ethical Funds showed scenes of child labour and people dying from cancer, presumably caused by smoking. The ad asked, "Do you know where your money goes?"

John Linthwaite, president of Ethical Funds, Inc., says its emphasis is on research. It digs deep to weed out companies that do not meet its ethical standards while ensuring financially sound investments. Ethical Funds has grown from $100 million in assets to more than $2 billion over the last decade.[18]

Deciding on Media and Measuring Effectiveness

After choosing the message, the advertiser's next task is to choose media to carry it. The steps here are deciding on desired reach, frequency, and impact; choosing among major media types; selecting specific media vehicles; deciding on media timing; and deciding on geographical media allocation. Then the results of these decisions need to be evaluated.

Deciding on Reach, Frequency, and Impact

Media selection is finding the most cost-effective media to deliver the desired number and type of exposures to the target audience. What do we mean by the desired number of exposures? Presumably, the advertiser is seeking a specified advertising objective and response from the target audience—for example, a target level of product trial. The rate of product trial will depend, among other things, on level of brand awareness. Suppose the rate of product trial increases at a diminishing rate with the level of audience awareness, as shown in Figure 18.2(a). If the advertiser seeks a product trial rate of (say) T^*, it will be necessary to achieve a brand awareness level of A^*.

FIGURE 18.2

Relationship Among Trial, Awareness, and the Exposure Function

The next task is to find out how many exposures, E^*, will produce a level of audience awareness of A^*. The effect of exposures on audience awareness depends on the exposures' reach, frequency, and impact:

- *Reach (R).* The number of different persons or households exposed to a particular media schedule at least once during a specified time period.

- *Frequency (F).* The number of times within the specified time period that an average person or household is exposed to the message.

- *Impact (I).* The qualitative value of an exposure through a given medium (thus a food ad in *Canadian Living* would have a higher impact than in *Canadian Business*).

Figure 18.2(b) shows the relationship between audience awareness and reach. Audience awareness will be greater the higher the exposures' reach, frequency, and impact. There are important trade-offs among reach, frequency, and impact. Suppose the planner has an advertising budget of $1 000 000 and the cost per thousand exposures of average quality is $5. This means the advertiser can buy 200 000 000 exposures ($1 000 000 ÷ [$5/1000]). If the advertiser seeks an average exposure frequency of 10, then the advertiser can reach 20 000 000 people (200 000 000 ÷ 10) with the given budget. But if the advertiser wants higher-quality media costing $10 per thousand exposures, it will be able to reach only 10 000 000 people unless it is willing to lower the desired exposure frequency.

The relationship between reach, frequency, and impact is captured in the following concepts:

- *Total number of exposures (E).* This is the reach times the average frequency; that is, $E = R \times F$. This measure is referred to as the gross rating points (GRP). If a given media schedule reaches 80 percent of the homes with an average exposure frequency of 3, the media schedule is said to have a GRP of 240 (80×3). If another media schedule has a GRP of 300, it is said to have more weight, but we cannot tell how this weight breaks down into reach and frequency.

- *Weighted number of exposures (WE):* This is the reach times average frequency times average impact, that is $WE = R \times F \times I$.

The media planner has to figure out the most cost-effective combination of reach, frequency, and impact. Reach is most important when launching new products, flanker brands, extensions of well-known brands, or infrequently purchased brands; or going after an undefined target market. Frequency is most important where there are strong competitors, a complex story to tell, high consumer resistance, or a frequent-purchase cycle.[19]

Many advertisers believe a target audience needs a large number of exposures for the advertising to work. Others doubt the value of high frequency. They believe that after people see the same ad a few times, they either act on it, get irritated by it, or stop noticing it.[20]

Another factor arguing for repetition is that of forgetting. The job of repetition is partly to put the message back into memory. The higher the forgetting rate associated with a brand, product category, or message, the higher the warranted level of repetition. However, repetition is not enough; ads wear out and viewers tune out. Advertisers should not coast on a tired ad but insist on fresh executions by their advertising agency.

Choosing Among Major Media Types

The media planner has to know the capacity of the major advertising media types to deliver reach, frequency, and impact. The major advertising media along with their costs, advantages, and limitations are profiled in Table 18.1.

Media planners make their choices by considering the following variables:

- *Target-audience media habits.* Radio and television are the most effective media for reaching teenagers.

- *Product characteristics.* Media types have different potential for demonstration, visualization, explanation, believability, and colour. Women's dresses are best shown in colour magazines, and Polaroid cameras are best demonstrated on television.

- *Message characteristics.* Timeliness and information content will influence media choice. A message announcing a major sale tomorrow will require radio, TV, or newspaper. A message containing a great deal of technical data might require specialized magazines or mailings.

- *Cost.* Television is very expensive, whereas newspaper advertising is relatively inexpensive. What counts is the cost-per-thousand exposures.

TABLE 18.1	PROFILES OF MAJOR MEDIA TYPES	
Medium	**Advantages**	**Limitations**
Newspapers	Flexibility; timeliness; good local market coverage; broad acceptance; high believability	Short life; poor reproduction quality; small "pass-along" audience
Television	Combines sight, sound, and motion; appealing to the senses; high attention; high reach	High absolute cost; high clutter; fleeting exposure; less audience selectivity
Direct mail	Audience selectivity; flexibility; no ad competition within the same medium; personalization	Relatively high cost; "junk mail" image
Radio	Mass use; high geographic and demographic selectivity; low cost	Audio presentation only; lower attention than television; nonstandardized rate structures; fleeting exposure
Magazines	High geographic and demographic selectivity; credibility and prestige; high-quality reproduction; long life; good pass-along readership	Long ad purchase lead time; some waste circulation; no guarantee of position
Outdoor	Flexibility; high repeat exposure; low cost; low competition	Limited audience selectivity; creative limitations
Yellow Pages	Excellent local coverage; high believability; wide reach; low cost	High competition; long ad purchase lead time; creative limitations
Newsletters	Very high selectivity; full control; interactive opportunities; relative low costs	Costs could run away
Brochures	Flexibility; full control; can dramatize messages	Overproduction could lead to runaway costs
Telephone	Many users; opportunity to give a personal touch	Relative high cost unless volunteers are used
Internet	High selectivity; interactive possibilities; relatively low cost	Relatively new media with a low number of users in some countries

Given the abundance of media, the planner must first decide how to allocate the budget to the major media types (see Table 18.2). In launching a new biscuit, Pillsbury might decide to allocate $3 million to daytime network television, $2 million to women's magazines, $1 million to daily newspapers in 20 major markets, $500 000 to various grassroots cooking events and competitions, and $50 000 to maintaining its homepage on the Internet.

TABLE 18.2	MARKETING COMMUNICATION REVENUES BY MEDIUM (CANADA, 2000, MILLIONS OF DOLLARS)	
	$	**% of Total**
Newspapers	2552	27%
TV	2456	26%
Direct Mail	1200	13%
Radio	1014	11%
Yellow Pages	1000	11%
Magazines	729	7%
Out-of-Home	293	3%
Internet	110	1%
Other	50	1%
Total	9404	

Source: Canadian Media Director's Council, *2002–2003 Media Digest* (Toronto: Marketing Magazine, 2002), p. 8.

The distribution must be planned with the awareness that people are increasingly time-starved. They are assaulted daily by ads and information from traditional media plus e-mail, voice mail, and instant messages. There is little time for thinking about experiences, let alone for hobbies and other diversions. Attention is becoming a scarce currency, and advertisers need strong devices to capture people's attention.[21] In deciding on the ad budget, marketers must also recognize that consumer response can be S-shaped: An ad threshold effect exists where some positive amount of advertising is necessary before any sales impact can be detected, but sales increases eventually flatten out.[22]

Alternative Advertising Options

For a long time, television was the dominant media. In recent years, researchers have noticed reduced effectiveness due to increased commercial clutter (advertisers beaming shorter and more numerous commercials at the audience), increased "zipping and zapping" of commercials (aided by the arrival of new TV systems such as TiVo and Replay TV), and lower viewing owing to the growth in cable and satellite TV and DVD/VCRs.[23] Furthermore, television advertising costs have risen faster than other media costs. Many marketers are looking for alternative advertising media.[24] One brewer, Molson, is taking an even more innovative tack by putting catchy phrases right on the bottles:

Molson

Crispin, Porter + Bogusky's campaign for Canadian brewer Molson won *Adweek's* award for Media Plan of the Year spending less than US$10 million. CP+B was hired to revitalize Molson's brand in the United States and renew its relevance among its core target of men aged 21 to 27 who are not sitting in front of the TV waiting for 30-second beer commercials. CP+B made a radical suggestion: Don't spend more ad money; dress up your beer bottles. The CP+B team came up with the idea of bottle label as badge, to let the product help men say something about themselves—mostly to the opposite sex. They designed clever labels featuring icebreakers guaranteed to get barflies buzzing. Used only on bottles sold in bars, the labels included such catchy phrases as "100% Available," "Hottie Magnet," "On the Rebound," "Guess Where My Tattoo Is?," "Wealthy Industrialist" and, perhaps most to the point, "I'm Not Wearing Any Underwear."[25]

PLACE ADVERTISING **Place advertising**, also called out-of-home advertising, is a broadly defined category that captures many different alternative advertising forms. Marketers are using creative and unexpected ad placements to grab consumers' attention. The rationale often given is that marketers are better off reaching people in other environments, such as where they work, play, and, of course, shop. Some of the options available include billboards, public places, product placement, and point-of-purchase.

Using place advertising to increase brand exposure and goodwill: The Oscar Mayer Wienermobile.

Billboards Billboards have been transformed over the years and now use colourful, digitally produced graphics, backlighting, sounds, movement, and unusual—even three-dimensional—images.[26] Some ads are even human. Adidas hoisted human billboards in Tokyo and Osaka, Japan. Two soccer players competed for shots during 15-minute matches scheduled five times a day while they and a ball dangled from ropes 12 storeys above ground.[27] Billboards do not even necessarily have to stay in one place. Marketers can buy ad space on billboard-laden trucks that are driven continuously all day in selected areas. Oscar Mayer sends six "Wiener-mobiles" travelling across North America each year to increase brand exposure and goodwill. Software company Oracle used a boat to tow a floating banner bearing the company's logo across San Francisco Bay.

The Burger Baron

In the age of discount fast food and super-sized marketing budgets, little independent restaurants don't have much of a chance—right? Wrong! If you are the Burger Baron of Regina, that is. Founded in 1958, the restaurant took pride in the quality and taste of its food. Its advertising, however, was failing to bring enough customers to its door. The restaurant also faced a location challenge. It is located in Regina's north end—one of the city's less desirable areas. The lack of buzz ended, however, when the Burger Baron hired Brown Communications, a local advertising and communications agency. With a budget of only $50 000, the creative team decided to use a billboard strategy to reach out to the city. The billboards featured messages such as "Making vegetarians reconsider since 1958," "Finally. A reason to go to the north end," and "Hey Ronald, you want a piece of me?" In the first year of the campaign, the restaurant experienced a 6 percent increase in sales. Readers of a local Regina newspaper, the *Prairie Dog*, voted Burger Baron as "home of Regina's best burger" two years running. The campaign recently won two International Association of Business Communicators ACE Awards. The biggest impact, however, was on the brand image and awareness—so much so that another Burger Baron is scheduled to be built in the city's south end.[28]

Public Spaces Advertisers are placing traditional TV and print ads in unconventional places such as movies, airlines, and lounges, as well as classrooms, sports arenas, office and hotel elevators, and other public places. Billboard-type poster ads are showing up everywhere. Transit ads on buses, subways, and commuter trains—around for years—have become a valuable way to reach working women. "Street furniture"—bus shelters, kiosks, and public areas—is another fast-growing option. Coca-Cola, for example, mounted illuminated rectangular displays called "light boxes" on New York subway tunnel walls to advertise its Dasani brand water.

Advertisers can buy space in stadiums and arenas and on garbage cans, bicycle racks, parking meters, airport luggage carousels, elevators, gasoline pumps, the bottom of golf cups, airline snack packages, and supermarket produce in the form of tiny labels on apples and bananas. Advertisers can even buy space in toilet stalls and above urinals, which, according to research studies, office workers visit an average of three to four times a day for roughly four minutes per visit.[29]

PRODUCT PLACEMENT   Product placement has expanded from movies to all types of TV shows. Marketers pay fees of $50 000 to $100 000 and even higher so that their products make cameo appearances in movies and on television. The exact sum depends on the amount and nature of the brand exposure. Sometimes placements are the result of a larger network advertising deal, but other times they are the work of small product placement shops that maintain close ties with prop masters, set designers, and production executives.[30]

Product placements can be combined with special promotions to publicize entertainment tie-ins. Aston Martin, 7-UP, Finlandia, VISA, and Omega all initiated major promotional pushes based on product placement tie-ins with the James Bond film *Die Another Day*.[31] With over US$100 million paid for product placement rights, some critics called the film "Buy Another Day."

Despite a small budget, Brown Communications developed an award-winning billboard campaign that drove hungry customers to Burger Baron's door.

Product placement: The Omega–James Bond tie-in ad for *Die Another Day*.

Some firms get product placement at no cost by supplying their product to the movie company (Nike does not pay to be in movies but often supplies shoes, jackets, bags, etc.).[32] Firms sometimes just get lucky and are included in shows for plot reasons. FedEx, for example, received lots of favourable exposure from the movie *Cast Away*.[33] Some television shows revolve around a central product placement: Ford and the WB network created a commercial-free program in 2001 called *No Boundaries*, which features Ford SUVs.

Marketers are finding other inventive ways to advertise during actual television broadcasts. Sports fans are familiar with the virtual logos networks add digitally to the playing field. Invisible to spectators at the event, these ads look just like painted-on logos to home viewers. Ads also appear in best-selling paperback books and movie videotapes. Written material such as annual reports, data sheets, catalogues, and newsletters increasingly carry ads. **Advertorials** are print ads that offer editorial content that reflects favourably on the brand and is difficult to distinguish from newspaper or magazine content. Many companies include advertising inserts in monthly bills. Some companies mail audiotapes or videotapes to prospects.

Other firms are exploring **branded entertainment** such as online mini-films. For its American Express client, Ogilvy and Digitas are creating a series of three to five-minute "Webisodes" starring its pitchman Jerry Seinfeld in "The Adventures of Seinfeld and Superman," and also using teaser TV spots.[34] Automakers are promoting cars with exciting online videos with special effects that pack more punch than the typical car ad.

bmwfilms.com

BMW was one of the first automakers to launch a successful video campaign. In 2001, the company hired some of Hollywood's top action movie directors such as John Woo, Guy Ritchie, and Ang Lee to create short films featuring the company's cars and starring actors such as Mickey Rourke and Madonna. To build traffic to the bmwfilms.com Web site, BMW used television spots that mirrored movie trailers. According to BMW's ad agency, 55.1 million people viewed "The Hire" series. Mazda has followed suit with its "Venus Flytrap" video promoting its RX-8, while Ford's "Evil Twin" video advertises the Sportka. As might be evident from their names, these online videos are designed to cater to 18- to 34-year-old men who are spending less and less time watching television and more and more time online.[35]

POINT-OF-PURCHASE   There are so many ways to communicate with consumers at the **point-of-purchase (P-O-P)**. In-store advertising includes ads on shopping carts, cart straps, aisles, and shelves, as well as promotion options such as in-store demonstrations, live sampling, and instant coupon machines. Some supermarkets are selling floor space for company logos and experimenting with talking shelves. P-O-P radio provides FM-style programming and commercial messages to thousands of food stores and drugstores nationwide. Programming includes a store-selected music format, consumer tips, and commercials. Ads on Wal-Mart TV run in 2500 stores and appear three times an hour. Airtime costs between US$50 000 and US$300 000 for a four-week flight of ads, depending on frequency. The impact can be considerable: According to one research study, more than half of shoppers visit a Wal-Mart at least once a month and one-third go once a week.[36]

The appeal of point-of-purchase advertising lies in the fact that numerous studies show that in many product categories consumers make the bulk of their final brand decisions in the store. One study suggested that 70 percent of all buying decisions are made in the store. In-store advertising is designed to increase the number of spontaneous buying decisions.

EVALUATING ALTERNATIVE MEDIA Alternative media present some interesting options for marketers. Ads now can appear virtually anywhere consumers have a few spare minutes or even seconds and thus enough time to notice them. The main advantage of nontraditional media is that a very precise and—because of the nature of the setting involved—captive audience often can be reached in a cost-effective manner. The message must be simple and direct. In fact, outdoor advertising is often called the "15-second sell." Strategically, out-of-home advertising is often more effective at enhancing brand awareness or reinforcing brand image than creating new brand associations.

The challenge with nontraditional media is demonstrating its reach and effectiveness through credible, independent research. These new marketing strategies and tactics must be ultimately judged on how they contribute, directly or indirectly, to brand equity. Unique ad placements designed to break through clutter may also be perceived as invasive and obtrusive. There has been some consumer backlash when people see ads in traditionally ad-free spaces, such as in schools, on police cruisers, and in doctor's waiting rooms. U.S. consumer advocate Ralph Nader says, "What these people on Madison Avenue don't understand is consumers will reach a saturation point."

But not all North Americans are turned off by the proliferation of advertising. One marketing consultant says, "Kids 18 and under aren't thinking twice about it. Branded merchandise is just the landscape of their lives." Perhaps because of the sheer pervasiveness of advertising, consumers seem to be less bothered by nontraditional media now than in the past.

Consumers must be favourably affected in some way to justify the marketing expenditures for nontraditional media. Some firms offering ad placement in supermarket checkout lines, fast food restaurants, physicians' waiting rooms, health clubs, and truck stops have suspended business at least in part because of a lack of consumer interest. The bottom line, however, is that there will always be room for creative means of placing the brand in front of consumers. The possibilities are endless: "Marketing Insight: Playing Games with Brands" describes the emergence of yet another new media trend.

Selecting Specific Vehicles

The media planner must search for the most cost-effective vehicles within each chosen media type. The advertiser who decides to buy 30 seconds of advertising on U.S. network television can pay around US$100 000 for a new show, over US$400 000 for a popular prime-time show such as *Will & Grace*, *ER*, or *Survivor*, or over US$2 million for an event like the Super Bowl.[37] Advertising on Canadian networks is a bargain in comparison. Thirty-second commercials on CBC range from $100 to $52 000 (averaging $6500), while those on Global range from $150 to $48 009 (averaging $7000). On specialty channels, the average rates can be even lower—$450 on Bravo! and $1250 on YTV.[38]

In making choices, the planner has to rely on measurement services that provide estimates of audience size, composition, and media cost. Audience size has several possible measures:

- *Circulation*. The number of physical units carrying the advertising.
- *Audience*. The number of people exposed to the vehicle. (If the vehicle has pass-on readership, then the audience is larger than circulation.)
- *Effective audience*. The number of people with target audience characteristics exposed to the vehicle.
- *Effective ad-exposed audience*. The number of people with target audience characteristics who actually saw the ad.

MARKETING INSIGHT

Playing Games with Brands

Doom. Halo. Half Life. To some they may just be the names of popular video games, but to others they represent the sound of cash registers ringing up sales. The industry is also growing rapidly. In the one-year period between October 2003 and 2004, video-game sales in Canada reached $446 million, a 6.5 percent increase over the previous year. PricewaterhouseCoopers thinks the worldwide video game industry will reach US$55.6 billion by 2008.

Not surprisingly, a 2004 survey of 25 000 Canadians confirms that the most frequent players (people who play seven days a week) are males between the ages of 12 and 24. However, when it comes to infrequent play averaging once a week, 35- to 49-year-olds lead the pack at 27 percent, and the gender split is 50:50. "It challenges people's assumptions about the industry," says Danielle LaBossiere, executive director of the Entertainment Software Association of Canada. "Everyone assumes it's 10-year-old boys playing games in their parents' basements but really people are choosing this as their entertainment option over movies and TV." People in the industry are paying a lot of attention to this trend. Jennifer Lee, director of corporate communications at game developer and distributor Hip Interactive in Mississauga, Ontario, notes, "Basically you're looking at people who were gamers in the '80s and are growing up and still playing video games."

Millions of people worldwide are playing online games. Massively multiplayer online games (MMOGs) in particular are growing in popularity. These types of computer games enable hundreds or thousands of players to simultaneously interact in a game world they are connected to via the Internet. EverQuest®, one of the most popular MMOGs, owned by Sony Entertainment, for example, is estimated to have 500 000 subscribers. The market for online games is evenly split between men and women. Women seem to prefer puzzles and collaborative games, whereas men seem more attracted to competitive or simulation games. A top-notch "advergame" can cost between US$100 000 and US$500 000 to develop. The game can be played on the sponsor's corporate homepage, on gaming portals, or even at restaurants. The NTN iTV Network is an out-of-home interactive entertainment network that delivers entertainment and sports games in approximately 3600 North American restaurants and bars.

Given the explosive popularity of video games with younger consumers, many advertisers have adopted an "if you can't beat them, join them" attitude. Simon Crowther, managing director of Vancouver-based Alias, a youth marketing consultancy, notes that 60 percent of youth (unprompted) think product placement in video games is acceptable. Porsche, 7-Up, and McDonald's have all been featured in games. Honda developed a game that allowed players to choose a Honda and zoom around city streets plastered with Honda logos. In the first three months 78 000 people played for an average of eight minutes. The cost per thousand (CPM) of US$7 compared favourably to a primetime TV commercial CPM of US$11.65. Marketers collect valuable customer data upon registration and often seek permission to send e-mail. Of game players sponsored by Ford Escape SUV, 54 percent signed up to receive e-mail.

The U.S. Army may seem like an unlikely fan of gaming, but with the war in Iraq creating major recruiting challenges, it has added games to its marketing arsenal. Recognizing that 90 percent of the target audience was online at least once a week, the U.S. Army decided to put its Web site at the head of its new "Army of One" campaign. The centrepiece was a game titled "America's Army: Operations," which half a million people play each weekend.

Sources: Sarah Dobson, "Me, Mom and Master Chief," *Marketing Magazine*, December 6, 2004; Keith Ferrazzi, "Advertising Shouldn't Be Hard Work, but Lately the Game Has Changed," *Wall Street Journal*, April 30, 2002; Marc Weingarten, "It's an Ad! It's a Game! It's . . . Both!" *Business 2.0*, March 2002, p. 102; Thomas Mucha, "Operation Sign 'Em Up," *Business 2.0*, April 2003, pp. 43–45; Dorothy Pomerantz, "You Play, They Win," *Forbes*, October 14, 2002, pp. 201–202; Suzanne Vranica, "Y&R Bets on Videogame Industry," *Wall Street Journal*, May 11, 2004; Hassan Fattah and Pamela Paul, "Gaming Gets Serious," *American Demographics*, May 2002, pp. 39–43; Lisa D'Innocenzo, "Plugging Into the Digital Revolution," *Strategy Magazine*, August 23, 2004, p. 12.

Media planners calculate the cost per thousand persons reached by a vehicle. A one-page, four-colour ad in *Maclean's* costs $31 960 and *Maclean's* estimated readership is 3.1 million people (the magazine's circulation is just over 500 000, with an estimated 6.2 readers per copy), so the cost of exposing the ad to 1000 persons is just over $10. The same ad in *Western Living* costs $19 700, but since it only reaches 820 000 persons (210 000 circulation, with an average of 3.9 readers per copy), the cost per thousand is about $24.[39] The media planner ranks each magazine by cost-per-thousand and favours magazines with the lowest cost-per-thousand for reaching target consumers. The magazines themselves often put together a "reader profile" for their advertisers, summarizing the charac-

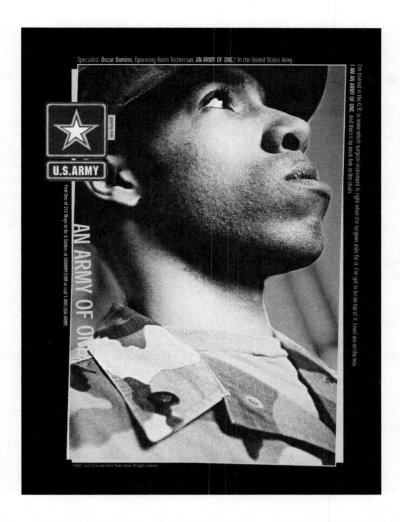

The U.S. Army used an online game accompanied by a print advertising campaign to improve its recruiting efforts.

teristics of the magazine's readers with respect to age, income, residence, marital status, and leisure activities.

Several adjustments have to be applied to the cost-per-thousand measure. First, the measure should be adjusted for *audience quality*. For a baby lotion ad, a magazine read by 1 million young mothers would have an exposure value of 1 million; if read by 1 million teenagers, it would have almost a zero exposure value. Second, the exposure value should be adjusted for the *audience-attention probability*. Readers of *Flare* may pay more attention to ads than do readers of *Canadian Business*. A "happy" commercial placed within an upbeat television show is more likely to be effective than a downbeat commercial in the same place.[40] Third, the exposure value should be adjusted for the magazine's *editorial quality* (prestige and believability). In addition, people are more likely to believe a TV or radio ad and to become more positively disposed toward the brand when the ad is placed within a program they like.[41] Fourth, the exposure value should be adjusted for the magazine's *ad placement policies and extra services* (such as regional or occupational editions and lead-time requirements).

Media planners are increasingly using more sophisticated measures of effectiveness and employing them in mathematical models to arrive at the best media mix. Many advertising agencies use a computer program to select the initial media and then make further improvements based on subjective factors.[42]

Deciding on Media Timing and Allocation

In choosing media, the advertiser faces both a macro-scheduling and a micro-scheduling problem. The *macro-scheduling problem* involves scheduling the advertising in relation to seasons and the business cycle. Suppose 70 percent of a product's sales occur between June and September. The firm can vary its advertising expenditures to follow the seasonal pattern, to oppose the seasonal pattern, or to be constant throughout the year.

The *micro-scheduling problem* calls for allocating advertising expenditures within a short period to obtain maximum impact. Suppose the firm decides to buy 30 radio spots in the month of September. Figure 18.3 shows several possible patterns. The left side shows that advertising messages for the month can be concentrated ("burst" advertising), dispersed continuously throughout the month, or dispersed intermittently. The top side shows that the advertising messages can be beamed with a level, rising, falling, or alternating frequency.

The most effective pattern depends on the communication objectives in relation to the nature of the product, target customers, distribution channels, and other marketing factors. The timing pattern should consider three factors. *Buyer turnover* expresses the rate at which new buyers enter the market; the higher this rate, the more continuous the advertising should be. *Purchase frequency* is the number of times during the period that the average buyer buys the product; the higher the purchase frequency, the more continuous the advertising should be. The *forgetting rate* is the rate at which the buyer forgets the brand; the higher the forgetting rate, the more continuous the advertising should be.

In launching a new product, the advertiser has to choose among continuity, concentration, flighting, and pulsing:

- *Continuity* is achieved by scheduling exposures evenly throughout a given period. Generally, advertisers use continuous advertising in expanding market situations, with frequently purchased items, and in tightly defined buyer categories.

- *Concentration* calls for spending all the advertising dollars in a single period. This makes sense for products with one selling season or holiday.

- *Flighting* calls for advertising for a period, followed by a period with no advertising, followed by a second period of advertising activity. It is used when funding is limited, the purchase cycle is relatively infrequent, and with seasonal items.

- *Pulsing* is continuous advertising at low-weight levels reinforced periodically by waves of heavier activity. Pulsing draws on the strength of continuous advertising and flights to create a compromise scheduling strategy.[43] Those who favour pulsing feel that the audience will learn the message more thoroughly, and money can be saved.

A company has to decide how to allocate its advertising budget over space as well as over time. The company makes "national buys" when it places ads on national TV networks or in nationally circulated magazines. It makes "spot buys" when it buys TV time in just a few markets or in regional editions of magazines. These markets are called *areas of dominant influence* (ADIs) or *designated marketing areas* (DMAs). Ads reach a market 60 to 100 kilometres from a city centre. The company makes "local buys" when it advertises in local newspapers, radio, or outdoor sites. Consider the following example:

FIGURE 18.3

Classification of Advertising Timing Patterns

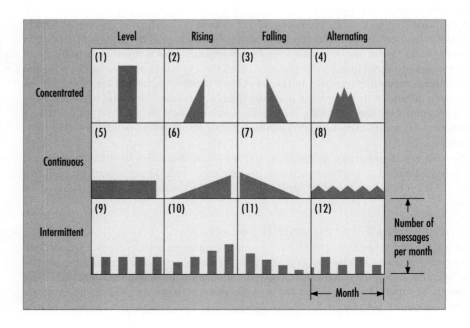

Pizza Hut

Pizza Hut levies a 4 percent advertising fee on its franchisees. It spends half of its budget on national media and half on regional and local media. Some national advertising is wasted because of low penetration in certain areas. Even though Pizza Hut may have a 30 percent share of the franchised pizza market nationally, this share may vary from 5 percent in some cities to 70 percent in others. The franchisees in the higher market-share cities want much more advertising money spent in their areas, but Pizza Hut does not have enough money to cover the whole nation by region. National advertising offers efficiency but fails to address the different local situations effectively.

Evaluating Advertising Effectiveness

Good planning and control of advertising depend on measures of advertising effectiveness. Most advertisers try to measure the communication effect of an ad—that is, its potential effect on awareness, knowledge, or preference. They would also like to measure the ad's sales effect.

COMMUNICATION-EFFECT RESEARCH   **Communication-effect research** seeks to determine whether an ad is communicating effectively. Called *copy testing*, it can be done before an ad is put into media and after it is printed or broadcast.

There are three major methods of pretesting. The *consumer feedback method* asks consumers for their reactions to a proposed ad. They respond to questions such as these:

1. What is the main message you get from this ad?
2. What do you think they want you to know, believe, or do?
3. How likely is it that this ad will influence you to undertake the action?
4. What works well in the ad and what works poorly?
5. How does the ad make you feel?
6. Where is the best place to reach you with this message? Where would you be most likely to notice it and pay attention to it? Where are you when you make decisions about this action?

Portfolio tests ask consumers to view or listen to a portfolio of advertisements. Consumers are then asked to recall all the ads and their content, aided or unaided by the interviewer. Recall level indicates an ad's ability to stand out and to have its message understood and remembered.

Laboratory tests use equipment to measure physiological reactions—heartbeat, blood pressure, pupil dilation, galvanic skin response, perspiration—to an ad; or consumers may be asked to turn a knob to indicate their moment-to-moment liking or interest while viewing sequenced material.[44] These tests measure attention-getting power but reveal nothing about impact on beliefs, attitudes, or intentions. Table 18.3 describes some specific advertising research techniques.

Pretest critics maintain that agencies can design ads that test well, but may not necessarily perform well in the marketplace. Proponents of ad pretesting maintain that useful diagnostic information can emerge and that pretests should not be used as the sole decision criterion anyway. Widely acknowledged as being one of the best advertisers around, Nike is notorious for doing very little ad pretesting. "Marketing Memo: How to Sell in Hard Times" offers some communication insights from its ad agency, Weiden & Kennedy.

Many advertisers use post-tests to assess the overall impact of a completed campaign. If a company hoped to increase brand awareness from 20 percent to 50 percent and succeeded in increasing it to only 30 percent, then the company is not spending enough, its ads are poor, or some other factor has been ignored.

SALES-EFFECT RESEARCH   What sales are generated by an ad that increases brand awareness by 20 percent and brand preference by 10 percent? Advertising's sales effect is generally harder to measure than its communication effect. Sales are influenced by many factors, such as features, price, and availability, as well as competitors' actions. The fewer or more controllable these other factors are, the easier it is to measure effect on sales. The sales impact is easiest to measure in direct-marketing situations and hardest to measure in brand or corporate image-building advertising.

Companies are generally interested in finding out whether they are overspending or underspending on advertising. One approach to answering this question is to work with the formulation shown in Figure 18.4.

FIGURE 18.4

Formula for Measuring Sales Impact of Advertising

TABLE 18.3	ADVERTISING RESEARCH TECHNIQUES

For Print Ads. Starch and Gallup & Robinson, Inc., are two widely used print pretesting services. Test ads are placed in magazines, which are then circulated to consumers. These consumers are contacted later and interviewed. Recall and recognition tests are used to determine advertising effectiveness.

For Broadcast Ads. *In-home tests:* A videotape is taken or downloaded into the homes of target consumers, who then view the commercials.

Trailer tests: In a trailer in a shopping centre, shoppers are shown the products and given an opportunity to select a series of brands. They then view commercials and are given coupons to be used in the shopping centre. Redemption rates indicate commercials' influence on purchase behaviour.

Theatre tests: Consumers are invited to a theatre to view a potential new television series along with some commercials. Before the show begins, consumers indicate preferred brands in different categories; after the viewing, consumers again choose preferred brands. Preference changes measure the commercials' persuasive power.

On-air tests: Respondents are recruited to watch a program on a regular TV channel during the test commercial or are selected based on their having viewed the program. They are asked questions about commercial recall.

Marketing Memo

How to Sell in Hard Times

With one of the best ad campaigns of the last decade ("Just Do It"), Nike's ad agency Weiden & Kennedy (W&K) knows a lot about what works in good economic times as well as bad. Here are six tips:

1. *Make noise.* During boom times, no one can be heard above the din. In slower times, anyone with a creative message will stand out—and gain an advantage on competitors who have gone quiet.

2. *Open up.* Customers look for brands they can trust. You have to give people an insight into who you really are as a brand—what you believe and stand for.

3. *Trust your gut.* Nike and W&K never show their ads to focus groups because they often will reject original or unconventional ideas simply because they are different.

4. *Look past the tube.* Television is expensive and not always necessary. W&K trusts street-level guerrilla advertising such as ad messages on sandwich boards, custom-made magazines, and toys to spread the word.

5. *Target the tribes.* To reach small, influential customer groups, or "tribes," W&K hits them where they live. Messages are projected on sidewalks and the sides of buildings, and CDs and DVDs that promote Nike shoes are handed out at parties and live events.

6. *Lure them to the Web.* W&K uses intrigue to draw customers to the brand's Web site—the most efficient marketing tool. The agency has used cliff-hanger commercials that started on TV but whose endings could be found only on the Nike Web site, as well as print ads, billboards, and even window displays as teasers.

Source: Warren Berger, "Just Do It Again," *Business 2.0* (September 2002): 81.

A company's *share of advertising expenditures* produces a *share of voice* (i.e., proportion of company advertising of that product to all advertising of that product) that earns a *share of consumers' minds and hearts* and ultimately, a *share of market*.

Researchers try to measure the sales impact through analyzing historical or experimental data. The *historical approach* involves correlating past sales to past advertising expenditures using advanced statistical techniques.[45] Other researchers use an *experimental design* to measure advertising's sales impact. Here is an example:

Information Resources, Inc.

Information Resources offers a service called BehaviorScan that provides marketers in North America with data about advertising effectiveness by tracking consumer purchases tied to specific advertising. Consumers in test markets who sign up to be members of IRI's "Shoppers Hotline" panel agree to have microcomputers record when the TV set is on and to which station it is tuned, while electronic scanners record UPC codes of their household purchases at supermarkets. IRI has the capability to send different commercials to different homes. The company also conducts in-store tests in many North American markets to study the effects of promotions, displays, coupons, store features, and packaging.[46]

"Marketing Insight: Understanding the Effects of Advertising and Promotion" provides a summary of a meta-analysis of IRI research studies.

A growing number of researchers are striving to measure the sales effect of advertising expenditures instead of settling for communication-effect measures.[47] Millward Brown International has conducted tracking studies in the United Kingdom for many years to provide information to help advertisers decide whether their advertising is benefiting their brand.[48]

Sales Promotion

Sales promotion, a key ingredient in marketing campaigns, consists of a collection of incentive tools, mostly short term, designed to stimulate quicker or greater purchase of particular products or services by consumers or the trade.[49]

Whereas advertising offers a *reason* to buy, sales promotion offers an *incentive* to buy. Sales promotion includes tools for *consumer promotion* (samples, coupons, cash refund offers, prices off, premiums, prizes, patronage rewards, free trials, warranties, tie-in promotions, cross-promotions, point-of-purchase displays, and demonstrations); *trade promotion* (prices off, advertising and display allowances, and free goods); and *business* and *sales-force promotion* (trade shows and conventions, contests for sales reps, and specialty advertising).

Objectives

Sales-promotion tools vary in their specific objectives. A free sample stimulates consumer trial, whereas a free management-advisory service aims at cementing a long-term relationship with a retailer.

Sellers use incentive-type promotions to attract new triers, to reward loyal customers, and to increase the repurchase rates of occasional users. Sales promotions often attract brand switchers, who are primarily looking for low price, good value, or premiums. Sales promotions generally are unlikely to turn them into loyal users, although they may be induced to make some subsequent purchases.[50] Sales promotions used in markets of high brand similarity can produce a high sales response in the short run but little permanent gain in market share. In markets of high brand dissimilarity, sales promotions may be able to alter market shares permanently. In addition to brand switching, consumers may engage in stockpiling—purchasing earlier than usual (purchase acceleration) or purchasing extra quantities.[51] But sales may then hit a post-promotion dip.[52]

A number of sales-promotion benefits flow to manufacturers and consumers.[53] Sales promotions enable manufacturers to adjust to short-term variations in supply and demand. They enable manufacturers to test how high a list price they can charge, because they can always discount it. They induce consumers to try new products instead of never straying from current ones. They lead to more varied retail formats, such as the everyday-low-price store and the promotional-pricing store. For retailers, promotions may increase sales of complementary categories (cake mix promotions may help to drive frosting sales) as well as induce some store-switching by consumers. They promote greater consumer awareness of prices. They permit manufacturers to sell more than they would normally sell at the list price. They help the manufacturer adapt programs to different consumer

MARKETING INSIGHT

Understanding the Effects of Advertising and Promotion

Information Resources Institute (IRI) has provided a unique, in-depth examination into how advertising works. IRI reviewed the results of 389 research studies conducted over a seven-year period and offered the following general principles concerning advertising and promotion effectiveness:

1. *TV advertising weight alone is not enough.* Only roughly half of TV advertising heavy-up plans have a measurable effect on sales, although when they do have an effect it is often large. The success rate is higher on new products or line extensions than on established brands.

2. *TV advertising is more likely to work when there are changes in copy or media strategy* (a new copy strategy or an expanded target market).

3. *When advertising is successful in increasing sales, its impact lasts beyond the period of peak spending.* Recent evidence shows the long-term positive effects of advertising lasting up to two years after peak spending. Moreover, the long-term incremental sales generated are approximately double the incremental sales observed in the first year of an advertising spending increase.

4. *About 20 percent of advertising plans pay out in the short term.* However, when the long-term effect of advertising is considered, it is likely that most advertising plans that show a significant effect in a split cable experiment would pay out.

5. *Promotions almost always have a measurable impact on sales. However, the effect is usually purely short term.*

6. *Payout statistics on promotions are dismal.* Roughly 16 percent of trade promotions are profitable. Furthermore, promotions' effects are often purely short term, except for new products.

7. *The above statistics on advertising and promotion payouts show that many brands are overspending on marketing support.* Many classes of spending can be reduced at an increase in profits.

8. *Allocating marketing funds involves a continuous search for marketing programs that offer the highest return on the marketing dollar.* Trade-offs between advertising, trade, and consumer promotions can be highly profitable when based on reliable evaluation systems measuring this productivity at any point in time.

9. *The current trend toward promotion spending is not sound from a marketing productivity standpoint.* When the strategic disadvantages of promotions are included—that is, losing control to the trade and training consumers to buy only on deal—the case is compelling for a re-evaluation of current practices and the incentive systems responsible for this trend.

A 2004 IRI study of 23 brands reinforced these findings, finding that advertising often didn't increase sales for mature brands or categories in decline.

Source: Leonard M. Lodish, Magid Abraham, Stuart Kalmenson, Jeanne Livelsberger, Beth Lubetkin, Bruce Richardson, and Mary Ellen Stevens, "How T.V. Advertising Works: A Meta Analysis of 389 Real World Split Cable T.V. Advertising Experiments," *Journal of Marketing Research*, 32 (May 1995): 125–139; Jack Neff, "TV Doesn't Sell Package Goods, *Advertising Age*, May 24, 2004, pp. 1, 30.

segments. Consumers themselves enjoy some satisfaction from being smart shoppers when they take advantage of price specials.

Service marketers also employ sales promotions to achieve marketing objectives. Some service firms use promotions to attract additional sales:

McDonald's Canada

McDonald's is well known for employing sales promotions to elicit additional sales. Recently, McDonald's Canada created a campaign using Canada's obsession with hockey and the NHL. They created a product called the "Hockey Hero Sandwich," a three-beef-patty sandwich, and added a unique promotion to encourage people to purchase it. With the purchase of the Hockey Hero, and any size fries, hash browns, or drink, customers could buy one of six official, doll-sized NHL jerseys for $2.69. Customers who purchased the mini-jerseys also received a $30 coupon toward the purchase of an actual NHL jersey at SportChek or Sports Experts.[54]

Advertising versus Promotion

A decade ago, the advertising-to-sales-promotion ratio was about 60:40. Today, in many consumer packaged-goods companies, sales promotion accounts for 75 percent of the combined budget (roughly 50 percent is trade promotion and 25 percent is consumer promotion). Sales-promotion expenditures have been increasing as a percentage of budget expenditure annually for the last two decades. Several factors contribute to this rapid growth, particularly in consumer markets.[55]

Promotion is now more accepted by top management as an effective sales tool; more product managers are qualified to use sales-promotion tools; and product managers are under greater pressure to increase current sales. In addition, the number of brands has increased; competitors use promotions frequently; many brands are seen as similar; consumers are more price-oriented; the trade has demanded more deals from manufacturers; and advertising efficiency has declined because of rising costs, media clutter, and legal restraints.

There is a danger, however, in letting advertising take too much of a back seat to promotions, because advertising typically builds brand loyalty. The question of whether or not sales promotion weakens brand loyalty is subject to interpretation. Sales promotion, with its incessant prices off, coupons, deals, and premiums, may devalue the product offering in buyers' minds. However, before jumping to any conclusion, we need to distinguish between price promotions and added-value promotions. Certain types of sales promotion can actually enhance brand image. The rapid growth of sales-promotion media has created clutter similar to advertising clutter. Manufacturers have to find ways to rise above the clutter—for instance, by offering larger coupon-redemption values or using more dramatic point-of-purchase displays or demonstrations.

Usually, when a brand is price promoted too often, the consumer begins to devalue it and buy it mainly when it goes on sale. So there is risk in putting a well-known brand on promotion over 30 percent of the time.[56] Automobile manufacturers turned to 0 percent financing and hefty cash rebates to ignite sales in the soft economy of 2000–2001 but have found it difficult to wean consumers from all the discounts since then: Two-thirds of Americans indicated that the timing of their next vehicle purchases will be affected by the level of sales incentives and one-third said they wouldn't buy without them.[57]

Dominant brands offer deals less frequently, because most deals subsidize only current users. Prior research has shown that sales promotions yield faster and more measurable responses in sales than advertising does but do not tend to yield new, long-term buyers in mature markets. Loyal brand buyers tend not to change their buying patterns as a result of competitive promotion. Advertising appears to be more effective at deepening brand loyalty.[58]

There is also evidence that price promotions do not build permanent total-category volume. One study of more than 1000 promotions concluded that only 16 percent paid off.[59] Small-share competitors find it advantageous to use sales promotion, because they cannot afford to match the market leaders' large advertising budgets; nor can they obtain shelf space without offering trade allowances or stimulate consumer trial without offering incentives. Price competition is often used by a small brand seeking to enlarge its share, but it is less effective for a category leader whose growth lies in expanding the entire category.[60] The upshot is that many consumer packaged-goods companies feel they are forced to use more sales promotion than they wish. They blame the heavy use of sales promotion for decreasing brand loyalty, increasing consumer price-sensitivity, brand-quality-image dilution, and a focus on short-run marketing planning.

Major Decisions

In using sales promotion, a company must establish its objectives, select the tools, develop the program, pretest the program, implement and control it, and evaluate the results.

ESTABLISHING OBJECTIVES   Sales-promotion objectives are derived from broader promotion objectives, which are derived from more basic marketing objectives developed for the product. For consumers, objectives include encouraging purchase of larger-sized units, building trial among nonusers, and attracting switchers away from competitors' brands. Ideally, promotions with consumers would have short-run sales impact as well as long-run brand equity effects. For retailers, objectives include persuading retailers to carry new items and higher levels of inventory, encouraging off-season buying, encouraging stocking of related items, offsetting competitive promotions, building brand loyalty, and gaining entry into new retail outlets. For the sales force, objectives include encouraging support of a new product or model, encouraging more prospecting, and stimulating off-season sales.[61]

SELECTING CONSUMER-PROMOTION TOOLS   The promotion planner should take into account the type of market, sales-promotion objectives, competitive conditions, and each tool's cost-effectiveness. The main consumer-promotion tools are summarized in Table 18.4. We can distinguish between *manufacturer promotions* and *retailer promotions*. The former are illustrated by the auto industry's frequent use of rebates, gifts to motivate test-drives and purchases, and high-value trade-in credit. The latter include price cuts, feature advertising, retailer coupons, and retailer contests or premiums.

We can also distinguish between sales-promotion tools that are *consumer-franchise building* and reinforce the consumer's brand preference, and those that do not. The former impart a selling message along with the deal, as in the case of free samples, frequency awards, coupons when they include a selling message, and premiums when they are related to the product. Sales-promotion tools that typically are not brand-building include price-off packs, consumer premiums not related to a product, contests and sweepstakes, consumer refund offers, and trade allowances.

Consumer franchise-building promotions offer the best of both worlds—they build brand equity while moving product. Here's an example of a highly effective consumer-franchise building promotion:

DiGiorno

Kraft has advertised its DiGiorno frozen pizza with the tagline, "It's Not Delivery. It's DiGiorno." The "Be a DiGiorno Delivery Guy" promotion contest was based on the fact that the pizza was not actually delivered but instead made fresh at home. The sweepstakes winner was given "nothing to do" in terms of a US$100 000 salary (to do nothing), a Ford Mustang GT convertible (which winners were not required to drive), and a Hawaiian vacation (to do nothing). The effort was backed with a national TV and print campaign, coupons on 10 million marked pizza boxes, and entry via an 800-number. It led to a 90 percent hike in incremental sales volume and resulted in an 18.1 percent market share, the highest in DiGiorno's history.[62]

Sales promotion seems most effective when used together with advertising. In one study, a price promotion alone produced only a 15 percent increase in sales volume. When combined with feature advertising, sales volume increased 19 percent; when combined with feature advertising and a point-of-purchase display, sales volume increased 24 percent.[63]

Many large companies have a sales-promotion manager whose job is to help brand managers choose the right promotional tool. Some marketers such as Colgate-Palmolive and Hershey Foods are also going online with their coupons, aided by various online coupon sites.

TABLE 18.4	MAJOR CONSUMER-PROMOTION TOOLS

Samples: Offer of a free amount of a product or service delivered door-to-door, sent in the mail, picked up in a store, attached to another product, or featured in an advertising offer.

Coupons: Certificates entitling the bearer to a stated saving on the purchase of a specific product: mailed, enclosed in other products or attached to them, or inserted in magazine and newspaper ads.

Cash Refund Offers (rebates): Provide a price reduction after purchase rather than at the retail shop: consumer sends a specified "proof of purchase" to the manufacturer who "refunds" part of the purchase price by mail.

Price Packs (cents-off deals): Offers to consumers of savings off the regular price of a product, flagged on the label or package. A *reduced-price pack* is a single package sold at a reduced price (such as two for the price of one). A *banded pack* is two related products banded together (such as a toothbrush and toothpaste).

Premiums (gifts): Merchandise offered at a relatively low cost or free as an incentive to purchase a particular product. A *with-pack premium* accompanies the product inside or on the package. A *free in-the-mail premium* is mailed to consumers who send in a proof of purchase, such as a box top or UPC code. A *self-liquidating premium* is sold below its normal retail price to consumers who request it.

Frequency Programs: Programs providing rewards related to the consumer's frequency and intensity in purchasing the company's products or services.

Prizes (contests, sweepstakes, games): *Prizes* are offers of the chance to win cash, trips, or merchandise as a result of purchasing something. A *contest* calls for consumers to submit an entry to be examined by a panel of judges who will select the best entries. A *sweepstakes* asks consumers to submit their names in a drawing. A *game* presents consumers with something every time they buy—bingo numbers, missing letters—which might help them win a prize.

Patronage Awards: Values in cash or in other forms that are proportional to patronage of a certain vendor or group of vendors.

Free Trials: Inviting prospective purchasers to try the product without cost in the hope that they will buy.

Product Warranties: Explicit or implicit promises by sellers that the product will perform as specified or that the seller will fix it or refund the customer's money during a specified period.

Tie-in Promotions: Two or more brands or companies team up on coupons, refunds, and contests to increase pulling power.

Cross-Promotions: Using one brand to advertise another noncompeting brand.

Point-of-Purchase (P-O-P) Displays and Demonstrations: P-O-P displays and demonstrations take place at the point-of-purchase or sale.

Valpak

The Valpak blue envelope is the most recognizable form of direct mail advertising in Canada. People anticipate the blue envelope because they know it delivers great savings from national and regional businesses—everything from dining and entertainment to home improvement to dry cleaning and auto services. Consumers can also access Valpak.com—the largest local Web site on the Internet, with more than 10 000 local and national offers—any time they need savings. Born in 1986, the company operates a network of more than 200 active franchises in Canada, the United States, and Puerto Rico.[64]

SELECTING TRADE-PROMOTION TOOLS Manufacturers use a number of trade-promotion tools (Table 18.5). Surprisingly, a higher proportion of the promotion pie is devoted to trade-promotion tools (46.9 percent) than to consumer promotion (27.9 percent). Manufacturers award money to the trade (1) to persuade the retailer or wholesaler to carry the brand; (2) to persuade the

TABLE 18.5	MAJOR TRADE-PROMOTION TOOLS

Price-Off (off-invoice or off-list): A straight discount off the list price on each case purchased during a stated time period.

Allowance: An amount offered in return for the retailer's agreeing to feature the manufacturer's products in some way. An *advertising allowance* compensates retailers for advertising the manufacturer's product. A *display allowance* compensates them for carrying a special product display.

Free Goods: Offers of extra cases of merchandise to intermediaries who buy a certain quantity or who feature a certain flavour or size.

Source: For more information, see Betsy Spethman, "Trade Promotion Redefined," *Brandweek*, March 13, 1995, pp. 25–32.

retailer or wholesaler to carry more units than the normal amount; (3) to induce retailers to promote the brand by featuring, display, and price reductions; and (4) to stimulate retailers and their sales clerks to push the product.

The growing power of large retailers has increased their ability to demand trade promotion at the expense of consumer promotion and advertising.[65] These retailers depend on promotion money from the manufacturers. No manufacturer could unilaterally stop offering trade allowances without losing retailer support. The company's sales force and its brand managers are often at odds over trade promotion. The sales force says that the local retailers will not keep the company's products on the shelf unless they receive more trade-promotion money, whereas the brand managers want to spend the limited funds on consumer promotion and advertising.

Manufacturers face several challenges in managing trade promotions. First, they often find it difficult to police retailers to make sure they are doing what they agreed to do. Manufacturers are increasingly insisting on proof of performance before paying any allowances. Second, more retailers are doing *forward buying*—that is, buying a greater quantity during the deal period than they can sell during the deal period. Retailers might respond to a 10-percent-off-case allowance by buying a 12-week or longer supply. The manufacturer has to schedule more production than planned and bear the costs of extra work shifts and overtime. Third, retailers are doing more diverting, buying more cases than needed in a region in which the manufacturer offered a deal, and shipping the surplus to their stores in nondeal regions. Manufacturers are trying to handle forward buying and diverting by limiting the amount they will sell at a discount, or producing and delivering less than the full order in an effort to smooth production.[66]

All said, manufacturers feel that trade promotion has become a nightmare. It contains layers of deals, is complex to administer, and often leads to lost revenues.

SELECTING BUSINESS- AND SALES-FORCE-PROMOTION TOOLS Companies spend billions of dollars on business- and sales-force-promotion tools (Table 18.6). These tools are used to gather business leads, impress and reward customers, and motivate the sales force to greater effort. Companies typically develop budgets for each business-promotion tool that remain fairly constant from year to year.

DEVELOPING THE PROGRAM In planning sales-promotion programs, marketers are increasingly blending several media into a total campaign concept.

TABLE 18.6	MAJOR BUSINESS- AND SALES-FORCE-PROMOTION TOOLS

Trade Shows and Conventions: Industry associations organize annual trade shows and conventions. Business marketers may spend as much as 35 percent of their annual promotion budget on trade shows. Thousands of trade shows take place every year, drawing millions of attendees. Trade show attendance can range from a few thousand people to over 70 000 for large shows held by the restaurant or hotel-motel industries. Participating vendors expect several benefits, including generating new sales leads, maintaining customer contacts, introducing new products, meeting new customers, selling more to present customers, and educating customers with publications, videos, and other audiovisual materials.

Sales Contests: A sales contest aims at inducing the sales force or dealers to increase their sales results over a stated period, with prizes (money, trips, gifts, or points) going to those who succeed.

Specialty Advertising: Specialty advertising consists of useful, low-cost items bearing the company's name and address, and sometimes an advertising message that salespeople give to prospects and customers. Common items are ballpoint pens, calendars, key chains, flashlights, tote bags, and memo pads.

Samsung and *Matrix Reloaded*

Eager to make a mark with 19- to 49-year-olds, Samsung leveraged its unique hand phone from the *Matrix Reloaded* movie sequel to launch a global, multi-media promotion. Designed to reinforce brand values of being advanced and fashionable, the promotion was seen as cool and relevant by the target market. A US$100 million global budget was set for TV, print, outdoor, and online ads, customized for each global market (30 different languages were used). Among the unprecedented efforts: purchasing all the signage in the trains and train stations in Tokyo for two days, wrapping a ten-storey building in Singapore with Samsung visuals; and a slew of billboards in 50+ markets from Paris to Paraguay. In-store merchandising featured gifts and posters with purchase at Best Buy and Radio Shack stores. An online sweepstakes helped to increase site visits by 65 percent. All this marketing effort resulted in a 25 percent jump in sales during the promotional period from April to June 2003.[67]

In deciding to use a particular incentive, marketers have several factors to consider. First, they must determine the *size* of the incentive. A certain minimum is necessary if the promotion is to succeed. Second, the marketing manager must establish *conditions* for participation. Incentives might be offered to everyone or to select groups. Third, the marketer has to decide on the *duration* of the promotion. According to one researcher, the optimal frequency is about three weeks per quarter, and optimal duration is the length of the average purchase cycle.[68] Fourth, the marketer must choose a *distribution vehicle*. A 25-cents-off coupon can be distributed in the package, in stores, by mail, or in advertising.

Fifth, the marketing manager must establish the *timing* of promotion. Finally, the marketer must determine the *total sales-promotion budget*. The cost of a particular promotion consists of the administrative cost (printing, mailing, and promoting the deal) and the incentive cost (cost of premium or cents-off, including redemption costs), multiplied by the expected number of units that will be sold on the deal. In the case of a coupon deal, the cost would take into account the fact that only a fraction of the consumers will redeem the coupons.

PRETESTING, IMPLEMENTING, CONTROLLING, AND EVALUATING THE PROGRAM
Although most sales-promotion programs are designed on the basis of experience, pretests can determine if the tools are appropriate, the incentive size optimal, and the presentation method efficient. Consumers can be asked to rate or rank different possible deals, or trial tests can be run in limited geographic areas.

Marketing managers must prepare implementation and control plans for each individual promotion that cover lead time and sell-in time. *Lead time* is the time necessary to prepare the program prior to launching it: initial planning, design, and approval of package modifications or material to be mailed or distributed; preparation of advertising and point-of-sale materials; notification of field sales personnel; establishment of allocations for individual distributors; purchasing and printing of special premiums or packaging materials; production of advance inventories in preparation for release at a specific date; and, finally, the distribution to the retailer.[69] *Sell-in time* begins with the promotional launch and ends when approximately 95 percent of the deal merchandise is in the hands of consumers.

Manufacturers can evaluate the program using three methods: sales data, consumer surveys, and experiments. The first method involves scanner sales data. Marketers can analyze the types of people who took advantage of the promotion, what they bought before the promotion, and how they behaved later toward the brand and other brands. Did the promotion attract new triers and also stimulate more purchasing by existing customers?

In general, sales promotions work best when they attract competitors' customers who then switch. If the company's product is not superior, the brand's share is likely to return to its pre-promotion level. *Consumer surveys* can be conducted to learn how many recall the promotion, what they thought of it, how many took advantage of it, and how the promotion affected subsequent brand-choice behaviour.[70] Sales promotions can also be evaluated through *experiments* that vary such attributes as incentive value, duration, and distribution media. For example, coupons can be sent to half of the households in a consumer panel. Scanner data can be used to track whether the coupons led more people to buy the product and when.

There are additional costs beyond the cost of specific promotions. First, promotions might decrease long-run brand loyalty. Second, promotions can be more expensive than they appear. Some are inevitably distributed to the wrong consumers. Third, there are the costs of special production runs, extra sales-force effort, and handling requirements. Finally, certain promotions irritate retailers, who may demand extra trade allowances or refuse to cooperate.[71]

Creating a brand experience: Everything Coca-Cola in Las Vegas, with a 30-metre lighted Coke bottle as part of the front of the building.

Events and Experiences

According to the IEG Sponsorship Report, US$11.14 billion was predicted to be spent on sponsorships in North America during 2004, with 69 percent of this going to sports, another 10 percent to entertainment tours and attractions, 7 percent to festivals, fairs, and annual events, 5 percent to the arts, and 9 percent to cause marketing. By becoming part of a special and more personally relevant moment in consumers' lives, involvement with events can broaden and deepen the relationship with their target market.

At the same time, daily encounters with brands may also affect consumers' brand attitudes and beliefs. *Atmospheres* are "packaged environments" that create or reinforce leanings toward product purchase. Law offices decorated with Oriental rugs and oak furniture communicate "stability" and "success."[72] A five-star hotel will use elegant chandeliers, marble columns, and other tangible signs of luxury.

Recognizing that it can now reach only 15 percent of the population with a primetime ad as compared to 40 percent as recently as the mid-1980s, Coca-Cola has diverted money into new initiatives that allow it to embed itself into the favourite activities of its target audience. The company has created "teen lounges" in major cities where kids can hang out and buy Cokes from see-through vending machines, placed downloadable songs on its myCokeMusic.com Web site in Britain, and blended its brand into the content of TV shows from the United States to Venezuela.[73]

Coca-Cola is not alone. More firms are creating on-site and off-site product and brand experiences. There is Everything Coca-Cola in Las Vegas, M&M World in Times Square in New York, and General Mills Cereal Adventure in Mall of America in Minnesota.[74] Small brands, of necessity, are even more likely to take less obvious and less expensive paths in sponsorship and communications. With a limited budget, Yoo-hoo chose to target teens by sponsoring the Warped Tour, an alternative music festival, via free samples and off-the-wall contests. For example, concert-goers could get free products if they were willing to chug the chocolate drink out of a boot (dubbed a "shoe-hoo").[75]

Guinness Canada

Guinness, the maker of the famous Irish stout beer, has created a unique and ultimately successful campaign using special event marketing initiatives. Guinness was behind the effort to make St. Patrick's Day a national holiday in Canada. The company hosted a series of bar events across the country where people were encouraged to vote for St. Patrick's Day becoming a national holiday. The objective of the Guinness rally is to raise awareness and sales for the Irish ale by recruiting members to the "Guinness Party of Canada" through guinnessvote.ca. By 2004, there were 92 000 people who voted, some of whom have been selected for invitation-only beer-themed events. The company has even hosted an election for the "Minister of Good Times" and a highly publicized, staged lobby event held at Parliament Hill in Ottawa, where members held signs to promote the cause. The initiative is said to have contributed a whopping 20 percent increase in sales for the brand.[76]

Events Objectives

Marketers report a number of reasons why they sponsor events:

1. *To identify with a particular target market or lifestyle.* Customers can be targeted geographically, demographically, psychographically, or behaviourally according to events. Events can be chosen based on attendees' attitudes toward and usage of certain products or brands. Advertisers such as Sony, Gillette, and Pepsi have advertised during ESPN's twice-yearly X Games to reach the elusive 12- to 19-year-old audience.[77]

2. *To increase awareness of company or product name.* Sponsorship often offers sustained exposure to a brand, a necessary condition to build brand recognition. By skillfully choosing sponsorship events or activities, identification with a product and thus brand recall can also be enhanced, such as Guinness Canada's St. Patrick's Day initiative.

3. *To create or reinforce consumer perceptions of key brand image associations.* Events themselves have associations that help to create or reinforce brand associations.

4. *To enhance corporate image dimensions.* Sponsorship is seen as a means to improve perceptions that the company is likable, prestigious, and so on, so that consumers will credit the company and favour it in later product choices.

5. *To create experiences and evoke feelings.* The feelings engendered by an exciting or rewarding event may also indirectly link to the brand. Marketers can use the Web to provide further event support and additional experiences.

Guinness Canada uses event marketing. It held a rally on Parliament Hill in Ottawa to make St. Patrick's Day a national holiday.

6. *To express commitment to the community or social issues.* Sponsorship that involves corporate tie-ins with nonprofit organizations and charities is often called cause-related marketing. Firms such as Timberland, Home Depot, Starbucks, and American Express have made cause-related marketing an important cornerstone of their marketing programs.

7. *To entertain key clients or reward key employees.* Many events include lavish hospitality tents and other special services or activities that are only available for sponsors and their guests. Involving clients with the event in these and other ways can engender goodwill and establish valuable business contacts. From an employee perspective, events can build participation and morale or be used as an incentive.

8. *To permit merchandising or promotional opportunities.* Many marketers tie in contests or sweepstakes, in-store merchandising, direct response, or other marketing activities with an event. L'Oréal Canada used its sponsorship of the hit TV show *Canadian Idol* in this way.

Despite these potential advantages, there are a number of potential disadvantages to sponsorship. The success of an event can be unpredictable and out of the control of the sponsor. Although many consumers will credit sponsors for providing the financial assistance to make an event possible, some consumers may still resent the commercialization of events.

Major Decisions

Developing successful sponsored events involves choosing the appropriate events, designing the optimal sponsorship program for the event, and measuring the effects of sponsorship.[78]

CHOOSING EVENT OPPORTUNITIES Because of the huge amount of money involved and the number of event opportunities that exist, many marketers are becoming much more strategic about the events with which they will get involved and the manner in which they will do so.

The marketing objectives and communication strategy that have been defined for the brand must be met by the event. The audience delivered by the event must match the target market of the brand. The event must have sufficient awareness, possess the desired image, and be capable of creating the desired effects with that target market. Consumers must make favourable attributions to the sponsor for its event involvement. An "ideal event" might be one (1) whose audience closely matches the desired target market, (2) that generates much favourable attention, (3) that is unique but not encumbered with many sponsors, (4) that lends itself to ancillary marketing activities, and (5) that reflects or enhances the brand or corporate image of the sponsor.

More and more firms are also using their names to sponsor the arenas, stadiums, and other venues that actually hold the events.[79] From 1999 to 2004, over US$2 billion was spent for naming rights to major North American sports facilities. For example, Air Canada agreed to pay Maple Leaf Sports and Entertainment $40 million over 20 years for the rights to have the Toronto Raptors' and Maple Leafs' arena named the Air Canada Centre.[80]

Air Canada agreed to pay $40 million over 20 years to name the Air Canada Centre.

DESIGNING SPONSORSHIP PROGRAMS Many marketers believe that it is the marketing program accompanying an event sponsorship that ultimately determines its success. A sponsor can strategically identify itself at an event in a number of ways, including banners, signs, and programs. For more significant impact, sponsors typically supplement such activities with samples, prizes, advertising, retail promotions, and publicity. At least two to three times the amount of the sponsorship expenditure should be spent on related marketing activities. Jamba Juice augments its running race sponsorships with bunches of runners in banana costumes. Any runner who finishes the race before a banana gets free smoothies for a year. Jamba Juice banners are displayed all around and smoothies are sampled by race finishers and onlookers.[81]

Event creation is a particularly important skill in publicizing fund-raising drives for nonprofit organizations. Fund-raisers have developed a large repertoire of special events, including anniversary celebrations, art exhibits, auctions, benefit evenings, bingo games, book sales, cake sales, contests, dances, dinners, fairs, fashion shows, parties in unusual places, phonathons, rummage sales, tours, and walkathons. No sooner is one type of event created, such as a walkathon, than competitors spawn new versions, such as readathons, bikeathons, and jogathons.[82]

MEASURING SPONSORSHIP ACTIVITIES As with public relations, measurement of events is difficult. There are two basic approaches to measuring the effects of sponsorship activities: The *supply-side* method focuses on potential exposure to the brand by assessing the extent of media coverage; and the *demand-side* method focuses on reported exposure from consumers. We examine each in turn.

Supply-side methods attempt to approximate the amount of time or space devoted to media coverage of an event. For example, the number of seconds that the brand is clearly visible on a television screen or the column inches of press clippings covering an event that mention the brand can be estimated. This measure of potential "impressions" is then translated into an equivalent "value" in advertising dollars according to the fees associated in actually advertising in the particular media vehicle. Some industry consultants have estimated that 30 seconds of TV logo exposure can be worth 6 to 10 or as much as 25 percent of a 30-second TV ad spot.

Although supply-side exposure methods provide quantifiable measures, their validity can be questioned. The difficulty lies in the fact that equating media coverage with advertising exposure ignores the content of the respective communications consumers receive. The advertiser uses media space and time to communicate a strategically designed message. Media coverage and telecasts only expose the brand and don't necessarily embellish its meaning in any direct way. Although some public relations professionals maintain that positive editorial coverage can be worth 5 to 10 times the advertising equivalency value, it is rare that sponsorship provides such favourable treatment.[83]

The "demand side" method attempts to identify the effects sponsorship has on consumers' brand knowledge. Tracking or customized surveys can explore the ability of the event sponsorship to affect awareness, attitudes, or even sales. Event spectators can be identified and surveyed to measure sponsor recall of the event as well as resulting attitudes and intentions toward the sponsor.

Public Relations

Not only must the company relate constructively to customers, suppliers, and dealers, it must also relate to a large number of interested publics. A **public** is any group that has an actual or potential interest in or impact on a company's ability to achieve its objectives. **Public relations (PR)** involves a variety of programs designed to promote or protect a company's image or its individual products.

The wise company takes concrete steps to manage successful relations with its key publics. Most companies have a public-relations department that monitors the attitudes of the organization's publics and distributes information and communications to build goodwill. The best PR departments spend time counselling top management to adopt positive programs and to eliminate questionable practices so that negative publicity does not arise in the first place. They perform the following five functions:

1. *Press relations.* Presenting news and information about the organization in the most positive light.

2. *Product publicity.* Sponsoring efforts to publicize specific products.

3. *Corporate communication.* Promoting understanding of the organization through internal and external communications.

4. *Lobbying.* Dealing with legislators and government officials to promote or defeat legislation and regulation.

5. *Counselling.* Advising management about public issues and company positions and image during good times and bad.

Marketing Public Relations

Many companies are turning to **marketing public relations (MPR)** to support corporate or product promotion and image making. MPR, like financial PR and community PR, serves a special constituency, the marketing department.[84]

The old name for MPR was **publicity**, which was seen as the task of securing editorial space—as opposed to paid space—in print and broadcast media to promote or "hype" a product, service, idea, place, person, or organization. MPR goes beyond simple publicity and plays an important role in the following tasks:

- *Assisting in the launch of new products.* The amazing commercial success of toys such as Teenage Mutant Ninja Turtles, Mighty Morphin' Power Rangers, Beanie Babies, and Pokémon owes a great deal to clever publicity.

- *Assisting in repositioning a mature product.* New York City had extremely bad press in the 1970s until the "I Love New York" campaign.

- *Building interest in a product category.* Companies and trade associations have used MPR to rebuild interest in declining commodities such as eggs, milk, beef, and potatoes, and to expand consumption of such products as tea, pork, and orange juice.

- *Influencing specific target groups.* The Vancouver Olympic Bid Committee leveraged public relations to build public support for the games as well as to win the right to hold the Olympics and Paralympics in Vancouver in 2010.

- *Defending products that have encountered public problems.* PR professionals must be adept at managing crises, such as the Coca-Cola incident in Belgium over allegedly contaminated soda, and Firestone's crisis with regard to the tire tread separation problem.

- *Building the corporate image in a way that reflects favourably on its products.* Bill Gates's speeches and books have helped to create an innovative image for Microsoft Corporation.

As the power of mass advertising weakens, marketing managers are turning to MPR to build awareness and brand knowledge for both new and established products. MPR is also effective in blanketing local communities and reaching specific groups. In several cases, MPR proved more cost-effective than advertising. Nevertheless, it must be planned jointly with advertising.[85] In addition, marketing managers need to acquire more skill in using MPR resources. Gillette is a trendsetter here: Each brand manager is required to have a budget line for MPR and to justify not using it. Done right, the impact can be substantial.

Clearly, creative public relations can affect public awareness at a fraction of the cost of advertising. The company does not pay for the space or time obtained in the media. It pays only for a staff to develop and circulate the stories and manage certain events. If the company develops an interesting story, it could be picked up by the media and be worth millions of dollars in equivalent advertising. Some experts say that consumers are five times more likely to be influenced by editorial copy than by advertising. Here's an example of a powerful PR campaign:

See You in Athens Fund

The not-for-profit organization called the See You in Athens Fund is an organization with a mission to help provide financial support to Canadian amateur athletes. Its principal objective is to fight the erroneous public perception that athletes are taken care of by government, family, and/or sponsors, when in fact 70 percent of Canada's Olympic contenders actually live below the poverty line. It wasn't until 2003 that the Fund turned to public relations to get its message across. Using a provocative and controversial public service announcement (PSA) created by Taxi of Toronto, the Fund exposed the athletes' struggle. The print ads and television commercials that were part of the campaign showed Canadian athletes begging for money (in contrast to the "feel good" podium shots). Using a public relations campaign to encourage inclusion of the PSA spots that resulted in different media proved to be the key to success. Every major newspaper in Canada ran the print ads (at no cost to the organization). The CBC produced a 12-minute documentary on the See You in Athens Fund, which aired several different times on *The National*. Most importantly, corporate partners couldn't wait to sign up. Molson, Beachcomber Hot Tubs, and the Maple Leaf Alumni joined the Fund, and when MasterCard joined the Fund, it made a $500 000 donation! The campaign is widely regarded as one of the most successful athletic fund-raising efforts in Canadian history.[86]

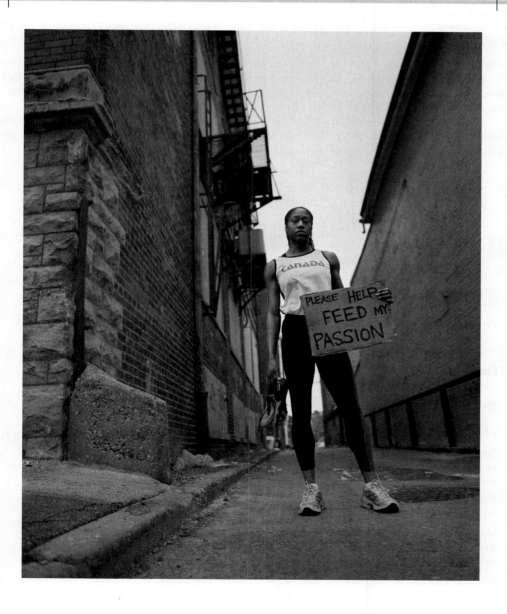

The See You in Athens Fund used public relations to create one of the most successful athletic fund-raising efforts in Canadian history.

Major Decisions in Marketing PR

In considering when and how to use MPR, management must establish the marketing objectives, choose the PR messages and vehicles, implement the plan carefully, and evaluate the results. The main tools of MPR are described in Table 18.7.[87]

ESTABLISHING OBJECTIVES MPR can build *awareness* by placing stories in the media to bring attention to a product, service, person, organization, or idea. It can build *credibility* by communicating the message in an editorial context. It can help boost sales-force and dealer enthusiasm with stories about a new product before it is launched. It can hold down *promotion cost* because MPR costs less than direct-mail and media advertising.

Whereas PR practitioners reach their target publics through the mass media, MPR is increasingly borrowing the techniques and technology of direct-response marketing to reach target audience members one-on-one.

CHOOSING MESSAGES AND VEHICLES The MPR manager must identify or develop interesting stories about the product. Suppose a relatively unknown university wants more visibility. The MPR practitioner will search for stories. Do any faculty members have unusual backgrounds, or are any working on unusual projects? Are any new and unusual courses being taught? Are any interesting events taking place on campus? If there are no interesting stories, the MPR practitioner should propose newsworthy events the university could sponsor. Here the challenge is to create news. PR ideas include hosting major academic conventions, inviting expert or celebrity speakers, and developing news conferences. Each event is an opportunity to develop a multitude of stories directed at different audiences.

IMPLEMENTING THE PLAN AND EVALUATING RESULTS MPR's contribution to the bottom line is difficult to measure, because it is used along with other promotional tools. The three most commonly used measures of MPR effectiveness are number of exposures; awareness, comprehension, or attitude change; and contribution to sales and profits.

The easiest measure of MPR effectiveness is the number of *exposures* carried by the media. Publicists supply the client with a clippings book showing all the media that carried news about the product and a summary statement such as the following:

> Media coverage included 3500 column inches of news and photographs in 350 publications with a combined circulation of 79.4 million; 2500 minutes of airtime of 290 radio stations and an estimated audience of 65 million; and 660 minutes of air time on 160 television

TABLE 18.7	MAJOR TOOLS IN MARKETING PR

Publications: Companies rely extensively on published materials to reach and influence their target markets. These include annual reports, brochures, articles, company newsletters and magazines, and audiovisual materials.

Events: Companies can draw attention to new products or other company activities by arranging special events like news conferences, seminars, outings, trade shows, exhibits, contests and competitions, and anniversaries that will reach the target publics.

Sponsorships: Companies can promote their brands and corporate name by sponsoring sports and cultural events and highly regarded causes.

News: One of the major tasks of PR professionals is to find or create favourable news about the company, its products, and its people, and get the media to accept press releases and attend press conferences.

Speeches: Increasingly, company executives must field questions from the media or give talks at trade associations or sales meetings, and these appearances can build the company's image.

Public-Service Activities: Companies can build goodwill by contributing money and time to good causes.

Identity Media: Companies need a visual identity that the public immediately recognizes. The visual identity is carried by company logos, stationery, brochures, signs, business forms, business cards, buildings, uniforms, and dress codes.

stations with an estimated audience of 91 million. If this time and space had been purchased at advertising rates, it would have amounted to $1 047 000.[88]

This measure is not very satisfying because it contains no indication of how many people actually read, heard, or recalled the message and what they thought afterward; nor does it contain information on the net audience reached, because publications overlap in readership. Because publicity's goal is reach, not frequency, it would be more useful to know the number of unduplicated exposures.

A better measure is the change in product awareness, comprehension, or attitude resulting from the MPR campaign (after allowing for the effect of other promotional tools). For example, how many people recall hearing the news item? How many told others about it (a measure of word of mouth)? How many changed their minds after hearing it?

Sales-and-profit impact is the most satisfactory measure. For example, 9 Lives Cat Food sales increased 43 percent by the end of the Morris the Cat PR campaign. However, advertising and sales promotion had also been stepped up. Suppose total sales have increased $1 500 000, and management estimates that MPR contributed 15 percent of the total increase. Then the return on MPR investment is calculated as follows:

Total sales increase	$1 500 000
Estimated sales increase due to PR (15 percent)	225 000
Contribution margin on product sales (10 percent)	22 500
Total direct cost of MPR program	210 000
Contribution margin added by PR investment	$12 500
Return on MPR investment ($12 500/$10 000)	125%

SUMMARY

1. Advertising is any paid form of nonpersonal presentation and promotion of ideas, goods, or services by an identified sponsor. Advertisers include not only business firms but also charitable, nonprofit, and government agencies.

2. Developing an advertising program is a five-step process: (1) set advertising objectives; (2) establish a budget; (3) choose the advertising message and creative strategy; (4) decide on the media; and (5) evaluate communication and sales effects.

3. Sales promotion consists of a diverse collection of incentive tools, mostly short term, designed to stimulate quicker or greater purchase of particular products or services by consumers or the trade. Sales promotion includes tools for consumer promotion, trade promotion, and business and sales-force promotion (trade shows and conventions, contests for sales reps, and specialty advertising). In using sales promotion, a com-

pany must establish its objectives, select the tools, develop the program, pretest the program, implement and control it, and evaluate the results.

4. Events and experiences are a means to become part of special and more personally relevant moments in consumers' lives. Involvement with events can broaden and deepen the relationship of the sponsor with its target market, but only if managed properly.

5. Public relations (PR) involves a variety of programs designed to promote or protect a company's image or its individual products. Many companies today use marketing public relations (MPR) to support the marketing department in corporate or product promotion and image making. MPR can affect public awareness at a fraction of the cost of advertising, and is often much more credible. The main tools of PR are publications, events, news, speeches, public-service activities, and identity media.

APPLICATIONS

Marketing Debate: Has TV Advertising Lost Power?

Long deemed the most successful advertising medium, television advertising has received increased criticism as being too expensive and, even worse, no longer as effective as it once was. Critics maintain that consumers tune out too many ads by zipping and zapping and that it is difficult to make a strong impression. The future, some claim, is with online advertising. Supporters of TV advertising disagree, contending that the multi-sensory impact of TV is unsurpassed and that no other media option offers the same potential impact.

Take a position: TV advertising has faded in importance versus TV advertising is still the most powerful advertising medium.

Marketing Discussion

What are some of your favourite TV ads? Why? How effective are the message and creative strategies? How are they building brand equity?

Marketing Spotlight: Virgin Group

Flamboyant iconoclast Richard Branson roared onto the British stage in the 1970s with his innovative Virgin Records. He signed unknown artists that no one would touch and began a marathon of publicity that continues to this day. He has since sold Virgin Records (to Thorn-EMI for nearly US$1 billion in 1992), but he has created over 200 companies worldwide whose combined revenues exceed US$5 billion.

The Virgin name—the third most respected brand in Britain—and the Branson personality cement the 200 companies. The Virgin name appears on diverse products and services such as planes, trains, finance, soft drinks, music, mobile phones, holidays, cars, wines, publishing, and even bridal wear. Despite the diversity, all connote value for money, quality, innovation, fun, and a sense of competitive challenge. The Virgin Group looks for new opportunities in markets with underserved, overcharged customers and complacent competition. Branson called these customer-hostile competitors "big bad wolves." "Wherever we find them, there is a clear opportunity area for Virgin to do a much better job than the competition. We introduce trust, innovation and customer friendliness where they don't exist," Branson said.

For example, Branson launched Virgin Atlantic Airways to take on stodgy, overpriced British Airways. A master of the strategic publicity stunt, Branson announced the new airline in a way guaranteed to gain free advertising. Wearing World War I–era flying gear, he announced the formation of Virgin Atlantic Airways on February 29, 1984. The first Virgin flight, on June 22, 1984, took off laden with celebrities and media. The flight came equipped with a brass band, waiters from Maxim's in white tie and tails, and free-flowing champagne. The airborne party enjoyed international press coverage and millions of dollars' worth of free publicity. Branson knew that photographers have a job to do and they'd turn up at his events if he gave them a good reason.

Similarly, when Branson launched Virgin Cola in the United States in 1998, he steered an army tank down Fifth Avenue in New York, garnering interviews on each of the network morning TV shows as a result.

When Virgin Mobile entered Canada in March 2005, Branson, dressed as a superhero, slid down a cable from the top of a building into the middle of Toronto's Dundas Square. He then hopped onto the back of a monster truck, drove over three cars, and proceeded to save three nurses who were chained to the vehicles. The medical theme is part of the broader marketing campaign that is comparing phone plans from rival service providers Bell Mobility, Telus Mobility, and Rogers Wireless to a fictitious venereal disease called "The Catch." The theme was designed to bring home the message that Virgin is bringing competition back to the Canadian market by offering Canadian customers a mobile phone service with no catches: great rates, no hidden fees, and no contracts to sign.

The launch wasn't without controversy. The "nurses" were bleach-blonde models wearing white stilettos and very short skirts. Life-size cut-outs instantly began appearing in shopping malls and other retail outlets selling Virgin Mobile phones. The 21 000-member Registered Nurses' Association of Ontario demanded a public apology from Branson and an end to the campaign. Virgin Mobile spokeswoman Paula Lash said the company was not about to pull the advertising. "It's really meant to be quite tongue-in-cheek," she said. "We've taken this comic-strip approach to everything. Virgin's marketing is about being fun, edgy and irreverent. We apologize if it was offensive to some people, but for the most part, we think it will really connect with our target market"—mostly teenagers and young adults. The controversy succeeded in generating even more press for Virgin.

The Virgin Group evolves with each new business venture. "The brand is regenerated, rather than extended in the conventional sense, by each business we become involved in," Branson said. "We are in essence an unusual venture capital organization: a branded one." Rather than simply offering financial backing, the Virgin Group offers powerful branding and management resources to stagnant organizations that Branson acquires. Branson usually retains 51 percent control of all Virgin-branded businesses, but he insists on a highly decentralized and flat management structure so that employees are empowered to make decisions.

Although Branson avoids traditional market research for a "screw it, let's do it" attitude, he stays in touch through constant customer contact. When he first set up Virgin Atlantic, he called 50 customers every month to chat and get their feedback. He appeared in airports to rub elbows with customers, and if a plane was delayed, he handed out gift certificates to a Virgin Megastore or discounts on future travel.

Virgin's marketing campaigns include press and radio ads, direct mail, and point-of-sale material. Virgin Mobile, for example, rolled out a postcard advertising campaign offering consumers discounted offers on new phones.

To identify where listeners to Virgin's Web-based Virgin Radio reside, the company created a VIP club. Listeners join the club by giving their postal code, which then lets Virgin Radio target promotions and advertising to specific locations, just as a local radio station would.

Once known as the "hippie capitalist," now knighted by the Queen of England, Sir Richard Branson continues to look for new businesses and generate publicity in his characteristic charismatic style. Remembering the advice of his friend about publicity—"If you don't give them a photograph that will get them on the front page, they won't turn up at your next event"—Branson always gives them a reason.

DISCUSSION QUESTIONS

1. What have been the key success factors for Virgin?

2. Where is Virgin vulnerable? What should it watch out for?

3. What recommendations would you make to Virgin's senior marketing executives going forward? What should they be sure to do with the company's marketing?

Sources: "Virgin Mobile Launches in Canada—Branson Delivers the Cure for the 'Catch'," Virgin Mobil Press Release, Toronto, March 1, 2005, **www.virginmobile.ca/web/pages/media_02_e.htm**; "Nurses to Boycott 'Demeaning' Virgin Mobile Ads," Canadian Press, March 5, 2005, **www.ctv.ca/servlet/ArticleNews/story/CTVNews/1109982330327_18/?hub=Canada**; Sean Hargrave, "Making Waves," *New Media Age*, January 15, 2004, pp. 24–27; Adam Lashinsky, "Shootout In Gadget Land," *Fortune*, November 10, 2003, p. 74; Sam Hill and Glenn Rifkin, *Radical Marketing* (New York: Harper Business, 1999); "Virgin Holiday Store Hires HHM for Major Push." *Precision Marketing*, January 23, 2004, pp. 3–4; "Virgin Mobile Postcards Offer Discounts," *Precision Marketing*, January 23, 2004, pp. 5–6; **www.virgin.com**.

19

IN THIS CHAPTER, WE WILL ADDRESS THE FOLLOWING QUESTIONS:

- How can companies use integrated direct marketing for competitive advantage?

- How can companies do effective e-marketing?

- What decisions do companies face in designing a sales force?

- How do companies manage a sales force efficiently?

- How can salespeople improve selling, negotiating, and relationship marketing skills?

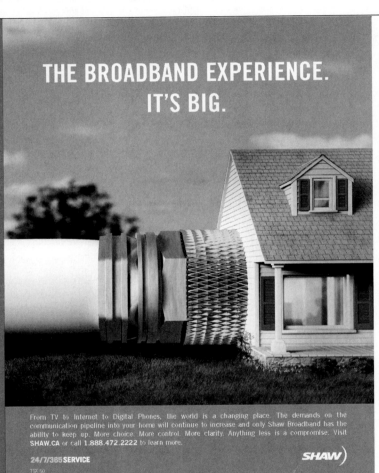

THE BROADBAND EXPERIENCE. IT'S BIG.

From TV to Internet to Digital Phones, the world is a changing place. The demands on the communication pipeline into your home will continue to increase and only Shaw Broadband has the ability to keep up. More choice. More control. More clarity. Anything less is a compromise. Visit **SHAW.CA** or call **1.888.472.2222** to learn more.

24/7/365 SERVICE

SHAW)

TSt 50

CHAPTER 19

Managing Personal Communications: Direct Marketing and Personal Selling

PROFILE: CANADIAN MARKETING EXCELLENCE

In an era of information superhighways, many marketers may believe that door-to-door selling to effectively reach consumers has gone the way of the dinosaurs. However, firms as diverse as Avon and Shaw Communications are proving how wrong such assumptions can be.

Shaw Communications Inc. is a diversified Canadian telecommunications company whose core business is providing broadband cable television, Internet, and satellite direct-to-home (DHT) services. It was founded in 1966 in Edmonton as the Capital Cable Television Co Ltd. Today it owns Star Choice (its satellite television arm) and Calgary-based Shaw Cable, the leading residential broadband service provider in western Canada, with approximately 2.1 million cable television customers and over 1 million Internet customers. The company prides itself on the quality of its products and its "customer care" services.

Shaw Cable, which has been using door-to-door sales since 1971, still generates 15 to 50 percent of its business (depending on the product and season) by using this technique, according to Phil Murray, vice-president of sales. "It's an incremental channel whereas in the past it was viewed as more of a primary channel," says Murray, adding that "any incremental sale is a good sale."

While Shaw uses a wide variety of direct marketing techniques, including direct mail and tele-marketing, the company relies on door-to-door sales because it has some advantages over other forms of marketing. Person-to-person marketing is still one of the most effective ways of starting a relationship and allows prospective customers to connect with a company in a way that can't be replicated by phone or via direct mail. For example, Shaw uses door-to-door sales to demonstrate digital technology to prospective customers on the spot. Such demonstrations allow the firm to instantly hook the customer up, whereas a telephone sales call might result in something like "Oh it sounds like a great offer, but I'm going to pass" because potential customers don't want to bother with the inconvenience of scheduling a visit and installation.

Personal sales forces can be hugely expensive, but Shaw keeps its costs relatively low by double-tasking its representatives. They work as commission-based independent contractors and double as technicians who can install cable or Internet service. Shaw's multi-pronged strategy has proven successful, and it has been able to ward off competition by the much larger national players.

Sources: Samson Okalow, "Knock on Wood," *Strategy Magazine*, January 12, 2004, p. 9; Samson Okalow, "Who'll Control the Future of Digital TV?" *Strategy Magazine*, December 1, 2003, p. 2; Shaw Communications Web site, **www.shaw.ca/en-ca/AboutShaw**.

Personalizing communications—and saying and doing the right thing to the right person at the right time—is critical. In this chapter, we consider how companies personalize their marketing communications to have more of an impact. We begin by evaluating direct marketing; then we consider personal selling and the sales force.

Direct Marketing

Direct marketing is the use of consumer-direct (CD) channels to reach and deliver goods and services to customers without using marketing intermediaries. These channels include direct mail, catalogues, telemarketing, interactive TV, kiosks, Web sites, and mobile devices.

Direct marketers seek a measurable response, typically a customer order. This is sometimes called **direct-order marketing**. Today, many direct marketers use direct marketing to build a long-term relationship with the customer.[1] They send birthday cards, information materials, or small premiums to certain customers. Airlines, hotels, and other businesses build strong customer relationships through frequency award programs and club programs.

Direct marketing is one of the fastest growing avenues for serving customers. More and more business marketers have turned to direct mail and telemarketing in response to the high and increasing costs of reaching business markets through a sales force. Figure 19.1 provides a breakdown of the various types of direct marketing.

One of the most pervasive loyalty marketing programs in Canada is the AIR MILES program run by the Loyalty Group. Over 100 sponsor firms belong to the program, which allows a whopping 70 percent of Canadian households to collect points they can use toward travel and other reward options. See how *Chatelaine* magazine used a direct marketing campaign centred on the AIR MILES program to build new relationships and strengthen existing ones:

Chatelaine and the AIR MILES® Reward Program

Using a genie-in-a-bottle concept as a basis for its "What Women Want" contest, *Chatelaine* asked women to make three wishes. Choices included "Buns of steel" and "Room full of orchids." In return for sharing their wishes, women could win prizes as high as 50 000 AIR MILES reward miles—enough for five flights around the world or 2000 movie passes. Awareness of the contest was established by initially e-mailing a targeted group of AIR MILES collectors and Chatelaine.com users who had opted in to receive online communication from either of the two companies. Using viral marketing, recipients were then encouraged to pass the e-mail along to friends and family for additional chances to win. In addition to information at www.chatelaine.com and www.airmiles.ca, a magazine ad in *Chatelaine* drove users online to enter the contest and send the e-mail to a friend. When contestants went to the contest Web site, *Chatelaine* was able to make a brand statement and show women the different areas of the magazine, while educating consumers as to how AIR MILES sponsors help women achieve a breadth of rewards faster and more easily while fulfilling some of their wishes at the same time. The response to this online marketing effort was huge: 98 000 entries from 65 000 entrants. Chatelaine believed its success resulted from what it learned from previous efforts. Given Chatelaine's and AIR MILES' commitment to privacy, it was very important to "raise it up a notch" and clearly promise that friends and family would not be contacted unless they opted in.[2]

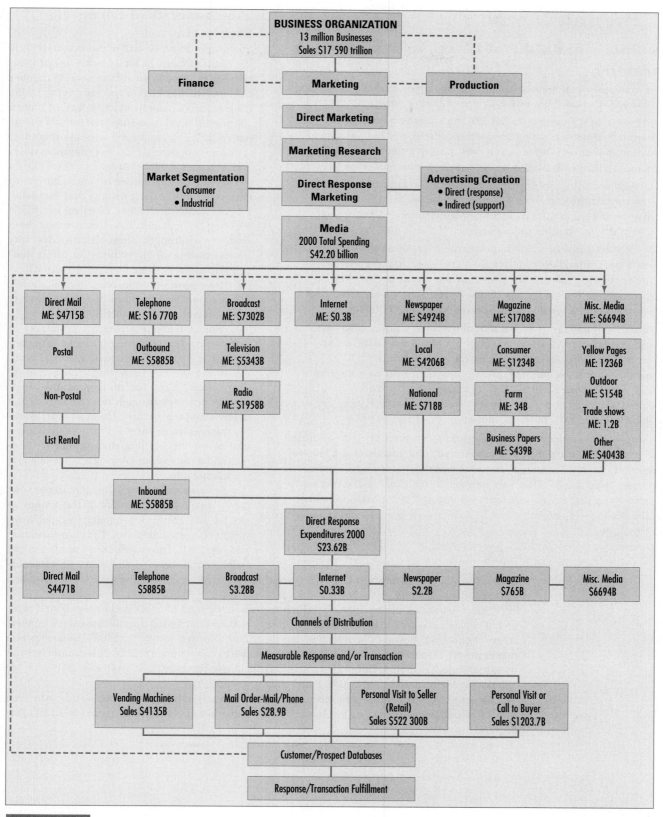

FIGURE 19.1

Direct Marketing Flow Chart

Source: Adapted from *Direct Marketing* magazine, 224 Seventh Street, Garden City, New York, 11530-5771.

Marketing Memo

The Public and Ethical Issues in Direct Marketing

Direct marketers and their customers usually enjoy mutually rewarding relationships. Occasionally, however, a darker side emerges:

- *Irritation.* Many people do not like the increasing number of hard-sell direct-marketing solicitations. Especially bothersome are dinnertime or late-night phone calls, poorly trained callers, and computerized calls placed by auto-dial recorded-message players.

- *Unfairness.* Some direct marketers take advantage of impulsive or less sophisticated buyers. TV shopping shows and infomercials may be the worst culprits with their smooth-talking hosts and claims of drastic price reductions.

- *Deception and fraud.* Some direct marketers design mailers and write copy intended to mislead buyers. They may exaggerate product size, performance claims, or the "retail price." The Competition Bureau and its Phone Busters hotline reported over $2 million in losses due to telephone fraud in 2003 alone.

- *Invasion of privacy.* It seems that almost every time consumers order products by mail or telephone, enter a sweepstakes, apply for a credit card, or take out a magazine subscription, their names, addresses, and purchasing behaviour may be added to several company databases. Critics worry that marketers may know too much about consumers' lives, and that they may use this knowledge to take unfair advantage.

People in the direct-marketing industry are attempting to address these issues. They know that, left unattended, such problems will lead to increasingly negative consumer attitudes, lower response rates, and calls for greater regulation. In the final analysis, most direct marketers want the same thing that consumers want: honest and well-designed marketing offers targeted only to those consumers who appreciate hearing about the offer.

The Benefits of Direct Marketing

The extraordinary growth of direct marketing is the result of many factors. *Market demassification* has resulted in an ever-increasing number of market niches. Higher costs of driving, traffic congestion, parking headaches, lack of time, a shortage of retail sales help, and lines at checkout counters all encourage at-home shopping. Consumers appreciate toll-free phone numbers and Web sites available 24 hours a day, 7 days a week, and direct marketers' commitment to customer service. The growth of next-day delivery via FedEx and other couriers has made ordering fast and easy. In addition, many chain stores have dropped slower-moving specialty items, creating an opportunity for direct marketers to promote these items to interested buyers. The growth of the Internet, e-mail, mobile phones, and fax machines has made product selection and ordering much simpler.

Direct marketing benefits customers in many ways. Home shopping can be fun, convenient, and hassle-free. It saves time and introduces consumers to a larger selection of merchandise. They can do comparative shopping by browsing through mail catalogues and online shopping services. They can order goods for themselves or others. Business customers also benefit by learning about available products and services without tying up time in meeting salespeople.

Sellers benefit as well. Direct marketers can buy a mailing list containing the names of almost any group: left-handed people, overweight people, millionaires. They can customize and personalize messages. Direct marketers can build a continuous relationship with each customer. The parents of a newborn baby will receive periodic mailings describing new clothes, toys, and other goods as the child grows.

Direct marketing can be timed to reach prospects at the right moment and receive higher readership because it is sent to more interested prospects. Direct marketing permits the testing of alternative media and messages in search of the most cost-effective approach. Direct marketing also makes the direct marketer's offer and strategy less visible to competitors. Finally, direct marketers can measure responses to their campaigns to decide which have been the most profitable. (However, see "Marketing Memo: Public and Ethical Issues in Direct Marketing.")

Direct marketers can use a number of channels to reach individual prospects and customers: direct mail, catalogue marketing, telemarketing, TV and other direct-response media, kiosk marketing, and e-marketing.

Moosehead Breweries

Saint John, New Brunswick–based Moosehead uses direct marketing as part of its strategy. Having developed an extensive consumer database, as part of an overall customer intimacy program, Moosehead is able to use direct mail and e-mail marketing campaigns to further engage its customers. Consumers receive mailings that contain thank-you messages, birthday and holiday greetings, reward/bonus mailings, advanced notice of events, and special offers. The program involves all major brands under the Moosehead family umbrella, both nationally and regionally, and encourages customers to visit the new Moosehead Lager merchandise site (www.mooseheadcountrystore.com), where a variety of products are available.[3]

Direct Mail

Direct-mail marketing involves sending an offer, announcement, reminder, or other item to a person. Using highly selective mailing lists, direct marketers send out millions of mail pieces each year—letters, flyers, foldouts, and other "salespeople with wings." Some direct marketers mail audiotapes, videotapes, CDs, and computer diskettes to prospects and customers.

Direct mail is a popular medium because it permits target market selectivity, can be personalized, is flexible, and allows early testing and response measurement. Although the cost per thousand people reached is higher than with mass media, the people reached are much better prospects. Direct mail may be paper-based and handled by Canada Post, telegraphic services, or for-profit mail carriers such as FedEx, Purolator, or UPS. Alternatively, marketers may employ fax mail, e-mail, or voice mail to sell direct.

Direct-mail marketing has passed through a number of stages:

- *"Carpet bombing."* Direct mailers gather or buy as many names as possible and send out a mass mailing. Usually the response rate is very low.
- *Database marketing.* Direct marketers mine the database to identify prospects who would have the most interest in an offer.
- *Interactive marketing.* Direct marketers include a telephone number and Web address, and offer to print coupons from the Web site. Recipients can contact the company with questions. The company uses the interaction as an opportunity to up-sell, cross-sell, and deepen the relationship.
- *Real-time personalized marketing.* Direct marketers know enough about each customer to customize and personalize the offer and message.
- *Lifetime value marketing.* Direct marketers develop a plan for lifetime marketing to each valuable customer, based on knowledge of life events and transitions.

Moosehead Breweries uses direct-mail campaigns both regionally and nationally to engage its customers.

One company long recognized for its strong, beneficial focus on customers is Mountain Equipment Co-op (MEC), which sells outdoor/casual clothing and equipment through mail order, online catalogues, and retail stores. To maximize customer satisfaction, MEC has an unequivocal, 100 percent "rock solid" guarantee for all purchases. MEC goes one step further, however. Unlike most retailers, it also guarantees the product selection advice offered through its catalogue, Web site, and staff; if an item you've purchased based on this advice turns out to be unsuitable, you can bring it back![4]

In constructing an effective direct-mail campaign, direct marketers must decide on their objectives, target markets, and prospects; offer elements, means of testing the campaign, and measures of campaign success.

ANZ Bank

Australia's ANZ Bank's "Change Your Home to Suit Your Life" campaign was chosen winner of the 2003 Direct Marketing Association award as top international direct and interactive marketing campaign. Direct response agency M&C Saatchi used sophisticated data analysis to identify and tailor a campaign to raise interest in home loans. Database profiling was used to select customers from 16 distinct groups of targets. Direct mail then offered information specific to each target audience, reflecting the recipient's situation and specific needs. As a result of the campaign, ANZ received a record number of calls to its home buyers line—an 83 percent year-on-year increase—a 3 percent rise in home loan applications, and a 47 percent increase in campaign recognition. The direct mail campaign specifically resulted in 4922 new accounts or mortgages with a conversion rate of 6 percent.[5]

OBJECTIVES Most direct marketers aim to receive an order from prospects. A campaign's success is judged by the response rate. An order-response rate of 2 percent is normally considered good, although this number varies with product category and price. Direct mail can achieve other communication objectives as well, such as producing prospect leads, strengthening customer relationships, informing and educating customers, reminding customers of offers, and reinforcing recent customer purchase decisions.

TARGET MARKETS AND PROSPECTS Direct marketers need to identify the characteristics of prospects and customers who are most able, willing, and ready to buy. Most direct marketers apply the R-F-M formula (*recency, frequency, monetary amount*) for rating and selecting customers. For any proposed offering, the company selects customers according to how much time has passed since their last purchase, how many times they have purchased, and how much they have spent since becoming a customer. Suppose the company is offering a leather jacket. It might make this offer to customers who made their last purchase between 30 and 60 days ago, who make three to six purchases a year, and who have spent at least $100 since becoming customers. Points are established for varying R-F-M levels, and each customer is scored. The higher the score, the more attractive the customer. The mailing is sent only to the most attractive customers.[6]

Prospects can also be identified on the basis of such variables as age, sex, income, education, and previous mail-order purchases. Occasions provide a good departure point for segmentation. New parents will be in the market for baby clothes and baby toys; students entering university will buy computers and small television sets; newlyweds will be looking for housing, furniture, appliances, and bank loans. Another useful segmentation variable is consumer lifestyle or "passion" groups, such as computer buffs, cooking buffs, and outdoor buffs. For business markets, Dun & Bradstreet operates an information service that provides a wealth of data.

In B2B direct marketing, the prospect is often not an individual but a group of people or a committee that includes both decision makers and multiple decision influencers. See "Marketing Memo: When Your Customer Is a Committee" for tips on crafting a direct-mail campaign aimed at business buyers.

Once the target market is defined, the direct marketer needs to obtain specific names. The company's best prospects are customers who have bought its products in the past. Additional names can be obtained by advertising some free offer. The direct marketer can also buy lists of names from list brokers, but these lists often have problems, including name duplication, incomplete data, and obsolete addresses. The better lists include overlays of demographic and psychographic information. Direct marketers typically buy and test a sample before buying more names from the same list.

Marketing Memo

When Your Customer Is a Committee

One of the many advantages of database marketing and direct mail is that they allow you to tailor format, offer, and sell messages to the target audience(s). Business marketers can create a series of interrelated and reinforced mailings to decision makers and decision influencers. Here are some tips for increasing success in selling to a customer-by-committee:

- When creating lead generation and follow-up mailings, remember that most business mailings are screened once, twice, or even more before reaching your targeted audience.
- Plan and budget for a series of mailings to each of your customer-by-committee members. Timing and multiple exposures are critical in reaching these audiences.
- Whenever possible, mail to individuals by name and title. Using the title helps the in-office mail screener reroute your mailing if the individual addressed has moved on to another job.
- Do not necessarily use the same format and size for reaching all your targeted audiences. A more expensive-looking envelope may reach the president or CEO, but it may be equally effective to use a less expensive, less personal format to reach other decision influencers.
- Tell your customer-by-committee that you are communicating with others in the organization.
- Make your decision influencers feel important. They can be your biggest advocates.
- When communicating with different audiences, make sure you anticipate—and address—their individual buying objectives and objections.
- When your database or mailing lists cannot help you reach all the key people, ask the individual you are addressing to pass along your information.
- When doing a lead-generation mailing, make sure to ask for the names and titles of those who might be interested and involved in the buying decision. Enter this information into your database.
- Even though it may seem like a lot of work (and expense) to write different versions of the same letter and create different offers, there is a big payoff. The final decision maker may be interested in having a payback calculated, but others may be interested in day-to-day benefits such as safety, convenience, and time savings. Tailor your offer to your targets.

Source: Adapted from Pat Friesen, "When Your Customer Is a Committee," *Target Marketing* (August 1998): 40.

OFFER ELEMENTS Nash sees the offer strategy as consisting of five elements—the *product*, the *offer*, the *medium*, the *distribution method*, and the *creative strategy*.[7] Fortunately, all of these elements can be tested.

In addition to these elements, the direct-mail marketer has to decide on five components of the mailing itself: the outside envelope, sales letter, circular, reply form, and reply envelope. Here are some findings:

1. The outside envelope will be more effective if it contains an illustration, preferably in colour, or a catchy reason to open the envelope, such as the announcement of a contest, premium, or benefit. Envelopes are more effective when they contain a colourful commemorative stamp, when the address is hand-typed or handwritten, and when the envelope differs in size or shape from standard envelopes.[8]

2. The sales letter should use a personal salutation and start with a headline in bold type. The letter should be printed on good-quality paper and be brief. A computer-typed letter usually outperforms a printed letter, and the presence of a pithy P.S. increases the response rate, as does the signature of someone whose title is important.

3. In most cases, a colourful circular accompanying the letter will increase the response rate by more than its cost.

4. Direct mailers should feature a toll-free number and also send recipients to their Web site. Coupons should be printed out at the Web site.

5. The inclusion of a postage-free reply envelope will dramatically increase the response rate.

Direct mail should be followed up by an e-mail, which is less expensive and less intrusive than a telemarketing call.

TESTING ELEMENTS One of the great advantages of direct marketing is the ability to test, under real marketplace conditions, different elements of an offer strategy, such as products, product features, copy platform, mailer type, envelope, prices, or mailing lists.

Direct marketers must remember that response rates typically understate a campaign's long-term impact. Suppose only 2 percent of the recipients who receive a direct-mail piece advertising Samsonite luggage place an order. A much larger percentage became aware of the product (direct mail has high readership), and some percentage may have formed an intention to buy at a later date (either by mail or at a retail outlet). Furthermore, some of them may mention Samsonite luggage to others as a result of the direct-mail piece. To derive a more comprehensive estimate of the promotion's impact, some companies are measuring direct marketing's impact on awareness, intention to buy, and word of mouth.

MEASURING CAMPAIGN SUCCESS: LIFETIME VALUE By adding up the planned campaign costs, the direct marketer can figure out in advance the needed break-even response rate. This rate must be net of returned merchandise and bad debts. Returned merchandise can kill an otherwise effective campaign. The direct marketer needs to analyze the main causes of returned merchandise (late shipment, defective merchandise, damage in transit, not as advertised, incorrect order fulfillment).

By carefully analyzing past campaigns, direct marketers can steadily improve performance. Even when a specific campaign fails to break even in the short run, it can still be profitable in the long run if customer lifetime is factored in (see Chapter 5). A customer's ultimate value is not revealed by a purchase response to a particular mailing. Rather, it is the expected profit made on all future purchases net of customer acquisition and maintenance costs. For an average customer, one would calculate the average customer longevity, average customer annual expenditure, and average gross margin, minus the average cost of customer acquisition and maintenance (properly discounted for the opportunity cost of money).[9]

Catalogue Marketing

In catalogue marketing, companies may send full-line merchandise catalogues, specialty consumer catalogues, and business catalogues, usually in print form but also sometimes as CDs, videos, or online. Zellers and Canadian Tire send general merchandise catalogues. Victoria's Secret sends specialty clothing catalogues to the upper-middle-class market. Through its catalogues, Avon sells cosmetics and IKEA sells furniture. Many of these direct marketers have found that combining catalogues and Web sites can be an effective way to sell. Thousands of small businesses also issue specialty catalogues. Large businesses such as Staples, Merck, and others send catalogues to business prospects and customers.

Catalogue marketing has a long history in Canada. Since the 1880s, Canadians living in isolated regions waited anxiously for catalogues to arrive. So beloved was the Eaton's catalogue, for example, that it was affectionately known by many nicknames, including the "Bible" and the "Wish Book."[10]

Catalogues are a huge business in North America. The Direct Marketing Association estimates that there are currently up to 10 000 mail-order catalogues of all kinds. Canadian Gardening, for example, lists over 500 catalogues for its gardening enthusiasts. However, the number of catalogues streaming into consumers' mailboxes is not the only measure of growth in this business. Cataloguers have gotten a big boost from the Internet—about three-quarters of catalogue companies present merchandise and take orders over the Internet. Some catalogue marketers, like Canadian Tire, are integrating their print editions with online editions. Others, like Nike Canada, are totally replacing their print catalogues with virtual versions.

Nike Canada

Every spring Nike Canada mailed catalogues to fitness instructors, offering them the latest aerobic gear at discount prices in the hope they would buy the merchandise and inspire their students to do the same. However, because only limited numbers of catalogues were produced, they were very expensive to print and distribute. CyberSight Canada, an Internet marketing services firm, offered a solution to the problem by creating a Web site that would serve as a virtual catalogue (www.nikeinp.ca). Members of the Instructor Network are mailed passwords to gain access to the site. Julia Maughan, national sports marketing coordinator for Nike Canada, says, "Our objectives were to simplify the ordering process, reduce the cost of the catalogue, and increase the number of orders from instructors." The effort has been a huge success. Online orders exceeded those generated by the print catalogue, and the company's expectations for its new digital program were surpassed![11]

Market research conducted by Canada Post suggests, however, that Canadians overwhelmingly prefer hard-copy catalogues to online versions, and would rather receive catalogues through the mail than pick them up from a store.[12] The success of a catalogue business also depends on the company's ability to manage its customer lists carefully so that there is little duplication or bad debts, to control its inventory carefully, to offer quality merchandise so that returns are low, and to project a distinctive image. See how one Canadian company has achieved success with its catalogues:

Awesome Ewe

Launched in 1999, this online mail-order business, which sells fine wool to the knitting community, began simply as a test site for a family of e-commerce software that Len and Marge Stalker developed. The site originally featured 4000 "brand-recognized" products aimed at knitters. Today Awesome Ewe's product line has grown to 18 000 products. Clients can purchase wool and patterns or redeem gift certificates in a couple of clicks. The company's e-mail newsletter has 9000 opt-in subscribers, and the Web site gets between 500 and 900 unique visitors a day. Stalker's online survey response rate from opt-in subscribers is 7 to 10 percent. Sales have been doubling yearly and the owners expect to reach $500 000 in 2004. The site has been so successful that it is featured as a case study on B.C.'s Ministry of Small Business and Economic Development's eBusiness Connection Web site.[13]

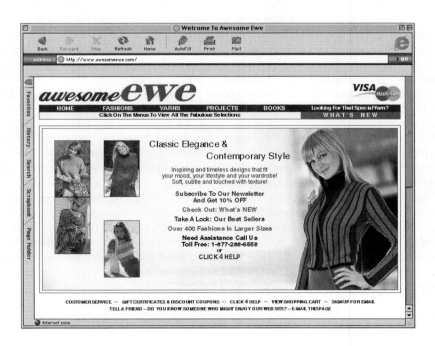

The Awesome Ewe built its entire business online by providing high-quality products and service to its niche market.

Global consumers in Asia and Europe are catching on to the catalogue craze. In the 1990s, North American catalogue companies such as L.L. Bean, MEC, Eddie Bauer, and Patagonia began setting up operations in Europe and Japan—and with great success. In just a few years, catalogues have won 5 percent of the US$20 billion Japanese mail-order catalogue market. A full 90 percent of L.L. Bean's international sales come from Japan.

Business marketers are making inroads as well. Sales to overseas (mainly European) markets have driven earnings increases at Viking Office Products and computer and network equipment cataloguer Black Box Corporation. Viking has had success in Europe because it has fewer superstores and is very receptive to mail order. Black Box owes much of its international growth to its customer service policies, which are unmatched in Europe.[14] By putting their entire catalogues online, catalogue companies have better access to global consumers than ever before, and save considerable printing and mailing costs in the process. By clicking on the appropriate icon, international shoppers can use Canadian-based Tilley Endurables Web site (**www.tilley.com**) to order products using their own currencies.

Telemarketing

Telemarketing is the use of the telephone and call centres to attract prospects, sell to existing customers, and provide service by taking orders and answering questions. Telemarketing helps companies increase revenue, reduce selling costs, and improve customer satisfaction.

Companies use call centres for *inbound telemarketing* (receiving calls from customers) and *outbound telemarketing* (initiating calls to prospects and customers). In fact, companies carry out four types of telemarketing:

- *Telesales.* Taking orders from catalogues or ads and also doing outbound calling. They can cross-sell the company's other products, upgrade orders, introduce new products, open new accounts, and reactivate former accounts.

- *Telecoverage.* Calling customers to maintain and nurture key account relationships and give more attention to neglected accounts.

- *Teleprospecting.* Generating and qualifying new leads for closure by another sales channel.

- *Customer service and technical support.* Answering service and technical questions.

Telemarketing is increasingly used in business as well as consumer marketing. Raleigh Bicycles uses telemarketing to reduce the amount of personal selling needed for contacting its dealers. In the first year, sales-force travel costs were reduced by 50 percent and sales in a single quarter went up 34 percent. With the increased diffusion of videophones, telemarketing will increasingly replace or supplement more expensive field sales calls. An increasing number of salespeople have made five- and six-figure sales without ever meeting the customer face-to-face. Effective telemarketing depends on choosing the right telemarketers, training them well, and providing performance incentives.

Telemarketing is a major industry in Canada, employing more than 270 000 people across the country. Marketers spend approximately twice the amount on telemarketing as they do on advertising, which isn't surprising since it generates approximately $16 billion in sales. Despite its importance as a major direct-marketing tool, it can be intrusive. Many Canadians have run out of patience with some unethical telemarketers who do not follow the Canadian Marketing Association's (CMA) code of ethics. In response, the Canadian Radio-television and Telecommunications Commission (CRTC) developed new regulations in 2004 to help Canadians ward off unwanted telemarketing and faxes. Among the changes is the requirement that telemarketers give their name and identify their organization before they begin their sales pitch, and give a toll-free telephone number that people can call with questions or complaints. Companies must also maintain lists of people who don't want their numbers called. The CRTC is also contemplating a national "Do Not Call" list similar to the one recently established in the United States. Even though the CMA has maintained a voluntary do not call list since 1988, which contains about 340 000 names, many believe a national list is needed since the list only applies to companies that are members of the CMA. While the CMA supported the development of "Do Not Call" lists, as an advocate for the telemarketing industry, it expressed concern about the other regulations, claiming they would put an enormous financial burden on business. In response to these concerns, the CRTC suspended enforcement of the new rules in September 2004 and is reviewing the potential impact of the regulations.[15]

Other Media for Direct-Response Marketing

Direct marketers use all the major media to make offers to potential buyers. Newspapers and magazines carry abundant print ads offering books, articles of clothing, appliances, vacations, and other goods and services that individuals can order by dialling a toll-free number. Radio ads present offers to listeners 24 hours a day.

TELEVISION Television is used by direct marketers in several ways:

1. *Direct-response advertising.* Some companies prepare 30- and 60-minute infomercials that attempt to combine the sell of commercials with the draw of educational information and entertainment. *Infomercials* can be seen as a cross between a sales call and a television ad and cost roughly US$250 000 to US$500 000 to make. A number of people have become famous with late-night channel switchers (e.g., Tony Robbins, Victoria Principal, and Kathy Smith). Increasingly, companies selling products that are complicated, technologically advanced, or simply require a great deal of explanation are turning to infomercials (Callaway Golf, Carnival Cruises, Mercedes, Microsoft, Philips Electronics, Universal Studios, and even the online job search site, Monster.com).[16] They share the product's story and benefits with millions of additional prospects at a cost-per-lead or cost-per-order that usually matches or beats direct mail or print ads.[17]

2. *At-home shopping channels.* Some television channels are dedicated to selling goods and services. On the Shopping Channel, which broadcasts 24 hours a day, the program's hosts offer bargain prices on such products as clothing, jewellery, lamps, collectible dolls, and power tools. Viewers call in orders on a toll-free number and receive delivery within 48 hours. Millions of adults watch home shopping programs, and close to half of them buy merchandise.

3. *Videotext and interactive TV.* The consumer's TV set is linked with a seller's catalogue by cable or telephone lines. Consumers can place orders via a special keyboard device connected to the system. Much research is now going on to combine TV, telephones, and computers into interactive TV.

The Hospital for Sick Children Foundation

The fund-raising arm of Toronto's Hospital for Sick Children uses direct marketing as a cornerstone of its overall marketing strategy. Recently, it began making direct-response television (DRTV) a key part of the foundation's efforts, which typically has fund-raising goals in excess of $50 million. The foundation created a one-hour DRTV program called *Place of Miracles: Inside the Hospital for Sick Children* in order to boost support and raise funds for its Miracle Club, a monthly donation program. The program, produced by EagleCom in Toronto, used a combination of individual patient stories and appeals from Canadian celebrities to support the hospital. Results from the one-hour program (along with its half-hour version and three two-minute segments) have showed considerable success; 61 percent of callers pledged donations, compared to the average for DRTV efforts of 45 percent.[18]

KIOSK MARKETING A kiosk is a small building or structure that might house a selling or information unit. The name describes newsstands, refreshment stands, and freestanding carts whose vendors sell watches, costume jewellery, and other items. The carts appear in bus and rail stations and along aisles in a mall. The term also covers computer-linked vending machines and "customer-order-placing machines" in stores, airports, and other locations. All of these are direct-selling tools. Some marketers have adapted the self-service feature of kiosks to their businesses. McDonald's found that customers who used its kiosks to order spent 30 percent more per order.[19]

Interactive Marketing

The newest channels for direct marketing are electronic.[20] The Internet provides marketers and consumers with opportunities for much greater *interaction* and *individualization*. Companies in the past would send standard media—magazines, newsletters, ads—to everyone. Today these companies can send individualized content and consumers themselves can further individualize the content. Today companies can interact and dialogue with much larger groups than ever in the past.

The exchange process in the age of information, however, has become increasingly customer-initiated and customer-controlled. Marketers and their representatives must wait until customers agree to participate in the exchange. Even after marketers enter the exchange process, customers define the rules of engagement, and insulate themselves with the help of agents and intermediaries if they so choose. Customers define what information they need, what offerings they are interested in, and what prices they are willing to pay.[21]

Electronic marketing is showing explosive growth. According to 24/7 Canada, Internet ad spending is expected to grow the fastest of all advertising mediums, reaching $306 million in 2008, an increase of 15.5 percent over 2003 figures.[22] More than half of online Canadians have broadband capabilities (a rate that far outpaces our U.S. neighbours) necessary for swift downloading of dense digital video and music files.[23] These new capabilities will spur the growth of rich media ads that combine animation, video, and sound with interactive features.

Axe Deodorant

Winner of *Business 2.0*'s 2003 Sweet Spot Award for Most Innovative Campaign, Unilever's Axe Deodorant body spray was launched in 2002 targeting a younger 18- to 24-year-old male audience interested in improving their appeal to the opposite sex. The centrepiece of the effort, designed by ad agency Bartle Bogle Hegarty, was a set of commercials purporting to be home videos and playing only on Axe's Web site (www.theaxeeffect.com). In each, an attractive young woman is instantly attracted by a whiff of Axe deodorant. In one 25-second clip, a high school cheerleader sprints onto a football field to tackle an Axe-saturated ball carrier. The agency's assumption was that this demographic group—95 percent of whom spent at least four hours online—preferred to discover brands, not to be sold them. The campaign bypassed conventional TV ads in favour of banner ads on Web sites of men's magazines *Maxim* and *FHM* as well as on AtomFilms, a repository of quirky short movies. The banners clicked through to a flashy Web site where surfers could view the video clips. The campaign ROI exceeded all expectations. The site received seven times as many hits as expected. Four months into the campaign, 1.7 million people had visited the site and a third of them reported that they had been sent there by friends.[24]

Benefits of Interactive Marketing

Interactive marketing offers many unique benefits.[25] It is highly accountable and its effects can be easily traced. Eddie Bauer cut its marketing cost per sale by 74 percent by concentrating on higher-performing ads.[26] The Web offers the advantage of "contextual placements." Marketers can buy ads from sites that are related to their offerings, as well as place advertising based on contextual keywords from online search outfits like Google. In that way, the Web can reach people when they have actually started the buying process. Light consumers of other media, especially television, can be reached. The Web is especially effective at reaching people during the day. Young, high-income, high-education consumers' total online media consumption exceeds that of TV.[27]

Designing an Attractive Web Site

Clearly all companies need to consider and evaluate e-marketing and e-purchasing opportunities. A key challenge is designing a site that is attractive on first viewing and interesting enough to encourage repeat visits.

Rayport and Jaworski have proposed that effective Web sites feature seven design elements that they call the 7Cs:[28]

- *Context*. Layout and design.
- *Content*. Text, pictures, sound, and video the site contains.
- *Community*. How the site enables user-to-user communication.
- *Customization*. Site's ability to tailor itself to different users or to allow users to personalize the site.
- *Communication*. How the site enables site-to-user, user-to-site, or two-way communication.
- *Connection*. Degree that the site is linked to other sites.
- *Commerce*. Site's capabilities to enable commercial transactions.

To encourage repeat visits, companies need to pay special attention to context and content factors and also embrace another "C"—constant change.[29]

Visitors will judge a site's performance on its ease of use and its physical attractiveness. Ease-of-use breaks down into three attributes: (1) the Web site downloads quickly, (2) the first page is easy to understand, and (3) the visitor finds it easy to navigate to other pages that open quickly. Physical attractiveness is determined by the following factors: (1) the individual pages are clean looking and not overly crammed with content, (2) the typefaces and font sizes are very readable, and (3) the site makes good use of colour (and sound).

Context factors facilitate repeat visits, but they do not ensure that this happens. Returning to a site depends on content. The content must be interesting, useful, and continuously changing. Certain types of content function well to attract first-time visitors and to bring them back again: (1) deep information with links to related sites, (2) changing news of interest, (3) changing free offers to visitors, (4) contests and sweepstakes, (5) humour and jokes, and (6) games.

Companies are also paying attention to how people buy once they are shopping online. See "Marketing Memo: Just Your Type" for a look at five categories of online buyers.

Marketing Memo

Just Your Type

Marketers have analyzed customers and markets in terms of gender, age, ethnicity, and other characteristics for decades. But demographics aren't the only tools for slicing up an online market. Market research firm Miller-Williams Inc. splits online buyers into five categories:

> *Sensibles*, at 37%, are the most numerous of all online shoppers, the easiest to satisfy and probably the best customers. *Agonizers*, representing 10%, do lots of comparison shopping, but aren't as price oriented as *Hagglers*, who make up 34%. *Loaners*, representing 15%, emphasize ease of use in their shopping experience. About 5% of online shoppers are Web-savvy but fickle *Techies*.

The takeaway message of this segmentation is that you need to know who your customers are and make sure you aren't offering something they don't want or need. "If you know your buyers are hagglers," reasons Amy Ferraro, director of research for Miller-Williams Inc., "you know you need to target them with coupons."

Source: Adapted from Mark Henricks, "Net Meeting," *Entrepreneur* (February 2003): 55.

Placing Ads and Promotion Online

A company has to decide which forms of Internet advertising will be most cost-effective in achieving advertising objectives. **Banner ads** are small rectangular boxes containing text and perhaps a picture. Companies pay to place banner ads on relevant Web sites. The larger the audience reached, the more the placement will cost. Some banners on Web sites are not paid for, but instead are accepted on a barter basis. In the early days of the Internet, viewers clicked on roughly 2 to 3 percent of the banner ads they saw, but that percentage quickly plummeted and advertisers began to explore other forms of communication.

Many companies get their name on the Internet by sponsoring special content on Web sites that carry news, financial information, and so on. **Sponsorships** are best placed in well-targeted sites where they can offer relevant information or service. The sponsor pays for showing the content and in turn receives acknowledgment as the sponsor of that particular service on the Web site.

A **microsite** is a limited area on the Web managed and paid for by an external advertiser/company. Microsites are particularly relevant for companies selling low-interest products such as insurance. People rarely visit an insurance company's Web site. However, the insurance company can create a microsite on used-car sites that offers advice for buyers of used cars and at the same time a good insurance deal.

Interstitials are advertisements, often with video or animation, that pop up between changes on a Web site. Ads for Johnson & Johnson's Tylenol headache reliever pop up on brokers' Web sites whenever the stock market falls by 100 points or more. Because consumers found pop-up ads intrusive and distracting, many computer users install software to block these ads.[30]

The hottest growth area has been **search-related ads**.[31] Thirty-five percent of all searches are reportedly for products or services. Search terms are used as a proxy for the consumer's consumption interests and relevant links to product or service offerings are listed alongside the search results from Google, Yahoo!, and MSN. Advertisers pay only if people click on the links. The cost per click depends on how high the link is ranked and the popularity of the keyword searched. Average click-through is about 2 percent, much more than comparable online ads.[32] At an average of 35 cents, paid search is a lot cheaper than the $1-per-lead for Yellow Pages listings. One Samsung executive estimated that it was 50 times cheaper to reach 1000 people online than on TV. The company now spends 10 percent of its advertising budget online.[33] A newer trend, **content-target advertising**, links ads not to keywords but to the content of Web pages.

Companies can set up **alliances** and **affiliate programs**. When one Internet company works with another one, they end up advertising each other. AOL has created many successful alliances with other companies. Amazon has almost 1 million affiliates that post Amazon banners on their Web sites. Companies can also undertake guerrilla-marketing actions to publicize the site and generate word of mouth. When Yahoo! started its Denmark site, it distributed apples at the busiest train station in Denmark with the message that in the next hours a trip to New York could be won on the Yahoo! site; it also managed to get this mentioned in Danish newspapers. Companies can offer to push content and ads to targeted audiences who agree to receive them and are presumably more interested in the product or product category.

Web advertising is showing double-digit growth. Costs are reasonable compared with those of other advertising media. For example, ESPN.com (**www.espn.com**), the number-one Internet sports site, attracts more than 5 million Web surfers a week. Based on current advertising rates, running advertising on the site for an entire year may range from US$500 000 to US$1 000 000 (depending on impression levels).[34] Yahoo! employs 100 salespeople who demonstrate how online ads can reach people with certain interests or who live in specific regions.

E-Marketing Guidelines

If a company does an e-mail campaign right, it can not only build customer relationships, but also reap additional profits. E-mail involves only a fraction of the cost of a "d-mail," or direct-mail, campaign. For example, Microsoft spent approximately US$70 million a year on paper-driven campaigns. Now, it sends out 20 million pieces of e-mail every month at a significant savings over the cost of paper-based campaigns. Also, compared to other forms of online marketing, e-mail is a hands-down winner. Click-through rates for ad banners have dropped to less than 1 percent, whereas click-through rates for e-mail are running around 80 percent.

Here are some important guidelines followed by pioneering e-mail marketers:[35]

- *Give the customer a reason to respond.* Companies should offer surfers powerful incentives for reading e-mail pitches and online ads, like e-mail trivia games, scavenger hunts, and instant-win sweepstakes.

- *Personalize the content of your e-mails.* IBM's iSource is distributed directly to customers' office e-mail each week, delivering only "the news they choose" in terms of announcements and weekly updates. Customers who agree to receive the newsletter select from topics listed on an interest profile.

- *Offer something the customer could not get via direct mail.* Because e-mail campaigns can be carried out quickly, they can offer time-sensitive information. Travelocity sends frequent e-mails pitching last-minute cheap airfares. Club Med uses e-mail to pitch unsold, discounted vacation packages to prospects in its database.

- *Make it easy for customers to "unsubscribe."* It is important that online customers have a positive exit experience. According to a Burston-Marsteller and Roper Strach Worldwide study, the top 10 percent of Web users who communicate much more often online typically share their views by e-mail with 11 friends when satisfied, but contact 17 friends when they are dissatisfied.[36]

Online merchants face many challenges in expanding the public's use of e-commerce. Customers will have to feel that the information they supply is confidential and not to be sold to others. Customers will need to trust that online transactions are secure. Companies must encourage communication by inviting prospects and customers to send in questions, suggestions, and even complaints via e-mail. Some sites include a call-me button—the customer clicks on it and his or her phone rings with a customer representative ready to answer a question. Customer service representatives can in principle respond quickly to these messages. Smart online marketers will answer quickly by sending out newsletters, special product or promotion offers based on purchase histories, reminders of service requirements or warranty renewals, or announcements of special events.

Direct marketing must be integrated with other communication and channel activities.[37] IBM and Ford have used integrated direct marketing to build profitable relations with customers over the years. Retailers such as Sears, IKEA, and Tilley Endurables regularly send catalogues to supplement in-store sales. Veseys, a mail-order and online gardening company based in Prince Edward Island, has been successfully serving Canadians for 65 years. Eddie Bauer made its fortune in the direct-marketing mail-order and phone-order business before opening its retail stores, after establishing strong brand name as a direct marketer. Such companies cross-promote their stores, catalogues, and Web sites, for example, by putting their Web addresses on their shopping bags.

Virgin Mobile

In a campaign that received top prize at the 2004 Cannes Lion awards, Virgin Mobile created a wireless phone service campaign in Australia to sell 5-cent text messaging that combined TV and outdoor ads and a Web page, all based on Warren, a fictitious, love-hungry character. Outdoor ads with Warren's text address and photo read, "Be my text kitten" and "Tell me your favourite text position." During the ten-week campaign, Warren got 600 000 text responses, and the Web site got 3 million hits. Sales increased by over 35 percent month-on-month, with existing users making 15 percent more calls and sending 20 percent more text messages.[38]

Designing the Sales Force

The original and oldest form of direct marketing is the field sales call. Today most industrial companies rely heavily on a professional sales force to locate prospects, develop them into customers, and grow the business; or they hire manufacturers' representatives and agents to carry out the direct-selling task. In addition, many consumer companies use a direct-selling force: insurance agents, stockbrokers, and distributors work for direct-sales organizations such as Amway, Mary Kay, and Tupperware. According to Statistics Canada's 2001 Census data, almost 25 percent of the total workforce works in sales or service occupations.[39] Sales forces are found in nonprofit as well as for-profit organizations. Hospitals and museums, for example, use fund-raisers to contact donors and solicit donations.

No one debates the importance of the sales force in marketing programs. However, companies are sensitive to the high and rising costs (salaries, commissions, bonuses, travel expenses, and benefits) of maintaining a sales force. Because the average cost of a personal sales call ranges from $200 to $300, and closing a sale typically requires four calls, the total cost can range from $800 to $1200.[40] Not surprisingly, companies are trying to increase the productivity of the sales force through better selection, training, supervision, motivation, and compensation.

The term *sales representative* covers a broad range of positions. Six can be distinguished, ranging from the least to the most creative types of selling:[41]

1. *Deliverer*—A salesperson whose major task is the delivery of a product (water, fuel, oil).

2. *Order taker*—A salesperson who acts predominantly as an inside order taker (the salesperson standing behind the counter) or outside order taker (the soap salesperson calling on the supermarket manager).

3. *Missionary*—A salesperson who is not expected or permitted to take an order but whose major task is to build goodwill or to educate the actual or potential user (the medical "detailer" representing an ethical pharmaceutical house).

4. *Technician*—A salesperson with a high level of technical knowledge (the engineering salesperson who is primarily a consultant to the client companies).

5. *Demand creator*—A salesperson who relies on creative methods for selling tangible products (vacuum cleaners, cleaning brushes, household products) or intangibles (insurance, advertising services, or education).

6. *Solution vendor*—A salesperson whose expertise is in the solving of a customer's problem, often with a system of the company's products and services (e.g., computer and communications systems).

Sales personnel serve as the company's personal link to the customers. The sales representative is the company to many of its customers. It is the sales rep who brings back much-needed information about the customer. Therefore, the company needs to carefully consider issues in sales-force design—namely, the development of sales-force objectives, strategy, structure, size, and compensation. (See Figure 19.2.)

FIGURE 19.2

Designing a Sales Force

Enbridge Home Services

Enbridge Home Services is a full-service energy company, currently operating across Ontario. It has over 150 years of experience in the energy industry, offering sales, installation, and service on heating and air-conditioning equipment and water heaters. It takes pride in selling reputable products, backed by a service guarantee. Its goal is to become the leader in residential home-comfort and business energy services. To accomplish this goal, Enbridge must have enthusiastic and motivated salespeople, whom Enbridge calls energy management consultants. They help their customers diagnose problems and find optimal solutions. Enbridge believes that its employees, including its sales force, are the most important component of its business success. Enbridge Home Services has a rich history of speaking with its customers face-to-face. It has been talking to consumers in their homes about their needs for as long as Enbridge has been in business. It believes face-to-face consultation is one of the best ways to build long-term relationships with customers. While some firms are abandoning personal, door-to-door selling in favour of telemarketing or e-mail marketing, Enbridge believes personal sales and consultation is pivotal to its ongoing success. As David Ainslie, marketing manager at Enbridge, notes, "Modern door-to-door campaigns offer a rare opportunity for companies to engage in one-on-one dialogue with their customers."[42]

Sales-Force Objectives and Strategy

The days when all the sales force would do was "sell, sell, and sell" are long gone. Sales reps need to know how to diagnose a customer's problem and propose a solution. Salespeople show a customer-prospect how their company can help a customer improve profitability.

Companies need to define the specific objectives they want their sales force to achieve. For example, a company might want its sales representatives to spend 80 percent of their time with current customers and 20 percent with prospects, and 85 percent of their time on established products and 15 percent on new products. The specific allocation scheme depends on the kind of products and customers, but regardless of the selling context, salespeople will have one or more of the following specific tasks to perform:

- *Prospecting*—Searching for prospects, or leads.
- *Targeting*—Deciding how to allocate their time among prospects and customers.
- *Communicating*—Communicating information about the company's products and services.
- *Selling*—Approaching, presenting, answering objections, and closing sales.
- *Servicing*—Providing various services to the customers—consulting on problems, rendering technical assistance, arranging financing, expediting delivery.
- *Information gathering*—Conducting market research and doing intelligence work.
- *Allocating*—Deciding which customers will get scarce products during product shortages.

Because of the expense, most companies are moving to the concept of a *leveraged sales force*. A sales force focuses on selling the company's more complex and customized products to large accounts, while low-end selling is done by inside salespeople and Web ordering. Tasks such as lead generation, proposal writing, order fulfillment, and post-sale support are turned over to others. Salespeople handle fewer accounts, and are rewarded for key account growth. This is far different from expecting salespeople to sell to every possible account, which is usually the weakness of geographically based sales forces.[43]

Companies must deploy sales forces strategically so that they call on the right customers at the right time and in the right way. Today's sales representatives act as "account managers" who arrange fruitful contact between various people in the buying and selling organizations. Selling increasingly calls for teamwork requiring the support of other personnel, such as *top management*, especially when national accounts or major sales are at stake; *technical people*, who supply technical information and service to the customer before, during, or after product purchase; *customer service representatives*, who provide installation, maintenance, and other services; and an *office staff*, consisting of sales analysts, order expediters, and assistants.

To maintain a market focus, salespeople should know how to analyze sales data, measure market potential, gather market intelligence, and develop marketing strategies and plans. Sales

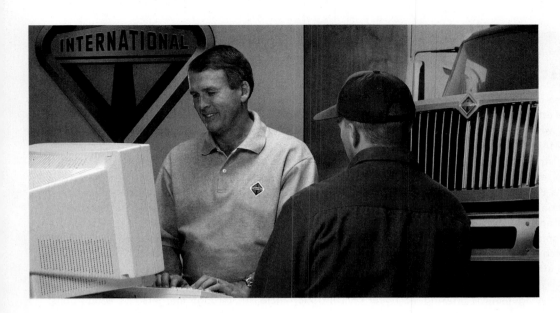

A service representative provides personalized, customized service to a customer purchasing a Navistar truck.

representatives need analytical marketing skills, and these skills become especially important at the higher levels of sales management. Marketers believe that sales forces will be more effective in the long run if they understand marketing as well as selling.

Once the company decides on an approach, it can use a direct or a contractual sales force. A **direct (company) sales force** consists of full- or part-time paid employees who work exclusively for the company. This sales force includes inside sales personnel who conduct business from the office using the telephone and receive visits from prospective buyers, and field sales personnel who travel and visit customers. A **contractual sales force** consists of manufacturers' reps, sales agents, and brokers, who are paid a commission based on sales.

Sales-Force Structure

The sales-force strategy has implications for the sales-force structure. A company that sells one product line to one end-using industry with customers in many locations would use a territorial structure. A company that sells many products to many types of customers might need a product or market structure. Some companies need a more complex structure. Motorola, for example, manages four types of sales forces: (1) a strategic market sales force composed of technical, applications, and quality engineers and service personnel assigned to major accounts; (2) a geographic sales force calling on thousands of customers in different territories; (3) a distributor sales force calling on and coaching Motorola distributors; and (4) an inside sales force doing telemarketing and taking orders via phone and fax.

Established companies need to revise their sales-force structure as market and economic conditions change. SAS, seller of business intelligence software, reorganized its sales force into industry-specific groups such as banks, brokerages, and insurers and saw revenue soar by 14 percent.[44] "Marketing Insight: Major Account Management" discusses major account management, a specialized form of sales-force structure.

Sales-Force Size

Once the company clarifies its strategy and structure, it is ready to consider sales-force size. Sales representatives are one of the company's most productive and expensive assets. Increasing their number will increase both sales and costs.

Once the company establishes the number of customers it wants to reach, it can use a *workload approach* to establish sales-force size. This method consists of the following five steps:

1. Customers are grouped into size classes according to annual sales volume.

2. Desirable call frequencies (number of calls on an account per year) are established for each class.

Major Account Management

Major accounts (also called key accounts, national accounts, global accounts, or house accounts) are typically singled out for special attention. Important customers who have multiple divisions in many locations are offered major account contracts, which provide uniform pricing and coordinated service for all customer divisions. A major account manager (MAM) supervises field reps calling on customer plants within their territories. Large accounts are often handled by a strategic account management team with cross-functional personnel who handle all aspects of the relationship. For example, in 1992 Procter & Gamble stationed a strategic account management team to work with Wal-Mart in its Bentonville, Arkansas, headquarters. By 1998, P&G and Wal-Mart had already jointly saved US$30 billion through supply chain improvements. Today, the P&G team in Bentonville consists of approximately 100 staffers dedicated to serving Wal-Mart.

The average company manages about 75 key accounts. If a company has several such accounts, it is likely to organize a major account management division, in which the average MAM handles nine accounts. MAMs typically report to the national sales manager who reports to the vice-president of marketing and sales, who in turn reports to the CEO.

Major account management is growing. As buyer concentration increases through mergers and acquisitions, fewer buyers account for a larger share of a company's sales. Many buyers are centralizing their purchases for certain items, which gives them more bargaining power. Sellers in turn need to devote more attention to these major buyers. Still another factor is that as products become more complex, more groups in the buyer's organization become involved in the purchase process. The typical salesperson might not have the skill, authority, or coverage to be effective in selling to the large buyer.

In selecting major accounts, companies look for accounts that purchase a high volume (especially of more profitable products), purchase centrally, require a high level of service in several geographic locations, may be price-sensitive, and may want a long-term partnering relationship. Major account managers have a number of duties: acting as the single point of contact; developing and growing customer business; understanding customer decision processes; identifying added-value opportunities; providing competitive intelligence; negotiating sales; and orchestrating customer service. MAMs are typically evaluated on their effectiveness in growing their share of the account's business and on their achievement of annual profit-and-sales volume goals. One MAM said, "My position must not be as a salesman, but as a 'marketing consultant' to our customers and a salesman of my company's capabilities as opposed to my company's products."

Major accounts normally receive more favourable pricing based on their purchase volume, but marketers cannot rely exclusively on this incentive to retain customer loyalty. There is always a risk that competitors can match or beat a price or that increased costs may necessitate raising prices. Many major accounts look for added value more than for a price advantage. They appreciate having a single point of dedicated contact; single billing; special warranties; EDI links; priority shipping; early information releases; customized products; and efficient maintenance, repair, and upgraded service. In addition to these practical considerations, there is the value of goodwill. Personal relationships with personnel who value the major account's business and who have a vested interest in the success of that business are compelling reasons for being a loyal customer.

Sources: S. Tubridy, "Major Account Management," in *AMA Management Handbook* (3rd ed.), edited by John J. Hampton (New York: Amacom, 1994), pp. 3–25, 3–27; Sanjit Sengupta, Robert E. Krapfel, and Michael A. Pusateri, "The Strategic Sales Force," *Marketing Management* (Summer 1997): 29–34; Robert S. Duboff and Lori Underhill Sherer, "Customized Customer Loyalty," *Marketing Management* (Summer 1997): 21–27; Tricia Campbell, "Getting Top Executives to Sell," *Sales & Marketing Management* (October 1998): 39; "Promotion Marketer of the Decade: Wal-Mart," *Promo*, December 1, 1999; Noel Capon, *Key Account Management and Planning: The Comprehensive Handbook for Managing Your Company's Most Important Strategic Asset* (New York: Free Press, 2001); Sallie Sherman, Joseph Sperry, and Samuel Reese, *The Seven Keys to Managing Strategic Accounts* (New York: McGraw-Hill Trade, 2003). More information can be obtained from NAMA (National Account Management Association), **www.nasm.com**.

3. The number of accounts in each size class is multiplied by the corresponding call frequency to arrive at the total workload for the country, in sales calls per year.

4. The average number of calls a sales representative can make per year is determined.

5. The number of sales representatives needed is determined by dividing the total annual calls required by the average annual calls made by a sales representative.

Suppose the company estimates that there are 1000 A accounts and 2000 B accounts in the nation. A accounts require 36 calls a year, and B accounts require 12 calls a year. The company needs a sales force that can make 60 000 sales calls a year. Suppose the average rep can make 1000 calls a year. The company would need 60 full-time sales representatives.

Sales-Force Compensation

To attract top-quality sales reps, the company has to develop an attractive compensation package. Sales reps want income regularity, extra reward for above-average performance, and fair payment for experience and longevity. Management wants control, economy, and simplicity. Some of these objectives will conflict. No wonder compensation plans exhibit a tremendous variety from industry to industry and even within the same industry.

The company must determine the four components of sales-force compensation—a fixed amount, a variable amount, expense allowances, and benefits. The *fixed amount*, a salary, is intended to satisfy the need for income stability. The *variable amount*, which might be commissions, bonus, or profit sharing, is intended to stimulate and reward effort. *Expense allowances* enable sales reps to meet the expenses involved in travel and entertaining. *Benefits*, such as paid vacations, sickness or accident benefits, pensions, and life insurance, are intended to provide security and job satisfaction.

Fixed compensation receives more emphasis in jobs with a high ratio of nonselling to selling duties and in jobs where the selling task is technically complex and involves teamwork. Variable compensation receives more emphasis in jobs where sales are cyclical or depend on individual initiative. Fixed and variable compensation give rise to three basic types of compensation plans—straight salary, straight commission, and combination salary and commission. Three-quarters of firms use a combination of salary and commission, though the relative proportion varies widely.[45]

Straight-salary plans provide sales reps with a secure income, make them more willing to perform nonselling activities, and give them less incentive to overstock customers. From the company's perspective, they provide administrative simplicity and lower turnover. Straight-commission plans attract higher performers, provide more motivation, require less supervision, and control selling costs. On the negative side, commission plans overemphasize getting the sale rather than building the relationship. Combination plans feature the benefits of both plans while reducing their disadvantages.

With compensation plans that combine fixed and variable pay, companies may link the variable portion of a salesperson's pay to a wide variety of strategic goals. Some see a new trend toward de-emphasizing volume measures in favour of factors such as gross profitability, customer satisfaction, and customer retention. For example, IBM now partly rewards salespeople on the basis of customer satisfaction as measured by customer surveys.[46] Other companies are basing the rep's reward partly on a sales team's performance or even companywide performance. This should get reps to work more closely together for the common good.

Managing the Sales Force

Once the company has established objectives, strategy, structure, size, and compensation, it has to recruit, select, train, supervise, motivate, and evaluate sales representatives. Various policies and procedures guide these decisions (see Figure 19.3).

Recruiting and Selecting Representatives

At the heart of a successful sales force is the selection of effective representatives. One survey revealed that the top 27 percent of the sales force brought in over 52 percent of the sales. Beyond differences in productivity is the great waste in hiring the wrong people. The average annual turnover rate for all industries is almost 20 percent. Sales force turnover leads to lost sales, costs of finding and training replacements, and often a strain on existing salespeople to pick up the slack.

Selecting sales reps would be simple if one knew what traits to look for. One good starting point is to ask customers what traits they prefer. Most customers say they want the rep to be honest, reliable, knowledgeable, and helpful. Finding what traits will actually lead to sales success, however, is challenging. Numerous studies have shown little relationship between sales performance on one hand, and background and experience variables, current status, lifestyle, attitude, personality, and skills on the other hand. More effective predictors have been composite tests and assessment centres where the working environment is simulated and applicants are assessed in an environment similar to the one in which they would work.[47]

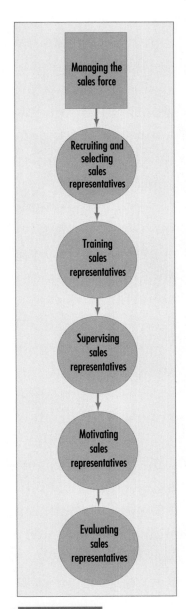

FIGURE 19.3

Managing the Sales Force

Xerox Canada

Xerox Canada has very specific sales-force criteria with respect to diversity. The company believes that it is crucially important to have a sales force that represents the different environments in which the company operates. As a result, Xerox Canada's sales force has employees from around the globe. The company believes that this strategy is critical to its success, particularly in Canada where there is such a diverse population of potential customers. Xerox was not surprised that it had breakthrough sales in its public-sector operations in 2003 as a result. Visible minorities account for nearly 10 percent of Xerox Canada's total workforce, and Aboriginal people make up another 1 percent.[48]

After management develops its selection criteria, it must recruit. The human resources department seeks applicants by soliciting names from current sales representatives, using employment agencies, placing job ads, and contacting university and college students. Selection procedures can vary from a single informal interview to prolonged testing and interviewing. Many companies give sales applicants formal tests. Although test scores are only one information element in a set that includes personal characteristics, references, past employment history, and interviewer reactions, they are weighted quite heavily by such companies as IBM, Prudential, and Procter & Gamble. Gillette claims that tests have reduced turnover and correlated well with the subsequent progress of new reps in the sales organization.

Training and Supervising Sales Representatives

Today's customers expect salespeople to have deep product knowledge, to add ideas to improve the customer's operations, and to be efficient and reliable. These demands have required companies to make a much higher investment in sales training.

New reps may spend a few weeks to several months in training. The median training period is 28 weeks in industrial-products companies, 12 in service companies, and 4 in consumer-products companies. Training time varies with the complexity of the selling task and the type of person recruited into the sales organization.

IBM

At IBM, new reps receive extensive initial training and may spend 15 percent of their time each year in additional training. IBM has now switched 25 percent of the training from classroom to e-learning, saving a great deal of money in the process. It uses a self-study system called Info-Window that combines a personal computer and a laser videodisc. A trainee can practise sales calls with an on-screen actor who portrays a buying executive in a particular industry. The actor-buyer responds differently depending on what the trainee says.

New methods of training are continually emerging, such as role-playing and sensitivity training; the use of cassette tapes, videotapes, and CD-ROMs; and programmed learning, distance learning, and films on selling.

Whirlpool

In order to increase its sales reps' understanding of its appliances, Whirlpool rented an eight-bedroom farmhouse near its headquarters in Benton Harbor, Michigan, and outfitted it with Whirlpool dishwashers, microwaves, washers, dryers, and refrigerators. It sent eight new salespeople to live in the house, to cook and do laundry and household chores. When they emerged, they knew a great deal about Whirlpool appliances and gained more confidence than if they had taken the traditional two-week classroom training course.[49]

Companies vary in how closely they supervise sales reps. Reps paid mostly on commission generally receive less supervision. Those who are salaried and must cover definite accounts are likely to receive substantial supervision. With multilevel selling, used by Avon, Sara Lee, Virgin, AOL Time Warner, and others, independent distributors are also in charge of their own sales force selling company products. These independent contractors or reps are paid a commission not only on their own sales but also on the sales of people they recruit and train.[50]

Sales Rep Productivity

How many calls should a company make on a particular account each year? Some research has suggested that today's sales reps are spending too much time selling to smaller, less profitable accounts when they should be focusing more of their efforts on selling to larger, more profitable accounts.[51]

NORMS FOR PROSPECT CALLS Companies often specify how much time reps should spend prospecting for new accounts. Spector Freight wants its sales representatives to spend 25 percent of their time prospecting and to stop calling on a prospect after three unsuccessful calls.

Companies set up prospecting standards for a number of reasons. Left to their own devices, many reps will spend most of their time with current customers, who are known quantities. Reps can depend on them for some business, whereas a prospect might never deliver any business. Some companies rely on a missionary sales force to open new accounts.

Whirlpool uses local households to train salespeople and to help its researchers develop intelligent major appliances.

USING SALES TIME EFFICIENTLY Studies have shown that the best sales reps are those who manage their time effectively.[52] One planning tool is *time-and-duty analysis*, which helps reps understand how they spend their time and how they might increase their productivity. In the course of a day, sales reps spend time planning, travelling, waiting, selling, and in administrative tasks (report writing and billing, attending sales meetings, and talking to others in the company about production, delivery, billing, sales performance, and other matters). With so many duties, it is no wonder that actual face-to-face selling time amounts to as little as 29 percent of total working time![53]

Companies are constantly seeking ways to improve sales-force productivity. Their methods take the form of training sales representatives in the use of "phone power," simplifying record keeping and administrative time, and using the computer and the Internet to develop call and routing plans, supply customer and competitive information, and automate the order preparation process.

Owens-Corning

Owens-Corning put its sales force online with FAST—its Field Automation Sales Team system. FAST empowers salespeople to make more of their own decisions by giving them a constant supply of information about the company and the people they are dealing with. Using laptop computers, each salesperson can access valuable product and customer information. With a few keystrokes, salespeople can prime themselves on backgrounds of clients; call up prewritten sales letters; transmit orders and resolve customer service issues on the spot during customer calls; and have samples, pamphlets, brochures, and other materials sent to clients.

To cut costs, reduce time demands on their outside sales force, and take advantage of computer and telecommunications innovations, many companies have increased the size and responsibilities of their inside sales force.[54]

Inside salespeople are of three types. There are *technical support people*, who provide technical information and answers to customers' questions. There are *sales assistants*, who provide clerical backup for the outside salespersons. They call ahead and confirm appointments, carry out credit checks, follow up on deliveries, and answer customers' questions. *Telemarketers* use the phone to find new leads, qualify them, and sell to them. Telemarketers can call up to 50 customers a day, compared to the four an outside salesperson can contact.

The inside sales force frees the outside reps to spend more time selling to major accounts, identifying and converting new major prospects, placing electronic ordering systems in customers' facilities, and obtaining more blanket orders and systems contracts. The inside salespeople spend more time checking inventory, following up orders, and phoning smaller accounts. The outside sales reps are paid largely on an incentive-compensation basis, and the inside reps on a salary or salary plus bonus pay.

Another dramatic breakthrough is the new high-tech equipment—desktop and laptop PCs, PDAs, videocassette recorders, videodiscs, automatic diallers, e-mail, fax machines, and teleconferencing and videophones. The salesperson has truly gone "electronic." Not only is sales and inventory information transferred much faster, but specific computer-based decision support systems on CDs have been created for sales managers and sales representatives.

One of the most valuable electronic tools for the sales rep is the company Web site, and one of its most useful applications is as a prospecting tool. Company Web sites can help define the firm's relationships with individual accounts and identify those whose business warrants a personal sales call. The Web site provides an introduction to self-identified potential customers. Depending on the nature of the business, the initial order may even take place online. For more complex transactions, the site provides a way for the buyer to contact the seller. Pall Corporation, a manufacturer of fluid filtration and purification technologies, has all e-mail directed to company headquarters, with leads going directly to the appropriate sales rep.[55]

Selling over the Internet supports relationship marketing by solving problems that do not require live intervention and thus allows more time to be spent on issues that are best addressed face-to-face.

Motivating Sales Representatives

The majority of sales representatives require encouragement and special incentives. This is especially true of field selling: Reps usually work alone, their hours are irregular, and they are often away from home. They confront aggressive, competing sales reps; they have an inferior status relative to the buyer; they often do not have the authority to do what is necessary to win an account; and they sometimes lose large orders they have worked hard to obtain.[56]

Most marketers believe that the higher the salesperson's motivation, the greater the effort and the resulting performance, rewards, and satisfaction—and thus further motivation. Such thinking is based on certain assumptions:

- *Sales managers must be able to convince salespeople that they can sell more by working harder or by being trained to work smarter.* But if sales are determined largely by economic conditions or competitive actions, this link is undermined.

- *Sales managers must be able to convince salespeople that the rewards for better performance are worth the extra effort.* But if the rewards seem to be set arbitrarily or are too small or of the wrong kind, this link is undermined.

To increase motivation, marketers reinforce intrinsic and extrinsic rewards of all types. One research study that measured the importance of different rewards found that the reward with the highest value was pay, followed by promotion, personal growth, and sense of accomplishment.[57] The least-valued rewards were liking and respect, security, and recognition. In other words, salespeople are highly motivated by pay and the chance to get ahead and satisfy their intrinsic needs, and less motivated by compliments and security. However, the researchers also found that the importance of motivators varied with demographic characteristics: Financial rewards were mostly valued by older, longer-tenured people and those who had large families. Higher-order rewards (recognition, liking and respect, sense of accomplishment) were more valued by young salespeople who were unmarried or had small families and usually more formal education.

Many companies set annual sales quotas. Quotas can be set on dollar sales, unit volume, margin, selling effort or activity, and product type. Compensation is often tied to degree of quota fulfillment. Sales quotas are developed from the annual marketing plan. The company first prepares a sales forecast that becomes the basis for planning production, workforce size, and financial requirements. Management then establishes quotas for regions and territories, which typically add up to more than the sales forecast to encourage managers and salespeople to perform at their best levels. If they fail to make their quotas, the company nevertheless might reach its sales forecast.

Each area sales manager divides the area's quota among the area's reps. Sometimes a rep's quotas are set high, to spur extra effort, or more modestly, to build confidence. One general view is that a salesperson's quota should be at least equal to the person's last year's sales plus some fraction of the difference between territory sales potential and last year's sales. The more favourably the salesperson reacts to pressure, the higher the fraction should be.

Conventional wisdom is that profits are maximized by sales reps focusing on the more important products and more profitable products. Reps are not likely to achieve their quotas for established products when the company is launching several new products at the same time. The company will need to expand its sales force for new product launches.

Setting sales quotas creates problems. If the company underestimates and the sales reps easily achieve their quotas, the company has overpaid its reps. If the company overestimates sales potential, the sales people will find it very hard to reach their quotas and be frustrated or quit. Another downside is that quotas can drive reps to get as much business as possible—often resulting in their ignoring the service side of the business. The company gains short-term results at the cost of long-term customer satisfaction.

Some companies are dropping quotas.[58] Siebel, the leading supplier of sales automation software, judges its sales reps using a number of metrics, such as customer satisfaction, repeat business, and profitable revenues. Almost 40 percent of incentive compensation is based on customers' reported satisfaction with service and product. The company's close scrutiny of the sales process leads to satisfied customers: Over 50 percent of Siebel's revenue comes from repeat business.[59] Nortel and AT&T Worldnet also prefer to use a larger set of measures for motivating and rewarding sales reps. Even hard-driving Oracle has changed its approach to sales compensation:

Oracle

Finding sales flagging and customers griping, Oracle, the second-largest software company in the world, overhauled its sales department in 2002. Oracle's rapidly expanding capabilities, with diverse applications such as human resources, supply chain, and CRM, made its account management system difficult. One rep could no longer be responsible for selling all Oracle products to certain customers. Reorganization resulted in reps' specializing in a few particular products. To try to tone down the sales force's reputation as overly aggressive, the commission structure was changed to a flat 4 to 6 percent, as compared to a wider range of 2 to 12 percent depending on how close to the end of the quarter the sale was made.[60]

Evaluating Sales Representatives

We have been describing the *feed-forward* aspects of sales supervision—how management communicates what the sales reps should be doing and motivates them to do it. But good feed-forward requires good *feedback*, which means getting regular information from reps to evaluate performance.

SOURCES OF INFORMATION The most important source of information about reps is sales reports. Additional information comes through personal observation, salesperson self-reports, customer letters and complaints, customer surveys, and conversations with other sales representatives.

Sales reports are divided between *activity plans* and *write-ups of activity results*. The best example of the former is the salesperson's work plan, which reps submit a week or month in advance. The plan describes intended calls and routing. This report forces sales reps to plan and schedule their activities and inform management of their whereabouts. It provides a basis for comparing their plans and accomplishments. Sales reps can be evaluated on their ability to "plan their work and work their plan."

Many companies require representatives to develop an annual territory marketing plan in which they outline their program for developing new accounts and increasing business from existing accounts. This type of report casts sales reps into the role of market managers and profit centres. Sales managers study these plans, make suggestions, and use them to develop sales quotas. Sales reps write up completed activities on *call reports*. Sales representatives also submit expense reports, new-business reports, lost-business reports, and reports on local business and economic conditions.

These reports provide raw data from which sales managers can extract key indicators of sales performance: (1) average number of sales calls per salesperson per day, (2) average sales call time per contact, (3) average revenue per sales call, (4) average cost per sales call, (5) entertainment cost per sales call, (6) percentage of orders per hundred sales calls, (7) number of new customers per period, (8) number of lost customers per period, and (9) sales-force cost as a percentage of total sales.

FORMAL EVALUATION The sales force's reports along with other observations supply the raw materials for evaluation. There are several approaches to conducting evaluations. One type of evaluation compares current performance to past performance. An example is shown in Table 19.1.

The sales manager can learn many things about a rep from this table. Total sales increased every year (line 3). This does not necessarily mean that the person is doing a better job. The product breakdown shows that he has been able to push the sales of product B further than the sales of product A (lines 1 and 2). According to his quotas for the two products (lines 4 and 5), his success in increasing product B sales could be at the expense of product A sales. According to gross profits (lines 6 and 7), the company earns more selling A than B. The rep might be pushing the higher-volume, lower-margin product at the expense of the more profitable product. Although he increased total sales by $1100 between 2001 and 2002 (line 3), the gross profits on total sales actually decreased by $580 (line 8).

Sales expense (line 9) shows a steady increase, although total expense as a percentage of total sales seems to be under control (line 10). The upward trend in total dollar expense does not seem to be explained by any increase in the number of calls (line 11), although it might be related to success in acquiring new customers (line 14). There is a possibility that in prospecting for new customers, this rep is neglecting present customers, as indicated by an upward trend in the annual number of lost customers (line 15).

The last two lines show the level and trend in sales and gross profits per customer. These figures become more meaningful when they are compared with overall company averages. If this rep's average gross profit per customer is lower than the company's average, he could be concentrating on the wrong customers or not spending enough time with each customer. A review of annual number of calls (line 11) shows that he might be making fewer annual calls than the average salesperson. If distances in the territory are similar to other territories, this could mean that he is not putting in a full workday, he is poor at sales planning and routing, or he spends too much time with certain accounts.

The rep might be quite effective in producing sales but not rate high with customers. Perhaps he is slightly better than the competitors' salespeople, or his product is better, or he keeps finding new customers to replace others who do not like to deal with him. The customers' opinion of the salesperson, product, and service can be measured by mail questionnaires or telephone calls.

Evaluations can also assess the salesperson's knowledge of the company, products, customers, competitors, territory, and responsibilities. Personality characteristics can be rated, such as general

TABLE 19.1	FORM FOR EVALUATING SALES REPRESENTATIVE'S PERFORMANCE			
Territory: Midland Sales Representative: John Smith	2001	2002	2003	2004
1. Net sales product A	$251 300	$253 200	$270 000	$263 100
2. Net sales product B	423 200	439 200	553 900	561 900
3. Net sales total	674 500	692 400	823 900	825 000
4. Percent of quota product A	95.6	92.0	88.0	84.7
5. Percent of quota product B	120.4	122.3	134.9	130.8
6. Gross profits product A	$50 260	$50 640	$54 000	$52 620
7. Gross profits product B	42 320	43 920	55 390	56 190
8. Gross profits total	92 580	94 560	109 390	108 810
9. Sales expense	$10 200	$11 100	$11 600	$13 200
10. Sales expense to total sales (%)	1.5	1.6	1.4	1.6
11. Number of calls	1 675	1 700	1 680	1 660
12. Cost per call	$6.09	$6.53	$6.90	$7.95
13. Average number of customers	320	324	328	334
14. Number of new customers	13	14	15	20
15. Number of lost customers	8	10	11	14
16. Average sales per customer	$2 108	$2 137	$2 512	$2 470
17. Average gross profit per customer	$289	$292	$334	$326

manner, appearance, speech, and temperament. The sales manager can review any problems in motivation or compliance.[61] Sales reps can provide attributions as to the success or failure of a sales call and how they would propose to improve the odds on subsequent calls. Possible explanations for their performance could be related to internal (effort, ability, and strategy) and external (task and luck) factors.[62]

Principles of Personal Selling

Personal selling is an ancient art. It has spawned a large literature and many principles. Effective salespersons have more than instinct; they are trained in methods of analysis and customer management. Today's companies spend hundreds of millions of dollars each year to train salespeople in the art of selling. Sales-training approaches try to convert a salesperson from a passive order taker into an active order getter who engages in customer problem solving. An active order getter learns how to listen and question in order to identify customer needs and come up with sound product solutions. This approach assumes that customers have latent needs that constitute opportunities and that they will be loyal to sales reps who can analyze their needs and have their long-term interests at heart. "Marketing Insight: Principles of Customer-Oriented Selling" offers some guidelines.

Most sales-training programs agree on the major steps involved in any effective sales process. We show these steps in Figure 19.4, and discuss their application to industrial selling next.[63]

The Six Steps

PROSPECTING AND QUALIFYING   The first step in selling is to identify and qualify prospects. More companies are taking responsibility for finding and qualifying leads so that the salespeople can use their expensive time doing what they can do best: selling. Companies can qualify the leads by contacting them by mail or phone to assess their level of interest and financial capacity. The leads can be categorized, with "hot" prospects turned over to the field sales force and "warm" prospects turned over to the telemarketing unit for follow-up. Even then, it usually takes about four calls on a prospect to consummate a business transaction.

PRE-APPROACH   The salesperson needs to learn as much as possible about the prospect company (what it needs, who is involved in the purchase decision) and its buyers (personal characteristics and buying styles). The salesperson should set call objectives: to qualify the prospect, gather information, make an immediate sale. Another task is to decide on the best contact approach, which might be a personal visit, a phone call, or a letter. Finally, the salesperson should plan an overall sales strategy for the account.

PRESENTATION AND DEMONSTRATION   The salesperson now tells the product "story" to the buyer, following the AIDA formula of gaining *attention*, holding *interest*, arousing *desire*, and obtaining *action*. The salesperson uses a *features, advantages, benefits,* and *value* approach (FABV). Features describe physical characteristics of a market offering, such as chip processing speeds or memory capacity. Advantages describe why the features provide an advantage to the customer. Benefits describe the economic, technical, service, and social benefits delivered by the offering. Value describes the worth (often in monetary terms) of the offering. Too often, salespeople spend too much time dwelling on product features (a product orientation) and not enough stressing the offering's benefits and value (a customer orientation).

OVERCOMING OBJECTIONS   Customers typically pose objections during the presentation or when asked for the order. *Psychological resistance* includes resistance to interference, preference for established supply sources or brands, apathy, reluctance to giving up something, unpleasant associations created by the sales rep, predetermined ideas, dislike of making decisions, and neurotic attitude toward money. *Logical resistance* might consist of objections to the price, delivery schedule, or certain product or company characteristics.

To handle these objections, the salesperson maintains a positive approach, asks the buyer to clarify the objection, questions the buyer in a way that the buyer has to answer his or her own objection, denies the validity of the objection, or turns the objection into a reason for buying. Handling and overcoming objections is a part of the broader skills of negotiation.

One potential problem is for salespeople to give in too often when customers demand a discount. One company recognized this as a problem when its sales revenue went up by 25 percent but its profit had remained flat. The company decided to retrain its salespeople to "sell the price," rather

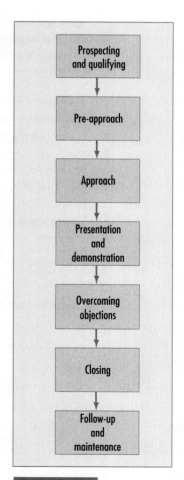

FIGURE 19.4

Major Steps in Effective Selling

MARKETING INSIGHT

Principles of Customer-Oriented Selling

Two vocal exponents of a customer-oriented approach to selling are Neil Rackham and Sharon Drew Morgen. Rackham has developed a method that he calls *SPIN selling* (Situation, Problem, Implication, Need-Payoff). Gone is the script of the slick salesperson, and in its place is the salesperson who knows how to raise good questions and listen and learn. Rackham trains salespeople to raise four types of questions with the prospect:

1. *Situation questions.* These ask about facts or explore the buyer's present situation. For example, "What system are you using to invoice your customers?"

2. *Problem questions.* These deal with problems, difficulties, and dissatisfactions the buyer is experiencing. For example, "What parts of the system create errors?"

3. *Implication questions.* These ask about the consequences or effects of a buyer's problems, difficulties, or dissatisfactions. For example, "How does this problem affect your people's productivity?"

4. *Need-payoff questions.* These ask about the value or usefulness of a proposed solution. For example, "How much would you save if our company could help reduce the errors by 80 percent?"

Rackham suggests that companies, especially those selling complex products or services, should have their salespeople move from *preliminaries*, to *investigating* the prospect's problems and needs, to *demonstrating* the supplier's superior capabilities, and then *obtaining* a long-term commitment. This approach reflects the growing interest of many companies in moving from pursuing an immediate sale to developing a long-term customer relationship.

Sharon Drew Morgen takes Rackham's approach a step further with what she calls the Buying Facilitation Method. She holds that the job of a salesperson is to help prospects go through a process to decide first whether their company's performance can be improved, and second whether the seller's offering would provide a solution. Prospects only buy when they realize they have a problem, that they lack resources to solve their problem, and that the seller's offering can add value.

Sales guru Tom Hopkins offers some additional tips to help close a deal:

1. *Ask questions that don't leave room for no.* "I could visit you today at 3, or would tomorrow at 9 be better?"

2. *Never use the word "price" or "cost."* Say investment.

3. *Never ask for "an appointment."* It suggests a serious time commitment. Say "I'll be in the area, and I was hoping I could just pop by and visit."

4. *Don't ask, "May I help you?"* They'll reply, "We're just looking." Ask instead what brought them into the store today.

5. *Isolate areas of agreement.* You need a lot of "little yeses" on the way to get a "big yes."

Sources: Neil Rackham, *SPIN Selling* (New York: McGraw-Hill, 1988). Also see his *The SPIN Selling Fieldbook* (New York: McGraw-Hill, 1996); Neil Rackham and John De Vincentis, *Rethinking the Sales Force* (New York: McGraw-Hill, 1996); Sharon Drew Morgen, *Selling With Integrity: Reinventing Sales Through Collaboration, Respect, and Serving* (New York: Berkeley Books, 1999); James Lardner, "Selling Salesmenship," *Business 2.0* (December 2002/January 2003): 66.

than "sell through price." Salespeople were given richer information about each customer's sales history and behaviour. They received training to recognize value-adding opportunities rather than price-cutting opportunities. As a result, the company's sales revenue climbed and so did its margins.[64]

CLOSING Now the salesperson attempts to close the sale. Salespeople need to know how to recognize closing signs from the buyer, including physical actions, statements or comments, and questions. There are several closing techniques. They can ask for the order, recapitulate the points of agreement, offer to help the secretary write up the order, ask whether the buyer wants A or B, get the buyer to make minor choices such as the colour or size, or indicate what the buyer will lose if the order is not placed now. The salesperson might offer the buyer specific inducements to close, such as a special price, an extra quantity, or a token gift.

FOLLOW-UP AND MAINTENANCE Follow-up and maintenance are necessary if the salesperson wants to ensure customer satisfaction and repeat business. Immediately after closing, the salesperson should cement any necessary details on delivery time, purchase terms, and other matters that are important to the customer. The salesperson should schedule a follow-up call when the initial order is received to make sure there is proper installation, instruction, and servicing. This visit or call will detect any problems, assure the buyer of the salesperson's interest, and reduce any cognitive dissonance that might have arisen. The salesperson should also develop a maintenance and growth plan for the account.

Negotiation

Marketing is concerned with exchange activities and the manner in which the terms of exchange are established. In *routinized exchange*, the terms are established by administered programs of pricing and distribution. In *negotiated exchange*, price and other terms are set via bargaining behaviour, in which two or more parties negotiate long-term binding agreements. Although price is the most frequently negotiated issue, other issues include contract completion time; quality of goods and services offered; purchase volume; responsibility for financing, risk taking, promotion, and title; and product safety.

Marketers who find themselves in bargaining situations need certain traits and skills to be effective. The most important are preparation and planning skill, knowledge of subject matter being negotiated, ability to think clearly and rapidly under pressure and uncertainty, ability to express thoughts verbally, listening skill, judgment and general intelligence, integrity, ability to persuade others, and patience.[65]

Relationship Marketing

The principles of personal selling and negotiation we have described are largely transaction-oriented because their purpose is to close a specific sale. But in many cases the company is not seeking an immediate sale, but rather to build a long-term supplier–customer relationship. The company wants to demonstrate that it has the capabilities to serve the account's needs in a superior way. Today's customers are large and often global. They prefer suppliers who can sell and deliver a coordinated set of products and services to many locations; who can quickly solve problems that arise in different locations; and who can work closely with customer teams to improve products and processes.

Salespeople working with key customers must do more than call when they think customers might be ready to place orders. They should call or visit at other times, take customers to dinner, and make useful suggestions about the business. They should monitor key accounts, know customers' problems, and be ready to serve them in a number of ways.

CIBC

The Canadian Imperial Bank of Commerce sales force practises relationship marketing regularly. Through mining its data warehouses and tracking leads generated from branch and call-centre staff, the company finds information related to events in its customers' lives, such as marriages or home purchases. For example, CIBC launched an initiative that locates customers with overdrawn accounts. Within 48 hours, CIBC makes contact with the customer to offer them overdraft protection. The bank found that customers bought overdraft protection, which protected the customer, created additional revenue, and reduced risk for the bank.[66]

When a relationship management program is properly implemented, the organization will begin to focus as much on managing its customers as on managing its products. At the same time, companies should realize that while there is a strong and warranted move toward relationship marketing, it is not effective in all situations. Ultimately, companies must judge which segments and which specific customers will respond profitably to relationship management.

SUMMARY

1. Direct marketing is an interactive marketing system that uses one or more media to effect a measurable response or transaction at any location. Direct marketing, especially electronic marketing, is showing explosive growth.

2. Direct marketers plan campaigns by deciding on objectives, target markets and prospects, offers, and prices. This is followed by testing and establishing measures to determine the campaign's success.

3. Major channels for direct marketing include face-to-face selling, direct mail, catalogue marketing, telemarketing, interactive TV, kiosks, Web sites, and mobile devices.

4. Interactive marketing provides marketers with opportunities for much greater interaction and individualization through well-designed Web sites as well as online ads and promotions.

5. Sales personnel serve as a company's link to its customers. The sales rep is the company to many of its customers, and it is the rep who brings back to the company much-needed information about the customer.

6. Designing the sales force requires decisions regarding objectives, strategy, structure, size, and compensation. Objectives may include prospecting, targeting, communicating, selling, servicing, information gathering, and allocating. Determining strategy requires choosing the most effective mix of selling approaches. Choosing the sales-force structure entails dividing territories by geography, product, or market (or some combination of these). Estimating how large the sales force needs to be involves estimating the total workload and how many sales hours (and hence salespeople) will be needed. Compensating the sales force entails determining what types of salaries, commissions, bonuses, expense accounts, and benefits to give, and how much weight customer satisfaction should have in determining total compensation.

7. There are five steps involved in managing the sales force: (1) recruiting and selecting sales representatives; (2) training the representatives in sales techniques and in the company's products, policies, and customer-satisfaction orientation; (3) supervising the sales force and helping reps to use their time efficiently; (4) motivating the sales force, and balancing quotas, monetary rewards, and supplementary motivators; (5) evaluating individual and group sales performance.

8. Effective salespeople are trained in the methods of analysis and customer management, as well as the art of sales professionalism. No approach works best in all circumstances, but most trainers agree that selling is a seven-step process: prospecting and qualifying customers, pre-approach, approach, presentation and demonstration, overcoming objections, closing, and follow-up and maintenance.

APPLICATIONS

Marketing Debate: Are Great Salespeople Born or Made?

One difference of opinion with respect to sales concerns the potential impact of training versus selection in developing an effective sales force. Some observers maintain that the best salespeople are "born" that way and are effective due to their personalities and all the interpersonal skills they have developed over a lifetime. Others contend that application of leading-edge sales techniques can make virtually anyone a sales star.

Take a position: The key to developing an effective sales force is selection versus The key to developing an effective sales force is training.

Marketing Discussion

Pick a company and go to the Web site. How would you evaluate the Web site? How well does it score on the 7Cs design elements—context, content, community, customization, communication, connection, and commerce?

Marketing Spotlight: Yahoo!

Yahoo! grew from a tiny upstart surrounded by Silicon Valley heavyweights to a major contender in Internet media. David Filo and Jerry Yang, two computer science Ph.D. students at Stanford University, created a simple search engine in 1994. Using a homemade filing system, the pair catalogued sites on the newly created World Wide Web and published the directory on the Internet. The original version was called Jerry and David's Guide to the World Wide Web.

Filo and Yang named their effort Yahoo! after they left school to devote their full attention to the business. At the time, the company's search engine was unique because in addition to the standard word search features, Yahoo! offered its users a massive searchable index. Surfers could search for sites in broad categories like Business and Economy or Arts and Humanities. They could organize the results by country or region and look at results from within just one category. Since Yahoo! was among the first such Internet guides, the site attracted hundreds of thousands of surfers within a year of its introduction. This early attention attracted investors, and in April 1995 founders Filo and Yang raised US$1 million in first-round venture capital.

From its start, Yahoo! conveyed an irreverent attitude. The Yahoo! attitude came from the top of the corporate ladder, in the personalities of founders Filo and Yang. The two had conceived of Yahoo! while housed "in trailers full of pizza boxes," and each of their business cards bore the title "Chief Yahoo!" Even the name contains a hidden joke—Yahoo is a self-deprecating acronym meaning "Yet Another Hierarchical Officious Oracle." Yahoo!'s marketing reflected the company's style as well: In one ad, Inuit ordered a hot tub online. Each ad closed with the tagline "Do You Yahoo!?" and the signature "Yahoo! yodel," an audio cue designed to reinforce customer recall of the brand.

Yahoo's most recent step into interactive marketing is to offer contextual advertising on its site. Contextual advertising means that the commercial links on a Yahoo page are tied to the particular content on that page. For example, a visitor at caranddriver.com reading a review of the Acura MDX will see paid text links advertising the Acura Web site and the Edmunds auto comparison site, rather than unrelated cell phone ads. Contextual advertising shows the same links users would see if they typed "Acura MDX" into the Yahoo! search engine.

Contextual advertising appeals to advertisers who are moving away from mass marketing toward more targeted approaches. Yahoo's new ad server creates contextual relevance, catching a consumer or decision maker reading material directly related to the advertised topic.

Although most users consider Yahoo! to be a search engine, Yahoo! sees itself as a place that packages experiences for consumers. A large percentage of revenues come from advertising, but the company continues to supplement its revenue through subscription sources such as online personal ads, premium e-mail products, and services for small businesses. For example, Yahoo! teamed with telecom company SBC to sell branded high-speed Internet service bundled with Yahoo services and premium e-mail. SBC Communications pays Yahoo! an estimated US$2.10 per month for every customer on the service. This lets Yahoo! increase its revenues without having to sell premium services one customer at a time. Jordan Rohan, an analyst at Schwab Soundview Capital Markets, estimates that Yahoo!'s non-search advertising grew by 22 percent in the fourth quarter of 2003, twice the rate of other specialized content sites.

Yahoo!'s two main advantages over search engine rival Google are its vast array of original content and a database with information about its 133 million registered users. By knowing where searchers live and what their interests are, Yahoo believes it can present them with both more relevant search results and more focused advertising.

Yahoo! is also attracting traditional advertisers like Pepsi and Ford. Yahoo!'s ad for the Ford Explorer, for example, featured sound effects simulating an engine with animation that made the Web browser appear to shake. To announce its new Ford F-150 Truck, Ford created an interactive 3-D ad and purchased roadblocks (ads that browsers must click through to reach other content) on the first day of its launch at Yahoo! as well as at MSN and AOL.

DISCUSSION QUESTIONS

1. What have been the key success factors for Yahoo!?

2. Where is Yahoo! vulnerable? What should it watch out for?

3. What recommendations would you make to senior marketing executives going forward? What should the company be sure to do with its marketing?

Sources: Saul Hansell, "The Search Engine That Isn't a Verb, Yet," *New York Times*, February 22, 2004; John Battelle, "Putting Online Ads in Context," *Business 2.0*, June 2003; Roger Slavens, "Contextual Search Heats Up," *B to B*, November 10, 2003, p. 25; "What Works" *Brandweek*, November 24, 2003, p. S12.

CREATING SUCCESSFUL LONG-TERM GROWTH

IN THIS CHAPTER, WE WILL ADDRESS THE FOLLOWING QUESTIONS:

- What challenges does a company face in developing new products?

- What organizational structures are used to manage new-product development?

- What are the main stages in developing new products?

- What is the best way to set up the new product development process?

- What factors affect the rate of diffusion and consumer adoption of newly launched products?

CHAPTER 20

Introducing New Market Offerings

PROFILE: CANADIAN MARKETING EXCELLENCE

Companies need to grow their revenue over time by developing new products and expanding into new markets. New product development shapes the company's future: improved or replacement products will maintain or build sales. Some companies put product innovation at the forefront of all they do. 3M Canada is one of the most innovative companies in the country. Creating innovative products and services that respond to customer needs has always been a way of life at 3M.

With this history of innovation, 3M makes more than 50 000 products, including sandpaper, adhesives, optical films, and fibre optic connectors. 3M's culture has fostered creativity and has given its employees the freedom to take risks and try new ideas. It invests more than US$1 billion annually in research and development, with a staff of more than 6000 scientists worldwide, and launches scores of new products every year. 3M's policy of allowing all employees to spend up to 15 percent of their time working on projects of personal interest helped to produce Post-it® notes, masking tape, and 3M's micro-replication technology. At the same time, 3M carefully monitors the commercialization potential for new product candidates, making sure scientists and marketers collaborate early in the process and putting more resources behind the likely winners. 3M's Golden Step Award program honours 3M employees and team members who have developed significant new products, product lines, or markets, and successfully generated at least US$10 million in annual global sales within three years of product introduction.

3M Canada was established in 1951 as the first international subsidiary of the global 3M Company. Today 3M has offices in more than 60 countries around the world. In 2004, it generated $US20 billion worldwide in sales revenues. 3M Canada employs more than 2000 people and has total annual sales of more than $1 billion. Its head offices are located in London, Ontario, and it has manufacturing operations and sales offices across the country.

3M Canada's vision statement puts customers and innovation at the centre of its business: "We will grow by helping our customers win—through the ingenuity and responsiveness of people who care." It stresses that it is committed to satisfying its customers with superior quality and value, while respecting the social and physical environment.

Take just one of its new products—one that is based on a perennial favourite—duct tape. No matter how successful the product, 3M is always seeking ways to make it better. 3M knew that the problem with repairing something using duct tape has always been "the ugly factor." Thus, the company developed a new version of the product that can handle almost any repair almost invisibly. Was the new product a success? Undoubtedly! When 3M surveyed Canadian consumers, over half of them said they would increase their use of duct tape now that the new product is available. Transparency isn't the only advantage to the new tape, however. It last six times longer than traditional duct tape, and it comes off the roll easily.

In early 2005, headlines in Canadian newspapers told of the problem hospitals were having fighting bacteria. While the surgical scrub process was effective, it often damaged the skin in the process of quelling bacteria. Surveys of operating room nurses revealed that 80 percent of them experienced problems with their hands, including dry, scaly, cracked skin; red, blotchy skin; or stinging resulting from hand-washing and scrubbing with anti-microbial agents. 3M again found a solution with a new product, 3M™ Avagard™, which not only kills bacteria but also protects the integrity of the skin. The emollient-rich formula makes it gentle on hands. Its waterless, scrubless properties spare hands the damage and, since it is applied via a foot pump, there is no contamination of the dispenser or recontamination of the hands.

As these two examples show, 3M is a powerhouse of problem solving through innovation!

Sources: "3M Canada's What's New Stories," "3M Canada's Visions, Values & Goals," "The 3M Canada Story," **http://solutions.3m.com/wps/portal/_s.155/110903/_l/en_CA/**; Michael Arndt, "3M's Rising Star," *BusinessWeek*, April 12, 2004, pp. 62–74.

Marketers play a key role in the new-product process by identifying and evaluating new product ideas and working with R&D and others in every stage of development. This chapter provides a detailed analysis of the new product development process. Chapter 21 considers how marketers can tap into global markets as another source of long-term growth.

Challenges in New Product Development

A company can add new products through acquisition or development. The acquisition route can take three forms. The company can buy other companies, it can acquire patents from other companies, or it can buy a licence or franchise from another company. Swiss food giant Nestlé increased its presence in North America via its acquisition of such diverse brands as Carnation, Hills Brothers, Stouffer's, and Ralston Purina.[1]

The development route can take two forms. The company can develop new products in its own laboratories, or it can contract with independent researchers or new-product development firms to develop specific new products. We can identify six categories of new products:[2]

1. *New-to-the-world products*—New products that create an entirely new market.
2. *New product lines*—New products that allow a company to enter an established market for the first time.
3. *Additions to existing product lines*—New products that supplement established product lines (package sizes, flavours, and so on).
4. *Improvements and revisions of existing products*—New products that provide improved performance or greater perceived value and replace existing products.
5. *Repositionings*—Existing products that are targeted to new markets or market segments.
6. *Cost reductions*—New products that provide similar performance at lower cost.

Less than 10 percent of all new products are truly innovative and new to the world. These products involve the greatest cost and risk because they are new to both the company and the marketplace. W. L. Gore, best known for its durable Gore-Tex outdoor fabric, has innovated breakthrough new products in a number of diverse areas—guitar strings, dental floss, medical devices, and fuel cells. It has adopted several principles to guide its new product development:[3]

1. *Work with potential customers.* Its thoracic graft designed to combat heart disease was developed in close collaboration with physicians.

2. *Let employees choose projects.* Few actual product leaders and teams are appointed. Gore likes to nurture "passionate champions" who convince others a project is worth their time and commitment. The development of the fuel cell rallied over 100 of the company's 6000 research associates.

3. *Give employees "dabble" time.* All research associates spend 10 percent of their work hours developing their own ideas. Promising ideas are pushed forward and judged according to a "Real, Win, Worth" exercise. Is the opportunity real? Can we win? Can we make money?

4. *Know when to let go.* Sometimes dead ends in one area can spark an innovation in another. Elixir acoustic guitar strings were a result of a failed venture into bike cables. Even successful ventures may have to move on. Glide shred-resistant dental floss was sold to Procter & Gamble because Gore-Tex knew that retailers would want to deal with a company selling a whole family of health-care products.

Most new-product activity is devoted to improving existing products. At Sony, over 80 percent of new-product activity is actually modifying and improving existing products. Gillette frequently updates its razor systems, launching the new M3Power wet shaver for men and Venus Divine for women in 2004.[4] In many categories, it is becoming increasingly difficult to identify blockbuster products that transform a market. But continually innovating to better satisfy consumer needs can force competitors to play catch-up.[5]

BlackBerry

Indispensable to subscribers including Sarah Jessica Parker and Jack Welch, Waterloo Ontario–based Research in Motion's (RIM) BlackBerry, introduced in 1999, has become almost synonymous with wireless e-mail. E-mail is automatically directed to BlackBerry as it is going to the desktop and can be answered with an intuitive thumb-operated keyboard. The corporate goal is to "enable wireless e-mail whenever and on whatever device people want." Adding new features such as voice and speakerphones, brighter colour screens, backlit keyboards, and international roaming has fuelled explosive growth. Its fanatical appeal has led some to dub the product "CrackBerries." With a subscriber base reaching 3 million in 2005, it's no surprise the stock price increased tenfold during the previous year.[6]

Launching new products as brand extensions into related product categories is one means of broadening the brand meaning. Nike started as a running shoe manufacturer but now competes in the sports market with all types of athletic shoes, clothing, and equipment. Armstrong World Industries moved from selling floor coverings to ceilings to total interior surface decoration. Product innovation and effective marketing programs have allowed these firms to expand their "market footprint."

In an economy of rapid change, continuous innovation is necessary. Most companies rarely innovate, some innovate occasionally, and a few innovate continuously. In the last category, McCain, Sony, 3M, Dell Computer, Maple Leaf, Oracle, Maytag, Costco, and Microsoft have been stock-price gain leaders in their respective industries.[7] These companies have created a positive attitude toward innovation and risk taking, they have routinized the innovation process, they practise teamwork, and they allow their people to experiment and even fail.

Companies that fail to develop new products are putting themselves at risk. Their existing products are vulnerable to changing customer needs and tastes, new technologies, shortened product life cycles, and increased domestic and foreign competition. New technologies are especially threatening.

Most established companies focus on *incremental innovation.* Newer companies create *disruptive technologies* that are cheaper and more likely to alter the competitive space. Established companies can be slow to react or invest in these disruptive technologies because they threaten their investment. Then they suddenly find themselves facing formidable new competitors, and many fail.[8]

Improving existing products: print ad for the new Gillette M3Power shaver for men.

To ensure that they don't fall into this trap, incumbent firms must carefully monitor the preferences of both customers and noncustomers over time and uncover evolving, difficult-to-articulate customer needs.[9]

PepsiCo

Determined to develop new products to reflect changing consumer tastes and demographics, food and beverage giant PepsiCo adds more than 200 product variations to its global portfolio each year, ranging from Quaker Soy Crisps to Gatorade Xtremo Thirst Quencher. Chairman and CEO Steven Reinmund believes that innovation is the key to consistent double-digit earnings growth: "Innovation is what consumers are looking for, particularly in the small, routine things of life." PepsiCo emphasizes new flavours and healthier ingredients with existing brands. It has also successfully launched new product lines in the United States such as Sabritas chips, a US$100 million success brought over from its Mexican subsidiary, and Propel fitness water, which achieved similar sales success only a year after its launch.[10]

At the same time, new-product development can be quite risky. Texas Instruments lost US$660 million before withdrawing from the home computer business; RCA lost US$500 million on its videodisc players; FedEx lost US$340 million on its Zap mail; DuPont lost an estimated US$100 million on a synthetic leather called Corfam; and the British-French Concorde aircraft never recovered its investment.[11] Even these amounts are paltry compared to the US$5 billion Iridium fiasco (see "Marketing Insight: Iridium Disconnects with Global Customers").

MARKETING INSIGHT

Iridium Disconnects with Global Customers

In the late 1990s, Motorola and several partners launched Iridium, a US$5 billion global satellite-based wireless telephone system. Motorola's engineers envisioned 66 telecommunications satellites that would circle the earth and make it possible for consumers to place and receive calls with one phone anywhere in the world. Motorola's aim was to establish a universal standard for wireless telephony.

Yet in August 1999, Iridium had to file for bankruptcy because it was unable to meet a US$90 million bond payment, and in March 2000, a judge ordered that the bankrupt system be shut down. Motorola was forced to pull the plug on the project. Now, it's clear that the project's sponsors did a poor job of thinking through the marketing issues:

1. The Iridium handset weighed about half a kilogram; most cell phones weigh considerably less. The handset was shaped like a brick and was awkward to carry or pack in a briefcase. The user had to carry a bag of attachments to achieve full functionality. Transmission problems included frequent incomplete calls and lost calls, and the voice quality was poorer than callers were used to on their cellular phones.

2. Iridium was originally launched at US$3000 and eventually came down to US$1500. Worse, airtime charges ranged from US$4 to US$9 a minute, whether the caller was phoning in his or her own city or calling from a Borneo jungle.

3. Although the phone was touted to be workable anywhere, it could not be used inside buildings or in moving cars. Users had to have a clear path between the handset and the orbiting satellites. Furthermore, large areas in Europe, Asia, and Africa lacked service.

4. Iridium budgeted US$180 million for promotion. Its advertising campaign showed a man in a heavy parka pulling a sled in a desolate snowbound place. His phone suddenly rings: He has contact with the outside world. This ad campaign was supplemented with a direct-mail campaign and a strong public relations program, but all this promotion needed to be followed up by competent personal selling. This was the hardest challenge, because prospects would raise questions about price, service breakdowns, and the bulky handset, and often conclude that the benefits were not worth the price.

5. Motorola chose selling partners in other parts of the world who often lacked marketing skills. Although the promotion campaign generated about 1.5 million inquiries, most were not answered or not answered quickly enough.

Senior management set a drop-dead launch date of September 23, 1998, but had to delay this until November 1. Even then, the company still had problems with the product, service, distribution, support, and finances. With all these complications, no wonder the project never attracted more than 50 000 buyers. The lesson: No amount of promotion can make a success out of a poorly designed product plagued with poor quality and poor service.

Sources: Jonathan Sidener, "Iridium's Adventure over Satellite Phone System Ordered Shut Down," *Arizona Republic*, March 18, 2000; Kevin Maney, "$3,000 Gadget Might Be Globe-Trotters Best Friend," *USA Today*, September 17, 1998; Leslie Cauley, "Iridium's Downfall," *Wall Street Journal*, August 18, 1999; Eric M. Olson, Stanley F. Slater, and Andrew J. Czaplewski, "The Iridium Story: A Marketing Disconnect?" *Marketing Management* (Summer 2000): 54–57.

New products designed for consumers and businesses continue to fail at a disturbing rate. Recent studies put the rate at 95 percent in the United States and 90 percent in Europe. In Canada, according to most industry estimates, 80 percent of new consumer products fail, with 20 percent remaining on shelves after two years.[12] New products can fail for many reasons: ignoring or misinterpreting market research; overestimating market size; high development costs; poor design; incorrect positioning, ineffective advertising, or wrong price; insufficient distribution support; and competitors who fight back hard.

Several factors also tend to hinder new product development:

- *Shortage of important ideas in certain areas.* There may be few ways left to improve some basic products (such as steel or detergents).

- *Fragmented markets.* Companies have to aim their new products at smaller market segments, and this can mean lower sales and profits for each product.

- *Social and governmental constraints.* New products have to satisfy consumer safety and environmental concerns.

- *Cost of development.* A company typically has to generate many ideas to find just one worthy of development, and often faces high R&D, manufacturing, and marketing costs.

- *Capital shortages.* Some companies with good ideas cannot raise the funds needed to research and launch them.

- *Faster required development time.* Companies must learn how to compress development time by using new techniques, strategic partners, early concept tests, and advanced marketing planning.

- *Shorter product life cycles.* When a new product is successful, rivals are quick to copy it. Sony used to enjoy a three-year lead on its new products. Now Matsushita will copy the product within six months, leaving hardly enough time for Sony to recoup its investment.

What can a company do to develop successful new products? Cooper and Kleinschmidt found that the number-one success factor is a unique, superior product. Such products succeed 98 percent of the time, compared to products with a moderate advantage (58 percent success) or minimal advantage (18 percent success). Another key factor is a well-defined product concept. The company carefully defines and assesses the target market, product requirements, and benefits before proceeding. Other success factors are technological and marketing synergy, quality of execution in all stages, and market attractiveness.[13] (See "Marketing Memo: Lessons for New Product Success.")

In 2004, *Marketing Magazine* debuted its Best New Product award. All the winners clearly demonstrate the new-product success factors described above. Five thousand Canadians voted on the appeal of the new products and whether or not they would repurchase them. Consider just two of the 2004 award winners:

Marketing Memo

Lessons for New Product Success

Strolling the aisles at Robert McMath's New Product Showcase and Learning Center is like being in some nightmare version of a supermarket. There is Gerber food for adults (pureed sweet-and-sour pork and chicken Madeira), microwaveable ice cream sundaes, parsnip chips, aerosol mustard, Ben-Gay aspirin, and Miller Clear Beer. How about Richard Simmons Dijon Vinaigrette Salad Spray, garlic cake in a jar, and Farrah shampoo?

McMath's unusual showcase represents US$4 billion in product investment. Behind each of the 80 000 products on display are squandered dollars and hopes. From them he has distilled dozens of lessons for an industry that, by its own admission, has a very short memory. McMath, a former marketer for Colgate-Palmolive, has now put his unique insights into a book called *What Were They Thinking?* Here are a few of the marketing lessons McMath espouses:

- *The value of a brand is its good name, which it earns over time.* People trust it to deliver a consistent set of attributes. Do not squander this trust by attaching your good name to something totally out of character. Louis Sherry No Sugar Added Gorgonzola Cheese dressing was everything that Louis Sherry, known for its rich candies and ice cream, should not be: sugarless, cheese, and salad dressing.

- *Me-too marketing is the number-one killer of new products.* Pepsi is one of the few survivors among dozens of other brands that have challenged Coke for more than a century. Ever hear of Toca-Cola? Coco-Cola? Yum-Yum Cola? French Wine of Cola? How about King-Cola, "the royal drink"?

- *People usually do not buy products that remind them of their shortcomings.* Gillette's For Oily Hair Only shampoo flopped because people did not want to confess that they had greasy hair; nor do they wish to advertise their faults and foibles to other people by carrying such products in their grocery carts.

- *Some products are too different from the products, services, or experiences consumers normally purchase.* You can tell that some innovative products are doomed as soon as you hear their names: Toaster Eggs, Cucumber Antiperspirant spray, Health-Sea Sea Sausage.

Sources: Paul Lukas, "The Ghastliest Product Launches," *Fortune*, March 16, 1996, p. 44; Jan Alexander, "Failure Inc." *Worldbusiness* (May–June 1996): 46; Ted Anthony, "Where's Farrah Shampoo? Next to the Salsa Ketchup," *Marketing News*, May 6, 1996, p. 13. Bulleted points are adapted from Robert M. McMath and Thom Forbes, *What Were They Thinking? Marketing Lessons I've Learned from Over 80,000 New-Product Innovations and Idiocies* (New York: Times Business, 1998), pp. 22–24, 28, 30–31, and 129–130.

Maple Leaf Prime Naturally Chicken

Maple Leaf Prime Naturally chicken won, in part, because of its lean, clean, and additive-free branding. As a product that tapped into Canadians' health and nutrition concerns, it became a sure-fire hit. Moreover, its clear packaging allows the consumers to see the quality of the chicken. As one consumer noted, "I trust the name 'Maple Leaf' and I like knowing that my foods aren't fed a bunch of chemicals."

Knorr 30-Minute Marinade (Unilever Canada)

This new product was another winner. With more and more two-income families, time is of the essence when it comes to preparing meals. Knorr coupled great taste with convenience, making its new marinade a must-have for Canadian consumers. Consumers were quick to sing its praises: "It makes everything you put in it taste fantastic." "The short time to marinate means a lot less preparation time. I don't have to plan ahead."

Organizational Arrangements

Once a company has carefully segmented the market, chosen its target customers, identified their needs, and determined its market positioning, it is better able to develop new products. Many companies today use *customer-driven engineering* to design new products. Customer-driven engineering attaches high importance to incorporating customer preferences in the final design.

New-product development requires senior management to define business domains, product categories, and specific criteria. General Motors has a hefty US$400 million benchmark it must apply to new car models—this is what it costs to get a new vehicle into production.[14] One company established the following acceptance criteria:

- The product can be introduced within five years.
- The product has a market potential of at least $50 million and a 15 percent growth rate.
- The product would provide at least 30 percent return on sales and 40 percent on investment.
- The product would achieve technical or market leadership.

Maple Leaf Prime Naturally chicken and Knorr 30-Minute Marinade were two of the 2004 *Marketing Magazine* New Product Award winners. These unique, superior products each offered consumers a new, distinct benefit.

Budgeting for New-Product Development

Senior management must decide how much to budget for new-product development. R&D outcomes are so uncertain that it is difficult to use normal investment criteria. Some companies solve this problem by financing as many projects as possible, hoping to achieve a few winners. Other companies apply a conventional percentage of sales figures or spend what the competition spends. Still other companies decide how many successful new products they need and work backward to estimate the required investment.

Table 20.1 shows how a company might calculate the cost of new product development. The new-products manager at a large consumer packaged-goods company reviewed the results of 64 ideas. Only one in four, or 16, passed the screening stage. It cost $1000 to review each idea at this stage. Half of these ideas, or eight, survived the concept-testing stage, at a cost of $20 000 each. Half of these, or four, survived the product-development stage, at a cost of $200 000 each. Half of these, or two, did well in the test market, at a cost of $500 000 each. When these two ideas were launched, at a cost of $5 million each, only one was highly successful. Thus the one successful idea cost the company $5 721 000 to develop.

In the process, 63 other ideas fell by the wayside. The total cost for developing one successful new product was $13 984 000. Unless the company can improve the pass ratios and reduce the costs at each stage, it will have to budget nearly $14 million for each successful new idea it hopes to find. If top management wants four successful new products in the next few years, it will have to budget at least $56 million (4 × $14 million) for new-product development.

Organizing New-Product Development

Companies handle the organizational aspect of new-product development in several ways.[15] Many companies assign responsibility for new-product ideas to *product managers*. But product managers are often so busy managing existing lines that they give little thought to new products other than line extensions. They also lack the specific skills and knowledge needed to develop and critique new products. Kraft and Johnson & Johnson have *new-product managers* who report to category managers. Some companies have a *high-level management committee* charged with reviewing and approving proposals. Large companies often establish a *new-product department* headed by a manager who has substantial authority and access to top management. The department's major responsibilities include generating and screening new ideas, working with the R&D department, and carrying out field-testing and commercialization.

3M, Dow, and General Mills often assign new-product development work to *venture teams*. A **venture team** is a cross-functional group charged with developing a specific product or business. These "intrapreneurs" are relieved of their other duties and given a budget, a time frame, and a "skunkworks" setting. *Skunkworks* are informal workplaces, sometimes garages, where intrapreneurial teams attempt to develop new products.

Cross-functional teams can collaborate and use concurrent new-product development to push new products to market.[16] Concurrent product development resembles a rugby match rather than a relay race, with team members passing the new product back and forth as they head toward the goal. Using this system, the Allen-Bradley Corporation (a maker of industrial controls) was able to develop a new electrical control device in just two years, as opposed to six years under its old system.

TABLE 20.1	FINDING ONE SUCCESSFUL NEW PRODUCT (STARTING WITH 64 NEW IDEAS)			
Stage	Number of Ideas	Pass Ratio	Cost per Product Idea	Total Cost
1. Idea screening	64	1:4	$ 1 000	$ 64 000
2. Concept testing	16	1:2	20 000	320 000
3. Product development	8	1:2	200 000	1 600 000
4. Test marketing	4	1:2	500 000	2 000 000
5. National launch	2	1:2	5 000 000	10 000 000
			$5 721 000	$13 984 000

Cross-functional teams help to ensure that engineers are not just driven to create a "better mousetrap" when potential customers do not really need or want one. Some possible criteria for staffing cross-functional new-product venture teams include:[17]

- *Desired team leadership style and level of expertise.* The more complex the new-product concept, the greater the desired expertise.

- *Team member skills and expertise.* New-venture teams for Aventis, part of a pharmaceutical, agricultural, and chemical conglomerate, contain people with expertise in chemistry, engineering, market research, financial analysis, and manufacturing.

- *Level of interest in the particular new-product concept.* Is there interest or, even better, a high level of ownership and commitment (a "concept champion")?

- *Potential for personal reward.* What motivates individuals to want to participate in this effort?

- *Diversity of team members.* This includes race, gender, nationality, breadth of experience, depth of experience, and personality. The greater the diversity, the greater the range of viewpoints and decision-making potential.

3M, Hewlett-Packard, Lego, and many other companies use the *stage-gate system* to manage the innovation process.[18] The process is divided into stages, and at the end of each stage is a gate or checkpoint. The project leader, working with a cross-functional team, must bring a set of known deliverables to each gate before the project can pass to the next stage. To move from the business plan stage into product development requires a convincing market research study of consumer needs and interest, a competitive analysis, and a technical appraisal. Senior managers review the criteria at each gate to judge whether the project deserves to move to the next stage. The gatekeepers make one of four decisions: *go, kill, hold,* or *recycle.* Stage-gate systems make the innovation process visible to all involved and clarify the project leader's and team's responsibilities at each stage.[19]

The stages in the new-product development process are shown in Figure 20.1. Many firms have multiple, parallel sets of projects working through the process, each at a different stage.[20] The process can be depicted as a *funnel:* a large number of initial new product ideas and concepts are winnowed down to a few high-potential products that are ultimately launched. But the process is not always linear. Many firms use a *spiral development process* that recognizes the value of returning to an earlier stage to make improvements before moving forward.

FIGURE 20.1

The New-Product
Development Decision Process

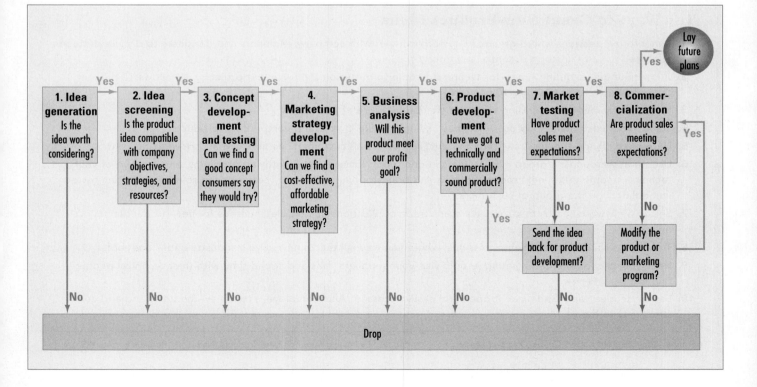

Eli Lilly

Recognizing that 90 percent of experimental drugs fail, Eli Lilly has established a corporate culture that looks at failure as an inevitable part of discovery. If a drug fails at its intended use, Lilly scientists are taught to look for new uses. Lilly often assigns a team of doctors and scientists to analyze every compound that fails at any stage in a human clinical trial. Many of Lilly's drug successes actually started out as failures. Evista was a failed contraceptive that became a US$1 billion-a-year drug for osteoporosis. Stattera was unsuccessful as an anti-depressant, but became a top seller for attention deficit/hyperactivity disorder. One promising cardiovascular drug in development started as an asthma project.[21]

We now look at the marketing challenges arising at each of the eight stages.

Managing the Development Process: Ideas

Idea Generation

The new product development process starts with the search for ideas. Some marketing experts believe that the greatest opportunities and highest leverage with new products are found by uncovering the best possible set of unmet customer needs or technological innovation.[22] New product ideas can come from interacting with various groups and from using creativity-generating techniques. (See "Marketing Memo: Ten Ways to Great New-Product Ideas.")

INTERACTING WITH OTHERS Ideas for new products can come from many sources, such as customers, scientists, competitors, employees, channel members, and top management.

Customer needs and wants are the logical place to start the search. One-on-one interviews and focus-group discussions can explore product needs and reactions. Griffin and Hauser suggest that conducting 10 to 20 in-depth experiential interviews per market segment often elicits the vast majority of customer needs.[23]

Marketing Memo

Ten Ways to Great New-Product Ideas

1. Run informal sessions where groups of customers meet with company engineers and designers to discuss problems and needs and brainstorm potential solutions.

2. Allow time off—scouting time—for technical people to putter on their own pet projects. 3M allows 15 percent time off; Rohm & Haas allows 10 percent.

3. Make a customer-brainstorming session a standard feature of plant tours.

4. Survey your customers: Find out what they like and dislike in your and competitors' products.

5. Undertake "fly-on-the-wall" or "camping out" research with customers, as do Fluke and Hewlett-Packard.

6. Use iterative rounds: a group of customers in one room, focusing on identifying problems, and a group of your technical people in the next room, listening and brainstorming solutions. The proposed solutions are then tested immediately on the group of customers.

7. Set up a keyword search that routinely scans trade publications in multiple countries for new-product announcements.

8. Treat trade shows as intelligence missions, where you view all that is new in your industry under one roof.

9. Have your technical and marketing people visit your suppliers' labs and spend time with their technical people—find out what is new.

10. Set up an idea vault, and make it open and easily accessed. Allow employees to review the ideas and add constructively to them.

Source: Adapted from Robert Cooper, *Product Leadership: Creating and Launching Superior New Products* (New York: Perseus Books, 1998).

Procter & Gamble emphasizes observational techniques with its customers. Brand marketers there spend at least 12 hours a month with consumers in their homes—watching how they clean dishes, wash floors, and brush teeth—and asking them about their habits and sources of frustration. They also have on-site labs such as a diaper-testing centre where dozens of parents bring their babies to be studied. This close scrutiny has led to several new product successes.

Procter & Gamble

To develop its Cover Girl Outlast all-day lip colour, P&G tested the product on nearly 30 000 women, inviting 500 of them to come to its labs each morning to apply the lipstick, record their activities, and return eight hours later so it could measure remaining lip colour. The activities, dubbed "torture tests" by P&G, ranged from eating spaghetti to kickboxing to showering. The product comes with a tube of glossy moisturizer that women can reapply on top of their colour—without having to look at a mirror. The blockbuster product quickly became the market leader.[24]

Technical companies can learn a great deal by studying customers who make the most advanced use of the company's products and who recognize the need for improvements before other customers do.[25] Microsoft studied 13- to 24-year-olds—the NetGen—and developed its threedegrees software product to satisfy their instant-messaging needs.[26] (For the special case of high-tech products, see "Marketing Insight: Developing Successful High-Tech Products.")

Employees throughout the company can be a source of ideas for improving production, products, and services. Toyota claims its employees submit 2 million ideas annually (about 35 suggestions per employee), over 85 percent of which are implemented. Kodak, Milliken, and other firms give monetary, holiday, or recognition awards to employees who submit the best ideas.

Companies can also find good ideas by researching competitors' products and services. They can find out what customers like and dislike about competitors' products. They can buy their competitors' products, take them apart, and build better ones. Company sales representatives and intermediaries are a particularly good source of ideas. These groups have firsthand exposure to customers and are often the first to learn about competitive developments.

Top management can be another major source of ideas. Some company leaders, such as the late Edwin H. Land, former CEO of Polaroid, or Andy Grove of Intel, took personal responsibility for technological innovation in their companies. New-product ideas can also come from inventors, patent lawyers, university and commercial laboratories, industrial consultants, advertising agencies, marketing research firms, and industrial publications. However, although ideas can flow from many sources, their chances of receiving serious attention often depend on someone in the organization taking the role of product champion.

CREATIVITY TECHNIQUES   Here is a sampling of techniques for stimulating creativity in individuals and groups:[27]

- *Attribute listing.* List the attributes of an object, such as a screwdriver. Then modify each attribute, such as replacing the wooden handle with plastic, providing torque power, adding different screw heads, and so on.

- *Forced relationships.* List several ideas and consider each one in relation to each other one. In designing new office furniture, for example, consider a desk, bookcase, and filing cabinet as separate ideas. One can then imagine a desk with a built-in bookcase or a desk with built-in files or a bookcase with built-in files.

- *Morphological analysis.* Start with a problem, such as "getting something from one place to another via a powered vehicle." Now think of dimensions, such as the type of platform (cart, chair, sling, bed), the medium (air, water, oil, rails), and the power source (compressed air, electric motor, magnetic fields). By listing every possible combination, one can generate many new solutions.

A blockbuster product: Cover Girl Outlast all-day lip colour. The product comes with a tube of moisturizer to be applied on top of the colour.

Developing Successful High-Tech Products

High tech covers a wide range of industries—telecommunications, computers, consumer electronics, biotech, software. Radical innovations carry a high level of risk and typically hurt the company's bottom line at least in the short run. The good news is that success can create a greater sustainable competitive advantage than might come from more ordinary products.

One way to define the scope of high tech is by its common characteristics:

- *High technological uncertainty.* Scientists working on high-tech products are never sure they will function as promised and be delivered on time.

- *High market uncertainty.* Marketers are not sure what needs the new technology will meet. How will buyers use Interactive TV? Which DVD format will prevail after Toshiba's introduction of HD (high definition) DVD?

- *High competitive volatility.* Will the strongest competition come from within the industry or from outside? Will competitors rewrite the rules? What products will this new technology replace?

- *High investment cost, low variable cost.* Many high-tech products require a large up-front investment to develop the first unit, but the costs fall rapidly on additional units. The cost of developing a new piece of software is very high, but the cost of distributing it in a CD-ROM is relatively low.

- *Short life.* Most high-tech products must be constantly upgraded. Competitors will often force the innovator to produce a second generation before recouping its investment on the first generation.

- *Finding funding sources for such risky projects is not easy.* Companies must create a strong R&D/marketing partnership to pull it off. Few reliable techniques exist for estimating demand for radical innovations. Focus groups will provide some perspectives on customer interest and need, but high-tech marketers will have to use a probe and learn approach based on observing early users and collecting feedback on their experiences.

High-tech marketers also face difficult questions related to the marketing mix:

- *Product.* What features and functions should they build into the new product? Should manufacturing be done in-house or be outsourced?

- *Price.* Should the price be set high? Would a low price be better in order to sell more quickly and go down the experience curve faster? Should the product be almost given away to accelerate adoption?

- *Distribution.* Is the product best sold through the company's own sales force or should it be put in the hands of agents, distributors, and dealers? Should the company start with one channel or build multiple sales channels early?

- *Communication.* What are the best messages to convey the basic benefits and features of the new product? What are the best media for communicating these messages? What sales-promotion incentives would drive early interest and purchase?

Source: For further ideas, see Jakki Mohr, *Marketing of High-Technology Products and Innovations*, 2nd ed. (Upper Saddle River, NJ: Prentice Hall, 2005).

- *Reverse assumption analysis.* List all the normal assumptions about an entity and then reverse them. Instead of assuming that a restaurant has menus, charges for food, and serves food, reverse each assumption. The new restaurant may decide to serve only what the chef bought that morning and cooked; may provide some food and charge only for how long the person sits at the table; and may design an exotic atmosphere and rent out the space to people who bring their own food and beverages.

- *New contexts.* Take familiar processes, such as people-helping services, and put them into a new context. Imagine helping dogs and cats instead of people with daycare service, stress reduction, psychotherapy, animal funerals, and so on. As another example, instead of hotel guests going to the front desk to check in, greet them at curbside and use a wireless device to register them.

- *Mind-mapping.* Start with a thought, such as a car, write it on a piece of paper, then think of the next thought that comes up (say Mercedes), link it to car, then think of the next association (Germany), and do this with all associations that come up with each new word. Perhaps a whole new idea will materialize.

Increasingly, new product ideas arise from *lateral marketing* that combines two product concepts or ideas to create a new offering. Here are some successful examples:

- Gas station stores = gas stations + food
- Cyber cafés = cafeteria + Internet
- Cereal bars = cereal + snacking
- Kinder Surprise = candy + toy
- Sony Walkman = audio + portable

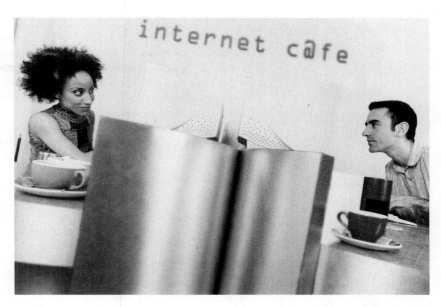

A cyber café = cafeteria + Internet.

Idea Screening

A company should motivate its employees to submit new ideas to an *idea manager* whose name and phone number are widely circulated. Ideas should be written down and reviewed each week by an *idea committee*. The company then sorts the proposed ideas into three groups: promising ideas, marginal ideas, and rejects. Each promising idea is researched by a committee member, who reports back to the committee. The surviving ideas then move into a full-scale screening process. In screening ideas, the company must avoid two types of errors.

A *DROP-error* occurs when the company dismisses an otherwise good idea. It is extremely easy to find fault with other people's ideas (Figure 20.2). Some companies shudder when they look back at ideas they dismissed or breathe sighs of relief when they realize how close they came to dropping what eventually became a huge success. This was the case with the television show *Friends*:

Friends

The NBC situation comedy *Friends* enjoyed a ten-year run from 1994 to 2004 as a perennial ratings powerhouse. But the show almost didn't see the light of day. According to an internal NBC research report, the pilot episode was described as "not very entertaining, clever, or original" and was given a failing grade, scoring 41 out of 100. Ironically, the pilot for an earlier hit sit-com, *Seinfeld*, also was rated as "weak," although the pilot for the medical drama *ER* scored a healthy 91. Courtney Cox's Monica was the *Friends* character that scored best with test audiences, but characters portrayed by Lisa Kudrow and Matthew Perry were deemed to have marginal appeal, and the Rachel, Ross, and Joey characters scored even lower. Adults 35 and over in the sample found the characters, as a whole, "smug, superficial, and self-absorbed."[28]

A *GO-error* occurs when the company permits a poor idea to move into development and commercialization. An *absolute product failure* loses money; its sales do not cover variable costs. A *partial product failure* loses money, but its sales cover all its variable costs and some of its fixed costs. A *relative product failure* yields a profit that is less than the company's target rate of return.

The purpose of screening is to drop poor ideas as early as possible. The rationale is that product-development costs rise substantially with each successive development stage. Most companies require new-product ideas to be described on a standard form that can be reviewed by a new-product committee. The description states the product idea, the target market, and the competition, and roughly estimates market size, product price, development time and costs, manufacturing costs, and rate of return.

The executive committee then reviews each idea against a set of criteria. Does the product meet a need? Would it offer superior value? Can it be distinctively advertised? Does the company have the necessary know-how and capital? Will the new product deliver the expected sales volume, sales growth, and profit?

"I've got a great idea!"

"It won't work here."

"We've tried it before."

"This isn't the right time."

"It can't be done."

"It's not the way we do things."

"We've done all right without it."

"It will cost too much."

"Let's discuss it at our next meeting."

FIGURE 20.2

Forces Fighting New Ideas

Source: With permission of Jerold Panas, Young & Partners, Inc.

The surviving ideas can be rated using a weighted-index method like that in Table 20.2. The first column lists factors required for successful product launches, and the second column assigns importance weights. The third column scores the product idea on a scale from 0 to 1.0, with 1.0 the highest score. The final step multiplies each factor's importance by the product score to obtain an overall rating. In this example, the product idea scores 0.69, which places it in the "good idea" level. The purpose of this basic rating device is to promote systematic evaluation and discussion. It is not supposed to make the decision for management.

As the idea moves through development, the company will constantly need to revise its estimate of the product's overall probability of success, using the following formula:

Overall probability of success	=	Probability of technical completion	×	Probability of commercialization given technical completion	×	Probability of economic success given commercialization

For example, if the three probabilities are estimated as 0.50, 0.65, and 0.74, respectively, the overall probability of success is 0.24. The company then has to judge whether this probability is high enough to warrant continued development.

Managing the Development Process: Concept to Strategy

Attractive ideas must be refined into testable product concepts. A *product idea* is a possible product the company might offer to the market. A *product concept* is an elaborated version of the idea expressed in consumer terms.

Concept Development and Testing

CONCEPT DEVELOPMENT Let us illustrate concept development with the following situation: A large food-processing company gets the idea of producing a powder to add to milk to increase its nutritional value and taste. This is a product idea, but consumers do not buy product ideas; they buy product concepts.

A product idea can be turned into several concepts. The first question is: Who will use this product? The powder can be aimed at infants, children, teenagers, young or middle-aged adults, or older adults. Second, what primary benefit should this product provide? Taste, nutrition, refreshment, energy? Third, when will people consume this drink? Breakfast, mid-morning, lunch, mid-afternoon, dinner, late evening? By answering these questions, a company can form several concepts:

- *Concept 1.* An instant breakfast drink for adults who want a quick nutritious breakfast without preparation.
- *Concept 2.* A tasty snack drink for children to drink as a midday refreshment.
- *Concept 3.* A health supplement for older adults to drink in the late evening before they go to bed.

TABLE 20.2	PRODUCT–IDEA RATING DEVICE		
Product Success Requirements	**Relative Weight (a)**	**Product Score (b)**	**Product Rating (c = a × b)**
Unique or superior product	0.40	0.8	0.32
High performance-to-cost ratio	0.30	0.6	0.18
High marketing dollar support	0.20	0.7	0.14
Lack of strong competition	0.10	0.5	0.05
Total	1.00		0.69[a]

[a]Rating scale: 0.00–0.30 poor; 0.31–0.60 fair; 0.61–0.80 good. Minimum acceptance rate: 0.61.

Each concept represents a *category concept* that defines the product's competition. An instant breakfast drink would compete against bacon and eggs, breakfast cereals, coffee and pastry, and other breakfast alternatives. A tasty snack drink would compete against soft drinks, fruit juices, and other thirst quenchers.

Suppose the instant-breakfast-drink concept looks best. The next task is to show where this powdered product would stand in relation to other breakfast products. Figure 20.3(a) uses the two dimensions of cost and preparation time to create a *product-positioning map* for the breakfast drink. An instant breakfast drink offers low cost and quick preparation. Its nearest competitor is cold cereal or breakfast bars; its most distant competitor is bacon and eggs. These contrasts can be utilized in communicating and promoting the concept to the market.

Next, the product concept has to be turned into a *brand concept.* Figure 20.3(b) is a brand-positioning map showing the current positions of three existing brands of instant breakfast drinks. The company needs to decide how much to charge and how calorific to make its drink. The new brand would be distinctive in the medium-price, medium-calorie market or in the high-price, high-calorie market. The company would not want to position it next to an existing brand, unless that brand is weak or inferior.

(a) Product-positioning Map (Breakfast Market)

(b) Brand-positioning Map (Instant Breakfast Market)

FIGURE 20.3

Product and Brand Positioning

CONCEPT TESTING   Concept testing involves presenting the product concept to target consumers and getting their reactions. The concepts can be presented symbolically or physically. The more the tested concepts resemble the final product or experience, the more dependable concept testing is.

In the past, creating physical prototypes was costly and time-consuming, but computer-aided design and manufacturing programs have changed that. Today firms can use *rapid prototyping* to design products (e.g., small appliances or toys) on a computer, and then produce plastic models of each. Potential consumers can view the plastic models and give their reactions.[29] Companies are also using *virtual reality* to test product concepts. Virtual reality programs use computers and sensory devices (such as gloves or goggles) to simulate reality.

Concept testing entails presenting consumers with an elaborated version of the concept. Here is the elaboration of concept 1 in our milk example:

> Our product is a powdered mixture that is added to milk to make an instant breakfast that gives the person all the needed nutrition along with good taste and high convenience. The product would be offered in three flavours (chocolate, vanilla, and strawberry) and would come in individual packets, six to a box, at $2.49 a box.

After receiving this information, researchers measure product dimensions by having consumers respond to the following questions:

1. *Communicability and believability*—Are the benefits clear to you and believable? If the scores are low, the concept must be refined or revised.

2. *Need level*—Do you see this product solving a problem or filling a need for you? The stronger the need, the higher the expected consumer interest.

3. *Gap level*—Do other products currently meet this need and satisfy you? The greater the gap, the higher the expected consumer interest. The need level can be multiplied by the gap level to produce a *need-gap score.* A high need-gap score means that the consumer sees the product as filling a strong need that is not satisfied by available alternatives.

4. *Perceived value*—Is the price reasonable in relation to the value? The higher the perceived value, the higher the expected consumer interest.

5. *Purchase intention*—Would you (definitely, probably, probably not, definitely not) buy the product? This would be high for consumers who answered the previous three questions positively.

6. *User targets, purchase occasions, purchasing frequency*—Who would use this product, and when and how often will the product be used?

Respondents' answers indicate whether the concept has a broad and strong consumer appeal, what products this new product competes against, and which consumers are the best targets. The need-gap levels and purchase-intention levels can be checked against norms for the product category to see whether the concept appears to be a winner, a long shot, or a loser. One food manufacturer rejects any concept that draws a definitely-would-buy score of less than 40 percent.

CONJOINT ANALYSIS Consumer preferences for alternative product concepts can be measured through **conjoint analysis**, a method for deriving the utility values that consumers attach to varying levels of a product's attributes.[30] Respondents are shown different hypothetical offers formed by combining varying levels of the attributes, and are then asked to rank the various offers. Management can identify the most appealing offer and the estimated market share and profit the company might realize. See how the technique is used at Bell Canada:[31]

Bell Canada

As competition in the $20 billion Canadian telecommunications industry heats up and the major telephone companies such as Telus, Bell Canada, and Rogers expand into each other's territories, the rivals are starting to provide new "bundles" of services. Each company is betting that the key to success is higher-value offers achieved by providing one "bundled" package. Bundling is a marketing strategy that involves combining different products and services in a package at a discount. The trick, of course, is to match these combinations to the right customers. As part of BCE's labyrinth of media companies, Montreal-based Bell Canada has the potential to bundle a wide range of products. For example, "The combination of wireless and the Internet with the ExpressVu satellite system brings a lot of value," says Myrianne Collin, Bell's general manager of integrated offers. Its first bundled offer achieved sales 140 percent above the objectives set for the campaign. The key to Bell's success has been careful market research. Bell uses conjoint analysis to test different bundles of services, and then derives optimal groupings that can be aimed at key market segments. One such bundle is Bell Security Solutions Inc. (BSSI), which provides network and information security for communications networks to Canadian business and government.

Green and Wind have illustrated this approach in connection with developing a new spot-removing carpet-cleaning agent for home use.[32] Suppose the new-product marketer is considering five design elements:

- Three package designs (A, B, C—see Figure 20.4)
- Three brand names (K2R, Glory, Bissell)
- Three prices ($1.19, $1.39, $1.59)
- A possible *Good Housekeeping* seal (yes, no)
- A possible money-back guarantee (yes, no)

Bell Canada, Convergent Media Systems, and Sony of Canada Ltd. joined forces to offer new in-store digital advertising, which the partners believe will revolutionize the way in-store advertising is done in Canada. Careful testing of new bundled offerings has been one key to Bell's success.

Although the researcher can form 108 possible product concepts ($3 \times 3 \times 3 \times 2 \times 2$), it would be too much to ask consumers to rank 108 concepts. A sample of, say, 18 contrasting product concepts can be chosen, and consumers would rank them from the most to the least preferred.

The marketer now uses a statistical program to derive the consumer's utility functions for each of the five attributes (see Figure 20.5). Utility ranges between zero and one—the higher the utility, the stronger the consumer's preference for that level of the attribute. Looking at packaging, we see that package B is the most favoured, followed by C and then A (A hardly has any utility). The preferred names are Bissell, K2R, and Glory, in that order. The consumer's utility varies inversely with price. A *Good Housekeeping* seal is preferred, but it does not add that much utility and may not be worth the effort to obtain it. A money-back guarantee is strongly preferred.

The consumer's most desired offer would be package design B, with the brand name Bissell, selling at the price of $1.19, with a *Good Housekeeping* seal and a money-back guarantee. We can also determine the relative importance of each attribute to this consumer—the difference between the highest and lowest utility level for that attribute. The greater the difference, the more important the attribute. Clearly, this consumer sees price and package design as the most important attributes, followed by money-back guarantee, brand name, and a *Good Housekeeping* seal.

When preference data are collected from a sufficient sample of target consumers, the data can be used to estimate the market share any specific offer is likely to achieve, given any assumptions about competitive response. The company, however, may not launch the market offer that promises to gain the greatest market share because of cost considerations. The most customer-appealing offer is not always the most profitable offer to make.

Under some conditions, researchers will collect the data not with a full-profile description of each offer, but by presenting two factors at a time. For example, respondents may be shown a table with three price levels and three package types and asked which of the nine combinations they would like most, followed by which one they would prefer next, and so on. They would then be shown a further table consisting of trade-offs between two other variables. The trade-off approach may be easier to use when there are many variables and possible offers. However, it is less realistic in that respondents are focusing on only two variables at a time.

Conjoint analysis has become one of the most popular concept-development and testing tools. Marriott designed its Courtyard hotel concept with the benefit of conjoint analysis. Other applications have included airline travel services, ethical drug design, and credit card features.

FIGURE 20.4

Samples for Conjoint Analysis

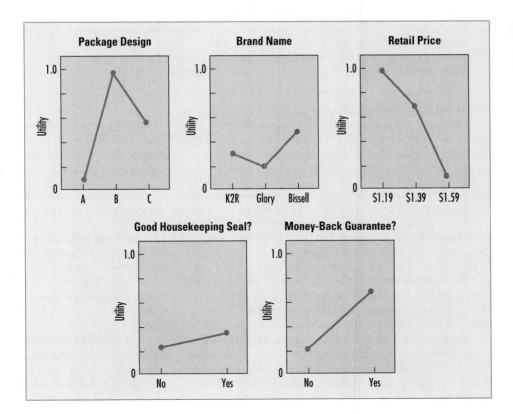

FIGURE 20.5

Utility Functions Based on Conjunct Analysis

Marketing Strategy

Following a successful concept test, the new-product manager will develop a preliminary strategy plan for introducing the new product into the market. The plan consists of three parts. The first part describes the target market's size, structure, and behaviour; the planned product positioning; and the sales, market share, and profit goals sought in the first few years:

> The target market for the instant breakfast drink is families with children who are receptive to a new, convenient, nutritious, and inexpensive form of breakfast. The company's brand will be positioned at the higher-price, higher-quality end of the instant-breakfast-drink category. The company will aim initially to sell 500 000 cases or 10 percent of the market, with a loss in the first year not exceeding $1.3 million. The second year will aim for 700 000 cases or 14 percent of the market, with a planned profit of $2.2 million.

The second part outlines the planned price, distribution strategy, and marketing budget for the first year:

> The product will be offered in chocolate, vanilla, and strawberry in individual packets of six to a box at a retail price of $2.49 a box. There will be 48 boxes per case, and the case price to distributors will be $24. For the first two months, dealers will be offered one case free for every four cases bought, plus cooperative-advertising allowances. Free samples will be distributed door to door. Coupons for 20 cents off will appear in newspapers. The total sales-promotional budget will be $2.9 million. An advertising budget of $6 million will be split 50:50 between national and local. Two-thirds will go into television and one-third into newspapers. Advertising copy will emphasize the benefit concepts of nutrition and convenience. The advertising-execution concept will revolve around a small boy who drinks instant breakfast and grows strong. During the first year, $100 000 will be spent on marketing research to buy store audits and consumer-panel information to monitor market reaction and buying rates.

The third part of the marketing-strategy plan describes the long-run sales and profit goals and marketing-mix strategy over time:

> The company intends to win a 25 percent market share and realize an after-tax return on investment of 12 percent. To achieve this return, product quality will start high and be improved over time through technical research. Price will initially be set at a high level and lowered gradually to expand the market and meet competition. The total promotion budget will be boosted each year about 20 percent, with the initial advertising–sales promotion split of 65:35 evolving eventually to 50:50. Marketing research will be reduced to $60 000 per year after the first year.

Business Analysis

After management develops the product concept and marketing strategy, it can evaluate the proposal's business attractiveness. Management needs to prepare sales, cost, and profit projections to determine whether they satisfy company objectives. If they do, the concept can move to the development stage. As new information comes in, the business analysis will undergo revision and expansion.

ESTIMATING TOTAL SALES Total estimated sales are the sum of estimated first-time sales, replacement sales, and repeat sales. Sales-estimation methods depend on whether the product is a one-time purchase (such as an engagement ring or retirement home), an infrequently purchased product, or a frequently purchased product. For one-time purchased products, sales rise at the beginning, peak, and later approach zero as the number of potential buyers is exhausted (see Figure 20.6[a]). If new buyers keep entering the market, the curve will not go down to zero.

Infrequently purchased products—such as automobiles, toasters, and industrial equipment—exhibit replacement cycles dictated by physical wearing out or by obsolescence associated with changing styles, features, and performance. Sales forecasting for this product category calls for estimating first-time sales and replacement sales separately (see Figure 20.6[b]).

Frequently purchased products, such as consumer and industrial nondurables, have product life-cycle sales resembling Figure 20.6(c). The number of first-time buyers initially increases and then decreases as fewer buyers are left (assuming a fixed population). Repeat purchases occur soon, providing that the product satisfies some buyers. The sales curve eventually falls to a plateau representing a level of steady repeat-purchase volume; by this time, the product is no longer a new product.

FIGURE 20.6

Product Life-Cycle Sales for Three Types of Products

In estimating sales, the manager's first task is to estimate first-time purchases of the new product in each period. To estimate replacement sales, management has to research the product's *survival-age distribution*—that is, the number of units that fail in year one, two, three, and so on. The low end of the distribution indicates when the first replacement sales will take place. The actual timing will be influenced by a variety of factors. Because replacement sales are difficult to estimate before the product is in use, some manufacturers base the decision to launch a new product solely on the estimate of first-time sales.

For a frequently purchased new product, the seller has to estimate repeat sales as well as first-time sales. A high rate of repeat purchasing means that customers are satisfied; sales are likely to stay high even after all first-time purchases take place. The seller should note the percentage of repeat purchases that take place in each repeat-purchase class: those who rebuy once, twice, three times, and so on. Some products and brands are bought a few times and dropped.[33]

ESTIMATING COSTS AND PROFITS Costs are estimated by the R&D, manufacturing, marketing, and finance departments. Table 20.3 illustrates a five-year projection of sales, costs, and profits for the instant breakfast drink.

Row 1 shows the projected sales revenue over the five-year period. The company expects to sell $11 889 000 (approximately 500 000 cases at $24 per case) in the first year. Behind this sales projection is a set of assumptions about the rate of market growth, the company's market share, and the factory-realized price. *Row 2* shows the cost of goods sold, which hovers around 33 percent of sales revenue. This cost is found by estimating the average cost of labour, ingredients, and packaging per case. *Row 3* shows the expected gross margin, which is the difference between sales revenue and cost of goods sold.

Row 4 shows anticipated development costs of $3.5 million, including product-development cost, marketing-research costs, and manufacturing-development costs. *Row 5* shows the estimated marketing costs over the five-year period to cover advertising, sales promotion, and marketing research and an amount allocated for sales force coverage and marketing administration. *Row 6* shows the allocated overhead to this new product to cover its share of the cost of executive salaries, heat, light, and so on.

Row 7, the gross contribution, is found by subtracting the preceding three costs from the gross margin. *Row 8*, supplementary contribution, lists any change in income from other company products caused by the introduction of the new product. It has two components. *Dragalong income* is additional income on other company products resulting from adding this product to the line. *Cannibalized income* is the reduced income on other company products resulting from adding this product to the line.[34] Table 20.3 assumes no supplementary contributions. *Row 9* shows the net contribution, which in this case is the same as the gross contribution. *Row 10* shows the discounted contribution—that is, the present value of each future contribution discounted at 15 percent per annum. For example, the company will not receive $4 716 000 until the fifth year. This amount is worth only $2 346 000 today if the company can earn 15 percent on its money through other investments.[35]

TABLE 20.3	PROJECTED FIVE-YEAR CASH-FLOW STATEMENT (IN THOUSANDS OF DOLLARS)					
	Year 0	Year 1	Year 2	Year 3	Year 4	Year 5
1. Sales revenue	$ 0	$11 889	$15 381	$19 654	$28 253	$32 491
2. Cost of goods sold	0	3 981	5 150	6 581	9 461	10 880
3. Gross margin	0	7 908	10 231	13 073	18 792	21 611
4. Development costs	–3 500	0	0	0	0	0
5. Marketing costs	0	8 000	6 460	8 255	11 866	13 646
6. Allocated overhead	0	1 189	1 538	1 965	2 825	3 249
7. Gross contribution	–3 500	–1 281	2 233	2 853	4 101	4 716
8. Supplementary contribution	0	0	0	0	0	0
9. Net contribution	–3 500	–1 281	2 233	2 853	4 101	4 716
10. Discounted contribution (15%)	–3 500	–1 113	1 691	1 877	2 343	2 346
11. Cumulative discounted cash flow	–3 500	–4 613	–2 922	–1 045	1 298	3 644

Finally, *row 11* shows the cumulative discounted cash flow, which is the accumulation of the annual contributions in row 10. Two things are of central interest. The first is the maximum investment exposure, which is the highest loss that the project can create. We see that the company will be in a maximum loss position of $4 613 000 in year 1. The second is the payback period, which is the time when the company recovers all of its investment, including the built-in return of 15 percent. The payback period here is approximately three and a half years. Management therefore has to decide whether to risk a maximum investment loss of $4.6 million and a possible payback period of three and a half years.

Companies use other financial measures to evaluate the merit of a new-product proposal. The simplest is **break-even analysis**, in which management estimates how many units of the product the company would have to sell to break even with the given price and cost structure. Or the estimate may be in terms of how many years it will take to break even. If management believes sales could easily reach the break-even number, it is likely to move the project into product development.

The most complex method of estimating profit is **risk analysis**. Here three estimates (optimistic, pessimistic, and most likely) are obtained for each uncertain variable affecting profitability under an assumed marketing environment and marketing strategy for the planning period. The computer simulates possible outcomes and computes a rate-of-return probability distribution showing the range of possible rates of returns and their probabilities.[36]

Managing the Development Process: Development to Commercialization

Up to now, the product has existed only as a word description, a drawing, or a prototype. This next step involves a jump in investment that dwarfs the costs incurred in the earlier stages. At this stage the company will determine whether the product idea can be translated into a technically and commercially feasible product. If it cannot, the accumulated project cost will be lost except for any useful information gained in the process.

Product Development

The job of translating target customer requirements into a working prototype is helped by a set of methods known as *quality function deployment* (QFD). The methodology takes the list of desired *customer attributes* (CAs) generated by market research and turns them into a list of *engineering attributes* (EAs) that the engineers can use. For example, customers of a proposed truck may want a certain acceleration rate (CA). Engineers can turn this into the required horsepower and other engineering equivalents (EAs). The methodology permits measuring the trade-offs and costs of providing the customer requirements. A major contribution of QFD is that it improves communication between marketers, engineers, and the manufacturing people.[37]

PHYSICAL PROTOTYPES The R&D department will develop one or more physical versions of the product concept. Its goal is to find a prototype that embodies the key attributes described in the product-concept statement, that performs safely under normal use and conditions, and that can be produced within the budgeted manufacturing costs. Developing and manufacturing a successful prototype can take days, weeks, months, or even years. Sophisticated virtual-reality technology is speeding the process. By designing and testing product designs through simulation, for example, companies achieve the flexibility to respond to new information and to resolve uncertainties by quickly exploring alternatives.

Boeing

Boeing designed its 777 aircraft on a totally digital basis. Engineers, designers, and more than 500 suppliers designed the aircraft on a special computer network without ever making a blueprint on paper. Its partners were connected by an extranet enabling them to communicate, share ideas, and work on the design at a distance. A computer-generated "human" could climb inside the three-dimensional design on-screen to show how difficult maintenance access would be for a live mechanic. Such computer modelling allowed engineers to spot design errors that otherwise would have remained undiscovered until a person began to work on a physical prototype. Avoiding the time and cost associated with building physical prototypes reduced development time and scrappage and rework by 60 to 90 percent.[38]

With the emergence of the Web, there is a need for more rapid prototyping and more flexible development processes. Michael Schrage, research associate at MIT's media lab, has correctly predicted: "Effective prototyping may be the most valuable 'core competence' an innovative organization can hope to have."[39] This has certainly been true for software companies such as Microsoft, Netscape, and the hundreds of Silicon Valley start-ups. Although Schrage says that specification-driven companies require that every "i" be dotted and "t" be crossed before anything can be shown to the next level of management, prototype-driven companies—such as Yahoo!, Microsoft, and Netscape—cherish quick-and-dirty tests and experiments.

Lab scientists must not only design the product's functional characteristics, but also communicate its psychological aspects through physical cues. How will consumers react to different colours, sizes, and weights? In the case of a mouthwash, a yellow colour supports an "antiseptic" claim (Listerine), a red colour supports a "refreshing" claim (Lavoris), and a green or blue colour supports a "cool" claim (Scope). Marketers need to supply lab people with information on what attributes consumers seek and how consumers judge whether these attributes are present.

Boeing's 777, designed digitally without a physical prototype, takes its first "flight" across the world's largest building, the Boeing assembly plant in Everett, Washington.

CUSTOMER TESTS When the prototypes are ready, they must be put through rigorous functional tests and *customer tests*. *Alpha testing* is the name given to testing the product within the firm to see how it performs in different applications. After refining the prototype further, the company moves to *beta testing* with customers.[40] It enlists a set of customers to use the prototype and give feedback. Table 20.4 shows some of the functional tests products go through before they enter the marketplace.

Consumer testing can take several forms, from bringing consumers into a laboratory to giving them samples to use in their homes. In-home placement tests are common with products ranging

TABLE 20.4	EXAMPLES OF CUSTOMER PRODUCT TESTS

Shaw Industries

At Shaw Industries, temps are paid US$5 an hour to pace up and down five long rows of sample carpets for up to eight hours a day, logging an average of 22.5 kilometres each. One regular reads three mysteries a week while pacing and shed 18 kilograms in two years. Shaw Industries counts walkers' steps and figures that 20 000 steps equal several years of average wear.

Apple Computer

Apple Computer assumes the worst for its PowerBook customers and submits the computers to a battery of indignities: It drenches the computers in Pepsi and other sodas, smears them with mayonnaise, and bakes them in ovens at temperatures of 60°C or more to simulate conditions in a car trunk.

Gillette

At Gillette, 200 volunteers from various departments come to work unshaven each day, troop to the second floor of the company's South Boston manufacturing and research plant, and enter small booths with a sink and mirror. There they take instructions from technicians on the other side of a small window as to which razor, shaving cream, or aftershave to use, and then they fill out questionnaires. "We bleed so you'll get a good shave at home," says one Gillette employee.

Source: Faye Rice, "Secrets of Product Testing," *Fortune*, November 28, 1994, pp. 172–74; Lawrence Ingrassia, "Taming the Monster: How Big Companies Can Change: Keeping Sharp: Gillette Holds Its Edge by Endlessly Searching for a Better Shave," *Wall Street Journal*, December 10, 1992, p. A1.

from ice cream flavours to new appliances. When DuPont developed its new synthetic carpeting, it installed free carpeting in several homes in exchange for the homeowners' willingness to report their likes and dislikes about the product.

Consumer preferences can be measured in several ways. Suppose a consumer is shown three items—A, B, and C, such as three cameras, three insurance plans, or three advertisements.

- The *rank-order* method asks the consumer to rank the three items in order of preference. The consumer might respond with A > B > C. Although this method has the advantage of simplicity, it does not reveal how intensely the consumer feels about each item nor whether the consumer likes any item very much. It is also difficult to use this method when there are many objects to be ranked.

- The *paired-comparison* method calls for presenting pairs of items and asking the consumer which one is preferred in each pair. Thus the consumer could be presented with the pairs AB, AC, and BC and say that she prefers A to B, A to C, and B to C. Then we could conclude that A > B > C. People find it easy to state their preference between two items, and this method allows the consumer to focus on the two items, noting their differences and similarities.

- The *monadic-rating* method asks the consumer to rate liking of each product on a scale. Suppose a seven-point scale is used, where 1 signifies intense dislike, 4 indifference, and 7 intense like. Suppose the consumer returns the following ratings: A = 6, B = 5, C = 3. We can derive the individual's preference order (i.e., A > B > C), and even know the qualitative levels of the person's preference for each and the rough distance between preferences.

Products must also undergo rigorous testing to ensure their safety.

Underwriters' Laboratories of Canada

Underwriters' Laboratories of Canada is an independent, not-for-profit product-safety testing and certification organization. From its birth in 1920, it has grown to become one of the most recognized, reputable conformity-assessment providers in the world. It helps companies ensure that their products meet safety standards both in Canada and abroad. It prides itself on its ability to evaluate more than 17 000 types of products worldwide, from home appliances and fire-fighting equipment to ultra-sound machines and plumbing. It also independently tests products to ensure public safety and provides warnings to consumers if it uncovers unsafe products.[41]

Market Testing

After management is satisfied with functional and psychological performance, the product is ready to be dressed up with a brand name and packaging, and put into a market test. The new product is introduced into an authentic setting to learn how large the market is and how consumers and dealers react to handling, using, and repurchasing the product.

Canada is becoming the "ultimate" test market for many U.S.-based multinationals that also have operations in Canada. Not only are they testing new products, they are testing the marketing campaigns that support the new product launch. The strategy of such firms is "Let the Canadian subsidiary come up with something a little more innovative and daring. Then, if it works here, roll it out in the United States." Pfizer's New York–based parent and Montreal-based subsidiary are setting the pace with everything from their award-winning "Good Morning" and "Champions" ads for Viagra (developed by Taxi Advertising of Toronto) to the launch of Listerine PocketPaks and Benylin DM Medicated Freezer Pops for children.[42]

Not all companies undertake market testing. A company officer at Revlon, Inc., stated: "In our field—primarily higher-priced cosmetics not geared for mass distribution—it would be unnecessary for us to market test. When we develop a new product, say an improved liquid makeup, we know it's going to sell because we're familiar with the field. And we've got 1500 demonstrators in department stores to promote it." Many companies, however, believe that market testing can yield valuable information about buyers, dealers, marketing program effectiveness, and market potential. The main issues are: How much market testing should be done, and what kind(s)?

The amount of market testing is influenced by the investment cost and risk on the one hand, and the time pressure and research cost on the other. High-investment–high-risk products, where the

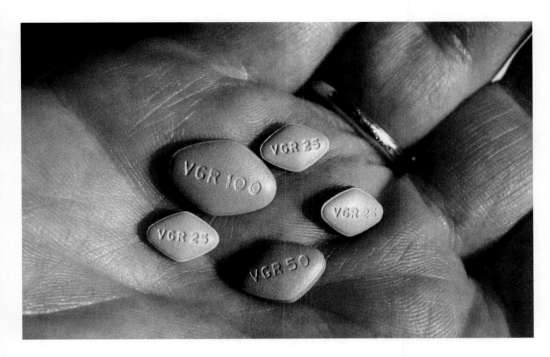

Canada is becoming the "ultimate" test market for products like Viagra.

chance of failure is high, must be market tested; the cost of the market tests will be an insignificant percentage of the total project cost. High-risk products—those that create new-product categories (first instant breakfast drink) or have novel features (first gum-strengthening toothpaste)—warrant more market testing than modified products (another toothpaste brand).

The amount of market testing may be severely reduced if the company is under great time pressure because the season is just starting or because competitors are about to launch their brands. The company may therefore prefer the risk of a product failure to the risk of losing distribution or market penetration on a highly successful product.

CONSUMER-GOODS MARKET TESTING In testing consumer products, the company seeks to estimate four variables: *trial, first repeat, adoption,* and *purchase frequency.* The company hopes to find all these variables at high levels. In some cases, it will find many consumers trying the product but few rebuying it; or it might find high permanent adoption but low purchase frequency (as with gourmet frozen foods).

Here are four major methods of consumer-goods market testing, from the least to the most costly.

Sales-Wave Research In *sales-wave research*, consumers who initially try the product at no cost are reoffered the product, or a competitor's product, at slightly reduced prices. They might be reoffered the product as many as three to five times (sales waves), with the company noting how many customers selected that product again and their reported level of satisfaction. Sales-wave research can also expose consumers to one or more advertising concepts to see the impact of that advertising on repeat purchase.

Sales-wave research can be implemented quickly, conducted with a fair amount of security, and carried out without final packaging and advertising. However, it does not indicate the trial rates that would be achieved with different sales-promotion incentives, because the consumers are preselected to try the product; nor does it indicate the brand's power to gain distribution and favourable shelf position.

Simulated Test Marketing Simulated test marketing calls for finding 30 to 40 qualified shoppers and questioning them about brand familiarity and preferences in a specific product category. These people are then invited to a brief screening of both well-known and new commercials or print ads. One ad advertises the new product, but it is not singled out for attention. Consumers receive a small amount of money and are invited into a store where they may buy any items. The company notes how many consumers buy the new brand and competing brands. This provides a measure of the ad's relative effectiveness against competing ads in stimulating trial. Consumers are asked the reasons for their purchases or nonpurchases. Those who did not buy the new brand are given a free sample. Some weeks later, they are reinterviewed by phone to determine product attitudes, usage, satisfaction, and repurchase intention and are offered an opportunity to repurchase any products.

This method gives fairly accurate results on advertising effectiveness and trial rates (and repeat rates if extended) in a much shorter time and at a fraction of the cost of using real test markets. Pretests often take only three months and may cost US$250 000.[43] The results are incorporated into new-product forecasting models to project ultimate sales levels. Marketing research firms report surprisingly accurate predictions of sales levels of products that are subsequently launched in the market.[44]

Controlled Test Marketing In this method, a research firm manages a panel of stores that will carry new products for a fee. The company with the new product specifies the number of stores and geographic locations it wants to test. The research firm delivers the product to the participating stores and controls shelf position; number of facings, displays, and point-of-purchase promotions; and pricing. Sales results can be measured through electronic scanners at the checkout. The company can also evaluate the impact of local advertising and promotions.

Controlled test marketing allows the company to test the impact of in-store factors and limited advertising on buying behaviour. A sample of consumers can be interviewed later to give their impressions of the product. The company does not have to use its own sales force, give trade allowances, or "buy" distribution. However, controlled test marketing provides no information on how to sell the trade on carrying the new product. This technique also exposes the product and its features to competitors' scrutiny.

Test Markets The ultimate way to test a new consumer product is to put it into full-blown test markets. The company chooses a few representative cities, and the sales force tries to sell the trade on carrying the product and giving it good shelf exposure. The company puts on a full advertising and promotion campaign similar to the one it would use in national marketing. Test marketing also permits testing the impact of alternative marketing plans by varying the marketing program in different cities: A full-scale test can cost over US$1 million, depending on the number of test cities, the test duration, and the amount of data the company wants to collect.

Management faces several decisions:

1. *How many test cities?* Most tests use between two and six cities. The greater the maximum possible loss, the greater the number of contending marketing strategies, the greater the regional differences, and the greater the chance of test-market interference by competitors, the greater the number of cities that should be used.

2. *Which cities?* Each company must develop selection criteria such as having good media coverage, cooperative chain stores, and average competitive activity.

3. *Length of test?* Market tests last anywhere from a few months to a year. The longer the average repurchase period, the longer the test period.

4. *What information?* Warehouse shipment data will show gross inventory buying but will not indicate weekly sales at the retail level. Store audits will show retail sales and competitors' market shares but will not reveal buyer characteristics. Consumer panels will indicate which people are buying which brands and their loyalty and switching rates. Buyer surveys will yield in-depth information about consumer attitudes, usage, and satisfaction.

5. *What action to take?* If the test markets show high trial and repurchase rates, the product should be launched nationally; if they show a high trial rate and a low repurchase rate, the product should be redesigned or dropped; if they show a low trial rate and a high repurchase rate, the product is satisfying but more people have to try it. This means increasing advertising and sales promotion. If trial and repurchase rates are both low, the product should be abandoned.

In spite of its benefits, many companies today skip test marketing and rely on faster and more economical testing methods. General Mills now prefers to launch new products in an area too large for rivals to disrupt. Managers review retail scanner data, which tell them within days how the product is doing and what corrective fine-tuning to do. Colgate-Palmolive often launches a new product in a set of small "lead countries" and keeps rolling it out if it proves successful.

BUSINESS-GOODS MARKET TESTING Business goods can also benefit from market testing. Expensive industrial goods and new technologies will normally undergo alpha testing (within the company) and beta testing (with outside customers). During beta testing, the vendor's technical people observe how test customers use the product, a practice that often exposes unanticipated problems of safety and servicing and alerts the vendor to customer training and servicing requirements. The vendor can also observe how much value the equipment adds to the customer's operation as a clue to subsequent pricing.

The vendor will ask the test customers to express their purchase intention and other reactions after the test. Vendors must carefully interpret the beta test results because only a small number of test customers are used, they are not randomly drawn, and the tests are somewhat customized to each site. Another risk is that test customers who are unimpressed with the product may leak unfavourable reports about it.

A second common test method for business goods is to introduce the new product at trade shows. The vendor can observe how much interest buyers show in the new product, how they react to various features and terms, and how many express purchase intentions or place orders.

New industrial products can be tested in distributor and dealer display rooms, where they may stand next to the manufacturer's other products and possibly competitors' products. This method yields preference and pricing information in the product's normal selling atmosphere. The disadvantages are that the customers might want to place early orders that cannot be filled, and those customers who come in might not represent the target market.

Industrial manufacturers come close to using full test marketing when they give a limited supply of the product to the sales force to sell in a limited number of areas that receive promotion support and printed catalogue sheets.

Commercialization

If the company goes ahead with commercialization, it will face its largest costs to date. The company will have to contract for manufacture or build or rent a full-scale manufacturing facility. Plant size will be a critical decision. When Quaker Oats launched its 100 Percent Natural breakfast cereal, it built a smaller plant than called for by the sales forecast. The demand so exceeded the forecast that for about a year it could not supply enough product to stores. Although Quaker Oats was gratified with the response, the low forecast cost it a considerable amount of profit.

Another major cost is marketing. To introduce a major new consumer packaged good into the North American market, the company may have to spend from US$25 million to as much as US$100 million in advertising, promotion, and other communications in the first year. In the introduction of new food products, marketing expenditures typically represent 57 percent of sales during the first year. Most new-product campaigns rely on a sequenced mix of market communication tools.

WHEN (TIMING) In commercializing a new product, market-entry timing is critical. Suppose a company has almost completed the development work on its new product and learns that a competitor is nearing the end of its development work. The company faces three choices:

1. *First entry*. The first firm entering a market usually enjoys the "first mover advantages" of locking up key distributors and customers and gaining leadership. But if the product is rushed to market before it is thoroughly debugged, the first entry can backfire.

2. *Parallel entry*. The firm might time its entry to coincide with the competitor's entry. The market may pay more attention when two companies are advertising the new product.

3. *Late entry*. The firm might delay its launch until after the competitor has entered. The competitor will have borne the cost of educating the market, and its product may reveal faults the late entrant can avoid. The late entrant can also learn the size of the market.

The timing decision involves additional considerations. If a new product replaces an older product, the company might delay the introduction until the old product's stock is drawn down. If the product is seasonal, it might be delayed until the right season arrives;[45] often a product waits for a "killer application" to occur. Complicating new product launches, many companies are encountering competitive "design-arounds"—rivals are imitating inventions but making their own versions just different enough to avoid patent infringement and the need to pay royalties.

WHERE (GEOGRAPHIC STRATEGY) The company must decide whether to launch the new product in a single locality, a region, several regions, the national market, or the international market. Most will develop a planned market rollout over time.

Company size is an important factor here. Small companies will select an attractive city and put on a blitz campaign. They will enter other cities one at a time. Large companies will introduce their product into a whole region and then move to the next region. Companies with national distribution networks, such as auto companies, will launch their new models in the national market.

Most companies design new products to sell primarily in the domestic market. If the product does well, the company considers exporting to neighbouring countries or the world market, redesigning if necessary. Cooper and Kleinschmidt, in their study of industrial products, found that domestic products designed solely for the domestic market tend to show a high failure rate, low market share, and low growth. In contrast, products designed for the world market—or at least to include neighbouring countries—achieve significantly more profits, both at home and abroad. Yet only 17 percent of the products in Cooper and Kleinschmidt's study were designed with an international orientation.[46] The implication is that companies should adopt an international focus in designing and developing new products.

In choosing rollout markets, the major criteria are market potential, company's local reputation, cost of filling the pipeline, cost of communication media, influence of area on other areas, and competitive penetration. The presence of strong competitors will influence rollout strategy. Suppose McDonald's wants to launch a new chain of fast-food pizza parlours. Pizza Hut, a formidable competitor, is strongly entrenched on the East Coast. Another pizza chain, Boston Pizza, founded in Edmonton in 1964, is entrenched on the West Coast. The Prairies are a battleground between the two other chains. The Ontario market, with its large population, is the most competitive of all with chains large and small competing for market share. McDonald's faces a complex decision in choosing a geographic rollout strategy but could launch in the West given that is where it perceives competition to be the least formidable.

With the Web connecting far-flung parts of the world, competition is more likely to cross national borders. Companies are increasingly rolling out new products simultaneously across the globe, rather than nationally or even regionally. However, masterminding a global launch provides challenges.

Companies will increasingly add the Web as another advertising medium to launch and describe each important new product:

Philips

Philips, the Dutch electronics company, recently launched Pronto, an "Intelligent Remote Control" to replace all other devices that receive infrared signals. Its Web site, www.pronto.philips.com, contains several features: About Pronto, A Virtual Tour, Where to Buy, Pronto News, Pronto Communities, and FAQs and Contacts. This is much richer information than any ad could offer.

TO WHOM (TARGET-MARKET PROSPECTS) Within the rollout markets, the company must target its initial distribution and promotion to the best prospect groups. Presumably, the company has already profiled the prime prospects, who would ideally have the following characteristics: They would be early adopters, heavy users, and opinion leaders, and they could be reached at a low cost.[47] Few groups have all these characteristics. The company should rate the various prospect groups on these characteristics and target the best group. The aim is to generate strong sales as soon as possible to attract further prospects.

HOW (INTRODUCTORY MARKET STRATEGY) The company must develop an action plan for introducing the new product into the rollout markets. In 1998, Apple Computer staged a massive marketing blitz to launch the iMac, its re-entry into the computer PC business after a hiatus of 14 years. Five years later, Apple struck gold again with the launch of the iPod:

Apple iPod

As with virtually all its products, Apple's design for their iPod MP3 player is striking. Sleek and cool, the product also offers much functionality. Apple paired iPod with the legitimate download song service iTunes through catchy TV commercials featuring black silhouettes of people listening to music with N.E.R.D.'s remix of "Rock Star" in the background. To target Gen Y, Apple created the Web site www.ipodrocks.com in November 2003. It touts the iPod as a gift for the holidays and offers suggestions to convince parents to buy one ("Ask nicely," "Stake your grades on it," "Do a good deed," and "Subliminal advertising"). Apple also initiated marketing collaborations with corporate icons America Online and Volkswagen. Just how strong is demand for the iPod? When compared to early sales of the revolutionary Sony Walkman, iPod's strength is astounding. Its sales are approximately 1 million units ahead of same-period Walkman sales levels after 2.5 years on the market. That comparison is especially impressive given iPod's price. It captured more than 50 percent of the new market. In 2004, Apple sold over 2 million iPods in the last quarter alone and consumer demand continues to be intense.[48]

A Web ad from the Philips Pronto site for the TSU7000 model Pronto Pro.

To coordinate the many activities involved in launching a new product, management can use network-planning techniques such as critical path scheduling. **Critical path scheduling (CPS)** calls for developing a master chart showing the simultaneous and sequential activities that must take place to launch the product. By estimating how much time each activity takes, the planners estimate completion time for the entire project. Any delay in any activity on the critical path will cause the project to be delayed. If the launch must be completed earlier, the planner searches for ways to reduce time along the critical path.[49]

The Consumer-Adoption Process

Adoption is an individual's decision to become a regular user of a product. How do potential customers learn about new products, try them, and adopt or reject them? *The consumer-adoption process* is later followed by the *consumer-loyalty process*, which is the concern of the established producer. Years ago, new-product marketers used a *mass-market approach* to launch products. This approach had two main drawbacks: It called for heavy marketing expenditures, and it involved many wasted exposures. These drawbacks led to a second approach, *heavy-user target marketing*. This approach makes sense, provided that heavy users are identifiable and are early adopters. However, even within the heavy-user group, many heavy users are loyal to existing brands. New-product marketers now aim at consumers who are early adopters.

The theory of innovation diffusion and consumer adoption helps marketers identify early adopters.

Stages in the Adoption Process

An **innovation** is any good, service, or idea that is *perceived* by someone as new. The idea may have a long history, but it is an innovation to the person who sees it as new. Innovations take time to spread through the social system. Rogers defines the **innovation diffusion process** as "the spread of a new idea from its source of invention or creation to its ultimate users or adopters."[50] The consumer-adoption process focuses on the mental process through which an individual passes from first hearing about an innovation to final adoption.[51]

Adopters of new products have been observed to move through five stages:

1. *Awareness*—The consumer becomes aware of the innovation but lacks information about it.
2. *Interest*—The consumer is stimulated to seek information about the innovation.
3. *Evaluation*—The consumer considers whether to try the innovation.
4. *Trial*—The consumer tries the innovation to improve his or her estimate of its value.
5. *Adoption*—The consumer decides to make full and regular use of the innovation.

The new-product marketer should facilitate movement through these stages. A portable electric-dishwasher manufacturer might discover that many consumers are stuck in the interest stage; they do not buy because of their uncertainty and the large investment cost. But these same consumers would be willing to use an electric dishwasher on a trial basis for a small monthly fee. The manufacturer should consider offering a trial-use plan with option to buy.

Factors Influencing the Adoption Process

Marketers recognize the following characteristics of the adoption process: differences in individual readiness to try new products, the effect of personal influence, differing rates of adoption, and differences in organizations' readiness to try new products.

READINESS TO TRY NEW PRODUCTS AND PERSONAL INFLUENCE Everett Rogers defines a person's level of innovativeness as "the degree to which an individual is relatively earlier in adopting new ideas than the other members of his social system." In each product area, there are pioneers and early adopters. Some people are the first to adopt new clothing fashions or new appliances; some doctors are the first to prescribe new medicines; and some farmers are the first to adopt new farming methods.[52] People can be classified into the adopter categories shown in Figure 20.7. After a slow start, an increasing number of people adopt the innovation, the number reaches a peak, and then it diminishes as fewer nonadopters remain. The five adopter groups differ in their value orientations and their motives for adopting or resisting the new product.[53]

- *Innovators* are technology enthusiasts and are venturesome and enjoy tinkering with new products and mastering their intricacies. In return for low prices, they are happy to conduct alpha and beta testing and report on early weaknesses.
- *Early adopters* are opinion leaders who carefully search for new technologies that might give them a dramatic competitive advantage. They are less price-sensitive and willing to adopt the product if given personalized solutions and good service support.
- *Early majority* are deliberate pragmatists who adopt the new technology when its benefits are proven and a lot of adoption has already taken place. They make up the mainstream market.
- *Late majority* are skeptical conservatives who are risk averse, technology shy, and price sensitive.
- *Laggards* are tradition-bound and resist the innovation until they find that the status quo is no longer defensible.

Each of the five groups must be approached with a different type of marketing if the firm wants to move its innovation through the full product life cycle.[54]

Personal influence is the effect one person has on another's attitude or purchase probability. Although personal influence is an important factor, its significance is greater in some situations and for some individuals than for others. Personal influence is more important in the evaluation stage of the adoption process than in the other stages. It has more influence on late adopters than early adopters. It also is more important in risky situations.

Companies often target innovators and early adopters with product rollouts. For Vespa scooters, Piaggio hired models to go round cafés and clubs to talk up the brand.[55] When Nike decided to enter the skateboarding market, it recognized that an anti-establishment, big company bias from the teen target skater market could present a sizable challenge. To gain some "street cred," it sold exclusively

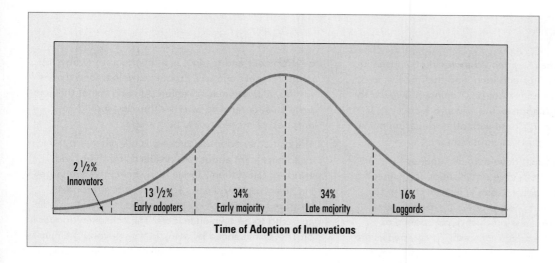

FIGURE 20.7

Adopter Categorization on the Basis of Relative Time of Adoption of Innovations

Source: Redrawn from Everett M. Rogers, *Diffusion of Innovations* (New York: The Free Press, 1983).

to independent shops, advertised nowhere but skate magazines, and gained sponsorships from well-admired pro riders by incorporating them into product design.[56]

CHARACTERISTICS OF THE INNOVATION Some products catch on immediately (roller blades), whereas others take a long time to gain acceptance (diesel engine autos). Five characteristics influence the rate of adoption of an innovation. We will consider them in relation to the adoption of personal video recorders (PVRs) for home use, as exemplified by TiVo.[57]

The first is *relative advantage*—the degree to which the innovation appears superior to existing products. The greater the perceived relative advantage of using a PVR, say, for easily recording favourite shows, pausing live TV, or skipping commercials, the more quickly personal computers will be adopted. The second is *compatibility*—the degree to which the innovation matches the values and experiences of the individuals. PVRs, for example, are highly compatible with avid television watchers. Third is *complexity*—the degree to which the innovation is relatively difficult to understand or use. PVRs are somewhat complex and will therefore take a slightly longer time to penetrate into home use. Fourth is *divisibility*—the degree to which the innovation can be tried on a limited basis. This provides a sizable challenge for PVRs—sampling can only occur in a retail store or perhaps a friend's house. Fifth is *communicability*—the degree to which the beneficial results of use are observable or describable to others. The fact that PVRs have some clear advantages can help create interest and curiosity.

Other characteristics that influence the rate of adoption are cost, risk and uncertainty, scientific credibility, and social approval. The new-product marketer has to research all these factors and give the key ones maximum attention in designing the new-product and marketing program.[58]

ORGANIZATIONS' READINESS TO ADOPT INNOVATIONS The creator of a new teaching method would want to identify innovative schools. The producer of a new piece of medical equipment would want to identify innovative hospitals. Adoption is associated with variables in the organization's environment (community progressiveness, community income), the organization itself (size, profits, pressure to change), and the administrators (education level, age, sophistication). Other forces come into play in trying to get a product adopted into organizations that receive the bulk of their funding from the government, such as public schools. A controversial or innovative product can be squelched by negative public opinion.

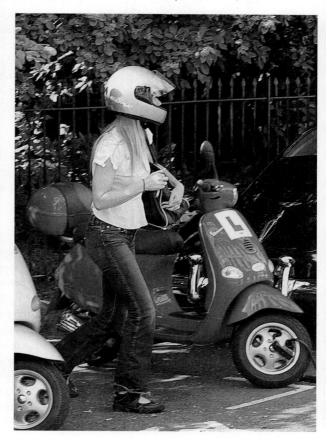

Gwyneth Paltrow with her Vespa. *In Style* magazine ran this photo in its October 2003 issue with the caption, "**Downsizing** Gas-guzzling, out. Fuel-efficient modes of transport, in. Gwyneth Paltrow (here), Matthew Broderick, and Sandra Bullock ride Vespas, which get up to 65 mpg [23 km/l] (from [US]$3000; vespa.usa.com)."

SUMMARY

1. Once a company has segmented the market, chosen its target customer groups and identified their needs, and determined its desired market positioning, it is ready to develop and launch appropriate new products. Marketing should participate with other departments in every stage of new-product development.

2. Successful new-product development requires the company to establish an effective organization for managing the development process. Companies can choose to use product managers, new-product managers, new-product committees, new-product departments, or new-product venture teams. Increasingly, companies are adopting cross-functional teams and developing multiple product concepts.

3. Eight stages are involved in the new-product development process: idea generation, screening, concept development and testing, marketing-strategy development, business analysis, product development, market testing, and commercialization. At each stage, the company must determine whether the idea should be dropped or moved to the next stage.

4. The consumer-adoption process is the process by which customers learn about new products, try them, and adopt or reject them. Today many marketers are targeting heavy users and early adopters of new products, because both groups can be reached by specific media and tend to be opinion leaders. The consumer-adoption process is influenced by many factors beyond the marketer's control, including consumers' and organizations' willingness to try new products, personal influences, and the characteristics of the new product or innovation.

APPLICATIONS

Marketing Debate: Who Should You Target with New Products?

Many firms target lead users or innovators with their new products, with the assumption that their adoption will trickle down to influence the broader market. Others disagree with this approach and contend that the most efficient and quickest route is to target the broader or even mass market directly.

Take a position: New products should always target new adopters versus New products should target the broadest market possible.

Marketing Discussion

Think about the last new product you bought. How do you think its success will be affected by the five characteristics of an innovation: relative advantage, compatibility, complexity, divisibility, and communicability?

Marketing Spotlight: Nokia

Nokia, originally a Finnish forestry products company formed in 1865, is now the world's top seller of mobile phones. Over the years, Nokia has made everything from toilet paper to televisions and tires. But in 1992, incoming CEO Jorma Ollila focused all of the company's resources on telecommunications.

Nokia's first digital phones appeared on the market in 1993. At the time, Nokia expected to sell only about 400 000 units. Instead, it sold 20 million. By 1998, Nokia was selling 40 million mobile phones per year, surpassing Motorola to become the world's biggest mobile phone company. Nokia now has nearly 40 percent market share in a global market.

How did Nokia get so successful? Back in the 1990s, cell phone companies like Motorola were following the Henry Ford motto of "You can have a car (or phone) in any colour as long as it's black." Cell phones were black, business-like, and boring. Nokia realized that cell phones were personal accessories and that many consumers wanted more than just a utilitarian phone. So it introduced phones with a sense of style, a riotous profusion of interchangeable faceplates, and a growing list of ring-tones. In 2001, Nokia's Mobile Phones (NMP) division launched 15 new products. In 2002, it launched 30 new products. In 2003, just ten years after its entry in the market, Nokia outsold Motorola, its nearest rival, by a two-to-one margin.

The new products sell well because they're more than just minor tweaks in colour or case design. Nokia was the first company to mass-market a cell phone with the antenna inside, the first to offer a user-changeable faceplate, the first to feature a built-in camera, and the first with a unique short-message chat function. The latest model features a rubberized case, flashlight, thermometer, calorie counter, stopwatch, and radio. Another comes with a foldout QWERTY keyboard that looks like wings on a large colour screen.

Why all these innovations? Because the market demands it. Customers' desire for fashion, new features, and small size drives Nokia to invest heavily in R&D. And an ever-expanding set of technical standards like WCDMA, GPRS, 3G, and IPv6 drive Nokia to innovate the internal components and network infrastructure that give next year's cell phone more features than last year's cell phone. The company ploughs 10 percent of revenues back into R&D—giving Nokia a US$3 billion per year budget for pushing the envelope and getting outside the box.

Nokia's secret to creating products that people will buy lies in how it organizes for innovation. One-third of Nokia's 52 000 employees work in R&D. But they don't work in a central lab. They work as small, autonomous teams. Nokia has some 69 R&D teams located throughout the world. Nokia gives these small teams the power to create new ideas for new market needs. "Big companies lose sensitivity," said Matti Alahuhta, president of NMP. "People need to feel they can make a difference. And they need to have the power to make their ideas happen. We've created a small-company soul inside a big-company body."

Although Nokia does maintain a central research lab for basic technology and product design, each small unit has P&L responsibility to create its own business model and do its own advanced R&D and marketing. "Ninety percent of the time, it feels like I'm running my own company," said Iikka Raiskinen,

head of Nokia's Entertainment and Media Business Unit. "We've been given the freedom to decide what the rules are, what the value chain is.... I consult the Nokia board the same way that a startup would consult its investors."

From its humble beginnings in the far north of Europe, Nokia made the shift from a natural resources company of the nineteenth century to become a high-tech leader in the twenty-first century. Now some 300 million people across 130 countries use Nokia phones. Nokia's ability to reinvent itself and unleash the creativity of its people has made Nokia the sixth most recognized brand in the world. But the company cannot rest on its laurels and must continue to innovate. When Nokia missed the boat on clamshell phones early in 2004, causing a rare drop in revenue, the firm accelerated the introduction of new models for the latter half of the year.

DISCUSSION QUESTIONS

1. What have been the key success factors for Nokia?

2. Where is Nokia vulnerable? What should it watch out for?

3. What recommendations would you make to senior marketing executives going forward? What should they be sure to do with the company's marketing?

Sources: Ian Wylie, "Calling for a Renewable Future," *Fast Company*, May 2003, pp. 46–48; Paul Kaihla, "Nokia's Hit Factory," *Business 2.0* (August 2002): 66–70; Jorma Ollila, "Nokia at the Forefront of Mobility," Nokia Annual General Meeting, March 27, 2003; **www.Nokia.com**; Andy Reinhardt, "Can Nokia Get the Wow Back?" *BusinessWeek*, May 31, 2004, pp. 48–49.

21

- What factors should a company review before deciding to go abroad?

- How can companies evaluate and select specific foreign markets to enter?

- What are the major ways of entering a foreign market?

- To what extent must the company adapt its products and marketing program to each foreign country?

- How should the company manage and organize its international activities?

CHAPTER 21

Tapping into Global Markets

PROFILE: CANADIAN MARKETING EXCELLENCE

In 2005, Montreal's Mega Bloks Inc. was named the winner of Canada's Export Awards. This is the second time the firm was an Export Award winner, also taking the top spot in 2003. As International Trade Minister Pierre Pettigrew noted, "Mega Bloks is an excellent choice for Exporter of the Year. This is a family-run business that has been exporting its construction toys since the mid-1980s. Today, thousands of children in over 100 countries enjoy playing with their top-quality products. Companies like Mega Bloks represent the exporting spirit and innovation that define the global success of Canadian businesses." The Canada Export Awards were established in 1983 by the Department of Foreign Affairs and International Trade (DFAIT) to recognize the success of Canadian exporters in the global marketplace and their contribution to Canada's economic growth. Over the past 20 years, over 230 companies have received Canada Export Awards.

Marc Bertrand, the company's president and CEO, sums up the firm's winning strategy with the following words: "No matter where kids live, they love to build, create and learn." Having a global market with a common need is certainly one of the keys to success. Its products have universal appeal and are known worldwide as safe, high-quality toys designed to help children learn, discover, and have fun. Other factors contributing to the firm's success are its affordable price, dynamic and dedicated local sales teams, and a step-by-step strategic approach to international expansion. Innovative retail partnerships are also at the heart of its strategy. As noted on the company's Web site, "We foster strong relationships with leading retailers and distributors, based on a consistent track record of reliability, service quality and attractive gross margins."

Mega Bloks is the maker of a broad range of construction toys that feature the company's own interlocking plastic blocks. The company was founded by Bertrand's mother and father in 1967 as a local toy distributor. It wasn't until 1985 that Mega Bloks began to evolve into a full-fledged toy manufacturer and exporter. Today, the company is the world's second-largest maker of construction toys, and Canada's most important toy company. Its vision is to be the most dynamic and innovative toy company, building quality products that are expandable and universal.

When the company decided to make the move from distributor to manufacturer, Bertrand surveyed the landscape, looking for a hole in the marketplace. He found one in the construction-toy niche. While the segment was practically synonymous with Denmark-based Lego, Betrand discovered that it offered no blocks for really small kids (two years and under). He designed his own line of snap-together, large building blocks—bigger than anything Lego had made—that would be easy for toddlers to manipulate and put together. The marketplace jumped on his innovation!

Betrand's timing was optimal as well. In 1988, Lego's patent for its large Duplo blocks expired in the United States. Lego was also a high-cost manufacturer. Mega Bloks, on the other hand, kept its costs low due to the type of plastic it used, so it wasn't long before Bertrand was shipping low-cost, "might-as-well-be-Lego blocks" to his retail contacts south of the border. Lego didn't take this onslaught lying down, and its legal battle with Mega Bloks over trademarks has gone many rounds. However, Mega Bloks is surging ahead, and it has become a major supplier to Wal-Mart.

Today, Mega Bloks sells its toys in over 100 countries through 11 offices located around the world. It employs approximately 1000 people, and 75 percent of the company's products are made in Montreal, using cost-efficient manufacturing technologies. While its sales throughout North America still account for the dominant share of its revenues (70 percent), international sales are growing steadily. The company has also expanded its product line. While Mega Bloks still sells bags of plastic bricks and Probuilder vehicles composed of thousands of pieces, its new Dragons line consists of fine-moulded action figures that happen to snap together. The company also makes remote-control cars and Sound Stackers, which bleat or moo when they're put together. It has been very cautious when it comes to licensed products (like merchandise associated with the *Harry Potter* books and films). "When we look at licensing, when we look at new product, we're always looking to make a three-to-five-year business plan on that line," Marc Bertrand says. If there is any chance a licensed product looks like a fad, the company backs away. Finally, the company has kept its product line diversified and no one item accounts for more than 5 percent of its revenues. Thus, if one toy flops, the company is still secure.

Mega Bloks' success is remarkable given how rapidly the toy business has evolved. In the early days, Canadian toy firms could almost guarantee success by picking up the distribution rights to a couple of lines from the big American producers. However, as the U.S. industry consolidated, manufacturers decided they could handle Canada on their own. Retailers also consolidated. Once you could find numerous mom-and-pop operations in every Canadian city. Today distribution is in the hands of behemoths that squeeze manufacturers on price. To add to the domestic industry's woes, manufacturers must fend off low-cost competition from Asia. Finally, you have to take into account that kids today are a challenging demographic when it comes to traditional toys. Kids like video games, and many traditional toy manufacturers have suffered as a result. For example, Mattel's profits fell 5 percent in the third quarter of 2004 and Hasbro laid off workers just before Christmas that year.

Mega Bloks continues to swim in a very different direction than other toy manufacturers. While other companies are fleeing to Asia, Mega Bloks retains half of its work in its highly automated Montreal plant. It does send the other half to China—anything that involves serious handwork or electronics.

Mega Bloks still faces many challenges. The toy market is in a slump and major retailers like Toys "R" Us, one of Mega Bloks' best customers, are up for sale. The high Canadian dollar is gnawing at Mega Bloks' margins, while the rising costs of plastic resins are driving up costs. Marc Bertrand is still optimistic, however. Its international sales are made in other currencies (euros for example) and the company has new markets to explore. It is eyeing the girls market and the counter-seasonal arts-and-crafts business while it continues its international expansion. It looks pretty certain that Mega Bloks will continue to construct an international success story uniquely its own.

Sources: "Minister Pettigrew Presents Exporter of the Year Award," Canada Export Awards Press Release No. 180, November 24, 2003, **www.infoexport.gc.ca/awards-prix**; Mega Bloks Web site **www.megabloks.com**; 2005 Canada Export Awards, **www.infoexport.gc.ca/awards-prix/mega_bloks-e_win.htm**; Chris Nuttall-Smith, "How to Make Mega Bucks," *Globe and Mail Report on Business*, April 2005, pp. 56–61.

With faster communication, transportation, and financial flows, the world is rapidly shrinking. Products developed in one country—Gucci purses, Mont Blanc pens, McDonald's hamburgers, Japanese sushi, Chanel suits, German BMWs—are finding enthusiastic acceptance in others. A German businessman may wear an Armani suit to meet an English friend at a Japanese restaurant, and later return home to drink Russian vodka and watch an American soap on TV. Consider the international success of Red Bull:

Red Bull

A billion-dollar brand in less than 15 years, Red Bull has gained 70 percent of the worldwide energy drink market by skillfully connecting with global youth. Founded in Austria by Dietrich Mateschitz, Red Bull was introduced into its first foreign market, Hungary, in 1992 and is now sold in over 100 countries. Red Bull consists of amino acid taurine, B-complex vitamins, caffeine, and carbohydrates. The drink was sold originally in only one size—the silver 250 mL can—and received little traditional advertising support beyond animated television commercials with the tagline "Red Bull Gives You Wiiings." Red Bull built buzz about the product through its "seeding program": The company micro-targets "in" shops, clubs, bars, and stores, gradually moves from bars and clubs to convenience stores and restaurants, and finally enters supermarkets. It targets "opinion leaders" by making Red Bull available at sports competitions, in limos before award shows, and at exclusive after-parties. Red Bull also built its cool image through sponsorship of extreme sports and unique grassroots efforts. In cities throughout the world, for example, the company sponsors an annual *Flugtag* where contestants build flying machines that they launch off ramp into water, true to the brand's slogan![1]

Although the opportunities for companies to enter and compete in foreign markets are significant, the risks can also be high. Companies selling in global industries, however, really have no choice but to internationalize their operations. In this chapter, we review the major decisions in expanding into global markets.

Competing on a Global Basis

Two hundred giant corporations, most of them larger than many national economies, have sales that in total exceed a quarter of the world's economic activity. On that basis, the Altria Group Inc., which is the parent company of Kraft Foods, Philip Morris International, Philip Morris USA, Philip Morris Capital Corporation, and SABMiller (the world's second-largest brewer), is larger than New Zealand and operates in 170 countries.

Trade is Canada's primary engine of economic growth. Our domestic market is relatively small, thus we depend on trade for the creation of jobs and the generation of wealth. As Trade Minister Pettigrew notes, "Canadians throughout the country profit from the dynamism and success of Canada's export companies." In 2004, the value of Canadian exports rose 7.6 percent (over 2003 levels) to a record $430.4 billion, spurred partly by strong energy prices and demand for metals and minerals. Exports represent approximately 45 percent of our gross domestic product (GDP). This was the highest percentage of any of the G-8 economies. In comparison, the United States' international sales account for only 25 percent of its GDP, while Japan exports approximately 15 percent of its GDP.[2]

Red Bull is a true global success story, achieving over 70 percent of world sales in just 15 years.

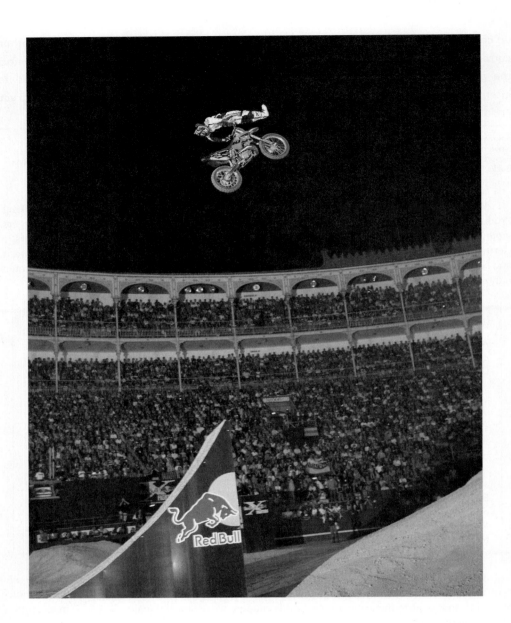

Many companies have conducted international marketing for decades—McCain Foods, Nortel, Nestlé, Shell, Bayer, and Toshiba are familiar to consumers around the world. But global competition is intensifying. Domestic companies who never thought about foreign competitors suddenly find them in their backyards. Newspapers report on the gains of Japanese, German, Swedish, and Korean car imports in the North American market, and the loss of textile and shoe markets to imports from developing countries in Latin America, Eastern Europe, and Asia.

A **global industry** is an industry in which the strategic positions of competitors in major geographic or national markets are fundamentally affected by their overall global positions.[3] A **global firm** is a firm that operates in more than one country and captures R&D, production, logistical, marketing, and financial advantages in its costs and reputation that are not available to purely domestic competitors.

Global firms plan, operate, and coordinate their activities on a worldwide basis. Ford's "world truck" has a European-made cab and a North American–built chassis, is assembled in Brazil, and is imported into the North American market for sale. Otis Elevator gets its door systems from France, small geared parts from Spain, electronics from Germany, and special motor drives from Japan; it uses the United States for systems integration. One of the most successful global companies is ABB, formed by a merger between the Swedish company ASEA and the Swiss company Brown Boveri:[4]

ABB

ABB's products include power transformers, electrical installations, instrumentation, auto components, air-conditioning equipment, and railroad equipment. The company has annual revenues of US$32 billion and 200 000 employees. Its motto: "ABB is a global company local everywhere." English is its official language (all ABB managers must be conversant in English), and all financial results must be reported in U.S. dollars. ABB aims to reconcile three contradictions: to be global and local; to be big and small; and to be radically decentralized with centralized reporting and control. It has fewer than 200 staff at company headquarters in Switzerland, compared to the 3000 people who populate the Siemens headquarters. The company's many product lines are organized into 8 business segments, 65 business areas, 1300 companies, and 5000 profit centres, with the average employee belonging to a profit centre of around 50 employees. Managers are regularly rotated among countries and mixed-nationality teams are encouraged. Depending on the type of business, some units are treated as superlocal businesses with lots of autonomy, while others are governed with major central control and are considered global businesses.[5]

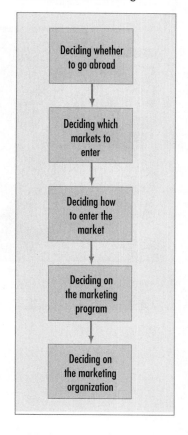

FIGURE 21.1

Major Decisions in International Marketing

- Deciding whether to go abroad
- Deciding which markets to enter
- Deciding how to enter the market
- Deciding on the marketing program
- Deciding on the marketing organization

A company need not be large, however, to sell globally. Small and medium-sized firms can practise global nichemanship. The Poilane Bakery sells 15 000 loaves of old-style bread each day in Paris—2.5 percent of all bread sold in that city—via company-owned delivery trucks. But each day, Poilane-branded bread is also shipped via FedEx to loyal customers in roughly 20 countries around the world.[6]

For a company of any size to go global, it must make a series of decisions (see Figure 21.1). We'll examine each of these decisions here.

Deciding Whether to Go Abroad

Most companies would prefer to remain domestic if their domestic market were large enough. Managers would not need to learn other languages and laws, deal with volatile currencies, face political and legal uncertainties, or redesign their products to suit different customer needs and expectations. Business would be easier and safer. Yet several factors are drawing more and more companies into the international arena:

- The company discovers that some foreign markets present higher profit opportunities than the domestic market.
- The company needs a larger customer base to achieve economies of scale.
- The company wants to reduce its dependence on any one market.
- Global firms offering better products or lower prices can attack the company's domestic market. The company might want to counterattack these competitors in their home markets.
- The company's customers are going abroad and require international servicing.

Before making a decision to go abroad, the company must weigh several risks:

- The company might not understand foreign customer preferences and fail to offer a competitively attractive product.
- The company might not understand the foreign country's business culture or know how to deal effectively with foreign nationals.
- The company might underestimate foreign regulations and incur unexpected costs.

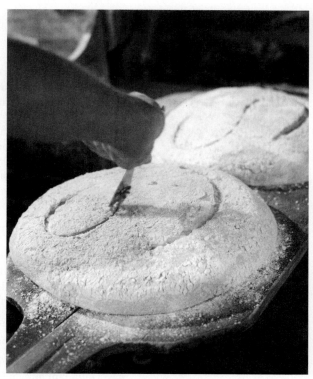

The company logo being carved into a loaf of Poilane bread, which is shipped daily via FedEx to loyal customers in countries around the world.

ExportSource.ca is the portal for Team Canada—a network of more than 20 federal government departments and agencies whose aim is to help Canadian businesses succeed in world markets.

- The company might realize that it lacks managers with international experience.

- The foreign country might change its commercial laws, devalue its currency, or undergo a political revolution and expropriate foreign property.

Because of the competing advantages and risks, companies often do not act until some event thrusts them into the international arena. Someone—a domestic exporter, an international importer, a foreign government—solicits the company to sell abroad, or the company is saddled with overcapacity and must find additional markets for its goods.

Most countries lament that too few of their companies participate in international trade. This keeps the country from earning foreign exchange to pay for needed imports. It also raises the spectre of domestic companies eventually being hurt or taken over by foreign multinationals. Many countries sponsor aggressive export-promotion programs to get their companies to export. These programs require a deep understanding of how companies become internationalized. The Canadian government works hard to convince companies to export and provides services and information essential to their success. In 1997, to better coordinate these efforts, Team Canada Inc. was born. Its aim is to increase the capabilities, preparedness, and international market development success of Canadian businesses. It was formed from a network of more than 20 federal government departments and agencies working with the provinces, territories, and other partners to provide a single window of access to export information and services.

The *internationalization process* has four stages:[7]

1. No regular export activities.
2. Export via independent representatives (agents).
3. Establishment of one or more sales subsidiaries.
4. Establishment of production facilities abroad.

The first task is to get companies to move from stage 1 to stage 2. This move is helped by studying how firms make their first export decisions.[8] Most firms work with an independent agent and enter a nearby or similar country. A company then engages further agents to enter additional countries. Later, it establishes an export department to manage its agent relationships. Still later, the company replaces its agents with its own sales subsidiaries in its larger export markets. This increases the company's investment and risk, but also its earning potential.

To manage these subsidiaries, the company replaces the export department with an international department. If certain markets continue to be large and stable, or if the host country insists on local production, the company takes the next step of locating production facilities in those markets. This means a still larger commitment and still larger potential earnings. By this time, the company is operating as a multinational and is engaged in optimizing its global sourcing, financing, manufacturing, and marketing. According to some researchers, top management begins to pay more attention to global opportunities when they find that over 15 percent of revenues comes from foreign markets.[9]

Deciding Which Markets to Enter

In deciding to go abroad, the company needs to define its marketing objectives and policies. What proportion of foreign to total sales will it seek? Most companies start small when they venture abroad. Some plan to stay small; others have bigger plans. Ayal and Zif have argued that a company should enter fewer countries when:

- Market entry and market control costs are high.
- Product and communication adaptation costs are high.
- Population and income size and growth are high in the initial countries chosen.
- Dominant foreign firms can establish high barriers to entry.[10]

How Many Markets to Enter

The company must decide how many countries to enter and how fast to expand. Consider Amway's experience:

Amway

Amway Corp., one of the world's largest direct-selling companies, markets its products and services through independent business owners worldwide. Amway expanded into Canada in the 1950s, and into Australia in 1971. By 2004, Amway had evolved into a multinational juggernaut with a sales force of more than 3.6 million independent distributors hauling in US$4.5 billion in sales. Established in 1998, Amway India quickly grew to 200 000 active Amway distributors by 2004. Amway currently sells products in 80 countries and territories worldwide. The corporate goal is to have overseas markets account for 80 percent of its sales. This is not unrealistic or overly ambitious considering that Amway already gains 70 percent of its sales from markets outside North America.[11]

Companies' entry strategy typically follows one of two possible approaches: a *waterfall* approach, in which countries are gradually entered sequentially; or a *sprinkler* approach, in which many countries are entered simultaneously within a limited period of time. Increasingly, especially with technology-intensive firms, they are *born global* and market to the entire world right from the outset.[12]

Generally speaking, companies such as Matsushita, BMW, and General Electric, or even newer companies such as Dell, Nortel, and The Body Shop, follow the waterfall approach. Expansion can be carefully planned and is less likely to strain human and financial resources. When first-mover advantage is crucial and a high degree of competitive intensity prevails, the sprinkler approach is preferred, as when Microsoft introduces a new form of Windows software. The main risk is the substantial resources involved and the difficulty of planning entry strategies in so many potentially diverse markets.

The company must also decide on the types of countries to consider. Attractiveness is influenced by the product, geography, income and population, political climate, and other factors. Kenichi Ohmae recommends that companies concentrate on selling in the "triad markets"—North America, Western Europe, and the Far East—because these markets account for a large percentage of all international trade.[13]

Developed versus Developing Markets

Although Ohmae's position makes short-run sense, it can spell disaster for the world economy in the long run. The unmet needs of the emerging or developing world represent huge potential markets for food, clothing, shelter, consumer electronics, appliances, and other goods. Many market leaders are rushing into Eastern Europe, China, and India. Colgate now draws more personal and household products business from Latin America than North America.[14]

The developed nations and the prosperous parts of developing nations account for less than 15 percent of the world's population. Is there a way for marketers to serve the other 85 percent, which has much less purchasing power? Successfully entering developing markets requires a special set of skills and plans. Consider how the following companies are pioneering ways to serve these consumers:[15]

- Grameen-Phone markets cell phones to 35 000 villages in Bangladesh by hiring village women as agents who lease phone time to other villagers, one call at a time.
- Colgate-Palmolive rolls into Indian villages with video vans that show the benefits of toothbrushing; it expects to earn over half of its Indian revenue from rural areas by 2003.
- An Indian-Australian car manufacturer created an affordable rural transport vehicle to compete with bullock carts rather than cars. The vehicle functions well at low speeds and carries up to two tonnes.
- Fiat developed a "third-world car," the Palio, that far outsells the Ford Fiesta in Brazil and that will be launched in other developing nations.
- Corporacion GEO builds low-income housing in Mexico. The two-bedroom homes are modular and can be expanded. The company is now moving into Chile and southern U.S. communities.

A Russian ad for Nestlé's Nescafé. As consumer spending has risen in Russia, the market for products of major multinationals like Nestlé has boomed.

These marketers are able to capitalize on the potential of developing markets by changing their conventional marketing practices to sell their products and services more effectively.[16] It cannot be business as usual when selling into developing markets. Economic and cultural differences abound; a marketing infrastructure may barely exist; and local competition can be surprisingly stiff. In China, PC maker Legend and mobile phone provider TCL have thrived despite strong foreign competition. Besides their close grasp on Chinese tastes, they also have their vast distribution networks, especially in rural areas.[17]

Smaller packaging and lower sales prices are often critical in markets where incomes are limited. Unilever's 4-cent sachets of detergent and shampoo have been a big hit in rural India, where 70 percent of the country's population still lives. When Coke moved to a smaller 200 mL bottle in India, selling for 10 to 12 cents in small shops, bus-stop stalls, and roadside eateries, sales jumped.[18] A Western image can also be helpful, as Coke discovered in China. Part of its success against local cola brand Jianlibao was due to its symbolic values of modernity and affluence.[19]

Recognizing that its cost structure made it difficult to compete effectively in developing markets, Procter & Gamble devised cheaper, clever ways to make the right kinds of products to suit consumer demand. It now uses contract manufacturers in certain markets and gained eight share points in Russia for Always feminine protection pads by responding to consumer wishes for a thicker pad.[20] Due to a boom in consumer spending, Russia has been the fastest-growing market for many major multinationals, including Nestlé, L'Oréal, and IKEA.[21]

The challenge is to think creatively about how marketing can fulfill the dreams of most of the world's population for a better standard of living. And many companies are betting that they can do just that.

General Motors

After launching Buick in China in 1999, GM poured more than US$2 billion into the region over the next five years, expanding the lineup to 14 models, ranging from the US$8000 Chevrolet Spark mini-car to high-end Cadillacs. Although competition in the third-largest car market is fierce, GM was able to secure 11 percent market share in 2004 and reap sizable profits.[22]

Regional Free Trade Zones

Regional economic integration—trading agreements between blocs of countries—has intensified in recent years. This development means that companies are more likely to enter entire regions at the same time. Certain countries have formed free trade zones or economic communities—groups of nations organized to work toward common goals in the regulation of international trade. One such community is the European Union (EU).

THE EUROPEAN UNION Formed in 1957, the European Union set out to create a single European market by reducing barriers to the free flow of products, services, finances, and labour among member countries, and by developing trade policies with nonmember nations. Today, the European Union is one of the world's single largest markets. The 15 member countries making up the EU increased by 10 in May 2004 with the addition of Cyprus, the Czech Republic, Estonia, Hungary, Latvia, Lithuania, Malta, Poland, Slovakia, and Slovenia. The EU now contains more than 454 million consumers and accounts for 23 percent of the world's exports. It has a common currency, the euro monetary system.

European unification offers tremendous trade opportunities for non-European firms. However, it also poses threats. European companies will grow bigger and more competitive. Witness the competition in the aircraft industry between Europe's Airbus consortium and Boeing in the United States. Perhaps an even bigger concern, however, is that lower barriers inside Europe will only create thicker outside walls. Some observers envision a "fortress Europe" that heaps favours on firms from EU countries but hinders outsiders by imposing obstacles such as stiffer import quotas, local content requirements, and other nontariff (nontax) barriers.

Also, companies that plan to create "pan-European" marketing campaigns directed to a unified Europe should proceed with caution. Even as the EU standardizes its general trade regulations and currency, creating an economic community will not create a homogeneous market. Companies marketing in Europe face 14 different languages, 2000 years of historical and cultural differences, and a daunting mass of local rules.

NAFTA   Closer to home, in North America, the United States and Canada phased out trade barriers in 1989. In January 1994, the North American Free Trade Agreement (NAFTA) established a free trade zone among the United States, Mexico, and Canada.

How effective has the trade agreement been a decade after its birth? The answer will depend on whom you ask, and the agreement has continued to be controversial. In 2004, ten years after NAFTA's initiation, trilateral trade among the three countries has doubled to $US620 billion yearly. The United States is our largest trade partner and Canada now enjoys an unprecedented $139 billion annual trade surplus with the United States. Our exports to Mexico have tripled since the agreement's launch, and Canada is now Mexico's second-biggest export market, while Mexico is Canada's sixth. The investment landscape has also changed. Canadian investment in Mexico has surged to almost $4 billion, 16 times what it was in 1990. Canadian investment in the United States has more than tripled to $198 billion over the same time period, while U.S. investment in Canada soared 150 percent to $215 billion. The Canadian government reports that the economy has grown by an average of 3.8 percent annually since the agreement came into force, generating 2.1 million jobs. The Canadian Labour Congress, however, doesn't share the government's enthusiasm. It estimates that total employment in manufacturing is now 10 percent below the pre-NAFTA levels while wages in the manufacturing sector have stayed the same or declined. Another critic, the Canadian Auto Workers union, claims that 7000 auto assembly jobs have shifted to Mexico from Canada. The recent softwood lumber dispute has caused further criticism of the agreement. In late 2004, the "binding" dispute resolution mechanism in NAFTA proved to be anything but binding when a ruling about unfair subsidies went in Canada's favour. The United States refused to agree and remove the tariffs on the industry, which accounts for approximately 3 percent of Canada's exports to the United States. Nonetheless, analysts agree that over its history, the agreement has largely been strong and dispute-free.[23]

Since the agreement has been so successful, Canada is taking a leadership role in trying to extend it to countries throughout South America. The envisioned free trade zone extending from Nunavut to Tierra del Fuego would have a combined GDP of more than US$20 trillion, or about 40 percent of the world's economic activity. This would position Canada to compete more effectively with the growing power of the European economic community.

MERCOSUL   Other free trade areas are forming in Latin America. For example, MERCOSUL now links Brazil, Argentina, Paraguay, and Uruguay. Chile and Mexico have formed a successful free trade zone. It is likely that NAFTA will eventually merge with this and other arrangements to form an all-Americas free trade zone.

It is the European nations that have tapped Latin America's enormous potential. As efforts to extend NAFTA to Latin America have stalled, European countries have moved in with a vengeance. When Latin American countries instituted market reforms and privatized public utilities, European companies rushed in to grab up lucrative contracts for rebuilding Latin America's infrastructure. Spain's Telefonica de Espana spent US$5 billion buying phone companies in Brazil, Chile, Peru, and Argentina. In Brazil, seven of the ten largest private companies are European owned, compared to two controlled by Americans. Among the notable European companies operating in Latin America are automotive giants Volkswagen and Fiat, the French supermarket chain Carrefours, and the Anglo-Dutch personal-care products group Gessy-Lever.

APEC   Twenty-one Pacific Rim countries, including the NAFTA member states, Japan, and China, form the Asian Pacific Economic Cooperation forum (APEC). As a founding member, Canada has been involved in the organization since its creation in 1989. Canada's participation is important given that the Asia-Pacific region represents about 45 percent of global trade and 55 percent of world income. Unlike the other agreements, APEC is not a free trade agreement. Its mandate is to ease the movement of goods, services, and people across borders. For example, an average trade transaction currently requires 40 documents. To eliminate this time-consuming red tape, APEC is aiming at paperless trading by 2005 for developed economies and 2010 for developing economies.[24]

Evaluating Potential Markets

Yet, however much nations and regions integrate their trading policies and standards, each nation still has unique features that must be understood. A nation's readiness for different products and services and its attractiveness as a market to foreign firms depend on its economic, political-legal, and cultural environments.

Suppose a company has assembled a list of potential markets to enter. How does it choose among them? Many companies prefer to sell to neighbouring countries because they understand these countries better and can control their costs more effectively. It is not surprising that Canada's largest export market is the United States. As of 2004, 82 percent of our merchandise export trade went south of the border (compare this to our second-largest export market, the European Union, which gets only 3 percent of our merchandise exports).[25]

Psychic proximity also helps determine export market choice. Many Canadian firms believe the United States is much like Canada, as are England and Australia—thus, they seek these markets rather than markets such as Germany and France because they feel more comfortable with the language, laws, and culture. Companies should be careful, however, in choosing markets according to cultural distance. Besides the fact that potentially better markets may be overlooked, it also may result in a superficial analysis of some very real differences among the countries. It may also lead to predictable marketing actions that would be a disadvantage from a competitive standpoint.[26]

Regardless of how chosen, it often makes sense to operate in fewer countries with a deeper commitment and penetration in each. In general, a company prefers to enter countries (1) that rank high on market attractiveness, (2) that are low in market risk, and (3) in which it possesses a competitive advantage. Here is how Bechtel Corporation, the construction giant, goes about evaluating overseas markets:

Bechtel Corporation

Bechtel provides premier technical, management, and directly related services to develop, manage, engineer, build, and operate installations for customers in nearly 60 countries worldwide. Before Bechtel ventures into new markets, the company starts with a detailed strategic market analysis. It looks at its markets and tries to determine where it should be in four or five years' time. A management team does a cost-benefit analysis that factors in the position of competitors, infrastructure, regulatory and trade barriers, and the tax situation (both corporate and individual). Ideally, the new market should be a country with an untapped need for its products or services, a quality, skilled labour pool capable of manufacturing the product, and a welcoming environment (governmental and physical).

Are there countries that meet Bechtel's requirements? Although Singapore has an educated, English-speaking labour force, basks in political stability, and encourages foreign investment, it has a small population. Although many countries in central Europe possess an eager, hungry-to-learn labour pool, their infrastructures create difficulties. The team evaluating a new market must determine whether the company could earn enough on its investment to cover the risk factors or other negatives.[27]

Deciding How to Enter the Market

Once a company decides to target a particular country, it has to determine the best mode of entry. Its broad choices are *indirect exporting, direct exporting, licensing, joint ventures,* and *direct investment.* These five market-entry strategies are shown in Figure 21.2. Each succeeding strategy involves more commitment, risk, control, and profit potential.

Indirect and Direct Export

The normal way to get involved in an international market is through export. *Occasional exporting* is a passive level of involvement in which the company exports from time to time, either on its own initiative or in response to unsolicited orders from abroad. *Active exporting* takes place when the company makes a commitment to expand into a particular market. In either case, the company produces its goods in the home country and might or might not adapt them to the international market.

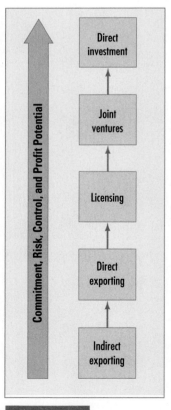

FIGURE 21.2

Five Models of Entry into Foreign Markets

Companies typically start with *indirect exporting*—that is, they work through independent inter- mediaries. *Domestic-based export merchants* buy the manufacturer's products and then sell them abroad. *Domestic-based export agents* seek and negotiate foreign purchases and are paid a commis- sion. Included in this group are trading companies. *Cooperative organizations* carry on exporting activities on behalf of several producers and are partly under their administrative control. They are often used by producers of primary products such as fruits or nuts. *Export-management companies* agree to manage a company's export activities for a fee.

Indirect export has two advantages. First, it involves less investment; the firm does not have to develop an export department, an overseas sales force, or a set of international contacts. Second, it involves less risk; because international-marketing intermediaries bring know-how and services to the relationship, the seller will normally make fewer mistakes.

Companies eventually may decide to handle their own exports.[28] The investment and risk are somewhat greater, but so is the potential return. A company can carry on direct exporting in several ways:

- *Domestic-based export department or division.* Might evolve into a self-contained export department operating as a profit centre.

- *Overseas sales branch or subsidiary.* The sales branch handles sales and distribution and might handle warehousing and promotion as well. It often serves as a display and customer service centre.

- *Travelling export sales representatives.* Home-based sales representatives are sent abroad to find business.

- *Foreign-based distributors or agents.* These distributors and agents might be given exclusive rights to represent the company in that country, or only limited rights.

Whether companies decide to export indirectly or directly, many companies use exporting as a way to "test the waters" before building a plant and manufacturing a product overseas. See how one successful Canadian exporter has expanded its product market:

Clearwater

Frozen, shell-off raw lobster meat is the latest export in a line of new products offered by Clearwater, a successful Nova Scotia–based seafood company. It is the world's largest exporter of fresh, live lobster and has become an industry leader by expanding markets for traditional seafood products. Previously, the only way to obtain raw meat was to buy live lobsters. However, the time and costs of cooking, shucking, storage, and waste dissuaded chefs from offering multiple menu offerings or serving lobster to large banquet functions. The company leveraged the Canadian embassies in Brussels, Copenhagen, Paris, Stockholm, and Oslo. They hosted demonstrations conducted by Clearwater's corporate chef, Stephan Czapalay, of this new product to top-level chefs and seafood importers and distributors. This highly targeted, personal campaign was much more successful than the traditional trade show approach. The European market was a particularly attractive target because the demand for seafood has been traditionally high, but local supplies are in decline.[29]

Using a Global Web Strategy

One of the best ways to initiate or extend export activities used to be to exhibit at an overseas trade show. With the Web, it is not even necessary to attend trade shows to show one's wares: Electronic communication via the Internet is extending the reach of companies large and small to worldwide markets.

Major marketers doing global e-commerce range from automakers (GM) to direct-mail compa- nies (Tilley Endurables) to running-shoe giants (Nike and Reebok) to Amazon.com. Marketers like these are using the Web to reach new customers outside their home countries, to support existing cus- tomers who live abroad, to source from international suppliers, and to build global brand awareness.

These companies adapt their Web sites to provide country-specific content and services to their best potential international markets, ideally in the local language. The number of Internet users is ris- ing quickly as access costs decline, local-language content increases, and infrastructure improves.

Upscale retailer and cataloguer The Sharper Image now gets more than 25 percent of its online business from overseas customers.[30]

The Internet has become an effective means of everything from gaining free exporting information and guidelines to conducting market research and offering customers several time zones away a secure process for ordering and paying for products. "Going abroad" on the Internet does pose special challenges. The global marketer may run up against governmental or cultural restrictions. In Germany, a vendor cannot accept payment via credit card until two weeks after an order has been sent. German law also prevents companies from using certain marketing techniques like unconditional lifetime guarantees. On a wider scale, the issue of who pays sales taxes and duties on global e-commerce is murkier still.

Finding free information about trade and exporting has never been easier. Here are some places to start a search:

- The Department of Foreign Affairs and International Trade (**www.dfait-maeci.gc.ca/menu-en.asp**)
- Team Canada Inc. (**http://exportsource.ca/gol/exportsource/site.nsf**)
- Export Development Canada (**www.edc.ca**)
- The Trade and Investment Section of Industry Canada (**http://strategis.ic.gc.ca/sc_mrkti/engdoc/homepage.html?categories=e_tra**)

In addition, most provincial governments provide information to facilitate international trade (e.g., for Ontario, see Ontario Exports Inc. at **www.ontarioexportsinc.com/oei**).

Licensing

Licensing is a simple way to become involved in international marketing. The licensor licenses a foreign company to use a manufacturing process, trademark, patent, trade secret, or other item of value for a fee or royalty. The licensor gains entry at little risk; the licensee gains production expertise or a well-known product or brand name.

Licensing has potential disadvantages. The licensor has less control over the licensee than it does over its own production and sales facilities. Furthermore, if the licensee is very successful, the firm has given up profits; and if and when the contract ends, the company might find that it has created a competitor. To avoid this, the licensor usually supplies some proprietary ingredients or components needed in the product (as Coca-Cola does). But the best strategy is for the licensor to lead in innovation so that the licensee will continue to depend on the licensor.

There are several variations on a licensing arrangement. Companies such as Hyatt and Marriott sell *management contracts* to owners of foreign hotels to manage these businesses for a fee. The management firm may even be given the option to purchase some share in the managed company within a stated period.

In *contract manufacturing*, the firm hires local manufacturers to produce the product. When Sears opened department stores in Mexico and Spain, it found qualified local manufacturers to produce many of its products. Contract manufacturing gives the company less control over the manufacturing process and the loss of potential profits on manufacturing. However, it offers a chance to start faster, with less risk and with the opportunity to form a partnership or buy out the local manufacturer later.

Finally, a company can enter a foreign market through *franchising*, which is a more complete form of licensing. The franchisor offers a complete brand concept and operating system. In return, the franchisee invests in and pays certain fees to the franchisor. McDonald's, KFC, and Avis have entered scores of countries by franchising their retail concepts and making sure their marketing is culturally relevant.

KFC Corporation

KFC is the world's largest fast-food chicken chain, owning or franchising 12 800 outlets in about 90 countries. KFC had a number of obstacles to overcome when it entered the Japanese market. The Japanese saw fast food as artificial, made by mechanical means, and unhealthy. To build trust in the KFC brand, advertising showed scenes depicting Colonel Sanders' beginnings in Kentucky that conveyed southern hospitality, old American tradition, and authentic home cooking. The campaign was hugely successful, and in less than eight years KFC expanded its presence from 400 locations to more than 1000. KFC is China's largest, oldest, and most popular quick-service restaurant chain, also with over 1000 locations. KFC is the most popular international brand throughout China, ranking higher than all others, according to a consumer survey conducted by AC Nielsen. China operations offer such fare as an "Old Beijing Twister"—a wrap modelled after the way Peking duck is served, but with fried chicken inside.[31]

Joint Ventures

Foreign investors may join with local investors to create a **joint venture** company in which they share ownership and control. For instance:[32]

- CAE of Montreal and China Southern Airlines formed a joint venture in January 2003 to provide aviation-training solutions for Asian carriers.
- Vancouver-based Cummins-Westport Inc. is a joint venture between leading diesel engine manufacturer Cummins Inc. and alternative fuels engine technology company Westport Innovations Inc. Cummins-Westport develops and markets the world's widest range of high-performance, low-emission engines for transit and commercial vehicles, as well as advanced alternative fuel system technologies for electrical power generation.
- Coca-Cola and Nestlé joined forces to develop the international market for "ready to drink" tea and coffee, which they currently sell in significant amounts in Japan.

A joint venture may be necessary or desirable for economic or political reasons. The foreign firm might lack the financial, physical, or managerial resources to undertake the venture alone; or the foreign government might require joint ownership as a condition for entry. Even corporate giants need joint ventures to crack the toughest markets. When it wanted to enter China's ice cream market, Unilever joined forces with Sumstar, a state-owned Chinese investment company. The venture's general manager says Sumstar's help with the formidable Chinese bureaucracy was crucial in getting a high-tech ice cream plant up and running in just 12 months.[33]

Joint ownership has certain drawbacks. The partners might disagree over investment, marketing, or other policies. One partner might want to reinvest earnings for growth, and the other partner might want to declare more dividends. Joint ownership can also prevent a multinational company from carrying out specific manufacturing and marketing policies on a worldwide basis.

Direct Investment

The ultimate form of foreign involvement is direct ownership of foreign-based assembly or manufacturing facilities. The foreign company can buy part or full interest in a local company or build its own facilities. General Motors, for example, has invested billions of dollars in auto manufacturers around the world, such as Shanghai GM, Fiat Auto Holdings, Isuzu, Daewoo, Suzuki, Saab, Fuji Heavy Industries, Jinbei GM Automotive Co., and AvtoVAZ.[34]

If the market appears large enough, foreign production facilities offer distinct advantages. First, the firm secures cost economies in the form of cheaper labour or raw materials, foreign-government investment incentives, and freight savings. Second, the firm strengthens its image in the host country because it creates jobs. Third, the firm develops a deeper relationship with government, customers, local suppliers, and distributors, enabling it to adapt its products better to the local environment. Fourth, the firm retains full control over its investment and therefore can develop manufacturing and marketing policies that serve its long-term international objectives. Fifth, the firm assures itself access to the market in case the host country starts insisting that locally purchased goods have domestic content. To realize these advantages, Canada and China are forging closer ties:

China

China now rivals the United States as Canada's most popular destination for foreign direct investment. In 2003, China became Canada's second-largest trading partner after the United States. The two-way trade grew to some $25 billion in 2003 and trade expanded by 50 percent throughout 2004. The Canadian government has been encouraging increased trade with China. Two successful "Team Canada" trade missions to China were completed in 1994 and 2001. Both countries are investing in operations in the other, particularly in the mining and energy sectors. According to Statistics Canada, Canadian direct investment in China has been growing by at least 12 percent per year and totalled $667 million in 2002 alone. Canada is also benefiting from Chinese investment, which totalled $224 million in 2002. While China is still largely a rural society, the urban middle class already exceeds 200 million people and is expected to grow to 400 million by 2010. With aging populations in Europe, Japan, and North America, Chinese middle-class consumers are increasingly attractive targets. According to *Canadian Business* magazine, the ability of Canadian firms to reach these consumers will depend on our direct investment success, and exporting alone won't cut it.[35]

The main disadvantage of direct investment is that the firm exposes a large investment to risks such as blocked or devalued currencies, worsening markets, or expropriation. The firm will find it expensive to reduce or close down its operations, because the host country might require substantial severance pay to the employees. Many Canadian retailers have used direct investment to attack the U.S. marketplace. However, they often find the competition more intense and change more rapid than they expected. Moreover, U.S. retailers often have the advantage of larger size and name recognition over their Canadian rivals. Until recently, only 20 percent of retailers entering the U.S. market succeeded. Mark's Work Wearhouse, Second Cup Ltd., Canadian Tire, and People's Jewellers have all tested the U.S. waters only to withdraw in defeat. Today, however, the success rate has risen to 50 percent. Retailers like Harry Rosen, Tim Hortons, Club Monaco, and Jean Coutu have led the charge. The more successful entrants have tended to be smaller, specialized retailers that aim at niche markets where they don't have to challenge U.S. competitors head on.[36]

Deciding on the Marketing Program

International companies must decide how much to adapt their marketing strategy to local conditions.[37] At one extreme are companies that use a globally *standardized marketing mix* worldwide. Standardization of the product, communication, and distribution channels promises the lowest costs. Table 21.1 summarizes some of the pros and cons of standardizing the marketing program. At the other extreme is an *adapted marketing mix*, where the producer adjusts the marketing program to each target market. For a discussion of the main issues, see "Marketing Insight: Global Standardization or Adaptation?"

Between the two extremes, many possibilities exist. Most brands are adapted to some extent to reflect significant differences in consumer behaviour, brand development, competitive forces, and the legal or political environment. Satisfying different consumer needs and wants can require different marketing programs. Cultural differences can often be pronounced across countries. Hofstede identifies four cultural dimensions that can differentiate countries:[38]

1. *Individualism vs. collectivism.* In collectivist societies, such as Japan, the self-worth of an individual is rooted more in the social system than in individual achievement.

2. *High vs. low power distance.* High power distance cultures tend to be less egalitarian.

3. *Masculine vs. feminine.* How much the culture is dominated by assertive males versus nurturing females.

4. *Weak vs. strong uncertainty avoidance.* How risk tolerant or aversive people are.

Even global brands, such as Pringles, Always, and Toyota, will undergo some changes in product features, packaging, channels, pricing, or communications in different global markets. (See "Marketing Memo: The Ten Commandments of Global Branding.") Marketers must make sure that their marketing is relevant to consumers in every market.

TABLE 21.1	GLOBAL MARKETING PROS AND CONS

Advantages

Economies of scale in production and distribution

Lower marketing costs

Power and scope

Consistency in brand image

Ability to leverage good ideas quickly and efficiently

Uniformity of marketing practices

Disadvantages

Differences in consumer needs, wants, and usage patterns for products

Differences in consumer response to marketing-mix elements

Differences in brand and product development and the competitive environment

Differences in the legal environment

Differences in marketing institutions

Differences in administrative procedures

Walt Disney Co.

When Walt Disney launched the Euro Disney theme park outside Paris in 1992, it was harshly criticized as being an example of American cultural imperialism. A number of local French customs and values, such as serving wine with meals, were ignored. As one Euro Disney executive noted, "When we first launched, there was the belief that it was enough to be Disney. Now we realize our guests need to be welcomed on the basis of their own culture and travel habits." Renamed Disneyland Paris, the theme park eventually became Europe's biggest tourist attraction—even more popular than the Eiffel Tower—by making a number of changes and adding more local touches.[39]

Product

Some types of products travel better across borders than others—food and beverage marketers have to contend with widely varying tastes.[40] "Marketing Insight: Establishing Global Service Brands" describes some of the special concerns for marketing services globally. Warren Keegan has distinguished five strategies for adapting product and communications to a foreign market (see Figure 21.3).[41]

Straight extension means introducing the product in the foreign market without any change. Straight extension has been successful with cameras, consumer electronics, and many machine tools. In other cases, it has been a disaster. General Foods introduced its standard powdered Jell-O in the British market only to find that British consumers prefer the solid wafer or cake form. Campbell Soup Company lost an estimated US$30 million in introducing its condensed soups in England; consumers saw expensive small-sized cans and did not realize that water needed to be added. Straight extension is tempting because it involves no additional R&D expense, manufacturing retooling, or promotional modification; but it can be costly in the long run.

Disneyland Paris, Europe's biggest tourist attraction.

Global Standardization or Adaptation?

The marketing concept holds that consumer needs vary and that marketing programs will be more effective when they are tailored to each target group. This also applies to foreign markets. Yet in 1983, in a groundbreaking article in the *Harvard Business Review*, Harvard professor Theodore Levitt challenged this view and supplied the intellectual rationale for global standardization: "The world is becoming a common marketplace in which people—no matter where they live—desire the same products and lifestyles."

The development of the Web, the rapid spread of cable and satellite TV around the world, and the global linking of telecommunications networks have led to a convergence of lifestyles. The convergence of needs and wants has created global markets for standardized products, particularly among the young middle class.

Levitt favours global corporations that try to sell the same product the same way to all consumers. They focus on similarities across world markets and "sensibly force suitably standardized products and services on the entire globe." These global marketers achieve economies through standardization of production, distribution, marketing, and management. They translate their efficiency into greater value for consumers by offering high quality and more reliable products at lower prices.

Coca-Cola, McDonald's, Marlboro, Nike, the NBA, and Gillette are among the companies that have successfully marketed global products. Consider Gillette: Some 1.2 billion people use at least one Gillette product daily, according to the company's estimates. Gillette enjoys huge economies of scale by selling a few types of razor blades in every single market.

Many companies have tried to launch their version of a world product. Yet, most products require some adaptation. Toyota's Corolla will exhibit some differences in styling. McDonald's offers a ham and cheese "Croque McDo" in France, a variation of the French favourite croque monsieur. Coca-Cola is sweeter or less carbonated in certain countries. Rather than assuming that its domestic product can be introduced "as is" in another country, the company should review the following elements and determine which would add more revenue than cost:

- Product features
- Brand name
- Labelling
- Packaging
- Colours
- Advertising execution
- Materials
- Prices
- Sales promotion
- Advertising themes
- Advertising media

Consumer behaviour can dramatically differ across markets. Take beverages. One of the highest per capita consumptions of carbonated soft drinks is the United States at 203.9 litres; Italy is among the lowest. But at 164.4 litres Italy is one of the highest per capita drinkers of bottled water, compared to the United Kingdom at only 20 litres. When it comes to beer, Ireland and the Czech Republic lead the pack at over 150 litres per capita, with France among the lowest at 35.9 litres.

Besides demand-side differences, other types of supply-side differences can also prevail. Levitt's critics pointed out that flexible manufacturing techniques made it easier to produce many different product versions, tailored to particular countries. One study showed that companies made one or more marketing-mix adaptations in 80 percent of their foreign products and that the average number of adapted elements was four. So perhaps Levitt's globalization dictum should be rephrased. Global marketing, yes. Global standardization, not necessarily.

Sources: Theodore Levitt, "The Globalization of Markets," *Harvard Business Review* (May–June 1983): 92–102; Bernard Wysocki Jr., "The Global Mall: In Developing Nations, Many Youths Splurge, Mainly on U.S. Goods," *Wall Street Journal*, June 26, 1997, p. A1; "What Makes a Company Great?" *Fortune*, October 26, 1998, pp. 218–226; David M. Szymanski, Sundar G. Bharadwaj, and P. Rajan Varadarajan, "Standardization versus Adaptation of International Marketing Strategy: An Empirical Investigation," *Journal of Marketing* (October 1993), pp. 1–17; "Burgers and Fries a la Française," *The Economist*, April 17, 2004, pp. 60–61; Johny K. Johansson, "Global Marketing: Research on Foreign Entry, Local Marketing, Global Management" in *Handbook of Marketing*, edited by Bart Weitz and Robin Wensley (London: Sage Publications), pp. 457–483.

Marketing Memo

The Ten Commandments of Global Branding

For many companies, global branding has been both a blessing and a curse. A global branding program can lower marketing costs, realize greater economies of scale in production, and provide a long-term source of growth. If not designed and implemented properly, however, it may ignore important differences in consumer behaviour and/or the competitive environment in the individual countries. These suggestions can help a company retain many of the advantages of global branding while minimizing the potential disadvantages:

1. *Understand similarities and differences in the global branding landscape.* International markets can vary in terms of brand development, consumer behaviour, competitive activity, legal restrictions, and so on.

2. *Do not take shortcuts in brand-building.* Building a brand in new markets should be done from the bottom up, both strategically (building awareness before brand image) and tactically (creating sources of brand equity in new markets).

3. *Establish a marketing infrastructure.* A company must either build marketing infrastructure from scratch or adapt to existing infrastructure in other countries.

4. *Embrace integrated marketing communications.* A company must often use many forms of communication in overseas markets, not just advertising.

5. *Establish brand partnerships.* Most global brands have marketing partners in their international markets that help companies achieve advantages in distribution, profitability, and added value.

6. *Balance standardization and customization.* Some elements of a marketing program can be standardized (packaging, brand name); others typically require greater customization (distribution channels).

7. *Balance global and local control.* Companies must balance global and local control within the organization and distribute decision-making between global and local managers.

8. *Establish operable guidelines.* Brand definition and guidelines must be established, communicated, and properly enforced so that marketers everywhere know what they are expected to do and not do. The goal is to set rules for how the brand should be positioned and marketed.

9. *Implement a global brand equity measurement system.* A global brand equity system is a set of research procedures designed to provide timely, accurate, and actionable information for marketers so they can make the best possible short-run tactical decisions and long-run strategic decisions.

10. *Leverage brand elements.* Proper design and implementation of brand elements (brand name and trademarked brand identifiers) can be an invaluable source of brand equity worldwide.

Source: Adapted from Kevin Lane Keller and Sanjay Sood, "The Ten Commandments of Global Branding," *Asian Journal of Marketing*, 8, no 2 (2001): 97–108.

	Product		
	Do Not Change Product	Adapt Product	Develop New Product
Do Not Change Communications	Straight extension	Product adaptation	Product invention
Adapt Communications	Communication adaptation	Dual adaptation	

(Communications — vertical axis label)

FIGURE 21.3

Five International Product and Communications Strategies

Product adaptation involves altering the product to meet local conditions or preferences. There are several levels of adaptation.

■ A company can produce a *regional version* of its product, such as a Western European version. Finnish cellular phone superstar Nokia customized its 6100 series phone for every major market. Developers built in rudimentary voice recognition for Asia, where keyboards are a problem, and raised the ring volume so the phone could be heard on crowded Asian streets.

Establishing Global Service Brands

The world market for services is growing at double the rate of world merchandise trade. Large firms in accounting, advertising, banking, communications, construction, insurance, law, management consulting, and retailing are pursuing global expansion. Price Waterhouse, American Express, Citigroup, Club Med, Hilton, and Thomas Cook are known worldwide. U.S. credit-card companies have streamed across the Atlantic to convince Europeans of the joys of charge cards. In Britain, industry heavyweights Citibank and American Express have wrested a lot of business from big British banks like Barclay's.

Many countries, however, have erected entry barriers or regulations. Brazil requires all accountants to possess a professional degree from a Brazilian university. Many Western European countries want to limit the number of U.S. television programs and films shown in their countries. Many U.S. states bar foreign bank branches. At the same time, the United States is pressuring South Korea to open its markets to U.S. banks. The World Trade Organization, consisting of 147 countries, and the General Agreement on Tariffs and Trade (GATT), consisting of 110 countries, continue to press for more free trade in international services and other areas.

Retailers who sell books, videos, and CD-ROMs, and entertainment companies have also had to contend with a culture of censorship in countries such as China and Singapore. In Singapore, for example, book retailers must submit potentially "hot" materials to the Committee on Undesirable Publications.

Sources: Charles P. Wallace, "Charge!" *Fortune*, September 28, 1998, pp. 189–196; **www.wto.org**; Ben Dolven, "Find the Niche," *Far Eastern Economic Review*, March 26, 1998, pp. 58–59.

- A company can produce a *country version* of its product. In Japan, Mister Donut's coffee cup is smaller and lighter to fit the hand of the average Japanese consumer; even the doughnuts are a little smaller. Kraft blends different coffees for the British (who drink their coffee with milk), the French (who drink their coffee black), and Latin Americans (who want a chicory taste).

- A company can produce a *city version* of its product—for instance, a beer to meet Munich tastes or Tokyo tastes.

- A company can produce different *retailer versions* of its product, such as one coffee brew for the Migros chain store and another for the Cooperative chain store, both in Switzerland.

Product invention consists of creating something new. It can take two forms. **Backward invention** is reintroducing earlier product forms that are well adapted to a foreign country's needs. The National Cash Register Company reintroduced its crank-operated cash register at half the price of a modern cash register and sold substantial numbers in Latin America and Africa.

Forward invention is creating a new product to meet a need in another country. There is an enormous need in less developed countries for low-cost, high-protein foods. Companies such as Quaker Oats, Swift, and Monsanto are researching these countries' nutrition needs, formulating new foods, and developing advertising campaigns to gain product trial and acceptance. Toyota produces vehicles specifically designed, with the help of local employees, to suit the tastes of these markets.[42]

Product invention is a costly strategy, but the payoffs can be great, particularly if a company can parlay a product innovation into other countries. In globalization's latest twist, North American companies are not only inventing new products for overseas markets, but also lifting products and ideas from their international operations and bringing them home.

Häagen-Dazs

Häagen-Dazs had developed a flavour for sale solely in Argentina, called "dulce de leche." Translated as "sweet of milk," it was named for the caramelized milk that is one of the most popular flavours in Argentina. Just one year later, the company rolled out dulce de leche in supermarkets from Boston to Los Angeles to Paris. The co-opted flavour soon did US$1 million a month in the United States, becoming one of the top ten flavours. It was particularly popular in Miami, where it sold twice as fast as any other flavour.[43]

In launching products and services globally, certain brand elements may have to be changed. When Clairol introduced the "Mist Stick," a curling iron, into Germany, it found that *mist* is slang for manure. Few Germans wanted to purchase a "manure stick." Brand slogans or ad taglines sometimes have to be changed too:[44]

- When Coors put its brand slogan "Turn it loose" into Spanish, it was read by some as "suffer from diarrhea."
- A laundry soap ad claiming to wash "really dirty parts" was translated in French-speaking Quebec to read "a soap for washing private parts."
- Perdue's slogan—"It takes a tough man to make a tender chicken"—was rendered into Spanish as "It takes a sexually excited man to make a chick affectionate."
- Electrolux's British ad line for its vacuum cleaners—"Nothing sucks like an Electrolux"—would certainly not lure customers in North America!

Table 21.2 lists some other famous blunders in this arena.

Communications

Companies can run the same marketing communications programs as used in the home market or change them for each local market, a process called **communication adaptation**. If it adapts both the product and the communication, the company engages in **dual adaptation**.

Consider the message. The company can use one message everywhere, varying only the language, name, and colours.[45] Exxon used "Put a tiger in your tank" with minor variations and gained international recognition. Colours can be changed to avoid taboos in some countries. Purple is associated with death in Burma and some Latin American nations; white is a mourning colour in India; and green is associated with disease in Malaysia.[46]

The second possibility is to use the same theme globally but adapt the copy to each local market. For example, a Camay soap commercial showed a beautiful woman bathing. In Venezuela, a man was seen in the bathroom; in Italy and France, only a man's hand was seen; and in Japan, the man waited outside. The positioning stays the same, but the creative execution reflects local sensibilities, as with Unilever:

TABLE 21.2	BLUNDERS IN INTERNATIONAL MARKETING

- Hallmark cards failed when they were introduced in France. The French dislike syrupy sentiment and prefer writing their own cards.
- Philips began to earn a profit in Japan only after it had reduced the size of its coffeemakers to fit into smaller Japanese kitchens and its shavers to fit smaller Japanese hands.
- Coca-Cola had to withdraw its two-litre bottle in Spain after discovering that few Spaniards owned refrigerators with large enough compartments to accommodate it.
- General Foods' Tang initially failed in France because it was positioned as a substitute for orange juice at breakfast. The French drink little orange juice and almost none at breakfast.
- Kellogg's Pop-Tarts failed in Britain because the percentage of British homes with toasters was significantly lower than in North America, and the product was too sweet for British tastes.
- Procter & Gamble's Crest toothpaste initially failed in Mexico when it used the U.S. campaign. Mexicans did not care as much for the decay-prevention benefit, nor did scientifically oriented advertising appeal to them.
- General Foods squandered millions trying to introduce packaged cake mixes to Japanese consumers. The company failed to note that only 3 percent of Japanese homes were equipped with ovens.
- S. C. Johnson's wax floor polish initially failed in Japan. The wax made the floors too slippery, and Johnson had overlooked the fact that Japanese do not wear shoes in their homes.

Unilever

Global marketing powerhouse Unilever decided to base the positioning of its detergent brands around the world on the consumer insight that parents universally saw dirty clothes and stains as a favourable sign of their children's experiences. The pitch in Europe for Omo detergent was a sentimental 60-second spot themed "Dirt Is Good" that exhorted viewers to love their dirt. In North America, a different pitch was used. The ad slogan for Wisk detergent was "Go Ahead. Get Dirty," and communications featured a sponsorship with baseball legend Cal Ripken.[47]

The third approach consists of developing a global pool of ads, from which each country selects the most appropriate one. Coca-Cola and Goodyear have used this approach. Finally, some companies allow their country managers to create country-specific ads—within guidelines, of course. Kraft uses different ads for Cheez Whiz in different countries, given that household penetration is 95 percent in Puerto Rico, where the cheese is put on everything, and 65 percent in Canada, where it is spread on morning breakfast toast. In the United States, it is considered a junk food.

The use of media also requires international adaptation because media availability varies from country to country. Norway, Belgium, France, the United States, and Canada do not allow cigarettes to be advertised on TV. Like Quebec, Austria and Italy regulate TV advertising to children. Saudi Arabia does not want advertisers to use women in ads. India taxes advertising. Magazines vary in availability and effectiveness; they play a major role in Italy and a minor one in Austria.

Marketers must also adapt sales-promotion techniques to different markets. Several European countries have laws preventing or limiting sales-promotion tools such as discounts, rebates, coupons, games of chance, and premiums. In Germany, Lands' End could not advertise its money-back guarantee, although it does accept returned merchandise. American Express could not award points based on charges to its card for redeeming merchandise. A German store could not advertise that it would contribute a small sum to the fight against AIDS for each transaction; a German law limits discounts to 3 percent of list price. However, these restrictions are under attack and are beginning to crumble.

Personal selling tactics may have to change too. The direct, no-nonsense approach favoured by North Americans (characterized by more of a "let's get down to business" stance) may not work as well in Europe, Asia, and other places where a more indirect, subtle approach can be more effective.[48] With younger, more worldly employees, however, such cultural differences may be less pronounced.

Price

Multinationals face several pricing problems when selling abroad. They must deal with price escalation, transfer prices, dumping charges, and grey markets.

When companies sell their goods abroad, they face a **price escalation** problem. A Gucci handbag may sell for half as much in Italy as in North America. Why? Gucci has to add the cost of transportation, tariffs, importer margin, wholesaler margin, and retailer margin to its factory price. Depending on these added costs, as well as the currency-fluctuation risk, the product might have to sell for two to five times as much in another country to make the same profit for the manufacturer. Because the cost escalation varies from country to country, the question is how to set the prices in different countries. Companies have three choices:

■ *Set a uniform price everywhere.* Coca-Cola might want to charge 75 cents for Coke everywhere in the world, but then Coca-Cola would earn quite different profit rates in different countries. Also, this strategy would result in the price being too high in poor countries and not high enough in rich countries.

A Lands' End ad for Germany. Because Germany has a number of laws preventing or limiting the use of sales-promotion tools, Lands' End cannot advertise its money-back guarantee, though it can accept merchandise returns.

LANDS'END
DIRECT MERCHANTS

Ihre Vorteile im Überblick:
- Wetterfestes Rauleder
- Komfor table Elastik-Einsätze
- Atmungsaktives Futter
- Leichte Zwischensohle
- Trittsicher profilierte Laufsohle

Für nur €39 halten Sie jedem Wetter Schritt

Gratis-Katalog ☎ 0800-9090800

www.landsend.de

- *Set a market-based price in each country.* Here Coca-Cola would charge what each country could afford, but this strategy ignores differences in the actual cost from country to country. Also, it could lead to a situation in which intermediaries in low-price countries reship their Coca-Cola to high-price countries.

- *Set a cost-based price in each country.* Here Coca-Cola would use a standard markup of its costs everywhere, but this strategy might price Coca-Cola out of the market in countries where its costs are high.

Another problem arises when a company sets a **transfer price** (the price it charges another unit in the company) for goods that it ships to its foreign subsidiaries. If the company charges too high a price to a subsidiary, it may end up paying higher tariff duties, although it may pay lower income taxes in the foreign country. If the company charges too low a price to its subsidiary, it can be charged with dumping. **Dumping** occurs when a company charges either less than its costs or less than it charges in its home market, in order to enter or win a market. In 2000, Stelco, a Canadian steel-maker, successfully fought dumping of steel products by steel-makers in Brazil, Finland, India, Indonesia, Thailand, and Ukraine. A Canadian tribunal found that cut-price steel imports from these countries caused "material injury to Canadian producers, including Stelco."[49] Various governments are watching for abuses and often force companies to charge the **arm's-length price**—that is, the price charged by other competitors for the same or a similar product.

Many multinationals are plagued by the grey-market problem. The **grey market** consists of branded products diverted from normal or authorized distributions channels in the country of product origin or across international borders. Dealers in the low-price country find ways to sell some of their products in higher-price countries, thus earning more. Industry research suggests that worldwide grey market activity accounts for over US$40 billion in revenue each year. In 2004, 3Com successfully sued several companies in Canada for a total of US$10 million after these companies provided written and oral misrepresentations to get deep discounts on 3Com networking equipment. The equipment, worth millions of dollars, was to be sold to a U.S. education software company and sent to China and Australia, but instead ended up back in the United States.[50]

Very often a company finds some enterprising distributors buying more than they can sell in their own country and reshipping the goods to another country to take advantage of price differences. Multinationals try to prevent grey markets by policing the distributors, by raising their prices to lower-cost distributors, or by altering the product characteristics or service warranties for different countries. In the European Union, the grey market may disappear altogether with the transition to the Euro. Once consumers recognize price differentiation by country, companies will be forced to harmonize prices throughout the countries that have adopted the single currency. Companies and marketers that offer the most innovative, specialized, or necessary products or services will be least affected by price transparency.[51]

The Internet also reduces price differentiation between countries. When companies sell their wares over the Internet, price becomes transparent: Customers can easily find out how much products sell for in different countries. Take an online training course, for instance. Whereas the price of a classroom-delivered day of training can vary significantly from Canada to France to Thailand, the price of an online-delivered day of training would have to be similar.[52]

Another global pricing challenge that has arisen in recent years occurs when countries with overcapacity, cheap currencies, and the need to export aggressively have pushed prices down and devalued their currencies. For multinational firms this poses challenges: Sluggish demand and reluctance to pay higher prices make selling in these emerging markets difficult. Instead of lowering prices and taking a loss, some multinationals have found more lucrative and creative means of coping.[53]

General Electric Company

Rather than striving for larger market share, GE's power systems unit focused on winning a larger percentage of each customer's expenditures. The unit asked its top 100 customers what services were most critical to them and how GE could provide or improve them. The answers prompted the company to cut its response time for replacing old or damaged parts from 12 weeks to 6. It began advising customers on the nuances of doing business in the diverse environments of Europe and Asia and providing the maintenance staff for occasional equipment upgrades. By adding value and helping customers reduce their costs and become more efficient, GE was able to avoid a move to commodity pricing and was actually able to generate bigger margins. These margins led to record revenues of US$15 billion in 2000, a 50 percent rise from the previous year.[54]

FIGURE 21.4

Whole-Channel Concept for International Marketing

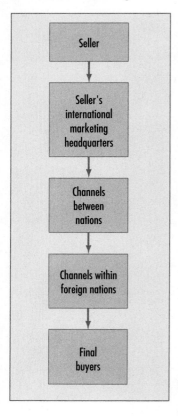

Distribution Channels

Too many manufacturers think their job is done once the product leaves the factory. They should pay attention to how the product moves within the foreign country. They should take a whole-channel view of the problem of distributing products to final users. Figure 21.4 shows the three major links between seller and ultimate buyer. In the first link, *seller's international marketing headquarters*, the export department or international division makes decisions on channels and other marketing-mix elements. The second link, *channels between nations*, gets the products to the borders of the foreign nation. The decisions made in this link include the types of intermediaries (agents, trading companies) that will be used, the type of transportation (air, sea), and the financing and risk arrangements. The third link, *channels within foreign nations*, gets the products from their entry point to final buyers and users.

Distribution channels within countries vary considerably. To sell soap in Japan, Procter & Gamble has to work through one of the most complicated distribution systems in the world. It must sell to a general wholesaler, who sells to a product wholesaler, who sells to a product-specialty wholesaler, who sells to a regional wholesaler, who sells to a local wholesaler, who finally sells to retailers. All these distribution levels can mean that the consumer's price ends up double or triple the importer's price. If P&G takes the soap to tropical Africa, the company might sell to an import wholesaler, who sells to several jobbers, who sell to petty traders (mostly women) working in local markets.

Another difference lies in the size and character of retail units abroad. Large-scale retail chains dominate the North American scene, but much foreign retailing is in the hands of small, independent retailers. In India, millions of retailers operate tiny shops or sell in open markets. Their markups are high, but the real price is brought down through haggling. Incomes are low, and people must shop daily for small amounts; they are limited to whatever quantity can be carried home on foot or on a bicycle. Most homes lack storage space and refrigeration. Packaging costs are kept low in order to keep prices low. In India, cigarettes are often bought singly. Breaking bulk remains an important function of intermediaries and helps perpetuate the long channels of distribution, which are a major obstacle to the expansion of large-scale retailing in developing countries.

When multinationals first enter a country, they prefer to work with local distributors who have good local knowledge, but friction often arises later.[55] The multinational complains that the local distributor does not invest in business growth, does not follow company policy, or does not share enough information. The local distributor complains of insufficient corporate support, impossible goals, and confusing policies. The multinational must choose the right distributors, invest in them, and set up performance goals to which they can agree.[56]

Some companies choose to invest in infrastructure to ensure they benefit from the right channels. Peruvian cola company Kola Real has been able to survive despite competing with Coca-Cola and Pepsi-Cola in Mexico by setting up its own distribution network of 600 leased lorries, 24 distribution centres, and 800 salespeople.[57]

Many retailers are trying to make inroads into global markets. France's Carrefour, Germany's Metro, and the United Kingdom's Tesco have all established global positions. Germany's Aldi follows a simple formula globally. It stocks only about 700 products (compared with more than 20 000 at a traditional grocer such as Royal Ahold's Albert Heijin), almost all on its own exclusive label. Because it sells so few products, Aldi can exert strong control over quality and price and can simplify shipping and handling, leading to large margins. Retail experts expect Aldi to have 1000 stores in the United States by 2010, with as much as 2 percent of the U.S. grocery market. American retail giant Wal-Mart is also expanding overseas, although sometimes to mixed results.[58]

Wal-Mart

Wal-Mart has more than 1000 stores in Mexico, Canada, Germany, Argentina, China, Britain, South Korea, Brazil, and Puerto Rico. By 2003, Wal-Mart received 20 percent of its revenue from overseas, up from 12 percent in 2000. The company has learned along the way. While its Canadian launch was a major success, German operations encountered a number of obstacles. When Wal-Mart opened its stores in Latin America, sales were disappointing. Wal-Mart designed its Latin American stores like those in the United States: narrow aisles crowded with merchandise, huge parking lots, many products with red, white, and blue banners, and so on. However, Latin American shoppers expect wider aisles since they come with larger families; many do not have a car and need door-to-door bus transportation, and the red, white, and blue banners seem like Yankee imperialism.[59]

Country-of-Origin Effects

In an increasingly connected, highly competitive global marketplace, government officials and marketers are concerned with how attitudes and beliefs about their country affect consumer and business decision making. *Country-of-origin perceptions* are the mental associations and beliefs triggered by a country. Government officials want to strengthen their country's image to help domestic marketers who export and to attract foreign firms and investors. Marketers want to use country-of-origin perceptions in the most advantageous way possible to sell their products and services.

Building Country Images

Governments now recognize that the image of their cities and countries affects more than tourism and has important value in commerce. Attracting foreign business can improve the local economy, providing jobs and improving infrastructure. City officials in Kobe, Japan, were able to entice multinationals Procter & Gamble, Nestlé, and Eli Lilly to locate their Japanese headquarters in the city through traditional marketing techniques, with careful targeting and positioning.[60] Hong Kong officials also developed a symbol—a stylized dragon—to represent their city's core brand values.[61]

Countries all over the world are being marketed like any other brand. In some cases, negative perceptions must be overcome. Research by the British Council in 2000 revealed that young opinion leaders in 28 countries saw Britons as weak on creativity and innovation, class-ridden, racist, and cold.[62] Relying partly on the global success of Nokia, Finland launched a campaign to enhance its image as a centre of high-tech innovation.[63] A number of initiatives have been undertaken to improve Canada's image both as prime place for direct investment and as a source of high-quality products.[64]

Branding Canada

In 2001, Investment Partnerships Canada (IPC) commissioned a qualitative research study of American executives' perceptions of Canada as a prime place for investment. Attracting investment is important since one out of every ten jobs in Canada depends directly on foreign investment. The IPC needed a knowledge base to guide Canada's future marketing and branding efforts. The research led to some valuable insights. While Canada was well regarded and reasonably well known by 74 percent of the respondents, it was not high on the radar screens of almost half of the sample (49 percent) as an investment destination. The results suggest a three-part brand proposition that Canada can claim:

- *A thriving marketplace*—Investors can find all the infrastructure and support required to succeed and be profitable.
- *A talented labour pool*—Canada has an abundance of qualified people with the skills to help a company achieve its objectives.
- *An environment almost like home*—Canada's business environment and culture are similar to those of the United States, while it poses lower risks and offers higher returns than other investment options.

In 2004, *Brand Canada* was unveiled at the International Boston Seafood Show as the new logo for Canadian aquaculture. Bob Speller, the minister of agriculture, noted, "Exports drive Canada's economy, so it is important that our high-quality products be easily identifiable anywhere in the world. The new *Brand Canada* trade logo appearing on packaging will help promote the overall excellence of Canadian fish and seafood products in the minds of international consumers and commercial buyers." The initiative is part of a long-term strategy designed to differentiate Canada's aquaculture products from those of competitor countries by assuring buyers that Canadian aquaculture products are safe and environmentally sustainable.

Consumer Perceptions of Country-of-Origin

Global marketers know that buyers hold distinct attitudes and beliefs about brands or products from different countries.[65] These country-of-origin perceptions can affect consumer decision making directly and indirectly. The perceptions may be included as an attribute in decision making or influence other attributes it the process ("If it's French, it must be stylish"). The mere fact that a brand is perceived as being successful on a global stage may lend credibility and respect.[66] Several studies have found the following:[67]

Hong Kong's trademark, a stylized dragon with the tagline "Asia's world city."

- People are often ethnocentric and favourably predisposed to their own country's products, unless they come from a less developed country.

- The more favourable a country's image, the more prominently the "Made in . . ." label should be displayed.

- The impact of country of origin varies with the type of product. Consumers want to know where a car was made but not the lubricating oil.

- Certain countries enjoy a reputation for certain goods: Japan for automobiles and consumer electronics; the United States for high-tech innovations, soft drinks, toys, cigarettes, and jeans; France for wine, perfume, and luxury goods.

- Sometimes country-of-origin perception can encompass an entire country's products. In one study, Chinese consumers in Hong Kong perceived American products as prestigious, Japanese products as innovative, and Chinese products as cheap.

The favourability of country-of-origin perceptions must be considered both from a domestic and foreign perspective. In the domestic market, country-of-origin perceptions may stir consumers' patriotic notions or remind them of their past. As international trade grows, consumers may view certain brands as symbolically important in their own cultural heritage and identity. Patriotic appeals have been the basis of marketing strategies all over the world. Patriotic appeals, however, can lack uniqueness and even be overused. For example, Molson recently dropped its famous "I AM Canadian" campaign because it was no longer driving sales.

A company has several options when its products are competitively priced but their place of origin turns consumers off. The company can consider co-production with a foreign company that has a better name: South Korea could make a fine leather jacket that it sends to Italy for finishing; or the company can adopt a strategy to achieve world-class quality in the local industry, as is the case with Belgian chocolates, Polish ham, and Colombian coffee.

As progress is made, companies can start to build local roots to increase relevance, as exemplified by Toyota, which has made sales in North America a top priority. BMW has been following a similar strategy.[68]

Deciding on the Marketing Organization

Companies manage their international marketing activities in three ways: through export departments, international divisions, or a global organization.

Export Department

A firm normally gets into international marketing by simply shipping out its goods. If its international sales expand, the company organizes an export department consisting of a sales manager and a few assistants. As sales increase, the export department is expanded to include various marketing services so that the company can go after business more aggressively. If the firm moves into joint ventures or direct investment, the export department will no longer be adequate to manage international operations.

International Division

Many companies become involved in several international markets and ventures. Sooner or later they will create international divisions to handle all their international activity. The international division is headed by a division president, who sets goals and budgets and is responsible for the company's international growth.

The international division's corporate staff consists of functional specialists who provide services to various operating units. Operating units can be organized in several ways. First, they can be *geographical organizations*. Reporting to the international-division president might be regional vice-presidents for North America, Latin America, Europe, Africa, the Middle East, and the Far East. Reporting to the regional vice-presidents are country managers who are responsible for a sales force, sales branches, distributors, and licensees in the respective countries. The operating units may be *world product groups,* each with an international vice-president responsible for worldwide sales of each product group. The vice-presidents may draw on corporate-staff area specialists for expertise on different geographical areas. Finally, operating units may be *international subsidiaries*, each headed by a president. The various subsidiary presidents report to the president of the international division.

Many multinationals shift between types of organization.

IBM

Part of IBM's massive reorganization strategy has been to put 235 000 employees into 14 customer-focused groups such as oil and gas, entertainment, and financial services. This way a big customer will be able to cut one deal with a central sales office to have IBM computers installed worldwide. Under the old system, a corporate customer with operations in 20 countries had to contract with 20 little Big Blues, each with its own pricing structure and service standards.[69]

Global Organization

Several firms have become truly global organizations. Their top corporate management and staff plan worldwide manufacturing facilities, marketing policies, financial flows, and logistical systems. The global operating units report directly to the chief executive or executive committee, not to the head of an international division. Executives are trained in worldwide operations. Management is recruited from many countries; components and supplies are purchased where they can be obtained at the least cost; and investments are made where the anticipated returns are greatest.

These companies face several organizational complexities. For example, when pricing a company's mainframe computers to a large banking system in Germany, how much influence should the headquarters' product manager have? And the company's market manager for the banking sector? And the company's German country manager?

Bartlett and Ghoshal have proposed circumstances under which different approaches work best. In *Managing Across Borders*, they describe forces that favour "global integration" (capital-intensive production, homogeneous demand) versus "national responsiveness" (local standards and barriers, strong local preferences). They distinguish three organizational strategies:[70]

1. *A global strategy treats the world as a single market.* This strategy is warranted when the forces for global integration are strong and the forces for national responsiveness are weak. This is true of the consumer electronics market, for example, where most buyers will accept a fairly standardized pocket radio, CD player, or TV. Matsushita has performed better than GE and Philips in the consumer electronics market because Matsushita operates in a more globally coordinated and standardized way.

2. *A multinational strategy treats the world as a portfolio of national opportunities.* This strategy is warranted when the forces favouring national responsiveness are strong and the forces favouring global integration are weak. This is the situation in the branded packaged-goods business (food products, cleaning products). Bartlett and Ghoshal cite Unilever as a better performer than Kao and P&G because Unilever grants more decision-making autonomy to its local branches.

3. *A "glocal" strategy standardizes certain core elements and localizes other elements.* This strategy makes sense for an industry (such as telecommunications) where each nation requires some adaptation of its equipment, but the providing company can also standardize some of the core components. Bartlett and Ghoshal cite Ericsson as balancing these considerations better than NEC (too globally oriented) and ITT (too locally oriented).

Many firms seek a blend of centralized global control from corporate headquarters with input from local and regional marketers. Finding that balance can be tricky. Coca-Cola's "think local, act local" philosophy, which decentralized much of the power and responsibility to design marketing programs and activities, fell apart when many local managers lacked the necessary skills or discipline. Decidedly un-Coke-like ads appeared—such as skinny-dippers streaking down a beach in Italy—and sales stalled. The pendulum swung back, and Coke executives in Atlanta began to play a stronger strategic role again.[71]

SUMMARY

1. Despite the many challenges in the international arena (shifting borders, unstable governments, foreign-exchange problems, corruption, and technological pirating), companies selling in global industries need to internationalize their operations. Companies cannot simply stay domestic and expect to maintain their markets.

2. In deciding to go abroad, a company needs to define its international marketing objectives and policies. The company must determine whether to market in a few countries or many countries. It must decide which countries to consider. In general, the candidate countries should be rated on three criteria: market attractiveness, risk, and competitive advantage. Developing countries offer a unique set of opportunities and risks.

3. Once a company decides on a particular country, it must determine the best mode of entry. Its broad choices are indirect exporting, direct exporting, licensing, joint ventures, and direct investment. Each succeeding strategy involves more commitment, risk, control, and profit potential.

4. In deciding on the marketing program, a company must decide how much to adapt its marketing program—product, communications, distribution, and price—to local conditions. At the product level, firms can pursue a strategy of straight extension, product adaptation, or product invention. At the communication level, firms may choose communication adaptation or dual adaptation. At the price level, firms may encounter price escalation and grey markets. At the distribution level, firms need to take a whole-channel view of the challenge of distributing products to the final users. In creating all elements of the marketing program, firms must be aware of the cultural, social, political, technological, environmental, and legal limitations they face in other countries.

5. Country-of-origin perceptions can affect consumers and businesses alike. Managing those perceptions in the most advantageous way possible is an important marketing priority.

6. Depending on the level of international involvement, companies manage their international marketing activity in three ways: through export departments, international divisions, or a global organization.

APPLICATIONS

Marketing Debate: Is the World Coming Closer Together?

Many social commentators maintain that youth and teens are becoming more and more alike across countries as time goes on. Others, while not disputing that fact, point out that the differences between cultures at even younger ages by far exceed the similarities.

Take a position: People are becoming more and more similar versus The differences between people of different cultures far outweigh their similarities.

Marketing Discussion

Think of some of your favourite brands. Do you know where they come from? Where and how they are made or provided? Do you think it would affect your perceptions of quality or satisfaction?

Marketing Spotlight: Starbucks

Starbucks opened in 1971, at a time when coffee consumption in North America had been declining for a decade. The decline stemmed from rivalry among the major coffee brands, which were competing on price. As a result, they were using cheaper coffee beans to reduce costs, compromising the quality of the coffee. Starbucks' founders decided to experiment with a new concept: a store that would sell only the finest imported coffee beans and coffee brewing equipment. The original store did not sell coffee by the cup, only beans. You could get a good cup of coffee, but you had to make it yourself at home.

Howard Schultz came to Starbucks in 1982 and saw a new possibility for the company. While in Milan on business, Schultz walked into an Italian coffee bar and had an epiphany with his espresso. "There was nothing like this in America. It was an extension of people's front porch. It was an emotional experience," he said. He knew right away that he wanted to bring this concept to the United States. Schultz set about creating an environment for Starbucks coffeehouses that would reflect Italian elegance melded with American informality. Schultz envisioned that Starbucks would become a "personal treat" for its customers, a "Third Place"—a comfortable, sociable gathering spot bridging the workplace and the home.

Starbucks' geographical expansion throughout the United States was carefully planned. The management team agreed that all stores would be owned and operated by the company rather than as a franchise. In building a strong brand, Schultz knew that he and his executive team needed complete control to cultivate an unparalleled image of quality. In too many other companies, franchisees did business their own way. Franchisees could potentially sacrifice Starbucks' commitment to excellence in order to turn higher profits. Starbucks did not want to allow the corner-cutting that had caused the original decline in Americans' consumption of coffee.

Starbucks employed a "hub" expansion strategy, in which coffeehouses entered a new market in a clustered group. For each region, a large city served as the hub. Teams of trained professionals supported the new cluster of stores. In the large hub market, the company rapidly opened 20 or more stores within the first two years. From the established hub, Starbucks stores then spread to new "spoke" markets: smaller satellite cities and nearby suburban locations.

The joke about two Starbucks across the street from each other reflects Starbucks' strategy. The deliberate saturation often cannibalizes 30 percent of one store's sales by introducing a store nearby. But this drop in revenue is offset by efficiencies in marketing and distribution costs, and the enhanced image of convenience. A typical customer stops by Starbucks 18 times a month. No American retailer has a higher frequency of customer visits.

Starbucks expanded into Canada (opening a store in Vancouver) in 1987 and into Tokyo in 1996. Although detractors said that fastidious tea-drinking Japanese would never buy coffee in paper cups, Starbucks proved them wrong. Locations in Japan have two-and-a-half times the annual sales of those in the United States. There are now over 500 Starbucks locations in Japan, and the country is the company's most profitable region anywhere.

When expanding globally, Starbucks also used acquisitions. In 1998, it gained a foothold in the British coffee market by buying the London-based Seattle Coffee Company. In 2001, it made its first foray onto the European continent, opening locations in Switzerland and Austria and then Spain, Germany, and Greece. Interestingly, Starbucks is bucking the typical European coffeehouse trend by making its coffeehouses nonsmoking. About 40 percent of Europeans smoke. Critics said Starbucks would lose half of its market by prohibiting smoking at its coffeehouses, but Starbucks was unfazed. The first store in Vienna had 100 000 guests in the first two months. The controversial nonsmoking policy received a positive response because Starbucks couched it in terms of the coffee, not health. Signs in stores say "Aroma protection through smoke-free space" and then thank customers for not smoking.

Howard Schultz stepped down as CEO in 2000, but he remains chairman and "Chief Global Strategist." Starbucks currently has over 7400 stores, 1460 of which are outside the United States in over 30 countries. Schultz eventually sees having 25 000 stores worldwide. He wants to see a Starbucks in every country in the world. But there's one country that especially has his eye: Italy, where the whole Starbucks concept began.

DISCUSSION QUESTIONS

1. What have been the key success factors for Starbucks?

2. Where is Starbucks vulnerable? What should it watch out for?

3. What recommendations would you make to its senior marketing executives going forward? What should the company be sure to do with its marketing?

Sources: Andy Serwer, "Hot Starbucks to Go," *Fortune*, January 26, 2004, pp. 61–74; Cora Daniels, "Mr. Coffee: The Man Behind the $4.75 Frappuccino Makes the 500," *Fortune*, April 14, 2003, p. 139; Steven Erlanger, "An American Coffeehouse (or 4) in Vienna," *New York Times*, June 1, 2002, p. A1.

22

IN THIS CHAPTER, WE WILL ADDRESS THE FOLLOWING QUESTIONS:

- What are important trends in marketing practices?

- What are the keys to effective internal marketing?

- How can companies be responsible social marketers?

- How can a company improve its marketing implementation skills?

- What tools are available to help companies monitor and improve their marketing activities?

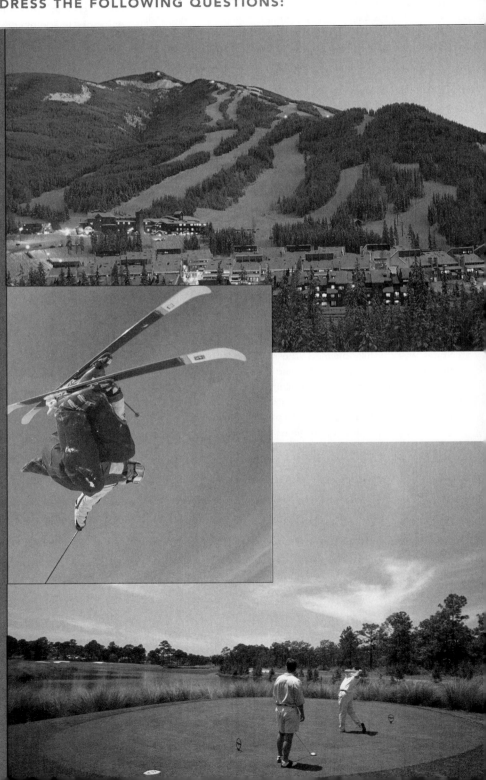

CHAPTER 22

Managing a Holistic Marketing Organization

PROFILE: CANADIAN MARKETING EXCELLENCE

Some companies don't sell products; they market experiences. In fact, this idea is at the heart of Vancouver-headquartered Intrawest's mission, which it defines as one of delivering "memorable, unique, ultimately body-and-soul satisfying experiences . . . again and again." Intrawest is a world leader in destination resorts and adventure travel. Its network of premier resorts ranges from the tops of towering mountains to championship golf courses and pristine beaches. Its resorts have captured the hearts of a loyal and growing customer base. With over 8 million annual skier visits on ten mountains, thousands of golfers on 36 championship golf courses, and thousands more visiting lakeside and ocean beaches, Intrawest is positioned among the leaders in the leisure industry. Its recent acquisition of Abercrombie & Kent (the world's leading luxury adventure-travel company operating in over 100 countries throughout the world) and Alpine Helicopters Ltd. (the parent company of Canadian Mountain Holidays) now allows Intrawest to offer adventure travel around the globe. Intrawest also has land on which to build 19 811 more units to create the most vibrant resort villages in the world.

Intrawest was founded in 1976 by Joe Houssian, the company's chairman, president, and CEO. He began the firm as a residential and urban real estate company. However, in the mid-1980s, he met Hugh Smythe, then president of Blackcomb. The two joined forces, marrying resort operations with real estate expertise. Today, Intrawest owns or is involved in 14 mountain resorts in North America and Europe, including Whistler and Panorama in British Columbia, Tremblant in Quebec, Copper in Colorado, and Mammoth in California. It also owns two warm-weather resorts in the United States.

All of Intrawest's actions are guided by its mission combined with a set of ethical principles and standards of conduct. Intrawest's standards of conduct include compliance with the law and acting with integrity, avoiding conflicts of interest, protecting the privacy of the personal data of its clients, and respecting the communities in which it operates. It notes, however, that "no standards of business conduct can replace the thoughtful behaviour of an ethical employee."

Much of Intrawest's success is due to its ability to attract great employees, and then motivate them through its strong internal marketing program. Its 24 800 employees have a passion for service excellence, ensuring that Intrawest resorts are the most animated and exciting playgrounds in the world. Gary Raymond is one of these employees. Raymond is CEO of Intrawest's resort development group, and you can often find him chatting about the intricacies of resort design—or "placemaking," as the title on his business card proclaims. For example, in designing Sandestin, Intrawest's gated golf and beach resort in Florida, Intrawest created a full storyline and history for every building. Through the power of Intrawest's imagination, Sandestin has been transformed from what had recently been undeveloped land into a historic fishing village.

While some decry the artificiality and fabricated nature of the resorts, others believe that Intrawest has now set a global standard that few others can match. There is no doubt that the resorts draw extremely loyal customers back year after year. While unseasonable weather in the winter of 2005 dampened the firm's profitability, it was largely insulated from disaster just by the fact that it has so many resorts. When the peaks are bare in one area, there is sure to be snow in another. Furthermore, Intrawest has developed its resorts so that they are busy during at least two seasons of the year.

Intrawest's development process begins with "envisioning." The team includes not only Intrawest employees, but also community members and outside experts. Such a team transformed the worn and dated Tremblant ski area in Quebec. The old lodges were shabby and out of date. Even their locations were unworkable. Again a story was developed in which the buildings formed the core of a nineteenth-century Quebec village. New foundations were poured, and the old structures were moved into place, forming a rambling streetscape more typical of a European village. Over the years, Intrawest has learned that such streets are a key to success. An Intrawest street always separates people from traffic and is never straight. "Otherwise, people will see what's coming up and won't need to walk there." The pedestrian walkways encourage milling and interaction. Every aspect of the village is designed to appeal to one of the five senses. There is no question that the scent of fresh baked bread wafting through the air is there by deliberate design.

Intrawest believes its true competitive advantage, however, doesn't reside in its choice properties, but rather in the intellectual capital it has accumulated—its ability to invent new places that people want to visit and buy into. The ability to design this type of resort rests on its deep understanding of its customers—largely affluent boomers. The depth of Intrawest's customer knowledge is astounding. For example, the average Intrawest customer didn't merely go to university—he or she went away to university. The firm can pinpoint the few neighbourhoods within the dozen or so large North American cities where its customers are likely to live. Furthermore, they are part of the "time-starved" generation that has built considerable affluence but often has little time to enjoy it. Thus, Intrawest's strategy is to fulfill their every leisure-time desire and make their scarce vacation decisions easy—stay within the Intrawest family.

However, just knowing the average consumer isn't enough. Intrawest's research led to the identification of six distinct segments defined around common needs, attitudes, and behaviours. For example, its "valuable detached experts" are regular skiers, who may own a home at an Intrawest. They make up 14 percent of the customer base and respond best to clear and direct communications with strong value positioning. The "family value vacationers," who make up 17 percent of their customers, are people who comparison-shop and look for bargains. They respond to images of social experiences and offers of ski, spa, and restaurant packages.

Using a page out of books written by Club Med and Disney, Intrawest uses permission-based marketing and its precise segmentation to cross-sell to its loyal clientele, turning winter skiers into summer golfers, mountain bikers, and concert-goers. "We've got a number of different resorts across North America and the idea is to try and leverage them and introduce our customers to some of the other opportunities that are out there," says Linda Denis, vice-president of customer relationship marketing.

There's no doubt that careful targeting of marketing messages to its distinct segments is a powerful revenue-generating tool. Recently, Intrawest sent a direct mail offer to some of its lapsed "savvy passionate experts." Losing these people could have had big implications because the group represented big spenders who ski at any time of the year or in any conditions and are willing to trade up to season passes, heli-skiing, or advanced lessons. The direct mail campaign used "steep and deep" imagery and copy that read "awesome terrain and four high alpine bowls open for business." It was a huge success, leading to a 78 percent increase in purchases and an 81 percent jump in revenues.

Creating a total customer experience requires total control by management. The company runs everything from the lifts to the development plan for the real estate, the reservations systems, the commercial space, and many of the stores and visitor services. This need for control has its downside. As one Whistler resident noted, there is a love/hate relationship between the town and the company. He likened this relationship to one where the serfs depend on the landlord for their livelihood. Even though the landlord has been responsible for their success, they resent him nonetheless. To minimize such criticisms, Intrawest limits its retail involvement to soft goods and ski gear and services. By attracting an increasing number of visitors to its resorts, Intrawest creates opportunities for all area businesses.

Intrawest's strategic edge lies in its ability to integrate three sectors of the leisure industry: resort operations (skiing, golfing, hiking, mountain biking, retail, food and beverage), resort real estate development, and its vacation club (or timeshare) business. Controlling all aspects of the business also allows the company to achieve certain economies of scale.

Intrawest isn't shy about its formula for success, which it publishes right on its Web page (see www.intrawest.com/about/overview/successformula.asp). Like many businesses that focus on customer relationship management, it knows that retaining a customer and cross-selling to that person over a lifetime of interactions creates a win–win situation for both the firm and the client. As the Web site notes, "Each gear of Intrawest's revenue clock produces increased guest visits, increased revenue per visit and higher real estate values at every turn." See how the company spells out the formula:

1. We start with a resort and enhance the experience.
2. Then build an animated village so people stay longer.
3. All this attracts more visitors who come more often, spend more money, and bring their friends.
4. More real estate is built and attractions are added, drawing yet more people.
5. More people, more often, leads to the expansion of year-round facilities, maximizing use of shops, hotels, convention facilities, and restaurants.
6. As occupancy and room rates climb, so does demand for resort real estate, creating a surge in real estate sales.
7. All this results in a total resort experience which brings year-round destination visitors, generating financial critical mass, which . . .
8. Leads to more resorts. Network synergy results in a compounding effect on the company's revenue streams and growth through time.

As you can see, Intrawest is a company that fully understands how to manage the total marketing effort!

Sources: Intrawest Web site, **www.intrawest.com/index.asp**; Jim Sutherland, "It Takes a Village," *Globe and Mail Report on Business*, March 24, 2005, pp. 26–34; Eve Lazarus, "Intrawest Digs Deep," *Marketing Magazine*, **www.marketingmag.ca/magazine/current/in_context/article.jsp;jsessionid=KBHCGBJONCLM?content= 20040531_61684_61684**, May 31, 2004; Ann Gibbon, "Big Seen as Best for Ski Resorts," *Globe and Mail*, September 17, 1996, pp. B1, B4; Patti Summerfield, "Special Report: Top Database Marketers," *Strategy Magazine*, July 21, 1997, p. DR12.

Healthy long-term growth for a brand requires that the marketing organization be managed properly. Holistic marketers, like Intrawest, must embrace the complexity of marketing. They must engage in a host of carefully planned, interconnected marketing activities.[1] Successful holistic marketing requires effective relationship marketing, integrated marketing, internal marketing, and social marketing. Previous chapters addressed the first two topics and the strategy and tactics of marketing.[2] In this chapter, we consider internal and social marketing and how marketing should be administered and conducted responsibly. In our discussion, we look at how firms organize, implement, evaluate, and control marketing activities. We also discuss the increased importance of social responsibility. We begin by examining changes in how companies conduct marketing today.

Trends in Marketing Practices

Chapters 1 and 3 describe some important changes in the marketing macroenvironment, such as globalization, deregulation, technological advances, customer empowerment, and market fragmentation. In response to this rapidly changing environment, companies have restructured their business and marketing practices in some of the following ways:

- *Re-engineering*. Appointing teams to manage customer-value-building processes and break down walls between departments.
- *Outsourcing*. Greater willingness to buy more goods and services from outside domestic or foreign vendors.
- *Benchmarking*. Studying "best practice companies" to improve performance.
- *Supplier partnering*. Increased partnering with fewer but better value-adding suppliers.
- *Customer partnering*. Working more closely with customers to add value to their operations.
- *Merging*. Acquiring or merging with firms in the same or complementary industries to gain economies of scale and scope.
- *Globalizing*. Increased effort to "think global" and "act local."
- *Flattening*. Reducing the number of organizational levels to get closer to the customer.
- *Focusing*. Determining the most profitable businesses and customers and focusing on them.
- *Accelerating*. Designing the organization and setting up processes to respond more quickly to changes in the environment.
- *Empowering*. Encouraging and empowering personnel to produce more ideas and take more initiative.

The role of marketing in the organization is also changing.[3] Traditionally, marketers have played the roles of intermediaries, charged with understanding customer needs and transmitting the voice of the customer to various functional areas in the organization. In a networked enterprise, every functional area can interact directly with customers. Marketing no longer has sole ownership of customer interactions; rather, marketing needs to integrate all the customer-facing processes so that customers see a single face and hear a single voice when they interact with the firm.

Internal Marketing

Internal marketing requires that everyone in the organization buy into the concepts and goals of marketing and engage in choosing, providing, and communicating customer value. Over the years, marketing has evolved as it has grown from work done by the sales department into a complex group of activities spread through the organization.[4] Because simple sales departments were unable to conduct important functions such as marketing research, new product development, advertising, sales promotion, and customer service, firms began to create marketing departments. When conflict arose between marketing and sales departments, many firms merged the two.

A company can have an excellent marketing department, however, and yet fail at marketing. Much depends on how other company departments view customers. If they point to the marketing department and say, "They do the marketing," the company has not implemented effective marketing. Only when all employees realize that their jobs are to create, serve, and satisfy customers does the company become an effective marketer.[5] "Marketing Memo: Characteristics of Company Departments That Are Truly Customer-Driven" presents a measurement tool that can be used to evaluate which company departments have fully embraced the importance of being customer-driven.[6]

Many companies are now focusing on key processes rather than departments because departmental organization is viewed as a barrier to the smooth performance of fundamental business processes. To achieve customer-related outcomes, companies appoint process leaders who manage cross-disciplinary teams. Marketing and sales people spend an increasing percentage of their time as process team members. As a result, marketing personnel may have a solid-line responsibility to their teams and a dotted-line responsibility to the marketing department. The marketing department is also responsible for training marketing personnel, assigning them to new teams, and evaluating their overall performance.

Let's look at how marketing departments are being organized, how they can work effectively with other departments, and how firms can foster a creative marketing culture within the entire organization.

Organizing the Marketing Department

Modern marketing departments may be organized in a number of different, sometimes overlapping ways:[7] functionally, geographically, by product or brand, by market, in a matrix, and by corporate division.

FUNCTIONAL ORGANIZATION   The most common form of marketing organization consists of functional specialists reporting to a marketing vice-president, who coordinates their activities. Figure 22.1 shows five specialists. Additional specialists might include a customer service manager, a marketing planning manager, a market logistics manager, a direct marketing manager, and an Internet marketing manager.

The main advantage of a functional marketing organization is its administrative simplicity. However, it can be quite a challenge to develop smooth working relations within the marketing department.[8] This form also can lose its effectiveness as products and markets increase. A functional organization often leads to inadequate planning for specific products and markets. Products that are not favoured by anyone are neglected. Then, each functional group competes with others for budget and status. The marketing vice-president constantly has to weigh the claims of competing functional specialists and faces a difficult coordination problem.

GEOGRAPHIC ORGANIZATION   A company selling in a national market often organizes its sales force (and sometimes other functions, including marketing) along geographic lines. The national sales manager may supervise four regional sales managers, who each supervise six zone managers, who in turn supervise eight district sales managers, who supervise ten salespeople.

Several companies are now adding *area market specialists* (regional or local marketing managers) to support the sales efforts in high-volume markets. One such market might be Toronto, where 10.2 percent of the population are of South Asian descent.[9] The specialist would know the distinct

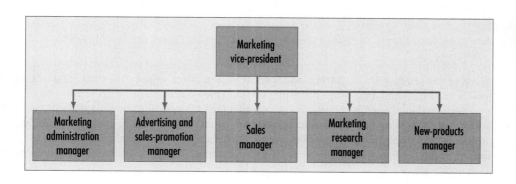

FIGURE 22.1

Functional Organization

Marketing Memo

Characteristics of Company Departments That Are Truly Customer-Driven

R&D	____ They spend time meeting customers and listening to their problems.
	____ They welcome the involvement of marketing, manufacturing, and other departments on each new project.
	____ They benchmark competitors' products and seek "best of class" solutions.
	____ They solicit customer reactions and suggestions as the project progresses.
	____ They continuously improve and refine the product on the basis of market feedback.
Purchasing	____ They proactively search for the best suppliers rather than choose only from those who solicit their business.
	____ They build long-term relations with fewer but more reliable high-quality suppliers.
	____ They do not compromise quality for price savings.
Manufacturing	____ They invite customers to visit and tour their plants.
	____ They visit customer factories to see how customers use the company's products.
	____ They willingly work overtime when it is important to meet promised delivery schedules.
	____ They continuously search for ways to produce goods faster and/or at lower costs.
	____ They continuously improve product quality, aiming for zero defects.
	____ They meet customer requirements for "customization" where this can be done profitably.
Marketing	____ They study customer needs and wants in well-defined market segments.
	____ They allocate marketing effort in relation to the long-run profit potential of the targeted segments.
	____ They develop winning offerings for each target segment.
	____ They measure company image and customer satisfaction on a continuous basis.
	____ They continuously gather and evaluate ideas for new products, product improvements, and services to meet customers' needs.
	____ They influence all company departments and employees to be customer-centred in their thinking and practice.
Sales	____ They have specialized knowledge of the customer's industry.
	____ They strive to give the customer "the best solution."
	____ They make only promises that they can keep.
	____ They feed back customers' needs and ideas to those in charge of product development.
	____ They serve the same customers for a long period of time.
Logistics	____ They set a high standard for service delivery time and they meet this standard consistently.
	____ They operate a knowledgeable and friendly customer service department that can answer questions, handle complaints, and resolve problems in a satisfactory and timely manner.
Accounting	____ They prepare periodic "profitability" reports by product, market segment, geographic areas (regions, sales territories), order sizes, and individual customers.
	____ They prepare invoices tailored to customer needs and answer customer queries courteously and quickly.
Finance	____ They understand and support marketing expenditures (e.g., image advertising) that represent marketing investments that produce long-term customer preference and loyalty.
	____ They tailor the financial package to the customers' financial requirements.
	____ They make quick decisions on customer creditworthiness.
Public Relations	____ They disseminate favourable news about the company and they "damage control" unfavourable news.
	____ They act as an internal customer and public advocate for better company policies and practices.
Other Customer Contact Personnel	____ They are competent, courteous, cheerful, credible, reliable, and responsive.

needs of this group, help marketing managers at headquarters adjust their marketing mix, and prepare local annual and long-range plans for selling all the company's products in Toronto.

Improved information and marketing research technologies have spurred regionalization. Data from retail-store scanners allow instant tracking of product sales, helping companies pinpoint local problems and opportunities. Retailers themselves strongly prefer local programs aimed at consumers in their cities and neighbourhoods. To keep retailers happy, manufacturers now create more local marketing plans.

Some companies have shifted to a greater regional marketing emphasis. McDonald's, for example, now spends about 50 percent of its total advertising budget regionally. Other companies, such as Air Canada, have moved away from regional brands in favour of corporate brands.

PRODUCT- OR BRAND-MANAGEMENT ORGANIZATION Companies producing a variety of products and brands often establish a product- (or brand-) management organization. The product-management organization does not replace the functional organization, but serves as another layer of management. A product manager supervises product category managers, who in turn supervise specific product and brand managers.

A product-management organization makes sense if the company's products are quite different, or if the sheer number of products is beyond the ability of a functional organization to handle. Kraft has used a product-management organization in its Post division, with separate product category managers in charge of cereals, pet food, and beverages. Within the cereal product group, Kraft has had separate subcategory managers for nutritional cereals, children's presweetened cereals, family cereals, and miscellaneous cereals.

Product and brand management is sometimes characterized as a *hub-and-spoke* system. The brand or product manager is figuratively at the centre with spokes emanating out to various departments (see Figure 22.2). Some of the tasks that product or brand managers may perform include:

- Developing a long-range and competitive strategy for the product.
- Preparing an annual marketing plan and sales forecast.
- Working with advertising and merchandising agencies to develop copy, programs, and campaigns.
- Increasing support of the product among the sales force and distributors.
- Gathering continuous intelligence on the product's performance, customer and dealer attitudes, and new problems and opportunities.
- Initiating product improvements to meet changing market needs.

The product-management organization has several advantages. The product manager can concentrate on developing a cost-effective marketing mix for the product; he or she can react more quickly to new products in the marketplace. The company's smaller brands have a product advocate. However, this organization has some disadvantages too:

- Product managers and specifically brand managers are not given enough authority to carry out their responsibilities. They have to rely on persuasion to get the cooperation of other departments.

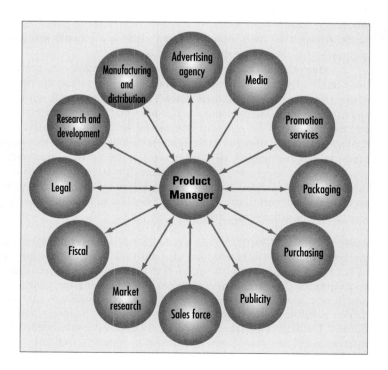

FIGURE 22.2

The Product Manager's Interactions

PM

APM

PA

(a) Vertical Product Team

PM

R   C

(b) Triangular Product Team

PM

R   C   S   D   F   E

(c) Horizontal Product Team

PM = product manager
AP = associate product manager
PA = product assistant
R = market researcher
C = communication specialist
S = sales manager
D = distribution specialist
F = finance/accounting specialist
E = engineer

FIGURE 22.3

Three Types of Product Teams

- Product and brand managers become experts in their product area but rarely achieve functional expertise. They vacillate between acting as experts and having to defer to real experts.

- The product-management system often turns out to be costly. One person is appointed to manage each major product or brand. Soon managers are appointed to manage even minor products and brands.

- Brand managers normally manage a brand for only a short time. Short-term involvement leads to short-term planning and plays havoc with building long-term strengths.

- The fragmentation of markets makes it harder to develop a national strategy from headquarters. Brand managers must increasingly please regional and local sales groups, resulting in a transfer of power from marketing to sales.

- Product and brand managers cause the company to focus on building market share rather than building the customer relationship. Yet the customer relationship, not the brand, may be the primary lever for value creation.

A second alternative with a product-management organization is to switch from product managers to *product teams*. There are three types of potential product-team structures: vertical product team, triangular product team, and the horizontal product team (see Figure 22.3).

The triangular and horizontal product team approaches are favoured by those who advocate brand-asset management. They believe that each major brand should be run by a *brand asset management team (BAMT)* consisting of key representatives from major functions affecting the brand's performance. The company is comprised of several BAMTs, which periodically report to a BAMT directors committee, which itself reports to a chief branding officer. This is quite different from the way brands have traditionally been handled.

A third alternative for product-management organization is to eliminate product manager positions for minor products and assign two or more products to each remaining manager. This is feasible where two or more products appeal to a similar set of needs. A cosmetics company does not need separate product managers for each product because cosmetics serve one major need—beauty. A toiletries company needs different managers for headache remedies, toothpaste, soap, and shampoo, because these products differ in use and appeal.

A fourth alternative for product-management organization is to introduce *category management*, in which a company focuses on product categories to manage its brands. Procter & Gamble, pioneers of the brand-management system, and several other top firms have made a significant shift in recent years to category management.[10]

P&G cites a number of advantages to a category-management structure. By fostering internal competition among brand managers, the traditional brand-management system created strong incentives to excel, but also much internal competition for resources and a lack of coordination. Whereas a smaller share category might have become relatively neglected before (e.g., in product categories such as "hard surface cleaners"), the new scheme was designed to ensure that all categories would be able to receive adequate resources.[11]

Another rationale for category management is the increasing power of the trade. Because the retail trade has tended to think in terms of product categories and the profitability derived from different departments and sections of their stores, P&G felt it only made sense for them to deal with the trade along similar lines. Retailers such as Wal-Mart and regional grocery chains such as Dominick's have embraced category management themselves as a means to define a particular product category's strategic role within the store and to address such operating issues as logistics, the role of private-label products, and the trade-offs between offering product variety and avoiding inefficient duplication.[12]

Category management is not a panacea. It is still a product-driven system. Colgate has moved from brand management (Colgate toothpaste) to category management (toothpaste category) to a new stage called "customer-need management" (mouth care). This last step finally focuses the organization on a basic customer need.[13]

MARKET-MANAGEMENT ORGANIZATION   Many companies sell their products to different markets. Canon sells its fax machines to consumer, business, and government markets. Dofasco sells its flat rolled steel and tubular products to manufacturers of automobiles, steel framing, food cans, and appliances. When customers fall into different user groups with distinct buying preferences and practices, a *market-management organization* is desirable. A market manager supervises several market managers (also called market-development managers, market specialists, or industry specialists). The market managers draw on functional services as needed. Market managers of important markets might even have functional specialists reporting to them.

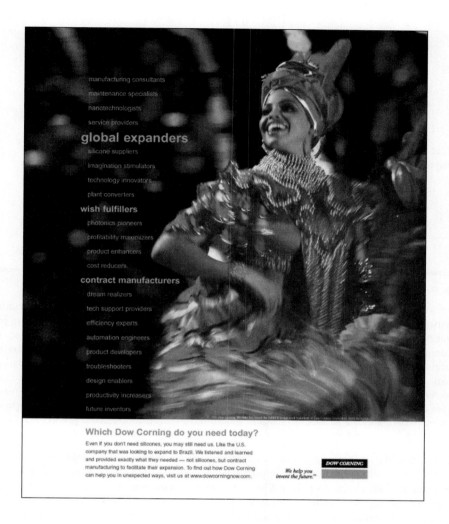

manufacturing consultants
maintenance specialists
nanotechnologists
service providers
global expanders
silicone suppliers
imagination stimulators
technology innovators
plant converters
wish fulfillers
photonics pioneers
profitability maximizers
product enhancers
cost reducers
contract manufacturers
dream realizers
tech support providers
efficiency experts
automation engineers
product developers
troubleshooters
design enablers
productivity increasers
future inventors

Which Dow Corning do you need today?

Even if you don't need silicones, you may still need us. Like the U.S. company that was looking to expand to Brazil. We listened and learned and provided exactly what they needed — not silicones, but contract manufacturing to facilitate their expansion. To find out how Dow Corning can help you in unexpected ways, visit us at www.dowcorningnow.com.

We help you invent the future.™   DOW CORNING

A print ad spells out the services Dow Corning can provide for customers. Dow Corning uses a horizontal product team organization. Teams consist of from five to eight people, and each team manages a specific product, market, and process.

Market managers are staff (not line) people, with duties similar to those of product managers. Market managers develop long-range and annual plans for their markets. Their performance is judged by their market's growth and profitability. This system carries many of the same advantages and disadvantages of product-management systems. Its strongest advantage is that the marketing activity is organized to meet the needs of distinct customer groups rather than being focused on marketing functions, regions, or products. Many companies are reorganizing along market lines and becoming *market-centred organizations*. Xerox has converted from geographic selling to selling by industry, as have IBM and Hewlett-Packard.

In a *customer-management organization*, companies can organize themselves to understand and deal with individual customers rather than with the mass market or even market segments.

MATRIX-MANAGEMENT ORGANIZATION   Companies that produce many products flowing into many markets may adopt a matrix organization. DuPont was a pioneer in developing the matrix structure (see Figure 22.4):

FIGURE 22.4

Product-/Market-Management
Matrix System

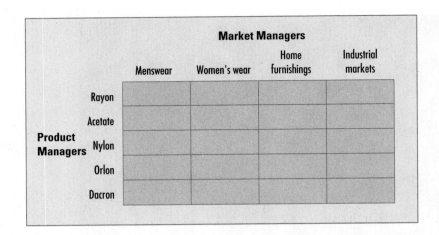

DuPont

Before being spun off, DuPont's textile fibres department consisted of separate product managers for rayon, acetate, nylon, orlon, and dacron; and separate market managers for menswear, women's wear, home furnishings, and industrial markets. The product managers planned the sales and profits for their respective fibres. They asked market managers to estimate how much of their fibre they could sell in each market at a proposed price. Market managers, however, were generally more interested in meeting their market's needs than pushing a particular fibre. In preparing their market plans, they asked each product manager about the fibre's planned prices and availabilities. The final sales forecast of the market managers and the product managers should have added to the same grand total.

Companies like DuPont can go one step further and view the market managers as the main marketers, and their product managers as suppliers. The menswear market manager, for example, would be empowered to buy textile fibres from DuPont's product managers or, if DuPont's price is too high, from outside suppliers. This system would force DuPont product managers to become more efficient. If a DuPont product manager could not match the "arm's length pricing" levels of competitive suppliers, then perhaps DuPont should not continue to produce that fibre.

A matrix organization would seem desirable in a multi-product, multi-market company. The rub is that this system is costly and often creates conflicts. There is the cost of supporting all the managers. There are also questions about where authority and responsibility should reside.

Matrix management gained advocates because companies provide the context in which a matrix can thrive—flat, lean team organizations focused around business processes that cut horizontally across functions.[14]

CORPORATE-DIVISIONAL ORGANIZATION As multi-product, multi-market companies grow, they often convert their larger product or market groups into separate divisions. The divisions set up their own departments and services. This raises the question of what marketing services and activities should be retained at company headquarters. Divisionalized companies have reached different answers to this question:

- *No corporate marketing.* Some companies lack a corporate marketing staff. They do not see any useful function for marketing at the corporate level. Each division has its own marketing department.

- *Moderate corporate marketing.* Some companies have a small corporate marketing staff that performs a few functions, primarily (1) assisting top management with overall opportunity evaluation, (2) providing divisions with consulting assistance on request, (3) helping divisions that have little or no marketing, and (4) promoting the marketing concept throughout the company.

- *Strong corporate marketing.* Some companies have a corporate marketing staff that, in addition to the preceding activities, provides various marketing services to the divisions, such as specialized advertising services, sales-promotion services, marketing research services, and sales-administration services.

Regardless of how formalized corporate marketing is, certain activities must occur within the organization in a "top-down" fashion. Webster sees the role of marketing at the corporate level as:[15]

1. To promote a culture of customer orientation and to be an advocate for the customer in the deliberations of top-management strategy formulators.

2. To assess market attractiveness by analyzing customer needs and wants and competitive offerings.

3. To develop the firm's overall value proposition, the vision and articulation of how it proposes to deliver superior value to customers.

Relations with Other Departments

In principle, all business functions should interact harmoniously to pursue the firm's overall objectives. In practice, however, interdepartmental relations are often characterized by deep rivalries and distrust. Some conflict stems from differences of opinion as to what is in the company's best interests, some from real trade-offs between departmental well-being and company well-being, and some from unfortunate stereotypes and prejudices.

In the typical organization, each business function has a potential impact on customer satisfaction. Under the marketing concept, all departments need to "think customer" and work together to satisfy customer needs and expectations. The marketing department must drive this point home. The marketing vice-president, or CMO, has two tasks: (1) to coordinate the company's internal marketing activities and (2) to coordinate marketing with finance, operations, and other company functions to serve the customer.

Yet, there is little agreement on how much influence and authority marketing should have over other departments. Typically, the marketing vice-president must work through persuasion rather than authority. Other departments often resist changing their way of working to fulfill the customer's interests. Inevitably, departments define company problems and goals from their viewpoint. Conflicts of interest are unavoidable. Breakdowns in communication further exacerbate the problem. Consider the following potential negative reactions that marketing can receive from different functional groups:

- *Engineering* comes into conflict with marketing executives when the latter want several models produced, often with product features requiring custom components. Engineers often think of marketing people as inept technically, as continually changing priorities, and as not fully credible or trustworthy.

- *Purchasing executives* see marketing executives pushing for several models in a product line, which requires purchasing small quantities of many items rather than large quantities of few items. They think that marketing insists on too high a quality for materials and components. They also dislike marketing's forecasting inaccuracy, which causes them to place rush orders at unfavourable prices or to carry excessive inventories.

- *Financial executives* suspect that marketing forecasts are self-serving. They think marketers are too quick to slash prices to win orders, instead of pricing to make a profit. They claim that marketers "know the value of everything and cost of nothing."

- *Accountants* see marketing people as lax in providing sales reports on time. They dislike the special deals salespeople make with customers because these require special accounting procedures. Credit officers evaluate potential customers' credit standing and deny or limit credit to the more doubtful ones. They think marketers will sell to anyone, including those from whom payment is doubtful.

Companies need to develop a balanced orientation in which marketing and other functions jointly determine what is in the company's best interests. Solutions include joint seminars to understand each other's viewpoints, joint committees and liaison personnel, personnel exchange programs, and analytical methods to determine the most profitable course of action.[16]

Perhaps the best solution is for marketing to periodically propose a *function-to-function* meeting with departments where greater understanding and collaboration is warranted. Even if each function indulges in stereotypical charges and complaints about the other, such a meeting can lead to a clearing of the air and a basis for a more constructive collaboration. Each department needs to understand the operating logic of the other departments. When departments work together toward common goals, marketing is more effective.

Procter & Gamble

With 19 of their 20 largest brands gaining share and a stock price that doubled, Procter & Gamble was clearly on a roll during 2002–2004. Organic growth in core businesses provided much of the impetus. P&G's new product hit rate, defined in terms of when returns exceeded the cost of capital, was 70 percent to 90 percent. Although this extraordinary performance was due to many factors, close interactions between marketing and 7500 R&D personnel worldwide was critical. To facilitate interaction, problems and solutions are posted on an internal Web site and "communities of practice" dedicated to particular expertise (e.g., "whiteners") meet frequently. Joint collaboration between different units of P&G has produced such diverse products as Crest Whitestrips teeth whiteners, Iams Dental Defense tartar-fighting pet food, and Olay Daily facials cleansing cloths. Mr. Clean AutoDry carwash system was designed with input from R&D experts who worked on the Pur water purification and Cascade automatic dishwasher powder brands.[17]

Building a Creative Marketing Organization

Many companies are beginning to realize that they are not really market- and customer-driven—they are product-and-sales driven. Companies such as Nortel, Baxter, General Motors, and Imperial Oil (Esso) are attempting to transform themselves into true market-driven companies. This will require:

1. Developing a companywide passion for customers.

2. Organizing around customer segments instead of around products.

3. Developing a deep understanding of customers through qualitative and quantitative research.

The payoffs are considerable. Two researchers recently concluded: "We found that the more aggressive a company's customer-focused strategy, the higher its productivity. Those with a customer focus were almost 7 percent more productive than their competitors."[18]

The task is not easy. It will not happen as a result of the CEO making speeches and urging every employee to "think customer." The change will require a change in job and department definitions, responsibilities, incentives, and relationships. See "Marketing Insight: The Marketing CEO" for actions a CEO can take to improve marketing capabilities.

Although it is necessary in a hypercompetitive economy that an organization be customer-oriented, it is not enough. The organization must also be creative. Companies today copy each other's advantages and strategies with increasing speed. Differentiation gets harder to achieve, let alone maintain. Margins fall when firms become more alike. The only answer is for the firm to build a capability in strategic innovation and imagination (see "Marketing Insight: Fuelling Strategic Innovation"). This capability comes from assembling tools, processes, skills, and measures that will enable the firm to generate more and better new ideas than its competitors.[19]

Companies must watch trends and be ready to capitalize on them. Motorola was 18 months late in moving from analogue to digital cellular phones, giving Nokia and Ericsson a big lead. Barnes & Noble was late in recognizing online ordering of books and music, giving Amazon the lead. Nestlé was late in recognizing the trend toward coffeehouses such as Starbucks. Coca-Cola was slow in recognizing beverage trends toward fruit-flavoured drinks such as Snapple, energy drinks such as Gatorade, and designer water brands. The company is now fiercely playing catch-up, using innovation to challenge these category leaders with Fruitopia noncarbonated fruit beverage, POWERade energy drink, and Dasani water. Its success is remarkable. Its Diet Coke with Lime won *Marketing Magazine's* best new product award in 2004 in the health and calorie-reduced beverage category. In March 2005, it introduced new mini cans of its most popular soft drinks. The 237 mL cans are about one-third smaller than traditional cans.[20]

MARKETING INSIGHT

The Marketing CEO

What steps can a CEO take to create a market- and customer-focused company?

1. *Convince senior management of the need to become customer-focused.* The CEO personally exemplifies strong customer commitment and rewards those in the organization who do likewise. For example, former CEOs Jack Welch of GE and Lou Gerstner of IBM are said to have spent 100 days a year visiting with customers, in spite of their many strategic, financial, and administrative burdens; and IBM's top 470 executives are personally responsible for more than 1300 customer accounts.

2. *Appoint a senior marketing officer and marketing task force.* The marketing task force should include the CEO; the vice-presidents of sales, R&D, purchasing, manufacturing, finance, and human resources; and other key individuals.

3. *Get outside help and guidance.* Consulting firms have considerable experience in helping companies move toward a marketing orientation.

4. *Change the company's reward measurement and system.* As long as purchasing and manufacturing are rewarded for keeping costs low, they will resist accepting some costs required to serve customers better. As long as finance focuses on short-term profit, it will oppose major investments designed to build satisfied, loyal customers.

5. *Hire strong marketing talent.* The company needs a strong marketing vice-president who not only manages the marketing department but also gains respect from and influence with the other vice-presidents. A multidivisional company would benefit from establishing a strong corporate marketing department.

6. *Develop strong in-house marketing training programs.* The company should design well-crafted marketing training programs for corporate management, divisional general managers, marketing and sales personnel, manufacturing personnel, R&D personnel, and others. GE, Motorola, and Accenture run these programs.

7. *Install a modern marketing planning system.* The planning format will require managers to think about the marketing environment, opportunities, competitive trends, and other forces. These managers then prepare strategies and sales and profit forecasts for specific products and segments and are accountable for performance.

8. *Establish an annual marketing excellence recognition program.* Business units that believe they have developed exemplary marketing plans should submit a description of their plans and results. The winning teams would be rewarded at a special ceremony. The plans would be disseminated to the other business units as "models of marketing thinking." Such programs are carried on by Accenture, Becton-Dickenson, and DuPont.

9. *Shift from a department focus to a process-outcome focus.* After defining the fundamental business processes that determine its success, the company should appoint process leaders and cross-disciplinary teams to re-engineer and implement these processes.

10. *Empower the employees.* Progressive companies encourage and reward their employees for coming up with new ideas. They also empower them to settle customer complaints in order to save the customer's business. IBM, for example, lets its front-line employees spend up to US$5000 to solve a customer problem on the spot.

Fuelling Strategic Innovation

Professor Stephen Brown of Ulster University has challenged a number of fundamental assumptions underlying the marketing concept. He thinks that marketers make too much of researching and satisfying consumers, and as a result, risk losing marketing imagination and significant consumer impact. Here are his criticisms:

1. If marketers pay too much attention to what consumers say they need or want, marketers will simply make products similar to those that already exist. Consumers normally start from what they know, not from what might be possible. For example, they might say they want a smaller cellular phone but would not ask for one that includes a Palm Pilot or voice recognition. It is the marketer's job to go beyond what customers say they want.

2. The marketing concept assumes that consumers have clear goals and pursue them rationally. But consumers are buffeted by all kinds of forces. Many respond to hyped products and stories. Therefore marketers need skills beyond APIC—analysis, planning, implementation, and control. Marketers need to be able to create dramas, new realities, artificial scarcities, celebrations, and the like.

3. The marketing concept implies that marketers must be submissive to customers, and go all out to please them. Any suggestion that marketers might "play" with the customer, even manipulate the public, is taboo. Yet some of the greatest marketers of the past, such as P. T. Barnum, teased the public and overdramatized offerings, and the public loved it. Why should the customer be dominant and the marketer always be submissive?

How can companies build a capability for strategic innovation? Here are some approaches:

- Hire some marketers who are unusually creative to counterbalance the majority who do marketing by the textbook. These people may be more unconventional, more rule-breaking, more risk-taking, and even more argumentative, but their ideas will at least present a challenge.

- Train your employees in the use of creativity techniques, including group techniques (brainstorming, synectics) and individual techniques (visualization, attribute listing, forced relationships, morphological analysis, mind-mapping).

- List observable trends such as longer working hours, single parents, and new lifestyles, and tease out their implications for your firm.

- List unmet needs and imagine new offerings or solutions: how to help people lose weight, stop smoking, relieve stress, meet others, and so on.

- Set up rewards and prizes for new ideas. Run a "best idea" competition once a month. Give a cash reward, extra vacation time, or travel awards to those who come up with the best ideas.

- Senior managers should take small sets of employees out to lunch or dinner once a week to discuss ideas they might have for improving the business. Sometimes take them into new settings, such as a wrestling match, a drug rehabilitation centre, or a poor neighbourhood.

- Set up groups of employees to critique the company's and competitors' products and services. Also have them critique the company's cherished beliefs and consider turning them upside down.

- Occasionally hire creative resources from outside the firm. Many large advertising agencies, such as Leo Burnett, run a creativity service for clients.

Source: For more on Brown's views, see Stephen Brown, *Marketing—The Retro Revolution* (Thousand Oaks, CA: Sage Publications, 2001). For more on creativity, see Michael Michalko, *Cracking Creativity: The Secrets of Creative Genius* (Berkeley, CA: Ten Speed Press, 1998); James M. Higgins, *101 Creative Problem Solving Techniques* (New York: New Management Publishing Company, 1994); and all of the books by Edward DeBono.

POWERade

Challenging leader Gatorade in the energy drink market has been a tough task. After introducing several innovations subsequent to POWERade's launch in 1990, such as sports cap packaging and offbeat flavours, Coca-Cola found the brand was stagnating. Relaunched in 2001, POWERade was positioned on the basis of active consumer lifestyles as "Fuel for Life." The logo was completely revamped to feature a snake-like "P," and the product was reformulated with B vitamins. Ads themed "Very Real Power" showed athletes doing seemingly impossible feats by virtue of realistic special effects. Innovation has continued to drive a turnaround in sales. In the summer of 2003, the company introduced special edition Matrix Reloaded POWERade with a custom-shaped package and new flavour to create a tie-in with the blockbuster movie franchise. Other special editions tied to the Olympics, NASCAR, and NHRA followed. September 2004 saw the launch of sourberry-flavoured POWERade FLAVA23, backed by an integrated marketing program that featured a DC Comics depiction of NBA star and POWERade spokesman LeBron James.[21]

Market leaders tend to miss trends when they are risk-averse, obsessed about protecting their existing markets and physical resources, and more interested in efficiency than innovation.

Socially Responsible Marketing

Effective internal marketing must be matched by a strong sense of social responsibility.[22] Companies need to evaluate whether they are truly practising ethical and socially responsible marketing. Several forces are driving companies to practise a higher level of corporate social responsibility: rising customer expectations, changing employee expectations, government legislation and pressure, investor interest in social criteria, and changing business procurement practices.[23]

Business success and continually satisfying the customer and other stakeholders are closely tied to adoption and implementation of high standards of business and marketing conduct. The most admired companies in the world abide by a code of serving people's interests, not only their own. Canada's *Corporate Knights* is the world's first mass-market magazine with an explicit focus on corporate social responsibility. In each edition it makes the case that good corporate citizenship and solid financial performance go hand-in-hand. Each year, it provides a ranking of Canada's 50 best corporate citizens. In 2004, Zenon Environmental Inc., Alcan, Dofasco, the Royal Bank, Transalta Corporation, and Suncor Energy were listed among the top ten firms.[24]

Business practices are often under attack because business situations routinely pose tough ethical dilemmas. The issues are complicated: Drawing a clear line between normal marketing practice and unethical behaviour is not easy. At the same time, certain business practices are clearly unethical or illegal. These include bribery or stealing trade secrets; false and deceptive advertising; exclusive dealing and tying agreements; quality or safety defects; false warranties; inaccurate labelling; price-fixing or undue discrimination; and barriers to entry and predatory competition.

Today companies that do not perform ethically or well are at greater risk of being exposed, thanks to the Internet. In the past, a disgruntled customer might bad-mouth a manufacturer or merchant to 12 other people; today he or she can reach thousands of people on the Internet. Microsoft, for example, has attracted scores of anti-Microsoft sites, including Hate Microsoft and Boycott Microsoft. Well-managed PR campaigns can also have an effect. The Rainforest Action Network launched

Canada's *Corporate Knights* is the world's first mass-market magazine with an explicit focus on corporate social responsibility.

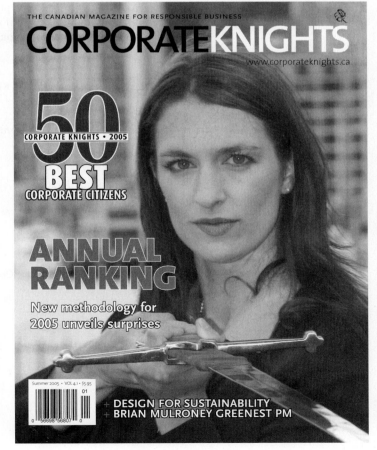

THE CANADIAN MAGAZINE FOR RESPONSIBLE BUSINESS

CORPORATEKNIGHTS

www.corporateknights.ca

50 CORPORATE KNIGHTS · 2005

BEST CORPORATE CITIZENS

ANNUAL RANKING

New methodology for 2005 unveils surprises

Summer 2005 · VOL 4.1 · $5.95

+ DESIGN FOR SUSTAINABILITY
+ BRIAN MULRONEY GREENEST PM

a punishing PR campaign in 1997 to stop Home Depot from selling old-growth lumber. After two years of bad publicity and resistance to new store locations, Home Depot agreed to have its suppliers work with environmental and forestry groups to certify that its wood products are not from endangered areas.[25]

Corporate Social Responsibility

Raising the level of socially responsible marketing calls for a three-pronged attack that relies on proper legal, ethical, and social responsibility behaviour.

LEGAL BEHAVIOUR Society must use the law to define, as clearly as possible, those practices that are illegal, antisocial, or anticompetitive. Organizations must ensure that every employee knows and observes any relevant laws. For example, sales managers can check that sales representatives know and observe the law, such as the fact that it is illegal for salespeople to lie to consumers or mislead them about the advantages of buying a product. Salespeople may not offer bribes to government officials in Canada or abroad as stipulated by the Corruption of Foreign Public Officials Act. They may not obtain or use competitors' technical or trade secrets through bribery or industrial espionage. Finally, salespeople must not disparage competitors or competing products by suggesting things that are not true. Every sales representative must understand these laws and act accordingly.[26]

ETHICAL BEHAVIOUR Companies must adopt and disseminate a written code of ethics, build a company tradition of ethical behaviour, and hold its people fully responsible for observing ethical and legal guidelines.[27] A 1999 poll by Environics International, a public-opinion research firm, found that 67 percent of North Americans are willing to buy or boycott products on ethical grounds. In response to heightened consumer sensitivity on the topic, KPMG's 1999 survey of 1100 global companies found that 24 percent produce annual "sustainability" reports.[28]

SOCIAL RESPONSIBILITY BEHAVIOUR Individual marketers must practise a "social conscience" in specific dealings with customers and stakeholders.[29] Increasingly, people say that they want information about a company's record on social and environmental responsibility to help decide which companies to buy from, invest in, and work for.[30] Table 22.1 lists the companies that *Corporate Knights* ranked as the ten best corporate citizens in 2005.

Companies around the world are becoming more sensitive to matters of social responsibility. Fetzer Vineyards is one such company that has fully embraced such issues:

TABLE 22.1	*CORPORATE KNIGHTS'* TOP TEN CORPORATE CITIZENS, 2005
1. Bank of Montreal	
2. Shoppers Drug Mart Corporation	
3. IGM Financial Inc.	
4. Laurentian Bank of Canada	
5. Husky Injection Moldings Systems Ltd.	
6. Torstar Corporation	
7. TELUS Corporation	
8. Interface Inc.	
9. Toronto-Dominion Bank	
10. Canadian Imperial Bank of Commerce	

Source: "The 2005 Best 50 Corporate Citizens," **www.corporateknights.ca/best50/2005best50.asp** (viewed September 5, 2005).

Fetzer Vineyards

The sixth-largest winery in the United States and winner of many product quality awards, Fetzer has transformed its business according to the triple bottom line—measuring corporate success by social and environmental impact as well as profit and loss. Every one of the 2000 acres owned by Fetzer is certified as organic and the vineyards are designated a "zero waste" business by the state of California. Their philosophy even extends to product packaging. To spare trees, labels are made from a plant fibre known as kenaf and printed with soy-based inks; the corks aren't sanitized with chlorine; and the cases are made from recycled cardboard. The winery uses alternative solar and biodiesel energy sources and broke convention with extensive programs and benefits for part-time workers as well as full-time employees. Even though it belongs to the highly competitive wine industry, Fetzer believes that business and social progress should go hand-in-hand. Its financial and marketing success has led the Wine Institute, a trade group for the California wine industry, to introduce the first statewide sustainable wine-growing practices.[31]

Deciding how to communicate corporate attitudes and behaviours toward social responsibility can be difficult. Corporate philanthropy, for example, may go unrecognized.[32] The financial service sector contains some of Canada's largest corporate donors. Canada's leading six financial service firms contributed almost $171 million to charities and nonprofit organizations in 2003 alone.[33] Although companies can be credited for good deeds, the deeds can be easily overlooked if not publicized and easily resented if the company is seen as being exploitative or fails to live up to a "good guys" image.[34] Philip Morris Company's US$250 million ad campaign touting its charitable activities was met with skepticism because of its negative corporate image.

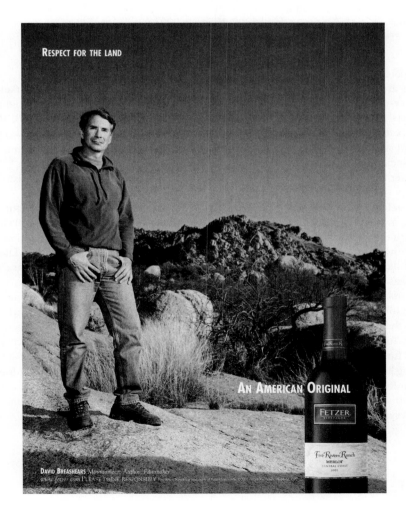

This Fetzer ad reinforces the company's commitment to social responsibility. David Breashears is an author, filmmaker, and world-renowned climber who has ascended Everest several times.

Socially Responsible Business Models

The future holds a wealth of opportunities for companies.[35] Technological advances in solar energy, online networks, cable and satellite television, biotechnology, and telecommunications promise to change the world as we know it. At the same time, forces in the socioeconomic, cultural, and natural environments will impose new limits on marketing and business practices. Companies that are able to innovate new solutions and values in a socially responsible way are the most likely to succeed.[36]

Many companies such as The Body Shop, Vancity Credit Union, and Pfizer Canada are giving social responsibility a more prominent role. Other companies are demonstrating their responsibility through innovative partnerships. Microsoft Canada and the Canadian National Institute for the Blind partnered to provide more than 3 million blind, visually impaired, and print disabled Canadians with access to a new world of information.[37] Another example of a company with social responsibility at the core of its business model is Working Assets:

Working Assets

Working Assets was established in 1985 to help people support causes through everyday activities like talking on the phone. Every time customers use one of Working Assets' donation-linked services (Long Distance, Local, Wireless, Credit Card or Online), the company donates a portion of the customer's bill to nonprofit groups. Working Assets donates at least 1 percent of annual revenues to charity and lets customers vote on which nonprofit groups receive money. To date, US$40 million has been raised by the company for causes including Greenpeace, Oxfam America, Rainforest Action Network, Human Rights Watch, Planned Parenthood, Stand for Children, and Doctors Without Borders, among many others. The customers addressed in the company's clever tagline "We make your voice heard" are people who identify themselves as supporters of progressive causes. Working Assets' corporate idealism has had a favourable effect on the bottom line. Revenue shot up from US$2 million in 1991 to roughly US$300 million in 2003.[38]

Cause-Related Marketing

Many firms are blending their corporate social responsibility initiatives with their marketing activities.[39] **Cause-related marketing** is marketing that links the firm's contributions to a designated cause to customers' engaging directly or indirectly in revenue-producing transactions with the firm.[40] Cause marketing has also been called a part of *corporate societal marketing* (CSM), which Drumwright and Murphy define as marketing efforts "that have at least one non-economic objective related to social welfare and use the resources of the company and/or of its partners."[41] They also include other activities such as traditional and strategic philanthropy and volunteerism as part of CSM.

Cause-related marketing began in earnest in the 1980s. Many observers credit American Express with raising awareness of the mutual benefits of cause-related marketing through its 1983 campaign to help restore the Statue of Liberty. By donating a penny for every credit-card transaction and a dollar for each new card issued, American Express gave US$1.7 million to the Statue of Liberty—Ellis Island Foundation. In the process, transactions for American Express rose 30 percent, and new cards issued increased by 15 percent during this period.

Cause-related marketing comes in many forms. Tesco, a leading U.K. retailer, has created a "Computer for Schools" program: Customers receive vouchers for every £10 spent, which can be donated to the school of their choice; the school can then exchange the vouchers for new computer equipment. Tupperware Canada Ltd. ran a fund-raising program in March 2002. For every item sold during this fund-raiser, Tupperware Canada Ltd. donated a dollar to MADD Canada. Dawn, the top dishwashing liquid in the United States, launched a campaign highlighting the fact that the product's grease-cleaning power had an unusual side benefit—it could be used to clean birds caught in oil spills. A Web site, **www.saveaduck.com**, outlines its financial donations and educational program. British Airways has a particularly successful and highly visible program:

British Airways

British Airways partnered with UNICEF and developed a cause-marketing campaign called Change for Good. Passengers on British Airways flights are encouraged to donate leftover foreign currency from their travels. The scheme is simple: Passengers deposit their surplus currency in envelopes provided by British Airways, which collects the deposits and donates them directly to UNICEF. British Airways advertises its program during an in-flight video, on the backs of seat cards, and with in-flight announcements. The company also developed a television ad that featured a child thanking British Airways for its contribution to UNICEF. Because Change for Good can be directly targeted to passengers and can produce immediate results, it does not require extensive advertising or promotion and is highly cost-efficient. Since 1994, almost US$40 million has been raised and distributed around the world.[42]

CAUSE MARKETING BENEFITS AND COSTS A successful cause marketing program can produce a number of benefits: improving social welfare; creating differentiated brand positioning; building strong consumer bonds; enhancing the company's public image with government officials and other decision makers; creating a reservoir of good will; boosting internal morale and galvanizing employees; and driving sales.[43]

By humanizing the firm, consumers may develop a strong, unique bond with the firm that transcends normal marketplace transactions.[44] Some of the specific means by which cause marketing programs can build brand equity with consumers include (1) building brand awareness, (2) enhancing brand image, (3) establishing brand credibility, (4) evoking brand feelings, (5) creating a sense of brand community, and (6) eliciting brand engagement.[45] Liz Claiborne has exhibited strong commitment to its cause:

Liz Claiborne

In 1991, at a time when domestic violence was often a taboo or "hot potato" issue, Liz Claiborne developed its Women's Work program against domestic violence, now dubbed "Love Is Not Abuse." Prior to starting the campaign, the company had conducted research which revealed that 96 percent of its customers believed domestic violence was a problem and 91 percent of those same customers would have a positive opinion of a company that started an awareness campaign about the issue. The major fund-raising event is an annual charity shopping day every October at Liz Claiborne stores. The company donates 10 percent of sales to local domestic violence organizations. Liz Claiborne also contributes proceeds from the sale of T-shirts, jewellery, and other products related to the campaign. Additionally, the company pays for public service campaigns that appear on television, radio, billboards, and bus shelters and distributes awareness posters, brochures, and mailings. Over the years, Liz Claiborne has also sponsored workshops, surveys, celebrity-endorsed awareness campaigns, and other events.[46]

The danger, however, is that the promotional efforts behind a cause-related marketing program could backfire if cynical consumers question the link between the product and the cause and see the firm as being self-serving and exploitative.[47] For example, Bristol-Meyers Squibb (BMS) supports the Tour de Cure, which funds diabetes research and prevention. On the official Web page of the tour, the BMS logo includes the statement that BMS is "A leader in Type 2 Diabetes Care." This potentially profitable connection between the sponsor and the event may lead some consumers to view BMS's support for the Tour de Cure as opportunistic.[48]

A number of decisions must be made in designing and implementing a cause marketing program, such as how many and which cause(s) to choose and how to brand the cause program.

CHOOSING A CAUSE Some experts believe that the positive impact on a brand from cause-related marketing may be lessened by sporadic involvement with numerous causes. For example, Cathy Chizauskas, Gillette's director of civic affairs, states: "When you're spreading out your giving in fifty-dollar to one-thousand-dollar increments, no one knows what you are doing. . . . It doesn't make much of a splash."[49]

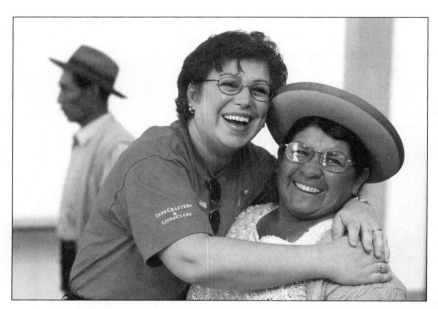

LensCrafters' Give the Gift of Sight program in action.

Many companies choose to focus on one or a few main causes to simplify execution and maximize impact. One of the more focused cause marketers is McDonald's. Ronald McDonald Houses in more than 20 countries offer more than 5000 rooms each night to families needing support while their child is in the hospital. Ronald McDonald House program has provided a "home away from home" for nearly 4 million family members since its beginning in 1974.

Limiting support to a single cause, however, may limit the pool of consumers or other stakeholders who could transfer positive feelings from the cause to the firm. In addition, many popular causes already have numerous corporate sponsors. Reportedly, over 300 companies, including Avon, Ford, Estée Lauder, Revlon, Lee Jeans, Polo Ralph Lauren, Yoplait, Saks, BMW, and American Express, currently associate themselves with breast cancer as a cause in some way.[50] As a consequence, the brand may find itself "lost in the shuffle," overlooked in a sea of symbolic pink ribbons.

Opportunities can potentially be greater with "orphan causes"—causes such as diseases that afflict fewer than 200 000 people.[51] Another option is overlooked diseases, such as pancreatic cancer, which is the fourth deadliest form of cancer behind skin, lung, and breast and yet has received little or no corporate support.

Most firms tend to choose causes that fit their corporate or brand image and matter to their employees and shareholders. LensCrafters' Give the Gift of Sight program is a family of charitable vision-care programs that has provided free eye exams and glasses to more than 3 million needy people throughout North America and in developing countries around the world.

BRANDING THE CAUSE MARKETING PROGRAM There are three potential options for branding a cause marketing program:

1. *Self-branded: Create own cause program.* The firm takes ownership of a cause and develops an entirely new organization to deliver benefits associated with the cause. The newly created self-branded cause could be branded with the parent brand or an individual product brand. The Ronald McDonald House Charities and the Avon Breast Cancer Crusade are classic examples of self-branded cause entities.

2. *Co-branded: Link to existing cause program.* The firm partners with an existing cause. Typically, the identification of the brand affiliation with the cause is only in the form of its designation as a sponsor or supporter—the actual involvement is not branded as a program in any way. Currently, co-branding relationships with causes are the most popular type of activity. KitchenAid Canada's "Cook for the Cure," which is entering its sixth year, is a grassroots effort that encourages consumers across the country to host parties at home. This not only raises funds (instead of bringing a hostess gift, such as a bottle of wine, people donate money), but also enlists guests to become cure ambassadors. At **www.cookforthecure.ca**, hosts browse the party guide, search recipes, and submit the funds they've raised. In addition to its online presence, the program is supported by television and print advertising, point-of-purchase materials, co-promotions at liquor stores, and cooking schools and PR activities.[52]

3. *Jointly branded: Link to existing cause program.* In this hybrid approach, firms partner with an existing cause but explicitly brand the program that links to the cause. An example is the CrownLife ParticipACTION Challenge, which pits active cities against each other. It is a classic example of a community event that is both the message and the medium.

Co-branding with an existing cause is a means for firms to complement their existing brand image with specific associations that are "borrowed" or "transferred" from a cause. Self-branding can be useful when a firm is trying to augment existing consumer associations via emotional and imagery appeals. Joint branding may permit the best of both worlds by establishing a strong connection with an existing cause but maintaining a distinct identity at the same time. "Marketing Memo: Making a Difference" provides some tips from a top cause marketing firm.

Marketing Memo

Making a Difference

One of the most accomplished cause marketing consultants is Cone, Inc. It offers the following perspectives on the current state of cause marketing and how it should best be practised:

> With new vigor, consumers, customers, employees, investors and communities are closely watching how companies behave in relation to them and to society. Influential groups such as Business for Social Responsibility, Dow Jones Sustainability Index, *Fortune* magazine and others are judging companies based on a complex series of global standards. Business practices such as governance, philanthropy, sourcing, the environment, employee relations and community relations have moved from behind the scenes to center stage. For executives today, appropriately defining, executing and communicating corporate social responsibility (CSR) has never been more important.

To help execute and communicate CSR more effectively, Cone offers the following considerations:

- *Define CSR for your company.* Make sure that your senior executives are all talking about the same thing. CSR includes a broad range of complex internal and external business practices. Although they are vital components of the CSR mix, corporate philanthropy and community relations don't define CSR alone.

- *Build a diverse team.* The development and execution of CSR strategies require a collaborative, concerted team effort. Create a decision-making task force that integrates and brings together a range of expertise and resources, including marketing, public affairs, community relations, legal, human resources, manufacturing, and others. Put a formal process in place to approach CSR strategy development, ongoing implementation, and continuous improvement.

- *Analyze your current CSR-related activities and revamp them if necessary.* Do your due diligence at the outset to understand CSR gaps and risks specific to your company. Research industry examples and cull best practices from leading case studies. Make sure to consider global trends, as Europe is far advanced of North America.

- *Forge and strengthen NGO relationships.* The more than 300 000 nongovernmental organizations (NGOs) around the world are a powerful force on corporate policies and behaviour, serving as both advocates and loud critics. Forge sincere partnerships with organizations that can offer you independent, unbiased insight into and evaluation of your CSR activities, provide expertise on social issues and developing global markets, and offer access to key influentials.

- *Develop a cause branding initiative.* Create a public face for your citizenship activities through a signature cause branding initiative that integrates philanthropy, community relations, marketing and human resources assets. ConAgra Foods; Feeding Children Better program, for example, is a multi-year initiative created to feed millions of hungry children through innovative partnerships, grant-making, employee volunteerism, and education and awareness.

- *Walk your talk.* Critics often assert that companies exploit CSR as a PR smokescreen to conceal or divert attention from corporate misdeeds and blemishes. Before introducing any new CSR initiative or drawing attention to good corporate behaviour, make sure that your company is addressing stakeholder expectations of CSR at the most basic level.

- *Don't be silent.* Not only do North Americans expect businesses to behave socially, the majority want companies to tell them how they are doing so. An overwhelming majority also say they prefer to find out about CSR activities from a third-party source, particularly the media.

- *Beware.* Greater public awareness for your corporate citizenship record can be double-edged. Claims of socially responsible behaviour, even sincere ones, often invite public scrutiny. Be prepared. Even if your company is not ready to proactively communicate about your CSR activities, be ready to respond to public inquiries immediately. Don't let the threat of public scrutiny keep you mute, though. More often than not, silence regarding CSR issues is translated as indifference, or worse, inaction.

Sources: Cone Buzz, April 2004. See also Carol L. Cone, Mark A. Feldman, and Alison T. DaSilva, "Cause and Effects," *Harvard Business Review* (July 2003): 95–101.

Social Marketing

Some marketing is conducted to directly address a social problem or cause. Cause-related marketing is done by a company to support a cause. **Social marketing** is done by a nonprofit or government organization to further a cause, such as "say no to drugs" or "exercise more and eat better."[53] The need for social marketing is evident; consider the following recent facts and figures:[54]

- More than 1 million Canadian children—nearly one in six—live in families experiencing poverty.

- Teen pregnancy is considered a major public health problem in Canada, where there are over 20 000 live births annually to mothers aged 15 to 19 years, and over 225 babies born to mothers aged 10 to 14 years. Canada's teenage pregnancy rates are higher than rates in Japan, Switzerland, Sweden, and Finland, but lower than those in New Zealand and the United States.

- Car crashes are the number-one cause of death among Canadian teens, and studies suggest about 40 percent are alcohol-related.

- Gamblers Anonymous says that gambling is a progressive and incurable illness. Statistics Canada reports that 6.3 percent of the population are thought to be "at risk gamblers and problem gamblers." People who are compulsive gamblers allocate large amounts of time to gambling and little time for family, friends, or other interests. They place larger and larger bets despite the fact they have growing debt.

Social marketing is a global phenomenon that goes back for years. In the 1950s, India started family-planning campaigns. In the 1970s, the Australian government ran "Wear Your Seat Belt" campaigns. In the late 1970s, the Canadian government launched campaigns to "Say No to Drugs," "Stop Smoking," and "Exercise for Health." In the 1980s, the World Bank, World Health Organization, and U.S. Centers for Disease Control and Prevention started to use the term and promote interest in social marketing. Notable global social marketing successes include the following:

- Oral rehydration therapy in Honduras significantly decreased deaths from diarrhea in small children under the age of five.

- Social marketers created booths in marketplaces where Ugandan midwives sold contraceptives at affordable prices.

- Population Communication Services created and promoted two extremely popular songs in Latin America, "Stop" and "When We Are Together," to help young women "say no."

ParticipACTION

Health and Welfare Canada and one of its dynamic directors, Jim Mintz, have one of the longest records of any social marketing organization in the world. More than 125 companies, nonprofit organizations, and other government agencies formed partnerships that contributed close to $60 million in financial, human, and material resources to key causes. One of its most famous programs is the ParticipACTION initiative. ParticipACTION was established the same year the first definition of social marketing was published. For the past quarter century, ParticipACTION has promoted physical activity, and its work is recognized around the world. The program's success has been attributed to its clear and specific objectives, ability to foster corporate partnerships, and its focused media strategy and high-quality messages. The latter created so much goodwill that ParticipACTION never paid a cent for media coverage valued at an estimated $15 million per year.[55]

Choosing the right goal or objective for a social marketing program is critical. Should a family-planning campaign focus on abstinence or birth control? Should a campaign to fight air pollution focus on ride-sharing or mass transit? Social marketing campaigns may have objectives related to changing people's cognitions, values, actions, or behaviours. The following examples illustrate the range of possible objectives.

Cognitive campaigns

- Explain the nutritional value of different foods
- Explain the importance of conservation

Action campaigns

- Attract people for mass immunization

- Motivate people to vote "yes" on a certain issue
- Motivate people to donate blood
- Motivate women to take a pap test

Behavioural campaigns

- Demotivate cigarette smoking
- Demotivate hard drug usage
- Demotivate excessive consumption of alcohol

Value campaigns

- Alter ideas about abortion
- Change attitudes of bigoted people

Social marketing may employ a number of different tactics to achieve its goals.[56] The social marketing planning process follows many of the same steps as for traditional products and services (see Table 22.2). Some key success factors in developing and implementing a social marketing program include:

- Study the literature and previous campaigns.
- Choose target markets that are most ready to respond.
- Promote a single, doable behaviour in clear, simple terms.
- Explain the benefits in compelling terms.
- Make it easy to adopt the behaviour.
- Develop attention-grabbing messages and media.
- Consider an education-entertainment approach.

Given the complexity and challenges of the issues involved with social marketing, it is important to take a long-run view. Social marketing programs take time and may involve a series of phased programs or actions. For example, take the sequence of actions that have been involved in discouraging smoking: cancer reports, labelling of cigarettes, banning cigarette advertising, education about secondary smoke effects, no smoking in homes, no smoking in restaurants, no smoking on planes, raising taxes on cigarettes to pay for anti-smoking campaigns, lawsuits against cigarette companies.

TABLE 22.2	SOCIAL MARKETING PLANNING PROCESS

Where Are We?
- Determine program focus.
- Identify campaign purpose.
- Conduct an analysis of Strengths, Weaknesses, Opportunities, and Threats (SWOT).
- Review past and similar efforts.

Where Do We Want to Go?
- Select target audiences.
- Set objectives and goals.
- Analyze target audiences and the competition.

How Will We Get There?
- Product: Design the market offering.
- Price: Manage costs of behaviour change.
- Distribution: Make the product available.
- Communications: Create messages and choose media.

How Will We Stay on Course?
- Develop a plan for evaluation and monitoring.
- Establish budgets and find funding sources.
- Complete an implementation plan.

The actual success of the social marketing program must be evaluated in terms of the program objectives. Criteria might include the following: high incidence of adoption, high speed of adoption, high continuance of adoption, low cost per unit of adoption, and no major counterproductive consequences.

Marketing Implementation

Table 22.3 summarizes the characteristics of a great marketing company. A marketing company is great not by "what it is," but by "what it does."[57] **Marketing implementation** is the process that turns marketing plans into action assignments and ensures that such assignments are executed in a manner that accomplishes the plan's stated objectives.[58]

A brilliant strategic marketing plan counts for little if it is not implemented properly. Consider the following example:

> A chemical company learned that the customers were not getting good service from any of the competitors. The company decided to make customer service its strategic thrust. When this strategy failed, a post-mortem revealed a number of implementation failures. The customer service department continued to be held in low regard by top management; it was understaffed; and it was used as a dumping ground for weak managers. Furthermore, the company's reward system continued to focus on cost containment and current profitability. The company had failed to make the changes required to carry out its strategy.

Strategy addresses the *what* and *why* of marketing activities; implementation addresses the *who*, *where*, *when*, and *how*. Strategy and implementation are closely related: One layer of strategy implies certain tactical implementation assignments at a lower level. For example, top management's strategic decision to "harvest" a product must be translated into specific actions and assignments.

Thomas Bonoma identified four sets of skills for implementing marketing programs:

1. *Diagnostic skills.* When marketing programs do not fulfill expectations, was it the result of poor strategy or poor implementation? If implementation, what went wrong?

2. *Identification of company level.* Implementation problems can occur in three levels: the marketing function, the marketing program, and the marketing policy level.

3. *Implementation skills.* To implement programs successfully, marketers need other skills: *allocating skills* for budgeting resources, *organizing skills* to develop an effective organization, and *interaction skills* to motivate others to get things done.

4. *Evaluation skills.* Marketers also need monitoring skills to track and evaluate marketing actions.[59]

Companies today are striving to make their marketing operations more efficient and their return on marketing investment more measurable (see Chapter 4). Marketing costs can amount to 20 to 40 percent of a company's total operating budget. Companies recognize the high amount of waste in many practices: too many meetings lasting too long, undue time spent in looking for documents, delays in receiving approvals, and difficulties in coordinating vendor partners.

TABLE 22.3	CHARACTERISTICS OF A GREAT MARKETING COMPANY

- The company selects target markets in which it enjoys superior advantages, and exits or avoids markets where it is intrinsically weak.
- Virtually all the company's employees and departments are customer- and market-minded.
- There is a good working relation between marketing, R&D, and manufacturing.
- There is a good working relation between marketing, sales, and customer service.
- The company has installed incentives designed to lead to the right behaviours.
- The company continuously builds and tracks customer satisfaction and loyalty.
- The company manages a value-delivery system in partnership with strong suppliers and distributors.
- The company is skilled in building its brand name(s) and image.
- The company is flexible in meeting customers' varying requirements.

Most marketing departments use a limited number of unconnected technology tools such as e-mail, spreadsheets, project management software, and customer databases. But unconnected tools cannot deal with the increasingly complex nature of business, the increased number of collaborators, and the global scope of operations. Companies use information technology to improve the management of their marketing resources. They need better templates for marketing processes, better management of marketing assets, and better allocation of marketing resources. Certain repetitive processes can be automated. This drive is going under such names as *marketing resource management* (MRM), *enterprise marketing management* (EMM), and *marketing automation systems* (MAS).[60]

Several software companies now offer software packages to help companies better manage their marketing processes, assets, and resources. The packages are customized so different marketing managers—vice-president of marketing, product and brand managers, field sales managers, marketing communications managers—can do their planning, implementation, and control.

Marketing resource management (MRM) software provides a set of Web-based applications that automate and integrate such activities as project management, campaign management, budget management, asset management, brand management, customer relationship management, and knowledge management. The knowledge management component consists of process templates, how-to wizards, and best practices.

The software packages are Web-hosted and available to users with passwords. They add up to what some have called *desktop marketing* in that marketers can find whatever information and decision structures they need on their computers. The computer will host a dashboard on which marketers can manage their activities. In the next few years, MRM software will enable marketers to greatly improve spending and investment decisions, bring new products to market more quickly, and reduce decision time and costs.

Evaluation and Control

In spite of the need to monitor and control marketing activities, many companies have inadequate control procedures. A study of 75 companies turned up these findings:

- Smaller companies do a poorer job of setting clear objectives and establishing systems to measure performance.
- Less than half the companies studied knew their individual products' profitability. About one-third had no regular review procedures for spotting and deleting weak products.
- Almost half of the companies failed to compare their prices with those of the competition, to analyze their warehousing and distribution costs, to analyze the causes of returned merchandise, to conduct formal evaluations of advertising effectiveness, and to review their sales force's call reports.
- Many companies take four to eight weeks to develop control reports, which are occasionally inaccurate.

Table 22.4 lists four types of marketing control needed by companies: annual-plan control, profitability control, efficiency control, and strategic control. Chapter 4 described how companies can use marketing metrics to analyze marketing plans and their profitability. Annual-plan control aims to ensure that the company achieves the sales, profits, and other goals established in its annual plan. The heart of annual-plan control is management by objectives. Four steps are involved (see Figure 22.5). First, management sets monthly or quarterly goals. Second, management monitors its performance in the marketplace. Third, management determines the causes of serious performance deviations. Fourth, management takes corrective action to close the gaps between goals and performance.

This control model applies to all levels of the organization. Top management sets annual sales and profit goals that become specific goals for lower levels of management. Each product manager is committed to attaining specified levels of sales and costs; each regional district and sales manager and each sales representative is also committed to specific goals. Each period, top management reviews and interprets the results.

FIGURE 22.5

The Control Process

TABLE 22.4	TYPES OF MARKETING CONTROL		
Type of Control	**Prime Responsibility**	**Purpose of Control**	**Approaches**
I. Annual-plan control	Top management Middle management	To examine whether the planned results are being achieved	■ Sales analysis ■ Market share analysis ■ Sales-to-expense ratios ■ Financial analysis ■ Market-based scorecard analysis
II. Profitability control	Marketing controller	To examine where the company is making and losing money	Profitability by: ■ product ■ territory ■ customer ■ segment ■ trade channel ■ order size
III. Efficiency control	Line and staff management Marketing controller	To evaluate and improve the spending efficiency and impact of marketing expenditures	Efficiency of: ■ sales force ■ advertising ■ sales promotion ■ distribution
IV. Strategic control	Top management Marketing auditor	To examine whether the company is pursuing its best opportunities with respect to markets, products, and channels	■ Marketing-effectiveness rating instrument ■ Marketing audit ■ Marketing excellence review ■ Company ethical and social responsibility review

Efficiency Control

Suppose a profitability analysis reveals that the company is earning poor profits in certain products, territories, or markets. Are there more efficient ways to manage the sales force, advertising, sales promotion, and distribution in connection with these marketing entities?

Some companies have established a *marketing controller* position to improve marketing efficiency. Marketing controllers work out of the controller's office but specialize in the marketing side of the business. At companies such as General Foods, DuPont, and Johnson & Johnson, they perform a sophisticated financial analysis of marketing expenditures and results. They examine adherence to profit plans, help prepare brand managers' budgets, measure the efficiency of promotions, analyze media production costs, evaluate customer and geographic profitability, and educate marketing personnel on the financial implications of marketing decisions.[61]

SALES-FORCE EFFICIENCY Sales managers need to monitor the following key indicators of efficiency in their territories:

- Average number of calls per salesperson per day.
- Average sales call time per contact.
- Average revenue per sales call.
- Average cost per sales call.
- Entertainment cost per sales call.
- Percentage of orders per 100 sales calls.
- Number of new customers per period.
- Number of lost customers per period.
- Sales-force cost as a percentage of total sales.

When a company starts investigating sales-force efficiency, it often finds areas for improvement. General Electric reduced the size of one of its divisional sales forces after discovering that its salespeople were calling on customers too often. When a large airline found that its salespeople were both selling and servicing, it transferred the servicing function to lower-paid clerks. Another company conducted time-and-duty studies and found ways to reduce the ratio of idle-to-productive time.

ADVERTISING EFFICIENCY Many managers believe it is almost impossible to measure what they are getting for their advertising dollars; but they should try to keep track of at least the following statistics:

- Advertising cost per thousand target buyers reached by media vehicle.
- Percentage of audience who noted, saw, or associated and read most of each print ad.
- Consumer opinions on the ad's content and effectiveness.
- Before and after measures of attitude toward the product.
- Number of inquiries stimulated by the ad.
- Cost per inquiry.

Management can take a number of steps to improve advertising efficiency, including doing a better job of positioning the product, defining objectives, pretesting messages, using computer technology to guide the selection of media, looking for better media buys, and doing post-testing.

SALES-PROMOTION EFFICIENCY Sales promotion includes dozens of devices for stimulating buyer interest and product trial. To improve sales-promotion efficiency, management should record the costs and sales impact of each promotion. Management should watch the following statistics:

- Percentage of sales sold on deal.
- Display costs per sales dollar.
- Percentage of coupons redeemed.
- Number of inquiries resulting from a demonstration.

A sales-promotion manager can analyze the results of different promotions and advise product managers on the most cost-effective promotions to use.

DISTRIBUTION EFFICIENCY Management needs to search for distribution economies in inventory control, warehouse locations, and transportation modes. It should track such measures as:

- Logistics costs as a percentage of sales.
- Percentage of orders filled correctly.
- Percentage of on-time deliveries.
- Number of billing errors.

Management should strive to reduce inventory while at the same time speeding up the order-to-delivery cycle. That both can be done simultaneously is shown by Dell Computer:

Dell

A customer-customized computer that is ordered from Dell's Web site at 9:00 A.M. on Wednesday can be on the delivery truck by 9:00 P.M. Thursday. In that short period, Dell electronically orders the computer components from its suppliers' warehouses. Equally impressive, Dell gets paid electronically within 24 hours, while Compaq, supplying its computers to retailers, receives payment days later.

One problem is that distribution efficiency declines when the company experiences strong sales increases. Peter Senge describes a situation in which a strong sales surge causes the company to fall behind in meeting delivery dates (see Figure 22.6).[62] This leads customers to bad-mouth the company and eventually sales fall. Management responds by increasing sales-force incentives to secure more orders. The sales force succeeds, but once again the company slips in meeting delivery dates. Management needs to identify the real bottleneck and invest in more production and distribution capacity.

Strategic Control

From time to time, companies need to undertake a critical review of overall marketing goals and effectiveness. Each company should periodically reassess its strategic approach to the marketplace

FIGURE 22.6

Dynamic Interactions Between Sales Orders and Distribution Efficiency

Source: Adapted from Peter M. Senge, *The Fifth Discipline.* ©1990 by Peter M. Senge. Used by permission of Doubleday, a division of Bantam Doubleday Dell Publishing Group, Inc.

with marketing effectiveness reviews and marketing audits. Companies can also perform marketing excellence reviews and ethical/social responsibility reviews.

THE MARKETING EFFECTIVENESS REVIEW A company's or division's marketing effectiveness is reflected in the degree to which it exhibits the five major attributes of a marketing orientation: *customer philosophy, integrated marketing organization, adequate marketing information, strategic orientation,* and *operational efficiency* (see "Marketing Memo: Marketing Effectiveness Review Instrument"). Most companies and divisions receive scores in the fair-to-good range.[63]

Marketing Memo

Marketing Effectiveness Review Instrument

(Check One Answer to Each Question)

Customer Philosophy

A. *Does management recognize the importance of designing the company to serve the needs and wants of chosen markets?*

   0 ___ Management primarily thinks in terms of selling current and new products to whomever will buy them.

   1 ___ Management thinks in terms of serving a wide range of markets and needs with equal effectiveness.

   2 ___ Management thinks in terms of serving the needs and wants of well-defined markets and market segments chosen for their long-run growth and profit potential for the company.

B. *Does management develop different offerings and marketing plans for different segments of the market?*

   0 ___ No.   1 ___ Somewhat.   2 ___ To a large extent.

C. *Does management take a whole marketing-system view (suppliers, channels, competitors, customers, environment) in planning its business?*

   0 ___ No. Management concentrates on selling and servicing its immediate customers.

   1 ___ Somewhat. Management takes a long view of its channels, although the bulk of its effort goes to selling and servicing the immediate customers.

   2 ___ Yes. Management takes a whole marketing-systems view, recognizing the threats and opportunities created for the company by changes in any part of the system.

Integrated Marketing Organization

D. *Is there high-level marketing integration and control of the major marketing functions?*

   0 ___ No. Sales and other marketing functions are not integrated at the top and there is some unproductive conflict.

   1 ___ Somewhat. There is formal integration and control of the major marketing functions but less than satisfactory coordination and cooperation.

   2 ___ Yes. The major marketing functions are effectively integrated.

E. *Does marketing management work well with management in research, manufacturing, purchasing, logistics, and finance?*

   0 ___ No. There are complaints that marketing is unreasonable in the demands and costs it places on other departments.

   1 ___ Somewhat. The relations are amicable, although each department pretty much acts to serve its own interests.

   2 ___ Yes. The departments cooperate effectively and resolve issues in the best interest of the company as a whole.

F. *How well organized is the new-product development process?*

   0 ___ The system is ill-defined and poorly handled.

   1 ___ The system formally exists but lacks sophistication.

   2 ___ The system is well structured and operates on teamwork principles.

Adequate Marketing Information

G. *When were the latest marketing research studies of customers, buying influences, channels, and competitors conducted?*

   0 ___ Several years ago.   2 ___ A few years ago.   3 ___ Recently.

H. *How well does management know the sales potential and profitability of different market segments, customers, territories, products, channels, and order sizes?*

   0 ___ Not at all.   1 ___ Somewhat.   2 ___ Very well.

I. *What effort is expended to measure and improve the cost-effectiveness of different marketing expenditures?*

   0 ___ Little or no effort.   1 ___ Some effort.   2 ___ Substantial effort.

Strategic Orientation

J. *What is the extent of formal marketing planning?*
0 ___ Management conducts little or no formal marketing planning.
1 ___ Management develops an annual marketing plan.
2 ___ Management develops a detailed annual marketing plan and a strategic long-range plan that is updated annually.

K. *How impressive is the current marketing strategy?*
0 ___ The current strategy is not clear.
1 ___ The current strategy is clear and represents a continuation of traditional strategy.
2 ___ The current strategy is clear, innovative, data-based, and well reasoned.

L. *What is the extent of contingency thinking and planning?*
0 ___ Management does little or no contingency thinking.
1 ___ Management does some contingency thinking but little formal contingency planning.
2 ___ Management formally identifies the most important contingencies and develops contingency plans.

Operational Efficiency

M. *How well is the marketing strategy communicated and implemented?*
0 ___ Poorly.   1 ___ Fairly.   2 ___ Successfully.

N. *Is management doing an effective job with its marketing resources?*
0 ___ No. The marketing resources are inadequate for the job to be done.
1 ___ Somewhat. The marketing resources are adequate but they are not employed optimally.
2 ___ Yes. The marketing resources are adequate and are employed efficiently.

O. *Does management show a good capacity to react quickly and effectively to on-the-spot developments?*
0 ___ No. Sales and market information is not very current and management reaction time is slow.
1 ___ Somewhat. Management receives fairly up-to-date sales and market information; management reaction time varies.
2 ___ Yes. Management has installed systems yielding highly current information and fast reaction time.

Total Score

The instrument is used in the following way. The appropriate answer is checked for each question. The scores are added—the total will be somewhere between 0 and 30. The following scale shows the level of marketing effectiveness:

0–5 = None	11–15 = Fair	21–25 = Very good
6–10 = Poor	16–20 = Good	26–30 = Superior

Source: Philip Kotler, "From Sales Obsession to Marketing Effectiveness," *Harvard Business Review* (November–December 1977): 67–75.
Copyright © 1977 by the President and Fellows of Harvard College; all rights reserved.

THE MARKETING AUDIT The average North American corporation loses half of its customers in five years, half of its employees in four years, and half of its investors in less than one year. Clearly, this points to some weaknesses. Companies that discover weaknesses should undertake a thorough study known as a marketing audit.[64] A **marketing audit** is a comprehensive, systematic, independent, and periodic examination of a company's or business unit's marketing environment, objectives, strategies, and activities with a view to determining problem areas and opportunities and recommending a plan of action to improve the company's marketing performance.

Let us examine the marketing audit's four characteristics:

1. *Comprehensive.* The marketing audit covers all the major marketing activities of a business, not just a few trouble spots. It would be called a functional audit if it covered only the sales force, pricing, or some other marketing activity. Although functional audits are useful, they sometimes mislead management. Excessive sales-force turnover, for example, could be a symptom not of poor sales-force training or compensation but of weak company products and promotion. A comprehensive marketing audit usually is more effective in locating the real source of problems.

2. *Systematic.* The marketing audit is an orderly examination of the organization's macro- and micro-marketing environments, marketing objectives and strategies, marketing systems, and specific activities. The audit indicates the most-needed improvements, which are then incorporated into a corrective action plan involving both short-run and long-run steps to improve overall effectiveness.

3. *Independent.* A marketing audit can be conducted in six ways: self-audit, audit from across, audit from above, company auditing office, company task-force audit, and outsider audit. Self-audits, in which managers use a checklist to rate their own operations, lack objectivity and independence.[65] The 3M Company has made good use of a corporate auditing office, which provides marketing audit services to divisions on request.[66] Generally speaking, however, the best audits come from outside consultants who have the necessary objectivity, broad experience in a number of industries, some familiarity with the industry being audited, and the undivided time and attention to give to the audit.

4. *Periodic.* Typically, marketing audits are initiated only after sales have turned down, sales-force morale has fallen, and other problems have occurred. Companies are thrown into a crisis partly because they failed to review their marketing operations during good times. A periodic marketing audit can benefit companies in good health as well as those in trouble.

A marketing audit starts with a meeting between the company officer(s) and the marketing auditor(s) to work out an agreement on the audit's objectives, coverage, depth, data sources, report format, and time frame. A detailed plan regarding who is to be interviewed, the questions to be asked, the time and place of contact, and so on is prepared so that auditing time and cost are kept to a minimum. The cardinal rule in marketing auditing is: Do not rely solely on company managers for data and opinions. Customers, dealers, and other outside groups must also be interviewed. Many companies do not really know how their customers and dealers see them, nor do they fully understand customer needs.

The marketing audit examines six major components of the company's marketing situation. The major questions are listed in Table 22.5.

TABLE 22.5	COMPONENTS OF A MARKETING AUDIT

Part I. Marketing Environment Audit

Macroenvironment

A. Demographic	What major demographic developments and trends pose opportunities or threats to this company? What actions has the company taken in response to these developments and trends?
B. Economic	What major developments in income, prices, savings, and credit will affect the company? What actions has the company been taking in response to these developments and trends?
C. Environmental	What is the outlook for the cost and availability of natural resources and energy needed by the company? What concerns have been expressed about the company's role in pollution and conservation, and what steps has the company taken?
D. Technological	What major changes are occurring in product and process technology? What is the company's position in these technologies? What major generic substitutes might replace this product?
E. Political	What changes in laws and regulations might affect marketing strategy and tactics? What is happening in the areas of pollution control, equal employment opportunity, product safety, advertising, price control, and so forth, that affects marketing strategy?
F. Cultural	What is the public's attitude toward business and toward the company's products? What changes in customer lifestyles and values might affect the company?

Task Environment

A. Markets	What is happening to market size, growth, geographical distribution, and profits? What are the major market segments?
B. Customers	What are the customers' needs and buying processes? How do customers and prospects rate the company and its competitors on reputation, product quality, service, sales force, and price? How do different customer segments make their buying decisions?
C. Competitors	Who are the major competitors? What are their objectives, strategies, strengths, weaknesses, sizes, and market shares? What trends will affect future competition and substitutes for the company's products?
D. Distribution and Dealers	What are the main trade channels for bringing products to customers? What are the efficiency levels and growth potentials of the different trade channels?
E. Suppliers	What is the outlook for the availability of key resources used in production? What trends are occurring among suppliers?

TABLE 22.5	*(continued)*

F. Facilitators and Marketing Firms — What is the cost and availability outlook for transportation services, warehousing facilities, and financial resources? How effective are the company's advertising agencies and marketing research firms?

G. Publics — Which publics represent particular opportunities or problems for the company? What steps has the company taken to deal effectively with each public?

Part II. Marketing Strategy Audit

A. Business Mission — Is the business mission clearly stated in market-oriented terms? Is it feasible?

B. Marketing Objectives and Goals — Are the company and marketing objectives and goals stated clearly enough to guide marketing planning and performance measurement? Are the marketing objectives appropriate, given the company's competitive position, resources, and opportunities?

C. Strategy — Has the management articulated a clear marketing strategy for achieving its marketing objectives? Is the strategy convincing? Is the strategy appropriate to the stage of the product life cycle, competitors' strategies, and the state of the economy? Is the company using the best basis for market segmentation? Does it have clear criteria for rating the segments and choosing the best ones? Has it developed accurate profiles of each target segment? Has the company developed an effective positioning and marketing mix for each target segment? Are marketing resources allocated optimally to the major elements of the marketing mix? Are enough resources or too many resources budgeted to accomplish the marketing objectives?

Part III. Marketing Organization Audit

A. Formal Structure — Does the marketing vice-president have adequate authority and responsibility for company activities that affect customers' satisfaction? Are the marketing activities optimally structured along functional, product, segment, end-user, and geographical lines?

B. Functional Efficiency — Are there good communication and working relations between marketing and sales? Is the product-management system working effectively? Are product managers able to plan profits or only sales volume? Are there any groups in marketing that need more training, motivation, supervision, or evaluation?

C. Interface Efficiency — Are there any problems between marketing and manufacturing, R&D, purchasing, finance, accounting, and/or legal that need attention?

Part IV. Marketing Systems Audit

A. Marketing Information System — Is the marketing intelligence system producing accurate, sufficient, and timely information about market-place developments with respect to customers, prospects, distributors and dealers, competitors, suppliers, and various publics? Are company decision makers asking for enough marketing research, and are they using the results? Is the company employing the best methods for market measurement and sales forecasting?

B. Marketing Planning Systems — Is the marketing planning system well conceived and effectively used? Do marketers have decision support systems available? Does the planning system result in acceptable sales targets and quotas?

C. Marketing Control System — Are the control procedures adequate to ensure that the annual plan objectives are being achieved? Does management periodically analyze the profitability of products, markets, territories, and channels of distribution? Are marketing costs and productivity periodically examined?

D. New-Product Development System — Is the company well organized to gather, generate, and screen new-product ideas? Does the company do adequate concept research and business analysis before investing in new ideas? Does the company carry out adequate product and market testing before launching new products?

PART V. Marketing Productivity Audit

A. Profitability Analysis — What is the profitability of the company's different products, markets, territories, and channels of distribution? Should the company enter, expand, contract, or withdraw from any business segments?

B. Cost-Effectiveness Analysis — Do any marketing activities seem to have excessive costs? Can cost-reducing steps be taken?

Part VI. Marketing Function Audits

A. Products — What are the company's product-line objectives? Are they sound? Is the current product line meeting the objectives? Should the product line be stretched or contracted upward, downward, or both ways? Which products should be phased out? Which products should be added? What are the buyers' knowledge and attitudes toward the company's and competitors' product quality, features, styling, brand names, and so on? What areas of product and brand strategy need improvement?

TABLE 22.5	*(continued)*
B. Price	What are the company's pricing objectives, policies, strategies, and procedures? To what extent are prices set on cost, demand, and competitive criteria? Do the customers see the company's prices as being in line with the value of its offer? What does management know about the price elasticity of demand, experience-curve effects, and competitors' prices and pricing policies? To what extent are price policies compatible with the needs of distributors and dealers, suppliers, and government regulation?
C. Distribution	What are the company's distribution objectives and strategies? Is there adequate market coverage and service? How effective are distributors, dealers, manufacturers' representatives, brokers, agents, and others? Should the company consider changing its distribution channels?
D. Advertising, Sales Promotion, Publicity, and Direct Marketing	What are the organization's advertising objectives? Are they sound? Is the right amount being spent on advertising? Are the ad themes and copy effective? What do customers and the public think about the advertising? Are the advertising media well chosen? Is the internal advertising staff adequate? Is the sales-promotion budget adequate? Is there effective and sufficient use of sales-promotion tools such as samples, coupons, displays, and sales contests? Is the public relations staff competent and creative? Is the company making enough use of direct, online, and database marketing?
E. Sales Force	What are the sales force's objectives? Is the sales force large enough to accomplish the company's objectives? Is the sales force organized along the proper principles of specialization (territory, market, product)? Are there enough (or too many) sales managers to guide the field sales representatives? Do the sales-compensation level and structure provide adequate incentive and reward? Does the sales force show high morale, ability, and effort? Are the procedures adequate for setting quotas and evaluating performance? How does the company's sales force compare to competitors' sales forces?

THE MARKETING EXCELLENCE REVIEW Companies can use another instrument to rate their performance in relation to the best practices of high-performing businesses. The three columns in Table 22.6 distinguish among poor, good, and excellent business and marketing practices. Management can place a checkmark to indicate its perception of where the business stands. The resulting profile exposes weaknesses and strengths, highlighting where the company might make changes to become a truly outstanding player in the marketplace.

The Future of Marketing

Top management has recognized that past marketing has been highly wasteful and is demanding more accountability from marketing. "Marketing Memo: The Major Marketing Weaknesses" summarizes the major deficiencies that companies have in marketing, how to spot these deficiencies, and what to do about them.

Going forward, there are a number of imperatives to achieve marketing excellence. Marketing must be "holistic" and less departmental. Marketers must achieve larger influence in the company if they are to be the main architect of business strategy. Marketers must continuously create new ideas if the company is to prosper in a hypercompetitive economy. Marketers must strive for customer insight and treat customers differently but appropriately. Marketers must build their brands through performance, more than through promotion. Marketers must go electronic and win through building superior information and communication systems.

In these ways, modern marketing will continue to evolve and confront new challenges and opportunities. As a result, the coming years will see:

- The demise of the marketing department and the rise of holistic marketing.
- The demise of free-spending marketing and the rise of ROI marketing.
- The demise of marketing intuition and the rise of marketing science.
- The demise of manual marketing and the rise of automated marketing.
- The demise of mass marketing and the rise of precision marketing.

To accomplish these changes and become truly holistic with marketing, a new set of skills and competencies is needed. Proficiency will be demanded in areas such as:

- Customer relationship management (CRM).

TABLE 22.6	A MARKETING EXCELLENCE REVIEW: BEST PRACTICES	
Poor	**Good**	**Excellent**
Product-Driven	Market-Driven	Market-Driving
Mass-Market Oriented	Segment Oriented	Niche Oriented and Customer Oriented
Product Offer	Augmented Product Offer	Customer Solutions Offer
Average Product Quality	Better than Average	Legendary
Average Service Quality	Better than Average	Legendary
End-Product Oriented	Core-Product Oriented	Core-Competency Oriented
Function Oriented	Process Oriented	Outcome Oriented
Reacting to Competitors	Benchmarking Competitors	Leapfrogging Competitors
Supplier Exploitation	Supplier Preference	Supplier Partnership
Dealer Exploitation	Dealer Support	Dealer Partnership
Price-Driven	Quality-Driven	Value-Driven
Average Speed	Better than Average	Legendary
Hierarchy	Network	Teamwork
Vertically Integrated	Flattened Organization	Strategic Alliances
Shareholder-Driven	Stakeholder-Driven	Societally Driven

- Partner relationship management (PRM).
- Database marketing and data-mining.
- Contact centre management and telemarketing.
- Public relations marketing (including event and sponsorship marketing).
- Brand building and brand asset management.
- Experiential marketing.
- Integrated marketing communications.
- Profitability analysis by segment, customer, and channel.

It is an exciting time for marketing. In the relentless pursuit of marketing superiority and dominance, new rules and practices are emerging. The benefits of successful twenty-first-century marketing are many, but will only come with hard work, insight, and inspiration. The words of nineteenth-century American author Ralph Waldo Emerson may never be more true: "This time like all times is a good one, if we but know what to do with it."

Marketing Memo

Major Marketing Weaknesses

A number of "deadly sins" signal that the marketing program is in trouble. Here are ten deadly sins, the signs, and some solutions.

Deadly Sin: The company is not sufficiently market focused and customer driven.

Signs: Poor identification of market segments, poor prioritization of market segments, no market segment managers, employees who think it is the job of marketing and sales to serve customers, no training program to create a customer culture, no incentives to treat the customer especially well.

Solutions: Use more advanced segmentation techniques, prioritize segments, specialize the sales force, develop a clear hierarchy of company values, foster more "customer consciousness" in employees and company agents, make it easy for customers to reach the company and respond quickly to any communication.

Deadly Sin: The company does not fully understand its target customers.

Signs: Latest study of customers is three years old, customers are not buying your product like they once did, competitors' products are selling better, high level of customer returns and complaints.

Solutions: Do more sophisticated consumer research, use more analytical techniques, establish customer and dealer panels, use customer relationship software, do data mining.

Deadly Sin: The company needs to better define and monitor its competitors.

Signs: The company focuses on near competitors, misses distant competitors and disruptive technologies, no system for gathering and distributing competitive intelligence.

Solutions: Establish an office for competitive intelligence, hire competitors' people, watch for technology that might affect the company, prepare offerings like competitors'.

Deadly Sin: The company does not properly manage relationships with stakeholders.

Signs: Employees, dealers, and investors are not happy; good suppliers do not come.

Solutions: Move from zero-sum thinking to positive-sum thinking; do a better job of managing employees, supplier relations, distributors, dealers, and investors.

Deadly Sin: The company is not good at finding new opportunities.

Signs: The company has not identified any exciting new opportunities for years, the new ideas the company has launched have largely failed.

Solutions: Set up a system for stimulating the flow of new ideas.

Deadly Sin: The company's marketing planning process is deficient.

Signs: The marketing plan format does not have the right components, there is no way to estimate the financial implications of different strategies, there is no contingency planning.

Solutions: Establish a standard format including situational analysis, SWOT, major issues, objectives, strategy, tactics, budgets, and controls; ask marketers what changes they would make if they were given 20 percent more or less budget; run an annual marketing awards program with prizes for best plans and performance.

Deadly Sin: Product and service policies need tightening.

Signs: Too many products and many are losing money, the company is giving away too many services, the company is poor at cross-selling products and services.

Solutions: Establish a system to track weak products and fix or drop them, offer and price services at different levels, improve processes for cross-selling and up-selling.

Deadly Sin: The company's brand-building and communication skills are weak.

Signs: The target market does not know much about the company, the brand is not seen as distinctive, the company allocates its budget to the same marketing tools in about the same proportion each year, there is little evaluation of the ROI impact of promotions.

Solutions: Improve brand-building strategies and measurement of results, shift money into effective marketing instruments, require marketers to estimate the ROI impact in advance of funding requests.

Deadly Sin: The company is not organized for effective and efficient marketing.

Signs: Staff lacks twenty-first-century marketing skills, bad vibes between marketing/sales and other departments.

Solutions: Appoint a strong leader and build new skills in the marketing department, improve marketing's relations with other departments.

Deadly Sin: The company has not made maximum use of technology.

Signs: Minimal use of the Internet, outdated sales automation system, no market automation, no decision-support models, no marketing dashboards.

Solutions: Use the Internet more, improve the sales automation system, apply market automation to routine decisions, develop formal marketing decision models and marketing dashboards.

Source: Philip Kotler, *Ten Deadly Marketing Sins: Signs and Solutions* (Hoboken, NJ: John Wiley & Sons, 2004).

SUMMARY

1. The modern marketing department has evolved through the years from a simple a sales department to an organizational structure where marketing personnel work mainly on cross-disciplinary teams.

2. Modern marketing departments can be organized in a number of ways. Some companies are organized by functional specialization, while others focus on geography and regionalization. Still others emphasize product and brand management or market-segment management. Some companies establish a matrix organization consisting of both product and market managers. Finally, some companies have strong corporate marketing, others have limited corporate marketing, and still others place marketing only in the divisions.

3. Effective modern marketing organizations are marked by a strong cooperation and customer focus among the company's departments: marketing, R&D, engineering, purchasing, manufacturing, operations, finance, accounting, and credit.

4. Companies must practise social responsibility through their legal, ethical, and social words and actions. Cause marketing can be a means for companies to productively link social responsibility to consumer marketing programs. Social marketing is done by a nonprofit or government organization to directly address a social problem or cause.

5. A brilliant strategic marketing plan counts for little if it is not implemented properly. Implementing marketing plans calls for skills in recognizing and diagnosing a problem, assessing the company level where the problem exists, implementation skills, and skills in evaluating the results.

6. The marketing department has to monitor and control marketing activities continuously. Efficiency control focuses on finding ways to increase the efficiency of the sales force, advertising, sales promotion, and distribution. Strategic control entails a periodic reassessment of the company and its strategic approach to the marketplace, using the tools of the marketing effectiveness and excellence reviews and the marketing audit.

APPLICATIONS

Marketing Debate: Is Marketing Management an Art or a Science?

Some marketing observers maintain that good marketing is something that is more than anything an art and does not lend itself to rigorous analysis and deliberation. Others strongly disagree and contend that marketing management is a highly disciplined enterprise that shares much in common with other business disciplines.

Take a position: Marketing management is largely an artistic exercise and therefore highly subjective versus Marketing management is largely a scientific exercise with well-established guidelines and criteria.

Marketing Discussion

How does cause or corporate societal marketing affect your personal consumer behaviour? Do you ever buy or not buy any products or services from a company because of its environmental policies or programs? Why or why not?

Marketing Spotlight: Microsoft

Microsoft was founded in 1975, when Bill Gates dropped out of Harvard at age 19 to work with high school friend Paul Allen on a version of the BASIC programming language. After moving the company from Albuquerque, New Mexico, to Seattle, Washington, in 1979, Gates and Allen began writing operating system software. What happened to the company since its founding is a well-known and oft-told story. Here are a few of the key strategies that enabled Microsoft to achieve such remarkable growth in the very competitive computer industry.

Product Innovation: Microsoft achieved early success because of a single product innovation. In 1980, IBM gave Microsoft a contract to write the operating system for its new PCs, which led to the creation of Microsoft Disk Operating System (MS-DOS). Because other computer manufacturers wanted compatibility with IBM machines, Microsoft was soon adopted as the standard PC operating system.

Brand-Extension Strategy: Microsoft used its strong brand name to launch new software products such as Microsoft Word, Microsoft Office, and Microsoft Internet Explorer. In 1989, Microsoft became the world's largest software seller, boasting the broadest array of software products and applications as well as the highest profit margin in the industry (close to 25 percent). Launching a new product under a strong existing brand name gives the new product instant recognition and credibility with much less advertising outlay. Microsoft currently has the second most valuable brand (worth US$103 billion) behind Procter & Gamble.

Heavy Advertising: As the company matured and sought new avenues for growth, it increased both product and brand advertising. In 1994, the company made two major moves: It hired the head of marketing and advertising from Procter & Gamble, and it developed its first global advertising campaign. The campaign doubled the company's ad budget to US$100 million, and the following year that figure ballooned to US$200 million for the Windows 95 launch. Today, Microsoft routinely spends US$50 million to market a single product. The company recently spent US$150 million to promote its newest version of Microsoft Office. Its ads emphasize the latent potential to achieve more when customers use Microsoft products with campaigns entitled "Yes You Can," "Software for the Agile Business," and "Realize Your Potential."

Competitive Toughness: Microsoft's aggressive competitive practices enabled the company to establish a leadership role in many product categories, but they also led to legal battles. Microsoft settled an antitrust lawsuit from the U.S. Justice Department over claims that it had limited consumer choice and stifled competition in part by bundling software, such as Internet Explorer, with its operating system. Similar lawsuits in Europe, Japan, and with various U.S. State Attorneys General are pending. Given how Microsoft supplanted IBM in the industry that IBM created, many potential business partners in media, technology, and communications are now wary of Microsoft.

Product Expansion: Microsoft quickly expanded its business beyond operating systems. The company moved from desktops to servers, from desktops to portables, and into consumer electronics. After overcoming initial reluctance to embrace the Internet, Microsoft developed the Internet Explorer Web browser as an answer to Netscape and the Web portal Microsoft Network (MSN) to compete with Yahoo! and AOL. MSN is the second-largest Internet service provider, but it has only about one-third the subscribers of leader AOL. Expanding into media, Microsoft formed a joint venture with NBC to create the cable station MSNBC, which features news, financial, and talk-show programming. The company rolled out a video game console called Xbox intended to compete with advanced game systems from Sony and Nintendo.

Product Integration: Microsoft uses integration between its products to boost cross-selling. The company's enterprise software integrates with its desktop software, and its desktop Windows platform integrates with its PocketPC PDA platform. A wristwatch with Microsoft software can receive messages from the desktop version of Microsoft Outlook. Microsoft recently gave away copies of its newest Microsoft Office Suite to enterprise clients. Every time users of the free copy tried to access some of the more innovative collaborative features of Office, they got a notice telling them that they needed Microsoft Exchange Server (an expensive enterprise product that helps Microsoft solidify its hold on the customer).

Microsoft is continuing on the path of deeper integration. Its .NET (pronounced "dot-net") concept is designed to merge Windows with the Internet directly. Microsoft.Net will allow multiple devices—PCs, wireless phones, pagers, digital cameras, PDAs, and other "smart devices"—to work together over Web connections with unprecedented ease. The company is also working on its Trustworthy Computing initiative to help increase the security of computers and prevent unauthorized access to files and computers. Meanwhile, the company continues to expand in new ways with forays into online music sales, search engines, and cell phones.

DISCUSSION QUESTIONS

1. What have been the key success factors for Microsoft?

2. Where is Microsoft vulnerable? What should it watch out for?

3. What recommendations would you make to senior marketing executives going forward? What should the company be sure to do with its marketing?

Sources: "What's in a Name?" *Forbes*, April 19, 2004, p. 59; Adam Lashinsky, "Shootout in Gadget Land," *Fortune*, November 10, 2003, p. 74; Morag Cuddeford Jones, "IT's a Lifestyle for Nick Barley at Microsoft," *Brand Strategy*, March 2004, pp. 18–19.

NOTES

Chapter 1

1. Norma Ramage, "Big Rock Brewery Campaign Looks Back to Go Forward," *Marketing Magazine*, July 7, 2005.

2. "AMA Adopts New Definition of Marketing," *Marketing News*, www.marketingpower.com/content21257.php, September 15, 2004 (viewed August 22, 2005).

3. Peter Drucker, *Management: Tasks, Responsibilities, Practices* (New York: Harper and Row, 1973), pp. 64–65.

4. Statistics Canada, "Gross Domestic Product at Basic Prices, Primary Industries," www.statcan.ca/english/Pgdb/prim03.htm (viewed June 14, 2004).

5. Industry Canada, "Gross Domestic Product (GDP) by Industry by Services-Producing Sectors of the Canadian Economy 1997–2003," http://strategis.ic.gc.ca/sc_ecnmy/sio/cis41-91gdpe.html (viewed June 14, 2004).

6. Philip Kotler, "Dream Vacations: The Booming Market for Designed Experiences," *The Futurist* (October 1984): 7–13; B. Joseph Pine II and James Gilmore, *The Experience Economy* (Boston: Harvard Business School Press, 1999); and Bernd Schmitt, *Experience Marketing* (New York: Free Press, 1999).

7. Irving J. Rein, Philip Kotler, and Martin Stoller, *High Visibility* (Chicago: NTC Publishers, 1998).

8. Philip Kotler, Irving J. Rein, and Donald Haider, *Marketing Places: Attracting Investment, Industry, and Tourism to Cities, States, and Nations* (New York: Free Press, 1993); and *Marketing Places Europe* (London: Financial Times Prentice-Hall, 1999).

9. Carl Shapiro and Hal R. Varian, "Versioning: The Smart Way to Sell Information," *Harvard Business Review* (November–December 1998): pp. 106–114.

10. John R. Brandt, "Dare to Be Different," *Chief Executive* (May 2003): pp. 34–38.

11. Jeffrey Rayport and John Sviokla, "Managing in the Marketspace," *Harvard Business Review* (November–December 1994): pp. 141–150. Also see their "Exploring the Virtual Value Chain," *Harvard Business Review* (November–December 1995): pp. 75–85.

12. Mohan Sawhney, *Seven Steps to Nirvana* (New York: McGraw-Hill, 2001).

13. Jean-Marie Dru, *Beyond Disruption: Changing the Rules in the Marketplace*, John Wiley & Sons, 2002; Sam Hill and Glenn Rifkin, *Radical Marketing* (New York: HarperBusiness, 1999).

14. Lisa D'Innocenzo, "A Market of One: Whether You Market Cars, Clothes or Credit, If You're Not Customizing for Customers, You're Not Keeping Up," *Strategy Magazine*, January 26, 2004, www.strategymag.com/articles/magazine/20040126/customization.html?word=customization (viewed June 15, 2004).

15. Adam Lashinsky, "Shootout in Gadget Land," *Fortune*, November 10, 2003, pp. 77–86.

16. Gerry Khermouch, "Breaking into the Name Game," *Business Week*, April 7, 2003, p. 54; Anonymous, "China's Challenge," *Marketing Week*, October 2, 2003, pp. 22–24.

17. Bruce I. Newman, ed., *Handbook of Political Marketing* (Thousand Oaks, CA: Sage Publications, 1999); and Bruce I. Newman, *The Mass Marketing of Politics* (Thousand Oaks, CA: Sage Publications, 1999).

18. John B. McKitterick, "What Is the Marketing Management Concept?" In *The Frontiers of Marketing Thought and Action* (Chicago: American Marketing Association, 1957), pp. 71–82; Fred J. Borch, "The Marketing Philosophy as a Way of Business Life," *The Marketing Concept: Its Meaning to Management* (Marketing series, no. 99) (New York: American Management Association, 1957), pp. 3–5; Robert J. Keith, "The Marketing Revolution," *Journal of Marketing* (January 1960): 35–38.

19. Levitt, "Marketing Myopia," *Harvard Business Review*, (July–August 1960), p. 50.

20. Ajay K. Kohli and Bernard J. Jaworski, "Market Orientation: The Construct, Research Propositions, and Managerial Implications," *Journal of Marketing* (April 1990): pp. 1–18; John C. Narver and Stanley F. Slater, "The Effect of a Market Orientation on Business Profitability," *Journal of Marketing* (October 1990): pp. 20–35; Stanley F. Slater and John C. Narver, "Market Orientation, Customer Value, and Superior Performance," *Business Horizons*, March–April 1994, 22–28; A. Pelham and D. Wilson, "A Longitudinal Study of the Impact of Market Structure, Firm Structure, Strategy and Market Orientation Culture on Dimensions of Business Performance," *Journal of the Academy of Marketing Science* 24, no. 1, (1996): pp. 27–43; Rohit Deshpande and John U. Farley, "Measuring Market Orientation: Generalization and Synthesis," *Journal of Market-Focused Management* 2 (1998): 213–232.

21. John C. Narver, Stanley F. Slater, and Douglas L. MacLachlan, "Total Market Orientation, Business Performance, and Innovation," Working Paper Series, Marketing Science Institute, Report No. 00-116, 2000, pp. 1–34. See also Ken Matsuno and John T. Mentzer, "The Effects of Strategy Type on the Market Orientation—Performance Relationship," *Journal or Marketing* (October 2000): pp. 1–16.

22. Helen Branswell, "Children with Nut Allergies Get Bitter Lesson in Commerce from Nestlé," *Canadian Press*, April 24, 2000; and "Nestlé Reverses Decision, Will Continue to Make Nut-Free Chocolate Bars," *Canadian Press*, from the Ottawa Anaphylaxis Support Group Web site, www.ottawaasg.com/media/nestle424.htm and www.ottawaasg.com/media/cp.htm.

23. Christian Honburg, John P. Workman Jr., and Harley Krohmen, "Marketings Influence Within the Firm," *Journal of Marketing* (January 1999): pp. 1–15.

24. Jochen Zeitz, "This Shoe's One Cool Cat," *Brandweek*, October 20, 2003, pp. M58–M61; Kevin J. O'Brien, "Focusing On Armchair Athletes, Puma Becomes a Leader," *New York Times*, March 12, 2004.

25. Evert Gummesson, *Total Relationship Marketing* (Boston: Butterworth-Heinemann, 1999); Regis McKenna, *Relationship Marketing* (Reading, MA: Addison-Wesley, 1991); Martin Christopher, Adrian Payne, and David Ballantyne, *Relationship Marketing: Bringing Quality, Customer Service, and Marketing Together* (Oxford, U.K: Butterworth-Heinemann, 1991). "Imports, exports and trade balance of goods on a balance-of-payment basis, by country or country grouping, " Statistics Canada, November 10, 2005, www40.statcan.ca/101/cst01/gblec02a.htm.

26. James C. Anderson, Hakan Hakansson, and Jan Johanson, "Dyadic Business Relationships within a Business Network Context," *Journal of Marketing* (October 15, 1994): 1–15.

27. Laura Mazur, "Personal Touch Is Now Crucial to Growing Profits," *Marketing*, November 27, 2003, p. 18.

28. Samson Okalow, "Packaged Goods Go Direct," *Strategy Magazine*, June 2, 2003, www.strategymag.com/articles/d+i/20030602/packaged.html?word=relationship%20marketing (viewed June 15, 2004).

29. Neil H. Borden, "The Concept of the Marketing Mix," *Journal of Advertising Research* 4 (June): 2–7. For another framework, see George S. Day, "The Capabilities of Market-Driven Organizations," *Journal of Marketing* 58, no. 4 (October 1994): 37–52.

30. E. Jerome McCarthy, *Basic Marketing: A Managerial Approach*, 12th ed. (Homewood, IL: Irwin, 1996). Two alternative classifications are worth noting. Frey proposed that all marketing decision

variables could be categorized into two factors: the offering (product, packaging, brand, price, and service) and methods and tools (distribution channels, personal selling, advertising, sales promotion, and publicity). See Albert W. Frey, *Advertising*, 3rd ed. (New York: Ronald Press, 1961), p. 30. Lazer and Kelly proposed a three-factor classification: goods and services mix, distribution mix, and communications mix. See William Lazer and Eugene J. Kelly, *Managerial Marketing: Perspectives and Viewpoints*, rev. ed. (Homewood, IL: Irwin, 1962), p. 413.

31. Robert Lauterborn, "New Marketing Litany: 4P's Passé; C-Words Take Over," *Advertising Age*, October 1, 1990, p. 26.

32. Gregory Solman, "Trailers, Bots and Emails Tout Gory Movies to Teens," *Adweek*, October 6, 2003, p. 10.

33. William Greider, "Victory at McDonald's," *The Nation*, August 18, 2003.

34. Hanish Pringle and Marjorie Thompson, *Brand Soul: How Cause-Related Marketing Builds Brands* (New York: John Wiley & Sons, 1999); Richard Earle, *The Art of Cause Marketing* (Lincolnwood, IL: NTC, 2000).

35. CIBC Web site, www.cibc.com (viewed June15, 2004); Canadian Breast Cancer Foundation Run for the Cure Website, www.cbcfrunforthecure.org (viewed June 15, 2004).

36. Private conversation with Carpenter.

37. Larry Selden and Geoffrey Colvin, *Angel Customers & Demon Customers*, Portfolio (Penguin), 2003.

38. Goran Svensson, "Beyond Global Marketing and the Globalization of Marketing Activities," *Management Decision*, 2002, 40 (6), pp. 574–583.

39. Jonathan Glancey, "The Private World of the Walkman," *The Guardian*, October 11, 1999.

40. Joann Muller, "Ford: Why It's Worse Than You Think," *Business Week*, June 25, 2001; Ford *1999 Annual Report*; Greg Keenan, "Six Degrees of Perfection," *The Globe and Mail*, December 20, 2000.

Chapter 2

1. Keith H. Hammonds, "Michael Porter's Big Ideas," *Fast Company*, March 2001, pp. 150–154.

2. www.H&M.com and Eric Sylvers, "Cut-Rate Swedish Retailers Enters the Italian Market," *The New York Times*, August 27, 2003, p. W.1.

3. Scott Gardiner, "Old Navy Sails to Canada's Shores," *Marketing Magazine*, April 9, 2001; Lisa D'Innocenzo, "Niche Marketing Key to Successful Stateside Retail Expansion," *Strategy Magazine*, March 11, 2002, pp 1–2; Gap Inc. Web page, www.gap.com/asp/home_gap.html?wdid=0.

4. Nirmalya Kumar, *Marketing as Strategy: The CEO's Agenda for Driving Growth and Innovation* (Boston: Harvard Business School Press, 2004).

5. Frederick E. Webster, Jr., "The Future Role of Marketing in the Organization," in *Reflections on the Futures of Marketing*, edited by Donald R. Lehmann and Katherine Jocz (Cambridge, MA: Marketing Science Institute, 1997), pp. 39–66.

6. Michael E. Porter, *Competitive Advantage: Creating and Sustaining Superior Performance* (New York: The Free Press, 1985).

7. Robert Hiebeler, Thomas B. Kelly, and Charles Ketteman, *Best Practices: Building Your Business with Customer-Focused Solutions* (New York: Simon and Schuster, 1998).

8. Michael Hammer and James Champy, *Reengineering the Corporation* (New York: HarperBusiness, 1993).

9. George Stalk, "Competing on Capability: The New Rules of Corporate Strategy," *Harvard Business Review* (March–April 1992): 57–69; Benson P. Shapiro, V. Kasturi Rangan, and John J. Sviokla, "Staple Yourself to an Order," *Harvard Business Review* (July–August 1992): 113–122.

10. Jon R. Katzenbach and Douglas K. Smith, *The Wisdom of Teams: Creating the High-Performance Organization* (Boston: Harvard Business School Press, 1993); Hammer and Champy, *Reengineering the Corporation*.

11. Michael Johnsen, "Profiting from a First-Place Focus," *Drug Store News*, January 20, 2003, p. 26.

12. Myron Magnet, "The New Golden Rule of Business," *Fortune*, November 28, 1994, pp. 60–64.

13. "Canadian Tire and NAPA Canada Enter into Product Supply and Technology Agreement for Select Automotive Hard Parts," UAP Press Release, November 4, 2002, www.uapinc.com (viewed July 5, 2004).

14. C. K. Prahalad and Gary Hamel, "The Core Competence of the Corporation," *Harvard Business Review*, (May–June 1990): 79–91.

15. John Menary "Institutional Report Form Questions (for the Year April 2002–March 2003)," Canada Foundation for Innovation Web site, www.innovation.ca (viewed July 7, 2004); Hospital for Sick Children Web site, www.sickkids.on.ca (viewed July 7, 2004).

16. George S. Day, "The Capabilities of Market-Driven Organizations," *Journal of Marketing* (October 1994): 38.

17. *Pew Internet and American Life Project Survey*, November–December 2000.

18. Kasuaki Ushikubo, "A Method of Structure Analysis for Developing Product Concepts and Its Applications," *European Research*, 14 (4), 1986, 174–175.

19. Jesus Sanchez, "Kodak Cuts Dividend; Shifts Strategy," *Los Angeles Times*, September 26, 2003, p. C.3.

20. Susan Kuchinskas, "The Tao of Wow," *Adweek Magazines' Technology Marketing*, June 2003, p. 10.

21. Yoram J. Wind and Vijay Mahajan with Robert E. Gunther, *Convergence Marketing: Strategies for Reaching the New Hybrid Consumer* (Upper Saddle River, NJ: Prentice Hall PTR, 2002).

22. Peter Drucker, *Management: Tasks, Responsibilities and Practices* (New York: Harper and Row, 1973), ch. 7.

23. Ralph A. Oliva, "Nowhere to Hide," *Marketing Management*, July/August 2001, pp. 44–46.

24. "DRAXIS Granted U.S. Patent for Bifunctional Compounds," Company news release, October 1, 2003, www.draxis.com/news/2003/news01102003.asp.

25. *Pew Internet and American Life Project Survey*, November–December 2000.

26. Chuck Martin, *Net Future* (New York: McGraw-Hill, 1999).

27. Leah Nathans Spiro, "Pitney Goes for Growth," *Chief Executive*, October 2003, pp. 38–42.

28. Jeffrey F. Rayport and Bernard J. Jaworski, *e-commerce* (New York: McGraw-Hill, 2001), p. 116.

29. Tilman Kemmler, Monika Kubicová, Robert Musslewhite, and Rodney Prezeau, "E-Performance II—The Good, the Bad, and the Merely Average," an exclusive to *mckinseyquarterly.com*, 2001.

30. The same matrix can be expanded into nine cells by adding modified products and modified markets. See S. J. Johnson and Conrad Jones, "How to Organize for New Products," *Harvard Business Review* (May–June 1957): 49–62.

31. www.starbucks.com; Howard Schultz, *Pour Your Heart into It* (New York: Hyperion, 1997); Andy Serwer, "Hot Starbucks to Go," *Fortune*, January 26, 2004, pp. 60–74.

32. Tim Goodman, "NBC Everywhere?" *San Francisco Chronicle*, September 4, 2003, p. E. 1.

33. CanWest Global Communications Corp., *2003 Annual Report*; "CanWest Sells Shares of Ulster Television Plc. (UTV) for Pnds. Stlg. 59 Million," CanWest Global Press Release, June 30, 2004 (viewed as posted on the CanWest Global Web site, www.canwest.com, July 6, 2004).

34. "Business: Microsoft's Contradiction," *The Economist* (January 31, 1998): 65–67; Andrew J. Glass, "Microsoft Pushes Forward,

Playing to Win the Market," *Atlanta Constitution*, June 24, 1998, p. D12.

35. Ben Elgin, "Yahoo! Act Two," *Business Week*, June 2, 2003, pp. 70–76.

36. Daniel Howe, "Note to DaimlerChrysler: It's Not a Small World after All," *Detroit News*, May 19, 1998, p. B4; Bill Vlasic, "The First Global Car Colossus," *BusinessWeek*, May 18, 1998, pp. 40–43; Pamela Harper, "Business 'Cultures' at War," *Electronic News*, August 3, 1998, pp. 50, 55.

37. Bill Vlasic, and Bradley Stertz. "Taken for a Ride," *Business Week*, June 5, 2000; Jeffrey Ball and Scott Miller, "DaimlerChrysler Isn't Living Up to Its Promise," *Wall Street Journal*, July 26, 2000; Eric Reguly, "Daimler, Chrysler Still a Cutture Clash," *The Globe and Mail*, January 30, 2001.

38. E. Jerome McCarthy, *Basic Marketing: A Managerial Approach*, 12th ed. (Homewood, IL: Irwin, 1996).

39. Ian Wylie, "Calling for a Renewable Future," *Fast Company*, May 2003, pp. 46–48.

40. Paul J. H. Shoemaker, "Scenario Plannning: A Tool for Strategic Thinking," *Sloan Management Review* (Winter 1995): 25–40.

41. Philip Kotler, *Kotler on Marketing*, Free Press: New York, NY, 1999.

42. Kotler, *Kotler on Marketing*.

43. Phil Connell interview with Executive Producer Megan McCoy, July 6, 2004; Toolkit Productions Web site, www.toolkitproductions.com.

44. George Stalk, Philip Evans, and Lawrence E. Shulman, "Competing Capabilities: The New Rules of Corporate Strategy," *Harvard Business Review* (March–April 1992): 57–69.

45. Ram Charan and Noel M. Tichy, *Every Business Is a Growth Business: How Your Company Can Prosper Year after Year* (New York: Times Business, Random House, 1998).

46. Michael E. Porter, *Competitive Strategy: Techniques for Analyzing Industries and Competitors* (New York: The Free Press, 1980), ch. 2.

47. Michael E. Porter, "What Is Strategy?" *Harvard Business Review* (November–December 1996): 61–78.

48. "Michelin Begins Grand Prix Promotion," *Adnews On-Line Daily*, May 21, 2002.

49. For some readings on strategic alliances, see Peter Lorange and Johan Roos, *Strategic Alliances: Formation, Implementation and Evolution* (Cambridge, MA: Blackwell, 1992); Jordan D. Lewis, *Partnerships for Profit: Structuring and Managing Strategic Alliances* (New York: The Free Press, 1990); John R. Harbison and Peter Pekar Jr., *Smart Alliances: A Practical Guide to Repeatable Success* (Jossey-Bass, 1998); *Harvard Business Review on Strategic Alliances* (Cambridge, MA: Harvard Business School Press, 2002).

50. Anonymous, "Trends Report: Looking for the Pharmaceutical-Biotechnology Alliance Creates a Win-Win," *Health and Medicine Week*, December 29, 2003, p. 726.

51. Robin Cooper and Robert S. Kalpan, "Profit Priorities from Activity-Based Costing," *Harvard Business Review* (May–June 1991): 130–135.

52. Robert S. Kaplan and David P. Norton, *The Balanced Scorecard: Translating Strategy into Action* (Boston: Harvard Business School Press, 1996), as a tool for monitoring stakeholder satisfaction.

53. Thomas J. Peters and Robert H. Waterman Jr., *In Search of Excellence: Lessons from America's Best-Run Companies* (New York: Harper and Row, 1982), pp. 9–12.

54. Terrence E. Deal and Allan A. Kennedy, *Corporate Cultures: The Rites and Rituals of Corporate Life* (Reading, MA: Addison-Wesley, 1982); "Corporate Culture," *BusinessWeek*, October 27, 1980, pp. 148–160; Stanley M. Davis, *Managing Corporate Culture* (Cambridge, MA: Ballinger, 1984); John P. Kotter and James L. Heskett, *Corporate Culture and Performance* (New York: The Free Press, 1992).

55. Nitin Nohria, William Joyce, and Bruce Roberson, "What Really Works," *Harvard Business Review*, 81, no. 7 (2003): 42–53.

56. Lawrence M. Fisher, "With a New Smart Suite, Lotus Catches Its Rivals' Success," *New York Times*, June 15, 1998, p. 6.

57. Sarah Ellison, "Kraft's Stale Strategy: Endless Extensions of Oreos, Chips-Ahoy and Jell-O Brands Created a New-Product Void," *Wall Street Journal*, December 18, 2003, p. B1.

58. Marian Burk Wood, *The Marketing Plan: A Handbook* (Upper Saddle River, NJ: Prentice Hall, 2003).

59. Donald R. Lehmann and Russell S. Winer, *Product Management*, 3rd ed (Boston, MA: McGraw-Hill/Irwin, 2001).

60. Reproduced from Marian Burk Wood, *The Marketing Plan: A Handbook* (Upper Saddle River, NJ: Prentice Hall, 2003).

Chapter 3

1. Susan Warren, "Pillow Talk: Stackers Outnumber Plumpers; Don't Mention Drool," *Wall Street Journal*, January 8, 1998, p. B1.

2. Steve Weinstein, "Realistic Partnering: How to Do Business Better," *Progressive Grocer*, 71 (February 1992): 80–85; Charles Fishman, "The Wal-Mart You Don't Know," *Fast Company* (December 2003): 68–80.

3. Kevin Helliker, "Smile: That Cranky Shopper May Be a Store Spy," *Wall Street Journal*, November 30, 1994, pp. B1, B6; and Edward F. McQuarrie, *Customer Visits: Building a Better Market Focus*, 2nd ed. (Newburey Park, CA: Sage Press, 1998).

4. Lesley Young, "When Three Heads Are Better Than One," *Marketing Magazine Online*, www.marketingmag.ca, December 8, 2003 (viewed November 1, 2004).

5. Julie Forster, "You Deserve a Better Break Today," *BusinessWeek*, September 30, 2002, p. 42.

6. Kevin Helliker, "Smile: That Cranky Shopper May Be a Store Spy," *Wall Street Journal*, November 30, 1994, pp. B1, B6; Edward F. McQuarrie, *Customer Visits: Building a Better Market Focus*, 2nd ed. (Newbury Park, CA: Sage Press, 1998).

7. Kim Girard, "Strategies to Turn Stealth Into Wealth," *Business 2.0*, May 2003, p. 66.

8. Andy Serwer, "P&G's Covert Operation," *Fortune*, September 17, 2001, pp. 42–44.

9. Statistics Canada, www.statscan.ca (viewed November 1, 2004).

10. Kim Girard, "Strategies to Turn Stealth Into Wealth," *Business 2.0*, May 2003, p. 66.

11. Robin T. Peterson and Zhilin Yang, "Web Product Reviews Help Strategy," *Marketing News*, April 7, 2004, p. 18.

12. See www.badfads.com for examples of fads and collectibles through the years.

13. Andrea Zoe Aster, ". . . and the Grooms Wore Pink," *Marketing Magazine Online*, www.marketingmag.ca, May 10, 2004 (viewed November 7, 2004).

14. John Naisbitt and Patricia Aburdene, *Megatrends 2000* (New York: Avon Books, 1990).

15. World POPClock, U.S. Census Bureau, www.census.gov, September 1999.

16. Statistics Canada, "A Profile of the Canadian Population: Where We Live," 2001 Census-Release 1, March 12, 2002, www.geodepot.statscan.ca/Diss/Highlights/Highlights_e.cfm (viewed June 5, 2002); and *The Daily*, "Latest Indicators: Population Estimate (as of July 2004)," www.statcan.ca/start.html (viewed November 1, 2004).

17. Although over 10 years old, this breakdown provides useful perspective. See Donella H. Meadows, Dennis L. Meadows, and Jorgen Randers, *Beyond Limits* (Chelsea Green Publishing Company, 1993), for some commentary.

18. Sally D. Goll, "Marketing: China (Only) Children Get the Royal Treatment," *Wall Street Journal*, February 8, 1995, p. B1.

19. "Survey: Forever Young," *The Economist*, March 27, 2004, pp. 53–54.

20. Statistics Canada Web site, "Canadian Statistics: Population by Age and Sex, (as of July 1, 2004)," www.statcan.ca/english/Pgdb/demo10a.htm.

21. Astrid Van Den Broek, "Brand Makeovers," *Marketing*, April 26, 1999, p. 21.

22. "Further Along the X Axis," *American Demographics* (May 2004): 21–24.

23. Daren Fonda, "A Pitch to the Rich," *Time*, November 24, 2003; but see Neal E. Boudette, "As VW Tries to Sell Pricier Cars, Everyman Image Holds It Back," *Wall Street Journal*, May 13, 2004.

24. David Leonhardt, "Hey Kids, Buy This," *BusinessWeek*, June 30, 1997, pp. 62–67; Don Tapscott, "*Growing Up Digital; The Rise of the Net Generation* (New York: McGraw Hill 1997); Statistics Canada, "Canadian Statistics: Population by Age and Sex, (as of July 1, 2004)," www.statcan.ca/english/Pgdb/demo10a.htm.

25. Material for this section was drawn from: Jo Marney, "Counting Ethnic Canadians," *Marketing Magazine Online*, www.marketingmag.ca, June 4, 2001; Statistics Canada, "Top 25 Ethnic Origins in Canada (1)," 1996 Census, www.statscan.ca/english.census96/feb17/eolan.htm; Malcolm Dunlop and Christine Comi, "Multicultural Explosion," *Strategy: The Canadian Marketing Report*, February 11, 2002, p. 25; Astrid Van Den Broek, "Fighting Cultural Fade," *Strategy: The Canadian Marketing Report*, February 22, 2002, p. 21; and Statistics Canada, *The Daily*, "Demographic Statistics: As of July 2002 (Preliminary)," September 26, 2002, www.statscan.ca/daily/english/020926/d020926b.htm (viewed September 30, 2002). All statistics from these sources were updated with new data from: Statistics Canada, "2001 Census: Highlight Tables and Topic-Based Tabulations," www12.statcan.ca/english/census01/Products/Standard/Index.cfm (viewed November 1, 2004).

26. Bobby Siu, "Ethnic Marketing: Demographic Wave Well Worth Riding," *Strategy: The Canadian Marketing Report*, July 6, 1998, p. 15; and David Todd, "Special Report: Multicultural Marketing: Nike Takes It to the Streets," *Strategy: The Canadian Marketing Report*, August 17, 1998, p. 26.

27. Siu, "Ethnic Marketing: Demographic Wave Well Worth Riding"; Todd, "Special Report: Multicultural Marketing: Nike Takes It to the Streets."

28. Statistics Canada, "Canadians with Disabilities," Canadian Centre for Justice Statistics Profile Series, June 2001, www.statscan.ca/english/freepub/850033MIE01002.pdf (viewed May 26, 2002).

29. Statistics Canada, "Population 15 Years and Over by Highest Degree, Certificate or Diploma (1986–2001 Censuses)," 2001 Census, http://canadaonline.about.com/gi/dynamic/offsite.htm?zi=1/XJ&sdn=canadaonline&zu=www.statcan.ca/english/Pgdb/educat.htm (viewed January 27, 2005).

30. Statistics Canada, "Recent Trends in Adult Education and Training in Canada," www.statcan.ca/english/freepub/81-004-XIE/200412/aets.htm (viewed January 27, 2005).

31. ABC Canada, "Adult Literacy Canada," www.abc-canada.org/literacy_facts/ (viewed January 27, 2005); Statistics Canada, "Canadians with Literacy Problems," Canadian Centre for Justice Statistics Profile Series, June 2001, www.statscan.ca/english/freepub/85F0033MIE/85F0033MIE01003.pdf (viewed May 26, 2002); Statistics Canada, "Population 15 Years and Over by Highest Level of Schooling, by Provinces and Territories (2001 Census)," www.statcan.ca/english/Pgdb/educ43a.htm (viewed November 1, 2004); Statistics Canada, "Population 15 Years and Over by Highest Degree, Certificate or Diploma, by Provinces and Territories (2001 Census)," www.statcan.ca/english/Pgdb/educ41a.htm (viewed November 1, 2004).

32. Statistics Canada, "Household Type, in Private Households, 2001 Counts, for Canada, Provinces and Territories—20% Sample Data," www12.statcan.ca/english/census01/products/highlight/PrivateHouseholds/Page.cfm?Lang=E&Geo=PR&View=1a&Table=1&StartRec=1&Sort=2&B1=Counts.

33. Statistics Canada, "2001 Census, Topic-based Tabulations: Number of Children at Home (8) and Family Structure (7A) for Census Families in Private Households, for Canada, Provinces and Territories, 1981 to 2001 Censuses—20% Sample Data," www12.statcan.ca (viewed November 2, 2004); Statistics Canada, "Canada at a Glance 2003," p. 1 (viewed November 2, 2004).

34. Angela Phillips, "Friends Are the New Family," *The Guardian*, December 12, 2003, p. 1.

35. Kris Oser, "Friendster Uses Imaginary Pals to Lure Real Ones," *Advertising Age*, July 19, 2004, pp. 3, 33; Vanessa Hua, "Bound Together," *San Francisco Chronicle*, June 27, 2003, p. B1.

36. Statistics Canada, *The Daily*, "Canadian Community Health Survey," Tuesday, June 15, 2004, www.statcan.ca/Daily/English/040615/d040615b.htm (viewed November 2, 2004).

37. Rebecca Gardyn, "A Market Kept in the Closet," *American Demographics* (November 2001): 37–43.

38. Michelle Halpern, "They're Here, They're Queer, and They Love to Shop," *Marketing Magazine Online*, www.marketingmag.ca, September 20, 2004 (viewed November 2, 2004).

39. Statistics Canada, "A Profile of the Canadian Population: Where We Live," 2001 Census-Release 1, March 12, 2002, www.geodepot.statcan.ca/Diss/Highlights/Highlights_e.cfm (viewed June 5, 2002); Statistics Canada, Ross Finnie, "The Effects of Inter-Provincial Mobility on Individuals' Earnings: Panel Model Estimated for Canada," Analytical Studies Branch Research Paper Series, Report 163, Catalogue No. 11F0019MIE200163, October 2001, www.collection.nlc-bnc.ca/100/20/301/statscan/research_paper_analytical _11f0019-e/no163/11Foo19MIE011163.pdf (viewed September 22, 2002).

40. Lauri J. Flynn, "Not Just a Copy Shop Any Longer, Kinko's Pushes Its Computer Services," *New York Times*, July 6, 1998, p. D1; www.kinkos.com.

41. Manjeet Kripalani and Pete Engardio, "The Rise of India," *Business Week*, December 8, 2003, pp. 66–76; Joanna Slater, "Call of the West," *Wall Street Journal*, January 2, 2004, p. A1.

42. Statistics Canada, "Income of Canadian Families," 2001 Census: Analysis Series, May 13, 2003, www12.statcan.ca/english/census01/Products/Analytic/companion/inc/pdf/96F0030XIE2001014.pdf (viewed November 3, 2004).

43. Louise Lee, "The Gap Has Reason to Dance Again," *BusinessWeek*, April 19, 2004, p. 42.

44. Chris Daniels, "Almost Rich," *Marketing Magazine Online*, www.marketingmag.ca, April 26, 2004 (viewed November 3, 2004).

45. Statistics Canada, "Recent Trends in Household Net Worth," Latest Developments in the Canadian Economic Accounts, June 24, 2004, www.statcan.ca/english/freepub/13-605-XIE/2003001/chronology/2004networth/index.htm (viewed November 3, 2004); "Credit Card Statistics," October 2003, Canadian Bankers Association, www.cba.ca/en/ViewDocument.asp?fl=6&sl=110&tl=&docid=421 (viewed November 3, 2004).

46. Stephen Baker and Manjeet Kripalani, "Software: Will Outsourcing Hurt America's Supremacy?" *Business Week*, March 1, 2004, pp. 84–94; Jennifer Reingold, "Into Thin Air," *Fast Company* (April 2004): 76–82.

47. Alison Stanley and Paul Argenti, "Starbucks Coffee Company," case study, Tuck School of Business at Dartmouth, www.starbucks.com/aboutus/StarbucksAndFairTrade.pdf.

48. Pamela Paul, "Corporate Responsibility," *American Demographics* (May 2002): 24–25.

49. Paul Wenske, "You Too Could Lose $19,000!" *Kansas City Star*, October 31, 1999; "Clearing House Suit Chronology," Associated Press, January 26, 2001.

50. "LCBO and Shoppers Drug Mart Offer Good Host Kit for Unexpected Overnight Guests; MADD Canada Benefits," LCBO

Media Release, November 12, 2004, www.madd.ca/english/news/stories/n041112.htm (viewed January 27, 2005).

51. Michael Adams, *Fire and Ice: The United States, Canada and the Myth of Converging Values* (Toronto: Penguin Canada, 2003).

52. David MacDonald and Michael Adams, "We Are What We Drive," *Marketing Magazine*, March 15, 2004; Lynn Fletcher, "UNDER SIEGE, but Still Upbeat," *Marketing Magazine Online*, www.marketingmag.ca, October 27, 2003 (viewed November 3, 2004).

53. Laura Zinn, "Teens: Here Comes the Biggest Wave Yet," *BusinessWeek*, April 11, 2004, pp. 76–86.

54. Rebecca Gardyn, "Eco-Friend or Foe," *American Demographics*, October 2003, pp. 12–13. See also Rebecca Gardyn, "Being Green," *American Demographics*, September 2002, pp. 10–11.

55. Environment Canada, www.ec.gc.ca/EnviroRegs/eng/ceparegs.cfm (viewed November 3, 2004).

56. Keith McArthur, "Canadians Put the Environment First," *The Globe and Mail*, June 23, 1997, p. A4.

57. Brad Stone, "Your Next Computer," *Newsweek*, June 7, 2004, p. 65.

58. Statistics Canada, *The Daily*, "Are There High-Tech Industries or Only High-Tech Firms?" December 10, 1998, www.statcan.ca/English/981210/d981210.htm (viewed September 22, 2002); Statistics Canada, "Abstract: Canadian agriculture at a glance," www.statcan.ca:8096/bsolc/english/bsolc?catno=96-325-X20010006959 (viewed November 3, 2004).

59. Moon Ihlwan, "Wireless Wonders: Samsung Gets Wired on Wireless," *BusinessWeek*, April 26, 2004; Richard Shim and Michael Kannelos, "Networked Homes Move Closer to Reality," CNET News.com, May 28, 2004.

60. National Research Council of Canada, "GERD as a % of GDP for Selected OECD Countries 2001," September 2, 2004, www.nserc.gc.ca/about/stats/2002-2003/en/slides/slide82.htm (viewed January 27, 2005).

61. Research Info Source, "Canada's Top 100 Corporate R&D Spenders 2002," www.researchinfosource.com/2002-top100.pdf (viewed January 27, 2005).

62. See Dorothy Cohen, *Legal Issues on Marketing Decision Making* (Cincinnati: South-Western, 1995).

63. Rebecca Gardyn, "Swap Meet," *American Demographics* (July 2001): 51–55.

64. Pamela Paul, "Mixed Signals," *American Demographics* (July 2001): 45–49.

Chapter 4

1. Thomas Kinnear and Ann Root, eds., *1994 Survey of Market Research* (Chicago: American Marketing Association, 1994).

2. Emily Sweeney, "Karmaloop Shapes Urban Fashion by Spotting Trends Where They Start," *Boston Globe*, July 8, 2004, p. D3.

3. Kevin J. Clancy and Robert S. Shulman, *Marketing Myths That Are Killing Business*, (New York: McGraw-Hill, 1994), p. 58; Phaedra Hise, "Comprehensive CompuServe," *Inc.* (June 1994): 109; "Business Bulletin: Studying the Competition," *Wall Street Journal*, p. A1–5.

4. Kate Maddox, "The ROI of Research," *B to B*, April 5, 2004, pp. 25, 28.

5. For some background information on in-flight Internet service, see "In-Flight Dogfight," *Business2.Com*, January 9, 2001, pp. 84–91; John Blau, "In-Flight Internet Service Ready for Takeoff," *IDG News Service*, June 14, 2002; "Boeing In-Flight Internet Plan Goes Airborne," *The Associated Press*, April 18, 2004.

6. For a discussion of the decision-theory approach to the value of research, see Donald R. Lehmann, Sunil Gupta, and Joel Steckel, *Market Research* (Reading, MA: Addison-Wesley, 1997).

7. Allison Stein Wellner, "Look Who's Watching," *Continental* (April 2003): 39–41; Linda Tischler, "Every Move You Make," *Fast Company* (April 2004): 73–75.

8. Dennis W. Rook, "Loss of Vision: Focus Groups Fail to Connect Theory, Current Practice," *Marketing News*, September 15, 2003, p. 40.

9. Bruce Nussbaum, "The Power of Design," *Business Week*, May 17, 2004, pp. 86–94.

10. Roger D. Blackwell, James S. Hensel, Michael B. Phillips, and Brian Sternthal, *Laboratory Equipment for Marketing Research* (Dubuque, IA: Kendall/Hunt, 1970); Wally Wood, "The Race to Replace Memory," *Marketing and Media Decisions* (July 1986): 166–167. See also Gerald Zaltman, "Rethinking Market Research: Putting People Back In," *Journal of Marketing Research* 34, no. 4 (November 1997): 424–437; Andy Raskin, "A Face Any Business Can Trust," *Business 2.0*, December 2003, pp. 58–60; Louise Witt, "Inside Intent," *American Demographics* (March 2004): 34–39.

11. Adam Froman, "Real Time Research," *Marketing Magazine Online*, www.marketingmag.ca, June 7, 2004 (viewed November 5, 2004).

12. Maddox, "The ROI of Research."

13. Peter Fuller, "A Two-Way Conversation," *Brandweek*, February 25, 2002, pp. 21–27.

14. Catherine Arnold, "Hershey Research Sees Net Gain," *Marketing News*, November 25, 2002, p. 17.

15. Ipsos-Reid Canada, www.ipsos-reid.com/ca/index.cfm (viewed May 22, 2002); Terry Poulton, "Givin' It Away," *Strategy: The Canadian Marketing Report*, January 28, 2002, p. 24.

16. Joe Dysart, "Cutting Market Research Costs with On-Site Surveys," *The Secured Lender*, March/April 2004, pp. 64–67.

17. Suzy Bashford, "The Opinion Formers," *Revolution*, May 2004, pp. 42–46.

18. Bob Lamons, "Eureka! Future of B-to-B Research Is Online," *Marketing News*, September 24, 2001, pp. 9–10.

19. Witt, "Inside Intent."

20. Lisa D'Innocenzo, "Focus Groups for a New Age?" *Strategy Magazine Online*, www.strategymag.com, August 23, 2004 (viewed November 5, 2004).

21. Kevin J. Clancy and Peter C. Krieg, *Counterintuitive Marketing: How Great Results Come from Uncommon Sense* (New York: The Free Press, 2000).

22. John D. C. Little, "Decision Support Systems for Marketing Managers," *Journal of Marketing* (Summer 1979): 11. See "Special Issue on Managerial Decision Making," *Marketing Science*, 18, no. 3 (1999) for some contemporary perspectives.

23. Leonard M. Lodish, "CALLPLAN: An Interactive Salesman's Call Planning System," *Management Science* (December 1971): 25–40.

24. Christine Moorman, Gerald Zaltman, and Rohit Deshpandé, "Relationships Between Providers and Users of Market Research: The Dynamics of Trust Within and Between Organizations," *Journal of Marketing Research*, 29 (August 1992): 314–328.

25. Quote excerpted from Arthur Shapiro, "Let's Redefine Market Research," *Brandweek*, June 21, 2004, p. 20.

26. John McManus, "Stumbling Into Intelligence, *American Demographics* (April 2004): 22–25.

27. John Gaffney, "The Buzz Must Go On," *Business 2.0* (February 2002): 49–50.

28. Tim Ambler, *Marketing and the Bottom Line: The New Metrics of Corporate Wealth* (London: FT Prentice-Hall, 2000).

29. Bob Donath, "Employ Marketing Metrics with a Track Record," *Marketing News*, September 15, 2003, p. 12.

30. Kusum L. Ailawadi, Donald R. Lehmann, and Scott A. Neslin, "Revenue Premium as an Outcome Measure of Brand Equity, *Journal of Marketing*, 67 (October 2003): 1–17.

31. Tim Ambler, *Marketing and the Bottom Line: The New Metrics of Corporate Wealth* (London: FT Prentice-Hall, 2000); Tim Ambler, "What Does Marketing Success Look Like?," *Marketing Management* (Spring 2001): 13–18.

32. Fred Vogelstein, "Mighty Amazon," *Fortune*, May 26, 2003, pp. 60–74.

33. Samson Okalow, "What's in Your Wallet?" *Strategy Magazine Online*, www.strategymag.com, September 17, 2004 (viewed November 5, 2004).

34. Robert S. Kaplan and David P Norton, *The Balanced Scorecard* (Boston: Harvard Business School Press, 1996).

35. Richard Whiteley and Diane Hessan, *Customer-Centered Growth* (Reading, MA: Addison-Wesley, 1996), pp. 87–90; Adrian J. Slywotzky, *Value Migration: How to Think Several Moves Ahead of the Competition* (Boston: Harvard University Press, 1996), pp. 231–235.

36. Marion Debruyne and Katrina Hubbard, "Marketing Metrics," working paper series, Conference Summary, Marketing Science Institute, Report No. 00-119, 2000.

37. Alfred R. Oxenfeldt, "How to Use Market-Share Measurement," *Harvard Business Review* (January–February 1969): 59–68.

38. There is a one-half chance that a successive observation will be higher or lower. Therefore, the probability of finding six successively higher values is given by (1/2) to the sixth, or 1/64.

39. Alternatively, companies need to focus on factors affecting shareholder value. The goal of marketing planning is to increase shareholder value, which is the present value of the future income stream created by the company's present actions. Rate-of-return analysis usually focuses on only one year's results. See Alfred Rapport, *Creating Shareholder Value*, rev. ed. (New York: The Free Press, 1997).

40. For additional reading on financial analysis, see Peter L. Mullins, *Measuring Customer and Product Line Profitability* (Washington, DC: Distribution Research and Education Foundation, 1984).

41. The MAC Group, *Distribution: A Competitive Weapon* (Cambridge, MA: MAC Group, 1985), p. 20.

42. Robin Cooper and Robert S. Kaplan, "Profit Priorities from Activity-Based Costing," *Harvard Business Review* (May–June 1991): 130–135.

43. Jack Neff, "P&G, Clorox Rediscover Modeling," *Advertising Age*, March 29, 2004, p. 10.

44. Laura Q. Hughes, "Econometrics Take Root," *Advertising Age*, August 5, 2002, p. S4.

45. Lisa D'Innocenzo, "Corus Research into What Women Want Sparks Younger, Bolder WTN," *Strategy: The Canadian Marketing Report*, March 25, 2002, p. 1; Sarah Smith, "More Fun, Less Earnest," *Marketing Magazine*, May 8, 2002, pp. 13–14.

46. For a good discussion and illustration, see Roger J. Best, *Market-Based Management*, 2nd ed. (Upper Saddle River, NJ: Prentice Hall, 2000), pp. 71–75.

47. Ipsos Reid, "Almost 70 Per Cent of Canadian Home Owners Opt for Conservative Fixed Rate Mortgage Strategy According to New BMO Bank of Montreal Survey," www.ipsos-na.com/news/pressrelease.cfm?id=2434, October 29, 2004 (viewed November 6, 2004).

48. Telecommunications Canada, www.tc.ca/tc-vision.html.

49. For further discussion, see Gary L. Lilien, Philip Kotler, and K. Sridhar Moorthy, *Marketing Models* (Upper Saddle River, NJ: Prentice Hall, 1992).

50. www.naics.com; www.census.gov/epcd/naics02.

51. Brian Sternthal and Alice M. Tybout, "Segmentation and Targeting," in *Kellogg on Marketing*, Dawn Iacobucci, ed. (New York: John Wiley & Sons, 2001), pp. 3–30.

52. Norman Dalkey and Olaf Helmer, "An Experimental Application of the Delphi Method to the Use of Experts," *Management Science* (April 1963): 458–467. Also see Roger J. Best, "An Experiment in Delphi Estimation in Marketing Decision Making," *Journal of Marketing Research* (November 1974): 447–452. For an excellent overview of market forecasting, see Scott Armstrong, ed., *Principles of Forecasting: A Handbook for Researchers and Practitioners* (Norwell, MA: Kluwer Academic Publishers, 2001)

and his Web site: http://fourps.wharton.upenn.edu/forecast/handbook.html.

Chapter 5

1. Glen L. Urban, "The Emerging Era of Customer Advocacy," *MIT Sloan Management Review* (Winter 2004): 77–82; Robert D. Hof, "The eBay Economy," *Business Week*, August 25, 2003, pp. 125–128; http://pages.ebay.ca/community/aboutebay/index.html?ssPageName=STRK:STMP:245 (viewed September 30, 2004).

2. Urban, "The Emerging Era of Customer Advocacy."

3. Irwin P. Levin and Richard D. Johnson, "Estimating Price-Quality Tradeoffs Using Comparative Judgments," *Journal of Consumer Research* (June 11, 1984): 593–600. Customer perceived value can be measured as a difference or as a ratio. If total customer value is $20 000 and total customer cost is $16 000, then the customer perceived value is $4000 (measured as a difference) or 1.25 (measured as a ratio). Ratios that are used to compare offers are often called *value-price ratios*.

4. For more on customer perceived value, see David C. Swaddling and Charles Miller, *Customer Power* (Dublin, OH: The Wellington Press, 2001).

5. Gary Hamel, "Strategy as Revolution," *Harvard Business Review* (July–August 1996): 69–82.

6. Michael J. Lanning, *Delivering Profitable Value* (Oxford, UK: Capstone, 1998).

7. Larry Selden and Geoffrey Colvin, "What Customers Want," *Fortune*, July 7, 2003, pp. 122–127.

8. Simon Knox and Stan Maklan, *Competing on Value: Bridging the Gap Between Brand and Customer Value* (London, UK: Financial Times, 1998). See also Richard A. Spreng, Scott B. MacKenzie, and Richard W. Olshawskiy, "A Reexamination of the Determinants of Consumer Satisfaction," *Journal of Marketing*, no. 3 (July 1996): 15–32.

9. Fred Crawford and Ryan Mathews, *The Myth of Excellence: Why Great Companies Never Try to Be the Best of Everything* (New York: Crown Business), pp. 85–100.

10. For some provocative analysis, see Susan Fournier and David Glenmick, "Rediscovering Satisfaction," *Journal of Marketing* (October 1999): pp. 5–23.

11. For an interesting analysis of the effects of different types of expectations, see William Boulding, Ajay Kalra, and Richard Staelin, "The Quality Double Whammy," *Marketing Service*, 18, no. 4 (1999): 463–484.

12. www.saturn.com; "Saturn Illustrates Value of Customer Loyalty," *Louisville Courier-Journal*, September 5, 1999.

13. Sally B. Donnelly, "Friendlier Skies," *Time*, January 26, 2004, pp. 39–40; Arlyn Tobias Gahilan, "The Amazing JetBlue," *FSB: Fortune Small Business* (May 2003): 50–60.

14. Lesley Young, "Taking Marketing to the Bank," *Marketing Magazine*, February 11, 2002, pp. 4–7; Bernadette Johnson, "Bankers' Online Offerings Reflect Today's Savvy Consumers," *Strategy: The Canadian Marketing Report*, February 25, 2002, p. D2.

15. Thomas O. Jones and W. Earl Sasser, Jr., "Why Satisfied Customers Defect," *Harvard Business Review* (November–December 1995): 88–99.

16. Companies should also note that managers and salespeople can manipulate customer satisfaction ratings. They can be especially nice to customers just before the survey. They can also try to exclude unhappy customers. Another danger is that if customers know the company will go out of its way to please customers, some may express high dissatisfaction in order to receive more concessions.

17. Anne Chen, "Customer Feedback Key for Theme Park; Inquisite Lets Visitors Sound Off," *eWeek*, December 15, 2003, p. 58.

18. Frederick K. Reichheld, "The One Number You Need to Grow," *Harvard Business Review* (December 2003): 46–54.

19. Alex Taylor III, "Mercedes Hits a Pothole," *Fortune*, October 27, 2003, pp. 140–146.

20. Andy Holloway, "I'm Down Here, Guys," *Canadian Business Magazine Online*, www.canadianbusiness.com, October 28, 2002 (viewed July 8, 2004).

21. "The Gurus of Quality: American Companies Are Heading the Quality Gospel Preached by Deming, Juran, Crosby, and Taguchi," *Traffic Management* (July 1990): 35–39.

22. Cyndee Miller, "U.S. Firms Lag in Meeting Global Quality Standards," *Marketing News*, February 15, 1993.

23. J. Daniel Beckham, "Expect the Unexpected in Health Care Marketing Future," *The Academy Bulletin* (July 1992): 3.

24. "Quality: The U.S. Drives to Catch Up," *Business Week*, November 1982, pp. 66–80. For a more recent assessment of progress, see "Quality Programs Show Shoddy Results," *Wall Street Journal*, May 14, 1992, p. B1. See also Roland R. Rust, Anthony J. Zahorik, and Timothy L. Keiningham, "Return on Quality (ROQ): Making Service Quality Financially Accountable," *Journal of Marketing* 59, no. 2 (April 1995): 58–70.

25. Robert D. Buzzell and Bradley T. Gale, *The PIMS Principles: Linking Strategy to Performance* (New York: The Free Press, 1987), ch. 6. (PIMS stands for Profit Impact of Market Strategy.)

26. David Greising, "Quality: How to Make It Pay," *Business Week*, August 8, 1994, pp. 54–59; Roland R. Rust, Anthony J. Zahorik, and Timothy L. Keiningham, "Return on Quality (ROQ): Making Service Quality Financially Accountable," *Journal of Marketing* 59, no. 2 (April 1995): 58–70.

27. Roland T. Rust, Christine Moorman, and Peter R. Dickson, "Getting Return on Quality: Revenue Expansion, Cost Reduction, or Both," *Journal of Marketing*, 65 (October 2002): 7–24.

28. Quoted in Don Peppers and Martha Rogers, *The One-to-One Future: Building Relationships One Customer at a Time* (New York: Currency Doubleday, 1993), p. 108.

29. William A. Sherden, *Market Ownership: The Art and Science of Becoming #1* (New York: Amacom, 1994), p. 77.

30. Robert J. Bowman, "Good Things, Smaller Packages," *World Trade*, 6, no. 9 (October 1993): 106–110.

31. Werner J. Reinartz and V. Kumar, "The Impact of Customer Relationship Characteristics on Profitable Lifetime Duration," *Journal of Marketing*, 67 (January 2003): 77–99; Werner J. Reinartz and V. Kumar, "On the Profitability of Long-Life Customers in a Noncontractual Setting: An Empirical Investigation and Implications for Marketing," *Journal of Marketing*, 64 (October 2000): 17–35.

32. Rakesh Niraj, Mahendra Gupta, and Chakravarthi Narasimhan, "Customer Profitability in a Supply Chain," *Journal of Marketing* (July 2001): 1–16.

33. Thomas M. Petro, "Profitability: The Fifth 'P' of Marketing," *Bank Marketing* (September 1990): 48–52; "Who Are Your Best Customers?" *Bank Marketing* (October 1990): 48–52.

34. Ravi Dhar and Rashi Glazer, "Hedging Customers," *Harvard Business Review* (May 2003): 86–92.

35. Sara Minogue, "Customer Profitability Management," *Strategy Magazine Online*, www.strategymag.com, February 9, 2004 (viewed July 8, 2004).

36. Michael E. Porter, *Competitive Strategy: Techniques for Analyzing Industries and Competitors* (New York: Free Press, 1980).

37. Carl Sewell and Paul Brown, *Customers for Life* (New York: Pocket Books, 1990), p. 162.

38. Greg Farrel, "Marketers Put a Price on Your Life." *USA Today*, July 7, 1999.

39. Stephan A. Butscher, "Welcome to the Club: Building Customer Loyalty," *Marketing News*, September 9, 1996, p. 9.

40. Cited in Don Peppers and Martha Rogers, *The One-to-One Future* (New York: Currency, 1993), pp. 37–38.

41. Ian Gordon, *Relationship Marketing* (Toronto: John Wiley & Sons Canada Ltd., 1998), p. 9.

42. Robert C. Blattberg and John Deighton, "Manage Marketing by the Customer Equity Test," *Harvard Business Review* (July–August 1996): 136–144.

43. Roland T. Rust, Valerie A. Zeithaml, and Katherine A. Lemon, *Driving Customer Equity* (New York: Free Press 2000).

44. Mohan Sawhney, "Beyond CRM: Managing Relational Equity," from talk given at "Managing Customer Relationships in the Network Economy," September 20, 2000. For a broad discussion of the term "equity," see Roderick J. Brodie, Mark S. Glynn, Joel Van Durme, "Towards a Theory of Marketplace Equity," *Marketing Theory*, 2, no. 1 (2000): 5–28.

45. Nicole E. Coviello, Roderick J. Brodie, Peter J. Danaher, and Wesley J. Johnston, "How Firms Relate to Their Markets: An Empirical Examination of Contemporary Marketing Practices," *Journal of Marketing*, 66 (July 2002): pp. 33–46.

46. Michael J. Lanning, *Delivering Profitable Value* (Oxford, UK: Capstone, 1998).

47. Samson Okalow, "Courting the First-Time Buyers," *Strategy Magazine Online*, www.strategymag.com, May 31, 2004 (viewed July 9, 2004).

48. Nora A. Aufreiter, David Elzinga, and Jonathan W. Gordon, "Better Branding," *The McKinsey Quarterly*, no. 4 (2003): 29–39.

49. Michael J. Lanning, *Delivering Profitable Value* (Oxford, UK: Capstone, 1998).

50. Example based on the personal experiences of one of the authors.

51. Peppers and Rogers, *The One-to-One Future*; Don Peppers and Martha Rogers, *Enterprise One to One: Tools for Competing in the Interactive Age* (New York: Currency, 1997); Don Peppers and Martha Rogers, *The One-to-One Manager: Real-World Lessons in Customer Relationship Management* (New York: Doubleday 1999); Don Peppers, Martha Rogers, and Bob Dorf, *The One-to-One Fieldbook: The Complete Toolkit for Implementing a 1to1 Marketing Program* (New York: Bantam, 1999); Don Peppers and Martha Rogers, *One-to-One B2B: Customer Development Strategies for the Business-to-Business World* (New York: Doubleday, 2001).

52. Katherine O'Brien, "Differentiation Begins with Customer Knowledge," *American Printer* (July 2003): p. 8.

53. Alan W. H. Grant and Leonard A. Schlesinger, "Realize Your Customer's Full Profit Potential," *Harvard Business Review* (September–October 1995): 59–72; Art Friedman, "Harley-Davidson Motorcycles Posts Record Revenue, Earnings for 2003, Motorcycle Cruiser," *Motorcycle Cruiser*, www.motorcyclecruiser.com/newsandupdates/hd4q03/ (viewed September 30, 2004).

54. Jeffrey Gitomer, *Customer Satisfaction Is Worthless; Customer Loyalty Is Priceless: How to Make Customers Love You, Keep Them Coming Back and Tell Everyone They Know* (Austin, TX: Bard Press, 1998).

55. Technical Assistance Research Programs (TARP), *U.S Office of Consumer Affairs Study on Complaint Handling in America*, 1986.

56. Karl Albrecht and Ron Zemke, *Service America!* (Homewood Il: Dow Jones-Irwin, 1985), pp. 6–7; Roland T. Rust, Bala Subramanian, and Mark Wells, "Making Complaints a Management Tool," *Marketing Management*, 1, no. 3 (1992): 40–45; Ruth Bolton and Tina M. Bronkhorst, "The Relationship Between Customer Complaints to the Firm and Subsequent Exit Behavior," *Advances in Consumer Research*, vol. 22 (Provo, Utah: Association for Consumer Research, 1995); Stephen S. Tax and Stephen W. Brown, "Recovering and Learning from Service Failure," *Sloan Management Review*, 40, no. 1 (1998): 75–88.

57. Maryfran Johnson, "Colliding with Customers," *Computerworld*, December 15, 2003, p. 20; Bob Brewin, "User Complaints Push Dell to Return PC Support to U.S.," *Computerworld*, December 1, 2003, p. 6.

58. Frederick F. Reichheld, *The Loyalty Effect* (Boston: Harvard Business School Press, 1996).

59. Robert Blattberg, Byung-Do Kim, and Scott Neslin, *Database Marketing: Theory and Practice* (in press).

60. Sara Minogue, "Random Acts of Kindness," *Strategy Magazine Online*, www.strategymag.com, August 25, 2003 (viewed July 9, 2004).

61. Michael Totty, "E-Commerce (A Special Report); Business Solutions," *Wall Street Journal*, October 20, 2003, p. R4.

62. Jeffrey Pfeffer, "The Face of Your Business," *Business 2.0* (December 2002–January 2003): 58.

63. Frederick F. Reichheld, "Learning from Customer Defections," *Harvard Business Review* (March–April 1996): 56–69.

64. Reichheld, "Learning from Customer Defections."

65. Leonard L. Berry and A. Parasuraman, *Marketing Services: Computing through Quality* (New York: The Free Press, 1991), pp. 136–142. See also Richard Cross and Janet Smith, *Customer Bonding: Pathways to Lasting Customer Loyalty* (Lincolnwood, IL: NTC Business Books, 1995).

66. For a review, see Grahame R. Dowling and Mark Uncles, "Do Customer Loyalty Programs Really Work?" *Sloan Management Review*, 38, no. 4 (1997): 71–82.

67. Samson Okalow, "Auditing Loyalty," *Strategy Magazine Online*, www.strategymag.com, April 21, 2003 (viewed July 8, 2004).

68. www.apple.com.

69. www.hog.com.

70. James H. Donnelly Jr., Leonard L. Berry, and Thomas W. Thompson, *Marketing Financial Services—A Strategic Vision* (Homewood, IL: Dow Jones–Irwin, 1985), p. 113.

71. Susan Stellin, "For Many Online Companies, Customer Service Is Hardly a Priority," *New York Times*, February 19, 2001; Michelle Johnson, "Getting Ready for the Onslaught," *Boston Globe*, November 4, 1999.

72. www.warp9inc.com/Newsletter/06_2001/ShoppingCarts.htm.

73. *BW Online*, July 22, 2002, Talk Show.

74. www.veseys.com/sub.cfm (viewed September 30, 2004).

75. From a privately circulated paper, Lester Wunderman, "The Most Elusive Word in Marketing," June 2000. Also see Lester Wunderman, *Being Direct* (NewYork: Random House 1996).

76. Ian Mount, "Marketing," *Business 2.0* (August/September 2001): 84.

77. Peter R. Peacock, "Data Mining in Marketing: Part 1," *Marketing Management* (Winter 1998): 9–18, and "Data Mining in Marketing: Part 2," *Marketing Management* (Spring 1998): 15–25; Ginger Conlon, "What the !@#!*?!! Is a Data Warehouse?" *Sales & Marketing Management* (April 1997): 41–48; Skip Press, "Fool's Gold? As Companies Rush to Mine Data, They May Dig Up Real Gems—Or False Trends," *Sales & Marketing Management* (April 1997): 58, 60, 62; John Verity, "A Trillion-Byte Weapon," *BusinessWeek*, July 31, 1995, pp. 80–81.

78. James Lattin, Doug Carroll, and Paul Green, *Analyzing Multivariate Data* (Florence, KY: Thomson Brooks/Cole, 2003); Simon Haykin, *Neural Networks: A Comprehensive Foundation*, 2nd edition (Upper Saddle River, NJ: Prentice-Hall, 1998); Michael J. A. Berry and Gordon Linoff, *Data Mining Techniques: For Marketing, Sales, and Customer Support* (New York: John Wiley & Sons, 1997).

79. Werner Reinartz and V. Kumar, "The Mismanagement of Customer Loyalty," *Harvard Business Review* (July 2002): 86–94; Susan M. Fournier, Susan Dobscha, and David Glen Mick, "Preventing the Premature Death of Relationship Marketing," *Harvard Business Review* (January–February 1998): 42–51.

80. Jon Swartz, "Ebay Faithful Expect Loyalty in Return," *USA TODAY*, July 1, 2002, pp. B1–B2.

81. George S. Day, "Creating a Superior Customer-Relating Capability," *Sloan Management Review*, 44, no. 3 (2003): 77–82.

82. Darrell K. Rigby, Frederick F. Reichheld, and Phil Schefter, "Avoid the Four Perils of CRM," *Harvard Business Review* (February 2002): 101–109.

83. Marlene Milczarek, "Database Diamond Mining: Marketers Are Increasingly Turing to Their Customer Information Bank for Research," *Marketing Magazine Online*, www.marketingmag.com, August 13, 2001 (viewed July 8, 2004).

Chapter 6

1. "Real Men Get Waxed," *The Economist*, July 5, 2003, p. 57; Robyn Meredith and Melanie Wells, "Today's Man," *Forbes*, September 1, 2003, p. 52.

2. For discussions of Canadian values, see Reginald W. Bibby, *The Bibby Report: Social Trends Canadian Style* (Toronto: Stoddart, 1995) and Michael Adams, *Sex in the Snow: Canadian Social Values at the End of the Millennium* (Toronto: Viking, 1997). See also Leon G. Schiffman and Leslie Lazar Kanuk, *Consumer Behavior*, 6th ed. (Upper Saddle River, NJ: Prentice Hall, 1997).

3. Shawna Steinberg, "Oh Canada in the Spotlight," *Marketing Magazine*, November 2, 1998, pp. 10–11.

4. Sara Minogue, "Reaching New Canadians: Multicultural Experts Offer Their Best Practice Advice to Niche Marketers," *Strategy Magazine Online*, www.strategymag.com, September 22, 2003 (viewed July 13, 2004); Caribana Festival Web site, www.caribana.com (viewed July 13, 2004).

5. The Centre for Canadian Studies, *The Political Voice of Canadian Regional Identities*, 2001, www.mta.ca/faculty/arts/canadian_studies/english/about/study_guide/regional/index.html (viewed October 16, 2004).

6. Schiffman and Kanuk, *Consumer Behavior*.

7. Anonymous, "Nestlé Uses SMS Campaign to Create a Buzz for KitKat Kubes," *Revolution* (October 2003): 5

8. Norihiko Shirouzu, "Japan's High School Girls Excel in Art of Setting Trends," *Wall Street Journal*, April 27, 1998, pp. B1–B6.

9. Rosann L. Spiro, "Persuasion in Family Decision Making," *Journal of Consumer Research* (March 1983): 393–402; David J. Burns, "Husband–Wife Innovative Consumer Decision Making: Exploring the Effect of Family Power," *Psychology & Marketing* (May–June 1992): 175–189; Robert Boutilier, "Pulling the Family's Strings," *American Demographics* (August 1993): 44–48; Elizabeth S. Moore, William L. Wilkie, and Richard J. Lutz, "Passing the Torch: Intergenerational Influences as a Source of Brand Equity," *Journal of Marketing* (April 2002): 17–37. For cross-cultural comparisons of husband–wife buying roles, see John B. Ford, Michael S. LaTour, and Tony L. Henthorne, "Perception of Marital Roles in Purchase-Decision Processes: A Cross-Cultural Study," *Journal of the Academy of Marketing Science* (Spring 1995): 120–131.

10. Kay M. Palan and Robert E. Wilkes," Adolescent–Parent Interaction in Family Decision Making," *Journal of Consumer Research*, 24, no. 2 (1997): 159–169; Sharon E. Beatty and Salil Talpade, "Adolescent Influence in Family Decision Making: A Replication with Extension," *Journal of Consumer Research*, 21 (1994): 332–341.

11. Lyle V. Harris, "Men Rule the Aisles," *The Globe and Mail*, May 6, 1999, p. C5.

12. Marilyn Lavin, "Husband-Dominant, Wife-Dominant, Joint: A Shopping Typology for Baby Boom Couples?" *Journal of Consumer Marketing* 10, no. 3 (1993): 33–42.

13. Jim Hopkins, "Financial Firms Cater to Powerful Women," *USA TODAY*, June 18, 2002, p. 3B.

14. Anonymous, "Retailers Learn That Electronics Shopping Isn't Just a Guy Thing," *Wall Street Journal*, January 15, 2004, p. D3.

15. Hillary Chura, "Failing to Connect: Marketing Messages for Women Fall Short," *Advertising Age*, September 23, 2002, pp. 13–14.

16. Betty Wood, "A Royal Reward," *Marketing Magazine Online*, www.marketmag.ca, June 17, 2000; Chris Daniels, "Pulling No

Punches," Report on Market Shares: Financial Services, *Marketing Magazine*, May 7, 2002, p. 11.

17. James U. McNeal, "Tapping the Three Kids' Markets," *American Demographics* (April 1998): 37–41.

18. Chris Powell, "Under the Influence," *Marketing Magazine*, February 16, 2004; Media Awareness Network, "How Marketers Target Kids," www.media-awareness.ca/english/parents/marketing/marketers_target_kids.cfm.

19. Jennifer Bayot, "The Teenage Market; Young, Hip and Looking for a Bargain," *The New York Times*, December 1, 2003, p. C8.

20. Stephanie Whittaker, "Tweens and Teens Lobby for High-Speed Access," *Marketing Magazine Online*, www.marketmag.ca, May 21, 2001 (viewed July 13, 2004)

21. Corus Entertainment, www.corusent.com/tv/ytv/index.asp (viewed October 16, 2004).

22. Courtney Kane, "TV and Movie Characters Sell Children's Snacks," *New York Times*, December 8, 2003, p. C.7.

23. Peter Diekmeyer, "Get 'Em While They're Still Young: Mouvement Desjardins Uses School Program to Market Savings Accounts to Students," *Strategy: The Canadian Marketing Report*, March 11, 2002, p. 25.

24. Lawrence Lepisto, "A Life Span Perspective of Consumer Behavior," in Elizabeth Hirshman and Morris Holbrook (eds.), *Advances in Consumer Research*, vol. 12 (Provo, UT: Association for Consumer Research, 1985), p. 47. Also see Gail Sheehy, *New Passages: Mapping Your Life Across Time* (New York: Random House, 1995).

25. See Frederick Herzberg, *Work and the Nature of Man* (Cleveland: William Collins, 1966); Henk Thierry and Agnes M. Koopman-Iwerna, "Motivation and Satisfaction," in P. J. Drenth (ed.), *Handbook of Work and Organizational Psychology* (New York: John Wiley, 1984), pp. 141–142.

26. Harold H. Kassarjian and Mary Jane Sheffet, "Personality and Consumer Behavior: An Update," in Harold H. Kassarjian and Thomas S. Robertson (eds.), *Perspectives in Consumer Behavior* (Glenview, IL: Scott, Foresman, 1981), pp. 160–180.

27. Jennifer Aaker, "Dimensions of Measuring Brand Personality," *Journal of Marketing Research* 34 (August 1997): 347–356.

28. M. Joseph Sirgy, "Self Concept in Consumer Behavior: A Critical Review," *Journal of Consumer Research*, 9 (December 1982), pp. 287–300.

29. Timothy R. Graeff, "Consumption Situations and the Effects of Brand Image on Consumers' Brand Evaluations," *Psychology & Marketing*, 1997, 14 (1): 49–70; Timothy R. Graeff, "Image Congruence Effects on Product Evaluations: The Role of Self-Monitoring and Public/Private Consumption," *Psychology & Marketing*, 13, no. 5 (1996): 481–499.

30. Jennifer L. Aaker, "The Malleable Self: The Role of Self-Expression in Persuasion," *Journal of Marketing Research*, 36, no. 2 (1999): 45–57.

31. Amy Cortese, "They Care About the World (and They Shop Too)," *The New York Times*, July 20, 2003, pp. 3–4.

32. Anthony Banco and Wendy Zellner, "Is Wal-Mart Too Powerful?" *Business Week*, October 6, 2003, p. 100.

33. Toby Weber, "All Three? Gee," *Wireless Review* (May 2003): 12–14.

34. Noel C. Paul, "Meal Kits in Home," *Christian Science Monitor*, June 9, 2003, p. 13.

35. Thomas J. Reynolds and Jonathan Gutman, "Laddering Theory, Method, Analysis, and Interpretation," *Journal of Advertising Research* (February–March 1988): 11–34.

36. Ernest Dichter, *Handbook of Consumer Motivations* (New York: McGraw-Hill, 1964).

37. Jan Callebaut et al., *The Naked Consumer: The Secret of Motivational Research in Global Marketing* (Antwerp, Belgium: Censydiam Institute, 1994).

38. Melanie Wells, "Mind Games," *Forbes*, September 1, 2003, p. 70.

39. Abraham Maslow, *Motivation and Personality* (New York: Harper and Row, 1954), pp. 80–106.

40. See Frederick Herzberg, *Work and the Nature of Man* (Cleveland: William Collins, 1966); Henk Thierry and Agnes M. Koopman-Iwerna, "Motivation and Satisfaction," in P. J. Drenth (ed.), *Handbook of Work and Organizational Psychology* (New York: John Wiley, 1984), pp. 141–142.

41. Bernard Berelson and Gary A. Steiner, *Human Behavior: An Inventory of Scientific Findings* (New York: Harcourt, Brace Jovanovich, 1964), p. 88.

42. J. Edward Russo, Margaret G. Meloy, T.J. Wilks, "The Distortion of Product Information During Brand Choice," *Journal of Marketing Research*, 35 (1998): 438–452.

43. Leslie de Chernatony and Simon Knox, "How an Appreciation of Consumer Behavior Can Help in Product Testing," *Journal of Market Research Society*, (July 1990): 333. See also Chris Janiszewski and Stiju M. J. Osselar, "A Connectionist Model of Brand-Quality Association," *Journal of Marketing Research*, August 2000, pp. 331–351.

44. Florida's Chris Janiszewski has developed a fascinating research program looking at preconscious processing effects. See Chris Janiszewski, "Preattentive Mere Exposure Effects," *Journal of Consumer Research*, 20 (December 1993): 376–392, as well as some of his earlier and subsequent research.

45. See Timothy E. Moore, "Subliminal Advertising: What You See Is What You Get," *Journal of Marketing*, 46, 1982, pp. 38–47 for an early classic and Andrew B. Aylesworth, Ronald C. Goodstein, and Ajay Kalra, "Effect of Archetypal Embeds on Feelings: An Indirect Route to Affecting Attitudes?" *Journal of Advertising*, 28, no. 3 (1999): 73–81 for a more current treatment.

46. John R. Anderson, *The Architecture of Cognition* (Cambridge, MA: Harvard University Press, 1983); Robert S. Wyer, Jr. and Thomas K. Srull, "Person Memory and Judgment," *Psychological Review*, 96, no. 1 (1989): 58–83.

47. Marc Gobe, "Emotional Identity," *Global Cosmetic Industry*, 171, no. 2 (February 2003): pp. 26–27; Fara Warner, "Upscale Chocolates Not Hot, So Godiva Does a Makeover" *Brandweek*, July 4, 1994, p. 21.

48. For additional discussion, see John G. Lynch Jr. and Thomas K. Srull, "Memory and Attentional Factors in Consumer Choice: Concepts and Research Methods," *Journal of Consumer Research*, 9 (June 1982): 18–36, and Joseph W. Alba, J. Wesley Hutchinson, and John G. Lynch, Jr., "Memory and Decision Making," in *Handbook of Consumer Theory and Research*, Harold H. Kassarjian and Thomas S. Robertson (eds.) (Englewood Cliffs, NJ: Prentice-Hall, Inc., 1992), pp. 1–49.

49. Fergus I. M. Craik and Robert S. Lockhart, "Levels of Processing: A Framework for Memory Research," *Journal of Verbal Learning and Verbal Behavior*, 11 (1972): 671–684; Fergus I. M. Craik and Endel Tulving, "Depth of Processing and the Retention of Words in Episodic Memory," *Journal of Experimental Psychology*, 104, no. 3 (1975): 268–294; Robert S. Lockhart, Fergus I. M. Craik, and Larry Jacoby, "Depth of Processing, Recognition, and Recall," in *Recall and Recognition*, John Brown, ed. (New York: John Wiley & Sons, Inc., 1976).

50. Leonard M. Lodish, Magid Abraham, Stuart Kalmenson, Jeanne Livelsberger, Beth Lubetkin, Bruce Richardson, and Mary Ellen Stevens, "How T.V. Advertising Works: A Meta Analysis of 389 Real World Split Cable T.V. Advertising Experiments," *Journal of Marketing Research*, 32 (May 1995): 125–139.

51. Elizabeth F. Loftus and Gregory R. Loftus, "On the Permanence of Stored Information in the Human Brain," *American Psychologist*, 35 (May 1980): 409–420.

52. Benson Shapiro, V. Kasturi Rangan, and John Sviokla, "Staple Yourself to an Order," *Harvard Business Review* (July–August 1992): 113–122. See also Carrie M. Heilman, Douglas Bowman, and Gordon P. Wright, "The Evolution of Brand Preferences and Choice Behaviors of Consumers New to a Market," *Journal of Marketing Research* (May 2000): 139–155.

53. Alison Stein Wellner, "Research on a Shoestring," *American Demographics* (April 2001): 38–39.

54. Marketing scholars have developed several models of the consumer buying process. See John A. Howard and Jagdish N. Sheth, *The Theory of Buyer Behavior* (New York: Wiley, 1969); James F. Engel, Roger D. Blackwell, and Paul W. Miniard, *Consumer Behavior*, 8th ed. (Fort Worth, TX: Dryden, 1994); Mary Frances Luce, James R. Bettman, and John W. Payne, *Emotional Decisions: Tradeoff Difficulty and Coping in Consumer Choice*, (Chicago, IL: University of Chicago Press, 2001).

55. William P. Putsis Jr. and Narasimhan Srinivasan, "Buying or Just Browsing? The Duration of Purchase Deliberation," *Journal of Marketing Research* (August 1994): 393–402.

56. Earle Eldridge, "Many Car Shoppers First Stop Is 'Consumer Reports,'" *USA Today*, September 16, 2003, pp. 1B–2B.

57. Adrienne Sanders, "Yankee Imperialism," *Forbes*, December 13, 1999, p. 56.

58. Norma Ramage, "Ending the Online Free Ride," *Marketing Magazine Online*, www.marketmag.ca, January 12, 2004 (viewed July 14, 2004).

59. Chem L. Narayana and Rom J. Markin, "Consumer Behavior and Product Performance: An Alternative Conceptualization," *Journal of Marketing* (October 1975): 1–6. See also Wayne S. DeSarbo and Kamel Jedidi, "The Spatial Representation of Heterogeneous Consideration Sets," *Marketing Science* 14, no. 3, pt. 2 (1995): 326–342; Lee G. Cooper and Akihiro Inoue, "Building Market Structures from Consumer Preferences," *Journal of Marketing Research* 33, no. 3 (August 1996): 293–306.

60. Virginia Postrel, "The Lessons of the Grocery Shelf Also Have Something to Say About Affirmative Action," *New York Times*, January 30, 2003, p. C2.

61. David Krech, Richard S. Crutchfield, and Egerton L. Ballachey, *Individual in Society* (New York: McGraw-Hill, 1962), ch. 2.

62. "Biotech Council Breaks Toronto Transit Shelter Campaign," *Adnews On-Line Daily*, June 10, 2002.

63. See Paul E. Green and Yoram Wind, *Multiattribute Decisions in Marketing: A Measurement Approach* (Hinsdale, IL: Dryden, 1973), ch. 2; Leigh McAlister, "Choosing Multiple Items from a Product Class," *Journal of Consumer Research* (December 1979): 213–224; Richard J. Lutz, "The Role of Attitude Theory in Marketing," in Kassarjian and Robertson (eds.) *Perspectives in Consumer Behavior*, 317–339.

64. This expectancy-value model was originally developed by Martin Fishbein, "Attitudes and Prediction of Behavior," in Martin Fishbein (ed.), *Readings in Attitude Theory and Measurement* (New York: John Wiley, 1967), pp. 477–492. For a critical review, see Paul W. Miniard and Joel B. Cohen, "An Examination of the Fishbein-Ajzen Behavioral-Intentions Model's Concepts and Measures," *Journal of Experimental Social Psychology* (May 1981): 309–339.

65. Michael R. Solomon, *Consumer Behavior: Buying, Having and Being* (Upper Saddle River, NJ: Prentice-Hall, 2001).

66. James R. Bettman, Eric J. Johnson, and John W. Payne, "Consumer Decision Making," in *Handbook of Consumer Theory and Research*, Harold H. Kassarjian and Thomas S. Robertson (eds.) (Englewood Cliffs, NJ: Prentice-Hall, Inc., 1992), pp. 50–84.

67. Jagdish N. Sheth, "An Investigation of Relationships among Evaluative Beliefs, Affect, Behavioral Intention, and Behavior," in John U. Farley, John A. Howard, and L. Winston Ring (eds.), *Consumer Behavior: Theory and Application* (Boston: Allyn & Bacon, 1974), pp. 89–114.

68. Fishbein, "Attitudes and Prediction of Behavior."

69. Raymond A. Bauer, "Consumer Behavior as Risk Taking," in Donald F. Cox (ed.), *Risk Taking and Information Handling in Consumer Behavior* (Boston: Division of Research, Harvard Business School, 1967); James W. Taylor, "The Role of Risk in Consumer Behavior," *Journal of Marketing* (April 1974): 54–60.

70. Priscilla A. La Barbera and David Mazursky, "A Longitudinal Assessment of Consumer Satisfaction/Dissatisfaction: The Dynamic Aspect of the Cognitive Process," *Journal of Marketing Research* (November 1983): 393–404.

71. Ralph L. Day, "Modeling Choices among Alternative Responses to Dissatisfaction," *Advances in Consumer Research*, 11 (1984): 496–499. Also see Philip Kotler and Murali K. Mantrala, "Flawed Products: Consumer Responses and Marketer Strategies," *Journal of Consumer Marketing* (Summer 1985): 27–36.

72. Barry L. Bayus, "Word of Mouth: The Indirect Effects of Marketing Efforts," *Journal of Advertising Research* (June–July 1985): 31–39.

73. Albert O. Hirschman, *Exit, Voice, and Loyalty* (Cambridge, MA: Harvard University Press, 1970).

74. Mary C. Gilly and Richard W. Hansen, "Consumer Complaint Handling as a Strategic Marketing Tool," *Journal of Consumer Marketing* (Fall 1985): 5–16.

75. James H. Donnelly Jr. and John M. Ivancevich, "Post-Purchase Reinforcement and Back-Out Behavior," *Journal of Marketing Research* (August 1970): 399–400.

76. John D. Cripps, "Heuristics and Biases in Timing the Replacement of Durable Products," *Journal of Consumer Research*, 21 (September 1994): 304–318.

77. Richard E. Petty and John T. Cacioppo, *Attitudes and Persuasion: Classic and Contemporary Approaches* (New York: McGraw-Hill, 1981); Richard E. Petty, *Communication and Persuasion: Central and Peripheral Routes to Attitude Change* (New York: Springer-Verlag, 1986).

78. Herbert E. Krugman, "The Impact of Television Advertising: Learning without Involvement," *Public Opinion Quarterly* (Fall 1965): 349–356.

79. Frank R. Kardes, *Consumer Behavior and Managerial Decision-Making*, 2nd ed. (Upper Saddle River, NJ: Prentice-Hall, 2003).

80. See Richard Thaler, "Mental Accounting and Consumer Choice," *Marketing Science*, 4, no. 3 (1985): 199–214 for a seminal piece, and Richard Thaler, "Mental Accounting Matters," *Journal of Behavioral Decision-Making*, 12, no. 3 (1999): 183–206 for more contemporary perspectives.

81. Gary L. Gastineau and Mark P. Kritzman, *Dictionary of Financial Risk Management*, 3rd ed. (New York: John Wiley & Sons, 1999).

82. Example adapted from Daniel Kahneman, and Amos Tversky, "Prospect Theory: An Analysis of Decision Under Risk," *Econometrica*, 47 (March 1979): pp. 263–291.

83. Harper W. Boyd Jr. and Sidney Levy, "New Dimensions in Consumer Analysis," *Harvard Business Review* 163 (November–December): 129–140.

84. Sandra Vandermerwe, *Customer Capitalism: Increasing Returns in New Market Spaces* (London: Nicholas Brealey Publishing), ch. 11.

85. Patricia B. Seybold, "Get Inside the Lives of Your Customers," *Harvard Business Review* (May 2001): 81–89.

Chapter 7

1. Janet Guyon, "The Man Who Mooned Larry Ellison," *Fortune*, July 7, 2003, pp. 71–74.

2. James C. Anderson and James A. Narus, *Business Market Management: Understanding, Creating and Delivering Value* (Upper Saddle River, NJ: Prentice Hall, 1998).

3. Frederick E. Webster Jr. and Yoram Wind, *Organizational Buying Behavior* (Upper Saddle River, NJ: Prentice Hall, 1972), p. 2.

4. Jennifer Gilbert, "Small but Mighty," *Sales & Marketing Management* (January 2004): pp. 30–35.

5. Michael Collins, "Breaking into the Big Leagues," *American Demographics* (January 1996): 24.

6. Industry Canada, *Report on "Key Small Business Statistics,"* www.strategis.ic.gc.ca, April 2004 (viewed July 19, 2004).

7. Patrick J. Robinson, Charles W. Faris, and Yoram Wind, *Industrial Buying and Creative Marketing* (Boston: Allyn & Bacon, 1967).

8. Daniel H. McQuiston, "Novelty, Complexity, and Importance as Causal Determinants of Industrial Buyer Behavior," *Journal of Marketing* (April 1989): 66–79; Peter Doyle, Arch G. Woodside, and Paul Mitchell, "Organizational Buying in New Task and Rebuy Situations," *Industrial Marketing Management* (February 1979): 7–11.

9. Urban B. Ozanne and Gilbert A. Churchill Jr., "Five Dimensions of the Industrial Adoption Process," *Journal of Marketing Research* (August 1971): 322–328.

10. Magna International, www.magna.com (viewed July 19, 2004); Magna International *2003 Annual Report* (viewed July 19, 2004).

11. Donald W. Jackson Jr., Janet E. Keith, and Richard K. Burdick, "Purchasing Agents' Perceptions of Industrial Buying Center Influence: A Situational Approach," *Journal of Marketing* (Fall 1984): 75–83.

12. Webster and Wind, *Organizational Buying Behavior*, p. 6.

13. Webster and Wind, *Organizational Buying Behavior*, p. 6.

14. Frederick E. Webster Jr. and Yoram Wind, "A General Model for Understanding Organizational Buying Behavior," *Journal of Marketing*, 36 (April 1972): 12–19; Webster and Wind, *Organizational Buying Behavior*.

15. Frederick E. Webster Jr. and Kevin Lane Keller, "A Roadmap for Branding in Industrial Markets," working paper, Amos Tuck School of Business, Dartmouth College.

16. Scott Ward and Frederick E. Webster Jr., "Organizational Buying Behavior" in *Handbook of Consumer Behavior*, edited by Tom Robertson and Hal Kassarjian (Upper Saddle River, NJ: Prentice-Hall, 1991), pp. 419–458.

17. Webster and Wind, *Organizational Buying Behavior*, p. 6.

18. CN Web site, "CN Announces New Sales and Marketing Structure to Improve Customer Service," CN News Release, April 14, 2004 (viewed July 23, 2004).

19. Nirmalya Kumar, *Marketing as Strategy: Understanding the CEO's Agenda for Driving Growth and Innovation* (Boston: Harvard Business School Press, 2004).

20. Kumar, *Marketing as Strategy*.

21. Sara Lorge, "Purchasing Power," *Sales & Marketing Management* (June 1998): 43–46.

22. David Hannon, "Lockheed Martin: Negotiators Inc.," *Purchasing*, February 5, 2004, pp. 27–30.

23. Anderson and Narus, *Business Market Management: Understanding, Creating and Delivering Value*.

24. Adapted from Peter Kraljic, "Purchasing Must Become Supply Management," *Harvard Business Review* (September–October 1993): 109–117.

25. Tim Minahan, "OEM Buying Survey—Part 2: Buyers Get New Roles but Keep Old Tasks," *Purchasing*, July 16, 1998, pp. 208–209.

26. Robinson, Faris, and Wind, *Industrial Buying and Creative Marketing*.

27. Ceridian Canada, "New Branding Campaign from Ceridian Canada Offers Businesses 'The Freedom to Succeed,'" News Release, February 12, 2002, www.ceridian.ca (viewed June 8, 2002).

28. Rajdeep Grewal, James M. Comer, and Raj Mehta, "An Investigation into the Antecedents of Organizational Participation in Business-to-Business Electronic Markets," *Journal of Marketing*, 65 (July 2001): pp. 17–33.

29. "The Digital Economy in Canada: Canadian e-Commerce Statistics," http://e-com.ic.gc.ca/epic/internet/inecic-ceac.nsf/en/gv00163e.html (viewed September 3, 2005).

30. Industry Canada, "Key Small Business Statistics," http://strategis.ic.gc.ca/sbstatistics, July 2005 (viewed August 23, 2005).

31. David Hannon, "Owens Corning Plans to Go 80% Paperless by End-2004," *Purchasing*, January 15, 2004, pp. 16, 18.

32. Kate Maddox, "#1 Hewlett-Packard Co., www.hp.com," *BtoB*, August 11, 2003, pp. 1, 23.

33. Robert Hiebeler, Thomas B. Kelly, and Charles Ketteman, *Best Practices: Building Your Business with Customer-Focused Solutions* (New York: Arthur Andersen/Simon & Schuster, 1998), pp. 122–124.

34. "Xerox Multinational Supplier Quality Survey," *Purchasing*, January 12, 1995, p. 112.

35. Daniel J. Flint, Robert B. Woodruff, and Sarah Fisher Gardial, "Exploring the Phenomenon of Customers' Desired Value Change in a Business-to-Business Context," *Journal of Marketing*, 66 (October 2002): 102–117.

36. Donald R. Lehmann and John O'Shaughnessy, "Differences in Attribute Importance for Different Industrial Products," *Journal of Marketing* (April 1974): 36–42.

37. Minahan, "OEM Buying Survey–Part 2: Buyers Get New Roles but Keep Old Tasks."

38. See James A. Narus and James C. Anderson, "Turn Your Industrial Distributors into Partners," *Harvard Business Review* (March–April 1986): 66–71; William Atkinson, "Now That's Value Add," *Purchasing*, December 11, 2003, p. 26.

39. Arnt Buvik and George John, "When Does Vertical Coordination Improve Industrial Purchasing Relationships," *Journal of Marketing*, 64 (October 2000): 52–64.

40. Shankar Ganesan, "Determinants of Long-Term Orientation in Buyer–Seller Relationships," *Journal of Marketing*, 58 (April 1994): 1–19; Patricia M. Doney and Joseph P. Cannon, "An Examination of the Nature of Trust in Buyer–Seller Relationships," *Journal of Marketing*, 61 (April 1997): 35–51.

41. John H. Sheridan, "An Alliance Built on Trust," *Industry Week*, March 17, 1997, pp. 66–70.

42. William W. Keep, Stanley C. Hollander, and Roger Dickinson, "Forces Impinging on Long-Term Business-to-Business Relationships in the United States: An Historical Perspective," *Journal of Marketing*, 62 (April 1998): 31–45.

43. Joseph P. Cannon and William D. Perreault Jr., "Buyer–Seller Relationships in Business Markets," *Journal of Marketing Research*, 36 (November 1999): 439–460.

44. Joseph P. Cannon and William D. Perreault Jr., "Buyer–Seller Relationships in Business Markets, *Journal of Marketing Research*, 36 (November 1999): 439–460.

45. Thomas G. Noordewier, George John, and John R. Nevin, "Performance Outcomes of Purchasing Arrangements in Industrial Buyer–Vendor Arrangements," *Journal of Marketing*, 54 (October), 80–93; Arnt Buvik and George John, "When Does Vertical Coordination Improve Industrial Purchasing Relationships," *Journal of Marketing*, 64 (October 2000): 52–64.

46. Akesel I. Rokkan, Jan B. Heide, and Kenneth H. Wathne, "Specific Investment in Marketing Relationships: Expropriation and Bonding Effects," *Journal of Marketing Research*, 40 (May 2003): 210–224.

47. Mrinal Ghosh and George John, "Governance Value Analysis and Marketing Strategy," *Journal of Marketing*, 63 (Special Issue, 1999): 131–145.

48. Sandy Jap, "Pie Expansion Effects: Collaboration Processes in Buyer–Seller Relationships," *Journal of Marketing Research*, 36 (November 1999): 461–475.

49. Arnt Buvik and George John, "When Does Vertical Coordination Improve Industrial Purchasing Relationships," *Journal of Marketing*, 64 (October 2000): 52–64.

50. Kenneth H. Wathne and Jan B. Heide, "Opportunism in Interfirm Relationships: Forms, Outcomes, and Solutions," *Journal of Marketing*, 64 (October 2000): 36–51.

51. Mary Walton, "When Your Partner Fails You," *Fortune*, 135, no. 10, pp. 87–89.

52. Mark B. Houston and Shane A. Johnson, "Buyer–Supplier Contracts Versus Joint Ventures: Determinants and Consequences

of Transaction Structure," *Journal of Marketing Research*, 37 (February 2000): 1–15.

53. Akesel I. Rokkan, Jan B. Heide, and Kenneth H. Wathne, "Specific Investment in Marketing Relationships: Expropriation and Bonding Effects," *Journal of Marketing Research*, 40 (May 2003): 210–224.

54. Contracts Canada, "The Basics of Selling to Government," www.contractscanada.gc.ca (viewed July 19, 2004).

55. Casey Mahood, "Bombardier Lands Huge Jet Order," *The Globe and Mail*, March 30, 2000, pp. B1, B15; Bombardier Web site, "Bombardier Wins Transportation Supply Contract Worth $7.9 Billion Cdn for the London Underground in U.K.," Press Release, April 7, 2003, www.aerospace.bombardier.com (viewed July 19, 2004); Helena Katz, "Hot Wheels! To Get Good Traction Brand in the Expanding All-Terrain Market, Newcomer Bombardier Must Build Its Brand," *Marketing Magazine Online*, www.marketingmag.com, June 14, 1999; Bombardier Web site, "Bombardier Aerospace Launches e-Business Customer Service Initiative," Press Release, October 10, 2000, www.aerospace.bombardier.com (viewed October 5, 2002).

Chapter 8

1. James C. Anderson and James A. Narus, "Capturing the Value of Supplementary Services," *Harvard Business Review* (January–February 1995): 75–83.

2. Greg Burns, "It Only Hertz When Enterprise Laughs," *Business Week*, December 12, 1994, p. 44.

3. Tevfik Dalgic and Maarten Leeuw, "Niche Marketing Revisited: Concept, Applications, and Some European Cases," *European Journal of Marketing* 28, no. 4 (1994): 39–55.

4. Craig Wilson, "Hallmark Hits the Mark," *USA TODAY*, June 14, 2001, pp. 1D–2D.

5. Ian Zack, "Out of the Tube," *Forbes*, November 26, 2001, p. 200.

6. Robert Blattberg and John Deighton, "Interactive Marketing: Exploiting the Age of Addressibility," *Sloan Management Review* 33, no. 1 (1991): 5–14.

7. David Stipp, "How Genetech Got It," *Fortune*, June 9, 2003, pp. 81–88.

8. Hermann Simon, *Hidden Champions* (Boston: Harvard Business School Press, 1996).

9. Paul Davidson, "Entrepreneurs Reap Riches from Net Niches," *USA Today*, April 20, 1998, p. B3.

10. www.ostrichesonline.com.

11. Lisa D'Innocenzo, "Death of the Canadian Ad?" *Strategy Magazine Online*, www.strategymag.com, March 22, 2004 (viewed August 3, 2004); Joe Hospodarec, "The Creative Eye," *Marketing Magazine Online*, www.marketingmag.ca, October 27, 2003 (viewed August 3, 2004).

12. Peter Post, "Beyond Brand—The Power of Experience Branding," *ANA/The Advertiser* (October–November 2000).

13. Joe Sharkey, "Attention Holiday Inn Towel Snatchers: All Is Forgiven," *New York Times*, July 15, 2003, p. C.7; Travel Almanac column, "Get Above It All, Ride a Balloon," *Houston Chronicle*, August 17, 2003, p. 3.

14. B. Joseph Pine and James H. Gilmore, *The Experience Economy: Work Is Theatre & Every Business a Stage*, Cambridge, MA: Harvard University Press, 1999.

15. Arlene Weintrub, "Chairman of the Board," *Business Week*, May 28, 2001, p. 96.

16. Don Peppers and Martha Rogers, *The One-to-One Future: Building Relationships One Customer at a Time* (New York: Currency/Doubleday, 1993).

17. Adrian J. Slywotzky and David J. Morrison, *How Digital Is Your Business?* (New York: Crown Business, 2000), p. 39.

18. Jerry Wind and A. Rangaswamy, "Customerization: The Second Revolution in Mass Customization," Wharton School Working Paper, June 1999.

19. James C. Anderson and James A. Narus, "Capturing the Value of Supplementary Services," *Harvard Business Review* (January–February 1995): 75–83.

20. Joann Muller, "Kmart Con Salsa: Will It Be Enough?" *Business Week*, September 9, 2002.

21. Chris Powell, "Globe Offers T.O. with I.Q.," *Marketing Magazine Online*, www.marketingmag.ca, September 15, 2003 (viewed August 3, 2004).

22. Kate Kane, "It's a Small World," *Working Woman* (October 1997): 22.

23. Other leading suppliers of geodemographic data are ClusterPlus (by Donnelly Marketing Information Services) and Acord (C.A.C.I., Inc.).

24. Becky Ebenkamp, "Urban America Redefined," *Brandweek*, October 6, 2003, pp. 12–13; Christina Del Valle, "They Know Where You Live: And How You Buy," *BusinessWeek*, February 7, 1994, p. 89.

25. www.claritas.com.

26. Michael J. Weiss, *The Clustering of America* (New York: Harper and Row, 1988); *Breaking Up Is Hard to Do: The Clustered World* (Boston: Little, Brown & Co., 2000).

27. "CANFAR Hires Zeppelin to Handle Have a Heart Campaign," *Adnews On-Line Daily*, June 11, 2002.

28. Michael J. Weiss, "To Be about to Be," *American Demographics*, September 2003, pp. 29–36.

29. Andrew Tilin, "Will the Kids Buy It?" *Business 2.0* (May 2003): 94–99; Sholnn Freeman and Norihiko Shirouzu, "Toyota's Gen Y Gamble—New Scion Line Sure Is Boxy but It's an Early Success as Youth Shun Dad's Camry," *Wall Street Journal*, July 30, 2003, p. B1; Keith Naughton, "Hip to Be Square," *Newsweek*, October 21, 2002, pp. 50–51.

30. Sarah Allison and Carlos Tejada," Mr., Mrs., Meet Mr. Clean," *The Wall Street Journal*, January 30, 2003, pp. B1, B3.

31. Jim Rendon, "Rear Window," *Business 2.0*, August 2003, p. 72.

32. Joanne Thomas Yaccato, "Through the Gender Lens," *Marketing Magazine Online*, www.marketingmag.ca, June 30, 2003 (viewed August 3, 2004); Lisa D'Innocenzo, "Maytag in Lingerie," *Strategy Magazine*, October 15, 2004, p. 6.

33. Samson Okalow, "BMO InvestorLine Hits the Links for RSP Season," *Strategy Magazine*, May 3, 2004, p. 13.

34. Gregory L. White and Shirley Leung, "Middle Market Shrinks as Americans Migrate toward the Higher End, *Wall Street Journal*, March 29, 2002, pp. A1, A8.

35. Michael Silverstein and Neil Fiske, *Trading Up: The New American Luxury* (Portfolio, 2003).

36. Linda Tischler, "The Price Is Right," *Fast Company*, November 2003, pp. 83–91; Statistics Canada 2001 Census, "Income of Families, Individuals and Households," www.statscan.ca (viewed August 3, 2004).

37. Geoffrey E. Meredith, Charles D. Schewe, and Janice Karlovich, *Defining Markets, Defining Moments* (New York: Hungrey Minds, Inc., 2002).

38. Andrew E. Serwer, "42,496 Secrets Bared," *Fortune*, January 24, 1994, pp. 13–14; Kenneth Labich, "Class in America," *Fortune*, February 7, 1994, pp. 114–126.

39. Leah Rickard, "Gerber Trots Out New Ads Backing Toddler Food Line," *Advertising Age*, April 11, 1994, pp. 1, 48.

40. Harold Thorkilsen, "Manager's Journal: Lessons of the Great Cranberry Crisis," *Wall Street Journal*, December 21, 1987, p. 20.

41. Pam Danziger, "Getting More for V-Day," *Brandweek*, February 9, 2004, p. 19.

42. Allana Sullivan, "Mobil Bets Drivers Pick Cappuccino over Parties," *Wall Street Journal*, January 30, 1995.

43. This classification was adapted from George H. Brown, "Brand Loyalty: Fact or Fiction?" *Advertising Age*, June 1952–January 1953, a series. See also Peter E. Rossi, R. McCulloch, and G. Allenby, "The Value of Purchase History Data in Target Marketing," *Marketing Science* 15, no. 4 (1996): 321–340.

44. Chip Walker, "How Strong Is Your Brand," Marketing Tools (January/February 1995): pp. 46–53.

45. www.conversionmodel.com.

46. Michele Marchetti, "Dell Computer," *Sales & Marketing Management* (October 1997): 50–53.

47. Industry Canada, "Key Small Business Statistics—April 2004," www.strategis.ic.gc.ca (viewed August 8, 2004).

48. Lisa D'Innocenzo, "Big Box Goes Downtown," *Strategy Magazine Online*, www.Strategymag.com, December 1, 2003 (viewed August 8, 2004).

49. Thomas S. Robertson and Howard Barich, "A Successful Approach to Segmenting Industrial Markets," *Planning Forum* (November–December 1992): 5–11.

50. Neil Rackham and John DeVincentis, *Rethinking the Sales Force: Redefining Selling to Create and Capture Customer Value* (New York: McGraw-Hill, 1999), ch. 1.

51. Wendell R. Smith, "Product Differentiation and Market Segmentation as Alternative Marketing Strategies," *Journal of Marketing* (July 1956): 4.

52. www.esteelauder.com.

53. Marc Gunther, "Tree Huggers, Soy Lovers, and Profits," *Fortune*, June 23, 2003, pp. 98–104.

54. Catherine Arns, "PC Makers Head for 'SoHo,'" *BusinessWeek*, September 28, 1992, pp. 125–126; Gerry Khermouch, "The Marketers Take Over," *Brandweek*, September 27, 1993, pp. 29–35.

55. For a market-structure study of the hierarchy of attributes in the coffee market, see Dipak Jain, Frank M. Bass, and Yu-Min Chen, "Estimation of Latent Class Models with Heterogeneous Choice Probabilities: An Application to Market Structuring," *Journal of Marketing Research* (February 1990): 94–101. For an application of means–end chain analysis to global markets, see Freakel Ter Hofstede, Jan-Benrlict E. M. Steenkamp, and Michel Wedel, "International Market Segmentation Based on Consumer–Product Relations," *Journal of Marketing Research* (February 1999): 1–17.

56. Bart Macchiette and Roy Abhijit, "Sensitive Groups and Social Issues," *Journal of Consumer Marketing* 11, no. 4 (1994): 55–64.

57. Barry Meier, "Data on Tobacco Show a Strategy Aimed at Blacks," *New York Times*, February 6, 1998, p. A1; Gregory Freeman, "Ads Aimed at Blacks and Children Should Exact a High Price," *St. Louis Post-Dispatch*, p. B1.

58. Patrick Lejtenyi, "Underlying Differences," *Marketing Magazine Online*, www.marketingmag.ca, June 5, 2000.

59. Caroline E. Mayer, "Nurturing Brand Loyalty; With Preschool Supplies, Firms Woo Future Customers—and Current Parents," *The Washington Post*, October 12, 2003, p. F1.

60. Concerned Children's Advertisers, www.cca-canada.com (viewed August 8, 2004).

Chapter 9

1. Interbrand Group, *World's Greatest Brands: An International Review* (New York: John Wiley, 1992).

2. Jacob Jacoby, Jerry C. Olson, and Rafael Haddock, "Price, Brand Name, and Product Composition Characteristics as Determinants of Perceived Quality," *Journal of Consumer Research*, 3, no. 4 (1971): 209–216; Jacob Jacoby, George Syzbillo, and Jacqueline Busato-Sehach, "Information Acquisition Behavior in Brand Choice Situations," *Journal of Marketing Research*, 11 (1977): 63–69.

3. Leslie de Chernatony and Gil McWilliam, "The Varying Nature of Brands as Assets," *International Journal of Advertising*, 8, no. 4 (1989): 339–349.

4. Constance E. Bagley, *Managers and the Legal Environment: Strategies for the 21st Century*, 2nd ed. (Cincinnati, OH: West Publishing, 1995).

5. Tulin Erdem, "Brand Equity as a Signaling Phenomenon," *Journal of Consumer Psychology*, 7, no. 2 (1998): 131–157.

6. Scott Davis, *Brand Asset Management* (San Francisco: Jossey-Bass, 2000); D. C. Bello and M. B. Holbrook, "Does an Absence of Brand Equity Generalize Across Product Classes?" *Journal of Business Research*, 34 (1996): 125–131; Mary W. Sullivan, "How Brand Names Affect the Demand for Twin Automobiles," *Journal of Marketing Research* 35 (1998): 154–165; Adrian J. Slywotzky and Benson P. Shapiro, "Leveraging to Beat the Odds: The New Marketing Mindset," *Harvard Business Review* (September–October 1993): 97–107.

7. The power of branding is not without its critics, however, some of whom reject the commercialism associated with branding activities. See Naomi Klein, *No Logo: Taking Aim at the Brand Bullies* (New York: Picador, 2000).

8. Charles Bymer, "Valuing Your Brands: Lessons from Wall Street and the Impact on Marketers," *ARF Third Annual Advertising and Promotion Workshop*, February 5–6, 1991.

9. Kevin Lane Keller, "The Brand Report Card," *Harvard Business Review* (January–February 2000): 147–157.

10. Other approaches are based on economic principles of signalling (e.g., Tulin Erdem, "Brand Equity as a Signaling Phenomenon," *Journal of Consumer Psychology*, 7, no. 2 (1998): 131–157), or more of a sociological, anthropological, or biological perspective (e.g., Grant McCracken, "Culture and Consumption: A Theoretical Account of the Structure and Movement of the Cultural Meaning of Consumer Goods," *Journal of Consumer Research*, 13 (1986): 71–83, or Susan Fournier, "Consumers and Their Brands: Developing Relationship Theory in Consumer Research," *Journal of Consumer Research*, 24, no. 3 (1998): 343–373).

11. David A. Aaker, *Managing Brand Equity* (New York: Free Press, 1991); David A. Aaker *Building Strong Brands* (New York: Free Press, 1996); David A. Aaker and Erich Joachimsthaler, *Brand Leadership* (New York: Free Press, 2000); Kevin Lane Keller, *Strategic Brand Management*, 2nd ed. (Upper Saddle River, NJ: Prentice-Hall, 2003).

12. Jean-Noel Kapferer, *Strategic Brand Management: New Approaches to Creating and Evaluating Brand Equity* (London: Kogan Page, 1992), p. 38; Jennifer L. Aaker, "Dimensions of Brand Personality," *Journal of Marketing Research* (August 1997): 347–356; Scott Davis, *Brand Asset Management: Driving Profitable Growth Through Your Brands* (San Francisco: Jossey-Bass, 2000). For an overview of academic research on branding, see Kevin Lane Keller, "Branding and Brand Equity," in *Handbook of Marketing*, edited by Bart Weitz and Robin Wensley (Sage Publications, 2002), pp. 151–178.

13. Kevin Lane Keller, *Strategic Brand Management*, 2nd ed. (Upper Saddle River, NJ: Prentice-Hall, 2003).

14. Alice Z. Cuneo, "Apple Transcends as Lifestyle Brand," *Advertising Age*, December 15, 2003, pp. S2, S6; "Big Apple Comes to Toronto," Media Briefs, *Marketing Magazine Online*, June 4, 2001.

15. Angela Scardillo, "Making Milk COOL," *Marketing Magazine*, August 11, 2003.

16. Melanie Wells, "Red Baron," *Forbes*, July 3, 2000, pp. 151–160; Kerry Capell with Wendy Zellner, "Richard Branson's Next Big Adventure," *BusinessWeek*, March 8, 2004, pp. 44–45; Kerry Capell, "Virgin Takes E-wing," *BusinessWeek e.biz*, January 22, 2001, pp. EB30–34.

17. David A. Aaker, *Building Strong Brands* (New York: Free Press, 1995).

18. GM Canada Press Release, "Canadian Alpine Ski Team and GM Canada Combine to Blow Away the Competition," Oshawa, Ontario (September 27, 2004); Aaker, *Building Strong Brands*.

19. Kevin Lane Keller, "Building Customer-Based Brand Equity: A Blueprint for Creating Strong Brands," *Marketing Management*, 10 (July/August 2001): 15–19.

20. Christine Bittar, "Old Spice Does New Tricks," *Brandweek*, June 2, 2003, pp. 17–18.

21. Paul Keegan, "The Rise and Fall (and Rise Again) of Joe Boxer, *Business 2.0* (December 2002/January 2003): 76–82.

22. Alex Taylor III, "VW Learns What's in a Name: Trouble," *Fortune*, August 11, 2003, p. 40.

23. Kim Robertson, "Strategically Desirable Brand Name Characteristics," *Journal of Consumer Marketing* (Fall 1989): 61–70; C. Kohli and D. W. LaBahn, "Creating Effective Brand Names: A Study of the Naming Process," *Journal of Advertising Research* (January/February 1997): 67–75.

24. Robert Salerno, "We Try Harder: An Ad Creates a Brand," *Brandweek*, September 8, 2003, pp. 32, 33.

25. Don E. Schultz, Stanley I. Tannenbaum, and Robert F. Lauterborn, *Integrated Marketing Communications* (Lincolnwood, IL: NTC Business Books, 1993).

26. Mohanbir Sawhney, "Don't Harmonize, Synchronize," *Harvard Business Review* (July–August 2001): 101–108.

27. David C. Court, John E. Forsyth, Greg C. Kelly, and Mark A. Loch, "The New Rules of Branding: Building Strong Brands Faster," *McKinsey Marketing Practice* 13; Scott Bedbury, *A New Brand World* (New York: Viking Press, 2002).

28. Sonia Reyes, "Cheerios: The Ride," *Brandweek*, September 23, 2002, pp. 14–16.

29. Ian Wylie, "These Lollies Are About to Go Pop," *Fast Company* (December 2002): 52–54.

30. Christopher Locke, Rick Levine, Doc Searls, David Weinberger, *The Cluetrain Manifesto: The End of Business as Usual* (Cambridge: Perseus Press, 2000).

31. Bruce Horovitz, "Gen Y: A Tough Crowd to Sell," *USA Today*, April 22, 2002, p. B1.

32. *Kellogg on Integrated Marketing*, edited by Dawn Iacobucci and Bobby Calder (New York: John Wiley & Sons, 2003).

33. Drew Madsen, "Olive Garden: Creating Value Through an Integrated Brand Experience," presentation at Marketing Science Institute Conference, *Brand Orchestration*, Orlando, FL, December 4, 2003.

34. Scott Davis and Michael Dunn, *Building the Brand Driven Business* (New York: John Wiley & Sons, 2002); Colin Mitchell, "Selling the Brand Inside," *Harvard Business Review* (January 2002): 99–105.

35. Stan Maklan and Simon Knox, *Competing on Value* (Upper Saddle River, NJ: Financial Times Prentice-Hall, 2000).

36. Lesley Young, "From the Inside Out," *Marketing Magazine Online*, www.marketingmag.ca, April 19, 2004 (viewed August 13, 2004).

37. Laurel Wentz, "Brand Audits Reshaping Images," *Ad Age International* (September 1996): pp. 38–41.

38. Keller, *Strategic Brand Management*; Todd Wasserman, "Sharpening the Focus," *Brandweek*, November 3, 2003, pp. 28–32.

39. Danny Kucharsky, "Employees Star in Standard Life Ads," *Marketing Magazine Online*, www.marketingmag.ca, September 30, 2002 (viewed August 13, 2004).

40. Gerry Khermouch and Diane Brady, "Brands in an Age of Anti-Americanism," *BusinessWeek*, August 4, 2003, pp. 69–78. The article ranks the 100 best global brands using the valuation method developed by Interbrand. See also "Marked by the Market," *The Economist*, December 1, 2001, pp. 59–60 for an illustration of Stern Stewart's Wealth Added Index.

41. Aaker, *Building Strong Brands*. Also see Patrick Barwise et al., *Accounting for Brands* (London: Institute of Chartered Accountants in England and Wales, 1990); Peter H. Farquhar, Julia

42. Y. Han, and Yuji Ijiri, "Brands on the Balance Sheet," *Marketing Management* (Winter 1992): 16–22.

42. Joann Muller, "Honey, I Shrank the Box," *Forbes*, November 10, 2003, pp. 82–86.

43. David Kiley, "To Boost Sales, Volvo Returns to Its Roots: Safety," *USA Today*, August 26, 2002, p. 6B.

44. Natalie Mizik and Robert Jacobson, "Trading Off Between Value Creation and Value Appropriation: The Financial Implications of Shifts in Strategic Emphasis," *Journal of Marketing*, 67 (January 2003): 63–76.

45. Mark Speece, "Marketer's Malady: Fear of Change," *Brandweek*, August 19, 2002, p. 34.

46. Keith Naughton, "Fixing Cadillac, *Newsweek*, May 28, 2001, pp. 36–37.

47. Tamara Kaplan, "The Tylenol Crisis: How Effective Public Relations Saved Johnson & Johnson,"1998, www.personal.psu.edu/users/w/x/wxk116/tylenol/crisis.html.

48. Norman Klein and Stephen A. Greyser, "The Perrier Recall: A Source of Trouble," Harvard Business School Case #9-590-104 and "The Perrier Relaunch," Harvard Business School Case #9-590-130.

49. Ronald Alsop, "Enduring Brands Hold Their Allure by Sticking Close to Their Roots," *Wall Street Journal Centennial Edition*, 1989.

50. Peter Farquhar, "Managing Brand Equity," *Marketing Research*, 1 (September 1989): 24–33.

51. Steven M. Shugan, "Branded Variants," 1989 AMA Educators' Proceedings (Chicago: American Marketing Association, 1989), pp. 33–38. See also M. Bergen, S. Dutta, and S. M. Shugan, "Branded Variants: A Retail Perspective," *Journal of Marketing Research*, 33 (February 1996): 9–21.

52. Constance L. Hays, "No More Brand X: Licensing of Names Adds to Image and Profit," *New York Times*, June 12, 1998, p. D1; Carleen Hawn, "What's in a Name? Whatever You Make It," *Forbes*, July 27, 1998, pp. 84–88; Carl Quintanilla, "Advertising: Caterpillar, Deere Break Ground in Consumer-Product Territory," *Wall Street Journal*, June 20, 1996, p. B2. Also see David A. Aaker, Building Strong Brands (New York: The Free Press, 1995).

53. Becy Ebenkamp, "The Creative License," *Brandweek*, June 9, 2003, pp. 36–40.

54. Theodore Levitt, "Marketing Success Through Differentiation—of Anything," *Harvard Business Review* (January–February 1980): 83–91.

55. Byung-Do Kim and Mary W. Sullivan, "The Effect of Parent Brand Experience on Line Extension Trial and Repeat Purchase," *Marketing Letters*, 9 (April 1998): 181–193.

56. Kevin Lane Keller and David A. Aaker, "The Effects of Sequential Introduction of Brand Extensions," *Journal of Marketing Research*, 29 (February 1992): 35–50; John Milewicz and Paul Herbig, "Evaluating the Brand Extension Decision Using a Model of Reputation Building," *Journal of Product & Brand Management*, 3, no 1 (1994): 39–47.

57. Mary W. Sullivan, "Brand Extensions: When to Use Them," *Management Science*, 38, no. 6 (June 1992): 793–806; Daniel C. Smith, "Brand Extension and Advertising Efficiency: What Can and Cannot Be Expected," *Journal of Advertising Research* (November/December 1992): 11–20. See also Daniel C. Smith and C. Whan Park, "The Effects of Brand Extensions on Market Share and Advertising Efficiency," *Journal of Marketing Research*, 29 (August 1992): 296–313.

58. Lesley Young, "New and Approved," *Marketing Magazine Online*, www.marketingmag.ca, April 5, 2004 (viewed August 13, 2004).

59. Subramanian Balachander and Sanjoy Ghose, "Reciprocal Spillover Effects: A Strategic Benefit of Brand Extensions," *Journal of Marketing*, 67, no. 1 (January 2003).

60. John A. Quelch and David Kenny, "Extend Profits, Not Product Lines," *Harvard Business Review* (September–October 1994): 153–160; Bruce G. S. Hardle, Leonard M. Lodish, James V. Kilmer,

and David R. Beatty et al., "The Logic of Product-Line Extensions," *Harvard Business Review* (November–December 1994): 53–62; J. Andrews and G. S. Low, "New but Not Improved: Factors That Affect the Development of Meaningful Line Extensions," Working Paper Report No. 98-124 (Cambridge, MA: Marketing Science Institute, November 1998); Maureen Morrin, "The Impact of Brand Extensions on Parent Brand Memory Structures and Retrieval Processes," *Journal of Marketing Research*, 36, no. 4 (1999): 517–525.

61. Al Ries and Jack Trout, *Positioning: The Battle for Your Mind* (New York: McGraw-Hill, 1981).

62. David A. Aaker, *Brand Portfolio Strategy: Creating Relevance, Differentiation, Energy, Leverage, and Clarity* (New York: Free Press, 2004).

63. Mary W. Sullivan, "Measuring Image Spillovers in Umbrella-Branded Products," *Journal of Business*, 63, no. 3 (1990): 309–329.

64. Barbara Loken and Deborah Roedder John, "Diluting Brand Beliefs: When Do Brand Extensions Have a Negative Impact?" *Journal of Marketing* (July 1993): 71–84; Deborah Roedder John, Barbara Loken, and Christopher Joiner, "The Negative Impact of Extensions: Can Flagship Products Be Diluted?" *Journal of Marketing* (January 1998): 19–32; Susan M. Broniarcyzk and Joseph W. Alba, "The Importance of the Brand in Brand Extension," *Journal of Marketing Research* (May 1994): 214–28 (this entire issue of *JMR* is devoted to brands and brand equity). See also R. Ahluwalia and Z. Gürhan-Canli, "The Effects of Extensions on the Family Brand Name: An Accessibility-Diagnosticity Perspective," *Journal of Consumer Research* 27 (December 2000): 371–381; Z. Gürhan-Canli and M. Durairaj, "The Effects of Extensions on Brand Name Dilution and Enhancement," *Journal of Marketing Research* 35 (1998): 464–473; S. J. Milberg, C. W. Park, and M. S. McCarthy, "Managing Negative Feedback Effects Associated with Brand Extensions: The Impact of Alternative Branding Strategies," *Journal of Consumer Psychology*, 6 (1997): 119–140.

65. Andrea Rothman, "France's Bic Bets U.S. Consumers Will Go for Perfume on the Cheap," *Wall Street Journal*, January 12, 1989, p. B6.

66. Philip Kotler, *Marketing Management*, 11th ed. (Upper Saddle River, NJ: Prentice-Hall, 2003): Patrick Barwise and Thomas Robertson, "Brand Portfolios," *European Management Journal*, 10, no. 3 (September 1992): 277–285.

67. Jack Trout, *Differentiate or Die: Survival in Our Era of Killer Competition* (New York: Wiley, 2000).

68. Nirmalya Kumar, "Kill a Brand, Keep a Customer," *Harvard Business Review* (December 2003): 87–95.

69. For a methodological approach for assessing the extent and nature of cannibalization, see Charlotte H. Mason and George R. Milne, "An Approach for Identifying Cannibalization within Product Line Extensions and Multi-Brand Strategies," *Journal of Business Research*, 31 (1994): 163–170.

70. Paul W. Farris, "The Chevrolet Corvette," Case UVA-M-320, The Darden Graduate Business School Foundation, University of Virginia, Charlottesville, Virginia.

Chapter 10

1. Kortney Stringer, "Hard Lesson Learned: Premium and No-Frills Don't Mix," *Wall Street Journal*, November 3, 2003, p. B1.

2. Al Ries and Jack Trout, *Positioning: The Battle for Your Mind* (New York: Warner Books, 1982).

3. Lesley Young, "Plucky Branding," *Marketing Magazine Online*, www.marketingmag.ca, October 6, 2003 (viewed August 29, 2004).

4. The concept of "points-of-parity" and "points-of-difference" and many of the other ideas and examples in this section were first developed by Northwestern University's Brian Sternthal and further refined in collaboration with Northwestern University's Alice Tybout.

5. Richard Heller, "Folk Fortune," *Forbes*, September 4, 2000, pp. 66–69.

6. Julia Boorstin, "How Coach Got Hot," *Fortune*, October 28, 2002, pp. 132–134.

7. "Adams Ads Push Natural Qualities of Peanut Butter," *Marketing Magazine Online*, www.marketingmag.ca, March 18, 2002 (viewed August 19, 2004).

8. Jim Hopkins, "When the Devil Is in the Design, *USA Today* December 31, 2001, p. 3B.

9. Keith Naughton, "Ford's 'Perfect Storm,'" *Newsweek*, September 17, 2001, pp. 48–50.

10. Dale Buss, "Sweet Success," *Brandweek*, May 12, 2003, pp. 22–23.

11. Lisa D'Innocenzo, "Moores: For Guys Who Hate to Shop," *Strategy Magazine Online*, www.strategymag.com, May 3, 2004 (viewed August 19, 2004).

12. WestJet Web site, http://c0dsp.westjet.com/internet/sky/about/index.jsp (viewed May 20, 2002); WestJet Annual Information Form 2001, March 20, 2002; Norma Ramage, "WestJet Revels in Rival's Shadow," *Marketing Magazine Online*, www.marketingmag.ca, May 6, 2002; Norma Ramage, "Clive's Flight Plan," *Marketing Magazine Online*, www.marketingmag.ca, September 10, 2001; Sarah Smith, "Flying Cluttered Skies," *Marketing Magazine Online*, www.marketingmag.ca, April 9, 2001; Peter Fitzpatrick, "Canadian Considers No-frills Flying," *The Financial Post*, April 12, 1999, p. C3; and Mathew Ingram, "WestJet on the Right Flight Path," *The Globe and Mail*, September 8, 1998, p. B2.

13. Bridget Finn, "Selling Cool in a Bottle—of Dish Soap," *Business 2.0*, December 2003, pp. 72–73.

14. Robert D. Buzzell and Bradley T. Gale, *The PIMS Principles: Linking Strategy to Performance* (New York: The Free Press, 1987).

15. "The 25 Best Sales Forces," *Sales & Marketing Management* (July 1998): 32–50.

16. For a similar list, see Leonard L. Berry and A. Parasuraman, *Marketing Services: Competing Through Quality* (New York: The Free Press, 1991), p. 16.

17. *Canada's 50 Best Managed Companies*, www.canadas50best.com/en/default.htm (viewed February 7, 2005); Personal Services, www.capitalcitysavings.ca/default.htm (viewed February 7, 2005).

18. William C. Symonds, "Working for Working Adults," *Business Week*, June 9, 2003, p. 86; www.uopxworld.com/Infopages/distance-education-canada.asp (viewed February 7, 2005).

19. Karen Axelrod and Bruce Brumberg, *Watch It Made in the U.S.A.* (Santa Fe: John Muir Publications, 1997).

20. The Bata Shoe Museum, www.batashoemuseum.ca (viewed August 20, 2004).

21. Some authors distinguished additional stages. Wasson suggested a stage of competitive turbulence between growth and maturity. See Chester R. Wasson, *Dynamic Competitive Strategy and Product Life Cycles* (Austin, TX: Austin Press, 1978). Maturity describes a stage of sales growth slowdown and saturation, a stage of flat sales after sales have peaked.

22. John E. Swan and David R. Rink, "Fitting Market Strategy to Varying Product Life Cycles," *Business Horizons* (January–February 1982): 72–76; Gerald J. Tellis and C. Merle Crawford, "An Evolutionary Approach to Product Growth Theory," *Journal of Marketing* (Fall 1981): 125–134.

23. William E. Cox Jr., "Product Life Cycles as Marketing Models," *Journal of Business* (October 1967): 375–384.

24. Jordan P. Yale, "The Strategy of Nylon's Growth," *Modern Textiles Magazine* (February 1964): 32; Also see Theodore Levitt, "Exploit the Product Life Cycle," *Harvard Business Review* (November–December 1965): 81–94.

25. Chester R. Wasson, "How Predictable Are Fashion and Other Product Life Cycles?" *Journal of Marketing* (July 1968): 36–43.

26. Chester R. Wasson, "How Predictable Are Fashion and Other Product Life Cycles?" *Journal of Marketing* (July 1968): 36–43.

27. William H. Reynolds, "Cars and Clothing: Understanding Fashion Trends," *Journal of Marketing* (July 1968): 44–49.

28. Patrick Butters, "What Biggest Selling Adult Game Still Cranks Out Vexing Questions?" *Insight on the News*, January 26, 1998, p. 39.

29. Robert D. Buzzell, "Competitive Behavior and Product Life Cycles," in *New Ideas for Successful Marketing*, edited by John S. Wright and Jack Goldstucker (Chicago: American Marketing Association, 1956), p. 51.

30. Rajesh J. Chandy, Gerard J. Tellis, Deborah J. MacInnis, and Pattana Thaivanich, "What to Say When: Advertising Appeals in Evolving Markets," *Journal of Marketing Research*, 38 (November): 399–414.

31. William T. Robinson and Claes Fornell, "Sources of Market Pioneer Advantages in Consumer Goods Industries," *Journal of Marketing Research* (August 1985): 305–317. Glen L. Urban et al., "Market Share Rewards to Pioneering Brands: An Empirical Analysis and Strategic Implications," *Management Science* (June 1986): 645–659.

32. Gregory S. Carpenter and Kent Nakamoto, "Consumer Preference Formation and Pioneering Advantage," *Journal of Marketing Research* (August 1989): 285–298.

33. William T. Robinson and Sungwook Min, "Is the First to Market the First to Fail? Empirical Evidence for Industrial Goods Businesses," *Journal of Marketing Research*, 39 (February 2002): 120–128.

34. Frank R. Kardes, Gurumurthy Kalyanaram, Murali Chankdrashekaran, and Ronald J. Dornoff, "Brand Retrieval, Consideration Set Composition, Consumer Choice, and the Pioneering Advantage," *Journal of Consumer Research* (June 1993): 62–75. See also Frank H. Alpert and Michael A. Kamins, "Pioneer Brand Advantage and Consumer Behavior: A Conceptual Framework and Propositional Inventory," *Journal of the Academy of Marketing Science* (Summer 1994): 244–253.

35. Thomas S. Robertson and Hubert Gatignon, "How Innovators Thwart New Entrants into Their Market," *Planning Review* (September–October 1991): 4–11, 48; Douglas Bowman and Hubert Gatignon, "Order of Entry as a Moderator of the Effect of Marketing Mix on Market Share," *Marketing Science*, 15, no. 3 (1996): 222–242.

36. Venkatesh Shankar, Gregory S. Carpenter, Lakshman Krishnamurthi, "Late Mover Advantage: How Innovative Late Entrants Outsell Pioneers," *Journal of Marketing Research*, 35 (February 1998): 54–70.

37. Steven P. Schnaars, *Managing Imitation Strategies* (New York: The Free Press, 1994). See also Jin K. Han, Namwoon Kim, and Hony-Bom Kin, "Entry Barriers: A Dull-, One-, or Two-Edged Sword for Incumbents? Unraveling the Paradox from a Contingency Perspective," *Journal of Marketing* (January 2001): 1–14.

38. Victor Kegan, "Second Sight: Second Movers Take All," *The Guardian*, October 10, 2002.

39. Peter N. Golder and Gerald J. Tellis, "Pioneer Advantage: Marketing Logic or Marketing Legend?" *Journal of Marketing Research* (May 1992): 34–46; Shizhang and Arthur B. Markman "Overcoming the Early Advantge: The Role of Alignable and Nanalignable Differences, *Journal of Marketing Research* (November 1998): 1–15.

40. Gerald Tellis and Peter Golder, *Will & Vision: How Latecomers Can Grow to Dominate Markets* (New York: McGraw-Hill, 2001); Rajesh K. Chandy and Gerald J. Tellis, "The Incumbent's Curse? Incumbency, Size, and Radical Product Innovation," *Journal of Marketing Research* (July 2000): 1–17.

41. Linda Himelstein, "Yahoo! The Company, the Strategy, the Stock," *BusinessWeek*, September 7, 1998, pp. 66–76; Marc Gunther, "The Cheering Fades for Yahoo," *Fortune*, November 12, 2001;

Ben Elgin, "Inside Yahoo! The Untold Story of How Arrogance, Infighting, and Management Missteps Derailed One of the Hottest Companies on the Web," *BusinessWeek*, May 21, 2001, p. 114; Ben Elgin, "The Search War Is About to Get Bloody," *Business Week*, July 28, 2003, pp. 72–73.

42. Himelstein, "Yahoo! The Company, the Strategy, the Stock"; Gunther, "The Cheering Fades for Yahoo"; Elgin, "Inside Yahoo!"; Elgin, "The Search War Is About to Get Bloody."

43. "The History of the Mini 1959 to 2003," www.outmotoring.com/mini_history.html (viewed February 9, 2005); 2004 Marketing Awards "Television Production—Under $50,000 Campaign," *Marketing Magazine*, March 29, 2004.

44. Sarah Ellison, "P&G to Buy Glide Dental Floss, A Popular Brand," *Wall Street Journal*, September 17, 2003, p. A.19; "What's Hot: Promoting Dental Floss," *Drug Store News*, September 8, 2003, p. 23.

45. Allen J. McGrath, "Growth Strategies with a '90s Twist," *Across the Board*, March 1995, pp. 43–46.

46. Jane Eisinger Rooney, "Brand New Day," *Association Management*, February 2003, pp. 46–51.

47. Lisa D'Innocenzo, "Fewer Diapers, More Dating at Life Network," *Strategy Magazine Online*, www.strategymag.com, August 25, 2003 (viewed August 20, 2004); Alliance Atlantis Web site, www.allianceatlantis.com (viewed August 20, 2004).

48. Brian Wansink and Michael L. Ray, "Advertising Strategies to Increase Usage Frequency," *Journal of Marketing* (January 1996): 31–46. Also see Brian Wansink, "Expansion Advertising," in *How Advertising Works*, edited by John Philip Jones (Thousand Oaks, CA: Sage Publications), pp. 95–103.

49. Stephanie Thompson, "Coffee Brands Think Outside of the Can," *Advertising Age*, July 28, 2003, p. 26.

50. Vanessa O'Connell, "Food: After Years of Trial and Error, a Pickle Slice That Stays Put," *Wall Street Journal*, October 6, 1998, p. B1; "Vlasic's Hamburger-Size Pickles," *Wall Street Journal*, October 5, 1998, p. A26; www.vlasic.com.

51. Kathryn Shattuck, "Mouthwash Without the Bottle," *New York Times*, July 7, 2002, p. 32; Michael Beirne and Aaron Baar, "Altoids Takes Offense in Breath Strips War," *Brandweek*, December 9, 2002, p. 17.

52. Stephen M. Nowlis and Itamar Simonson, "The Effect of New Product Features on Brand Choice," *Journal of Marketing Research* (February 1996): 36–46.

53. Philip Kotler, "Phasing Out Weak Products," *Harvard Business Review* (March–April 1965): 107–118; Richard T. Hise, A. Parasuraman, and R. Viswanathan, "Product Elimination: The Neglected Management Responsibility," *Journal of Business Strategy* (Spring 1984): 56–63; George J. Avlonitis, "Product Elimination Decision Making: Does Formality Matter," *Journal of Marketing* (Winter 1985): 41–52.

54. Kathryn Rudie Harrigan, "The Effect of Exit Barriers upon Strategic Flexibility," *Strategic Management Journal*, 1 (1980): 165–176.

55. Kathryn Rudie Harrigan, "Strategies for Declining Industries," *Journal of Business Strategy*, (Fall 1980): 27.

56. "Hot Cereal Is One Hot Commodity," *Prepared Foods*, January 2000.

57. Philip Kotler, "Harvesting Strategies for Weak Products," *Business Horizons* (August 1978): 15–22; Laurence P. Feldman and Albert L. Page, "Harvesting: The Misunderstood Market Exit Strategy," *Journal of Business Strategy* (Spring 1985): 79–85.

58. Claudia H. Deutsch, "Pitney Bowes Survives Faxes, E-Mail and the Internet," *New York Times*, August 18, 1998, p. D1; Matthew Lubanko, "Pitney Bowes Faces E-Foes Despite Lion's Share of the Market," *Hartford Courant*, March 18, 2000, p. E1.

59. Nariman K. Dhalla and Sonia Yuspeh, "Forget the Product Life Cycle Concept!" *Harvard Business Review* (January–February 1976): 105.

60. Robert D. Buzzell, "Market Functions and Market Evolution," *Journal of Marketing*, 63 (Special Issue), 1999, pp. 61–63.

61. For a discussion of the evolution of the minivan market between 1982 and 1998, see José Antonio Rosa, Joseph F. Porac, Jelena Runser-Spanjol, and Michael S. Saxon, "Sociocognitive Dynamics in a Product Market," *Journal of Marketing*, 63 (Special Issue, 1999): 64–77.

62. Daniel Fisher, "Six Feet Under," *Forbes*, July 7, 2003, pp. 66–68.

Chapter 11

1. Leonard M. Fuld, *The New Competitor Intelligence: The Complete Resource for Finding, Analyzing, and Using Information about Your Competitors* (New York: John Wiley, 1995); John A. Czepiel, *Competitive Marketing Strategy* (Upper Saddle River, NJ: Prentice Hall, 1992).

2. Michael E. Porter, *Competitive Strategy* (New York: The Free Press, 1980), pp. 22–23.

3. Michael Barbero, "Tougher Toy Game Takes Its Toll on KB," *The Washington Post*, January 15, 2004, p. E01; Constance L. Hays, "Toy Retailers Find Prices At Wal-Mart Tough to Beat," *The New York Times*, December 23, 2003, p. C1.

4. Michael Krantz, "Click Till You Drop," *Time*, July 20, 1998, pp. 34–39; Michael Krauss, "The Web Is Taking Your Customers for Itself," *Marketing News*, June 8, 1998, p. 8.

5. Jonathan Gaw, "Britannica Gives In and Gets Online," *Los Angeles Times*, October 19, 2000, p. A1.

6. Allan D. Shocker, "Determining the Structure of Product-Markets: Practices, Issues, and Suggestions," in *Handbook of Marketing*, edited by Barton A. Weitz and Robin Wensley (London: Sage Publications, 2002), pp. 106–125. See also Bruce H. Clark and David B. Montgomery, "Managerial Identification of Competitors," *Journal of Marketing*, 63 (July 1999): 67–83.

7. Patti Summerfield, "Canada's Top 12 Media Companies," *Strategy Magazine*, November 17, 2003; Tom Lowry, Ronald Grover, Catherine Yang, Steve Rosenbush, and Peter Burrows, "Mega Media Mergers: How Dangerous?" *Business Week*, February 23, 2004, pp. 34–42.

8. James Mcquire, "Corel Wins Market Share from Microsoft Office," October 16, 2002, Newsfactor Network, www.newsfactor.com/perl/story/19693.html (viewed October 17, 2002); "Corel Corporation Wins Two SmallBusinessComputing.com Excellence in Technology Awards," Corel Press Release, Ottawa, January 31, 2005, www.corel.com.

9. Kathryn Rudie Harrigan, "The Effect of Exit Barriers upon Strategic Flexibility," *Strategic Management Journal*, 1 (1980): 165–176.

10. Michael E. Porter, *Competitive Advantage* (New York: The Free Press, 1985), pp. 225, 485.

11. Porter, *Competitive Strategy*, ch. 13.

12. Theodore Levitt's classic article, "Marketing Myopia," *Harvard Business Review* (July–August 1960): 45–56.

13. Jeffrey F. Rayport and Bernard J. Jaworski, *e-Commerce* (New York: McGraw-Hill, 2001), p. 53.

14. Porter, *Competitive Strategy*, ch. 7.

15. William E. Rothschild, *How to Gain (and Maintain) the Competitive Advantage* (New York: McGraw-Hill, 1989), ch. 5.

16. Fairmont Hotels & Resorts Web site, www.fairmont.com (viewed August 26, 2004); Paul Fengler and Garric Ng, "Green Consumer Guide," *Corporate Knights*, 1, no. 2 (Fall 2002): 25–27.

17. Starbucks, www.starbucks.com/aboutus/overview.asp.

18. Brian Wansink, "Can Package Size Accelerate Usage Volume," *Journal of Marketing*, 60 (July 1996): 1–14.

19. Elizabeth Jensen, "Wine Gets a Makeover: A Complex Zinfandel Becomes a Power 'Zin,'" *Wall Street Journal*, October 14, 1997, pp. A1, A6.

20. John D. Cripps, "Heuristics and Biases in Timing the Replacement of Durable Products," *Journal of Consumer Research*, 21 (September 1994): 304–318.

21. "Business Bubbles," *The Economist*," October 12, 2002.

22. Carla Rapoport, "You Can Make Money in Japan," *Fortune*, February 12, 1990, pp. 85–92; Keith H. Hammonds, "A Moment Kodak Wants to Capture," *BusinessWeek*, August 27, 1990, pp. 52–53; Alison Fahey, "Polaroid, Kodak, Fuji Get Clicking," *Advertising Age*, May 20, 1991, p. 18; Peter Nulty, "The New Look of Photography," *Fortune*, July 1, 1991, pp. 36–41.

23. Bruce Upbin, "Sharpening the Claws," *Forbes*, July 26, 1999, pp. 102–105.

24. Akio Morita, *Made in Japan* (New York: Dutton, 1986), ch. 1.

25. Jonathan Glancey, "The Private World of the Walkman," *The Guardian*, October 11, 1999.

26. Guy Stevenson, lunch address, Canadian Marketing Association Conference on Customer Relationship Management, Toronto, February 27, 2002; Deborah Stokes, "Consumer Love 'Churn,'" *The Financial Post*, March 1, 1999, p. C13.

27. The intensified competition that takes place worldwide has sparked management interest in models of military warfare; see Sun Tsu, *The Art of War* (London: Oxford University Press, 1963); Miyamoto Mushashi, *A Book of Five Rings* (Woodstock, NY: Overlook Press, 1974); Carl von Clausewitz, *On War* (London: Routledge & Kegan Paul, 1908); B. H. Liddell-Hart, *Strategy* (New York: Praeger, 1967).

28. These six defence strategies, as well as the five attack strategies, are taken from Philip Kotler and Ravi Singh, "Marketing Warfare in the 1980s," *Journal of Business Strategy* (Winter 1981): 30–41. For additional reading, see Gerald A. Michaelson, *Winning the Marketing War: A Field Manual for Business Leaders* (Lanham, MD: Abt Books, 1987); Al Ries and Jack Trout, *Marketing Warfare* (New York: New American Library, 1986); Jay Conrad Levinson, *Guerrilla Marketing* (Boston: Houghton-Mifflin Co., 1984); and Barrie G. James, *Business Wargames* (Harmondsworth, England: Penguin Books, 1984).

29. Porter, *Competitive Strategy*, ch. 4; Jaideep Prabhu and David W. Stewart, "Signaling Strategies in Competitive Interaction: Building Reputations and Hiding the Truth," *Journal of Marketing Research*, 38 (February 2001): 62–72.

30. Jehoshua Eliashberg and Thomas S. Robertson, "New Product Preannouncing Behavior: A Market Signaling Study," *Journal of Marketing Research*, 25, no. 93 (1988): 282–292; Roger J. Calantone and Kim E. Schatzel, "Strategic Foretelling: Communication-Based Antecedents of a Firm's Propensity to Preannounce," *Journal of Marketing*, 64 (January 2000): 17–30.

31. Thomas S. Robertson, Jehoshua Eliashberg, and Talia Rymon, "New Product Announcement Signals and Incumbent Reactions," *Journal of Marketing*, 59 (July 1995): 1–15.

32. Barry L. Bayus, Sanjay Jain, and Ambar G. Rao, "Truth or Consequences: An Analysis of Vaporware and New Product Announcements, *Journal of Marketing Research*, 38 (February 2001): 3–13.

33. Charles Haddad, "FedEx: Gaining on Ground," *Business Week*, December 16, 2002, pp. 126–128; Kevin Kelleher, "Why FedEx Is Gaining Ground," *Business 2.0* (October 2003): 56–57.

34. Philip Kotler and Paul N. Bloom, "Strategies for High Market-Share Companies," *Harvard Business Review* (November–December 1975): 63–72. Also see Porter, *Competitive Advantage*, pp. 221–226.

35. John Burghardt, "Viewpoint: He Who Slings Mud Loses Ground," *Strategy Magazine Online*, August 3, 1998 (viewed August 26, 2004); Ian Edwards, "Federal Election Wars," *Strategy Magazine Online*, June 14, 2004 (viewed August 26, 2004).

36. Robert D. Buzzell and Frederick D. Wiersema, "Successful Share-Building Strategies," *Harvard Business Review* (January–February 1981): 135–144.

37. Robert J. Dolan, "Models of Competition: A Review of Theory and Empirical Evidence," in *Review of Marketing*, edited by Ben M. Enis and Kenneth J. Roering (Chicago: American Marketing Association, 1981), pp. 224–234.

38. Linda Hellofs and Robert Jacobson, "Market Share and Customer's Perceptions of Quality: When Can Firms Grow Their Way to Higher Versus Lower Quality?" *Journal of Marketing*, 63 (January 1999): 16–25.

39. Alex Taylor III, "Lord of the Air," *Fortune*, November 10, 2003, pp. 144–152.

40. Lisa D'Innocenzo, "Triumph of the Underdog," *Strategy Magazine Online*, October 20, 2003 (viewed August 26, 2004).

41. Holman W. Jenkins Jr., "Business World: On a Happier Note, Orange Juice," *Wall Street Journal*, September 23, 1998, p. A23; Robert J. O'Harrow Jr., "PepsiCo to Acquire Quaker for $14 Billion," *Washington Post*, December 5, 2000, p. E01.

42. Eryn Brown, "Sony's Big Bazooka," *Fortune*, December 30, 2002, pp. 111–114.

43. Alison Overholt, "The Google of Email?" *Fast Company*, March 2004, p. 36; Michael Bazeley, "New Software Product Is Called the Google of Email," *Knight Ridder Tribune Business News*, April 14, 2004, p. 1.

44. "Boots Counts the Cost of Not Counting Pennies," *Marketing Week*, February 5, 2004, pp. 30–31.

45. Jean-Marc Leger and Dave Scholz, "The Appeal of Beer Ads," *Marketing Magazine*, June 17, 2002, p. 24.

46. Henny Sender, "World Business (A Special Report) Back from the Brink: Samsung Electronics Got into Trouble by Being Like Many Asian Firms; It Survived by Being Different," *The Wall Street Journal*, September 22, 2003, p. R5.

47. Theodore Levitt, "Innovative Imitation," *Harvard Business Review* (September–October 1966): 63. Also see Steven P. Schnaars, *Managing Imitation Strategies: How Later Entrants Seize Markets from Pioneers* (New York: The Free Press, 1994).

48. Stuart F. Brown, "The Company That Out-Harleys Harley," *Fortune*, September 28, 1998, pp. 56–57.

49. Allen J. McGrath, "Growth Strategies with a '90s Twist," *Across the Board* (March 1995): 43–46; Antonio Ligi, "The Bottom Line: Logitech Plots Its Escape from Mouse Trap," *Dow Jones Newswire*, February 20, 2001.

50. Jayne O'Donnell, "Family Rolling to Success on Tire Rack," *USA Today*, December 8, 2003, p. 3B.

51. Kristen Vinakmens, "Small but Mighty," *Strategy Magazine Online*, December 15, 2003 (viewed August 26, 2004).

52. Reported in E. R. Linneman and L. J. Stanton, *Making Niche Marketing Work* (New York: McGraw-Hill, 1991).

53. Thomas A. Fogarty, "Keeping Zippo's Flame Eternal," *USA Today*, June 24, 2003, p. 3B.

54. Matthew Maier, "Hooking Up With Gen Y," *Business 2.0* (October 2003): 49–52.

55. "Virgin Group and Bell Mobility Announce Partnership to Bring Virgin Mobile to Canada," Bell Canada Enterprises Press Release, www.bce.ca/en/news/releases/bc/2004/03/30/71061.html, March 30, 2004 (viewed February 13, 2005); Gerry Khermouch, "Richard Branson: Winning Virgin Territory," *Business Week*, December 22, 2003, p. 45.

56. Robert Spector, *Amazon.com: Get Big Fast* (New York: HarperBusiness, 2000), p. 151.

Chapter 12

1. This discussion is adapted from Theodore Levitt, "Marketing Success through Differentiation: Of Anything," *Harvard Business Review* (January–February 1980): 83–91. The first level, core benefit, has been added to Levitt's discussion.

2. Harper W. Boyd Jr. and Sidney Levy, "New Dimensions in Consumer Analysis," *Harvard Business Review* (November–December 1963): 129–140.

3. Theodore Levitt, *The Marketing Mode* (New York: McGraw-Hill, 1969), p. 2.

4. Joe Iannarelli, "Jamestown Container Thinks Outside the Box," *Business First*, October 3, 2003, p. 4.

5. Steven Rosenbush, "Verizon's Gutsy Bet," *Business Week*, August 4, 2003, pp. 53–62.

6. For some definitions, see *Dictionary of Marketing Terms*, edited by Peter D. Bennett (Chicago: American Marketing Association, 1995). Also see Patrick E. Murphy and Ben M. Enis, "Classifying Products Strategically," *Journal of Marketing* (July 1986): 24–42.

7. CHC Helicopter Web site, www.chc.ca (viewed September 16, 2004); Kathleen Martin, "Where Rotors Rule," *Marketing Magazine Online*, www.marketingmag.ca, April 2, 2001.

8. Some of these bases are discussed in David A. Garvin, "Competing on the Eight Dimensions of Quality," *Harvard Business Review* (November–December 1987): 101–109.

9. Seth Godin, "In Praise of the Purple Cow," *Fast Company* (February 2003): 74–85.

10. Purdy's Chocolates Web site, www.purdys.com; "The 50 Best Companies to Work for (in Canada)," *R.O.B. Magazine* (January 2002): 42.

11. Elizabeth Corcoran, "The E Gang," *Forbes*, July 24, 2000, p. 145.

12. Bernd Schmitt and Alex Simonson, *Marketing Aesthetics: The Strategic Management of Brand, Identity, and Image* (New York: The Free Press, 1997).

13. Bruce Nussbaum, "The Power of Design," *BusinessWeek*, May 17, 2004, pp. 88–94; "Masters of Design," *Fast Company*, June 2004, pp. 61–75. Also, see Philip Kotler, "Design: A Powerful but Neglected Strategic Tool," *Journal of Business Strategy* (Fall 1984): 16–21.

14. Steam Whistle Brewing Company Web site, www.steamwhistle.ca (viewed September 17, 2004); Lisa D'Innocenzo, "Saving Canadian Beer," *Strategy Magazine Online*, www.strategymag.com, September 8, 2003 (viewed September 17, 2004); Kristen Vinakmens, "Steam Whistle Goes West," *Strategy Magazine Online*, www.strategymag.com, June 16, 2003 (viewed September 17, 2004).

15. For a comprehensive discussion of Cemex, see Adrian J. Slywotzky and David J. Morrison, *How Digital Is Your Business* (New York: Crown Business, 2000), ch. 5.

16. "Pac Bell to Offer DSL, You Can Install," *San Francisco Chronicle*, March 20, 2000.

17. Mark Sanchez, "Herman Miller Offers Training to Its Furniture Users," *Grand Rapids Business Journal*, December 2, 2002, p. 23.

18. Shoppers Drug Mart Web site, www.shoppersdrugmart.ca (viewed September 17, 2004).

19. Linda Knapp, "A Sick Computer?" *Seattle Times*, January 28, 2001, p. D8.

20. "Best Buy Turns on the Geek Appeal," *DSN Retailing Today*, February 24, 2003, p. 22.

21. Robert Bordley, "Determining the Appropriate Depth and Breadth of a Firm's Product Portfolio, *Journal of Marketing Research*, 40 (February), 2003, pp. 39–53; Peter Boatwright and Joseph C. Nunes, "Reducing Assortment: An Attribute-Based Approach, *Journal of Marketing*, 65 (July 2001): 50–63.

22. Adapted from a Hamilton Consultants White Paper, December 1, 2000.

23. This illustration is found in Benson P. Shapiro, *Industrial Product Policy: Managing the Existing Product Line* (Cambridge, MA: Marketing Science Institute, September 1977), pp. 3–5, 98–101.

24. *The Economist*, "Brand Challenge," April 6, 2002, p. 68.

25. David A. Aaker, "Should You Take Your Brand to Where the Action Is?" *Harvard Business Review* (September–October 1997):

135–143; A. Kirmani, S. Sood, and S. Bridges, "The Ownership Effect in Consumer Responses to Brand Line Stretches," *Journal of Marketing* 63 (1999): 88–101; T. Randall, K. Ulrich, and D. Reibstein, "Brand Equity and Vertical Product Line Extent," *Marketing Science* 17 (1998): 356–379; Samson Okalow, "Exploiting Atkins," *Strategy Magazine*, February 9, 2004, p. 3.

26. Igor Reichlin, "Racing to Stay Ahead," *Chief Executive*, November 2003, pp. 50–53.

27. Steuart Henderson Britt, "How Weber's Law Can Be Applied to Marketing," *Business Horizons* (February 1975): 21–29.

28. John Willman, "Leaner, Cleaner, and Healthier Is the Stated Aim," *Financial Times*, February 23, 2000; John Thornhill, "A Bad Time to Be in Consumer Goods," *Financial Times*, September 28, 2000; "Unilever's Goal: 'Power Brands,'" *Advertising Age*, January 3, 2000; "Unilever Axes 25,000 Jobs," *CNNfn*, February 22, 2000; "Unilever Sees 395 Mln. Eur. Cost Savings This Yearr from Brand Reduction," *AFX* (UK), May 9, 2001; "A Chat with Unilever's Niall FitzGerald," *Business Week Online*, August 2, 2001; Harriet Marsh, "Unilever a Year Down the 'Path,'" *Marketing*, February 22, 2001, p. 30.

29. Andy Reinhardt, "Who Says Intel's Chips Are Down?" *BusinessWeek*, December 7, 1998, pp. 103–104; Therese Poletti, "Computer-Chip Price War Breaks Out," *San José Mercury News*, April 17, 2001; Cliff Edwards, "Intel: What Is CEO Craig Barrett Up To?" *BusinessWeek*, March 8, 2004, pp. 56–60.

30. Lee Gomes, "Computer-Printer Price Drop Isn't Starving Makers," *Wall Street Journal*, August 16, 1996, p. B4; Simon Avery, "H-P Sees Room for Growth in Printer Market," *Wall Street Journal*, June 28, 2001, p. B6; Ben Elgin, "Can HP's Printer Biz Keep Printing Money?" *BusinessWeek*, July 14, 2003, pp. 68–70.

31. Robert E. Weigand, "Buy In—Follow On Strategies for Profit," *Sloan Management Review* (Spring 1991): 29–37.

32. See Gerald J. Tellis, "Beyond the Many Faces of Price: An Integration of Pricing Strategies," *Journal of Marketing* (October 1986): 155. This excellent article also analyzes and illustrates other pricing strategies. Also see Dilip Soman and John T. Gourville, "Transaction Decoupling: How Price Bundling Affects the Decision to Consume," *Journal of Marketing Research*, 38 (February 2001): 30–44.

33. Adapted from George Wuebker, "Bundles Effectiveness Often Undermined," *Marketing News*, March 18, 2002, pp. 9–12. See Stefan Stremersch and Gerard J. Tellis, "Strategic Bundling of Products & Prices, *Journal of Marketing*, 66 (January 2002): 55–72.

34. Akshay R. Rao and Robert W. Ruekert, "Brand Alliances as Signals of Product Quality," *Sloan Management Review* (Fall 1994): 87–97; Akshay R. Rao, Lu Qu, and Robert W. Ruekert, "Signaling Unobservable Quality through a Brand Ally," *Journal of Marketing Research*, 36, no 2 (1999): 258–268.

35. Bernard L. Simonin and Julie A. Ruth, "Is a Company Known by the Company It Keeps? Assessing the Spillover Effects of Brand Alliances on Consumer Brand Attitudes," *Journal of Marketing Research* (February 1998): 30–42. See also C. W. Park, S. Y. Jun, and A. D. Shocker, "Composite Branding Alliances: An Investigation of Extension and Feedback Effects," *Journal of Marketing Research* 33 (1996): 453–466.

36. Chris Daniels, "Rogers and Yahoo! Co-brand Their Broadband," *Marketing Magazine Online Daily News*, www.marketingmag.ca, July 15, 2004 (viewed September 17, 2004).

37. C. W. Park, S. Y. Jun, and A. D. Shocker, "Composite Branding Alliances: An Investigation of Extension and Feedback Effects, " *Journal of Marketing Research*, 33 (1996): 453–466; Lance Leuthesser, Chiranjier Kohli, and Rajneesh Suri, "2+2 = 5? A Framework for Using Co-branding to Leverage a Brand," *Journal of Brand Management*, 2, no. 1 (September 2003): pp. 35–47.

38. Based in part on a talk by Nancy Bailey, "Using Licensing to Build the Brand," Brand Masters conference, December 7, 2000.

39. Kalpesh Kaushik Desai and Kevin Lane Keller, "The Effects of Brand Expansions and Ingredient Branding Strategies on Host Brand Extendibility," *Journal of Marketing*, 66 (January): 73–93; D. C. Denison, "Ingredient Branding Puts Big Names in the Mix," *The Boston Globe*, May 26, 2002, p. E2.

40. www.dupont.com.

41. Gerry Khermouch, "Zona Sets Collectible Max-packs," *Brandweek*, April 20, 1998, p. 16.

42. www.arizonabev.com.

43. Judith Rosen, "Classics Strategies; Classics Sale," *Publishers Weekly*, October 6, 2003, pp. 16–18; Karen Springen, "Nancy's Still Nice," *Newsweek*, February 16, 2004, p. 9.

44. Seth Goldin, "In Praise of Purple Cows," *Fast Company*, February 2003, pp. 74–85.

45. Susan B. Bassin, "Value-Added Packaging Cuts Through Store Clutter," *Marketing News*, September 26, 1988, p. 21.

46. Trish Hall, "New Packaging May Soon Lead to Food That Tastes Better and Is More Convenient," *Wall Street Journal*, April 21, 1986, p. 25.

47. "Tetra Pak Opens Innovative Environmentally Friendly Corporate Headquarters," *PR Newswire*, September 1, 1999.

48. Kate Fitzgerald, "Packaging Is the Capper," *Advertising Age*, May 5, 2003, p. 22.

49. Pam Weisz, "Repackaging," *Brandweek*, February 27, 1995, pp. 25–27.

50. "Campbell Soup Co. Changes the Look of Its Famous Cans," *The Wall Street Journal*, August 26, 1999, p. B10; Kate Novack, "Tomato Soup with a Side of Pop Art," *Time*, May 10, 2004.

51. Jason Stein, "10-Year Mitsubishi Warranty Is Small Part of a Larger Plan," *Automotive News*, January 12, 2004, p. 16.

52. "More Firms Pledge Guaranteed Service," *Wall Street Journal*, July 17, 1991, pp. B1, B6; Barbara Ettore, "Phenomenal Promises Mean Business," *Management Review* (March 1994): 18–23. Also see Christopher W. L. Hart, *Extraordinary Guarantees* (New York: Amacom, 1993); Sridhar Moorthy and Kannan Srinivasan, "Signaling Quality with a Money-Back Guarantee: The Role of Transaction Costs," *Marketing Science*, 14, no. 4 (1995): 442–446.

Chapter 13

1. Statistics Canada, "Gross Domestic Product at Basic Prices, Primary Industries," www.statcan.ca/english/Pgdb/prim03.htm (viewed June 14, 2004).

2. Statistics Canada, Business Patterns Database, December 2003, viewed online through Industry Canada, strategis.ic.gc.ca/sc_ecnmy/sio/cis11-33este.html.

3. Mohanbir Sawhney, Sridhar Balasubramanian, and Vish V. Krishnan, "Creating Growth with Services," *MIT Sloan Management Review* (Winter 2004): pp. 34–43.

4. Theodore Levitt, "Marketing Intangible Products and Product Intangibles," *Harvard Business Review* (May–June 1981): 94–102; Leonard L. Berry, "Services Marketing Is Different," *Business* (May–June 1980): 24–30.

5. Further classifications of services are described in Christopher H. Lovelock, *Services Marketing*, 3rd ed. (Upper Saddle River, NJ: Prentice Hall, 1996). Also see John E. Bateson, *Managing Services Marketing: Text and Readings*, 3rd ed. (Hinsdale, IL: Dryden, 1995).

6. Valarie A. Zeithaml, "How Consumer Evaluation Processes Differ between Goods and Services," in *Marketing of Services*, edited by J. Donnelly and W. R. George (Chicago: American Marketing Association, 1981), pp. 186–190.

7. Amy Ostrom and Dawn Iacobucci, "Consumer Trade-offs and the Evaluation of Services," *Journal of Marketing* (January 1995): 17–28.

8. Theodore Levitt, "Marketing Intangible Products and Product Intangibles," *Harvard Business Review* (May–June 1981): 94–102; Berry, "Services Marketing Is Different."

9. B. H. Booms and M. J. Bitner, "Marketing Strategies and Organizational Structures for Service Firms," in *Marketing of Services*, edited by J. Donnelly and W. R. George (Chicago: American Marketing Association, 1981), pp. 47–51.

10. Lewis P. Carbone and Stephan H. Haeckel, "Engineering Customer Experiences," *Marketing Management* (Winter 1994): 17.

11. Sarah Smith, "Call of the Yukon," *Marketing Magazine*, May 13, 2002, pp. 13–16.

12. "Viva Cirque Du Soleil!," *CBS News.com*, Feb. 20, 2005 www.cbsnews.com/stories/2005/02/18/60minutes/main675104.shtml; Cirque du Soleil Web site, www.cirquedusoleil.com/CirqueDuSoleil/en/default.htm; "Cirque du Soliel's Solstrom," *CBC.ca* Program guide, www.cbc.ca/programguide/program/index.jsp?program=Cirque+du+Soleil's+Solstrom.

13. G. Lynn Shostack, "Service Positioning Through Structural Change," *Journal of Marketing* (January 1987): 34–43.

14. Debra Zahay and Abbie Griffin, "Are Customer Information Systems Worth It? Results from B2B Services," *Marketing Science Institute Working Paper*, Report No. 02-113, 2002.

15. W. Earl Sasser, "Match Supply and Demand in Service Industries," *Harvard Business Review* (November–December 1976): 133–140.

16. Seth Godin, "If It's Broke, Fix It," *Fast Company* (October 2003): 131.

17. Diane Brady, "Why Service Stinks," *BusinessWeek*, October 23, 2000, pp. 119–128.

18. Bruce Horovitz, "Whatever Happened to Customer Service? Automated Answering, Long Waits Irk Consumers," *USA Today*, September 26, 2003, p. A1.

19. Horovitz, "Whatever Happened to Customer Service?"

20. "Air Canada Reports Highest System Load Factor for Any Month Ever in July," Air Canada News Release, Montreal, August 4, 2005; "Air Canada Ranked Best Airline in North America in International Survey of Air Travelers," Air Canada News Release, Montreal, June 2, 2005; "Ace Aviation Holdings Inc. Releases First Quarter Results," Air Canada News Release, Montreal, May 13, 2005.

21. However, see Ellen Day and Richard J. Fox, "Extended Warranties, Service Contracts, and Maintenance Agreement: A Marketing Opportunity?" *Journal of Consumer Marketing* (Fall 1985): 77–86.

22. Susan M. Keaveney, "Customer Switching Behavior in Service Industries: An Exploratory Study," *Journal of Marketing* (April 1995): 71–82. See also Michael D. Hartline and O. C. Ferrell, "The Management of Customer-Contact Service Employees: An Empirical Investigation," *Journal of Marketing* (October 1996): 52–70; Lois A. Mohr, Mary Jo Bitner, and Bernard H. Booms, "Critical Service Encounters: The Employee's Viewpoint," *Journal of Marketing* (October 1994): 95–106; Linda L. Price, Eric J. Arnould, and Patrick Tierney, "Going to Extremes: Managing Service Encounters and Assessing Provider Performance," *Journal of Marketing* (April 1995): 83–97; Jaishankar Ganesh, Mark J. Arnold, and Kristy E. Reynolds, "Understanding the Customer Base of Service Providers: An Examination of the Differences Between Switchers and Sayers," *Journal of Marketing*, 64 (July 2000): 65–87.

23. Christian Gronroos, "A Service Quality Model and Its Marketing Implications," *European Journal of Marketing* 18, no. 4 (1984): 36–44.

24. Leonard Berry, "Big Ideas in Services Marketing," *Journal of Consumer Marketing* (Spring 1986): 47–51. See also Walter E. Greene, Gary D. Walls, and Larry J. Schrest, "Internal Marketing: The Key to External Marketing Success," *Journal of Services Marketing* 8, no. 4 (1994): 5–13; John R. Hauser, Duncan I. Simester, and Birger Wernerfelt, "Internal Customers and Internal Suppliers," *Journal of Marketing Research* (August 1996): 268–280; Jagdip Singh, "Performance Productivity and Quality of

Frontline Employees in Service Organizations," *Journal of Marketing*, 64 (April 2000): 15–34.

25. Anonymous, "What Makes Singapore a Service Champion?" *Strategic Direction* (April 2003): 26–28.

26. Gronroos, "A Service Quality Model," pp. 38–39; Michael D. Hartline, James G. Maxham III, and Daryl O. McKee, "Corridors of Influence in the Dissemination of Customer-Oriented Strategy to Customer Contact Service Employees," *Journal of Marketing* (April 2000): 35–50.

27. Nilly Landau, "Are You Being Served?" *International Business* (March 1995): 38–40.

28. Philip Kotler and Paul N. Bloom, *Marketing Professional Services* (Upper Saddle River, NJ: Prentice Hall, 1984).

29. Glenn B. Voss, A. Parasuraman, and Dhruv Grewal, "The Role of Price, Performance, and Expectations in Determining Satisfaction in Service Exchanges," *Journal of Marketing*, 62 (October 1998), pp. 46–61.

30. www.ritzcarlton.com.

31. A. Parasuraman, Valarie A. Zeithaml, and Leonard L. Berry, "A Conceptual Model of Service Quality and Its Implications for Future Research," *Journal of Marketing* (Fall 1985): 41–50. See also Susan J. Devlin and H. K. Dong, "Service Quality from the Customers' Perspective," *Marketing Research: A Magazine of Management & Applications* (Winter 1994): 4–13; Michael K. Brady and J. Joseph Cronin Jr., "Some New Thoughts on Conceptualizing Perceived Service Quality," *Journal of Marketing*, 65 (July 2001): 34–49.

32. Leonard L. Berry and A. Parasuraman, *Marketing Services: Competing Through Quality* (New York: The Free Press, 1991), p. 16.

33. A. Parasuraman, Valarie A. Zeithaml, and Leonard L. Berry, "A Conceptual Model of Service Quality and Its Implications for Future Research," *Journal of Marketing* (Fall 1985): 41–50.

34. Danny Kucharsky, "Convergence Redeemers," *Marketing Magazine Online*, www.marketingmag.ca, January 26, 2004 (viewed September 21, 2004).

35. John Helyar, "At E*Trade, Growing Up Is Hard to Do," *Fortune*, March 18, 2002, pp. 88–90.

36. James L. Heskett, W. Earl Sasser Jr., and Christopher W. L. Hart, *Service Breakthroughs* (New York: The Free Press, 1990).

37. William C. Copacino, *Supply Chain Management* (Boca Raton, FL: St. Lucie Press, 1997).

38. Ryan Starr, "Book Value: Amazon.ca Isn't Winning the War with Heather Reisman Yet," *Canadian Business*, October 28, 2002, pp. 13–14.

39. Leonard L. Berry, Kathleen Seiders, and Dhruv Grewal, "Understanding Service Convenience," *Journal of Marketing*, 66 (July 2002): 1–17.

40. Mary Jo Bitner, "Self-Service Technologies: What Do Customers Expect?" *Marketing Management* (Spring 2001): 10–11; Matthew L. Meuter, Amy L. Ostrom, Robert J. Roundtree, and Mary Jo Bitner, "Self-Service Technologies: Understanding Customer Satisfaction with Technology Based Service Encounters," *Journal of Marketing*, 64 (July 2000): 50–64.

41. John A. Martilla and John C. James, "Importance-Performance Analysis," *Journal of Marketing* (January 1977): 77–79.

42. Interestingly, research has shown that customers who switch service providers due to dissatisfaction are likely to exhibit elevated levels of loyalty with their new firm. See Jaishankar Ganesh, Mark J. Arnold, and Kristy E. Reynolds, "Understanding the Customer Base of Service Providers: An Examination of the Differences Between Switchers and Stayers," *Journal of Marketing*, 64 (July 2000): 65–87.

43. John Goodman, *Technical Assistance Research Program* (TARP), U.S. Office of Consumer Affairs Study on Complaint Handling in America, 1986; Albrecht and Zemke, *Service America!*; Berry and Parasuraman, *Marketing Services*; Roland T. Rust, Bala Subramanian, and Mark Wells, "Making Complaints a

Management Tool," *Marketing Management*, 1, no. 3 (1992): 41–45; Stephen S. Tax, Stephen W. Brown, and Murali Chandrashekaran, "Customer Evaluations of Service Complaint Experiences: Implications for Relationship Marketing," *Journal of Marketing* (April 1998): 60–76.

44. Stephen S. Tax and Stephen W. Brown, "Recovering and Learning from Service Failure," *Sloan Management Review* (Fall 1998): 75–88.

45. Robert Hiebeler, Thomas B. Kelly, and Charles Ketteman, *Best Practices: Building Your Business with Customer-Focused Solutions* (New York: Arthur Andersen/Simon & Schuster, 1997), pp. 184–185.

46. Tax, Brown, and Chandrashekaran, "Customer Evaluations of Service Complaint Experiences"; Tax and Brown, "Recovering and Learning from Service Failures."

47. James G. Maxham III and Richard G. Netemeyer, "Firms Reap What They Sow: The Effects of Shared Values and Perceived Organizational Justice on Customer's Evaluations of Complaint Handling," *Journal of Marketing*, 67 (January 2003): 46–62; Jagdip Singh, "Performance Productivity and Quality of Frontline Employees in Service Organizations," *Journal of Marketing*, 64 (April 2000): 15–34; Barry J. Rabin and James S. Boles, "Employee Behavior in a Service Environment: A Model and Test of Potential Differences Between Men and Women," *Journal of Marketing*, 62 (April 1998): 77–91.

48. Dale Buss, "Success from the Ground Up," *Brandweek*, June 16, 2003, pp. 21–22.

49. Hal F. Rosenbluth and Diane McFerrin Peters, *The Customer Comes Second* (New York: William Morrow, 1992).

50. Kirstin Downey Grimsley, "Service with a Forced Smile; Safeway's Courtesy Campaign Also Elicits Some Frowns," *Washington Post*, October 18, 1998, p. A1; Suzy Fox, "Emotional Value: Creating Strong Bonds with Your Customers," *Personnel Psychology*, April 1, 2001, pp. 230–234.

51. Simon Avery, "RIM Hits a Major Crossroad," *Globe and Mail Report on Business Online*, www.theglobeandmail.com, September 18, 2004 (viewed September 21, 2004). "Blackberry subscribers surpass 3m mark," Net Imperative, September 5, 2005, www.netimperative.com/2005/05/09/Blackberry_3m.

52. Carolyn Marconi and Donna MacFarland, "Growth By Marketing Under the Radar," presentation made at Marketing Science Institute Board of Trustees Meeting: Pathways to Growth, November 7, 2002.

53. Pizza Pizza Web site, www.pizzapizza.ca (viewed September 21, 2004).

54. Christopher Rowland, "The Pharmacist in Chains Promote Personal Touch to Keep Edge Over Mail-Order Firms," *Boston Globe*, December 10, 2003, p. D1.

55. Lisa D'Innocenzo, "Legal Firms Court Clients with Ads," *Strategy*, October 8, 2001, p. 4.

56. Kristen Vinakmens, "Push Feeds Their Sugo Cravings," *Strategy*, October 21, 2002, pp. 1–2.

57. Geoff Keighley, "The Phantasmagoria Factory," *Business 2.0* (February 2004): 102.

58. Milind M. Lele and Uday S. Karmarkar, "Good Product Support Is Smart Marketing," *Harvard Business Review* (November–December): 124–132.

59. For recent research on the effects of delays in service on service evaluations, see Shirley Taylor, "Waiting for Service: The Relationship between Delays and Evaluations of Service," *Journal of Marketing* (April 1994): 56–69; Michael K. Hui and David K. Tse, "What to Tell Consumers in Waits of Different Lengths: An Integrative Model of Service Evaluation," *Journal of Marketing* (April 1996): 81–90.

Chapter 14

1. Linda Tischler, "The Price Is Right," *Fast Company*, November 2003, pp. 83–89.

2. "The Price Is Wrong," *The Economist*, May 25, 2002.

3. David J. Schwartz, *Marketing Today: A Basic Approach*, 3rd ed. (New York: Harcourt Brace Jovanovich, 1981), p. 271; Confederation Bridge website, Frequently Asked Questions, www.confederationbridge.com/bridge/faqs.aspx?pageid=5&lang=en (viewed March 11, 2005).

4. Michael Menduno, "Priced to Perfection," *Business 2.0*, March 6, 2001, pp. 40–42.

5. Lisa D'Innocenzo, "Quiznos Slashes Price, Touts 20 New Low-Carb Subs," *Strategy Magazine Online*, www.strategymag.com, April 19, 2004 (viewed October 4, 2004).

6. For a thorough, up-to-date review of pricing research, see Chezy Ofir and Russell S. Winer, "Pricing: Economic and Behavioral Models," in *Handbook of Marketing*, edited by Bart Weitz and Robin Wensley (New York: Sage Publications, 2002), pp. 267–281.

7. Peter R. Dickson and Alan G. Sawyer, "The Price Knowledge and Search of Supermarket Shoppers," *Journal of Marketing* (July 1990): 42–53. For a methodological qualification, however, see Hooman Estalami, Alfred Holden, and Donald R. Lehmann, "Macro-Economic Determinants of Consumer Price Knowledge: A Meta-Analysis of Four Decades of Research," *International Journal of Research in Marketing*, 18 (December 2001): 341–355.

8. For a different point of view, see Chris Janiszewski and Donald R. Lichtenstein, "A Range Theory Account of Price Perception," *Journal of Consumer Research* (March 1999): 353–368.

9. K. N. Rajendran and Gerard J. Tellis, "Contextual and Temporal Components of Reference Price," *Journal of Marketing* (January 1994): 22–34; Goromurthy Kalyanaram and Rossell S. Winer, "Empirical Generalizations from Reference Price Research," *Marketing Science*, 14, no. 3 (1995): G161–G169.

10. Robert Strauss, "Prices You Just Can't Believe," *New York Times*, January 17, 2002, p. G1.

11. John T. Gourville, "Pennies-a-Day: The Effect of Temporal Reframing on Transaction Evaluation," *Journal of Consumer Research* (March 1998): 395–408.

12. Gurumurthy Kalyanaram and Russell S. Winer, "Empirical Generalizations from Reference Research," *Marketing Science* (Fall 1995): 161–169.

13. Glenn E. Mayhew and Russell S. Winer, "An Empirical Analysis of Internal and External Reference Price Effects Using Scanner Data," *Journal of Consumer Research* (June 1992): 62–70.

14. Gary M. Erickson and Johny K. Johansson, "The Role of Price in Multi-Attribute Product-Evaluations," *Journal of Consumer Research* (September 1985): 195–199.

15. Samson Okalo, "Vitamin Wars: A Market for the Taking?" *Strategy Magazine Online*, www.strategymag.com, April 5, 2004 (viewed October 1, 2004).

16. Jonathan Welsh, "A New Status Symbol: Overpaying for Your Minivan Despite Discounts, More Cars Sell Above the Sticker Price," *Wall Street Journal*, July 23, 2003, p. D1.

17. Christina Leadlay, "Taste of Mexico: More Than Just a Beverage, Tequila Is a Drink Whose History Incorporates Centuries of National Identity," *Embassy Culture Magazine*, www.embassymag.ca, August 4, 2004 (viewed October 1, 2004); Ian Chadwick, "Tequila in Canada," *Tequila Aficionado Magazine*, www.tequilaaficionado.com (viewed October 1, 2004).

18. Mark Stiving and Russell S. Winer, "An Empirical Analysis of Price Endings with Scanner Data," *Journal of Consumer Research* (June 1997): 57–68.

19. Eric Anderson and Duncan Simester, "The Role of Price Endings: Why Stores May Sell More at $49 Than at $44," an unpublished conference paper, April 2001.

20. Eric Anderson and Duncan Simester, "Mind Your Pricing Cues," *Harvard Business Review* (September 2003): 96–103.

21. Robert M. Schindler and Patrick N. Kirby, "Patterns of Rightmost Digits Used in Advertised Prices: Implications for Nine-Ending Effects," *Journal of Consumer Research* (September 1997): 192–201.

22. Eric Anderson and Duncan Simester, "Mind Your Pricing Cues," *Harvard Business Review* (September 2003): 96–103.

23. Robert C. Blattberg and Kenneth Wisniewski, "Price-Induced Patterns of Competition," *Marketing Science*, 8 (Fall 1989): 291–309.

24. Elliot B. Ross, "Making Money with Proactive Pricing," *Harvard Business Review* (November–December 1984): 145–155.

25. Shantanu Dutta, Mark J. Zbaracki, and Mark Bergen, "Pricing Process as a Capability: A Resource Based Perspective," *Strategic Management Journal*, no. 7 (2000): 615–630.

26. Kara Swisher, "Electronics 2001: The Essential Guide," *Wall Street Journal*, January 5, 2001.

27. Michael Silverstein and Neil Fiske, *Trading Up: The New American Luxury* (New York: Portfolio, 2003).

28. Christopher Lawton, "A Liquor Maverick Shakes Up Industry with Pricey Brands," *Wall Street Journal*, May 21, 2003, pp. A1, A9.

29. Sidney Bennett and J. B. Wilkinson, "Price-Quantity Relationships and Price Elasticity under In-Store Experimentation," *Journal of Business Research* (January 1974): 30–34.

30. Walter Baker, Mike Marn, and Craig Zawada, "Price Smarter on the Net," *Harvard Business Review* (February 2001): 122–127.

31. John R. Nevin, "Laboratory Experiments for Estimating Consumer Demand: A Validation Study," *Journal of Marketing Research* (August 1974): 261–268; Jonathan Weiner, "Forecasting Demand: Consumer Electronics Marketer Uses a Conjoint Approach to Configure Its New Product and Set the Right Price," *Marketing Research: A Magazine of Management & Applications* (Summer 1994): 6–11.

32. Thomas T. Nagle and Reed K. Holden, *The Strategy and Tactics of Pricing*, 3rd ed. (Upper Saddle River, NJ: Prentice-Hall, 2002).

33. For summary of elasticity studies, see Dominique M. Hanssens, Leonard J. Parsons, and Randall L. Schultz, *Market Response Models: Econometric and Time Series Analysis* (Boston: Kluwer Academic Publishers, 1990), pp. 187–191.

34. Gene Epstein, "Economic Beat: Stretching Things," *Barron's*, December 15, 1997, p. 65.

35. William W. Alberts, "The Experience Curve Doctrine Reconsidered," *Journal of Marketing* (July 1989): 36–49.

36. Robin Cooper and Robert S. Kaplan, "Profit Priorities from Activity-Based Costing," *Harvard Business Review* (May–June 1991): 130–135. For more on ABC, see ch. 24.

37. "Easier Than ABC," *The Economist*, October 25, 2003, p. 56

38. "Japan's Smart Secret Weapon," *Fortune*, August 12, 1991, p. 75.

39. "Price at the Heart of Sprint Ads," *Marketing Magazine Online Daily*, www.marketingmag.ca, May 16, 2002 (viewed October 4, 2004).

40. Tung-Zong Chang and Albert R. Wildt, "Price, Product Information, and Purchase Intention: An Empirical Study," *Journal of the Academy of Marketing Science* (Winter 1994): 16–27. See also G. Dean Kortge and Patrick A. Okonkwo, "Perceived Value Approach to Pricing," *Industrial Marketing Management* (May 1993): 133–140.

41. James C. Anderson, Dipak C. Jain, and Pradeep K. Chintagunta, "Customer Value Assessment in Business Markets: A State-of-Practice Study," *Journal of Business-to-Business Marketing*, 1, no. 1 (1993): 3–29.

42. Bill Saporito, "Behind the Tumult at P&G," *Fortune*, March 7, 1994, pp. 74–82. For empirical analysis of its effects, see Kusim L. Ailawadi, Donald R. Lehmann, and Scott A. Neslin, "Market Response to a Major Policy Change in the Marketing Mix: Learning from Procter & Gamble's Value Pricing Strategy," *Journal of Marketing*, 65 (January 2001): 44–61.

43. Stephen J. Hoch, Xavier Dreze, and Mary J. Purk, "EDLP, Hi-Lo, and Margin Arithmetic," *Journal of Marketing* (October 1994): 16–27; Rajiv Lal and R. Rao, "Supermarket Competition: The Case of Everyday Low Pricing," *Marketing Science*, 16, no. 1 (1997): 60–80.

44. Joseph W. Alba, Carl F. Mela, Terence A. Shimp, and Joel E. Urbany, "The Effect of Discount Frequency and Depth on Consumer Price Judgments," *Journal of Consumer Research* (September 1999): 99–114.

45. Chris Daniels, "The Bay Offers More Affordability," *Marketing Magazine Online*, www.marketingmag.ca, September 2, 2002 (viewed October 4, 2004); "Bay Puts a Price on Price," *Marketing Magazine Online Daily*, www.marketingmag.ca, May 12, 2003 (viewed October 4, 2004).

46. Becky Bull, "No Consensus on Pricing," *Progressive Grocer* (November 1998): 87–90.

47. Chris Nelson, "Ticketmaster Auction Will Let Highest Bidder Set Concert Prices," *New York Times*, September 1, 2003, p. C6.

48. "Royal Mail Drives Major Cost Savings Through Free Markets," Free Markets press release, December 15, 2003.

49. Paul W. Farris and David J. Reibstein, "How Prices, Expenditures, and Profits Are Linked," *Harvard Business Review* (November–December 1979): 173–184. See also Makoto Abe, "Price and Advertising Strategy of a National Brand against Its Private-Label Clone: A Signaling Game Approach," *Journal of Business Research* (July 1995): 241–250.

50. J. P. Morgan Report, "eTailing and the Five C's," March 2000.

51. Eugene H. Fram and Michael S. McCarthy, "The True Price of Penalties," *Marketing Management* (October 1999): 49–56.

52. Kissan Joseph, "On the Optimality of Delegating Pricing Authority to the Sales Force," *Journal of Marketing*, 65 (January 2001): 62–70.

53. Gary McWilliams, "How Dell Fine-Tunes Its PC Pricing to Gain Edge in a Slow Market," *Wall Street Journal*, June 8, 2001, p. A1; "Dell," http://company.monster.ca/dellca/ (viewed March 11, 2005).

54. Joel E. Urbany, "Justifying Profitable Pricing," *Journal of Product and Brand Management*, 10, no. 3 (2001): 141–157.

55. Charles Fishman, "The Wal-Mart You Don't Know," *Fast Company* (December 2003): 68–80.

56. Normandy Madden, "P&G Adapts Attitude Toward Local Markets," *Advertising Age*, February 23, 2004, pp. 28–29.

57. James Mehring, "Let the Markups Begin," *BusinessWeek*, May 19, 2003, p. 100.

58. Michael Rowe, *Countertrade* (London: Euromoney Books, 1989); P. N. Agarwala, *Countertrade: A Global Perspective* (New Delhi: Vikas Publishing House, 1991); Christopher M. Korth, ed., *International Countertrade* (New York: Quorum Books, 1987).

59. For an interesting discussion of a quantity surcharge, see David E. Sprott, Kenneth C. Manning, and Anthony Miyazaki, "Grocery Price Settings and Quantity Surcharges, *Journal of Marketing*, 67 (July 2003): 34–46.

60. Michael V. Marn and Robert L. Rosiello, "Managing Price, Gaining Profit," *Harvard Business Review* (September–October 1992): 84–94. See also Gerard J. Tellis, "Tackling the Retailer Decision Maze: Which Brands to Discount, How Much, When, and Why?" *Marketing Science* 14, no. 3, pt. 2 (1995): 271–299; Kusum L. Ailawadi, Scott A. Neslin, and Karen Gedeak, "Pursuing the Value-Conscious Consumer: Store Brands Versus National Brand Promotions," *Journal of Marketing*, 65 (January 2001): 71–89.

61. David Welch, "Ford Tames the Rebate Beast," *BusinessWeek*, May 5, 2003, p. 38.

62. Kevin J. Clancy, "At What Profit Price?" *Brandweek*, June 23, 1997.

63. Ramarao Deesiraju and Steven M. Shugan, "Strategic Service Pricing and Yield Management," *Journal of Marketing*, 63 (January 1999): 44–56; Robert E. Weigand, "Yield Management: Filling Buckets, Papering the House," *Business Horizons* (September–October 1999): 55–64.

64. Charles Fishman, "Which Price Is Right?" *Fast Company* (March 2003): 92–102; John Sviokla, "Value Poaching," *Across the Board* (March/April 2003): 11–12.

65. Mike France, "Does Predatory Pricing Make Microsoft a Predator?" *BusinessWeek,* November 23, 1998, pp. 130–132. Also see Joseph P. Guiltinan and Gregory T. Gundlack, "Aggressive and Predatory Pricing: A Framework for Analysis," *Journal of Advertising* (July 1996): 87–102.

66. Lara Mille, "The Price Is Wrong," *Marketing Magazine Online,* www.marketingmag.ca, February 4, 2002; "McDonald's Canada Announces Next Phase of Balanced Lifestyle Initiative," McDonald's press release, Toronto, March 8, 2005.

67. Margaret C. Campbell, "Perceptions of Pricing Unfairness: Antecedents and Consequences," *Journal of Marketing Research,* 36 (May 1999): 187–199.

68. Delroy Alexander, "Products, Profits Put Kraft, Leader in Pinch," *Chicago Tribune,* November 2, 2003, p. 5.

69. Eric Mitchell, "How Not to Raise Prices," *Small Business Reports* (November 1990): 64–67.

70. For a classic review, see Kent B. Monroe, "Buyers' Subjective Perceptions of Price," *Journal of Marketing Research* (February 1973): 70–80. See also, Z. John Zhang, Fred Feinberg, Aradhna Krishna,"Do We Care What Others Get? A Behaviorist Approach to Targeted Promotions," *Journal of Marketing Research,* 39 (August 2002): 277–291.

71. Adapted from Robert J. Dolan and Hermann Simon, "Power Pricers," *Across the Board* (May 1997): 18–19.

72. Kusim L. Ailawadi, Donald R. Lehmann, and Scott A. Neslin, "Market Response to a Major Policy Change in the Marketing Mix: Learning from Procter & Gamble's Value Pricing Strategy," *Journal of Marketing* 65 (January 2001): 44–61.

Chapter 15

1. Joann Muller, "Kmart: The Flood Waters Are Rising," *BusinessWeek,* January 28, 2002, p. 106. Note that Kmart later emerged from bankruptcy on May 6, 2003.

2. Anne T. Coughlan, Erin Anderson, Louis W. Stern, and Adel I. El-Ansary, *Marketing Channels,* 6th ed. (Upper Saddle River, NJ: Prentice Hall, 2001).

3. Louis W. Stern and Barton A. Weitz, "The Revolution in Distribution: Challenges and Opportunities," *Long Range Planning,* 30, no. 6 (1997): 823–829.

4. For an insightful summary of academic research, see Erin Anderson and Anne T. Coughlan, "Channel Management: Structure, Governance, and Relationship Management," in *Handbook of Marketing,* edited by Bart Weitz and Robin Wensley (London: Sage Publications, 2002), pp. 223–247. See also Gary L. Frazier, "Organizing and Managing Channels of Distribution," *Journal of the Academy of Marketing Sciences,* 27, no. 2 (1999): 226–240.

5. E. Raymond Corey, *Industrial Marketing: Cases and Concepts,* 4th ed. (Upper Saddle River, NJ: Prentice Hall, 1991), ch. 5.

6. Sarah Smith, "Curling Film Boosted by Hockey Gold," *Marketing Magazine Online,* www.marketingmag.ca, March 11, 2002.

7. For a technical discussion of how service-oriented firms choose to enter international markets, see M. Krishna Erramilli, "Service Firms' International Entry-Mode Approach: A Modified Transaction-Cost Analysis Approach," *Journal of Marketing* (July 1993): 19–38.

8. Kristen Vinakmens, "Digitizing the Experience," *Strategy Magazine Online,* www.strategymag.ca, December 1, 2003 (viewed October 5, 2004).

9. Paul F. Nunes and Frank V. Cespedes, "The Customer Has Escaped," *Harvard Business Review* (November 2003): 96–105.

10. John Helyar, "The Only Company Wal-Mart Fears," *Fortune,* November 24, 2003, pp. 158–166. See also Michael Silverstein and Neil Fiske, *Trading Up: The New American Luxury* (New York, NY Portfolio, 2003).

11. Mike Troy, "From Supply Chain to Demand Chain, a New View of the Marketplace," *DSN Retailing Today,* October 13, 2003, pp. 8–9.

12. Coughlan, Anderson, Stern, and El-Ansary, *Marketing Channels,* pp. 5–6.

13. Leon Goren, "Dealing Direct," *Marketing Magazine Online,* www.marketingmag.ca, May 13, 2002; Promotional Products Association of Canada Web site, www.promocan.com (viewed October 5, 2004).

14. For additional information on backward channels, see Marianne Jahre, "Household Waste Collection as a Reverse Channel: A Theoretical Perspective," *International Journal of Physical Distribution and Logistics* 25, no. 2 (1995): 39–55; Terrance L. Pohlen and M. Theodore Farris II, "Reverse Logistics in Plastics Recycling," *International Journal of Physical Distribution and Logistics* 22, no. 7 (1992): 35–37.

15. "Dell Recycling," www1.ca.dell.com/content/topics/segtopic.aspx/dell_recycling?c=ca&cs=CADHS1&l=en&s=dhs (viewed March 11, 2005).

16. Irving Rein, Philip Kotler, and Martin Stoller, *High Visibility* (New York: Dodd, Mead, 1987).

17. Taken from Anne T. Coughlan and Louis W. Stern, "Marketing Channel Design and Management," in *Kellogg on Marketing,* edited by Dawn Iacobucci (New York: John Wiley, 2001), p. 249.

18. Louis P. Bucklin, *Competition and Evolution in the Distributive Trades* (Upper Saddle River, NJ: Prentice Hall, 1972). Also see Stern and El-Ansary, *Marketing Channels.*

19. Louis P. Bucklin, *A Theory of Distribution Channel Structure* (Berkeley: Institute of Business and Economic Research, University of California, 1966).

20. Bridget Finn, "A Quart of Milk, a Dozen Eggs and a 2.6-GHz Laptop," *Business 2.0* (October 2003): 58.

21. "Trouser Suit," *The Economist,* November 24, 2001, p. 56.

22. "Exclusives Becoming a Common Practice," *DSN Retailing Today,* February 9, 2004, pp. 38, 44.

23. Andy Holloway, "Space Oddity," *Canadian Business Magazine Online,* www.canadianbusiness.com, September 9, 2002 (viewed October 5, 2004); Mootaxi Web site, www.moontaximedia.com (viewed October 5, 2004).

24. www.disney.com; Edward Helmore, "Media: Why House of Mouse Is Haunted by Failures," *The Observer,* February 11, 2001, p. 10.

25. For more on relationship marketing and the governance of marketing channels, see Jan B. Heide, "Interorganizational Governance in Marketing Channels," *Journal of Marketing* (January 1994): 71–85.

26. Lawrence G. Friedman and Timothy R. Furey, *The Channel Advantage: Going to Marketing with Multiple Sales Channels* (Woburn, MA: Butterworth-Heinemann, 1999). They suggest measuring a channel's profitability by the expense-to-revenue ratio, or E/R. E/R is the average transaction cost divided by the average order size. The average transaction cost is found by dividing the total expense in operating the channel by the total number of transactions. The lower the E/R, the more profitable the channel because less money is spent on selling cost for each dollar of revenue.

27. http://americas.kyocera.com/news.

28. Erin Anderson and Anne T. Coughlan, "Channel Management: Structure, Governance, and Relationship Management," in *Handbook of Marketing,* edited by Bart Weitz and Robin Wensley (London: Sage Publications, 2002), pp. 223–247.

29. These bases of power were identified in John R. P. French and Bertram Raven, "The Bases of Social Power," in *Studies in Social Power,* edited by Dorwin Cartwright (Ann Arbor: University of Michigan Press, 1959), pp. 150–167.

30. Bert Rosenbloom, *Marketing Channels: A Management View,* 5th ed. (Hinsdale, IL: Dryden, 1995).

31. Tobi Elkin, "Apple Gambles with Retail Plan," *Advertising Age,* June 24, 2001; www.apple.com/retail; www.apple.com/ca.

32. For an excellent report on this issue, see Howard Sutton, *Rethinking the Company's Selling and Distribution Channels,* research report no. 885, Conference Board, 1986, p. 26.

33. Russell Johnston and Paul R. Lawrence, "Beyond Vertical Integration: The Rise of the Value-Adding Partnership," *Harvard Business Review* (July–August 1988): 94–101. See also Judy A. Siguaw, Penny M. Simpson, and Thomas L. Baker, "Effects of Supplier Market Orientation on Distributor Market Orientation and the Channel Relationship: The Distribution Perspective," *Journal of Marketing* (July 1998): 99–111; Narakesari Narayandas and Manohar U. Kalwani, "Long-Term Manufacturer–Supplier Relationships: Do They Pay Off for Supplier Firms?" *Journal of Marketing* (January 1995): 1–16; Arnt Bovik and George John, "When Does Vertical Coordination Improve Industrial Purchasing Relationships," *Journal of Marketing* 64 (October 2000): pp. 52–64.

34. Interview with *Toronto Star* management on industry dynamics.

35. Rowland T. Moriarty and Ursula Moran, "Marketing Hybrid Marketing Systems," *Harvard Business Review* (November–December 1990): 146–155. Also see Gordon S. Swartz and Rowland T. Moriarty, "Marketing Automation Meets the Capital Budgeting Wall," *Marketing Management* 1, no. 3 (1992); Sridhar Balasubramanian, "Mail versus Mall: A Strategic Analysis of Competition Between Direct Marketers and Conventional Retailers," *Marketing Science* 17, no. 3 (1998): 181–195.

36. Mountain Equipment Co-op, www.mec.ca/Main/home.jsp?bmUID=1110726106451; Sports Check, www.sportchek.ca.

37. Anne T. Coughlan and Louis W. Stern, "Marketing Channel Design and Management," in *Kellogg on Marketing*, edited by Dawn Iacobucci (New York: John Wiley, 2001), pp. 247–269.

38. Rob Wheery, "Pedal Pushers," *Forbes*, October 14, 2002, pp. 205–206.

39. Fareena Sultan and Andrew J. Rohm, "The Evolving Role of the Internet in Marketing Strategy: An Exploratory Study," *Journal of Interactive Marketing* (Spring 2004): 6–19.

40. This section draws on Stern and El-Ansary, *Marketing Channels*, ch. 6. See also Jonathan D. Hibbard, Nirmalya Kumar, and Louis W. Stern, "Examining the Impact of Destructive Acts in Marketing Channel Relationships," *Journal of Marketing Research* 38 (February 2001): 45–61; Kersi D. Antia and Gary L. Frazier, "The Severity of Contract Enforcement in Interfirm Channel Relationships," *Journal of Marketing*, 65 (October 2001): 67–81; James R. Brown, Chekitan S. Dev, and Dong-Jin Lee, "Managing Marketing Channel Opportunism: The Efficiency of Alternative Governance Mechanisms," *Journal of Marketing*, 64 (April 2001): 51–65.

41. Allessandra Galloni, "Levi's Doesn't Fancy Selling with Cukes," *Wall Street Journal*, April 10, 2001, p. B10; "Trouser Suit," *The Economist*, November 24, 2001, p. 56; www.levistrauss.com.

42. William G. Zikmund and William J. Stanton, "Recycling Solid Wastes: A Channels-of-Distribution Problem," *Journal of Marketing* (July 1971): 34.

43. Steve Bodow, "The Care and Feeding of a Killer App," *Business 2.0* (August 2002): 76–78.

44. Ronald Abler, John S. Adams, and Peter Gould, *Spatial Organizations: The Geographer's View of the World* (Upper Saddle River, NJ: Prentice Hall, 1971), pp. 531–532.

45. Described in *Inside 1-to-1*, Peppers and Rogers Group newsletter, May 14, 2001.

46. Bob Tedeshi, "How Harley Revved Online Sales," *Business 2.0* (December 2002/January 2003): 44.

47. Gary McWilliams and Ann Zimmerman, "Dell Plans to Peddle PCs Inside Sears, Other Large Chains," *Wall Street Journal*, January 30, 2003, pp. B1, B3.

48. Kristen Vinakmens, "Digitizing the Experience," *Strategy Magazine Online*, www.strategymag.ca, December 1, 2003 (viewed October 5, 2004).

49. Pallavi Gogoi, "The Hot News in Banking: Bricks and Mortar," *BusinessWeek*, April 21, 2003, pp. 83–84.

50. "2001 Industry Forecasts," *Outdoor Power Equipment*, January 1, 2001.

Chapter 16

1. William R. Davidson, Albert D. Bates, and Stephen J. Bass, "Retail Life Cycle," *Harvard Business Review* (November–December 1976): 89–96.

2. ACNielsen, "In the News," March 2003, www.acnielsen.ca/Insights/IntheNews/March2003.htm.

3. Stanley C. Hollander, "The Wheel of Retailing," *Journal of Marketing* (July 1960): 37–42.

4. Margaret Webb Pressler, "Convenience, No Store; Vending Machines Are Being Stocked with More Than Snacks," *The Washington Post*, April 10, 2004, p. D12.

5. Anne D'Innocenzio, "Upscale Bloomingdale's Heads Down to SoHo," *New York Times*, April 23, 2004.

6. Amy Merrick, Jeffrey Trachtenberg, and Ann Zimmerman, "Department Stores Fight to Preserve Role That May Be Outdated," *Wall Street Journal*, March 12, 2002; Ann Zimmerman, "Dillard's Counts on House Brands to Recapture Reputation," *Wall Street Journal*, March 2001.

7. "Reinventing the Store—the Future of Retailing," *The Economist*, November 22, 2003, pp. 65–68.

8. Charles Fishman, "The Anarchist's Cookbook," *Fast Company*, July 2004, pp. 70–78.

9. "Better and Better, to Be "Mom's Store, Priced Right," Zellers report, August 2004, www.hbc.com/hbc/mediacentre/displayfile. asp?intAttachmentId=14&strLanguageVersion=hbc.

10. Jason Kirby, "Location, Location, Location?" *Canadian Business*, November 25, 2002, pp. 38–50; North West Company Web site, www.northwest.ca (viewed October 14, 2004).

11. Louis Lee, "Thinking Small at the Mall," *BusinessWeek*, May 26, 2003, pp. 94–95.

12. Kimberly L. Allers, "Retail's Rebel Yell," *Fortune*, November 10, 2003, pp. 137–142.

13. Laurence H. Wortzel, "Retailing Strategies for Today's Marketplace," *Journal of Business Strategy* (Spring 1987): 45–56.

14. Mark Tatge, "Fun & Games," *Forbes*, January 12, 2004, pp. 138–144.

15. Uta Werner, John McDermott, and Greg Rotz, "Retailers at the Crossroads: How to Develop Profitable New Growth Strategies," *Journal of Business Strategy*, 25, no 2 (2004): 10–17.

16. Cecilie Rohwedder, "Viva la Differenza," *Wall Street Journal*, January 29, 2003, pp. B1, B8.

17. Bernadette Johnson, "Counter Strategy," *Strategy Magazine Online*, www.strategymag.ca, May 31, 2004 (viewed October 14, 2004).

18. Rona Web site, www.rona.ca; Liza d'Innocenzo, "Big Box Goes Downtown," *Strategy Magazine*, December 1, 2003, p. 1.

19. Constance L. Hays, "Retailers Seeking to Lure Customers with Service," *The New York Times*, December 1, 2003, p. C13.

20. Piet Vroon et al., *Smell: The Secret Seducer* (New York: Farrar, Straus & Giroux, 1997).

21. West Edmonton Mall Web site, www.westedmontonmall.ca (viewed October 14, 2004).

22. Kenneth T. Rosen and Amanda L. Howard, "E-tail: Gold Rush or Fool's Gold?" *California Management Review*, April 1, 2000, pp. 72–100; Moira Cotlier, "Census Releases First E-commerce Report," *Catalog Age*, May 1, 2001; Associated Press, "Online Sales Boomed at End of 2000," *Star-Tribune of Twin Cities*, February 17, 2001; "Reinventing the Store," *The Economist*, November 22, 2003, pp. 65–68.

23. For more discussion, see Philip Kotler, "Atmospherics as a Marketing Tool," *Journal of Retailing* (Winter 1973–1974): 48–64;

Mary Jo Bitner, "Servicescapes: The Impact of Physical Surroundings on Customers and Employees," *Journal of Marketing* (April 1992): 57–71. Also see B. Joseph Pine II and James H. Gilmore, *The Experience Economy* (Boston: Harvard Business School Press, 1999).

24. Janet Eastman, "In the Latest Form of Retail Theater, Appliance Customers Who Come to Visit Are Making Themselves Right at Home," *The Los Angeles Times*, November 1, 2002, p. E32.

25. Frank Feather, *The Future Consumer* (Toronto: Warwick Publishing, 1994), p. 171. Also see Stephen J. Hoch, Xavier Dreeze, and Mary E. Purk, "EDLP, Hi-Lo, and Margin Arithmetic," *Journal of Marketing* (October 1994): 1–15; David R. Bell and James M. Lattin, "Shopping Behavior and Consumer Preference for Retail Price Format: Why 'Large Basket' Shoppers Prefer EDLP," *Marketing Science*, 17 (Spring 1998): 66–68.

26. Peter Vamos, "LCBO's Brandt Pours on Results," *Strategy Magazine Online*, www.strategymag.ca, July 16, 2001 (viewed October 14, 2004).

27. Forzani Group Investor Presentation, "Scotia Capital Back to School Conference," Forzani Group Web site, www.forzanigroup.com, September 21, 2004 (viewed October 14, 2004).

28. Carol Tice, "Anchors Away: Department Stores Lose Role at Malls," *Puget Sound Business Journal*, February 13, 2004, p. 1.

29. R. L. Davies and D. S. Rogers, eds., *Store Location and Store Assessment Research* (New York: John Wiley, 1984).

30. Sara L. McLafferty, *Location Strategies for Retail and Service Firms* (Lexington, MA: Lexington Books, 1987).

31. Theresa Howard, "Retail Stores Pop Up for Limited Time Only," *USA Today*, May 28, 2004, 1B.

32. Wendy Liebmann, "Consumers Push Back," *Brandweek*, February 23, 2004, pp. 19–20.

33. Liebmann, "Consumers Push Back," pp. 19–20.

34. Liebmann, "Consumers Push Back," pp. 19–20.

35. "Better and Better," Zellers, 2004 Report, www.hbc.com/hbc/mediacentre/displayfile. asp?intAttachmentId=14&strLanguageVersion=hbc.

36. "Sears Updates Its Operations," *USA Today*, October 29, 2001; Amy Merrick, "Sears to Overhaul Stores, Change Format, Cut 5,000 Jobs in Move to Boost Earnings," *Wall Street Journal*, October 25, 2001, p. B9.

37. Catherine Yang, "Maybe They Should Call Them Scammers," *BusinessWeek*, January 16, 1995, pp. 32–33; Ronald C. Goodstein, "UPC Scanner Pricing Systems: Are They Accurate?" *Journal of Marketing* (April 1994): 20–30.

38. For a listing of the key factors involved in success with an EDI system, see R. P. Vlosky, D. T. Wilson, and P. M. Smith, "Electronic Data Interchange Implementation Strategies: A Case Study," *Journal of Business & Industrial Marketing* 9, no. 4 (1994): 5–18.

39. "Business Bulletin: Shopper Scanner," *Wall Street Journal*, February 18, 1995, p. A1.

40. For further discussion of retail trends, see Louis W. Stern and Adel I. El-Ansary, *Marketing Channels*, 5th ed. (Upper Saddle River, NJ: Prentice Hall, 1996).

41. Shelley Donald Coolidge, "Facing Saturated Home Markets, Retailers Look to Rest of World," *Christian Science Monitor*, February 14, 1994, p. 7; Carla Rapoport with Justin Martin, "Retailers Go Global," *Fortune*, February 20, 1995, pp. 102–108.

42. Matthew Boyle, "Brand Killers," *Fortune*, August 11, 2003, pp. 88–100.

43. Gary McWilliams, "Retailers Create Own-Label PCs as Brand Names Dwindle," *Wall Street Journal*, May 3, 2002, pp. B1, B3.

44. Michelle Halpern, "Hip Huggers," *Marketing Magazine Online*, www.marketingmag.ca, August 23, 2004 (viewed October 16, 2004); Bluenotes Web site, www.blnts.com (viewed October 16, 2004).

45. Matthew Boyle, "Brand Killers," *Fortune*, August 11, 2003, pp. 88–100; William C. Copacino, *Supply Chain Management* (Boca Raton, FL: St. Lucie Press, 1997).

46. James A. Narus and James C. Anderson, "Contributing as a Distributor to Partnerships with Manufacturers," *Business Horizons* (September–October 1987). Also see James D. Hlavecek and Tommy J. McCuistion, "Industrial Distributors—When, Who, and How," *Harvard Business Review* (March–April 1983): 96–101.

47. Anthony Leong, Lara Kalins, Oren Levy, Marion De Marcillac, and Annekatrin Scholze, "The Film Distribution Industry in Canada," www.mediacircus.net/filmdis1.html.

48. Bert McCammon, Robert F. Lusch, Deborah S. Coykendall, and James M. Kenderdine, *Wholesaling in Transition* (Norman: University of Oklahoma, College of Business Administration, 1989).

49. Hoover's Company Profiles, 1999; and company Web sites.

50. Michael Liedtke, "Online Goes Offline at McKesson HBOC," *Pittsburgh Post-Gazette*, February 27, 2001, p. B4.

51. Holly Quan, "Grocery Programs Take Flight," *Marketing Magazine Online*, www.marketingmag.ca, July 8, 2002 (viewed October 16, 2004).

52. James A. Narus and James C. Anderson, "Contributing as a Distributor to Partnerships with Manufacturers." Also see James D. Hlavecek and Tommy J. McCuistion, "Industrial Distributors—When, Who, and How," *Harvard Business Review* (March–April 1983): 96–101.

53. William C. Copacino, *Supply Chain Management* (Boca Raton, FL: St. Lucie Press, 1997).

54. Ronald Henkoff, "Delivering the Goods," *Fortune*, November 28, 1994, pp. 64–78.

55. Henkoff, "Delivering the Goods," pp. 64–78.

56. Rita Koselka, "Distribution Revolution," *Forbes*, May 25, 1992, pp. 54–62.

57. The optimal order quantity is given by the formula $Q^* = 2DS/IC$, where D = annual demand, S = cost to place one order, and I = annual carrying cost per unit. Known as the economic-order quantity formula, it assumes a constant ordering cost, a constant cost of carrying an additional unit in inventory, a known demand, and no quantity discounts. For further reading on this subject, see Richard J. Tersine, *Principles of Inventory and Materials Management*, 4th ed. (Upper Saddle River, NJ: Prentice Hall, 1994).

58. William C. Copacino, *Supply Chain Management* (Boca Raton, FL: St. Lucie Press, 1997), pp. 122–123.

59. Renee DeGross, "Retailers Try eBay Overstocks, Returns For Sale Online," *The Atlanta Journal-Constitution*, April 10, 2004, p. E1.

Chapter 17

1. Some of these definitions are adapted from Peter D. Bennett, ed., *Dictionary of Marketing Terms* (Chicago: American Marketing Association, 1995).

2. "Online Is in the Mix for Traditional Marketers," Special Advertising Section, *Brandweek*, February 2003.

3. Joseph W. Alba and J. Wesley Hutchinson, "Dimensions of Consumer Expertise," *Journal of Consumer Research*, 13 (March 1987): 411–453.

4. Deborah L. Vence, "Marketing in Harmony: Boston Orchestra Tunes Up Net Campaign," *Marketing News*, June 23, 2003, p. 5.

5. For an alternative communication model developed specifically for advertising communications, see Barbara B. Stern, "A Revised Communication Model for Advertising: Multiple Dimensions of the Source, the Message, and the Recipient," *Journal of Advertising* (June 1994): 5–15. For some additional perspectives, see Tom Duncan and Sandra E. Moriarity, "A Communication-Based Marketing Model for Managing Relationships," *Journal of Marketing* (April 1998): 1–13.

6. Brian Sternthal and C. Samuel Craig, *Consumer Behavior: An Information Processing Perspective* (Upper Saddle River, NJ: Prentice Hall, 1982), pp. 97–102.

7. Demetrios Vakratsas and Tim Ambler, "How Advertising Works: What Do We Really Know," *Journal of Marketing*, 63, no. 1 (January 1999): 26–43.

8. Celeste Ward, "Goodby Pulls Haagen-Dazs Back from 1980s Limbo," *Adweek*, 45, no 24 (2004): 11.

9. This section is based on the excellent text, John R. Rossiter and Larry Percy, *Advertising and Promotion Management*, 2nd ed. (New York: McGraw-Hill, 1997).

10. James F. Engel, Roger D. Blackwell, and Paul W. Minard, *Consumer Behavior*, 9th ed. (Fort Worth, TX: Dryden, 2001).

11. Rossiter and Percy, *Advertising and Promotion Management*.

12. James F. Engel, Roger D. Blackwell, and Paul W. Minard, *Consumer Behavior*, 9th ed. (Fort Worth, TX: Dryden, 2001).

13. Ayn E. Crowley and Wayne D. Hoyer, "An Integrative Framework for Understanding Two-Sided Persuasion," *Journal of Consumer Research* (March 1994): 561–574.

14. C. I. Hovland, A. A. Lumsdaine, and F. D. Sheffield, *Experiments on Mass Communication*, vol. 3 (Princeton, NJ: Princeton University Press, 1948), ch. 8; Crowley and Hoyer, "An Integrative Framework for Understanding Two-Sided Persuasion." For an alternative viewpoint, see George E. Belch, "The Effects of Message Modality on One- and Two-Sided Advertising Messages," in *Advances in Consumer Research*, edited by Richard P. Bagozzi and Alice M. Tybout (Ann Arbor, MI: Association for Consumer Research, 1983), pp. 21–26.

15. Curtis P. Haugtvedt and Duane T. Wegener, "Message Order Effects in Persuasion: An Attitude Strength Perspective," *Journal of Consumer Research* (June 1994): 205–218; H. Rao Unnava, Robert E. Burnkrant, and Sunil Erevelles, "Effects of Presentation Order and Communication Modality on Recall and Attitude," *Journal of Consumer Research* (December 1994): 481–490.

16. Sternthal and Craig, *Consumer Behavior*, pp. 282–284.

17. Stuart Elliott, "Why a Duck? Because It Sells Insurance," *The New York Times*, June 24, 2002, p. C11.

18. Michael R. Solomon, *Consumer Behavior*, 6th ed. (Upper Saddle River, NJ: Prentice Hall, 2004).

19. Rick Thiessen and Mat Wilcox, "Quick Thinking," *Marketing Magazine Online*, www.marketingmag.ca, September 6, 2004 (viewed October 21, 2004).

20. "The Death of the Jingle," *The Economist*, February 8, 2003, p. 61.

21. Kevin Goldman, "Advertising: Knock, Knock. Who's There? The Same Old Funny Ad Again," *Wall Street Journal*, November 2, 1993, p. B10. See also Marc G. Weinberger, Harlan Spotts, Leland Campbell, and Amy L. Parsons, "The Use and Effect of Humor in Different Advertising Media," *Journal of Advertising Research* (May–June 1995): 44–55.

22. Herbert C. Kelman and Carl I. Hovland, "Reinstatement of the Communication in Delayed Measurement of Opinion Change," *Journal of Abnormal and Social Psychology* 48 (1953): 327–335.

23. David J. Moore, John C. Mowen, and Richard Reardon, "Multiple Sources in Advertising Appeals: When Product Endorsers Are Paid by the Advertising Sponsor," *Journal of the Academy of Marketing Science* (Summer 1994): 234–243.

24. Julie Sloane, "Gorgeous George," *Fsb: Fortune Small Business* (June 2003): 36.

25. C. E. Osgood and P. H. Tannenbaum, "The Principles of Congruity in the Prediction of Attitude Change," *Psychological Review* 62 (1955): 42–55.

26. Richard C. Morais, "Mobile Mayhem," *Forbes*, July, 6 1998, p. 138; "Working in Harmony," *Soap Perfumery & Cosmetics*, July 1, 1998, p. 27; Rodger Harrabin, "A Commercial Break for Parents," *Independent*, September 8, 1998, p. 19; Naveen Donthu, "A Cross Country Investigation of Recall of and Attitude toward Comparative Advertising," *Journal of Advertising* 27 (June 22, 1998): 111; "EU to Try Again on Tobacco Advertising Ban," Associated Press, May 9, 2001.

27. David Todd, "Multicultural Marketing: Bell ExpressVu Promises a Dose of 'Dishum Dishum,'" *Marketing Magazine Online*, www.marketingmag.ca, February 15, 1999 (viewed October 21, 2004).

28. "Rebirth of a Salesman," *The Economist*, April 14, 2001.

29. Michael Kiely, "Word-of-Mouth Marketing," *Marketing* (September 1993): 6. See also Aric Rindfleisch and Christine Moorman, "The Acquisition and Utilization of Information in New Product Alliances: A Strength-of-Ties Perspective," *Journal of Marketing* (April 2001): 1–18.

30. Ian Mount, "Marketing," *Business 2.0* (August/September 2001): 84.

31. J. Johnson Brown and P. Reingen, "Social Ties and Word-of-Mouth Referral Behavior," *Journal of Consumer Research* 14 (1987): 350–362; Jacqueline Johnson Brown, Peter M. Reingen, and Everett M. Rogers, *Diffusion of Innovations*, 4th ed. (New York: The Free Press, 1995).

32. Elizabeth Wellington, "Freebies and Chitchat Are Hot Marketing Tools," *Philadelphia Inquirer*, December 31, 2003; Bob Sperber, "Krispy Kreme Word-of-Mouth Tactics Continue to Go Against the Grain," *Brandweek*, October 21, 2002, p. 9.

33. Sarah Dobson, "Campbell Tries In-the-Box Approach," *Marketing Magazine Online*, www.marketingmag.ca, November 11, 2002 (viewed October 21, 2004).

34. Renée Dye, "The Buzz on Buzz," *Harvard Business Review* (November–December 2000): 139–146.

35. John Batelle, "The Net of Influence," *Business 2.0* (March 2004): 70.

36. Kenneth Hein, "Run Red Run," *Brandweek*, February 25, 2002, pp. 14–15.

37. Malcolm Macalister Hall, "Selling by Stealth," *Business Life* (November 2001): 51–55.

38. Ann Meyer, "Word-of-Mouth Marketing Speaks Well for Small Business," *Chicago Tribune*, July 28, 2003.

39. Emanuel Rosen, *The Anatomy of Buzz* (New York: Currency, 2000), ch. 12; "Viral Marketing," *Sales & Marketing Automation* (November 1999): 12–14; George Silverman, *The Secrets of Word-of-Mouth Marketing* (New York: Amacom, 2001).

40. Marian Salzman, Ira Matathia, and Ann O'Reilly, *Buzz: Harness the Power of Influence and Create Demand* (New York: Wiley 2003).

41. Linda Tischler, "Buzz Without Bucks," *Fast Company* (August 2003): 78.

42. Jack Neff, "Spam Research Reveals Disgust with Pop-Up Ads," *Advertising Age*, August 25, 2003, pp. 1, 21.

43. Thomson H. Davenport and John C. Beck, *The Attention Economy: Understanding the New Current of Business* (Boston: Harvard Business School Press, 2000).

44. Theodore Levitt, *Industrial Purchasing Behavior: A Study in Communication Effects* (Boston: Division of Research, Harvard Business School, 1965).

45. Adapted from G. Maxwell Ule, "A Media Plan for 'Sputnik' Cigarettes," *How to Plan Media Strategy* (American Association of Advertising Agencies, 1957 Regional Convention), pp. 41–52.

46. Thomas C. Kinnear and Kenneth L. Bernhardt, *Principles of Marketing*, 2nd ed. (Glenview, IL: Scott Foresman and Co., 1986).

47. Andrea Zoe Aster, "The Patient Princess," *Marketing Magazine Online*, www.marketingmag.ca, September 13, 2004 (viewed October 22, 2004).

48. Terrence Sing, "Integrated Marketing More Than Just an Internet Brochure," *Pacific Business News*, February 18, 2004, p. 23.

49. Amna Kirmani, "The Effect of Perceived Advertising Costs on Brand Perceptions," *Journal of Consumer Research*, 17 (September 17, 1990): 160–171; Amna Kirmani and Peter Wright,

"Money Talks: Perceived Advertising Expense and Expected Product Quality," *Journal of Consumer Research*, 16 (December 1989): 344–353.

50. Demetrios Vakratsas and Tim Ambler, "How Advertising Works: What Do We Really Know," *Journal of Marketing*, 63, no. 1 (January 1999): 26–43.

51. Wende Knapp and Andrew Berthoff, "The Power of Public Relations: Getting the Most from Your Marketing Communications Budget," Integrated Marketing Communications Summit, Canadian Institute, February 1, 2005, http://canadianinstitute.com/program_conference/conf_details_section.cfm?page=1&ID=2967&Mode=Normal.

52. *How Advertising Works in Today's Marketplace: The Morrill Study* (New York: McGraw-Hill, 1971), p. 4.

53. Theodore Levitt, *Industrial Purchasing Behavior: A Study in Communication Effects* (Boston: Division of Research, Harvard Business School, 1965).

54. Tourism Newfoundland and Labrador Web site, www.gov.nf.ca/tourism (viewed October 28, 2002).

55. Ernan Roman, *Integrated Direct Marketing: The Cutting Edge Strategy for Synchronizing Advertising, Direct Mail, Telemarketing, and Field Sales* (Lincolnwood, IL: NTC Business Books, 1995).

56. William T. Moran, "Insights from Pricing Research," in E. B. Bailey, ed., *Pricing Practices and Strategies* (New York: The Conference Board, 1978), pp. 7–13.

57. Raymond R. Burke and Thomas K. Srull, "Competitive Interference and Consumer Memory for Advertising," *Journal of Consumer Research*, 15 (June 1988): 55–68; Kevin Lane Keller, "Memory Factors in Advertising: The Effect of Advertising Retrieval Cues on Brand Evaluations," *Journal of Consumer Research*, 14 (December 1987): 316–333; Kevin Lane Keller, "Memory and Evaluations in Competitive Advertising Environments," *Journal of Consumer Research*, 17 (March 1991): 463–476; Robert J. Kent and Chris T. Allen, "Competitive Interference Effects in Consumer Memory for Advertising: The Role of Brand Familiarity," *Journal of Marketing*, 58 (July 1994): 97–105.

58. David Walker and Michael J. von Gonten, "Explaining Related Recall Outcomes: New Answers from a Better Model," *Journal of Advertising Research*, 29 (1989): 11–21.

59. Kevin Lane Keller, Susan Heckler, and Michael J. Houston, "The Effects of Brand Name Suggestiveness on Advertising Recall," *Journal of Marketing*, 62 (January 1998): 48–57.

60. Bob Tedeschi, "E-Commerce Report," *The New York Times*, June 24, 2002, p. C8.

61. Gerry Khermouch, "The Top 5 Rules of the Ad Game," *BusinessWeek*, January 20, 2003, pp. 72–73.

62. Dale Buss, "On Again, Off Again," *Brand Marketing*, February 2001, p. 51; Kenneth Hein, "Pepsi: This Time It's All About the Dew,'" *Brandweek*, January 19, 2004, p. 4.

63. Heather Green, "Online Ads Take Off Again," *BusinessWeek*, May 5, 2003, p. 75.

64. Maria Puente, "Online Experience Is Now a Much Better Fit," *USA Today*, December 4, 2002, p. 2E.

65. Don E. Shultz, Stanley I. Tannenbaum, and Robert F. Lauterborn, *Integrated Marketing Communications: Putting It Together and Making It Work* (Lincolnwood, IL: NTC Business Books, 1992); Don E. Schultz and Heidi Schultz, *IMC, The Next Generation: Five Steps for Delivering Value and Measuring Financial Returns* (New York: McGraw-Hill, 2003).

Chapter 18

1. Jack Neff and Lisa Sanders, "It's Broken," *Advertising Age*, February 16, 2004, pp. 1, 30.

2. Ellen Neuborne, "Ads That Actually Sell Stuff," *Business 2.0* (June 2004): 78.

3. Russell H. Colley, *Defining Advertising Goals for Measured Advertising Results* (New York: Association of National Advertisers, 1961).

4. William L. Wilkie and Paul W. Farris, "Comparison Advertising: Problem and Potential," *Journal of Marketing* (October 1975): 7–15.

5. Randall L. Rose, Paul W. Miniard, Michael J. Barone, Kenneth C. Manning, and Brian D. Till, "When Persuasion Goes Undetected: The Case of Comparative Advertising," *Journal of Marketing Research* (August 1993): 315–330; Sanjay Putrevu and Kenneth R. Lord, "Comparative and Noncomparative Advertising: Attitudinal Effects under Cognitive and Affective Involvement Conditions," *Journal of Advertising* (June 1994): 77–91; Dhruv Grewal, Sukumar Kavanoor, and James Barnes, "Comparative versus Noncomparative Advertising: A Meta-Analysis," *Journal of Marketing* (October 1997): 1–15; Dhruv Grewal, Kent B. Monroe, and P. Krishnan, "The Effects of Price-Comparison Advertising on Buyers' Perceptions of Acquisition Value, Transaction Value, and Behavioral Intentions," *Journal of Marketing* (April 1998): 46–59.

6. For a good discussion, see David A. Aaker and James M. Carman, "Are You Overadvertising?" *Journal of Advertising Research* (August–September 1982): 57–70.

7. Donald E. Schultz, Dennis Martin, and William P. Brown, *Strategic Advertising Campaigns* (Chicago: Crain Books, 1984), pp. 192–197.

8. Rajesh Chandy, Gerard J. Tellis, Debbie MacInnis, and Pattana Thaivanich, "What to Say When: Advertising Appeals in Evolving Markets," *Journal of Marketing Research* 38, no. 4 (November 2001); Gerard J. Tellis, Rajesh Chandy, and Pattana Thaivanich, "Decomposing the Effects of Direct Advertising: Which Brand Works, When, Where, and How Long?" *Journal of Marketing Research* 37 (February 2000): 32–46.

9. See George S. Low and Jakki J. Mohr, "Brand Managers' Perceptions of the Marketing Communications Budget Allocation Process" (Cambridge, MA: Marketing Science Institute, Report No. 98-105, March 1998); and their "The Advertising Sales Promotion Trade-Off: Theory and Practice" (Cambridge, MA: Marketing Science Institute, Report No. 92-127, October 1992). Also see Gabriel J. Beihal and Daniel A. Sheinen, "Managing the Brand in a Corporate Advertising Environment: A Decision-Making Framework for Brand Managers," *Journal of Advertising* 17 (June 22, 1998): 99.

10. "Rona: Faites Attention!" *Strategy Magazine Online*, www.strategymag.com, November 12, 2004 (viewed November 25, 2004).

11. James B. Amdorfer, "Absolut Ads Sans Bottle Offer a Short-Story Series," *Advertising Age*, January 12, 1998, p. 8; Shelly Branch, "Absolut's Latest Ad Leaves Bottle Behind," *Wall Street Journal*, May 3, 2001, p. B9.

12. Statistics Canada, *The Daily*, www.statcan.ca/Daily/English/040728/d040728b.htm, July 28, 2004 (viewed November 25, 2004).

13. David Ogilvy, *Ogilvy on Advertising* (New York: Vintage Books, 1983).

14. Patti Summerfield, "Heard Any Good Ads Lately? Radio: The Niche Broadcast Medium That's Highly Targetable, Effective, Cost-Efficient and Largely Ignored by the Innovator-Creators," *Strategy Magazine Online*, www.strategymag.com, November 12, 2004 (viewed November 25, 2004).

15. Kim Bartel Sheehan, *Controversies in Contemporary Advertising* (Thousand Oaks, CA: Sage Publications, 2003); Advertising Standards Canada, "CO2001 Ad Complaints Report," www.adstandards.com/en/standards.report.asp (PDF document, p. 15). For further reading, see Dorothy Cohen, *Legal Issues in Marketing Decision Making* (Cincinnati, OH; South-Westerm, 1995).

16. "Calvin Klein: A Case Study," Media Awareness Network, Ottawa, Ontario.

17. Suzanne Vranica, "Sirius Ad Is Best for Most Sexist," *Wall Street Journal*, April 1, 2004, p. B6.

18. Adapted from Sandra Cordon, "Where High Road Meets Bottom Line: Ethical Mutual Funds Avoid Companies Deemed Socially Irresponsible," *The London Free Press*, October 9, 1998, p. D3.

19. Schultz et al., *Strategic Advertising Campaigns*, p. 340.

20. Herbert E. Krugman, "What Makes Advertising Effective?" *Harvard Business Review* (March–April 1975): 98.

21. Thomas H. Davenport and John C. Beck, *The Attention Economy: Understanding the New Currency of Business* (Boston: Harvard Business School Press, 2000).

22. Demetrios Vakratsas, Fred M. Feinberg, Frank M. Bass, Gurumurthy Kalyanaram, "The Shape of Advertising Response Functions Revisited: A Model of Dynamic Probabilistic Thresholds," *Marketing Science*, 23, no. 1 (Winter 2004): 109–119.

23. Susan Thea Posnock, "It Can Control Madison Avenue," *American Demographics* (February 2004): 29–33.

24. James Betzold, "Jaded Riders Are Ever-Tougher Sell," *Advertising Age*, July 9, 2001; Michael McCarthy, "Ads Are Here, There, Everywhere," *USA Today*, June 19, 2001; Kipp Cheng, "Captivating Audiences," *Brandweek*, November 29, 1999; Michael McCarthy, "Critics Target 'Omnipresent' Ads," *USA Today*, April 16, 2001.

25. Nate Nickerson, "How About This Beer Label: "I'M IN ADVERTIS-ING," *Fast Company*, March 2004, p. 45; Tony Case, "Crispin, Porter + Bogusky," *Adweek*, June 21, 2004.

26. Sam Jaffe, "Easy Riders," *American Demographics* (March 2004): 20–23.

27. Theresa Howard, "Ads Seek Greatness," *USA Today*, June 23, 2004, p. 4B.

28. Clare Gagne, "Small Budget Miracle," *Marketing Magazine Online*, www.marketingmag.ca, November 15, 2004 (viewed November 26, 2004); Brown Communications, "Burger Baron Strikes Back!" www.browncommunications.com/default.aspx?DN=65,66,8,1,Documents.

29. Jeff Pelline, "New Commercial Twist in Corporate Restrooms," *San Francisco Chronicle*, October 6, 1986.

30. Brian Steinberg and Suzanne Vranica, "Prime-Time TV's New Guest Stars: Products," *Wall Street Journal*, January 13, 2004, pp. B1, B4.

31. Jane Weaver, "A License to Shill," November 17, 2002, MSNBC News.

32. Joanne Lipman, "Product Placement Can Be Free Lunch," *Wall Street Journal*, November 25, 1991; John Lippman and Rick Brooks, "Hot Holiday Flick Pairs FedEx, Hanks," *Wall Street Journal*, December 11, 2000, pp. B1, B6.

33. Warren Berger, "That's Advertainment," *Business 2.0* (March 2003): 91–95.

34. Catherine P. Taylor, "Digitas," *Brandweek IQ Quarterly*, February 23, 2004, pp. 24–25.

35. Jean Halliday, "Mazda Goes Viral to Tout New Cars," *Automotive News*, November 24, 2003, p. 42B.

36. Matthew Boyle, "Hey Shoppers: Ads on Aisle 7!" *Fortune*, November 24, 2003.

37. Richard Linnett, "'Friends' Tops TV Price Chart," *Advertising Age*, September 15, 2003, pp. 1, 46.

38. Canadian Media Director's Council, *2002-2003 Media Digest* (Toronto: Marketing Magazine, 2002), p. 19.

39. Canadian Media Director's Council, p. 43.

40. Michael A. Kamins, Lawrence J. Marks, and Deborah Skinner, "Television Commercial Evaluation in the Context of Program Induced Mood: Congruency versus Consistency Effects," *Journal of Advertising* (June 1991): 1–14.

41. Kenneth R. Lord and Robert E. Burnkrant, "Attention versus Distraction: The Interactive Effect of Program Involvement and Attentional Devices on Commercial Processing," *Journal of Advertising* (March 1993): 47–60; Kenneth R. Lord, Myung-Soo Lee, and Paul L. Sauer, "Program Context Antecedents of Attitude Toward Radio Commercials," *Journal of the Academy of Marketing Science* (Winter 1994): 3–15.

42. Roland T. Rust, *Advertising Media Models: A Practical Guide* (Lexington, MA: Lexington Books, 1986).

43. Hani I. Mesak, "An Aggregate Advertising Pulsing Model with Wearout Effects," *Marketing Science* (Summer 1992): 310–326; Fred M. Feinberg, "Pulsing Policies for Aggregate Advertising Models," *Marketing Science* (Summer 1992): 221–234.

44. Josephine L.C.M. Woltman Elpers, Michel Wedel, and Rik G.M. Pieters, "Why Do Consumers Stop Viewing Television Commercials? Two Experiments on the Influence of Moment-to-Moment Entertainment and Information Value," *Journal of Marketing Research*, 40 (November), 2003, pp. 437–453.

45. Kristian S. Palda, *The Measurement of Cumulative Advertising Effect* (Upper Saddle River, NJ: Prentice Hall, 1964), p. 87; David B. Montgomery and Alvin J. Silk, "Estimating Dynamic Effects of Market Communications Expenditures," *Management Science* (June 1972): 485–501.

46. www.infores.com; Leonard M. Lodish, Magid Abraham, Stuart Kalmenson, Jeanne Livelsberger, Beth Lubetkin, Bruce Richardson, and Mary Ellen Stevens, "How T.V. Advertising Works: A Meta-Analysis of 389 Real World Split Cable T.V. Advertising Experiments," *Journal of Marketing Research*, 32 (May 1995): pp. 125–139.

47. In addition to the sources cited below, see David Walker and Tony M. Dubitsky, "Why Liking Matters," *Journal of Advertising Research* (May–June 1994): 9–18; Abhilasha Mehta, "How Advertising Response Modeling (ARM) Can Increase Ad Effectiveness," *Journal of Advertising Research* (May–June 1994): 62–74; Karin Holstius, "Sales Response to Advertising," *International Journal of Advertising* 9, no. 1 (1990): 38–56; John Deighton, Caroline Henderson, and Scott Neslin, "The Effects of Advertising on Brand Switching and Repeat Purchasing," *Journal of Marketing Research* (February 1994): 28–43; Anil Kaul and Dick R. Wittink, "Empirical Generalizations about the Impact of Advertising on Price Sensitivity and Price," *Marketing Science* 14, no. 3, pt. 1 (1995): G151–160; Ajay Kalra and Ronald C. Goodstein, "The Impact of Advertising Positioning Strategies on Consumer Price Sensitivity," *Journal of Marketing Research* (May 1998): 210–224; Gerard J. Tellis, Rajesh K. Chandy, and Pattana Thaivanich, "Which Ad Works, When, Where, and How Often? Modeling the Effects of Direct Television Advertising," *Journal of Marketing Research*, 37 (February 2000): 32–46.

48. Nigel Hollis, "The Link between TV Ad Awareness and Sales: New Evidence from Sales Response Modelling," *Journal of the Market Research Society* (January 1994): 41–55.

49. From Robert C. Blattberg and Scott A. Neslin, *Sales Promotion: Concepts, Methods, and Strategies* (Upper Saddle River, NJ: Prentice Hall, 1990). This text provides the most comprehensive and analytical treatment of sales promotion to date. An extremely up-to-date and comprehensive review of academic work on sales promotions can be found in Scott Neslin, "Sales Promotion," in *Handbook of Marketing*, edited by Bart Weitz and Robin Wensley (London: Sage Publications, 2002), pp. 310–338.

50. Kusum Ailawadi, Karen Gedenk, and Scott A. Neslin, "Heterogeneity and Purchase Event Feedback in Choice Models: An Empirical Analysis with Implications for Model Building," *International Journal of Research in Marketing*, 16 (1999): 177–198. See also Eric T. Anderson and Duncan Simester, "The Long-Run Effects of Promotion Depth on New Versus Established Customers: Three Field Studies," *Marketing Science*, 23, no. 1 (Winter 2004): 4–20.

51. Carl Mela, Kamel Jedidi, and Douglas Bowman, "The Long Term Impact of Promotions on Consumer Stockpiling," *Journal of Marketing Research* 35, no. 2 (May 1998): 250–262.

52. Harald J. Van Heerde, Peter S. H. Leeflang, and Dick Wittink, "The Estimation of Pre- and Postpromotion Dips with Store-Level

Scanner Data," *Journal of Marketing Research* 37, no. 3 (August 2000): 383–395.

53. Paul W. Farris and John A. Quelch, "In Defense of Price Promotion," *Sloan Management Review* (Fall 1987): 63–69.

54. "Promo Hits and Misses," *Marketing Magazine Online*, May 12, 2003 (viewed November 29, 2004).

55. Roger A. Strang, "Sales Promotion: Fast Growth, Faulty Management," *Harvard Business Review* (July–August 1976): 116–119.

56. For a good summary of the research on whether promotion erodes the consumer franchise of leading brands, see Blattberg and Neslin, *Sales Promotion*.

57. AutoVIBES, *AutoBeat Daily*, March 3, 2004; Karen Lundegaard and Sholnn Freeman, "Detroit's Challenge: Weaning Buyers from Years of Deals," *Wall Street Journal*, January 6, 2004, pp. A1, A2.

58. Robert George Brown, "Sales Response to Promotions and Advertising," *Journal of Advertising Research* (August 1974): 36–37. Also see Carl F. Mela, Sunil Gupta, and Donald R. Lehmann, "The Long-Term Impact of Promotion and Advertising on Consumer Brand Choice," *Journal of Marketing Research* (May 1997): 248–261; Purushottam Papatla and Lakshman Krishnamurti, "Measuring the Dynamic Effects of Promotions on Brand Choice," *Journal of Marketing Research* (February 1996): 20–35; Kamel Jedidi, Carl F. Mela, and Sunil Gupta, "Managing Advertising and Promotion for Long-Run Profitability," *Marketing Science* 18, no. 1 (1999): 1–22.

59. Magid M. Abraham and Leonard M. Lodish, "Getting the Most Out of Advertising and Promotion," *Harvard Business Review* (May–June 1990): 50–60. See also Shuba Srinivasan, Koen Pauwels, Dominique Hanssens, and Marnik Dekimpe, "Do Promotions Benefit Manufacturers, Retailers, or Both?" *Management Science*, 2004.

60. F. Kent Mitchel, "Advertising/Promotion Budgets: How Did We Get Here, and What Do We Do Now?" *Journal of Consumer Marketing* (Fall 1985): 405–447.

61. For a model for setting sales-promotions objectives, see David B. Jones, "Setting Promotional Goals: A Communications Relationship Model," *Journal of Consumer Marketing* 11, no. 1 (1994): 38–49.

62. Sonia Reyes, "Krafting the Total Promo Package," *Brandweek*, July 15, 2002, pp. 24–27.

63. See John C. Totten and Martin P. Block, *Analyzing Sales Promotion: Text and Cases*, 2nd ed. (Chicago: Dartnell, 1994), pp. 69–70.

64. Valpak Direct Marketing Systems, Inc., "A History of Results-Oriented Advertising," www.valpak.com/vpcol/corporate.do.

65. Paul W. Farris and Kusum L. Ailawadi, "Retail Power: Monster or Mouse?" *Journal of Retailing* (Winter 1992): 351–369.

66. "Retailers Buy Far in Advance to Exploit Trade Promotions," *Wall Street Journal* October 9, 1986, p. 35; Rajiv Lal, J. Little, and J. M. Vilas-Boas, "A Theory of Forward Buying, Merchandising, and Trade Deals," *Marketing Science* 15, no. 1 (1996): 21–37.

67. Kenneth Hein, "Samsung Decodes the *Matrix* Mania," *Brandweek*, March 22, 2004, p. R3.

68. Arthur Stern, "Measuring the Effectiveness of Package Goods Promotion Strategies" (paper presented to the Association of National Advertisers, Glen Cove, NY, February 1978).

69. Kurt H. Schaffir and H. George Trenten, *Marketing Information Systems* (New York: Amacom, 1973), p. 81.

70. Joe A. Dodson, Alice M. Tybout, and Brian Sternthal, "Impact of Deals and Deal Retraction on Brand Switching," *Journal of Marketing Research* (February 1978): 72–81.

71. Books on sales promotion include Totten and Block, *Analyzing Sales Promotion: Text and Cases*; Don E. Schultz, William A. Robinson, and Lisa A. Petrison, *Sales Promotion Essentials*, 2nd ed. (Lincolnwood, IL: NTC Business Books, 1994); John Wilmshurst, *Below-the-Line Promotion* (Oxford, England: Butterworth/Heinemann, 1993); Blattberg and Neslin, *Sales Promotion: Concepts, Methods, and Strategies*. For an expert systems approach to sales promotion, see John W. Keon and Judy Bayer, "An Expert Approach to Sales Promotion Management," *Journal of Advertising Research* (June–July 1986): 19–26.

72. Philip Kotler, "Atmospherics as a Marketing Tool," *Journal of Retailing* (Winter 1973–1974): 48–64.

73. Dean Foust, "Coke: Wooing the TiVo Generation," *Business Week*, March 1, 2004, pp. 77–78.

74. Kathleen Kerwin, "When the Factory Is a Theme Park," *BusinessWeek*, May 3, 2004, p. 94; Vanessa O'Connell, "'You-Are-There' Advertising," *Wall Street Journal*, August 5, 2002, pp. B1, B3.

75. Kenneth Hein, "The Age of Reason," *Brandweek*, October 27, 2003, pp. 24–28.

76. Sarah Dobson, "The Main Event," *Marketing Magazine Online*, www.marketingmag.ca, September 13, 2004 (viewed November 29, 2004).

77. Monte Burke, "X-treme Economics," *Forbes*, February 2, 2004, pp. 42–44.

78. The Association of National Advertisers has a useful source, *Event Marketing: A Management Guide*, which is available at www.ana.net/bookstore.

79. Ian Mount, "Exploding the Myths of Stadium Naming," *Business 2.0* (April 2004): 82.

80. "Air Canada Centre Name Likely to Stay," *Marketing Magazine Daily*, www.marketingmag.ca, April 4, 2003 (viewed November 29, 2004).

81. Kelley Gates, "Wild in the Streets," *Brand Marketing* (February 2001): 54.

82. Dwight W. Catherwood and Richard L. Van Kirk, *The Complete Guide to Special Event Management* (New York: John Wiley, 1992).

83. William L. Shankin and John Kuzma, "Buying That Sporting Image," *Marketing Management* (Spring 1992): 65.

84. For an excellent account, see Thomas L. Harris, *The Marketer's Guide to Public Relations* (New York: John Wiley, 1991). Also see Harris, *Value-Added Public Relations* (Chicago: NTC Business Books, 1998).

85. Tom Duncan, *A Study of How Manufacturers and Service Companies Perceive and Use Marketing Public Relations* (Muncie, IN: Ball State University, December 1985). For more on how to contrast the effectiveness of advertising with the effectiveness of PR, see Kenneth R. Lord and Sanjay Putrevu, "Advertising and Publicity: An Information Processing Perspective," *Journal of Economic Psychology* (March 1993): 57–84.

86. Julie Rusciolelli, "PR Discovers Metrics," *Marketing Magazine Online*, www.marketingmag.ca, March 29, 2004 (viewed November 29, 2004); Taxi Canada Web site, www.taxi.ca (viewed November 29, 2004); See You In Torino Web site, www.seeyouintorino.com (viewed November 29, 2004).

87. For further reading on cause-related marketing, see P. Rajan Varadarajan and Anil Menon, "Cause-Related Marketing: A Co-Alignment of Marketing Strategy and Corporate Philanthropy," *Journal of Marketing* (July 1988): 58–74.

88. Arthur M. Merims, "Marketing's Stepchild: Product Publicity," *Harvard Business Review* (November–December 1972): 111–112. Also see Katherine D. Paine, "There Is a Method for Measuring PR," *Marketing News*, November 6, 1987, p. 5.

Chapter 19

1. The terms *direct-order marketing* and *direct-relationship marketing* were suggested as subsets of direct marketing by Stan Rapp and Tom Collins in *The Great Marketing Turnaround* (Upper Saddle River, NJ: Prentice Hall, 1990).

2. Sarah Smith, "Women Want More Air Miles Reward Miles," *Marketing Magazine Online*, www.marketingmag.ca, February 18, 2002.

3. Michael J. Mcgovern, "The Precise Art of Direct Marketing," *Marketing Magazine Online*, www.marketingmag.ca, March 22, 2004 (viewed December 1, 2004).

4. See "Warranty and Returns," on Mountain Equipment Co-op's Web site, www.mec.ca/Main/content_text.jsp?FOLDER%3C%3Efolder_id=653315&bmUID=1111590669470.

5. www.directmarketingmag.com.

6. Bob Stone, *Successful Direct Marketing Methods*, 6th ed. (Lincolnwood, IL: NTC Business Books, 1996). Also see David Shepard Associates, *The New Direct Marketing*, 2nd ed. (Chicago: Irwin, 1995); Amiya K. Basu, Atasi Basu, and Rajeev Batra, "Modeling the Response Pattern to Direct Marketing Campaigns," *Journal of Marketing Research* (May 1995): 204–212.

7. Edward L. Nash, *Direct Marketing: Strategy, Planning, Execution*, 3rd ed. (New York: McGraw-Hill, 1995).

8. Rachel McLaughlin, "Get the Envelope Opened!" *Target Marketing* (September 1998): 37–39.

9. The *average customer longevity* (N) is related to the *customer retention rate* (CR). Suppose the company retains 80 percent of its customers each year. Then the average customer longevity is given by:

$$N = 1 / (1 - CR) = 1 / 0.2 = 5$$

10. "Canadian Mail Order Catalogues," Library and Archives Canada, www.collectionscanada.ca/mailorder/index-e.html.

11. Stephanie Whittaker, "Nike Catalogue Site Targets Instructors," *Marketing Magazine Online*, www.marketingmag.ca, May 21, 2001.

12. "Catalogue Mail: Frequently Asked Questions," Canada Post Web site, www.canadapost.ca/business/offerings/catalogue_mail/can/about_faqs-e.asp.

13. "Case Study: Awesome Ewe," www.e-bc.ca/casestudies_details.asp?id=2 (viewed March 23, 2005).

14. Mari Yamaguchi, "Japanese Consumers Shun Local Catalogs to Buy American," *Marketing News*, December 2, 1996, p. 12; Cacilie Rohwedder, "U.S. Mail-Order Firms Shake Up Europe— Better Service, Specialized Catalogs Find Eager Shoppers," *Wall Street Journal*, January 6, 1998; Kathleen Kiley, "B-to-B Marketers High on Overseas Sales," *Catalog Age* (January 1997): 8.

15. "Do Not Call: CRTC Rules," CBC News Online, www.cbc.ca/news/background/telemarketing/ (viewed December 13, 2004); "Ottawa Leans to DNC Registry as Flak Rises over CRTC Rules," *Direct Marketing News*, October 2004, www.dmn.ca/Articles/Articles/2004/Nov/dnc1104.htm; Telecom Decision CRTC 2004-63, Application by the Canadian Marketing Association to Stay Decision 2004-35, Reference: 8662-C131-200408543, Ottawa, 28 September 2004; Telecom Decision CRTC 2004-35, Review of Telemarketing Rules, Reference: 8665-C12-13/0, Ottawa, 21 May 2004.

16. Jim Edwards, "The Art of the Infomercial," *Brandweek*, September 3, 2001, pp. 14–19.

17. "Infomercial Offers Multiple Uses," *Direct Marketing* (September 1998): 11; Tim Hawthorne, When and Why to Consider Infomercials," *Target Marketing* (February 1998): 52–53.

18. Michelle Warren, "Sick Kids' Direct Drama," *Marketing Magazine Online*, www.marketingmag.ca, February 10, 2003 (viewed December 1, 2004).

19. Charles Fishman, "The Tool of a New Machine," *Fast Company*, May 2004, 92–95.

20. Tony Case, "Growing Up," *Interactive Quarterly*, April 19, 2004, pp. 32–34.

21. Asim Ansari and Carl F. Mela (2003), "E-Customization," *Journal of Marketing Research*, 40, no. 2 (May 2003): 131–145.

22. "Internet Ad Market Heating Up: Report," *The Banner*, August 2004, www.247canada.com/en/newsletter/newsletter-0408.html#article08.

23. Marketing Magazine Digital Marketing Report, "Logging On," *Marketing Magazine Online*, April 21, 2003 (viewed December 1, 2004).

24. Thomas Mucha, "Spray Here. Get Girl." *Business 2.0*, June 1, 2003.

25. David L. Smith and Karen McFee, "Media Mix 101: Online Media for Traditional Marketers," September 2003, http://advantage.msn.com/articles/MediaMix101_2.asp.

26. Paul C. Judge, "Will Online Ads Ever Click?" *Fast Company* (March 2001): 181–192.

27. Online Publisher's Association, "OPA Media Consumption Study" January 2002.

28. Jeffrey F. Rayport and Bernard J. Jaworski, *e-commerce* (New York: McGraw-Hill, 2001), p. 116.

29. Bob Tedeschi, "E-Commerce Report," *The New York Times*, June 24, 2002, p. C8

30. Stephen Baker, "Pop-Up Ads Had Better Start Pleasing," *BusinessWeek*, December 8, 2003, p. 40.

31. "Prime Clicking Time," *The Economist*, May 31, 2003, p. 65; Ben Elgin, "Search Engines Are Picking Up Steam," *BusinessWeek*, March 24, 2003, pp. 86–87.

32. Ned Desmond, "Google's Next Runaway Success," *Business 2.0*, November 2002, p. 73.

33. Heather Green, "Online Ads Take Off Again," *BusinessWeek*, May 5, 2003, p. 75.

34. These numbers reflect March 2004 figures and are based on ad impressions available on the homepage of 6MM per day and a rate card CPM (cost per thousand) for a standard 728×90 unit (the horizontal unit at the top of the page) of US$15 (although most major advertisers do not have to pay this price).

35. Seth Godin, *Permission Marketing: Turning Strangers into Friends and Friends into Customers* (New York: Simon & Schuster, 1999).

36. Chana R. Schoenberger, "Web? What Web?" *Forbes*, June 10, 2002, p. 132.

37. Rapp and Collins, *Maximarketing* (New York: McGraw-Hill, 1987).

38. Theresa Howard, "Ad Winners Able to Implement 'Total Communications Strategy,'" *USA Today*, June 22, 2004.

39. Statistics Canada Web site, Canadian Statistics: Labour and Unemployment Statistics, "Experienced Labour Force 15 Years and Over by Occupation and Sex, by Provinces and Territories (2001 Census)," www.statcan.ca (viewed December 1, 2004).

40. Bill Keenan, "Cost-per-call Data Deserve Scruitiny," *Industry Week*, Jan 10, 2000.

41. Adapted from Robert N. McMurry, "The Mystique of Super-Salesmanship," *Harvard Business Review* (March–April 1961): 114. Also see William C. Moncrief III, "Selling Activity and Sales Position Taxonomies for Industrial Salesforces," *Journal of Marketing Research* (August 1986): 261–270.

42. David Ainslie, "Willy Loman's Legacy," *Marketing Magazine*, August 20, 2001; Enbridge's Web site www.enbridgeservices.com/index.asp (viewed July 8, 2002).

43. Lawrence G. Friedman and Timothy R. Furey, *The Channel Advantage: Going to Marketing with Multiple Sales Channels* (Oxford, UK: Butterworth-Heinemann, 1999).

44. Michael Copeland, "Hits and Misses," *Business 2.0* (April 2004): 142.

45. Luis R. Gomez-Mejia, David B. Balkin, and Robert L. Cardy, *Managing Human Resources* (Upper Saddle River, NJ: Prentice Hall, 1995), pp. 416–418.

46. "What Salespeople Are Paid," *Sales & Marketing Management* (February 1995): 30–31; Power, "Smart Selling," pp. 46–48; William Keenan Jr., ed., *The Sales & Marketing Management Guide to Sales Compensation Planning: Commissions, Bonuses & Beyond* (Chicago: Probus Publishing, 1994).

47. Sonke Albers, "Salesforce Management—Compensation, Motivation, Selection, and Training," in *Handbook of Marketing*,

edited by Bart Weitz and Robin Wensley (London: Sage Publications, 2002), pp. 248–266.

48. Raizel Robin and Laura Bogomolny, "A Competitive Edge: How Minority Hiring Practices Help Keep Fedex, Xerox Canada and Call-Net on Top," *Canadian Business Magazine Online*, www.canadianbusiness.com, March 29, 2004 (viewed December 2, 2004).

49. "Welcome to the Real Whirled: How Whirlpool Training Forced Salespeople to Live with the Brand," *Sales & Marketing Management* (February 2001): 87–88.

50. Nanette Byrnes, "Avon Calling—Lots of New Reps," *BusinessWeek*, June 2, 2003, pp. 53–54.

51. Michael R. W. Bommer, Brian F. O'Neil, and Beheruz N. Sethna, "A Methodology for Optimizing Selling Time of Salespersons," *Journal of Marketing Theory and Practice* (Spring 1994): 61–75. See also Lissan Joseph, "On the Optimality of Delegating Pricing Authority to the Sales Force," *Journal of Marketing* 65 (January 2001): 62–70.

52. Thomas Blackshear and Richard E. Plank, "The Impact of Adaptive Selling on Sales Effectiveness within the Pharmaceutical Industry," *Journal of Marketing Theory and Practice* (Summer 1994): 106–125.

53. Dartnell Corporation, 30th Sales Force Compensation Survey. Other breakdowns show that 12.7 percent is spent in service calls, 16 percent in administrative tasks, 25.1 percent in telephone selling, and 17.4 percent in waiting/travelling.

54. James A. Narus and James C. Anderson, "Industrial Distributor Selling: The Roles of Outside and Inside Sales," *Industrial Marketing Management* 15 (1986): 55–62.

55. Charles Waltner, "Pall Corp. Wins Business with Info-Driven Web Site," *Net Marketing* (October 1996).

56. Willem Verbeke and Richard P. Bagozzi, "Sales Call Anxiety: Exploring What It Means When Fear Rules a Sales Encounter," *Journal of Marketing*, 64 (July 2000): 88–101.

57. Gilbert A. Churchill Jr., Neil M. Ford, and Orville C. Walker Jr., *Sales Force Management: Planning, Implementation and Control*, 4th ed. (Homewood, IL: Irwin, 1993). Also see Jhinuk Chowdhury, "The Motivational Impact of Sales Quotas on Effort," *Journal of Marketing Research* (February 1993): 28–41; Murali K. Mantrala, Prabhakant Sinha, and Andris A. Zoltners, "Structuring a Multiproduct Sales Quota-Bonus Plan for a Heterogeneous Sales Force: A Practical Model-Based Approach," *Marketing Science* 13, no. 2 (1994): 121–144; Wujin Chu, Eitan Gerstner, and James D. Hess, "Costs and Benefits of Hard-Sell," *Journal of Marketing Research* (February 1995): 97–102; Manfred Krafft, "In Empirical Investigation of the Antecedents of Sales Force Control Systems," *Journal of Marketing* 63 (July 1999): 120–134.

58. Eilene Zimmerman, "Quota Busters," *Sales & Marketing Management* (January 2001): pp. 59–63.

59. Melanie Warner, "Confessions of a Control Freak," *Fortune*, September 4, 2000, p. 30; Peter Burrows, "The Era of Efficiency," *BusinessWeek*, June 18, 2001, p. 92.

60. Ian Mount, "Out of Control," *Business 2.0* (August 2002): 38–44.

61. Philip M. Posdakoff and Scott B. MacKenzie, "Organizational Citizenship Behaviors and Sales Unit Effectiveness," *Journal of Marketing Research* (August 1994): 351–363. See also Andrea L. Dixon, Rosann L. Spiro, and Magbul Jamil, "Successful and Unsuccessful Sales Calls: Measuring Salesperson Attributions and Behavioral Intentions," *Journal of Marketing*, 65 (July 2001): 64–78; Willem Verbeke and Richard P. Bagozzi, "Sales Call Anxiety: Exploring What It Means When Fear Rules a Sales Encounter," *Journal of Marketing*, 64 (July 2000): 88–101.

62. Andrea L. Dixon, Rosann L. Spiro, and Maqbul Jamil, "Successful and Unsuccessful Sales Calls: Measuring Salesperson Attributions and Behavioral Intentions," *Journal of Marketing*, 65 (July 2001): 64–78.

63. Some of the following discussion is based on W. J. E. Crissy, William H. Cunningham, and Isabella C. M. Cunningham, *Selling: The Personal Force in Marketing* (New York: John Wiley, 1977), pp. 119–129.

64. Joel E. Urbany, "Justifying Profitable Pricing," Working Paper Series, Marketing Science Institute, Report No. 00-117, 2000, pp. 17–18.

65. For additional reading, see Howard Raiffa, *The Art and Science of Negotiation* (Cambridge, MA: Harvard University Press, 1982); Max H. Bazerman and Margaret A. Neale, *Negotiating Rationally* (New York: The Free Press, 1992); James C. Freund, *Smart Negotiating* (New York: Simon & Schuster, 1992); Frank L. Acuff, *How to Negotiate Anything with Anyone Anywhere Around the World* (New York: American Management Association, 1993); Jehoshua Eliashberg, Gary L. Lilien, and Nam Kim, "Searching for Generalizations in Business Marketing Negotiations," *Marketing Science* 14, no. 3 (pt. 1) (1995): G47–G60.

66. Kristen Vinakmens, "Timing Is Everything: Top Marketers Experiment with Systems That React to Customer Behaviour with Just the Right Offer at Just the Right Time," *Marketing Magazine Online*, www.marketingmag.ca, September 8, 2003 (viewed December 2, 2004).

Chapter 20

1. Deborah Ball and Sarah Ellison, "Nestlé's Appetite for Acquisitions Quickens," *Wall Street Journal*, August 7, 2002, p. B3.

2. Booz, Allen & Hamilton, *New Products Management for the 1980s* (New York: Booz, Allen & Hamilton, 1982).

3. Ann Harrington, "Who's Afraid of a New Product," *Fortune*, November 10, 2003, pp. 189–192; Brad Weiners, "Gore-Tex Tackles the Great Indoors," *Business 2.0* (April 2004): 32.

4. William Symonds, "Can Gillette Regain Its Edge," *BusinessWeek*, January 26, 2004, p. 46.

5. "Don't Laugh at Gilded Butterflies," *The Economist*, April 24, 2004, pp. 71–73.

6. Diane Brady, "The Brains Behind Blackberry," *BusinessWeek*, April 19, 2004, pp. 55–56; Alison Overholt, "Good to Great," *Fast Company* (May 2004): 45.

7. For details, see Thomas Kuczmarski, Arthur Middlebrooks, and Jeffrey Swaddling, *Innovating the Corporation: Creating Value for Customers and Shareholders* (Lincolnwood, IL: NTC, 2000).

8. Clayton M. Christensen, *The Innovator's Dilemma: When New Technologies Cause Great Firms to Fail* (Boston, MA: Harvard University Press, 1997).

9. Ely Dahan and John R. Hauser, "Product Development: Managing a Dispersed Process," in *Handbook of Marketing*, edited by Weitz and Robin Wensley, pp. 179–222.

10. Diane Brady, "A Thousand and One Noshes," *BusinessWeek*, June 14, 2004, pp. 54–56.

11. Christopher Power, "Flops," *BusinessWeek*, August 16, 1993, pp. 76–82.

12. Andrea Zoe Aster, "Consumer Research Goes Online," *Marketing Magazine*, June 7, 2004; Deloitte and Touche, "Vision in Manufacturing Study," Deloitte Consultng and Kenan-Flagler Business School, March 6, 1998; A. C. Nielsen, "New Product Introduction—Successful Innovation/Failure: Fragile Boundary," A. C. Nielsen BASES and Ernst & Young Global Client Consulting, June 24, 1999.

13. Robert G. Cooper and Elko J. Kleinschmidt, *New Products: The Key Factors in Success* (Chicago: American Marketing Association, 1990).

14. David Welch, "Can Stodgy GM Turn Stylish?" *BusinessWeek*, November 11, 2002, pp. 111–112.

15. David S. Hopkins, *Options in New-Product Organization* (New York: Conference Board, 1974); Doug Ayers, Robert Dahlstrom, and Steven J. Skinner, "An Exploratory Investigation of Organizational Antecedents to New Product Success," *Journal of Marketing Research* (February 1997): 107–116.

16. Rajesh Sethi, Daniel C. Smith, and C. Whan Park, "Cross Functional Product Development Teams, Creativity, and the

Innovativness of New Consumer Products," *Journal of Marketing Research*, 38 (February 2001): 73–85.

17. Don H. Lester, "Critical Success Factors for New Product Development," *Research Technology Management* (January–February 1998): 36–43.

18. Robert G. Cooper, "Stage-Gate Systems: A New Tool for Managing New Products," *Business Horizons* (May–June 1990): 44–54. See also "The New Prod System: The Industry Experience," *Journal of Product Innovation Management*, 9 (1992): 113–127.

19. Robert Cooper, *Product Leadership: Creating and Launching Superior New Products* (New York: Perseus Books, 1998).

20. Ely Dahan and John R. Hauser, "Product Development: Managing a Dispersed Process," in *Handbook of Marketing*, edited by Bart Weitz and Robin Wensley (London: Sage Publications), pp. 179–222.

21. Thomas N. Burton, "By Learning from Failures Lilly Keeps Drug Pipelines Full," *Wall Street Journal*, April 21, 2004, pp. A1, A12.

22. John Hauser and Gerard J. Tellis, "Research on Innovation: A Review and Agenda for Marketing," 2004, working paper.

23. Abbie J. Griffin and John Hauser, "The Voice of the Customer," *Marketing Science* (Winter 1993): 1–27.

24. Emily Nelson, "Stuck on You," *Wall Street Journal*, May 9, 2002, pp. B1, B4.

25. Eric von Hippel, "Lead Users: A Source of Novel Product Concepts," *Management Science* (July 1986): 791–805. Also see *The Sources of Innovation* (New York: Oxford University Press, 1988); and "Learning from Lead Users," in *Marketing in an Electronic Age*, edited by Robert D. Buzzell (Cambridge, MA: Harvard Business School Press, 1985), pp. 308–317.

26. Steven Levy, "Microsoft Gets a Clue from its Kiddie Corps," *Newsweek*, February 24, 2003, pp. 56–57.

27. Michael Michalko, *Cracking Creativity: The Secrets of Creative Genius* (Berkeley, CA: Ten Speed Press, 1998); James M. Higgins, *101 Creative Problem Solving Techniques* (New York: New Management Publishing Company, 1994); Darren W. Dahl and Page Moreau, "The Influence and Value of Analogical Thinking During New Product Ideation," *Journal of Marketing Research*, 39 (February 2002): 47–60.

28. www.smokinggun.com.

29. "The Ultimate Widget: 3-D 'Printing' May Revolutionize Product Design and Manufacturing," *U.S. News & World Report*, July 20, 1992, p. 55.

30. For additional information, also see Paul E. Green and V. Srinivasan, "Conjoint Analysis in Marketing: New Developments with Implications for Research and Practice," *Journal of Marketing* (October 1990): 3–19; Dick R. Wittnick, Marco Vriens, and Wim Burhenne, "Commercial Uses of Conjoint Analysis in Europe: Results and Critical Reflections," *International Journal of Research in Marketing* (January 1994): 41–52; Jordan J. Louviere, David A. Hensher, and Joffre D. Swait, *Stated Choice Models: Analysis and Applications* (New York: Cambridge University Press, 2000).

31. Lesley Young, "Peddling Telecom Bundles," *Marketing Magazine*, May 7, 2001, www.marketingmag.ca/magazine/current/feature/article.jsp?content=20010507_17481#; "Bell Canada Launches Bell Security Solutions Inc.," Bell Canada Press Release, (Ottawa), February 15, 2005, http://enterprise.bell.ca/en/default.asp?sid=256&did=807.

32. The full-profile example was taken from Paul E. Green and Yoram Wind, "New Ways to Measure Consumers' Judgments," *Harvard Business Review* (July–August 1975): 107–117.

33. Robert Blattberg and John Golany, "Tracker: An Early Test Market Forecasting and Diagnostic Model for New Product Planning," *Journal of Marketing Research* (May 1978): 192–202; Glen L. Urban, Bruce D. Weinberg, and John R. Hauser, "Premarket Forecasting of Really New Products," *Journal of Marketing* (January 1996): 47–60; Peter N. Golder and Gerald J. Tellis, "Will It Ever Fly? Modeling the Takeoff of Really New Consumer Durables," *Marketing Science*, 16, no. 3 (1997): 256–270.

34. Roger A. Kerin, Michael G. Harvey, and James T. Rothe, "Cannibalism and New Product Development," *Business Horizons* (October 1978): 25–31.

35. The present value (V) of a future sum (I) to be received t years from today and discounted at the interest rate (r) is given by $V5It/(11r)t$. Thus $4 761 000/(1.15)5 = $2 346 000.

36. David B. Hertz, "Risk Analysis in Capital Investment," *Harvard Business Review* (January–February 1964): 96–106.

37. John Hauser, "House of Quality," *Harvard Business Review* (May–June 1988): 63–73. Customer-driven engineering is also called "quality function deployment." See Lawrence R. Guinta and Nancy C. Praizler, *The QFD Book: The Team Approach to Solving Problems and Satisfying Customers through Quality Function Deployment* (New York: AMACOM, 1993); V. Srinivasan, William S. Lovejoy, and David Beach, "Integrated Product Design for Marketability and Manufacturing," *Journal of Marketing Research* (February 1997): 154–163.

38. Marco Iansiti and Alan MacCormack, "Developing Products on Internet Time," *Harvard Business Review* (September–October 1997): 108–117; Srikant Datar, C. Clark Jordan, and Kannan Srinivasan, "Advantages of Time-Based New Product Development in a Fast-Cycle Industry," *Journal of Marketing Research* (February 1997): 36–49; Christopher D. Ittner and David F. Larcker, "Product Development Cycle Time and Organizational Performance," *Journal of Marketing Research* (February 1997): 13–23.

39. Tom Peters, *The Circle of Innovation* (New York: Alfred A. Knopf, 1997), p. 96. For more general discussion, see also Rajesh Sethi, "New Product Quality and Product Development Teams," *Journal of Marketing* (April 2000): 1–14; Christine Moorman and Anne S. Miner, "The Convergence of Planning and Execution Improvisation in New Product Development," *Journal of Marketing* (July 1998): 1–20; Ravinchoanath MacChavan and Rajiv Graver, "From Embedded Knowledge to Embodied Knowledge: New Product Development as Knowledge Management," *Journal of Marketing* (October 1998): 1–12.

40. Tom Peters, *The Circle of Innovation* (New York: Alfred A. Knopf, 1997), p. 96. For more general discussion, see also Rajesh Sethi, "New Product Quality and Product Development Teams," *Journal of Marketing* (April 2000): 1–14; Christine Moorman and Anne S. Miner, "The Convergence of Planning and Execution Improvisation in New Product Development," *Journal of Marketing* (July 1998): 1–20; Ravinchoanath MacChavan and Rajiv Graver, "From Embedded Knowledge to Embodied Knowledge: New Product Development as Knowledge Management," *Journal of Marketing* (October 1998): 1–12.

41. Underwriters' Laboratories of Canada Web site, www.ulc.ca/index.asp (viewed March 25, 2005).

42. Jim McElgunn, "The Ultimate Test Market," *Marketing Magazine*, February 10, 2003, www.marketingmag.ca/magazine/current/editorial/article.jsp?content=20030210_24163.

43. Christopher Power, "Will It Sell in Podunk? Hard to Say," *Business Week*, August 10, 1992, pp. 46–47.

44. Kevin J. Clancy, Robert S. Shulman, and Marianne Wolf, *Simulated Test Marketing: Technology for Launching Successful New Products* (New York: Lexington Books, 1994); V. Mahajan and Jerry Wind, "New Product Models: Practice, Shortcomings, and Desired Improvements," *Journal of Product Innovation Management* 9 (1992): 129–139; Glen L. Urban, John R. Hauser, and Roberta A. Chicos, "Information Acceleration: Validation and Lessons from the Field," *Journal of Marketing Research* (February 1997): 143–153.

45. For further discussion, see Robert J. Thomas, "Timing: The Key to Market Entry," *Journal of Consumer Marketing* (Summer 1985): 77–87; Thomas S. Robertson, Jehoshua Eliashberg, and Talia Rymon, "New Product Announcement Signals and Incumbent Reactions," *Journal of Marketing* (July 1995): 1–15; Frank H. Alpert and Michael A. Kamins, "Pioneer Brand Advantages and Consumer Behavior: A Conceptual Framework and Propositional Inventory," *Journal of the Academy of Marketing Science* (Summer 1994): 244–236; Barry L. Bayos, Sanjay Jain, and Ambar

Rao, "Consequences: An Analysis of Truth or Vaporware and New Product Announcements," *Journal of Marketing Research* (February 2001): 3–13.

46. Cooper and Kleinschmidt, *New Products*, pp. 35–38.

47. Philip Kotler and Gerald Zaltman, "Targeting Prospects for a New Product," *Journal of Advertising Research* (February 1976): 7–20.

48. Peter Burrows, "Rock On, iPod," *BusinessWeek*, June 7, 2004, pp. 130–131; Jay Lyman, "Mini iPod Moving Quickly, Apple Says," *TechNewsWorld*, February 26, 2004; David Taylor, *Brand Stretch* (New York: Wiley, 2004); "iPod Now Outpacing Walkman Growth Rate," *Digital Music News*, December 1, 2004 www.digitalmusicnews.com/yesterday/december2004#120104ipod.

49. For details, see Keith G. Lockyer, *Critical Path Analysis and Other Project Network Techniques* (London: Pitman, 1984). Also see Arvind Rangaswamy and Gary L. Lilien, "Software Tools for New Product Development," *Journal of Marketing Research* (February 1997): 177–184.

50. The following discussion leans heavily on Everett M. Rogers, *Diffusion of Innovations* (New York: The Free Press, 1962). Also see his third edition, published in 1983.

51. C. Page Moreau, Donald R. Lehmann, and Arthur B. Markman, "Entrenched Knowledge Structures and Consumer Response to New Products," *Journal of Marketing Research*, 38 (February 2001): 14–29.

52. Steve Hoeffler, "Measuring Preferences for Really New Products," *Journal of Marketing Research*, 40 (November 2003): 406–420.

53. Rogers, *Diffusion of Innovations*, p. 192; Geoffrey A. Moore, *Crossing the Chasm: Marketing and Selling High-Tech Products to Mainstream Customers* (New York: HarperBusiness, 1999).

54. A. Parasuraman and Charles L. Colby, *Techno-Ready Marketing* (New York: The Free Press, 2001); Jakki Mohr, *Marketing of High-Technology Products and Innovations* (Upper Saddle River, NJ: Prentice Hall, 2001).

55. Malcolm Macalister Hall, "Selling by Stealth," *Business Life* (November 2001): 51–55.

56. Jordan Robertson, "How Nike Got Street Cred," *Business 2.0* (May 2004): 43–46.

57. Cliff Edwards, "Is TiVo's Signal Still Fading?" *BusinessWeek*, September 10, 2001, pp. 72–74; Cliff Edwards, "Will Souping Up TiVo Save It?" *BusinessWeek*, May 17, 2004, pp. 63–64.

58. Hubert Gatignon and Thomas S. Robertson, "A Propositional Inventory for New Diffusion Research," *Journal of Consumer Research* (March 1985): 849–867; Vijay Mahajan, Eitan Muller, and Frank M. Bass, "Diffusion of New Products: Empirical Generalizations and Managerial Uses," *Marketing Science* 14, no. 3, part 2 (1995): G79–G89; Fareena Sultan, John U. Farley, and Donald R. Lehman, "Reflection on 'A Meta-Analysis of Applications of Diffusion Models,'" *Journal of Marketing Research* (May 1996): 247–249; Minhi Hahn, Sehoon Park, and Andris A. Zoltners, "Analysis of New Product Diffusion Using a Four-segment Trial-repeat Model," *Marketing Science*, 13, no. 3 (1994): 224–247.

Chapter 21

1. Kevin Lane Keller, "Red Bull: Managing a High Growth Brand," in *Best Practice Cases in Branding*, (Upper Saddle River, NJ: Prentice Hall, 2003); "Selling Energy," *The Economist*, May 9, 2002.

2. Statistics Canada, "International Merchandise Trade: Annual Review," *The Daily*, August 11, 2005, www.statcan.ca/Daily/English/050811/d050811a.htm; www.ita.doc.gov; Export Forecast Summary, Fall 2004; Export Development Canada, www.edc.ca/docs.

3. Michael E. Porter, *Competitive Strategy* (New York: The Free Press, 1980), p. 275.

4. Charles Fleming and Leslie Lopez, "The Corporate Challenge—No Boundaries: ABB's Dramatic Plan to Recast Its Business Structure along Global Lines: It May Not Be Easy—or Wise," *Wall Street Journal*, September 28, 1998, p. R16; Richard Tomlinson, "Dethroning Percy Barnevik," *Fortune*, April 1, 2002.

5.   www.abb.com.

6. Ron Lieber, "Give Us This Day Our Global Bread," *Fast Company* (March 2001): 158.

7. Jan Johanson and Finn Wiedersheim-Paul, "The Internationalization of the Firm," *Journal of Management Studies* (October 1975): 305–322.

8. Stan Reid, "The Decision Maker and Export Entry and Expansion," *Journal of International Business Studies* (Fall 1981): 101–112; Igal Ayal, "Industry Export Performance: Assessment and Prediction," *Journal of Marketing* (Summer 1982): 54–61; Somkid Jatusripitak, *The Exporting Behavior of Manufacturing Firms* (Ann Arbor: University of Michigan Press, 1986).

9. Michael R. Czinkota and Ilkka A. Ronkainen, *International Marketing*, 5th ed. (New York: Harcourt Brace Jovanovich, 1999).

10. Igal Ayal and Jehiel Zif, "Market Expansion Strategies in Multinational Marketing," *Journal of Marketing* (Spring 1979): 84–94.

11. Yumiro Ono, "On a Mission: Amway Grows Abroad, Sending 'Ambassadors' to Spread the Word," *Wall Street Journal*, May 14, 1997, p. A1; www.amway.com.

12. For a timely and thorough review of academic research on global marketing, see Johny K. Johansson, "Global Marketing: Research on Foreign Entry, Local Marketing, Global Management," in *Handbook of Marketing*, edited by Bart Weitz and Robin Wensley (London: 2002 Sage Publications), pp. 457–483. Also see Johny K. Johansson, *Global Marketing*, 2nd ed. (New York: McGraw-Hill, 2003). For some global marketing research issues, see Susan Douglas and Samuel R. Craig, *International Marketing Research*, 2nd ed. (Upper Saddle River, NJ: Prentice Hall, 2000).

13. Kenichi Ohmae, *Triad Power* (New York: The Free Press, 1985); Philip Kotler and Nikhilesh Dholakia, "Ending Global Stagnation: Linking the Fortunes of the Industrial and Developing Countries," *Business in the Contemporary World* (Spring 1989): 86–97.

14. Jack Neff, "Submerged," *Advertising Age*, March 4, 2002, p. 14.

15. Adapted from Vijay Mahajan, Marcos V. Pratini De Moraes, and Jerry Wind, "The Invisible Global Market," *Marketing Management* (Winter 2000): 31–35.

16. Niraj Dawar and Amitava Chattopadhyay, "Rethinking Marketing Programs for Emerging Markets," *Long Range Planning*, 35, no 5 (October 2002).

17. Gabriel Kahn, "Local Brands Outgun Foreigners in China's Advertising Market," *Wall Street Journal*, October 8, 2003, p. B6A; "The Local Touch," *The Economist*, March 8, 2003, p. 58.

18. Manjeet Kripalani, "Finally, Coke Gets It Right," *BusinessWeek*, February 10, 2003, p. 47; Manjeet Kripalani, "Battling for Pennies in India's Villages," *BusinessWeek*, June 10, 2002, p. 22E7.

19. "Not So Fizzy," *The Economist*, February 23, 2002, pp. 66–67; Rajeev Batra, Venkatram Ramaswamy, Dana L. Alden, Jan-Benedict E. M. Steenkamp, and S. Ramachander, "Effects of Brand Local and Nonlocal Origin on Consumer Attitudes in Developing Countries," *Journal of Consumer Psychology* 9, no. 2 (2000): 83–95.

20. Patricia Sellers, "P&G: Teaching an Old Dog New Tricks," *Fortune*, May 31, 2004, pp. 167–180.

21. Catherine Belton, "To Russia, With Love: The Multinationals Song," *BusinessWeek*, September 16, 2002, pp. 44–46.

22. David Welch, "GM: Gunning It in China," *BusinessWeek*, June 21, 2004, pp. 112–115; Joann Muller, "Thanks, Now Move Over," *Forbes*, July 26, 2004, pp. 76–78.

23. "NAFTA—10 Years Later," *CBC News Online*, January 7, 2004, www.cbc.ca/news/background/summitofamericas/nafta.html; Rob Portman, "Washington Speaks: Good Neighbours Must Talk," *Globe and Mail*, September 3, 2005, p. A23; Norman Spector, "Old Fights, New Rounds, Same Politicization," *Globe and Mail*, September 5, 2005, p. A15.

24. "APEC Working for Canadians," Department of Foreign Affairs and International Trade, www.dfait-maeci.gc.ca/trade/canada-apec/working-e.asp (viewed March 25, 2005).

25. Statistics Canada Table "Population by sex and age group," 27 October, 2005 http://www40.statcan.ca/l01/cst01/demo10a.htm.

26. Johny K. Johansson, "Global Marketing: Research on Foreign Entry, Local Marketing, Global Management," in *Handbook of Marketing,* edited by Bart Weitz and Robin Wensley (London: Sage Publications, 2002), pp. 457–483.

27. Charlene Marmer Solomon, "Don't Get Burned by Hot Markets," *Workforce* (January 1998): 12–22.

28. For an academic review, see Leonidas C. Leonidou, Constantine S. Katsikeas, and Nigel F. Piercy, "Identifying Managerial Influences on Exporting: Past Research and Future Directions," *Journal of International Marketing* 6, no. 2 (1998): 74–102.

29. "Clearwater Launches New Lobster Product in Europe," Canada Export On-Line, Department of Foreign Affairs and International Trade, March 1, 2005, http://webapps.dfait-maeci.gc.ca/canadexport/view.asp?id=382293&language=E.

30. Brandon Mitchener, "E-Commerce: Border Crossings," *Wall Street Journal,* November 22, 1999, p. R41.

31. Cynthia Kemper, "KFC Tradition Sold Japan on Chicken," *Denver Post,* June 7, 1998, p. J4; Ted Anthony, "KFC Spreading Its Wings and More throughout China," *Associated Press,* January 16, 2004.

32. Laura Mazur and Annik Hogg, *The Marketing Challenge* (Wokingham, England: Addison-Wesley, 1993), pp. 42–44; Jan Willem Karel, "Brand Strategy Positions Products Worldwide," *Journal of Business Strategy* 12, no. 3 (May–June 1991): 16–19; Canadian Embassy Beijing Newsletter, February 2004, www.beijing.gc.ca/beijing/en/navmain/media/partnerships/1059.htm.

33. Paula Dwyer, "Tearing Up Today's Organization Chart," *Business Week,* November 18, 1994, pp. 80–90.

34. Joann Muller, "Global Motors," *Forbes,* January 12, 2004, pp. 62–68.

35. Glen Hodgson, "China—Get Used to It," *Canadian Business,* December 27, 2004; "Minister Peterson and Canadian Business Representatives Conclude Successful Trade Mission to China," *Team Canada Newsletter,* no. 16, January 25, 2005, www.teamcanada.gc.ca/china2005/menu-en.asp; "Address by Prime Minister Paul Martin to the Canada–China Business Council," Office of the Prime Minister, January 21, 2005, http://pm.gc.ca/eng/news.asp?id=399; "Canada-China Trade and Investment," Government of Canada, November 28, 2003, www.beijing.gc.ca/beijing/en/navmain/canada/602/index.htm.

36. Paul Brent, "It's Tough to Make It South of the Border," *Financial Post,* March 10, 1999, C6; Zena Olijnyk, "Plan to Quit U.S. Lifts Future Shop Stock 24%," *Financial Post,* March 10, 1999, p. C6.

37. Shaoming Zou and S. Tamer Cavusgil, "The GMS: A Broad Conceptualtization of Global Marketing Strategy and Its Effect on Firm Performance," *Journal of Marketing* 66 (October 2002): 40–56.

38. Geert Hofstede, *Culture's Consequences* (Beverley Hills, CA: Sage, 1980).

39. Paulo Prada and Bruce Orwall, "A Certain 'Je Ne Sais Quoi' at Disney's New Park," *Wall Street Journal,* March 12, 2003, p. B1.

40. Arundhati Parmar, "Dependent Variables: Sounds Global Strategies Rely on Certain Factors," *Marketing News,* September 16, 2002, p. 4.

41. Warren J. Keegan, *Multinational Marketing Management,* 5th ed. (Upper Saddle River, NJ: Prentice Hall, 1995), pp. 378–381.

42. "What Makes a Company Great?" *Fortune,* October 26, 1998, pp. 218–226.

43. David Leonhardt, "It Was a Hit in Buenos Aires—So Why Not Boise?" *BusinessWeek,* September 7, 1998, pp. 56–58; Marlene Parrish, "Taste Buds Tango at New Squirrel Hill Café," *Pittsburgh Post-Gazette,* February 6, 2003.

44. Richard P. Carpenter and the Globe Staff, "What They Meant to Say Was . . . ," *Boston Globe,* August 2, 1998, p. M6.

45. For an interesting distinction based on the concept of global consumer culture positioning, see Dana L. Alden, Jan-Benedict E. M. Steenkamp, and Rajeev Batra, "Brand Positioning Through Advertising in Asia, North America, and Europe: The Role of Global Consumer Culture," *Journal of Marketing,* 63 (January 1999): 75–87.

46. Thomas J. Madden, Kelly Hewett, and Martin S. Roth, "Managing Images in Different Cultures: A Cross-National Study of Color Meanings and Preferences," *Journal of International Marketing,* 8, no. 4 (2000): 90–107; Zeynep Gürhan-Canli and Durairaj Maheswaran, "Cultural Variations in Country of Origin Effects," *Journal of Marketing Research,* 37 (August 2000): 309–317.

47. Erin White and Sarah Ellison, "Unilever Ads Offer a Tribute to Dirt," *Wall Street Journal,* June 2, 2003.

48. John L. Graham, Alma T. Mintu, and Waymond Rogers, "Explorations of Negotiations Behaviors in Ten Foreign Cultures Using a Model Developed in the United States," *Management Science,* 40 (January 1994): 72–95.

49. Tony Van Alphen, "Some U.S. Makers Dumping Steel in Canada," *Toronto Star,* May 2, 2001, p. E01.

50. www.agmaglobal.org.

51. Maricris G. Briones, "The Euro Starts Here," *Marketing News,* July 20, 1998, pp. 1, 39.

52. Elliott Masie, "Global Pricing in an Internet World," *Computer Reseller News,* May 11, 1998, pp. 55, 58.

53. Ram Charan, "The Rules Have Changed," *Fortune,* March 16, 1998, pp. 159–162.

54. www.ge.com.

55. David Arnold, "Seven Rules of International Distribution," *Harvard Business Review* (November–December 2000): 131–137.

56. Arnold, "Seven Rules of International Distribution," 131–137.

57. "Cola Down Mexico Way," *The Economist,* October 11, 2003, pp. 69–70.

58. Jack Ewing, "The Next Wal-Mart?" *BusinessWeek,* April 26, 2004, pp. 60–62.

59. "How Big Can It Grow?" *The Economist,* April 17, 2004, pp. 67–69; Greg Masters, "Wal-Mart's Global Challenge," *Retail Merchandiser Magazine,* May 1, 2004.

60. "From Head & Shoulders to Kobe," *The Economist,* March 27, 2004, p. 64.

61. "A Dragon with Core Values," *The Economist,* March 30, 2002.

62. "The Shock of Old," *The Economist,* July 13, 2002, p. 49.

63. Jim Rendon, "When Nations Need a Little Marketing," *New York Times,* November 23, 2003.

64. "Regan Unveils New Brand Canada Aquaculture Logo," Fisheries and Oceans Canada, News Release, March 15, 2004, www.dfo-mpo.gc.ca/media/newsrel/2004/hq-ac19_e.htm; "Branding Canada," Canadian Embassy Washington, DC, News Release, March 2001, www.canadianembassy.org/invest/branding-en.asp.

65. Zeynep Gurhan-Canli and Durairaj Maheswaran, "Cultural Variations in Country of Origin Effects," *Journal of Marketing Research,* 37 (August 2000): 309–317.

66. Jan-Benedict, E. M. Steenkamp, Rajeev Batra, and Dana L. Alden, "How Perceived Brand Globalness Creates Brand Value," *Journal of International Business Studies,* 34 (2003): 53–65.

67. Johny K. Johansson, "Global Marketing: Research on Foreign Entry, Local Marketing, Global Management," pp. 457–483; Johny K. Johansson, "Determinants and Effects of the Use of 'Made In' Labels," *International Marketing Review (UK)* 6, no. 1 (1989): 47–58; Warren J. Bilkey and Erik Nes, "Country-of-Origin Effects on Product Evaluations," *Journal of International Business Studies* (Spring–Summer 1982): 89–99; "Old Wine in New Bottles," *The Economist,* February 21, 1998, p. 45; Zeynep

Gürhan-Canli and Durairaj Maheswaran, "Cultural Variations in Country of Origin Effects," pp. 309–317.

68. Alex Taylor III, "BMW Turns More American Than Ever," *Fortune*, February 23, 2004, p. 42.

69. Dwyer, "Tearing Up Today's Organization Chart," pp. 80–90.

70. Christopher A. Bartlett and Sumantra Ghoshal, *Managing Across Borders* (Cambridge, MA: Harvard Business School Press, 1989).

71. Betsy McKay, "Coke Hunts for Talent to Re-establish Its Marketing Might," *Wall Street Journal*, March 6, 2002, p. B4.

Chapter 22

1. Keith Fox, Katherine Jocz, and Bernard Jaworski, "A Common Language," *Marketing Management* (May/June 2003): 14–17.

2. For additional updates on the latest academic thinking on marketing strategy and tactics, see *Kellogg on Marketing*, edited by Dawn Iacobucci (New York: Wiley, 2001), and *Kellogg on Integrated Marketing*, edited by Dawn Iacobucci and Bobby Calder (New York: Wiley, 2003).

3. Frederick E. Webster, Jr., Alan J. Malter, and Shankar Ganesan, "Can Marketing Regain Its Seat at the Table?" *Marketing Science Institute Report No. 03-113*.

4. For a broad historical treatment of marketing thought, see D. G. Brian Jones and Eric H. Shaw, "A History of Marketing Thought," in *Handbook of Marketing*, edited by Barton A. Weitz and Robin Wensley (London: Sage Publications, 2002), pp. 39–65.

5. Frederick E. Webster Jr., "The Changing Role of Marketing in the Corporation," *Journal of Marketing* (October 1992): 1–17. Also see Ravi S. Achrol, "Evolution of the Marketing Organization: New Forms for Turbulent Environment," *Journal of Marketing* (October 1991): 77–93; John P. Workman Jr., Christian Homburg, and Kjell Gruner, "Marketing Organization: An Integrative Framework of Dimensions and Determinants," *Journal of Marketing* (July 1998): 21–41. For some contemporary perspectives, see Special Issue 1999 of *Journal of Marketing Fundamental Issues and Directions for Marketing*.

6. For an excellent account of how to convert a company into a market-driven organization, see George Day, *The Market-Driven Organization: Aligning Culture, Capabilities, and Configuration to the Market* (New York: The Free Press, 1989).

7. Frederick E. Webster Jr., "The Role of Marketing and the Firm," in *Handbook of Marketing*, edited by Barton A. Weitz and Robin Wensley (London: Sage Publications, 2002), pp. 39–65.

8. Frank V. Cespedes, *Concurrent Marketing: Integrating Product, Sales, and Service* (Boston: Harvard Business School Press, 1995); and *Managing Marketing Linkages: Text, Cases, and Readings* (Upper Saddle River, NJ: Prentice Hall, 1996).

9. "Visible Minorities and Ethnicity in Ontario: Factsheet 6," Census 2001 Highlights, Ministry of Finance, www.gov.on.ca/FIN/english/demographics/cenhi6e.htm.

10. Zachary Schiller, "The Marketing Revolution at Procter & Gamble," *BusinessWeek*, July 25, 1988, pp. 72–76; Laurie Freeman, "P&G Widens Power Base: Adds Category Managers," *Advertising Age*.

11. Michael J. Zenor, "The Profit Benefits of Category Management," *Journal of Marketing Research*, 31 (May 1994): 202–213.

12. Gerry Khermouch, "Brands Overboard," *Brandweek*, August 22, 1994, pp. 25–39.

13. For further reading, see Robert Dewar and Don Shultz, "The Product Manager, an Idea Whose Time Has Gone," *Marketing Communications* (May 1998): 28–35; "The Marketing Revolution at Proctor & Gamble," *BusinessWeek*, July 25, 1988, pp. 72–76; Kevin T. Higgins, "Category Management: New Tools Changing Life for Manufacturers, Retailers," *Marketing News*, September 25, 1989, pp. 2, 19; George S. Low and Ronald A. Fullerton, "Brands, Brand Management, and the Brand Manager System: A Critical Historical Evaluation," *Journal of Marketing Research* (May 1994): 173–190; Michael J. Zanor, "The Profit Benefits of

Category Management," *Journal of Marketing Research* (May 1994): 202–213.

14. Richard E. Anderson, "Matrix Redux," *Business Horizons* (November–December 1994): 6–10.

15. Frederick E. Webster Jr., "The Role of Marketing and the Firm," in *Handbook of Marketing*, edited by Barton A. Weitz and Robin Wensley (London: Sage Publications, 2002), pp. 39–65.

16. Benson P. Shapiro, "Can Marketing and Manufacturing Coexist?" *Harvard Business Review* (September–October 1977): 104–114. Also see Robert W. Ruekert and Orville C. Walker Jr., "Marketing's Interaction with Other Functional Units: A Conceptual Framework with Other Empirical Evidence," *Journal of Marketing* (January 1987): 1–19.

17. Patricia Sellers, "P&G: Teaching an Old Dog New Tricks," *Fortune*, May 31, 2004, pp. 167–180.

18. Erik Brynjolfsson and Lorin Hitt, "The Customer Counts," *Information Week*, September 9, 1996.

19. Gary Hamel, *Leading the Revolution* (Boston: Harvard Business School Press, 2000).

20. "Coca-Cola Expands Lime Flavour," *Marketing Magazine*, March 17, 2005, www.marketingmag.ca/magazine/marketingdaily/article.jsp?content=20050317_101536_5660.

21. Kenneth Hein, "Rohan Oza," *Brandweek*, April 8, 2002, p. 36; "POWERade Scores with LeBron," *Brandweek*, August 18, 2004.

22. William L. Wilkie and Elizabeth S. Moore, "Marketing's Relationship to Society," in *Handbook of Marketing*, edited by Barton A. Weitz and Robin Wensley (London: Sage Publications, 2002), pp. 1–38.

23. "Special Report: Corporate Social Responsibility," *The Economist*, December 14, 2002, pp. 62–63.

24. www.corporateknights.ca/best50/index.asp.

25. Don Tapscott and Anthony Williams, "What? Now We Have to Make a Profit *and* Be Ethical," *Business 2.0* (February 2002): 30.

26. For further reading, see Dorothy Cohen, *Legal Issues in Marketing Decision Making* (Cincinnati, OH: South-Western, 1995); Canada's Anti-corruption legislation, www.respondanet.com/english/anti_corruption/reports/compendio_en/Html%20Files/Canada.htm

27. Shelby D. Hunt and Scott Vitell, "The General Theory of Marketing Ethics: A Retrospective and Revision," in *Ethics in Marketing*, edited by John Quelch and Craig Smith (Chicago: Irwin, 1992).

28. Tapscott and Williams, "What? Now We Have to Make a Profit *and* Be Ethical," pp. 30–31.

29. Marc Gunther, "Tree Huggers, Soy Lovers, and Profits," *Fortune*, June 23, 200, pp. 98–104.

30. Ronald J. Alsop, "Perils of Corporate Philanthropy," *Wall Street Journal*, January 16, 2002, p. B1; Ronald J. Alsop, *The 18 Immutable Laws of Corporate Reputation: Creating, Protecting, and Repairing Your Most Valuable Asset* (New York: Free Press, 2004).

31. Paul Dolan, *True to Our Roots: Fermenting a Business Revolution* (New York: Bloomberg Press, 2003); Alison Overholt, "The Good Earth," *Fast Company* (December 2003): 86–88.

32. Michael E. Porter and Mark R. Kramer, "The Competitive Advantage of Corporate Philanthropy," *Harvard Business Review* (December 2002): 5–16.

33. "Imagine Recognizes Two Financial Companies for Corporate Citizenship Efforts," Imagine Press Release, December 2004, www.imagine.ca/content/media/media_articles.asp?item=1.

34. Dwane Hal Deane, "Associating the Corporation with a Charitable Event Through Sponsorship: Measuring the Effects on Corporate Community Relations," *Journal of Advertising* (Winter 2002): 77–87.

35. See Philip Kotler and Nancy Lee, *Corporate Social Responsibility: Doing the Most Good for Your Company and Your Cause* (New York: John Wiley, 2005).

36. For a discussion of some public health marketing issues and opportunities, see Michael L. Rothschild, "Carrots, Sticks, and Promises: A Conceptual Framework for the Management of Public Health and Social Issue Behaviors," *Journal of Marketing*, 63 (October 1999): 24–37.

37. "2004 New Spirit of Community Partnership Awards," Imagine Canada, www.imagine.ca/content/awards&recognition/partnership_awards.asp?section=awards.

38. Todd Wallack, "Conscience Calls," *San Francisco Chronicle*, September 21, 2000; www.workingassets.com.

39. Hamish Pringle and Marjorie Thompson, *How Cause Related Marketing Builds Brands* (New York: John Wiley & Sons, 1999); Christine Bittar, "Seeking Cause and Effect," *Brandweek*, November 11, 2002, pp. 19–24; "Marketing, Corporate Social Initiatives, and the Bottom Line," Marketing Science Institute Conference Summary, *MSI Report No. 01-106*, 2001.

40. Rajan Varadarajan and Anil Menon, "Cause-Related Marketing: A Co-alignment of Marketing Strategy and Corporate Philanthropy," *Journal of Marketing*, 52 (1988): 58–74.

41. Minette Drumwright and Patrick E. Murphy, "Corporate Societal Marketing," in *Handbook of Marketing and Society*, edited by Paul N. Bloom and Gregory T. Gundlach (Thousand Oaks, CA: Sage Publications, 2001), pp. 162–183. See also Minette Drumwright, "Company Advertising with a Social Dimension: The Role of Noneconomic Criteria," *Journal of Marketing*, 60 (October 1996): 71–87.

42. www.britishairways.com.

43. Pat Auger, Paul Burke, Timothy Devinney, and Jordan J. Loviere, "What Will Consumers Pay for Social Product Features?" *Journal of Business Ethics*, 42 (2003): 281–304.

44. C. B. Bhattacharya and Sankar Sen, "Consumer-Company Identification: A Framework for Understanding Consumers' Relationships with Companies," *Journal of Marketing*, 67 (April 2003): 76–88; Sankar Sen and C. B. Bhattacharya, "Does Doing Good Always Lead to Doing Better? Consumer Reactions to Corporate Social Responsibility," *Journal of Marketing Research*, 38, no. 2 (2001): 225–244; Dennis B. Arnett, Steve D. German, and Shelby D. Hunt, "The Identity Salience Model of Relationship Marketing Success: The Case of Nonprofit Marketing," *Journal of Marketing*, 67 (April 2003): 89–105.

45. Stephen Hoeffler and Kevin Lane Keller, "Building Brand Equity through Corporate Societal Marketing," *Journal of Public Policy and Marketing*, 21, no. 1 (Spring 2002): 78–89. See also Special Issue: Corporate Responsibility, *Journal of Brand Management* 10, nos. 4–5 (May 2003).

46. Hamish Pringle and Marjorie Thompson, *How Cause Related Marketing Builds Brands* (New York: John Wiley & Sons, 1999); www.loveisnotabuse.com.

47. Mark R. Forehand and Sonya Grier, "When Is Honesty the Best Policy? The Effect of Stated Company Intent on Consumer Skepticism," *Journal of Consumer Psychology*, 13, no. 3 (2003): 349–356; Dwane Hal Dean, "Associating the Corporation with a Charitable Event Through Sponsorship: Measuring the Effects on Corporate Community Relations," *Journal of Advertising*, 31, no. 4 (2002): 77–87.

48. Steve Hoeffler, Paul N. Bloom, and Kevin Lane Keller, "Achieving Social Change Through Corporate Societal Marketing: Incorporating a Consumer Orientation into CSR Programs," working paper, Kenan-Flagler School of Business, University of North Carolina at Chapel Hill, 2004.

49. Alsop, *The 18 Immutable Laws of Corporate Reputation: Creating, Protecting, and Repairing Your Most Valuable Asset*, p. 125.

50. Susan Orenstein, "The Selling of Breast Cancer," *Business 2.0* (February 2003): 88–94; H. Meyer, "When the Cause Is Just," *Journal of Business Strategy* (November–December 1999): 27–31.

51. Christine Bittar, "Seeking Cause & Effect," *Brandweek*, November 11, 2002, pp. 18–24.

52. Michelle Warren, "Cause Commotion," *Marketing Magazine*, October 6, 2003, www.marketingmag.ca/magazine/current/promo_report/article.jsp?content=20031006_57550_57550.

53. Philip Kotler, Ned Roberto, and Nancy Lee, *Social Marketing: Improving the Quality of Life* (London: Sage, 2002).

54. Laurel Rothman and Peter Bleyer, "Premiers Must Make Poverty History," *Toronto Star*, August 10, 2005; "Teen Pregnancy," Public Health Agency of Canada, www.phac-aspc.gc.ca/publicat/meas-haut/mu_ee_e.html; Mothers Against Drunk Drivers, "In the News," Canada News Release, www.madd.ca/english/news/stories/n05jun23.htm; "Betting the Farm: An Overview of Gambling Addiction," *CBC News Online*, www.cbc.ca/news/background/gambling/addiction.html, November 18, 2003.

55. "Best Practices and Prospects for Social Marketing in Public Health," Health Canada, Speech by François Lagarde, Social Marketing and Communications Consultant, www.hc-sc.gc.ca/english/socialmarketing/social_marketing/tutorial/appendix.html.

56. See Michael L. Rothschild, "Carrots, Sticks, and Promises: A Conceptual Framework for the Management of Public Health and Social Issue Behaviors," *Journal of Marketing* (October 1999): 24–37.

57. For more on developing and implementing marketing plans, see H. W. Goetsch, *Developing, Implementing, and Managing an Effective Marketing Plan* (Chicago: NTC Business Books, 1993).

58. Goetsch, *Developing, Implementing, and Managing an Effective Marketing Plan*.

59. Thomas V. Bonoma, *The Marketing Edge: Making Strategies Work* (New York: The Free Press, 1985). Much of this section is based on Bonoma's work.

60. C. Marcus, "Marketing Resource Management: Key Components," *Gartner Research Note*, August 22, 2001.

61. Sam R. Goodman, *Increasing Corporate Profitability* (New York: Ronald Press, 1982), ch. 1. Also see Bernard J. Jaworski, Vlasis Stathakopoulos, and H. Shanker Krishnan, "Control Combinations in Marketing: Conceptual Framework and Empirical Evidence," *Journal of Marketing* (January 1993): 57–69.

62. Peter M. Senge, *The Fifth Discipline: The Art and Practice of the Learning Organization* (New York: Doubleday Currency, 1990), ch. 7.

63. For further discussion of this instrument, see Philip Kotler, "From Sales Obsession to Marketing Effectiveness," *Harvard Business Review* (November–December 1977): 67–75.

64. Philip Kotler, William Gregor, and William Rodgers, "The Marketing Audit Comes of Age," *Sloan Management Review* (Winter 1989): 49–62.

65. Useful checklists for a marketing self-audit can be found in Aubrey Wilson, *Aubrey Wilson's Marketing Audit Checklists* (London: McGraw-Hill, 1982); Mike Wilson, *The Management of Marketing* (Westmead, England: Gower Publishing, 1980). A marketing audit software program is described in Ben M. Enis and Stephen J. Garfein, "The Computer-Driven Marketing Audit," *Journal of Management Inquiry* (December 1992): 306–318.

66. Kotler, Gregor, and Rodgers, "The Marketing Audit Comes of Age," pp. 49–62.

GLOSSARY

A

activity-based cost (ABC) accounting procedures that can quantify the true profitability of different activities by identifying their actual costs.

adoption an individual's decision to become a regular user of a product.

advertising any paid form of nonpersonal presentation and promotion of ideas, goods, or services by an identified sponsor.

advertising goal (objective) a specific communication task and achievement level to be accomplished with a specific audience in a specific period of time.

advertorials print ads that offer editorial content that reflects favourably on the brand and resemble newspaper or magazine content.

alliances (or affiliate programs) situation where a company agrees to cooperate with another firm to accomplish a particular objective. For example, one Internet company works with another one, and they end up advertising each other's products or services.

anchoring and adjustment heuristic when consumers arrive at an initial judgment and then make adjustments of their first impressions based on additional information.

arm's-length price the price charged by other competitors for the same or a similar product.

aspirational groups groups a person hopes or would like to join.

associative network memory model a conceptual representation that views memory as consisting of a set of nodes and interconnecting links where nodes represent stored information or concepts and links represent the strength of association between this information or concepts.

attitude a person's enduring favourable or unfavourable evaluation, emotional feeling, and action tendencies toward some object or idea.

augmented product a product that includes features that go beyond consumer expectations and differentiate the product from competitors.

availability heuristic when consumers base their predictions on the quickness and ease with which a particular example of an outcome comes to mind.

available market the set of consumers who have interest, income, and access to a particular offer.

average cost the cost per unit at a given level of production; it is equal to total costs divided by production.

B

backward invention reintroducing earlier product forms that can be well adapted to a foreign country's needs.

banner ads (Internet) small, rectangular boxes containing text and perhaps a picture to support a brand.

basic product what specifically the actual product is.

belief a descriptive thought that a person holds about something.

brand a name, term, sign, symbol, or design, or a combination of them, intended to identify the goods or services of one seller or group of sellers and to differentiate them from those of competitors.

brand associations all brand-related thoughts, feelings, perceptions, images, experiences, beliefs, attitudes, and so on that become linked to the brand node.

brand audit a consumer-focused exercise that involves a series of procedures to assess the health of the brand, uncover its sources of brand equity, and suggest ways to improve and leverage its equity.

brand awareness consumers' ability to identify the brand under different conditions, as reflected by their brand recognition or recall performance.

brand contact any information-bearing experience a customer or prospect has with the brand, the product category, or the market that relates to the marketer's product or service.

brand development index (BDI) the index of brand sales to category sales.

brand dilution when consumers no longer associate a brand with a specific product or highly similar products or start thinking less favourably about the brand.

brand elements those trademarkable devices that serve to identify and differentiate the brand such as a brand name, logo, or character.

brand equity the added value endowed to products and services.

brand extension a company's use of an established brand to introduce a new product.

brand image the perceptions and beliefs held by consumers, as reflected in the associations held in consumer memory.

brand knowledge all the thoughts, feelings, images, experiences, beliefs, and so on that become associated with the brand.

brand line all products, original as well as line and category extensions, sold under a particular brand name.

brand mix the set of all brand lines that a particular seller makes available to buyers.

brand personality the specific mix of human traits that may be attributed to a particular brand.

brand portfolio the set of all brands and brand lines a particular firm offers for sale to buyers in a particular category.

brand promise the marketer's vision of what the brand must be and do for consumers.

brand valuation an estimate of the total financial value of the brand.

brand value chain a structured approach to assessing the sources and outcomes of brand equity and the manner in which marketing activities create brand value.

branded entertainment using sports, music, arts, or other entertainment activities to build brand equity.

branded variants specific brand lines uniquely supplied to different retailers or distribution channels.

branding strategy the number and nature of common and distinctive brand elements applied to the different products sold by the firm.

branding endowing products and services with the power of a brand.

break-even analysis a means by which management estimates how many units of the product the company would have to sell to break even with the given price and cost structure.

brick-and-click existing companies that have added an online site for information and/or e-commerce.

business database complete information about business customers' past purchases; past volumes, prices, and profits.

business market all the organizations that acquire goods and services used in the production of other products or services that are sold, rented, or supplied to others.

C

capital items long-lasting goods that facilitate developing or managing the finished product.

captive products products that are necessary to the use of other products, such as razor blades or film.

category extension using the parent brand to brand a new product outside the product category currently served by the parent brand.

category membership the products or sets of products with which a brand competes and which function as close substitutes.

cause-related marketing marketing that links a firm's contributions to a designated cause to customers' engaging directly or indirectly in revenue-producing transactions with the firm.

channel advantage when a company successfully switches its customers to lower-cost channels, while assuming no loss of sales or deterioration in service quality.

channel conflict when one channel member's actions prevent the channel from achieving its goal.

channel coordination when channel members are brought together to advance the goals of the channel, as opposed to their own potentially incompatible goals.

channel power the ability to alter channel members' behaviour so that they take actions they would not have taken otherwise.

co-branding situation in which two or more well-known existing brands are combined into a joint product and/or marketed together in some fashion.

communication adaptation changing marketing communications programs for each local market.

communication-effect research determining whether an ad is communicating effectively.

company demand the company's estimated share of market demand at alternative levels of company marketing effort in a given time period.

company sales forecast the expected level of company sales based on a chosen marketing plan and an assumed marketing environment.

competitive advantage a company's ability to perform in one or more ways that competitors cannot or will not match.

conformance quality the degree to which all the produced units are identical and meet the promised specifications.

conjoint analysis a method for deriving the utility values that consumers attach to varying levels of a product's attributes.

conjunctive heuristic the consumer sets a minimum acceptable cutoff level for each attribute and chooses the first alternative that meets the minimum standard for all attributes.

consumer behaviour the study of how individuals, groups, and organizations select, buy, use, and dispose of goods, services, ideas, or experiences to satisfy their needs and wants.

consumer involvement the level of engagement and active processing undertaken by the consumer in responding to a marketing stimulus.

consumerist movement an organized movement of citizens and government to strengthen the rights and powers of buyers in relation to sellers.

consumption system the way the user performs the tasks of getting and using products and related services.

containerization putting the goods in boxes or trailers that are easy to transfer between two transportation modes.

content-target advertising links ads not to keywords but to the contents of Web pages.

contractual sales force manufacturers' reps, sales agents, and brokers, who are paid a commission based on sales.

convenience goods goods the consumer purchases frequently, immediately, and with a minimum of effort.

conventional marketing channel an independent producer, wholesaler(s), and retailer(s).

core benefit the service or benefit the customer is really buying.

core competency attribute that (1) is a source of competitive advantage in that it makes a significant contribution to perceived customer benefits, (2) has applications in a wide variety of markets, (3) is difficult for competitors to imitate.

core values the belief systems that underlie consumer attitudes and behaviour, and that determine people's choices and desires over the long term.

corporate culture the shared experiences, stories, beliefs, and norms that characterize an organization.

corporate retailing corporately owned retailing outlets that achieve economies of scale, greater purchasing power, wider brand recognition, and better-trained employees.

critical path scheduling (CPS) developing a master chart showing the simultaneous and sequential activities that must take place to launch the product.

cues stimuli that determine when, where, and how a person responds.

culture the fundamental determinant of a person's wants and behaviour.

customer churn high customer defection.

customer consulting data, information systems, and advice services that the seller offers to buyers.

customer database an organized collection of comprehensive information about individual customers or prospects that is current, accessible, and actionable for marketing purposes.

customer equity the total of the discounted lifetime values of all of the firm's customers.

customer lifetime value (CLV) the net present value of the stream of future profits expected over the customer's lifetime purchases.

customer mailing list a set of names, addresses, and telephone numbers.

customer perceived value (CPV) the difference between the prospective customer's evaluation of all the benefits and all the costs of an offering and the perceived alternatives.

customer profitability analysis (CPA) a means of assessing and ranking customer profitability through accounting techniques such as activity-based costing (ABC).

customer relationship management (CRM) the process of managing detailed information about individual customers and carefully managing all customer "touch points" to maximize customer loyalty.

customer training training the customer's employees to use the vendor's equipment properly and efficiently.

customer value analysis report of the company's strengths and weaknesses relative to various competitors.

customer value hierarchy five product levels that must be addressed by marketers in planning a market offering.

customer-based brand equity the differential effect that brand knowledge has on a consumer response to the marketing of that brand.

customerization combination of operationally driven mass customization with customized marketing in a way that empowers consumers to design the product and service offering of their choice.

customer-performance scorecard how well the company is doing year after year on particular customer-based measures.

D

data warehouse a collection of current data captured, organized, and stored in a company's contact centre.

database marketing the process of building, maintaining, and using customer databases and other databases for the purpose of contacting, transacting, and building customer relationships.

datamining the extracting of useful information about individuals, trends, and segments from the mass of data.

delivery how well the product or service is delivered to the customer.

demand chain planning the process of designing the supply chain based on adopting a target market perspective and working backward.

design the totality of features that affect how a product looks and functions in terms of customer requirements.

direct (company) sales force full- or part-time paid employees who work exclusively for the company.

direct marketing the use of consumer-direct (CD) channels to reach and deliver goods and services to customers without using marketing intermediaries.

direct product profitability (DDP) a way of measuring a product's handling costs from the time it reaches the warehouse until a customer buys it in the retail store.

direct-marketing channel channel in which the manufacturer sells directly to the final customer.

direct-order marketing marketing in which direct marketers seek a measurable response, typically a customer order.

discrimination the process of recognizing differences in sets of similar stimuli and adjusting responses accordingly.

dissociative groups those groups whose values or behaviour an individual rejects.

distribution programming building a planned, professionally managed, vertical marketing system that meets the needs of both manufacturer and distributors.

drive a strong internal stimulus impelling action.

dual adaptation adapting both the product and the communications to the local market.

dumping situation in which a company charges either less than its costs or less than it charges in its home market, in order to enter or win a market.

durability a measure of a product's expected operating life under natural or stressful conditions.

e-business the use of electronic means and platforms to conduct a company's business.

e-commerce a company or site offers to transact or facilitate the selling of products and services online.

elimination-by-aspects heuristic situation in which the consumer compares brands on an attribute selected probabilistically, and brands are eliminated if they do not meet minimum acceptable cutoff levels.

e-marketing company efforts to inform buyers, communicate, promote, and sell its products and services over the Internet.

environmental threat a challenge posed by an unfavourable trend or development that would lead to lower sales or profit.

e-purchasing purchase of goods, services, and information from various online suppliers.

everyday low pricing (EDLP) in retailing, a constant low price with few or no price promotions and special sales.

exchange the process of obtaining a desired product from someone by offering something in return.

exclusive distribution severely limiting the number of intermediaries, in order to maintain control over the service level and outputs offered by resellers.

expectancy-value model consumers evaluate products and services by combining their brand beliefs—positive and negative—according to their weighted importance.

expected product a set of attributes and conditions buyers normally expect when they purchase this product.

experience curve (learning curve) a decline in the average cost with accumulated production experience.

fad a craze that is unpredictable, short-lived, and without social, economic, and political significance.

family brand situation in which the parent brand is already associated with multiple products through brand extensions.

family of orientation parents and siblings.

family of procreation spouse and children.

features things that enhance the basic function of a product.

fixed costs (overhead) costs that do not vary with production or sales revenue.

flexible market offering (1) a naked solution containing the product and service elements that all segment members value, and (2) discretionary options that some segment members value.

focus group a gathering of six to ten people who are carefully selected based on certain demographic, psychographic, or other considerations and brought together to discuss various topics of interest.

forecasting the art of anticipating what buyers are likely to do under a given set of conditions.

form the size, shape, or physical structure of a product.

forward invention creating a new product to meet a need in another country.

frequency programs (FPs) designed to provide rewards to customers who buy frequently and in substantial amounts.

generics unbranded, plainly packaged, less expensive versions of common products.

global firm a firm that operates in more than one country and captures R&D, production, logistical, marketing, and financial advantages in its costs and reputation that are not available to purely domestic competitors.

global industry an industry in which the strategic positions of competitors in major geographic or national markets are fundamentally affected by their overall global positions.

goal formulation the process of developing specific goals for the planning period.

going-rate pricing price based largely on competitors' prices.

grey market branded products diverted from normal or authorized distributions channels in the country of product origin or across international borders.

heuristics rules of thumb or mental shortcuts in the decision process.

high-low pricing charging higher prices on an everyday basis but then running frequent promotions and special sales.

holistic marketing a concept based on the development, design, and implementation of marketing programs, processes, and activities that recognizes their breadth and interdependencies.

horizontal marketing system two or more unrelated companies put together resources or programs to exploit an emerging market opportunity.

hybrid channels use of multiple channels of distribution to reach customers in a defined market.

image the set of beliefs, ideas, and impressions a person holds regarding an object.

industry a group of firms that offer a product or class of products that are close substitutes for one another.

ingredient branding a special case of co-branding that involves creating brand equity for materials, components, or parts that are necessarily contained within other branded products.

innovation diffusion process the spread of a new idea from its source of invention or creation to its ultimate users or adopters.

innovation any good, service, or idea that is perceived by someone as new.

installation the work done to make a product operational in its planned location.

institutional market schools, hospitals, nursing homes, prisons, and other institutions that must provide goods and services to people in their care.

integrated logistics systems (ILS) materials management, material flow systems, and physical distribution, abetted by information technology (IT).

integrated marketing communications (IMC) a concept of marketing communications planning that recognizes the added value of a comprehensive plan.

integrated marketing mixing and matching marketing activities to maximize their individual and collective efforts.

intensive distribution the manufacturer placing the goods or services in as many outlets as possible.

internal branding activities and processes that help to inform and inspire employees.

interstitials advertisements, often with video or animation, that pop up between changes on a Web site.

joint venture a company in which multiple investors share ownership and control.

learning changes in an individual's behaviour arising from experience.

lexicographic heuristic consumer choosing the best brand on the basis of its perceived most important attribute.

licensed product one whose brand name has been licensed to other manufacturers who actually make the product.

life stage part of the life cycle; defines a person's major concern, such as going through a divorce or taking care of an older parent.

life-cycle cost the product's purchase cost plus the discounted cost of maintenance and repair less the discounted salvage value.

lifestyle a person's pattern of living in the world as expressed in activities, interests, and opinions.

line extension the parent brand is used to brand a new product that targets a new market segment within a product category currently served by the parent brand.

line stretching a company lengthens its product line beyond its current range.

long-term memory (LTM) a permanent repository of information.

loyalty a commitment to rebuy or repatronize a preferred product or service.

maintenance and repair the service program for helping customers keep purchased products in good working order.

market demand the total volume of a product that would be bought by a defined customer group in a defined geographical area in a defined time period in a defined marketing environment under a defined marketing program.

market forecast the market demand corresponding to the level of industry marketing expenditure.

market logistics planning the infrastructure to meet demand, then implementing and controlling the physical flows or materials and final goods from points of origin to points of use, to meet customer requirements at a profit.

market opportunity analysis (MOA) system used to determine the attractiveness and probability of success.

market partitioning the process of investigating the hierarchy of attributes consumers examine in choosing a brand if they use phased decision strategies.

market penetration index a comparison of the current level of market demand to the potential demand level.

market potential the upper limit to market demand whereby increased marketing expenditures would not be expected to stimulate further demand.

market share a company's share of a total market expressed as a percentage of the revenues the firm earns as a portion of total market revenues or the volume it sells as a portion of the total volume sold in the marketplace.

market-buildup method method in which a firm identifies all the potential buyers in each market and estimates their potential purchases.

marketer someone who seeks a response (attention, a purchase, a vote, a donation) from another party, called the prospect.

marketing audit a comprehensive, systematic, independent, and periodic examination of a company's or business unit's marketing environment, objectives, strategies, and activities.

marketing channel system the particular set of marketing channels employed by a firm.

marketing channels sets of interdependent organizations involved in the process of making a product or service available for use or consumption.

marketing communications mix advertising, sales promotion, events and experiences, public relations and publicity, direct marketing, and personal selling.

marketing communications the means by which firms attempt to inform, persuade, and remind consumers—directly or indirectly—about products and brands that they sell.

marketing decision support system (MDSS) a coordinated collection of data, systems, tools, and techniques with supporting software and hardware by which an organization gathers and interprets relevant information from business and the environment and turns it into a basis for marketing action.

marketing implementation the process that turns marketing plans into action assignments and ensures that such assignments are executed in a manner that accomplishes the plan's stated objectives.

marketing information system (MIS) people, equipment, and procedures to gather, sort, analyze, evaluate, and distribute information to marketing decision makers.

marketing intelligence system a set of procedures and sources managers use to obtain everyday information about developments in the marketing environment.

marketing management the art and science of choosing target markets and getting, keeping, and growing customers through creating, delivering, and communicating superior customer value.

marketing metrics the set of measures that helps firms to quantify, compare, and interpret their marketing performance.

marketing network the company and its supporting stakeholders, with whom it has built mutually profitable business relationships.

marketing opportunity an area of buyer need and interest in which there is a high probability that a company can profitably satisfy that need.

marketing plan written document that summarizes what the marketer has learned about the marketplace, indicates how the firm plans to reach its marketing objectives, and helps direct and coordinate the marketing effort.

marketing public relations (MPR) publicity and other activities that build corporate or product image to facilitate marketing goals.

marketing research the systematic design, collection, analysis, and reporting of data and findings relevant to a specific marketing situation facing the company.

marketing process of planning and executing the conception, pricing, promotion, and distribution of ideas, goods, and services to create exchanges that satisfy individual and organizational goals.

market-penetration pricing pricing strategy where prices start low to drive higher sales volume from price-sensitive customers and produce productivity gains.

market-skimming pricing pricing strategy where prices start high and are slowly lowered over time to maximize profits from less price-sensitive customers.

markup pricing an item by adding a standard increase to the product's cost.

mass customization the ability of a company to meet each customer's requirements—to prepare on a mass basis individually designed products, services, programs, and communications.

mass marketing situation in which the seller engages in the mass production, mass distribution, and mass promotion of one product for all buyers.

materials and parts goods that enter the manufacturer's product completely.

media selection finding the most cost-effective media to deliver the desired number and type of exposures to the target audience.

megamarketing the strategic coordination of economic, psychological, political, and public relations skills, to gain the cooperation of a number of parties in order to enter or operate in a given market.

megatrends large social, economic, political, and technological changes that are slow to form, and once in place, have an influence for seven to ten years or longer.

membership groups groups having a direct influence on a person.

memory encoding how and where information gets into memory.

memory retrieval how and from where information gets out of memory.

mental accounting the manner by which consumers code, categorize, and evaluate financial outcomes of choices.

microsales analysis examination of specific products and territories that fail to produce expected sales.

microsite a limited area on the Web managed and paid for by an external advertiser/company.

mission statements statements that organizations develop to share with managers, employees, and (in many cases) customers.

mixed bundling the seller offers goods both individually and in bundles.

motive a need that is sufficiently pressing to drive a person to act.

multi-channel marketing a single firm uses two or more marketing channels to reach one or more customer segments.

multitasking doing two or more things at the same time.

net price analysis analysis that encompasses company list price, average discount, promotional spending, and co-op advertising to arrive at net price.

noncompensatory models in consumer choice, when consumers do not simultaneously consider all positive and negative attribute considerations in making a decision.

opinion leader the person in informal, product-related communications who offers advice or information about a specific product or product category.

ordering ease how easy it is for the customer to place an order with the company.

organization a company's structures, policies, and corporate culture.

organizational buying the decision-making process by which formal organizations establish the need for purchased products and services and identify, evaluate, and choose among alternative brands and suppliers.

overall market share the company's sales expressed as a percentage of total market sales.

overhead costs that do not vary with production or sales revenue.

packaging all the activities of designing and producing the container for a product.

parent brand an existing brand that gives birth to a brand extension.

partner relationship management (PRM) activities the firm undertakes to build mutually satisfying long-term relations with key partners such as suppliers, distributors, ad agencies, and marketing research suppliers.

penetrated market the set of consumers who are buying a company's product.

perceived value the value promised by the company's value proposition and perceived by the customer.

perception the process by which an individual selects, organizes, and interprets information inputs to create a meaningful picture of the world.

performance quality the level at which the product's primary characteristics operate.

personal communications channels two or more persons communicating directly face-to-face, person-to-audience, over the telephone, or through e-mail.

personal influence the effect one person has on another's attitude or purchase probability.

personality a set of distinguishing human psychological traits that lead to relatively consistent responses to environmental stimuli.

place advertising (also out-of-home advertising) ads that appear outside of home and where consumers work and play.

point-of-purchase (P-O-P) the location where a purchase is made, typically thought of in terms of a retail setting.

positioning the act of designing the company's offering and image to occupy a distinctive place in the mind of the target market.

potential market the set of consumers who profess a sufficient level of interest in a market offer.

potential product all the possible augmentations and transformations the product or offering might undergo in the future.

price discrimination a company sells a product or service at two or more prices that do not reflect a proportional difference in costs.

price escalation an increase in the price of a product due to added costs of selling it in different countries.

primary groups groups with which a person interacts continuously and informally, such as family, friends, neighbours, and co-workers.

principle of congruity psychological mechanism that states that consumers like to see seemingly related objects as being as similar as possible in their favourability.

private label brands brands that retailers and wholesalers develop and market.

product adaptation altering the product to meet local conditions or preferences.

product assortment the set of all products and items a particular seller offers for sale.

product invention creating something new via product development or other means.

product mix see product assortment.

product penetration percentage the percentage of ownership or use of a product or service in a population.

product system a group of diverse but related items that function in a compatible manner.

product anything that can be offered to a market to satisfy a want or need.

profitable customer a person, household, or company that over time yields a revenue stream that exceeds by an acceptable amount the company's cost stream of attracting, selling, and servicing that customer.

prospect theory when consumers frame decision alternatives in terms of gains and losses according to a value function.

prospect person or group from whom a marketer is seeking a response (e.g., attention, a purchase, a vote, a donation).

psychographics the science of using psychology and demographics to better understand consumers.

public any group that has an actual or potential interest in or impact on a company's ability to achieve its objectives.

public relations (PR) a variety of programs designed to promote or protect a company's image or its individual products.

publicity the task of securing editorial space—as opposed to paid space—in print and broadcast media to promote something.

pull strategy when the manufacturer uses advertising and promotion to persuade consumers to ask intermediaries for the product, thus inducing the intermediaries to order it.

purchase probability scale a scale to measure the probability of a buyer making a particular purchase.

pure bundling a firm only offers its products as a bundle.

pure-online companies that have launched a Web site without any previous existence as a firm.

push strategy when the manufacturer uses its sales force and trade promotion money to induce intermediaries to carry, promote, and sell the product to end users.

quality the totality of features and characteristics of a product or service that bear on its ability to satisfy stated or implied needs.

R

reference groups all the groups that have a direct or indirect influence on a person's attitudes or behaviour.

reference prices pricing information a consumer retains in memory which is used to interpret and evaluate a new price.

relational equity the cumulative value of the firm's network of relationships with its customers, partners, suppliers, employees, and investors.

relationship marketing building mutually satisfying long-term relationships with key parties, in order to earn and retain their business.

relative market share market share in relation to a company's largest competitor.

reliability a measure of the probability that a product will not malfunction or fail within a specified time period.

reparability a measure of the ease of fixing a product when it malfunctions or fails.

representativeness heuristic when consumers base their predictions on how representative or similar an outcome is to other examples.

retailer (or retail store) any business enterprise whose sales volume comes primarily from retailing.

retailing all the activities involved in selling goods or services directly to final consumers for personal, nonbusiness use.

risk analysis a method by which possible rates of returns and their probabilities are calculated by obtaining estimates for uncertain variables affecting profitability.

role the activities a person is expected to perform.

S

sales analysis measuring and evaluating actual sales in relation to goals.

sales budget a conservative estimate of the expected volume of sales, used for making current purchasing, production, and cash flow decisions.

sales promotion a collection of incentive tools, mostly short term, designed to stimulate quicker or greater purchase of particular products or services by consumers or the trade.

sales quota the sales goal set for a product line, company division, or sales representative.

sales-variance analysis a measure of the relative contribution of different factors to a gap in sales performance.

satisfaction a person's feelings of pleasure or disappointment resulting from comparing a product's perceived performance or outcome in relation to his or her expectations.

scenario analysis developing plausible representations of a firm's possible future that make different assumptions about forces driving the market and include different uncertainties.

search-related ads ads in which search terms are used as a proxy for the consumer's consumption interests and relevant links to product or service offerings are listed alongside the search results.

secondary groups groups that tend to be more formal and require less interaction than primary groups, such as religious, professional, and trade-union groups.

selective attention the mental process of screening out certain stimuli while noticing others.

selective distortion the tendency to interpret product information in a way that fits consumer perceptions.

selective distribution the use of more than a few but less than all of the intermediaries who are willing to carry a particular product.

selective retention good points about a product that consumers like are remembered and good points about competing products are forgotten.

served market share a company's sales expressed as a percentage of the total sales to its served market.

served market all the buyers who are able and willing to buy a company's product.

service any act or performance that one party can offer to another that is essentially intangible and does not result in the ownership of anything.

share penetration index a comparison of a company's current market share to its potential market share.

shopping goods goods that the consumer, in the process of selection and purchase, characteristically compares on such bases as suitability, quality, price, and style.

short-term memory (STM) a temporary repository of information.

social classes homogeneous and enduring divisions in a society, which are hierarchically ordered and whose members share similar values, interests, and behaviour.

social marketing marketing done by a nonprofit or government organization to further a cause, such as "say no to drugs."

specialty goods goods that have unique characteristics or brand identification for which a sufficient number of buyers are willing to make a special purchasing effort.

sponsorship financial support of an event or activity in return for recognition and acknowledgment as the sponsor.

stakeholder-performance scorecard a measure to track the satisfaction of various constituencies who have a critical interest in and impact on the company's performance.

status one's position within his or her own hierarchy or culture.

straight extension introducing a product in a foreign market without any change in the product.

strategic brand management the design and implementation of marketing activities and programs to build, measure, and manage brands to maximize their value.

strategic business units (SBUs) a single business or collection of related businesses that can be planned separately from the rest of the company, with its own set of competitors and a manager who is responsible for strategic planning and profit performance.

strategic group firms pursuing the same strategy directed to the same target market.

strategic marketing plan laying out the target markets and the value proposition that will be offered, based on analysis of the best market opportunities.

strategy a company's game plan for achieving its goals.

style a product's look and feel to the buyer.

sub-brand a new brand combined with an existing brand.

subcultures subdivisions of a culture that provide more specific identification and socialization, such as nationalities, religions, racial groups, and geographical regions.

subliminal perception receiving and processing subconscious messages that affect behaviour.

super-segment a set of segments sharing some exploitable similarity.

supplies and business services short-term goods and services that facilitate developing or managing the finished product.

supply chain management (SCM) procuring the right inputs (raw materials, components, and capital equipment); converting them efficiently into finished products; and dispatching them to the final destinations.

supply chain see value-delivery network.

tactical marketing plan marketing tactics, including product features, promotion, merchandising, pricing, sales channels, and service.

target costing deducting the desired profit margin from the price at which a product will sell, given its appeal and competitors' prices.

target market the part of the qualified available market the company decides to pursue.

target-return pricing determining the price that would yield the firm's target rate of return on investment (ROI).

telemarketing the use of telephone and call centres to attract prospects, sell to existing customers, and provide service by taking orders and answering questions.

total costs the sum of the fixed and variable costs for any given level of production.

total customer cost the bundle of costs customers expect to incur in evaluating, obtaining, using, and disposing of the given market offering, including monetary, time, energy, and psychic costs.

total customer value the perceived monetary value of the bundle of economic, functional, and psychological benefits customers expect from a given market offering.

total quality management (TQM) an organizationwide approach to continuously improving the quality of all the organization's processes, products, and services.

tracking studies collecting information from consumers on a routine basis over time.

transaction a trade of values between two or more parties: A gives X to B and receives Y in return.

transfer price the price a company charges another unit in the company for goods it ships to foreign subsidiaries.

transfer in the case of gifts, subsidies, and charitable contributions: A gives X to B but does not receive anything tangible in return.

trend a direction or sequence of events that has some momentum and durability.

two-part pricing a fixed fee plus a variable usage fee.

tying agreements agreements in which producers of strong brands sell their products to dealers only if dealers purchase related products or services, such as other products in the brand line.

unsought goods those the consumer does not know about or does not normally think of buying, like smoke detectors.

value chain a tool for identifying ways to create more customer value; identifies strategically relevant activities that create value and cost in a specific business.

value-delivery network a company's supply chain and how it partners with specific suppliers and distributors to make products and bring them to markets.

value network a system of partnerships and alliances that a firm creates to source, augment, and deliver its offerings.

value pricing winning loyal customers by charging a fairly low price for a high-quality offering.

value proposition the whole cluster of benefits the company promises to deliver.

value-delivery system all the expectancies the customer will have on the way to obtaining and using the offering.

variable costs costs that vary directly with the level of production.

venture team a cross-functional group charged with developing a specific product or business.

vertical integration situation in which manufacturers try to control or own their suppliers, distributors, or other intermediaries.

vertical marketing system (VMS) producer, wholesaler(s), and retailer(s) acting as a unified system.

viral marketing using the Internet to create word of mouth effects to support marketing efforts and goals.

wholesaling all the activities involved in selling goods or services to those who buy for resale or business use.

yield pricing situation in which companies offer (1) discounted but limited early purchases, (2) higher-priced late purchases, and (3) the lowest rates on unsold inventory just before it expires.

zero-level channel (direct-marketing channel) a manufacturer selling directly to the final customer.

NAME INDEX

COMPANY/BRAND INDEX

SUBJECT INDEX

Credits

CHAPTER 1 2 Reprinted by permission of Kraft Canada; 6 Courtesy of Big Rock Brewery; 7 Courtesy of Rainer Stratmann for Lexus; 9 Courtesy U.S. Department of Transportation. This ad was created pro bono on behalf of the Ad Council's Drunk Driving campaign; 10 © Queen's Printer for Ontario, 2005. Reproduced with permission.; 13 Courtesy of Corbis/Bettmann; 15 Courtesy of Shiseido Co., Ltd. Tokyo, Japan; 24 Reprinted by permission of CIBC; 25 Courtesy of Volvo Cars of North America, LLC.

CHAPTER 2 4 Mike Cassese/Reuters/Landov; 39 Courtesy of Nike; 41 (top) Steven E. Frischling/Bloomberg News/Landov; 41 (bottom) Steve White/CP Photo Archive; 48 Reprinted courtesy of Caterpillar, Inc.; 51 Courtesy of AP Wide World Photos; 55 Courtesy of Ken Cedeno Photography; 60 Courtesy of Star Alliance;

CHAPTER 3 2 Daniel Acker/Bloomberg News/Landov; 82 Courtesy of DeBoer's Furniture Ltd.; 85 HOT WHEELS is a trademark owned by and used with permission from Mattel , Inc. © 2005 Mattel, Inc. All rights reserved.; 86 Reprinted by permission of Chatelaine; 91 Courtesy of Getty Images, Inc–Liaison; 99 Courtesy of Getty Images/Time Life Pictures; 100 (left) Courtesy of PhotoEdit; 100 (right) Courtesy of Bruce Coleman, Inc.

CHAPTER 4 104 Reprinted by permission of Delvinia Interactive; 110 Courtesy of PhotoEdit; 116 Courtesy of PhotoEdit; 132 GLADWARE® is a registered trademark of The Glad Products Company. Used with permission. © 2004 The Glad Products Company. Reprinted with permission.; 135 Courtesy of PhotoEdit; 139 Courtesy of The Conference Board of Canada.

CHAPTER 5 144 Norm Betts/Bloomberg News/Landov; 149 Courtesy of The Image Works; 151 Courtesy of Saturn; 152 © Alene M. McNeill; 154 Courtesy of Countrywide Finance Corporation; 158 Courtesy of Getty Images, Inc–Liaison; 161 Courtesy of Rogers Communications Inc.; 162 Steve White/CP Photo Archive; 166 Reprinted by permission of Grocery Gateway; 170 Courtesy of Corbis/Bettmann; 175 Courtesy of Enterprise Rent-a-Car Company.

CHAPTER 6 178 © PASCAL LAUENER/Reuters/Corbis; 181 Courtesy of Corbis/Bettmann; 186 BMO Bank of Montreal; 188 Courtesy of the Sherwin-Williams Co.; 189 Courtesy of Shaw Cablesystems G.P.; 192 Courtesy of Levi Strauss and Co.; 196 Courtesy of PepsiCo International; 201 Courtesy of Corbis/Bettmann; 204 Courtesy of the Council for Biotechnology Information; 209 KELLOGG'S®, ALL-BRAN®, and SMART START® are registered trademarks of Kellogg Company. © 2004 Kellogg NA Co. KASHI® and HEART TO HEART™ are trademarks of Kashi Company. Used with permission.

CHAPTER 7 214 Courtesy of Vancity; 220 Courtesy of Magna; 221 Courtesy of Corbis/Bettmann; 223 Courtesy of CN; 228 Ceridian Canada Marketing Department.

CHAPTER 8 240 lululemon athletica; 243 Courtesy of Henry Ford Museum and Greenfield Village; 245 Courtesy of Brunico Communications Inc.; 246 Courtesy of Tom's of Maine, and Josh Royte, Maine Chapter of The Nature Conservancy; 249 Courtesy of VANS Inc.; 253 Courtesy of CANFAR; 258 Courtesy of Ocean Spray Cranberries, Inc.; 267 Gregory Boissy/MAXPPP/Landov; 268 Courtesy of PepsiCo International; 269 Courtesy of Colgate-Palmolive Company.

CHAPTER 9 272 CPimages.ca/Phototake; 277 Courtesy of The Australian Tourist Commission; 283 Courtesy of The Great-West Life Assurance Company; 286 Courtesy of Olive Garden® Italian Restaurants and Darden Corporation; 294 Courtesy of Campbell Soup Company; 300 Dick Hemingway; 302 © The Proctor & Gamble Company. Used by permission.

CHAPTER 10 308 Reprinted by permission of the Canadian Tourism Commission; 313 Courtesy of Maple Leaf Foods; 319 Noah Berger/Bloomberg News/Landov; 321 Courtesy of Getty Images, Inc.–Agence France Presse. Roslan Rahman/Agence France Presse/Getty Images; 322 Courtesy of Corbis/Bettmann; 327 Courtesy of Getty Images, Inc.–Hulton Archive Photos. Mario Tama/Hulton Archive/Getty Images; 328 Courtesy of Alliance Atlantis Communications Inc.; Courtesy of Pinnacle Foods Corporation. © Bill Truran Productions; 333 LEGO, the LEGO logo, and PLAY ON are trademarks of the LEGO GROUP, which does not sponsor or endorse this publication. © 2004 The LEGO Group and used here with permission.

CHAPTER 11 338 Courtesy of Bombardier; 345 © 2006 Corel Corporation. All rights reserved; 346 Courtesy of Shell Oil Company; 353 Courtesy of AP Wide World Photos; 358 Courtesy of the Quaker Oats Company; 361 Courtesy of S&S Cycle, Inc.; 363 (top) Courtesy of A.T. Cross Company; 363 (bottom) Courtesy of The Running Room.

CHAPTER 12 368 Courtesy of Rumba Games; 374 Courtesy of the Cattlemen's Beef Board; 376 Director of Communications. CHC Helicopter Corporation; 378 Steam Whistle Brewing; 380 Courtesy of Woodfin Camp & Associates; 383 Courtesy of palmOne, Inc.; 386 Courtesy of Gallo of Sonoma, Healdsburg, Sonoma County; 389 Reprinted by permission of Intel Corporation, Copyright Intel Corporation, 2003; 391 © 2005 Starbucks Corporation. All rights reserved. Used with permission.; 393 courtesy of E. I. Dupont de Nemours and Company. Corian® is a registered trademark of DuPont or its affiliates.; 395 © The Procter & Gamble Company. Used by permission.

CHAPTER 13 400 Reprinted by permission of ING DIRECT; 407 Andreu Dalmau/EPA/Landov; 409 Courtesy of PhotoEdit; 414 Reprinted by permission of Via Rail Canada Inc.; 423 Courtesy of RE/MAX®; 425 Pizza Pizza Limited; 426 (top) RBC Corporate Archives; 426 (bottom) Creative: Andy Shortt & Jason Sweet, Push.

CHAPTER 14 432 KIA Canada; 435 Courtesy of Whirlool Corporation; 448 Courtesy of Pearson Learning Group Photo Studio; 451 Courtesy of PhotoEdit; 463 Courtesy of GlaxoSmithKline.

CHAPTER 15 466 Courtesy of Mediagrif; 474 Courtesy of Nautilus; 477 Citizens Bank of Canada; 484 Courtesy of Corbis/Bettmann; 485 Courtesy of Navistar/International Truck Intellectual Property Company, LLC; 495 Courtesy of STIHL Canada.

CHAPTER 16 498 Courtesy of The Running Room; 505 Courtesy of AP Wide World Photos; 507 The North West Company; 509 Courtesy of Hot Topic and Converse; 517 Boris Spremo/CP Photo Archive; 518 Courtesy of Getty Images, Inc.–Liaison, Heinz–Getty Images, Inc.; 522 Steve White/CP Photo Archive; 525 Courtesy of Xerox; 527 Courtesy of Corbis/SABA Press Photos, Inc.

CHAPTER 17 532 © L'Oreal Canada Inc. All rights reserved. Every reproduction of the picture is strictly prohibited without obtaining first the written approval of L'Oreal Canada Inc. and CTV's Canadian Idol.; 538 © Kimberly-Clark Worldwide, Inc. Reprinted with permission; 543 TILEX® is a registered trademark of The Clorox Company. Used with permission. © 2004 The Clorox Company. Reprinted with permission.; 550 Lisa Brant; 557 Daniel Acker/Bloomberg News/Landov; 559 Newfoundland and Labrador Tourism; 561 © 2004 Accenture. All rights reserved. Reprinted with permission.; 563 © 2004 The Dannon Company, Inc. All rights reserved. Reprinted with permission.

CHAPTER 18 568 Courtesy of DDB Canada; 575 Under permission by V&S Vin & Sprit AB (publ). ABSOLUT COUNTRY OF; SWEDEN VODKA & LOGO, ABSOLUT, ABSOLUT BOTTLE DESIGN AND ABSOLUT CALLIGRAPHY ARE TRADEMARKS OWNED BY V&S VIN & SPRIT AB (publ). © 2004 V&S VIN & SPRIT AB (publ). Copyright The Andy Warhol Foundation for the Visual Arts by V&S Vin & Sprit Aktiebolag under exclusive license.; 580 Courtesy of Corbis/Bettmann; 581 Brown Communications Group; 582 Courtesy of Omega; 585 Courtesy of the U.S. Army; 596 Courtesy of Corbis/Bettmann; 597 Courtesy of Guinness; 598 © Ron Stroud/Masterfile; 601 This marketing campaign was created, designed and donated by TAXI. Reprinted by permission of See You in Canadian Athletes Fund.

CHAPTER 19 606 Courtesy of Shaw Cablesystems G.P.; 611 Moosehead Breweries; 615 Courtesy of ShopSmart Online Inc.; 623 Courtesy of Navistar/International Truck Intellectual Property Company, LLC.

CHAPTER 20 636 Courtesy of 3M; 640 Courtesy of Gillette Blades and Razors; 643 Courtesy of Maple Leaf Foods; 647 Courtesy of Procter & Gamble Cosmetics/Noxell Corporation; 649 Courtesy of Corbis Digital Stock; 652 Courtesy of Sony of Canada Limited and Bell World; 657 Courtesy of The Boeing Company; 659 Jerzy Dabrowski/DPA/Landov; 663 © Koninklijke Philips Electronics N.V. All rights reserved.; 665 Courtesy of Retna Ltd.

CHAPTER 21 668 Reprinted by permission of Toni Hafkenscheid; 672 Courtesy of Red Bull. © Flo Hagena/Red Bull 2004; 673 © Ethan Hill; 674 Reprinted by permission of the Government of Canada; 676 Courtesy of Societé des Produits Nestle S.A., Vevey, Switzerland; 683 Courtesy of Corbis/Sygma; 688 Lands' End, Inc. Used with permission.; 692 Logo: © Copyright Brand Hong Kong Management Office. a) Courtesy of Corbis Digital Stock, b) Courtesy of Corbis Digital Stock, c) Courtesy of Corbis/Bettmann.

CHAPTER 22 696 Courtesy of Intrawest; 705 Courtesy of Dow Corning; 711 Courtesy of Corporate Knights Inc.; 713 Courtesy of Bown-Forman Wines/Fetzer Vineyards. Photo used by permission of Albert Watson and David Breashears; 716 Courtesy of LensCrafters' Give the Gift of Sight/© Lyons Photography.